D1407768

See citation page 727

726

BUSINESS AND ECONOMICS PUBLICATIONS

WILLIAM HOMER SPENCER, *Editor*

Dean of The School of Business
The University of Chicago

THE ECONOMICS OF LABOR
Volume III

ORGANIZED LABOR

This book is produced in full compliance with the government's regulations for conserving paper and other essential materials.

THE ECONOMICS OF LABOR

THIS VOLUME

VOLUME III: *Organized Labor*

OTHER VOLUMES

VOLUME I: *Labor's Progress and Some Basic Labor Problems*

Background: Problems at Issue and Methods of Attack—
The Trend of Real Earnings—Share of the Workers in the
Increasing National Income—A Survey of Wage Theory:
Some Explanations of the Trends—Distribution of In-
come among Persons and Families: Poverty and Inade-
quate Earnings: Distribution of Wealth—Governmental
Regulation of Wages—Women in Industry—Child Labor
—Hours of Work.

VOLUME II: *Labor's Risks and Social Insurance*

The Problem of Unemployment: Amount, Causes and
Effects—The Problem of Unemployment: Methods of
Dealing with the Problem—The Problem of Unemploy-
ment: Unemployment Insurance—The Problem of Work
Injuries: Industrial Accidents and Occupational Dis-
ease—The Problem of Sickness and Non-Industrial
Accident Among Wage Earners—Compulsory Health
Insurance Abroad—The Compulsory Health Insurance
Movement in the United States and a Suggested Plan—
The Problem of the Industrially Old Worker.

ORGANIZED LABOR

BY

HARRY A. MILLIS

*Professor and Chairman Emeritus of the Department of
Economics, The University of Chicago; Chairman
of the National Labor Relations Board*

AND

ROYAL E. MONTGOMERY

Professor of Economics, Cornell University

FIRST EDITION

McGRAW-HILL BOOK COMPANY, Inc.

NEW YORK AND LONDON

1945

64G106X

HD
6508
M58

M65e
v.3

331

ORGANIZED LABOR

COPYRIGHT, 1945, BY THE
McGRAW-HILL BOOK COMPANY, INC.

PRINTED IN THE UNITED STATES OF AMERICA

*All rights reserved. This book, or
parts thereof, may not be reproduced
in any form without permission of
the publishers.*

THE MAPLE PRESS COMPANY, YORK, PA.

PREFACE

This volume on organized labor is the concluding one of a series of three dealing with the economics of labor. Like the two preceding volumes, it probably does not constitute a "textbook" in the ordinary meaning of that word. The treatment—again as in the first two volumes —is more exhaustive than would have been possible within ordinary textbook limitations; more of detailed analysis, more descriptive material, and—perhaps here and there—freer expression of opinion have entered into the chapters than would have been the case in textbook writing; and the emphasis upon, and space devoted to, matters that we have regarded as constituting the core of the subject of organized labor are different from what they would have been in another type of treatise. We hope, nevertheless, that the volume will not be without value as an instructional aid.

Considerable time has elapsed since the publication of the first two volumes of this series. The fact that duties of public service, teaching, and other character have made this lapse of time unavoidable does not lessen the regret of the authors that the publication of *Organized Labor* could not more shortly have followed that of *Labor's Progress and Problems* and *Labor's Risks and Social Insurance*. Most of those parts of the book that were drafted some time ago have been rewritten or revised to bring the factual material and the account of developments to comparatively recent date, although—partly for the obvious reasons inherent in the fact that one of the authors is occupying a public position which bears an intimate relation to some of the matters discussed—this has not been done throughout.

As was observed in the preface to Volume I, the writing of, and primary responsibility for, different segments of a treatise of the length of these three volumes necessarily had to be assumed by one or the other of the authors; and inclusion there and in the preface to Volume II of a word about the division of labor seemed not to be inappropriate. In the present volume the first five chapters, on the history of the trade-union movement, were drafted by Mr. Montgomery, and the remaining ten by Mr. Millis. However, in the final outcome all chapters are the result of numerous consultations between us, each author contributed sections to some of the chapters the preparation of which was the primary responsibility of the other, and the book is a joint product for which joint responsibility is assumed.

v

The great obligation of the authors to the contributions that have been made by many students of the problems with which this book is concerned is indicated by the number of names appearing in the text and footnotes of the various chapters. Many persons and organizations have aided us in a somewhat more direct manner. While these persons and organizations are so numerous that individual mention of them is impossible, it is our pleasant duty to acknowledge our indebtedness to those whose help has been greatest. Mandal R. Segal rendered valuable aid in the preparation of the chapter on employee representation plans. The help of Joseph Rosenfarb in connection with parts of the two chapters on the law of labor and of Jacob Karro in connection with the discussion of the legal status of collective-bargaining agreements in the second of these chapters was invaluable. We are greatly indebted, also, to Alexander B. Motenko for the preparation of notes on the jurisdiction and policies of the National Labor Relations Board, discussed in the first chapter on the law of labor, and to Phillips Garman for assistance in preparation of the chapter on trade-union institutionalism. General assistance has been rendered at different times by Natalie Pannes Allen, Robert K. Burns, Lily Mary David, and Louis Lazaroff. Among these rendering general assistance, special mention should be made of Mrs. Allen, whose assistance extended over the longest period of time and found place in virtually all parts of the chapters.

HARRY A. MILLIS,
ROYAL E. MONTGOMERY.

CONTENTS

CHAPTER VIII

CHAPTER IX

CHAPTER X

CHAPTER XIV

CHAPTER XV

LIST OF TABLES

ORGANIZED LABOR

CHAPTER I

AN INTRODUCTORY STATEMENT

Organizations of wage earners and collective determination of the terms and conditions of employment have become, as everyone aware of the economic and social forces of modern life knows, integral and powerful factors in our contemporary system of producing and distributing goods and services. They affect, in one way or another, the sharing of the product of industry among persons and economic classes, the allocation of social resources, the attitudes of millions of persons toward existing social and economic arrangements, the volume of employment and of unemployment, the rate and direction of social change, the character of legal rights and prerogatives, the material status of large parts of the population, the stability or instability of business activity, the technical processes of production, and the policies of government. The implications in the realm of economic analysis of the policies they pursue and the methods to which they resort are both numerous and profound.

In this volume, the third of a series on the economics of labor, some acquaintance on the part of the reader with the nature of this powerful social force, organized labor, and with the problems to which its emergence and development have given rise will be presupposed; and preliminary survey will be of abbreviated character. Nevertheless, it is in point at the outset to mention the more elementary facts entering into explanation of the existence of the organized labor movement, to allude to some of the environmental factors initiating it and determining its character, and to refer in brief preview manner to some of the more basic of the issues with which this volume is concerned.

SOME INTRODUCTORY CONSIDERATIONS

A statement of the nature, in its more elemental aspects, of the organized labor movement is, for the most part, a statement of the apparent and fairly obvious. Concerted action on the part of wage earners, the substitution of collective for individual attack upon the problems confronting them, patently is an outgrowth of their consciousness or conviction that these problems are of common or group character, of a more or less common interpretation—its basis in both the experiences

1

of men and in the doctrines and ideologies with which they have become acquainted—of these problems and of their position in the economic and social fabric, and of a common conviction as to remedial expedients.[1] So regarded, organization of labor is merely one aspect of the ages-old effort of men to remake their environment, to remove disabilities, to conserve and extend the scope of their opportunity.

Equally patent are two other facts: that modern unionism, a rank-and-file reaction to economic conditions as men see and interpret these conditions, has been largely, although not entirely, a product of those changes in the organization of industry that separated the workers from the ownership and marketing of their products and, for the most part, from ownership of the instruments of production; and, second, that the reaction in group interpretations and concomitant programs of action would be expected to, and does, vary greatly among different groups of workers. Only when, in the evolution of the economy, changes dividing the workers and the business enterprisers into separate classes, possessed of different and frequently conflicting interests, had occurred were the circumstances precedent to that basic ingredient of unionism, common or group interpretation of needs and problems, present. The various groups reacting to these changes in industrial organization have, however, differed in size, in industrial coverage, in economic and social theories adopted, in ultimate aims, and in specific policies and methods. Sometimes they have been confined to a single craft, sometimes they have been inclusive of all workers in an industry, and sometimes they have extended beyond industrial boundaries. Their economic interpretations have ranged from a simple bargain theory of wages—with consequent emphasis upon the union's function, as a cooperative selling organization, of placing a reserve price upon labor power—to an elaborate doctrine of economic determinism and of labor's "historic mission" in the process of social change. Nor, indeed, has it been necessary that all members of the group be convinced of the permanency of their status as wage earners, of the validity of the "once a laborer, always a laborer" concept. The necessity, rather, has been the conviction that for the present and the immediate future their problems possess sufficient mutuality or commonness to dictate group rather than individual attack upon them. Out of this conviction economic creeds, with their logical implications in policies, methods, and tactics, have evolved.

One other obvious fact may be mentioned here: that the organized-labor movement, an attempt on the part of men to advance their economic interests as they understand them, has aims, policies, and methods that run more or less counter to those of other social and economic groups. In its very character and composition, organized labor has encroached

[1] Cf. R. F. Hoxie, *Trade Unionism in the United States,* D. Appleton-Century Company, Inc., New York (1917), Chap. 1.

upon vested interests, has run counter to prevailing mores, has more than once forced the sacrifice of prerogatives theretofore taken for granted; and its development, in consequence, has been accompanied by turmoil and conflict. Like every movement at once arousing the hopes of some men and exciting the fears of others, it has more often been either the subject of uncritical acceptance and laudation or else the object of bitter denunciation than the subject matter of dispassionate and critical survey and analysis. This has been inevitable, for labor's organizations and concerted efforts owe their inception and growth to one of the most basic of the problems of social life, the struggle for possession of material things, and to some of the most powerful of human motivations.

INITIATING AND CONDITIONING FACTORS

The fact just referred to, that unionism, a manifestation of the wage earners' interpretation of the situation confronting them and a concomitant program of action, is not a consistent or unitary thing, carries with it the implication that no single or unitary interpretation of it is adequate. It would be comforting to find some one formula of explanation and interpretation of the rise of the movement, of its policies and its creeds, and of its development into the powerful and articulate force that (with the exception of totalitarian countries) it is today in the industrially advanced nations; but the comfort would be that of oversimplification and of an ignoring of the realities. The elements entering into the various group interpretations and the ensuing programs of action have, on the contrary, been myriad and protean in character. Changes in environmental conditions from time to time, and differences at the same time among different regions and branches of the economy, have produced diversified and frequently conflicting programs of action; the type of unionism dominant in one decade has sometimes receded into the background during the next; and workers quite similarly situated in respect to the external environment have not always reached the same interpretation of the social and economic situation in which they have found themselves. Merely because the character of group interpretations has been dependent upon subjective as well as upon objective factors—upon the temperaments, inherited social theories, apperceptive qualities, racial and class traditions, memory imprints, and experiences of men—one finds throughout the history of the movement the concurrent existence of different and rival "functional" types of unionism,[1] even though they

---

[1] See the late Professor Hoxie's discussion of "functional" types (*i.e.*, different types classified according to purpose, interpretations, and mode of operation) *ibid.*, pp. 44–78. The extent to which the above paragraphs are indebted to Professor Hoxie's conceptions of unionism will be apparent to anyone familiar with his pioneering work, the influence of which has proved to be permanent.

have often been included within the same organic or structural unit.

Reminder of the diversified and conflicting factors that have gone into the making of labor movements, and of the nonunitary character of these movements themselves, should not, however, be permitted to obscure the factors of fairly fundamental and permanent character that have had enduring influence. Differentiation between these fundamental and more-or-less permanent causes of unionism and determinants of its character, on the one hand, and the more casual and ephemeral ones, on the other, is, indeed, a requisite to intelligent study of the phenomenon. The questions then arise: What have been the more fundamental and permanent forces determining the character of unionism? What generalizations with respect to the effects of these forces and environmental circumstances appear to be warranted? What have been significant differences in the effects of the same or similar environmental circumstances upon the behavior and purposes of various groups?

The answers to these questions are, of course, to be found chiefly in a study of the evolution of the movement; and our task in the four chapters immediately following is to glean from a historical survey some comprehension of the forces that have nurtured the movement and given to it character and color. At the same time, it will be helpful to approach these facts of history with preliminary reference to the more basic of the circumstances and developments that have brought unionism into being and have influenced its philosophies, theories, ultimate aims, policies, methods, numerical strength, and effectiveness.

An explanation in terms of differentiation of economic functions, of changes in the organization of industry, is, as has already been implied, inescapable. That basic prerequisite, recognition by the workers of a common or group interest, can occur only when men's interests as wage earners are stronger than their economic ties with other groups; and clear differentiation of employer functions and worker functions is obviously precedent to such a recognition. This does not mean that the impulse toward combination and concerted action was first manifested by workers conscious of, or convinced as to, the permanency of their economic status; on the contrary, as is indicated in the chapters immediately following, the early organizations in both England and the United States were those of skilled craftsmen many of whom might reasonably expect some day to become masters. With changes in the organization of industry, particularly the appearance of middlemen and greater separation of the workers from the marketing of their products, however, employer and employee functions became more clearly differentiated. Conflicts of economic interest and the tendency toward debasement of wages and conditions led to combinations among the artisans for the purpose of preventing the group from being injured by the competitive underbidding of its own members.

In the development of the factory system and of large-scale production is found another of the forces bringing unionism into existence and conditioning its functional character. While it is true, as Sidney and Beatrice Webb have observed,[1] that trade unions would have emerged out of the wage system and asserted their place as permanent parts of our institutional life had the Industrial Revolution never occurred, the factory system has both stimulated the development of labor organizations and influenced their character, aims, policies, and structural forms. With its impersonality and its subdivision of labor, it has deepened the rift between employers and workers, made more apparent the conflicts of interest between them, and rendered less certain the opportunity of skilled artisans to earn their livelihoods throughout the active period of life in given occupations or trades. The technological changes that accompanied the development of the factory system have, as is developed in detail later in this volume, affected profoundly the structural form, the policies, and the tactics of trade unionism.

Still a third of the explanations of the development of unionism and of the bent it has taken at one time or another is to be found in the widening of the areas within which have been determined the exchange value of goods and therefore the demand price for labor. In the United States this factor has been of especial importance. "The vast area of the United States," Professor Commons has written, "coupled with free trade within that area and a spreading network of transportation, has developed an unparalleled extension of the competitive area of markets, and thereby has strikingly distinguished American movements from those of other countries. . . . For it is not so much the mechanical inventions and the growth of industrial technique . . . that have given character to American industrial movements as it is the development and concentration of bargaining power over immense areas."[2] Overemphasis upon the importance of the expansion of market areas is possible, but at the same time this influence must be accorded the serious consideration it deserves. In the United States, unionism did not become a truly national movement until the nation had developed national markets.

Other factors entering into determination of the purposes, economic theories, and immediate programs of labor organizations merit mention in this introductory statement. Where, as in nineteenth-century America, opportunity to attain proprietorship status has been comparatively great and social classes have been relatively fluid, wage earners have been psychologically predisposed against being compressed into

---

[1] Sidney and Beatrice Webb, *History of Trade Unionism* (1897 ed.), Longmans, Green and Company, New York, pp. 25–27.

[2] J. R. Commons in Commons and Associates, *History of Labor in the United States* (1918), vol. 1, The Macmillan Company, New York, pp. 4–6.

a single class, reluctant to subordinate personal and individual efforts to those of their own economic group, and prone to identify themselves in interest and outlook with the propertied middle class. They have envisaged the collective battles dictated for them by social arrangements as being—in alignment with the farmers, small businessmen, and all the economically less favored classes—battles against monopolists, land grabbers, invisible governments and empires of big business, and all who would curb their opportunities to become independent proprietors, rather than against employers for higher wages and better employment conditions here and now. Where, on the other hand, social classes have been relatively fixed and the notion of permanency of economic status has been more widespread within the working class, ultimate objectives of the labor organizations, and their resultant policies, methods, and structural forms, have differed. Conservation and improvement of immediate job opportunities or else—at the other extreme—abolition of capitalistic arrangements and contrivances and establishment of collective ownership of the instruments of production and distribution, rather than the individualistic panaceas of a movement predicated upon the assumption of an abundance of opportunity, have, under such circumstances, appeared to be the logically dictated programs.

Price movements, the composition of the wage-earning class, the extent to which standards of living have been competitive rather than customary, the activities of labor organizers, and governmental and political factors also have played important roles in stimulating or retarding, as the case may have been, the organization of labor and in determining organized labor's aims and policies. During periods of rising prices and business activity, both the lag of money wage rates behind the cost of living and the enhanced ability of business enterprise to pay higher wages if forced to do so have encouraged workers to organize. These conditions have also influenced the functional character of unionism. Pragmatism, concentration of effort upon immediate "business" objectives, recognition of the unions, and improvement in working conditions, rather than espousal of all-embracing "uplift" programs, have generally been characteristic—although of course by no means the sole characteristics—of periods of rising prices and enlivened business activity. When, on the other hand, prices have been falling, business depressed, and employers able "to bring labor to its senses," the tactics and aims of "pure and simple" trade unionism have more often been looked upon with a degree of skepticism, and labor has been more disposed to harken to the plea of those promising, if only they are listened to and followed, fundamental reconstruction of the social order and an economic hereafter from which the trials and hardships of the present would be permanently excluded.

The composition of a nation's wage-earning population—whether it is culturally, ethnically, linguistically, religiously, and racially homogeneous or heterogeneous—is likewise a factor of importance in determining the bent taken by its organized-labor movement. In the United States the differences among the workers, on all of these grounds, have been greater than in any other industrially advanced country, and the effects of these differences have been profound, even though not uniform in character. Development of cohesiveness within economic groups has, to a considerable extent, been impeded; foreign ideologies transplanted to the American soil in consequence of the large volume of immigration, on the other hand, have engendered sympathy for collectivism and concerted action on the part of the wage earners; and, in ways indicated in the following chapters, the philosophical basis of the labor movement, the labor policies of business enterprise, the structural form of unionism, and the extent of labor organization in different branches of industry have reflected the heterogeneous character of the working population. Both the composition of the American wage-earning class and the already mentioned relative abundance of opportunity and comparative fluidity of social classes have caused standards of living here to be competitive rather than customary and therefore have constituted an incentive for labor to organize and wrest from the incumbent owners of industry the monetary prerequisites of a higher standard of life.

Two other factors deserve mention. The organization of many thousands of workers cannot be fully explained without reference to the activities of union organizers in inducing prospective unionists to affiliate and then in attempting to keep them in the union. Obvious as this fact may appear to be, it is one essential in explaining the dimensions of the labor movement, particularly in the United States. Detailed material included in the chapters that follow affords examples of the importance of this factor. In the second place, and of somewhat more fundamental character, have been the effects of governmental and political conditions and arrangements. The legal and constitutional systems within which labor movements have operated—systems of jurisprudence, judicial codes, the structure of government, and the extent to which the powers of sovereignty have been centralized or diffused—have influenced greatly and inevitably, again as is developed in detail in later chapters, both the emphasis placed upon political as contrasted to purely economic methods and the inclusiveness of the objectives of labor groups.

A PREVIEW OF PROBLEMS AND ISSUES

The foregoing paragraphs may, it is hoped, contribute a little toward understanding and a point of view, but they fall far short of suggesting all the issues entering into a study of organized labor or all the tasks of analysis and mastery of detailed material that such a study entails. Some preliminary mention of these issues and tasks is desirable.

A historical survey of the organized-labor movement is indispensable. Only through detailed account of the vicissitudes of unionism can its fundamental nature be understood, the various interpretations of it—of which the literature is prolific—be tested realistically, and the character and importance of the various determinants of its functional character, as suggested in the preceding paragraphs, be subjected to verification. The growth of American unionism, from a movement inclusive of less than half a million workers shortly before the turn of the century to one including some 13,000,000 of the nation's employed persons at the end of 1943, the abandonment of indigenously American upliftism and the adoption of the economic creed of pragmatic "job-conscious" unionism, the policies and methods upon which primary reliance has been placed for more than half a century, and latter-day internal cleavages can be understood and properly appraised only in the light of their historical setting.

The aims, philosophies, theories, and economic programs of the trade-union movement obviously demand scrutiny, for they are expressions of the economic convictions of millions of men—convictions that are, in the aggregate, a potent factor with which realistic economic analysis must reckon. Critical evaluation of these theories and assumptions is, of course, an inescapable task, but first they should be examined sympathetically and with sincere effort to understand their genesis and their persistence in the experiences of wage earners.

At the same time, some effort to evaluate the economic efficacy of unionism and such examination as can be made of its effects upon the operation of the economy as a whole necessarily constitute major tasks before us. While organization of labor has arisen as a more or less spontaneous reaction of the workers to the problems confronting them, and by its tenacity and growth has given proof that it is a response of fundamental character to the social relations of production bringing it into existence, classical and neoclassical economic theory has not accorded to it a place comparable in importance to the one it has found in the real economic world. Accordingly, an important task is that of grappling with the question of economic efficacy from the point of view of unionism's own purposes and aims and with the question of economic effects from the point of view of the operation of our industrial organization as a whole.

Irrespective of the conclusions that may ensue from a juxtaposition of organized labor's economic theories and aims and the postulates of orthodox economics, however, trade unionism and collective bargaining must, as a practical matter, be regarded as institutions of assured survival. In democratic countries, the acceptance—and, indeed, a considerable amount of encouragement—of collective bargaining have become integral components of public policy. Moreover, it may be mentioned in passing, some form of collective agreement almost necessarily has to be the chief goal of a unionism that accepts the present system of producing goods and services and of utilizing labor power and seeks the improvement of the material status of its own members within this system. The relevance therefore, in a volume on organized labor, of a survey of the processes of collective bargaining—of how collective bargaining works—is fairly apparent.

Likewise, the various policies and methods to which labor organizations resort—policies in respect to wages, hours, limitation of employment opportunities to union men, conditions of work, output, jurisdiction, apprenticeship training, and other matters—and the problem of their structural form demand consideration. Trade-union policies and methods are, from one point of view, merely the instrumentalities that the group adopts for achieving its ends and rendering effective its larger program; but, from another point of view, they are the warp and woof of day-to-day industrial relations in unionized industries. Outgrowths or logical concomitants of the theories and assumptions of the organized group, these policies, methods, and working rules necessarily vary in character and in the emphasis that is placed upon one as against another of them, according to the differences in the circumstances in which unions seeking basically the same ends operate and also according to differences in the ultimate ends of different functional groups. Trade-union structure, also, is to be regarded, when placed in proper perspective, as a means to the end, but the problem of structure is inseparably interwoven with that of achievement of larger purposes, and it is obvious that no adequate understanding of the organized-labor movement can be had without examination of its structural forms and its government. In the United States, as indicated later, the emergence and entrenchment toward the end of the nineteenth century of a federated craft unionism, rather than of an industrial union movement, were an organizational manifestation of ideas and an economic creed incubated by nearly a hundred years of experience. Trade-union structure is, indeed, a more or less accurate reflection of both the purposes of the organized group and the conditions within which it operates; and frequently one measure of the weakness of a labor movement is the tardiness with which it succeeds in effecting structural adaptations to changes in environmental conditions.

Organization of labor is, of course, not exclusively an effort to improve conditions and enlarge the scope of group opportunity in the framework of the system of capitalistic free enterprise. Within the "official" movement, as well as without it, the influence of those conceiving the

proper function of organized labor to be that of serving as a vehicle of
social change has constantly made itself felt. While left-wing unionism,
owing to the inseparability of its activities and purposes from the major
strands of the story of the development of the labor movement, is not
treated in a separate chapter in this volume, its importance in the picture
as a whole becomes apparent as one threads one's way through the history
of British and American unionism. Nor must the purely economic
efforts of organized labor be permitted to obscure those of political
character. Labor's political programs and ventures can be divorced from
other phases of its history and activities only in an artificial way; and in
this volume they are, like the subject of left-wing unionism, discussed
chiefly in connection with the historical treatment of organized labor.
The importance, however, of the emphasis placed upon political in contrast to purely economic efforts, of the factors entering into determination
of labor's political "line," and of the differences in larger aims and interpretations that a strong political bent manifests is almost self-evident.

Two other of the issues and problems with which the following
chapters are concerned call for brief mention here. To many members
of the general public, industrial disputes are—unfortunately and inaccu-
rately—the phenomena most frequently associated with unionism. They
engender fears and animosities, encourage the ever-present latent disposition to let feelings and emotions take the place of dispassionate
appraisal of the merits of conflicting positions and patient efforts to
understand given situations. Placed in proper perspective, resort to
strikes or lockouts has been evidence that the processes of collective
bargaining have failed to function in a given set of circumstances or that,
when efforts to organize theretofore nonunionized industries or trades
have been under way, acquiescence in the demand for union recognition
and collective bargaining has been deemed less palatable than economic
resistance. The social costs of industrial disputes must not, however,
be minimized. The relative importance of different causes of strikes
and lockouts, the reasoning of the courts about them, the successes and
failures of different types of machinery for their prevention and settlement, and the effect of different patterns of employer-worker contractual
relations upon the number of man-hours lost in consequence of industrial
disputes are among the matters deserving careful and somewhat detailed
consideration.

Finally, we shall attempt to probe the field of public policy toward
labor combinations, an area where controversy and uncertainty have in
the past been predominant elements. For decades, lawmakers and
jurists have been puzzled by the problems arising out of the association
of men to improve their material status by concerted action. What is
and what is not an indictable or a restrainable conspiracy, the evaluation
of the rights of parties engaged in industrial controversy and application

of the "just cause" calculus, the financial responsibility properly to be attached to unincorporated associations, and the trenchment upon personal rights occasioned by invocation of the legal instrumentalities for protection of long-recognized property rights have been among the most difficult—and at the same time among the most imperative in their demand for solution—of public-policy questions. To many wage earners, the law of labor, particularly in the United States, has seemed to be an instrument that, under the guise of equality and freedom of contract, has deprived them of real equality. Certainly they have had ample evidence that it has been contradictory as between one jurisdiction and another. In no other of the areas surveyed in this volume, however, have changes in this country been more rapid, and in some respects unprecedented, during comparatively recent years than in public policy toward labor combinations. Federal and state legislation has curbed the power of the courts to extend their equity arm to restrain trade-union activities; Supreme Court decisions have given a somewhat different substance to the relation of the Antitrust Act to the activities of organized labor; and the old right of workers to organize and bargain collectively through representatives of their own choosing has been rendered real and dynamic by prohibition of employer interference, restraint, or coercion when employees engage in self-organization activities, employer sponsorship of labor organizations, discrimination in hire or tenure because of union membership or activities, and refusal to bargain collectively. Federal administrative and quasijudicial machinery now assists such self-organization and collective bargaining as stems from the volition of the workers by determining units appropriate for collective bargaining, conducting elections and in other ways determining who are the majority choices as bargaining representatives, and deciding cases of alleged unfair labor practices. Such a public policy stands out in sharp contrast to that of past decades.

Understanding and intelligent consideration of all the problems and issues enumerated in the foregoing paragraphs are, as has already been said, dependent upon some knowledge of the genesis and development of the organized labor movement. The immediate task, therefore, is a historical survey of American trade unionism, together with very brief reference to the evolution of the British labor movement.

CHAPTER II

NINETEENTH CENTURY AMERICAN UNIONISM

In all industrially advanced countries, the story of trade-union development is a story of successive adaptations to changing conditions and problems. The kind of unionism dominant in one decade has frequently been overshadowed by another kind in the following decade; in the case of no labor movement is a single or unitary explanation of the bent taken at any given time sufficient.

While various developments, problems, and relations of government to organized labor in other countries, particularly England, are discussed in later chapters, the historical account of organized labor is, in this volume, limited to the American movement. Summary reminder of some of the differences in the substantive character of unionism in the two great English-speaking countries is, however, in point at the outset.[1] "Upliftism" rather than conservation of job opportunity long played a greater part in determining the character of the theorizing and objectives of trade unionism in this country; on the other hand, determined adherence to economic methods and the trade-union means of improving the material status of the workers, rather than adoption of broad programs of political and social reform, were on the whole more characteristic of American than of British unionism after about the turn of the century. Labor organization here was, in the past, more limited in extent, more predominately representative of the upper strata of labor rather than of the semiskilled and unskilled. In contrast to the English situation—in which unionism's foothold was in the heavy industries dependent upon export and accordingly subject to the uncertainties of international political and economic relations—organization in this country was to a greater extent confined to the "sheltered" industries producing for the domestic market. For years less disposed than was its British counterpart to seek modification of property rights by exercise of the coercive power of the state, American unionism has nevertheless been harder hitting when concentrating its attention upon the attainment of job control and more intolerant of overlapping jurisdictions. Adaptation

[1] Among the many works on the British labor movement that may be consulted are Sidney and Beatrice Webb, *History of Trade Unionism*, G. D. H. Cole, *A Brief History of the British Working Class*, H. A. Marquand and Others, *Organized Labor on Four Continents*, and Carl Brand, *British Labour's Rise to Power*.

of trade-union structure to changes in the economy and in technical conditions of production has, on the whole, been a more acute problem in this country. "Pure and simple" unionism triumphed here less by emancipation from the influence of left-wing intellectuals than by the abandonment of middle-class philosophy. Other contrasts between the character and problems of organized labor in these two countries appear in connection with various of the problems discussed later.

FACTORS IN THE MAKING OF AMERICAN UNIONISM

That the forces, environmental circumstances, and trends in social and economic evolution giving rise to the American labor movement and determining its character and color have been numerous, diverse in kind, and sometimes of conflicting or antithetical nature goes without saying. Some of them have been, indeed, a trifle elusive, difficult to classify or characterize with satisfactory particularity; evaluation of their relative importance can be made only in most general terms. One fact, however, emerges clearly from the story of trade-union development recorded in the following pages of this chapter: that the relative lack of class consciousness on the part of the great majority of American workers was for long a dominant factor in the history of American labor. To this factor are attributable in large part the ever-recurring nineteenth-century tendency of the workers to ally themselves with the producing classes generally and to aspire toward the attainment of proprietorship status rather than improvement of the lot of wage earners as wage earners, the susceptibility to programs promising economic equality within the capitalistic system rather than looking, on the one hand, toward collective ownership of productive instruments or accepting, on the other hand, the premise of permanent wage-earner status, and the narrow scope to which unionism confined itself after the stabilization of the late nineteenth century.

Nor is great difficulty encountered in discovering the reasons for the reluctance of the workers of this country to accept the tenets of a proletarian-conscious labor movement. So long as individuals feel that they have reasonable opportunity to become independent producers, just so long are they likely to be more concerned in keeping the door to this opportunity open rather than in improving the conditions of the wage earners as a class. One characteristic of American economic evolution, until near the close of the nineteenth century, was the abundance of free land and the opportunity to attain proprietorship status consequent upon it. There were thousands of acres of fertile land awaiting the labor of man; there was adopted—largely in consequence of working-class agitation—a policy of making private ownership of this land easily available to him who would undergo the hardships of pioneering; and there resulted a tendency on the part of the workers to identify themselves in interest and outlook with the propertied classes. The presence of free land—combined with the dynamic character of American industry and other conditions mentioned later—made, moreover, for a fluidity of social classes, for less permanency of status in fact as well as in the minds of the workers. The economically oppressed envisaged as the way out, not concerted action on the part of the whole proletariat, but rather the prevention of those monopolistic tendencies which would result in the solidification of class lines; the psychology of their movements for common betterment tended to be middle class rather than proletarian; and their collective battles for many years were against monopolies, land grabbers, those believed to be in control of the credit resources of the nation, quite as much as—perhaps more than—against employers for higher wages, shorter hours, and better working conditions.

Other factors, some of them closely related to the one just mentioned, inhibited development of consciousness of common or group character of needs and problems on the part of the workers, and accordingly retarded the growth of a purely wage-earning-class movement. The industry of this new continent—a continent blessed with abundant resources awaiting exploitation—was extraordinarily dynamic, and it became geared to an exceptionally rapid rate of growth. As a result, entrepreneurial opportunities were relatively great, and the rise of individuals out of the working class was facilitated; at the same time there was an immigrant labor force—not, for reasons indicated later, on the whole prone to organize along the lines that appealed so greatly to the native-born—to take the place of the native-born workers who looked toward, and often attained, proprietorship and entrepreneurial status. In other words, America had, both in group interpretation and in fact, less of a settled laboring population than had England or Germany. Moreover, trends in the national development had on the whole the effect of obscuring rather than magnifying class disputes and interests. With the westward movement proceeding steadily during the nineteenth century, sectional rather than class interests attracted and held the attention of the population, including its labor segments. Such post-Civil War issues as the tariff, subsidies to and regulation of the railways, and money and the banking system were in large part sectional in character, and labor frequently found itself aligned with other economic classes on these questions. On the money question, it found itself fighting with the Western agrarians, and not a few of the trade unionists felt their interest in the tariff protection desired by their employers to be so great that they supported high-tariff candidates for Congress regardless of all else.

Immigration and the heterogeneous character of the labor force likewise account for the comparative weakness of class feeling, for the fact that the great problem of organized labor so much of the time has been that of how to stay organized. Nowhere else, in the past, were there such great differences—ethnical, linguistic, religious, and cultural—among the wage earners, and the mixture of races and nationalities, the transplanting of old-world hates and antagonisms, prevented individual points of view from becoming crystallized into group attitudes. In some ways, it is true, the admixture in the American labor force of men of different races and of many nationalities furthered rather than inhibited the development of class distinctions. The fact that in this country employers and workers were separated from each other not only by the economic line of demarcation, but also, to a considerable extent, by racial and nationalistic differences caused them to think in different terms to a greater extent than they otherwise would have done. Moreover, the traditional open-door policy with reference to immigration brought to the United States many men of great native abilities who were prevented by unfamiliarity with the English language or by philosophies acquired in Europe from acquiring and holding managerial or political positions. The organized-labor movement often was, in consequence, the beneficiary of the talents of such men, while American-born workers of no greater talents rose to managerial, entrepreneurial, or political positions. Coming to America with a background of European socialism and of racial or class oppression, many of the immigrants were more sympathetic toward collectivism and concerted action than were the individualistic Anglo-Saxons whose ancestors had lived here for generations, more cynical about indigenously American uplift schemes; and they were prone to lend their heartiest support to the organized-labor movement when its creed was strictly wage-earner in character, not an admixture of wage-earner and lower middle-class aspirations and interpretations. The contribution of the foreign workers has therefore been substantial, both in furthering organization and in determining union assumptions and policies.

It is probable, however, that the aggregate consequence of the heterogeneity of the working force in the United States was adverse to the crystallization of class consciousness and to the development of labor organization. Antagonisms of races and nationalities, misunderstandings growing out of language differences and conflicts of cultures, and ability of employers to use these conditions to their own advantage by mixing in the same production units workers of different and antagonistic nationalities, all had the effect of retarding organization of labor. The habits of docility with which many immigrants arrived in the United States caused them to be less prone to revolt against the "drive" method of procuring output and against autocratic managerial policies. Since many of the immigrants were, particularly after the 1880's, unskilled workers, management frequently introduced a technique suited to their capacities; it adapted jobs to the limited capacities of men, rather than men to jobs. Skilled workers organized into trade unions regarded the immigrants as a competitive menace, and their insistence upon the closed shop proceeded in part from the feeling that barriers must be established against this competitive menace.

In the character of our political institutions and in the reverence with which the American community has regarded the institution of private property are to be found additional reasons for the lack of class consciousness on the part of the workers and for ultimate arrival—so far as the majority of organized groups were concerned—at the conclusion that attempts to infringe too greatly upon traditional property rights were likely to redound to labor's detriment. Workers here were early granted the ballot, with resultant absence of a factor that in other countries set them off as a class separate from the rest of the community. The fact that participation in political life was not, as elsewhere, reserved for the upper economic classes had its inevitable effect in retarding the development of a strictly wage-earning class consciousness, while the discouragement to independent party action on the political front, inherent in our system of government, tended to minimize the importance of one field of action where the common character of the problems of all labor might be brought into clearer relief. Likewise the entrenchment in the thinking of the American people, as well as in the legal foundations of our capitalism, of the notion of inviolability of property rights dictated, according to the convictions reached by thousands of unionists, that it was dangerous or futile to encroach too far upon these rights; that organized labor, a minority group, dare not antagonize the great middle class by threatening the safety of the institution.

Emphasis upon the community conditions that for so long caused organized labor to seek those remedies, and to adopt those modes of procedure, which were expected to keep it from becoming compressed into a single class should not, however, obscure the forces constantly impelling purely wage-earner action for immediate material betterment. Basically these forces were, of course, those operative in any nation whose economy is developing into one of industrial capitalism: differentiation of employer and employee functions and separation of workers from the marketing of their products; increasing impersonality of relations between workers, on the one hand, and the owners and managers of industry, on the other; the weakness of individual workers as bargainers; and mechanization of industry and the growth of large-scale production. A few of the more peculiarly American conditions and developmental trends should, however, receive special mention.

The extremely rapid widening of the competitive areas within which have been determined the prices of goods, and therefore the exchange value of labor, has played an important part in fostering trade-union development in the United States. In the 1830's, as is indicated later, the city federation of various local craft or trade unions (then called the city "trades' union") was sufficient in most cases to protect the organized workers aga nst competitive underbidding, since the competitive menace at that ime was not so much the out-of-town product made under lower labor costs selling in the same market as the products of unionized labor as the low-paid out-of-town mechanic coming to the city and underbidding the union members. When, however, goods made in one locality competed actively with those produced elsewhere, equalization of competitive conditions in various localities became necessary, and national trade unions were the obvious remedial expedient. It was not, in fact, until the nation had become a national market that unionism became a truly national movement.[1] To the rapidity of market area expansion and to the vastness of these market areas are attributable a not unimportant part of the trends in, and characteristics of, the movement noted in the following pages.

To an extraordinary extent, standards of living of the American workers have been competitive, not customary; and in this fact is found another of the forces inducing them to organize and determining the objectives and the character of wage-earner organizations. Thousands of the immigrants who turned their eyes and directed their footsteps toward America were actuated primarily by the motive of improvement in material status; the relative fluidity of social classes had the effect, as has already been implied, of encouraging individuals of one economic status to seek to attain higher status; and the fact that a higher wage level obtained in a country where labor was favorably circumstanced relative to land and other natural resources caused business enterprise to direct aggressive sales methods toward the wage earners to a greater extent than business in other countries found it profitable to do. This essentially competitive standard of living inhibited to no inconsiderable degree the development of a purely working-class consciousness, but it also encouraged the more highly skilled and better paid of the working force to organize on a "business" basis and to seek aggressively those bargaining advantages which would result in elevation of the standard of living.

Many of America's basic industries, as everyone knows, have developed the utmost degree of mechanization, and in this mechanization— with its concomitant large-scale production and minute subdivision of operations—is to be found still another factor explaining the developments recorded in this and the immediately following chapters. In

---

[1] It must be borne in mind, as Professor Slichter has pointed out [S. H. Slichter, "The Worker in Modern Economic Society," *Journal of Political Economy*, vol. 34 (1926), pp. 100–124] that the development of a national market, on the other hand, in several respects hampers labor organization as well as stimulates it. The wide area of markets in the United States is partly responsible for the technique that has kept so many of our workers in the semiskilled class. Also, the fact that the market is often larger than can be economically served by one plant has caused many enterprises to have several; and such firms have been notoriously hard to organize.

part, as has already been said, the degree of mechanization introduced
in many of the basic industries was a consequence of the character of the
labor supply, particularly of the immigrant portions of it during the
final decades of the nineteenth century; but other conditions of American
economic life also entered into the determination of the technological
arrangements in some of the industries employing the larger number of
wage earners. There was, in America, an expanding internal market,
unhampered by trade barriers and accelerated in its development by the
rapid increase of population. From one side of the country to the other,
people demanded the same standardized goods, and accordingly large-
scale enterprise, with its mechanization and its specialization and its
machines, developed most rapidly. Effects upon the labor movement
were various. In no little degree, organization of the mass of production
workers was retarded. Partly in consequence of this retardation,
unionism after the stabilization of the late nineteenth century adhered to
structural arrangements that, in turn, made it difficult for these millions
of semiskilled production workers to find a place within the organized-
labor movement.

THE PERIOD OF THE BEGINNINGS, 1790–1827

When George Washington, in April of 1788, swore to preserve,
protect, and defend the new Constitution of the United States, the labor
supply of the United States included persons of differing economic and
legal status: farmer-craftsmen who produced articles for immediate
consumption or for exchange, indentured servants, slaves, free unskilled
laborers, itinerant skilled craftsmen, and a sprinkling of skilled craftsmen
who had settled permanently in the towns. Guildlike organizations,
characterized by cooperation between masters and journeymen, had
existed and in some cases flourished in Colonial America, and such
attributes of modern unionism as wage scales applicable to all in a given
group, benefit features, exclusion from employment of nonmembers, and
—occasionally—resort to the strike are to be found in annals of these
bodies.[1] Charitable and benefit societies were also formed by the

[1] For an account of these colonial associations, see David J. Saposs in Commons and
Associates, *History of Labor in the United States*, vol. 1, pp. 25–49. One of the earliest
societies of craftsmen was the Carpenters Society of Philadelphia, organized in 1724 (Norman Ware, *Labor in Modern Industrial Society*, p. 27, D. C. Heath and Company, Boston).
This society originally included both masters and journeymen, engaged in both charitable
and bargaining activities, and imposed fines for disclosing the "price list" (wage scale) to
outsiders. "Charitable" societies that sometimes interpreted the word "charity" so
broadly as to include prices of wares, wages of journeymen, apprenticeship, and unfair
competition were formed in other trades by the masters, or by masters and journeymen,
and in some cases—like those of the printers, carpenters, shoemakers, tailors, hatters,
bricklayers, and coopers—journeymen established their own charitable societies, "and
they too may have turned from charity to bargaining" (*ibid.*). The first American labor

journeymen alone. Both types of organization—those including masters and journeymen and those composed entirely of the latter—were confined to the skilled trades, and neither constituted trade unions in the contemporary sense of the term.

By the 1790's, however, organizations the membership of which was exclusively wage-earner, and the purposes of which were primarily protection or advancement of the economic interests of employees, appeared as institutions with which the masters must reckon. The Philadelphia shoemakers organized in 1792, and although the society lived only a year, a second organization, formed in 1794 under the name of Federal Society of Journeymen Cordwainers, maintained its existence until 1806.[1] The carpenters and cordwainers of Boston organized in 1793 and 1794, respectively, the printers of New York in 1794 and of Philadelphia in 1802,[2] and the shoemakers of Pittsburgh and the printers of Boston in 1809. During the period 1810–1815 printers' societies were also formed in Albany, Washington, and New Orleans, and a continuous organization was maintained in Baltimore between 1800 and 1805. The bakers, tailors, and other groups affiliated in organizations that attained some permanency in the larger cities; and in the smaller towns, also, organizations sprang up, some of which were able to raise appreciably the rate of wages then obtaining.

These early organizations of town craftsmen in the consumption-goods industries were, it is hardly necessary to say, not those of individuals who were conscious of permanency of wage-earner status, nor were the circumstances bringing about the separation of journeymen from the masters the same in every case. In some trades a new functionary, the "merchant capitalist," who sought to buy where he could buy most cheaply and to sell where he could sell most dearly, had appeared, and his appearance broadened the area within which competition worked out its effects. Placed, in a sense, within the control of this merchant middleman to whom they sold their wares, the masters were practically forced to reduce costs by lowering wages, and the workers organized in self-defense. In other cases, however, workers were not in danger of suffering

---

strike is sometimes given as that of the New York bakers in 1741, but in fact this was really a protest of the master bakers against a municipal regulation of the price of bread. Selig Perlman, *History of Trade Unionism in the United States*, p. 2, (1922).

[1] S. Perlman, *History of Trade Unionism in the United States*, p. 4.

[2] The New York printers, organized in 1794 under the name of Typographical Society, maintained their organization for ten years and six months. The New York Typographical Society maintained itself from 1794 to 1799, reorganized as the Franklin Society in 1799, and continued in existence to 1804. A second New York Typographical Society was formed in 1809 and continued until 1818 (N. Ware, *op. cit.*, p. 128). The Philadelphia printers had struck for higher wages as early as 1786 but had neglected to keep up an organization after winning their demands. S. Perlman, *History of Trade Unionism in the United States*, p. 4.

retrogression of their standards of living, but they were peculiarly advantaged because of their scarcity, intelligence, and facility of communication. During the years preceding 1790 the artisans and mechanics had found their skills to be in increasing demand, and organization to force payment in accordance with this strengthening of demand appeared to be the obvious mode of procedure. The mobility of some of the skilled craftsmen, like the printers, resulted in the formation of town organizations to protect the artisans against the "foreigner," and the contacts established among locals of different towns or cities was more a protection against the migratory journeyman than against the competition of goods made elsewhere. A number of the societies, it is true, worked in close collaboration with the masters,[1] but their formation was in response to the economic conviction expressed by the New York printers in 1817 when they declared that "the interests of the journeymen are separate and in some respects opposite to those of the employers."[2]

As would be expected in view of the circumstances giving rise to the pre-1827 labor organizations, the demands upon employers were those of a simple business unionism having, for the most part, a purely local basis. A price list or scale of wages was presented to individual employers or occasionally to associations of the masters; incorporation into the joint agreement of a code of working rules frequently was sought; union control of apprenticeship was regarded as a necessary part of job protection; and in some cases a closed shop was demanded. "The first step toward collective action was taken when the journeymen selected a committee to visit individual employers with the price list. The Philadelphia Typographical Society followed this practice as early as 1802. The shoemakers, both in Philadelphia and Pittsburgh, followed a similar practice."[3] The strike was, of course, the chief weapon of these early societies, and the issue in the majority of them was that of

---

[1] This was particularly true of the compositors, who were reluctant to turn against the small master. In Mease's *Picture of Philadelphia* it was said of the Philadelphia Typographical Society that "so much celebrity has this society obtained that employers, not only in the city but in all parts of the United States, when in want of good workmen, apply to the president to recommend them." Quoted by N. Ware, *op. cit.*, p. 129.

[2] Quoted by S. Perlman, *History of Trade Unionism* . . . , p. 5. This statement was made in connection with a decision that employers could no longer remain members of journeymen organizations. Policy with reference to permitting employers to remain members of the unions differed somewhat among the various groups. The shoemakers generally excluded them. The printers, on the other hand, were more liberal in this respect, employers being members of some of the printers' societies and journeymen who became employers being allowed to retain their membership. But toward the end of the second decade of the nineteenth century, the printers' policy seems to have become, in general, that manifested by the 1817 action of the New York group.

[3] D. J. Saposs, in Commons and Associates, *op. cit.*, vol. 1, p. 121, The Macmillan Company, New York.

wages.[1] In addition, sympathetic strikes,[2] strikes for the ten-hour day, and strikes for the closed shop are interwoven with the history of early American trade unionism. Payment of strike benefits dates from the first authenticated strike in 1786. A few instances of violence and intimidation, and of physical attacks upon "scab" workers, are on record, but ordinarily the strikes seem to have been of peaceful character.

Formation of these trade unions and the aggressive tactics they adopted in turn brought into being a number of militant employers' associations.[3] In their capacity as merchants, the masters often had been organized prior to the appearance of the journeymen's societies; and as the questions of wages, acceptance of union working rules, and the closed shop became more serious, the masters' associations assumed the function of dealing with labor. Working rules and the closed-shop demand appear, on the whole, to have been more influential in solidifying opposition of the employers than was the wage issue. Occasionally the organized employers consented to negotiate with the unions, but in other cases they sought, by refusal to negotiate and by creating through advertising a force of nonunion workers, "to break them up altogether, root and branch."[4] In 1809 the employing printers of New York "accepted the terms of the union merely to gain time to recruit a sufficient force of workmen to take the place of members when an opportune time arrived,"[5] and immediately thereafter they distributed circular letters throughout Pennsylvania, Connecticut, and Massachusetts urging nonunion printers to seek employment in New York. Earlier the Philadelphia master printers had through newspaper advertising sought to induce "sober young men from the country" to augment the supply of unorganized labor, and the journeymen had replied in print that these advertisements were "often delusive" and calculated wrongly to influence the "undutiful and thoughtless."[6] The tactical

---

[1] The first genuine labor strike, it is believed, was that of the Philadelphia printers, who in 1786 "turned out" for a minimum wage of $6 a week. Another strike—probably the second in American trade-union history—occurred in 1791, when the Philadelphia house carpenters quit work in support of their demand for the ten-hour day. In 1799 the Philadelphia Federal Society of Journeymen Cordwainers conducted an organized strike that lasted nine or ten weeks. S. Perlman, *History of Trade Unionism* . . . , pp. 4–5.

[2] The first sympathetic strike on record is that of the Philadelphia shoemakers in 1799. Those striking had no grievance of their own, but apparently they succumbed to pressure to strike for higher wages for the makers of boots. *Ibid.*

[3] For a factual account of these early employers' associations, see Commons and Associates, *History of Labor in the United States*, vol. 1, pp. 132–134.

[4] From the record of the "Philadelphia trial" of the following year, quoted by D. J. Saposs, *op. cit.*, p. 133.

[5] From the minutes of the New York Typographical Society, Nov. 11 and Dec. 16, 1809, quoted by G. E. Stevens in *History of Typographical Union No. 6*, and by D. J. Saposs, *op. cit.*, p. 134.

[6] *Ibid.*

procedure of employers in the shoemaking industry included, in addition, resort to the courts on the ground that the activities and purposes of journeymen societies rendered the members guilty of the common-law offense of conspiracy.[1] These early conspiracy trials, symptomatic of early American attitude toward combinations that tended to restrain trade or to monopolize the market for labor power or for goods, merit brief recapitulation.

Between 1806 and 1815,[2] at least six conspiracy cases were tried before juries that were judges of both law and fact, four of them resulting in verdicts adverse to the journeymen; and during the years between the lifting in 1820 of the depression and 1827 still other indictments were returned. In the Philadelphia Cordwainers case of 1806[3] the court, with untroubled simplicity, declared that "a combination of workmen to raise their wages may be considered from a twofold point of view; one is to benefit themselves, the other to injure those who do not join their society. The rule of law condemns both." Some years later Judge Roberts, in a case involving the Pittsburgh shoemakers,[4] for the first time brought injury to the community resulting from trade-union activities within the scope of judicial contemplation when he declared that "the human mind spontaneously revolts at the idea of oppression," that "where divers persons confederate together by indirect means to impoverish or prejudice a third person, or to do acts unlawful or prejudicial to the community" they are indictable at common law for a conspiracy, and that while the question might appear to be whether "the journeymen were oppressed and the masters the oppressors," this question really was irrelevant to the case. Cognizance of the legitimate purpose of improvement of working conditions, and therefore of the necessity to evaluate the rights of contending persons and apply

---

[1] It is interesting to note that no conspiracy indictments were returned against the printers, although activities of the cordwainers were distinctly hampered by the courts. There are, as Professor Ware has suggested (op. cit., p. 128), several reasons for this. The printers were not as strong bargainers as were the cordwainers, and accordingly the policy of combing the market for non-union workers more frequently sufficed so far as attainment of employer objectives were concerned. The absence of violence in the printers' strikes and the failure of these craftsmen greatly to advance wages are other explanations. There was—and always has been—a strong benefit sentiment among the printers, and their demands upon the employers were usually conciliatory in tone.

[2] For an account of these conspiracy cases see D. J. Saposs in Commons and Associates, History of Labor in the United States, vol. 1, pp. 138–149. The Documentary History of American Industrial Society, by J. R. Commons and Others, vol. 3, Arthur H. Clark Company, Glendale, Calif., includes a fairly large number of decisions rendered in the early conspiracy cases. See also A. Mason, Organized Labor and the Law, pp. 61–66, Duke University Press, Durham, N. C.

[3] Recorded in J. R. Commons and Others, op. cit., vol. 3, p. 59, and A. Mason, op. cit.

[4] For details, see N. Ware, op. cit., pp. 139–140.

a "just cause" calculus, did begin to be taken, it is true, by some of the jurists; but prior to the clarifying decision in the 1842 case of *Common-wealth v. Hunt*,[1] the labor organizations were never certain when their purposes or methods would encounter judicial disapproval.

None of these early societies had attained enough strength or stability to withstand the impact of severe industrial depression, and when, after the conclusion of the Napoleonic wars and the lifting of the embargo, foreign traders and manufacturers threw their products upon the American market, a prolonged business depression for a time brought American trade unionism almost to an end. Those workers' organizations like the printers', which had emphasized mutual insurance, survived as benefit institutions; but trade unionism *as trade unionism* virtually ceased to function. The depression reached its depth in 1820, and the immediately following years, years of improvement in business conditions, were characterized by the reappearance of aggressive unionism in a number of the branches of industry. Organizations surviving into the next period—a period characterized by demands for "equal rights," for the stifling of monopolistic tendencies, and for "citizenship rights"— appeared among the hatters, the tailors, the weavers, the nailers, and the cabinetmakers, and for the first time factory workers—many of whom in the textile industry were women—organized into labor unions.[2] Prices advanced rapidly during 1824 and 1825; strikes for higher wages, the ten-hour day, and the closed shop occurred in a number of important industrial centers; and with the renewed trade-union activities there came a fresh crop of trials for conspiracy. Moreover, "signs of the awakening,"[3] of resentment against an institutional order denying to the working class social and economic prerogatives and opportunities enjoyed by other classes, were a characteristic of the industrial atmosphere of the second half of the 1820's.

The Awakening, 1827–1834

The real beginning of the American labor movement—if a "labor movement" is so defined as to presuppose a feeling of solidarity on the part of the workers extending beyond a single occupation or trade— occurred during the second half of the 1820's, when causes of both economic and broadly social character ushered in an era of trade unionism, reform agitation, and local labor parties. Renewed industrial depression after the business revival of the first half of the decade brought discontent and conviction that the wage earners in various branches of industry were

---

[1] 4 *Metcalf* [Mass.] 111.

[2] For details see S. Perlman, *History of Trade Unionism* . . . , pp. 6–8, and Commons and Associates, *History of Labor in the United States*, pp. 153–169.

[3] This is the term used by D. J. Saposs in Commons and Associates, *op. cit.*, to character-ize the period from 1820 to 1827.

victims of the same economic and political conditions; broadening of markets and competitive areas stimulated trade unionism; and toward the end of the 1827–1834 period rising prices, as almost always, had the same effect. The causes of a social character were various. The prevailing spirit of the time was that of rampant Jacksonian democracy, with its emphasis upon the rights of the common man. In politics the party of Alexander Hamilton, who had declared in the Constitutional Convention of 1787 that "all communities divide themselves into the few and the many, the first rich and well born and the other the mass of the people who seldom judge or determine right,"[1] had been displaced in 1800 by that of the philosophical Jefferson, who loved to speculate about the rights of man; and in 1828, when Jackson triumphed over John Quincy Adams, the "common people" felt that they had come into their own and that the rule of New England bourgeoisie and Virginia planters had entered its twilight. Primarily agrarian rather than urban and wage-earning though the Jacksonian movement was, its emphasis upon social equality and the rights of man in general drew into its vortex a wage-earning class but recently endowed with the franchise.[2]

Specific grievances of the wage earners were numerous—economic and political inequality between citizens of different classes, the length of the work day,[3] imprisonment for debt,[4] absence of mechanics' lien laws to protect wages in case of the bankruptcy of employers, the Pennsylvania compulsory militia system under which the wealthy could avoid service,[5] lack of free public education for the children of the poor,[6] governmental favoritism toward the banks and other corporations, the issue of banknote currency of unstable purchasing power and the monopoly of credit

---

[1] Charles and Mary Beard, *The Rise of American Civilization*, vol. 1, p. 316. The original source is, of course, the Madison Diary.

[2] Massachusetts granted suffrage to workmen (*i.e.*, removed property qualifications for voting) in 1820, and New York in 1822. The Pennsylvania constitution of 1790 extended the right of suffrage to those who paid any kind of state or county tax, however small.

[3] The first argument advanced by American workers in support of their demand for a shorter work week was not primarily economic in character but was to the effect that the shorter work period was necessary if the workers were to be competent citizens. The sun-to-sun working day was regarded as incompatible with competent citizenship, since workers were precluded from the leisure necessary for consideration of public questions and were therefore condemned to an inferior position in the state. For accounts of the shorter-hours movement as part of the crusade for "citizenship" see D. D. Lescohier in vol. 3 of Commons and Associates, *History of Labor in the United States*, pp. 97–99, and vol. 1, of this series, pp. 489–490.

[4] In 1829 the Boston Prison Discipline Society estimated that about 75,000 persons were imprisoned for debt annually in the United States. S. Perlman, *op. cit.*, p. 11.

[5] All citizens were liable for service in the state militia, but the rich were able to avoid it by paying "fines," which in fact became a recognized purchase of immunity.

[6] A labor paper as late as 1837 estimated that 250,000 of the 400,000 children in Pennsylvania of school age were not in any school. S. Perlman, *History of Trade Unionism*, p. 14.

maintained by the banks, and in general the failure of the government to protect the poorer citizens' right to "life, liberty, and the pursuit of happiness."[1] The Declaration of Independence, with its enunciation of the doctrine of unalienable rights, must be taken seriously; and to take it seriously could mean nothing other than equal opportunity for poor and rich alike, removal of the power of the wealthy to oppress the economically submerged, and more equal distribution of the material things of life. Workers in the growing urban centers began to try to extricate themselves from existing party organizations and to agitate for a series of reforms intended to emphasize personal rights as against property rights: free education supported by taxes on property, public guardianship of the Robert Dale Owen brand, correction of unequal distribution of wealth, mechanics' liens on property to secure the wage earner as a creditor, prohibition of the seizure for debt by the capitalist of the body of the propertyless worker, exemption of wages and tools from execution for the wage earner's debt. "These were the new jurisprudence by which, for the first time in the modern world, manhood suffrage created personal rights superior to property rights."[2]

Part of this "new jurisprudence" doubtless embodied potentialities of change in social conventions and economic institutions of which the majority of the workers hardly had cognizance. Robert Dale Owen's program of "state guardianship,"[3] which for a time became the battle cry of the Workingmen's Party in New York, was nurtured in the aspirations of the poor for the education of their children, but in its expanded form it looked toward state support of all children and governmental assumption of virtually all the functions of guardianship or parenthood. Owen himself had been educated at a progressive school at

---

[1] The teachings of Thomas Skidmore, an agrarian reformer of the period whose equal-division program is discussed on page 27, are symbolic of the temper of the working-class "citizenship" aspirations of the late 1820's and early 1830's. Skidmore, a student of Thomas Jefferson and a disciple of the English Spenceans, believed that the unalienable rights of which the Declaration of Independence spoke could become real and dynamic only when concentration of ownership of property had been abolished. Jefferson, so Skidmore believed, had been guilty of a logical and literary lapse when he wrote that all men were endowed by their Creator with the rights of "life, liberty, and the pursuit of happiness." This logical and literary delinquency on Jefferson's part appears to have perturbed Skidmore greatly. Life and liberty were, he believed, rights that meant something, but the *pursuit* of happiness, as contrasted to happiness itself, is not a "right." In place of "pursuit of happiness" Skidmore would have substituted the word "property." From detail in N. Ware, *op. cit.*, pp. 157–158 (D. C. Heath and Company, Boston).

[2] J. R. Commons in Commons and Associates, *op. cit.*, vol. 1, p. 12.

[3] The state-guardianship movement espoused by the labor organizations of this time is traced by Helen L. Sumner in vol. 3 of J. R. Commons and Associates, *op. cit.*, pp. 246–260. R. D. Owen's autobiography, *Threading My Way*, gives his own account of the development and crystallization of the philosophy underlying the movement. See also *The Incorrigible Idealist*, by Elinor Pancost and Anne E. Lincoln (1940).

Hofwyl, Switzerland, and he was steeped in the cooperationist and human-character doctrines of his more famous father. Looking upon the failure of the New Harmony communistic experiment, he concluded that this failure was imputable to the antisocial habits the members had acquired before they embarked upon the life in which friendly cooperation, not self-aggrandizement and ruthless competition, was to be the rule.[1] Obviously, the preventive medicine consisted of a system of "rational" education of the young. With his friend and fellow reformer, Frances Wright,[2] Owen evolved a plan whereby state boarding schools would be established at which all children would receive the same general and industrial education, and equal food and clothing. An Association for the Protection of Industry and for the Promotion of National Education, founded by Owen, proposed that the state should become "the guardian of all her children," and requested an appropriation of $100,000 from the legislature to endow a Model National School. But many of the workingmen were skeptical. The Cook faction within the New York Workingmen's Party was opposed to all things Owenite,[3] and the New York Typographical Society (which included both masters and journeymen) characterized state guardianship as being "entirely visionary" and the views of Owen as "entirely at variance" with those of the Society. The state-guardianship movement ran its course. In Philadelphia and elsewhere, the establishment of free public education—particularly the kind of education that would "combine a knowledge of the practical arts with that of the useful sciences"—became a major objective of the labor groups, with Owenism a far-from-absent ingredient; but state guardianship *per se* rapidly became a discarded part of the educational program.

[1] Robert Owen, the father of Robert Dale Owen, bought the New Harmony, Ind., property in 1825, and the community continued as an Owenite experiment for three years. Since the New Harmony experiment is properly to be regarded as a forerunner of the communist or associationist schemes of the 1840's, account of it is deferred until later in this chapter (see *infra*, pp. 35–37).

[2] Frances Wright, suffragist and social reformer, was born in Scotland and was reared by Jeremy Bentham. Prior to coming to the United States, where she became the first agitator for "women's rights" as well as for improved material status of the working class, she had spent some time with the Lafayettes in France, and had delved into the doctrines of the French Revolution of four decades before. Miss Wright was one of the original New Harmony group; and after the breakup of that community she attempted for a time to emancipate negroes in an Owen-like community at Nashoba, Tenn., then returned to New Harmony, where she and Robert Dale Owen edited the *Nashoba and New Harmony Gazette*. Later a Fanny Wright sect was established in an old New York church, renamed the Hall of Science, and the *New Harmony Gazette* was thereafter issued in New York as the *Free Enquirer* (N. Ware, *Labor in Modern Industrial Society*, p. 153). This publication for some time functioned as the organ of the educational and social reformers and expressed the point of view of those factions of the New York labor movement which were most enamored of the doctrines of Owen.

[3] For details, see H. L. Sumner, *op. cit.*, pp. 248–250.

In another of the short-lived crusades into which the aspiration toward "equality" and "citizenship" resolved itself, the slightly misnamed "agrarianism" of Thomas Skidmore, the demands of the workers went beyond the immediate removal of economic disabilities; for a little while, indeed, it appeared that by "equality" the laboring groups meant equal division of property. Skidmore, a self-educated mechanic, in 1829 set forth his doctrines in a book published under the (not unrevealing) title: *The Rights of Man to Property: being a Proposition to make it Equal among the Adults of the Present Generation: and to Provide for its Equal Transmission to Every Individual of Each Succeeding Generation, on Arriving at the Age of Maturity.* "Let the poor and middling classes understand that their oppressions come from the overgrown wealth that exists among them, on the one hand, and from entire destitution on the other; and that as this overgrown wealth is continually augmenting its possessions in a rapid ratio, the public sufferings are continually augmenting also, and must continue to augment, until the equal and unalienable rights of the people shall order them otherwise."[1]   A constitutional convention was to be called for the purpose of redistributing wealth, and in the meantime, Skidmore believed, it might be necessary to set up a Committee of Safety to see that the rich did not abscond with their wealth.   Skidmore's appeal was directly to the dispossessed, his following class-conscious and proletarian. The New York workmen endorsed the agrarian[2] proposals and went into politics on an agrarian platform; but rather quickly the mass of the workers dropped the scheme. Possibly they had raised the question of "the nature of the tenure by which men hold title to their property" merely as a stratagem intended to forestall efforts of the employers to increase the length of the workday from ten to eleven hours;[3] if this was the purpose, the stratagem worked, for the employers abandoned their demand that hours be lengthened. As a brief excursion into a type of radicalism that could not command widespread or permanent

---

[1] From *The Rights of Man to Property*, p. 388, quoted by N. Ware, *op. cit.*, p. 158.

[2] Probably the name Agrarianism became attached to the Skidmore movement because of the title of Thomas Paine's 1797 book, *Agrarian Justice*, which advocated equal division by means of inheritance taxation.   The term "agrarianism" of course derives from a time when land was the chief form of wealth and it had come to be one implying a belief in equal distribution of wealth.

[3] Under Skidmore's guidance, meetings of the New York mechanics were held in April, 1829, called primarily to avert action by employers to extend the workday beyond ten hours. A Committee of Fifty was named to suggest means of warding off the lengthening of hours. In October this Committee proposed that labor go into politics on an agrarian platform, and it nominated candidates for the state legislature. The Cook faction in New York, which opposed this action, succeeded in getting control of the ward organizations that had been established by the workingmen in this, their initial political effort in New York; and Skidmore then established a rival party. Meanwhile, employers had dropped the eleven-hour issue. In April, 1830, Skidmore began to publish his *Friend of Equal Rights*. He died in 1832.

wage-earner adherence, the Skidmore episode was of only transitory
importance; but some of its repercussions were of profound significance.
The demand for redistribution of wealth really constituted the first of a
long series of "tests" of the strength of the institution of private property
in individualistic America, and the reaction of the community was of a
character not capable of misinterpretation. Public alarm and the manifest disposition to resist with ferocity any encroachment upon the sacred
rights of property convinced many of the workers that they could attack
the institution of private property only at their peril.

The character of the objectives of the labor groups during the period
with which we are immediately concerned, as set forth in some detail in
the preceding paragraphs, makes explanation of what had been happening
in the American labor world comparatively easy. It is clear that the
reforms sought were not so much the trade-union program of a later
day as the individualistic panaceas of a group unwilling to recognize or
accept the position in the economic scheme in which industrial evolution
was placing them. Competitive forces and changing market organization
had broken down, to an extent, craft and community lines; they had
created a group that was conscious of the common character of the needs
and problems of its members but that at the same time was unwilling
to accept the pessimistic conclusion of permanency of status. The
issue—the fundamental antagonism of interest—envisaged by the workers was not between functional classes, the employers and the employees,
but rather it was between the rich and the poor, between the beneficiaries
of the capitalism of the day and the economically dispossessed. The
measures they therefore sought—encouraged in so doing by manhood
suffrage and the spirit of the time—were of an individualistic, antimonopoly, personal rights, uplift character, rather than protection of the
job and security of tenure.

Structurally, this movement manifested itself in labor parties, in
local trade unions, in city centrals, and in attempts to bring all workers
and "real producers" together in general associations.[1] What is believed
to be the first coordinated movement of several trades in the United
States was launched in Philadelphia in 1827 when, as a result of the
strike of building-trades mechanics for the ten-hour day, there was
formed the Philadelphia Mechanics' Union of Trade Associations.
Trade-union in inception, this city central nevertheless was more representative in ideological character of the ferment of the time. A manifesto
possibly—but not probably—penned by a journeyman, the verbiage of

---

[1] Detailed account of the workingmen's parties of the period is to be found in Commons
and Associates, *History of Labor in the United States*, vol. 1, pp. 231–285, and of the Philadelphia city central and of the New England Association of Farmers, Mechanics, and Other
Workmen on pp. 185–231 and 302–326 of the same volume. *Cf.* also S. Perlman, *History
of Trade Unionism* . . . , pp. 9–18, and N. Ware, *The Industrial Worker.*

which was strongly suggestive of Robert Owen and Robert Dale Owen, demanded equality and a more just balance of "mental, moral, political, and scientific" power "among the various classes which constitute society at large," and postulated the thesis that the insufficiency of the wage earners' purchasing power accounted for industrial depressions and unemployment. This city central, in turn, gave birth in May, 1828, to the first labor party in the modern world,[1] the Workingmen's Labor Party of Philadelphia, which polled 2,400 votes in the fall election of that year and gained the balance of power in the city council. The New York workers embarked upon their first political venture the following year, when the Workingmen's Party, compounded of Skidmore agrarianism and other elements, garnered 4,000 votes out of a total of 21,000;[2] and in Boston, upstate New York, and elsewhere labor parties and city centrals sprang up.[3] New England, where the manufacturing industries were becoming dominant, was the scene of an attempt to bring within one organization not only the farmers and skilled mechanics—groups who found place within the labor parties of Pennsylvania and New York —but also the factory operatives. The New England Association of Farmers, Mechanics, and Other Workmen, a new type of labor organization, was partly political and partly economic. Emerging in 1831 out of the ten-hour movement, it rapidly embraced within the range of its objectives other matters, the majority of which necessitated action on the political front. The inclusiveness and catholicity of its membership turned it toward broad social reform, upliftism, and "redress of the wrongs of the producing class by resort to the ballot." Entering state politics in 1833 and 1834, the Association supported several candidates, but it became engrossed chiefly in presentation of its various memorials to the legislatures of the several New England states.

For a time, this general industrial union and the various labor parties were forces with which it was necessary for the "nonproducing" classes to reckon. Their importance, however, lies not in the immediate strength they attained, for this was soon dissipated; rather it lies in the breaking down of the narrow craft-consciousness that had characterized the earlier unions and in preparing the way for the broader forms of organization that were to follow. The labor parties were led by inexperienced men whose idealism and devotion to "principles" exceeded their

[1] Not until nearly forty years later did the Labour Representation Leagues emerge in England as the first bodies representative in politics solely of labor.

[2] S. Perlman, *History of Trade Unionism* . . . , p. 17. This New York movement, as has already been said, originated in resistance to the lengthening of the workday but quickly took on a political coloration.

[3] In 1830, Farmers, Mechanics, and Workingmen's Parties are known to have been in existence in Albany, Troy, Rochester, Utica, Syracuse, Schenectady, Ithaca, Batavia, and other upstate New York places.

ability to compromise or to practice the useful art of political manipulation;[1] on the other hand, the "designing men" in the older parties rapidly espoused as their own the labor-party proposals that appealed most to the wage earners. Tammany Hall became a proponent of mechanics' lien laws. By 1831 the Philadelphia party had become virtually moribund, and in New York and elsewhere the political movements passed into history shortly thereafter. The New England Association of Farmers, Mechanics, and Other Workmen held a final convention in October, 1834, listened to a florid and highly indefinite address by its president,[2] and adjourned never to meet again. But the trade unions, even though supporting with varying degrees of enthusiasm the independent party movement, centered their attention upon methods of job control during the years when "equality" and "citizenship" were labor's more emphasized demands, and it was to them that the workers turned during the period when rising prices relegated the idea of political action and one big union into the background.

ATTEMPTS AT NATIONAL FEDERATION, 1834–1837

The species of unionism obtaining from 1834 until the panic of 1837 was distinctly modern in character. Disillusioned by the failure of their political programs and forced by the economic situation—especially the rising prices that accompanied speculation—to concentrate upon the less grandiose matters of wages, hours, and conditions, the workers appeared to be content to fight their battle on the economic front. Certainly they had not abandoned the ingrained American antimonopoly complex that was to inspire or to plague—according as one looks at the matter—the labor movement (as a purely *labor* movement) for decades to come, and such consciousness of permanency of status as obtained was probably still more a fear than a recognition. The immediate situation, however, encouraged the growth of a type of unionism not greatly different from the "pure and simple" brand brought forward by the fathers of the American Federation of Labor nearly half a century later. Multiplication of state banks and circulation of irredeemable wildcat currency caused the cost of living to soar, and protection of material status dictated that the workers content themselves with the restricted solidarity of the isolated trade society and of city centrals that eschewed independent party action. Trade unions therefore multiplied rapidly. In 1833, when the workers began to turn back to simple trade unionism, there were twenty-nine organized trades in New York, twenty-one in Philadelphia, seventeen in Baltimore, and smaller numbers else-

---

[1] In New York, for example, the Owenites would have nothing to do with the Skidmoreites, nor the Skidmoreites with the Owenites, and the Cook faction was both scornful of, and anathema to, both.

[2] *Cf.* H. L. Sumner, *op. cit.*, p. 315.

where. Among the organized groups in Philadelphia were the hand-loom weavers, plasterers, bricklayers, blacksmiths and tinsmiths, cigar makers, plumbers, milliners, and manual workers.[1] Several trades, like the Pennsylvania printers and tailors, which had formerly been organized on a benevolent basis, reorganized as trade societies. The wave of organization continued, and by 1836 Philadelphia had fifty-eight trade unions, New York fifty-two, Newark sixteen, Pittsburgh thirteen, Cincinnati fourteen, and Louisville seven.[2] For the first time, also, women workers organized in appreciable numbers. These labor organizations were, for the most part, composed of skilled craftsmen who demanded increases in wages, the ten-hour day, union control of apprenticeship, and the closed shop.

Together with the formation of local craft unions went four other developments of significance: the combination once more of trade unions of the various cities into city centrals (or "trades' unions" as they were designated), organization of employers' associations, affiliation of locals of the various trades into national trade unions, and an attempt to federate all labor organizations into one general body. The New York Trades' Union was organized on Aug. 14, 1833, as a result of an alliance of fifteen trades with the carpenters in their strike for higher wages, and relatively quickly city centrals appeared in Baltimore, Philadelphia, Boston, and elsewhere. These local federations of trade unions, unlike those of the preceding period, repudiated active politics and concentrated their efforts upon the rendering of financial and moral support to member locals during strikes, the boycott of nonunion goods, the organization of unorganized trades, and warfare against scab workers. Repudiation of active politics did not, however, involve condemnation of legislative action, or lobbying; indeed, the campaign by the New York Trades' Union for suppression of the competition from prison-made goods constituted "the first sustained legislative campaign that was ever conducted by a labor organization."[3] The strength and cohesion given to the local trade unions by the city centrals, combined with the fact that the locals of the various cities were forming national trades unions, led in turn to a rather profuse growth of employers' associations, especially in the building trades of the cities. As during the first quarter of the century, the employers sought the aid of the courts, in addition to attempting to maintain open shops and black-listing men with union affiliation or sympathies. Between 1829 and 1842 there were eight recorded prosecutions of labor organizations for conspiracy.[4] But the

[1] S. Perlman, *History of Trade Unionism* . . . , p. 19.

[2] *Ibid.*, p. 19. For detailed account of the growth of this unionism, see Edward Mittleman in Commons and Associates, *op. cit.*, vol. 1, pp. 335–337.

[3] S. Perlman, *History of Trade Unionism* . . . , p. 21.

[4] These cases are discussed by Edward Mittleman in Commons and Associates, *op. cit.*, vol. 1, pp. 401–412.

judicial tide was beginning to turn, and the percentage of convictions in conspiracy cases was lower than it had been during the previous periods of employer resort to the courts.[1]

This organized opposition on the part of the employers was one cause of the several attempts to federalize the workers in all crafts into one national organization; the other cause of greatest importance was the desire for still wider solidarity that was engendered by the unity of action of the several trades in the various city centrals. In 1834 the General Trades' Union of New York invited delegates from the city centrals elsewhere[2] to attend a convention called "to advance the moral and intellectual condition and pecuniary interests of the laboring class . . . and . . . promote the establishment of trade unions in every section of the United States" and as a result of action taken by the convention there was established the National Trades' Union—the first federated body in the United States attempting to bring within its membership all local unions, nationals, and city centrals.[3] Headed by Ely Moore, then labor candidate for Congress as well as president of the New York Trades' Union, the National Trades' Union nevertheless squelched at the outset the attempts of the intelligentsia to turn it primarily into the political arena. Its functions were, it is true, never any too clearly defined, and it apparently was able to exercise only such power as the member bodies chose to let it have. For a time it undertook for the member unions the administration and payment of strike benefits, attempted to restrict the entrance of women and children into the labor market, and carried on propaganda for free public schools and factory legislation. Its most important single achievement was the final securing of the ten-hour day for government employees.[4] It never, however, became a truly effective coordinator of the efforts of the member national unions and city centrals.

The attempt to establish an all-inclusive federation having failed to realize the optimistic expectations originally underlying it, the organized

[1] Of the eight recorded prosecutions between 1829 and 1842, the workingmen were convicted in two cases, in two others the courts sustained demurrers to the indictments, in three the defendants were acquitted after jury trials, and the outcome of the eighth case is unknown. S. Perlman, *History of Trade Unionism* . . . , p. 25.

[2] The delegates actually attending this meeting were from the trades' unions, or city centrals, of New York, Philadelphia, Boston, Brooklyn, Poughkeepsie, and Newark.

[3] Probably needless to say, the New England Association of Farmers, Mechanics, and Other Workmen of the preceding period cannot be regarded as an attempt to federalize all unions, since it was based upon the idea of one big union inclusive of all manual workers rather than upon the idea of federation of units sovereign except in so far as they voluntarily delegated power to the central body.

[4] President Van Buren signed the order establishing the ten-hour day for government employees and persons employed by contractors doing government work, on Mar. 31, 1840, after the National Trades' Union had gone out of existence.

labor movement in 1835 and 1836 began to fall back upon job control and national organization along craft lines. During 1835 and 1836, at least five trades held national conventions and organized on a national basis.[1] Both the widening of competitive areas as a result of improvement in the means of transportation[2] and rising prices necessitated organization. Then, in 1837 came the financial panic and within a short time almost every form of labor organization—from the local trades societies to the National Trades' Union—was wiped out. Moreover, the depression brought a readiness on the part of the workers to listen to, and to follow, a group of reformers and intellectuals who were all too ready to depreciate the virtues of business unionism and to dangle before the masses the particular "ism" that would bring emancipation from industrial slavery. It was the heyday of the intellectual; never again did he find the labor movement quite so willing to accept, without question or qualification, his pronunciamentos as to its manifest destiny.

HUMANITARIAN ASPIRATIONS: THE ISMS OF 1837–1852

An era of frenzied speculation and monetary instability culminated in the panic of 1837; then, for more than a decade, depression darkened the economic landscape, relieved by only occasional and sporadic periods of prosperity. Economic conditions prompted the wage earners to search for a better type of economic order, and a concurrence of social, intellectual, and religious unrest rendered fertile the soil for propagation of schemes promising speedy advent of a new social system. Out of the conjunction of humanitarianism, utopias, economic stargazing, and bizarre reforms characterizing the period 1837–1852, several generalizations of significance in the interpretation of the history of the American labor movement emerge.

As has been said, this period more than any other was characterized by the superimposition of the ideology of the intellectual upon the labor movement; it was dominated, for a while, by men and women of the educated class—persons keenly sensitive to the inequalities of the economic system and the hardships of the workers and prone to regard abolition of these inequalities and hardships as a personal responsibility. Indeed, an enumeration of the men and women who became proponents of the Fourier gospel of Association, accepted by thousands of the laboring people, is an enumeration of "many of the leading historians, essayists, orators, journalists, poets, and artists of America at that

---

[1] National Cooperative Association of Journeymen Cordwainers, National Typographical Society, the Comb Makers, the Carpenters, and the Hand Loom Weavers. From Commons and Associates, *op. cit.*

[2] It will be recalled that the Erie Canal was completed in 1825, for the first time making possible transportation of goods by water from the Great Lakes to the Atlantic.

time."[1] But of the long-run effects of the espousal of the programs of the intellectuals there can be little question. Labor looked upon the promised land, was allured by the bird's-eye view, but upon closer scrutiny found it was not altogether congenial to American predispositions. Moreover, discovery quickly emerged that the intellectuals had become so immersed in the massive structure of their schemes that they had given little thought to the prosaic and practical details necessary to effect their realization or else, equally bad, that the plans had been developed in such manifold and overwhelming detail as to inhibit wage-earner disposition to adopt them. Out of the experience there emerged the conviction—adhered to for a time, but only for a time—that labor must develop its own home-grown philosophy and programs.

In the second place, the strongly individualistic predilections of the American worker, the desire to restore equality of economic opportunity for all members of all classes, rather than to perfect rigid job control, came into clear relief during this period, especially in the agitation for land reform and in the establishment of producers' cooperative workshops. The current discontent of the masses manifested itself, in no small part, in their attempts to extricate themselves from the wage system by one means or another—a manifestation the moral of which was that the workers were ready to approach their problems as wage earners, rather than as potential small-scale proprietors, or owners of self-governing workshops, or members of model communities, only when the scope of group or class action was distinctly limited. In the third place, the experience of this period demonstrated, even if in somewhat less unmistaken fashion than a later one, the fear with which the people of nineteenth-century America regarded any movement encroaching upon the rights of property. George Henry Evans's agrarianism, centering around the vast American domain, was indeed free from some of the more alarming implications of Thomas Skidmore's earlier agrarianism, and the growing American community, immensely pleased with itself, found little cause for alarm in the utopian indiscretions of Charles A. Dana or Horace Greeley; but assertion of the inalienable rights of propertyless men—not of the railroad stock companies or the promoters of new enterprise—to part of the national domain was a bit disturbing to men of property, and some phases of producers' cooperation were regarded as subversive. The militant resistance elicited by movements to curb the rights of property was impressed forcefully upon the American workers. Finally, in this period, as in so many others, there was to be noted the effect of business depression upon the attitudes and policies of organized labor. The panic of 1837 brought an end to most of the existing trade unionism, and during the depression years that followed the workers were

[1] H. E. Hoagland in Commons and Associates, *History of Labor in the United States,* vol. 1, p. 502.

more ready to turn to panaceas and schemes of universal reform than to rehabilitation of their job-control organizations.

The Association movement of the 1840's, the effort to establish a mode of social and economic life in which an all-compelling principle of attraction would draw men together in cooperative effort, eliminate industrial chaos and wasteful competition, and multiply tremendously the physical output of goods and services, had its antecedents in earlier attempts to effect, via the model-community route, reorganization of society.   Robert Owen's scheme of communistic societies flowered briefly during the New Harmony days of the mid-1820's, but during the ten years preceding 1837 its influence upon the labor movement—aside from the furnishing of such personalities as Robert Dale Owen and Frances Wright—was slight.   But while Owenism appeared to have failed, not all of Owen's followers were willing to admit failure, and after the panic in 1837 Owenite societies sprang up in numerous places, and several communities of the species Owen had envisaged were projected.[1]   This community movement made little headway, but the Owen ideal of a reorganized society remained and found its expression in the Fourier program of Association,[2] a most unusual conjunction of fantastic notions and homely common sense.   Glaring wastes and inefficiencies were, Fourier held, an inevitable concomitant of the competitive system, psychic disharmonies resulted from the antagonism of the institutions of modern civilization to the free play of man's natural impulses, and the ever-present principle of "attraction"—a force impelling men to cooperative effort rather than to competition with each other—was being thwarted. For the socialism of Robert Owen, which was characterized by paternalism, concentration of authority, and the idea of a community of goods, Fourier and his more fundamentalist followers had little sympathy.[3]

[1] In fact, some of the phalanxes established by the Fourierites, whose philosophy on some points differed appreciably from Owenism, were to be regarded in part as being also Owenite experiments.   In January, 1841, the *Herald of the New Moral World and Millenial Harbinger* appeared in New York as the organ of a revived Owenism, and an "Owen Society of Rational Religionists" was established about the same time.   The most prominent leader of this revived Owenite movement was John A. Collins, who founded the Skaneateles (New York) Community, an antislavery experiment based upon Owen's principles.   H. E. Hoagland, *op. cit.*, p. 504.

[2] Fourier was born in 1772 and died in 1837.   The best volume in English setting forth his doctrines is *Selections from the Works of Charles Fourier*, edited by Charles Gide (Julia Franklin, trans., 1901).

[3] Fourier once observed that Owen's plan for "a community of goods is so pitiful that it is not worthy of repudiation."   He also wrote: "A sect directed by Mr. Owen claims to have founded the associative state.   The facts are all to the contrary.   His group, by false methods which are in every respect contrary to the nature of attraction, is working to discredit the idea of association.   Moreover, the Owenite sect has attracted neither savage nor civilized neighbors; not a tribe or province in the United States has been willing to adopt this monastic regime of community of goods, this semi-atheism or avoidance of

Rather, their emphasis was placed upon the efficiency that would be attained when human impulses or "passions" were given full sway, and when society had been so organized that the instincts or impulses of men were combined into a mechanism producing "coincidence in every respect between individual interest and collective interest." The unit of organization in the new and better social system was to be the phalanx, a community of about 1,500 people living a primarily agricultural life; within each phalanx individuals were to be associated with each other in "series" composed of those having common interests, and formal government would be little needed. All producers' goods and land were to be the property of the phalanx, but private property and inheritance would not be abolished, for individuals could buy, continue to own, and bequeath stock in the phalanx, and consumer goods would be privately owned.[1]

The promise of a society in which man's productive powers would be multiplied, in which poverty would be abolished and leisure increased, in which evil would disappear and culture would become more spacious, in which the sordidness of mechanical work would be superseded by the beauty of self-expression, and in which wealth would become the servant rather than the master of man was alluring to the intellectual leaders of a decade of social and economic ferment, and from them the idea of Association filtered down to the labor organizations. The paternalistic and authoritarian character of Robert Owen's plans had never appealed greatly to the skeptical and restive ones of America's middle-class intelligentsia—which rejected the notion of the "natural rights" philosophers that the troubles of the wage earners and other real producers were due to control by monopolists of natural rights—but the Fourier notion that society was suffering from the pernicious effects of free competition[2] did. Possibly the wage earners were not aware of the extent to which political action and the thesis of class antagonism had been by implication repudiated by the espousal of Fourierism; in any event, they harkened to the voice of the intellectual, and for a time the appeal of the Association program to a group economically submerged but psychologically opposed to accepting the tenets of proletarianism was powerful. During the early 1840's, more than forty phalanxes were

---

religion, and other monstrosities which Mr. Owen dignifies by the name of association." From *Œuvres complètes*, vol. 2, quoted by Donald Wagner in *Social Reformers*, p. 219, The Macmillan Company, New York.

[1] Among the many good brief accounts of the doctrines of Fourier and of the spread of Fourierism in the United States during the 1840's are those to be found in J. H. Noyes, *History of Socialism in the United States*, Donald Wagner, *Social Reformers*, Gustavus Myers, *History of American Idealism*, Harry W. Laidler, *History of Socialist Thought*, and Lewis Mumford, *Story of the Utopias*.

[2] For fuller discussion of this difference between the doctrines of Owenism and those of Fourierism, see H. E. Hoagland, *op. cit.*, pp. 498–499.

established, and as many more were proposed, in localities as widely separated as Illinois and Massachusetts.[1]

But the mortality rate was terrific. Bad financing appears to have been a characteristic rather than an exceptional feature; constant friction over wage arrangements gave eloquent proof of how hateful practitioners of friendly cooperation could be to one another; the leadership of professional reformers was on the whole a handicap rather than an asset; trade-union support of an idea merely espoused by, not germinated within, the labor bodies could not be counted upon with certainty; and the nonconformist character of the people who always participate first in such a movement proved to be a drawback. On the average, each phalanx survived only a little more than three years, and by the early 1850's the movement had for the most part run its course.

From the point of view of trade unionism, the effects were of a character hardly to be mistaken. Attention of the workers was distracted from real remedies, and the development of a stable union movement was impeded. On the other hand, the temporary indiscretion had the effect of convincing many wage earners that they must face their problems as wage earners, not as potential members of a social order that had no wage system; and the concentration of effort upon trade-union activities between 1852 and the Civil War reflected this conviction. In the third place, the remoteness of the movement from the thinking of the great American middle class, which labor had never dared completely to alienate, redounded adversely to organized labor. While Associationism was sponsored by intellectuals who were, at least in point of birth and early environment, of the middle class, the mass of business and professional people either looked upon their efforts with tolerant cynicism or else regarded them as something threatening the *status quo*. Neither attitude brought to labor any support from an economic and social class whose support it greatly needed. Finally, the digression from trade unionism to utopianism demonstrated the falsity of the notion that there was enough class consciousness among the workers to make them ready to set about building the structure of a new society via the model community route. While the very lack of proletarian consciousness among the American workers was one reason why a movement of this type appealed so strongly to them for a time, this psychology had its limits as well as its possibilities for action. The rank and file found, very shortly, that they were more interested in pre-emption acts and abundant credit for their cooperative enterprises—means of elevating their status within the existing social framework—than in peaceably building another social order.

[1] For details see H. E. Hoagland in Commons and Associates, vol. 1, pp. 501–506.

Producers' and consumers' cooperation, which taken together can be regarded as the second major "ism" of the period, may be placed, a bit arbitrarily, halfway between the idealistic reform philosophies and "pure and simple" trade unionism. Both reflected the influence of the intellectuals, but both stemmed in part, also, from the reaction of the workers to inadequate incomes and increasing difficulty in the attainment of proprietorship status. Especially did producers' cooperation harmonize well with the equality-of-opportunity, antimonopoly bent of the typical wage earner.[1] If the capitalist boss would not otherwise be got rid of, and if immediate attainment of the status of individual proprietorship seemed impossible, then the best alternative was a cooperative system of "self-bossing." In fact, "so well did the quest for an individualistic alternative to the wage system by the route of 'cooperative individualism' harmonize with the basic character traits of the American worker that a crop of cooperative failures in one decade would prove futile as a warning to the next, down to the middle of the eighties, when the Knights of Labor made their experiment, the most far-reaching yet attempted."[2] When in 1836 the trade societies began to lose their strikes, and then in and after 1837 found themselves relatively helpless in the face of financial panic and business depression, it was accordingly rather in the expected course of events that they would turn to producers' cooperation.[3] The cordwainers working on ladies' shoes opened a "manufactory" of their own in Philadelphia in June, 1836, and the movement spread to other trades and other cities.[4] During the decade of the forties similar attempts were made by the molders and other trade unionists, and following the failure of strikes in 1850 and 1851 the cooperative ventures multiplied. The German elements of the working population, influenced by the cooperationist doctrines of Wilhelm

[1] As is indicated later (cf. infra, pp. 52–53, 67), producers' cooperation continued to appeal strongly to the American workers until the turn of the century. Since the stabilization of the labor movement, characterized by the decline of the Knights of Labor and the rise of the American Federation of Labor, however, the ideal of the self-governing workshop has played a relatively small part in determining the objectives and methods of labor organizations. On the other hand, enthusiasm for consumers' cooperation has more or less periodically revived after periods when the movement has been relatively quiescent.

[2] S. Perlman, A Theory of the Labor Movement, pp. 191–192.

[3] Producers' cooperation was not an original contribution of the period here under survey, although prior to the second half of the 1830's its importance in the labor movement as a whole had been small. The earliest American self-governing workshop is believed to have been the one established in Philadelphia in 1791, when striking house carpenters retaliated against their employers by offering to undertake contracts for 25 per cent less than the price charged by the masters. S. Perlman, History of Trade Unionism . . . , p. 30.

[4] For details, see ibid., p. 31, and H. E. Hoagland in Commons and Associates, op. cit., pp. 506–519.

Weitling,[1] were particularly sympathetic toward the self-governing workshop.

Producers' cooperation proved to be no satisfactory substitute for trade unionism. It competed strongly for the interest, support, and financial resources of the labor organizations, and to the extent that it was successful in its appeal it rendered the trade unions weaker when they faced the employer on bargain day. Moreover, there seemed to develop between the two movements a grave incompatibility. A cooperative, to be successful, had to cut costs and undersell other producers; indirectly, therefore, the effect was to underbid other labor. Also, the majority of those cooperative workshops which did attain a modicum of success really ceased to be cooperatives and worked with hired labor. The producers' cooperation movement for a time receded into the background, although only to re-emerge, more vigorous and vocal, in the 1870's and 1880's.

Consumers' cooperation, first tried on a large scale in the forties, carried with it the appeal of a lower cost of living and of elimination of wastes in distribution, rather than the promise of escape from wage-earner to proprietorship status. Several factors combined during the fifth decade of the century to give impetus to the movement.[2] The idealism that quickly attached to the 1840 experiment of the Rochdale pioneers in England fired the imagination of some of the workers and of perhaps more of their middle-class friends. There was, it became apparent, no fundamental incompatibility between trade unionism and consumers' cooperation such as the vicissitudes of producers' cooperation were beginning to indicate obtained between it and trade unionism. Industrial conditions were also favorable to the movement, particularly in New England. A series of strikes during 1843 and 1844 had been unsuccessful, and this failure, combined with the fact that thousands of women and girls were employed under most unsatisfactory conditions, stimulated the interest of humanitarians in the lot of the workers. Many of these humanitarians seized upon the idea of consumers' cooperation as a means of alleviating the distress then so prevalent. A New

---

[1] A well-known German communist who settled in America about 1850. The cooperative movement among the Germans was to a great extent identified with the name of Weitling.

[2] Consumers' cooperation efforts had appeared sporadically before the 1840's. What is believed to have been the first attempt occurred in Philadelphia in 1829. The New England Association of Farmers, Mechanics, and Other Workmen (cf. supra, pp. 29–30) in 1831 discussed distributive cooperation at length, and half a dozen attempts were mentioned in the *Cooperator*, published in Utica, in 1832 (S. Perlman, *History of Trade Unionism* . . . , p. 33). In general, the cooperatives prior to the middle of the 1840's sought to effect a saving by purchasing in large quantities goods that were then broken up and distributed at a slight advance over original cost to meet expenses.

England Protective Union[1] was established under the stimulus of the agitation for consumers' cooperation, with ultimate objectives more far-reaching than minor economies in the purchase of goods, and in 1852 this organization embraced 403 consumer-cooperative divisions, 167 of which reported a capital of $241,712 and 165 of which announced annual sales of $1,696,825.[2] The American cooperative movement incorporated the British principles of open membership, equal voting by members irrespective of shares, sales for cash, and federation of the various societies for wholesale purposes, but it differed from it in that goods were ordinarily sold at cost (or at enough above cost to cover operation expenses) instead of at market prices. Had the Civil War not interrupted[3] the progress of the cooperative movement, the tradition that consumers' cooperation and trade unionism are two almost coordinate arms of the labor movement might have become firmly entrenched; but the disturbed social and economic conditions of the War years very nearly annihilated the consumer-cooperative movement.

Model communities might have proved to be a delusion and producers' workshops a source of friction rather than of labor solidarity, but there still remained thousands of acres of fertile land, awaiting the labor of man. To it the American worker looked for ultimate protection of his superior status and for elevation out of the wage-earning class. So long as a section of land could be had practically for the taking, wages in urban occupations would have to approximate roughly the productivity of labor as applied to land, and transition from wage-earning to proprietorship status would be easy. But the villain of the piece was the monopolistic land grabber. Ever since the adoption of the Constitution in 1787, speculators and slave owners had found it comparatively easy to secure ownership of large tracts of the Western lands;[4] the mission of the wage-earning class and its friends accordingly was a reform in public policy with reference to the national domain that would insure to the common man his inalienable right to this gift of nature.

Land Reform—sometimes designated as the "new agrarianism of the forties"—stemmed in part from Spencean antecedents. George Henry

---

[1] This union, established in 1845, was called the Working Men's Protective Union until 1849. A schism, based chiefly upon personal differences, resulted in 1853 in the formation of a separate secessionist organization, the American Protective Union.

[2] From detail presented in S. Perlman, *History of Trade Unionism* . . . , pp. 33–34.

[3] Interrupted it for reasons that are fairly apparent: the withdrawal of men into the military establishment, the influx of foreigners, who replaced the native-born, into New England towns as a result of the wartime demand for labor and the exodus of Americans who enlisted, and the uncertain state of trade, which frightened shareholders and made them willing to see the cooperative enterprises pass into the hands of private tradesmen.

[4] The conflict among different groups wishing opportunity to control the Western lands was, of course, an important issue in the Constitutional Convention, where the will of the "men of property" finally prevailed. The entire story is excellently traced in Charles A. Beard's *An Economic Interpretation of the Constitution*.

Evans had been temporarily associated with Thomas Skidmore, and his paper, the *Workingmen's Advocate*, had for a while been vocal on behalf of the equal-division program, but with the passing of time his early radicalism became tempered with consciousness of political actualities and of the inherent conservatism of the American community when property interests were at stake.   Moreover, it so happened that in the United States there was no necessity to break up great estates or seize on behalf of the economically submerged land already held by private owners; there was government land in abundance.   Evans's program accordingly resolved itself into homestead laws under which the public lands would become the property of settlers without price, limitation on the size of farms to prevent concentration of ownership in the hands of monopolists, and exemption of homesteads from seizure for debt.   The public domain was to be divided into "rural republican townships," and the individual's right to the resources of nature was even to be protected against himself by governmental edict that the homestead should be inalienable.

In its ideology, the land-reform movement of this period lacked the nicely seasoned theoretical substance that, under Henry George, it acquired in the seventies; it never so thoroughly captivated those who are ever intrigued by propositions that must be reasoned out on a theoretical plane.   Evans apparently sensed only vaguely (although Ricardo's *Principles of Political Economy* was available for him who chose to read) the significance of unearned increment in land.   Certainly mathematical illustrations of intensive and extensive margins of cultivation, of rent land and no-rent land, were of minor importance in the agitational loquacity of the day.   To Evans it was sufficient that man's right to life implied his right to use the materials necessary for existence, and the message his program conveyed to the workers was one they wanted to hear: that opportunity existed in abundance, but that sinister interests were singling them out as a group to be denied participation in it.

Like producers' cooperation, land reform harmonized well with the character traits of the American worker.   Its appeal was individualistic, not collectivist; its promise was economic equality within a system of private property, not conservation of the limited opportunity of a permanent wage-earning group.   Labor papers espoused Evans's doctrines with alacrity; Horace Greeley's *New York Tribune* endorsed the homestead movement in 1845; a National Reform Convention in New York that same year resulted in the creation of an Industrial Congress and local Industrial Brotherhoods to promote land reform; and petitions and memorials were showered upon Congress.   Evans and his followers were convinced that labor could not achieve its objectives through a party of its own, and the nonpartisan policy of bargaining with individual

candidates irrespective of their party affiliation was accordingly adopted.[1]
To a very real extent the political tactics were successful. Tammany
harkened, then bargained, then endorsed the program;[2] the Tennessee
congressman, Andrew Johnson, introduced the first homestead bill in
1845; and by supporting the Free Soilers and others who formed the
Republican Party, the land reformers as a reward secured the Homestead
Act of 1862. Not all that they wanted was conceded to them when
President Lincoln affixed his signature to the 1862 bill, and the granting
of free homesteads was accompanied by huge land grants to the railroads. Nevertheless, land was made available to the propertyless of the
nation, and the principle of homestead exemption became almost universally adopted. The tendency toward concentration of land ownership
was checked, and of the fact that the change in land policy aided in
protecting the superior status of the workers there can be little question.

Yet it is possible that this very strengthening of the economic position
of the workers as individuals retarded the development of a stable trade-
union movement. As Professor Perlman has persuasively contended,[3]
trade unionism and land reform include elements of basic incompatibility.
The former starts from the premise that institutional arrangements have
limited the opportunities of individual workers and that therefore they
must practice solidarity in conserving and protecting such as are available
for the group as a whole; the latter proceeds from a premise of abundance
of opportunity that is inhibitory of collective action and subordination of
individual immediate interests to those of the group. The point of
incompatibility between the two movements can, of course, easily be
overworked, but recognition must be given the fact that trade unionism
often seemed less attractive to workers of the individualistic American
environment than did private ownership of small segments of property,
and that land reform entrenched—so long as there was free land—the
latter alternative.

[1] Professor Ware (*Labor in Modern Economic Society*, p. 170) has said: "George Henry
Evans may be regarded as the inventor of what later became the 'non-partisan' political
policy of the American Federation of Labor." To characterize him as "the inventor" of
the policy is perhaps going a trifle too far; certainly, however, the success attained by the
movement—even though the Homestead Act of 1862 did not carry out the broad principles
of inalienability and land limitations—constituted as important a demonstration as had
yet been given of the efficacy of the nonpartisan method.

[2] In May, 1851, a mass meeting was held in Tammany Hall "of all those in favor of
land and other industrial reform, to be made elements in the presidential campaign of
1852" and a platform proclaiming man's right to the soil and urging that freedom of public
lands be endorsed by the Democratic Party was adopted. This meeting nominated as
the Democratic candidate (*i.e.* endorsed, for consideration of the coming Democratic
convention) Senator Isaac A. Walker of Wisconsin. S. Perlman, *History of Trade Unionism* . . . , p. 38.

[3] See *A Theory of the Labor Movement*, pp. 182–187.

The dominance of the isms during this period should not, however, obscure from view the unostentatious trade unions that operated throughout. Some of the old locals that survived the panic of 1837 showed signs of renewed life as the period progressed, and toward the end of the 1840's new ones began appearing a bit more frequently. For the most part these locals were small affairs, often failing to make their voices heard in the confusion of tongues that accompanied phalanxism, cooperation, and land reform. No very serious attempt to federate all craft locals into one national organization appears to have been made, and not until after 1850 were attempts to bring the locals of the crafts or trades into national craft unions rewarded with any success. But one great movement of the period, the struggle for the ten-hour day, was primarily trade union rather than uplift, humanitarian, or utopian. It sprang from the mentality of the trade unionist, not from that of the intellectual. In part, to be sure, the movement proceeded along the legislative route, aiming at limitation of the hours of women workers in order to eliminate their competition for jobs, but in part it took the form of economic pressure upon the employers. Outside of the building industry, where craftsmen in the larger Eastern cities had secured the ten-hour day by 1835 and where the shorter work day began during the 1840's to be attained in smaller places, the ten-hour crusade did not immediately affect the work period of a large number of employees.[1] Average daily hours of factory workers in 1840 have been estimated at 11.4,[2] and in spite of the ten-hour agitation and the strikes accompanying it, no pronounced downward trend began to manifest itself until the middle of the 1850's.

"SAFE AND SANE" UNIONISM, 1852–1860

It is not difficult to explain the abandonment of the broad philosophies of the humanitarian period and the revival of trade unionism during the early 1850's. The workers had had enough, for a time, of the intellectuals and their "isms"; they were resentful of the paucity of practical accomplishment; they looked upon depleted treasuries that were painful reminders of effort that had come to little or nothing. They became convinced that the battle must be fought out on the economic front, with the strategy that of trade unionism and the ideology that incubated by labor's own bitter experience. This conviction was strengthened, in turn, by the industrial developments of the decade just preceding the Civil War. The American industrial revolution may be said, with a little dogmatism, to have begun about 1840, when the use of anthracite coal gave impetus

---

[1] For details about the ten-hour movement of the 1840's see H. E. Hoagland in Commons and Associates, *op. cit.*, pp. 536–547.

[2] See vol. I of this series, pp. 465–485, where facts about trends in the length of the work day and week are summarized. The early legislation limiting the hours of women workers is discussed on pp. 527–528 of the same volume.

to the iron and steel industry. By 1855 the Bessemer process had become commercially feasible. Textiles had been on a factory basis since the 1820's. Between 1840 and 1860—Sumner's "golden age"—the wealth of the people of the United States is estimated to have increased 126 per cent,[1] while population increased from 17,000,000 to 31,000,000, and the number of men engaged in manufactures having an output of $500 a year or more from 791,000 to 1,311,000. According to the Census of 1840, the total value of manufactured products was $483,278,000; in 1850 it was $1,019,106,000; and in 1860, $1,885,861,000. Along with industrialization of the country went increasing urbanization, the percentage of the total population living in places of 8,000 or more inhabitants increasing from 8.5 in 1840 to 12.5 in 1850 and 16.1 in 1860.

Inevitably this industrialization drew sharper lines of demarcation between the propertyless workers and employer-capitalists, and made excursions into the realm of utopianism and humanitarianism inexpedient for workers who wanted to protect their immediate economic interests. Rising prices[2] rendered the efforts of the wage earners to keep wages from lagging behind living costs a more than sufficient task, and the business depressions that accompanied the industrialization of the "golden age" were not long enough once more to turn the thoughts of the workers to grandiose panaceas and schemes of universal reform. Improved transportation was another factor dictating that unionism, in its own interest, eschew the glittering and all-embracing programs that would distract from business efficacy. The first railroad in the modern sense, the Baltimore and Ohio, had commenced operation in 1830, and although the last tie of the Union Pacific, connecting Chicago and the Pacific Coast, was not to be laid until 1869, the railway mileage of the country increased from 2,800 in 1840 to 30,600 in 1860. The broadening of the market that came under the influence of improved transportation strengthened the movement toward national organization of labor along craft lines, since the widening of the competitive area undermined the ability of local organizations to control wages and conditions in the face of underbidding elsewhere.

To writers of American social history, the unionism of this period has seemed to be of scant significance, probably because of the way it was obscured by the absorbing premonitions of the Civil War. And, indeed, its effect upon the general level of wages and upon conditions in general

---

[1] Absolute, not per capita.

[2] *Cf.* vol. I of this series, pp. 80–82. The cost of living, as is indicated by the data there presented, rose from 73 in 1850 to 82 in 1860 (1913 = 100), or about 12 per cent. During this period money wages rose from 43 to 47 (same base year), or failed to increase quite as rapidly as the cost of living. Professor Hansen's index numbers, which are utilized in the data here summarized, showed real wages to have been 59 (1913 base) in 1850 and 57 in 1860.

cannot have been great. It was confined to the more skilled trades, and scarcely had it got under way when its power was undermined, first by the panic of 1857 and then by the outbreak of war. But its vigor for a time is beyond question. Locals were formed in the skilled trades of most of the cities, and—as a revival on a larger scale of a tendency manifest between 1834 and 1837[1]—these locals of the various trades joined together in nationwide organizations. The National Typographical Union saw the light of day in 1852, the Locomotive Engineers and the Hat Finishers in 1854, the United Cigarmakers' Union and the National Protective Association in 1856, and the Iron Molders and the Machinists and Blacksmiths in 1859.[2] In at least half a dozen other trades attempts at national organization were made, and collective bargaining was established on a firmer basis than during the previous period of "pure and simple" unionism (1834–1837). But at the first impact of business depression in 1857 the weaker nationals disintegrated and many of the locals became ineffective.

CIVIL WAR UNIONISM, 1860–1867

The initial effects of the Civil War upon unionism were, naturally, extremely adverse. In the face of the dislocation of industry, the paralysis of business that accompanied the outbreak of hostilities and the temporary increase in unemployment, the introduction of machinery under the pressure for increased production and the consequent displacement of workers, the movement of trade-union members from their normal pursuits into the military establishment, and the rise of prices with an accompanying decline in real wages, the labor organizations found themselves virtually incapable of effective defensive action. Nearly all of those that had survived the depression of 1857 disappeared. By 1863, however, war conditions had begun to have the opposite effect. Prices continued to soar as the printing presses turned out more greenbacks, and by 1865 the cost of living was perhaps 75 per cent above its 1860 level. Real earnings, on the other hand, were approximately (as an average for all industrial groups) one-third lower.[3] Labor was

---

[1] It will be recalled (*supra*, p. 33) that five nationals are known to have been formed during these years, and possibly there were more.

[2] From detail presented by H. E. Hoagland, *op. cit.*, pp. 620–623, and S. Perlman, *History of Trade Unionism* . . . , pp. 40–41. Among other national unions formed or attempted before the Civil War, of which Mr. Hoagland found evidence, were the Upholsterers' National Union, the Plumbers' National Union, the National Union of Building Trades, the Mechanics' Trades Union Association of the United States, the Lithographers' National Union, the National Convention of Silver Platers, the Painters' National Union, the Cordwainers' National Union, the National Cotton Mule Spinners' Association of America, and the Journeymen Stone Cutters' Association of the United States and Canada.

[3] For details concerning the movement of real earnings during the Civil War period, see vol. I of this series, p. 82.

driven to organize along trade-union lines. The abnormal demand for goods, combined with a shortage of man power, put the workers in a distinctly more strategic position, and the trade-union movement gained momentum.[1]

In its pattern and development, the unionism of the Civil War years followed the unionism of the 1830's. Local organizations appeared in the skilled trades; these locals were combined into city centrals, or trades' assemblies; and national organization along trade lines experienced substantial growth after about 1863. Some of these nationals were able to maintain their existence throughout the years of depression and very spotty prosperity of the 1870's, calmly treading the trade-union way while political excursions and uplift aberrations were at their height, and it was around them that there was built, some eighteen or twenty years later, a federated unionism, standing for business tactics and conservation of job opportunity, as against the more grandiose type, predicated upon the notion of a community of economic interests throughout the working class and attempting to weld all the producing masses into a single organization. By the end of the 1860's at least thirty national trade unions were in existence, a few being holdovers from the preceding period but the majority new during the years of the conflict between the states. An attempt was made in 1864 to federate the several trades' assemblies (city centrals) into an International Industrial Assembly of North America, but "the time had passed for a national federation of city centrals"[2] and the Assembly lived only a short time. Total trade-union membership during the last years of the decade probably fell not far short of 300,000.[3]

EMERGENCE OF A NATIONAL LABOR MOVEMENT

To unravel all the strands that went into the making of the American labor movement from 1867 to 1886 still remains—in spite of the abundance of careful historical research and the excellence of numerous synthesizing accounts—a task of first magnitude. The period was, like that of the thirties and forties, one of contradictions and contrasts, working themselves out in a wider competitive area and on a bigger scale of prosperity and depression. Everything seemed pronounced, yet nothing very clear-cut. Trade unionism, demoralized though it was by the depressions of the 1870's, became on the whole increasingly vigorous and assertive, but it was interwoven—more closely and more inextricably than in the forties—with the imposing "isms" of the day. Utopianism

[1] See John B. Andrews in Commons and Associates, *History of Labor in the United States*, vol. 2, pp. 13–42, for detailed account of the trade-union developments of the Civil War period, here recorded only in summary form.

[2] S. Perlman, *History of Trade Unionism* . . . , p. 43.

[3] In addition to the permanent contribution of a few nationals that, some years later, formed the nucleus of a federated business unionism, the period of the Civil War also con-

and job-consciousness, German socialism and American trade unionism, the anarchism of the Black International and the religiosity of the Knights of Labor, Molly Maguires setting forth at midnight in the coal fields and East Side cigar makers vehemently debating the controverted points in Marx, federal troops squelching labor disturbances and a national labor organization asking for compulsory arbitration and enforcement of decisions, the pragmatic idealism of Mr. Samuel Gompers and the business pragmatism of Mr. Jay Gould, free land and free silver, Greenbackism and an Americanized version of the "economic labor" concept,[1] trade-union deprecation of strikes and trade-union instigation of some of the most bitter strikes in the nation's history, consumers' cooperation and the eight-hour day, producers' cooperation and Mr. Henry George, wage-earner support of private property and schemes to draw the fangs of capitalism, demands for labor legislation and tirades against the political state—all these enter into the confused picture.

The confusion of the labor movement during this period was, however, only a manifestation of the confusion of American economic and social life. The decades immediately following the Civil War were those of the growing pains of a young and husky industrialism, overfed and pampered by its doting governmental guardian. Southern agrarianism was, for a time, politically impotent, and Northern industrial interests made the most of their opportunity. Stimulated, first by the war demand for goods and then by protective tariffs and all manner of governmental aid, manufacturing enterprises expanded enormously—sometimes in excess of justification afforded by the expansion of the market for particular products. In economic life it was Charles A. Beard's period of "the triumph of business enterprise"; in politics it was Claude Bowers's

---

tributed the economic ideology of Ira Steward, which is to say that it contributed a doctrine destined to permeate the movement during the remainder of the nineteenth and on into the twentieth century. Steward's philosophy of the economic effects of the shorter working day has been discussed in an earlier volume of this series (vol. I, pp. 494–495), but it may be recalled here that the doctrine his name came to epitomize was much more than a bit of theorizing about the relationship between the standard of living, as affected by leisure, and worker incomes. Although Steward shared with some of his contemporary reformers a skepticism about the efficacy of trade unionism, and possibly never sensed all the implications of his own doctrine, it was impossible to espouse his panacea for economic ills, the eight-hour day, without seeing its corollary: concerted action on the economic front by those whose employment opportunities were subject to the same market forces. The spreading of the idea was, therefore, an important contribution in the building of the kind of unionism that finally survived in the United States, even though Stewardism itself may have been "only a half-way station between the antimonopoly individualism of the past and the self-confident trade unionism of the future." S. Perlman, *A Theory of the Labor Movement*, p. 194.

[1] That is, the notion that exclusively labor—not labor and the other real producers— organizations should be formed, functioning as economic, not political or broadly educational, bodies.

"the tragic era." Increasing industrialization was accompanied by—and was, of course, both cause and consequence of—the widening of competitive areas. The first transcontinental railroad was completed in 1869, and railroad mileage of the United States increased from 30,625 in 1860 to 167,191 in 1890. Both industrialization and widening of the competitive areas impressed upon the workers the need for group or class action, even if they did not immediately make clear the exact direction the group or class action should take.

Other developments were stimulating collective action on the part of the workers, bringing into clearer relief an antagonism of interest between the "plain people" and the beneficiaries of the industrialism of the era, and giving rise to philosophies that paraded in verbal wardrobes of many colors. While the wealth of the country was increasing, both absolutely and per capita,[1] concentration of ownership and control proceeded apace. Prices were falling, and the business depression of the seventies, as well as the halting character of the prosperity of the eighties, bred discontent. The impact of declining prices fell with particular force upon the debtor farmers[2] and brought into being a series of agrarian movements with which the urban labor movement became entangled, with retarding effect so far as development of a stable unionism was concerned. The growth of cities and the gradual appropriation, under the Homestead Acts, of the more desirable farm land brought to the fore the element of unearned increment in land, and made the program of Henry George—which was not job-conscious or trade-union in character—more appealing to many of the economically submerged than "pure and simple" unionism. The paucity of labor legislation encouraged the use of the political instrument as a means of ameliorating the conditions of the workers; immigration brought into the American working community the seeds of European socialism and at the same time created barriers—language difficulties, nationalistic hatreds, misunderstood folkways—to inclusive organization; mechanization of industrial processes increased the number of unskilled workers ready to assume a place in the labor movement.

At the end of the Civil War, the national unions were gaining strength and increasing in number, while almost every important city had its trade assembly. The Brotherhood of Locomotive Engineers had been formed in 1863, the Order of Railway Conductors saw the light of day in 1868, and the Brotherhood of Firemen and Enginemen in 1873. Outside of the transportation field, the carpenters, bricklayers, typographical workers, machinists, and other groups of craftsmen either formed national unions, reorganized existing nationals, or strengthened and

[1] *Cf.* vol. I, of this series, pp. 261–269.

[2] Real wages of industrial workers increased appreciably during this period, even though gains in the purchasing power of hourly rates and full-time weekly earnings were offset to an extent by widespread unemployment. See vol. I of this series, pp. 82–85.

extended—as in the case of the cigar makers—those already established
during the previous period. Although the Railroad Brotherhoods were
founded primarily as mutual benefit associations and evolved into business institutions, these national craft organizations were for the most
part bargaining institutions, with benefit features of secondary importance. During the three years 1870–1873 nine new national unions
appeared, and previously organized unions experienced substantial
growth.[1] Overshadowed both within and without the ranks of labor by
the National Labor Union and its individualistic panaceas though the
trade unions were, they constituted the real strength of the American
labor movement. Hours began to be limited by agreements with
employers, and the eight-hour movement reached its climax in the summer of 1872, when New York City experienced a general eight-hour
strike.[2]

Financial panic, then business depression, overtook the country
in 1873, and in the face of underlying economic forces the craft unions
found themselves comparatively helpless. To an extent, labor's reaction
was the same as during other periods of depression: a turning to panaceas,
an imbibing of the medicines that economic doctors prescribed as the
cure-all for economic ills, a search for the villains who were crushing
down upon the brow of labor its crown of thorns. But the spirit of
resentment expressed itself in a more militant economic movement,
as well as in espousal of the current isms. Between 1873 and 1878
strikes were frequent and sometimes violent,[3] the Molly Maguires[4]
terrorized the community with a success entirely disproportionate to
their strength and numbers; the judiciary came to the protection of

---

[1] S. Perlman, *History of Trade Unionism* . . . , p. 44. Estimates of trade-union
membership during this period varied greatly. In 1869 the *New York Herald* estimated it
to be about 170,000, and a labor leader at the same time claimed that the total was as high
as 600,000 (*ibid.*). As was stated earlier (*supra*, p. 46), probably trade-union membership
at the end of the 1860's fell not far short of 300,000.

[2] J. B. Andrews in Commons and Associates, *op. cit.*, vol. 3, pp. 42–84, and S. Perlman,
History of Trade Unionism . . . , p. 50.

[3] For an excellent account of these strikes, see S. Perlman, *op. cit.*, pp. 58–60, and for
more detailed account see J. B. Andrews in vol. 2 of Commons and Associates, *op. cit.*,
pp. 185–195.

[4] The Molly Maguires was an organization of terrorists—a kind of labor Ku Klux Klan.
Between 1871 and 1879 the Pennsylvania coal strikes gravitated, to a considerable extent,
into the hands of the Molly Maguires, and several of the Mollies, in turn, gravitated into
the hands of the Pinkerton detectives. The first national miners' organization, the
National Association of Miners, organized by John Siney in 1873, was destroyed in 1875
when the Molly Maguires got control (N. Ware, *Labor in Modern Industrial Society*, p. 320).
The terroristic activities of the Molly Maguires reached their climax in the railroad strikes
of 1877. The most authentic account of this organization is J. Walter Coleman's *The
Molly Maguire Riots* (1936). See also Louis Adamic's *Dynamite, The Story of Class Violence
in America*.

private property with injunctions against railroad strikes; and federal troops intervened in industrial disputes.[1] In general, the strikes failed, and for a time the workers seemed more interested in Greenbackism and consumers' cooperation. About 1879, however, trade-union membership again showed a tendency to increase substantially, and the year 1883 found nearly fifty nationals in existence, with a combined membership, it has been estimated,[2] of between 200,000 and 225,000. Early in 1885 total union membership probably was not greatly below 300,000. Collective bargaining began to be put upon a more stable basis, with sliding scales and systems of local and district conciliation and arbitration operative in the coal fields and elsewhere.

It is, however, in the attempts to consolidate all labor forces into a single organization that the mixture of trade unionism and uplift unionism characterizing the period comes into clearest relief. The National Labor Union, a politico-reform and trade-union society, was founded in 1866, and during the six tempestuous years of its existence it voiced an ideology that was more expressive of the purposes of uplift or anti-monopoly unionism than of the less romantic business type. Structurally, this organization was a loosely built federation of city trades' assemblies, national trade unions, local trade unions, and reform organizations ranging from those dominated by philosophical anarchists to those of the socialists and woman suffragists; and as a loose federation it was ill adapted to effective representation of the craft-union point of view.[3] Labor and the farmers—all the plain people of the nation—should become affiliated in one general organization; strikes should be regarded only as weapons of last resort and abolished entirely as soon as possible; easy money should be provided for the farmers and for the producers' cooperatives by an increase in the volume of United States notes outstanding and by provision for their redemption in government bonds rather than in specie; interest rates should be reduced by law and the procuring of profits above the wages of management made a conspiracy; the political instrument should be used to rectify the shortcomings of the national banking system and to protect American standards of

---

[1] Outbreaks of physical violence were fairly frequent, and in some cases order was restored only when federal troops arrived. The greatest of the strikes was on the Pennsylvania line, in and around Pittsburgh. The railroad yards were set on fire and damages of about $5,000,000 were caused. Order was restored in this case by patrols of citizens. Violence also characterized the southwestern railroad strikes, in spite of the industrially pacificist proclivities of the leader, Martin Irons. *Cf.* Terence V. Powderly's *The Path I Trod* (1940).

[2] By Commons and Associates, vol. 2, pp. 302–331, and by S. Perlman, *History of Trade Unionism* . . . , p. 82.

[3] For account of the National Labor Union, see J. B. Andrews in Commons and Associates, *op. cit.*, vol. 2, pp. 85–156, and Lewis Lorwin, *The American Federation of Labor*, pp. 7–9.

living from the competition of Oriental labor; both political action and trade agreements should be the means of protecting women workers and preventing their underbidding of adult males, maintaining the apprenticeship system, making the eight-hour day universal, and hastening the advent of a cooperative industrial system. As a movement seeking attainment of these ends, the National Labor Union reflected the aspirations and ideals of labor during the years immediately following the conflict between the states. A bit of detail concerning a few of the crusades expressive of these aspirations and ideals is in point.

When the first convention was held in 1866, unemployment was widespread. War industries were closing their plants, the economic dislocations incident to readjustment to peacetime conditions were disturbing the economy, and demobilized soldiers were being absorbed only slowly into gainful pursuits. Emphasis accordingly was placed upon the eight-hour day, to be attained chiefly by legislation. In part, the simple work-sharing and "lump of labor" or "work fund" notions actuated the eight-hour movement, but to a greater extent the philosophy of Ira Steward—with its intermingling of the ideas of higher standards of living as a causal factor in increasing wages and the demand for labor, of increased purchasing power to lift off the market the increased output of goods that was resulting from technological advances, and of increased physical productivity consequent upon the shorter work day or week[1]—predominated in the thinking of the leaders and of the rank and file.[2] The eight-hour day for employees of the Federal Government was attained in 1868, largely as a result of the propagandistic activities of the National Labor Union, and although expectation that the eight-hour day would quickly spread to private employment failed to materialize, the achievement encouraged resort to political tactics; it demonstrated that when labor concentrated upon a modest objective and exerted steady pressure, prospects securing desired legislation were not entirely hopeless. But the effort to bring about enactment of general eight-hour laws in the several industrialized states failed.[3]

[1] *Cf.* vol. I of this series, pp. 494–497.

[2] Ira Steward himself had a fundamental skepticism concerning the efficacy of trade unionism, and he preferred legislation to trade-union activity as a means of achieving the eight-hour day. In 1866, the year of the founding of the National Labor Union, Steward organized the Grand Eight-hour League of Massachusetts as a special propagandist organization (S. Perlman, *History of Trade Unionism* . . . , pp. 46–47). The League was a secret body, intended as the central organization of a chain of subordinate leagues in the state, and its establishment was followed by the appearance of Eight-hour Leagues in states other than Massachusetts.

[3] Eight-hour laws were, in fact, enacted in a number of the states, but they were largely ineffective because they permitted longer hours than the legal maxima when the contract of employment so specified and because they lacked provisions for effective enforcement. Several of the states enacted laws limiting the hours of women workers, although these

Other panaceas meanwhile engrossed the National Labor Union and its constituent organizations. Cooperative workshops were the next best thing to individual proprietorship, and an organization with such a strong producer-conscious, uplift bent could not but succumb to the lure. The motto of the Order of the Knights of St. Crispin,[1] then the largest trade union of the country, epitomized the place occupied by the self-governing workshop in the ultimate objectives of the wage earners of the late 1860's: "The present demand of the Crispin is steady employment and fair wages, but his future is self-employment."[2] Unsuccessful strikes during 1867 and 1868 only served to strengthen the conviction that in the establishment of cooperative shops rather than in trade-union activities lay the salvation of the workers. The Iron Molders, under the leadership of W. H. Sylvis,[3] opened ten or more cooperative foundries, all of which quickly found themselves in financial difficulties, and the bakers, coachmakers, collar makers, coal miners, shipwrights, machinists and blacksmiths, foundry workers, nailers, ship carpenters, calkers,

---

laws were subject, even if in somewhat lesser degree, to the shortcomings of the general eight-hour laws. For details concerning the hours legislation of this period, see J. B. Andrews in Commons and Associates, *op. cit.*, vol. 3, pp. 102–111, Commons and Andrews, *Principles of Labor Legislation* (1936 ed.), pp. 101–102, S. Perlman, *History of Trade Unionism . . .* , pp. 49–50, and vol. I of this series, pp. 527–529.

[1] For accounts of the Order of St. Crispin, see D. D. Lescohier, "The Knights of St. Crispin, 1867–1874," University of Wisconsin *Bulletin 355;* J. R. Commons and Others, *Documentary History of American Industrial Society*, vol. 3, pp. 51–54; and J. B. Andrews in Commons and Associates, *History of Labor in the United States*, vol. 2, pp. 76–79. This union of shoemakers was organized as a secret order early in 1867. Its numerous strikes were chiefly for the purpose of protecting the journeymen from the competition of "green hands" and apprentices, rather than to advance wages and shorten hours. Throughout its brief but meteoric career, however, it was strongly wedded to the ideal of cooperative self-employment. Defeated in a majority of its strikes and unsuccessful for the most part in its cooperative stores and cooperative workshops, the order went out of existence in 1874. A number of the Crispins later became leaders in the Knights of Labor.

[2] From the *American Workman*, June, 1869, quoted by J. B. Andrews, *op. cit.*, p. 79.

[3] W. H. Sylvis really deserves more than footnote mention in an account of American labor during the post-Civil War period, both because he symbolized the conviction of so many of the economically submerged that in political action and cooperation rather than in trade unionism were to be found their economic salvation and because of the enormous practical influence he exercised. He became president of the Iron Molders National Union in 1864, and the following year toured the country, preaching cooperation, the formation of a general national assembly, and independent political action. He was convinced that "pure and simple" trade unions were at best defensive organizations only, and that permanent reform would have to come through political action. Nonpartisan political action he definitely repudiated. "We have tried the balance of power or make-weight expedient of questioning candidates and throwing our votes in favor of such as endorsed or were pledged to our interests. How vain and futile this expedient has proven is known to all" (from James Sylvis, *The Life, Speeches, and Essays of William H. Sylvis*, p. 72, quoted by Norman Ware in *Labor in Modern Industrial Society*, p. 178). Monetary reform, he came to believe, "could so change the whole face of society as to do away with the necessity of trade unions entirely" (*ibid.*).

glass blowers, hatters, boilermakers, plumbers, tailors, printers, needle-women, and others joined in the movement.[1] A large proportion were the aftermath of unsuccessful strikes. But the sum-total effect of the ventures was much the same as in the forties: the cooperatives competed too strongly for the meager financial resources of the trade unions, they frequently found it necessary to cut prices and thus indirectly to underbid labor employed by capitalistic enterprises, and when successful they generally ceased to be real cooperatives and worked with hired labor. A movement for consumers' cooperation, preceding in point of time the height of enthusiasm for producers' cooperation, likewise ran its course during the six years of the life of the National Labor Union.[2]

Experience with producers' cooperation convinced many of the trade-union leaders that labor could not secure its "natural rights" while the credit system of the nation enabled "nonproducers" to accumulate wealth more rapidly than labor could create it, and this experience was in part responsible for the embracing, as one of the most revered isms, of monetary reform. Greenbackism had as its motivating force the desire to give the man without capital an opportunity in business equal to that of his rich competitor; as a labor movement, it was another mani-festation of the individualistic disposition of the nineteenth-century American wage earner. The bankers and the middlemen controlled the credit resources of the nation and restricted, in consequence, the oppor-tunity of the submerged. Patently, then, the remedy lay in govern-mental aid in furnishing capital and credit to the producers of physical products. The means, moreover, were already at hand.[3] The govern-ment need not resort to exercise of the power to tax in order to furnish capital to the workers, as Ferdinand Lassalle had advocated,[4] for the

---

[1] From the enumeration given by Professor Perlman, *History of Trade Unionism* . . . , p. 53. See also vol. 2 of Commons and Associates, *op. cit.*, pp. 111–119.

[2] The upswing of prices during the Civil War gave rise to a luxuriant crop of consumers' cooperatives. Thomas Phillips, a shoemaker, arrived in the United States from England in 1852, fired with evangelistic zeal for Rochdale principles, and under his inspiration the Union Cooperative Association was established in Philadelphia in 1862. By 1866 almost every industrial town between Boston and San Francisco had some form of distributive cooperation. After that year, the one of the founding of the National Labor Union, the movement for a time became less important. For details, see James P. Warbasse, *Cooperative Democracy*, J. B. Andrews, *op. cit.*, pp. 38–41, and S. Perlman, *History of Trade Unionism* . . . , pp. 52–53.

[3] For an account of Greenbackism as a labor movement, *cf.* J. B. Andrews, *op. cit.*, 118–124.

[4] Lassalle, Karl Marx's great contemporary, would have had the state lend its credit to cooperative associations of workmen, the funds being raised by taxation. The Lassallean socialist program, which is sometimes—with general but not strict accuracy—said to have differed from that of Marx in its greater emphasis upon political methods, was an important influence in the United States when the International Workingmen's Association was set-ting out to capture the American labor movement. For an account of the life and doctrines

enormous public debt consequent upon the Civil War was already available for that purpose. The United States notes, instead of remaining
what they then were, irredeemable promises to pay in specie, were to be
made convertible into government bonds bearing a rate of interest
reduced to 3 per cent, and the bonds in turn were to be convertible into
legal-tender currency. The quantity of circulating media could accordingly be inflated to the amount of the outstanding bonds, but the danger
of retrogression of real earnings consequent upon inflation seems to have
been given little thought by a labor movement closely allied with the
Western agrarians, who wanted higher prices and whose interests as "real
producers" were assumed by the leaders of the labor segments of the
Greenback movement to be fundamentally harmonious with those of the
urban workers. Of overshadowing immediate appeal was the fact that
the workingmen, the trade-union cooperatives, and the farmers would be
able to secure capital at only slightly more than 3 per cent instead of at
the much higher interest rates charged by the banks.[1]

Greenbackism accentuated the already strong political bent of the
National Labor Union, and political action, in turn, was in large part
responsible for the demise of the organization. The 1872 convention
convened as a political convention, to nominate a national ticket upon a
Greenback platform, and with the failure of this project the National
Labor Union disintegrated.[2] The cheap-money cause continued, it is
true, to command the allegiance of the workers, centering upon govern-
ment-issued paper money until the resumption of specie payments
(1879),[3] and then, during the 1880's, upon righting of the "crime of 1873"

---

of Lassalle, see Arnold Shirokauer, *Lassalle* (Eden and Cedar Paul, trans. 1932). The
biographies of Karl Marx by Franz Mehring and Otto Rühle are also illuminating in their
exposition of Lassalle's theories and in their account of the cleavage in the international
socialist movement between the Marxian and Lassallean formulations.

[1] This would follow from the fact that the bonds would bear this rate of interest and
from the convertibility of bonds into greenbacks and vice versa. When a bondholder could
secure slightly more than 3 per cent by lending to a borrower—a workman, a businessman,
a farmer, a producers' cooperative—he would convert his bonds into greenbacks and lend
them.

[2] As early as 1866, when the eight-hour demand was still uppermost, the National
Labor Union had resolved upon independent party action, and its history—particularly
after the embracing of Greenbackism in 1867—became largely the history of labor's first
attempt on a national scale to play a lone political hand. At the 1872 convention a Greenback platform was adopted and the new party there formed, the National Labor and Reform
Party, nominated Judge David Davis of Illinois for the presidency. When the Democrats
nominated Horace Greeley, Judge Davis withdrew; the party was a failure, and with its
failure the National Labor Union collapsed. From detail presented by S. Perlman, *History
of Trade Unionism* . . . , pp. 56–57, and J. B. Andrews, *op. cit.*, 153–156.

[3] Throughout the depressed 1870's Greenbackism continued to be popular with the
working people, chiefly because the rise of prices that would accompany currency inflation
was believed to foreshadow prosperity and fuller employment. During the mid-1870's
many of the organized wage earners seemed to lose their enthusiasm, practically all of the

and free coinage of silver at the ratio of sixteen to one. Likewise consumers' cooperation to an extent came back into its own after the death of the National Labor Union.[1] But the organization itself was defunct in 1872, after six years of turbulent existence.

As in the earlier period of political activity, the chief effect of labor's participation in politics was to force upon the old parties an acceptance of its demands, some of which were eventually enacted into law. The Bland-Allison Act of 1878, the decision to leave permanently outstanding, even though redeemable in gold, $346,000,000 in United States notes, the already recorded establishment of the eight-hour day upon government works, and the Chinese Exclusion Act were at least partly attributable to the political activities of this organization. When, however, the trade unions contemplated the superiority of business unionism over political and uplift methods, they found the National Labor Union cumbersome and ineffective when seeking to give expression to the trade-union point of view, and before the disastrous political adventure of the fall of 1872 the "pure and simple" unionists had manifested disposition to leave it to the political reformers. For a time job-conscious unionism found expression in a National Industrial Congress, established in 1873 upon a platform of straight unionism, with resort to politics only when industrial methods proved to be ineffective; but the establishment of the Congress, an event that marked "the first appearance of an organization similar in object and structure to the present American Federation of Labor,"[2] was followed in two months by business depression, and almost from the start it was doomed to failure. Another attempt at organization on a national basis was made in 1876, when a National Labor

---

[1] 100,000 votes Peter Cooper received as the Greenback Party candidate in 1876 coming from rural districts; but in the political labor upheaval that followed the strikes of 1877 Greenbackism assumed formidable proportions. It then became primarily a labor movement. In the congressional elections of 1878 the aggregate Greenback vote was not far short of a million, and fourteen representatives pledged to the Greenback program were returned to Congress. Late in 1878, however, the date for the redemption of greenbacks in gold was set as Jan. 1, 1879, the premium on gold disappeared, and Greenbackism as an issue became a matter of historical record.

[1] Consumers' cooperation of the middle and late seventies was a movement organized by the Sovereigns of Industry, a secret order, in 1874. "The Order of the Sovereigns of Industry," read its Declaration of Purposes, "is an association of the industrial or laboring classes, without regard to race, sex, color, nationality, or occupation; not founded for the purpose of waging any war of aggression upon any other class, or for fostering any antagonism of labor against capital, or of arraying the poor against the rich; but for mutual assistance in self-improvement and self-protection." The chief strength of this organization, which for a few years enjoyed considerable success, was in the New England and the Middle Atlantic states. The Order began to decline in 1878 and was dissolved in 1880. For details see J. B. Andrews, op. cit., pp. 171–174, and E. M. Chamberlin, The Sovereigns of Industry.

[2] J. B. Andrews, op. cit., p. 156.

Congress was held in Pittsburgh, but the participants were largely Green-backers and socialists, who could not agree among themselves, and the attempt came to nothing. Not until the rapid rise of the Knights of Labor some years later did the attempt to consolidate all labor forces into one organization again give promise of success.

In the meantime, at least three distinct ideas regarding the form and objectives of a national labor association continued to struggle with each other for supremacy, blurred and interwoven as the ideas and their organizational forms sometimes became. The unions of the skilled workers[1] continued to look toward a combination the functions of which would be the attainment of trade-union—not uplift or socialistic—objectives and assistance to each other in strikes; other groups of organized workers were more concerned, as the American workers had so long been concerned, with those panaceas which would enable wage earners to rise out of their class and restore equality of opportunity, and they concerned themselves chiefly with the broad program of social reform for which the National Labor Union had stood; while further to the left a few unions and propagandist groups, composed largely of immigrant workers, sought to establish a national labor association built upon a firm basis of class-conscious socialism. The last-named movement, failing though it did as an immediate effort, deserves a few words of separate mention, for it was of profound influence in bringing forth—ironically enough from one point of view—a national association of trade unions that might, upon superficial scrutiny, be regarded as its conditioned opposite.

The International Workingmen's Association, established in London in 1864, had almost been rent asunder by the split between the Marxian socialists and the anarchist followers of Bakunin,[2] and in 1872 the head-

---

[1] For a tabular summary of the unions formed or reorganized during these years, see L. Lorwin, *The American Federation of Labor*, pp. 474–475.

[2] Michael Bakunin (1814–1876), a revolutionist whose antecedents were those of the Russian nobility, differed from Marx on a number of grounds. "He hated the state, industrialism, and therefore state socialism" (N. Ware, *Labor in Modern Economic Society*, p. 233). Bakunin tried to get control of the International, and Marx feared that he would. "Marx began a violent and more or less secret campaign against . . . [Bakunin] accusing him of trying to dominate the movement and of acting as an agent of the Russian government. Bakunin for his part professed to believe that Marx was a tool of Bismarck" (Donald Wagner, *Social Reformers*, p. 538). Accusations and cross accusations developed. The rumor circulated that Marx had been told that Bakunin was a Russian spy. Marx accused Bakunin of embezzling a small sum of money advanced for the translation of the (then completed) first volume of *Das Kapital*. The London (*i.e.*, Marxian) clique controlled the General Council of the International, and Marx called a "conference" in London in 1871, instead of the regular meeting provided for in the constitution. A protest from beyond London, where the membership was more under the anarchist influence of Bakunin, immediately made itself heard, chiefly in protest against choice of The Hague as the place of the 1872 meeting. In 1872 at The Hague meeting, where the issues were the nature, aims,

quarters were moved—at the instigation of Marx and his followers—to New York. Prior to that time the First International had, to be sure, attempted to permeate the American labor movement,[1] but the methods had been those of persuasion and of "boring from within" the National Labor Union. During the second half of the 1870's, with the International—now no longer a truly "international" organization—having its directing center on American soil, tactics changed; "sections" were established under the New York headquarters of Marx's American lieutenant, F. A. Sorge;[2] and aggressive efforts were made to capture American labor. When the socialists failed in 1876 to capture a Congress called in Tyrone, Pa., for the purpose of uniting all interested "in the elevation of labor," they formed a Workingmen's Party of the United States, which one year later took its present name of Socialist-Labor Party. For years, this Party tried to become the dominating force in the American labor movement and to create an American labor (*i.e.*, socialist) party that could command the primary allegiance of the working-class people. Neither the Marxists affiliated with the various American sections of the International nor the Lassallean socialists, whose appeal seemed for a time, during the depressed middle seventies, to reach more responsive ears than did that of the followers of Marx,[3] ever attained those positions

---

and methods of revolutionary activity and permission for a secret organization to function within the International, the Marxists put through a resolution that headquarters of the General Council be moved to New York. The last congress of the First International was held in Geneva in 1873, with the American section not represented. Another international organization, popularly known as the "Black International," was formed by the followers of Bakunin and drew to itself some wage-earning followers in the United States, particularly the group active in propagandist activities during the years immediately preceding the Haymarket riot of 1886. From detail in N. Ware, *op. cit.* (D. C. Heath and Company) and Donald Wagner, *op. cit.* (The Macmillan Company).

[1] Between 1866 and 1870 the International had no important organization of its own on American soil, but it tried to establish itself and spread its doctrines through affiliation with the National Labor Union, which it promised, as an inducement, international regulation of immigration (S. Perlman, *History of Trade Unionism in the United States*, p. 75). Membership had increased appreciably by 1870, however, and after headquarters of the General Council had been established in this country the International had its "sections" in nearly every large city. New York and Chicago were the two most important centers.

[2] F. A. Sorge, a music teacher of New York City and Hoboken, had emigrated from Germany in the mid-1850's. He was a fundamentalist Marxist, incapable of being secured by the political socialism of the Lassallean faction or the anarchism of the Bakunists, and Marx turned to him when looking for a leader of the International in America.

[3] As a matter of fact, a majority of the German socialists who arrived in the United States during the late 1860's and early 1870's were Lassalleans rather than Marxists. Ferdinand Lassalle, magnetic orator and brilliant popular leader, had a following among the German working people that Karl Marx, living a semi-impoverished life in London and working in his lonely way upon the great treatise, never possessed. The Lassalleans, as has been said earlier, tended to subordinate the economic organization of the working class in trade unions to political action; the Marxists in the International, on the other hand, were

of dominance and leadership which they sought and which—from the Marxist point of view at least—it was their "historic mission" to attain. Nevertheless, the socialistic influence of this period was important in determining the bent taken by American unionism before the turn of the century.

Characterization of this influence carries with it, however, distinct hazard of overfacile generalization. Socialistic ideology's vicissitudes in American manualist thinking fit into no pattern of ultimate logic. The federated trade unionism that gained ascendency after 1886 was in functional character an amalgam of diverse elements: of business-union theorizing incubated by labor's own hard experience, without benefit of reasoned conviction that organization for job protection was in America the only workable application of the Marxist principle of economic organization of labor; of socialistic aspirations that bred impatience with the narrow job-conscious variety of "applied socialism" practiced by the trade unions; of much social meliorism; of vigorous, even if somewhat subordinated, political consciousness. It was far from constituting a clear-cut, simon-pure expression of socialistic class consciousness. Yet the profound importance of socialism in bringing into being a federated "business" unionism should not, on the other hand, be understated. The workers imbued with the philosophy of the International were, *ipso facto*, unsympathetic toward the individualistic American idea of self-employment, and they were cynical about antimonopoly political movements; their very fidelity to socialistic tenets restrained them from pursuing the gaudy siren of antimonopoly, uplift unionism.[1] Within the trade-union movement, particularly as it began to be grouped around the Cigarmakers' Union, the leaders thought and argued and meditated; they studied Marx while working on the job,[2] and they also studied realisti-

---

convinced that trade unionism must be prior to, and the substructure of, political action. The political predilections of the Lassalleans in America probably were a not negligible factor in shunting the Internationalists into trade-union activity.

[1] As Professor Perlman, imputing perhaps more direct cause-and-effect relationship between the socialistic movement and the emergence of a "job-conscious" unionism than the above paragraph does, has phrased it: "[The leaders] had grasped the idea, supremely correct for American labor conditions, that the economic front was the only front on which the labor army could stay united. . . . But this discovery . . . could not have been hit upon . . . if the class-consciousness of these 'philosophers-organizers' had not rendered them immune . . . against being swept off their feet by the 'producer-consciousness' of the individualistic panaceas of the native American labor movement." *A Theory of the Labor Movement*, pp. 197–198.

[2] For an account of the efforts of the group that came to be designated as the "philosopher-organizers" to arrive at some working creed for the American labor movement, see the interesting account in Mr. Gompers's memoirs, *My Seventy Years of Life and Labor*, vol. 1. The cigar makers in the shops on the east side of Manhattan Island developed the practice of designating one of their number to read from *Capital* or from various socialistic tracts while the others worked, the group as a whole contributing the wages of the reader

cally the American labor scene; and they arrived at some rather definite conclusions. The socialistic movement was in part—although only in part—the training school of the leaders who finally arrived at a creed of "pure and simple" trade unionism;[1] and the class-consciousness imbibed in this training school made itself manifest as they became absorbed in practical, day-to-day problems. They became, it is true, more pragmatic, more opportunist, but they retained the International's conception of *economic* labor organization, and this conception dictated a species of labor movement differing markedly from the native individualistic variety, with its hankering for self-employment and its periodic antimonopoly crusades. While overemphasis upon the socialistic strands that went into the making of a job-conscious, business unionism would do violence to historical accuracy, it is equally true that failure to recognize the importance of the background in socialism of some of the trade-union leaders would be to ignore one of the most real and vital of the constituents of the unionism of the decades after about 1890.

Yet the American worker needed more than the propaganda of the Internationalists and the failure of the National Labor Union to prove to him the superiority of business unionism over the more romantic type; his individualistic yearnings still prompted him to enlist under the banners of antimonopoly politics and uplift associations. The arousing of a great hope, accompanied by proportionately great disappointment, was perhaps necessary before he was willing to abandon the type of unionism for which he had manifested profound affection over a period of almost a century. The rise of a movement like the Knights of Labor— a movement that may, in one sense, be regarded as the last great fling at a reformist type of unionism—could no more have been prevented in the United States than could the movement of population westward have been halted or the demand for free silver reasoned out of court.

In the year 1869, while the wise men and the voluble men of the nation were pointing to the joining of the Union Pacific and the Central Pacific at Promontory Point as proof that the star of Manifest Destiny hung high

---

during the hours lost from work. Mr. Gompers, whose vocal intonations were apparently superior to those of some of his colleagues, seems frequently to have been the one designated as the reader.

[1] The various "sections" of the International in the United States, it has been estimated (S. Perlman, *History of Trade Unionism* . . . , p. 78), probably never had more than 1,000 members, most of whom were immigrants. Nevertheless, these "sections" became a preparatory school in trade-union leadership for many of the later organizers and leaders of the American Federation of Labor. Among the outstanding leaders who had their training in this preparatory school were Adolph Strasser, a German-born cigar maker whose union became a kind of "new model" in the United States, P. J. McGuire, an American-born carpenter who founded the Brotherhood of Carpenters and Joiners, and Mr. Gompers, who was grounded in practical trade-union experience, in class-consciousness derived from the study of Marx, and in a great deal of practical idealism.

in the heavens, seven tailors met one evening at the home of Uriah
Stephens in Philadelphia.[1] The residue of a garment cutters' benefit
society that had found the standards of its trade undermined during the
Civil War by cheap work upon government contracts for army supplies,
these men were convinced that the narrow craft sentiment of the trade
unions brought division among the workers where unity was essential;
they wanted a labor organization that would include all wage earners and
real producers (*i.e.*, farmers and members of the lower middle class as
well as wage earners) irrespective of craft, race, nationality, sex, or creed.
They formed such an organization,[2] a secret society that for a time grew
only slowly.[3] Early in the 1870's, however, the Order of the Knights
of Labor had extended westward through Reading and to Pittsburgh,
and northward as far as Massachusetts; and during the depression years
it was able, as a secret society, to expand as an open trade-union movement probably could not have done.[4] By 1878, when the General
Assembly met for the first time and national organization became a
reality, the Knights included about fifteen districts in Pennsylvania,
Ohio, West Virginia, Indiana, Illinois, and New York. It completed its

[1] Uriah Stephens, founder of the Knights of Labor, approached labor problems from the
point of view of a kind of semi-religious humanitarianism. Trained for the Baptist ministry, he was motivated by evangelistic zeal, by a desire to improve the lot of the economically submerged everywhere, that made him impatient of the narrow and—as it seemed to
him—the selfish purposes of the craft unions. Stephens continued to head the Knights
until 1878, when he was succeeded by Terence V. Powderly.

[2] The organization that became Assembly No. 1 of the Knights of Labor when, in 1871,
the name by which the organization is known in American labor history was adopted.

[3] The literature pertaining to the Knights of Labor is voluminous. In the standard
American history of labor, Commons and Associates, *History of Labor in the United States*,
the story of this organization is told by Selig Perlman in vol. 1, pp. 301–521. Norman
Ware's *The Labor Movement, 1865–1897* is in considerable part a history of the Knights of
Labor. Years ago (1893) Terence V. Powderly's *Thirty Years of Labor* was published, and
in 1940 a second Powderly memoir, based upon a manuscript the existence of which at the
time of Powderly's death was known only to his widow, and in recent years only to a few,
was edited by Henry David and others and published by the Columbia University Press
under the title *The Path I Trod*. Richard T. Ely's pioneering work, *The Labor Movement in
America* (1886) is illuminating in its portrayal of the impression the Knights of Labor made
at the time of its greatest strength upon an observant young American economist. *The
Labor Movement, The Problem of Today*, edited by George E. McNeill (with a group of
associate editors including such diverse persons as Terence V. Powderly, Dr. Edmund J.
James of the University of Pennsylvania, P. J. McGuire of the Carpenters' Union, Henry
George, the Rev. R. Heber Newton of New York, and John J. O'Neill of Missouri) and
published in 1887, is a contemporary publication by labor leaders and organized labor's
friends that is well worth consulting for the light it throws upon the broadly social and
humanitarian objectives of the Order of the Knights of Labor. These, however, are only a
few of the many tracts and books dealing with the Knights.

[4] The Order, able to avoid notice because it was a secret organization, benefited from
the misfortunes the depressions of the 1870's inflicted upon the trade unions. As the open
unions disintegrated, many of their members affiliated with the Knights.

national organization in time for the upturn of business, and with the dropping of its secrecy numerous workers theretofore skeptical or distrustful of the organization found no reason for not affiliating with it.[1]

For a time the new assemblies, or local units, that were established had a trade basis, but as the idea of labor or plain-people solidarity began to express itself more strongly, a greater number of the local units began to be mixed in character, including persons of different trades or (with exceptions mentioned later) gainful occupations, of both sexes, and irrespective of race or color. By the beginning of the second decade of its existence the Knights was, theoretically and to a certain extent in practice, a hierarchy contemplating the welding together of all the labor forces of the nation. At the head was the General Assembly, given by the constitution "full and final jurisdiction in all matters pertaining to local and district assemblies"; then came the district assemblies, which possessed power within their districts "to decide all appeals and settle all controversies within or between local assemblies"; and finally there were the local assemblies, to which workers belonged as individuals. In practice, however, this high degree of centralization frequently was lacking, the local and district assemblies disregarding more than once the decisions of the General Assembly and its officers. Although the number of "mixed" assemblies increased after the organization was established on a national basis, with a new constitution, in 1878, the majority of the local assemblies appear always to have been trade and industrial units.[2] Often the Order accepted local craft unions without a change in their structure, and a number of the national craft unions were admitted as district assemblies, generally under the name of "trade districts." In consequence of this practice, the national unions were able to maintain their structure and existence intact and at the same time to become integral parts of this all-embracing labor, plain-people organization.

It can be seen that by the early 1880's the Knights of Labor—in accordance with the hope and expectation of the founders—had ceased to be primarily a trade society, and the evolution in structure was of course a consequence of evolution in functional character. The aim of

---

[1] The secret "vow" had been contributed by Uriah Stephens, the founder of the Order. When Powderly became General Master Workman in 1879 he insisted that the vow be replaced by a promise and undertook to prove to Cardinal Gibbons, who had been opposed to an Order that was not only secret but also was believed to harbor socialistic purposes, that there was nothing socialistic about the Knights. Cardinal Gibbons in turn persuaded the Vatican to this effect, and Catholics felt free to join the Order.

[2] On Jan. 1, 1882, the Knights of Labor included 484 local assemblies, and only 116 were mixed locals. Four years later, when the Knights of Labor reached its peak in membership and in strength—and included by far the largest number of workers who had ever been affiliated with an American labor organization—there were 1,499 local assemblies, of which 836 were trade locals and the rest were mixed. Edward Berman, in Stein, Davis, and Others, *Labor Problems in America*, p. 155.

the Order and of the leaders of the mixed assemblies was, in spite of the
trade-union character of most of the local and some of the district assemblies, to weld the labor movement into a single disciplined army, subject
to orders from a central office, rather than to promote the interests of
the craft unions; and this aim inevitably led both to catholicity of membership and to a broadly political and uplift program. Although three-
fourths of the members of each assembly were required to be wage-earners,
all gainfully employed persons except lawyers, bankers, professional
gamblers or stockbrokers, saloonkeepers, and (prior to 1881) physicians
were eligible to membership. To such an organization the unskilled
workers flocked in hordes, joined by many of the economically submerged
of the self-employed,[1] and for a time membership increased almost beyond
the expectations of the most optimistic. There was, however, little
stability in personnel; many came, some remained only a little while and
then lost interest, and the whole was, in the words of Professor Commons,
"more nearly a procession than an organization, so rapidly did the
membership change."[2] But the years of its spectacular rise were years
that have properly been characterized[3] as those of "the great upheaval,"
and the Knights of Labor became the most important labor organization
that had yet developed on American soil.

Various factors contributed to the remarkable growth of the Order.
The abolition of secrecy and the completion of national organization in
1878 synchronized, as has already been said, with the beginning of an
upward trend of business. During the years from 1879 to 1882, to be
sure, the labor movement was typical of any period of rising prices; it was
confined in large part to the skilled, it did not press aggressively for class
solidarity, and it was predominately trade-union rather than political
and uplift in color and purpose. Nevertheless, the Order as it had been
reconstituted merely awaited conditions that in 1885 and 1886 were
literally to hurl people—skilled and unskilled workers alike—into its local
assemblies. Depression again overtook the nation's economy in 1884–
1885, the trade unions were defeated in their strikes against wage reduc-

---

[1] Throughout its history, there was a major division within the Knights between the
East and the West, in spite of the basic assumption of harmony of interest among all the
"real producers" of the nation. The farmers and the small-town elements of the West were
on the whole more politically minded than were the trade unionists of the East, then turning their attention—partly as a result of the already discussed socialistic influences—
toward purely economic organization of labor. Within the city assemblies, also, there was
more or less constant cleavage. In New York City the two groups that struggled for
ascendency were the Irish-American politicians in the district organization and the various
socialist cliques. For details, see N. Ware, *The Labor Movement*, 1865–1897.

[2] In *History of Labor in the United States*, vol. 1, p. 13.

[3] By S. Perlman (*History of Trade Unionism* . . . , pp. 89–90), by J. B. Andrews in
Commons and Associates, *op. cit.*, vol. 2, pp. 356–395, and various other labor historians.

tions,[1] unemployment became widespread, and trade-union members manifested a disposition to turn from the empty larder of business unionism to the attractive menu of an uplift association. Protests against political corruption and concentration of property ownership also stimulated the growth of an organization permeated with reform idealism. In 1886 economically submerged social classes of the country were electrified by a political campaign in New York City, where Henry George was almost elected mayor (just possibly was elected, but counted out in the tabulation of votes) upon a platform not altogether different in its broader philosophical basis from that of the Knights of Labor.[2] Radical sentiment, nurtured in the economic conditions of the mid-1880's, induced men to affiliate with a movement whose program seemed to promise a kindlier and more equitable social system. The Haymarket riot of May 4, 1886,[3] a consequence of the eight-hour movement, aroused public

[1] For details concerning these strikes, see S. Perlman, *ibid.*, pp. 82–84, and Commons and Associates, *op. cit.*, vol. 2, pp. 356–386, and N. Ware, *The Labor Movement, 1865–1897.*

[2] Henry George was the candidate of the United Labor Party of New York City, an admixture of liberals, reformers, trade unionists, Knights of Labor, socialists, and single-taxers. Abram S. Hewitt, the Democratic organization candidate, polled 90,000 votes, and Henry George 68,000. The third candidate, who received the vote of 60,000, was a young "good-government" reformer named Theodore Roosevelt. For accounts of this campaign, see Henry George, Jr., *Life of Henry George,* Louis Post, *Henry George, The Prophet of San Francisco,* and S. Perlman in Commons and Associates, *op. cit.*, pp. 450–454. Dr. Perlman concluded that "there is sufficient ground for the belief that George was counted out by thousands of votes."

[3] In 1884 the Federation of Organized Trades and Labor Unions, formed three years earlier (*cf. infra,* p. 72), resolved to initiate eight hours as the legal workday on May 1, 1886. The movement was endorsed by the anarchistic International Working Peoples' Association, popularly known as the Black International. Powderly, head of the Knights of Labor, opposed participation in the May 1 demonstrations, but many of the members and local officers of the Knights were eager to demonstrate for the shorter workday. May 1 for the most part passed peacefully, but on May 3 August Spies, one of the revolutionists supporting the May 1 demonstrations, addressed a group of workers near the plant of the McCormick Harvester Co., in Chicago, where a strike had been in progress since early in the year. Some of the striking McCormick employees attacked strikebreakers leaving the factory; police were called; and in the resulting riot one person was killed. The radical leaders (chiefly those affiliated with the Black International) called a meeting the following night (May 4) in Haymarket Square to protest against "police brutality." The number attending the meeting did not exceed 1,300, and when rain began to fall the crowd dwindled to about one-fourth of the number originally assembled. Testimony at the time and subsequent research have established that the speeches made by the members of the Black International were less provocative than many they had given before in Chicago. Mayor Carter Harrison observed the meeting in person, concluded that there was no danger of physical violence, and departed. Just as Samuel Fielden, one of the social revolutionists, was on the point of closing his speech, police appeared and ordered dispersion of the meeting. Then a bomb, hurled by an unknown person at the first rank of the police, exploded. The police reformed their ranks and began to fire; the crowd fled. One policeman was killed

antagonism to the Knights and to the labor movement generally, but the following trial and execution of four radical leaders—believed by many to be "labor martyrs"—inculcated a frame of mind not entirely irrelevant to the "great upheaval," and accordingly to growth of the Knights of Labor. Aggressive efforts on the part of the national officers were another factor stimulating the expansion of the Order. Lecturers and recruiters were sent throughout the country, bringing to thousands its doctrines and its promises. The unskilled found the warm welcome accorded them by the Knights in marked contrast to the frigidity of the trade unions. Perhaps most important of all, however, was the success —a trifle ironical, in view of its deep-rooted antipathy toward industrial strife—of the Order in conducting strikes. During 1885 and 1886 ordinary strikes over wages and hours, sympathetic strikes, and boycotts[1]

---

during the encounter, six died of their wounds, and possibly a hundred persons were injured. Public opinion at once placed the blame for the bombing upon the "anarchists" affiliated with the Black International. Upon a theory of conspiracy advanced in the court of Judge Joseph E. Gary, eight of them were found guilty of murder, and four—August Spies, Albert Parsons, Adolph Fischer, and George Engle—were executed on Nov. 11, 1887. Six years later John Peter Altgeld, governor of Illinois, defied still-hysterical public opinion by pardoning the three convicted men who were then in prison (another, sentenced to be hanged, had committed suicide in his cell), and issued a statement concerning the conduct of the trial by Judge Gary that remains one of the most damning—and convincing— characterizations of judicial partiality in American history. The identity of the bomb thrower has never been learned, and almost certainly it now never will be learned; but all the evidence that has come to light in the years since the 1880's exculpates the accused from any direct responsibility for the crime. The case became a *cause célèbre* during the years immediately following 1886. Labor organizations in Europe as well as in the United States protested against the executions, and the four "Chicago anarchists" became revolutionary labor's symbol of martyrdom. The affair had other consequences. The middle-class hysteria that gripped the country convinced the trade-union leaders of the danger inherent in identification of their movement with the more extreme forms of radicalism and was probably a factor of no little importance in shunting the federated trade unionism that succeeded the Knights of Labor into a position of conservatism with respect to property rights. Mr. Gompers always said that the eight-hour movement was set back at least ten years by the Haymarket bomb. The most detailed and careful investigation of the Haymarket incident is that of Henry David, who has told the story in *The History of the Haymarket Affair* (Farrar & Rinehart, Inc., New York, 1936), a book to which this footnote is indebted for the factual material presented. In the Commons and Associates *History*, the details of the tragedy and an appraisal of its significance in the history of the American labor movement are presented by Selig Perlman, vol. 2, pp. 386–395. Louis Adamic's *Dynamite, The Story of Class Violence in America* and Robert Hunter's *Violence and the Labor Movement* also set forth the essential facts, and C. O. Johnson's *Carter Harrison I, A Study in Political Leadership* gives the Chicago setting at the time as well as circumstantial evidence that there was no danger of physical violence at the time Mayor Harrison left the meeting shortly before the—never fully explained—arrival of police and the throwing of the bomb.

[1] In 1885 the number of boycotts was nearly seven times as large as it had been in 1884. Nearly all of these boycotts either originated with, or else were taken up by, the Knights of Labor (S. Perlman, *History of Trade Unionism* . . . , p. 85).

became increasingly common. National officers of the Knights of Labor generally, it is true, tried to avoid these strikes, but they found themselves unable to do so; and it is likely that in the turmoil of industrial warfare the educational and humanitarian objectives tended to recede into the background, even in the minds of idealistic leaders with anti-strike predilections. Sometimes the Knights gave the impression of having won victories for striking workers that the trade unions were unable to achieve, and, in more cases than one, the workers joined the Order after they already had struck; but some of its victories—achieved in spite of the inadaptability to strike prosecution of an organization composed of mixed assemblies—were substantial and spectacular. They galvanized the labor movement into militant action. When Jay Gould, perhaps the most powerful capitalist in the United States, was forced to recognize the Order as a power equal to himself,[1] there was literally a stampede to organize under the banner of the Knights of Labor.

As a result of all these influences and conditions, the membership of the Knights increased by approximately 600,000 within one year, while the trade unions likewise experienced substantial gains. In 1879 only 20,151 workers were affiliated with the Knights, and four years later the estimated membership was 51,914.[2] The summer of 1885 found the organization possessed of a paid-up membership of 104,000; then, during

---

[1] On Feb. 27 and Mar. 9, 1885, strikes against wage reductions occurred on two of the Gould railways, the Wabash and the Missouri, Kansas, and Texas. The men on the third Gould road, the Missouri Pacific, joined those of the other two at all points where the lines touched. The wage reductions had applied to the shopmen, but the locomotive engineers, firemen, brakemen, and conductors supported the strikers. The strike was won; wage rates were restored and the strikers were reinstated. Six months later, however, a second strike occurred—one that resulted in probably the most publicized victory in the history of the Knights of Labor. The Wabash, then in the hands of a receiver, reduced the force in the shops at Moberly, Mo., to a point that virtually constituted a lockout of members of the Knights of Labor in violation of the settlement of the preceding strike. The General Executive Board of the Knights declared a boycott on Wabash rolling stock—an order that would have affected over 20,000 miles of railway. Jay Gould (who was then engaged in stock manipulations and wanted to maintain the price of Wabash stock) capitulated. At a conference of the Executive Board of the Knights and the managers of the Missouri Pacific and the Wabash railroads, he threw his influence in favor of making concessions to the men. The receiver of the Wabash road, under pressure from Mr. Gould, issued an order conceding all the demands of the Knights: discharge of all new men hired in Wabash shops since the beginning of the lockout, reinstatement of all discharged men, and assurance that no discrimination against the members of the Order would be made in the future. Mr. Gould also assured the Knights that he believed in labor organization and arbitration, that he wanted the employees to come to him directly in all difficulties, and that in the future he "would always endeavor to do what was right." From details presented by S. Perlman, ibid., pp. 86–88, and in Commons and Associates, op. cit., vol. 1, pp. 362–374.

[2] Estimated membership for each of the years 1879–1883 inclusive was: 1879, 20,151; 1880, 28,136; 1881, 19,422; 1882, 42,417; 1883, 51,914. S. Perlman, History of Trade Unionism . . . , pp. 82–83.

the following fourteen months, it increased to perhaps more than 700,000.[1]
The trade unions that same year (1886) included at least 250,000 members.[2]   The "great upheaval" had reached its peak, and this upheaval
"meant more than the mere quickening of the pace of the movement
begun in previous years and decades. . . . It signalled the appearance
on the scene of a new class which had not hitherto found a place in the
labor movement, namely the unskilled. . . . This movement, rising as
an elemental protest against oppression and degradation, could be but
feebly restrained by any considerations of expediency and prudence; nor,
of course, could it be restrained by any lessons from experience."[3]

The functional character of the Knights of Labor—the purposes, the
social and economic assumptions and theories, the remedial policies and
methods—has necessarily been touched upon in the preceding paragraphs,
but more particularity is called for at this point.   When the Order was
established, as has been said, the purpose was broadly reformist, the
methods contemplated educational rather than militant, even though
during the early years the organization functioned chiefly as a trade
society and during the years 1884–1886 it became increasingly aggressive
and militant.   "Education" meant, it is true, different things to different
leaders, but to Powderly and his followers, at least, it connoted planning
and propaganda for an economic system in which self-employment and
ownership of small parcels of property by the great mass of the producers
would supplant the wage system.[4]   Reliance upon educational methods,
in turn, dictated deprecation of strikes.   "Strikes should be avoided

---

[1] The books of the Order showed 702,824 members in 1886, although some officials
claimed a membership of more than 730,000.   Terence V. Powderly in his *Thirty Years of
Labor*, p. 641, on the other hand, says that membership never rose above 600,000.   *Cf.* also
the Powderly memoirs published in 1940, *The Path I Trod*.   The constantly changing composition, and hence the inevitability that at any one time large numbers would be included
who had really dropped out, is chiefly responsible for the wide variation in the estimates of
membership in 1886, the year when the order attained its greatest strength.

[2] All of these 250,000 cannot, of course, be added to the same 700,000 Knights to obtain
a figure of total union membership in 1886, since some of the union members were also
included within the Knights of Labor total, either because trade-union locals were accepted
as local assemblies or because the national trade unions were given the status of "district
trade assemblies" of the Knights of Labor.

[3] S. Perlman, *History of Trade Unionism* . . . , p. 80.

[4] To Uriah Stephens, founder of the Order, the word "education" probably did not
denote peaceful means of attaining such far-reaching ends as those contemplated when the
constitution of 1878 was adopted and Powderly became General Master Workman; rather
the term denoted a vague kind of semireligious humanitarianism.   *Cf.* Powderly's *Thirty
Years of Labor* and *The Path I Trod* and N. Ware's *The Labor Movement*, 1865–1897.   As
Professor Perlman (*History of Trade Unionism*, p. 71) has characterized the purposes
and attitudes of Powderly: "Powderly bore unmistakeably the stamp of this sort of idealism
throughout all the time when he was the foremost labor leader in the country [the idealism
set forth in the Preamble of the Order, as summarized later in this paragraph].   Unlike
Samuel Gompers . . . he was foreign to that spirit of combative unionism which accepts

whenever possible," the constitution declared. "Strikes at best only afford temporary relief, and members should be educated to depend upon thorough organization, cooperation, and political action, and through these the abolishment of the wage system. Our mission cannot be accomplished in a day or a generation. Agitation, education, and organization are all necessary." And when establishing an assistance fund for district and local assemblies, the General Assembly was careful to guard against the use of money for strike purposes. "We declare that strikes are deplorable in their effect and contrary to the best interests of the Order." Instead, the Order looked—in spite of its involvement in the strikes which it deprecated—toward propaganda politics, legislative action, land reform, producers' cooperation,[1] and those weapons which were aimed at the "money power" and the corporations, at a concentration of wealth ownership that "unless checked" would "inevitably lead to the pauperisation and hopeless degradation of the toiling masses," at inequality of economic opportunity.

The Preamble adopted in 1878 in place of the former secret ritual, setting forth the cardinal "First Principles," and the reiteration of these in the 1884 platform are worthy of paraphrase: direct representation and legislation, the initiative and referendum, establishment of bureaus of labor statistics, taxation of unearned increment in land, abrogation of all legislation not resting equally upon employers and employees, laws to further health and safety and to prevent accidents and occupational diseases, laws to compel corporations to pay their workers weekly, abolition of the contract system on public works, compulsory arbitration and enforcement of the decisions, prohibition of the employment of children less than fifteen years of age, compulsory schooling and free textbooks, income and inheritance taxes, prohibition of the hiring out of convict labor, retention of the greenbacks as a permanent part of the nation's circulating media, free coinage of silver at the ratio of sixteen

---

the wage system but concentrates on a struggle to wrest concessions from the employers. Even when circumstances which were largely beyond his control made Powderly a strike leader on a huge scale, his heart lay elsewhere—in circumventing the wage system by opening to the worker an escape into self-employment through cooperation."

[1] Producers' cooperation of course appealed strongly to workers whose yearnings for self-employment and ownership of property were so strong, and the Knights instituted cooperative experiments more extensive than those of the National Labor Union period. Also, the work was carried on by the Order as a whole, not by the scattered initiative of national and local unions. The plan was to start an organization of consumers, somewhat along Rochdale lines, these consumers being the members of the Order; but it differed from the English model in that consumers' cooperation did not have as its primary object the reduction of costs in distribution and saving of money for consumers but was intended primarily to create a market for the products of the producers' cooperatives. Consumers' cooperation, in other words, was to be merely a steppingstone to producers' cooperation, or self-employment.

to one, government ownership of the railroads and telegraph systems, a merit basis of appointment and promotion in the government service, a cooperative industrial system, the eight-hour day, and equal rights (including equal pay for equal work) for both sexes. For reforms such as these the Knights endeavored to bring the whole of the producing masses within its all-inclusive organization, engaged incessantly in propagandist and educational work, lobbied at Washington and the state capitols, and aligned itself with the Greenback and Populist parties, and then with the Bryan Democrats in 1896 and 1900.

A generalization as to the character of these objectives may be made, even if doing so involves some repetition. The Knights was clearly proceeding upon the assumption that no fundamental disharmony of interest obtained between employers and workers as such and that the interests of all workers were basically the same. The real conflict was between the producing and the nonproducing classes. Only on these assumptions could the deprecation of strikes, the emphasis upon educational and political methods, and the ignoring of the separate trade interests be regarded as consistent. It was a plain-people crusade, based upon the premise of an abundance of opportunity to be shared among all workers of hand and brain; the mission of the producing classes was to regain for themselves, and to protect, this opportunity.

These broadly reformist objectives and the all-embracing structural character soon brought the Order into conflict with the trade unions, even as workers were turning by the thousands to it. For a while, to be sure, it looked as if an amicable adjustment might be made.[1] Thousands of the trade unionists were attracted by the idealism of spirit and purpose motivating the Knights, and the latter in turn had found the aid of the skilled workers essential for victory in many of the strikes that had been precipitated by the unskilled and semiskilled workers.[2] But the plain-people objectives of the Order sometimes required subordination of the immediate interests of those seeking better control of their jobs, and its structural arrangements prevented exercise of group pressure where such pressure could most effectively be exercised.[3] The monetary proposals, having their immediate inception, to no inconsiderable extent, in the financial difficulties of the cooperatives and their *rationale* in the thesis that many of the evils of contemporary society sprang from the fact that credit went to privileged middlemen rather than to individual producers or groups of producers, brought subordination of the wage-earner point of view to that of the debtor agrarian classes. Likewise

---

[1] The facts about the negotiations between the Knights and the trade unions and the final break are sketched *infra*, pp. 73, 74–75.

[2] *Cf.* L. Lorwin, *The American Federation of Labor*, pp. 17–18.

[3] The reasons for this structural inadaptability are discussed in some detail *infra*, pp. 69, 74–75.

the political crusades distracted attention from immediate improvement of working conditions of skilled workers. Producers' cooperation bore much the same fruits that it had borne during earlier periods: competition for the interest, enthusiasm, and financial resources of the labor organizations, antagonism between the small group of cooperators and the mass of the workers who remained in private employment, and ultimate failure.[1]

The growing indifference of the trade unions toward the Knights of Labor, even while the latter was steadily becoming more powerful, was not, however, so much a result of the Order's interest in intellectual, social, and political improvement as of its ineffectiveness as a trade union device. It must be remembered that while on the one side the Knights was an idealistic movement, it always tried to maintain control over collective bargaining. Moreover, it is possible to overstate the differences between the Knights of Labor and the federated organization of trade unions that had appeared on the industrial horizon in 1881.[2] While in theory, and to a considerable extent in practice, the Knights stood opposed to the principle that the primary unit of organization should be a local composed of artisans following a single vocation, most of the local assemblies were composed exclusively of workers in a single trade.[3] On the other hand, the organizers of the Federation of Organized Trades and Labor Unions (after 1886 the American Federation of Labor) frequently found it necessary to assimilate into one local union workers of miscellaneous crafts—"federal labor unions." Nevertheless, the sum-total effect of the concurrent presence of the trade unions and the Knights of Labor was to create dual authority and divided loyalty on the part of individual members, and to tempt those skilled workers who were wedded much more strongly to their unions than to the Order to abandon the least effective protector of immediate job interests. In spite of the success in winning victories over employers during the days of the great upheaval, the centralized character of the organization and the mixture in some local assemblies of workers of miscellaneous trades were impediments to effective concentration of economic strength where it was most needed that neither spectacular short-run success nor moralizing about the ultimate viciousness of strikes could obliterate.

[1] The story of, and reasons for, this failure are recorded by S. Perlman, *History of Trade Unionism in the United States*, pp. 125–129, and in Commons and Associates, *History of Labor in the United States*, vol. 1, pp. 430–439.

[2] The Federation of Organized Trades and Labor Unions, formed in Pittsburgh in 1881. *Cf. infra*, pp. 72–73.

[3] Also, it will be remembered, some of the national unions were admitted to the Knights as district assemblies. In addition, some of the influential trade-union leaders, like Adolph Strasser, P. J. McGuire, Frank K. Foster, and Samuel Gompers, were members of the Order.

Trade unionists accordingly began to abandon the Order; and by 1887 the great upheaval of the unskilled and semiskilled had subsided. After that year the Knights for the most part lost its hold upon the wage-conscious and largely foreign population of the great cities and became predominantly an organization of country folk, of mechanics in the smaller towns, and of small merchants and farmers. Membership in good standing had fallen to 222,000 by midsummer of 1888, to a claimed 100,000 in 1890, and to 75,000 in 1893. By 1890 the American Federation of Labor had the allegiance of the majority of the national trade unions, and by the turn of the century the Knights had become only a shadow of its former self. The causes of its decline should be discussed in a little more detail, for they are of profound significance in an interpretation of the bent taken by the American labor movement.

Factors of a more or less immediate and circumstantial character, such as the unsuccessful outcome of the strikes in which the Order became engaged after 1886, internal dissension, the opposition of employers, churches, and the judiciary, and the failure of the cooperative efforts, of course contributed to the rapid decline in membership and influence of the Knights, but for the most part these immediate and circumstantial causes were merely symptomatic of more fundamental factors. The more basic causes are to be found in the inadaptability of its structure to the economic needs of the workers, in the fallacy of some of the assumptions adopted, and in the failure to take into account some highly significant characteristics of the American community and of American working-class psychology.

The structural arrangements of the Order were in large part, of course, a consequence of its basic assumptions. Proceeding upon the notion of a harmony of interests among all workers of hand and brain, and minimizing or ignoring the ever-present conflict over division of the value product of industry between employers and employees, the Knights built its centralized heirarchy and its system of mixed local and district units, and thus invited difficulties with the trade unions. As a matter of fact, the skilled craftsmen sometimes found their affiliation with the Order a positive handicap, since immediate self-interest often dictated restrictions of numbers through apprenticeship rules and other devices and the pressing of an advantage that reacted detrimentally to the unskilled. Nor did these unskilled find the mixed assemblies permanently congenial. Immigrants in large part, they had come to the land where—they had been told—opportunity and individual enterprise abounded; and the shock of their first contact with the American industrialism of the 1880's, of their discovery of its autocratic systems of management and its ugly harshness, resulted in the "great upheaval" of 1884–1886. But after the first violent reaction, expressing itself in the organization movement of these two years, they tended to abandon the Order, some because they sought channels of life that would lead to individual gain, others merely because they sensed the indifference of the skilled to their needs and problems. There could, in any event, be little unity of purpose, except when uplift legislation was being approved or magnificently platitudinous resolutions were being passed, within mixed assemblies. Trade or craft consciousness was increasing among the workers but there was not enough strictly wage-earning class consciousness to make possible the organization of the entire wage-earning population into a mixed industrial assembly. The heterogeneity of the Order became greater— and the inadaptability of the structure in the meeting of practical, every-day problems on the economic front accordingly became more apparent— when the organization spread to the agricultural regions, and its membership became diluted with farmers, shopkeepers, and small employers— groups possessed of little interest in the problems that were agitating the urban wage earners. The Knights, however, proceeded upon the assumption, and built up a structure compatible with the assumption, that organization could be successful and permanent when inclusive of both wage earners and other members of the "productive classes." This mistake about the class cohesiveness of the employed, and of the economically underprivileged self-employed, masses was one of the greatest mistakes made by the Knights, and the judgment of the socialists, who were turning their attention to the trade unions, was on this point superior. The leaders of the Order never quite sensed the fact that those individualistic traits with which their philosophy harmonized so well inhibited fighting solidarity except where the workers were held together by the common purpose of protecting and extending job opportunity.

Nor did the Knights take sufficient cognizance of two characteristics of the American community: the limitations placed by the governmental structure upon labor's successful exercise of the political weapon and the property-mindedness of the powerful middle class. In spite of the fact that "education"—a vague and blessed word, meaning different things to different leaders—and not politics was originally contemplated as the foremost means of achieving the idealistic and humanitarian objectives, the Knights more and more found itself drawn into the whirlpool of politics. Subordination of the purposes and objectives of wage earners to the broad vistas of social reform promised through political action, as well as practical demonstration of the difficulties of purely wage-earner political action, were the consequence; and those workers with a narrow but substantial job interest to protect became more and more enamored of the idea of purely economic organization of labor. Failure to take into account the property-mindedness of public opinion (which meant, in large part, middle-class opinion) likewise contributed to the decline of the Order. An age that considered John Hay's *The Breadwinners* a daring bit of economic radicalism, and that denounced as an anarchist the Governor of Illinois who possessed the courage to pardon men wrongly convicted of responsibility for the Haymarket riots, was not ready to tolerate the encroachments upon vested interests contemplated by the Knights' political and social program. The situation was, it is true, a trifle anomalous. The period was one of prevailing discontent, a condition that itself rendered attractive the Order's program; even though the ultimate objective, to be achieved through peaceful and nonrevolutionary means, was nothing short of abolition of the wage system, no movement along the German socialistic route toward abolition of the institution of private property was included in the plans for a better social order;[1] and, indeed, the rank and file of the membership tended to revere private property and fervidly hoped to get some of it. The evangelical zeal of the leaders and the religious humanitarianism of their appeal brought, for a time, also, a considerable amount of middle-class support, and middle-class people were affiliated with the organization. The essential fact, however, is that the Knights' program for bringing to the masses the benefits of the wealth of the nation encroached upon the interests of dominant property groups and made them determined that their grip on what they possessed should not be weakened. The socialists in the trade unions, unlike many of the Knights, had no particular reverence for the institution of private property, but they had great reverence for practical facts, and they therefore evolved a program of worker control of jobs that was in important respects less alarming to the more influential groups in American social and economic life.

Advent of the Era of Federated Trade Unions

Even before the years that marked the sudden growth of the Order of the Knights of Labor, the trade unions had, for reasons already mentioned, manifested a disposition to draw away from the weaker elements of unskilled and semiskilled workers and to concentrate their efforts upon the building up of organizations, coextensive with trade competitive areas, that would be strong enough to win recognition from employers, establish collective bargaining and stable trade agreements, and retain their memberships during periods of depression. Expressive of this disposition was the formation, in November, 1881, of the Federation of Organized Trades and Labor Unions of the United States and Canada, the forerunner of the American Federation of Labor.[2]　Between 1881 and

---

[1] Of course, socialists affiliated with the Order and tried to get control of it. Assembly No. 49 (the New York City assembly) was in particular the scene of conflict between socialists and others. The story of the attempt of Daniel DeLeon and the Socialist-Labor Party to seize control of Assembly No. 49 is told in the following chapter (*infra*, pp. 107–113). But fundamentally, as has been said or implied more than once in the preceding pages, the Knights envisaged as the route to abolition of the wage system self-employment and ownership of small parcels of property, not an attack on the institution of private property.

[2] *Cf.* L. Lorwin, *op. cit.*, pp. 17–21.

1886, as the Knights grew in numbers and power, the growth of the Federation was moderate, some years witnessing losses rather than gains;[1] and efforts to work out a *modus vivendi* between the two organizations were pushed aggressively by its leaders.   By 1885, however, relations between the Knights and the craft unions (both those that were included within the Federation and those that were not) had become increasingly strained, and the events of 1886 widened the rift.[2]   When a proposed "treaty," under the terms of which the Knights would have ceased organizing trades in which there were unions without the consent of the latter, disbanded their trade assemblies, and refrained from interfering in strikes or issuing labels in competition with the unions,[3] was rejected by the Order,[4] a trade-union committee of five[5] issued a call to all trade unions

[1] Within a year following the Pittsburgh convention of 1881, the Federation had dwindled to such an extent that it had become an insignificant body.   Samuel Gompers, who assumed chairmanship of the Legislative Committee of the Federation in 1883, was constantly active in its behalf, but the Federation made little progress.   Its annual income between 1882 and 1885 varied between $400 to $725.   *Ibid.*, p. 17.

[2] For a time it looked as if an amicable settlement might be reached.   Events of 1885 and 1866, however, rendered less probable the reaching of any compromise satisfactory to both the trade unions and the Knights.   With the rapid growth of the Order, the unions lost in both numbers and cohesion, and the Knights—intoxicated a bit, perhaps, by their success in strikes, boycotts, and collective bargaining—were becoming more certain that the unions could be forced into the Order, even against their will.   Activities of the socialists, who tried to control both the Order and the trade unions, intensified the friction. The rift was accentuated by the eight-hour movement of the mid-1880's.   The Knights opposed the resolution of the Federation of Organized Trades and Labor Unions that labor strike for the eight-hour day on May 1, 1886 (*cf. supra*, p. 63), in spite of the favor with which the project was regarded by some of the local assemblies and by many of the individual members of the Order.   While the agitation for the eight-hour day was increasing, five trade-union officials (P. J. McGuire, Adolph Strasser, W. H. Foster, and two others) issued a circular calling attention to the damage done the trade unions by a "malicious" element within the Knights of Labor, and summoning the unions to send delegates to a convention in Philadelphia on May 18, 1886, for the purpose of considering the situation.   The delegates attending declared—in language savoring of the influence of the International Workingmen's Association upon trade-union ideology—that the craft unions had a "historical basis" and "were best qualified to regulate their own internal concerns" (L. Lorwin, *op. cit.*, p. 20).   But they still professed faith in "the solidarity of all labor interests," and appointed a committee of five to draft the "treaty" referred to above.   For fuller details, see L. Lorwin, *ibid.*, pp. 18–21.

[3] Patently the effect of this agreement would have been to deprive the Order of its industrial features and to make it a subsidiary of the unions.

[4] The rejection took place at the General Assembly of the Knights (then at the height of its power, with perhaps 700,000 members), which convened in Richmond, Va., on Oct. 4, 1886.   The Knights added insult to injury by admitting to membership the Progressive Cigarmakers' Union, a rival of the established Cigarmakers' Union, and expelling all cigar makers affiliated with the latter.   L. Lorwin, *ibid.*, p. 21.

[5] The same committee that had issued the call for the Philadelphia convention of May 18, 1886.

of the United States to send representatives to a convention in Columbus, Ohio, on Dec. 8, 1886, for the purpose of drawing "the bonds of unity much closer together between all trades unions of America" by means of "an American federation or alliance of all national and international trades unions." The convention acted in accordance with the purpose set forth in the summons. At the same time, the Federation of Organized Trades and Labor Unions of the United States and Canada met at Columbus and decided to merge with the new Federation. Thus was born the American Federation of Labor.[1]

Based upon national and international unions, and pledged to a "strict recognition of the autonomy of each trade," the Federation proceeded to tread the straight and narrow path of business unionism. It lacked the idealistic and emotional appeal of the Knights, and for a time after 1886 its progress was slow. Negotiations were, indeed, raised once more with the Knights in 1888, but these negotiations, like those of 1886, were merely demonstrative of the irreconcilability of the points of view of the two organizations.[2] The Federation refused to recede from the substance of its position that the interests of labor could be best advanced through the mechanism of trade unions, that these unions should have complete control over all trade matters, that dualism therefore could not

[1] At its 1889 convention the American Federation of Labor decided to regard the Federation of Organized Trades and Labor Unions of the United States and Canada as an earlier stage of its own history, and to date its origin from 1881; hence the "Founded in 1881" that appears on all the official publications of the Federation.

[2] The Knights, in the 1888 negotiations, proposed mutual recognition of working cards and labels, and mutual exclusion of suspended or expelled members, while the Federation demanded that the Order revoke the charters of its trade districts and become a purely benevolent, educational, and humanitarian society. Were the Knights thus reconstituted, the Federation was perfectly willing to have all working people become members of the Order. It insisted, however, that there must be only one jurisdiction in each trade or craft and that the unions could not share control of trade matters with other organizations. It is most apparent that each organization felt that its very existence depended upon the capitulation of the other to its point of view. The Knights realized that if the Federation did not recognize the mixed assemblies as *bona fide* locals, the members were not union men and could not work with union men in closed shops; the Federation realized that to respect the working card of the Knights would, as a practical matter, be to surrender the fight for trade autonomy. The story of the negotiations between the Knights and the Federation has been traced by a number of writers. An excellent summary account is that of William Kirk in Hollander and Barnett, *Studies in American Trade Unionism*, pp. 345–380. L. Lorwin's *The American Federation of Labor*, pp. 8–24, also presents a most excellent and authoritative account. An account is also given in G. G. Groat's *Organized Labor in America*, pp. 73–99. Among other works to which reference may be made are Commons and Associates, *History of Labor in the United States*, vol. 2, pp. 482–495, N. Ware, *The Labor Movement*, 1865–1897, pp. 187–193, and S. Perlman, *History of Trade Unionism in the United States*, pp. 106–129. Mr. Gompers's *My Seventy Years of Life and Labor* and T. V. Powderly's *The Path I Trod* should also be consulted by one wishing to investigate the matter in more detail.

be tolerated, and that the national trade unions should become affiliated with each other only in voluntary federation; the Knights could not consider these proposals, the manifest consequence of which would have been surrender of the Order's industrial features. Each went its way— the Federation to grow only slowly for a time, the Knights to continue to decline rapidly.

By 1890 the federation of autonomous trade unions overshadowed the Knights of Labor. But the advent of this new unionism signified more than merely the supersession of a highly centralized organization by a federation of autonomous trade unions. It marked a change in the tactics and ultimate objectives of the labor movement, an abandonment of the idea that all workers had the same economic interests, and a departure from the old "producing classes" point of view. After seventy-five years of oscillation between trade unionism and utopianism, craft-consciousness and humanitarianism, job control and uplift of the masses, the American manualists seemed to have made a choice. They did not deny the abstract principle of a common labor cause, but they had become convinced that the mechanism through which the interests of all could best be promoted was the craft union, with as much voluntary federation as was necessary to protect craft interests and administer those phases of labor's program not coming easily within the scope of autonomous trade bodies.

Chapter III

AMERICAN TRADE-UNION HISTORY, 1890–1920

In functional character, the unionism that slowly achieved predominance during the latter years of the nineteenth century, as the Knights of Labor declined in numbers and influence, was no consistent or unitary thing. On the contrary, its group interpretation and its program of action stemmed from various sources, each of which contributed to the composite whole: from practical lessons learned during a century of oscillations between one set of objectives and another, from the socialist concept of class conflict, from indigenously American antimonopoly and uplift predispositions, from the disillusionment of many wage earners with the all-embracing organizations into which these very predispositions had led them, from observation of the readiness of the American community ferociously to resist encroachments upon the institution of private property, from demonstration by skilled workers of the superiority of economic methods and trade-union organization in the achievement of immediate ends, from a group egotism born of the battles waged by craftsmen on the economic front.

But diversified and antithetical in character though the sources of this unionism were, its basic economic assumptions and convictions had crystallized by the second half of the 1880's; and during the years of stabilization, between 1886 and 1897, these convictions—although challenged constantly by strong minorities within the movement—became clearer and stronger. Brief recapitulation of these assumptions and a reminder of their implications in union policies and methods are here in point.

Primarily, the leaders of federated trade unionism were convinced, reliance must be placed upon economic methods and trade organization. The principle that economic power transcends all other kinds of power found substantiation in the experience of the American workers as well as in socialist theory, and the logical deduction from this principle was the principle of economic methods; while decades of alliances between the wage earners and other members of the "productive classes" had engendered the conviction that the workers must have their own distinctive organization, that the fiction of harmony of economic interests among all the "real producers" must be sternly rejected. Moreover, organization for economic—not political, or uplift, or broadly humanitarian, or "educational"—action must be spontaneous and voluntary.

76

There was not enough class consciousness, there was too much identification in interest and outlook with the propertied classes, on the part of the American workers to permit successful and permanent organization save when the urge to organize originated in their own consciousness of the common or group character of their needs and problems. Nor was the socialist concept of antagonism of interest between the workers and the property owners employing them absent from the philosophy of the unionism that is the concern of the present chapter. A fundamental conflict of interest was inherent in capitalistic institutionalism,[1] but this conflict need not assume a violent character; shorn of its more extreme character, the socialist notion of class struggle became a demand for mutual agreement about those matters on which the interests of employers and workers clashed.

This trade-union creed carried with it concrete implications. Since the great unifying element, the one common denominator, in the functional type of unionism dominated by the American Federation of Labor was control of the workers' immediate economic opportunity—*i.e.*, control of jobs—the "natural" unit of organization was that of men in the same occupations, possessed of approximately the same skill and technical knowledge and potential underbidders of each other in the absence of collective selling of labor power. Such a unionism appealed mightily to the skilled workers. "It embodied the idea of skill, craft solidarity, monopolistic power, and protection against insecurity due either to scarcity of jobs or to arbitrariness of employers. It promised quick returns for limited obligations."[2] Implicit also in the assumptions that have been stated was the policy of stressing immediate improvements rather than ultimate aims. The American worker, experience of many years had demonstrated, was willing to subordinate his individualistic urges to purely wage-earner solidarity only when immediate gains in the matters of wages, hours, and working conditions, not the ultimate building of the structure of a new society within the shell of the old, was the promise placed before him. Still another of the implications of the trade-

[1] The preamble of the constitution of the American Federation of Labor reads: "Whereas, A struggle is going on in all the nations of the civilized world between the oppressors and the oppressed of all countries, a struggle between the capitalist and the laborer, which grows in intensity from year to year, and will work disastrous results to the toiling millions if they are not combined for mutual protection and benefit;

"It, therefore, behooves the representatives of the Trade and Labor Unions of America, in Convention assembled, to adopt such measures and disseminate such principles among the mechanics and laborers of our country as will permanently unite them to secure the recognition of rights to which they are justly entitled.

"We, therefore, declare ourselves in favor of the formation of a thorough Federation, embracing every Trade and Labor Organization in America, organized under the Trade Union system."

[2] Lewis Lorwin, *The American Federation of Labor* (Brookings Institution, Washington, D. C., 1933), p. 53.

union working creed was ruthless suppression of dualism. The internal solidarity of labor groups being a thing of most fragile character—the overshadowing problem of organized labor in America being, indeed, the problem of how to stay organized—anything tending to undermine this solidarity must be severely suppressed. Motivated by this opposition to dual unionism, the American Federation of Labor insisted that only its charter should give to an individual union its rights and privileges and that the principle of strict trade autonomy should be religiously observed. Nor could the unions too rapidly push on toward solidarity inclusive of more than the craft group, for worker solidarity, as understood by the leaders, was a "solidarity with a quickly diminishing potency as one passed from the craft group—which looks upon the jobs in a craft as its common property for which it is ready to fight long and bitterly—to the widening concentric circles of related fields, the industry, the American Federation of Labor, and the world labor movement."[1]

Specific techniques dictated by the economic assumptions of the kind of unionism that superseded the Knights of Labor type were restrained militancy; caution in resort to strikes and boycotts; centralized authority within each union in order to enforce discipline, negotiate successfully with employers, and carry out the terms of joint agreements; high dues and large strike funds; sustained efforts to bring within the trade-union fold the unorganized segments of different crafts or trades; and the obtaining of public approval of unionism. Finally, there must be sought, as a kind of ultimate end, written trade agreements. Some form of trade agreement—the outcome of direct negotiation between employers and workers, negotiation that constitutes the essence of "recognition" of the union—has, indeed, almost necessarily to be the chief objective of a unionism that accepts the institutional characteristics of a system of quasi-competitive capitalism, rejects, at least for the immediate future, the more fundamentalist versions of the Marxian conception of class struggle and its concomitant belief in an inevitable cataclysm eventuating in socialism, and tries merely to improve as much as possible the material conditions of its members here and now.

From the 1890's to the World War

The decline in the membership and strength of American labor organizations after the upheaval that culminated in 1886 was reassuring to men whose fears had been excited and disheartening to men whose hopes had been aroused; and to many of both groups there came the conviction that organized labor could not occupy the place in American

---

[1] Selig Perlman and Philip Taft in "Labor Movements," vol. 4 of Commons and Associates, *History of Labor in the United States* (The Macmillan Company, New York, 1932), pp. 8–9.

economy that for a time it had seemed destined to occupy.   Others, however, regarded the decline either as a temporary reaction or as demonstration that the unionism of the post-Civil War years was to be supplanted by another species.   "A reaction appears to have set in," wrote Professor Ely of Johns Hopkins University, "but a change will again come, and the unions and various associations will once more report an increasing membership.   The progress of the labor movement may be compared to the incoming tide.   Each wave advances a little further than the previous one; and he is the merest tyro in social science, and an ignoramus in the history of his country, who imagines that a permanent decline has overtaken organized labor, whatever his talents or acquisitions may be in other respects."[1]   Likewise the leaders of the trade unions were confident that ultimately their kind of labor organization would demonstrate renewed vitality and unquestionable survival capacity.   They set about the development of their techniques and the strengthening of their organizations and a decade later were able to point to a "stabilization" of the labor movement upon the solid foundations of trade unionism. This decade of stabilization (1887–1897) was a crucial one, and it invites brief examination.

The "Stabilization" Years, 1887–1897.—Comparative economic tranquility characterized the years between 1887 and 1892, while the Knights lost the greater part of their membership and the A. F. of L., patiently plodding ahead, enjoyed some modest gains.   Strikes of 1888 and 1889 failed to reach the proportions of those that had occurred a few years earlier,[2] and a renewed eight-hour movement attained little success outside of the building trades.[3]   But new trade unions were being formed each year.[4]   In the majority of cases, memberships were small and the

[1] Richard T. Ely, *The Labor Movement in America* (1886), p. 90.

[2] For details about the railroad and other strikes of these two years see S. Perlman in *History of Trade Unionism in the United States*, pp. 130–131, and in vol. 2 of Commons and Associates, *History of Labor in the United States*, pp. 498–501.

[3] The failure of the earlier eight-hour movement has been discussed in the preceding chapter (*supra*, pp. 63–64).   At the 1888 convention of the A. F. of L. a resolution that a general demand for an eight-hour day should be made on May 1, 1890, was adopted.   Chief advocates of the resolution were the delegates of the Carpenters' Union, which had experienced rapid growth during the preceding two years and was the largest union affiliated with the Federation.   The strategy called first for a drive to obtain the eight-hour day for the carpenters, then for a centering upon the coal miners.   The carpenters achieved considerable success and claimed that they had won the eight-hour day in 137 cities, but the miners' union was then in a weak position and not more than one-tenth of the miners were organized.   Little progress toward the shorter work period was made after the victories achieved by the carpenters, and for a time the eight-hour movement came to an end.

[4] Between 1886 and 1890 the following national unions, some of which later became powerful labor organizations, were formed or reorganized: Maintenance of Way Employees, Order of Railroad Telegraphers, Brotherhood of Lake Engineers, Bakers' National Union, National Union of Brewers of the United States (1886); Brotherhood of Painters and

high dues and benefit features regarded as essentials in a solid trade-union movement were lacking; but a few of the organizations emerged from the 1880's with centralized power and control over considerable sections of their respective trades[1] and were able to lend indispensable aid to the Federation in its work of unifying the scattered elements of organized labor. The Federation itself, in 1892, was a loose association of some forty nationals, of which twenty-five or thirty paid dues and sent delegates to the annual conventions.[2] In the year ending October 31, 1892, eight new national unions were chartered, and the total number of charters issued to local unions, city centrals, and state federations in thirty-two states was 277.[3]

Events of the second half of the decade 1887–1897 were of a character challenging the progress of federated trade unionism, but the failure of these events to shake the labor movement from the chosen groove of "pure and simple" unionism, as like events had shaken it in the past, constituted impressive evidence that the trade-union economic creed and form of organization had secured the permanent allegiance of at least a majority of America's skilled workers. In the Homestead strike of 1892, the Association of Iron and Steel Workers lost its control over important segments of the industry,[4] and the labor movement as a whole had brought home to it the power of the modern corporation. Then, in 1893, financial panic, followed by a business depression that continued for three years, challenged trade unionism and no doubt caused many

---

Decorators, Stone Cutters' Union, Pattern Makers' League, Order of Railway Conductors (incorporated), American Brotherhood of Steamboat Pilots, Paving Cutters' Union (1887); United Brotherhood of Carpenters and Joiners of America (result of amalgamation, the United Brotherhood of Carpenters having been formed in 1881), United Machinists and Mechanical Engineers of America, Tin, Sheet Iron, and Cornice Workers' Association, Metal Polishers (Knights of Labor Trade Assembly 252), Brotherhood of Railway Car Repairers (1888); Operative Plasterers' International Union (change of name), United Association of Journeymen Plumbers and Steamfitters, National Association of Machinists (change of name), National Progressive Miners' Union, National Association of Letter Carriers (1889); International Brotherhood of Brass Molders, United Mine Workers of America, United Green Glass Workers' Association (1890). From L. Lorwin, *op. cit.*, pp. 474–475.

[1] The United Brotherhood of Carpenters and Joiners in 1892 had a membership of 57,000, the Cigarmakers' Union 27,000, the Iron and Steel Workers' Union more than 24,000, the Iron Molders' Union 23,000, and the Typographical Union 28,000. Also, several smaller unions, like the Granite Cutters, had achieved stability and centralized power. From detail presented by L. Lorwin, *ibid.*, p. 32.

[2] *Ibid.*, p. 31.

[3] *Ibid.*, p. 33.

[4] For details about the Homestead strike, see S. Perlman in *History of Trade Unionism* . . . , pp. 133–135, and in Commons and Associates, *History of Labor in the United States*, vol. 2, pp. 495–497, and L. Lorwin, *op. cit.*, pp. 33–34. The defeat of the union meant not only the loss of the Carnegie Homestead plant, but, as other steel companies followed the lead of the Carnegie corporation, of the majority of mills in the Pittsburgh district.

workers to wonder whether the trade-union idea, rather than the panaceas of political action and social meliorism, really was correct.   The number of employees on strike in 1894, about 750,000, surpassed even the mark that had been set in 1886; the majority of these strikes were defensive in character, not aggressive, as they had been eight years earlier; and in general the workers lost.   The Pullman strike of 1894[1] demonstrated—in the opinion of President Gompers and the other trade-union leaders—the danger of general strikes, which would inevitably disrupt the unions and array public opinion against them, and it impressed upon the union leadership with unmistakable force the fact that the employers had a powerful ally in the courts.   Demands for socialistic and political action became more insistent during the years 1893–1896.[2]

Nevertheless, the trade unions held their membership, the aggregate figure of all unions affiliated with the Federation remaining nearly 275,000 throughout the years 1893–1897; and the success in withstanding the conditions of the depression period proved that trade unionism had won over political action and all-embracing uplift organizations.   In his presidential address of 1899 Samuel Gompers characterized as "noteworthy" the fact that "while in every previous industrial crisis the trade unions were literally mowed down and swept out of existence, the unions

---

[1] The Pullman strike of 1894 constituted the first attempt to stage a strike on the continental European model, and its apparent potentialities alarmed both the trade-union leaders, who feared that a general strike would disrupt the unions and the Federation, and the property-minded middle class, who regarded the strike as an attack upon the entire social order.   In March, 1894, the Pullman Palace Car Co. employees (employed at the plant in Pullman, Ill., south of Chicago) had voted to join Eugene V. Debs's American Railway Union, an organization formed the preceding year under the leadership of Debs to unite all railroad workers in one organization.   The Pullman strike, growing out of a demand of certain employees in the shops at Pullman for a restoration of wages paid the preceding year, began on May 11, 1894.   The American Railway Union unanimously voted at its June, 1894, convention that members should stop handling Pullman cars, and sympathetic strikes began on June 26.   The strike soon spread over a wide territory.   The Knights of Labor endorsed it, the Farmers' Alliance offered to feed the strikers, and many members of the Railroad Brotherhoods participated, even though their organizations were opposed to the strike.   An injunction restraining Debs and the other principal officers of the American Railway Union from compelling or inducing railway employees to strike by threats was issued, and these officers were charged with contempt of court for disobeying this injunction.   Pressure upon President Gompers to lend Federation support to the American Railway Union resulted in a conference of about twenty-five of the officers of national and international unions affiliated with the Federation.   Gompers persuaded the conference to endorse a statement advising the unions affiliated with the A. F. of L. to refrain from participating in any general or local strikes.   Federal troops were sent to Chicago by President Cleveland, in spite of the protest of Governor Altgeld, to protect the United States mails, and the strike collapsed.   For details concerning the Pullman strike, see the standard American history of organized labor, Commons and Associates, *History of Labor in the United States*, vol. 2, pp. 502–507, Norman Ware, *Labor in Modern Industrial Society*, pp. 275–291, and S. Perlman, *History of Trade Unionism* . . . , pp. 136–139.

[2] See *infra*, pp. 107–115.

now in existence have manifested not only the power of resistance, but of stability and permanency . . . . As a result of the trade-union form of organization membership is maintained; the organization remains intact during dull periods of industry, and is prepared to take advantage of the first sign of an industrial revival."[1] As the depression of the 1890's lifted, the species of unionism that had demonstrated its stability and survival capacity, in spite of frequent defeats on the economic front, and had convinced the skilled workers that it was the most appropriate instrument for achievement of their purposes entered upon its first great expansion.

Trade-union Growth, 1897-1914.—From the 1886 peak of possibly 1,000,000, the membership of all American labor organizations had shrunk to less than 450,000 in 1897;[2] then, during the seven-year period 1897-1904 it increased to more than 2,000,000, and in 1914, the year of the outbreak of the First World War, it had attained a level in excess of 2,600,000. The following tabular summary indicates the year-by-year trend in both estimated total trade-union membership and reported[3] A. F. of L. membership.

Several of the facts indicated by the foregoing data deserve comment. (1) The substantial growth experienced by American unionism during these seventeen years is apparent. Trade unionism entered the War period with a membership of 2,687,000, and in 1913 its membership had exceeded this figure by 29,000. The average annual increase was approximately 125,000. In only four of these seventeen years did membership decline, and in none of the four was the drop as great as 10 per cent. (2) The gains, it will be noted, took place to a great extent in the years

---

[1] American Federation of Labor, *Convention Proceedings*, 1899, quoted by S. Perlman in *History of Trade Unionism* . . . , pp. 135–136.

[2] It will be recalled (*supra*, pp. 65–66) that in 1886 the Knights of Labor perhaps had more than 700,000 members, and that there was considerable independent trade unionism. Estimates of actual membership in 1886 vary, but the conclusion of "possibly 1,000,000," with emphasis upon the "possibly," appears to be the one accepted by the majority of labor historians. In 1897, according to the estimates of Prof. Wolman (*Growth of American Trade Unions*, p. 33, and *Ebb and Flow in Trade Unionism*, p. 16) total trade-union membership was an estimated 447,000. That same year (1897) reported membership of the A. F. of L. was 264,825.

[3] The membership reported by member unions at the conventions of the A. F. of L. has probably exceeded to an extent actual membership. See L. Lorwin's *The American Federation of Labor*, p. 484, where estimates of annual average membership of a selected group of unions in 1931 (made by Dr. Leo Wolman for the President's Committee on Recent Social Changes) are compared with reported membership. The data there presented show reported membership of these selected unions to have been 1,119,200, and the estimated membership only 847,300. Since there is no reason for assuming that the same ratio should be applied to all the A. F. of L. unions, or for all years included in the table, however, the authors have presented reported membership in Table 1.

TABLE 1.—AMERICAN TRADE UNIONS, TOTAL MEMBERSHIP AND AMERICAN FEDERATION OF LABOR MEMBERSHIP, 1897–1914[1]

Year	Average annual trade-union membership	Average annual American Federation of Labor membership
1897	447,000	264,825
1898	500,700	278,016
1899	611,000	349,422
1900	868,500	548,321
1901	1,124,700	787,537
1902	1,375,900	1,024,399
1903	1,913,900	1,465,300
1904	2,072,700	1,676,200
1905	2,022,300	1,494,300
1906	1,907,300	1,454,200
1907	2,080,400	1,538,970
1908	2,130,600	1,586,885
1909	2,005,600	1,482,872
1910	2,140,500	1,562,112
1911	2,343,400	1,761,835
1912	2,452,400	1,770,145
1913	2,716,300	1,996,004
1914	2,687,100	2,020,671

[1] Data on total trade union membership have been taken from p. 16 of Prof. Wolman's *Ebb and Flow in Trade Unionism*, (National Bureau of Economic Research Inc., New York, 1936), and those on A. F. of L. membership from the *Reports of Proceedings* of the conventions. Both series of data are here presented in order that the increasing influence of the Federation in American unionism as a whole may be expressed with a modicum of quantitative precision.

1897–1904. During the period 1904–1910, on the other hand, the increase in membership was small, and three of the four years that witnessed declines in both total union membership and A. F. of L. membership during the whole seventeen-year period 1897–1917 were between 1904 and 1910.[1] Between 1910 and 1913, however, union membership increased by almost 600,000. (3) The increased percentage of all American unionists who by 1914 were members of organizations affiliated with the A. F. of L. should also be noted. In 1897 total membership of the Federation was 264,825, or about 60 per cent of the 447,000 trade unionists in the country; in 1904 the Federation included 1,676,200 out of a total of 2,072,700, or about 80 per cent; six years later (1910) the figures were 1,562,112 and 2,140,500, respectively, or 75 per cent; and in

[1] Factors accounting for the less-accelerated progress between 1904 and 1910 are alluded to in the following sections of the chapter. Brief summary mention of the more important of them is sufficient at this point. By 1904 the zest for organization had, to an extent, spent itself. Employer opposition, as is indicated later, solidified about 1902 and became relatively effective by 1904. To an extent, the immediate limits of craft-union development had been reached by 1904, the unions having asserted their jurisdictional claims to areas of industry they regarded as organizable.

1914 the Federation included about 77 per cent of the 2,678,100 trade-
union members.[1]

By 1914, then, organized labor was more than twice as strong, numerically, as it had been in 1886, when the great organization movement of
the Knights of Labor period reached its peak, and it was appreciably
stronger even when allowance has been made for the increase in population and in the number of gainfully employed and potentially organizable
persons. A few important questions concerning the nature of this
growth between 1897 and 1914 suggest themselves. Was it chiefly a
consequence of an expansion of existing unions, or did it reflect an increase
in the number of functioning labor organizations? Was trade-union
membership, in spite of the increase that has just been summarized, concentrated in a comparatively small number of categories of employment,
or had it penetrated fairly generally the occupations in which the American wage earners found employment? Was it confined to the urban
centers, or had it intruded itself into the smaller cities and towns of the
United States? Data are available that make possible reasonably
accurate answers to all three of these questions.

Statistics of the number of national and international unions affiliated
with the A. F. of L. each year and of the total number of charters issued
by, and surrendered to, both the Federation and the international unions
afford the best available—although not conclusive—evidence as to whether
the 1897–1914 growth was chiefly a consequence of the expansion of
existing unions or of an increase in the number of functioning organizations.[2] The conclusion to which examination of both sets of evidence
points is that prior to 1904 the growth in union membership was in considerable part a consequence of an increase in the number of trade unions,
but that thereafter it was much more attributable to expansion of those
already in existence. During the seven-year period 1897–1904 the number of national and international unions affiliated with the Federation

---

[1] The most important groups outside the Federation in 1914 were the "Big Four" Rail-
road Brotherhoods (the Brotherhood of Locomotive Engineers, the Brotherhood of Railroad
Firemen and Enginemen, the Brotherhood of Railway Trainmen, and the Brotherhood of
Railway Conductors), groups that as late as the 1940's still remained independent, the
Industrial Workers of the World, which had been formed in 1906 (cf. infra, pp. 115–118),
and the Bricklayers' Union. The last-named union affiliated with the Federation in 1917.

[2] The data on number of affiliated unions quoted in this paragraph and the following
footnote are from L. Wolman's Ebb and Flow in Trade Unionism, p. 18, and those on the net
number of charters granted each year are from Selig Perlman and Philip Taft, "Labor
Movements," in Commons and Associates, History of Labor in the United States, vol. 4,
p. 14. Professor Wolman's data for 1897 and 1898 were compiled from the Proceedings
of the annual conventions of the American Federation of Labor, and his data for other
years are from L. Lorwin's The American Federation of Labor, p. 488. Professors Perlman
and Taft have taken their data from the Proceedings of the American Federation of Labor
for the various years covered. As the above sentence says, the evidence is not conclusive.
Many of the organizations affiliating had existed for some time.

increased from 58 to 120,[1] and the excess of charters granted over charters surrendered from 1,979 in 1899 to 6,211 in 1903, although in 1904 the figure fell to 1,367.[2]   In only one year during the decade following 1904, however, did the number of nationals and internationals in the Federation equal the 1904 figure, and in 1914 ten fewer were reported than had been ten years earlier.[3]   In part the decline in the number of nationals and internationals after 1904 was a consequence of amalgamations of existing organizations; but, in conjunction with the increase in total union membership and the annual ratios of charters granted to charters surrendered, it was also a reflection of the fact that during the decade 1904–1914 the growth was due to expansion of existing unions rather than to formation of new ones.   Data on the excess of charters granted over those surrendered show that with the exception of one year (1907) the net annual increase was less than 1,000.[4]

In spite of the increase in membership between 1897 and 1914 and of the increase in number of functioning unions between the former year and 1904, American unionism remained concentrated in a comparatively small number of categories of employment.   More than half of the total increase of 2,240,100 during the seventeen-year period was due to the growth of three groups of unions—those of the coal miners, the railroad workers, and the building trades workers[5]—and except for the miners the great mass of semiskilled and unskilled workers remained unorganized. In 1910, 27.8 per cent of the employees in mining, quarrying, and crude petroleum and gas production are estimated to have been organized;[6] 11.4 per cent of those in manufacturing and mechanical industries (including the construction industries); 19.5 per cent of those in transportation and communication; and only 2.0 per cent of those in the service industries.[7]

[1] The number during each of these years was as follows: 1897, 58; 1898, 67; 1899, 73; 1900, 82; 1901, 87; 1902, 97; 1903, 113; 1904, 120.

[2] Perlman and Taft, op. cit., p. 14.   The excess of charters granted by both the Federation and the international unions over charters surrendered to them during each of the years 1899–1904 was as follows: 1899, 1,979; 1900, 3,300; 1901, 2,906; 1902, 4,185; 1903, 4,185; 1904, 1,367.

[3] L. Wolman, Ebb and Flow in Trade Unionism, p. 18.   The number of nationals and internationals affiliated with the Federation each year was: 1905, 118; 1906, 119; 1907, 117; 1908, 116; 1909, 119; 1910, 120; 1911, 115; 1912, 112; 1913, 111; 1914, 110.

[4] Excess of charters granted by both the Federation and the international unions over charters surrendered to them for each of the years 1905–1910: 1905, 253; 1906, 415; 1907, 1,285; 1908, 815; 1909, 131; 1910, 929.   Perlman and Taft, op. cit., p. 14.

[5] From L. Wolman, Ebb and Flow in Trade Unionism, pp. 19 and 20.

[6] Ibid., p. 118.

[7] In some of the subdivisions within these main industrial groups, however, the percentages were considerably higher.   In coal mining 36.8 per cent of the workers were organized in 1910; 27.6 per cent of the employees of steam railroad companies were that year members of trade unions; and 33.2 per cent of the employees in water transportation held membership in trade unions.   Ibid., p. 118.

Trade-union penetration of the less urban sections of the country was another characteristic of the years 1897–1904. According to the analysis of Professors Perlman and Taft,[1] who have examined the data for seven states,[2] the driving force of organized labor prior to 1904 was confined to no one region; indeed, the small-town trade-union membership in some states increased more than did that of the urban centers. After 1904, however, the tendency toward geographical dispersion appears to have run its course. In nonurban communities such as those of the coal industry, trade unionism remained entrenched and sometimes expanded; but for the most part it withdrew to the more hospitable environment of the larger cities, and the outbreak of the European War in 1914 found it, on the whole, with comparatively small representation in the rural regions.[3]

Economic and Social Background.—The years of the trade-union growth summarized in the immediately preceding paragraphs were years when the American economy and American social life were undergoing changes the import of which was profound. Summary mention of some of these changes and reference to the environmental determinants of the unionism of 1897–1914 is imperative at this point, for it is in the light of these changes and environmental determinants that the phases of trade-union history discussed in the following pages must be examined and interpreted.

By 1900, the economic and social United States had, in some respects, reached a turning point. The last frontier had disappeared, and with its disappearance one great epoch in American cultural and economic history came to an end. From the fact that part of the population, all through the nineteenth century, had been migrating westward, carving out anew its mode of life, wresting with primitive and elemental forces, and attaining ownership of small parcels of property had proceeded a spirit of individualism, a buoyancy, a colorful and exuberant culture, that became enduring parts of the American heritage; but these forces operated less powerfully when they ceased to be nurtured by the activism of the frontier.[4] Free land ceased to be the "natural" regulator of wages that it had been during the nineteenth century, and opportunity to attain proprietorship status, fairly real so long as desirable land could be had for the taking, became less abundant. Wage earners were consequently not so prone to think of themselves as future property owners rather than as persons who must act collectively to enhance their job opportunities, and agrarian movements ceased to have their nineteenth-

---

[1] *Op. cit.*, pp. 15–19.

[2] New York, New Hampshire, Maine, Missouri, Minnesota, Michigan, and Iowa.

[3] For detail, see Perlman and Taft, *op. cit.*, pp. 15–20.

[4] For the standard treatise on the influence of the frontier, see F. J. Turner, *The Frontier in American History*.

century lure for urban craftsmen.   A smaller percentage of the nation's population was dependent upon agriculture for livelihood as the twentieth century entered its second decade than had been during the years that witnessed the rise and decline of the Knights of Labor and the stabilization of federated trade unionism; more found place in industrial pursuits.[1] These changes in the relative importance of different sources of livelihood were accompanied by an increase in the relative number of wage earners and lower salaried persons in the gainfully occupied part of the population.[2]   Along with the changes that have just been mentioned went increasing urbanization of the population,[3] another trend of significance in accounting for the trade-union expansion of these years.   The kind of unionism that succeeded the nineteenth-century "plain people" varieties was, in spite of the expansion into rural areas before 1904, more indigenous to, and found a more hospitable environment in, the cities and larger towns.   As urban dwellers, the wage earners were confronted by various kinds of economic insecurity, they were more—in the majority of cases entirely—dependent upon the wages they earned for livelihood, and they discovered that their economic ties with others working in the same occupations or trades were exceedingly strong.   To many of them the proper remedial expedient, organization and collective dealing with employers, seemed to be obvious.

As industrialization and urbanization were proceeding, the rising tide of immigration reached its peak.   Net annual immigration during the decade 1881–1890 had been 524,661; then, during the 1890's, a decade that included a prolonged depression, the annual average dropped to

[1] Agriculture, which in the 1880's had been the most important source of livelihood, absorbing 44.4 per cent of the gainfully occupied persons of the United States, according to the Census of 1880, had by 1900 come to include only 35.7 per cent of them, and by 1910 only 32.6 per cent.   Manufacturing, on the other hand, included 21.8 per cent of the gainfully occupied in 1880, 24.4 per cent in 1900, and 29.3 per cent in 1910 (*Abstract of the Fifteenth Census of the United States*, p. 305).   For a more detailed summary and for discussion of the changes in sources of livelihood, see vol. I of this series, pp. 21–23.

[2] For a breakdown of the census data to show changes in the absolute and relative size of different economic groups (*i.e.*, farmers, farm laborers, proprietors and officials, professional persons, lower-salaried persons, servants, and industrial wage earners), made by A. H. Hansen and T. M. Sogge, *cf. Journal of the American Statistical Association*, vol. 28 (June, 1933), pp. 199–203.   Professor Leo Wolman's classification of the working population into three major groups—employees, professional workers, and proprietors, managers, officials, salaried workers, and commission workers—is to be found in *Ebb and Flow in Trade Unionism*, p. 113.   For a summary of both of these studies and for discussion of changes in the economic status of the working population, see vol. I of this series, pp. 32–38.

[3] In 1890, 35.4 per cent of the American people lived in "urban territory" (places of 2,500 or more population), and 64.6 per cent in "rural territory"; in 1910 the figures were 45.8 and 54.2, respectively.   In the former year 15.0 per cent of the people lived in cities of 100,000 or more population, and 18.2 per cent in cities of 50,000 or more, while in 1910 the respective figures were 21.6 and 26.1.   *Abstract of the Fifteenth Census of the United States*, p. 14.

367,856; but during the first ten years of the 1900's it mounted to 869,536. More than 750,000 persons from other countries arrived in the United States during the year prior to the outbreak of war in Europe.[1] As significant as the increase in the volume of immigration were the changes in its sources. In the early 1880's, more than five-sixths of the European immigration was from Northern and Western Europe and less than one-sixth from Southern and Eastern Europe; by 1914 the proportions had been almost exactly reversed.[2] The older immigrants had frequently brought with them a "craft mastery," far from all of them were unfamiliar with the theories and methods of trade unionism, and some brought to the American working class doctrines that, as has been indicated in the preceding chapter, contributed not a little to the building of a strictly wage-earner movement for improvement of material conditions.

That the effects upon the trade unionism of the early twentieth century of both the large volume of immigration and of the changes in its sources were fundamental and pervasive goes without saying. To the leaders of the federated craft unionism, the newer immigrant workers constituted a competitive menace that must be guarded against both by the attainment of a trade-union "job ownership" excluding from participation in the opportunities of the craft these competitive under-bidders and by governmental restriction of immigration. Frequently the consequence of abundant immigration was the undermining of the jobs of skilled workers, since—particularly as the "new" immigrants took the place of the "old"—many employers found it more economical to adapt jobs to the limited capacities of men than to assume the expense of developing, through costly training programs, skilled workers. They could not buy skill ready-made in the European market to so great an extent as they had formerly been able to buy it and accordingly they introduced technological conditions reducing the proportion of all wage earners who must possess craft knowledge and skill. As a result, the cleavage between the skilled and the unskilled was widened, and the organized segments of the former set about perfecting their control over job opportunities through a system of working rules that sometimes had little application to the employment conditions of employees whose jobs were unskilled or semiskilled. The fact that many of the newer immigrants, arriving in the United States with backgrounds of racial or class oppression, had developed habits of docility rendered easier the introduction of employer policies in which there was little place for collective dealing and labor organization and at the same time sincerely convinced many of the trade-union leaders that to attempt to organize the unskilled

---

[1] From *Annual Reports* of the United States Commissioner of Immigration.

[2] In 1882 the "old" immigration constituted 86.9 per cent of all European immigration, and the "new" 13.1 per cent. In 1914 the proportions were: "old," 15.5 per cent; "new," 84.5 per cent.

was, save in exceptional cases, a task of insurmountable difficulty. As was indicated in the preceding chapter, racial and nationalistic differences between the skilled and the unskilled were a barrier to crystallization of the conviction that they should attack their economic problems together; and the fact that workers and employers in the United States were to a considerable extent of different racial and nationalistic stock was a force accentuating the differences in points of view and the fundamental antagonisms that were already inherent in employer-worker relations. Unlike the older immigrants from England or Germany, some of whom had contributed so greatly to the building of a federated trade unionism, the majority of those who turned their eyes and directed their footsteps to America during the decade and a half before 1914 were possessed of little acquaintance with labor organization, and they less frequently brought with them a clearly developed or articulated philosophy of labor's position in a system of capitalism.

Other developmental trends deserve brief mention. The competitive areas within which were determined the prices of commodities continued to expand, and the trade unions, in consequence, found imperative the organization of theretofore unorganized regions, in order to prevent undermining of their standards by competition of goods produced under lower labor costs. As union-produced and nonunion-produced goods came to compete to a greater extent, the temptation to resort to the boycott—legally hazardous as judicial construction of the Antitrust Act of 1890 proved this to be before the end of the first decade of the century—became stronger. With the expansion of market areas, industry became larger of scale,[1] and it made more extensive application of industrial inventions. While the majority of factories remained comparatively small and while the prevalence of small-scale establishments continued to be one of the important problems confronting some of the trade unions,[2] the dominant trend during the years that are the concern of these pages was, particularly in manufacturing, toward larger scale

---

[1] Between 1899 and 1909 the number of manufacturing establishments in the United States increased by 29.4 per cent, the number of wage earners by 40.4 per cent, wages (in dollars) by 70.6 per cent, value product by 81.2 per cent, and value added by manufacture by 76.5 per cent (*Biennial Census of Manufactures*, 1933, pp. 18–19). In other words, the number of wage earners increased much more rapidly than the number of establishments, while gross value of products and value added by manufacture increased much more rapidly than the number of wage earners. In 1904 manufacturing establishments the value of whose product was $100,000 or more constituted 11.2 per cent of all manufacturing establishments; a decade later, in 1914, such establishments constituted 19.2 per cent of all manufacturing establishments (*Statistical Abstract of the United States*, 1920, p. 190). For a fuller account of the development of large-scale production and discussion of its effects upon the position of labor, see vol. I of this series, pp. 6–13.

[2] For a brief discussion of some of the problems to which continued prevalence of small-scale production has given rise, see vol. I of this series, pp. 12–13.

establishments.   Relatively fewer workers, in other words, found place in employing units where "individual bargaining" could be much more than an empty phrase.   Changes in basic production processes and techniques accompanied the development of large-scale industry, the quantity of capital and nonhuman power utilized in the processes of production increased much more rapidly than did the quantity of labor,[1] and in the majority of lines of enterprise physical output per employee became greater.[2]   Mechanization, the increase in the quantity of capital and nonhuman power, and simplification of task in large-scale establishments—the last-named trend being encouraged, as has already been pointed out, by the character of the immigrant labor supply—often operated to undermine the jobs of skilled workers.   The labor organizations did not, in the majority of cases, take a position of long-run opposition to technological changes and the introduction of machinery,[3] but they did insist that their employment opportunities be protected in some manner when innovations and laborsaving machinery were introduced, and they looked more than ever to trade-union working rules as the short-run protectors of craft opportunity.

The increasing importance of the corporate form of business organization also deserves mention.   By 1909 only 25.9 per cent of the nation's manufacturing establishments were owned by corporations, but this 25.9 per cent of the establishments employed 75.6 per cent of all wage

[1] In manufacturing, for example, the number of wage earners employed (average for the year) was 4,713,000 in 1899 and 6,888,000 in 1914.   The amount of horsepower devoted to productive operations, on the other hand, increased from 10,098,000 to 22,264,000 (*Statistical Abstract of the United States*, 1936, p. 733).   The quantity of fixed capital devoted to manufacturing is estimated to have increased by 144 per cent during this period (P. H. Douglas, *The Theory of Wages*, pp. 113–121).   See vol. I of this series, pp. 19–21, where data on wage earners, horsepower, total fixed capital, and relative fixed capital, as compiled from various sources, are given for the years 1869–1929.

[2] Although physical output per employee perhaps did not increase as much during these years as one might be led to expect in view of the really great increase in nonhuman power and fixed capital.   Professor Douglas's index of physical productivity in all manufacturing (see *Real Wages in the United States*, p. 510) shows the index number for 1914 (on the 1899 base of 100) to have been 116.   For estimates of the trend of physical product per employee in specific manufacturing industries and in nonmanufacturing lines of enterprise, see the same study, pp. 509–524, and vol. I of this series, pp. 151–157.   The reason physical product per employee did not increase to a greater extent than it did during these years is probably to be found in part in the fact that in the majority of plants and industries not a great deal was done to increase the efficiency of labor.   During these years markets were fairly "easy," prices were rising, and cheap immigrant labor was available; consequently the interest in increasing productivity, while far from absent, perhaps did not reach the proportions that it would have reached under other conditions.   In some sections of industry the average level of efficiency in 1914 was much lower than it was a decade later.

[3] See *infra*, pp. 429–437, where trade-union position on these matters is discussed in some detail, and S. H. Slichter, *Union Policies and Industrial Management*, Chaps. 7, 8, and 9.

earners attached to manufacturing enterprises.[1] Possessing unity of action and employing thousands of workers, the large corporation was obviously in better position to resist the demands of workers than was the small firm. Together with the rise of the corporation as the dominant (in point of number of wage earners employed, capital, and value of product) form of business organization went horizontal and vertical combination of industry.[2] In some respects the development of business combinations—the old technical "trusts," holding companies, mergers, and then more subtle forms—redounded to the benefit of labor. Less subject to the nibbling of competition, these combinations were frequently able to maintain better terms and conditions of employment, dictated by unions with which they must deal, than were attainable in sharply competitive industries of many units. But the majority of them were antiunion in their labor predilections, and they frequently were able to recruit nonunion labor from a rather wide area and to set and maintain wage rates, even in the face of trade-union pressure, when competitive forces in industries where labor was unorganized—or trade-union pressure upon numerous smaller competing employers—would have forced readjustment upward.

The wealth and income of the American people increased appreciably between the late 1890's and 1914, but neither concentration of property ownership nor inequality in the distribution of income showed signs of giving way to wider diffusion,[3] and real earnings advanced but little.[4] A majority of the semiskilled and unskilled workers—perhaps a majority of all wage earners—continued to receive incomes insufficient to support families of average or "standard" size at a minimum health and decency level.[5] Awareness of these facts was one of the motivations of the "progressive revolt"—of the "quest for social justice"—of the years between 1909 and 1912, with its accompanying crusade for labor legislation. Convinced that *laissez faire* must be modified, but with the basic institutions of capitalism retained, the reformers pictured the worker as the chief victim of the conditions it was their mission to analyze and expose; and the intellectual climate engendered by the various "social justice" movements was favorable to collective self-help efforts on the part of the wage earners. The remedies sought by the reformers were, it is true, to be achieved in large part by political methods, and their

---

[1] *Abstract of the Fourteenth Census of the United States*, p. 1021.

[2] For a discussion of the significance, from the point of view of the position of labor, of the development of the corporate form of business organization and of business combinations, see vol. I of this series, pp. 14–19.

[3] For estimates of the increase in the absolute and per capita national wealth, and of its distribution, see vol. I of this series, pp. 261–271, and for data on the increase in the absolute and per capita national income, see pp. 137–157 and 219–227 of the same volume.

[4] See *ibid.*, pp. 85–115.

[5] See *ibid.*, pp. 233–239.

proponents were generally middle-class people actuated by strongly humanitarian motives; but to a not-negligible extent the labor organizations were the beneficiaries of the social temper of the time. The job-conscious unionists of the Federation and the members of nonaffiliated conservative organizations like the railroad brotherhoods did not revert to the nineteenth-century habit of abandoning, so far as primary emphasis was concerned, the "pure and simple" variety of unionism, of permitting the distinctively labor organizations to be submerged in the broader reform movements. But with the help of their middle-class friends, they did—while continuing to tread the straight and narrow path of trade unionism—make the American public much more familiar with labor's grievances and with its aspirations.

Stabilization of Contractual Relations.—A unionism eschewing, for the most part, political tactics and adhering tenaciously to the thesis that the economic basis of labor organization was superior to any other necessarily had as its chief aspiration the attainment of trade agreements with employers. These agreements, the outcome of direct negotiation between organized workers and organized employers (or between organized workers and individual employers), were in themselves the ultimate form of "recognition" of the union. To the extent that they embodied those rules and protective regulations that had been sought by the labor organizations, job ownership had been conceded to the wage earners as a group. Such agreements, specifying the basic conditions of employment and ordinarily outlining procedures for enforcement and renewal, were evidence that collective bargaining had succeeded in its purpose. The increasing number of trade agreements during the late 1890's and the early 1900's is an important part of the story of trade-union development during those years.

Prior to the 1890's trade agreements had, of course, resulted from employer-union negotiations,[1] but they still remained the exceptional,

---

[1] The early "bill of prices" or "price list" (*cf. supra*, pp. 20–21) was the precursor of the modern trade agreement. The earliest known trade agreement in the United States, "a simple wage agreement of a very primitive type," appeared in the printing industry in 1795 (Division of Economic Research, National Labor Relations Board, *Written Trade Agreements in Collective Bargaining*, Government Printing Office, 1940, p. 20). By the 1830's written agreements covering matters other than wages and hours existed, and by the middle of the nineteenth century they had become longer and somewhat complicated documents. The agreements of that time were, however, almost entirely those of local craft unions and the employers. With the industrialization of the country, the coverage tended to be extended, both geographically and industrially. During the 1870's written agreements were maintained and in some areas even advanced, in spite of business depression. In the iron industry, where there had been a written wage scale since 1866, the trade agreements were extended during the 1870's, and the first written agreements in the bituminous coal industry were also introduced during this period. Trade agreements were introduced in the anthracite coal industry in 1869, although they were temporarily abandoned a few years

not the ordinary, outcome of trade-union activity. In 1890 a system of national agreements and annual conferences was established in the glass-container industry; and the following year the National Union of Iron Molders and the Stove Founders Defense Association entered into a national agreement that has frequently been characterized as the beginning of the modern trade agreements.[1] Depression during and after 1893 retarded somewhat the application of the trade-agreement system, but about 1897, as the business cycle turned upward, this normal concomitant of successful collective-bargaining relationships appeared in an increasing number of trades and industries. The 1897 strike of the bituminous coal miners led to the agreement of 1898 and to establishment of the Interstate Joint Conference as an instrument of collective bargaining, and shortly thereafter the anthracite miners secured an agreement incorporating part of their demands upon the operators.[2] In the building trades agreements between the unions in particular trades and their employers, frequently incorporating plans for conciliation and arbitration of disputes, had been entered into as early as the 1880's, and uniformity in the main provisions of the agreements of the various trades began to

---

later. With the expansion of industry and the extension of the factory system in the 1880's, trade agreements multiplied, especially beginning about 1887, but still they remained the exception (*Ibid.*, pp. 20–22). See also J. R. Commons, *Trade Unionism and Labor Problems* (1905 ed.).

[1] A few words about the agreement in the stove industry—one of the first national agreements and for years one of the most successful—are merited at this point. Three decades of strife, discontent, and unstabilized competitive conditions preceded the institution of peaceful collective bargaining. The first step toward achieving a national agreement was taken at the Union convention of 1890, when a conference was proposed to the employers. At the conference of March, 1891, a joint committee (three representatives of the employees and three of the employers) was set up. The three basic clauses in the agreement were: (1) disputes that could not be settled directly were to be submitted to the presidents of the two associations; (2) should they fail to reach an agreement, the question in dispute was to be placed before the Conference Committee, whose majority decision was to be binding for twelve months; and (3) no change was to be made in the *status quo* while a dispute was pending. The agreement has been renewed periodically, and on the whole it has functioned successfully in the solving of long-standing problems as well as of new ones. During the postwar period the competition of factory-made central-heating systems and loss of membership by the Association occasioned considerable difficulties in the operation of the system, but the conference method has been continued. By the early 1940's, the agreement contained twenty-eight clauses that had been added from time to time to the original three. For accounts of this interesting agreement, see Philip Taft in the Twentieth Century Fund Volume, *How Collective Bargaining Works* (1942), S. Perlman, *History of Trade Unionism . . . ,* pp. 143–144, and Frey and Commons, "Conciliation in the Stove Industry," *Bulletin of the Bureau of Labor,* January, 1906, pp. 138–150.

[2] See A. E. Suffern, *Conciliation and Arbitration in the Coal Industry of America* and *The Coal Miner's Struggle for Industrial Status,* Perlman and Taft, vol. 4 of *History of Labor in the United States,* pp. 20–50, Chris Evans, *History of the United Mine Workers of America,* Isador Lubin, *Miners' Wages and the Cost of Coal,* and Elsie Gluck, *John Mitchell, Labor Leader.*

be attained in the various cities.[1] The printers, a group always most adept in the practices of conservative business unionism, in 1898 entered into the "Syracuse agreement" with the United Typothetae, an agreement providing for gradual reduction in hours from ten to nine, the unions promising to do all they could to equalize wage scales in the various competitive districts.[2] Organized workers engaged in the operation of trains had secured agreements with individual carriers, in a few cases, more than a decade before 1890.[3] Among other industries in which collective agreements were established during the years immediately following 1898 were iron molding, newspaper publishing, stove mounting, brass polishing, machine shop, pottery, overalls manufacture, and shipping on the Great Lakes.[4] "The clarification of the conception of the trade agreement was perhaps the main achievement of the nineties. Without the trade agreement, the labor movement could hardly come to eschew 'panaceas' and to reconstitute itself upon the basis of opportunism. The coming in of the trade agreement, whether national, sectional, or local, was also the chief factor in stabilizing the movement against industrial depressions."[5]

[1] See William Haber, *Industrial Relations in the Building Industry*, pp. 346–463.

[2] This agreement was between the United Typothetae, representing the employers, and three labor organizations, the International Typographical Union, the International Printing Pressmen and Assistants' Union, and the International Brotherhood of Bookbinders. Attempts to reach a national agreement with the employers, primarily as a means of equalizing wages among competitive districts and of shortening hours, had been made by the organized printers a decade before the Syracuse agreement of 1898. The 1888 convention of the International Typographical Union appointed a committee to visit the national session of the United Typothetae and discuss a "basis of cooperation between the two organizations" (Perlman and Taft, "Labor Movements," in Commons and Associates, *History of Labor in the United States*, vol. 4, p. 53). The Typothetae rejected the suggestion and recommended that differences between employers and employees be settled locally. By 1897, however, the Typographical Union had secured the support of the Pressmen and of the Bookbinders, and the Typothetae received union representatives at its 1898 convention and in the fall of that year entered into the Syracuse conference that produced the agreement. The union continued its shorter-hours campaign, seeking now the eight-hour day. The Typothetae in 1902 offered to sign an agreement with the International Typographical to pay the union scale and maintain union conditions, provided the employer was granted the right to employ whomever he chose, regardless of union affiliation (*ibid.*, p. 56). The Typographical Union rejected this proposal, although the Pressmen accepted it. It was not until 1908 that the Union won on the eight-hour-day issue. For details in connection with the agreements in the printing industry, see George Barnett, *The Printers*, Leona M. Powell, *History of the United Typothetae of America*, and George A. Tracy, *History of the Typographical Union*.

[3] With enactment of the legislation of 1888, and then of the Erdman Act of 1898, terms and conditions of employment of railway employees of course became more subject to governmental influence. See *infra*, pp. 730–750, where the machinery of dispute adjustment on railways, as provided for in successive legislative enactments, is discussed in some detail.

[4] Division of Economic Research, National Labor Relations Board, *op. cit.*, p. 23.

[5] S. Perlman, *History of Trade Unionism*, p. 145.

Opposition of Employers.—Between 1897 and 1904, as has already been indicated, the membership of American trade unions increased from less than 500,000 to more than 2,000,000. Concurrently with this increase in numerical strength, the national and international organizations—to which the locals became more subordinated—acquired greater power, more centralized control, and enhanced elasticity and unity of action. Treasuries came to hold funds sufficient to finance expensive strikes. Trade-union strength sometimes necessitated the surrender, under the terms of trade agreements, of employer prerogatives that had been regarded as sacred. In the face of these developments, the alarm of many employers increased and their opposition to trade unionism increased, even while collective bargaining and agreements incorporating jointly determined rules and practices were becoming the accepted mode of industrial relations in important trades and industries.

Conditions toward the end of 1901 appeared to be favorable for an open-shop drive that, many business interests hoped, would prevent the spread of unionism, if not eradicate it where a foothold had already been secured. Those industries in which employers, for one reason or another, were comparatively willing to enter into collective agreements had by that year been fairly well organized, and the mere fact that unionism had advanced to a certain extent rendered further advances more difficult, opposition to them more promising. Although opposition to trade unionism seems to have been more bitter among the owners of small- and medium-sized firms,[1] the use of the corporation as the dominant form of business organization on the whole lent sustenance to the antiunion activities of the period. Not only were they in better position to utilize the weapons of discharge for union activities, espionage, propaganda, and paternalistic welfare work, but the necessity that their labor policies

---

[1] While the large employers in steel, the metal trades, Great Lakes shipping, and elsewhere were antiunion, it probably was the smaller employers—men who owned and managed their own businesses—who were most reluctant to permit any curbing of individual initiative, freedom of contract, and competition. These smaller enterprises were vigorously opposed to "trusts," and their opposition to trusts of course included opposition to "labor trusts." Also, the real strength of the movement seems to have centered in the West rather than in the East, in spite of the fact that its financial nourishment was in the latter part of the country and that the headquarters of the various associations participating in the drive were generally in New York City or one of the other eastern cities. Nevertheless, the rise of giant corporations and of industrial combinations, antiunion in their labor predilections, was a most potent factor in the open-shop drive of the years following 1901, even though the feeling against unions ran higher, was more personal in character, and tended to express itself more in terms of the indignities of invasion of "rights," among the smaller businessmen of the country than among the managers of large corporations and the bankers who frequently controlled these corporations. For an excellent discussion of the sources of this opposition to unions, see L. Lorwin, *The American Federation of Labor*, pp. 76–84.

be accepted by fairly large portions of the labor supply implemented tremendously the open-shop movement.

Various organizations participated in the drive.[1] Between 1900, when John Kirby, Jr., organized an association of employers in Dayton, Ohio—the first "completely open-shop city" of any appreciable size in the United States—and 1906, employers' associations unalterably opposed to the closed shop, and in some cases refusing to have any dealings with labor organizations, were formed in a number of large and medium-sized cities. The National Association of Manufacturers[2] had by 1903 adopted an aggressive open-shop policy, and it, in turn, promoted the organization of the Citizens' Industrial Association of America, a body of more inclusive membership.[3] Still a third of the general associations, the American Anti-boycott Association, organized in 1902, devoted its energies in large part to bringing restraint of trade prosecutions against the unions, and in 1908 its efforts were rewarded with an unqualified Supreme Court declaration that labor combinations came within the purview of the Sherman Antitrust Act of 1890.[4] The efforts of these general associations were supplemented by those of several trade associations. The National Metal Trades Association in 1901 broke off relations with the Machinists' Union, with which it had entered into a national agreement the year before, and from then on maintained a consistently open-shop policy. The National Founders Association refused in 1904 to deal longer with the Molders Union; and in 1905 a break between the National Erectors Association and the Bridge and Structural Iron Workers Union caused the former to espouse the cause of the open

[1] For more detailed account of the open-shop drive of this period, see Perlman and Taft, op. cit., pp. 129–137, and L. Lorwin, op. cit., pp. 76–84.

[2] The National Association of Manufacturers, organized in 1895, had originally been concerned chiefly with questions of trade expansion, but by 1903 it had definitely become converted to a policy of belligerent open-shopism. For a detailed account of the history, policies, philosophy, and propaganda and other methods of the N.A.M., see A. G. Taylor, "The National Association of Manufacturers," University of Illinois Studies in the Social Sciences, vol. 15 (1927).

[3] This association included employers in branches of industry other than manufacturing and devoted its energies in large part to arousing public opinion against unions and making the public aware of the "pitfalls of unionism." The Association brought patronage pressure against businessmen in the various cities where its branches were formed to force them to become members, and when necessary attempt was made to mobilize the purchasing power of the general public. L. Lorwin, op. cit., p. 77.

[4] Loewe v. Lawlor, 208 U. S. 274 (1908). The Supreme Court reasoning in this, the famous Danbury Hatters case, is discussed later in this volume (infra, pp. 568–569). The American Anti-boycott Association was in part the creation of Daniel Davenport, a Bridgeport, Conn., lawyer. D. E. Loewe, one of the manufacturers boycotted by the United Hatters of America, took the first step in organizing the American Anti-boycott Association, and it was he who enlisted the efforts of Mr. Davenport. The name of the American Anti-boycott Association has since been changed to League for Industrial Rights.

shop.[1] The National Council for Industrial Defense, an inclusive organization with primarily political and lobbying functions, was organized at the instigation of the National Association of Manufacturers in 1907. Organized and disciplined national leadership was given the movement when, in October of 1903, a number of open-shop propagandists met in convention and formed the Citizens' Industrial Association.[2]

Various tactics were employed by these antiunion associations. Members were exhorted to maintain open shops, not to become "traitors to their class" or "traitors to America"; in some cases membership itself involved a virtual pledge not to enter into closed-shop agreements; financial assistance was extended to employers engaged in trade disputes; black lists were maintained; joint support was given in cases involving litigation; legislation sponsored by the trade unions was opposed; and directly or indirectly attempts were made to mold public opinion in favor of the open shop.[3] Constantly the thesis that the interests of the employing class were the interests of society as a whole, including the wage earners, was reiterated,[4] and the moral duty of the employer to defend, in the name of society, the "right" of the nonunion man to work was emphasized.

The drive produced results. While unionism continued to maintain the foothold it had acquired in some of the most important industries and trades, there is little doubt that the already noted slowing down of the

---

[1] See Luke Grant, *The Bridge and Structural Iron Workers Union* (one of the studies prepared for the United States Commission on Industrial Relations of 1914–1915).

[2] In April, 1903, a number of the leaders of the open-shop movement met, at the call of D. M. Parry, president of the National Association of Manufacturers, to formulate plans and to provide cohesion and unity on a national scale for the open-shop drive. It was this action that in fact constituted the turning point in the history of the National Association of Manufacturers, which had formerly concerned itself primarily with trade problems, the tariff, and the like. The April, 1903, conference issued a call for a convention to be held on October 29, 1903. At this convention, attended by 250 delegates from 124 employers' organizations, the Citizens' Industrial Association was launched. An executive committee, a kind of general staff of the open-shop campaign, was appointed; a statement attacking the closed shop as contrary to the principles of American government and institutions was issued; and formation of local associations in each craft and affiliation of local associations with the National Association of Manufacturers were urged. Conventions were held annually for several years thereafter. From detail in Perlman and Taft, *op. cit.*, pp. 133–136.

[3] A number of individuals of influence, the purity of whose motives is beyond question, were enlisted in the open-shop drive. One of these, President Charles W. Eliot of Harvard University, characterized the scab worker as being in fact "a very good type of modern hero."

[4] An extreme statement of employer position, quoted many times during the years since it was made, is that of George F. Baer, president of the Philadelphia and Reading Company: "The rights and interests of the laboring man will be protected and cared for not by labor agitators but by Christian men to whom God in His infinite wisdom has given control of the property interests of the country."

rate of growth after 1904[1] was in part imputable to the concerted efforts of employers to halt the advance that began in 1897 and to maintain or re-establish the open shop. Public opinion was influenced by the crusade against unionism in general as it had not been by the employers' resistance to particular unions on specific fronts.[2] Particularly in the primarily agricultural states did trade unions become increasingly suspect. "The concerted campaign of open-shop employers . . . had stopped unionism in its tracks, as [is] borne out by the aggregate membership figures of the labor organizations. The liquidation of unionism in the smaller communities that accompanied this general repulse of the labor movement possessed a significance beyond mere loss in membership. It was as if non-urbanized America, still the nation's political and social stronghold, had tried unionism and rejected it as an alien growth."[3] About 1908 a rising political progressivism reinculcated in the public mind a somewhat more liberal attitude on labor questions, and the influence of the Citizens' Industrial Association and other labor-opposing organizations waned. Equally important in explaining the decline in their influence and aggressiveness, however, was the fact that to no inconsiderable extent their purpose of checking the growth of unionism had been achieved.

Organized labor's reaction to the employers' offensive followed no consistent or unitary pattern. To the socialists within the Federation and to the western radical elements, some of whom in 1906 united in forming the Industrial Workers of the World,[4] the appreciable success of the open-shop crusade and the public support it elicited were evidence of the fatuity of expecting that unionism, if it confined its objectives to a narrow range and did not seek to deprive the incumbent owners of industry of their property rights, would be able to entrench itself as the protector of the workers' job interests in all or a majority of the branches of American economic life. The business interests of the individualistic

[1] Cf. supra, p. 83.

[2] During the anthracite strike of 1902, public opinion was on the whole favorable to the miners, and this favorable opinion inevitably extended to an extent to organized labor in general. But by 1904 or 1905 a distinct change in the public temper could be noted. At the 1906 convention of the Citizens' Industrial Association, C. W. Post, then its head, was able to say that "two years ago the press and pulpit were delivering platitudes about the oppression of the workingman. Now this all has been changed since it has been discovered that the enormous Labor Trust is the heaviest oppressor of the independent workingman as well as the common American citizen. The people have become aroused and are now acting. It has been the duty of this Association to place the facts before the people by various forms of publicity in the work of moulding public opinion to a point of active self-defense." Citizens' Industrial Association, Proceedings of the Fourth Convention, pp. 6–9, quoted by Perlman and Taft, in Commons and Associates, op. cit., vol. 4, pp. 136–137 (The Macmillan Company, New York, 1932).

[3] Ibid., p. 136 (The Macmillan Company, New York, 1932).

[4] Cf. infra, pp. 116–118.

United States, these left-wing groups contended, had demonstrated their unyielding opposition to even such minor encroachments upon property prerogatives as were contemplated by the program of the trade unions and their unwillingness to be lured into recognition of the unions and collective bargaining by protestations of reverence for private property and promises of stability and good faith in contractual relations.   Obviously, then, the moral of the employers' offensive was the need to revitalize the trade-union movement into an instrumentality for hastening the collapse of the social relations of production that, in their aggregate, constituted capitalism.   Conservative trade unionism, the dominant type both within and without the Federation, had impressed upon it the fact that it would be accepted as part of the permanent institutionalism of many industries only when employers could do no other than accept it, and its conviction that hard-hitting tactics on the economic front—tactics dictating centralized control on the part of the national organizations, discipline, strike funds, and those auxiliary features which would aid in holding the membership in days of adversity as well as in days of triumph and improvement in material status—were a prime essential was deepened and solidified.   Legislation emancipating organized labor from the fetters of judicial interference was sought, but only as a means of rendering the unions stronger in achieving by economic action their limited objectives. The conviction that the opposition of employers dictated more, not less, militancy and aggressiveness on the economic front was, however, accompanied by a greater consciousness that the unions must demonstrate to employers and to the public their determination to abide in good faith by the terms of agreements once entered into and that hasty and ill-considered strikes must be prevented.   To an extent the open-shop drive had been precipitated, the leadership and many of the rank and file became aware, by the irresponsibility of some of the organizations and, particularly, by their readiness to strike regardless of unexpired agreements if opportunity for attainment of immediate advantages presented itself; and the offspring of this awareness was an enhanced feeling of responsibility.

Still another phase of labor's defense, or counteroffensive, was the qualified adoption of a policy of interclass collaboration on a scale wider than merely that of joint negotiation and mutual effort to arrive at satisfactory trade agreements.   This policy—anathema to the radical elements, a crass violation, from their point of view, of the principles of the class struggle—is best typified by the alignment of Mr. Gompers and other labor leaders with the National Civic Federation.   It left its imprint upon American unionism during the years on through, and after, the World War of 1914–1918, and its adoption was symptomatic of developments in the economic theorizing and social outlook of the leadership that—in spite of adherence to the fundamentals of the economic creed formulated during the years the trade unions were superseding the Knights of Labor—had been taking place.

A product of the industrial turmoil of the 1890's, the National Civic Federation[1] was predicated upon the assumption that the employers, workers, capitalists, philanthropists, and intellectuals of the country could, and should, be brought into agreement on a number of broad industrial principles, the acceptance of which was dictated by the mutual interdependence of labor and capital and by the public interest in the maintenance of tranquil industrial relations. As applied to the development of labor policies, the Civic Federation's program was threefold: convincing the public that strikes and lockouts could be avoided, inducing employers and workers to enter into trade agreements, and maintaining machinery for the mediation and adjudication of industrial disputes.

Samuel Gompers,[2] John Mitchell, James O'Connell, and a number of other outstanding trade unionists affiliated with the Civic Federation, and from the point of view of an opportunistic and pragmatic business unionism their action was far from lacking in reasonable basis. Well-financed employer associations were actively engaged in molding the kind of public opinion on labor questions that they wanted, and in the Civic Federation the trade-union leaders thought they saw an instrumentality for putting their case before the public. Moreover, a pro-collective-bargaining organization that itself included representatives of the employing and investing classes might be most helpful in inducing employers to recognize unions and enter into trade agreements without the preceding pressure of strikes. Since the financial strain imposed by the employers' offensive upon both the American Federation of Labor and the national and international unions had been very great, the possibility of warding off preventable struggles and of procuring through the mediational machinery of the Civic Federation at least part of the gains that might—or might not—result from costly struggles was appealing. It was recognized, also, that with the markets for the products of many manufacturers expanding, and expected to continue to expand, employers might often be ready to make rather appreciable concessions to the trade unions if they were assured, in return, of trade-union responsibility in carrying out the terms of collective agreements and of immunity from strikes.

Considerations such as these, rather than desertion of any essential part of trade unionism's assumptions and theories, accounted for the

[1] For a more detailed account of the National Civic Federation, see L. Lorwin, *The American Federation of Labor*, pp. 64–65, and 82–84.

[2] See Samuel Gompers's *My Seventy Years of Life and Labor*, vol. I, pp. 105–118, for his own account of the motives underlying his affiliation with the Civic Federation.

alignment of trade-union leaders with the employing interests[1] and with socially minded citizens of the upper wealth and income brackets.[2]   To an extent, the anticipated benefits were realized.   Unionism was able to "enlighten" the less prejudiced and already better informed portions of the citizenry concerning its principles and its aspirations.   Employers in some cases recognized and dealt with labor organizations when, had it not been for labor's participation in a movement like the National Civic Federation, they might not have done so.   The National Association of Manufacturers found its open-shop propaganda vigorously combated by the National Civic Federation,[3] even though the latter included among its members some of the outstanding protagonists of the open shop.   Nor did labor's expectation that strikes would be averted or settled more quickly prove to be without foundation.[4]   In realization through the interventionist activities of a public-spirited organization friendly to collective bargaining, instead of through costly strikes, of improved terms and conditions of employment, the trade unionists found

[1] The employing interests were a minority within the Civic Federation.   Under the plan of organization adopted in 1900, when the National Civic Federation appeared as an outgrowth of the Chicago Civic Federation, established in 1893, employers, labor, and the public had separate representation on the leading committees.   Dr. Lorwin (*op. cit.*, pp. 82–83), after his careful analysis, concluded that there were two main reasons why the Civic Federation could be used as it was by the American Federation of Labor: sectional differences within it, and differences in the occupations of its members.   Although it originated in Chicago, the National Civic Federation was in considerable part an Eastern institution, and the intellectual and industrial climate of the East was more favorable to unionism than was that of the West.   The occupations of the members were diverse. Clergymen, editors, sociologists, social workers, economists, and other professional persons, as well as employers, capitalists, and representatives of organized labor, found place within the organization.   "The men who owned and managed their own businesses were in a minority.   On the other hand, it contained many men of great wealth with large holdings and responsible positions in great corporations. . . . The bankers and men of Wall Street, more remote from the scene of industrial struggles, seemed readier at times to concede, at least in general terms, the justice of organized labor's claims."   *Ibid.*, p. 83.

[2] Mark Hanna was chairman of the Civic Federation and Samuel Gompers vice-chairman.   Among the public representatives were such men as August Belmont, Grover Cleveland, and Charles W. Eliot.

[3] The 1900 preamble of the National Civic Federation declared: "Organized labor cannot be destroyed without debasement of the masses. . . . Organized labor can correct its errors."   Quoted by Perlman and Taft, "Labor Movements," in Commons and Associates. *op. cit.*, vol. 4, p. 48 (The Macmillan Company, New York, 1932).

[4] The National Civic Federation maintained a Division of Mediation and Conciliation, and it also promoted permanent local boards of conciliation that sought to avert and to settle strikes.   The conciliation work if 1905 and 1906 extended to twenty-two states. The years 1900–1905 were those of the National Civic Federation's greatest influence as a force making for conciliation, mediation, and arbitration of labor disputes, as well as in other matters coming within the scope of its program.   From detail presented by Professors Perlman and Taft, *ibid.*, pp. 48–49.

vindication of their policy of interclass collaboration; and such part
of the stabilization of industrial relations under trade agreements
during the early years of the century as was attributable to the
policies and activities of the group with which they had become
associated could be pointed to as corroborative evidence of the wisdom
of the leaders.

Yet debit, as well as credit, items appeared on the balance sheet of
this new policy. The National Civic Federation, endorsing collective
bargaining and trade agreements though it did, had in common with the
antiunion employers' associations the desire to curb the more aggressive
aspects of unionism. Alignment with groups antipathetic to aggressiveness and militancy hardly provided the nourishment necessary for completion of unionism's task of organizing the workers in a country where
so little of this task had been accomplished, so much still remained to be
done. In all likelihood, Mr. Gompers and the other leaders overestimated the value of hearings before distinguished audiences; probably
they underestimated, on the other hand, the sedative and lethargic
effect upon the American labor movement of alliance with the employing
interests. The craft unions felt, in many cases, that the community
had accepted them as necessary and desirable institutions, and this
feeling dulled their consciousness of the reservations with which they had
been accepted and at the same time dampened their latent fervor to
extend a helping hand to those further down in the economic scale,
rendered them more unwilling to permit, if immediate cost in job opportunity were involved, those structural readjustments which would make
possible inclusion within the organized labor movement of the millions
of unskilled workers. The kind of unionism represented by the American
Federation of Labor experienced no clearcut and complete metamorphosis of policy and social outlook as a result of entering into an *entente*
with employers, corporation magnates, and intellectuals, but its aggressiveness was curbed to an extent and the conservative components of its
economic and political philosophy came to bulk larger.[1]

Problems of Structure.—The "naturalness" of the craft form of
organization, except where craft lines of demarcation were virtually non-

[1] In consequence of the fight with the socialists in the American Federation of Labor
(*cf. infra*, pp. 107–112), Mr. Gompers and his colleagues may have become, in fact, more
receptive to the politically and economically conservative implications of alignment with the
employer and public factions of the National Civic Federation than they realized. The
1900 preamble of the National Civic Federation set forth the dictum that "the twin foes of
industrial peace are the anti-union employers and the socialists." Mr. Gompers did not
need to be persuaded that both were foes, and—the struggle to prevent the socialists from
gaining control of the Federation perhaps having pushed him into a somewhat more conservative position than he would have taken had this struggle not occurred—he was not
likely to eschew the social philosophy of a movement directing its ammunition against both
socialism and the antiunion employers.

existent, was, for reasons indicated in the preceding chapter,[1] one of the important notions impressed upon the unionists, whose experience with the Knights of Labor had convinced them that an all-embracing organization was an ineffective protector of immediate job interests. Not only must the organization of labor have a basis primarily, if not exclusively, economic in character, but it must recognize that the solidarity and cohesion of the labor movement stemmed from the common concern of men about the same jobs, and it must build its structure accordingly. This meant craft unionism where distinct crafts obtained. The rise of the federated trade unionism of the late nineteenth century is, again as was pointed out in the preceding chapter, to be explained largely in terms of the interests and outlook of the skilled workers, and these interests and this outlook had as a logical implication the preservation of the form of organization that would protect the immediate job opportunity of skilled craftsmen.

Prior to about the turn of the century the deficiencies of, and the problems inherent in, this form of organization occasioned little difficulty. But as membership increased, and as theretofore unorganized sectors of industry were brought within the trade-union fold, the question of structural arrangements, particularly as this question centered upon the boundaries of different crafts and the settlement of demarcation disputes,[2] became increasingly acute. Disputes between or among unions as to what work belonged to each multiplied; attack upon problems of common interest to the members of several crafts was inhibited by the absence of satisfactory forms of intercraft organization; uniformity in the more general terms of agreements of different craft unions, desirable in cases like building construction, where several distinct crafts are usually employed simultaneously on the same product, was difficult to attain; and organization by separate crafts of the skilled workers of an industry usually meant, as a practical matter, that the unskilled remained unorganized.[3] Recognition of the threat to trade unionism's growth and

[1] Cf. supra, p. 77. The entire problem of structure is discussed in Chap. VI, here we are concerned with the problem only in so far as it is inseparable from a historical account and an understanding of the forces that have made American trade-union history what it has been.

[2] The problem of jurisdictional disputes is discussed in some detail infra, pp. 272–279.

[3] Although the last-named consequence of the structure unionism had assumed was not the primary motivation of the readjustments of the period that is the concern of this section of the chapter. Efforts during the years prior to 1914 were focused for the most part upon the development of interorganizations that would make possible common attack by a number of craft or compound-craft organizations when their problems were of common character and upon devising machinery for the avoidance of inter-union disputes over jurisdiction. With the development of the mass-production industries, employing large numbers of unskilled or production workers and relatively few craftsmen, the practical exclusion of part of the labor supply from the organized labor movement of course became a structural problem of greater proportions and the need of interorganizations of craftsmen

health that was inherent in these conditions gave rise to various attempts to surmount the structural shortcomings: amalgamation of related crafts, widening by more liberal rules of admission the base of different craft unions, and interorganizations of crafts with common problems.[1]

Initiative in these attempts had to come, in part, from the national federation of trade unions.[2] The smaller unions looked with no little fear upon the possibility of absorption by the larger ones, and some sacrifice of trade autonomy was likely to be involved in participation in machinery for the settlement of jurisdictional disputes and in membership in quasi-industrial federations; pressure from above was accordingly necessary. But the American Federation of Labor was a voluntary organization, and in the determination of policy it could make no departures from past practices, and no changes in past organizational forms, except those the member unions controlling it willed to permit. Pronouncements of the annual conventions and the Executive Council on the problem of craft-union claims and on structural arrangements in general were, in consequence, frequently vague and calculated to please all, and policy as a whole often seemed vacillating. Nevertheless, steps were taken to remedy the deficiencies of the craft form of organization. At the 1900 convention of the Federation, the delegates urged abandonment of the narrower conceptions of craft autonomy, recommended that disputes between unions be settled by amalgamation, and specifically instructed the Executive Council to grant no charter in the future without a clear definition of the jurisdiction of the recipient union.[3] The convention of the following year, while reiterating the principle of craft or trade organization and again calling for amalgamations, conceded the existence of exceptional cases in which all workers—temporarily at least—should be enrolled in the "paramount organization" in the industry. Compulsory methods of enforcing such deviations from

---

and of machinery for the settlement of jurisdictional disputes among craftsmen relatively less important.

[1] The interorganizations discussed in the present section of the chapter are, perhaps needless to say, those formed for attainment of the economic ends of business unionism— recognition by employers, collective bargaining, trade agreements, improvement in terms and conditions of employment—and not those the function of which was the advancement, by methods not primarily economic as well as by economic methods, of the interests of labor generally, such as the city centrals and state federations.

[2] In the case of the National Departments, as is indicated later, the suggestion seems to have come from some of the national unions before the American Federation became enthusiastic about the idea; but without the efforts of the Federation it is most unlikely that they would have been formed.

[3] This was the so-called "Scranton Declaration." For details, see L. Lorwin, The American Federation of Labor, pp. 68–69. One year earlier (1899) a resolution introduced by James O'Connell, head of the Machinists' Union, had expressed the disposition of the convention to guarantee to each craft "absolute self-government and complete jurisdiction over its members wherever employed."

craft-union principles were, however, specifically rejected. These resolutions bespoke the difficulties inherent in effecting necessary changes in trade-union structure. To ignore the problem would be perilous; to grapple with it in a thoroughgoing fashion would involve a treading upon the interests of the various unions, a treading that they were unwilling to permit and generally were in position to prevent.

Discovery of ways and means to eliminate the weaknesses arising in the trade-union movement as a whole from the predominance within it of the craft form of organization and at the same time to preserve the autonomy and protect the rights of craft unions continued, therefore, to be one of the most acute, and at the same time one of the most baffling, of problems. In the opportunistic manner of business unionists, however, the leaders of the Federation and of the constituent nationals and internationals were able to devise expedients and institute policies that— at a time when fewer workers were employed in the mechanized, mass-production industries than are today—succeeded to an appreciable extent. Beginning in 1905 the Executive Council of the Federation became more cautious in the granting of charters, and the resultant check upon increase in the number of unions was that overlapping jurisdictions were less numerous than they otherwise would have been and jurisdictional disputes less frequent. Trades councils bringing together the different craft unions, formation of which was advocated by the 1901 convention of the Federation, were established with increasing frequency during the early years of the 1900's.[1] Amalgamations were effected, and some of the craft unions, particularly during the last four or five years before the outbreak of the war of 1914–1918, when the "new" (Southeastern European) immigrants had come to constitute a majority of the employees in a number of the larger industries, showed greater readiness to make common cause with the semiskilled or unskilled workers and to modify their structures accordingly.[2] With the formation of the Departments of the American Federation of Labor,[3] beginning in 1908, however, the most important step was taken to solve the problem of structure for the organizations affiliated with the Federation.[4] These

[1] In the building construction industry, the metal trades, and elsewhere some of these local trades councils had in fact been established during the 1890's or—in a few cases— earlier.

[2] The Machinists, the Carpenters, and a few other craft unions lowered initiation fees and sought to broaden their jurisdictions, and in a few cases, like that of the International Ladies Garment Workers Union, reorganizations on a wider trade and industrial basis were effected. The I.L.G.W.U., formed in 1890, was reorganized as a semi-industrial or amalgamated union in 1910.

[3] For the most complete account of these Departments, see A. T. Hebbing, *The Departments of the American Federation of Labor*, (1931).

[4] It will be recalled (*supra*, p. 83) that in 1908, when the first of the Departments (the Building Trades Department) was formed, the A. F. of L. included 1,586,885 of the coun-

Departments, indebted for their existence partly to the efforts of leaders
of the Federation to work out some kind of *modus vivendi* that would
preserve craft autonomy and at the same time provide industrial unity
where it was needed, and partly to the efforts of member unions,[1] were
national federations of the craft and compound craft unions within the
industries for which they were established. Functioning as the formu-
lators of policies of common concern to all member unions[2] and especially
as agencies for the avoidance and settlement of jurisdictional disputes,
the Departments constituted the craft unions' answer to criticisms of the
industrial unionists—an answer the substance of which was that a substitute retaining the advantages of craft unionism and at the same time
able to present a united industrial front when necessary had been evolved.

Challenges from the Left.—The "pure and simple" unionism that
was engrossed, during the pre-1914 years, in remodeling to some extent
its structure, resisting open-shop drives, securing recognition and collective agreements, convincing the American community of its nonsub-
versive character, and meeting the problem of adverse court decisions,
was indebted for part of its economic creed, as has necessarily been said
more than once, to the socialist movement of the 1870's and 1880's. Two
notions in particular had their sources in doctrinaire socialism rather
than in American uplift and "producer-conscious" movements: that
labor must have its own distinctive organizations, inclusive of none but

---

try's 2,130,600 trade unionists. The organization and functions of the Departments of the
Federation are discussed later in this volume, and reference here is confined to those
aspects which are an essential part of the historical record. In 1943 the Federation had
four Departments: the Building Trades Construction Department, the Metal Trades
Department, the Railway Employees Department, and the Union-label Trades Department. A Mining Department was organized in 1911 and abolished in 1922.

[1] In spite of the fact that the craft unions were fearful of affiliations with other craft
unions in the same industry when such affiliations might threaten their jurisdiction, the
movement for interorganization on this basis appears to have originated with some of the
member unions and for a time to have received a rather frigid reception from the Federation itself. Mr. Gompers, it is true, had suggested the idea as early as 1888, but when in
1897 the unions in the building trades set up an international building trades council the
A. F. of L. refused, on the ground that it trespassed upon the rights and authority of the
national unions, to recognize it. At the 1907 convention, however, President Gompers
sponsored a plan to continue a Structural Building Trades Alliance, which had been established by the Brotherhood of Carpenters and Joiners in 1903. The charter was issued to
the Building Trades Department (now called the Building Trades Construction Department) on Mar. 20, 1908. That same year the Metal Trades Department was chartered,
while in 1909 the Railway Employees Department and the Union-label Department came
into existence.

[2] This statement in fact applies to only the first three of the four Departments now in
existence, as enumerated in a foregoing footnote. The Union-label Department differs
from the others in that its function is the aiding of unionism in general by promoting the
affirmative use of labor's purchasing power—*i.e.*, the purchase by union members and others
of goods carrying the union label.

wage earners, and that the primacy of economic methods must ever be kept in mind. From these premises, the labor movement proceeded along the trade-union route, its social outlook becoming a little more conservative and its militancy a bit more restrained.

To the orthodox followers of Marx in the United States, however, the applied socialism of the Gompers group was an illegitimate and highly disreputable offspring of socialism—a brazen denial of labor's "historic mission," crass treachery to the class struggle. The misleaders of labor must be ejected from the movement; the labor organizations must be transformed from instrumentalities for attainment of the palliatives of collective bargaining and job control into the vanguards of the society of tomorrow.

Socialist members abounded, it is true, in the unions affiliated with the A. F. of L., but the apostles of doctrinaire purity were impatient of their policy of slow penetration; and the Socialist Labor Party, under the leadership of Daniel DeLeon, set about the task of injecting true socialism into the life blood of the organized labor movement. Founded in 1876,[1] and possessed of some real influence during the height of the struggle between the Knights of labor and the A. F. of L. by virtue of the fact that it held a certain balance of power, the Socialist Labor Party had declined in strength and influence by 1889, when Daniel DeLeon affiliated with it.[2]   But it was the sole political representative of unadul-

---

[1] See *supra*, p. 57, where the circumstances bringing the Socialist Labor Party into being and the elements composing it at the outset are discussed. The name "Socialist Labor Party" was not taken until 1877, and that year is sometimes given as the one of the actual establishment of the Party.

[2] Daniel DeLeon was born on the island of Curaçao, off Venezuela, in 1852, was educated in Germany and at Columbia University, taught mathematics for a time at a school in Westchester County, New York, lectured on international law at Columbia University, and in 1889 resigned his university post and definitely aligned himself with the socialist movement. He was instrumental in the establishment, that same year, of the New York Central Labor Federation as a rival of the old Central Labor Union of New York (*cf. infra*, p. 108). In 1892 he became editor of the Socialist Labor paper *The People*, in the columns of which he employed his consummate art of vituperation to denounce Mr. Gompers and the other leaders of the A. F. of L. A man of erudition, possessed of a command of several languages, steeped in the Marxian classics, DeLeon to a considerable extent fitted the specifications of "the intellectual of the labor movement." But his influence upon the great mass of American trade unionists was both temporary and slight. As is indicated shortly, he split the socialist movement and probably caused many of the socialists within the American Federation to move closer to the Gompers position in respect to economic creed and methods. By not a few of his contemporary Socialists, DeLeon was regarded as not being a "true" or "sound" Marxist. He adhered, they said, to the "iron law of wages" Marx had repudiated, lacked real faith in the capacity of the working class to function as a vehicle of social change, and really wanted a program of direction of revolutionary activity by a selected few in the party that would logically have displaced the self-governing trade unions. Learned though he was, he never had the intuitive appreciation of the American scene, of the responses different kinds of appeals and tactics would elicit from the wage

terated Marxism in the United States, and it set out to capture the American labor movement. A campaign would be launched to infuse with socialistic doctrines, objectives, and methods both the A. F. of L. and the declining Knights of Labor; should it fail, there remained more drastic methods.

The trade unionists won the first engagement. At the 1890 convention of the A. F. of L., President Gompers's refusal to grant a charter to the socialistic Central Labor Federation of New York, a refusal based not upon the socialism of the petitioning organization but upon the contention that it was allied with a political party, was sustained 1,574 to 496.[1] In the opinion of the socialists, the issue had been clearly drawn. Their party was a workers' party; as such it was different from other parties, and it should accordingly be regarded differently by a federation purporting to represent the wage-earning masses of the country. The contention of Gompers, P. J. McGuire,[2] and others that to admit, even in this indirect manner, the Socialist Labor Party would in effect be to open the door to other political parties, with possible submergence of the unions in politics as an ultimate result, was a red herring; the real motivation was opposition to a truly socialistic labor movement. Encouraged by the support accorded their position on the floor of the convention,[3]

---

earners and the middle class, that Samuel Gompers possessed. Disagreement with his interpretations of economic forces and with his decisions he regarded as tantamount to betrayal of the cause of labor. For an excellent brief characterization of DeLeon, see Perlman and Taft in vol. 4 of Commons and Associates, *History of Labor in the United States*, pp. 217–219. See also Morris Hillquit's *History of Socialism in the United States*, and Olive M. Johnson's *Daniel DeLeon* (publication of National Executive Committee of the Socialist Labor Party, 1923).

[1] The Central Labor Federation of New York was organized by the socialists, who were supported by unions of German and Russian-Jewish immigrants, as a rival of the Central Labor Union (the A. F. of L. affiliate) in 1889. Unfriendliness of the latter organization to the Socialist Labor Party in the local political campaigns of 1887 and 1888 appears to have been the immediate reason for the organization of the Central Labor Federation. Gompers issued a charter to the new organization upon its formation in 1889; then a compromise between the two New York unions was worked out, the Central Labor Federation member unions re-entering the Central Labor Union and returning their charter; but in 1890 they again withdrew and asked the A. F. of L. for a return of the Central Labor Federation charter. Gompers refused on the ground that the Central Labor Federation, by virtue of its having admitted to membership the English-speaking section of the Socialist Labor Party, was a political organization. The issue came before the 1890 convention of the A. F. of L. when Lucien Sanial, sent as a delegate to contest Gompers's decision, sought to gain a seat as the representative of the Central Labor Federation. For accounts of this episode, see Perlman and Taft, *op. cit.*, pp. 219–220, L. Lorwin, *op. cit.*, pp. 30–31, and Norman Ware, *Labor in Modern Industrial Society*, pp. 264–265.

[2] McGuire had been one of the original (1876) members of the Socialist Labor Party, but he dropped out in 1881 when, largely as a result of his efforts, the Carpenters' Union was organized.

[3] The chief support of the socialist position in the 1890 convention came from the miners, who at that time were divided about equally between the A. F. of L. and the Knights of

even though the defeat had been decisive, the DeLeon socialists launched their campaign—in the columns of *The People* and elsewhere—against the "labor lieutenants of capitalism," attempted to "bore from within" the Federation's unions, and in 1892 submitted their first presidential ticket for the approval of the American electorate.[1]

Conditions of 1893 and 1894 were favorable to those seeking to bestow upon the organized labor movement the proper—in their opinion—doctrinaire inspiration and political methodology, to convert the A. F. of L. from a mere economic organization of limited objectives to an economic-political one of far-reaching objectives. The beginning of depression and increasing unemployment, defeat of the unions in strikes, a rapidly shrinking labor market, the political-mindedness and radicalism of the Populist movement, and court prosecutions all combined to aid powerfully the socialist and radical leaders within the Federation in their attempts to remake it into something more to their liking. In this atmosphere the delegates to the 1893 convention, by a vote of 2,244 to 67,[2] submitted to the affiliated unions an eleven-point "political programme," adoption of which would have committed the Federation to political action and to "collective ownership by the people of all means of production and distribution."[3] The program proved attractive to the

---

Labor, and from the German unions. Groups other than the miners that supported the socialist cause were the bakers, brewery workers, furniture workers, and boot and shoe workers. From detail in N. Ware, *op. cit.*, p. 264, and L. Lorwin, *op. cit.*, p. 31.

[1] Simon Wing of Massachusetts and Charles H. Matchett of New York. The ticket polled 21,532 votes, almost all of which were from New York City, out of a total popular vote of 12,040,384. James B. Weaver, candidate of the Populist Party, an expression of the unrest that was sweeping the West in 1892, received 1,040,886 votes, in contrast to the Marxist party's 21,532.

[2] Probably the temper of the convention was not so radical, however, as this overwhelming vote in favor of submission of the "political programme" would indicate. In the first place, the delegates were merely voting on "submission" to the member unions for their consideration and ratification or rejection, not necessarily taking a stand on the merits of the proposals. In the second place, the vote for the political-socialistic program was increased as a result of the attempt to prevent the re-election of Mr. Gompers as president. Some of the delegates opposed to him on personal grounds started a movement to bring about his defeat, and both sides solicited votes of the socialist delegates. With the aid of some of the socialists, Gompers was re-elected over John McBride of the United Mine Workers by the close vote of 1,314 to 1,222, and the socialists in turn received support from some of the nonsocialists for their "political programme" and its controversial Plank Ten. For details about the fight against Gompers, see L. Lorwin, *op. cit.*, p. 36.

[3] The proposal for independent political action referred to the recent action of the British Trade Union Congress in endorsing political action, reciting that the English trade unions had entered the field of independent politics "as auxiliary to their economic action." This political plank, by referring to the example of the British unions, in effect constituted a proposal for independent political action. The eleven points of the program demanded: compulsory education, popular initiation of legislation, a legal eight-hour day, governmental inspection of mines and workshops, abolition of the sweating system, employers' liability laws, abolition of the contract system upon public work, municipal ownership of

memberships of the affiliated unions during the following months, as business activity declined and unemployment and labor unrest mounted, and before the convention of 1894 assembled in Denver a majority of the member organizations had given their endorsement.[1] Opposition manifested itself somewhat tardily, but the seriousness of the situation was apparent. Adoption of Plank Ten, the one calling for "collective ownership by the people of all the means of production and distribution," would be tantamount to subordination of job-conscious, business union-ism to class-conscious socialism, so feared by the middle class, whose antagonism the trade-union leaders felt they must avoid as much as possible; endorsement of political action might result in submergence of the instruments of economic action in the whirlpool of politics.

Socialists and antisocialists debated for five days at the Denver con-vention of 1894,[2] and through a series of parliamentary maneuvers the

---

electric light, gas, street railway, and water systems, nationalization of the people of all means of production and distribution, and the referendum upon all legislation. The most controversial parts were, of course, the endorsement of political action and Plank Ten, the one calling for "collective ownership by the people of all means of production and distribu-tion." The other planks, it may be noted, bore a coloration that was Knights of Labor as much as A. F. of L. While Plank Ten of course met with the approval of the Socialist Labor Party, its adoption for submission to the member unions was not the achievement of this party or of DeLeon's propaganda, but of those trade unionists who were content to move more slowly than was DeLeon, quietly boring from within but not expecting that the transformation of the Federation into a socialistic organization could take place in any but piecemeal manner—if, indeed, it could take place at all, and if, indeed, transformation into a thoroughgoing socialistic organization was to be desired. The 1893 "political pro-gramme" was introduced by Thomas J. Morgan, a machinist by trade and a delegate from the Central Labor Union of Chicago.

[1] Indicative of the disposition of trade unionists to depart somewhat from the narrow "economism" of the Federation during these years of depression and labor unrest was the active participation of the unions in politics in 1894. The *American Federationist* (official organ of the Federation) of November, 1894, listed more than 300 union members who were candidates for some elective office. Only half a dozen of these were elected, and Mr. Gompers was able to point, in the presidential address of 1894, to these failures as persuasive argument against adoption of the political program. S. Perlman, *History of Trade Union-ism* . . . , p. 140.

[2] The convention of 1894 was the first one farther west than Chicago, and the selection of Denver was in the nature of a gesture to the West on the part of the Federation. The appearance of the Western Federation of Miners (which was organized in 1893 but did not affiliate with the A. F. of L. until 1896) and the Populist sentiment within the Federation also influenced the choice of the convention city. Undoubtedly, also, the influence of the silver-mine owners, who were anxious that the Federation support strongly the movement for remonetization of silver at the old sixteen-to-one ratio, was another factor bringing the convention westward. Free-silver sentiment ran high among the trade-union memberships at that time. "The delegates . . . were royally entertained. They were shown the silver mines and were able to pick up 'souvenirs.' They were addressed by a Populist governor in true Populist style" (N. Ware, *op. cit.*, p. 266, D. C. Heath and Company, Boston, 1935). The location of the convention and the atmosphere in which it was held were distinctly favorable to adoption of a political and broadly reformist program.

proposal to endorse collective ownership and independent political action was defeated.[1]   The action of the convention appeared to be contrary to the disposition of the trade-union members, as expressed when they approved the "political programme,"[2] and it was made possible only because many delegates voted contrary to the instructions of their organizations to support the resolution.   But the Federation had gone on record as officially opposed to both independent political action and participation in efforts to hasten the advent of the socialist commonwealth, and in doing so it had made a decision the effect of which was important and lasting.   The federated trade unions, in spite of the politically and socialistically minded portions of their memberships, became increasingly wary of the pitfalls of independent party action and of espousal of radical objectives that would dissipate the energy needed for achieving the immediate objectives of business unionism.   While the socialists of course did not abandon their efforts to capture the Federation,[3] many of them—particularly those of the doctrinaire DeLeon faction—became pessimistic about the possibility of molding the Federation into an organ for the advancement of socialism and directed more of their

[1] The first nine of the eleven planks in the program that had been submitted to the member unions the preceding year were adopted with modifying amendments.   When Plank Ten was reached the antisocialists introduced a series of absurd amendments, intended to make both the plank and the consideration of it ridiculous, and in what the records indicate must have been considerable parliamentary confusion Plank Ten was defeated.   The preamble calling for independent political action was defeated, on motion of Adolph Strasser, by the close delegate vote of twenty-nine to twenty-seven (1,345 to 861 as votes were cast on the basis of the size of the unions represented by the delegates). From detail presented in S. Perlman, *History of Trade Unionism* . . . , pp. 140–141, Commons and Associates, *History of Labor in the United States*, vol. 2, pp. 511–514, L. Lorwin, *op. cit.*, pp. 38–39, and N. Ware, *op. cit.*, pp. 267–268.

[2] In the debate Mr. Gompers declared that "the submission of this program to our organizations was largely accepted by the membership as an endorsement of political action," thus implying that an erroneous impression was responsible for the endorsements. The logical corollary of this view was, of course, that the delegates were not bound by endorsements and instructions given under a wrong impression—*i.e.*, that the 1893 convention had expressed approval of the program instead of merely approval of its submission to the unions.   But it is likely that in this case Mr. Gompers was performing chiefly in his role of tactician, a role that he always played superbly.   The member unions did not have to endorse the program if they did not want to, and it is questionable how much an impression that the Federation convention had approved it would have influenced them.

[3] At the next (1895) convention of the A. F. of L., a resolution seeking to pledge it to independent political action for the achievement of socialistic objectives was introduced, but instead the convention, by a vote of 1,460 to 158, adopted the following resolution: "That it is clearly the duty of union workingmen to use their franchise so as to protect and advance the class interests of the men and women of labor and their children; that the interests of the workers as a class are of paramount importance to party interests; that the class interests of labor demand labor measures in preference to party measures, and, we, therefore, recommend to the workers more independent voting outside of party lines." Quoted in Commons and Associates, *op. cit.*, vol. 2, pp. 513–514.

efforts to the building of dual organizations that would be true expressions of the class struggle. Mr. Gompers, defeated for the presidency in 1894 but re-elected in 1895,[1] had permanently alienated the socialists; and the socialists, in turn, had permanently alienated Mr. Gompers.

The Knights of Labor, as well as the A. F. of L., had been included as an object of frontal attack in the campaign plans of the DeLeon socialists, and by the capture of District Assembly 49 (the New York City Assembly) a short-lived victory was achieved.[2] It proved, however, to be of little consequence in advancement of the cause of socialism; the Knights of Labor was rapidly becoming decrepit, and in spite of the catholicity of social outlook it included and of the affiliation of some of its members with the Socialist Labor Party,[3] it never was imbued with truly socialistic (in the Marxian sense) class consciousness. DeLeon was denied control of the *Journal of the Knights of Labor,* allegedly promised him in return for socialist support of the winning candidate for head of the Order in 1894, and then, in 1895, he was even refused a seat in the General Assembly. The moral—its impressiveness increased by the re-election of Gompers as president of the Federation in 1895—was obvious: the cause of the proletariat must be carried forward by a new national organization, destined ultimately to displace both of the existing "buffers of capitalism against whom every intelligent effort of the working class for emancipation has hitherto gone to pieces."[4] But the Socialist Trade and Labor Alliance[5] was a failure from the start. Its

---

[1] Deprived of the socialist vote that had retained him in office in 1893 (*cf. supra,* p. 109), Gompers was defeated in 1894 by John McBride, a United Mine Workers socialist, 1,170 to 976. The following year, Gompers defeated McBride, although only by the close vote of 1,041 to 1,023. The year 1894–1895 was the only one between 1886 and his death in 1925 that Samuel Gompers was not president of the Federation.

[2] Under orders from DeLeon, the socialist unions, including the influential United Hebrew Trades, joined and captured District Assembly 49, and at the General Assembly of 1894 the socialists combined with the supporters of James R. Sovereign to defeat Terence V. Powderly for Grand Master Workman. For a summary account of the efforts to capture the Knights and of the alliance of the DeLeonites and the Soverign supporters, see Perlman and Taft, *op. cit.,* pp. 220–221.

[3] Charles H. Matchett, the New York telephone mechanic who was candidate for the vice-presidency on the first (1892) Socialist Labor Party national ticket and for president in 1896, had been a prominent Knights of Labor man, and others of the Order had become active Socialist Labor Party workers by the early 1890's. The eight socialist delegates to the 1894 convention of the Knights held the balance of power, and Sovereign defeated Powderly as a result of the deal he made with DeLeon for socialist support.

[4] Words of DeLeon at the 1896 convention of the Socialist Labor Party, quoted from the convention *Proceedings* by Professors Perlman and Taft, *op. cit.,* p. 222.

[5] The Socialist Trade and Labor Alliance came into existence as a result of DeLeon's control of District Assembly 49 of the Knights of Labor. This Assembly repudiated the national officers the year DeLeon was denied a seat in the General Assembly (1895) and issued an appeal to local assemblies and trade unions to join in forming a rival of the A. F. of L. that would be a true exponent of international socialism; and at a meeting attended

membership, variously estimated in 1898 at between 15,000 and 30,000,[1] was confined almost entirely to a few unions of socialistic bent in and near New York City. From the standpoint of socialism, as many of the socialists, increasingly impatient with DeLeon and his leadership, themselves concluded, the step was unfortunate, since the socialists were stamped as destroyers of the unity of labor at a time when, owing to experience of the unions in the struggle with the Knights of Labor, feeling against dualism ran high. Socialist trade unionists, aware of the economic ineffectiveness of a movement devoid of "organization conscious" labor representatives, in many cases came to the support of Mr. Gompers.

Lacking, then, the support of a majority of the radical trade unionists, both the Alliance and the Socialist Labor Party became little more than select societies of rigid doctrinarians, and a new social-democratic party, rooted in the native American strain of social and political radicalism as well as in Marxian tenets and recognizing that "trade unions are by historical necessity organized on neutral grounds so far as political affiliation is concerned,"[2] came into being. In 1899 the anti-DeLeon faction of the Socialist Labor Party openly revolted[3] and, headed by Morris Hillquit,[4] departed for Rochester and held a convention of its own early in 1900. Two midwestern movements had in the meantime developed. Eugene V. Debs, idealistic, nontheoretical, humanitarian,[5] had left the Populist Party, after voting for Bryan in 1896, and established his Social Democracy of America and his Brotherhood of the Cooperative Commonwealth, organizations in which the strands of utopianism and indigenously American populism were extremely strong; and then, with others, had launched the Social Democratic Party in 1898.[6] Victor

---

by representatives of the few unions responding to the call, the Socialist Trade and Labor Alliance was formed. Perlman and Taft, *op. cit.*, pp. 221–222.

[1] L. Lorwin, *The American Federation of Labor*, p. 57.

[2] From a resolution adopted at the "unity convention" of 1901, where the Socialist Party of America was founded. Quoted by S. Perlman, *History of Trade Unionism* . . . , p. 212.

[3] The immediate issue on which the final break took place was that of election of delegates to the General Committee of Section New York. This Committee had absolute power over selection of the National Secretary and National Executive Committee. For details of the break, see Perlman and Taft, *op. cit.*, 223–224.

[4] Morris Hillquit, a Russian Jew who came to the United States in 1888, was a lawyer and leading socialist at the time of the 1889 split within the Party. In 1917 he polled the largest vote a Socialist has ever received for the mayoralty of New York City. Mr. Hillquit's *History of Socialism in the United States* (1903) is an able historical record.

[5] For an interpretative account of Debs's life and influence, see McAlister Coleman, *Eugene V. Debs.*

[6] The Brotherhood of the Cooperative Commonwealth advocated a colonization scheme. The membership of the Brotherhood would gradually settle in colonies in one of the Western states, capture control of the state, and then transform it into a socialistic commonwealth. By the time of the Rochester Convention (1900) the colonization scheme had been aban-

Berger of Milwaukee, newspaper editor, student of Marx, and proponent
of a kind of revisionist socialism that was anticipatory of Eduard Bernstein, differed from the socialists who had arrived via the populistic route
on more points than one, but he and his group had broken with the
Socialist Labor Party and its doctrinaire orthodoxy and they found
cooperation with other reform groups far from impossible.[1] The two
midwestern movements became known as the Debs-Berger socialism, and
in 1900 they joined with the secessionist Socialist Labor Party group in
nominating the same presidential ticket.[2] The vote polled that November, 97,730, was nearly three times as large as that of DeLeon's candidate,
and it constituted a compelling argument for fusion of the Debs-Berger
Social Democracy and the secessionists from the twenty-four year-old
socialist party.[3] At a Unity Convention in 1901 the Socialist Party of
America was founded upon a platform stressing a series of immediate
demands[4] but having as its ultimate goal "the organization of the working class and those in sympathy with it into a political party, with the

---

doned and both the Brotherhood and the Social Democracy of America had ceased to
function.

[1] In fact, the Berger socialists cooperated with the Populists in 1894, and in 1896 Berger
organized a presidential boom for Debs at the People's Party (Populist) convention. Debs
supported Bryan on the Populist ticket, but the Milwaukee group decided that Bryan's
nomination proved there was no point in longer cooperating with the Populists. Both
before and after 1896, however, there was cooperation between the two men in their
socialistic-populistic-reformist activities. Berger had visited Debs when the latter was in
the Woodstock jail and has been referred to as Debs's "socialist god-father." *Cf.* Perlman
and Taft, *op. cit.*, pp. 225–226.

[2] For president, Eugene V. Debs; for vice-president, Job Harriman.

[3] A motion to unite was defeated in 1900, when the common presidential ticket was
nominated, 1,213 to 939. The question of the name of the new party was one obstacle to
amalgamation. Also, the westerners were suspicious of any group that had been affiliated
with DeLeon, and Hillquit and his followers were not enthusiastic about Debs's former
colonizing socialism. But, as was indicated earlier, this scheme had been abandoned
before 1900, and all recognized the necessity of a socialism that regarded accomplishment
in the American scene as more important than rigid doctrinaire orthodoxy, and the results
of the 1900 election were too encouraging to permit postponement of unification.

[4] Among others: Public ownership of all means of transportation and all other public
utilities, as well as all industries controlled by monopolies, trusts, and combines, the revenue
from these publicly owned industries being applied to "the increase of wages and shortening
of hours, to the improvement of service and the lowering of prices to consumers"; progressive reduction of the hours of labor and increase of wages; state or national insurance
of working people in case of accidents, unemployment, sickness, and want in old age, the
funds for this purpose "to be collected from the capitalist class"; inauguration by employment of public credit of a system of public industries "in order that the workers may be
secured the full product of their labor"; education for all with state and municipal aid for
books, clothing, and food; equal civil and political rights for both sexes; the initiative and
referendum, proportional representation, and recall of representatives. From the summary of the 1901 Socialist platform in Earl R. Sikes, *Contemporary Economic Systems*
(Henry Holt and Company, Inc., New York, 1940), p. 208.

object of conquering the powers of government and using them for the purpose of transforming the present system of private ownership of means of production and distribution into collective ownership by the entire people."

Repudiation by the new Socialist Party of the extremes of doctrinaire orthodoxy insisted upon by the Socialist Labor Party and recognition of the "neutral grounds," so far as political affiliation was concerned, upon which the trade unions were "by historical necessity" organized did not, of course, involve abandonment of efforts to convert the membership of the A. F. of L. to socialism and to elicit from it a declaration of ultimate purposes socialistic in character, and after 1901 the "boring from within" tactics were continued.[1] The socialist offensive did not, however, become so great a threat to the established precepts of federated trade unionism as it had been during the 1890's. During the second half of the decade 1900-1910 the challenge was different in character, and it emerged not from the citadel of finance and industrial capitalism in the East, where the Marxian "inevitabilities" should by all principles of economic determinism have worked themselves out most fully, but from the conditions of labor and the robust activism of the American West. It found its organizational expression in the Industrial Workers of the World.[2]

The American West of the closing years of the nineteenth and the early years of the twentieth century afforded fertile soil for the rise of a revolutionary industrial unionism. Industrial disputes had been bitter and prolonged, and frequently they had partaken more of the nature of civil war than of ordinary labor struggles. In a number of the western states the restraining influence of a dominant middle class was absent. Facing a capitalism that was, on the whole, more ruthless than the finance

---

[1] At the 1902 convention of the A. F. of L. a resolution directing it to advise the working people of America to organize their economic and political power "to secure for labor the full equivalent of its toil" failed to carry by a vote of 4,899 to 4,171 (L. Lorwin, op. cit., p. 73), and substantially the same resolution failed of adoption, by a wider margin, at the 1903 convention. That year the socialist candidate for the presidency of the Federation received only 1,236 votes, as against 12,449 for Mr. Gompers (ibid., p. 74). After 1903 the socialists changed their tactics for a time, and merely urged the trade unionists "to study economic conditions" (ibid.). In 1912, for the first time after 1903, the socialists nominated one of their leaders, Max Hayes, for the presidency, and he mustered 27 per cent of the votes of the convention.

[2] The most detailed account of the I.W.W. during the first fifteen years of its history is Paul F. Brissenden's The I.W.W., A Study in American Syndicalism (1920). The following fifteen years of its history are traced in John Gambs, The Decline of the I.W.W. (1932). David J. Saposs' Left Wing Unionism (1926) includes an excellent interpretative account of the policies and tactics of the I.W.W., and Carleton Parker's The Casual Laborer and Other Essays (1920) sets forth vividly the sociopsychological basis of the movement. Extremely good accounts, more summary in form, are those of Perlman and Taft, op. cit., pp. 169-217, and L. Lorwin, op. cit., pp. 84-87.

capitalism of the East, more primitive in the methods it adopted to oppose labor, and more insistent upon maintenance of individualistic prerogatives, was a working force that often tended to be impetuous, impatient of restraint and slow-moving processes, contemptuous of property rights, and cynical about the trade-agreement form of interclass collaboration. The mining industry of the Rockies had attracted men who necessarily had to be self-assertive and daring, men to whom the acquisition of wealth was often a matter of sheer luck and whose reverence for property rights was consequently slight. In the lumber camps of the Northwest, the hop fields of California, the fruit- and wheat-producing areas on both sides of the mountains, the Pacific Coast marine industry, and elsewhere, thousands of migratory workers—men divorced from the stabilizing influence of permanent employment connections, property ownership, home life, social status, and the conventional forms of approbation, men who saw no reason why they should feel indebted to the established order of things—were ready to fight capitalism with the first weapons at hand. An anarcho-syndicalistic program harmonized with the predispositions of such workers, and the socialistic analysis that found its way into the official philosophy of the I.W.W. probably came to them as a consistent explanation of their own experiences. Moreover, the craft unions of the A. F. of L. had failed to make those adjustments and to take those steps prerequisite to the organization of these workers, and at the same time the conservative economic doctrines and limited objectives of the Federation made little appeal to men sometimes employed under quasi-feudalistic industrial conditions and keenly cognizant of the ferocity with which Western capitalism opposed their concerted efforts to deprive it of its industrially autocratic powers.

Conviction of the miners of the West that their salvation lay in industrial unionism and aggressive tactics expressed itself in 1893 in the formation of the Western Federation of Miners, a union attempting to include all employees of the metal mines and smelters, and for a brief period (1896–1897) this organization held membership in the American Federation. But between the two federations there was a basic incompatibility of structure and an irreconcilable conflict of policy and program, and the Western organization went its own way.[1] Seeking to establish a national labor organization that would reflect its own militant spirit and

---

[1] As is indicated shortly (*infra*, pp. 117–118), the Western Federation of Miners was the only group of any considerable membership represented in the convention that in 1905 gave birth to the I.W.W. Two years later, however, after a defeat in the coal-mining industry that followed an earlier defeat at Cripple Creek, the Western Federation of Miners became bitterly opposed to the I.W.W. under the leadership of William D. Haywood and withdrew from it. In 1911 it rejoined the American Federation, and in 1916 changed its name to International Union of Mine, Mill, and Smelter Workers. By that time it had become a respectable industrial union. In 1935 this union was one of the original members of the Committee for Industrial Organization.

function throughout the entire West, the Miners' Federation in 1898 established a rival of the A. F. of L., the American Labor Union.[1] Both the new organization and the parent body, of which William D. Haywood[2] was elected secretary-treasurer in 1900, became increasingly militant and radical, more impelled to expand and unite all laboring groups of revolutionary disposition in one big union. Defeat of the Western Federation of Miners in its industrial struggles likewise encouraged the movement for amalgamation with other groups.[3] Conferences looking toward formation of a new national organization were held in 1904 and early 1905, originally without benefit of official socialist participation,[4]

[1] Originally the new organization was called the Western Labor Union, the name American Labor Union being taken in 1902. This organization endorsed socialism, the cooperative commonwealth, and collective ownership of the instruments of production and distribution, but it was primarily a nondoctrinaire and militant labor union exercising centralized control over strikes and deriving its revolutionary fervor from the industrial background and experience of the membership rather than from theoretical socialism. By 1905, the year of the formation of the I.W.W., this organization had a membership of about 16,000, in addition to about 27,000 in the parent Western Federation of Miners (S. Perlman, *History of Trade Unionism* . . . , p. 214).

[2] William D. Haywood, for years regarded by thousands of the economically submerged unskilled workers as their champion, was born in Salt Lake City in 1869, went to work in the mines at the age of nine, joined the Western Federation of Miners in 1896, and became secretary-treasurer of that organization in 1900. About 1901 he became converted to socialism, and he had already arrived at the conclusion that craft unionism of the A. F. of L. species could be only a stumbling block to working-class progress. After his acquittal in 1907 on the charge of murdering Governor Steunenberg of Idaho he became a national figure in radical circles. He was for a time active in the Socialist Party, and in 1915 he became secretary-treasurer of the I.W.W. In 1918 he was sentenced to twenty years of imprisonment on the charge of conspiracy to obstruct the progress of the War, and in 1920, when his sentence was sustained upon appeal, he escaped to Russia, where he died in 1928. *Cf. Bill Haywood's Book, An Autobiography* (1929), P. F. Brissenden, *op. cit.*, J. F. Gambs, *op. cit.*, and Perlman and Taft, in vol. 4 of Commons and Associates, *History of Labor in the United States*, pp. 270–272.

[3] By the summer of 1904 the Western Federation of Miners had been entirely wiped out of the Cripple Creek district of Colorado, and the officers became convinced that survival of the organization depended upon amalgamation with other groups, in order that the miners could count on having allies in their own Western territory.

[4] The participants in a conference held in Chicago in the fall of 1904 were the editor of the official organ of the United Brewery Workmen, the president and secretary-treasurer of the United Brotherhood of Railway Employees, the American representative of the Amalgamated Society of Engineers of Great Britain, and two officials of the American Labor Union (N. Ware, *op. cit.*, p. 305; cf. also P. R. Brissenden, *op. cit.*). The American Labor Union and the United Brotherhood of Railway Employees were satellites of the Western Federation of Miners, which was the dominant factor in the conference. The Brewers, affiliated with the A. F. of L., although originally a Knights of Labor organization, was dissatisfied because of its constant jurisdictional disputes with the Federation's craft unions. It is important, as Professor Ware has pointed out (*op. cit.*, pp. 305–306), to remember that in spite of the emphasis that has been placed upon the syndicalistic and socialistic character of the I.W.W., this "original group" was brought together by the needs and circumstances of trade and industrial unions. But the trade-union character and immediate needs and

and at a convention in Chicago, June, 1905, the Industrial Workers of the World was launched upon its tempestuous career.

A heterogeneous group assembled at this first convention. There were representatives of the Western Federation of Miners, the only well-organized group with any considerable numerical strength, and its American Labor Union, of the Socialist Trade and Labor Alliance, and of dissatisfied A. F. of L. locals.[1] A number of individuals, not authorized to represent any organizations, participated: intellectuals, disgruntled trade unionists, members of the Socialist Party and the Socialist Labor Party, and ordinary wage earners. William D. Haywood was there, as were Mother Jones, ardent defender of the rights of the coal miners, Daniel DeLeon, and Eugene V. Debs. In addition to those attending as individuals, 186 delegates from 34 state, district, and national organizations took part in the convention.[2] No national union affiliated with the A. F. of L. was represented.

From the outset, the I.W.W. was divided upon the question of the relative emphasis to be placed upon political action and industrial action, or whether all political action should not—as the syndicalist followers of Sorel in France averred—be sternly repudiated.[3] But there was agreement upon certain fundamentals: the idea of a struggle, inherent in the capitalism, between the capitalists and the proletariat; abhorrence of the conservative aims of the American Federation of Labor; adoption of the revolutionary watchword "abolition of the wage system" instead of the conservative motto "a fair day's wage for a fair day's work"; repudiation of a craft unionism that "pitted one set of workers against another in the same industry" and acceptance of the principle of industrial organization; the necessity that the structure of the organization be such as to provide a framework of the workers' cooperative commonwealth of the future; and the desirability that the new movement function as a dual organization rather than merely as a propaganda and edu-

circumstances should not, on the other hand, be overemphasized, as there is danger of their being in a "revisionist" interpretation of the origins of the I.W.W. The Western Federation of Miners and the American Labor Union (which had little existence apart from the Western Federation of Miners) were both class-conscious and revolutionary organizations, even if they were not politically minded, and a second preliminary conference (convening Jan. 2, 1905) was participated in by Eugene V. Debs of the Socialist Party and Daniel DeLeon, recognized leader of the Socialist Labor Party and the Socialist Trade and Labor Alliance. *Ibid.*, p. 308.

[1] Among others, locals of the miners, brewers, printers, hotel and restaurant workers, switchmen, street-railway employees, barbers, metal polishers, carpenters, and tailors. N. Ware, *ibid.*, p. 311; P. F. Brissenden, *op. cit.*, pp. 68–73.

[2] *Proceedings of First Annual Convention*, quoted by Perlman and Taft, *op. cit.*, p. 232.

[3] This issue caused a split in the organization in 1908. At its first convention the I.W.W. endorsed independent working-class political action but did not mention a specific party.

cational agency.[1]   A preamble expressive of these fundamentals and ringing with the terminology of the class struggle was adopted,[2] and an elaborate form of industrial organization, in which all industry would be divided into thirteen departments, was set forth.[3]   Immediate tactics were to include aggressive organization drives, sustained militancy, continual emphasis upon the spirit of revolutionary solidarity in contrast to the supine spirit of business unionism, and, as a kind of natural consequence of these, "direct action"—strikes, sympathetic strikes, the "strike on the job," restriction of output, and the various methods of imposing obstacles upon the employers' conduct of industrial operations and interfering with capitalistic procedures in general.   Direct action did not mean that contractual relations might never be entered into, but it did mean

[1] Although disagreement on this point developed later, it is likely that at the outset the socialists who were parties to the establishment of the I.W.W.—both those of Debs and those of DeLeon persuasion—really expected that it would function chiefly as a propagandist, "boring from within," and political agency, even though rigidly "dual" at the outset. During the period 1911–1913, the question of whether the I.W.W. should adhere to the basic strategy of dualism became acute.   William Z. Foster had returned from Europe, converted to the idea that in "boring from within," not in the establishment of rival or dual organizations, lay the really effective tactic of radical unionism, and he wanted the I.W.W. to become a kind of propagandist league.   While the "Wobblies" (workers carrying I.W.W. cards or regarding themselves as connected with the organization) almost instinctively took to the "boring from within" tactic, they never regarded this as a substitute for the maintenance and extension of their organization, but only as an adventitious adjunct.   William Z. Foster left the organization and established a Syndicalist League in 1912.

[2] The full preamble of the I.W.W. reads: "The working class and the employing class have nothing in common.   There can be no peace so long as hunger and want are found among millions of working people and the few, who make up the employing class, have all the good things of life.   Between these two classes a struggle must go on until the workers of the world organize as a class, take possession of the earth and the machinery of production, and abolish the wage system.   We find that the centering of management of the industries into fewer and fewer hands makes the trade unions unable to cope with the ever-growing power of the employing class.   The trade unions foster a state of affairs which allows one set of workers to be pitted against another set of workers in the same industry, thereby helping defeat one another in wage wars.   Moreover, the trade unions aid the employing class to mislead the workers into the belief that the working class have interests in common with their employers.   These conditions can be changed and the interest of the working class upheld only by an organization formed in such a way that all its members in any one industry, or in all industries if necessary, cease work whenever a strike or lockout is on in any department thereof, thus making an injury to one an injury to all.   Instead of the conservative motto, 'A fair day's wage for a fair day's work,' we must inscribe on our banner the revolutionary watchword, 'Abolition of the wage system.'   It is the historic mission of the working class to do away with capitalism.   The army of production must be organized, not only for the every-day struggle with capitalists, but also to carry on production when capitalism shall have been overthrown.   By organizing industrially we are forming the structure of the new society within the shell of the old."

[3] For the details of this departmental organization, see P. F. Brissenden, op. cit., pp. 98–101.

that reliance could not be placed upon these palliatives except as immediate strategic devices.

Internal dissension arose within the I.W.W. almost at the start, particularly between the politically minded and theoretical socialists and the nontheoretical Westerners who, while willing to have the organization bestow verbal benediction upon the analyses and program of the revolutionary theoreticians, were more concerned about building effective industrial organizations and by direct action wresting from capitalism as many of the prerogatives it had been exercising as possible. Daniel DeLeon wanted to fight capitalism, to employ his own phrase, "on a civilized plane," but the lives and social thinking of the Western miners and lumber-camp employees, as has been observed[1], were little complicated by "civilized" inhibitions.[2] Socialist ideology failed to influence them as its proponents were confident that it would; on the other hand, they were greatly influenced by fear of dualism and division within the organization. At the 1906 convention disagreement between the "conservatives" (those concerned chiefly with more effective organization of labor) and the "radicals" resulted in withdrawal of the charter members of the I.W.W. who were identified with the Socialist Party,[3] and at the same time the westerners launched a vigorous campaign against DeLeon and the Socialist Labor Party faction. The Western Federation of Miners, the only member union of any considerable numerical strength, had been torn between the "radical" and "conservative" factions, but its disposition to favor the latter was accentuated by an unfortunate strike experience in 1907, and it withdrew, a sobered and more job-conscious organization and an embittered foe of the movement it had done so much to initiate.[4] In 1908 DeLeon was expelled from the convention, the direct-actionists from the West developing a sudden respect for parliamentary procedure and a devout constitutionalism and voting DeLeon out on the technical ground that he was a delegate from a union in an industry different from his own.[5]

[1] By Professors Perlman and Taft, op. cit., p. 235.

[2] For an account of these differences in points of view and objectives, see ibid., pp. 233–236.

[3] Ibid., p. 235.

[4] The Western Federation of Miners was itself split between the radical socialist faction of the I.W.W. and the faction seeking the immediate building of effective and militant labor organizations, but the latter won. In the 1907 conflict between the miners and the employers in Goldfield, Nev., the Western Federation found that the support accorded it by the nonminer I.W.W. contingent had, if anything, increased the improbability of winning against the employers, because of the accentuation of community hostility toward the union. This experience solidified the conviction expressed by Acting Secretary-treasurer Kirwan at the 1907 convention of the Western Federation of Miners (ibid., p. 234), that the I.W.W. had become a "millstone around the neck" of the Western Federation of Miners.

[5] The DeLeonites formed a rival I.W.W. with headquarters in Detroit, an organization generally referred to as the "Detroit Branch" or the "Detroit I.W.W." In 1915 the

With both socialist factions eliminated, the I.W.W. became in a true sense the representative of the unskilled and migratory workers of the West and the exponent of their brand of radicalism.[1] It initiated, or intervened in, strikes of workers on construction jobs, in agriculture and fruit growing, in the lumber camps, in the Wheatland hop fields, in the shipping industry, and in other segments of Western industry; and beginning about 1909 it offered its leadership to the unorganized immigrant workers of the East, many of whom were employed in fields that the A. F. of L. unions had either neglected or found beyond their ability to organize. The success attained in some of these Eastern strikes, particularly those at McKees Rocks, Pa., and Lawrence, Mass., advertised the I.W.W. favorably among foreign-language wage earners, and its "free speech" campaigns, a practical necessity in view of the fact that the agitational and propagandist activities so often took the form of street meetings,[2] frequently enabled it to appear in the role of defender, against an alliance of employing interests and local government officials, of labor's constitutional rights. Rarely, however, did permanent organizations of stable memberships result from success in the conduct of strikes, and after the unsuccessful Paterson textile disputes of 1912 and 1913 total membership of the I.W.W. declined.[3]

The A. F. of L. regarded the I.W.W. as a potential menace. Craft autonomy had been challenged by "industrialism," business unionism by the revolutionary kind. Mr. Gompers and his associates remembered the "Great Upheaval" of 1885–1887, and, in the widely heralded appearance of the I.W.W. in the East, as well as in its organizing of the casual and migratory workers of the West, they envisaged the possibilities of another upheaval threatening the established trade-union order. Moreover, the program of industrial unionism was likely to appeal to the two large industrial unions within the Federation, the United Mine Workers

---

Detroit I.W.W. changed its name to "Workers' International Industrial Union." It never developed into a movement of any importance.

[1] Perhaps needless to say, however, schisms continued to develop within the I.W.W. during the pre-1914 period. As is indicated in an earlier footnote (*supra*, p. 119), the question of whether the tactics of dualism should be subordinated to those of propaganda and "boring from within" resulted in the withdrawal of William Z. Foster and the group he led. Another issue upon which the I.W.W. divided was whether control should be centralized or decentralized. The issue came before the eighth (1912) convention, where the proposals of the decentralizers, although strongly supported, were defeated.

[2] For an account of the free-speech fight, in which the I.W.W. engaged most actively between 1909 and 1912, see Perlman and Taft, *op. cit.*, pp. 236–247 and P. F. Brissenden, *The I.W.W., A Study in American Syndicalism*, Chap. 11.

[3] Total membership of the I.W.W. has always been difficult to estimate. Claims of officials during the years of its rise were, of course, extravagant, but it is probable that the total never reached 60,000. It must be remembered, however, that paid-up membership or the number of workers carrying cards is not a measure of the importance and influence of such an organization to the extent that it is of an organization like the A. F. of L.

and the Brewery Workers.[1] An inevitable counterattack, the components of which were vehement denunciation and a hurling of the
epithet "socialist," on the one hand, and plans to meet the I.W.W. on its
own ground by organizing within the Federation those elements to which
the rival addressed itself, on the other, was launched.[2] Probably the rise
of a revolutionary opponent after 1905 entrenched even more the conservative social and economic philosophy of the leaders of the A. F. of L.,
just as the efforts of the socialists to capture it had done a few years
before, but the threat of the I.W.W. did prod the dominant labor movement into giving more consideration to the problem of organizing the
unskilled.

The failure of the I.W.W. to materialize as a real rival of the A. F. of
L. is attributable, however, not to the kind of attack the Gompers group
made upon it, but rather to its own inherent weaknesses and to the
incompatibility of its policies and purposes with both the immediate
needs of the workers and the attitudes of the great American middle
class. By its more extreme direct-action tactics it aroused the fear of the
farmers, the small tradesmen, and the self-employed, as well as the
antagonism of conservative unionists; to thousands of middle-class
Americans the organization appeared to be a mysterious, incalculable
force, likely to appear any time and work destruction. It was not
accorded to the ordinary protections of due process of law, and vigilance
committees were organized to see that it did not get them. As a purely
industrial union, the I.W.W. harbored weaknesses that prevented it from
building permanently and extensively. Inspired by a semianarchist
philosophy—a philosophy that in its nature tends to cast suspicion on
attempts to build permanently and therefore paralyzes the disposition
to build—the leaders concerned themselves more with furthering revolutionary propaganda in industrial centers under the guise of unionism than
with performing the day-to-day tasks that a successful and enduring
unionism must perform; and revolutionary propaganda in itself was not

---

[1] It will be recalled (*supra*, pp. 117–118) that locals of both of these unions had been
represented at the 1905 Chicago convention at which the I.W.W. was formed.

[2] The Executive Council of the Federation instructed the constituent unions to oppose
the I.W.W., and Mr. Gompers indiscriminately identified all socialists with the movement.
"In vain did Max Hayes, representing the moderate socialists inside the trade unions, plead
that no socialist would indorse the 'revolutionary and almost unintelligible' preamble of
the I.W.W. and that the majority of socialist trade unionists, like himself, were determined
to remain loyal to the A. F. of L." (L. Lorwin, *The American Federation of Labor*, p. 87).
The leaders of the Federation were aware, however, that denunciation and application of
the socialist label were not in themselves sufficient and that the best way to meet the enemy
was by competing for the allegiance of the unskilled, to which it addressed much of its appeal.
At the 1912 Rochester convention of the A. F. of L., the organization of the unskilled was
near the head of the list of problems considered. S. Perlman, *History of Trade Unionism*
. . . , p. 216.

sufficient to attract and hold the majority of immigrant and other unskilled workers.[1] Ideals the fulfillment of which lay in the distant future overshadowed immediate economic needs. The I.W.W. did, to be sure, win strikes, but after a strike had been won it generally reverted to propaganda activities, neglecting to lay the foundations of permanent unions. On the other hand, its revolutionary zeal caused it to believe that once a strike was started it must be fought out to the end without compromise, irrespective of the probable outcome.[2] Finally, the obstacles to permanent organization in situations in which the I.W.W. operated—the fear and in some cases the docility of foreign workers, nationalistic antagonisms within the labor force, frequent absence of as permanent and substantial a job interest as that possessed by members of the Federation's constituent units, the strength of employers' associations, the alliance with employers of "law and order" agencies and the "respectable" elements of the community, the attitude of the courts toward a revolutionary and direct-actionist movement—were so great as to render difficult the task of an organization not hampered by the I.W.W.'s inherent weaknesses.

Trade Unionism and Politics, 1897-1914.—Efforts of the socialists to commit the Federation to endorsement of an independent labor party had apparently failed by the early 1900's,[3] and the primacy of economic efforts was a firmly ingrained tenet of the federated trade unionism.[4] Nevertheless, events were conspiring to force the trade unions to participate somewhat more actively in politics, even though this participation be of the nonpartisan or bipartisan variety. The antiunion offensive of the employers[5] caused many of the rank and file to question whether

[1] For an excellent critical discussion of the reasons for the failure of the I.W.W. to maintain permanent organizations with substantial membership, the thought of which is followed to an extent in the above lines, see David J. Saposs, *Left Wing Unionism*, pp. 144-162 (International Publishers Co., Inc., New York, 1923).

[2] Dr. Saposs summarizes the indictments of the immigrant and unskilled workers against the I.W.W. (*ibid.*, pp. 148-149) as follows: (1) Except in strike periods, it only indirectly concerned itself with furtherance of the immediate material interests of its adherents. (2) Even during strikes, leaders frequently subordinated immediate issues to propagating their doctrines. (3) It failed to establish continually functioning local organizations. (4) By withdrawing prominent leaders after strikes and diverting their energies to propaganda, it deprived local leaders of necessary counsel and guidance. (5) Its policy of denouncing accumulation of strike funds and of discouraging retention of a staff of paid officials was a handicap. (6) After the automatic poststrike disbanding of the local strike organization, no organization remained to protect the workers in maintaining the gains they had wrested from the employers. (7) When a new crisis developed, the organizing work had to be done over again.

[3] *Cf. supra*, pp. 107-112.

[4] *Cf. supra*, pp. 76-77. The subject of labor and politics and the political activities of trade unionism are not, in this volume, discussed in a separate chapter, but are treated as matters inseparable from a historical survey of the trade-union movement.

[5] *Cf. supra*, pp. 95-102.

the potentialities of purely economic action had not been overestimated; unorganized workers, many of whom did not fit into the craft system that formed the basis of the dominant movement, tended to look toward ameliorative legislation for improvement of their working and living conditions; the "progressive revolt" of the years preceding 1912[1] carried with it an intellectual climate conducive to a program of broad legislative reform; and the success of the British independent political movement in the election of 1905, followed as it was by enactment of the Trades Disputes Act of 1906,[2] stimulated a desire on the part of many American unionists to follow the example of their English fellows. Even more important was the disposition of the courts to issue injunctions restricting or entirely preventing resort to the methods the unions regarded as essential to the prosecution of strikes,[3] and to regard unions as coming within the application of the Sherman Antitrust Act of 1890.[4]

By 1906 the pressure of some of the international unions and the manifest concern of some of labor's friends over the lethargy of the Federation in the political arena resulted in a conference, summoned by President Gompers, of the executive heads of the international unions. A Bill of Grievances was submitted to the President and to both houses of the national legislature[5] and a program of labor legislation and political and economic reforms was formulated. Some of the demands incorporated in this Bill and the program formulated—child-labor laws, free schools and textbooks, votes for women, and issue of money by the government free from the manipulation of private bankers for gain—were reminiscent of the "upliftism" of the Knights of Labor; others were expressive of the progressive and reformist spirit of the time; but to a considerable extent they were trade union in character. Immigration must be restricted, the government must prohibit or curb the manufacture and sale of products made by convict labor, the eight-hour-day

---

[1] *Cf. supra*, pp. 91–92.

[2] *Cf. infra*, p. 496.

[3] The common-law bases of the conspiracy doctrine upon which injunctions were issued with increasing frequency during the late 1880's and the 1890's is discussed *infra*, pp. 499–509 and the nature and problems arising out of the application of this legal instrument are discussed *infra*, pp. 629–651.

[4] It was not until 1908 that the Supreme Court, in the historic Danbury Hatters case (*Loewe v. Lawlor*, 208 U. S. 274), clearly established that trade unions come within the purview of the Antitrust Act, but lower federal courts had taken this position some years before. The Danbury Hatters decision is summarized and discussed in some detail *infra* pp. 568–569.

[5] For detailed discussion of the 1906 Bill of Grievances see L. Lorwin, *op. cit.*, pp. 88–90, Perlman and Taft, in vol. 4 of Commons and Associates, *History of Labor in the United States*, pp. 152–153, and Mollie Ray Carroll, *Labor and Politics*. The entire Bill is to be found in the *Proceedings* of the Twenty-sixth Annual Convention of the A. F. of L., 1906.

standard must be maintained and prevailing wage rates paid on government work, and most of all the misuse of the injunction in labor disputes must be ended and trade unions exempted from operation of the Antitrust Act. There was, in addition, a threat to appeal over the heads of elected representatives to the electorate itself, should the demands not be heeded. "Labor brings these, its grievances, to your attention because you are the representatives responsible for legislation and for failure of legislation. . . . Labor now appeals to you, and we trust it may not be in vain. But if perchance you may not heed us, we shall appeal to the conscience and support of our fellow citizens."

When a bill regulating the issuance of injunctions in labor disputes, introduced in the House of Representatives at A. F. of L. instigation, failed to receive serious consideration, and congressional indifference to the other demands of the Bill of Grievances became apparent, the Federation entered politics in a nonpartisan capacity. A Labor Representation Committee[1] of the Executive Council circularized organized labor and its friends in 1906, urging nomination by the Democratic and the Republican parties of candidates favorable to labor's demands and recommending that wherever both major parties ignored these demands a straight labor ticket be nominated. The candidates whose records the various affiliated units—city centrals, state federations, and local unions—found to be unsatisfactory were, in the majority of cases, re-elected in November of 1906, but with reduced pluralities; Congressman Littlefield of Maine, upon whom the Federation's attack had been centered, was returned to the House with a plurality only one-fourth that he had received two years earlier; and six trade-union members were elected to Congress.[2] Mr. Gompers characterized the results of the Federation's excursion into politics as "magical,"[3] but the House of Representatives elected in 1906 proved to be more unsympathetic toward labor's legislative program than its predecessor had been.

The 1906 political activities of the trade-union movement were significant. They did not constitute a step toward independent labor-party action, and lest they be so construed Mr. Gompers at the 1906 convention of the Federation emphasized that there had been no deviation from the political policy endorsed by previous conventions. The delegates to this convention, still fearful of the disruptive effects of independent political efforts upon the economic strength of the trade unions and perhaps influenced by the old horror that the labor movement might fall into the hands of the socialists, officially sanctioned the nonpartisan policy. Nevertheless, the Federation had actively entered politics to reward its friends and punish its enemies, and this step was itself recogni-

[1] Samuel Gompers, Frank Morrison, and James O'Connell.
[2] Perlman and Taft, op. cit., p. 154.
[3] L. Lorwin, op. cit., p. 90.

tion that in the developing American economic and social structure greater emphasis had to be placed upon political methods. For the first time, city and state central bodies and local organizations had been placed under pressure to elect delegates to conferences or conventions called to formulate plans for effecting the defeat of legislators indifferent or hostile to labor's demands, and perhaps even more important was the instruction of the Labor Representation Committee that a straight labor ticket be nominated where both parties ignored the trade-union legislative program. Nor did events of the years immediately after 1906 permit the Federation to return to the relatively quiescent political policy of earlier years. Early in 1908 the Danbury Hatters decision was rendered, and a conference of trade-union officers and representatives of several farm organizations, called by the Executive Council of the A. F. of L., urged the calling of meetings in protest against the labor injunction and against application of the Sherman Act to the "legitimate" activities of labor organizations. Labor's first entry into a national campaign took place that year, when the influence and support of the Federation were thrown to Bryan.[1] Two years later organized labor's participation in the congressional elections produced results regarded by the leaders as satisfactory,[2] and then, in 1912, a party of distinctly prolabor predilections came into power. In 1914, President Wilson signed the Clayton Amendment to the Antitrust Act,[3] and organized labor believed that its greatest legislative objectives—freedom from the writ of injunction, exemption from the Antitrust Act, statutory enunciation of its

---

[1] A series of demands, formulated by the American Federation of Labor, was presented to the Resolutions Committees of both the Democratic and the Republican parties in 1908, the antiinjunction plank being, of course, the one most stressed. The more important of the demands were: statutory enunciation of the right of labor to organize; prohibition of the issuance of injunctions in labor disputes where such injunctions would not apply in the absence of a labor dispute and in cases where there already existed a remedy at law; trial by jury in contempt cases when the contempt was not committed in the presence of the court or so near as to obstruct the administration of justice; extension of the eight-hour day to all public works, both those carried on directly by the government and those done by private contractors; endorsement of an employers' liability law; a constitutional amendment granting suffrage to women; and creation of a department of labor and a bureau of mines. From Perlman and Taft, *op. cit.*, p. 157. *Cf.* also L. Lorwin, *op. cit.*, pp. 116–122, and Mollie Ray Carroll, *op. cit.*

[2] More active efforts to obtain state labor legislation also characterized the developing political policy of the Federation during the seven or eight years prior to 1914. The Federation fell in line with, then actively supported, the movement for workmen's compensation laws. With some apparent misgivings, it also took an attitude more favorable to old-age pensions. Legal limitations upon the hours of women workers were also supported, although the Gompers group apparently remained skeptical concerning the desirability of minimum wage laws for women. The development of these types of labor legislation and the forces active in support of them are discussed in vol. I of this series, pp. 301–323 and 527–534, and in vol. II, pp. 187–205 and 378–382.

[3] 38 Stat. L. 730.

lawfulness per se and of its right to utilize without judicial interference its traditional and revered techniques—had been achieved.

When the president of the A. F. of L. could proclaim that a "new magna charta" and a "bill of rights" for labor had been written upon the statutes of the United States, critics of the nonpartisan political policy found themselves at an argumentative disadvantage. But the magna charta as construed by the Supreme Court between 1914 and the end of the 1930's[1] made lawful nothing that had been unlawful prior to its enactment. As vitiating—from the point of view of labor's expectations—constructions began to be placed upon the "exemption" from the operation of the Antitrust law, the declaration that nothing in these laws should prevent labor organizations from "lawfully" carrying out their "legitimate" objects, and the immunities from injunctive interference in cases of concerted cessation of work or patronage and of peaceful persuasion,[2] the exuberance over this political achievement gave way to sober recognition of the ever-present danger of judicial nullification or emasculation of the gains labor had achieved through political action.

In view of the decades-old disagreement among courts as to what did and what did not constitute an actionable conspiracy, what was lawful and what was unlawful when the motives of combinations were probed, the confidence of the trade-union leadership that the Clayton Act had wrought a substantive change in the law of labor is revealing. There was little or no anticipation of the judicial pitfalls inherent in the words of the Act, and apparently there was entire assurance that a mere declaration of the permissibility under the Antitrust laws of the "existence and operation" of labor organizations and of the "lawfully carrying out of their legitimate objects" necessarily rendered lawful activities that

---

[1] The interpretation placed upon the Sherman Act and the Clayton Amendment in the early 1940's (especially in *Milk Drivers Local v. Lake Valley Products Co.*, 61 Sup. Ct. 122, and *U. S. Hutcheson*, 61 Sup. Ct. 463) are discussed *infra*, pp. 575–581.

[2] The story of the Clayton Act's judicial vicissitudes is recorded later in this volume (*infra*, pp. 569–570, 578–580, 615–616, 622–624), and mention of its main provisions and of the aggregate import of the Supreme Court constructions suffices for the purposes of this chapter. Section 6 enunciated the amiable principle that "the labor of a human being is not a commodity or article of commerce" and declared that nothing in the Antitrust laws should be construed to forbid the existence and operation of labor organizations or to prevent their lawfully carrying out their legitimate objects. Section 20, the other most important labor section, provided that no injunction should be granted in any case "between employers and employees, or between employees, or between persons employed and persons seeking employment" growing out of a dispute concerning terms and conditions of employment, "unless necessary to prevent irreparable injury to property or a property right," and that no injunction should be issued preventing persons, singly or in concert, from ceasing to work, or from persuading others "by peaceful and lawful means" to do so, or from ceasing to patronize, or from "peaceably" assembling in a "lawful" manner and for "lawful" purposes. In the tortuous field of labor law, it of course still remained for the courts to decide what was "lawful," "legitimate," "peaceful," etc.

theretofore had been regarded as unlawful restraint of trade. A unionism forced into political action largely in consequence of judicial prevention of what it wanted to do—center its activities in the economic area—was not so cognizant of political hurdles to be taken as it was of the familiar economic hurdles, and its traditional patterns of thought caused it to regard the political victory as an achievement no more subject to the refereeship of a higher power than were its victories over employers in trade disputes. In any event, the fact that the legislation achieved after years of effort to be exempted from the operation of the Antitrust laws and "emancipated" from judicial interference did not (in Supreme Court contemplation) introduce any real change in the substantive law (and would have been in violation of constitutional guarantees if it had to be construed as so doing) was not apparent until some years after 1914; and with the "magna charta" still apparently a magna charta, and with other legislative achievements to which to point,[1] the Federation was able to declare that, given a sympathetic administration, labor-sponsored measures could be enacted into law without unionism's having to assume the risks of independent party action.

WARTIME UNIONISM, 1914–1920

Not more than one of every nine of the nonagricultural employees of the United States was a trade-union member when, in 1914, the nations of Europe faced each other in a life-and-death struggle,[2] but the unionism that had emerged out of the turmoil of the 1880's found reason to assert

---

[1] Among which were the prohibition in government arsenals and naval establishments of the so-called "scientific management" systems (U. S. Laws, 1914–1915, C. 83 and C. 143), the Lloyd-LaFollette Act, granting to public employees the right of lobbying and affiliating with labor organizations and the "LaFollette Seamen's Act" (38 Stat. L. 1164, signed by the President in 1915), under which some of the worst of the working conditions of men employed in marine transportation were eradicated.

[2] It will be recalled (*supra*, pp. 82–86) that in 1910, according to the estimates of Professor Wolman, less than one-tenth (9.9 per cent) of the nonagricultural employees were trade-union members. Between 1910 and 1914, trade-union membership increased, according to the same source, from 2,140,500 to 2,687,100, or by more than half a million. The total number of nonagricultural employees in 1910 is estimated by Professor Wolman to have been 20,140,904, and it seems safe to assume that in 1914 the total number did not exceed 24,000,-000. (Professor Wolman's estimate of the total number of nonagricultural employees in 1920 is 27,359,660, and if a "straight-line" method of estimating the increase during the intercensal years is used—*i.e.*, if the increase of 6,549,756 is assumed to have occurred in annual increments of 654,975—the number of nonagricultural employees in 1914 was 23,429,800. There can, however, be no doubt that more of the total 1910–1920 increase took place during the first half of the decade than did during the second half, when immigration was curtailed and the cityward migration was not exceeding the farmward migration as it did during the 1920's; and probably in 1914 the total number of nonagricultural workers was considerably greater than 23,500,000 but still less than 24,000,000.) Hence the percentage of organization was probably less than 11 (or "one of every nine") that year.

that it had proved its superiority to other kinds of labor organization. In spite of the criticism that both progressive unionists within its ranks and intellectuals outside were wont to hurl, the federated trade unionism had demonstrated its stability and survival capacity. Membership had increased from less than 500,000 in 1897 to more than 2,500,000 in 1914.[1] Recognition had been attained; trade agreements had been entered into and enforced. Attacks of open-shop employers and of left-wing elements had retarded and checked, not prevented, substantial growth and expansion. With the subordination of locals to the national and international unions, necessary coordination and unity of action had been attained. Structural modifications—departments, amalgamations, widening of craft bases, trades' councils—had been effected without sacrifice of the virtues of the craft form of organization, and the Federation had demonstrated an adaptability and a catholicity of outlook that enabled it to include such diverse groups as the United Mine Workers, the Brotherhood of Carpenters and Joiners, the Photo Engravers, the Western Federation of Miners, and the Brewery Workers. The trade-union leadership believed that the primacy of economic action policy and the tenet of nonpartisanship had been vindicated.

Other phases of the 1914 trade-union situation were, however, less favorable. Structural modifications had not kept pace with the increasing need for them. After the first great increase in membership, between 1897 and 1905, the rate of growth had been much slower. Save for anthracite coal, the "trustified" industries remained unconquered; the unskilled and semiskilled workers, with few exceptions, were still unorganized. Industrial unrest mounted during the two or three years before the outbreak of the European War, and the voluminous testimony taken and published by the United States Commission on Industrial Relations[2] revealed how much of unionism's task of substituting its kind of "industrial government" for managerial autocracy remained to be accomplished. Business activity decreased during the twelve months prior to the beginning of the war, and the accompanying decline in trade-union membership, while not great, was a little ominous. But the impact of war abroad upon conditions in the American labor market, and then the manifold repercussions upon the labor movement of American participation in the conflict, rendered academic for a time any ques-

---

[1] *Cf. supra*, p. 83.

[2] This Commission was created by Act of Congress in 1912, largely in response to the mounting industrial unrest. Strikes, such as the one in the Colorado coal fields, had been characterized by a great deal of violence, and incidents, such as the bombing of the *Los Angeles Times* building, an act growing out of a strike, aroused public apprehension. The *Report* of the Commission rejected the compulsory arbitration proposal of its employer members and advocated strongly an extension of trade unionism and collective agreements. The *Final Report and Testimony of the Commission on Industrial Relations* was published in twelve volumes in 1915.

tion of whether the A. F. of L. kind of unionism had approached the
natural limits of its growth and strength.

The Wartime Background.—During the six-year period 1914–1920
trade-union membership increased by almost 2,500,000—a gain in excess
of that of the seventeen-year period 1897–1914. Industries and regions
heretofore almost entirely unorganized were penetrated, "recognition"
was secured from employers who had been unbending in their opposition
to unionism, discrimination against workers because of union affiliations
or activities was in effect prohibited in industries essential to wartime
efforts, and union standards of wages, hours, and conditions became the
accepted norm in governmental labor policies. Concessions were
wrested from employers and gains were achieved that probably would
have been unattainable under normal conditions for years. A brief
summary of the causes of this advance should precede detailed discussion of it.

Business depression turned into prosperity as European orders for
munitions and other goods—the purchase of which was made possible,
to a considerable extent, by loans of American financial institutions—
began to reach the United States in increasing numbers. Widened
profit margins caused employers to be less reluctant to grant wage
increases and to be more unwilling to risk interruptions in production
that might result from failure to negotiate with the unions. The war
abroad reduced to a small fraction of its pre-1914 proportions the volume
of immigration,[1] and unemployment diminished. By 1916 the labor
market was much more a "sellers' market," much less a "buyers'," than
it had been two years before. Strikes for higher wages and recognition
increased in number, and frequently the A. F. of L. affiliates emerged
from them with enhanced prestige and larger memberships.[2] All of the
losses in numerical strength during the minor depression of 1913–1914
had been, as is indicated shortly,[3] retrieved by 1916. That same year
the Railroad Brotherhoods, under threat of strike, were able to bring
about enactment of the Adamson Act,[4] establishing the basic eight-hour
day, and—partaking of the nature of an official declaration of the acceptance of trade unionism as an integral part of the American commonwealth

---

[1] *Cf.* vol. I of this series, pp. 29–31.

[2] The A. F. of L. affiliates gained significantly from strikes involving the munitions
workers, which were led by the International Association of Machinists, and from those of
the New York longshoremen, the building trades unions, the streetcar employees of Chicago,
and the women's garment workers of Philadelphia. In another series of strikes, the Federation was able to capture from the I.W.W. leadership of a number of groups of unskilled
and, for the most part, foreign-born workers. For details see L. Lorwin, *The American
Federation of Labor*, pp. 132–134.

[3] *Cf. infra*, p. 132.

[4] U. S. Laws, 1916, C. 436. Constitutionality of the Act was sustained by the Supreme
Court in 1917 (*Wilson v. New*, 243 U. S. 332).

—President Wilson stated that in the future no President would be able to ignore the organized labor movement.[1]

Organized labor's great opportunity came, however, when the United States entered the war. Increased output in all the basic industries was imperative, and, since unmitigated cooperation of labor was one of the conditions essential to its attainment, both employers and the government were willing to make concessions. As small industries expanded rapidly and new industries experienced a mushroom growth, competition for labor became extremely keen, while on the supply side the curtailment of immigration synchronized with withdrawal of more than 5,000,000 able-bodied men into the military establishment. Willingness to bid wages upward and reluctance to risk strikes were increased by the "cost-plus" terms of many of the government contracts,[2] while the practical suspension of the Antitrust laws for the duration of the war, which meant that combination and the pooling of trade data were permissible, was an inducement to employers to make concessions to organized labor in return for labor's promise to cooperate and hold in abeyance the strike weapon. The conservative position of the A. F. of L. with reference to property rights and its comparative indifference to far-reaching plans for social reorganization[3] likewise rendered the government and undoubtedly no negligible number of employers more ready to enter into arrangements with the unions involving concessions they had sought for years.

Still another force operating powerfully to advance trade unionism and collective bargaining was the official policy of the Federal Administration. When the government undertook operation or administration of basic industries like the railroads and coal mining, it gave official recognition to collective bargaining with labor, and the various government boards established to unify the labor policy of the country and prevent strikes adopted as a basic canon the right of workers to organize and bargain collectively free from discrimination because of union membership or activity. Finally, the social and political atmosphere of the War period was far from irrelevant to the spread of unionism and the new power it attained. The war was professedly one for "democracy," and the democratic claims of a labor movement that itself refused to challenge the basic precepts of capitalistic democracy could not with consistency be ignored. In the fervor and emotionalism of the time,

[1] At the dedication of the new A. F. of L. building in Washington, July 4, 1916.

[2] That is, the government agreed to pay those with whom it entered into contracts the cost of the work (including, of course, labor cost) plus a certain percentage of the costs, which would constitute a "fair" profit.

[3] The postarmistice Reconstruction Program of the A. F. of L. (cf. infra, pp. 141–143) and British labor's program for a new social order stand out in marked contrast to each other, and the former is expressive of a social and economic attitude that employers found not intolerable, even though many of them were awaiting the end of the war to put labor in its place in respect of the "right to organize."

employers refusing to cooperate with boards and commissions established to adjust labor disputes and develop a national labor policy, merely because these boards had adopted policies and enunciated principles antithetical to traditional open-shop predilections, were likely to be labeled "obstructionists"; and many of them, convinced of the righteousness of the government's war efforts, did not want either to be or to be labeled obstructionists. Moral conviction joined with "cost-plus" contracts to accord to trade unionism a new status and a new opportunity.

Increase in, and Distribution of, Trade-union Membership.—The story of the increase in total trade-union membership and in membership of the A. F. of L. is told, in quantitative terms, in Table 2. The growth revealed was without precedent. Between 1914 and 1920, total mem-

TABLE 2.—TOTAL MEMBERSHIP OF AMERICAN TRADE UNIONS AND OF UNIONS AFFILIATED WITH THE AMERICAN FEDERATION OF LABOR, AND ANNUAL CHANGES IN BOTH, 1914–1920[1]

Year	All unions		American Federation of Labor	
	Average annual membership	Increase or decrease over preceding year	Average annual membership	Increase or decrease over preceding year
1914	2,687,100		2,020,700	
1915	2,582,600	−104,500	1,946,300	− 74,400
1916	2,772,700	+190,100	2,072,700	+126,400
1917	3,061,400	+288,700	2,371,400	+298,700
1918	3,467,300	+405,900	2,726,500	+355,100
1919	4,125,200	+657,900	3,260,100	+533,600
1920	5,047,800	+922,600	4,078,700	+818,600

[1] Compiled from Leo Wolman, *Ebb and Flow in Trade Unionism*, p. 26, and from the *Proceedings* of the American Federation of Labor for the various years.

bership increased from 2,687,100 to 5,047,800, and between 1915, when membership was less than in 1914, and 1920 the increase was 2,465,200—almost a 100 per cent increase in five years. In one year, 1919–1920, the gain fell not far short of a million (922,600). It will be noted, also, that the increase in A. F. of L. membership about kept pace with the increase in total union membership and that the percentage of all unionists included within the Federation's affiliates did not change appreciably.[1] Relative to the total number of wage earners in the United States, trade unionism was almost twice as strong when it reached its 1920 peak as it had been ten years earlier. In 1910 only 8.6 per cent of all employees,

[1] It will be noted that in 1917 total A. F. of L. membership, according to the foregoing data, increased by 10,000 more than did membership of all unions. This would indicate losses on the part of some of the nonaffiliated organizations. It is likely, however, that the fact that A. F. of L. figures on "paid-up" membership are not exactly comparable to the more refined figures resulting from Professor Wolman's statistical investigation accounts chiefly for the difference.

and 9.9 per cent of all nonagricultural employees, were, according to the most competent estimates, members of trade unions.[1]   Ten years later, the respective percentages were 17.5 and 19.4.[2]

The wartime expansion of unionism was, on the whole, confined to a relatively restricted class of workers, the building and transportation groups, together with the unions in the metal, machinery, shipbuilding, and clothing industries, accounting for about three-fourths of the total 1915–1920 increase in membership.[3]   Unions in industries most essential to the prosecution of the war experienced, as would have been expected, the greatest growth.[4]   In contrast to the next period of great expansion, that of the post-1933 years,[5] the gains of the War period were less widely diffused among industries and occupations, and they constituted to a greater extent a development of unionism where it already had a foothold rather than a conquering of theretofore almost entirely unorganized

[1] L. Wolman, *op. cit.*, p. 116.

[2] *Ibid.*   It may be noted in passing that there was nothing especially unique about the development of labor organization in the United States during the war and early postwar periods.   In all countries affected by similar conditions, the membership trends were much the same.   For example, total membership of English trade unions in 1920 is estimated to have been 8,346,000, as contrasted to 4,145,000 in 1914 (from data in the *Ministry of Labour Gazette*, October, 1935, as summarized by Professor Wolman, *op. cit.*, p. 31).   The real uniqueness of trade-union growth during this period lay in the fact that in spite of the traditional antiunion attitude in major sectors of industry, an attitude much stronger than in England, and of the failure of unionism prior to the war to be accepted and recognized as it had been in England, the growth here was relatively as great as it was there.

[3] The total increase in membership of these four groups of unions and of all unions has been estimated by Professor Wolman (*op. cit.*, p. 28) as follows:

Group of Unions	Increase 1915–1920
Building construction	355,200
Metals, machinery, shipbuilding	634,600
Transportation and communication	680,100
Clothing	200,800
Total above groups	1,870,700
Total all unions	2,465,200

[4] As examples: The Seamen's Union included 21,700 members in 1916, 65,000 in 1920, and 103,300 in 1921.   The Longshoremen's Union increased from 25,000 in 1916 to 74,000 in 1920, the Maintenance of Way Employees from 8,900 in 1916 to 54,200 in 1919; the Teamsters' Union from 59,000 in 1916 to 110,800 in 1920.   Metal trades unions began, as a result of the manufacture of munitions for the Allies, to expand prior to entrance of the United States into the war.   Within this group, the Machinists' Union numbered 71,900 in 1915, 112,500 in 1917, and 330,800 in 1920; the Boiler Makers' membership jumped from 31,200 in 1917 to 103,000 in 1920; and the Blacksmiths' Union from 12,000 in 1917 to 48,300 in 1920.   Within the building trades, the Carpenters' Union included 331,500 in 1920 as contrasted to 231,700 in 1917, and the Electricians' membership increased from 41,500 to 139,200.   From data compiled by Perlman and Taft, in vol. 4 of Commons and Associates, *History of Labor in the United States*, p. 410.   The sources of the data are the 1919 *Proceedings* of the American Federation of Labor, pp. 30–31, and Professor Wolman's *Growth of American Trade Unions*, pp. 110–116.

[5] *Cf. infra*, pp. 192–201.

industries and trades.[1] Industrial unionism was no stronger, relative
to craft unionism, in 1920 than it had been in 1914; on the contrary, a
slightly smaller percentage of all unionists seem to have been affiliated
with organizations having an industrial basis.[2] As a sum-total consequence of the war-period increase in union membership, almost twice
as large a proportion of the employees of manufacturing and mechanical
industries (including construction) were organized in 1920 as had been
ten years before (22.2 per cent, as contrasted to 11.4 per cent in 1910),
slightly more than twice as large a proportion in transportation and
communication (39.6 per cent in 1920 as contrasted to 19.5 per cent in
1910) and in the service industries (4.9 and 2.0 per cent in these two years
respectively).[3] In mining, quarrying, and gas and petroleum production,
the percentage of trade-union organization among employees increased
from 28.8 to 39.6 per cent.[4]

Distribution of the total membership of American labor organizations
among different industries and trades of course changed to an extent
during these years of expansion. Some unions largest in 1914 found
themselves constituting a smaller percentage of the total organized labor

[1] It will be noted that the Miners were not one of the groups, listed in footnote 3,
p. 133, as contributing most to the expansion of unionism during this period. The reason
was that the United Mine Workers had already become one of the largest American unions
by 1914, and with its capacity for further development limited, it gained only 55,000 members between 1914 and 1920. The building and the transportation and communication
groups, which together contributed 963,300 to the total 1915–1920 increase of 1,870,700,
had been of substantial size at the beginning of the War period, but they had included
many small unions and had claimed jurisdiction over numerous occupations that were
hardly organized. These small unions grew during the War period, and at the same time
substantial memberships were acquired in occupations where the jurisdictional claims had
theretofore been chiefly paper claims. While the building industry proper failed to share
proportionately in the general prosperity of American industry during this period, and
some of the strictly building-trades organizations (like the Bricklayers' Union) failed to
increase in membership, the membership of unions like the Carpenters, which has always
had jurisdiction over a substantial number of craftsmen in other industries, increased
greatly and accounted for a considerable part of the increase of 355,200 credited in footnote
3, p. 133, of the building-construction unions. The 200,800 increase in the clothing
industry group was largely due to the founding in 1915 of the Amalgamated Clothing
Workers of America and to the rapid growth of this union during the five years
thereafter. The observations in this footnote are based upon and follow closely the
analysis of Professor Wolman in *Ebb and Flow in Trade Unionism*, pp. 26–32.

[2] Professor Wolman's estimate (*Ebb and Flow in Trade Unionism*, p. 92) is that 75 per
cent of the total union membership found place in craft or compound-craft organizations
in 1914 and 78 per cent in 1920. These percentages were arrived at by subtracting from
total union membership the membership of all mining, clothing, and shoe unions and of the
United Textile Workers, the Amalgamated Textile Workers, the Associated Silk Workers,
the Brewery Workers, the Marine and Shipbuilding Workers, the Iron and Steel Workers,
and the Electrical Industry Employees Union.

[3] The estimates of Professor Wolman, *ibid.*, p. 118.

[4] *Ibid.*

movement in 1920 than they had constituted six or ten years earlier, even though contributing greatly to the absolute increase.[1] The unions in the building-construction industry contributed an estimated 355,200 to the total increase in the union membership of 2,465,200,[2] but in 1920 they included more nearly one-sixth of the total of all organized workers than the one-fifth they had included in 1914. The mining and quarrying industry, in which 27.8 per cent of the employees were organized in 1910 and 39.6 per cent in 1920, employed only between one-eleventh and one-twelfth of all the country's unionists in 1920, as contrasted to more than one-eighth in 1910 and more than one-seventh in 1914. The metals, machinery, and shipbuilding unions, on the other hand, included in 1920 nearly twice as large a proportion of all organized workers as in 1910 and more than twice as large a proportion as in 1914. Transportation and communication unions, which are estimated to have increased in membership by 680,000 during the 1915–1920 period, had the affiliation of nearly one-quarter of all American unionists in 1920, as against a little more than one-fifth in 1914. On the whole, however, no startling change in the distribution of trade-union membership occurred during the years of wartime expansion. The essential facts are set forth in the following table.

TABLE 3.—MEMBERSHIP OF AMERICAN TRADE UNIONS, PERCENTAGE IN EACH INDUSTRIAL GROUP, 1910, 1914, 1920[1]

Industrial group	1910	1914	1920
Mining, quarrying, and oil	12.8	14.1	8.7
Building construction	21.4	20.2	17.6
Metals, machinery, shipbuilding	9.2	8.4	17.0
Textiles	1.0	1.1	3.0
Leather and shoes	2.2	2.2	2.2
Clothing	4.6	5.9	7.4
Lumber and woodworking	1.3	0.9	0.5
Paper, printing, bookbinding	4.2	4.1	3.2
Chemicals, clay, glass, stone	2.8	2.1	1.0
Food, liquor, tobacco	5.7	4.6	3.6
Transportation and communication	22.5	20.9	24.9
Public service	2.7	3.4	3.2
Theater and music	2.8	3.4	2.0
Trade	0.7	0.6	0.4
Hotel and restaurant service	1.7	2.7	1.2
Domestic and personal service	1.4	1.4	1.0
Miscellaneous	3.0	3.2	3.1
Total	100.0	100.0	100.0

[1] Compiled from the data presented by Professor Wolman, *op. cit.*, Appendix, Table II, pp. 198–199.

[1] As a consequence, of course, of the fact that their memberships had bulked large in total trade-union membership at the beginning of the period and that the absolute increases were not as great relative to the membership at the beginning as were those of the unions in branches of the economy where labor organization had included much smaller percentages of the total working force.

[2] *Cf. supra*, p. 133, footnote 3.

Labor's Attitude toward the War.—In the United States, as in all countries, the first reaction of the wage-earning masses toward the War was a recoil at the horror of it all, and pressure to mobilize labor opinion against American participation was strong. The leadership of organized labor, however, was reluctant to sanction a declaration that in no event would labor support American involvement, and as the War progressed pro-Ally feeling became stronger in the officialdom and also among the rank and file.[1] During the latter part of 1915 and 1916, the leadership of the Federation participated actively in the preparedness campaign, and Mr. Gompers was among the National Civic Federation members who drafted a resolution calling upon Congress to create a Council of National Defense. Official proclamation of organized labor's position on the war was made at a conference, held on Mar. 12, 1917, when war seemed inevitable, of 148 officers of various national unions, including the Railroad Brotherhoods.[2] A resolution interpreted as an unconditional pledge that organized labor would support the government should the United States enter the war was adopted,[3] but "the government must recognize the organized labor movement as the agency through which it must cooperate with the wage-earners." Specific safeguards of the interests of trade unionism, demanded in return for the pledge to support the government in waging a war, included: representation of organized labor on all agencies determining or administering policies of national defense; conformity to trade-union standards in government and private employment; agreement "by representatives of the government and those engaged and employed in the industry" as a prerequisite to "whatever changes in the organization of industry are necessary"; imposition of the same demands for service upon property as upon labor and limitation of profits; and maintenance of industrial and commercial service

---

[1] The story of the various forces brought to bear upon the leadership of the A. F. of L. is told in excellent fashion in L. Lorwin, *The American Federation of Labor*, pp. 136–143. Mr. Gompers's *My Seventy Years of Life and Labor*, vol. II, pp. 322–387, should also be consulted by one seeking to disentangle the numerous forces that went into the making of the final war position of the dominant labor faction.

[2] The conference was called by Mr. Gompers, who was concerned lest the trade-union movement fail to be put before the public in a "patriotic light." The only important international unions not represented were the International Ladies' Garment Workers, the Western Federation of Miners, the Journeymen Barbers, and the International Typographical Union. L. Lorwin, *op. cit.*, p. 143.

[3] "We . . . hereby pledge ourselves, in peace or in war, in stress or in strain, to stand unreservedly by the standards of liberty and the safety and preservation of the institutions and ideals of our Republic. . . . Should our country be drawn into the maelstrom of European conflict, we, with these ideals of liberty and justice, . . . offer our services to our country in every field of activity to defend, safeguard, and preserve the Republic of the United States of America against its enemies whomsoever they may be, and call upon our fellow workers and fellow citizens in the holy name of labor, justice, freedom, and humanity devotedly and patriotically to give like service."

upon a nonmilitary basis, since "the same voluntary institutions that organized industrial, commercial, and transportation workers in times of peace will best take care of the same problems in time of war."[1]   The reception the trade unions accorded this resolution, and the demands it incorporated, was decidedly lukewarm, but the country as a whole accepted it as a statement of organized labor's official position.

The A. F. of L. accordingly was—on the conditions just enumerated—strongly committed to a prowar position by April of 1917, and the opposition of the traditionally obstructionist—from its point of view—Socialist Party and the I.W.W. only solidified this position and convinced it that it must put the labor movement before the American people in the proper light.[2]   An "American Alliance for Labor and Democracy" was formed—at the instigation of the Executive Council of the Federation and with the financial aid of the Creel Committee on Public Information—[3] to

[1] From the summary of the demands in S. Perlman, *History of Trade Unionism* . . . , pp. 233–234.

[2] The story of left-wing opposition to the War and to the Federation's prowar position must here be confined to a brief summary.   A referendum of Socialist Party membership, shortly after the declaration of war, overwhelmingly endorsed resolutions condemning the entry of the United States into the War, characterizing the conflict as an outgrowth of commercial and financial rivalry, and pledging the Party's opposition to conscription and censorship.   In spite of the withdrawal of some prowar socialists (like Upton Sinclair and John Spargo), the War gave the party a new cause and membership increased from 67,788 to 81,172 during the two months between April and June, 1917 (Perlman and Taft, *op. cit.*, p. 422).   Government reprisals were of course visited upon the socialists, and a number of prominent members, including Eugene V. Debs, Victor Berger, and Adolph Germer, were sentenced to prison for violation of the espionage act.   The I.W.W. had probably alarmed the business interests of the country more than had the Socialist Party, and it was the chief object of a campaign the immediate purpose of which was to stifle sedition and disloyalty but the roots of which had been nurtured in industrial conflict.   Raids were made by agents of the Department of Justice upon I.W.W. headquarters in Pittsburgh, New York, Boston, Baltimore, Detroit, San Francisco, Milwaukee, Los Angeles, Spokane, Portland, Ore., Omaha, Minneapolis, and Lincoln, Neb., even while the President was appointing a liberal jurist to make an impartial survey of the activities of the organization; 166 members were indicted for violation of the espionage act; local authorities sprang to the defense of the industrial *status quo* and unofficial vigilante organizations took law and order into their own hands.   Of the 166 leaders and members arrested during the federal raids of Sept. 5, 1917, an even 100 were convicted of conspiracy to obstruct and hamper the military program (from detail in Perlman and Taft, *op. cit.*, pp. 416–419).   The government's wartime attack upon the I.W.W. had the effect of virtually bringing about the end of that organization as an effective economic force, although the organization continued its existence and at the time of the writing of these lines (1943) still maintained a national headquarters in Chicago and published a weekly paper.   The government's antisedition campaign removed the I.W.W. leaders who had been most adept in "organizing on the job," and the less stable and mature leadership that succeeded them were more concerned with propaganda and a vague "revolutionary cause" than with building a militant but stable industrial unionism.

[3] For accounts of the somewhat checkered career of this prowar labor organization see L. Lorwin, *op. cit.*, pp. 149–153 and Perlman and Taft, *op. cit.*, pp. 403–406.   The leaders of the Alliance were social reformers, pro-war socialists, and various heads of national and

combat subversive elements and prove to all that American labor was unqualifiedly in favor of vigorous prosecution of the military program. As a further evidence of labor's position, various semiofficial trade-union committees went abroad to win the support by European trade-union and socialist organizations of America's war aims. More important than the propagandist activities of the Federation and its Alliance for Labor and Democracy, however, were the trade-union policies of cooperation with the government to maintain uninterrupted production and the concessions granted to unionism in return for its adoption of these policies.

Government Labor Policies and Unionism.—The proviso in organized labor's agreement to support the war that it be represented on all government agencies and commissions concerned with labor matters was accepted and adhered to faithfully by the administration. When the Council of National Defense was formed in 1916, unionism was represented on the Advisory Council by Mr. Gompers, who in turn headed a committee of his own choosing to formulate and recommend to the government and to the labor organizations those phases of labor policy it deemed desirable; and labor was represented on, among other agencies, the Emergency Construction Board, the Fuel Administration, the Food Administration Board, and the powerful War Industries Board, the last-named being the recognized arbiter of the country's industries for the duration of the War. The President's Mediation Commission was established in the summer of 1917 and was followed by similar tripartite bodies. In April, 1918, the most important single agency of the War period in the field of industrial relations, the War Labor Board, was established.[1] Having as its primary function the settlement by mediation and conciliation of controversies in fields of production that were directly or indirectly necessary for effective conduct of the War, this Board inevitably had to establish standards, develop policies, and apply canons the effect of which was profound.

---

international unions. The organization declared that "a sturdy defense of the interests of labor is wholly compatible with loyalty to the government," demanded conscription of wealth as well as of men, and accompanied its ringing defense of free speech with the qualification that "all those whose expressions are obstructive to the government in its conduct of the war, or who are capable of giving aid or comfort to the nation's foes, should be suppressed by the authorities." Support of the Alliance was officially voted at the 1917 convention of the A. F. of L., and its pronunciamentos became official expressions of the war position of the Federation.

[1] The War Labor Board consisted of five representatives of the employers, five of labor, and two (William Howard Taft and Frank P. Walsh) of the public. When the War Labor Board was established it was decided that agencies already operating were to be continued, but that the War Labor Board should act as a court of appeal for cases under the jurisdiction of these boards as well as a court of first resort in cases involving war production.

Basic in these principles and canons was the right of the workers to bargain collectively through representatives of their own choosing, a tenet to which the Board and the other governmental agencies adhered consistently, and this in turn dictated the principle—necessary to make the general right to organize and bargain collectively real and dynamic — that workers were not to be discharged for membership in trade unions or in any way be subjected to discrimination because of such membership. Labor, on the other hand, must not exercise "coercion" in attempting to induce nonunion men to affiliate or employers to enter into agreements, and specific declaration was made that in establishments where both union and nonunion workers were employed continuation of this situation should not be deemed a grievance; the *status quo* with reference to the union or closed shop was, in other words, to be maintained for the duration of the War.   Union rates of wages were to be paid where they had been customary in the past, and the living-wage principle was to be made applicable to all workers, including common laborers.   The basic eight-hour day was to be recognized as applying in all cases in which the existing law required it, while in other cases the question of hours was to be settled "with due regard to government necessities and the welfare, health, and proper comfort of the workers."[1]   Finally, the principle was established that strikes and lockouts should be abandoned as methods of achieving the purposes of the workers and of the employers during the period of the War, although no penalties were provided in the case of breaches of the rule.[2]

The public policy toward labor combinations expressed in these principles and policies was, needless to say, the most favorable from the point of view of unionism that had ever been adopted and it was, in addition, an enforceable policy to all intents and purposes.   Organized labor made only one real concession—relinquishment of the right to strike— but it made this concession in general terms, with no penalties attached.[3] In such a setting, the trade-union growth that has already been summarized was almost inevitable.

[1] Quoted from the statement of "Principles and Policies" by S. Perlman in *History of Trade Unionism* . . . , p. 238.   See also L. Lorwin, *op. cit.*, p. 165.

[2] Establishment of the War Labor Board of course did not constitute adoption of the principle of compulsory arbitration, since the Board could not force a party to a dispute to submit to its arbitration or to that of its designated umpire.   Nevertheless, public opinion was so strongly against any interruptions of production in the war industries and the government possessed such far-reaching powers by virtue of its orders and the priority of its right to materials and labor that in almost every instance the decision of the War Labor Board was accepted without strikes or lockouts.

[3] The agreement to maintain the *status quo* with reference to the open or closed shop can hardly be called a concession, since labor was protected in maintenance of the closed or union shop where it had already been attained and was only postponing exercise of the new strength that government policies and war conditions generally brought to it in seeking this particular objective where it had not already been attained.

THE POSTARMISTICE YEARS, 1918–1920

Business went into a brief downswing after the armistice of November, 1918, then quickly revived, and, during the prosperity that continued until the summer of 1920, union membership increased, as has already been said, by nearly a million and a half.[1] But even as the organized labor movement was attaining a numerical strength greater than ever before, and not again to be equaled for fifteen years, it found itself confronted with challenges and beset by problems that it was in some ways ill prepared to meet and solve. Under the exhilarating influence of wartime conditions, the outlook and programs of many of the unions had expanded, had come to include the ends connoted by the rather vague but extremely popular terms "industrial citizenship" and "constitutional government in industry" as well the ends—even if not substantively different in the last analysis—traditionally sought through recognition, trade agreements, and exercise of "job control." In a period of rapidly evaporating national idealism, withdrawal of government protection of labor's right to organize, and entrepreneurial disposition to reassert prewar managerial prerogatives and return as quickly as possible to *laissez faire*, however, the programs and expectations engendered by War conditions were rudely challenged. The cost of living mounted rapidly,[2] and the lag of money wage rates, combined with the manifest tendency of employers to withdraw the "recognition" accorded to unions during the War, accentuated industrial unrest and increased the number of industrial disputes; adverse court decisions,[3] even though only a prelude

[1] Estimated annual average membership: 1918: 3,467,300; 1919, 4,125,200; 1920, 5,047,800. *Cf. supra*, p. 132.

[2] In midsummer of 1918 the Bureau of Labor Statistics cost-of-living index stood at 163 on the 1913 base of 100; by the summer of 1920 it was 206.

[3] In 1905, before the United States entered the War, the Supreme Court ruled (*Coppage v. Kansas*, 236 U. S. 1) that a state could not, in view of the interdictions of the Fourteenth Amendment, prohibit employers from exacting, as a condition of employment, a promise from workers that they would not affiliate with a labor organization, and in 1917 it ruled (*Hitchman Coal and Coke Co. v. Mitchell*, 245 U. S. 229) that employers had a property right or property interest in antiunion contracts of employment *protectible* against union organizers by writ of injunction. The ominous implication of these decisions seems, however, to have been obscured by the prounion policies of the various government boards and commissions of the War period. Also, legislation intended to improve terms, and conditions of employment did not fare badly in the courts during the years immediately preceding 1920. In 1915 the Supreme Court of the United States sustained a state statute limiting the hours of employment of adult males (*Bunting v. Oregon*, 243 U. S. 246), and in 1917 it held that workmen's compensation laws were a proper exercise of the police power of the state (*New York Central R. R. v. White*, 243 U. S. 188, and *Mountain Timber Co. v. Washington*, 243 U. S. 219) and by an even division left in force state minimum-wage laws applicable to women and minors (*Stettler v. O'Hara*, 243 U. S. 629). These favorable decisions on legislation regulating terms and conditions of employment, combined with

to those that were to come during the 1920's, and an apparently changed attitude on the part of the national administration, brought to some of the trade-union leaders and to many of the rank and file uneasy doubt concerning the permanency of the advantages that had resulted from organized labor's wartime position; the broad reconstructionist program of the British Labour Party excited the admiration of that part of the Federation's membership which yearned for a labor movement possessed of broadly collectivist, if not strict Marxist, objectives, while the Russian revolution inspired those farther to the left. In such a setting, the federated trade unionism that had "fitted" well into the economic and social conditions of wartime America, and had profited greatly therefrom, groped for some kind of permanent labor policy which would preserve the gains that had been, and still were being, made, accord with the circumstances and temper of the "new day," and yet preserve in their fundamentals the revered forms of organization and the tested modes of economic action.

The Reconstruction Program of the American Federation of Labor, approved by the Executive Council late in 1918 and then by the convention of the Federation in 1919,[1] expressed the disposition to adapt traditional policies to new conditions and to the rising tide of liberalism and radicalism without abandonment of their fundamentals. "Democracy in industry" should and must mean the right of workers to be represented through trade unions; interference by employers with the right of workers to organize and bargain collectively must be prohibited; the right to a living wage must be conceded and trade-union activity recognized as the most effective method of obtaining and maintaining such a wage; and public employees must be conceded the right to organize. The forty-four-hour week with higher overtime rates, greater legal protection of women in industry, consumers' cooperation, and removal of restrictions on freedom of speech were approved, and child labor was denounced. A series of political reforms included effective government regulation or else government ownership of "public and semi-public utilities," reforms in federal and state taxation, the institution of government housing systems, complete suspension of immigration for two years, and the recall

---

the favorable attitude of the boards and commissions appointed during the War period, probably had the effect of obscuring from the vision of trade-union leadership the danger to its normal activities of decisions like those in the Coppage and Hitchman cases during the period of hostilities.

[1] The Reconstruction Program was drafted by a special "reconstruction committee" appointed at the June, 1918, convention and was approved by the Executive Council on Dec. 28, 1918 (L. Lorwin, *The American Federation of Labor*, p. 174). Approval of the entire convention of the Federation was given in June, 1919.

of judicial decisions.[1] While some concessions to the militant and increasingly radical spirit of postwar labor were embodied in this Program, the underlying purposes differed not greatly from those of the Bill of Grievances of 1906;[2] the A. F. of L. still stood as a bulwark of conservatism.

Between the adoption of the Program by the Executive Council late in 1918 and the convention of June, 1919, however, developments were of a character forcing the adoption of a more advanced position. Mounting labor unrest and a sharp increase in the number and severity of industrial disputes, an apparently less favorable attitude toward unionism on the part of the national administration, and widespread feeling that labor's services during the War were not sufficiently appreciated and that the implied promises made to it by government and industry were not being kept made themselves felt when the 1919 convention assembled, and approval of the Reconstruction Program was accompanied by endorsement of the Plumb Plan for worker and public participation in management of the railroads and eventual amortization of private ownership[3] and by resolutions demanding the release of political prisoners and freedom for Tom Mooney. At the same time, however, the government of Soviet Russia and its motivating political-economic philosophy were condemned, the right of city centrals—more militant than many of the international trade unions and more prone to espouse

---

[1] From the summary made by Dr. Lorwin. *ibid.*, pp. 174–175. The full text of *Labor's Program of Reconstruction Aims to Secure a Better and Brighter Day* may be found in the *American Federationist*, February, 1919, pp. 129*ff.*, and in David J. Saposs, *Readings in Trade Unionism* (1926), pp. 45–59.

[2] *Cf. supra*, pp. 124–126.

[3] This plan, advocated in 1919 by Glenn E. Plumb, attorney for some of the railroad unions, involved the taking over of the railroads by the government, payment to incumbent owners of an amount equivalent to a court-determined "fair valuation" which must exclude capitalization of rights and privileges not granted in the charters that had been issued by the states, and issuance of government bonds to finance the purchase. Management of the roads would then be in the hands of a board of fifteen members—five appointed by the President of the United States to represent the public, five elected by classified railroad employees to represent labor, and five elected by the railroad officials to represent management. Gradual amortization of the bonds would take place through reduction of the outstanding indebtedness at the rate of 1 per cent per annum, and an automatic economy-sharing scheme (*i.e.*, reduction of passenger and freight rates whenever the government's share of the profits exceeded a fixed percentage of operating revenue) was provided for. The plan was, as Professor Perlman has observed (*History of Trade Unionism* . . . , p. 60), similar to land reform and other panaceas of American labor history in that it proposed to equalize the opportunities of labor and capital in using economic power to obtain "just rewards" for service rendered the public, but it differed from the earlier producer-conscious movements in that it made the trade unions the organized representatives of producers' interests and entitled them to participate in the direct management of industry. "An ideal copartnership and self-employment were thus set up, going beyond the bonds of self-help to which organized labor had limited itself in the eighties" (*ibid.*).

the liberal and radical doctrines of the time—to conduct strikes was curtailed, and several proposals for changes in the constitution of the Federation, such as election of officers by referendum vote, were rejected.[1] Continued criticism of the comparatively conservative position of the Federation spurred its Executive Council to call a conference late in 1919[2] participated in by the Railroad Brotherhoods, in which a report adopted under the title Labor's Bill of Rights reiterated the main proposals of the Reconstruction Program of 1918, censured the United States Steel Corporation for its attitude in the great steel strike of 1919,[3] called for deflation of the currency and disclosure by the government of the costs and profits of corporations, professed willingness of organized labor to cooperate with scientific management in lowering costs of production,[4] and endorsed the League of Nations and the International Labour Organization.[5] The concessions to the radicals embodied in this Bill of Rights were patently of little magnitude, and indicative of adherence by the Federation to its traditional precepts and methods were the refusal to have part in an independent political party, the failure to offer any immediate measures for general economic reconstruction, the withholding of endorsement of those progressive movements which voiced current discontent, and the refusal at the 1920 convention to readapt the old policy of trade autonomy through reorganization of the various departments.[6]

These attempts of the Federation to evolve formulas that would entrench the policies and methods it believed to have been vindicated by experience and at the same time placate sufficiently the radical and militant elements were made in an environment of industrial unrest, increasing employer and community impatience with the restraints imposed by unionism and collective bargaining, and rapidly changing government policy. The trade unions emerged from their wartime experience with a new sense of power, and when employing interests indicated unmistakably that the truce of the period of hostilities was over, bitterness and a disposition to resort to economic force inevitably

[1] From L. Lorwin, *op. cit.*, p. 191.

[2] The Conference convened on Dec. 13, 1909.

[3] *Cf. infra*, pp. 145–146.

[4] This position was prophetic of the "new wage policy" of the middle 1920's, with its offer to cooperate with management in eliminating wastes and increasing the efficiency of industry (*cf. infra*, pp. 171–173). It will be recalled that no mention of cooperation to increase efficiency or of the relation of wages to productivity was made in the 1918 Reconstruction Program.

[5] From the summary of Dr. Lorwin, *op. cit.*, p. 193.

[6] The proposal before the 1920 convention was that of reorganizing the Federation's unions into twelve departments. Instead, the convention adopted a resolution that was in essence the Scranton Declaration of 1901.

ensued. Other factors contributed to the increase in the number of strikes and lockouts. Money earnings frequently failed to advance as rapidly as did the cost of living. Leadership of many locals and some internationals had gravitated into the hands of men whose trade-union creed constituted substantial departure from the precepts of Gomperism; and the newly recruited memberships, lacking the discipline and training of the long-organized craft unionists, were eager to take aggressive action. Wartime emotionalism found its outlet, after the Armistice, in middle-class hysteria against the "reds," with accompanying disposition to regard ordinary strikes as being motivated by revolutionary or subversive purposes, as well as in wage-earner proneness to resort to more primitive militancy. With the liquidation of the various "prolabor" government agencies, a restraining influence was removed. As a consequence of all these circumstances, the number of strikes and lockouts increased from 3,353 in 1918 to 3,630 in 1919 and 3,411 in 1920, and the number of wage earners involved from 1,239,989 during the first-named year to 4,160,348 in 1919 and 1,463,054 in 1920. The experience of the employees of the railroads,[1] as well as the strikes of the miners[2] and

---

[1] The railroad shopmen in the summer of 1919 demanded an increase in wages to offset the increase in the cost of living, and a number of unauthorized strikes took place. Under pressure of the international officials and in response to the plea of President Wilson, the strikers returned to work, and the President in turn promised to use all the powers of government immediately to reduce the cost of living. In September of that year the United States Railroad Administration and the shopmen's unions entered into national agreements embodying the practices that had been in vogue during the War period under the Railroad Administration, including "recognition" and some of the working rules regarded by the unions as most important, but no wage increase was granted during 1919 and the cost of living, instead of declining, continued to soar. Early in 1920 the Esch-Cummins Bill was passed by Congress and signed by the President, who announced that the roads would be returned to the owners on Mar. 1 of that year. Under the terms of this Act, a Board representing the public, the owners, and the unions was established and empowered to investigate in the case of disputes and to issue awards, but the right to strike was left unimpaired. For detailed account and excellent analysis of the labor provisions of the Esch-Cummins Act and of the operation between 1920 and 1926 of the Railway Labor Board, see H. D. Wolf, *The Railway Labor Board.* Shortly after the roads had been returned to the private owners, and prior to appointment of the Board provided for by the 1920 legislation, a large number of switchmen and yardmen went on an "outlaw" strike, and the Board, after its appointment, announced that no "outlaw" organizations would have any standing before it. A wage award of the Board on July 20, 1920, increased the railroad wage bill appreciably but failed to satisfy the unions. S. Perlman, *History of Trade Unionism* . . . , pp. 246 and 252.

[2] The 1919 strike of the bituminous coal miners revealed, even more than did the experiences of the railroad workers summarized in the preceding footnote, the changed attitude of the government toward organized labor after the period of hostilities was over. In this case, a wartime law (the Lever Act), regarded as practically abrogated although not actually repealed, was invoked against the strikers, and an injunction restraining the officers of the United Mine Workers and "all other persons whomsoever" from doing any-

steel-industry workers[1] were especially indicative of the changed public temper toward organized labor, of the end of the wartime truce, and of the failure of the Federation's loyalty to the national cause during the War and its relatively conservative utterances and policies thereafter to induce acceptance of collective bargaining without first subjecting employers to the pressure of the old-fashioned kind of industrial disputes. With the failure of a National Industrial Conference, convened at the

---

thing in connection with the strike was issued.   In October, 1917, the United Mine Workers entered into a contract with the United States Fuel Administration, covering wages, hours, and other matters, which was to continue for the duration of the War but in no case later than Apr. 1, 1920.   During the postarmistice months, as the cost of living advanced and the real earnings of the miners declined, the United Mine Workers took the position that the War was over and that the—now disadvantageous—contract had therefore automatically expired.   The September, 1919, convention of the U.M.W. demanded wage increases averaging about 60 per cent and a thirty-hour (five-day) work week, and authorized a strike if satisfactory agreement with the mine owners could not be reached.   The strike order was issued on October 15, effective October 31.   One week before the date set for the lockout, the President issued a proclamation that the United States was still at war and that the strike was unlawful, and appealed to the United Mine Workers to prevent the impending stoppage.   The United States Fuel Administration (then in process of dissolution) intervened and attempted to bring about a settlement at a 14 per cent wage increase, and the President offered to appoint an investigating tribunal.   Under pressure from the administration, with which he had been so closely identified during the War, Mr. Gompers on October 29 attempted to induce President Lewis of the United Mine Workers to agree to a postponement on the understanding that a conference with the operators could be arranged, and Attorney General Palmer that same day issued a statement that the strike was illegal in view of the fact that the Lever Act, creating the United States Fuel Administration, was still in force.   Nevertheless about 425,000 miners, 250,000 of whom were in the Central Competitive District, struck on Oct. 31.   Judge Anderson of the Federal District Court in Indianapolis, on motion of the Attorney General, the same day issued the injunction referred to above, and on Nov. 8 a permanent injunction, in effect ordering the United Mine Workers to cancel the strike, was issued.   A conference of United Mine Worker officials (Nov. 10) decided that a strike implying (in view of the injunction issued under the wartime act) defiance of the government could not be continued, and John L. Lewis ordered its discontinuance.   But organized labor bitterly resented the injunction and the attitude of the administration in general.   The Executive Council of the A. F. of L. issued a statement justifying the strike and accusing the government of bad faith in the matter of the Lever Act.   When the strike order was rescinded, the majority of the miners returned to work, although the strike continued in many places for about a month longer.   The United Mine Workers agreed to accept the Fuel Administration's proposal of a 14 per cent wage increase pending the investigation and findings of the tripartite coal commission President Wilson had promised.   The Bituminous Coal Commission that was appointed finally settled the wage dispute by granting a 27 per cent increase but not the thirty-hour week. From detail in L. Lorwin, *op. cit.*, pp. 184–187, and S. Perlman, *History of Trade Unionism* . . . , pp. 250–252.

[1] The great steel strike of 1919, a strike against perhaps the most powerful capitalist aggregation in the world, demonstrated with unmistakable clarity the determination of the steel companies to prevent unionization of the industry, the ease with which employing interests could utilize the fanatical hysteria of the time to prevent organization efforts, and the ineffectiveness of a multiplicity of cooperating labor organizations, instead of one indus-

invitation of President Wilson on Oct. 6, 1919, to agree that "collective bargaining"—approved in principle and *per se* by public and employer representatives as well as by those of organized labor—should mean bargaining between employers and representatives of trade unions independent of any employer influence or control, the fact that employers were not going to permit continued expansion of unionism if they could help it became unmistakably apparent.[1]

---

trial union, in organizing an industry like steel. The refusal of Judge Elbert Gary, chairman of the board of directors of the United States Steel Corporation, to confer with the leaders of the striking unions was in a sense the culminating postwar gesture indicating how unfounded had been the expectations of permanent recognition and collective bargaining entertained by the cooperative and "truly American" trade unionism during the War period. The facts about the disastrous steel strike of 1919 should be recorded in a little detail. The Amalgamated Association of Iron and Steel workers had continued to sign wage agreements with a number of the companies since 1901 but its membership, which was confined to the skilled workers, had been declining, and the great mass of semiskilled and unskilled workers in the industry remained unorganized. At the 1918 convention of the A. F. of L. a resolution, introduced by William Z. Foster, authorized an organizing campaign and established a National Organizing Committee composed of the presidents of the twenty-four international unions that had jurisdiction in the industry. Demands upon the steel companies included recognition, abolition of the twelve-hour day (*cf.* vol. I of this series, pp. 475–476), wage increases sufficient to guarantee "an American standard of living," the right of collective bargaining, the checkoff, and abolition of company unions. Organizing work started in the Chicago district in September, 1918, and by the spring of 1919 some organization obtained in the majority of steel centers. The National Organizing Committee met in July, 1919, formally enunciated the demands enumerated above, and submitted a strike vote to the unions. The memberships voted overwhelmingly for the strike; the heads of the United States Steel Corporation refused to negotiate; and on September 22 the strike, of which William Z. Foster was the guiding spirit, began. Probably 300,000 men left work. (The unions claimed that 367,000 were out by October 9, while the companies declared that the number never exceeded 200,000 at any one time.) The strike failed for a number of reasons. It was pictured in the press as the American counterpart of the Russian Revolution, and the report (returned Nov. 9, 1919) of a Senate investigating committee, which confirmed the validity of the workers' complaints as to long hours and censured the companies for not permitting selection of wage-earning representatives to present grievances, even though affirming a "red" element in the strike, had little influence upon the unbalanced public opinion. Gompers and the Executive Council of the Federation were distrustful of Foster, whose radical record was invoked against the strike; there were jealousies among, and there was lack of coordination on the part of, the twenty-four unions; and the companies were powerful and determined. Early in November the strike showed signs of weakening, and on Jan. 9, 1920, it was abandoned. From detail in S. Perlman, *op. cit.*, pp. 248–250, and L. Lorwin, *The American Federation of Labor*, pp. 180–184.

[1] This Conference, modeled upon the British gathering held earlier, included seventeen employer representatives, fifteen participants representing the A. F. of L. and the Railroad Brotherhoods, and twenty-one public representatives. Under the rules adopted, a majority of each group had to agree to any proposal or resolution if it were to be regarded as the decision or recommendation of the Conference. Held while the potency of wartime spirit was rapidly diminishing, and with the great steel strike as a background, the Conference was probably foredoomed from the outset. Labor's representatives insisted upon recog-

As industrial warfare spread to new fronts and the officialdom of the A. F. of L., fighting to retain and extend the gains of the War years, temporized to an extent with the liberal and radical forces abroad in the land and at the same time refused to alter in their fundamentals its outlook and policies, political and economic radicalism became stronger and more vocal, both within and without the organized labor movement. Inspired by the Russian Revolution, one faction of the Socialist Party seceded upon the issue of acceptance of the Moscow version of Marxism and affiliation with the Third International. The Socialist Party, after its internal troubles of 1919-1920, changed its tactics to an extent, refrained from attacking the trade unions because they refused to be socialistic, expressed its yearning for cooperation and a uniting of the labor organizations and the progressive forces of the country, and envisaged itself as the American labor party of the future in a position comparable to that of the Independent Labour Party in England; but the Communist Party that emerged out of the schisms and vicissitudes of the radical movement during the early postwar years plagued the trade unions, not by open candidacies for office but by a tactic more difficult to combat, "boring from within."[1] The I.W.W., already

---

nition of the right of workers to be represented by delegates of their own choosing in collective negotiations with employers and insisted that collective bargaining would be futile were workers not privileged to choose as their spokesmen representatives of the national trade unions; employer representatives insisted that no employer must be obligated to meet for purposes of collective bargaining with other than his own employees and that collective bargaining be so defined as to include negotiations with shop committees and employee-representation organizations as an alternative to trade unions. When agreement was obviously impossible, the labor group left and the Conference broke up. President Wilson later (Nov. 16, 1919) called a second conference, nominally composed solely of representatives of the public. The report of this President's Second Industrial Conference, issued on Dec. 29, 1919, avoided the controversial issue of the form of collective bargaining (i.e., the right of employers to refuse to meet with representatives of other than their own employees) and defined collective bargaining to include shop committees as well as independent trade unions, proposed an elaborate system of tribunals for investigation and adjustment of disputes, and recommended government restriction of strikes in industries vested with a public interest. For a brief period, the report of this second conference was rather widely discussed in labor, business, and academic circles, but it had little if any effect upon the long-run course of American industrial realtions.

[1] The Socialist Party, as has already been pointed out, experienced a revitalization as a result of its espousal of an antiwar position and its position as the only important proponent of economic and political dissent and radicalism during those years. After the War, the conservatives within the Party demanded that the United States and other nations permit the Soviet experiment to continue unhampered by outside influences but refused to permit the American socialist movement to be submerged by the doctrines and policies of the Third International, established in 1919. The left-wingers within the Party, on the other hand, criticized what they regarded as the moderate reformist program of the right-wing leaders, and insisted upon affiliation with the newly established Communist (Third) International. Left-wing locals were suspended from the Party by the New York State Executive Committee, and the Michigan State organization was suspended by the

deprived of many of its more capable leaders by the government's policy toward it during the War, sought to give expression to, and lead in the attainment of, the revolutionary objectives of the workers of the world; but in the social, psychological, and industrial environment of 1918–1920 it found the American public disposed ferociously and ruthlessly to exterminate it. I.W.W. halls were demolished, conflicts with officers and self-appointed guardians of law and order, of which the Centralia, Wash., episode was most important, took place, criminal syndicalism laws were enacted, and perhaps 2,000 members of the organization were jailed on charges of vagrancy, criminal syndicalism, and sedition.[1] As an active force, the I.W.W. was practically eliminated from the Northwest, and elsewhere it ceased to possess sufficient strength to make it a force with which either employing interests or the trade unions need reckon seriously.

Efforts of the communists to "bore from within" the trade unions were accompanied by continued criticism of the refusal of the A. F. of L. to include within its purposes more of the liberal and progressive programs of the time than had found place in the Reconstruction Program and the Bill of Rights[2] and by movements for an independent party representing the wage earners, the farmers, and the "forward-looking" elements generally. A National Labor Party emerged, joined with the middle-class, liberal Committee of Forty-eight, and entered the 1920 presidential

---

National Executive Committee. The left-wing elements held a convention of their own in June, 1919, split on the question of whether to organize a communist party immediately or to continue to try to capture the Socialist Party, and then those adhering to the former position formed the National Organizing Committee. Out of the factional struggles and maneuvers there emerged, toward the end of the summer of 1919, the Communist Party and the Communist Labor Party, and on order of the Communist International these two parties were merged in the spring of 1920. At the 1920 convention of the Socialist Party the question of affiliation with the Communist International was considered, but a twenty-one-point program insisted upon by the latter was unsatisfactory to the convention, and the affiliation did not materialize. At a 1921 conference of the Socialist Party, acceptance of the twenty-one points again was rejected, and decision was made to lift the ban on cooperation with other radical and liberal groups. Affiliation with the Conference for Progressive Political Action, activities of which are recorded in the following chapter (infra, pp. 183–187), was thereby made possible. In 1921 the communists, finding underground activity not entirely satisfactory, created a Workers' Party as a kind of open and aboveboard representative. The Communist International thereafter orderedt he entire movement to emerge from underground, and during the early 1920's the party bore the official name Workers' Party. The "boring from within" tactics during this period were conducted chiefly by the Trade Union Educational League, a creation of William Z. Foster For a full account of events within the American socialist movement during the two years following the armistice of 1918, see Perlman and Taft in vol. 4 of *History of Labor in the United States*, pp. 421–427, an account to which this footnote is indebted for the factual material recorded.

[1] For details, see *ibid.*, pp. 527–432.
[2] *Cf. supra*, pp. 141–143.

campaign as the Farmer-Labor Party.[1]   The vote polled in November
of that year by this new party was not sufficiently large to forbode
effective challenge to the nonpartisan political policy of the Federation,[2]
but the leadership took seriously the collectivist program it advocated
and the manifest disposition of many city centrals and some state federations to support it.   A committee consisting of the Executive Council
of the Federation and the officers of the Departments was formed to
combat the sentiment among the trade unionists for an independent labor
party, widespread publicity was given to the virtues of the nonpartisan
policy, and the demands of the Reconstruction Program of 1918 and the
Bill of Rights of 1919 were energetically voiced in the effort to elect
representatives and senators favorable to them.[3]   In point of positive
gains, the 1920 political activities of the A. F. of L. were almost negligible,
but they did succeed to no inconsiderable extent in frustrating the forces
working to bring into being a truly effective labor party.   Under fear
of incurring the displeasure—and possibly the reprisals—of the officialdom, many city centrals and some state federations dissociated themselves from the movement for independent political action.[4]   In spite of
the ferment, radicalism, and progressivism of the two years immediately
following the end of the War, the federated trade unionism of the United
States was adhering as tenaciously as ever to its traditional political
tenets when, during the second half of 1920, business depression brought
unemployment and trade-union membership began to decline.

[1] These independent political movements emerged in different parts of the country.
The Nonpartisan League, founded in North Dakota as early as 1915, was primarily an
agrarian movement but it predicated its success upon the bringing about of common
political action on the part of labor and the organized farmers.   Various state farmer-
labor parties stemmed, with varying degrees of directness, from the Nonpartisan League.
A Minnesota party founded at its instigation first worked through the Republican Party,
and then in conjunction with the State Federation of Labor through a Farmer-Labor Party.
In Illinois a Labor Party of Cook County, formed under the leadership of John Fitzpatrick
and Edward Nockles of the Chicago Federation of Labor, was endorsed by the Illinois
State Federation of Labor, becoming the Labor Party of Illinois.   The Chicago and Illinois
State Federations and their political offspring convoked a conference to form a national
labor party, inviting participation on the part of the Nonpartisan League and the Committee of Forty-eight; and at this conference a National Labor Party was formed.   Later,
at a convention held in Chicago during the early summer of 1920, the National Labor
Party and the Committee of Forty-eight amalgamated in the Farmer-labor Party.   From
detail presented by Perlman and Taft, op. cit., pp. 525–530.
[2] Parley P. Christensen, the Western lawyer nominated for the presidency after Robert
M. La Follette, Sr., had refused to be the candidate, received approximately 300,000 votes,
or slightly less than one-third the number Eugene V. Debs polled on the Socialist ticket.
[3] From L. Lorwin, op. cit., p. 194.
[4] Ibid., p. 195.

Chapter IV

AMERICAN UNIONISM OF THE 1920'S

The 1920's stand out, for more reasons than one, as a period unique in the history of American trade unionism. During an industrial expansion the proportions of which were, in some ways, unprecedented, organized labor failed to hold its own;[1] an era of prosperity that should, according to historical precedents, have witnessed labor militancy, aggressiveness in conquering unorganized areas and in entrenching more strongly job control already obtained, found old and established unions experiencing difficulty in maintaining past gains and something akin to inertia, pacifism, or disillusionment pervading the movement as a whole. In the face of changes in the technological and market structure of business enterprise, trade-union structure remained much what it had been; ideologically, the movement seemed bent upon adjusting itself to the superficially dominant economic thought of the "new capitalism." Until the early 1930's, when depression experiences produced a new government policy and a new public attitude toward trade unionism and a bitterly cynical wage-earner outlook toward both the panaceas of "enlightened" employers and some of the arrangements within the house of labor, organized labor appeared to have been stopped in its tracks. Brief reminder of some of the environmental circumstances of the time is a prerequisite to interpretive examination of trade-union vicissitudes between the relatively brief postwar depression and the great depression of the 1930's.

Conditioning and Determining Factors of the Decade

American economic life of the 1920's was experiencing—so said many of the more vocal of the economic commentators of the time—a "new industrial revolution," and of the fact that changes occurred whose effects upon the functional and structural kind of unionism that emerged from the War period were both profound and generally of adverse character there can be no question. Capital and management exercised an increasingly important influence, relative to labor, in productive processes, and technological developments proceeded rapidly.[2] New lines

[1] *Cf. infra*, pp. 162–165.

[2] *Cf.* vol. I of this series, pp. 19–21, for data on number of wage earners, the increase in the use of nonhuman power, and changes in the quantity of fixed capital. For factual material concerning the increase in physical and value product per worker, see *ibid.*, pp. 38–

of enterprise, like the young automobile, chemical, and electrical industries in the manufacturing group, expanded rapidly, contributing a share of total output, employment, and payrolls entirely disproportionate to their contribution of the pre-1920 era, and substantial new sources of employment were created in the public utility and service industries and in the distributive trades. The movement toward formation of combinations—both vertical and horizontal—became accelerated in manufacturing, banking, and distribution, with resultant formation of mergers, chain stores, and combinations on a large scale;[1] in utilities, iron and steel, banking, machinery, textiles, foodstuffs, and other branches of production, the giant corporation came into a new position of power and importance;[2] geographical migrations of industry became more important than theretofore, and a larger proportion of the country's wage earners found employment in large-scale plants.[3]

These changes in the structure of American industry had inevitable reflection in the capacity of unionism to maintain its established position or move forward, in the tactics adopted, and in the economic ideas or theories espoused. The development of mechanical appliances, the introduction of new kinds of machinery, and the adoption of mass-production methods where market and technological conditions permitted rendered difficult, for several reasons, the task of extending union organization. With the partial destruction of important crafts, the ratio of semiskilled and unskilled to skilled workers increased, and, even where craftsmen remained in their trades, they often found that the technological changes were such that they no longer fitted into the jurisdictional framework of existing unions. Displacement of part of the craftsmen, with resultant underbidding by the unemployed reserves, made harder the maintenance of organization by those not displaced. In addition, the wage earners thrown out of jobs were, by and large, those most prone to become or remain members of unions.[4] Likewise the increasing

---

40 and 136–161, A. R. Burns, *Production Trends in the United States*, Paul H. Douglas, *Real Wages in the United States*, Harry Jerome, *Mechanization in Industry*, and National Resources Committee, *Technological Trends and National Policy*.

[1] *Cf.* vol. I of this series, pp. 17–19.

[2] *Cf. ibid.*, pp. 14–17.

[3] *Cf. ibid.*, pp. 6–13.

[4] Some of the workers displaced in industries experiencing technological changes undoubtedly were absorbed in the service industries and elsewhere, but—rapidly as did radios and gasoline filling stations become part of the American culture pattern—there seems to be no question that the reabsorption process failed to manifest sufficient speed and magnitude of those displaced. The theoretical aspects of technological displacement are discussed in vol. I of this series, pp. 508–513, and in vol. II, pp. 27–39. One fact of extreme importance is that the service industries, which produced (or received) more of the nation's total purchasing power in 1930 than in 1920, are considerably less "capital intensive" (*i.e.*, the ratio of value of capital employed to value of output) but at the same time

relative importance as sources of employment of the newer industries redounded adversely to the kind of unionism that was dominant during the 1920's, since these industries—representing on the whole the more prosperous segments of the American economy—operated on a basis of mechanization rendering inapplicable the craft form of labor organization. On the other hand, several of the older and, before 1920, strongly organized industries experienced prolonged depression, amidst the fairly general and loudly proclaimed prosperity of the time, and in the depression of these industries, as in the increasing importance and the prosperity of the newer ones, is to be found an explanation of unionism's failure to continue its prewar and wartime expansion.[1]

Migration of industry also contributed to organized labor's difficulties by reducing employment of union members in the partially abandoned regions as well as by furnishing unused reserves of labor in the regions in which the migrating industries established their new plants.[2] Of similar import, so far as unionism's capacity to continue its earlier expansion was concerned, were the continued trend toward large-scale production, the increased dominance of the corporate form of organization, and the acceleration of the business-combination movement. Both technical conditions of production in, and the labor policies pursued by, enterprises whose plants each employed large numbers of workers imposed obstacles to the securing or maintaining of union footholds. The managers of large corporations—who by the 1920's, more than ever before, had become a distinct functional group, separate from the investors—were impatient of union working-rule restrictions even if not so prone as the old-fashioned entrepreneur to resent such encroachments upon ownership incidents as a personal affront, maintained sturdy opposition to trade unionism in areas where it had not yet effectively penetrated,[3] and, in

---

not more "labor intensive" (*i.e.*, the ratio of labor hours employed in a given period to value of output) than other industries. This meant that an increase in the relative importance of the service industries had the effect of diminishing employment opportunities.

[1] Clothing manufacture and bituminous coal production, for example, were depressed during a considerable part of the decade, and many unionists in these industries were thrown out of work without being absorbed elsewhere. The New England sections of the textile industry, for years the scene of industrial turmoil, likewise suffered a depression that was an obstacle to union recovery from the 1921–1922 losses.

[2] In textiles, clothing manufacture, printing, photoengraving, and other lines of enterprise, many firms moved their production units from centers where they had been located for years to nonunion regions. For a time, the southward migration seemed to insure to the textile industry immunity from trade unionism. Generally adverse conditions in the bituminous coal industry, where sources of supply are scattered over Pennsylvania, Illinois, Oklahoma, Ohio, and other states, caused appreciable change in the relative importance of different centers of production, with aggregate consequences distinctly adverse to the United Miners of America.

[3] As is said in somewhat greater detail in an earlier volume of this series (vol. I, pp. 16–17), control of many business enterprises had oscillated, by the earlier years of the

accordance with the "enlightened" precepts of the "new economic era," they instituted employment policies in which welfare work, company unions, employee-representation plans, and in general an interclass harmony program played large part. Business combinations—effectuated through holding companies, mergers, and more subtle devices—were frequently able to dominate the employment situation and exercise no little control over wages, hours, and conditions; the majority of them were antiunion in their labor predilections; and frequently the motive of speculation—accessory or supplementary to the motive of economy and lower unit-production costs—underlying their formation was a factor causing the purchasers of securities, primarily concerned in the yield and the enhancement of value of these securities, to be resentful of union rules and demands for a larger share of the value product.

In the increase in the real income of the wage earners and of the American people as a whole during the 1920's is to be found another explanation of the failure of unionism to penetrate new areas or—relative to the size of the working class as a whole—to hold its own. By the end of the decade, per capita real income realized from all sources in the United States was approximately 50 per cent, and income from current production approximately 40 per cent, greater than at the turn of the century. More than two-thirds of this three-decades increase occurred during the years between 1920 and 1930.[1] To a not inconsiderable extent, the wage earners participated in this material advancement in the form of substantial increase in real earnings,[2] even though hundreds of thousands of them continued to receive wages insufficient to maintain for their families minimum health and decency standards of living.[3] Both the rise in real earnings and the increase in per capita real income retarded trade-union organization. Many more wage earners than

---

century, into the hands of investment bankers; then, when corporations were able to provide the capital necessary for expansion out of their own earnings, or when their credit ratings became so good that they were able to sell their securities directly to the public, control gravitated into the hands of professional managers. The remoteness of banker control from actual production operations made it more impersonal, but—in view of the primary interest in net earnings and market value of securities—not less impatient of union rules increasing production costs. One of the dominant trends of the 1920's, however, was the development of a separate functional group, the business managers. Frequently these managers had little stake as owners of the enterprises, but their authority generally was unchallenged so long as stockholders received dividends regularly. Like the bankers, they were less prone than the traditional entrepreneur to resent in a personal fashion employee criticisms of the conduct of business, and they were perhaps more prone than the latter to recognize the desirability of making financial investment in employee morale. But they were just as impatient as either the traditional entrepreneur or the investment banking house in control of a business of union restrictions that might increase production costs.

[1] Cf. vol. 1 of this series pp. 192–194.

[2] Cf. ibid., pp. 85–115.

[3] Cf. ibid., pp. 244–255.

theretofore were able to enjoy standards of living approximating those of the middle class; their thinking and economic outlook became, in consequence, not receptive to the appeals of labor leaders. In brief, the rise in real earnings spiked the most effective argument of organized labor.

The lethargic effect upon trade unionism of rising real earnings and increasing real national income was accentuated by a conjunction of interrelated, or consequential, factors. Many workers were convinced that unionism played little part in bringing about the rise in hourly and annual real earnings, and they observed that earnings frequently advanced as much in the unorganized trades and industries as in those that were unionized.[1] A bombardment of employer personnel policies based upon the interclass harmony hypothesis strengthened this conviction, and for other reasons the urge toward exclusively wage-earner concerted action was rendered feeble. Able, like members of the middle class, to purchase numerous new goods and services—cheap motorcars, radios, movie entertainment, and the like—many wage earners were diverted from their interest in unionism; under the impetus of improved and cheapened means of transportation and communication, different economic classes came to have more noneconomic phases of life in common than formerly, and trade-union affairs ceased to occupy the place as a phase of life extending beyond improvement of material conditions that they had occupied in the lives of many workers a decade or two earlier; the nineteenth-century conviction that individual opportunity was the peculiar heritage of America found emotional support in the upward surge of the stock market and in the constantly reiterated proclamation that American prosperity could not be other than permanent. In such an atmosphere, old-fashioned militant unionism found itself a bit bewildered, uncertain how to proceed, prone to resort to traditional economic-front tactics without effectuating the structural changes necessary to insure success of these tactics, groping to adjust itself to the more superficial aspects of current economic and social thought.

Nor did the curtailment of immigration, the increasing homogeneity of the nation's working force, that characterized the 1920's contribute to a furtherance of trade unionism.[2] The material welfare of the American wage earners undoubtedly was enhanced to an extent when the "rising tide of immigration" became a matter of history,[3] and for a

---

[1] See vol. I of this series, pp. 212–214, for a brief discussion of the probable influence of unionism in advancing real earnings, or in maintaining gains already attained, during this period.

[2] See vol. I of this series, pp. 29–32, for the statistics of the volume and sources of immigration prior to and during the 1920's.

[3] Among other reasons because competitive underbidding of workers accustomed to the lower standards of living of laborers in other countries was lessened and because the curtailment of the labor supply raised the marginal productivity of labor.

number of reasons the cause of unionism might have been expected to receive impetus. The "new" immigrants who came to the United States during the early years of the century, for reasons already pointed out,[1] found rather little place in the dominant labor movement, really constituted no potentially organizable group for the federated trade unionism; redundancy of the labor supply consequent upon immigration and the competitive underbidding of immigrant workers had been effective aids to the efforts of employers to prevent unionism from gaining a foothold where it was not already established; the presence of unskilled and relatively cheap labor had furnished an incentive for corporations to mechanize their establishments—to adapt jobs to the limited capacities of men as much as possible—with a resultant narrowing of the fields of employment in which the workers were most adept in organizing on the craft basis and utilizing the tactics of craft unionism. The fact that during the immediate prewar period many of the larger industries were manned so largely by immigrants or first-generation Americans—workers separated from their employers by racial and nationalistic lines of demarcation as well as by economic function—had accounted in considerable part for the fact that here, more than in other countries, the middle class was frequently to be found energetically and militantly on the side of employers during labor disputes. For these reasons, unionism might have been expected to receive stimulus from the curtailment of immigration.

These favorable consequences did not, however, materialize. The improvement in material status of the workers, imputable in part to the dwindling of the number of those who turned their eyes and directed their footsteps to this continent, had the effect—in an era of the social and economic characteristics enumerated in the present section of the chapter—of engendering less rather than more consciousness of the common character of their needs and problems. Also, employers found a partial substitute for immigrant labor in the Mexicans and Negroes who migrated northward and found employment in the steel mills, in meat-packing establishments, and elsewhere. Geographical migration of many firms—a migration motivated primarily by the desire to tap new sources of cheap and docile labor—likewise contributed to a nullification of some of the beneficial effects of immigration restriction that might have accrued to unionism. Mechanization of industry had been encouraged during the prewar years, as has already been pointed out, by the presence of immigrant labor; but during the 1920's the curtailment of the supply of foreign-provided unskilled and semiskilled workers was accompanied by even greater mechanization, increase in the ratio of capital to labor, and introduction of laborsaving machinery. The dominant type of labor organization, adhering as it did to the revered

[1] *Cf. supra*, pp. 88–89.

principles of craft organization, provided little if any more place for a native-born group of semiskilled operatives than it had for the foreign workers of a quarter of a century earlier.

Changes in the relative importance of different sources of livelihood and in the economic status of the gainfully employed persons of the United States were also of fundamental importance in determining the progress and functional character of unionism. One of the marked trends of the 1920's was that relatively fewer persons were attached to manufacturing and agriculture as the years passed and that a larger proportion of the gainfully employed found place in transportation and communication, the clerical occupations, and the service occupations.[1] Changes of profound import to the organized labor movement accompanied—and were consequences of—the decline in the importance of some sources of livelihood and the rise in the importance of others.[2] Industrial wage earners, the group most immediately thought of when the term "the proletariat" is mentioned, declined in relative importance, for the first time in half a century, during the 1920's;[3] the number of lower-salaried workers, on the other hand, increased to an unprecedented extent;[4] the numerical importance of professional persons likewise increased during these ten years;[5] while farm laborers, a little more than holding their own in absolute numbers, declined as a percentage of all gainfully employed, and the number of independent farmers declined both absolutely and relatively.[6] The period was not one in which changes in economic status strongly corroborated the thesis that the

[1] For statistical detail, see Fifteenth Census of the United States, vol. 2, *Population*, Table II, p. 6, and vol. I of this series, pp. 21–24.

[2] *Cf.* vol. I of this series, pp. 32–38.

[3] In 1920, according to the estimates of A. H. Hansen and T. M. Sogge (*cf. ibid.*, pp. 32–35) 17,684,072 persons, or 42.4 per cent of the gainfully employed of the nation, were industrial wage earners; in 1930, 18,512,640 persons, or 37.9 per cent of all gainfully employed, came within this class. The absolute increase in the number of industrial wage earners was less than the absolute increase in the number of salaried persons, professional workers, or proprietors and officials.

[4] In 1920 the salaried workers are estimated to have numbered 3,385,306 and to have constituted 9.6 per cent of all gainfully employed persons; ten years later they numbered 7,116,814 and constituted 14.6 per cent of all persons engaged in productive activity. In absolute figures, in other words, there was an increase of 3,131,508 in the number of salaried workers, as compared with an increase of only 864,568 in the number of industrial wage earners (*ibid.*). Phrased still differently, there was an increase of 62 per cent in the relative importance of the lower-salaried class during the decade, and a decline of the relative importance of the number of industrial wage earners.

[5] See *ibid.*, pp. 35–36. In 1920, 2,760,190, or 6.6 per cent of all gainfully employed; in 1930, 3,845,559, or 7.9 per cent of all gainfully employed. *Cf. ibid.*, p. 32 and pp. 37–38.

[6] Farm laborers numbered 4,178,637 in 1920 and 4,392,764 in 1930, the percentages (of all gainfully employed) being 10.0 in the former year and 9.9 in the latter. Independent farmers numbered 6.463,708 in 1920 and 6,079,234 in 1930, and the percentage of all gainfully occupied was 15.5 the former year and 12.4 the latter.

wage-earning class—those of proletarian status, inevitably propelled by economic determinism into group or class action—is destined, as one of the "inevitabilities" of capitalistic evolution, to become a larger part of the total population.[1]

The effects of these changes upon the trade-union history of the period were important.   In the absence of appreciable increase in the size of those classes most prone to organize and attempt by common action protect their job opportunities, the disposition to organize diminished in intensity.   The urban upper and middle class (proprietors and officials, professional persons, and salaried workers), was comprised of persons whose economic thinking and outlook, while not exactly proceeding from nineteenth-century individualistic premises, had little in common with the economic thinking of the more class-conscious of the urban workers, and this group became a larger segment of the American gain-fully occupied population while the latter decreased as a percentage of the gainfully employed.   Salaried workers, the group increasing most rapidly during the decade, had been a notoriously unorganizable group, little susceptible to the pleas of the trade-union organizer and possessed of tastes and social predilections more like those of small businessmen and professional persons than of wage earners.

Labor policies of the larger employers, adapted skillfully to circum-stances and developments already operating to check the advance of unionism, were still another important part of the industrial relations picture of the 1920's.   With some important exceptions, management curbed its frontal attack upon the principles of collective bargaining, became less audible in enunciating that staple of the open-shop argument, the appeal to individualism; instead, it professed acceptance of the doctrine of high wages, thus blunting the edge of unionism's appeal, and proclaimed the advent of an era of "welfare capitalism" based upon

---

[1] Farm laborers, lower-salaried persons, industrial wage earners, and servants may be grouped together as the "dependent" class, and farmers, proprietors and officials, and pro-fessional persons as members of the "independent" class.   A comparison of these two economic groups [cf. A. H. Hansen and T. M. Sogge, "Industrial Classes in the United States," *Journal of the American Statistical Association*, vol. 28 (June, 1933), pp. 199–203, and vol. I of this series, p. 32 and pp. 36–37] shows that the independent and dependent groups were about the same size in 1930 as they had been a decade before.   The four classes grouped above as dependent classes constituted 65.1 per cent of all gainfully employed in 1920, and 65.6 per cent in 1930.   Attention may be called, also, to one other grouping of economic classes: a grouping into "the urban upper and middle class" and "urban workers" (cf. vol. I of this series, p. 36).   For this purpose, proprietors and officials, professional persons, and the lower-salaried persons may be designated by the former term, and ser-vants and industrial wage earners by the latter.   Such a grouping (*ibid.*) reveals that urban workers comprised 45.5 per cent of all gainfully occupied in 1920 and only 42.0 per cent in 1930, while during these ten years the urban upper and middle classes increased from 23.8 per cent to 31.1 per cent of all gainfully occupied.

scientific management, elimination of wastes in industry, long-range planning, and acceptance—in its company-union formulation—of the principle of collective bargaining. Particularly in the expanding mass-production industries, where the workers were in the main without trade-union tradition, was the soil of union growth rendered barren by a conjunction of rising real earnings and employer policies professing to substitute direct benefits and emoluments for the indirect guarantees of unionism. In specific content, the labor policies of welfare capitalism took various forms and included various devices. The older type of welfare work—improvement in physical conditions of employment, insurance against sickness and accidents and institution of death benefits, pension plans, social, recreational, and educational activities, company housing projects, and health and safety work—was continued and expanded, and its appeal was especially great among the rapidly increasing number of clerical workers, persons who are not relatively well paid but who value physical comfort highly. Profit-sharing plans continued to manifest their traditionally high birth rate as well as their equally high death rate, and employee stock ownership, introduced on a wider scale than ever before,[1] was expected to (and frequently did) cement the faith of the workers in the existing order, entrench their reverence for the institution of private property, inculcate the belief that strikes against the firms employing them were strikes against themselves, and convince them that the economic interests of the wage earners were fundamentally harmonious with those of the employing and investing class.

Most important of the employer policies retarding the advancement of unionism during the decade, however, were "scientific" personnel administration and company unionism. Departments of personnel administration multiplied, and "the personnel officer became a combination disciplinarian and father confessor . . . modern industry's substitute for the personal relationship between employer and employee which had been [undermined] by large-scale production."[2] New methods of job administration were introduced; centralized hiring and transfer-and-promotion systems, based upon job analysis and specification and rating techniques, became common; and numerous systems of wage payment stemming from Frederick Taylor's "scientific" management—the Gantt, Emerson, Rowan, Halsey, Merrick, Bedaux, Baum, Priestman, and others—were inaugurated to overcome the deficiencies of straight time and piece rates. From the point of view of effect upon worker

[1] See National Industrial Conference Board, *What Employers Are Doing for Employees* and *Employee Stock Ownership*, Division of Industrial Relations, Princeton University, *Employee Stock Ownership in the United States*, Robert S. Brookings, *Industrial Ownership in the United States*, and Thomas N. Carver, *Present Industrial Revolution in the United States.*

[2] Philip Taft in *How Collective Bargaining Works*, p. 906 (The Twentieth Century Fund, New York, 1942).

attitudes, the centralization of employment functions and the minimizing of the petty prerogatives of foremen were probably the most significant of the personnel policies characteristic of the decade.[1] Hiring and firing tended, in the establishments introducing the more elaborate and formalized personnel administration policies, to become a function of one department, concerned primarily with labor-management matters, instead of being, as under traditional rule-of-thumb managerial policies, a function of the foreman; frequently the directive powers of foremen were minimized; and in many cases provision was made that before workers could be discharged (not laid off because of lack of work) they were entitled to a hearing before an allegedly impartial individual or committee. The consequence was a greater sense of security on the part of the employees and an elimination of the irritations engendered by the exasperating tyranny of the petty boss. Not a little cynical about some of the other components of scientific personnel administration and the more elaborate forms of welfare work though thousands of the workers may have been, they were anything but indifferent to the kind of treatment they received during their working hours or to the extent to which their job security depended upon the prejudice or whim of an individual. Their urge toward militant trade-union action was weakened appreciably by job administration policies insuring them—seemingly at least—a modicum of tenure security and protection against unfair and arbitrary treatment.

Bulking as large, certainly, as personnel administration in the streamlined labor policies of the twenties was company unionism.[2] During the War period, as has already been said, a mushroom growth of shop committees, representation plans, and "employees' associations" had developed. Cessation of hostilities was followed by the speedy—and generally unlamented—demise of the majority of these employer-instituted and -controlled organizations, but during the following decade organizations formed on the plant or employing-unit basis, unconnected in any way with the independent labor movement, and ordinarily financed and controlled by management and investors, became one of the most characteristic features of the "new era" offensive against unionism. Particularly was the company union congenial to conditions of employment in the technologically advanced mass-production industries. Seldom affording the substance of collective bargaining, these plant organizations served as a means of handling minor complaints and developing *esprit d'corps* on the part of the wage earners, of causing them

[1] See Sumner H. Slichter, "Labor Policies of American Corporations," *Quarterly Journal of Economics*, vol. 43 (1929), pp. 393–435.

[2] Company unions and employee-representation plans are discussed in some detail in Chap. XV. Reference to them at this point is confined to general characterization and to allusion to their influence upon the independent trade-union movement.

to be company-conscious rather than craft-conscious or class-conscious, and of converting them to the notion that the best kind of collective bargaining was that carried on by workers and employers possessed of a common interest, without the intervention of "dues-hungry" outsiders.

The impact of management's new and "enlightened" labor policies was upsetting to the kind of unionism that had enjoyed such good health and rapid growth during the War years; it found itself perplexed, uncertain how to proceed, lacking any vigorous counter-offensive. When combating the pre- "new economic era" capitalism, it was not at a loss for proper strategy; frequently it was defeated in industrial struggles, but it at least knew what to do. When, however, capitalism "took the worker's own point of view," attempted to provide directly at least part of what trade unionism promised, and resorted to the method of inducement, the leaders of the organized labor movement found themselves without defensive formula or effective mode of procedure. Employer labor policies, combined with such antiunion weapons as "yellow-dog" contracts[1] and "employers' closed shops,"[2] proved to be powerful barriers to "outside" unions.

Three other factors exerting their influence upon the trade unionism of the years between the end of the war and the depression of the 1930's, each of which is discussed later, deserve brief mention at this point: the prevalent economic ideas to which unionism adjusted its utterances and policies, the ravages of the labor injunction and the retarding effect of adverse judicial decisions, and the structural arrangements to which the dominant segments of the union movement still adhered.

When the war ended, American capitalism had reason to assume its acceptance by a large majority of the people, and the economic doctrines and philosophy expressed by many businessmen entrenched this acceptance and rendered a bit out of harmony with the ideological atmosphere a unionism whose economic thinking proceeded in considerable part from a simple supply-and-demand analysis and whose chief tactic was aggressive effort to attain an ability to put a reserve price on labor's services. As unit costs of production declined and, under a fairly stable general price level, profit margins widened, reinvestment of earnings was accelerated and plant and equipment expanded enormously. Entrepreneurial contemplation of the possible long-run consequences of these tendencies, combined with widespread discussion of "underconsumption," "faulty flow of purchasing power," and "balancing greater production with greater consumption,"[3] produced innumerable protesta-

---

[1] *Cf. infra*, pp. 511–513.

[2] *Cf. infra*, pp. 472–479.

[3] The books by W. T. Foster and Waddill Catchings (*Money, Profits, Progress and Plenty, Business without a Buyer*, and *The Road to Plenty*) were symptomatic of some of the more articulate economic thought in business—and to an extent in academic—circles.

tions that business enterprise recognized the necessity and the economy of paying high wages and sensed the antediluvian character, in an age of planned welfare capitalism, of traditional supply and demand wage policies. From somewhat different intellectual soil came an emphasis upon the economic wastes existent in prevailing production and distribution processes, and accompanying this emphasis the conviction that—with management given the free hand that the social temper of the decade was disposed to accord it—the national income could be increased so greatly that poverty no longer would cast its shadow over American life.[1] Each of these economic ideas—that of balance between production and consumption and that of elimination of waste in industry—tended to gravitate toward the other, and in their merged form they came to imply that there must be a further rise in the national income accompanied by more widely diffused purchasing power. Unionism, a trifle foreign to its traditional thinking though the ideas were, adapted its utterances and demands to them; it would be the mechanism for preventing underconsumption; and in return for the higher wages enabling it to be such a mechanism it would cooperate with management in effectuating greater productive efficiency. The aggregate effect was to check its aggressiveness, for while the position taken in itself involved no necessary relinquishment of the methods and techniques of economic pressure, the

[1] The idea of elimination of waste in industry and that of increasing productive efficiency caught the imagination of the American people of the 1920's to the extent that the movement for achievement of these ends almost took upon itself the coloration of a moral crusade. The increase in physical production and real national income that began after the depression of 1921–1922 in itself stimulated interest in ways and means of still further increasing production; the persons in the lower income brackets, able to enjoy comforts and amenities theretofore beyond their purchasing power, were predisposed to harken to the message that in interclass collaboration to produce more, not in class conflict, was to be found the formula of still greater advancement of their standards of living; and the industrial engineers, preaching a modernized version of Taylorism, found themselves regarded as the foreordained agents of the age of plenty. The Federated Engineering Societies' *Waste in Industry* (1922), an attempt to describe and to measure quantitatively the extent and sources of industrial waste, had an influence extending far beyond the number of those who ever heard of the book itself, and Stuart Chase's *The Tragedy of Waste* reached a still wider audience (see also David Friday's *Profits, Wages, and Prices*). During the period when Herbert Hoover was Secretary of Commerce (1921–1929), collaboration between business enterprise and the Department of Commerce to eliminate wastes in, and enhance the productive efficiency of, American industry became one of the more widely proclaimed of the policies of the Federal Government. The relations of price factors to technological factors appear—in spite of the A. F. of L.'s concern about the relevance of greater productive efficiency to mass purchasing power—not to have entered to any appreciable extent into the thinking of those converted to the idea that the great desideratum was removal of the causes of industrial waste and greater physical output. Thorstein Veblen's *The Engineers and the Price System* was, it is true, published in 1919, but the ideas embodied within it commanded little popular attention until (after Veblen's death) they appeared in exaggerated and distorted form, during the winter of 1933, in that melancholy travesty on economic science, technocracy.

absorption with new economic ideas and the policies these ideas seemed to dictate in fact inhibited the militancy and the tendency of prewar unionism to push for material advantages unconcerned about the more sophisticated wage doctrines, increased the faith placed in conciliatory and persuasive methods and in middle-class demeanor, and contributed nothing toward penetration of the unorganized areas of industry.

Two other factors retarding the growth of the trade-union movement were a series of adverse court decisions, culminating in the Bedford ruling of 1927,[1] and the unsuitability of unionism's structural arrangements to the industrial conditions of the postwar years. Before the middle of the decade it was apparent that the "magna charta" of 1914, the Clayton Act, had made lawful nothing unlawful before its enactment,[2] and the number of injunctions and temporary restraining orders was appreciably greater, as an annual average, between 1921 and the end of the decade than it had been prior to the legislation of 1914. Picketing was severely limited in the majority of jurisdictions, and it appeared, after the important Supreme Court decision of 1927, that simple refusal of members of a trade-union local to work upon unfinished materials produced under open-shop conditions in another state constituted conspiracy in restraint of interstate commerce. The two factors retarding trade-union growth—adverse court decisions and structural deficiencies—were related to each other, different as they were in character. Craft unions, to a greater extent than those whose coverage is industrial, are prone to utilize those tactics—sympathetic strikes, secondary boycotts, exclusive rules "maliciously" injuring the employment opportunities or market expectations of others—than are those labor organizations whose basis is industrial; and the craft form of organization covered a larger percentage of the nation's employees in 1929 than it did in 1920.[3] It was, as has already been said more than once, ill adapted to trade-union progress in the most rapidly expanding sectors of American industry, but in spite of some amalgamations and a widening of the craft base here and there, the A. F. of L. had accomplished little in the direction of necessary structural readjustments by the end of the decade.

Trade-union Membership during the Decade

Total membership of American trade unions reached its peak, an estimated 5,047,800, in 1920, then declined to 3,622,000 in 1923 and failed to increase (except for the slight 1927 gain) during the following years of the 1920's. The essential facts are set forth in the following table.

[1] Cf. infra, pp. 587–589.
[2] Cf. supra, pp. 126–128.
[3] Professor Wolman (Ebb and Flow in Trade Unionism, p. 92) found craft-union membership to be 78 per cent of total union membership in 1920 and 83 per cent in 1929.

TABLE 4.—TOTAL MEMBERSHIP OF AMERICAN TRADE UNIONS AND OF THE AMERICAN FEDERATION OF LABOR, AND ANNUAL CHANGES IN TOTAL MEMBERSHIP OF ALL TRADE UNIONS, 1920–1930[1]

Year	All unions	American Federation of Labor	Increase or decrease for year
1920	5,047,800	4,078,740	
1921	4,781,300	3,906,528	−266,500
1922	4,027,400	3,195,635	−753,900
1923	3,622,000	2,926,468	−405,400
1924	3,536,100	2,865,799	− 85,900
1925	3,519,400	2,877,297	− 16,700
1926	3,502,400	2,803,966	− 17,000
1927	3,546,500	2,812,526	+ 44,100
1928	3,479,800	2,896,063	− 66,700
1929	3,442,600	2,933,545	− 37,200
1930	3,392,800	2,961,096	− 49,800

[1] This table has been compiled from data presented on pp. 16, 26, and 34 of Professor Wolman's *Ebb and Flow in Trade Unionism,* and from the *Annual Reports* of the Executive Council of the A. F. of L.

In 1930, it will be noted, total membership was 1,655,000 less than it had been ten years before. Since the bulk of the losses of the 1920's had occurred by the end of 1923, it is desirable to examine first the factors responsible for the 1920–1923 trend, and then to analyze the membership losses during the remainder of the decade.

During the period of growth from 1915 to 1920, it will be recalled,[1] approximately 75 per cent of the growth in total union membership occurred within four groups—building construction; metals, machinery, and shipbuilding; transportation and communication; and clothing. During the three-year period of great losses, 1920–1923, the same groups of unions were responsible for nearly four-fifths of the total decline.[2] These losses were not, however, evenly distributed among the various unions within these groups; and one of the important facts to be noted is that the losses of a few large unions were chiefly responsible for the great decline in total membership. The railroad organizations lost many members as a consequence of the shopmen's strike of 1922;[3] the International Ladies Garment Workers Union suffered greatly from the New York struggle between the communist and anticommunist factions; and the United Mine Workers, a union outside the four groups mentioned above, contributed a disproportionate share to the total membership shrinkage.[4]

[1] *Supra,* pp. 133–134.

[2] To be exact, Professor Wolman's estimates show that of a total union growth of 2,465,200 between 1915 and 1920, 1,870,700 represented the growth of these four groups of unions. In the 1920–1923 period, total union loss was 1,475,800, to which these four groups of unions contributed 1,128,200.

[3] *Cf. infra,* p. 164.

[4] The unevenness of the distribution of membership losses needs to be illustrated and explained in a little detail. Several of the individual unions in the metals, machinery, and

Lack of uniformity also characterized the experiences of the different unions during the 1923–1930 period, when total union membership losses were 230,000. There were losses in mining, metals, machinery, and shipbuilding, textiles, leather and shoes, clothing, chemical, clay, glass, and stone, the food industries, and transportation and communication, and gains in building construction, lumber and woodworking, the paper and printing group, public service, and the entertainment occupations.[1] By 1930 the percentage of the nation's nonagricultural

shipbuilding group, which had enjoyed the largest increases prior to 1920, were dependent for continuance of their prosperity upon the unprecedented employment in strictly war industry and on the permanence of a government policy not greatly different from that of the War period, and, when these sources of employment shrank and public control was removed, the unions suffered greatly. For statistical detail, see Leo Wolman, *op. cit.*, p. 30. The building-trades group, on the other hand, did not sustain losses comparable to those of the unions just mentioned. During the War, the Carpenters and Electrical Workers, classified as building-trades organizations but having jurisdiction over craftsmen employed in other important industries, experienced gains in such industries while the building industry proper was failing to share proportionately in the wartime prosperity; then, in the postwar period these unions sustained losses outside of building construction, but the expansion of the building industry during the early 1920's in considerable part offset these losses. Some of the transportation unions, like the railway clerks, expanded under the policies of the United States Railway Administration and then, like other groups the maintenance of whose gains depended upon the continuance of government War policy, contracted rapidly. The membership of ten typical unions in 1915, 1920, and 1923, as estimated by Professor Wolman (*ibid.*, p. 30) indicates the variety of experience among individual unions and the importance of relatively few unions in the labor movement as a whole:

Union group and name of union	Average annual membership		
	1915	1920	1923
Building construction....................................	532,700	887,900	789,500
Carpenters...	194,000	371,900	315,000
Electrical Workers..................................	36,200	139,200	142,000
Metals, machinery and shipbuilding....................	224,200	858,800	257,100
Boilermakers and Iron Shipbuilders....................	17,300	103,000	19,400
Machinists...	71,900	330,800	76,400
Railway Carmen....................................	29,300	182,100	76,700
Clothing...	173,700	374,500	295,200
Amalgamated Clothing Workers......................	38,000	177,000	134,000
Transportation and communication.....................	576,000	1,256,100	907,300
Railway Clerks....................................	5,000	186,000	96,100
Seamen..	16,000	65,900	17,900
Teamsters...	51,600	110,800	72,700
Longshoremen......................................	25,000	74,000	34,300
Total, above unions...............................	484,300	1,740,700	984,500
Total, all unions.................................	2,582,600	5,047,800	3,622,000

[1] Following are the statistics on 1923 and 1929 membership of thirteen groups of unions

employees having membership in labor organizations had dropped to an estimated 10.1, as compared with 19.4 in 1920 and 9.9 in 1910.[1] The trade-union losses of the 1920's, losses sustained while the number of potentially organizable persons was increasing each year, were sufficient, in other words, to bring the percentage that organized employees constituted of all employees down almost to that of twenty years before.[2]

THE OPEN-SHOP OFFENSIVE: BREAKING OF TRADE-UNION CONTROL

The "personnel administration offensive" of the 1920's[3] carried with it, as has already been said, a lessening of the reliance of employers upon the militancy and the appeal to individualism that had been characteristic of their opposition to unionism during the early years of the century; an acceptance of the principle of collective bargaining, with the principle finding its operative meaning in the activities of company unions and

and the increase or decrease over the period as a whole (from *ibid.*, p. 40):

Group of unions	Average annual membership		Increase or decrease over period
	1923	1929	
Mining, quarrying and oil.............................	529,600	270,800	−258,800
Building construction..............................	789,500	919,000	+129,500
Metals, machinery, and shipbuilding.....................	257,100	211,400	− 45,700
Textiles...	37,300	35,300	− 2,000
Leather and shoes.................................	55,900	46,600	− 9,300
Clothing...	295,200	218,100	− 77,100
Lumber and woodworking...........................	10,600	13,200	+ 2,600
Paper, printing, and bookbinding......................	150,900	162,500	+ 11,600
Chemicals, clay, glass, and stone.....................	49,500	37,900	− 11,600
Food, liquor, and tobacco...........................	76,300	64,600	− 11,700
Transportation and communication.....................	907,300	892,200	− 15,100
Public service....................................	179,800	246,600	+ 66,800
Theaters and music................................	103,600	135,000	+ 31,400

[1] In 1910, according to Professor Wolman's estimates, 8.6 per cent of all employees and 9.9 per cent of nonagricultural employees were organized. The 1920 corresponding percentages were 17.5 and 19.4, and those for 1930 were 9.3 and 10.1. *Ebb and Flow in Trade Unionism*, p. 116.

[2] Within the different branches of industry changes in the percentage, of course, varied. Thus: In mining, quarrying, and crude petroleum and gas production, 22.4 per cent of the workers are estimated to have been organized in 1930 as compared with 27.8 in 1910, and 39.6 in 1920. In manufacturing and mechanical industries, the estimated percentage of organization for 1930 was 12.2 as compared with 11.4 in 1910 and 22.2 in 1920. The 1930 transportation group percentage of organization was 22.1, as compared with 19.5 in 1910 and 39.6 in 1920. In the service industries 3.2 per cent of all employees were organized in 1930, while the 1910 and 1920 percentages were 2.0 and 4.9 respectively.

[3] *Cf. supra*, pp. 157–160.

employee-representation plans; and an increased emphasis upon welfare and job-administration policies whose underlying premise was that unionism could not flourish among contented workers. But nothing in these policies suggested, or involved, a disposition to accept as permanent organized labor's wartime gains or to tolerate the closed shop where it could be eradicated; indeed, some of the personnel and welfare plans, as well as the representation schemes, had as essential prerequisites to their functioning the absence of independent unionism and the kind of regulation of working conditions that independent unionism would bring with it. When, accordingly, government policies favorable to unionism were abandoned, a drive to re-establish the open shop where it previously had obtained gained momentum. By the end of 1920, a network of open-shop organizations covered the country, and early in 1921 the various local groups, which had been operating along common lines and manifesting the same types of inspiration, came together at a conference of twenty-two state employers' associations, adopted for the movement the name American Plan, and mobilized for the battle against the closed shop.[1]

To an extent, the American Plan campaign differed from the open-shop drive of the early 1900's. Strategy was concentrated on the front of ideals and sentiments, as contrasted to the purely industrial front, to a greater extent than it had been two decades earlier; propaganda for "industrial democracy" of the employee-representation-plan species provided a new kind of ammunition; and greater efforts were made to develop *esprit d' corps* and plant-consciousness among the employees, to convince them of the reasonableness—not infrequently of the kindliness—of management's disposition toward them, and of the fundamentally common economic interests of all parties to industry than were characteristic of the earlier antiunion efforts. Methods less redolent of the philosophy of the "new capitalism" were, however, not ignored.

[1] For an excellent account of the formation and tactics of these organizations, see Perlman and Taft, in vol. 4 of Commons and Associates, *History of Labor in the United States*, pp. 489–514. A more summary account is to be found in L. Lorwin's *The American Federation of Labor*, pp. 201–205. During the War period, as has already been said, many employers were restive, awaiting the cessation of hostilities for conditions that would permit them to become emancipated from trade-union restraints, and by 1920 conditions appeared to be auspicious for united action. Early that year, a number of associations in the metal trades entered into an agreement to support the open shop; a little later the United States Chamber of Commerce, in a referendum adopted by its members, stressed "the right of open shop operations by employers," and in the autumn of that year the National Association of Manufacturers established an open-shop department and commenced to issue special bulletins on the subject (L. Lorwin, *ibid.*, pp. 202–203). By the end of the year, few if any states were without active open-shop associations. New York had at least fifty, Massachusetts eighteen or more, and Illinois forty-six. The Middle West apparently outdid the East in fervor for the open shop. From detail in Perlman and Taft, *op. cit.*, pp. 491–495.

"Yellow-dog" contracts, held by earlier Supreme Court decisions to be constitutionally unprohibitable under either the commerce power of the Federal Government or the police power of the states,[1] were in 1917, when decision was rendered in the Hitchman case,[2] transformed from relatively ineffectual psychological weapons into potent legal and economic weapons, since federal courts must, under the Hitchman doctrine, issue injunctions restraining trade-union organizational efforts threatening the property right or property interest of the employer in such contracts.[3] The wartime policy of nondiscrimination in hire or tenure[4] prevented immediate capitalization of the Hitchman precedent by employers of antiunion predilections, but from 1920 on the "yellow-dog" contract was an important instrument for holding in check the organizational efforts of trade unions and forestalling the introduction of the closed shop.[5] Together with the policy of maintaining the "employer's closed shop,"[6] this contract proved to be one of the most effective devices for breaking unions or preventing their spread and for stopping in its tracks the closed-shop advance.

Powerfully favoring the "American Plan," also, were the postwar anti-"red" hysteria, which for a time furnished to millions of middle-class people a psychological outlet for the hysteria and emotionalism engendered during the War and which could easily be turned against labor organizations and their leaders, and the success of the appeal to farmers' organizations that they make common cause with the employers against the monopolistic closed shop. For the most part, the more aggressive tactics of the "employers' mass offensive" were directed against the unions of the metal trades and the building trades. In the

---

[1] *Adair v. U. S.*, 208 U. S. 161 (1908) and *Coppage v. Kansas*, 236 U. S. 1 (1915). *Cf. infra*, pp. 511–512.

[2] 245 U. S. 229. *Cf.* and *infra*, pp. 513–515.

[3] The majority of state courts followed the Hitchman precedent, although there were some notable exceptions like New York (in the doctrine set forth in the Exchange Bakery and Interborough cases). *Cf. infra*, p. 517.

[4] *Cf. supra*, p. 139.

[5] The effectiveness in many situations of the "yellow-dog" contract should be apparent. Frequently only a small percentage of employees in a given employing unit might be under such contracts (which were sometimes written and sometimes only oral), but when union organizers attempted to organize the unit, the employer could contend that such efforts threatened his rights (or legally enforceable interests) in the contracts with such employees as had entered into them and petition a court to extend its equity arm in protection.

[6] That is, the shop, or employing unit, that would not hire union men. It may be noted, in passing, that the National Association of Manufacturers' definition of the "open shop," adopted in 1923, excluded by implication the employer's closed shop. This definition was: "An establishment where employment relations are determined by individual right of contract, without arbitrary discrimination based on membership or non-membership in any lawful labor organization." But nice definitional implications did not prevent many employers from adopting the policy of hiring no union men.

New York and Chicago markets of the latter, the fight to an extent took the form of a public crusade against corrupt and uneconomic trade practices.

Some of the unions were able to withstand the open-shop offensive, experiencing little curtailment of their areas of job control or forced relinquishment of their closed-shop agreements, but the aggregate effect was to liquidate a considerable part of the wartime advances. Where the industry or trade had emerged from the War with its employees still poorly organized, as in the case of textile manufacture, the attack was centered mainly on wages and hours; in the more highly organized trades, union control bore the brunt of the attack. Efforts of many of the unions to maintain gains made prior to the middle of 1920, in the face of a declining price level, resulted in the loss of strikes against wage reductions, and these losses in turn undermined union control and hence aided the open-shop generally. In the printing industry and the needle trades, clothing manufacture, and elsewhere, the employers' attack was repulsed, although only at appreciable financial cost to the unions;[1] but such groups as the seamen,[2] the packing-house employees,[3] and members of the unions grouped together in the Railway Employees' Department of the A. F. of L. suffered either the loss of the preferential or closed shop or else found union control distinctly weakened. The Machinists' Union, which had succeeded in organizing the employees of numerous machine shops during the years immediately preceding 1920, sustained defeat in a number of important strikes and witnessed institution of the open shop in these machine shops as well as in the railway shops in which its members had found employment.[4] In the textile industry wages were slashed and the already relatively ineffective union control was still further undermined.[5] The United Mine Workers of America, the nation's largest industrial union, declined in membership, between 1923 and 1929, from 492,900 to 245,100,[6] union control in the Northern bituminous fields had to be in part surrendered, and in important soft-coal areas the system of collective bargaining that had obtained for some thirty years broke down.[7]

[1] For details, see Perlman and Taft, op. cit., pp. 497–498 and 501–504.

[2] See ibid., pp. 494–497.

[3] Ibid., pp. 500–501.

[4] Cf. L. Lorwin, op. cit., pp. 203–204.

[5] For details, see Perlman and Taft, op. cit., pp. 511–514.

[6] L. Wolman, Ebb and Flow in Trade Unionism, p. 229. In part, as Professor Taft has observed, this loss was due to the decrease in the number employed in the industry (from 862,536 in 1923 to 654,494 in 1929), but it was also due to loss of union control in the Northern bituminous fields other than those of Illinois. How Collective Bargaining Works, Chap. 1.

[7] Union control was maintained, for the most part, in Illinois, but a rival union, the Progressive Miners of America, was able to supplant the United Miners in important coal-

It was, however, in that citadel of trade unionism, the building trades, that the open-shop and antiunion movement probably manifested its greatest vigor, even though the breaking of union control attained in some cities proved to be only temporary and total membership of the building-trades labor organizations was—contrary to the situation in the majority of other trades and industries—greater in 1929 than it had been early in the decade.   Here, perhaps more than any place else, the American Plan assumed the coloration of a public movement against corruption, monopoly, and economic extortion.   The housing shortage of the early years of the postwar period was generally (and rather indiscriminately) attributed to the high wages received, and the working rules maintained, by the building-trades labor organizations; legislative commissions in New York and Illinois aroused public opinion by their "revelations" of graft, racketeering, and the strike-insurance form of extortion; and evidence of collusive agreements between the representatives of organized labor and the contractors was not lacking.[1]   Employers' associations and citizens' committees in the various urban centers set about breaking the strength of the unions, and to an extent succeeded in temporary attainment of their end.   Revelations of conditions in the New York building trades, made by a joint investigating committee of both houses of the New York legislature (the Lockwood Committee) produced convictions of a number of the building-trades labor leaders, a strengthening of the hand of antiunion employers' and citizens' groups, and an increase in the percentage of contracts fulfilled under open-shop conditions, but the foothold of the labor organizations in Manhattan and Brooklyn was maintained, as it was to a somewhat lesser extent in the other boroughs.[2]

In Chicago the effort to break the grip of organized labor was for a brief period more successful.   As a result of the refusal in 1921 of a number of the unions to accept an unpalatable wage award, accompanied by what they believed to be an unwarranted attempt of the arbitrator

---

producing parts of the state.   The whole Northern bituminous coal industry, where collective bargaining had existed since 1898, faced a serious situation in the early 1920's. Operators in the organized areas found themselves unable to meet the competition of the expanding nonunion Southern fields and demanded wage readjustments, but the union adhered to John L. Lewis's "No Backward Step" policy and for a time refused to make concessions.   Finally, when concessions had to be accepted, they did not prevent the breakdown of the system of collective bargaining that had obtained for about three decades.   As Professor Taft has observed (ibid.), "a more flexible wage policy might have saved the day for the union, although this is doubtful in view of the ability of the Southern operators to follow the wage cutting of their Northern competitors, and for that matter even to improve upon it."

[1] See William Haber, *Industrial Relations in the Building Industry*, F. L. Ryan, *Industrial Relations in the San Francisco Building Trades*, and R. E. Montgomery, *Industrial Relations in the Chicago Building Trades*.

[2] For details, see Perlman and Taft, *op. cit.*, pp. 504–506, and W. Haber, *op. cit.*, pp. 358–370.

to revise their working rules, a Citizens' Committee sponsored by the Chamber of Commerce "outlawed" the unions refusing to accept the award (the Landis Award) and attempted to introduce the open shop in those trades the unions of which refused to accept the award.[1] For a time, the unions accepting the award had to sacrifice one of the dearest of their traditional prerogatives, the right to refuse to work on buildings and jobs on which nonunion men of other trades were employed, but the Citizens' Committee made no attempt to conduct the trades whose unions had accepted the award upon an open-shop basis. The unions (assisted tacitly by not a few contractors who were resentful of "outside" intervention) finally won against the Citizens' Committee, and by 1927 the last traces of this episode had been liquidated.

But San Francisco, once the "union stronghold of America," saw a considerable part of its building industry put upon the open-shop basis. Employer motives there were less camouflaged as a fight in the public interest, and—*propter hoc* or not—the attack upon organized labor was more successful. The centralized organization of the various unions, the San Francisco Building Trades Council, was eliminated as an effective force, and the unions were told they must accept a dictated peace under the American Plan, providing that employers were to deal directly with their employees or with individual craft unions. Institution of the open shop followed the refusal of some of the more important unions to accept the terms of this dictated peace, and wage reductions occurred throughout the industry.[2] Conditions finally reverted to "normal," but even by the early 1930's the San Francisco building-trades unions had not succeeded in recovering all the losses sustained during the early 1920's. Experience in these three cities, where the open-shop drive in the building industry was best organized and financed, was not untypical of experience throughout the country. Trade-union control was sometimes broken, frequently it was undermined, but in the final outcome the building-trades unions maintained their pre-eminence in the organized-labor movement. In contrast to the really great loss in trade-union membership as a whole between 1920 and the end of the decade following that year,[3] total building-trades union membership rose—largely in consequence of the building boom—from 789,500 in 1923 to 919,000 in 1929.[4]

Re-establishment of the open shop in some of the areas of American industry and the weakening of union control in industries and trades where collective bargaining—with or without eligibility of nonunion men

---

[1] For details, see Perlman and Taft, *op. cit.*, pp. 506–509, W. Haber, *op. cit.*, pp. 387–400, and R. E. Montgomery, *op. cit.*, pp. 233–310.

[2] For details see Perlman and Taft, *op. cit.*, pp. 509–511, and F. L. Ryan, *op. cit.*, pp. 294–306.

[3] *Cf. supra*, p. 163.

[4] L. Wolman, *op. cit.*, p. 40.

to work—remained, combined with the already mentioned decline in union membership between 1920 and 1923[1] and the adverse environmental conditions discussed earlier in this chapter,[2] inevitably reduced the number of strikes during the years after 1923; and the rise in real earnings,[3] together with the employment policies and other trends and conditioning factors already mentioned,[4] had the same effect.[5] In 1919, 4,160,348 workers participated in 3,630 strikes, these figures marking a new peak.[6] Industrial disputes continued to be abnormally frequent during 1920 and 1921, then declined precipitately in number. During the years 1922–1925 the average number was only 37 per cent of that of the five-year period 1916–1921, and the number of workers involved was only 48 per cent of the 1916–1921 average.[7] The following half of the decade industrial relations continued to be characterized by a remarkable freedom from strikes.[8] Textiles, building construction, mining, lumber production, and the metal trades (listed in order of importance) were responsible for between one-half and three-fifths, while wages and hours were the predominating issues in about half of the strikes and union matters in between 20 and 30 per cent.[9] The unions lost more strikes than they won.[10] There was, in addition, marked diminution in the intensity, as well as in the frequency, of industrial disputes.

NEW POLICIES AND THEORIES: RESTATEMENT OF ECONOMIC AIMS

The widely heralded—at the time—"new wage policy" of American trade unionism, officially proclaimed at the 1925 convention of the

[1] *Cf. supra*, p. 163.

[2] *Supra*, pp. 150–162.

[3] *Cf.* vol. I of this series, pp. 85–115.

[4] *Cf. supra*, pp. 153–154.

[5] The strike statistics for this, and other, periods in the history of American trade unionism are summarized in Chap. XIII.

[6] Selig Perlman in H. A. Marquand and Others, *Organized Labour in Four Continents*, p. 327.

[7] L. Lorwin, *op. cit.*, p. 240. Dr. Lorwin made his computation from data of the U. S. Bureau of Labor Statistics, published in the *Monthly Labor Review* for June, 1931.

[8] The annual disputes per annum between 1926 and 1930, according to Dr. Lorwin's analysis of the U. S. Bureau of Labor Statistics data, was 791, or only 23 per cent of the average number between 1916 and 1921, and the average number of workers involved was only 13 per cent of the 1916–1921 average. *Ibid.*

[9] S. Perlman in Marquand and Others, *op. cit.*, pp. 327–328.

[10] To be more exact, Professor Perlman's analysis of the strike statistics shows that between 1919 and 1934 between one-fourth and one-third of the strikes ended in favor of the strikers, except for 1921, when only 17 per cent resulted in victories. During the same period, between 26 and 46 per cent were definitely lost, and between 14 per cent and 26 per cent ended in compromise—except in 1919, when 36 per cent were compromised (*ibid.*, p. 328). While these data pertain to the fifteen-year period 1919–1934, they are roughly indicative of the percentages of strikes won, lost, and compromised during the years here under consideration.

American Federation of Labor,[1] must be regarded, in retrospect, as a defensive reaction against conditions and developments with which the dominant type of unionism found itself unable to grapple successfully. Sustaining defeats on the industrial front, forced to relinquish the advantages of the closed shop in industries and trades that had been organized during the War period, finding its anatomical characteristics ill adapted to changes that were taking place in the American productive and distributive mechanisms, and a trifle bewildered by the confusing maze of ideological currents and cross currents, "business" unionism felt itself constrained to reformulate its appeal to both wage earners and employers. This appeal found expression in the "new wage policy." Wages must rise "in proportion to increased productivity" in order to insure both the industrial stability consequent upon mass purchasing power and a lessening of economic inequality; hours of work must be reduced (preferably to the forty-four-hour and five-day week) to prevent technological displacement;[2] and then, in return, organized labor would cooperate to eliminate wastes in, and increase the efficiency of, industry. The old objectives of "a living wage" and "a fair day's work for a fair day's pay" must be relegated to the archives of a more primitive industrial age; organized labor henceforth demanded a "social wage."[3] Concomitant with elucidation of this new wage policy went increased emphasis upon trade-union research and education and an expansion of the miscellaneous trade-union services and activities discussed later in this volume.[4]

Such a declaration of policy harmonized well with the economic and social thought of the mid-1920's. The problem of economic waste then bulked large in the thinking of business and professional groups, and the offer of organized labor to cooperate in eliminating waste and enhancing efficiency was appealing. It was, in addition, a demonstration of the fundamental conservatism of the labor movement; an affirmation of yearning to increase the efficiency of capitalistic enterprise was ideologically very remote from the thesis of class struggle.[1] The spirit of

---

[1] Cf. American Federation of Labor, Proceedings of the Forty-fifth Annual Convention, pp. 231–233 and 271.

[2] For statement of the trade-union position concerning the effect of reduction in the length of the work period upon the real remuneration of the workers, see vol. I of this series, pp. 493–497.

[3] In the words of the A. F. of L.: "Higher productivity without corresponding increase of real wages means that the additional product has to be bought by others than the wage earner. This means that the social position of the wage earner in relation to other consumers becomes worse, because his standard of living will not advance proportionately with those of other groups." American Federation of Labor, "Organized Labor's Modern Wage Policy," Research Series 17. See also "The Modern Wage Policy of the A. F. of L.," American Federationist, August, 1927, p. 922.

[4] Cf. Chap. VII.

the time was essentially conservative, and so was the position taken by the A. F. of L. Likewise the emphasis upon higher real earnings as a means of "balancing production and consumption"[2] and the concern about displacement of workers by laborsaving and output-increasing machinery were attuned to the economic and social thought of the period. Unable to sustain its vitality by the revered methods of craft unionism but unwilling to abandon as the fundamental ingredients these methods or this form of organization, the labor movement (its left-wing elements remaining characteristically cynical and contemptuous) took verbal ammunition from the arsenal of the employing and middle classes. Its task became that of convincing management that only the trade unions, the "custodians of skill and craft," were able to provide the labor cooperation necessary in achieving greater efficiency and higher quality of workmanship, in reducing personnel turnover, in attaining regularity of operation and employment, and in improving productive methods in general.

There is scant evidence that organized labor's new wage policy influenced appreciably the movement of money and real earnings during the 1920's. While the purchasing power of both hourly rates and average annual incomes of employed persons advanced more during these ten years than during the doubly long period 1900–1920,[3] little of this advance was imputable to entrepreneurial conviction born of the inexorable logic of labor's restated case for higher wages. As much was tacitly (or perhaps unconsciously) conceded by trade-union leaders during the economically melancholy years of the 1930's, when they pointed to the collapse of the price system as irrefutable vindication of the hypothesis that failure of real earnings to advance as their formula prescribed could lead only to economic collapse.

ORGANIZATIONAL EFFORTS AND TACTICS

It was recognized, however, that the new program of conciliatory and cooperative overtures, of seeking to convince management of the reason-

[1] Although it may be mentioned in passing that the widely acclaimed pledge to cooperate in improving productive efficiency really did no more than to approve for general adoption the plan that had been in operation in the shops of the Baltimore and Ohio Railroad for several years before the Federation's 1925 convention.

[2] The leaders of the Federation were, it must be said, not too clear in their utterances of the doctrine that wages must rise "in proportion to the rise in productivity" in order to provide a market for the goods the nation's workers and productive apparatus were turning out, and hence "save industry from itself." Nevertheless, the trade-union leaders had grasped the idea that in the lag of real earnings behind per capita production they had a talking point, and—pressed as they were for a new type of appeal and encouraged by the hospitality of businessmen to the theory of a sympathetic correlation between high wages and business stability—they made the most of the point.

[3] Cf. vol. I of this series, pp. 82–115.

ableness of recognizing unions pledged to aid in increasing efficiency, was no complete substitute for unionism's efforts to conquer theretofore unconquered areas. These unconquered areas were numerous and extensive when the American economy emerged from the postwar depression and began inhaling the exhilarating atmosphere of the new era. Steel, the nation's greatest industry in point of value of product and number of employees, remained largely unorganized, its rates of pay still relatively low and its anachronistic hours schedule, the twelve-hour day and the seven-day week,[1] still obtaining in blast-furnace operation and several other categories of employment; in the rapidly expanding motorcar industry the open shop remained pre-eminent; the textile industry, experiencing depression in the North amid the general prosperity of the time, began migrating to the Southern regions, where a redundant labor supply, accustomed to a low standard of living and unacquainted with trade unionism, was available; less than 5 per cent of the nation's gainfully employed women were members of trade unions.[2] Organizational campaigns were obviously the order of the day.

None of these campaigns succeeded. The attack upon the steel industry, launched in the summer of 1923 by the Executive Council of the American Federation, the Amalgamated Association of Iron, Steel, and Tin Workers, and the thirteen other unions maintaining jurisdictional claims in the industry, collapsed within a few months.[3] Organi-

[1] Cf. vol. I of this series, pp. 472–476.

[2] In 1920 8,549,511 women, or 21.1 per cent of the female population ten years of age or over, were gainfully employed, these women constituting 20.5 per cent of all gainfully employed persons (Fifteenth Census of the United States, Occupation Statistics, p. 8). That year, according to the estimates of Professor Wolman (Growth of American Trade Unions, p. 98) less than 400,000 women, or not quite 8 per cent of total trade-union membership, were members of trade unions. Professor Wolman doubts (to anticipate a bit the story of efforts to organize women workers during the 1920's) whether this ratio changed greatly during the following thirteen years. It is likely that in 1930—in view of the decline in the trade-union membership (supra, p. 163), and assuming the ratio to have remained approximately the same—not more than 340,000 women were members of labor organizations.

[3] For details see L. Lorwin, The American Federation of Labor, pp. 218–220, and Perlman and Taft, in vol. 4 of Commons and Associates, History of Labor in the United States, pp. 461–469. This postwar attempt to organize the steel industry is important enough in the labor history of the period to deserve a footnote of factual recapitulation. Conservative trade-union leaders resented bitterly the intrusion of William Z. Foster into the steel strike of 1919 (cf. supra, pp. 145–146), and, as business emerged from the 1920–1922 depression, the Executive Council of the Federation, which had frequently been petitioned to assist in organizing the industry, decided to assume leadership in an organization drive. Within a few months the failure of the effort was apparent, and the Amalgamated Association of Iron, Steel, and Tin Workers advised abandonment of the campaign. The factors accounting for the failure were various. The United States Steel Corporation (under pressure from the President of the United States and numerous private groups) introduced the eight-hour day, thereby depriving the unions of a persuasive argument; coordination among the organizers was poor; and the workers, enjoying an advance in real earnings as well as a

zation of the automobile industry, attempted in 1925 under A. F. of L.
leadership, likewise proved to be a task beyond the capacity of a unionism
unwilling to reverse enough its old methods and seemingly unable to
make the kind of appeals that would have elicited sympathetic response
on the part of workers who were engaged in straight-line production
operations. Concessions to the craft unions rendered impossible organization of the industry on an industrial basis;[2] and emphasis upon the
interdependent interests of unions and management, the duties and
obligations of each side in respect to collective agreements, and the need
for joint efforts in stabilizing employment and improving the quality of

---

reduction in hours, did not respond enthusiastically. More important was the inability
of a Federation composed largely of craft unions, its officialdom unable to set aside the
interests of the craft unions without their consent, to organize an industry like steel. In
1924, the Amalgamated Association asked the American Federation to request all other
organizations to relinquish jurisdiction over workers in the steel mills. Such action would
have made the Amalgamated Association in fact the industrial union of the industry.
However, the National Organizing Committee that had been appointed by the Federation
(representing the several craft unions maintaining jurisdictional claims in the industry)
rejected the request, and the Amalgamated Association, in turn, refused to undertake the
task of organizing when handicapped by the conflicting jurisdictional claims of other unions
(L. Lorwin, *op. cit.*, p. 220).

[2] Here, again, the story as told in general terms should be supplemented by a little
detail. The automobile industry, as has already been said, in some ways played a part in
the economy of the 1920's not unlike that of railways during the last quarter of the nineteenth century, particularly in providing an outlet for capital investment and in bringing
about the employment of a larger portion of the nation's working force where its value
productivity was greater, thus contributing to the rise of real earnings. This great industry, employing more than half a million persons, remained almost entirely unorganized.
Progressives within the A. F. of L. demanded organizational activity—and, of course, the
Communists pointed to motorcar production as a glaring example of the weakness of the
existent labor movement. At the 1925 convention of the Federation, a committee of
the Metal Trades Department was appointed to consider the problem of organizing the
industry. This committee recognized that the industrial form of organization was the only
workable one in view of both the character of the labor supply and the technology of the
industry. But the craft unions asserted their "rights," and a compromise program, submitted by President Green at a conference of the international unions with jurisdictional
claims in the industry, both recognized the immediate necessity of organizing on the industrial basis and promised ultimate protection of the jurisdictional prerogatives of the craft
unions. Even this suggestion was, however, too drastic for the craft unions. During
the year 1925–1926, little was accomplished beyond propaganda activity. In 1926,
the Metal Trades Department asked the Federation to undertake the campaign, and this
request was granted at the 1926 Detroit convention. This convention also recommended
that the question of trade jurisdiction be waived during the campaign. Conferences of
the international unions with jurisdictional claims in the automobile industry were subsequently held (seventeen unions participating at first, and later only nine), and on Mar. 12,
1927, the above-mentioned plan of President Green was adopted in substance. Another
concession to the craft unions was the provision that locals of workers already organized
by crafts, like the patternmakers, painters, and die setters, were not to be disturbed.
From detail in L. Lorwin, *op. cit.*, pp. 244–248.

work—an amplification of the "higher strategy" of cooperation with management[1]—failed to persuade the employing interests of the desirability of recognizing and dealing with the unions.

Another major A. F. of L. organizational effort of the decade was directed toward the millions of unorganized women workers. The decision adverse to minimum wage legislation for women in the District of Columbia case of 1923[2] rendered persuasive the argument that in unionization, not in state assistance, lay the hope for improvement in the material welfare of these workers, and at the 1923 convention that year President Gompers was authorized to prepare a plan for organizing the women wage earners of the country. This campaign, like those in the steel and the motor industry, ended in failure.[3] Plans for a Women's Department within the Federation failed to invoke enthusiastic response on the part of leaders of the national and international unions, and suggestions set forth at a conference of these leaders would have involved modification of the Federation's structure that neither its leaders nor the craft-union officials were willing to make. Toward the end of the summer of 1924, the Executive Council, finding that the plans to organize women workers did not meet with the approval of a sufficient number of unions, decided to terminate the effort.[4]

Other attempts to extend the scope of trade-union control in the majority of cases met with similar lack of success, while at the same time union membership was declining as the number of wage earners was increasing[5] and former strongholds of unionism, like the coal-mining industry[6] were afforded examples of the inadequacy of even the organizations that had formerly been strongest to resist the onslaught of employer opposition and the economic forces of the age of "new capitalism." Just as the decade ended, with stock-market premonitions of the great depression of the 1930's, the Federation and the United Textile Workers directed an attack upon the great unorganized Southern labor

[1] Cf. supra, pp. 172–173.

[2] 261 U. S. 525. Cf. vol. I of this series, pp. 324–342.

[3] For details see L. Lorwin, op. cit., pp. 220–221.

[4] Various factors, in addition to those suggested above, entered into the failure of the A. F. of L.'s 1923–1924 effort to organize women workers. Women have always constituted a notoriously unorganizable group (cf. vol. I of this series, pp. 391–397). The campaign appears not to have been well organized, and the trade-union leaders never were really enthusiastic about it. A considerable number of them had the feeling that the presence of women in industry undermines working standards and that to organize them would redound adversely to the interests of male wage earners. Nor is it improbable that some of the members of the trade-union hierarchy were convinced that woman's place is in the home anyway. The international unions also feared that a women's department would encroach upon their prerogatives. For this reason, the Gompers suggestion apparently was dropped shortly after it had been made.

[5] Cf. supra, pp. 163–164.

[6] Cf. supra, p. 165.

market, particularly the textile industry.[1] This campaign revealed the weakness of conciliatory and cooperative overtures to employers who had not had impressed upon them the ability of labor to wrest concessions by concerted action, the lack of sensitivity of the union leaders to conditions and attitudes of the community and the economic outlook of Southern Workers, and the inability of the trade unionism of the time to recapture the methods and practice the tactics of an early period when they were most needed; in point of positive accomplishment, it left the Southern labor picture little changed. Membership of the United Textile Workers increased some, it is true, new locals were established, and several firms entered into trade agreements, but even these modest gains were quickly dissipated during the early part of the depression of the 1930's.[2] The final failure of unionism to penetrate new areas was in

[1] For details see Perlman and Taft, *op. cit.*, pp. 603–610, and L. Lorwin, *op. cit.*, p. 248. Pressure upon the A. F. of L. to undertake the organization of Southern industry was strong during the late twenties. The number of wage earners employed in Southern manufacturing plants had increased by about 350 per cent between 1880 and 1920, numbering about a million and a half when the decade opened. Early in 1919 the United Textile workers invaded the Southern industrial areas, centering the campaign around the forty-eight-hour week, but this campaign succumbed during the postwar depression. During the 1920's Northern capital—attracted by low taxes, cheap power, proximity to raw materials, the paucity of state labor laws, the absence of effective trade unionism, and the presence of a labor supply accustomed to low standards of living and unlikely to manifest trade-union or collectivist proclivities—continued its southward migration at an accelerated pace. The dominant labor movement was being criticized for its inaction by both progressives within it and Communists without, and it could not afford permanently to ignore the grievances under which the workers in the textile mills of the South were smarting: long hours, low rates of pay, the "stretch-out," and discrimination against union organizers and sympathizers. Moreover, a series of strikes at Gastonia and Marion, N. C., Elizabethton, Tenn., and elsewhere (*cf.* Perlman and Taft, *op. cit.*, pp. 605–609, and Tom Tippitt, *When Southern Labor Stirs*) seemed to indicate underlying revolt against employment conditions and receptiveness to unionization on the part of the workers. At the 1929 convention of the A. F. of L., President Green was instructed to summon a conference of the international unions and to devise an organizing campaign.

[2] The failure cannot be attributed entirely to ineptitude of the leadership or inadaptability of the tactics and structure of the unions. Organization of the Southern textile workers was a task of magnitude and difficulty. The labor supply—especially those parts of it that had been recruited from among the "poor whites" in the mountain regions, accustomed to low standards of living and prone to be docile factory employees—was not predisposed toward labor organization. The beginning of general depression in November, 1929, of course added to the difficulties. Also, sufficient funds to care for strikers were lacking. Nevertheless, the conduct of the organization campaign and the character of the appeals that were made appear, in retrospect, to have almost been insurance against success from the start. The A. F. of L. and United Textile Workers at the start contemplated the concurrent following of two lines of attack: organization work and preaching the gospel of unionism to the workers, and appeals to employers to accept the union-management cooperation philosophy and the "mass consumption" doctrine. The admixture of advocacy of cooperation with management, on the one hand, and old-fashioned organizing methods, on the other, resulted in a somewhat vacillating policy, with the sum-total effect

conformity with its experiences during the whole of the "prosperity era" between the depression of 1920–1922 and the beginning of the 1930's.

LEFT-WING UNIONISM DURING THE 1920's

Progressivism was running high within many of the trade unions affiliated with the American Federation, as well as within the nonaffiliated Railroad Brotherhoods, during the early 1920's,[1] and the leadership of these unions was accordingly constrained to temporize, to adopt more liberal policies and tactics. Utilization by the Communists, for their own purposes, of the agitation and activities of the progressives within the trade unions resulted in ruthless suppression of Communist influence by the dominant factions,[2] but the predominant conservative elements realized, nevertheless, that some concessions to the radicals had to be made. The concessions actually made were, however, of mild and temporizing character, negatived from the point of view of the liberals and radicals by the emphasis—even before the promulgation of the "new wage policy" of 1925—placed upon cooperative solving of industrial problems by workers and management and by indifference to extension of state regulatory powers and reiteration of the traditional nonpartisan

---

of giving priority to the newer function of cooperation with management. But few Southern employers were really responsive to the union-management cooperation philosophy.

[1] The progressivism and discontent within long-established unions during the first part of the decade were a result of a number of conditions and forces. The "letdown" of the trade unions after the War, when their expectations had been raised high, the social temper of the War and postarmistice periods, realization on the part of more thoughtful leaders that traditional tactics must be supplemented by others, and here and there the attainment of control by a younger and more liberal leadership all had the effect of creating a demand for more progressive action. Likewise the criticisms of the Communists and the limited success they attained in the William Z. Foster "boring from within" program had the same effect. Indicative of the unrest both within and without the Federation were the introduction by the railroad unions at the 1921 convention of resolutions calling for nationalization of the roads, the demand of the electrical workers for measures to prevent the Federal Reserve System from lending money for speculative and nonproductive purposes, the old-age-pension program of the Machinists' Union and the United Mine Workers (cf. L. Lorwin, op. cit., p. 214), and the challenge to the candidacy of Mr. Gompers for re-election as President of the Federation in 1921 (cf. Perlman and Taft, op. cit., pp. 540–541).

[2] The Communists instigated agitation for amalgamation of existing craft unions into industrial unions in the International Ladies' Garment Workers' Union, the Machinists' Union, the Longshoremen's Union, the Maintenance of Way Workers, and others, and President Gompers and the Executive Council, while not objecting to voluntary amalgamation, realized that the methods of the Communists under the leadership of Mr. Foster were intended to promote rebellion against the men in office, to further the class struggle, and to supplement the "reactionary and official bureaucracy" by union delegates representative of the workers in the shops and on the jobs. Membership in organizations like Mr. Foster's Trade Union Educational League (later called the Trade Union Unity League) became ground for expulsion from the Federation and its constituent unions.

political policy.[1] As in earlier periods,[2] extreme left-wind sentiment and activities were to be found without rather than within the Federation.

Conservative unionism's old critic, the Socialist Party,[3] neither "bored from within" the trade unions nor challenged them from without as it had done years earlier,[4] and the I.W.W., adhering though it did to the philosophy proclaimed and the tactics adopted at the time of its formation,[5] failed to regain the strength that had been shattered by the wartime and postwar attacks upon it.[6] But the Communists took the place of the Socialists and I.W.W. of the earlier period. During the first half of the decade, official Party policy, as directed by William Z. Foster and his Trade Union Educational League, was that of endeavoring to capture the existing unions by activities of the Communists within them, a policy that proved to be most successful in the needle trades.[7] When

---

[1] Declarations at the 1921 and 1922 conventions of the Federation committed it to nationalization of the railroads, mines, and public utilities and to support of such social legislation as the Sheppard-Towner Maternity Bill and old-age pensions. At the 1923 convention the Executive Council Report submitted placed emphasis upon the undemocratic character of banking and the sinister influence of financial interests upon industrial relations. During 1923 and 1924 arrangements for carrying on educational work were made with the Workers' Educational Bureau. These concessions to the less conservative elements of the trade-union movement were, however, offset by the conservative positions taken. The Manifesto adopted at the 1923 convention manifested more interest in enhancement of productive efficiency than in trade-union or political liberalism, advocated closer contacts between "the science of industry and representatives of the organized workers" and (although in 1924 the Federation was to find itself supporting for the presidency an independent candidate who was also the beneficiary of official Socialist support) decried independent political action on the part of organized labor. From detail in L. Lorwin, *op. cit.*, pp. 213-221

[2] *Cf. supra*, pp. 106-123.

[3] After the cleavage within the Socialist Party and the formation of the Workers' (later Communist) Party (*cf. supra*, pp. 148-149), the socialists ceased criticizing the Federation as bitterly as theretofore because of its refusal to become converted to socialist ideology, and began to hope that the Party might attain somewhat the same relation to the federated trade unionism of the United States that the British Labour Party bore to the Trade Union Congress and its affiliated organizations. In 1924, as is indicated later (*cf. infra*, p. 184), the Party for the first time since 1900 did not nominate candidates of its own for the presidency and vice-presidency, but supported Senator LaFollette, who had both A. F. of L. and Railroad Brotherhood endorsement. The opposition of the Communists undoubtedly was a factor in pushing the Socialist Party into a somewhat more conservative position.

[4] *Cf. supra*, pp. 107-112.

[5] *Cf. supra*, pp. 118-120.

[6] *Cf. supra*, pp. 147-148.

[7] From 1922 on, the Communist faction was extremely active in the International Ladies' Garment Workers' Union, and it demanded that the Union affiliate with the Red Trade Union International (a Communist federation of unions of the various countries). The General Executive Board of the Union ruled that union members belonging to outside organizations that interfered with the affairs of the union were subject to expulsion. In Chicago members of the Trade Union Educational League were expelled, and in New York

the results of this policy proved to be slight, "boring from within" was superseded by dual unionism. Under inspiration (or orders) from the Red International, the Trade Union Educational League transformed itself from a propagandist and educational body, seeking by gradual infiltration of its doctrines to capture the established unions, into a center for independent trade unions, operating under the name of Trade Union Unity League,[1] and began aggressively to pursue the work of organizing independent unions. The National Needle Trades Industrial Union, the National Textile Workers' Union, and the National Miners' Union all presented challenges to the long-established and dominant labor organizations of a character distinctly different from those of the Socialists during the early years of the century; these were rival organizations operating upon the particular industrial fronts that had "belonged" to the anticommunist trade and industrial unions.

While these dual organizations occasioned annoyance and alarm for the unions affiliated with the American Federation, their concrete achievements were neither great nor enduring. The National Miners' Union scored some temporary victories in the Pittsburgh region and elsewhere; the National Textile Workers' efforts to organize the textile industry of the South were, as has already been implied,[2] a force prodding the United Textile Workers and the A. F. of L. into their 1929 efforts to unionize the workers in the Southern mills; and the Needle Trade Industrial Union conducted strikes of the furriers, cloakmakers, and dressmakers. Probably the most important consequence of the Communist activity of the 1920's was the retarding of the progressive movement within unions affiliated with the American Federation. Many of the younger members of these organizations, progressive but decidedly not Communist in their predilections, might have injected new vitality into the unions, forced structural and tactical readjustments, and in more cases than one displaced the old leadership; but the Communist offensive

---

some of the members were disqualified from holding office for a period of years. The internecine struggle between the international officers and the Communists continued in the International Ladies' Garment Workers' Union until the latter years of the decade, when the policy of "boring from within" gave way to the policy of dual unionism. Other unions, like the Furriers' Union, the Amalgamated Clothing Workers of America, and the United Mine Workers, also experienced the same struggle between the Communists and the anticommunist factions. For details, see Perlman and Taft, in vol. 4 of Commons and Associates, *History of Labor in the United States*, pp. 538–562, and Stein, Davis, and Others, *Labor Problems in America*, pp. 216–219.

[1] The Trade Union Unity League, successor to the Trade Union Educational League, was not formed until September, 1929, but the substitution of boring from within by dualism was under way the preceding year, when the communists in the International Ladies' Garment Workers' Union and the Furriers' Union organized the Needle Trades Industrial Union.

[2] *Cf. supra*, pp. 177–178.

forced them into a defensive alignment with the conservative leaders whose opponents they otherwise would have been.

Another leftist challenge to the dominant unionism of the decade was not Communist in inspiration and sustenance, nor was it entirely expressive of a movement of revolt within the unions. The Conference for Progressive Labor Action, which had its inception in the break between Brookwood Labor College and the American Federation of Labor,[1] was supported by liberal "intellectuals" as well as by some of the more progressive leaders of unions affiliated with the Federation, and it hoped to become a "militant rallying center" for the American labor movement. With a social and economic outlook of the left-wing socialist persuasion, the conference announced its intention of working within the unions of the American Federation of Labor without "making a fetish" of the latter, and of organizing new independent unions when it deemed such action necessary. Immediately it wanted a more aggressive and militant unionism, a broadened structural basis, the supplanting of narrow craft consciousness and job consciousness by a more radical labor consciousness, and greater reliance upon political action; its ultimate program predicated abolition of capitalism, the attainment of a socialist planned society, and acceptance of belief in the class struggle coupled with opposition to the dictatorial methods of the Communists. The Conference continued to be active during the early 1930's.

LABOR AND POLITICS DURING THE 1920'S

Impatience with the nonpartisan political policy of the American Federation and with its reluctance to engage in any political action beyond that embraced in the program of the early years of the century[2] ran high during the early 1920's. Middle-class liberals and progressives, who could not accept as the sole summation of ultimate verities in the field of capital-labor relations the theories and methods of "economism" and "job-consciousness," were caustically critical of the political policies of the Executive Council and the leaders of the craft unions; and both within and without the Federation organized workers were demonstrat-

---

[1] Brookwood Labor College, at Katonah, N. Y., was founded in 1921 and was supported by various of the Federation's affiliated unions. In 1928 several of these unions withdrew their support on the ground that the College's teachings were "left-wing," anti-American Federation of Labor, and even "flavored with Communism." After an investigation of Brookwood, conducted by Matthew Woll at the request of President Green, the Federation withdrew its support, but students from A. F. of L. unions continued, nevertheless, to attend the college. After the support of the Federation had been withdrawn, Brookwood became more critical in spirit and utterance, and in May, 1929, some of its guiding spirits summoned a conference of "labor progressives" in New York City. This conference, presided over by A. J. Muste, issued a "Challenge to Progressives" and organized the Conference for Progressive Labor Action.

[2] Cf. supra, pp. 123–128.

ing increased receptiveness to the idea of independent political action. The 1920 attempt to establish an enduring national Farmer-Labor Party[1] had, it is true, ended in failure, but some of the local and state organizations formed in 1919 and 1920 maintained their identity and continued to agitate for an American labor party that would have a relation to the trade unions roughly comparable to that of the British Labour Party to the trade unions in England. The beginning of a series of adverse Supreme Court decisions[2] convinced numerous trade unionists that a labor movement so devoid of political-mindedness as to believe that it had been given a free hand on the economic front by the ambiguous and question-begging terms of the Clayton Act[3] was inadequate to meet the problems confronting it in the postwar era and that a manifestation of labor's political strength would have wholesome effect upon both legislators and the judiciary. For a number of reasons, the railway unions were favorably disposed toward enlargement of the scope of organized labor's political activity. Under provisions of the legislation of 1920,[4] the wages and working conditions of employees of the railroads depended upon government decision, a circumstance the moral of which seemed to be the desirability that organized labor possess greater political strength; experience during the wartime government administration of the roads had served to remove some of the old fear of "statism"; and the immediate end of securing repeal or amendment of some of the unsatisfactory provisions of the Esch-Cummins Act likewise convinced the railway employees—those of both the train service Brotherhoods and the members of the unions constituting the Railway Employees' Department of the American Federation—that all organized labor should be united in a powerful political movement. Unions of socialistic antecedents, like those in the needle trades, joined the movement for a labor party from idealistic motives; and the Socialist Party—its former left-wing elements now largely within the Communist camp—believed that it could work most effectively toward its goal of production for service and not for profit through alignment with other dissident political groups and that it should capitalize the opportunity afforded by the upsurge of political-action sentiment within the strictly economic organizations of labor.

The sentiment in favor of independent political action or more aggressive participation in politics of the traditional nonpartisan variety, or both, found expression in various organizations and tactical adjustments during the first half of the decade, with its culmination in the presidential

---

[1] Cf. supra, pp. 148–149.

[2] Particularly in American Steel Foundries v. Tri-city Trade Council, 257 U. S. 184 (1921), Truax v. Corrigan, 257 U. S. 312 (1921), and Duplex Printing Co. v. Deering, 254 U. S. 443 (1921).

[3] Cf. supra, pp. 126–128.

[4] Cf. infra, pp. 735–737.

campaign of 1924.[1] At a conference sponsored by the Chicago Federation of Labor early in 1922,[2] the Conference for Progressive Political Action, intended as a political nucleus and clearinghouse of labor organizations and progressive elements generally, was established, and it entered the congressional campaign of 1922 with the purpose of supporting candidates favorable to labor measures. Local conferences were established by the Conference for Progressive Political Action, but the strategy was to leave these subordinate local bodies free either to work within the primaries of the old parties or to make third-ticket congressional nominations. The American Federation of Labor, not affiliated with the Conference, although some of its international unions and state federations were, also waged an active campaign prior to the November elections of that year, and in a number of cases it reached agreement with various farmers' organizations to support common candidates.[3]

Leaders of the trade unions were for the most part satisfied with the results of the 1922 elections, and were not disposed to perambulate farther along the route to an independent political labor movement, but the Chicago Federation group and others who had hoped that the 1922 activities of the Conference for Progressive Political Action would give birth to an American labor party continued their independent-party efforts. A Chicago conference, held in July, 1923, collapsed as a consequence of Communist participation and domination,[4] but the Farmer-Labor Party of Minnesota, which had held aloof from the political movement sponsored by the Chicago Federation, enjoyed increasing power and prestige, eclipsing the Democratic Party of that state and in 1922 and 1923 winning the two United States senatorships from Minnesota.[5] Dur-

[1] For more detailed account of organized labor's political activities during the 1920's, see Nathan Fine, *Labor and Farmer Parties in United States*, 1829–1928, Perlman and Taft, *op. cit.*, pp. 525–538, and L. Lorwin, *op. cit.*, pp. 221–226.

[2] At the Chicago gathering where the Conference for Progressive Political Action was formed, there were present representatives of eight international unions, eight state federations, the Chicago Federation of Labor, the Socialist Party, a number of farm organizations, the Non-partisan League, an organization of Single Taxers, the National Catholic Welfare Party, the Methodist Federation of Social Service, and a number of other organizations.

[3] *Cf.* Perlman and Taft, *op. cit.*, pp. 531–534.

[4] President Fitzpatrick of the Chicago Federation of Labor, acting for the remnants of the Farmer-Labor Party of 1920, called the conference of July, 1923. Members of the Workers' (later Communist) Party were invited, and, because of the presence of the Communists, the Socialist Party, the Socialist Labor Party, the invited international unions affiliated with the A. F. of L., and the Railroad Brotherhoods refused to participate. As a result, the genuine Farmer-Labor delegates (*i.e.*, the Fitzpatrick faction and others primarily interested in establishment of an independent party that was neither Communist nor merely a mechanism for aiding the Federation unions in their policy of working within the old parties) were outvoted, and left the conference. From detail in *ibid.*, pp. 529–531.

[5] Henrick Shipstead and Magnus Johnson were the two Farmer-Labor senators elected

ing the period between the congressional campaigns of 1922 and the first quarter of 1924, the Conference for Progressive Political Action remained apart from both the Chicago Federation and the Minnesota Farmer-labor party movements.

In the spring of 1924, however, the impeding independent presidential candidacy of Senator Robert M. La Follette forced the various labor and progressive groups to reach a decision on the question of uniting in their support of a third ticket. The Executive Council of the A. F. of L. procrastinated, weighed the advantages of its old policy of eschewing positions that might even savor of a class political movement, and for a time extended little encouragement to those within its ranks who wished it to become an active participant in an independent party effort. The Railroad Brotherhoods, on the other hand, favored endorsement of La Follette, as did many of the rank and file of the A. F. of L. unions and a considerable proportion of their more progressive leaders.[1] Likewise the Conference for Progressive Political Action—in spite of its recent aloofness from the Chicago and Minnesota third-party movements and of some sentiment within it for continuing to support the more desirable of the candidates of the old parties—felt that in 1924 its support of the national candidates of either of the old parties would be futile; and when the Democrats nominated a conservative corporation lawyer,[2] support of a third ticket became inevitable and endorsement of Senator La Follette almost equally so. The Conference summoned a Progressive Convention which convened in Cleveland July 4 and was attended by about 600 delegates representing national and international unions both within and without the Federation, city and state federations, some of the cooperative societies, the Socialist Party,[3] the Committee of Forty-eight,[4] the Progressive Party (Wisconsin La Follette faction), the Women's Committee on Political Action, "and 'miscellaneous university, educational, and third party groups,' together with a 'sprinkling of farmers'";[5] and a platform calculated to appeal to progressive nonlabor elements of

---

in 1922 and 1923, respectively. Senator Shipstead was re-elected in 1928, 1934, and 1940, although he stood as a Republican candidate for the term expiring in January, 1947.

[1] William H. Johnston, president of the International Association of Machinists, presided at the Cleveland convention of July, 1924, which was called by the Conference for Progressive Political Action and which nominated Senators La Follette and Wheeler.

[2] John W. Davis of New York and West Virginia.

[3] The year 1924 has been the only one since the first ticket was named in 1900 (*cf. supra*, pp. 113–115) that the Socialist Party has not nominated its own candidates. The Party of course maintained its identity in 1924, although represented in the Progressive Convention and subsequently endorsing the convention's nominees.

[4] An organization of progressives and liberals that had been active in the formation of the Farmer-Labor Party of 1920.

[5] L. Lorwin, *op. cit.*, p. 223.

the electorate as well as to organized labor was adopted.[1] Robert M. La Follette, progressive Republican, was formally nominated for the presidency in accordance with the already made arrangement, and the progressive Democrat, Burton K. Wheeler of Montana, became the vice-presidential nominee in accordance with Senator La Follette's wishes. In conformity with the presidential nominee's desires, the La Follette-Wheeler ticket was to be regarded as an "independent," not as a third-party, one, and no attempt was to be made to sponsor candidates other than those for the first two national offices. The actions of the Cleveland convention, in other words, involved no steps toward immediate formation of a third party.

The nomination of La Follette rendered the position of the American Federation of Labor, and particularly of its Executive Council, not a little difficult. Its old critic, the Socialist Party, had been an important part of the Conference for Progressive Political Action and of the Cleveland convention, and it had endorsed La Follette instead of nominating its own candidates. Moreover, support of an independent ticket, technically consistent with the Federation's traditional political policy though such support might be, would inevitably be interpreted as a step in the direction of formation of an American labor party. But, on the other hand, the rank-and-file pressure upon the Executive Council to support the La Follette ticket was strong; both the Republican and Democratic platform committees had been frigid toward the proposals of the representatives of organized labor appearing before them; the platform emerging from neither convention was satisfactory to the A. F. of L.; and the Cleveland Progressive Convention platform, in contrast, included the majority of labor's demands and no planks that were obnoxious to it. Considerations dictating support of the independent candidates were clearly more compelling than those dictating the contrary. The endorsement was, however, given with reluctance and, without doubt, not a little regret,[2] and President Gompers accompanied

[1] To a considerable extent the platform was aimed at monopolistic or specially privileged business. Except for the advocacy of improved child-labor laws and ratification of the child-labor amendment (*cf.* vol. I of this series, pp. 448–460), little was included about social legislation. There were, however, assertions of labor's right to organize and bargain collectively and condemnation of judicial interference with this right and of the issuance of injunctions in labor disputes calculated to make strong appeal to the trade-union part of the electorate. Among the more important of the platform planks were: the demand that private monopoly be crushed; denunciation of imperialistic foreign policies and demand that the Treaty of Versailles be revised; demand that the constitutional guarantees of freedom of speech, press, and assemblage be enforced; endorsement of the project of a publicly owned super-power system and of public control of all natural resources; advocacy of high progressive taxation, repeal of existing tariff duties, and more direct control of money and credit; and promise to create a government marketing corporation for farm products. From Dr. Lorwin's summary, *ibid.*, p. 224.

[2] Samuel Gompers, then a very sick man, apparently accepted the endorsement of an

his announcement of the endorsement by emphasis upon the fact that the Federation had neither committed itself to, nor identified itself with, any group supporting the La Follette candidacy (meaning the Socialists), and that the action in no way signified that the Federation had committed itself to a third party.[1]

About one voter in every six supported the labor-endorsed independent candidacy in the election of November, 1924.[2] For the most part, the third-party strength lay in the urban centers,[3] and there can be no doubt that in addition to the almost unqualified support of the railroad organizations both within and without the Federation, and of the Socialists, organized labor in general voted in accordance with the recommendation of the Executive Council.[4] Socialists and other advocates of a third party representing the labor, liberal, and radical forces of the nation regarded the outcome of the 1924 election as a promising beginning, but the leaders of the railroad unions and of the A. F. of L., measuring this outcome in terms of immediate results, were disappointed. The former turned their attention from independent party action to the reaching of understandings with management. The companies, like the unions, were

---

independent or third-party ticket as the only alternative, and it was not an alternative that made him happy. As Miss Florence Thorne, for years Mr. Gompers's secretary, has narrated the events in the Appendix she wrote for Mr. Gompers's memoirs: Mr. Gompers had for months before the national party conventions warned the leaders of the Democratic Party that unless it showed greater disposition to accept, and in good faith seek the realization of, labor's demands, organized labor would not continue to support it. Mr. Gompers went from the hospital to present labor's case to the Democratic platform committee, but the platform adopted was distinctly unsatisfactory. Miss Thorne records that when, back in his hospital room, Mr. Gompers heard the reading of the Democratic platform, which ignored his plea, he remarked: "It looks as if we were forced to turn to La Follette." After the nomination of John W. Davis as the Democratic candidate, he declared: "There is no other way." Since Mr. Gompers was physically unable to confer with Senator La Follette, he sent two of his colleagues as confidential representatives to outline the basis upon which the campaign was to be conducted. He also suggested to the Executive Council the endorsement of La Follette "as a protest against reaction and materialism in politics." From Appendix written by Miss Thorne in Samuel Gompers, *My Seventy Years of Life and Labor*, vol. 2, pp. 537–538.

[1] "Cooperation hereby urged is not a pledge of identification with an independent party movement or a third party, nor can it be construed as support for such a party, group or movement, except as such action accords with our non-partisan policy. We do not accept government as the solution of the problems of life. . . . Neither can this cooperation imply our support, acceptance, or endorsement of policies or principles advocated by any minority groups or organizations that may see fit to support their candidates." Executive Council statement, quoted by L. Lorwin, *op. cit.*, p. 225.

[2] La Follette's total vote was 4,826,352, or 16.5 per cent of the total popular vote.

[3] Although Cleveland was the largest city carried by the La Follette-Wheeler ticket. The electoral vote of only one state, Wisconsin, was secured.

[4] In the congressional districts, the A. F. of L. followed its old policy of supporting candidates of one or the other of the major parties. For the most part, also, the Conference for Progressive Political Action adhered to this policy in the congressional elections of 1924.

dissatisfied with the Railroad Labor Board that had been established by the legislation of 1920; and acting together the two groups secured the Railroad Labor Act of 1926.[1] Thereafter the unions refused to interest themselves further in a labor party movement. Likewise the 1924 convention of the A. F. of L., held after the election, endorsed continuation of the tried-and-true nonpartisan policy. The Conference for Progressive Political Action met and liquidated in February, 1925. During the remainder of the 1920's, the Minnesota Farmer-Labor Party was the only survivor of the third-party movements of the first half of that decade.

[1] *Cf. infra*, pp. 737–748.

CHAPTER V

AMERICAN UNIONISM SINCE 1930

In almost every significant phase, American trade-union history since 1930 stands out in sharp contrast to that of the 1920's. The downward trend of membership[1] reversed itself after 1932, and during the early 1940's approximately 12,000,000 wage earners—the largest percentage of the nation's employees, as well as the largest absolute number, up that time—were members of craft and industrial unions.[2] Old labor organizations expanded, new ones multiplied; and the great mass-production industries like steel, automobiles, electrical manufacturing, rubber, and aluminum—immune during the 1920's to appreciable trade-union penetration—found themselves adopting the collective-bargaining pattern of industrial relations. Dominance in the labor movement as a whole of the federated trade unionism represented by the Executive Council of the American Federation was rudely challenged during the second half of the 1930–1940 decade by an industrial union movement, and the rapid numerical growth and the expansion into new geographical and industrial areas were accompanied by the most bitter dissension and the widest cleavage within the ranks of organized labor since the 1860's.[3] Without abandoning two revered tenets—that economic power transcends all other power and that wage earners must have their own distinctive organizations—unionism to an extent changed in functional character; it became infused with a new militancy, it looked to the state to a greater extent to provide direct guarantees of economic security and material welfare as well as the rules and apparatus enabling workers to bargain collectively through representatives of their own choosing, and it minimized less the importance of action on the political front. In still other ways, post-1930 trade-union developments differ markedly from those recorded in the preceding chapters.

BACKGROUND FORCES AND DEVELOPMENTS

In 1929, as everyone knows, the business cycle entered into a precipitous downswing—a cyclical trend that did not reverse itself, except temporarily and slightly once or twice, until 1933. Employment in

[1] *Cf. supra*, p. 163, and *infra*, pp. 192–196.

[2] By the end of 1943, as is indicated later, probably 13,000,000 persons were members of independent labor organizations.

[3] *Cf. infra*, pp. 201–222.

manufacturing at the depth of the depression stood at only 59 per cent of the 1923–1925 average, and in spite of the fact that the decline in hourly wage rates for the most part kept within the decrease in the cost of living, widespread unemployment and part-time employment reduced by probably one-third the real income of the wage earners and salaried persons of the United States.[1] By January of 1935, after the Federal Government for almost two years had engaged in an extensive program of work relief and relief work, some 5,488,000 relief cases, involving 20,676,700 dependent persons, were being handled;[2] and with a shrinking national income,[3] persons of almost every walk of life experienced serious —frequently tragic—curtailment of their standards of living.

The effect of these changes in economic conditions upon the attitudes and group predispositions of the workers, upon the intellectual climate within which unionism operated, and upon the policy of the government toward labor organization was profound. Skepticism about the automatic beneficence of the system of free private enterprise appeared to increase in proportion to the decline in business activity. Disillusioned with the interclass harmony hypothesis and the expectation of permanent prosperity that during the twenties had checked any latent disposition to organize, cynical about the roseate promises of the preceding decade's "welfare capitalism," wage earners were now much more prone to assert a positive right to participate, through concerted action and representation by those of their own choosing, in the determination of terms and conditions of employment.[4] Meanwhile, the social and economic predispositions of members of other economic classes underwent modification or, in some cases, complete metamorphosis. The conviction engendered by the collapse of the price system that fundamentally pathological conditions obtained within the economic order carried with it greater middle-class tolerance of the objectives of organized labor, less disposition to regard the appurtenances of collective bargaining and job-control as unwarranted and pernicious intrusions into this economic order. Such economic notions as those of underconsumption, the necessity of economic

[1] See vol. I of this series, pp. 115–128.
[2] See vol. II of this series, pp. 89–103.
[3] See vol. I of this series, pp. 146–148.
[4] Of course, depression conditions also afforded fertile soil for the nurture of left-wing labor movements, but as a generalization it can be said that the radical and revolutionary movements manifested much less strength and capacity to expand than might have been expected. Had government policies after 1932 not removed old obstacles in the way of self-organization on the part of labor, and in fact positively assisted such organization (cf. infra, pp. 190–192), it is likely that movements looking toward the overthrow of the capitalistic system would have enlisted the support of many more wage earners than they did. The rapid development of protective legislation and social insurance after 1933 was also a factor holding in check the kind of labor unrest likely to manifest itself in more revolutionary movements. The Communist and other left-wing movements since 1930 are discussed infra, pp. 238–241.

planning, and the possibility of future contraction, or expansion at a less
rapid rate, of the economy as a whole obviously reflected increasing suspicion of the thesis that under a regime of profit making and competition
social resources will be utilized in such manner, except during temporary
maladjustments, as to afford full employment of the factors of production
and the maximum output of goods, in proper relative quantities, that
they are physically capable of turning out.   While the import of these
economically popular notions was not in every respect a reasoned justification of the extension of unionism,[1] their aggregate effect was to create
a community receptiveness to concerted efforts on the part of the worst
victims of the imperfections of the economic system.   The reinvigorated
disposition of the workers to organize, public attitudes and economic
thinking during the years immediately following 1929, and the government policies that are described shortly all afforded an opportunity for
trade unionism greater, even, than that it had enjoyed during the period
1917–1920.

But most important of all the factors explaining the revival and
growth of unionism after 1933,[2] in contrast to the trade-union lethargy
and inability to expand during the 1920's, was the changed policy of the
government.   Consequent largely upon the public frame of mind engendered by depression conditions, a new administration, more prolabor
than its immediate predecessors, more skeptical than they had been of
the rugged individualism of the past, and pledged to inaugurate a "New

[1] The notion that incomes received by consumers were inadequate to lift off the market
the goods industry was capable of turning out—a very old idea, given re-expression in the
mid-1920's by the American Federation of Labor but attaining very considerable popular
vogue during the depression of the 1930's—had as a logical corollary, of course, the idea
that organization of labor to wrest a larger share of the value product from those classes
who were more prone to save rather than spend their incomes quickly is eminently desirable
to provide "economic balance."   Congressional benediction was bestowed upon organization of labor as a means of increasing mass purchasing power and thereby minimizing
industrial depressions in the "Findings and Policy" set forth in the National Labor Relations Act (49 Stat. 449) of 1935 ("Inequality of bargaining power between employees who
do not possess full freedom of association or actual liberty of contract . . . tends to
aggravate recurrent business depressions, by depressing wage rates and the purchasing
power of wage earners in industry and by preventing the stabilization of competitive wage
rates and working conditions within and between industries . . . causing diminution of
employment and wages and in such volume as substantially to impair or disrupt the market
for goods.")   The implications of the notion that industry in the future would not expand
at its past geometrical rate of growth and that, indeed, the economy might be entering a
period of contraction were, however, not altogether in the nature of a reasoned justification
of the extension of unionism, since one obvious dictate was that restrictions upon technological change that retarded new investment must be removed.   Likewise, the belief of
many economists that current economic ills were in part attributable to the rigidity of
prices was a doctrine not all the implications of which were favorable to unionism.

[2] As is indicated later (infra, p. 192) trade-union membership declined in orthodox
depression fashion between 1929 and 1933; then the revival commenced.

Deal," assumed control after four years during which capitalism's "natural recuperative forces" had failed to operate. In the years immediately following, protective legislation and social insurance—so widely demanded by the workers and "liberals" of the country that the American Federation of Labor was forced to modify in substantial degree its traditional attitude toward state assistance—was enacted by the Federal Government, and, under federal encouragement and as a result of federal example, by the various states to an extent that the United States became a leading, not a laggard, nation in these phases of the government's relation to labor conditions. More important, from the point of view of the background in government policies of the trade unionism that has functioned since 1930 were the enactments freeing—as ultimately construed by the Supreme Court—organized labor from the ravages of the injunction, elucidating the wage earners' old right to organize and bargain collectively through representatives of their own choosing, rendering this right real and dynamic by prohibiting such practices and acts on the part of employers as had in the past often made it a merely nominal right, and providing for governmental assistance in the determination of units appropriate for collective bargaining and in the selection of bargaining representatives. Even before the advent of the new administration, the Norris-La Guardia Act of 1932[1] restrained the federal courts from extending their equity arm to protect "yellow-dog" contracts, declared in effect that workers have a stake or property interest in their collective activities that must be balanced against the rights and interests of employers and third parties when restraining orders are sought, and established procedural requirements and immunities from injunction that, as ultimately construed by the Supreme Court,[2] enlarged enormously the legally permissible area of labor's self-help program. Then, in 1933, the National Industrial Recovery Act[3] required the inclusion in every code of fair competition of the provision that employees had the right to organize and bargain collectively through representatives of their own choosing without interference, restraint, or coercion on the part of employers; and in 1935 the National Labor Relations Act reiterated this general right, placed such correlative restraints and obligations upon employers as were regarded as necessary to make the general right real and dynamic, and established machinery to prevent the enumerated unfair labor practices and to aid workers in units found to be appropriate for collective bargaining in the selection of their representatives for bargaining purposes.[4] Constituting to a considerable

[1] 47 Stat. 70.   The provisions of this legislation and the Supreme Court constructions of it are discussed *infra*, pp. 591–593, 643–650, as are also the "baby Norris-La Guardia Acts" of a number of the states.

[2] *Cf. infra*, pp. 578–581, 622–628.

[3] 48 Stat. 195; 15 U. S. C. 703.   *Cf.* vol. I of this series, pp. 356–370, and *infra*, pp. 521–522.

[4] 49 Stat. 449.   *Cf. infra*, pp. 522–523.

extent a revival of the principles enunciated by the War Labor Board of
more than fifteen years earlier,[1] the government's new labor policies
—policies that transformed the labor code of the United States from one
of the most restrictive among the industrially advanced nations to one of
the most liberal—were productive of both the rapid growth of old unions
and the establishment of new ones.   During the two-year period of the
National Recovery Administration, it is true, the provisions of Sec. 7
(a), designed to protect the workers' right to self-organization, were far
from effective in preventing either the establishment of company-
dominated labor organizations or discrimination against union members,[2]
and the National Labor Relations Act did not become really effective
until its constitutionality was sustained by the Supreme Court on Apr.
12, 1937.[3]   Nevertheless, neither the failure of the legislative enactments
to achieve with complete success the purposes to which the literal import
of their words pointed nor the developing cleavage within the organized-
labor movement prevented substantial revival of unionism during the
four years following 1933;[4] and after the spring of 1937, with the right
of the National Labor Relations Board to restrain antiunion practices
that were decades old definitely established, membership expanded and
trade unions multiplied even more rapidly, while old citadels of the open
shop succumbed to the demand that they bargain collectively.

TRADE-UNION EXPANSION: MEMBERSHIP TRENDS

With the exception of one year (1927), trade-union membership had
declined steadily during the 1920's,[5] and this trend continued, in orthodox
depression pattern, until 1933, when less than 3,000,000 workers were
members of trade unions.[6]   As in previous depressions, craft unions for

[1] Cf. supra, pp. 138–139.

[2] The reasons why Sec. 7 (a) failed to prevent either employer-dominated unions or
discrimination against members of and employee sympathizers with independent unions
are discussed in some detail infra, pp. 194–195, 522–523.   For an account of the operations of the labor boards of the NRA period, see Lewis L. Lorwin and Arthur Wubnig,
Labor Relations Boards (1935).

[3] National Labor Relations Board v. Jones and Laughlin Steel Corp., 301 U. S. 1; National
Labor Relations Board v. Fruehauf Trailer Co., 301 U. S. 49; National Labor Relations
Board v. Friedman-Harry Marks Clothing Co., 301 U. S. 58; Associated Press v. National
Labor Relations Board, 301 U. S. 103; Washington, Virginia, and Maryland Coach Co. v.
National Labor Relations Board, 301 U. S. 142.

[4] Cf. infra, pp. 193–196.

[5] Cf. supra, p. 163.

[6] Professor Wolman's data (Ebb and Flow in Trade Unionism, p. 16) show that total
trade-union membership during each of the years 1929–1933 was as follows: 1929, 3,442,600;
1930, 3,392,800; 1931, 3,358,100; 1932, 3,144,300; 1933, 2,973,000.   The American Federation of Labor paid-up membership during each of these years was: 1929, 2,933,545; 1930,
2,961,096; 1931, 2,889,550; 1932, 2,532,261; 1933, 2,126,796 (Proceedings of the Sixtieth
[1940] Convention, p. 44).

the most part maintained their footholds where they already were entrenched,[1] even while their membership was declining and thousands of the individuals affiliated with them were walking the streets looking for work, but—again as in previous depressions—the trade-union movement as a whole (far from an aggressive or powerful movement, as the previous chapter has indicated, when the prosperity days of the late twenties entered a sudden twilight) found itself relatively ineffective in the face of underlying economic conditions.

Beginning about the middle of 1933, however, the trend reversed itself. Under the impetus of the already mentioned government labor policies, the membership of established unions increased, and the American Federation of Labor, presented with a new opportunity, itself assumed the function of organization in industries or trades where little or no organization had theretofore obtained. Between June and October, 1933, the Federation chartered 584 directly affiliated federal unions with a membership of about 300,000, more than in any comparable period of the Federation's history.[2] In addition, its national and international unions, these same months, chartered 2,953 locals.[3] Total trade-union membership rose from an estimated 2,973,000 in 1933 to an estimated 3,608,600 in 1934,[4] and the reported dues-paying membership of the Federation from 2,126,796 to 2,608,011.[5] The gain during this one year,

---

[1] In 1933 the members of craft unions constituted, it is true, a somewhat smaller percentage of all unionists than they had in 1929, the percentages, according to Professor Wolman's estimates (*ibid.*, p. 92), having been 83 in 1929 and 73 in 1933. The corresponding increase in the importance of industrial unionism in the organized-labor movement as a whole was, however, a result of the "federal labor unions" formed as a temporary expedient under A. F. of L. inspiration and direction during the latter part of 1933 (*cf. infra*, pp. 203–205), and the generalization that until 1933 the established craft unions were the organizations able to withstand at all successfully the impact of depression conditions is correct.

[2] From *Proceedings of the Fifty-third* (1933) *Annual Convention of the American Federation of Labor*, p. 78. *Cf.* also Philip Taft, "Organized Labor and the New Deal" in the Twentieth Century Fund study, *How Collective Bargaining Works*, pp. 5–8.

[3] *Ibid.*

[4] L. Wolman, *op. cit.*, p. 16.

[5] American Federation of Labor, *Proceedings of the Sixtieth* [1940] *Convention*, p. 44. Although the convention reports showed a 1933 average of 2,126,796, the Federation in October, 1933, estimated its total membership, those not paying the per capita tax as well as those who were, at 3,926,798 (*United Mine Workers Journal*, Oct. 15, 1933, p. 9). This claimed membership of October, 1933, was divided as follows: paying per capita tax, 2,526,796; exempt from dues, 100,000; in new international local unions, 500,000; recruits in old international unions, 450,000; recruits in old federal locals, 50,000. This membership, of course, exceeded by nearly 1,300,000 the reported dues-paying membership at the following, 1934, convention. While many of the members of the new federal unions and of the "recruits" claimed in October, 1933, were dues-paying members of locals of national and international unions by October, 1934, when the Fifty-fourth Convention was held, and no excess approaching 1,400,000 (probably an optimistic guess, indeed, for October, 1933) can be added to the paid-up membership reported in 1934, inclusion of those not

in other words, was almost equal to the total loss of the decade 1923–1933.[1] Almost half a million more wage earners were within the fold of the A. F. of L. when the 1935 convention convened, reported membership that year being 3,045,347 in contrast to 2,608,011 in 1934, and total trade-union membership midyear in 1935 probably stood at about 4,400,000, or a gain of more than three-quarters of a million over the 3,608,600 estimated by Professor Wolman for 1934.[2]

This growth was, it is true, held in check by several factors. The partitioning of newly formed federal unions, discussed later[3] together with the policy of the Executive Council in granting new charters, undoubtedly prevented trade-union expansion from proceeding even more rapidly than it did between 1933 and 1935, and after two years of New Deal labor policies total trade-union membership was still substantially below that of the 1920 peak.[4] Concomitant with the growth of independent unionism during these two years went, also, a rapid multiplication of the form of labor organization that was anathema to independent unionism but vastly more congenial to many thousands of entrepreneurs, the company union. As has already been said, Sec. 7 (a) of the National Industrial Recovery Act did not prevent the introduction of employer-dominated labor organizations, with a plant or company basis, and between 1932 and 1935 the number of workers included within such organizations is estimated to have increased from 1,263,194 to about 2,500,000.[5] Company-union membership at the beginning of the latter year was approximately three-fifths as large as that of all independent trade unions.[6] Nevertheless, the trade-union

---

paying dues certainly would have raised the reported 2,608,011 of that year to substantially more than 3,000,000.

[1] *Cf. supra*, p. 163 and pp. 192–193.

[2] The estimate of total membership at midyear of 1935 is derived from the Twentieth Century Fund study, *Labor and the Government* (1935), p. 24, and the *Annual Reports of Labour Organization in Canada* of the Canadian Department of Labour. The former estimated trade-union membership in early 1935 at 4,200,000, but this estimate, unlike Professor Wolman's estimates, which have been used for the earlier years, did not include the membership of Canadian locals. Accordingly, the authors have added the estimate of the Canadian Department of Labour and have made allowance for the increase known to have taken place in trade unionism in the United States between April and midsummer of 1935. Hence the estimate of 4,400,000.

[3] *Cf. infra*, pp. 204–208.

[4] *Cf. supra*, pp. 132–133.

[5] National Industrial Conference Board, *Collective Bargaining through Employee Representation* (1933), p. 16, and Twentieth Century Fund, *Labor and the Government* (1935).

[6] Company unions and employee-representation plans are discussed in detail in Chap. XV of this volume. As indicative of the rapid growth of this form of labor organization during the two-year life of the NRA, it may be mentioned at this point that a study published by the U. S. Bureau of Labor Statistics in 1938 (*Bulletin* 634, "Characteristics of Company Unions"), showed that more than 60 per cent of those in existence in 1935 had been organized between 1933 and that year. They were widespread in the iron and

growth during these two years—a growth achieved in the face of wide-spread even though diminishing unemployment and a growing storm within the house of labor—was little short of phenomenal. Even more significant, perhaps, was the geographical and industrial spread of unionism. Labor organization penetrated localities theretofore regarded as impregnable open-shop strongholds, and striking gains were realized in some of the mass-production industries.[1]

The second half of the 1930's and of the first four years of the 1940's witnessed—partly as a very consequence of the dissension within the labor movement—an increase in total union membership to approximately 13,000,000, a larger percentage of all employees than had been organized in 1920. To an extent, this remarkable growth resulted from an increase in the size of existing unions; to a greater extent it reflected the formation of new unions and their penetration of theretofore unconquered geographical and industrial areas.

Membership of the American Federation of Labor, as reported to the 1936 convention—the convention held shortly after suspension by the Executive Council of the unions that late in 1935 formed the Committee for Industrial Organization[2]—was 3,422,398, a gain of only 377,051 over the preceding year, and between 1936 and 1937—chiefly in consequence of the loss of the unions that had formed the rival national organization—there was a decline for the first time in four years, the reported yearly membership for 1937 being 2,860,933. This loss was, however, much more than offset by the gains of the industrial unions outside the Federation, both the former member unions now in the C.I.O. and new unions formed under its inspiration. Prodded into more vigorous activity by the organizational efforts of the C.I.O., the A. F. of L. assumed leadership —in temporary departure from its old principle of "voluntarism" and its old belief in the necessity of spontaneity—in campaigns to organize the unorganized industries. International unions at the same time increased their organizational staffs, extended their jurisdictions, and received with open arms unskilled and semiskilled workers theretofore

---

steel, chemical, and transportation industries and in "miscellaneous manufactures." It is of significance, also, that while trade-union strength was then concentrated in plants employing fewer than 2,500 workers, the company union was very prevalent among firms employing 2,500 or more (*ibid.*, pp. 37, 48, and 51).

[1] The following examples, compiled by Professor Taft from the *Proceedings* of the Fifty-fourth (1934) A. F. of L. Convention, are indicative of the industrial spread of unionism: In rubber-tire manufacturing, 65 unions were functioning in 1934, almost all of which had been organized since the enactment of the NIRA. In June, 1933, there were no A. F. of L. unions in the automobile industry, but a little more than a year later 106 federal locals were active. Between July, 1933, and the same month of 1934, the number of locals in the aluminum industry increased from 1 to 20, and in the lumber industry (of 21 states and Canada) from 4 to 130. *Cf. How Collective Bargaining Works*, p. 6.

[2] *Cf. infra*, pp. 209-211.

not welcomed. In spite of the business recession that began in 1937, the Federation membership rose to 3,623,000 in 1938; and total trade-union membership that year, as estimated by the National Resources Committee, was about 8,000,000, in contrast to the 1933 figure of less than 3,000,000.[1] With the revival of business in 1939, the expansion continued, and by early 1940 between 8,500,000 and 9,000,000 workers in the United States and Canada[2] were attached to the A.F. of L., the C.I.O., and unaffiliated outside unions. The following year (1941) total membership was about 11,000,000.[3] In addition, perhaps 500,000 to 1,000,000 more workers were in "independent" organizations in fact more closely connected with management than with the organized-labor movement. The total number of wage earners and salaried workers attached to industry in 1940 was about 45,000,000, of whom about 35,000,000 were actually at work. In 1941 nearly 40,000,000 persons were actually at work. During 1942 and 1943 membership continued to increase, and early in 1944 perhaps more than 13,000,000 persons found place in the organized labor movement. Dues-paying membership of the A.F. of L., which had been 4,569,056 (including Canadian membership) on Aug. 31, 1941, rose to 5,482,581 for the same date in 1942, and to 5,939,020 for Aug. 31, 1943.[4] The president of the C.I.O. reported to the November, 1943, convention that dues-paying membership of C.I.O. unions had increased by 1,104,963 (1,135,368 with inclusion of Canadian locals) between August, 1942, and August, 1943.[5] Total membership claimed by the C.I.O. in the autumn of 1943 was 5,285,000.[6] Membership of the labor organizations affiliated with neither the A.F. of L. nor the C.I.O. likewise increased between 1941 and early 1944.

Four characteristics of the growth and expansion of labor organization between 1933 and the first half of the 1940's, as set forth in the immediately foregoing paragraphs, deserve a bit of detailed comment: the decline of independent unionism's rival, the company-dominated organization; the contributions of newly formed organizations, in contrast to those already established, to the aggregate numerical growth; the increasing importance of industrial or quasi-industrial unionism in the movement as a whole; and the extent to which collective bargaining had become established in

[1] National Resources Committee, *The Structure of the American Economy*, Part I, p. 118.

[2] The Canadian membership that year was about 200,000. Labor Research Association, *Labor Notes*, March, 1941, p. 9.

[3] Estimate of the Twentieth Century Fund study of collective bargaining. *Cf. How Collective Bargaining Works*, p. 13.

[4] From *Proceedings* of the Sixty-first, Sixty-second, and Sixty-third Annual Conventions.

[5] *Report of President Philip Murray to Sixth Constitutional Convention of the Congress of Industrial Organizations*, p. 17.

[6] *C.I.O.News*, Nov. 8, 1943, p. 2.

different segments of the American economy as the fifth decade of the century began.

During the period of the NRA, as has already been indicated,[1] employers manifested renewed enthusiasm for company-controlled employee-representation plans and company unions, but the 1937 decisions affirming the constitutionality of the National Labor Relations Act[2] resulted in a distinct curbing of the formation by firms of new company unions. Some of the previously established ones affiliated with regular trade unions during the organizational campaigns of 1937, and changes were effected in the structure and characteristics of others in order to render them compatible with the prohibition of the old (*i.e.*, company-dominated) type of company union embodied in the federal legislation.[3] Disestablishment orders issued by the National Labor Relations Board in the case of numerous plant organizations that it found still to be dominated by, interfered with, or financed by employers[4] produced many reorganizations of such character that the typical "company union" became a membership organization with more or less valid claims to be regarded as an agency for collective bargaining.[5] In 1941, there were perhaps 500,000 to 1,000,000 workers in "independent" organizations of this type. But although shorn of the less-subtle attributes of company domination, and in many cases entirely in accordance with the literal import of the words of the federal legislation, labor organizations of this type were in many cases more closely connected with management than with the organized-labor movement.[6]

With very few exceptions,[7] the majority of established unions grew in size and influence after 1933. Some of the "old" organizations, because of the fact that they already included a fairly large percentage in the trades or industries of their jurisdiction or for other reasons, experienced, it is true, only moderate gains,[8] but the membership of

[1] *Supra*, pp. 192, 194–195.

[2] *Cf. infra*, pp. 523–524.

[3] Section 8 (2) of the National Labor Relations Act: "It shall be an unfair labor practice for an employer to dominate or interfere with the formation or administration of any labor organization or contribute financial or other support to it."

[4] Between 1935 and 1940 approximately 340 company unions were ordered to be disestablished.

[5] *Cf.* Chap. XV.

[6] For this reason, the membership of these independents has not been included in the foregoing estimates of total trade-union membership.

[7] The Wood Carvers, the Metal Engravers, the Sleeping Car Conductors, the Rural Letter Carriers, the Plasterers, and the Stone Cutters suffered some membership loss during the post-1933 period (*cf. How Collective Bargaining Works*, p. 15). The majority of the unions in this group occupy only a minor place in the labor movement.

[8] Professor Taft (*ibid.*) cites as examples the Brotherhood of Railway Carmen, the Photo Engravers' Union, the pressmen's unions, the International Typographical Union, the Sheet Metal Workers' Union, and the National Federation of Post Office Clerks.

others doubled, quadrupled, and in at least three cases increased sixfold or more.[1]   More significant as a manifestation of the spread of organization consciousness among the American workers was the appearance of new unions in theretofore unorganized or almost unorganized industries and trades.   In the mass-production industries, like iron and steel, motor car production, electrical and radio manufacturing, and aluminum production, hundreds of thousands of workers were drawn into strong industrial unions.   Whereas there had been little effective labor organization in the iron and steel industry for years prior to 1933,[2] the Steel Workers Organizing Committee of the C.I.O. claimed in the summer of 1941 to have a membership of about 600,000, although the number paying dues was probably about 350,000; and among other new unions were the Automobile Workers with a claimed 600,000 in 1941, the United Electrical, Radio and Machine Workers, with a claimed membership of 300,000, the Rubber Workers, with 57,500 claimed members, the Aluminum Workers, with 31,000, the Glass, Ceramic, and Silica Sand Workers, with 22,500, the American Newspaper Guild, with 19,000, and the Cannery, Agricultural, Packing and Allied Workers, with more than 100,000. Approximately 60 per cent of the total increase in union membership recorded earlier in this section of the chapter[3] was a consequence of the growth of existing unions rather than of the appearance and expansion of the new organizations, but the latter, bringing within the labor movement hundreds of thousands of employees in sectors of the American economy theretofore regarded as immune to unionism, was probably more significant and striking.

A third of the characteristics of trade-union development during the years with which this chapter is concerned was the increasing importance of the industrial or quasi-industrial, as contrasted to the craft or compound-craft, form of organization.   Industrial unions, as has already been indicated, included only about 17 per cent of the organized workers in 1929, 27 per cent in 1933, and 33 per cent in 1934.[4]   Both the estab-

---

[1] For example, Professor Taft has estimated (*ibid.*, pp. 15–16) that the membership of the United Mine Workers increased from 300,000 to 600,000 between 1933 and 1942, that of the Amalgamated Clothing Workers from 125,000 to 275,000, that of the Brotherhood of Electrical Workers from 94,000 to 201,000, that of the Machinists from 65,000 to 222,000, that of the Bakery Workers fivefold (to 84,000 in 1942), and that of the Teamsters sixfold (to 400,000 in 1942).   During this period the membership of the Meat Cutters and Butcher Workmen increased from 11,000 to 85,000 or eightfold, and that of the Hotel and Restaurant Employees from 23,000 to 214,000, or ninefold.   The estimates are based chiefly upon the 1942 *Report* of the Executive Council of the A.F. of L.

[2] In the early years of the depression of the 1930's the old Amalgamated Association of Iron, Steel, and Tin Workers probably had a dues-paying membership of not more than 5,000.   Previous unsuccessful attempts to organize the steelworkers are discussed in an earlier chapter (*cf. supra*, pp. 145–146).

[3] *Supra*, pp. 192–196.

[4] The data are from Professor Wolman's *Ebb and Flow in Trade Unionism*, p. 92.

lishment of new unions, predominantly with an industrial or near-industrial basis, and the extension of the jurisdictions of established ones during the second half of the 1930's changed these percentages markedly. In early 1940 the Congress of Industrial Organizations, which had its inception in the demand for the industrial form of organization, included, as has already been said, some 3,500,000 workers, in contrast to the Federation's more than 4,000,000. While some of the member unions of the C.I.O. have not claimed jurisdiction over entire industries, the membership attained by this organization during only five years of existence is indicative of the rapidity of the increase in the proportion that industrial unionists constituted of all unionists. Also, established unions, both within and without the A.F. of L., extended their jurisdictions to related trades and industries or to the unskilled and semiskilled workers, their structural arrangements in consequence partaking less of those of craft or compound-craft unions and more of those of industrial unions.[1] While definitional questions are entangled with attempts to measure with quantitative precision the relative strength of craft or compound-craft unionism, on the one hand, and industrial unionism, on the other, the estimate is warranted that during the early 1940's more than 50 per cent of the nation's organized workers, in contrast to less than one-fifth in 1929, were affiliated with unions more accurately to be characterized as industrial or quasi-industrial than as craft or compound craft.

Finally, this summary of the growth and expansion of trade unionism during the period with which the chapter is concerned should include mention of the proportion of the workers covered by collective agreements among the various industries. The advance of collective bargaining, implied in the preceding account of membership trends and of the penetration of unionism into theretofore unorganized industries and geographical areas, was without doubt one of the major developments in the American economy of the 1930's. In contrast to the situation of the 1920's, where it has been confined largely to the building, printing, and

---

[1] As examples of the greater inclusiveness of long-established unions, Professor Taft (op. cit., p. 16) cites the following facts: Almost half of the membership of the Amalgamated Clothing Workers (a C.I.O. union) in the early 1940's was composed of journeymen tailors and shirt, neckwear, laundry, and cleaning and dyeing workers, whereas the membership of these groups in the Amalgamated before 1933 had been practically negligible; the Brotherhood of Electrical Workers, the membership of which prior to 1933 had been composed largely of electricians in the railroad and construction industries, after 1933 included employees of powerhouses and electrical manufacturing plants, some 105,000 of the union's 203,000 members being attached to the latter two industries in November, 1939; the Flint Glass Workers' Union received numerous unskilled "miscellaneous" workers; the Machinists began organization of workers in the aircraft industry on an industrial basis; and the Bakery Workers after 1936 began to seek bargaining rights in mechanized bread and cracker bakeries.

needle trades, coal mining, the railroads, and a comparatively small
number of other industries, collective bargaining obtained to some extent
in 1943 in almost every branch of industry.   More than 90 per cent of the
employees in such important industries or trades as railroads, longshore
work, acting on the legitimate stage, motion-picture operation, stagehand
work, coal mining, granite cutting, brewing, mechanical work in newspaper establishments, the fur trades, men's clothing, diamond cutting,
glass-container manufacture, and the flat-glass industry are estimated[1] to
have been covered by collective agreements that year; between three-
fourths and nine-tenths of the workers in aluminum production, the
automobile industry, the manufacture of caps and cloth hats, and the
women's clothing industry were working under the terms of collective
agreements;[2] more than 55 but less than 75 per cent of those employed
in intercity bus transportation, ship personnel work in salt-water transportation, urban transportation, building construction, meat packing,
electrical manufacturing, iron and steel, printing and publishing, hosiery
manufacture, neckwear, shirts, nightwear, and bathrobe production,
cooperage, and the flint glass industry had their terms and conditions of
employment determined by collective bargaining;[2] and about half (more
than 45 but less than 55 per cent) of the persons employed in quarrying,
flour milling and cereal manufacture, shipbuilding, bookbinding, litho-
graphing, and hat manufacture, or as airline pilots, were covered by
agreements negotiated by representatives of their own choosing.[2]   In
such industries as cement, laundry service, metal mining, baking, fishing,
aircraft production, farm-equipment manufacture, machine tools, paper
and pulp, boots and shoes, hat and cap materials, textiles, and die casting,
appreciable proportions (between 25 and 45 per cent) of the working
personnel came under collective agreements.   Less than one-fourth of
the employees in trucking, building service, hotels and restaurants,
mercantile establishments, the lime and gypsum industry, cigar
making, newspaper editorial and commercial employment, glove manufacture, chemicals, furniture manufacture, leather tanneries, lumber, and
petroleum refining were estimated to be covered by collective agreements
in 1941.[2]   Moreover, a number of strong craft unions had agreements
determining the remuneration and working conditions of a large number,
and in some cases practically all, the craftsmen within their respective
jurisdictions in industries that otherwise were poorly or only moderately
organized.   While the extent to which the agreements incorporated the
closed-shop arrangement and other mechanisms of job control that
business unionists usually seek to secure varied greatly from industry to

[1] Estimates of Philip Taft in *How Collective Bargaining Works*, pp. 18–22.
[2] *Ibid.*

industry, and also within given industries,[1] the advance of collective
bargaining on almost all industrial fronts is patent from the facts just
summarized. It was an advance characterized, also, by a spread of
unionism from the urban centers—for long a more hospitable habitat—
into the middle-sized and small manufacturing communities,[2] and by a
distinct tendency toward coverage by the collective agreements of a
wider geographical area.[3]

THE PROBLEM OF STRUCTURE: LABOR'S CIVIL WAR

During the second half of the 1930's, the organized-labor movement
of the United States was split asunder, and a civil war comparable in
bitterness to, although different in character from, that of the 1880's
accompanied—and indeed was in part responsible for—the unprecedented
growth and expansion that have been traced in the immediately preceding pages. Immediately induced by a conjunction of circumstances,
some of them almost fortuitous in character, peculiar to the years of the
depression and of the New Deal labor policies, the formation in 1935 of
the Committee for Industrial Organization, which three years later
reconstituted itself as a permanent organization rivaling the American
Federation of Labor, was in fact a consequence of conditions and developments some of which had been long in the making: technological, economic, and market trends that rendered the policies and anatomical
characteristics of federated trade unionism insufficient to effect the
inclusion of millions of semiskilled operatives; the impact of craft-union
unwillingness to relinquish jurisdictional "rights" in the mass-production
industries upon the organizational possibilities created by the govern-

---

[1] For the most part, the status of the unions in the various industries depended upon
the age of the organizations and the time collective bargaining had been in effect. Newly
organized unions almost always experience difficulty in obtaining the closed shop from
employers traditionally opposed to unionism. In the early 1940's the closed shop was most
prevalent in building construction, coal mining, the printing trades, men's and women's
clothing, and other industries where collective bargaining had long been the accepted mode
of industrial relations. In such industries as automobiles, rubber, and iron and steel, on
the other hand, the agreements generally granted exclusive bargaining rights to the recognized unions but did not provide for the closed shop. A relatively small proportion of the
agreements with newly formed labor organizations provided that the unions should bargain
for their own members only.

[2] As is pointed out in an earlier chapter (*cf. supra*, p. 86), the growth of unionism during the few years prior to 1904 was characterized by penetration of the less-urban regions
of the country, but after that year the number of organizations and total membership in
the towns and smaller cities dropped. During the three decades following 1904 no marked
tendency of unionism to gain a foothold in the less-urban centers manifested itself, except
temporarily during the War period, until the 1930's. The seeming inability of labor
organization to establish itself in the smaller places was, of course, one of the factors inducing migration of plants to such places during the 1920's.

[3] Although the local agreement, negotiated with single employers or local associations of
employers, still remained the most common type in the first half of the 1940's.

ment's labor policies and other circumstances discussed earlier in this chapter;[1] the character of the labor supply in both the organized and the unorganized sectors of American industry; dissatisfaction in the ranks of federated trade unionism with the policies and economic creed of those who had inherited the traditions and the ideologies of the founding fathers of the A. F. of L.; personal animosities and jealousies and tenacious adherence to vested interests; and still others. A brief prefatory mention of some of these background conditions, circumstances, and factors is in point.

Not much more than one-tenth of the nation's nonagricultural employees, it will be recalled,[2] were organized in 1930. Adherence by the A. F. of L. to the principle of "voluntarism"—the principle that the propulsive force for organization must come from the workers themselves, not be superimposed upon them by a federated or centralized organization—had seemingly justified itself, to be sure, from the point of view of the minority of skilled workers who were affiliated in strong craft organizations, particularly when applied in conjunction with trade councils, departments, and other quasi-industrial federations; but in the great unorganized sectors of industry, where large aggregations of capital rather than small industrial units frequently obtained and where the absence or weakness of capacity for self-organization on the part of the workers necessitated centralized direction of organizing campaigns, "voluntarism" and quasi-industrial federation proved insufficient to achieve realization of the opportunity afforded during and immediately after 1933. As a central body of autonomous unions, never having as its primary function the assumption of general responsibility for labor's organizing efforts,[3] the Federation lacked the equipment and the personnel for the organization campaign to which the Recovery Act and the new vitalization of American labor invited it; the craft and compound-craft member unions were not prepared to relinquish their jurisdictional rights in the mass-production industries, even though their memberships there were frequently of negligible size; and some of the leaders of the internationals were reluctant to risk defense funds in an effort to organize those who had seemed to them in the past to be indifferent to unionism's appeal. Only by the rendering of much more assistance than it had been in the habit of rendering and by the granting of unrestricted industrial charters, however, could the federated labor movement reasonably hope for speedy inclusion within its ranks of millions theretofore unorganized.

[1] *Cf. supra*, pp. 188–192.

[2] To be exact, 10.1 per cent, according to Professor Wolman's estimates. *Cf. supra*, p. 165.

[3] There had, of course, been instances, such as the automobile and textile-industry campaigns of the 1920's, when the Federation assumed general responsibility for organizing workers in particular industries. *Cf. supra*, pp. 173–178.

The semiskilled production workers were to a great extent unacquainted with the gospel of unionism, and they were prone to be company-conscious or plant-conscious rather than craft- or class-conscious; the self-organization disposition that needed nurture and direction from the general labor movement was a disposition to organize on the industrial basis, not because such employees possessed a knowledge of the history of the labor movement or a philosophy of its development but merely because for them it was the natural thing to do.[1]   The problem confronting the general labor movement was patently one of extreme difficulty: how to organize the workers in industries almost entirely untouched by unionism into the most suitable type of organization without encroaching upon the jurisdictions already claimed by, and conceded to, the national and international affiliates.   It was the failure of the A. F. of L. to solve this problem, more than anything else, that led to the civil war within the ranks of labor and to formation of a rival national organization.

The necessity of readjusting old policies and adopting—at least for a time—somewhat different methods was, however, clearly recognized. At its 1933 convention, the Federation authorized a conference of the various national and international unions for the purpose of devising a method of organizing the unorganized wage earners of the nation, and this conference, held in January, 1934, endorsed the strategy of establishing within each plant where organization had already developed,[2] or where the organizers were successful in establishing unions, local "federal unions," directly affiliated with the A. F. of L.[3]   But the ques-

---

[1] *Cf.* Philip Taft, "The Problem of Structure in American Unionism," *American Economic Review*, vol. 27 (March, 1937), pp. 11–21, and David Saposs, "The A. F. of L. and the C.I.O." in *Collective Bargaining for Today and Tomorrow*, pp. 16–24.   In addition to the fact that the contact with unionism of many of the production workers in the mass industries had been slight, the tendency to follow as guides their old company-union plans was another factor conductive to a disposition to organize on the plant (*i.e.*, industrial-union local unit) basis.

[2] An organizing movement was, in fact, under way before Sec. 7 (*a*) of the National Industrial Recovery Act became the law of the United States.   In the automobile industry the workers manifested disposition to organize into independent unions, and the United Automobile, Aircraft, and Vehicle Workers Union, an organization that had been expelled from the A. F. of L. because of its refusal to relinquish its claims to all workers in the industry, made some headway.   The A. F. of L. played little or no part in creating union sentiment during these early struggles in the automobile industry (*cf.* Philip Taft, *ibid.*, pp. 6–8). Also, some of the trade-union leaders had become aware of the organization impetus that would follow enactment of the NIRA and had laid the groundwork for organization drives. John L. Lewis brought together in Washington a staff of former United Mine Worker organizers.   By the time of the enactment of the Recovery Act and its Sec. 7 (*a*) (June, 1933), the organizing work of these men was well under way.

[3] "Local trade and federal labor unions," directly affiliated with the A. F. of L., had often been established in the past, of course, and the practice of establishing them afforded an organizational model that the Federation was able to follow in organizing immediately on the plant basis.   In the past, however, expectation had been that members of the directly

tion of whether these new federal locals would ultimately be brought together in national or international industrial unions, or whether the craftsmen within them would eventually find place in local units of the craft-union affiliates was not settled by the January, 1934, conference. Instead, the need to organize promptly was emphasized and the question of ultimate forms was avoided, albeit in language that appeared to be satisfactory to the craft unionists. "The paramount issue," affirmed the conference, "is not what particular form of organization shall be followed in this emergency and this unusual situation. The demand of the moment is to promote organization in whatever form or method is best designed to rally the wage earners to the cause of Organized Labor, bearing in mind that in pursuit of organization the present structure, rights and interests of affiliated National and International Unions must be followed, observed, and safeguarded."[1] No definite stand was taken, in other words, upon the crucial question of whether the craft unions were to surrender their jurisdictional claims.[2]

In consequence of the policy of establishing plant units as the best means of "taking immediate advantage of the situation," the number of

---

affiliated federal unions would before a great while find place in either existent nationals or in new national unions formed when the number of federal locals was large enough to warrant formation of a national union.

[1] The entire report of this conference is to be found in vol. 41 (February, 1934) of the *American Federationist*, pp. 138–140; *cf.* also American Federation of Labor, *Proceedings*, 1934, p. 41. To summarize in more detail the recommendations of this conference, they were, in addition to the general principle stated above: (1) "That the work of organizing by and through the national and international unions, supplemented by that of the American Federation of Labor through federal and local trade unions, proceed with increased vigor and determination; that the fullest possible latitude be exercised by the Executive Council in the granting of federal charters; and that where or whenever temporary infraction of the rights of national or international unions may be involved . . . the Executive Council adjust such difficulties in the spirit of taking full advantage of the immediate situation and with the ultimate recognition of the rights of all concerned." (2) That the Executive Council through the officers of the Federation arrange conferences among all concerned in the organization work—the Federation's organizers, the heads of the national and international unions, and officers of established federal unions—"for the purpose of creating complete understanding and harmony among those charged with organization work, to be followed in methods of promoting organization so as to avoid or lessen unnecessary friction, conflict, or limitations due to varying financial requirements of different national and international organizations and forms and character of organizations being promoted." (3) That periodic conferences be called by officers of the Federation to review progress, reconcile differences, and in general to further organizational endeavors. (4) That the Federation arrange for "mass meetings throughout the land" and in other ways supervise the public-relations aspect of the organizing campaign. It was in accordance with the purport of this report, as construed by the Executive Council, that a National Council of Automobile Workers, representing more than 150 federal locals, was organized in June, 1934.

[2] Obviously, "in the spirit of taking full advantage of the immediate situation" could

federal unions directly affiliated with the American Federation increased from 673 in 1933[1] to 1,788 in 1934;[2] and the majority of the members of these organizations unquestionably regarded themselves as industrial unionists whose locals would ultimately be affiliated with each other in permanent national industrial unions. The industrial-union faction within the Federation's established unions, also, while willing that the jurisdiction of craft unions be maintained, where already established, insisted that the mass-production industries be permanently recognized as the sphere of industrial organizations, with no subsequent "feeding" of the skilled craftsmen into locals of established craft or compound-craft internationals. But the craft unions began to assert their jurisdictional claims to workers in the newly organized plant unions; the fact that their efforts to bring within the fold such craftsmen in the past had frequently been of little more than nominal character deterred them not a bit from asserting claim to such workers once a considerable number of them had been included within the new plant-basis organizations. Nor, from their own point of view, was the position taken devoid of reason, for once craft-union jurisdictions were infringed upon, industrial unions might demand more and more, become voracious in their demands after having once experienced the thrill of organizational success.[3] Lack of uniformity in concrete application of the January, 1934, conference report inhibited not a little, in ways discussed in more detail shortly, the organizing efforts, and industrial unionists became increasingly critical of the tenderness with which craft-union interests were, from their point of view, being treated and of the failure, as they regarded it, of the Federation to press its organization work as vigorously as it might have done. When the 1934 convention of the A. F. of L. convened in San Francisco, in October of that year, an indication of the dissatisfaction and rising feeling was to be found in the introduction of fourteen resolutions on the

---

hardly be interpreted other than an expression of the policy of initial organization upon the industrial basis, but "with ultimate recognition of the rights of all concerned" was susceptible to different interpretations.

[1] American Federation of Labor, *Proceedings*, 1933, p. 34.

[2] American Federation of Labor, *Proceedings*, 1934, p. 33.

[3] There were other reasons why the craft unions were insistent upon recognition of their jurisdictional rights to newly organized workers within the federal locals.   They were aware that the unconquered areas lying ahead of industrial unionism were more extensive than those before craft unionism.   Give the industrial unions all the workers in the mass industries, the craft unionists reasoned, and ultimately they would be the dominant factor in the organized-labor movement.   Inevitably this would mean less emphasis upon, and less support for, the revered craft-union instruments of job control.   Also, craft unions are almost always prone to fear that any relinquishment of a traditional interest or right constitutes an ultimate undermining of their economic strength, even though the relinquishment be where the assertion of the interest or right has been of little economic effectiveness in the past.

subject of industrial unionism[1] and in the bitterness with which the Executive Council's policy during the latter part of 1933 and the first eight months of 1934 was debated.[2]

A compromise resolution finally adopted by this convention (a) reiterated the doctrine of craft interests,[3] (b) conceded, however, the need of a new basis of organization in some segments of industry,[4] (c) directed the Executive Council to issue charters for national unions in the automotive, cement, aluminum, "and such other mass-production and miscellaneous industries as in the judgment of the Executive Council may be necessary to meet the situation" and to inaugurate a campaign to organize the iron and steel industry "at the earliest practical date," and (d) declared that in order to protect and safeguard the interests of members of the newly chartered national and international unions, the American Federation should provisionally direct the policies, administer the business, and designate the administrative and financial officers of such organizations. The susceptibility of this resolution to different interpretations is patent; indeed, the convention debate upon it makes clear that members of the two factions were constrained—or determined —to construe it in accordance with their respective views on the question of industrial unionism and the jurisdictional claims of craft unions.[5] To the craft unionists the reiteration of the doctrine of craft interests meant, so they said, that they had been guaranteed jurisdiction over those skilled mechanics whom they had always claimed as "belonging" to them, that at most they had been asked to hold in abeyance for a little time their demands that eligible workers organized in consequence of the campaign be turned over to them.[6] Industrial unionists, on the other

[1] For the texts of these fourteen resolutions, see American Federation of Labor, *Proceedings*, 1934, pp. 581–582.

[2] *Cf.* the stenographic report of the running debate at this convention, *ibid.*, pp. 587–597.

[3] "We consider it our duty to formulate a policy which will fully protect the jurisdictional rights of all trade unions organized upon craft lines and afford every opportunity for development and accession of those workers engaged upon work over which these organizations exercise jurisdiction. Experience has shown that craft organization is most effective in protecting the welfare and advancing the interests of workers where the nature of the industry is such that the lines of demarcation between crafts are distinguishable." *Ibid.*, pp. 586–587.

[4] "However, it is realized that in many of the industries in which thousands of workers are employed a new condition exists requiring organization upon a different basis to be most effective." *Ibid.*, p. 587.

[5] *Cf.* the colloquy between Delegate Wharton of the Machinists and Delegate Lewis of the United Mine Workers on pp. 589 and 590 of the 1934 *Proceedings* and the remarks of Delegate Woll of the Photo Engravers and Delegate Franklin of the Boilermakers and Iron Shipbuilders, *ibid.*, pp. 533 and 534.

[6] The literal import of the words of the resolution would indicate that the craft unionists were making quite a liberal interpretation when they took this position. While the blessing bestowed upon the principle of craft unionism and the reference to affording "every opportunity for development and accession of those workers engaged upon work over which these

hand—both during the convention and eleven months thereafter—construed the resolution as an endorsement of the principle of industrial unionism in the mass-production and miscellaneous industries.[1] Each side was, of course, aware that the resolution was in the last analysis a compromise—an attempt to produce something palatable enough to all to avoid any immediate cleavage within the Federation, while the time-honored method of delay helped in the working out of the problem. But neither side would recede from the substance of its position, and the alleged ignoring by the Executive Council of the spirit and letter of the resolution was the immediate cause of the formation by the advocates of unrestricted industrial unionism in the mass-production industries, one year later, of the Committee for Industrial Organization.

As the organization campaign appeared to lose some of its momentum during the eleven months following the San Francisco (1934) convention, and as indications that the craft-unionist interpretation of the resolution there adopted would be given operative effect in many cases,[2] the proponents of the policy of granting unrestricted industrial-union charters to the new organizations formed on the plant basis became increasingly restive. They pointed out—exaggerating somewhat the extent to which parceling out was actually practiced—that not a few federal unions were disbanded or were suspended for failing to comply with A.F. of L. rulings,

---

organizations exercise jurisdiction" can be construed, when lifted from their context, as a blanket endorsement of all craft-union jurisdictional claims, the immediately following sentence of the resolution quoted in an earlier footnote allocated these virtues of craft unionism to those industries "where the nature of the industry is such that the lines of demarcation between crafts are distinguishable." On the other hand, the craft unionists were able to say that "lines of demarcation" between the minority of workers in an industry who belonged to the various crafts and the production workers were "distinguishable."

[1] The industrial unionists could, of course, point to the declaration that "in many of the industries in which thousands of workers are employed a condition exists requiring organization upon a different basis to be most effective" as indicating that literal interpretation and corresponding application of the resolution involved relinquishment by the craftsmen of their claims in the automotive, cement, aluminum, and other mass-production industries. This point of view was set forth on the convention floor by Charles P. Howard of the International Typographical Union, the probable drafter of the resolution as finally adopted by the convention. Conciliatory toward the craftsmen as were Mr. Howard's remarks on this occasion, the only losses against which he assured them, in the event of the passage of the resolution, were losses in "membership," not in their claims to workers then members of federal unions organized on a plant basis.

[2] Evidence of the extent to which the claims of the craft unionists were recognized is to be found in the decrease in the number of federal unions chartered by the Federation. The number of such organizations declined from 1,788 in 1934 to 1,354 in 1935, and 941 in 1936 (American Federation of Labor, *Proceedings*, 1934, p. 33; *ibid.*, 1935, p. 31; *ibid.*, 1936, p. 43). This decline reflected in no little part the dismembering of these unions and allotment of their members to locals of the national craft unions. It also reflected, in part, the mortality rate among federal unions consequent upon the removal of the stronger, though numerically the minority, elements.

that the "raids" of the craft unions left within the federal units only those who in the past had been most unorganizable,[1] that enthusiasm of newly organized plant—or company-conscious workers for unionism rapidly evaporated when they were told that they "belonged" in other organizations for reasons that their unfamiliarity with unionism rendered unintelligible to them, that the union gains of 1933 and 1934 were fast being destroyed,[2] and that too little was being accomplished in organizing the industries that were the objects of primary attack. Enraged because of what it professed to regard as a brazen flounting of the spirit and intent of the 1934 resolution—"a breach of faith and a travesty upon good conscience"[3]—and disheartened because of what it characterized as the Federation's failure to take full advantage of the opportunity to organize the former open-shop strongholds, the industrial-union faction introduced resolutions of protest at the Atlantic City convention of 1935, these protests crystallizing in the report submitted by a minority of the Committee on Resolutions.[4]

"In the great mass-production industries," this report declared, "and in those in which the workers are composite mechanics, specialized and engaged upon classes of work which do not qualify them for craft-union membership, industrial organization is the only solution. . . . It is not the intention of this declaration of policy to permit the taking away from the National or International craft unions of any part of their present membership or potential membership in establishments where the dominant factor is skilled craftsmen coming under a proper definition of the jurisdiction of such National or International unions. However, it is the declared purpose to provide for the organization of workers in mass production and other industries upon industrial and plant lines,

[1] The position of the craft-union leadership and of the majority of the Executive Council of the A. F. of L. was that the production workers (the semiskilled and unskilled who did not find place in any craft) were to be organized on the industrial basis. But this involved no concession on the part of the craft unions; there was not—and never had been—any question that the industrial form of organization was the appropriate one for such workers.

[2] Not all the failure of unionism to expand as might have been expected during the year 1934–1935 should, however, be attributed to the backwardness of craft-union organizing tactics and adherence to theories and policies of union organization that were outmoded in the newer industries. The new federal unions were not well equipped to meet the situations confronting them. They lacked leadership, contact with other unions, and the cohesiveness of older and longer-established groups. But the partitioning of the memberships did not lessen, but on the contrary accentuated, these elements of weakness. The failure of the National Recovery Administration to afford anticipated protection to newly organized groups was another factor responsible for the failure of unionism to grow more rapidly during this year.

[3] Words of John L. Lewis during the debate on the "minority report" at the 1935 convention of the A. F. of L. See *Proceedings*, 1935, pp. 512–575, for stenographic report of the entire debate.

[4] Charles P. Howard, David Dubinsky, Frank B. Powers, John L. Lewis, A. A. Myrup, and J. C. Lewis.

regardless of claims based upon the question of jurisdiction."[1] After prolonged and bitter debate, this declaration of policy[2] was rejected by the convention by a vote of 18,024 to 10,933,[3] and a majority report sustaining the position taken by the Executive Council during the preceding year and endorsing the policy of leaving production employees within the industrial unions but "protecting ultimately" the rights and jurisdictions embodied in the charters of the national and international unions became the expressed declaration of the Federation.[4] Industrial unionism had been rejected.

Acceptance of this decision by the industrial unionists hardly lay within the realm of the probable.[5] Even before adjournment of the

[1] Complete text of the "minority report" is to be found in the 1935 *Proceedings* of the Federation, pp. 523–525.

[2] The report also called for an aggressive organization campaign in those industries in which the great majority of workers were not organized and instructed the Executive Council to issue unrestricted charters to workers organized into independent unions, company-dominated unions, and "those organizations now affiliated with associations not recognized by the American Federation of Labor to be bona fide labor organizations."

[3] *Proceedings*, 1935, pp. 574–575. The craft-union domination of the Federation and the constitutional provisions in respect to voting, whereby the smaller unions had more votes in relation to their memberships than did the larger ones, made probable from the outset of the rejection of the industrial-union report, but the vote polled for the policy of organization on the industrial basis in the mass-production and other described industries regardless of jurisdictional claims (10,933 out of 29,957) was indicative of the extent to which resentment against the Executive Council's policies in its application of the 1934 resolution had developed.

[4] The report of the majority of the Committee on Resolutions, introduced by John P. Frey of the Metal Trades Department, declared that those taking the position that the spirit and intent of the 1934 resolution had been perverted by Executive Council policies "either misunderstood the declaration adopted last year . . . or desire that the policy established in that declaration be set aside and existing international unions [be] merged into industrial organizations organized for the several industries"; interpreted the San Francisco declaration as calling for ultimate recognition of the jurisdictional claims of craft unions, with the production workers being left in industrial unions; and reiterated the doctrine that to its craft-union basis was to be attributed the strength of the American labor movement.

[5] Nearly four years later (in the summer of 1939), Matthew Woll of the Executive Council declared that if the two sides (*i.e.*, the industrial unionists and the craft unionists on the Committee on Resolutions) had conferred with each other (presumably after the drafting of their antithetical reports) "they might have modified their respective reports and have presented a unanimous report." He also then observed that the minority "and perhaps the majority" were at fault at the Atlantic City (1935) convention (from an address of Mr. Woll at the 1939 convention of the United Hatters, Cap and Millinery Workers International Union of America, published in *The Hat Worker* of June 15, 1939). In view of the fact that the point at issue was whether the craft unions would or would not relinquish their jurisdictional claims in the mass industries—a point concerning which it is hard to imagine a workable compromise—however, the conclusion seems inescapable that a "unanimous report" would have had to be another 1934 document, couched in ambiguities that each side could interpret as it chose. Executive Council policy during 1935–1936 would then, in all probability, have been much what it was during 1934–1935.

1935 convention, an informal conference of the leaders of the cause of industrial unionism, just defeated on the convention floor, was held "for the purpose of discussing the advisability of keeping unions favoring the industrial form of organization for the mass production industries in contact with each other and cementing their forces for future AFL conventions,"[1] and at a second conference, held shortly thereafter (Nov. 10, 1935) by the officers of eight unions representing approximately 940,000 members, there was formed the Committee for Industrial Organization, a body the mission of which was the promotion of industrial organization in the mass-production industries and elsewhere. The original members of the Committee were the heads of the United Mine Workers of America, the Amalgamated Clothing Workers of America, the International Typographical Union,[2] the United Textile Workers, the United Hatters, Cap and Millinery Workers of America,[3] the International Union of Mine, Mill, and Smelter Workers,[4] the International Ladies' Garment Workers, and the Oil Field, Gas Well, and Refinery Workers. These eight were shortly joined by the Federation of Flat Glass Workers, the Amalgamated Association of Iron, Steel, and Tin Workers, the United Automobile Workers of America, and the United Rubber Workers of America, and then a little later by the United Electrical and Radio Workers and the International Union of Marine and Shipyard Workers.[5]

[1] International Ladies' Garment Workers' Union, *The Position of the International Ladies' Garment Workers' Union in Relation to CIO and AFL, 1934–1938, Chronicled in Documents and Records* (1938), pp. 12–13. Those participating in this conference were John L. Lewis, Charles P. Howard, Sidney Hillman, and David Dubinsky.

[2] The status of the International Typographical Union differed from that of the other unions, in that its connection consisted only of the fact that its president, Charles P. Howard, was a member. It is true that originally the C.I.O. was merely a more-or-less informal "junta" of heads of the international unions, but so far as those other than the International Typographical were concerned it rapidly became more than this; it became an affiliation of the unions themselves, with exception of the Typographical.

[3] Strictly speaking, only the Cap and Millinery department of the United Hatters, Cap and Millinery Workers of America was affiliated with the C.I.O., and for this reason (and also for reasons of diplomacy, tactics, and strategy) the United Hatters, Cap and Millinery Workers of America was not suspended when the other members of the C.I.O. were in September, 1936.

[4] See *supra*, pp. 116–118, for the earlier history of the International Union of Mine, Mill and Smelter Workers and its connection with the I.W.W.

[5] The electrical equipment and radio workers had been refused an independent charter by the A.F. of L., and consequently affiliated with the C.I.O. The automobile workers had been dissatisfied with the charter granted them by the A.F. of L., since it gave the craft unions the right to claim the men whose work fell within craft-union jurisdictional claims in the automobile industry. The fact that the Executive Council of the Federation had appointed the officers of the United Automobile Workers and had refused complete autonomy to the union was another cause of dissatisfaction with the A.F. of L. It should be noted, however, that the appointment of officers and the administration of financial and other affairs was in accordance with the instructions to the Executive Council of the 1935 resolution.

With the formation of this Committee, the industrial unionists had taken matters into their own hands.[1]

The effort was, however, to be made within the framework of the American Federation of Labor, according to the originally professed purposes, and the tactics were to be propagandistic and advisory in character; the Committee for Industrial Organization was not a "dual" movement. But since the Executive Council—inhibited by the craft-union predilections of those who controlled it—was unable or unwilling to organize the workers of the mass and miscellaneous industries on the only workable basis, the industrial form, efforts to achieve this end must come from elsewhere within the Federation. When the rank and file of the membership of the federated trade-union movement had become convinced of the logic and expediency of the 1935 minority report, they would relinquish the jurisdictional claims that were serving to prevent organization of millions of unorganized, and structural modifications of the A. F. of L. would follow. Two paragraphs from the program formulated at the conference of Nov. 10, 1935, epitomize the Committee's professed position:

"The purpose of the Committee is to be encouragement and promotion of organization of the unorganized workers in the mass production and other industries upon an industrial basis, as outlined in the minority report of the Resolutions Committee submitted to the convention of the American Federation of Labor at Atlantic City; to foster recognition and acceptance of collective bargaining in such industries; to counsel and advise unorganized and newly organized groups of workers; to bring them under the banner and in affiliation with the American Federation of Labor.

"The attitude of members of the Committee as unanimously expressed was that its work would be to make organization efforts more effective, avoid injury to established National and International and Federal Labor Unions, and modernize the organization policies of the American Federation of Labor to meet the requirements of workers under modern industrial conditions."[2]

To the leadership of the A. F. of L., however, the formation of the Committee constituted disregard of a decision "democratically arrived at," and as such was dualism and rebellion. The professed limitation of functions to the "educational and advisory" area was regarded, by at least some of the trade-union leaders, with skepticism,[3] and the program

---

[1] Two weeks after the November 10 meeting at which the C.I.O. was formed, John L. Lewis resigned as vice-president of the A.F. of L., an office to which he had been elected at the Atlantic City convention.

[2] International Ladies' Garment Workers' Union, *op. cit.*, p. 13.

[3] Inevitably, the question of the good faith of the original statement that the Committee intended to work within the framework of the Federation of Labor in an educational

of "encouragement and promotion" of organization was taken as a threat actively to engage in organization efforts in competition with the established unions—as, in other words, that cardinal sin in the American labor movement, dualism.[1] In letters to the leaders of the movement President Green expressed his "feeling of apprehension over the grave consequences of the formation of an organization within the American Federation, even though it might be claimed that said organization was formed for the achievement of a laudable purpose,"[2] and called for dissolution of the Committee. Shortly thereafter (January, 1936) the Executive Council expressed apprehension over the outcome of the activities of the Committee, set forth the opinion that it should be "immediately dissolved" and should abide by the resolutions of the 1935 convention, and at the same time appointed a committee of its own membership[3] to confer with the heads of the dissident unions.

Rejecting both the demand that it disband and the request for a conference, the C.I.O. taunted the Federation for its failure to organize the steel industry and offered to provide one-third of a $1,500,000 fund for a campaign there;[4] and President Green—after the Executive Council's inevitable rejection of this offer—requested the Committee's heads to meet with the Council on July 8 and succeeding days "for the purpose of learning from each of these representatives the reason for their refusal to

---

and advisory manner was raised. Apparently there can be no doubt that some of the original participants expected that the formation of the Committee would galvanize the Federation leadership into aggressive organization activity and persuade it of the desirability of adopting the policy expressed in the 1934 minority report, and perhaps all of them hoped that it would. On the other hand, the possibility of a division within the organized-labor movement can hardly have been absent from the consciousness of the original group. In 1939 Mr. Woll of the Executive Council said: "I believe that most of those who joined the Committee did so, originally, with the firm belief that it was designed solely for educational purposes. It is equally true, however, that there are those within the movement who readily saw the opportunity for turning it into a distinctive agency to carry out purposes without, rather than within, the Council of the American Federation of Labor." *The Hat Worker*, June 15, 1939, pp. 10–11.

[1] The Executive Council report for 1936 declared: "This organization is formed for the purpose of imposing its purposes through concentrated, organized effort on the part of the Committee for Industrial Organization. This constitutes a challenge to the majority rule and democratic procedure in the American Federation of Labor." American Federation of Labor, *Proceedings*, 1936, pp. 69–70.

[2] *Ibid.*, p. 71.

[3] Vice-presidents Harrison, Weber, and Bugniazet.

[4] When the Executive Council—of course—rejected this offer, the C.I.O. placed $500,000, the greater part of which was furnished by the now-rehabilitated United Mine Workers of America, at the disposal of the Amalgamated Association of Iron, Steel, and Tin Workers, under an agreement whereby the Steel Workers' Organizing Committee, a creation of the C.I.O., was to direct the organizing campaign in the steel industry. For the text of this agreement, see American Federation of Labor, *Proceedings*, 1936, pp. 92–93.

comply with the request . . . to terminate the affiliation of their respective international unions with the Committee for Industrial Organization."[1]   Again the officers of the industrial-union movement refused to comply; on July 15, 1936, John P. Frey filed with the Executive Council charges that the C.I.O. was a dual organization guilty of "fomenting insurrection" and of acts "constituting rebellion";[2] officers of the international unions were directed to "stand trial" on Aug. 3, 1936; and upon their refusal to appear for "trial" the Executive Council ordered the suspension, not the expulsion, of the C.I.O. unions unless they severed their connections before Sept. 5, 1936.[3]   Both the constitutionality of the suspension order[4] and the haste with which the suspension was consummated[5] were subject to caustic criticism both within and without the Federation, but at the 1936 convention, where the insurgent unions were not represented, the Council's action was overwhelmingly sustained.[6] Following this convention, the Executive Council appointed a committee to confer with the C.I.O., but the latter refused to do so until the suspension order had been rescinded.   Although the Committee did not become a permanent organization, bearing the name of Congress of Industrial Organizations, until two years later,[7] the labor movement had been divided into two rival groups.

Developments between 1936 and the early 1940's served to deepen and entrench the division within labor's ranks.   The C.I.O. established new unions, organized sections of industry that had been relatively

[1] For the text of this letter, see *ibid.*, pp. 76–77.

[2] *Cf. ibid.*, pp. 79–80.

[3] For the text of the "findings of fact" upon which the suspension order was based and the order itself, see *ibid.*, pp. 80–82.

[4] The constitution of the A. F. of L. at that time provided that member unions could be "expelled" only on vote of the convention, but it included nothing about "suspension." On the other hand, a lawyer's case can be made that the organizing campaign had been delegated by the last (1935) convention to the Executive Council, that the Executive Council was taking a necessary step to prevent abandonment of the kind of organizing campaign the convention had directed, and that accordingly the suspension order was a constitutional procedure.

[5] The fact that the Executive Council was "in such a hurry" to suspend the C.I.O. unions, and did not wait for the action of the approaching Tampa convention, was called to the attention of the delegates at that gathering by more than one of the participants in the floor discussion.   But constitutionalism was, after all, not the outstanding consideration.   Perhaps the point of view of the Executive Council was most accurately put by Mr. Woll when, in 1939, he said: "The fact is that if the Council had not acted, there would have been possible disintegration within the American Federation of Labor which would have been disastrous.   The Council acted not so much to punish those who had formed the C.I.O., but rather to prevent disintegration from within and perhaps a greater danger than confronted it.   Of course, the convention at Tampa followed, and the act of the Council was affirmed."   *The Hat Worker*, June 15, 1939, p. 11.

[6] 21,679 to 2,043.   For the Committee on Resolutions report, approving the suspension of the C.I.O. unions, approved by this vote, see *Proceedings*, 1936, pp. 502–503.

[7] *Cf. infra*, p. 219.

impregnable against A. F. of L. attack,[1] and became a permanent independent institution with functions paralleling those of the Federation.[2] Mutual recriminations and "raiding" of jurisdictions accentuated the differences between the two groups; conferences between authorized representatives failed to achieve an acceptable *modus vivendi;* and inevitably the factors of individual and group pride and fear of loss of prestige and influence handicapped reconciliation efforts. The developments of these years, an important part of the history of organized labor in America, merit at least summary treatment.

The Executive Council of the Federation, acting upon the authority granted by the 1936 convention, early in 1937 ordered the expulsion of all C.I.O. unions from the city centrals and state federations,[3] and in retaliation the Committee one month later announced the chartering of various subunits comparable to the city and state federations of the A. F. of Labor.[4] A special conference of the nationals and internationals, called by the Executive Council, thereupon announced the financing by a special assessment of one cent per member per month of "aggressive organizing campaigns within their jurisdictions," carried on by the organizing staffs of these nationals and internationals in coordination with the A. F. of L.,[5] and the C.I.O. continued its campaigns—now increasing in momentum—in steel and elsewhere.[6] Then, by a vote of 25,616 to 1,227,[7] the 1937 convention of the Federation authorized the Executive Council to revoke, in its discretion, the charters of the unions that had affiliated with the C.I.O. and refused to dissociate themselves from it and return to the fold, voted at the same time to continue the committee for negotiation with the rebellious organizations, called upon "all, whether among employers or among political leaders to have due regard for the conditions that exist, for the facts that have been presented, and . . . to choose for themselves which philosophy and practices to support," and declared that "if, with all efforts proving unavailing, the die is cast for war against autocracy, against rebellion, against alliance of American greed and alien Communism, then we pledge our movement to bring to a quick and decisive close so far as lies within our power this internecine warfare."[8] Concurrently with the charter-

[1] *Cf. infra*, pp. 222–230.

[2] *Cf. infra*, p. 219.

[3] American Federation of Labor, *Proceedings*, 1937, p. 100.

[4] *Ibid.*, p. 101, and Union News Service, Mar. 15, 1937.

[5] Decision to call this conference of the nationals and internationals was made by the Executive Council in April, 1937, and the conference program was announced on May 24, 1937.

[6] *Cf. infra*, pp. 220–230.

[7] American Federation of Labor, *Proceedings*, 1937, pp. 416–417.

[8] The entire debate upon the report of the Committee on Resolutions at the 1937 convention of the Federation and the report itself are to be found in *ibid.*, pp. 373–416.

revocation decision and the adoption of the militantly phrased resolutions, however, went acceptance of a suggestion received from the C.I.O., then meeting in Atlantic City, that the Federation send representatives to a conference called for the purpose of composing differences between the two organizations;[1] and on Oct. 25, 1937, leaders of what had now become two rival movements[2] convened in Washington to evolve a formula for composing the differences between them.

In spite of the fact that a mutually acceptable compromise appears at one time to have been reached, the conference failed.   Proposals unacceptable to the Federation were submitted by C.I.O. participants,[3] and initial A. F. of L. suggestions were equally unpalatable to the C.I.O.;[4]

[1] See American Federation of Labor, *Proceedings*, 1938, pp. 86–89, Congress of Industrial Organizations, *Proceedings of First Constitutional Convention*, 1938, p. 92, and International Ladies' Garment Workers' Union, *op. cit.*, p. 38.   On Oct. 12, 1937, a conference of the C.I.O. organizations, meeting in Atlantic City, wired the convention of the A. F. of L., then in session in Denver, suggesting that a committee of 100 persons representing it meet with an A. F. of L. committee of the same size to consider "methods whereby a united labor movement can be brought about in America."   The Federation convention replied, through the secretary, restating its position on dual unionism and objecting to the unwieldy number of conferees proposed.   After a further exchange of telegrams, it was agreed that a smaller number of conferees should meet in Washington on Oct. 25, 1937.

[2] For the A. F. of L., Vice-presidents George M. Harrison, Matthew Woll, and G. M. Bugniazet; for the C.I.O., Charles P. Howard, Philip Murray, David Dubinsky, Harvey C. Flemming, James B. Carey, Homer Martin, S. H. Dalrymple, Michael J. Quill, Abraham Flaxer, and Joseph P. Curran.   Sidney Hillman and Jacob Potofsky of the C.I.O. also participated in the conferences later.

[3] The original proposals of the C.I.O. were: (1) that the A.F. of L. declare as one of its basic policies the organization of workers in the mass-production, marine, public-utilities, service, and basic fabricating industries on a solely industrial basis; (2) that a department, bearing the name of C.I.O., completely autonomous and directed by its own designated officers under its own department constitution, be established and have sole jurisdiction in regard to the workers in these industries and any matters affecting its affiliated organizations and their members; (3) that a joint convention of affiliates of both the A.F. of L. and the C.I.O. be held to ratify and work out effectuation of this program.   Patently adoption of this proposal would either have involved recognition of the principle of industrial unionism in the mass industries and abandonment of craft-union jurisdictional claims where C.I.O. unions had been established, or else—if, as was most probable, the craft unions refused to relinquish their jurisdictional claims—would have established dual unionism within the Federation.   The voting strength of the industrial unions was also a major consideration from the point of view of the Federation representatives.   It is highly improbable that the C.I.O. representatives seriously expected that the proposal of a C.I.O. department within the A.F. of L. would receive serious consideration.

[4] These were: (1) That all national and international unions chartered by the Federation and holding membership in the C.I.O. return to, and resume active affiliation with, the former.   Immediately upon resumption of such affiliation, these organizations would be accorded all rights and privileges enjoyed by them prior to formation of the C.I.O.   (2) In respect to other organizations affiliated with the C.I.O., conferences should be held immediately between representatives of the Federation's affiliates and organizations chartered by the C.I.O., in any cases where such member unions were in conflict with each other,

but a compromise formula, proposed by the Federation representatives, for a time seemed not improbable of adoption. Under this formula, the twelve A. F. of L. unions then within the Committee were not to apply for admittance, or to be admitted, to the Federation until all matters affecting the twenty new C.I.O. unions had been adjusted; joint conference committees with equal representation of both the concerned Federation affiliates and the concerned C.I.O. organizations were to be established for each of the twenty new C.I.O. unions, to work out solutions of the jurisdictional conflicts; and, when these conflicts had been adjusted, the membership of all the C.I.O. unions would be admitted to the Federation concurrently with that of the suspended A. F. of L. organizations. A special convention of the reunited labor movement would be held within a reasonable time (sixty to ninety days) after all matters in conflict had been adjusted, with "all affiliated organizations . . . entitled to representation with all rights and privileges" of other A. F. of L. unions. The Federation representatives pledged that, if all other matters were adjusted, they "would consider" recommendation that the constitution of that organization be amended to provide that suspension or revocation of the charter of an affiliate could take place only upon direct authority of the convention. Finally, there was the promise that "we would agree to specify certain industries where the industrial form of organization would apply."

This proposal, responsibility for the rejection of which the Federation, supported by statements of the President of the International Ladies' Garment Workers, has placed squarely upon the C.I.O. representatives,

---

for the purpose of bringing adjustment of such conflicts and the memberships into the Federation "upon terms and conditions mutually agreeable." (3) Questions of organization and administrative policies not mutually agreed to should be referred to the next convention of the A.F. of L. for final decision. "In the meantime an aggressive organizing campaign shall be continued and carried forward among the unorganized workers along both industrial and craft lines as circumstances and conditions warrant." (4) "The foregoing contemplates the establishment of one united, solidified, labor movement in America, and the termination of the division and discord now existing within the ranks of organized labor. Therefore the Committee for Industrial Organization shall be immediately dissolved" (Committee of Industrial Organization, *Proceedings of First Constitutional Convention*, p. 93; American Federation of Labor, *Proceedings*, 1938, pp. 82–93; and International Ladies' Garment Workers' Union, *op. cit.*, pp. 43–44). Had the C.I.O. accepted this proposal, its unions would, of course, have returned to the Federation possessed of only the controverted jurisdiction they had prior to November, 1935, and the recently formed unions would have had to bargain with those Federation affiliated with whom they found themselves in jurisdictional conflict, with ultimate decision where mutual agreement was not attained resting with the convention. Accordingly, the C.I.O. members of the conference raised the question of whether the Federation was prepared to recognize industrial unions as the only proper type for certain specific industries and pointed out that the proposal of the A.F. of L. representatives in the conference involved, in substance, abandonment by the C.I.O. of its member industrial unions.

and particularly upon John L. Lewis,[1] contemplated in fact, it will be noted, the establishment of the basic principles for which the C.I.O. had stood up to that time.   In the negotiations between the joint conference committees, the twenty new unions almost assuredly would not have secured all that they asked in the way of jurisdictional recognition; but the agreement to negotiate about the matters in conflict was itself tacit admission that their claims could not be dismissed as entirely without validity, and the offer to "specify certain industries where the industrial form of organization would apply" involved concession on the part of the Federation on the initial point of controversy in the entire dispute. C.I.O. representatives claimed, it is true, that the Federation representatives were without power to designate the industries in which the industrial form of organization should apply and that they were in fact without

[1] The significant fact from the point of view of this account of the division in the ranks of organized labor is, of course, that the compromise formula was finally rejected, not that of who should be charged with responsibility for the rejection.   Nevertheless, the apparent circumstances of the rejection furnish a somewhat illuminating example of the way reluctance to make immediate concessions for the sake of larger ultimate gains, personal unwillingness to compromise, and a fortuitous combination of circumstances may play their part in important decisions.   The Executive Council reported to the 1938 convention that this compromise "basis for agreement" was first accepted, then the next day rejected, by the C.I.O. representatives.   According to the Council, the conferees agreed to accept the formula, but as a courtesy to Philip Murray of the Steel Workers' Organizing Committee, who was not present when this agreement was reached, postponed official ratification and press release of it.   Then, according to the Council's account, Mr. Murray at the next meeting refused to carry out the understanding and, after appointment of a subcommittee, John L. Lewis definitely vetoed it (American Federation of Labor, *Proceedings*, 1938, pp. 90–91; *cf.* also the address of David Dubinsky before the New York Local Union Executive Boards of the International Ladies' Garment Workers' Union, January 11, 1938, in the already quoted *Position of the International Ladies' Garment Workers' Union in Relation to C.I.O. and A.F.L.*, pp. 49–63).   Matthew Woll's account of what happened (*The Hat Worker*, June 15, 1939, pp. 11–12) also deserves inclusion in the record.   Mr. Woll declared flatly in 1939 that "they [the conferees] did unanimously reach an agreement."   According to Mr. Woll's account, Charles P. Howard of the International Typographical Union, who was presiding at the afternoon session where this agreement was reached, called attention to the fact that Mr. Murray was not present, and suggested that in courtesy to the latter public announcement be postponed until the following morning.   "We readily acquiesced in that.   It was a proper request."   When, however, the Federation representatives returned to the conference room the following morning, they were advised, according to Mr. Woll, that the C.I.O. group could not meet with them until later in the day, and fear that the basis of agreement might yet be rejected by the C.I.O. developed.   "They [these fears] became realities, and the agreement we had reached had been thrown overboard and of course our conference failed of agreement." The C.I.O. representatives, on the other hand, took the position that the A.F. of L. had been reluctant to designate the precise industries in which unrestricted industrial charters would be granted, that the representatives of the Federation were really without power to agree upon specific industries to be so designated, and that an agreement recognizing in principle industrial unionism and protecting the existing C.I.O. unions accordingly could not be reached.   "At this meeting the same problem [recognition of the unrestricted

real power to negotiate any agreement, but neither of these contentions
appears to have been compelling ground for rejection of the terms of the
compromise summarized in the immediately preceding paragraph. It
appears certain that the A. F. of L. representatives did refer to certain
industries that they would at least recommend to the Executive Council,
and through it to the Federal convention, as being the exclusive province
of industrial unions,[1] and the allegation that they were without power
to negotiate any agreement raises the question of whether negotiations
between rival labor groups, of course subject to subsequent ratification,
ever can be purposeful.[2]

---

jurisdictional rights of the C.I.O. industrial unions] arose in the discussion. The C.I.O.
representatives asked whether specific industries could be named for which the industrial
form of organization would be definitely recognized and the claims of the craft unions in
such industries eliminated. Both Mr. Green and Mr. Harrison admitted absence of
authority to agree on the specific industries where industrial unionism could be granted.
Mr. Green and Mr. Harrison merely suggested again the same procedure that had been
offered by the A.F. of L. committee. No agreement could, therefore, be reached that
provided for recognition in principle of industrial unionism and for the protection in fact
of the existing C.I.O. unions" (Congress of Industrial Organizations, *Proceedings of First
Constitutional Convention*, 1938, p. 95; see also the postconferences statement of Philip
Murray, issued on Dec. 21, 1937, in International Ladies' Garment Workers' Union, *op. cit.*,
p. 45). The preponderance of evidence seems to point to the conclusion that an understanding—probably oral—was reached, the import of which was acceptance of the "basis
for agreement," and that this agreement was the following day rejected by the C.I.O.
representatives. The Federation published (in the 1938 Executive Council report) the
text of the agreement, and the fact that at least tentative acceptance of it had been secured
was not denied in either the C.I.O. 1938 *Proceedings* or in Mr. Murray's statement issued
after the conference had adjourned. As the International Ladies' Garment Workers'
Union has observed (*op. cit.*, p. 45), the C.I.O. postconference statement failed to mention
that a compromise agreement basis was reached and ignored all points enumerated in it.
On the other hand, it should be noted that the compromise formula had not been agreed
to by all members of the conference and that in the absence of official affirmative vote and
presumably a public announcement it might be regarded as still a matter for consideration.

[1] The contention of the C.I.O. that the Federation representatives were without
authority to agree upon specific industries where unrestricted industrial unionism would
obtain has been mentioned in the immediately preceding footnote. The Federation
conferees did, however, agree "to specify" certain industries as coming within this category.
Moreover, it is almost certain that a considerable list of such industries was discussed during
the conferences. *Cf.* the account of Mr. Woll, *op. cit.*

[2] It must of course be recognized that some of the powerful A.F. of L. unions might
have been strongly disposed to reject the compromise agreed to by the conferees, but
there was in late 1937 increasing recognition on the part of the rank and file of Federation
unions that insistence upon jurisdictional claims in the mass industries—paper claims in
some cases—was merely perpetuating a situation the effect of which was adverse to the
entire organized-labor movement. It may be mentioned that Mr. Bugniazet of the
Electricians was one of the negotiators, and his union had an important stake in the outcome. Also, the question has been raised: "Why did Lewis show such unseemly haste in
killing the agreement" if the compromise would not have been accepted by the A.F. of L.
unions anyway?

With the failure of the peace negotiations, further postponement of the long-delayed expulsions of the rebellious unions would, from the A.F. of L. point of view, have been pointless, and on Jan. 24, 1938, the Executive Council, acting upon the authority granted by the preceding convention, officially revoked the charters of the United Mine Workers of America, the International Union of Mine, Mill, and Smelter Workers, and the Federation of Flat Glass Workers. Three months later similar action was taken with reference to the charters of the United Automobile Workers of America, the United Rubber Workers of America, the United Textile Workers of America, and the Oil Field, Gas Well, and Refinery Workers.[1] At the 1938 Federation convention there was only one vote against the recommendation of the Committee on Resolutions that "this convention authorize the Executive Council to continue to carry on the battle and at the same time stand ready to respond to any geniune appeal to peace or any honorable or sincere opportunity to reunite the labor movement."[2] Almost concurrently with this declaration of the Federation, the constitutionless Committee for Industrial Organization was replaced by the permanent Congress of Industrial Organizations.[3] The schism in labor's ranks appeared to be wider and more deeply entrenched than ever before.

Rank-and-file pressure for mutual acceptance of some workable formula that would reunite the labor movement,[4] as well as the efforts of

[1] It will be noted that three of the "original twelve" were not included in these two charter-revocation actions. The United Hatters, Cap and Millinery Workers, for reasons mentioned earlier (*supra*, p. 210) had not been included in the original suspension order of the summer of 1936, and accordingly this union was not expelled under the 1938 Executive Council order. The International Typographical Union had been affiliated with the C.I.O. only through the participation of its president, Charles P. Howard, and it, likewise, was not expelled in 1938. The International Ladies' Garment Workers' Union, and particularly its president, David Dubinsky, had for some time adopted a conciliatory attitude toward the Federation and had been critical of what it regarded as the too unbending attitude of the C.I.O., particularly during the late 1937 peace negotiations, and this union was not expelled in 1938. For a complete statement of the position of this union see the already referred to *Position of the International Ladies' Garment Workers' Union in Relation to C.I.O. and A.F.L., Chronicled in Documents and Records.*

[2] American Federation of Labor, *Proceedings*, 1938, p. 387.

[3] At a convention held in Pittsburgh, Nov. 14–18, 1938. *Cf.* Congress of Industrial Organizations, *Proceedings of First Constitutional Convention.*

[4] The impact of the 1937 business recession upon the C.I.O. was more adverse than it was upon the A.F. of L., since the membership of the former was in the "heavy" industries, which were most affected; and rank-and-file pressure, proceeding from the conviction that already achieved gains could best be consolidated were the labor movement united, was for a resumption of peace negotiations. The loss of the International Ladies' Garment Workers' in 1939 and the growth of a dual movement, of A.F. of L. predilections, within the United Automobile Workers of America, also were factors within the C.I.O. conducive to resumption of negotiations. On the side of the A.F. of L. unions, there appeared during 1938 to be increasing recognition that the growing independence of attitude on the part

the President of the United States,[1] resulted, however, in another conference—as unsuccessful as the preceding effort had been—between representatives[2] of the rival movements. The C.I.O.'s proposal for a united labor movement, made at this conference of early 1939, involved the formation of a new American Congress of Labor, the Executive Board of which was to be equally representative of the former C.I.O. and the former A.F. of L., agreed-upon ineligibility of either Mr. Lewis or Mr. Green for the presidency of this new Congress, selection at a special convention of delegates of the Federation, the C.I.O. and the Railroad Brotherhoods of one of the officers of the last-named group as president, and utilization of the services of the United States Department of Labor for the settlement of jurisdictional disputes. The seriousness with which this proposal was advanced may be subject to not a little question,[3] but its rejection by the Federation emissaries was inevitable, for had the C.I.O. had equal representation in the proposed new American Congress of Labor, unrestricted industrial unionism in industries where the A.F. of L. unions were determined to oppose it would have been almost certain. In turn, the Federation representatives advanced a proposal much the same in substance as the one made at the 1937 conference: that the original seceders be readmitted with their additional members prior to the holding of a series of conferences to settle the jurisdictional problems created by the formation of the new unions. Readmitting the original seceders with their additional members did not, C.I.O. officials pointed out, insure to these unions unrestricted jurisdictional rights in their own industries, and the "holding of a series of conferences to settle the jurisdictional problems created by the formation of

---

of the two organizations and the overlapping of jurisdictions would redound adversely to the great mass of organized workers unless steps were taken to heal the breach. In August, 1938, Mr. Dubinsky of the International Ladies' Garment Workers' Union again made efforts to initiate place negotiations. *Cf.* American Federation of Labor, *Proceedings,* 1938, pp. 86–92.

[1] On Feb. 25, 1939, President Roosevelt sent identical letters to Presidents Green and Lewis, asking for reconciliation and a reuniting of the organized-labor movement, "first, because it is right; second, because the responsible officers of both groups seem to me to be ready and capable of a negotiated peace; third, because your membership ardently desires peace and unity for the better ordering of their responsible life in trade unions and in their communities; and, fourth, because the Government of the United States and the people of America believe it to be a wise and almost necessary step for the further development of the cooperation of free men in a democratic system such as ours." (*New York Times,* Feb. 26, 1939, and Walter Galenson, *Rival Unionism in the United States.*)

[2] For the C.I.O., John L. Lewis, Philip Murray, and Sidney Hillman; for the A.F. of L., Matthew Woll, Daniel J. Tobin, Harry C. Bates, and Thomas A. Rickert.

[3] It is hardly conceivable that Mr. Lewis was altogether serious in putting forth this proposal, or that he believed there was any probability that the A.F. of L. representatives would accept it. To propose an inclusive labor movement without consulting the reluctant Railway Brotherhoods could, indeed, be regarded as good publicity and nothing else.

new unions" was far from assurance that these new unions would not have to abandon to the craft unions considerable segments of their membership. No further peace meetings between the two major labor organizations took place until 1942. Meanwhile the C.I.O. recouped the losses sustained in consequence of the 1937 depression, developed the structure that is described in a later chapter, and took unto itself more the functions and characteristics of a permanent and independent institution,[1] and the Federation attained a membership exceeding that of the 1920 peak. Entrance of the United States into the World War late in 1941 increased the pressure for reconciliation of the differences within the house of labor. The policy set forth by the President of the United States—supported by President Murray of the C.I.O. and by A.F. of L. officialdom—shortly after the United States officially became a belligerent nation, however, was that of negotiations between permanent representatives of the two organizations and conferences between them and the nation's Chief Executive on any controverted matters threatening continuous production. This program was followed during the first half of 1942; and in the summer of that year new "peace committees" were appointed by both the C.I.O. and the A.F. of L. Negotiations between these two committees had produced no formula acceptable to both by 1944.

The same year that the new "peace committees" were appointed (1942), the United Mine Workers withdrew from the C.I.O., in the formation of which its role had been so important, and in 1943 it petitioned through its president for reaffiliation with the Federation.[2] At the October, 1943, A.F. of L. convention, a committee was appointed to negotiate with the Mine Workers on conditions of re-entry and to report the results of the negotiations to the January, 1944, meeting of the Executive Council of the Federation, which in turn was authorized by the convention—with stipulations concerning settlement of jurisdictional questions—to act upon the petition. No formula satisfactory to both parties to the negotiations was evolved. The position of the A.F. of L. negotiating committee, under instructions from the convention, was that the questions arising in consequence of the encroachment of the expanded United Mine Workers upon the jurisdiction of some of its affiliates must be settled prior to readmission; the president of the Mine Workers, on the other hand, wished settlement of these questions to be postponed until the Miners were back in the Federation.[3] In January,

[1] In November, 1940, Philip Murray succeeded John L. Lewis to the presidency.

[2] The International Ladies' Garment Workers' Union, another of the original C.I.O. group, refused to join the permanent Congress of Industrial Organizations when the latter was formed in 1938, and it later reaffiliated with the Federation.

[3] By 1943 the United Mine Workers, with its composite District 50, maintained jurisdictional claims encroaching upon those of about twenty A.F. of L. unions. The number of chemical, cosmetics, and by-products workers within the mine workers' union had increased greatly during the immediately preceding years, and these workers were claimed

1944, the Executive Council rejected the proposal that the Mine Workers be returned with the greater part of its 1944 membership, although indicating approval of admission as the union was constituted in 1936. The negotiating committee was instructed to confer again with representatives of the miners for the purpose of "clarifying all questions that have not been settled."

ORGANIZING CAMPAIGNS

The facts concerning the numerical growth of trade unionism during the years after 1933, the establishment of labor organization in industries and trades where it had theretofore been almost nonexistent, and the approximate number of workers covered by collective agreements in different sectors of the economy in the early 1940's have been presented earlier in this chapter.[1] An account of trade-union development during the eventful years since 1930 should, however, include a brief résumé of a few of the organizing campaigns that constituted such an important part of the labor-relations picture of those years.

As has been indicated, organized labor's rapid strides during the period with which this chapter is concerned were a consequence in part of the establishment of new unions in industries where little or no organization had obtained, in part of the inclusion of more nearly all the eligible workers in industries and crafts theretofore only partially organized, and in part of the extension of the jurisdiction of established unions and inclusion within them of groups of semiskilled operatives who had theretofore received scant attention from the federated trade unionism. The organizational efforts impressing themselves most vividly upon the public consciousness were, of course, those of the C.I.O.; but the importance of the campaigns carried on by affiliates of the A.F. of L. and those directly under Federation auspices should not be minimized. Formation of a rival national organization in itself galvanized the Federation into action, and after the Supreme Court validation of the National Labor Relations Act[2] the organizing staff was enlarged, the special tax for organizing purposes of one cent per member per month was continued, new charters were granted,[3] and numerous white-collar, cement, beet-

---

by A.F. of L. unions as "belonging" to them. Some railroad, electrical, and building trades workers were affiliated with District 50, as were still other groups.

[1] *Cf. supra*, pp. 192–201.

[2] 301 U. S. 1–147.

[3] When the United Mine Workers of America became one of the original C.I.O. unions, the Federation turned to the Progressive Miners' Union, a dual organization, and granted a charter to it in 1937. That same year charters were granted to the International Association of Cleaning and Dyehouse Workers and to the International Ladies' Handbag, Pocketbook, and Novelty Workers' Union (American Federation of Labor, *Proceedings*, 1937, pp. 117–118). For charters granted during subsequent years, see *Convention Proceedings* of the respective years.

sugar, packing-house and cannery, aluminum, flour-, feed-, and cereal-mill, fabricated metal-goods, agricultural, cannery and citrus, chemical, distillery, and other groups of workers, some for the first time, found membership in locals of the Federation's affiliates.[1]

It was, however, in the organizing campaigns of the C.I.O. that the militancy and aggressiveness characteristic of the unionism of the 1930's manifested themselves most clearly and that the industrial form of organization, covering in 1930 not more than one-fourth of all organized workers,[2] attained an importance and a coverage equal to those of craft or compound-craft unionism. Three of these campaigns, selected for illustrative purposes, may be summarized in a bit of detail: in steel, where organization of labor antedated the days of the Homestead struggle, but where for four decades defeat had attended the efforts to organize the entire industry; in the young motorcar industry, where American mass-production methods found their utmost application and where the open shop had seemed to be firmly entrenched; and in the chaotic and competition-ridden textile industry.

Conditions in the steel industry were of a character presenting difficulties against which the old Amalgamated Association of Iron, Steel, and Tin Workers had found itself relatively helpless. Control was centered in large part in different groups of bankers, with more or less interlocking relations, but all strongly antiunion in their labor predilections. Jealousy of craft unions had impeded the previous efforts, under A. F. of L. leadership, to organize the industry,[3] and the institution of employer-sponsored plant organizations—particularly after the enactment of the National Industrial Recovery Act and its Sec. 7 (a) in 1933—had proved an effective barrier against unionism. Thousands of the workers lived in homes owned by their employers; steel towns were frequently "company towns"; the labor supply was heterogeneous in point of race and national origins; hourly wage rates and weekly earnings were below those of seven or eight other major industries; and the recollection of failure in previous organization efforts inhibited the latent disposition of the employees to form labor organizations. During the period of the NRA, it is true, more organization consciousness developed within the working force, but actual accomplishments were slight. A luxuriant crop of employer-sponsored organizations was, indeed, the chief product of the years 1933–1935.

With the formation of the C.I.O., however, lethargy was transformed into aggressive effort. Under an agreement of June 4, 1936, between the Steel Workers' Organizing Committee, a recently formed subsidiary

---

[1] For details of the organization efforts among these workers, see *ibid.*, 1938, pp. 81–86, and 1940, pp. 51–59.

[2] *Cf. supra*, pp. 193–199.

[3] *Cf. supra*, pp. 145–146.

of the C.I.O., and the Amalgamated Association of Iron, Steel, and Tin Workers, the former virtually took over, or became the receiver of, the latter,[1] the $500,000 that John L. Lewis had shortly before offered to the A.F. of L. as one-third of a campaign chest, provided the C.I.O. were granted direction of the organization drive,[2] was placed at the disposal of the Steel Workers Organizing Committee, and an organizing campaign that resulted in abandonment, at long last, of the nonunion policy of the United States Steel Corporation, even though it was less successful in "Little Steel," gained momentum.

Tactics employed during the drive, which was under the leadership of Philip Murray of the United Mine Workers, were somewhat novel. Old-fashioned high-pressure appeals to the workers were recognized as dangerous, and instead efforts were made by education and persuasion to win over the various company unions that had been established—and financed—by the employers. The organizers were, for the most part, relatively young persons with a mining-industry background. A research division undertook to acquaint the liberal middle-class elements of the population with the wages and standards of living of steelworkers, the character of the bargaining and negotiatory arrangements of the company unions, and other conditions that unionism sought to change. As the campaign progressed, one company union after another in the plants of Steel Corporation subsidiaries was won over,[3] and finally, after a series of conferences between Myron W. Taylor, chairman of the board of the Corporation, and John L. Lewis of the C.I.O., "Big Steel" recognized the union.[4] Under the terms of the agreement between the Carnegie-

[1] For the text of this agreement, see A.F. of L., *Proceedings*, 1936, pp. 92–93. See also International Ladies' Garment Workers, *op. cit.*, pp. 28–31.

[2] *Cf. supra*, pp. 212–213.

[3] Mr. Murray decided to try to win over these organizations as such, rather than to seek direct repudiation of the company unions by their memberships and then the affiliation of individuals with the steel-union locals; and the wisdom of this decision appears to be amply attested by the results. The drive formally began on June 29, 1936. A few weeks later, sixty employee representatives, speaking for 45,000 steelworkers, met with regional Steel Workers' Organizing Committee directors and endorsed the C.I.O. About a week later the largest company union west of Pittsburgh, that of the Carnegie-Illinois plant at South Chicago, affiliated with the Amalgamated Association, by that time a subsidiary of the Steel Workers' Organizing Committee. The revolt of company unions continued, and in December, 1936, representatives from forty-two plants met in Pittsburgh, formed a C.I.O. council, and proposed a national convention. By February, 1937, the Steel Workers' Organizing Committee claimed 150,000 members in 280 lodges, as compared with the 5,000 to 10,000 members of the Amalgamated Association shortly before.

[4] Various factors entered into the decision of the U. S. Steel Corporation to alter its traditional position toward unionism and collective agreements. The foothold the C.I.O. unions (chiefly company unions that had gone over to independent unionism during the organization drive) had gained in U. S. Steel plants was a factor that had to be reckoned with; there appeared to be little doubt that a strike for recognition would be at least partially successful. The upturn of business and the expectation (until the reversal in the

Illinois Co. and the Steel Workers Organizing Committee, signed in the spring of 1937, the company recognized the latter as the bargaining agency for its own members, raised wages 10 per cent, and granted the forty-hour work week with time and a half for overtime. Within three months after the signing of this contract, the Steel Workers' Organizing Committee had reached agreements, practically without resort to strikes, with approximately 140 companies, including fourteen U. S. Steel subsidiaries and the large Jones and Laughlin independent.[1] Union membership in the steel industry continued to expand, and in the early 1940's, as is indicated elsewhere in this volume, the claimed membership of the Steel Workers' Organizing Committee (which, as a permanent national union, in 1942 took the name of United Steel Workers of America) was more than 500,000, and about three-fifths of the workers employed in American steel plants were under collective agreements.

In "Little Steel," however, the organization campaign was far from being so immediately successful. Following the signing of the agreements with the U. S. Steel Corporation's subsidiaries, the Steel Workers' Organizing Committee called strikes against five of the large independents;[2] and—after some procrastination and apparent division of opinion —the employing interests decided not to follow the lead of the Corporation, but on the contrary to resist to the end enforced recognition of the union and the signing of collective agreements.[3] Aided to a great extent by the support of middle-class opinion and "party of the third part" organizations in the communities where strikes were called,[4] the

summer of 1937, after the Carnegie-Illinois and most of the other agreements had been consummated) that it would continue caused the Corporation to be desirous of avoiding a general and prolonged stoppage of work. On the assumption that the business cycle would continue its upward trend, the agreements would give the corporation an advantage over competitors subject to strikes for recognition.

[1] In the Jones and Laughlin case, there was a short strike prior to the signing of the agreement; the other companies entered into agreements without strikes.

[2] Republic, Youngstown Sheet and Tube, Inland, Bethlehem, and Wierton.

[3] The independents were, as would have been expected, highly indignant when the Corporation abandoned the "principle" of the open shop and by doing so seemed to gain a competitive advantage. Personal resentment of some of the heads of the larger independents probably was a factor influencing the decision to fight the union rather than to accept the order of things established in the plants of their largest competitor.

[4] A variety of tactics was resorted to by the employing interests, community groups representing the employer's point of view if not actually inspired by employing interests, and others. "Back to work" movements were organized, Citizens' Committees were formed to "protect the right of the nonunion man to work without interference from any source," Law and Order Leagues in some cases assumed the function of enforcing their conceptions of the rights and responsibilities of parties to industrial disputes, and strikebreakers were imported into the towns where disputes were in progress. The printed hearings of the "La Follette Committee" (Hearings before a Sub-committee of the Committee on Education and Labor, U. S. Senate, 75th Congress, 3d Session, Pursuant to Senate Resolution 266 of the 74th Congress) are illuminating as to the tactics used in

independent producers were able, in the majority of cases, to stop the Steel Workers' Organizing Committee in its tracks, and "Little Steel" was, for the most part, able to avoid collective bargaining until 1941. That year it, too, succumbed, the larger independents (with exceptions like the National Steel Company) entering into agreements, the terms of which were similar to those of the U. S. Steel Corporation's 1937 agreement.

When the C.I.O. and its affiliated United Automobile Workers attacked the great mechanized motorcar industry—an industry that had proved the despair of the A.F. of L.—it was both confronted with difficulties that appeared to be enormous and aided by a manifest disposition to organize, a disposition so strong that in some cases it resulted in the workers' taking things into their hands before the leadership regarded the time to strike or present demands opportune.[1] It was confronted by a small number of powerful corporations; three employing groups, General Motors, Chrysler, and Ford, produced approximately 90 per cent of all the automobiles sold in the United States. Without exception, they adhered to the policy of the open shop, and their capacity for resistance was enormous. The wage earners in many of the plants were, however, ready and often anxious to organize. Complaining of the speed-up, a complicated system of wage payment, absence of job security, an espionage system in some plants, and in general of policies they characterized as those of industrial autocracy, they possessed attitudes and a frame of mind that should be capitalized most effectively by union organizers. The United Automobile Workers' membership had been aggrieved by the restrictions included in the charter granted it by the A. F. of L., by the cases after 1933 in which craftsmen were transferred from plant unions to locals of the craft organizations, and by the failure of the Federation to manifest greater aggressiveness in helping with the organizing work; and after the affiliation with the C.I.O. these workers were in a mood to strike for recognition.

The tactics accompanying the drive in the motorcar industry differed appreciably from those followed in the steel industry; indeed, the campaign partook more, particularly in its early stages, of rank-and-file initiation of strikes in spite of the restraining influence of the leadership than of a planned and centrally controlled organization drive. On

---

breaking the strikes in "Little Steel."   Report 151 ("The 'Little Steel' Strike and Citizens' Committees," printed Mar. 31, 1941) is especially worth consultation.

[1] An account of the formation of the United Automobile Workers of America has been given earlier in this chapter (*supra*, pp. 203, 210) in connection with the story of the cleavage between the industrial and the craft unions and the organization of the C.I.O. It will be recalled that the United Automobile Workers, after being formed under A.F. of L. tutelage as a federation of the various plant organizations, joined the C.I.O. in 1936. See W. H. McPherson, *Labor Relations in the Automobile Industry* (1940).

Dec. 28, 1936, 8,000 workers in the Cleveland Fisher Body plant walked out, and by Jan. 1, 1937, the strike had spread to two other large Fisher Body factories. The movement spread rapidly to other plants, frequently taking the tactical form of the stay-in or sit-down strike, and finally practically all General Motors plants were involved.[1] Efforts of the Governor of Michigan to mediate were unsuccessful, the strikers insisting upon the pledge of recognition before returning to work or giving up the plants "captured" by stay-in strikes and the company insisting that unlawfully seized property be abandoned before that or any other issue could be discussed. By the end of January, 1937, about 140,000 automobile-industry workers, chiefly in the Detroit region, were on strike.

In spite of the unyielding position professed by each side, however, a series of conferences between the head of the C.I.O. and General Motors officials was initiated early in February, and on Feb. 11 trade unionism attained its first victory worth mentioning in the automobile industry. An agreement between the United Automobile Workers and the General Motors Corporation was signed under which the former was recognized by the management as the bargaining representative of its own members; the forty-hour week with time and a half pay for overtime was granted; a study of the speed-up with a view to its modification was promised; and (by a separate agreement) a method of grievance adjustment was instituted. Signing of this agreement was followed by a strike of between 60,000 and 70,000 employees of the Chrysler Corporation, two-thirds of the strikers occupying the company's plants; and on Apr. 6, 1937, this strike was ended by the signing of an agreement that in effect recognized the union[2] and followed closely in all details the General Motors model of two months earlier. These agreements, with some modifications, have been renewed since; and finally, in the summer of 1941 the Ford Motor Company, the only large manufacturer still not dealing with the union, surrendered and entered into agreement providing for the closed shop.[3]

The textile industry, organization of which was undertaken by the Textile Workers' Organizing Committee (a creation of the C.I.O. that annexed the old United Textile Workers in somewhat the same manner in which the Steel Workers' Organizing Committee had annexed the Amal-

---

[1] As has been implied, a considerable number of these strikes were almost runaway in character. Union officials apparently were not ready and felt that the memberships of the United Automobile Workers locals were not inclusive of enough employees to enable the union to submit its demands to a company so strongly opposed to organization in the past as General Motors had been.

[2] Mr. Chrysler refused to recognize the United Automobile Workers as the sole bargaining agent for all the employees, as the union had demanded, but he agreed to refrain from recognizing any dual organization.

[3] In a National Labor Relations Board election, held in April, 1941, the Ford employees, by a large majority, voted to be represented by the C.I.O.-United Automobile Workers.

gamated Association) only after the C.I.O. had been in existence for more than a year and a half, presented problems different from those in either steel or motorcar production. The industry included some five main branches—cotton goods, silk, woolens, synthetic fabrics, and knit goods— each of which was in fierce competition with the others, and within each of these branches were to be found several large corporations, on the one hand, and thousands of small factories and "family shops," on the other. Each of the various products had a seasonal market, and the distribution organization that had developed placed the producers, to a considerable extent, at the mercy of the "factors" (the various sales functionaries in the marketing hierarchy). The character of the labor supply varied with the geographical distribution of the industry. In the North, where in the majority of textile centers the United Textile Workers had not been able to maintain permanent foothold, elder immigrants from the "new" (i.e., Southeastern European) sources and first-generation Americans predominated; in the South, which had come to include a larger percentage of the industry's employees as a result of the Southward migration of Northern textile capital during the preceding twenty years, there was a redundant labor supply, composed of workers accustomed to a low standard of living and often not prone to revolt against paternalistic and quasi-feudalistic employment policies. These characteristics of the industry and of the labor supply seemed to dictate the necessity of an approach somewhat different from that followed elsewhere.

Numerous attempts—by the A.F. of L., by the I.W.W., by the Socialists, and by the Communists—had been made to organize the textile workers, but in 1933, when the textile code and its Sec. 7 (a) were adopted, only about 65,000 of the 1,250,000 employees in this industry were organized. With the opportunity afforded under the NRA, the union grew to be an organization of some 350,000 members; but after the national strike of 1934 it failed to procure any appreciable number of new agreements, and in 1937, two years after the demise of the Textile Board,[1] its membership was again down to about 65,000. Then the Textile Workers' Organizing Committee launched its organization campaign. Under direction of Sidney Hillman of the Amalgamated Clothing Workers the campaign envisaged a solving of the peculiar problems presented by the characteristics of the industry, as summarized above, by the Amalgamated's old policy of "rationalization," by "viewing the industry as a whole" instead of merely organizing workers. Headed largely by Amalgamated Clothing Workers' organizers, the Textile Workers' Organizing Committee set about the task of convincing employers of the stabilizing advantages of "placing a floor under wages and a ceiling

---

[1] For an account of the activities of this Board of the NRA period, see Lorwin and Wubnig, *Labor Relations Boards*, pp. 415–428.

over hours" and of putting all competitors upon the same footing so far as minimum labor standards were concerned. Education and conciliatory and negotiatory tactics were emphasized; the financial situation of every important mill, its indebtedness, its wage scales and labor policies, and all other relevant information were tabulated by a research staff; and the sympathy or opposition of civic organizations, church groups, mayors, sheriffs, and other public officials was ascertained. More than 500 men and women organizers were attached to the eight regional offices.

But the widely heralded campaign in the textile industry was, on the whole, far less successful than the campaigns in the steel and motorcar industries. In the silk branch, where a series of strikes occurred in the autumn of 1937, approximately 85 per cent of the workers were organized and an agreement providing for the forty-hour week and a minimum weekly wage of $14 was negotiated; likewise in rayon and synthetic yarns more than four-fifths of the workers were organized; and the knit-goods branch of the industry became in large part a unionized segment. Few strikes were, however, called in other branches, and the mills producing yarn and thread, cotton goods, and woolen fabrics remained for the most part without appreciable organization and with few collective agreements. Particularly in the South, where cotton-goods production predominated and where dislike of the C.I.O. was powerful and specific, unionization remained a development of the future. At its 1938 convention the C.I.O. claimed that the Textile Workers' Organizing Committee[1] included some 450,000 individual members,[2] but these figures included duplications and inflations.[3] As is indicated earlier in this chapter,[4] more than one-fourth but less than 45 per cent of all workers in the textile industry of the United States were organized during the early 1940's. The rationalization tactics that had been successful in the men's clothing industry, and were copied in the textile campaign, proved to be insufficient in a geographically diffused industry like textiles, where the labor supply was much more heterogeneous and lacked the almost intuitive bent in favor of unionism to be found among urban needle-trades workers; in many cases the effects of the policy of helping to "put manufacturers on their feet" undoubtedly were to make nominal union members of workers who had not really engaged in self-organization and to produce agreements that involved little concession by industry;[5]

[1] The Textile Workers' Organizing Committee has more recently taken the name of Textile Workers' Union of America.

[2] Congress of Industrial Organizations, *Proceedings of First Constitutional Convention.*

[3] One reason for the inflated figure of membership was that the Textile Workers' Organizing Committee included in its reports and public statements all employees of firms with which agreements had been signed—those who had joined the union and those who had not.

[4] *Cf. supra,* p. 200.

[5] There can be little question that the effect of the policy of trying to put on their feet

and the business recession and the unemployment accompanying it presented additional difficulties.

EMPLOYER POLICIES

Confronted by a militant trade-union movement capable of achieving the gains that have been noted in the preceding paragraphs, as well as by changed wage-earner and middle-class attitudes and by government policies prohibiting such long-practiced antiunion methods as "yellow-dog" contracts, discrimination against union members, and refusal to bargain collectively, employers found themselves impelled to readjust their employment and personnel policies in more ways than one during the years after 1930. The personnel programs that had been character-istic of the preceding decade of "new capitalism" underwent substantial modification, their paternalistic features becoming more subordinated and the various devices premised upon the interclass harmony hypothesis, such as employee stock ownership and profit sharing, frequently being dropped entirely.[1] Employee-representation plans, on the other hand, enjoyed increased popularity for a time after enactment of the National Industrial Recovery Act, since, as has already been pointed out,[2] these plans were frequently recognized by administrative officials as constitut-ing compliance with the requirement that employees be free to organize and bargain collectively; and during and immediately after 1933 business enterprise manifested much more disposition to cooperate with the government in its labor policies than might have been expected in view of the impact of these policies upon some of management's long-asserted and long-recognized prerogatives.[3]

---

the various manufacturers' associations in the industry was in many cases a quick half-organization, without real agitation or real conversion of the workers to unionism, in order that employees could be signed up wholesale with the various associations. The Textile Workers' Organizing Committee, in following this policy, was prone to sign almost any agreement it could obtain.

[1] These "welfare" and personnel-administration plans, so characteristic of the 1920's are described briefly in the preceding chapter (*supra*, pp. 157–160). As profit margins narrowed, many employers found their welfare work something of a luxury that could be dispensed with; it was not "going so well" with the workers during those economically melancholy years anyway. Wage earners inevitably became cynical about, for example, employee stock ownership when this ownership was, in consequence of the precipitous decline in stock-market prices, a cause of financial loss to them. On the whole, such per-sonnel-administration programs as selection tests, job analysis and specification, and efficiency ratings were maintained throughout the depression, but the mortality rate among indirect financial incentive plans, welfare plans, and the various devices expressive of the thesis that "the best union is a union of the employer and his employees" was extremely high.

[2] *Cf. supra*, p. 192; also Chap. XV.

[3] There were, of course, various reasons for management's willingness to accept labor policies restraining it from continuing some phases of its policies toward unionism. The

For the most part, however, the annals of employer labor policies during the years with which this chapter is concerned are an account of attempts on the part of many—although not all—important employing interests to utilize the methods of economic pressure that had proved efficacious in the past, and of the impact of both government policies and a revitalized and greatly expanded labor movement upon these attempts. By 1935, when the Recovery Act became inoperative in consequence of Supreme Court ruling that it was unconstitutional, business revival was well under way, and the cause of entrepreneurial freedom was both vocal and articulate. The National Labor Relations Act, reiterating the general right that had been enunciated by Sec. 7(a) and attempting to make this right real and dynamic by the imposition of correlative restraints upon employers and the establishment of administrative and quasi-judicial machinery, was enacted shortly after the invalidation of the NIRA, but not until April, 1937, when its constitutionality was sustained, did the measure become really effective. Meanwhile many firms, assured by a number of eminent lawyers that the Act would never receive Supreme Court sanction as compatible with the basic law of the nation, continued more or less openly to support their company unions, to discriminate against workers of union affiliation or sympathies, to engage in espionage work, and to carry on anti-union propaganda.

When the National Labor Relations Act was at last declared by the highest court to be constitutional—a declaration that synchronized with the victories of the C.I.O. in steel and elsewhere and with the changed labor policy of the nation's largest corporation—many employers became reconciled to the fact that, unless and until the law was changed by congressional action, they would have to adjust their policies to the new order. They ceased supporting company-based labor organizations and bargained in good faith with their employees. A very appreciable number of them discovered virtues in the collective-bargaining way of industrial relations theretofore unsuspected, and urged no substantial change in government labor policy; others, while conforming to the provisions of the Act, agitated vigorously for its repeal or for amendments that would vitiate seriously the achievement of its central purpose. There were, however, still other employers who were neither converted to the policy of the Labor Relations Act nor reluctantly reconciled to the fact that they must accept it while it remained on the statutes of the United States. Tactics pursued by such employers included recognition of "independent" unions, many of which the National Labor Relations

---

trade practices permitted by some of the NRA codes were frequently regarded as ample compensation for the concessions demanded by Sec. 7(a), especially as this Section found operative meaning in some of the codes. Also, many entrepreneurs were desperate after three years of heavy financial losses, and were willing to turn things over to the government —for a time.

Board found to be in fact company dominated and ordered disestablished, attempts to engage in the motions of collective bargaining but in fact to offer no concessions or make no effort to reach an agreement with representatives of the workers, refusal to put into writing[1] agreements alleged to have been reached, the dissemination of propaganda somewhat more subtle than that of decades past but of an import that was unmistakable, and the sponsorship of "third-party" organizations in communities that were the scene of industrial strife. By the late 1930's and early 1940's tactics of this character had been curbed to no little extent, both by the sustained cease-and-desist orders of the federal agency charged with enforcement of the Labor Relations Act and by victories on the economic front of a unionism strong enough to withstand them; but the attitudes and labor predilections in general of many employers remained much what they had been at the beginning of the great depression.

LABOR AND POLITICS SINCE 1930

Organized labor had departed more than once during the decades before 1930 from the restricted program of political action that had been formulated by the fathers of the American Federation of Labor,[2] and developments during the 1920's had intensified the pressure from within for more aggressive political activity, even if still of the nonpartisan or bipartisan variety.[3] It was, however, during the 1930's that labor's political line changed most appreciably. The postwar years had brought to many unionists the conviction that their organizations frequently

---

[1] It was not until 1941 that a Supreme Court ruling to the effect that agreements reached must be put into writing was forthcoming. *Heinz Products Co. v. National Labor Relations Board*, 311 U. S. 514.

[2] *Cf. supra*, pp. 76–77, 101, and 123–128.

[3] The injunctions and adverse court decisions were one factor during the 1920's convincing many conservative unionists that the problems facing organization were of a character demanding that tested and proved "economism" be supplemented by more aggression on the political front. The shifting of plants in various industries to nonunion areas possessed of a favorable wage differential was another factor increasing the demand for more participation in politics on the part of organized labor, since the governmental intervention that a politically aggressive labor movement would seek was necessary either to establish wage minima by legislative enactment or to make possible the freedom of labor to organize in the unorganized regions. Problems of the railway workers, particularly their increased dependence upon the government for settlement of disputes and enforcement of the right of self-organization and collective bargaining, had the effect of convincing these workers of the desirability of more active participation in politics. It will be recalled (*supra*, pp. 184–185) that the railroad employees were the group most active in the La Follette movement of 1924, when the movement for an independent party reached its peak. By the depression years of the 1930's, also, many unionists had undoubtedly become increasingly concerned about the fact that the nonpartisan policy divided the ranks of organized labor and tended to make the Federation unions and their leaders the associates of municipal and state machines.

could not successfully combat the strength of employers on the economic front without government action to restrain the antiunion methods that business enterprise was legally free to use, and virtually all the unions supported, during the 1930's, legislation and administrative machinery designed to render real and dynamic the decades-old right, but often in fact not much more than a nominal right, of workers to organize and bargain collectively through representatives of their own choosing. The Federation, it is true, was reluctant to look to the government for direct provision of the guarantees unionism had sought to gain for the upper stratum of labor by its own efforts, but the irresistible sweep of events brought to it, nevertheless, a new political consciousness;[1] and from workers in the industrial unions that were existent in 1930, from the memberships of the new unions organized in the decade following that year, and from hundreds of thousands of middle-class sympathizers with the notion of a new liberal party of trade-union basis came a vigorous demand for revision of labor's past political tactics and political philosophy.

Various influences nurtured and promoted the widening of labor's political perspective and the invigoration of its political efforts. Governmental activities from the time of the NRA code system of 1933–1935 on contemplated more or less representation of labor upon various boards and commissions, and participation in the formulation of government decisions and the determination of government policies brought with it both recognition of the necessity of participation in government and political affairs and consciousness of their possibilities. The distinctly "prolabor"—in comparison with its immediate predecessors—character of the Federal Administration that came into office in 1933 and the protection afforded labor's legal right to organize and bargain collectively inevitably undermined the former skepticism about the efficacy of the policy of seeking guarantees from, and enforcement of rights by, the state. Geographical migrations of industry were another factor breeding political-mindedness.[2] In addition to the wage-differential advantage enjoyed by producers in many of these newer industrial areas—a differential constituting a competitive menace to trade-union standards in the organized regions that the government, prompted by a politically strong labor movement, might be expected to correct—there was the fact that state labor codes in these regions were much less advanced than in the longer-

---

[1] Not until 1932, to be sure, did the Federation move so far in the direction of state assistance as to endorse compulsory unemployment insurance and during the years after 1935 it centered its political and lobbying activities, to no little extent, upon such matters as revision of the Wagner Act to protect the interests of craft unions, Works Progress Administration policies that would maintain union hourly rates, and the like.

[2] For an excellent discussion of this influence, see Philip Taft, "Labor's Changing Political Line," *Journal of Political Economy*, vol. 47 (1937), pp. 634–650.

industrialized sections of the country;[1] and the need of government protection against substandard conditions dictated increased reliance upon the political instrument. As important as any of these influences in the ripening of organized labor's political consciousness, however, was the rise of the C.I.O. and the formation of new unions in theretofore unorganized parts of the economy. Some of the original C.I.O. unions had for years been confronted by economic forces control of which, their leadership and rank and file had come to feel, could be achieved only by state intervention,[2] and this favorable disposition toward a participation in politics and an extension of government control beyond that tolerable in the past to the Federation's craft unions infused the entire C.I.O. Moreover, several million workers not possessed of a narrow but substantial craft interest were, as has already been said, organized during this period. Uninhibited by the preconceptions of the Gompers school of thought, or by long trade-union education inculcating the doctrine of "economism," these newer unionists were impatient with the antistatism of the earlier labor movement; the notions of economic planning, production control, and price control bulked large in their economic thinking, and the logical correlative was political pressure to entrench these notions as permanent government policies.

The post-1930 vitalization of the political side of the labor movement has manifested itself in the increased aggressiveness with which the national and international unions, particularly those of the C.I.O., have sought legislative protection, in the enlargement of the scope of labor's political objectives, and in the spread of the conviction that even in a country like the United States the class interests of labor dictate that it present a united political front, although this united front may function through established political parties. The first two of these manifestations have been discussed in this and other sections of the present chapter, but the steps in the direction of an extension of independent labor politics, and the organizational embodiments of a more independent

---

[1] By the end of the 1920's the majority of the more highly industrialized sections of the country had developed labor codes providing the main types of protection that organized labor had sought twenty or thirty years earlier, but the newer industrial areas, anxious to hold industries that had migrated to them and to attract new ones, were reluctant to impose upon business enterprise similar labor codes. It was among the unions facing the problem of interregional competition, in the form of both wage differentials and freedom of some regions from the labor codes in force elsewhere, that the NRA code system proved to be the most effective instrument for extending control into theretofore unorganized regions.

[2] For example, the overexpanded and highly competitive bituminous coal industry, leaders of the United Mine Workers felt, could be stabilized only through government control such as was provided for in the Guffey Coal Conservation Act (cf. vol. I of this series, pp. 371–374), and the unions in the needle trades and in the textile industry were active supporters of federal wage and hour legislation because of their experience in competing with low-wage and long-hour areas.

political movement like Labor's Non-partisan League and the later Political Action Committee deserve mention at this point.

Formed in 1936 by international unions affiliated with both the C.I.O. and the A.F. of L.,[1] Labor's Non-partisan League adopted a policy which, while not precluding the ultimate formation of an independent labor party, contemplated for the most part a functioning within and through the old political organizations. Those most active in its formation were representatives of organized groups that had profited most from the policies of the administration which assumed office in 1933, and they saw an opportunity to rally more effectively labor's support of its friends, capitalize for the cause of an independent political movement the popularity of the administration with the wage-earning masses, and thus lay the groundwork for a future labor party without sacrificing, but rather by enhancing, immediate gains. Although the League refrained from taking those steps which would make it a successor to the many third-party attempts with which the history of the United States is strewn, its appearance on the political scene constituted a distinct departure from the traditional bipartisan policy of American trade unionism. Instead of merely endorsing the more desirable (or less undesirable) candidates of the older parties, the League—following in this respect the example of the agrarian Non-partisan League of the preceding decade—entered candidates of its own in the various primary elections, becoming to this extent an independent political party operating within the primaries of the older parties, and in New York State it resorted to independent party action and appeared on the ballot as the American Labor Party, although supporting the Democratic candidate in the presidential elections of 1936, 1940, and 1944, and in the New York gubernatorial elections of 1936 and 1938.[2]

The independent political movement has been handicapped by the split within the ranks of organized labor,[3] attempts of the Communists

[1] Although from the start Labor's Non-partisan League and its New York State off-spring, the American Labor Party, was much more representative of the political animus of the C.I.O. than of the political frame of mind of the A.F. of L. Also, a considerable number of A.F. of L. leaders who originally were active participants have left the organization, particularly in New York State. When organized in 1936, the League was headed by George L. Berry of the Pressmen's Union, an A.F. of L. affiliate. Sidney Hillman of the C.I.O.'s Amalgamated Clothing Workers was treasurer, John L. Lewis chairman of the executive board, and E. O. Oliver executive secretary.

[2] In 1942, the American Labor Party nominated its own candidate, Dean Alfange, for the governorship of New York.

[3] Although originally representative of both factions of the organized-labor movement, the League has been weakened by the withdrawal of the more important A.F. of L. leaders who originally supported it. In 1938 Mr. George Meany, president of the New York State Federation of Labor and after 1940 secretary-treasurer of the A.F. of L., withdrew because of dominance of local American Labor Party clubs by the C.I.O. unions, and his withdrawal was symptomatic of the position and action of many A.F. of L. leaders about that time. In 1937 the League participated in the Detroit municipal elections, supporting

to capture its local units,[1] differences between trade-union leaders on the question of policies and candidates,[2] and deep-rooted differences of opinion on momentous national issues,[3] and its career has been somewhat checkered. In 1936 the League was placed on a permanent basis, with offices and with a permanent staff functioning in Washington, and its part in the national campaigns of 1936 and 1940 was far from negligible.[4] Its appeal outside of New York State was for the most part confined to trade-union issues, with consequent failure to elicit the support that a progressive general-welfare program would have commanded from nonwage-earner elements of the electorate. In the nation's most populous state, however, the League's offspring, the American Labor Party, avoided this mistake and endeavored to rally to its support various progressive-minded elements of the community, cooperating with ideologically sympathetic Democratic, Republican, "social democratic," civic, church, and other groups; and there it has demonstrated itself to be a factor with which politicians and the older political organizations must reckon. The aggregate of success attained by the organized political movement, in spite of the handicapping factors that have been mentioned, has been appreciable; and as an expression of a very real urge within the organized-labor movement to adopt both a more aggressive and a more independent political policy, the formation and activities of the League have been extremely significant. Both in theoretical basis and voting strength, it has been representative of wage earners who have sought, and in all likelihood will continue to seek in the future, government intervention not only to provide by exercise of the coercive powers of the state those securities and minimum living standards that the older unions sought through their self-help organizations, but also to make

---

the candidates for city office of the United Automobile Workers, and in consequence encountered the active opposition of the A.F. of L. unions in that city. The withdrawal of the leading Federation people in New York undoubtedly destroyed a very favorable opportunity to wean the city workers from their generations-old allegiance to Tammany.

[1] By 1941 the American Labor Party of New York State had been split between a right-wing and a left-wing faction, and Communist penetration of many of the local clubs was an important (although not the sole) cause of this cleavage. A left-wing "Committee to Rebuild the American Labor Party" was actively functioning after 1941. In 1944, after the left-wing faction had gained control, the right-wing faction formed a new party in New York State, the American Liberal Party.

[2] During the presidential campaign of 1940, John L. Lewis announced his support of the Republican candidate, although the Democratic candidate had the endorsement of the American Labor Party of New York and of Labor's Non-partisan League as a national organization.

[3] In 1940 and 1941 American foreign policy and attitude toward steps feared by many to lead to American involvement in the European War were issues bringing bitter differences of opinion within, and hence disunity to, the League and the American Labor Party.

[4] During the 1936 campaign, Labor's Non-partisan League expended, through its local, state, and national organizations, approximately $1,000,000. Statement of Mr. Oliver, executive vice-president, to Professor Philip Taft; cf. Journal of Political Economy, loc. cit., p. 641.

effective more governmental guidance and control of the processes of producing and distributing economic goods. The labor political movement assumed increased dimensions and became more aggressive with the establishment, in 1943, of the C.I.O. Political Action Committee.[1]

A few general comments upon the substantive character of the political program of the C.I.O. unions and the more politically minded A.F. of L. organizations are not irrelevant. It is clear that this program constituted a departure of appreciable distance from that of organized labor during the preceding decades, and that it involved much greater appeal to the lower middle class and to the nonwage-earner elements of the community; but it was far from being merely a readoption of the typically antimonopoly, plain-people political program for which the American workers during the nineteenth century manifested such liking. Antimonopolism of course plays its part, but little in the hardheaded and pragmatic approach gives basis for the conclusion that illusions are held as to the immediate common interests of all the real producers of the nation. While the programs of the National Labor Union and of the Knights of Labor were indigenous to a nation of free land and relatively abundant opportunity for individuals to elevate themselves out of the wage-earning class, the political theorizing and objectives of the labor

[1] The C.I.O. Political Action Committee was established by the Executive Board of the C.I.O. in July, 1943, having as its function the conducting of "a broad and intensive program of education for the purpose of mobilizing the five million members of the C.I.O. and enlisting the active support of all other trade unions, AFL, Railroad Brotherhoods, and unaffiliated, for effective labor action on the political front." *Report of President Philip Murray to Sixth Constitutional Convention of the Congress of Industrial Organizations*, p. 52. While specifically disclaiming intention to organize a third party, the C.I.O. took the position that the gains from economic action can be implemented and extended only if labor develops "a progressive program of legislation and secures its enactment through effective participation in the political life of the nation." *Ibid.*, p. 53. A "statement on political action," adopted by a series of regional conferences in 1943 set forth as objectives of the Political Action Committee (1) immediate mobilization of the full force of the C.I.O. for political action, particularly in the 1944 national campaign; (2) establishment of united political action with the A.F. of L. and the Railroad Brotherhoods, "preferably through united political committees or through other means of collaboration"; (3) inclusion in such united labor actions of "the broadest possible consumer, farmer, and progressive groups"; (4) welding "the unity of all forces who support the Commander in Chief behind a single progressive win-the-war candidate for each office" and (5) working toward formation of a national united labor league "which will include C.I.O., AFL, Railroad Brotherhoods, and unaffiliated labor unions who agree with our objectives and weld labor into the mighty political force which its numbers, strength, organizability, and program entitle it to play in the life of the nation." *Ibid.* Early in 1944 the C.I.O. Political Action Committee announced that it would hold a national convention prior to the Republican and Democratic conventions for the purpose of drafting and presenting to the American people "a specific set of principles for the general welfare." Then, after the Republican and Democratic conventions, "we can," as President Murray put it, "decide what action to take regarding the two parties and the individual candidates whether for state or national offices or for the presidency." *C.I.O. News*, Jan. 3, 1944, p. 5. The Committee actively supported President Roosevelt during the Presidential canvass of 1944.

political movement of the 1930's and 1940's were much more indigenous to a community of corporate organization, centralized financial control, and mechanized production methods.   In the second place, the nondoctrinaire basis of the program is deserving of comment.   Labor's Non-Partisan League and the Political Action Committee have been opportunistic, the political vehicles of a movement aggressively coping with immediate conditions but little troubled by the dictates of Marxian "inevitabilities."   As such, they have been much more congenial to the mentality of the average American worker—a political and economic mentality that on the whole, perhaps, had changed surprisingly little during the economically melancholy years of the 1930's, when millions of individual economic tragedies could not but engender bitterness toward existing economic arrangements and contrivances, and when the Marxists were pointing to the collapse of the price system as irrefutable vindication of the prophesies of *Das Kapital*.   The economics of the labor political movement since 1930 have, indeed, savored much more of the doctrines of John A. Hobson than of those of Karl Marx.

LEFT-WING UNIONISM SINCE 1930

Attempts of left-wing factions to capture the organized-labor movement made comparatively little progress, as was indicated in the preceding chapter,[1] during the decade preceding 1930.   The Socialist Party, hoping to become the nucleus of the American labor party of the future, ceased aggressively to attack the A.F. of L., the I.W.W. survived the War and the post-war periods of hysteria and suppression with almost negligible membership, and the Communists made little headway either in "boring from within" existent unions or in establishing dual organizations.   Economic conditions and social attitudes during the years following the depression of 1921–1922 were both adverse to the development of a vigorous and effective left-wing movement.

During the 1930's, on the other hand, both the intellectual climate and the economic environment were of a character nurturing skepticism about the more individualistic aspects of capitalism and the limited objectives of a "job-conscious" trade-union movement.   The tenets of finance capitalism ceased to command the middle-class reverence that had theretofore been theirs, and the interclass harmony hypothesis that had been accepted by many wage earners lost its appeal.   For the most part, however, the spirit of dissent and protest arising from the economic and ideological conditions of the time expressed itself—and effectively—in the demand for new public policies enlarging the area of labor's permissible self-help program and curbing the more flagrant abuses of the profit system that had developed and to which was imputed responsibility for the financial and economic debacle that followed 1929

[1] *Cf. supra*, pp. 178–181.

rather than in movements of distinctly revolutionary character. From the point of view of trade unionism as a purely economic instrument, the most significant left-wing developments of the 1930's, by far, centered around the attempt of the Communists to capture, first, the A.F. of L. and, then, the C.I.O. No more successful in the aggregate than had been the attempts of the Socialists to capture the Federation during the closing years of the nineteenth and early years of the twentieth centuries,[1] these attempts nevertheless were closely interwoven with some of the developmental trends that have been traced in earlier pages of this chapter, and their failure to change greatly the substantive character of the "business" Federation and C.I.O. unions does not mean that they were devoid of significance.

Communist efforts in the American labor arena since 1930 must be surveyed with reminder of their foreign inspiration. Prior to the death of Vladimir Ilich Ulianov (Nicolai Lenin) in 1942, the Communist (Third) International had adhered to the thesis of "permanent revolution," of the impossibility of establishment of lasting socialism in one country when the economic world consisted of various capitalistic countries of inextricably intertwined relationships. By the time of Lenin's death, however, an increasingly powerful faction of the 1917 revolutionists had become convinced that other capitalistic countries were not going to follow very quickly in the Russian footsteps; and under the leadership of Joseph Stalin the goal of international socialism was abandoned in favor of socialism in one country—to the extent, even, of abandoning revolution-fomenting activities outside of Russia that might affect adversely the Russian experiment.

American Communist policy reflected these shifts in the immediate program of the Communist International, and the Communists of this country demonstrated both eclecticism of ideas and versatility of tactics. During the years between the mid-1920's and 1940 they adopted such diverse tactics and policies, at one time or another, as cooperating with groups like the I.W.W., attempting to "bore from within" established unions and capture control of them, creating separate or dual organizations,[2] joining all labor and other receptive groups in a "popular front" against Fascism, support of the Berlin-Moscow understanding between 1939 and 1941, and support of the United Nations cause after 1941.

[1] *Cf. supra*, pp. 106–112.

[2] This policy was followed by American Communists chiefly during the period 1928–1934, the so-called "third period" of the Comintern (the Moscow or Third International). The Communist Party formed the Trade Union Unity League with which were affiliated the National Miners' Union, the Food Workers' Industrial Union, the National Textile Workers' Union, the Needle Trades Industrial League Union, the Building Trades Industrial League, the Metal and Steel Workers' Industrial Union, the Marine Workers' Industrial League, and the Auto Workers' Union. None of these attained appreciable membership.

Prior to 1928, while the policy of "socialism in one country" was in its initial stage in the Union of Socialist Soviet Republics, American Communists adhered to the "boring from within" policy decreed by Moscow; then, from 1928 on through 1934, the Communist Party in the United States, like communist parties elsewhere, was ordered to form its own unions and to have no connection with mass organizations of wage earners such as the A.F. of L. But the demonstrated futility of attempting to build an independent federation of labor—together with developments in Germany and the formation of the Rome-Berlin axis—resulted in a complete reversal of policies on the part of the International—and accordingly of the American-Communist movement about the middle of the 1930's. A plenum of the Central Committee of the American Communist Party in January, 1935, decided against dual unionism and in favor, once more, of the policy of working within existing organizations, and shortly thereafter (August, 1935) the Communist International officially prohibited dual unionism everywhere, ordered cooperation with other groups, and decreed again that the Communists attempt to capture from within the various unions.[1] This program of cooperating with other groups and attempting to gain control of the economic organizations of labor by penetration of the membership and leadership had, indeed, been operative in the United States some little time prior to the January, 1935, plenum and the August, 1935, orders of the International; and it is this program which is of primary concern in an account of left-wing influences in and upon trade unionism during the period with which we are concerned.

Until the C.I.O. was almost two years old, the Communists centered their efforts upon A.F. of L. unions, and without doubt—and in spite of the vigorous and sometimes violent anticommunist utterances of the Federation leadership—contributed to the organization work of A.F. of L. affiliates prior to 1937. By the middle of that year, however, the C.I.O. had grown to sufficient proportions to make concentration upon it attractive, and there was reason to believe that its membership—largely unskilled workers, unfamiliar in the past with unionism, untrained in the tenets of job-consciousness and limitation of the objectives of organized labor—would be more receptive to Communist doctrine and promises than were the memberships of the Federation unions. The

[1] There were other manifestations of the "popular front" policy. In politics, the Communists aligned themselves with liberal elements in their various communities, occasionally supporting candidates of the older parties and attempting (not without some success) to make themselves an influential factor in the American Labor Party of New York State. Revolutionary utterances were discarded for a verbal wardrobe of conformity and respectability; Mr. Earl Browder, head of the Party in the United States, uncovered the historical fact that the Communists were the real inheritors of American democracy, and spoke approvingly of Thomas Jefferson and Abraham Lincoln. "Fellow travelers" were recruited from all who—knowingly or unknowingly—chose to travel.

Party decided to work, through its trade-union organizers, primarily within the C.I.O.

The Communists did not succeed in capturing the C.I.O., nor was there ever any real possibility that they would. A number of locals did for a time, it is true, oscillate to Communist domination, and a few of the higher officials of some of the affiliated organizations formed after 1935 (not the top leadership of the C.I.O. itself) were possessed of more or less sympathy with Party purposes. But certainly three-fourths of the C.I.O. unions have been free of any vestige of Stalinist influence,[1] and the overwhelming majority of the rank and file have been both unsympathetic toward, and rather uninterested in, the doctrinaire aspects of modern communism. In the quest for organizers possessed of some knowledge and experience, the C.I.O. turned to a number of radical political groups, just as the Federation during its early years had recruited effective organizers from some of the Socialist organizations, and some of those chosen were Communists; these were, however, a minority of all the organizers, and the men at the head of the C.I.O.—John L. Lewis, Sidney Hillman, and David Dubinsky, for example—had eradicated Communist influence from their own unions prior to the formation of the C.I.O. They were aware that, as Professor Taft has phrased the matter, "it is questionable whether the economic organization [the trade union] can remain an autonomous body, functioning for the economic protection and improvement of its members, when its policies are made by a caucus dominated by an outside political group which may not be cognizant or concerned with the special and peculiar problems of the union."[2]

In spite of the fact that the Communists did not capture—or were ever within striking range of capturing—the C.I.O. or its important national affiliates, however, Communist influence should not be underestimated. From the point of view of a movement like the C.I.O.—on the whole nondoctrinaire, concerned primarily with organizing workers on the industrial basis, opportunistic, espousing a political program looking toward greater governmental control of economic life and the distribution of income but not, à la the Leninist version of Marxism, toward seizing the bourgeois state in order to abolish the bourgeois class—the influence was unfortunate almost in proportion to its magnitude. The Communists sometimes proved to be excellent organizers, but they were not primarily interested in the material welfare of American labor in the American capitalistic system. Their loyalty and allegiance were to the Party, not to trade unionism, and their devotion to the Cause was a factor redounding adversely to the policy of maintaining in good faith collective agreements, since strikes frequently tended to entrench them,

---

[1] Cf. Philip Taft, "New Unionism in the United States," *American Economic Review*, vol. 29 (June, 1939), pp. 313–325, and Herbert Harris, *American Labor* (1939) p. 411.

[2] *American Economic Review, loc. cit.,* p. 320.

and peaceful and stable contractual relations to weaken them, in their positions. Trade unions were for them effective "springboards" during organization campaigns or strikes for recognition, but they were not effective media or springboards after organization had been effected and recognition attained and the task of the union was the carrying out of the obligations embodied in its collective agreement. The dissension within the labor organizations that almost inevitably accompanied Communist membership or leadership was another unfortunate consequence from the trade-union point of view. Fundamentalist adherence to a dogma rendered the Communists incapable of tolerating a pluralism of economic ideas and objectives or of making the compromises necessary for successful pursuance of trade-union objectives. Finally, the adverse effect of Communist influence in the C.I.O. upon public opinion should be noted. This influence brought to the employing class the powerful ally of an appreciable part of middle-class opinion, and the grossly exaggerated popular notion of the extent and power of Communism within the C.I.O. was a handicap of no small proportions that organization had to sustain.

Chapter VI

TRADE-UNION STRUCTURE, GOVERNMENT, AND INTERRELATIONSHIPS

Divergent interests and objectives have produced a variety of structural types of unions. In some cases the craft interests, in others the interests of the employmental or industrial group, while in still others interests centering in the general strike or in reform measures have been most influential. Hence, in some instances the organization established has been of and for the members of the craft, as with the Locomotive Engineers and the Pattern Makers; in other instances the organization set up has been of and for all occupational groups of manual workers finding employment in the industry, as in the case of the United Mine Workers of America; in still other instances the organization has been of and for workingmen in the locality without regard to crafts or industries, as in the cases of the One Big Union organized in Winnipeg, Canada, two decades ago, and of many of our earlier antimonopoly labor organizations. Most of the modern American unions have been organized on the craft or a semicraft basis, but the miners and more than threescore other national groups are organized on the industrial basis. The general labor unions, on the other hand, have been relatively fewest, and the more important of them have now passed into history. The chief examples of this last form of organization in the United States in more recent years have been found in the mixed locals set up by the I.W.W. for recruiting purposes, preparatory to organization along industrial lines.

Craft, industrial, and general labor unions are, however, only the main structural types of labor organization that are generally recognized. Along with them a number of variants are found; most unions are neither pure craft nor pure industrial unions. A majority of the existing (international) unions have resulted from the unification (amalgamation) of two or more craft organizations, or from the original organization of two or more related crafts into one body, or from the extension of jurisdiction by craft organizations to related occupations appearing in a changing situation. The instances of amalgamation of two or more unions into one have been very numerous in the United States, this in order to end jurisdiction disputes and to remove other sources of waste and weakness. Many of the American international unions, such as the Plumbers and Steam Fitters, are of this amalgamated-craft type. The members of the related crafts may maintain separate locals, but these are placed under the common authority of one international. Thus, whether based upon original organization together of two or more crafts or resulting from amalgamation, there are many multiple-craft organizations. Related to but differing from these, because jurisdiction has been established over complementary groups differing in skill, are what, for want of a better term, may be called extended craft or trade unions. An example is found in the Hotel and Restaurant Employees' International Alliance and Bartenders' International League of America. Many have been the instances in which craft organizations have pushed their jurisdictions downward and outward,[1] becoming trade unions with members differing in skill, or probably a type of semiindustrial union, or, indeed, both craft and industrial unions. Differing historically and in other respects are several such quasi-industrial unions as the Amalgamated Clothing Workers of America. Here from the beginning there have been locals of cutters and trimmers and of other occupational or shop groups. Locals for Italians and other national groups are also to be found in this and in other cases, these resulting from language difficulties and from racial sympathies and antipathies. Hence, in such cases, the membership in the local is not without racial and craft or occupational interests. These unions fall just short of the pure industrial union; the locals are associated through their affiliations to the international and are also usually brought together through local "joint boards," which coordinate them and serve their common interests. Finally, there are a number of multiple industrial unions, with jurisdiction over two or more industries. Extension of jurisdiction has not been by craft organizations alone. The United Brewery Workers, for example, now have jurisdiction over soft-drink manufacture as well as over brewing. To cite a second example, the Amalgamated Clothing Workers has in recent years been establishing jurisdiction, among others, over laundries, cleaning and dying establishments, and the manufacture of neckties and shirts. A third example is to be found in the conspicuous extension of jurisdiction by the Auto Workers over the agricultural-implement and aircraft industries.

Careful study will reveal many structural types of unions. A great variety of arrangements have developed, and most rapidly in the last

[1] For example, the Brotherhood of Carpenters, once an organization of craftsmen engaged in building construction, has for years had jurisdiction over planing mills and sash, door, and blind factories. In 1935 the A.F. of L. gave it jurisdiction over loggers and lumbermen who were extensively organized along industrial lines in the Northwest. The International Typographical Union admits to membership not only trained craftsmen, but also machine tenders and assistants. Since 1935 the Electrical Workers and several other unions have, in competition with the C.I.O., reached out to organize all workers in plants, regardless of occupation, and have frequently given them only Class B memberships. In opposing industrial unionism some craft organizations have gone far toward becoming industrial unions themselves. A considerable number of the internationals are now both craft, or multiple-craft, and industrial unions in their different parts.

several years.[1] Perhaps as useful a general grouping of unions upon a structural basis as any is, however, into (1) craft and multiple-craft unions, (2) extended craft or trade unions, (3) quasi-industrial, industrial, and multiple-industrial unions, and (4) general labor unions.[2] The relative advantages and disadvantages of some of these forms of organization will be discussed presently by way of an introduction to a discussion of allied trades organizations.[3]

The Local Union and Its Government

The local is basic in union organization. Except in the cases of the Diamond Workers and the Actors' Equity Association,[4] whose memberships are in the national organizations, the American workers normally hold their membership in the locals. And the local has usually not been directly connected with the workplace or plant. Only still somewhat exceptionally, and chiefly among miners, certain types of railway workers, the steelworkers, the automobile workers, the rubber workers, the aluminum workers, the radio workers, and in the cases of true "company" and the new crop of so-called "independent" unions, do those working together as a unit have a local of their own.[5] Most frequently, but with more and more numerous exceptions, there is the detached local or locals in which those working in various plants in a community have membership, with a shop committee or a shop chairman or steward on the job

[1] These years have been marked by an extraordinary struggle for power. The international that is consistent in respect to jurisdiction claims almost seems to be exceptional. Some extended craft unions have at a given time petitioned the National Labor Relations Board for elections in craft, in departmental, in semiindustrial, and industrial units. On the other hand, seeking aid in doing its organizing work, an industrial union in the garment industry has petitioned for elections among cutters, among pressers, exclusive of cleaners and folders, and among other sectional groups. The Warehousemen on the Pacific Coast have, among other plants, organized wineries and, most recently, have organized drug clerks and related groups in two large drug chains in southern California. To give one more example from among many coming to mind, the C.I.O. Construction Workers have been granted an election among the employees of a Michigan manufacturer and distributor of soft drinks. Such developments are explained by the vigorous organization drives, A.F. of L. and C.I.O. rivalry, and the right any group has under the National Labor Relations Act to be represented for the purpose of collective bargaining by any organization or person. The organizational picture is now perhaps the weirdest in the world's history.

[2] *Cf.* David J. Saposs and Sol Davison, "Structure of A.F.L. Unions," *Labor Relations Reporter*, vol. 4, no. 11 (1939), pp. 6-9.

[3] *Infra*, pp. 272-278.

[4] True also of the Sheep Shearer's Union, but in 1939 this organization was amalgamated with the Meat Cutters.

[5] The constitution of the United Automobile Workers of America, as originally adopted, required local union organization by employing plant. This gave rise to a struggle between the International and a Toledo local, which admitted to membership workers employed in thirteen local plants. See the report of F. J. Dillon, then general president, to South Bend Convention, Apr. 27, 1936.

in the workplace. In the cigar factory and in the print shop, however, there are the chapel "father" and the chapel, which is subsidiary to the local and which exercises a certain amount of authority.

Local Government and Administration.—In terms of its constitution and by-laws, the local union has a most democratic government. In meetings held periodically—usually twice a month or monthly—or occasionally by referendum vote, its business is to be transacted. Subject to limitations imposed by the "international" with which it is very generally affiliated, the local amends its constitution, by-laws, and rules; it elects its officers (president, vice-president, recording secretary, financial secretary, treasurer, sergeant-at-arms, trustees, executive board, etc.) and instructs them and passes upon their work and reports; it provides for necessary committees on grievances, organization, and audit, and passes upon their work and reports; it formulates "demands," ratifies or rejects agreements with employers, and takes strike votes. With exceptions,[1] the rank and file, with every full-fledged member in good standing entitled to one vote, are vested with full power. Legislative, judicial, and administrative matters rest in their hands for delegation or for direct decision. No governmental arrangement could be more democratic.

Union constitutions and by-laws, however, picture actual union government only in a limited way. With union government it is very much as it is with local political bodies. Indeed, a rather close parallel is found between the problems arising in union government and those arising in our city and other local affairs.

Especially in unions of the business type, and most of the American unions are of that type and most of the members are "bread and butter" unionists, the actual government is commonly pretty much that of the leaders and a relatively small group of active followers. Elections, strike votes, and bitterly fought contests induce large attendance at meetings; usually nothing else does after the organization becomes well established,[2] and frequently ballots at elections and strike votes are taken otherwise than at meetings. On other occasions than those mentioned, an attendance of 25 per cent is regarded by the typical union as unusually good. Frequently it is much smaller, even less than 5 per cent. Hence, there is here, as in political government, the problem of seeming indiffer-

---

[1] The exceptions are such as these: (*a*) occasional locals of Negroes or of junior workers employed, say, in pressrooms attached to a "white local" or to a pressmen's local and having a very limited control over certain matters; (*b*) locals of automobile, steel, or other workers with such large memberships that the authoritative meetings are of representatives selected by departments or plants. This latter arrangement, closely related to that found in so many employee-representation plans, is exemplified in a considerable number of instances at this time.

[2] That is, no longer a new one.

ence on the part of the rank and file.[1] In spite of penalties sometimes imposed for nonattendance, in spite of appeals, and in spite of much effort on the part of some organizations to make their programs attractive, this problem of small attendance appears to be a growing one. In part this is accounted for by the fact that there are more places to go and more things to do. There has been a multiplication of automobiles, movies, radios, and the like, and these have absorbed an increasing amount of the time of those American workers who can afford them. More and more the union has been under the necessity of competing with other institutions in order to secure and to retain the active interest of its members. Most unions are governed most of the time by a limited number, because the majority function only intermittently or spasmodically.

In view of what has been said concerning the importance of the leaders in actual union government, it may be asked who they are, how they secure and maintain their positions, what their relations are to the general membership, and to what degree of accountability they are held.[2]

Here and there unions have been organized, controlled, and led from the start by those with a personal interest to further. Tim Murphy's Gas House Gang in Chicago years ago provides an example. This was one type of the racketeering union of which much has been said. Such instances are so rare, however, that they may be dismissed from serious consideration. Much more frequently, the racketeer or misleader develops in a union organized quite legitimately; the wrong group gains and retains power, possibly for years.[3] But to answer the questions raised, it may be said that typically those who come into active union leadership do so because they are the more active, the abler, and the most representative of the group. Where the rank and file are greatly interested in revolution or in reform, the powerful debater, the fluent speaker, or the man who has an attractive program tends to come to the fore. On the other hand, where there have been numerous strikes and much turmoil, a martyr to the cause or a stouthearted striker is likely to receive popular support.

---

[1] In some cases, as among janitors and milk-wagon drivers, it is exceedingly difficult for most of the members to attend union meetings.

[2] With reference to leaders and rank and file, see R. F. Hoxie, *Trade Unionism in the United States* (1924), Chap. 7; Bruce Minton and John Stuart, *Men Who Lead Labor* (1937); William Z. Foster, *Misleaders of Labor* (1927); Elsie Glück, *John Mitchell, Miner* (1929); George Soule, *Sidney Hillman, Labor Statesman* (1939); Herbert Harris, *American Labor* (1939); and Robert R. R. Brooks, *When Labor Organizes* (1937), Chap. 9.

[3] As in the notorious case of the president and an international representative of the International Alliance of Theatrical and Stage Employees charged with obtaining $100,000 from Paramount Pictures, Inc., in the course of several years.

In newly organized unions the emotional and the militant types of men are likely to come to the fore. When a union has become stable and has maintained acceptable bargaining relations with the employers, however, the successful bargainer and administrator is more likely to appeal. Again, the "good fellow" gains support as he does in any group, especially when militancy is at low ebb. As is implied in what has just been said, there is usually close kinship between management leaders and union leaders in the organized trades.[1] Fighters beget fighters, bargainers beget bargainers, appreciation of the other fellow's problems changes attitudes, demands, and behavior. Just as an unwanted unionism brings the militant leader, and a militant, restless rank and file, to the fore, so are acceptance by employers of the right to bargain collectively and square dealing usually followed by the development of suitable leadership. With exceptions, the rule, of course, "cuts both ways." Finally, racial and similar considerations may have much influence on the selection of leaders. That this is true is evidenced by the care sometimes exercised in slatemaking to give necessary consideration to the Polish, the Italian, and other votes. But whatever the definition of bigness may be in the given case, the "big men" tend strongly to become the recognized leaders.[2]

While the above is true, it is also true that the "machine" not infrequently develops in unions as in city and county governments. Here any proneness there may have been to pass offices around gives way. The machine may select and develop the new leaders; it is much more likely to keep the official class in power. However power is secured, those in important positions usually dislike to be displaced. Some of the offices may be very desirable because of the prestige they carry, or the emoluments they provide, or the use to which power can be put. It may be, too, that questions of union policy and the details connected with union administration are important; an opportunity is wanted to carry through.[3] In any event, it is difficult to displace leaders once they are in power. They have the advantage of superior knowledge of most issues raised; they can frequently down opposition as emanating from the "enemies of the union"; possibly it will "look bad" if they are turned out; perhaps assignments to committees and jobs can be used to gain support; there are possibilities of packing meeting halls when only a fraction of the members can find place in them; rough tactics can be used to frighten protesting minorities into submission; possibly the counting of ballots is controlled. Anyone at all familiar with union affairs can easily supply examples in point. Generally speaking, human

---

[1] See "Management Looks at the Labor Problem," in *Business Week*, Sept. 26, 1942, particularly p. 73.

[2] See R. F. Hoxie, *op. cit.*, Chap. 7.

[3] Of course, if efficient and trustworthy, continuity of leadership is very desirable.

nature works out in the union world very much as in municipal affairs. It cannot be denied that there is not a little misgovernment. Not infrequently leaders continue in office when a change would be desirable, and even when it is desired by those who have the best interests of the organization at heart.[1]

All of this is true. Yet certain things—in addition to an inclination to pass around among the deserving certain offices requiring little time— remain to be pointed out if an entirely accurate picture is to be sketched. There is truth in Hoxie's statement that a cleavage tends strongly to develop between the leader and the rank and file, imperiling the position of the leader. Charged with responsibility, he is sobered and broadened by his contacts. Very likely in the course of years he becomes more conservative and thinks in terms of the average and the longer run. This is the salvation of the union in its relations with the employer, but the rank and file tend to become suspicious. The leader may become unfamiliar with the techniques of the craft or industry as they change while he is away from the bench. This is likely to serve as evidence that he is becoming unfit. Finally, leaders have more or less responsibility for securing observance of working agreements with employers and for maintaining discipline. All these factors tend to bring about a cleavage and to beget change in leadership.[2]

In connection with the problem presented by union government, it is important to note also that as a rule the rank and file are better qualified to vote and to pass upon issues of men and measures than are the electors of a city, that issues raised are likely to be clear-cut and relatively simple, and that the union men and women have a more immediate and a more direct and personal interest in their union than the citizens have in their city. Hence, the leaders are held to a stricter responsibility in union than in municipal affairs. The problem of union misgovernment, though

---

[1] There have been not a few instances in which the elections called for by local union constitutions have not been held; the officers continued to function indefinitely. Until the spring of 1940, the Milk Wagon Drivers of Chicago had not held an election for twenty years. In the same city, only the death of Mike Carrazo, in August, 1940, released twenty-five local unions of street cleaners and related groups from his rule. Then, four of those unions held a joint meeting at which the vice-president was elevated to the presidency by standing vote. This done, it was voted that his term of office should be five years. Still another hod-carrier local has had the same officers since 1920, without re-election. The Constitution provides (Art. III, Sec. 4): "The election of officers shall be held once every five (5) years. Regularly elected officers shall retain their offices for the term of their election or *until their successors are duly elected and have qualified*" (italics supplied). A number of bills introduced in the 77th Congress have as an objective the elimination of such practices.

[2] Because of such factors, suspicion of leaders was more or less characteristic of the I.W.W. At the present time much suspicion is found in a considerable number of unions established in the upheaval in recent years. Such suspicion is more or less inevitable because it takes much time to develop thoroughgoing and stable union men.

not a small one, is at most times not so great as that in the public service.[1]

Directly connected with this problem is the further, larger problem of weak and inefficient leadership. Weak and inefficient leadership has been particularly prevalent in the United States,[2] partly because of the newness of a large share of the unions, partly because of the necessity of recognizing "national" groups, partly, also, because of little class consciousness, but perhaps more because of the graduation of leaders into something else. In considerable number the more ambitious go into business for themselves; some enter the professions; others secure political office; many are drafted into the employers' service as superintendents, commissioners, etc., as in the coal industry. The able leaders, because many will not continue in the union at considerable sacrifice to themselves, are as likely to be drained off as the weak ones are to be replaced.[3]

The Business Agent.—Comparatively few local union officers receive any remuneration, except, in some cases, allowances for wages lost while on special union work. It is chiefly the secretaries of large locals, and especially those of unions paying benefits of various kinds, and business agents (walking delegates) who are employed on salary.[4]

Most of the business unions large enough to afford to do so employ one or more "business agents," "deputies," or whatever they may be called. These agents are usually elected for a term of one year[5] and are found most conspicuously in the building trades, a fact explained by the

[1] It need hardly be said that union members participate very much more extensively and very much more effectively in the selection of their leaders and in the determination of policies than do stockholders in the government of large business corporations.

[2] This has been strikingly so during the last few years, when union organization has greatly expanded. Many of the leaders have been both "green" and awkward. Moreover, designing men have had more opportunity to worm themselves in than when the labor movement has not been divided and highly competitive. Frequently those displaced by one organization have been more or less readily accepted by another. The view may be expressed that there has been too much interest in acquiring members, too little in assimilating them and developing sound organization and good government.

[3] The loss of able leaders has been much greater in the United States than in Great Britain and most of the Continental European countries, where status, class consciousness, and related things have been important, and where the "best money" has not been so alluring.

[4] It cannot be denied, however, that there are here and there cases in which local union officers are paid handsome salaries. The salaries of officers of the Milk Wagon Drivers in Chicago have recently been drastically cut. Nevertheless, the president is paid $12,500 and the others in proportion. The president of the Musicians' Union in the same city has recently become president of the International at a salary of $20,000, which is $6,000 less than he has received as president of the local. The payment of such salaries may be questioned as not in line with sound union policy.

[5] Sometimes the president serves ex officio as business agent, and now and then a business agent, whose accomplishments have singled him out, is elected for life.

peculiar nature of the industry and the unusual mobility of the workers between one job and another, but they are to be found also in the clothing trades, the metal industries, the printing trades, and elsewhere. Where employed, the business agents commonly devote full time to their union duties and are paid a weekly salary. This, it may be noted, is generally little more than the standard rate for the trade or what would be earned on the job, but there have been not a few instances in which rather handsome salaries have been voted. The payment of $7,500 a year in one Chicago instance, of $200 per week in another, with automobile provided, may be cited as examples of the exceptional cases where relatively high salaries are paid to business agents.

Union organization (which is most frequently without reference to the work place) and union business being what they are, there is very generally need for a full-time administrator of matters other than office routine. It is the business affairs of the union other than those falling to the secretary and treasurer to which the business agent is presumed to devote most of his time.

Unless there is a specialized employment office maintained by the union, and sometimes even if there is, the business agent takes a hand in the placing of members available for jobs. In the piecework clothing industries, he participates in price making, much to the advantage of the workers immediately concerned, for the business agent is commonly well versed in piece rates being paid in the market and stands in no fear of losing his job when higgling with the representative of the employer. Moreover, he is usually an experienced and clever negotiator. He takes up disputes about the application of piece rates when the question is not disposed of within the shop and about hirings at less than the standard rate. He hears complaints from the workers of unjust treatment in work assignments, of unduly severe discipline, of discrimination against union men, and of the employment of nonunion men. In short, it is his business to adjust grievances not disposed of in the shop and to see to it that union working rules and the provisions of written or oral agreements between the union and the employer are observed. Put in other words, he is a union inspector and policeman. But this is only one phase of his work. In many cases he holds shop meetings, at times collects dues and assessments, and perhaps assists in getting the rank and file to attend union meetings. He busies himself as an organizer in the partially organized trades and in times of strike or lockout serves as a strike leader. Knowing many of the rank and file personally and being versed in the conditions of the trade and in agreements and working rules, he plays an important role when action is taken in union meetings or by union committees. Finally, the business agent may also participate in conferences when new agreements are being negotiated. He is the most important cog in local union administrative machinery and government.

There is usually plenty of useful, even indispensable, work to be done by the business agent where one is employed. An efficient, right-minded agent is of great value to the workers and their union and not infrequently to employers operating union shops as well. On the other hand, an inefficient, dishonest, or generally unfit business agent may present a real problem. Because of this, and at times because of his efficiency, one hears in many concrete cases more denunciation of the "walking delegate" than of all else.

Some of this denunciation comes from radicals and malcontents constituting protesting minorities in many unions. They and the business agent usually have different outlooks and different temperaments. Frequently, especially when there is widespread unemployment, the workers have exaggerated impressions of favoritism in placements and in other connections. Many of them feel aggrieved by the piece rates set for their operations. Not a little of the denunciation comes from businessmen who are unable or unwilling to "play the game" as required by agreements and union rules. In their minds the union may be identified largely with the business agent, for he is the administrative officer with whom they most frequently have to do. He is expected to try to prevent "chiseling." Many instances will be found where the honest and efficient business agent is the one most vigorously denounced. But by no means all of the denunciation is to be explained in these ways. Perhaps the business agent "bulldozes," as many employers do also; he may be a real troublemaker. In the building trades he has frequently been delegated a great deal of power, perhaps that of suspending work entirely when nonunion men are employed or a dispute of any kind arises. Possibly he becomes a grafter, accepting bribes from that type of employer who will try to purchase anything he wants or using his power to force the employer to purchase "strike insurance," "industrial counsel," or whatever it may be called, if the employer wishes to proceed with his business unmolested. That there has been not a little of this, chiefly in the building trades, has been shown by public and other investigations in Chicago, New York, and elsewhere.[1] It occurs most frequently where much power is vested in the business agent and where the rank and file are merely "bread and butter" unionists and care little how much the business agent profits so long as steady work at good wages is provided.

The great majority of business agents are honest, and a substantial majority of them are hardworking and fairly efficient. Yet exceptions are only too frequently found. There is therefore a problem which calls

---

[1] See, especially, reports of the Dailey Commission [*Report of Illinois Building Investigation Commission Authorized by the 52nd General Assembly*, 1921 (1923)]; the Lockwood Committee [New York (State) *Final Report of the Joint Legislative Committee on Housing* (Legislative Document 48, 1923)], and R. E. Montgomery, *Industrial Relations in the Chicago Building Trades* (1927), Chap. 9.

for solution;[1] but the problem finds parallels readily enough in business circles and in public affairs.

In this connection it should be pointed out that in the newly organized mass industries seldom is there a business agent except as the president of the local union acts as one.[2] There, organization is, for the most part, along industrial lines and by plant. Typically, the workers are aided or represented by grievance committeemen, these standing over against and matching management supervisors, and by a bargaining committee. Such abuses as sometimes occur in connection with business agents are largely avoided. On the other hand, there is no check, such as the outside business agent usually supplies, on precipitate action taken by the rank and file.

The International and Its Government

The local is commonly the basic unit in union organization. A great majority of the locals have, however, been drawn together into so-called "nationals" and "internationals,"[3] in order to meet the problems connected with widening markets and migrating workmen, to extend and protect organization of the craft or industry, and to increase the power of the locals in their struggles with the employers. This nationalization has been especially marked in the United States, where in 1942 there were more than 180 nationals and internationals, with affiliated locals having close to 90 per cent of the total trade-union membership of the country.[4]

[1] In the needle trades in certain localities care has been exercised to select and train good deputies. Almost always business agents are elected for periods of six months or a year by the rank and file, or serve ex officio because they hold a particular office, especially that of president. For a brief discussion, see J. M. Budish and George Soule, *The New Unionism* (1920), pp. 183–184.

[2] Locals of the industrial unions in the mass-production industries generally have a plant basis, and the work performed by the business agent of a craft union is assumed by a committee of employees in the plant.

[3] Most of these organizations are "international," *i.e.*, they have locals outside of the continental United States, chiefly in Canada, but in some cases in our insular possessions also. For example, the International Typographical Union recently had 621 locals in the United States, 45 in Canada, and 1 each in Hawaii, the Philippine Islands, and Puerto Rico.

[4] For a list of these and a statement of their jurisdictions, reported membership, etc., see "Handbook of American Trade-unions, 1936 Edition," U. S. Bureau of Labor Statistics, *Bulletin* 618; see also Leo Wolman, *Ebb and Flow in Trade Unionism* (1936). Wolman states that there were 141 nationals and internationals in 1934. They are listed, with membership, in Appendix Table I, pp. 172 *et seq.* The Bureau of Labor Statistics, in *Bulletin* 618, however, gives information on 156 nationals and internationals. The list does not include any internationals organized since March, 1936. By the end of 1939, the Industrial Relations Division of the Bureau of Labor Statistics recorded 175 internationals. In 1942 there were known to the Department of Labor 182 nationals, internationals, national councils, and national organizing committees. For the names and affiliations of these, see *Labor Relations Reporter*, vol. 10 (July 27, 1942), pp. 717–720.

In its government the international makes use of the representative principle, modified to a considerable extent by the principle of direct legislation. Conventions of delegates from affiliated locals are held annually, biennially, triennially, quadrennially, quinquennially, or on call.[1] The convention is both a constitutional assembly and a legislative body, for, subject to some limitations, it may amend the constitution, and it legislates within the powers vested in it. It determines policies, approves or disapproves of proposals for labor legislation at the hands of the Congress or the state legislatures, sometimes adopts shop rules to be observed by the member locals, has increasingly established by-laws for the government of the affiliated locals, and legislates on other matters.

A majority of the internationals have, however, made provision for the use of the referendum and the initiative. Frequently constitutional amendments and only less frequently other measures are referred by the convention to the locals for acceptance or rejection by their members.[2] Almost as frequently, provision is made for the initiation of measures by affiliated locals, which then call for action by a convention or for popular vote. Direct legislation has, in fact, been more prevalent in trade-union government than in the governments of our municipalities and states. For years together, in a few instances, measures have been put to a

---

[1] The old arrangement generally was for each local to have one delegate and one vote, but as a result of democracy and gradual reduction in the amount of local fear and local desire to retain power, this has become quite exceptional. At present the number of delegates almost always varies with, but not in proportion to, the paid-up memberships of the several affiliated locals. Most matters are disposed of in convention by a show of hands, etc., each delegate having one vote, but on roll call on closely contested issues it has become more and more the rule for the delegates to have votes varying directly with the membership of the locals they represent.

An examination of the constitutions of 143 internationals, effective in 1936, reveals the following frequencies of conventions: (a) annually (including one dependent on call by executive officers and one on referendum vote), 44; (b) biennially (including four subject to referendum vote), 41; (c) triennially (including one dependent upon referendum vote), 23; (d) quadrennially (including two dependent upon referendum vote), 19; (e) quinquennially (including one dependent upon referendum vote), 6; (f) on call by executive council, 4, or on referendum vote, 4; (g) on special provision for holding of conventions, 2.

It is to be noted, however, that because of financial strain or for other reason, it is not highly exceptional for conventions not to be held regularly. For example, it was reported in August, 1939, that the Machinists and the Carpenters had held no conventions since 1928, the Electrical Workers none since 1929, and the Wood Carvers none since 1930. Numerous other internationals, after necessary procedures, have postponed or omitted one or more "regular" conventions. In some cases a substitute has been found in the referendum, in others in action taken by the executive committee or executive board.

[2] In analysis of 126 international constitutions in effect in 1936 shows that 64 contained no provision for the referendum on amendments. In 18 of the 62 constitutions that had provisions for the use of rank-and-file vote, such use was both general and mandatory. In the other cases it was limited or optional, rank-and-file vote being complementary to or a partial substitute for convention action.

popular vote and no conventions held.[1] The strong appeal made by popular government in the case of the internationals is explained in part by the desire to have a check upon unrepresentative government, in part by the fact that it is the democratic thing, in part by the desire to stimulate, interest, and educate the rank and file, without which a strong, stouthearted, and progressive unionism cannot be maintained.

While the principle of direct legislation finds extensive application in the government of our international unions, enthusiasm for it is considerably less than it was twenty or thirty years ago. The few organizations that had employed the initiative and referendum only have resumed the holding of conventions. This waning of enthusiasm is the product of union experience with direct legislation. The number of popular votes taken has in some instances become burdensome; generally the interest aroused has not been great, and only a minority have voted on measures referred;[2] some initiated measures have been defectively worked or out of harmony with other laws or parts of the constitution; a law adopted by popular vote may be difficult to revise or repeal when it has proved to be undesirable, if revision or repeal requires rank-and-file vote; the discussions of measures in the official journal and in the local meetings may magnify differences, lead to misunderstanding, dissatisfaction, and dissension, while conventions are likely to go through a period of struggle and end in compromise and harmony. Certainly conventions, with committee reports, provide opportunity for a more thorough discussion of ideas on a given subject than do official journal presentations and referenda. Moreover, experience has shown that conventions may be helpful in other ways. Their by-products may be important. Personal contacts are there established and these further cooperative handling of issues as they arise; delegates fraternize and get suggestions as to how their special, local problems might best be solved; experiences are recounted and strategy and techniques improved; the selection of a delegate and decision upon instructions to be given him may arouse interest in the local union; at any rate, the delegate reports back to his local, usually in a stimulative way. Finally, conventions arouse interest and give added prestige and strength to organization in the cities in which they are held.[3]

While enthusiasm for direct legislation in the government of internationals has waned and while the value of conventions has become more

---

[1] An extreme example is found in the Granite Cutters, who, after their convention in 1881, did not hold another until 1912.

[2] For not untypical experience with referenda, see an article by John P. Frey in *International Molders' Journal*, June, 1924, pp. 359–360. The article has been quoted by David J. Saposs, in his *Reading in Trade Unionism* (1926), pp. 149–150.

[3] But the costs of entertainment, etc., frequently impose great financial strain upon the locals.

fully recognized, there remains an appreciation of the initiative and the referendum as instruments to be used as and when checks are needed on misrepresentative conventions. Provision for direct legislation is still being incorporated in a considerable proportion of constitutions as new internationals are established.

The officers of the international union are a president, one or more vice-presidents, a secretary, a treasurer, and others, and an executive board consisting of some or all of the officers mentioned and perhaps a number of other persons elected by convention or by popular vote. The old method of selection, three or four decades ago, was by vote of delegates in convention. This practice still obtains in a majority of instances, but an increasing minority of internationals have adopted the method of popular vote.[1] The latter method meets the desire for a democratic selection; more important, it removes from the convention the heat, logrolling, distraction, and disturbance incidental to selection by delegates. It may be added that, while at times popular vote has been accompanied by unfortunate campaigning through the official journal and questions of balloting and vote counting, it succeeds better here than in legislative matters, for personalities arouse more interest and call forth a larger vote than do most measures.

The officers of the international, of course, have immediate charge of the administrative functions indicated by their offices. Some of them devote much time to organizing work. Moreover, the officers have a large hand in matters of legislation, for they are almost always delegates to the convention, are most familiar with the affairs of the organization, and report to the convention, with suggestions that are referred to committees for consideration. Moreover, the important committees are likely to be selected by the official class so that their policies as well as their stewardship are generally reviewed by sympathetic hands. Finally, when necessary, the general executive board makes decisions between conventions.

Vested with much power and occupying an advantageous position, the leading officials play a large role in determining the policies and laws of the union. Strong leaders, such as Sidney Hillman of the Amalgamated Clothing Workers, George Harrison of the Railway Clerks, and John Mitchell, formerly president of the United Mine Workers, are invaluable to their organizations; the weak, also the occasionally more or less corrupt, leaders, sometimes able to retain power for years by controlling organizers, packing conventions, withdrawing charters of

---

[1] An examination of the constitutions of 144 internationals, in effect in 1936, shows that the general officers, at any rate the chief officers, are normally elected in convention in 103 cases, by popular vote in 41. In the event of popular election, nominations are made by convention or by affiliated locals.

locals, etc., are a great hindrance to their organizations and in some instances have virtually wrecked them.[1]

To have an able leader as its commander in chief, properly supported by a good executive board, means for an international union what a good President, aided and advised by a good cabinet, means for the citizenship of the United States.

THE WORK OF THE INTERNATIONAL AND OF THE LOCAL UNION

We turn from these phases of union government to a brief discussion of the division of function between the international and the local and the control exercised by the former over the latter in the interest of efficiency but at the expense of local autonomy.

It has been said that, though the local is the structural unit, the international has become the economic unit. This is a pardonable exaggeration, for while as regards the distribution of power and division of function there are unions and unions, the tendency in the United States has been to confer upon the international, or for it to take into itself, more and more power and to exercise more and more control over its affiliated locals. The widening area of markets, the increasing mobility of workers, the inauguration and conduct of strikes with the object in view of preventing unwise or inexpedient action and of limiting the number of suspensions to be conducted and financed at a given time, and several other factors enter into the explanation of this shift in power and control. Some of the additional factors require brief comment.

As has been indicated,[2] unions ordinarily provide benefits of one or more kinds, most frequently burial allowances, but in some cases sickness and accident and unemployment benefits, also. Partly for reasons of financial expediency, partly because of the desire to generalize and standardize the provision made, partly because of administrative considerations, these benefit systems are largely "international."

Problems connected with admission to membership have called into existence much "international law" relating to eligibility by race, sex, and training and have frequently led to the setting of a uniform or a maximum initiation fee.[3] Dues paid to the locals and in part transferred to the international are frequently regulated by "international law" in order to keep them low, or, much more frequently, to insure that they are

---

[1] The histories of the United Mine Workers, the International Typographical Union, and the International Photoengravers' Union, and of less fortunate organizations provide eloquent evidence of the difference between efficient leadership on the one hand and weak or corrupt leadership on the other.   For an exaggerated but interesting and helpful account of undesirable union leadership, see William Z. Foster, *Misleaders of Labor*. For a sympathetic account of the activities of a successful leader, see Elsie Glück, *John Mitchell, Miner*.

[2] Chaps. I, IV, VII, and VIII of vol. II.

[3] *Infra*, pp. 259–270.

adequate to finance a vigorous unionism. Some internationals have adopted a number of work rules to be observed by their constituent locals, though with most of the unions rule making is local. The laws of the International Typographical Union, for example, provide for the closed shop and lay down rules with reference to a variety of things such as the hiring and discharge of workers. A great majority of the craft internationals have apprentice rules that are to be enforced by their locals in so far as possible, with such further requirements as these locals may add. Some of the internationals—the Railroad Brotherhoods, the United Mine Workers, the Amalgamated Clothing Workers among others—are parties to agreements with employers covering all or a large part of the United States. These are exceptional, however, since most joint agreements are local; yet in the strongly organized trades the local representatives are advised and aided by the international officers when making contracts. Frequently, local contracts must include provisions set up by the international; in some cases, as in the newspaper industry, most of the agreements entered into locally are underwritten and guaranteed by the central organization.

Last to be mentioned, but perhaps most important, among the functions of the international is that of protecting, mending, extending, and invigorating the organization of its trade or industry.

The control and financing of strikes in many cases protects locals against being broken up.[1] Further protection is rather generally

---

[1] Control over the calling of strikes by the affiliated locals is very extensively exercised by the internationals. The objectives of the control are to make sure of the adequacy of the cause, to reduce the number of lost strikes and of broken unions, and to protect such internationals as finance strikes against unduly heavy financial burdens.

Not long after their inception a great majority of the internationals began to control the calling of strikes and then in only a smaller number of cases to participate in the financing of them. Dr. Glocker found thirty years ago that 113 of 130 constitutions examined provided for more or less extensive control of strikes, at any rate (in 81 of the cases) of those strikes involving financial support by the international. [See T. W. Glocker, *The Government of American Trade Unions*, Johns Hopkins University Studies, Series 31 (1913). For details, see G. M. Janes, *Control of Strikes in American Trade Unions*, Johns Hopkins University Studies, Series 33 (1916).] Though the proportion of new internationals is large at this time (1942) and some of them have only limited functions, no doubt an intensive study would show that the relative number of internationals controlling the calling of strikes is fully as large as it was twenty-five years ago. Indeed, the constitutions of very few internationals contain no provision for it.

With exceptions, the constitutions of the internationals provide that strikes may be called only with the approval of the international executive board or of the president, and many of them specify in more or less detail the procedure to be followed by the local and the international officers before a strike may be called "legally." While this procedure agrees more or less from international organization to international organization, that of the Molders' Union is fairly typical in most respects. The constitution of that organization, after stating "Strikes are not beneficial to our organization; and it would be to our interest to avoid, as much as possible, all strikes, and not to resort to them until all other means at

provided by requiring the bonding of officers, the proper handling and the periodic auditing of funds, etc. Most strong internationals not only publish a journal to extend the education and to improve and support the morale of their members, but also maintain a staff of organizers to organize and guide new locals, to restore harmony where dissension has developed, and to invigorate anemic locals as well as to cooperate in the conferences with employers and to participate in the conduct of strikes. The importance of these activities is shown by the fact that in spite of the efforts put forth to prevent losses, the unions affiliated with the A.F. of L., between 1899 and 1914, lost 23,930 locals, while acquiring 50,293. The mortality rate of local unions has been and still is high.

This section may be closed with the statement that, in contrast to the situation years ago when the international was a weak supplement to or a federation of the locals, the local has in most of the strongly organized trades become pretty much an agent of the central organization and stands in its relations to it very much as the municipality or county stands to the state.

Admission to Membership: Union Finance

Reference has been made to a number of matters which internationals have tended to standardize and to control. Some of these are discussed elsewhere in this volume, but this is not true of admission to union membership, or of dues and initiation fees. Because of their importance these subjects are briefly discussed at this point.

Admission to Membership.—The constitution of each international states its jurisdictional claims. Whether these claims are narrow or wide as tested by the occupational groups to be found in the industry, they establish the main rule of eligibility to membership to be observed by the affiliated locals. But various problems have frequently resulted in further detailed legislation by the internationals.

---

our disposal are exhausted," provides that when a local by a three-fourths majority shall vote to resist an employer's demand or to stand by its own demand, the molders shall continue at work; that a bill of grievances and statement of conditions shall be sent to the international headquarters; that, thereupon, the president or an aid shall investigate the dispute and try to effect a settlement; in the event a settlement is not effected, the international executive board approves or disapproves the proposed strike; if the strike is approved, the international pays strike benefits, in the case of full-fledged journeymen at a rate of $9.60 per week; the international reserves the right to end a strike on two weeks' notice; for engaging in an unapproved strike there is penalty of suspension of the members and/or the local.

A considerable number of the internationals, like the Molders' Union, require a three-fourths vote (and a few of them a four-fifths vote) to carry a strike motion, but a larger number require only a two-thirds vote or a mere majority. About two-thirds of the internationals, like the Molders', pay strike benefits out of their treasuries; only a minority of those exercising control do not. These payments are explained in part by the fact that effective control over strikes depends largely on the payment and withholding of financial aid.

Labor organizations generally claim to be guided by the principle of inclusiveness in their organizational activities. Yet there are exceptions and limitations. Under apprentice rules, discussed in a later chapter, a measure of training is required. In the absence of such apprentice training, competency, as shown by experience, quality of work done, or examination, may suffice for membership in the union. But the principle of inclusiveness of competent workers is not infrequently departed from by craft unions and in time of unemployment by many industrial unions as well. "Books" may be closed when there is a scarcity of jobs; indeed, as during the depression of the 1930's, not only has gaining entrance to unionized trades frequently been discouraged, but in some cases the initiation fees—and possibly dues—of the younger members (younger in terms of membership) have been returned to them and membership canceled. This has of course been in an effort to adjust the supply of labor to an inadequate demand for it under the conditions obtaining. Though relatively few in number, there have also been instances in which union books have been closed when there was really no job scarcity. For example, a local building-trades organization in San Francisco, during the building boom following the Great Fire of 1906, refused even to accept "cards" of members in good standing in sister locals, and its members for months earned double the normal wages by long hours and Sunday labor paid for at penal rates. Growing out of such episodes, here and there "international law" forbids affiliated locals to close their books.

The closing of union books does not always mean that nonmembers are denied employment in union shops. Work permits may, at a price, be issued. This sytem has been used in seasonal industries so as to limit the number of members to the normal needs of the trade, as in brewing and, most frequently, in building construction. It has in some cases led to serious abuses, as, for example, in Chicago, where during the twenties and early thirties officials of the Local Projectionists' Union assigned jobs to permit men at the expense of regular members. Not only were taxes on the former higher than union dues and thus a source of additional income, but the system could also be used to control stubborn voting members. Growing revolt led to violent action; in the early thirties a number of protesting union members were shot. Finally, however, the international stepped in to clean up the situation. After 1935 the permit system apparently was no longer used as a disciplinary device, and preference to union members in job assignments became the rule.

Closely related to the problems just mentioned are those connected with the migration of workmen. Barbers, printers, musicians, and others may migrate for economic or other reasons; not infrequently they seek employment in certain localities in unduly large numbers. A local union may attempt to secure job protection by declining to accept or by exacting a second initiation fee from those who have good standing in sister locals. In order to prevent such abuses and to have a well-recognized rule, a large proportion of the internationals have legislated on the acceptance of cards and have placed a ban on the collection of a fee from unionists "transferring in" from sister locals.[1] Sometimes, however, such prohibitions are not observed, largely because of a strong feeling on the part of old members of a local that those who seek to share work opportunities should, so to speak, buy into the valuable partnership that has perhaps been developed by much sacrifice and at considerable cost. The local organization may have built up large reserves or property holdings. And, added to this feeling of what justice calls for, the local can use the money. Thus job protection, established interests, and financial need enter into the explanation of attempted discriminations against migrating unionists. They also enter into the explanation of some restrictive practices, such as the exaction of high initiation fees from nonunionists seeking membership in unions in well-organized trades, a matter to which we shall refer presently.

Women and Negro workers have frequently been excluded from union membership or have otherwise been discriminated against. The problems presented have raised questions of policy and begotten legislation by internationals extensively controlling the practices of their affiliated locals.

Regulations concerning eligibility of women to membership have, of course, tended to run in terms of the classes of persons employed at the time. Unless women in appreciable number found employment at the time of union organization, many of the international constitutions provided for the admission of males only. In other cases the national constitutions established no specific rule bearing upon the particular point. As time passed, however, women increasingly found employment in many of the various trades and industries and the question inevitably arose as to admission to membership. Perhaps, as in the manufacture of cigars, when women secured employment in the shops they were objected to because of the fear of new competition and were in many cases excluded from membership in the local unions. The question then came before the international for decision upon policy. Some of the internationals concerned legislated to organize women workers, on the theory that it was better to have them in the union than to have them compete

---

[1] Not so the American Federation of Musicians. Its rules provide that all members must deposit transfer cards if they work more than a week within the jurisdiction of another local union. A local must admit any out-of-town member who presents such a card. He is only admitted to full membership, however, after six months' residence and payment of the regular initiation fee. In the meantime he pays dues to both his old local and the one to which he has transferred. "Stand-by" fees are also charged if a traveling musician plays an engagement reserved for local members. Finally, traveling members pay special taxes to the international.

from outside. Indeed, some of them, in an effort to organize women
workers, offered special inducements, such as lower dues or initiation fees
than were paid by men.[1] However, many of the internationals were slow
to revise their constitutions so as to make women eligible to membership
or to make specific rules to prevent affiliated locals from discriminating
against them.[2] At the beginning of the First World War, the doors of a
considerable number of unions remained closed. By the end of the War
period, (1919) however, all but a few of the internationals with jurisdiction in trades and industries in which women had found employment had
opened their doors to them. Yet this does not necessarily mean that
there have been no cases in which efforts to organize women have been
slow. Neglect in organizing efforts, combined with the occupational
distribution of the sexes, the fact that a much larger percentage of women
than of men have been unskilled while, until very recently, most union
organization has been of the skilled and along craft lines, the short-time
interest of most women workers in the employment they have, the handicap women are under in attending union meetings, etc., explain why a
much smaller percentage of women than of men have belonged to labor
unions.

The foregoing observations concerning admission of women to union
membership apply to a considerable extent, also, in the case of Negroes.
It should be added, however, that the discrimination against Negroes
has tended to be greater than that against women, because Negroes have
more frequently found entrance into an industry as strikebreakers and
because of racial antipathy—a rather general fact. In 1943 there were
seven A.F. of L. and six non-A.F. of L. internationals that excluded
Negroes by constitutional provision. A few other internationals, such as
the Boilermakers and the Machinists, were accomplishing the same result
by ritual—pledging members not to present for membership anyone who
was not of the white race. Furthermore, there have been numerous
instances in which local unions have kept their doors closed to Negroes
in violation of international rule.[3]

Discrimination of one kind or another falling short of exclusion has
also obtained. In the case of the Sheet Metal Workers, membership
is in auxiliary organizations. Here and there, separate city central

[1] A considerable minority of unions exact lower initiation fees and dues from women
than from men.

[2] Internationals usually acted slowly, when at all, to open the doors to women because
of the strong opposition of the locals. Nor was favorable action taken always successful.
For example, when the Cigar Makers in 1875 passed a law admitting women, several of
its locals withdrew in protest and remained outside for several years. See F. E. Wolfe,
Admission to American Trade Unions, Johns Hopkins University Studies, Series 30 (1912),
p. 18. For historical reviews of women and the labor movement, see Chap. III of this
volume and Alice Henry, *Women and the Labor Movement* (1923), Chaps. 2–6.

[3] The Plumbers of Chicago may be cited as one instance.

bodies have been maintained for "colored locals"; and it is probable that neglect to organize Negro workers eligible to membership has been of much more frequent occurrence than outright discrimination against or exclusion of them.

This adverse treatment of the Negro has, of course, generally been at the hands of well-meaning people. The facts are easily understandable in the light of racial differences, employment experience, and other factors. Nevertheless, the discrimination has been unfortunate from the point of view of a vigorous and sound labor movement. It has militated against a constructive solution of the "racial problem," which calls for occupational opportunity.

Seldom have newly organized C.I.O. unions drawn the color line. Naturally, industrial unions in the organizing stage seek to organize all persons in employment, except "blacklegs."[1] Though its efforts have met with only limited success, because it has been a mere federation, the general position taken by the A.F. of L. is to be approved. To start with, the Federation was not disposed to tolerate by its affiliated organizations any exclusion of or discrimination against Negroes but favored the organization of all workers without regard to creed or race. As a condition of affiliation of the Locomotive Firemen, in the late 1890's, it sought to require that organization to lift its ban on Negroes, but without success. By 1900 it had become clear that the Federation could do little more than exercise moral suasion; the internationals balked at dictation. Beginning with the turn of the century, the Federation issued charters to colored locals and central bodies. Separate organization was again emphasized at the conclusion of World War I, but the effort to organize on that basis was rather unsuccessful because of the ineffectiveness of the Federation as an incidental international.[2] It has not been able to provide its member locals with the aid and supervision needed. More recently the general policy of the Federation has been to refer Negroes to the regular craft and industrial unions and to use moral suasion as best it could in an effort to provide Negroes with a normal place in the organized labor movement.[3]

[1] It may be noted that Art. II (1) of the constitution of the C.I.O. states that one of its objects is "to bring about the effective organization of the working men and women of America regardless of race, creed, color, or nationality. . . . "

[2] Recently, however, the Federation has created machinery for the better protection and guidance of its directly affiliated locals.

[3] Cf. S. D. Spero and A. L. Harris, The Black Worker (1931); American Federation of Labor, Proceedings: 1932, pp. 216–223; 1933, pp. 269–270; 1934, pp. 330–334; 1935, pp. 808–819, 827, 829; 1936, p. 379. See also F. E. Wolfe, op. cit., Chap. 6, and Herbert R. Northrup, "Organized Labor and the Negro Worker, "Journal of Political Economy, vol. 51, pp. 206–221 and 550. Two states, and possibly others, have legislated against racial discrimination by trade unions. A Kansas statute passed in 1941 prohibits any union (except organizations under the Railway Labor Act) from acting as a collective-bargaining

Union Finance: Initiation Fees and Dues.—Historically, policy with respect to initiation fees and local dues was the concern of the locals, not of the international, but this has undergone very considerable change as the internationals have performed new functions and gained more power. The change is explained in part as incidental to the financing of the international, but more so by efforts to protect against weakness in this direction or that. While many of the internationals exercise no control over fees or dues, many others definitely fix them or establish maxima, or minima, or both.

A number of internationals definitely fix the initiation fee to be charged by their member locals. Most frequently this fee is a small one, say $1 to $5. In rather exceptional cases, however, the fee prescribed is a high one. The Stone Cutters charge $75, the Elevator Constructors $200. Other internationals, in the interest of standardization and to protect against restrictive practices by locals, limit the fees that may be exacted. Most frequently the maxima are moderate: $5 in the cases of the Locomotive Firemen and the Railway Conductors, and $10 in the case of the Amalgamated Clothing Workers, but with the Brewery Workers the maximum rises to $28. A large number of internationals, indeed the largest number exercising control, set minimum fees to be charged, unless waived during organizing campaigns, as initiation fees frequently are. These minima may be $1, as in the case of the Railroad Trainmen, $5, as in the cases of the Machinists, Glass Bottle Blowers, and Railroad Telegraphers, or $10, as in the cases of the Carpenters, the Longshoremen, and the Carmen. A considerable number of those regulating fees, however, set both minima and maxima and permit the locals to exercise their discretion within the limits set. The minima are usually low, for example, $1 or $5, but are occasionally rather high as in the cases of the Bricklayers and Asbestos Workers, where the fee is $25. Likewise the maxima set vary widely, from $5 in the case of the United Garment Workers, to $25 with the Bakery and Confectionery Workers and the Leather Workers, to $50 with the Hod Carriers and Musicians, to $100 with the Asbestos Workers and the Lathers.[1]

Usually some part of the local initiation fee is taken by the international as a source of revenue. In other cases, however, the international may impose an additional fee.

---

representative, if it discriminates against or excludes from membership any person because of his race. New York amended its civil rights law in 1940 to prohibit unions from excluding anyone because of race or creed or denying equal treatment in designation of members for promotion or dismissal by an employer.

[1] International constitutions are not always observed. For example, in 1940, a Chicago local of common laborers was exacting an initiation fee of $70, though the maximum set by the International Constitution was $50.

The details presented show that not a few of the internationals have so regulated initiation fees as to prevent the restrictive practices alluded to above. But such is by no means always the case. With some internationals prescribing high fees and with others permitting the locals to exact high fees because of the setting of minimum fees only or because of no control being exercised, there are not a few cases in which considerable restriction is practiced through burdensome initiation fees. If concrete instances may be cited, $50, $75, $100, $202.50, $250, or $500 is the price paid for membership in particular organizations. Such exactions are a part of the so-called "union problem." Prevention of the levy of heavy exactions is one of the things those who would license and regulate unions propose. In the exaction of high initiation fees many union leaders also see a problem, but one which, in their opinion, should be solved by the organized labor movement itself, not by legislative intervention.[1]

The greater part of union revenues is derived from dues, regularly exacted except perhaps from unemployed members, and from assessments levied now and then to finance strikes or organizing campaigns or to meet deficits incurred in some way or other. Two generations ago, dues levied by American unions, as a whole, were low compared to those being levied by British unions. The contrast was found to an extent even a generation ago. This contrast has, however, largely disappeared, because of the diminished importance of the "old model" unions in Britain, of the development of social insurance there, and of the tendency in the United States for those unions whose members can afford to pay more to increase dues from time to time. In the United States, fifty or sixty years ago, union dues levied were most frequently not very different from those collected—when any were collected—by company unions in recent years. Only exceptionally were they as much as $1 per month; frequently they were as low as 10 cents per week. At present, it is chiefly newly organized unions and most industrial unions, a part of whose members receive low wages, that levy low dues. In such cases the dues are most frequently $1 per month. While in union after union there has been stout opposition on the part of the membership to the levy of increased dues to improve union administration, or to strengthen the

---

[1] Partly because of newspaper publicity, partly because of a desire to provide easy access to jobs in a wartime economy, numerous bills have been introduced into the Congress during the recent sessions, these generally providing for reporting initiation fees, dues, and assessments as part of a system of annual union registration with the Department of Labor or some other agency of the Federal Government, but some of them prohibiting the exaction of any initiation fee from workers accepting employment in war industries. Some of the measures are receiving active consideration in Congress. It is not improbable that some registration measure will be enacted. Practically all these bills, it should be noted, apply only to labor organizations. In other countries, for example, Australia, both employers' associations and unions register.

defense fund, or to finance unemployment, sickness, disability, or old-age benefits, there has been a strong tendency to increase dues and to extend and improve the services of the unions.   Union leaders generally urge a high-dues policy; experience is interpreted as showing its wisdom. Adequate revenues add greatly to the strength and effectiveness of a labor organization.   Sometimes, however, a personal interest is also evident; the larger the revenues, the higher are the salaries that can be paid to salaried officers.

Most of the internationals that regulate local dues follow the policy of "adequate" dues and provide that these shall be not less than a stipulated sum per member.   The minima set are on the whole moderate (from 50 cents per month, as in the case of the Butchers, to $1.50, as in the case of the Upholsterers, Railway Carmen, and the Painters and Decorators), the most frequent minimum being $1 (for example, for the Barbers, the United Garment Workers, and the Operating Engineers). However, not a few prescribe higher minimum dues ($2, as in the case of the Teamsters and Metal Polishers, $2.75, as in the case of the Lithographers, or $3, as in the case of the Electrical Workers).   About a third as many set a uniform fee for all locals.   These fees range mainly from 40 cents (42 cents in the case of the Railway Mail Association) to $1 (as in the case of the Marine and Shipbuilding Workers), although there are instances of high fees (for example, $3.25 in the case of the Molders).   In contrast to these, a few unions, chiefly those with a propaganda interest and a desire to gain adherents, provide that dues shall not exceed a given sum.   Some unions, in an effort to encourage organization of helpers, unskilled workers, and women, provide for lower dues for these groups.

Further regulation of local dues is found in connection with financing of the international.   Like the local, the international relies mainly upon dues and assessments for its revenues, and a large majority of internationals take their dues out of the local fees.   Most of those receiving a share of local dues take from 30 cents to $1 per month [for example, 30 cents in the case of the Teamsters, 33 cents in the case of the Railway Mail Association, and $1 in the case of the Machinists, the Stone Cutters, and (for members earning under $5 a day) the Paper Makers].   A few take smaller or larger amounts (21 cents in the case of the United National Association of Post Office Clerks, $2 in the case of the Photo Engravers, $3 in the case of the Bridge, Structural, and Ornamental Iron Workers).

In a few cases, exceptions to the historical rule, union revenues have been the property of the international, which has divided them between itself and its locals.   The Cigar Makers charge $1, giving the locals 50 per cent of this amount, and the Boot and Shoe Workers return a third of their dues of $1.52 to their locals.   In a minority of cases the international collects a fee from the members in addition to that levied upon

TABLE 5.—INITIATION FEES AND DUES AS PRESCRIBED OR REGULATED AND BENEFITS AS PROVIDED IN TYPICAL UNION CONSTITUTIONS

Name of union	Initiation fees			Monthly dues			Benefits							Remarks
	National	Local	Total	National	Local	Total	Death	Disability	Old-age	Journal	Sickness	Strike	Unemployment	
Automobile, Aircraft and Agricultural Implement Workers.	25% of local. min. $1.00b	Min. $3.00 Max. $15.00	Min. $2.00 Max. $15.00	$0.40b	$1.00	$1.00				X				Subscription to journal voluntary
Cigar Makers.	$3.00	Keeps 50% of international	$3.00	$1.00	Keeps 50% of international	$1.00				X		X		
Amalgamated Clothing Workers.	No provision	Max. $10.00	Max. $10.00	$0.50a	No provision	No provision								Must buy at least one publication
Elevator Constructors.	$20.00b	$200.00	$200.00	$1.65b	No provision	No provision								
Flint Glass Workers.	$3.00a	No provision	No provision	2% of earnings	No provision	No provision								
United Garment Workers.	$0.50b	Min. $3.00 Max. $5.00 Higher if approved by G.E.B.	Min. $3.00	$0.50a	Min. $1.00	Min. $1.00	X					X		Women lower local dues
Granite Cutters.	$25.00a	No provision	No provision	$2.00a	5% of international plus max. of $1.00	Max. $3.10	X	X (loss of sight)		X		X		Apprentices lower international fees
Hod Carriers.	$5.00a	Min. $5.00 Max. $50.00	Min. $10.00 Max. $55.00	$0.35b	No provision	No provision								
Ladies' Garment Workers.	$1.50b	No provision	No provision	$0.73b	No provision	No provision	X			X		X (aid to locals)		

TABLE 5.—INITIATION FEES AND DUES AS PRESCRIBED OR REGULATED AND BENEFITS AS PROVIDED IN TYPICAL UNION CONSTITUTIONS.—(Continued)

Name of union	Initiation fees			Monthly dues			Benefits							Remarks
	National	Local	Total	National	Local	Total	Death	Disability	Journal	Old-age	Sickness	Strike	Unemployment	
Locomotive Firemen	$0.60b	Max. $5.00	Min. $0.60 Max. $5.00	$0.95a	No provision	No provision	X	X (additional payments)	X			X		
Machinists	$1.50b	Min. $5.00	Min. $5.00	$1.00b	Min. $1.75	Min. $1.75	X	X	X			X (also victimization)		Helpers and apprentices lower local fees and international dues. Beneficial higher international dues
Metal Polishers	$3.00b	Min. $5.00	Min. $5.00	$0.90b	Min. $2.00	Min. $2.00	X		X			X		Helpers and women lower fees. Beneficial higher international dues
United Mine Workers	No provision	$10.00	$10.00	$0.50a	Min. $0.75	Min. $0.75						X		Lower local initiation for inexperienced. None for sons 16–21
Molders	$2.00b	$5.00	$5.00	$2.17b	$3.25	$3.25	X		X		X (local but national constitution sets terms)	X (also victimization)	X	Non-journeymen lower fees

TABLE 5.—INITIATION FEES AND DUES AS PRESCRIBED OR REGULATED AND BENEFITS AS PROVIDED IN TYPICAL UNION CONSTITUTIONS. (Continued)

Name of union	Initiation fees			Monthly dues			Benefits							Remarks
	National	Local	Total	National	Local	Total	Death	Disability	Journal	Old-age	Sickness	Strike	Unemployment	
Operating Engineers	No provision	Min. $2.00	Min. $2.00	$0.75[b]	Min. $1.00	Min. $1.00	X		X			X		
Paper Makers	50 % of the local fee[b]	Earning under $6.00 a day: min. $5.00. Earning $6.00 or over a day: min. $10.00; max. $30.00	Min. $5.00–$10.00 Max. $50.00	$1.00[b]	No provision	No provision	X					X (aid to locals)		Women lower initiation and international dues
Photo-Engravers	No provision	No provision	No provision	$2.00[b]	No provision	No provision	X		X		X (tuberculosis)	X		Apprentices lower international dues
Printing Pressmen	$2.50 plus a day's pay	No provision	No provision	$2.15[b]	Specified increase for increase in wages	No provision	X			X	X (Home)	X		Lower international dues for assistants and apprentices
Rubber Workers	$1.00[b]	$2.00	$2.00	$0.45[b]	$1.00	$1.00			X			X		
Railroad Trainmen	No provision	Min. $1.00	Min. $1.00	$0.25[a]	No provision	No provision	X (on payment of additional premiums)	X (on payment of additional premiums)	X	X (with additional premiums)	X (tuberculosis)	X		Beneficial higher national dues
United Textile Workers (C.I.O.)	$1.00[b]	No provision	No provision	$0.50[b]	Min. $1.00	Min. $1.00								
Typographical Union	Those under $5, $5.00 Over $5, $10.	No provision	No provision	$0.70[b]	No provision	No provision	X (Home)	X (Home)	X	X	X (Home)	X		Beneficial higher international dues

[a] In addition to local fees.
[b] Taken out of local fees.

them by the local. These amounts vary from small ones to fairly high dues (25 cents in the case of the Railroad Trainmen, 95 cents in the case of the Locomotive Firemen and Engineers, $2 in the case of the Granite Cutters), a slight majority charging less than $1. In highly exceptional cases the international takes a certain percentage of the earnings of the members, in addition to fees paid to the locals, as in the 2 per cent of earnings taken by the Flint Glass Workers. The general rule, however, has been increasingly for the international to levy a per capita tax, as empowered by its constitution, and to collect this from each of its locals rather than from the members individually. With the ascendancy of the internationals and with the more frequent provision of benefits, these per capita taxes have increased and have become a larger fraction of the per capita taxes or dues paid by the rank and file as a condition of remaining members in good standing. The relationship between international and local dues and initiation fees and the benefits provided by the international are illustrated in Table 5.

TRADE COUNCILS: LOCAL, DISTRICT, AND STATE

An examination of the structure, government, and functions of different units in union organization calls next for brief mention of joint boards, district councils, state councils,[1] and other devices now rather generally sandwiched in between the American international and its affiliated locals. The development of these intermediate organizations is explained by the experience of the unions; there is a strong tendency to shape and to reshape union structure in order to meet problems as they arise.

Only such exceptional organizations as the compositors hold to the rule of one local[2] in a city without regard to the size of the area or the number of workers to be organized. Most of the unions permit two or more locals to develop in a locality in order to meet the needs and convenience of the workers. This prevalent policy has resulted in the maintenance in a large city of a number of locals of teamsters, clothing workers, cigar makers, and carpenters and other building tradesmen. Hence, most organized trades are under the necessity of bringing their several locals in a large city into an arrangement to secure uniformity in wages, hours, and working rules. Otherwise, anarchy would prevail. The arrangement made to meet this necessity is to set up a council or federation with delegates from the various locals of the trade or industry. There are in Chicago, in a total of some thirty of these councils or federa-

---

[1] In the case of the C.I.O., district councils and state councils may correspond closely to the A.F. of L.'s city central bodies and state federations discussed later in this chapter.

[2] Except for those on foreign-language papers, the several thousand compositors in Chicago belong to Local 16, the much larger number in New York to Big Six.

tions, the Carpenters' District Council, the Teamsters' Joint Council, and the Amalgamated Clothing Workers' Joint Board.

Many unions have also established state councils or district councils covering an area either larger or smaller than that of a state. The Carpenters and Printers afford examples.[1] The primary function of these bodies may be to carry forward the organizing work described above and to assist in securing legislation desired at the hands of the state legislatures. Sometimes, however, these councils are themselves the units that enter into contractual arrangements with the employers, as in the case of the district and subdistrict organizations of the United Mine Workers. From 1898 to 1927, the agreements in the bituminous coal industry were based upon that of the Central Competitive District, embracing Illinois, Indiana, Ohio, and western Pennsylvania.[2] The representatives of the miners and the operators entered into an agreement for mining in this district, determining piece rates at base points in each state, hours, and certain other matters. This agreement was then taken into a conference of miner representatives and operators, say of District 12 (Illinois), and more details worked out for that particular district. Following this there were conferences in each subdistrict in order to fill in necessary details of the contract, such as the actual piece rates to be paid for mining. The Railroad Brotherhoods have maintained an interesting system of committees. Other organizations have still other arrangements than have been here described, but what has been said is sufficient to explain why these intermediate organizations have been established and how they may share with locals and international in performing the functions and exercising the control for which the situation is thought to call.

ALLIED TRADES ORGANIZATIONS; DEMARCATION AND JURISDICTION DISPUTES; INDUSTRIAL UNIONISM

Not to be confused with these intermediate organizations within the trade or industry are the alliances set up locally by the various unions in the printing (allied printing-trades councils), building (building-trades councils), metal (metal-trades federations), and other industries, and the national alliances and the industrial departments of the American Federation of Labor.[3] The printing-trades council is a delegate body of

---

[1] The Carpenters had twenty-six state councils in good standing in 1936.

[2] A similar arrangement is in effect today.

[3] For studies of typical building trades councils, see R. E. Montgomery, *op. cit.*, Chap. 4, and William Haber, *Industrial Relations in the Building Industry* (1930), Chaps. 12–14. For a study of the several departments of the American Federation of Labor, see Albert T. Helbing, *The Departments of the American Federation of Labor*, in Johns Hopkins University Studies, Series 49 (1931), and Lewis Lorwin, *The American Federation of Labor* (1933), Chap. 14.

representatives of locals of compositors, pressmen, and other "mechanical trades"; the building-trades council includes representatives of locals of carpenters, plumbers, and other building tradesmen; the Building and Construction[1] Trades Department, the Metal Trades Department, and the Railway Employees Department of the A.F. of L. are organizations of building trades, metal trades, and railway internationals, respectively, affiliated to the A.F. of L. Whether local or national, these allied-trades organizations are designed to serve the common needs of the different craft or industrial organizations and to iron out differences among them. To understand them fully, one needs to understand the issue of industrial unionism, and to understand that issue fully in turn, one needs, among other things, to understand the problem of demarcation and jurisdiction disputes. Hence, industrial unionism and demarcation and jurisdiction disputes are discussed briefly in connection with allied-trades councils.

Craft versus Industrial Unionism.—Reference has been made to the main structural types of unions. The general labor union has made a strong appeal to those who have been interested chiefly in reform or antimonopoly legislation or in the general strike. Though this structural type has been frequently met with until in recent years in some of the European countries, it has become largely a matter of history in the United States, for most of our unionism has developed out of the anti-monopoly or political stage into that of business unionism, and the general or mass strike has ordinarily been quite ineffective. Most of the American unions, therefore, are either industrial or craft unions or variants closely related to the one or the other of these. The larger number are in fact multiple-craft or extended-craft unions, which are mere variants from the craft and for present purposes need not be distinguished from the craft union. The industrial union, with its variants, though of outstanding importance in such countries as Sweden and, prior to 1934, Germany, and though increasing in importance during the last eight years, has played a subordinate, but not an unimportant, role in the United States.[2] For decades there has been strong propaganda for the industrial form of organization in this country, and at times it has made distinct headway. At present, more than sixty of the internationals are organized on an industrial or quasi-industrial basis. Prominent among these are the Miners, the Textile Workers, the Boot and Shoe Workers, the Auto Workers, the Steel Workers, the Rubber Workers,

---

[1] Name changed from Building Trades Department in 1937 to conform to actual jurisdiction of the Department.

[2] During the twenty years or so ending with 1935 membership in industrial unions fluctuated between some 17 per cent and more than 30 per cent of the total. In 1936 it was approximately 32 per cent and, with the remarkable organizing success of the C.I.O., it was by the end of 1937 more than 50 per cent. *Cf.* Leo Wolman, *Ebb and Flow in Trade Unionism.*

the Maritime Workers' Union, and the several unions in the different branches of the needle trades. The I.W.W. should be mentioned, also, though for several years it has played a much less important role than it did a generation ago.

The industrial union has appealed to the socialists and other radicals generally. With occupational interests placed somewhat in the background, the industrial form is presumed to make for a new spirit—that of solidarity of all classes of workers. With larger groups brought together, it makes propaganda for a new economic order more successful. Moreover, it parallels the organization of industry and, as the socialists and other radicals see it, provides the type of organization of workers needed in a revolutionized economic order. Naturally a number of the industrial unions have been radical in ultimate objective.[1] But, on the other hand, there have been many industrial unions without radical objectives, and a strong case can be made for the industrial form of organization as the most effective "business" form within the existing economic order. Many unionists who are not radicals are proponents of a more extensive industrial unionism than has obtained.

The proponent of industrial unionism may point to the economy that might be effected by having fewer organizations to house and to operate. Possibly he will say something concerning the likelihood that a small group, when separately organized, will go its own way to the injury of others. Nowadays, he may point to the fact that employers who are really willing to bargain collectively generally prefer to deal with one union rather than with several. He will certainly contend that the mechanization of industry, with concomitant subdivision of labor, is undermining the crafts and destroying the craft basis of organization. In concrete cases, to cling to the craft form of organization is to lose out. Industrial change is making the interests of skilled and unskilled more nearly one. He will certainly emphasize the fact that, with exceptions like the Hod Carriers, the unskilled have little chance to organize effectively by themselves. The unskilled are too easily displaced and have too limited means to finance an independent organization. If they are to be effectively organized and not to menace the skilled workers' jobs, the unskilled

---

[1] Much has been said of the C.I.O. and Communism, but only a small number of C.I.O. internationals have been appreciably influenced by any Communist membership, and these no more so than were the Fur Workers and the International Ladies' Garment Workers some years ago when affiliated with the A.F. of L. Of course the Communists prefer industrial organization to craft organization and find a more congenial place in the C.I.O. than in the A.F. of L. Moreover, on occasion the A.F. of L. has taken drastic measures to free internationals from Communist pressure and problems. Corresponding action has been taken by few of the C.I.O. organizations, but this fact perhaps has no particular significance, for no organization can well conduct a purge when in the organizing stage. It should be added that some C.I.O. organizations, for example, the Amalgamated Clothing Workers and the Miners, have, at one time or another, conducted purges.

must have the help and cooperation of their stronger brothers. This is, moreover, only less true of the semiskilled workers. The problem of organizing the workers generally in mass industries, he asserts, is complicated and made difficult if craft organizations are claiming and competing for jurisdiction.[1] Furthermore, he contends that the crafts are largely outmoded in these mass industries. He points to the former experience of workers in railway shops and elsewhere, and contends that the industrial union is stronger than craft organizations in bargaining with the employer. When the several occupational groups in an industry are independently organized and each has its own agreement, perhaps expiring when the other agreements do not, and with these several agreements perhaps outlawing the sympathetic strike, the employer has only to subdue or break one organization at a time. It may be that the members of the other organizations can be used to assist him in doing so. And, finally, the proponent will contend that industrial unionism would eliminate or greatly minimize the jurisdiction disputes that develop so frequently when the different crafts are organized independently. This last-mentioned consideration—elimination of jurisdiction disputes—is so important, so interwoven with the whole problem of structure, that a brief discussion of jurisdictional disputes is here in point; then direct discussion of industrial versus craft unionism may be resumed.

Disputes over jurisdiction do not occur between craft unions alone. History of the labor movement shows that there have been numerous disputes and struggles between overlapping industrial unions, between industrial unions with different ultimate objectives, and between dual unions resulting from secessions.[2] The relations between the United Mine Workers and the Western Federation of Miners a generation ago, the struggle between the I.W.W. and the unions just mentioned and others, and the struggle between the United Garment Workers and the Amalgamated Clothing Workers,[3] which seceded from it, in 1914 are cases in point. Then, too, there was the long struggle between the Seamen and the Longshoremen as to where the work of the one should leave off and that of the other begin. The fact is that the boundaries of an industry are by no means definite. Where does the steel industry

[1] For discussion of organization in mass industries, see Chap. V.

[2] For an excellent, though old, discussion of conflicts between industrial unions, see Solomon Blum, *Jurisdictional Disputes Resulting from Structural Differences in American Trade Unions*, in University of California Publications in Economics, vol. 3 (1913). At the present time, of course, most interunion disputes are between labor organizations with different affiliations, or between affiliated and "independent" unions. The latter are not discussed at this point.

[3] Ended for the time being by agreement on jurisdiction in 1933 and affiliation of the Amalgamated with the A.F. of L.

leave off and the automobile industry begin? As business is organized and conducted, overlapping departments in two or more industries provide abundant opportunity for disputes between industrial unions, such as that now current between the Amalgamated Clothing Workers and the International Ladies' Garment Workers, involving jurisdiction over such articles as slacks, raincoats, and bathrobes. And such disputes are not likely to be so few in the future as they have been in the past. But after all most disputes have developed between craft union and craft union or between a craft union and the industrial union in the industry, and, had only the industrial form of organization been employed, the particular disputes could not have arisen. A few concrete examples may advantageously be cited.

It was only natural that disputes should arise between the Brewery Workers, who claimed jurisdiction over all workers employed in or about breweries, and the internationals claiming jurisdiction over carpenters or coopers or teamsters or engineers or firemen, whether employed in breweries or elsewhere.[1] In the middle 1930's there were renewed complaints of encroachment upon the jurisdiction of the metal-trades unions by the Oil Field Workers. There have been, and are, many such cases.

With changes in materials and methods, it was only to be expected that there should be disputes between craft organizations in the building trades and elsewhere, especially when one set of workers would work for less money than the other or when jobs became scarce.

Sheet-metal workers and carpenters for many years fought for the right to install certain sheet-metal products in building construction, the one claiming the right because of the nature of the material, the other because the material was being substituted for wood and because, it was said, its installation required the tools and experience of the carpenter. Carpenters and concrete workers disputed as to who should build necessary wooden forms, the one claiming the work because the forms were of wood and constructed with carpenters' tools, the other because the making of forms was a mere incident in concrete construction work. There have been hundreds of such disputes, the largest number occurring in the building trades.[2] Of course, such disputes are almost wholly a question of the control of jobs. But nonrevolutionary unions are chiefly concerned

[1] For an account of this longstanding controversy, see American Federation of Labor, *Proceedings*, 1934, pp. 144–152 and 447–459, and *Proceedings*, 1939, pp. 563–573 and 591–616.

[2] For detail concerning jurisdiction disputes, see G. G. Groat, *An Introduction to the Study of Organized Labor in America* (1916), Chap. 25; N. R. Whitney, *Jurisdiction in American Building-Trades Unions* in Johns Hopkins University Studies, Series 32 (1914); R. E. Montgomery, *op. cit.*, Chap. 8; William Haber, *op. cit.*, Chaps. 6 and 7; reports of convention proceedings of the American Federation of Labor and of the Building and Construction Trades Department; and A. T. Helbing, *op. cit.* See also discussion of American Federation of Labor departments, *infra*, pp. 279–301.

with jobs and the terms on which they shall be filled. The problem of machinery from the worker's point of view is largely one of jobs. Apprenticeship is largely the same. The job is the source of one's livelihood. When it is encroached upon, especially by another group accepting work at a lower rate of pay, a strong reaction occurs.

Sometimes, also, new methods give rise to a new craft that seeks recognition as such but whose jurisdiction cuts across that of established unions. Unwilling to lose members and dues, the latter may refuse to give up any of its jurisdictional claims to the new group. Welding, for example, has been under the jurisdiction of various A.F. of L. metal-trades unions. However, it long ago became more or less a distinct craft; certain types of welding require special training and cannot be done by other metal-trades workers. Until late in 1941, welders were forced to belong to several unions at once as they moved from one job to another, or to work on only those welding jobs over which their union had jurisdiction. Dissatisfied with such conditions, they unsuccessfully sought a separate national charter from the A.F. of L. The dispute developed into open warfare when Pacific Coast shipyard welders went on strike in the late summer of 1941. Temporary settlement was reached, with the aid of the Office of Production Management, in an agreement that welders had to have only one union card. But early in 1942 welders in Puget Sound defense industries went on strike as part of the drive to obtain independent status within the A.F. of L. It was charged that some welders had been dismissed for refusing to pay dues to A.F. of L. unions that had closed-shop agreements with Pacific Coast shipyards. Denounced by the War Production Board and other government officials the strike soon collapsed. The dispute, however, will probably continue until the welders are recognized as an autonomous unit.

There have been scores of jurisdiction wars, interfering with production, begetting impatience on the part of employers and the public as few other things do, undermining the interest of workers in unionism,[1] and sometimes resulting in the dissolution of the weaker union engaged in a struggle. These disputes have been due for the most part to the craft form of organization; they have presented and still present one of the major union problems in the United States.

In such terms as these the case for industrial and against craft unionism is made. It is a strong case and has made wide appeal. But the movement toward industrial unionism was retarded by the fact that for years it was advocated in season and out of season by the socialists, and then by the communists, who have been prone to denounce union official-dom as well as craft unionism and whose interest in industrial unionism stemmed from a revolutionary objective rather than from a desire to further the immediate economic interests of unions. This prejudiced

[1] Or begetting interest in "independent" unionism.

the cause. Again, remaking unionism is different from setting up a logical scheme on paper. Logic lies frequently with the industrial form of organization. But reorganization (even into amalgamated craft unions) jeopardizes the officeholders; it involves financial readjustments, especially where benefit systems have been operated; it runs counter to the sentiments of loyal members; it may let down the bars established by craftsmen and permit new types of workers to compete for the old craftsmen's jobs. The problem of uniting two or more unions into one is not unlike that of combining two or more churches or other social institutions. Indeed, it involves much more numerous difficulties.

Nor is this all that is to be said. Crafts have been and are being undermined, but there are well-defined crafts nevertheless, and a worker's craft may mean much more to him than the industry in which it is carried on. Teamsters may frequently shift from industry to industry, but only infrequently do they leave the occupation. Perhaps carpenters shift much more from industry to industry than from carpentry to other occupations. This is certainly true of the highly skilled patternmakers. The craft organization may give the most stable relationship; it may give the best service in securing a desirable job; it is most likely to provide needed training through apprenticeship and to control the supply of labor; wages to be standardized are those of the craft or occupation. Within the industrial union there is likely to be jealousy over rates of pay in different occupations; the industrial union is inclined to level up wages at the expense of the big differentials of the skilled workers; there may be problems aplenty when "demands" are being formulated by different locals joined in a quasi-industrial union and agreements are being negotiated for them. Minority groups in industrial unions frequently feel that they have not fared justly. The International Typographical Union was once *the* union of the printing industry, but minority group after minority group developed with changing techniques, the art of printing, and division of labor, and these groups eventually secured independence. It was in this way that the Pressmen, the Photo-Engravers, and other printing-trades unions came into existence.[1] And, parenthetically, attention may be called to the fact that the tendency for the crafts to disappear is not universal. One fact is that certain crafts are undermined; other facts are that old ones persist and that new crafts appear, and in large number, and that the craftsmen are prone to form into groups on the basis of the craft interest. This proneness to organize on the basis of craft interest is particularly strong in the United States,

[1] The several unions gained independence from the International Typographical Union by securing national charters as follows: Pressmen, 1889; Bookbinders, 1892; Photo-Engravers, 1900; Stereotypers, 1902. For some time locals of mailers have been restive in the International Typographical Union, and an agitation has been carried on for a mailers' international.

where the method of collective bargaining has been most emphasized and where there has been less class solidarity than prevails in most countries.

In addition to referring to the above, the defender of craft unionism will point to the possibility of setting up councils, federations, and departments for furthering the common interests of related trades and for solving the problems arising among them, of which the jurisdiction dispute has been the most important and of most frequent occurrence. Trade alliances have played an important part in the organizational plans of the A.F. of L. They have been regarded by it as a constructive answer to much of the case made for industrial unionism.

Amalgamation as a Constructive Answer.—The American Federation of Labor has always prided itself upon being practical and adaptable and upon disposing of things in a common-sense way. In 1901, it met resolutions calling for industrial unionism with its Autonomy Declaration. This position was reaffirmed in 1912 and has been held to fairly consistently to the present time. The Declaration stated:

"As the magnificent growth of the American Federation of Labor is conceded by all students of economic thought to be the result of organization on trade lines, and believing it neither necessary nor expedient to make any radical departure from this fundamental principle, we declare that, as a general proposition, the interests of the workers will be best conserved by adhering as closely to that doctrine as the recent great changes in methods of production and employment make practicable. However, owing to the isolation of some few industries from thickly populated centers where the overwhelming number follow one branch thereof, and owing to the fact that in some industries comparatively few workers are engaged over whom separate organizations claim jurisdiction, we believe that jurisdiction in such industries by the paramount organization would yield the best results to the workers therein, at least until the development of organization of each branch has reached a stage wherein these may be placed, without material injury to all parties in interest, in affiliation with their national trade unions. . . .

"We hold that the interests of the trade union movement will be promoted by closely allying the sub-divided crafts, giving consideration to amalgamation and to the organization of District and National Trade Councils to which should be referred questions in dispute, and which should be adjusted within allied crafts' lines."[1]

In general adherence to this policy the A.F. of L. has readily accepted the industrial unionism of the coal miners and has not frowned upon that of the needle trades.[2] As the A.F. of L. has seen it, however, the indus-

---

[1] American Federation of Labor, *Proceedings* 1901, p. 240; also in *ibid.*, 1912, pp. 114–115.

[2] In 1935, however, jurisdiction over engineers and other craftsmen in metal mining was given to the respective craft organizations. Likewise, when the Amalgamated Cloth-

trial union must establish its claim, especially in an industry where a part of the workers have membership in craft organizations, and must remain the exception; the craft union should be the predominant form of labor organization. Faced by problems, it has emphasized above all else the amalgamation here and there of weak and warring unions and the establishment of allied councils to keep peace in the family and to further mutual interests.[1]

Though less numerous than the instances in Germany during the 1920's, there have been many amalgamations of American international unions, chiefly to solve the problems of weakness and/or jurisdiction wars. A large proportion of these amalgamations have resulted from the good offices of the A.F. of L. and its industrial departments.[2] Amalgamations have occurred most frequently among the building trades, where the number of internationals is distinctly smaller than it was a generation ago. The Carpenters have absorbed other wood working organizations, the Plumbers and the Steamfitters have been brought together in one national organization, the Building Laborers organization has replaced a number of organizations. Some success has also been realized in other industries, such as the metal trades, where, years ago, the Molders and the Core-Makers merged into one organization.[3] As already pointed out, however, the problems involved in amalgamating two or more labor organizations are usually numerous and difficult, with the result that many attempts at amalgamation have not succeeded. Because of these difficulties and the lack of planning, the number of craft unions has remained considerably larger than a logical plan would call for.

The American Federation of Labor, Its Departments, and Their Subsidiaries.—What the A. F. of L. has done within the last thirty-five years has been chiefly to establish and to extend alliances among the trades, to standardize them, to remove weaknesses in them revealed by experience,

---

ing Workers affiliated with the A.F. of L., machinists, electricians, and others were to be transferred to their craft organizations. It may be noted, also, that when the very considerable number of industrial unions established in the lumber and logging camps, in 1935, requested the setting up of an overhead organization for guidance and support, the A.F. of L. placed them under the jurisdiction of the Carpenters' Union.

[1] The detailed story of the policies adopted by the Federation in meeting the problem of structural readjustments is told in connection with the historical development of the American labor movement. *Cf. supra*, pp. 102–106.

[2] It is also true that in a considerable number of cases stronger, aggressive unions have made continuous war upon weaker unions and simply "swallowed" them, in spite of awards made by the A.F. of L. *Cf.* William Haber, *op. cit.*, Chap. 6.

[3] In 1939 the A.F. of L. ordered the Foundry Employees to merge with the Molders.

and to increase the chances of their successful operation. It has set up
its Building and Construction Trades Department (1908), its Metal
Trades Department (1908), and its Railway Employees' Department
(1909),[1] in which each international in building, metals, and railways, in
so far as affiliated with the A. F. of L., is presumed or urged to find place,
and under which there are subordinate organizations (building-trades
councils, metal-trades councils, and railway systems) that every affiliated
local is expected to join. Speaking very generally, the main functions
of the departments have been to avoid or to settle troublesome jurisdiction disputes, to organize subordinate bodies so as to improve the organization of the affiliated trades, and to lay down rules to be observed by
these bodies. The subordinate bodies are expected to submit their
differences for settlement and to stand together in prosecuting matters of
common concern.

The Railway Employees' Department.—The Railroad Brotherhoods
have generally held aloof from the other railway unions[2] and have never
affiliated with the A. F. of L. The value of some means of coordinating
the activities of the various other craft unions among railway employees
was demonstrated as early as 1893, when the Machinists, Boilermakers,
and Blacksmiths organized system federations and conducted successful
strikes in the shops of the Santa Fe and Union Pacific railroads. Such
voluntary system federations developed only slowly, but by 1908 the
sentiment in favor of closer affiliation among railroad men had grown to
such an extent that the Denver convention of the A.F. of L. sanctioned a

---

[1] It also, in 1912, created a Mining Department, but this was disestablished in 1922,
when, with the organization of metal miners reduced to small proportions, and that of the
oil workers no longer of importance, the only important union in the mining group was the
United Mine Workers (see A. T. Helbing, *The Departments of the American Federation of
Labor*, Chap. 2). Certain other groups, such as the culinary arts, at times showed an
interest in an A.F. of L. department, but none was organized, presumably because the
reasons were inadequate or the problem to be solved was relatively unimportant. Most
of the needle-trades internationals, including the Amalgamated Clothing Workers, then
outside of the A.F. of L., some years ago sought to establish an alliance and did cooperate
in organizing work. Finally, the Railroad Brotherhoods have at times had understandings
and acted in concert. Now, of course, there is the Railway Labor Executives' Association,
with headquarters in Washington. It stands over against the Railway Association.
On occasion the bargaining has been between these two organizations.

[2] The Brotherhoods have, however, cooperated with the other unions on some matters
of common concern, such as legislation and general wage adjustments. The Brotherhoods
cooperated with the Railway Employees' Department of the A.F. of L. in handling common
issues during the period of federal control and in presenting issues before the Railway Labor
Board established under the Railway Transportation Act of 1920. The need for concerted action between affiliated unions and the Brotherhoods culminated in the formation
in 1926 of the Railway Labor Executives' Association, composed of the chief executives of
some twenty of the standard unions in railway transportation. This cooperation has been
particularly effective in urging reforms in federal legislation and in meeting the problem of
wage adjustments during the depression years, 1932–1935, and in 1938.

tentative organization of the Railway Employees' Department.[1] In 1909, a constitution was adopted and officers were elected. The Department, as then organized, had only limited legislative and educational functions, and in 1912 the craft representatives of some forty systems of railroads organized a Federation of Federations in order to carry out more effective collective bargaining. Following this the Railway Employees' Department was completely reorganized, accepting the laws and officers of the Federation of Federations but retaining the name of the former organization. The Department as thus organized has remained substantially unchanged to the present time. Each of the seven international craft unions[2] affiliated with the Department retains its craft autonomy but agrees to cooperate with the different crafts locally, and through system federations and the Department, in collective bargaining, in seeking legislation, and in court action under the federal laws. The success of this cooperation is attested by the favorable federal legislation obtained and by the fact that during the critical depression period of 1932–1933 the railway unions were able to thwart all attempts to cut wages by more than 10 per cent.

Under the protection of the revised Railway Labor Act,[3] which prohibits all discrimination against railway employees for union activity and also any support of company unions by employers, the Department has carried on a vigorous organizing campaign, especially in railway shops. Since 1933, company union agreements have been taken over by the unions on seventy railroads—all except the Pennsylvania, "Frisco," and Santa Fe. The increase in membership of the affiliated unions is unobtainable, for the dues are paid directly to the craft organization and the membership of railway employees is not separated from membership of workers employed in other industries. It is significant, however, that in this organizing campaign the card that new members signed read, "[I] hereby authorize my Craft Organization *and the Railway Employees'*

[1] For an excellent discussion of this department, see A. T. Helbing, *op. cit.*, Chap. 3. A history and review of accomplishments of craft cooperation as given by the Department itself may be found in the pamphlet *Why You Should Be a Member of the Standard Railway Union of Your Craft*, issued by the Railway Employees' Department of the A.F. of L., 1933.

[2] International Association of Machinists; International Brotherhood of Blacksmiths, Drop Forgers and Helpers; International Brotherhood of Boilermakers, Iron Shipbuilders, and Helpers of America; Sheet Metal Workers' International Association; International Brotherhood of Electrical Workers; Brotherhood of Railway Carmen of America; and International Brotherhood of Firemen and Oilers. Six A.F. of L. railroad unions are outside of the Department—Brotherhood of Maintenance of Way Employees; Order of Railroad Telegraphers; Switchmen's Union of North America; Brotherhood of Railway Clerks; Masters, Mates and Pilots of America; and International Longshoremen's Association. The Switchmen and Maintenance of Way Employees were formerly affiliated but withdrew in 1935 and 1936.

[3] Public no. 442, 73d Congress, 2d Session, Chap. 691 (H. R. 9861), June 21, 1934. This Act is discussed in Chap. XII.

Department[1] . . . to represent me. . . . " The authorization of the Department, as well as of the craft organization, to represent the worker directly illustrates the tendency of the Department to assume collective-bargaining functions reserved to the crafts in other industries; actually almost all important negotiations, especially those to establish new agreements, have been carried on directly by the Department through its officers.[2] The jurisdiction disputes that would ordinarily hamper the extension of craft organization are in large measure avoided in the shops in this way. Other jurisdiction disputes are prevented by the refusal of the Department to accept the affiliation of unions with overlapping claims, such as the Plumbers. Disputes as to jurisdiction between affiliated unions have been settled by agreement, or by methods devised by the Executive Council of the Railway Employees' Department. Settlement by the executives has not been altogether successful, however, so that a new plan has recently been adopted. Under this plan, to which six of the seven crafts are parties, disputes not settled by the chief executives of the organizations involved will be referred to a referee whose decision will be binding.[3]

The Metal Trades Department.—The Metal Trades Department[4] federates most of the internationals[5] with jurisdiction in the metal industry as over against railway shops and building construction, in which some of these unions find a more or less important place. Under the Department there were in March, 1942, seventy-three subordinate councils. These included twelve navy-yard councils, five district councils (three in shipbuilding, one in copper, one in oil), five Canadian councils, and fifty-one miscellaneous councils.

---

[1] Italics are the authors'.

[2] Extensive powers for concerted negotiation are granted by Art. VIII of the Constitution (1930). Section 4 of that article reads, "No organization having once agreed to a concerted program shall have the right to withdraw from said program." Article IX, Secs. 1 and 2, gives the Department power to conduct strike votes and levy strike assessments. For some years, however, the railway internationals, including the brotherhoods, have acted as a unit when the carriers have sought wage reductions. Owing to differences on retirement legislation, however, in 1938, the Trainmen acted independently of the other organizations in the general opposition to a 15 per cent wage cut. In 1937, the brotherhoods and the other internationals acted as two more or less independent units in their successful efforts to obtain wage increases.

[3] See *Labor*, Feb. 13, 1940.

[4] See annual reports of proceedings. An excellent account of the Department is found in A. T. Helbing, *op. cit.*, Chap. 2. See also L. Lorwin, *The American Federation of Labor*, pp. 385–390.

[5] The affiliated unions are the Blacksmiths, Boilermakers, Technical Engineers, Operating Engineers, Electrical Workers, Firemen and Oilers, Hod Carriers, Structural Iron Workers, Machinists, Metal Polishers, Molders, Pattern Makers, Plumbers, Sheet Metal Workers, and Stove Mounters. These fifteen unions in 1941 paid per capita taxes to the A.F. of L. on a total of 950,400 members.

The government of the Department is lodged in a president, a secretary-treasurer, and six vice-presidents, these eight constituting the Executive Council, and the convention that meets annually immediately in advance of the A.F. of L. convention. The affiliated internationals and the district and local councils are entitled to send delegates to the conventions, but the internationals occupy a dominant positions, for they are entitled to one delegate for each 4,000 members and these delegates, on roll call, have one vote for each 100 members they represent, while the delegates of the other organizations (each represented by one delegate) have only one vote each.

The Department was designed to further organization in the metal trades in general; to encourage the formation of local councils and to confer on these councils power to deal jointly with the employers; to control concerted movements; and to settle jurisdiction disputes along "practicable lines." The exact nature of the functions performed and the emphasis placed upon them have varied considerably from time to time. In pre-World War I years emphasis was placed, with some measure of success, upon the extension of membership in the different crafts and upon the formation of local councils; concerted movements were also guided. During the First World War the needs of the government were such that a tremendous growth in union membership was realized, and the Department cooperated closely and effectively in standardizing and improving wages, hours, and working conditions and in maintaining industrial peace and fairly continuous production in shipbuilding and other war industries. From the close of the War until the enactment of NIRA the Department and the unions busied themselves with the problem of declining membership and with wages, hours, and working rules in the navy yards and other government establishments. In the matter of organization it was not really successful, because of the shrinkage of work after the War ended, technological changes, which were accompanied by less need for experienced craftsmen and the employment of relatively increasing numbers of semiskilled men and of women, and the effective opposition of the national and local metal-trades associations. In fact, as the years passed, the unions were left with little organization and control except in government establishments, the stove industry, and such shops as were engaged largely in repair and made-to-order work in which skilled help was required and in which there were limited opportunities for subdividing labor and an absence of that competition which characterizes production for a wide market. The Department was, however, effective in its activities in behalf of government employees and in furthering its incidental legislative demands.

With the adoption of NIRA the Department entered into the fourth period in its history. The unions again experienced substantial increases in membership and their position in industry was strengthened, as was that of the unions in the organized trades generally. The outstanding feature of the period covered by the New Deal was the emphasis placed upon district councils for defense and for concerted action in organizing and in collective bargaining. For some years, navy-yard metal-trades councils had been maintained. In 1933, the Department approved a plan for other district councils "so that all metal working local unions employed in some division or subdivision of the manufacturing industries, would be able to jointly adopt such policies as seemed most advisable and then jointly negotiate and enter into agreements with the employers."[1] Organization of the Marine Workers' Metal Trades District Council for the Port of New York and of the Office Equipment Workers' District Council followed in March, 1934. The former represented, for the purpose of concerted action, all workers in the yards, whether engaged in a metal trade or otherwise. The latter effected a relationship between the general industrial unions affiliated with the A.F. of L. and local unions of machinists, molders, and metal polishers.[2] It devoted much of its efforts to improving conditions in plants engaged in the manufacture of typewriters and adding and addressograph machines. Both of these and the Gulf Metal Trades District Council and the Oil Industry Metal Trades Council of Southern California, more recently established, provided organizations with some aspects of industrial unionism. The Department also in certain industries represented the several internationals in collective bargaining, and, in 1934, it joined with the Building Trades Department in negotiating an agreement with the Anaconda Copper Company that had the effect of bringing to an end a badly conducted, months-old strike of the miners into which the craft organizations had been drawn.[3]

Under the Defense Program, beginning in 1941, the Metal Trades Department entered a fifth period, in most respects like that during World War I years. Union membership increased and governmental, union, and management officials cooperated to standardize wages and working conditions. The Department participated in the negotiations of the Shipbuilding Stabilization Committee, a body of union, government, and employer representatives formed in the fall of 1940 to establish

[1] *Proceedings of the Twenty-sixth Annual Convention of the Metal Trades Department* (1934), p. 7.

[2] It may be noted that in 1933, and the years immediately following, the A.F. of L. also organized councils among the unions of workers in the auto, rubber, and aluminum industries, match manufacture, optical manufacture, pearl-button manufacture, and radio and allied trades, and among the unions of gasoline service-station attendants. In part, these represented a step toward the establishment of internationals. In 1935, the councils were replaced by international unions in the auto and rubber industries. Shortly thereafter both of these internationals affiliated with the C.I.O.

[3] For the facts, charges, and countercharges in this episode, see American Federation of Labor, *Proceedings*, 1935, pp. 614–665.

shipbuilding zones with uniform wages and working rules and to prevent strikes and lockouts. The first zone conference, held on the Pacific Coast, resulted in 1941 in a master agreement for thirty-nine Pacific Coast shipyards. The provisions included a $1.12 an hour rate for first-class mechanics, time and a half for overtime, prohibition of strikes and lockouts, and arbitration of unsettled grievances.[1] Similar agreements were later negotiated for the Atlantic and Gulf coasts, and for the Great Lakes. The Metal Trades Department participated in the latter two negotiations, but not in those for the Atlantic Coast, in which the C.I.O. alone represented the employees.

The Department has also been helpful in adding to and then protecting membership in the crafts and to an extent in federal unions, especially the weaker ones. Again, it has been instrumental in setting up additional local councils, though most of the time, owing to the apathy of the local unions and some of the internationals, many urban communities with a sufficient number of locals to qualify have been without such local federations. Concerted movements have been launched or guided, but perhaps as much thought has been given to checking undesirable movements and to protecting the internationals against subversive developments on the part of the local unions. Sometimes wages, hours, and working rules have been worked out through the local councils, but frequently they have not been because of the proneness of some of the locals to proceed in their own way. Federation has not been altogether effective in giving the metal trades a unified, consistent unionism. And, except in so far as federal labor unions have developed and as some of the internationals have extended their jurisdictions downward, as they have in considerable number under the New Deal and with C.I.O. competition, adequate provision has not been made for the organization of common labor and a part of the semiskilled. On occasion, a desire for industrial unionism has been evidenced, particularly by locals of machinists and metal polishers, but for the most part the unions have remained craft-minded and have supported the federation idea.[2]

Jurisdiction disputes have not been so numerous in the metal trades as they have been in the building industry, but they have occurred between Sheet Metal Workers and Boilermakers, Machinists and Pattern

[1] The Pacific Coast agreement did not bring immediate peace. In May, 1941, 1,200 A.F. of L. and 700 C.I.O. machinists in eleven San Francisco area shipyards went on strike against the $1.12 wage scale and payment of only time and a half for overtime. Other machinists in that area were receiving $1.15 an hour and double time for overtime. The main grievance of the strikers, however, was Bethlehem's failure to sign the master contract. The strike did not end until late in June, when Bethlehem accepted the National Defense Mediation Board's recommendation and signed the coastwide agreement for its San Francisco shipyard with the Bay City Metal Trades Council.

[2] During the last several years (from 1935), the President of the Metal Trades Department has been very active in defending the crafts against the program of the C.I.O.

Makers, Machinists and Plumbers, and other groups. The Department has partially succeeded in settling such disputes by mediation. In 1920 it was proposed to introduce a system for the authoritative settlement of jurisdiction disputes, such as obtained in the building industry, but in the opinion of some of the internationals such a system would not be along "practicable lines." Instead, it was decided that the Executive Council should "constitute a standing board of conciliation in controversies between affiliated unions." Thus, as Dr. Helbing has said, "The Department has never assumed authority to dictate in the matter of demarcation disputes. It has merely insisted that local councils did not have the right to decide jurisdictional disputes, but must refer the matter to the national unions involved. If they could not mutually agree, the Department acted as a mediator or conciliator either by urging the national officers to get together, or by talking it over at meetings of the Executive Council."[1] The fact is that serious disputes between metal-trades organizations are now left to the A.F. of L. for settlement.

This same tendency for the unions to follow self-interest has frequently stood in the way of general concerted movements. In the early history of the Department, the constitution was amended in order to compel dissenting or hesitating internationals to cooperate in concerted movements when voted by a three-quarters majority. However, the opposition to this on the part of some of the crafts was so strong and so determined that the amendment was soon eliminated. Since then the Department has proceeded upon the basis of conference and voluntary cooperation.

The Building and Construction Trades Department.—The first of the departments to be organized, and the largest, the Building and Construction Trades Department[2] (formerly the Building Trades Department) has been the most important, and the most troublesome, of the four industrial departments established by the American Federation of Labor. It was designed to federate all the international building-trades unions affiliated with the A.F. of L.; internationals not so affiliated have of course been

---

[1] A. T. Helbing, *op. cit.*, p. 56.

[2] See reports of proceedings of annual conventions of the Department; reports of proceedings of annual conventions of the American Federation of Labor, especially that for 1934; A. T. Helbing, *op. cit.*, Chap. 1; L. Lorwin, *The American Federation of Labor*, pp. 374–385; William Haber, *Industrial Relations in the Building Industry*, Chaps. 6 and 7.

This Department had been preceded by two other organizations designed to settle jurisdiction disputes and in a measure to control the granting of charters to building trades unions. In 1897, the National Building Trades Council was formed to provide some kind of central machinery for the adjustment of disputes but it remained incomplete and was unsuccessful. Seven years later, in 1904, the Structural Building Trades Alliance was formed by nine leading internationals that had not sponsored the Council. This Alliance was opposed by the smaller unions, which feared they would be gobbled up and the A.F. of L. refused to support any organization not initiated by and subordinated to itself. The establishment of the Building Trades Department of the A.F. of L. followed in 1908.

ineligible to membership. Much of the time the Department has been only a partial federation, owing chiefly to suspensions of or withdrawals by a few important unions.[1] Confronted by perplexing problems and persistently craft-minded, a few of the internationals have not always been amenable to control or moral suasion, and internal fights have been numerous and fierce. Another factor, boding ill, has been fear and jealousy between the smaller and the larger internationals. In 1934, there was a split; for months two rival departments maintained headquarters in Washington, D. C.; mediation by the A.F. of L. failed and court proceedings were resorted to, but the court would not recognize one organization and the terms of the officers of the other had expired. Following the A.F. of L. convention of 1935, however, the Building Trades Department was united and it made a new start, only to become almost ineffective in the settlement of jurisdiction disputes until 1939, after which considerable success was achieved.

The Building and Construction Trades Department is a federation of internationals. Its government is lodged in the annual conventions held immediately prior to the conventions of the A. F. of L., a president and a secretary-treasurer—the two salaried officers, elected triennially—and an executive council consisting of the president and eight vice-presidents elected annually, with the limitation that no two shall be selected from the same craft. Under the Department and chartered and in a measure controlled by it, there were, a few years ago, 510 local building-trades and thirteen state building-trades councils.

Unlike the Metal Trades Department, the conventions of the Building and Construction Trades Department have seated delegates from the affiliated internationals only. Each international of less than 4,000 members is entitled to one delegate, one of 4,000 or more to two delegates, one of 8,000 or more to three, one of 16,000 or more to four, one of 32,000 or more to five, and so on. In order to satisfy the larger internationals, who complained of underrepresentation, the delegates of those unions with seven or more delegates have since 1913 been entitled to a double vote.[2]

---

[1] To note only the more important facts, the Bricklayers did not affiliate with the A.F. of L. and the Department until 1916; they withdrew in 1927. The Carpenters, the largest union, were suspended in 1910, affiliated again in 1915, withdrew in 1921 because of objection to a decision in favor of the Sheet Metal Workers, reaffiliated once more in 1927 as a part of a deal involving the disestablishment of the National Board for Jurisdictional Awards, and again withdrew in 1929. The Electrical Workers, in affiliation from the beginning, withdrew in 1931 after the National Board of Trade Claims had been established in 1930. The Bricklayers, Electrical Workers, and Carpenters made joint application for readmission to the Department in 1934 and this was approved by its Executive Council. Division followed upon this, but since 1936 the Department has had as members all A.F. of L. affiliated building-trades internationals.

[2] The amendment providing for this was eliminated from the constitution at the 1934 convention, but the entire proceedings of that convention were declared invalid and void by the A.F. of L.

Among the more or less incidental functions of the Department has been the granting of charters to new internationals and to state and local councils. This prerogative has enabled it to guard against dual unionism with a considerable measure of success.[1] Another incidental, although not an important, function is that of furthering legislation of interest. A third of these functions is to be found in the relations between the Department and the large building contractors engaged in construction work in many localities. The Department has been able to require unionization and observance of union conditions by such contractors, generally as a condition of using union help anywhere. But, as conceived, the primary functions of the Department were two: (1) to organize local councils, to guide and control them, and to make rules for their observance; and (2) to settle jurisdiction disputes between the affiliated organizations.

Local building-trades councils had been established in some cities even in the early 1880's, and by 1908 they were to be found in most of the larger and in many of the medium-sized cities. The 200 then in existence had increased to 267 by 1917, and to 411 by 1922. Following this, with the decline of the general labor movement, with inevitable failures of the Department to give entirely satisfactory service in the settlement of jurisdiction disputes, with the withdrawal of some important unions from affiliation and consequent partial dismemberment of local councils, and with depression after 1929, the number of local councils fell to 357 in 1933. By 1936, however, the number had increased to 381;[2] early in 1942 it had further increased to the peak figure 510.

In organization, government, rules, and practices there had been great differences among the local councils. Much favoritism and injustice and many bad trade practices were to be corrected by standardization and control from headquarters in Washington. Under the Constitution and By-laws to Govern Local Councils,[3] each member-local union is entitled to two delegates if it has 100 members or less, and to four delegates if it has 200 members or more, up to 400. From this point on, one delegate is added up to a maximum of ten as the basic membership is doubled (thus 400 members, five delegates; 800 members, six delegates; 12,800 members or more, ten delegates).[4] The graduated system of representation is designed to protect the weaker crafts as well as to standardize representation. The other rules laid down, in so far as they have sig-

---

[1] Of course the C.I.O. in 1939 began to organize in the construction industry. Except in a few cities, success in organization has been limited.

[2] Of these, 13 were in Canada, 368 in continental United States. "Handbook of American Trade-unions, 1936," U. S. Bureau of Labor Statistics, *Bulletin* 618, p. 68.

[3] These may be found in the *Report of Proceedings* of any annual convention of the Department.

[4] *Constitution and By-laws*, Sec. 6.

nificance for our purposes, have been summarized by Dr. Lorwin as follows:

"Certain rules for the conduct of these councils have been formulated. Some of the rules are that local councils must admit only local unions in good standing in international unions affiliated with the department, and that no local council can enter into an agreement with an employers' association providing for compulsory arbitration, against sympathetic strikes, or for union men to work with non-union men.

"Local building trades councils in their turn have certain powers over local unions. Demands for wage increases or for shorter hours must be endorsed by the local councils, as no strike is permitted without the council's consent. When a strike has been declared, the local building trades council is placed in complete charge. Another function of the local council is to distribute quarterly the working cards which are issued by the department to all members in good standing."[1]

The spirit of local autonomy has been, and remains, very strong in the building trades, and it has not been difficult to find examples of violation of these various rules. Indeed, in some of the larger cities the rules formulated have been notoriously disregarded. In Chicago, for example, trade agreements provide for compulsory arbitration of disputes, prohibit sympathetic strikes, and, in a few instances, provide for the preferential shop. The calling and conduct of strikes may or may not be in accord with the rules promulgated.

Perhaps the Department has been as much interested in protecting the internationals as in requiring that positive things be done in certain ways by the local councils and unions. The local building-trades councils have tended to limit and undermine the authority of the international unions. The problem thus presented has been an important factor in shaping the policies and proceedings of the Department. Obviously, it must function largely through local councils, but these, when established, may and frequently do challenge the supremacy of the international union.

With reference to the accomplishments of the Department, Dr. Lorwin has observed:

"It has not succeeded in harmonizing the interests of the stronger with those of the weaker unions or in reconciling 'nationalism' and 'localism.' But it has mitigated friction and helped the local councils to stand against the stronger unions. The officers of the department spend a great deal of time assisting local councils in adjusting disputes between local unions, between unions and employers, and between the councils themselves and the international unions. However, inasmuch as its structure recognizes only national unions and gives no representation to

[1] L. Lorwin, *op. cit.*, p. 376.

the councils, the department in fact strengthens the international unions."[1]

The most important function, and the function of most interest in the immediate connection, has been the settling of jurisdiction disputes, which have plagued the building industry as they have plagued no other. The reasons for the frequent occurrence of such disputes have been excellently stated, and the problem indicated, by Dr. Lorwin:

"The persistence and multiplicity of such disputes in the building trades are caused by the changes which have been going on in the industry affecting simultaneously tools, processes, and materials. Structural steel, electricity, concrete, imitation stone, the displacement of wood, changes in decoration and architecture, the assembling of factory-made units on the job, the cement or plaster gun, the paint spray, and other innovations have played havoc with old demarcation lines, long acquired skills, and comparative wage levels. Confusion has arisen because at times well-established unions would resist the introduction of certain processes or materials. New unions would be chartered of workmen who would do the work at less pay. The older unions would then decide that since they could not ward off the new methods, they would try to control them. A jurisdictional dispute would result which might continue for many years. An even more common cause of dispute occurs when unions reach out to take in new processes or materials which are far removed from the terms of their original jurisdictional claims. Differences in local custom might also flare up into a national dispute. These internecine fights have been stimulated by the number of specialized crafts seeking work, the short duration of each job, and the highly seasonal character of the industry. These factors offset the advantages of a rapidly expanding industry in which the unions have controlled the number of workers through apprenticeship rules. As a result, competition for the pay envelope has at all times been keen."[2]

The Department attacked the problem of jurisdiction disputes and, finding itself not wholly equal to the task, cooperated with the employers in the industry through, in turn, the National Board for Jurisdictional Awards (1919–1927), the National Board of Trade Claims (1930–1934), and the National Planning and Adjustment Board—under the NRA Construction Code. Following the decision in the Schechter case,[3] invalidating the NRA, the Planning and Adjustment Board was disestablished, in June, 1935. In 1936, a new arrangement, becoming effective with the reconstruction of the Building Trades Department in that year, was inaugurated.

[1] *Ibid.*, pp. 377–378.
[2] *Ibid.*, pp. 378–379. For an extended discussion, see N. R. Whitney, *Jurisdiction in the American Building Trades.*
[3] 295 U.S. 495.

In 1908, the Department placed a ban on strikes over jurisdiction and provided for the settlement of disputes under a system of conciliation and self-imposed compulsory arbitration. If local effort failed or if the dispute was between affiliated internationals, the case came to the Department (Executive Council and the convention), whose decision was to be final and binding, unless appealed to the Executive Council of the A.F. of L., with the possibility of the issues being carried to the convention of that organization.

Recognizing the "justice of trade jurisdiction" and aiming "to guarantee the various branches of the building industry control of such work as rightfully belong[ed] to them, and to which they [were] entitled," the Department began to function by requesting each affiliated international to submit a statement of its jurisdiction claims. When received, these statements were submitted to the other internationals for examination. In the absence of protest, the claims submitted were approved, and, in accord with its Constitution, the Department guaranteed that "no encroachment by other trades [would] be countenanced or tolerated." Naturally, a great many protests were filed. These protested claims and new disputes provided the cases for settlement.

A number of cases were settled by effecting amalgamations of the unions concerned. Mediation was effective in securing agreements on jurisdiction in other cases, but many remained for decision.[1] In the earlier years much was accomplished in clearing up conflicting claims and in bringing peace and order to the building trades. Yet, not all was well, for decisions might not be accepted by a losing international or applied in all localities. It was for failure to abide by a decision that the Carpenters were suspended in 1910. Moreover, cases sometimes returned for further consideration and decision. Then, too, by 1915, a number of the internationals became extremely restive and sought to substitute voluntary arbitration for (self-imposed) compulsory arbitration. From 1915 on, the machinery for settling disputes was almost at a standstill. The building trades unions could not govern themselves efficiently and iron out their disputes in a satisfactory manner.

Because of the rather chaotic condition that had come to prevail, the American Institute of Architects, in 1918, sent a committee to the Department to offer assistance in designing more effective machinery for settling jurisdiction disputes. The outcome of the conferences held was the organization of the National Board for Jurisdictional Awards. This was established in 1919 and functioned for some eight years.

[1] Each report of the Department contains details relating to agreements and decisions as well as a statement of jurisdiction by each international. In one not untypical year, ten agreements and seven decisions were reported. Besides mediation and Executive Council decision, beginning in 1911, decision by arbitration boards of three was tried for a time.

The Board established consisted of eight members, of whom three were national union officers selected by the Department, two chosen by the Associated Contractors, and one each chosen by the American Institute of Architects, the American Engineering Council, and the National Building Trades Employers' Association.[1] As summarized by Helbing: "The constitution provided that complaints must be submitted in writing through an organization signatory to the agreement, and that the Board should have power to investigate all disputes for the purpose of collecting data for its awards. Should it fail to make an award, an umpire was to be called in; if the Board could not, by a two-thirds majority, decide upon an umpire, it was agreed that it would call upon the Secretary of Labor to name an umpire. Article nine stated that 'each signatory to this agreement hereby agrees that the membership of that organization shall not take part in sympathetic strikes in any case of jurisdictional disputes.' It provided further that the national organization must enforce the awards, and that if any local organization refused to comply with the provisions and the awards, it should be suspended from its national union. It was obligatory upon the national unions to see that a job was manned. Article 10 provided that the decisions should govern the architects and engineers in writing specifications and the contractors in awarding contracts."[2]

The National Board for Jurisdictional Awards, especially in its earlier years, had a decidedly moderating influence on industrial strife and jurisdiction disputes. Besides approving a number of earlier decisions by the A.F. of L. or the Department, it made more than a hundred decisions of major or minor importance. But even within two years of its establishment, not all was well with the arrangement and it eventually broke down.

Decisions on jurisdiction cannot always be based upon well-defined principles.[3] Hence, disputes recurred. Some major decisions were not accepted nor was observance of accepted decisions universal. The Carpenters withdrew from the Department in 1921, to avoid a decision favorable to the Sheet Metal Workers. Aggrieved, the Bricklayers also withdrew in 1927. Inasmuch as these organizations were involved in a majority of the disputes, cases involving them could not be settled. Other unions, though they did not withdraw, became disaffected and critical. Moreover, building-trades unions generally were aggrieved by, and became suspicious of, the Institute of Architects which, in 1922,

---

[1] A two-thirds vote was required for a decision.

[2] A. T. Helbing, *op. cit.*, p. 30.

[3] For the nature of the decisions, and agreements, see the proceedings of annual conventions. Many, if not most, of the decisions award a part of the work in question to one organization, the rest of it to the other. Usually no principles are involved or established.

resolved in favor of the open shop.[1] For the building-trades unions, of all unions, adhere to the principle of the union closed shop.

"The Board also encountered difficulty in getting its awards adopted by employers who hesitated to antagonize powerful unions. The situation was made more difficult in February, 1927, when the Board renewed several recommendations (first made in 1922) which tended to strengthen its powers. These were that members of the two professional societies —the architects and engineers—should stipulate in all specifications and contracts drawn up by them that the work be done in accordance with the Board's decisions; that general contractors and employers should require of their sub-contractors the performance of work in accordance with these decisions; and finally that each international union which was a member of the department should instruct its locals not to work with locals of any union refusing to abide by its awards."[2] In addition to all this, it was important from the point of view of the A.F. of L. and the Department that the reaffiliation of the Carpenters should be effected. The Carpenters had all the while taken the position that as the price of reaffiliation the decisions against their claims must be vacated.

Thus it was that the Board was disestablished in 1927. Though the blame was affixed upon employers who had not cooperated, the disestablishment was very largely the result of dissatisfaction, criticism, and fear, and the price paid for the reaffiliation of the Carpenters and the hoped-for 100 per cent Building Trades Department.

For approximately three years (1927–1930), the Department operated as it had before the Board for Jurisdictional Awards was established. With the Carpenters affiliated once more and the federation fairly complete except for the nonaffiliation of the Bricklayers, it realized a measure of success. A number of settlements were effected. By 1929, however, depression had developed in the building industry, and, because of unemployment and job-consciousness, disputes began to multiply. A desire for more effective machinery for the prevention and settlement of disputes resulted in the creation, on Nov. 10, 1930, of the National Board of Trade Claims.

In establishing this new Board, the lessons of past experience were heeded; the professional societies were not represented and a measure of

---

[1] This was related to the general open-shop movement so active in 1921, the struggle incidental to the so-called Landis Award (Chicago, 1921–1922), and the breakdown of arbitration and the establishment of the open shop in San Francisco. For a discussion of the American Plan, see Selig Perlman and Philip Taft, *Labor Movements*, vol. 4 of J. R. Commons and Associates, *History of Labor in the United States*, 1896–1932 (1935), Chap. 37, and *supra*, pp. 165–171.

[2] Quoted from L. Lorwin, *op. cit.*, p. 380.

elasticity as against national uniformity was accepted. The Board was established by the Department and the National Association of Building Trades Employers.[1] It consisted of the Executive Council of the Department and an equal number of representatives of the National Association. It could entertain claims sent in by internationals only. Its function was not to arbitrate, but to formulate the question to be arbitrated, unless upon investigation it was found that the claim had already been disposed of.[2] Each party to a dispute was to name an arbitrator and these arbitrators were to select an umpire. In the event of failure to agree upon an umpire within the time allowed, the president of the Department was to submit three names from which a selection was to be made. An award made was to be examined by the Board and, if found to be concise, clear, and in line with the question as stated, it was to be approved by the Board and a date fixed upon which it should become effective. Any unsatisfactory award was to be referred back to the arbitration board making it for further consideration and correction.

Room for elasticity was provided. It was not the purpose of the Board "to disturb conditions which were satisfactory in any community," for example, New York or Chicago, and any decision rendered was not in any way to affect the conditions there obtaining.[3]

Provision was made also under which, in any locality in which a council and an employers' association existed, a conference board, arbitration board, or local board of trade claims might be established to determine temporarily[4] jurisdiction claims for the district, when they should arise between meetings of the National Board.

A local board, arbitration board, or board of trade claims was to meet within seventy-two hours of the presentation of a claim and was required to render a decision within seventy-two hours thereafter. There was to be no strike, abandonment of work, or refusal to do work or to go upon the job, because of jurisdiction claims. Should any local labor union fail, within twenty-four hours, to abide by and work under any decision arrived at as set forth in the constitution, then the international union with which the local was affiliated should be notified of the failure and

[1] For the provisions here summarized, see *Constitution, National Board of Trade Claims*.

[2] Section 6 provided that "the Board shall recognize and shall not allow to be reopened, except by consent of the trades involved, any past decision rendered by the American Federation of Labor or Building Trades Department or the former National Board for Jurisdictional Awards, which have been approved by the Building Trades Department, and which decisions shall be filed with the Board." Seventy-one effective agreements and decisions were published in *Decisions Rendered Affecting the Building Industry*, a booklet published by the Board in August, 1932.

[3] One difficulty all the while had been that New York and some other cities, because of their special situations, customs, and earlier settlements in which adjustments had been made, were prone not to observe national decisions handed down.

[4] Effective only until a decision was rendered by the National Board (Art. 24).

was thereupon within twenty-four hours to furnish skilled men to do the work. If the international failed to furnish the men required, the employer was at liberty to fill the places with such men, members of other unions, as in his judgment could perform the work, and the members of such unions were required to respond.

Under these regulations, the machinery set up operated with a considerable measure of success in preventing or settling jurisdiction disputes. Most of the settlements, however, were made by the local boards established. Yet the full possibilities of the system were by no means realized, for three important internationals and their locals had no part in it.[1] In fact, the Carpenters, Bricklayers, and Electrical Workers, outside of the Department, entered into a tripartite agreement to cooperate in disputes involving any one of them. Once more it was shown that compulsory arbitration provided for by the industry could function only in so far as the international unions would cooperate.

Entered into for a period of two years, the agreement establishing the National Board of Trade Claims was renewed for a further period of two years—to November, 1934. In 1933, however, a construction code was approved and a National Planning and Adjustment Board established, Jan. 31, 1934, to settle interunion disputes. This new machinery was in operation until the codes were declared invalid in the Schechter decision, May 27, 1935. Following that, the arrangement for the Board of Trade Claims having lapsed, the Department once more provided the machinery for settling jurisdiction disputes among the building-trades unions.

The several internationals, whether members of the Department or not, had cooperated in connection with construction problems under the New Deal. Then, urged to do so by the President of the A.F. of L., the Carpenters, Bricklayers, and Electrical Workers in June, 1934, applied for readmission to the Department, upon a basis of equal rights with the then affiliated organizations, and the application was accepted by the Executive Council of the Department. When the delegates of these three crafts appeared at the convention in October of that year, however, they were not seated.[2] This unfavorable action was taken, it was said, because the three unions planned to make changes in the Department and to elect new officers and had sought the cooperation of certain internationals to that end. In part this purpose was acknowledged, but it was claimed to be within the rights of cooperating organizations. The action taken by the Department was declared to be invalid by President Green

[1] As already stated, the Bricklayers had withdrawn from the Department in 1927, and the Carpenters, again, in 1929. The Electrical Workers objected to the arrangement, and, in April, 1931, also withdrew.

[2] For details concerning this whole unfortunate matter, see, particularly, American Federation of Labor, *Proceedings*, 1934, pp. 346–348, 358–362, 488–513, 514–541, and *Report of Proceedings of the Twenty-eighth Annual Convention of the Building Trades Department*, American Federation of Labor (Nov. 26, 27, 28, 1934).

and the A.F. of L. convention. The Department, however, stood its ground and maintained that it had power to determine who might affiliate, although the Department was an arm of the A.F. of L.[1] A few weeks later, in accordance with instructions given by this convention, which had declared all proceedings of the annual convention of the Department invalid, the President of the A.F. of L. called a special convention of the Department. The unions represented in this convention were the Bricklayers, Carpenters, Electrical Workers, Operating Engineers, Marble Polishers, Teamsters, and Hod Carriers, with a per capital tax-paying membership of approximately 540,000.[2] The twelve internationals not responding to the call and not participating in the convention were the Asbestos Workers, Boilermakers, Bridge and Structural Iron Workers, Elevator Constructors, Granite Cutters, Wood, Wire, and Metal Lathers, Sheet Metal Workers, Painters, Decorators and Paper Hangers, Plasterers, Plumbers and Steam Fitters, Roofers, and Stone Cutters, with a combined taxpaying membership of approximately 200,000. All attempts to mediate the difficulty failed. The officers and the Executive Council declined to turn over the books and records of the Department for use by the convention. The matter was contested in court, but the court, holding that the special convention had not been properly called, would not recognize as legitimate the organization established or the officers elected by it, nor could the other group be recognized because it no longer had officers, since the actions taken at the San Francisco convention had been declared invalid and their terms had expired Jan. 1, 1935. Thus, the warring groups remained deadlocked until, at the 1935 convention of the Federation, a procedure was agreed upon for re-establishing or reuniting the Department.[3]

This procedure called for a committee of six, representing the two factions equally, to work out a plan, with an arbitrator to decide in the event of deadlock. The committee finally reached an agreement on methods of settling jurisdiction disputes.[4] "All former bona fide

[1] Other charges were also made, and denied, such as that some of the organizations had falsely reported their membership.

[2] Figured from "voting strength," based upon average paid-up membership, American Federation of Labor, *Proceedings*, 1934, pp. 35–36.

[3] A meeting was held in Washington on Aug. 1, 1935, but the representatives of only seven unions appeared. At this meeting a new organization was established, with Williams as president. The seating of Williams as delegate to the A.F. of L. convention was protested. Action was deferred, no doubt because agreement upon a course of procedure to establish harmony was expected.

[4] The conferees were, however, unable to agree upon a president and a secretary. The arbitrator selected a president from one faction, a secretary from the other. At the Denver Convention in 1937, however, new officers were elected by the faction headed by the Carpenters, who for twenty-five years had done much to defeat the efforts made to settle jurisdiction disputes. The slow and uncertain operation of the machinery established in 1936 and 1937 is largely explained by the outcome of the contest at Denver.

decisions as well as agreements entered into between international organizations should stand."[1] It was also understood "that the many devices for adjusting local disputes would not be disturbed."[2] The national Tribunal for settling disputes was to consist of a standing referee selected by the committee of six. His decisions were to be accepted and to be binding upon all organizations affiliated with the Department. "Failure of any affiliated organization to accept and abide by such decisions or interpretations [should] constitute cause for suspension or expulsion from the . . . Department by the vote of the . . . Convention following the report of the Executive Council which shall act as a fact-finding court."[3]

[1] Building Trades Department of the A.F. of L., *Report of Proceedings of the Special Convention*, Mar. 25, 1936, p. 6. The agreements and decisions on jurisdiction, whether the decisions were rendered by the A.F. of L., the Building Trades Department, the Board of Jurisdictional Awards, or the 1936–1938 referee, are found in the *Report of Proceedings of the Thirty-second Convention* . . . 1938, pp. 323–360, and in booklets published from time to time by the Department under the title "Agreements and Decisions Rendered Affecting the Building Industry."

[2] Building Trades Department, *Proceedings, Special* 1936, p. 18.

[3] The procedure established was as follows:

"1. The referee shall hold meetings at least four times each year, and at other times when he, in his discretion, deems it necessary.

"2. The Referee shall receive only requests for decisions from the President of the Department and Presidents of National or International Unions of claims for jurisdiction over control of work to be done. All National and International Unions affiliated with the Department shall be notified and sent copy of any request for decision submitted to the Referee by registered mail and return receipt requested.

"3. The Referee shall investigate each claim and determine whether it has already been disposed of.

"4. The Referee shall not permit any controversy that has been settled, and an agreement accepted and agreed to by the organization involved, to be reopened.

"5. If claim has not been settled already by decision or agreement, the matter shall be set for hearing and decision.

"6. The Referee shall state the controversy which is to be considered and request the claimants to present their evidence at the next regular meeting, set by the Referee, when evidence may be presented in its case, orally, by brief, or both.

"7. Should there be two claimants, one of which fails to present its case within the stated time, the work in question shall be declared to be in the possession of the organization who presented its case before the Referee.

"8. Should there be more than two claimants, any organization which fails to present its case within the stated time shall be eliminated from further consideration in regard to work in dispute.

"9. The Referee shall in each instance consider all evidence relevant or pertaining to the controversy and render his decision within ten days after the hearing, if possible, and send the decision to the organizations involved and to the Secretary of the . . . Department, who shall compile and keep a correct record of same. The Secretary of the . . . Department shall send copies of all decisions to all International Organizations, Local and State . . . Councils.

"10. Any decision or interpretation rendered by the Referee, in which the procedures involved in arriving at such decision or interpretation have been consistent with the

In the first part of 1937, the building industry was beset with jurisdiction disputes.[1] Recourse to the referee was taken haltingly; although several of the local councils had submitted plans for the settlement of local jurisdiction disputes for approval by the Department, there was no uniform plan for settling disputes locally. Moreover, it is said that "a few of [the] affiliated international unions had directed their local officials not to recognize decisions rendered locally or by the officials of the . . . Department."[2] In view of this and of the absence of any uniform plan in effect, and in order to reduce disputes to a minimum, the Executive Council, "after thorough study unanimously approved a plan of procedure which local councils must adhere to in the determination of local disputes."[3] The plan, introduced and maintained by the Executive Council over the protest of the Carpenters, was essentially the same as that operative under the Board of Trade Claims described above.[4] The essential difference between the arrangement effected and the arrangement that preceded it lay in the fact that it employed a one-man board or referee[5] and was without cooperative relationship with the employers.

Though for a time the machinery worked fairly well and a number of important cases were successfully disposed of, the hopes entertained for it as an agency for avoiding delays in construction work and friction between unions were not realized. Beginning with local machinery long

---

Articles hereof, shall be accepted by and be binding upon all organizations affiliated with the . . . Department. Failure of any affiliated organization to accept and abide by such decisions or interpretations shall constitute cause for suspension or expulsion from the . . . Department by the vote of the . . . Convention following the report of the Executive Council which shall act as a fact-finding court."

[1] In his report to the annual convention, held in Denver, the President of the Department said, "The old time question of jurisdictional dispute is still the paramount issue in the Building and Construction Trades Department. During the early part of this year jurisdictional disputes were so prevalent that they were a real menace to the building and construction industry. A dispute would appear at the least provocation and the Department was besieged with complaints from all parts of the country requesting settlement of the same. National and international organizations were repeatedly requested to send representatives to the seat of trouble for the purpose of reaching an understanding that would permit the work on the project to proceed. This would cause delay in operations and a great deal of time was lost by the mechanics and laborers, and a great deal of expense was entailed by contractors and owners or promoters of the project." *Proceedings of the Thirty-first Convention* (1937), p. 67.

[2] *Ibid.*, p. 108.

[3] *Ibid.*

[4] Quoted in full in *Report of Thirty-first Convention*, pp. 108–109. In view of the protest by the Carpenters, the Executive Council did, however, recommend to the Convention that the entire subject matter of local joint boards be referred to the Council for further study, investigation, and action. *Ibid.*, p. 110.

[5] Dr. John A. Lapp was selected as referee and served from July, 1936, to September, 1938, when he resigned because two of the internationals had declined to observe awards made by him.

functioning successfully in Chicago, Milwaukee, and New York, and less well-recognized institutions in an equal number of other cities, corresponding arrangements, following April, 1937, were effected in perhaps more than thirty additional cities. But the protest of the Carpenters at the Denver Convention of that year was strong enough to cause the action taken by the Executive Committee to provide for the establishment of local adjustment boards to be referred back for further consideration. The final outcome was that the action that had been taken in the spring of 1937 was rescinded early in 1938. This was an unfortunate backward step, for only the boards that had been functioning in 1936 continued to be recognized, and only three of these with certainty. Under these circumstances, very few cases locally decided could come to the referee on appeal. With the limited amount of local adjustment machinery, jurisdiction disputes over jobs generally went to the office of the Department for rulings. Few rulings were made; complaints accumulated; and jurisdiction fights continued. With few appeals from local decisions and the absence of rulings by the President of the Department from which appeal might be taken, the referee had few cases for decision, for only now and then were claims submitted jointly to him by interested internationals. A number of important and troublesome disputes over jurisdiction were not brought up for authoritative decision. Through no fault of the main machinery established, the problem of jurisdiction disputes in the building and construction industry was in 1938 being only slowly and very uncertainly solved. Indeed, the settlement of disputes was then perhaps more bogged down than ever before, for the dominant element in the Department did not believe in self-imposed compulsory arbitration and some of the unions failed to observe or to enforce awards made against their international claims.[1] Because of this nonobservance—if not defiance—the first referee resigned and the machinery was left without one of the essential parts. Once more, the procedure became that of the earliest years of the Department. In August, 1939, however, in order to mend the chaotic situation a new referee was selected and an agreement entered into between the Department and the National Association of Building Trades Employers providing that while a decision was awaited on a jurisdiction dispute, work should not be suspended but should be performed by the craft in possession of it in the concrete case. The internationals were pledged to see to it that this was done.

The new referee heard no cases before his death in the fall of 1941. Indeed in the preceding spring the Executive Council postponed indefinitely all hearings scheduled by him, because of the President's illness and "other pressing matters."[2] Nevertheless, progress was apparently

[1] Particularly the Carpenters and the Operating Engineers.
[2] *Report of Proceedings to the Thirty-fifth Annual Convention* . . . (1941), pp. 104, 199.

made in solving the problem of jurisdiction disputes. The Department made some 750 decisions in the year preceding the 1940 convention, of which twenty were referred to the referee. In his report to the convention the President commented on the "marked reduction" in the number of disputes and the almost entire elimination of jurisdiction strikes. He added, however, in a somewhat contradictory vein: "While the results have been encouraging we are far from satisfactorily solving the problem of strikes over jurisdictional disputes and I recommend and urge that an earnest endeavor be made through cooperation on the part of National and International Unions to curtail further . . . [such] stoppages. . . . "[1] The following year the exigencies of national defense operated to minimize jurisdiction strikes. In the summer of 1941, the Department, the government agencies engaged in defense construction, and the Office of Production Management negotiated an agreement covering all defense projects, which, among other provisions, prohibited all work stoppages.

Trade Alliances: an Evaluation.—In view of the foregoing detail, summarized yet necessarily occupying much space, what is to be said for these alliances? Have they proved to be a good substitute for industrial unionism?

These alliances,[2] thus sponsored, have done not a little to protect all parties from injurious wars over jurisdiction and to enhance the chances for cooperative effort, yet the problem of jurisdiction disputes long remained a large one in the building trades and perhaps has not even yet been adequately solved. The position of the several groups of organizations has been improved when dealing with the employers, especially with the railway companies. This has always been an important objective in the building industry and was the reason for the organization of the earlier local building-trades councils. The number of unions has been reduced by a considerable number of amalgamations. But, on the other hand, it must be said that despite numerous amalgamations effected, the number of organizations remains unduly large and the expense of operation is greater than it might be. When all is said, it must be recognized that the federation plan has been a limited success. It finds logical place where craft unionism obtains in an industry, or an important and distinct department therein, as in the building industry and the railway shops. But it is equally true that federation is not the logical thing and an acceptable answer in such industries as steel, where there is no adequate basis for craft unionism and where organization by crafts

[1] *Ibid.*, 1940, p. 100.
[2] A Mining Department was established by the A.F. of L., but was abolished during the period following the First World War. The Union-Label Department's functions are in essence different from those departments which constitute, in effect, interorganizations of the various craft and compound-craft organizations.

stands in the way of a general, effective organization of the workers employed in an industry. Certain industries have been mechanized to that point where craft unions have little significance. The industrial union, perhaps with craft departments, must be substituted if the mass of workers in such industries are to be organized and to function in a concerted manner and without too much friction and uncertainty.

It is evident that the American Federation of Labor has given some thought to possible improvements in the form of labor organization and that its policy has recently undergone some change but without sacrificing the craft organizations that have held the whip hand. The organizational setup has been somewhat improved. Nevertheless, had the Federation taken its task more seriously, and undertaken it earlier, and had it worked along the lines of the British Trade Union Congress,[1] which had the whole field surveyed with reference to adjustments and amalgamations here and there, still greater improvements might have been realized and perhaps the present division and disunity would have been avoided.[2] More important, a stronger, more virile labor movement should have been forthcoming. In any event, it is evident from our experience that the trades-alliance movement has done little to enlarge or alter the objectives of organized labor—the wisdom of which will, of course, be debated by reasonable men. As to the craft-federation idea as against industrial unionism, it may be said that in the concrete situation there is no one form of organization that is always and inherently best, if the objectives are merely to get the most here and now for the organized groups and to permit special groups to follow their natural bent. But if, added to this, the object is to organize as extensively as possible, to secure the advantage of labor party action and legislation, and, more especially, to effect a substantial change in economic organization, the industrial form rather than the craft form of organization, however much the latter might be improved by the setting up of alliances, would seem to be increasingly called for.

CITY CENTRAL BODIES (AMERICAN FEDERATION OF LABOR)

From this discussion of the structure, government, functions, and problems centering in the organization of labor by trades and industries, we turn to a discussion of central bodies. Here we are concerned with (a) city centrals and district and local councils, (b) state federations of labor and state councils, (c) the American Federation of Labor, whose affiliated organizations had for years preceding the suspensions made in 1936 more than four-fifths of the entire American trade-union membership, and (d) the Congress of Industrial Organizations. An effect of the 1936 suspensions was temporarily to reduce the A.F. of L. membership to

[1] See *Committee Report* to the Edinburgh Congress, 1927.
[2] For an account of the A.F. of L.-C.I.O. struggle from 1935 to date, see Chap. V.

less than three-fifths of the grand total. As the allegiance of a few internationals was transferred from the A.F. of L. to the C.I.O. and with the progress of organization of the latter, the Federation now embraces perhaps slightly less than half of the union membership of the United States. The present division in the organized-labor movement makes it necessary to discuss first the A.F. of L. city centrals, state federations, and the A.F. of L. itself, then the C.I.O.

City central bodies are found with a variety of names—Federation of Labor, Trades and Labor Assembly, Trades and Labor Council, Central Labor Union, Trades Council, Trades Assembly, Industrial Council, and the like. But, whatever the city central may be called, it is a loose organization of delegates, representing the various local unions of the city and its environs.[1] Moreover, it is the local arm of the A.F. of L.; hence, it seldom, if ever, embraces all the locals within the area, for those not affiliated directly with the Federation or with internationals so affiliated are not eligible to membership in it. But all eligible unions are presumed to have membership in it, for both the Federation and its affiliates are expected to urge their affiliated locals to join. Moreover, locals without membership in the city central are not presumed to be accepted into membership in certain other bodies. Yet, in spite of the requirements of the A.F. of L., it is doubtful whether the typical city central has as active members much more than half of the eligible locals. Many of the locals have a narrow outlook and are concerned almost entirely with protecting or furthering their own immediate interests, and therefore remain out of affiliation with the city central body. No acceptable method has been devised for securing a close approach to complete local federation of eligible unions.

The existing network of city centrals is largely a product of the last forty-five years. In 1899, there was a total of seventy-nine, and forty of these had been organized since 1895. By 1902, there were 424 in the United States and Canada; by 1914, 623. The peak number was reached in 1921, when there were 973. During the 1920's and the earlier 1930's, with a smaller A.F. of L. membership, the number of city centrals decreased. In 1930, it was 804, of which 772 were in continental United States and twenty-seven in Canada. In 1936, the number of affiliated city centrals, including those in Canada, was 734; in 1938, in spite of inroads made by the C.I.O., it was 792; in 1941 it was 800. Making due allowance for the fact that two separate A.F. of L. centrals are maintained occasionally in the South, one for white persons, the other for

[1] Representation in central bodies has been standardized by the A.F. of L. Article XI, Sec. 11, of the Constitution of the A.F. of L. reads: "The representation of local unions entitled to affiliation in Central Labor Unions shall be as follows: Local unions having 50 members or less, 2 delegates; 100 members or less, 3 delegates; 250 members or less, 4 delegates; 500 members or less, 5 delegates; one additional delegate to be allowed for each additional 500 members or majority fraction thereof."

Negroes, this means that almost every city of any real industrial importance has a city central body affiliated with the A.F. of L., for the number of cities with populations of 10,000 or more in the United States in 1940 was 1,077.

The city centrals function in a variety of ways. The larger ones may publish a weekly paper to provide labor and other news from labor's point of view. In this way and through its meetings, the city central tries to create a favorable atmosphere and to develop and maintain good morale. If active, it interests itself in a wide range of public affairs—education, government ownership or the granting of safeguarded franchises for the private operation of public utilities, and taxation, as well as in those matters of legislation and local finance which bear directly upon the welfare of organized labor. It will, perhaps, make an effort to elect labor's friends to public office and to defeat its enemies, especially the "injunction judge," but usually with little apparent result. Until recently, there has seldom been much evidence of a united labor vote. Here and there, the city central becomes interested in a labor party, as in Chicago and many other places twenty years ago. Usually these local political movements have been unsuccessful and short-lived, because of both a lack of labor solidarity and the activities of astute politicians in the old parties.[1] The officers of the city central are available as counsel to the local unions generally. Moreover, they take a hand in local organization work, and occasionally this is supplemented by the efforts of a full-time salaried organizer. The city central has no power to call strikes; that is completely in the hands of the organized trades and industries, whose autonomy is respected. Nevertheless, it may be quite helpful in strike situations by giving moral support, by participating in conferences, and by aiding the strikers to secure needed financial resources. It plays a role in local boycotts, which must be endorsed and widely advertised if they are to be successfully prosecuted. The normal procedure[2] is that grievances submitted to a city central must be referred to an appropriate committee (grievance committee or executive board), which tries to effect a settlement. Adjustment is then frequently effected. If the effort at adjustment fails, the boycott is perhaps levied and given such effect as an appeal to labor's friends carries. And, of course, the union label is boomed—with limited effect, experience has shown, upon the demand for union-made goods.

STATE FEDERATIONS OF LABOR

The state federations of labor are another arm—the state arm—of the American Federation of Labor. In a general way, they function in the state as the city central does in the city.

[1] Cf. Chap. XV.
[2] That required by the A.F. of L. but not invariably observed.

Though they are now arms of the A.F. of L., a considerable number of the state federations dating from the eighties and nineties were organized independently and owed their inception to some important issue of the time, such as prison labor. General affiliation with the A.F. of L. and organization in a majority of the states occurred between 1900 and the early 1920's, proceeding concurrently with the rapid growth of the labor movement and the drawing together of local unions into internationals. Federations were established in the last two of the forty-eight states in the early 1920's.

Under the rules of the A.F. of L., only unions directly or indirectly affiliated with it are eligible to membership in a state federation, and all eligible locals and city centrals are presumably urged to secure such membership. As a matter of fact, many of the internationals have been apathetic in this connection and many of the eligible locals and city centrals have not joined and selected delegates, because of lack of interest or because they have not wished to pay the necessary per capita tax. One of the strongest federations is that of Illinois, but a few years ago less than half of the eligible locals, with about three-quarters of the membership in all eligible locals, were actually affiliated. In the absence of any adequate measure to effect complete organization, the state federations, like the city centrals, have been fractional federations.

These state organizations do a variety of things, and, as regards detail, somewhat different things because of different outlooks and because the situations in which they function differ the one from the other. Their important functions, however, are two. The first is organizing work. The president and perhaps other officials of the federation are available for this work and devote a part of their time to it. In addition, a few of the strongest federations may employ one or more full-time organizers to supplement the efforts of the organizers employed by the internationals. Far more important than this, however, is the political and legislative function of the federation. It is in matters of government that its main efforts have centered.

The state federation is presumed to develop a legislative program. This program in part comes from the A. F. of L., which may be stressing the enactment of a workmen's compensation bill, or an antiinjunction bill, or an old-age-pension bill, or an unemployment-insurance bill, or some other specific measure in which it is greatly interested. In part, also, it is developed out of the great variety of resolutions considered at the state convention held annually or every second year. A large number of resolutions calling for legislation are acted upon favorably in convention; from these a number of the most important, in view of the problems dealt with and the interests of the diverse groups in the federation, are selected to be actively pushed in the legislature. Of course, the subjects of bills urged have changed in a changing situation. Convict-labor bills, eight-hour bills, factory codes, child-labor bills, workmen's compensation bills, minimum-wage bills, have at times been leading measures, but in more recent years antiinjunction, anti-"yellow-dog" contract, old-age pension and unemployment-insurance bills, and industrial relations measures have been in the forefront.

The next step is to secure a favorable house, senate, and governor, so that labor's bills will be enacted and antilabor bills, presented in large number by manufacturers' and other associations, will be defeated. The legislative records of candidates for office are examined and evaluated, and the attitudes of candidates without such record are looked into. Here and there, labor's proposals are placed before candidates for office, in an effort to ascertain positions taken and to secure pledges. An attempt is made to place the results obtained before union men and women through their locals and the press and an appeal is made to vote for the friends of labor and against its enemies. This is done in both primary and regular elections. In some concrete cases labor has been successful in determining the result of the election, but this has not been generally true because of the multiplicity of issues almost always involved and the urge of party regularity. These divide the labor vote. At times, also, federations have attempted to set up state labor parties, but in nearly all instances only to fail.

With elections over, the next step is to work for labor's program during the legislative session. The labor representatives are then pitted against the representatives of other organizations. Usually each of the forces is strong enough to defeat most of the measures presented by the other. Each is much stronger in opposition than in offense. The politic thing in most cases, as seen by the average legislator, is to do nothing. Most labor and most antilabor measures are killed or permitted to die in committee or on the calendar. In the main, it is the measure agreed upon by the two sides, say a compensation bill, and the measures which have succeeded in gaining general public support or which are induced by federal subsidy or tax, that are enacted into law. In view of this fact, well substantiated by experience in the different states, it may well be asked whether greater progress would not be realized if organized labor devoted more effort to educating the public and thus gaining its support for measures with a wide appeal.

THE AMERICAN FEDERATION OF LABOR[1]

The origin and earlier history of the American Federation of Labor have been presented in earlier chapters.[2] In August, 1941, it brought

---

[1] For an excellent account and criticism of the A. F. of L., see L. Lorwin, *op. cit.*

[2] *Supra,* pp. 72-75 and Chap. III.

together in a federation internationals, federal labor unions, and independent locals with a dues-paying membership of 4,569,056,[1] or over 40 per cent of the membership of all American labor organizations. It then federated 106 of the more than 180 internationals, these 106 having attached to them some 33,000 locals. In addition, it served as an international for 1,441 local trade and federal labor unions, with an average membership of 198,605 for the fiscal year 1940–1941. Moreover, it had connected with it the various central bodies described in the immediately preceding sections, the several departments (the Label and three industrial), the 800 city central bodies and the forty-nine (including Puerto Rico) state federations of labor. The accompanying diagram gives a picture of the composition of the A.F. of L. and at the same time assists the reader in visualizing for his own purposes the different structures finding place in the main organized-labor movement of the United States prior to the formation of the C.I.O.

The government of the A. F. of L. is entirely in the hands of its annual conventions and of the Executive Council, consisting of the president, the thirteen[2] vice-presidents, and the secretary-treasurer, which Council makes such decisions between conventions as exigencies require. Direct legislation finds no place in the government of the A.F. of L. Even the executive officers are selected in convention, from year to year. Each affiliated international and independent local is entitled to send delegates to the convention according to membership upon which per capita taxes have been paid—one for the first 4,000 members, two for the first 8,000, three for the first 16,000, and so on indefinitely. Federal labor unions, city centrals, state federations, and the departments are entitled to one delegate each. The British Trade Union Congress sends two fraternal

---

[1] For the year ending Aug. 31, 1943, its dues-paying membership had increased to 5,909,020. In addition it had an estimated 500,000 nondues-paying members. These figures include Canadian members. A substantial part of Canadian trade-union membership is in locals affiliated with A.F. of L. internationals. More than half of the central labor bodies in Canada are also directly affiliated with the A.F. of L. Naturally, these affiliations have raised questions as to function and authority between the A.F. of L. and the Canadian Trades and Labor Congress. As issues were finally disposed of, the former organization was to lend support to the latter as a cooperating federation, to act positively in " . . . trade and jurisdictional controversies in the case of all bodies acknowledging allegiance to [it] . . . " and to leave legislative and political issues for independent consideration and action. For an account of the relationship, see H. A. Logan, *The History of Trade-union Organization in Canada* (1928), especially pp. 178–186 (the quotation is from p. 185).

[2] Increased from eight to fifteen at the San Francisco convention, 1934. The Executive Council then became a body of eighteen as against one of eleven, as theretofore. In 1935, however, the offices of secretary and treasurer were combined, with the result that the Executive Council had seventeen members. In 1941, with one position vacant by reason of death and another held by a man under indictment for racketeering, the number of vice-presidents was reduced by two. The Executive Council therefore now has fifteen members.

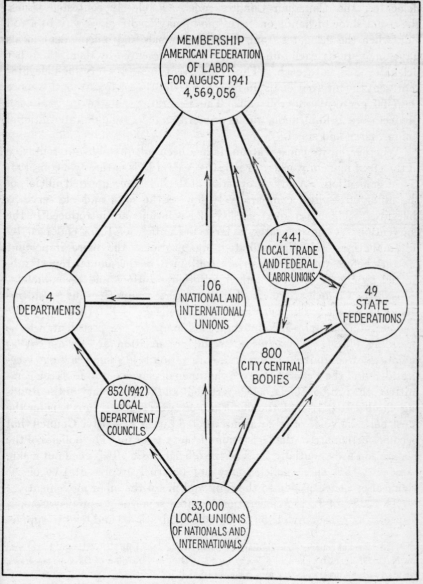

CHART A.[1]—The American Federation of Labor.

[1] Two years later, the total membership was larger, by approximately 1,500,000. The number of local trade and federal unions was 1,614, with a membership of 261,111, and the number of city central bodies was 758.

delegates, the Canadian Congress one. On closely contested issues, the usual show of hands or "aye" and "nay" vote gives way to a roll call, when the delegates from the internationals and independent locals have one vote for each hundred members represented by them, the other delegates one vote each. Thus, the great majority of the delegates represent the internationals; in their hands lies the voting strength—more than 90 per cent—on roll call. The Federation, unlike its American predecessors, is built upon, and is primarily a federation of, international unions, large and small.[1]

Whether, in its conservatism, it has been adequately representative of the great mass of workers or not, the A.F. of L. is naturally a conservative organization. A large proportion of the delegates are tried officials of the affiliated bodies; comparatively few of the rank and file serve as delegates. Though a great variety of resolutions are introduced in the convention by the delegates, a large percentage of them endorsed by or emanating from the affiliated organizations, the more important matters before the convention are contained in the annual report submitted by the Executive Council. Both resolutions and recommendations of the Council are referred to appropriate committees for consideration and report. The personnel of committees is determined by the convention, but upon recommendations made by the president, who is presiding officer. Those close to the organization are prominent as members of committees; thus in a convention held some years ago vice-presidents of the Federation were chairmen of eleven out of fourteen committees, the head of the Label Department and the Secretary of the Building Trades Department the chairmen of two others. Thus it is for the most part the voice of labor as interpreted by the Executive Council that becomes articulate in the legislation of the A.F. of L. The policies of the Federation are essentially those of the official class. This need not mean, of course, that these policies may not be truely representative of the views of or unacceptable to the rank and file of the labor movement.

The A.F. of L. is a federation;[2] unlike some of its predecessors, it respects the autonomy of the affiliated organizations[3] and tries to supple-

---

[1] There are, of course, some similarities between the American Federation of Labor and the National Trades Union. *Cf. supra*, p. 32. But, as rereading of those pages shows, the above generalization is true as a generalization.

[2] Incidentally, the A.F. of L. serves as an international for the affiliated local and federal labor unions, numbering, in 1943, as has been stated, 1,614, with approximately 260,000 members.

[3] This is particularly true of the affiliated internationals as over against state federations and city centrals. In its struggle with the C.I.O., however, the Executive Council has been given additional powers in dealing with affiliated organizations (Rule 2 adopted in May, 1936, and approved by the Tampa Convention). In recent years the president and the Executive Council have at times sought to prevent the expression of opposition to A.F. of L. policies and measures. For example, along with a dozen or more affiliated

ment their work and efforts in a variety of ways and to strengthen and lead the organized-labor movement. It functions in many ways, only the more important of which can be noted in this summary presentation. One of the functions of the A.F. of L. is to protect, mend, and extend labor organization. Not only has it established industrial departments to iron out jurisdiction disputes, among other things; it itself takes up disputes among member organizations and in conference or by decision disposes of them to the best of its ability. In this connection it has accomplished not a little, though the problem has been solved only to a limited extent. In granting charters it safeguards more or less[1] the jurisdiction rights of affiliated organizations and in this and other ways protects against dual unions. It is not too much to say that protection against dual unionism is one of the most important services rendered by the Federation. It also does something to remove weakness and waste by amalgamating unions, and to improve the organization of labor by the establishment of city centrals and other institutions already described. Finally, it cooperates with the affiliated internationals and supplements the work done by their organizers in organizing the non-union workers. In 1941 it spent over $1,000,000 for organizing purposes.

---

internationals, several state federations of labor, and many city centrals, the Cascade County Trades and Labor Assembly of Great Falls, Mont., resolved against any amendment of the Wagner Act. After consideration of the matter by the Council, President Green wrote the secretary and described the action as "traitorous." The resolution was said to be "in contradiction to action already taken by the highest authority within the American Federation. Central bodies chartered by the American Federation of Labor are required by the laws of the Federation to cooperate with the American Federation of Labor and to carry out the policies formulated by conventions of the American Federation of Labor." He added, "The American Federation of Labor cannot tolerate action on the part of a central body which attempts to set aside and contradict policies formulated and adopted by conventions of the American Federation of Labor," and threatened to take disciplinary action unless the resolution was rescinded.

Following a letter "from A.F. of L." to President Gramling of the Georgia State Federation of Labor, a delegate of Typographical Local No. 48 was at first denied a seat as a delegate unless he repudiated his official connection with the Georgia branch of Labor's Non-partisan League. Later an effort was made to require the taking of a special oath. *Typographical Journal*, June, 1939, pp. 643–645.

[1] The granting of charters to internationals with overlapping jurisdiction claims has occurred. Some years ago, disregarding craft rights, a 100 per cent charter was granted the "Martin faction" of the Auto Workers. This was objected to by two craft organizations. Among the older cases in which overlappping charters were granted is that of the Brewery Workers and the Teamsters. Some years ago the Brewery Workers were ordered to surrender their teamster and chauffeur members. This they refused to do and secured an injunction against the enforcement of the Federation decision. The lower court held that the Brewery Workers had been granted an inclusive charter and to deprive them of any of their charter rights would be to infringe upon a property right, but this decision was reversed. In 1941 the Brewery Workers were suspended from the Federation. The decades-old dispute continues, with the Teamsters inside and the Brewery Workers outside the A.F. of L.

It had nearly 200 regular salaried and about 1,900 volunteer organizers.[1]
The corresponding outlay in 1943 was $1,270,348.88, of which $605,802.52
was incurred in the formation and assistance of locals of internationals
and central bodies, the remainder in organizing and servicing directly
affiliated trade and federal labor unions. The number of paid organizers
was 178, of volunteer 1,956. These organizers have been operative in the
districts into which the country is divided for organizing purposes. At different
times special attention has been devoted to certain groups—migratory
workers, women workers, the steelworkers, the Negro, and, more
recently, the textile workers of the South, the auto and rubber workers in
the Middle West, the loggers and lumbermen of the Northwest, and shipbuilding,
aircraft, and other war industries. On occasion a special general
organizing campaign has been instituted, as when an effort was made several
years ago to mobilize the efforts of organized labor under the leadership
of the Union-Label Trades Department. Until 1938,[2] organizing work
was in the hands of the president and the Executive Council. Then,
an Organizing Department, with a director, was created, and organizing
activities centered in it.

In addition to the above functions and activities, the "booming"
of the union label is expected to stabilize organization and to add to the
effectiveness of collective bargaining between unions and employers.
Since 1909, the label efforts of the Federation have been coordinated
through the Label Department. This brings together fifty-six—formerly
more than sixty—internationals making use of labels, buttons, or shop
cards approved by the Federation. Under the Department are local
label leagues in 256 cities, including 10 in Canada. In addition, nearly
every city central has a label committee. Through their publications
and propaganda, these bodies seek to create a demand for union goods
and services, but this effort has been rather ineffective.[3]

Another function of the Federation is to support affiliated organizations
involved in industrial disputes. This it does not so much through
the levy of an assessment upon its membership to finance benefits,
which is within its power to do, as by making appeals for voluntary
contributions.

Still another service consists of its publications, such as the *American
Federationist, The Weekly News Letter*, a *Monthly Survey of Business*, and

---

[1] *Proceedings*, 1941, pp. 39, 43. This represented a tremendous increase over 1929,
when there were only thirty salaried organizers and about $125,000 was spent. The
increase, of course, reflects increased trade-union activity after 1933 and A.F. of L.-C.I.O.
rivalry.

[2] See *Proceedings*, 1938, p. 80. The Federation also levied an assessment of 1 cent per
month per member on affiliated organizations. This assessment was later abolished and
the per capita tax increased from 1 cent to 2 cents. In 1941 the tax was reduced to 1.5 cents
on all dues-paying members up to 300,000, 1 cent on those over 300,000.

[3] For an account of the Label Department, see A. T. Helbing, *The Departments of the
American Federation of Labor,* Chap. 4. See also L. Lorwin, *op. cit.*, pp. 367-374.

its propaganda pamphlets. The news, literature, and findings thus published are widely reprinted or quoted in labor papers, and assist in building up and maintaining morale as well as in molding union opinion and shaping union policy.

Omitting reference to the Legal Department[1] and other branches of its activities, we must emphasize the fact that the Federation is a policy-forming body and an instrument for securing desirable legislation. Inasmuch as the Federation's policies relative to union structure, wages, and other matters are noted elsewhere, its position with reference to the method of legislative enactment and types of labor legislation regarded as desirable alone need to be indicated here.

The Federation's philosophy, though influenced in its early history by critical socialists,[2] has for many years been individualistic, in the sense of limiting the scope of collectivism largely to the control of jobs, rather than socialistic. This philosophic characteristic has caused the Federation to stand in contrast to most of the central labor organizations in Europe. Of course, its individualism, like that of any rather conservative labor organization, has been modified to the extent necessary for group action. The group action on which emphasis has been placed has been that on the industrial field. In other words, the A.F. of L. has emphasized collective bargaining as against all other methods, even though a substantial change in the direction of securing state aid occurred under the New Deal. Political action and legislative enactment have been recognized as necessary, but of secondary importance. This long-time attitude toward political action and legislation is accounted for in part by the individualistic philosophy that dominates the Federation, in part by the extraordinary difficulty involved in securing, maintaining, and enforcing labor legislation in the United States. If control is to be exercised through legislation, it is necessary to push bills through Congress and forty-eight legislatures, which are usually dominated by the business and agricultural interests, then to defend the laws enacted in the courts when their validity is attacked under written constitutions on the ground that they, say, take property without due process of law, and, finally, in so far as the laws are not nullified or emasculated, to seek to have them adequately enforced in a country in which government has been notoriously weak in its administration.

But, however the fact is to be explained, the A.F. of L. has been conservative in its attitude toward labor legislation as compared to labor organizations in most countries, to the groups known as the "intelli-

---

[1] The Legal Department, maintained for several years, published valuable *Legal Information Bulletins*. This work was dropped during the depression. More recently the Federation has maintained a legal staff to draft bills and to serve as counsel in cases involving alleged violation of Sec. 7(a) of the NIRA and of the National Labor Relations Act.

[2] The contribution of socialist ideology to the economic creed of job-conscious "business" unionism is discussed *supra*, pp. 56–59.

gentsia," and even to no small number of its affiliated organizations.[1] Interested primarily in organization and collective bargaining, it has for more than forty years emphasized above all else that kind of legislation which would remove the shackles from labor, and, negatively, it has strongly opposed any legislation that would place new fetters upon its work on the industrial front. It has stood for freedom of assembly and of speech and publication; for the right to organize and against the "yellow-dog" contract and therefore for Sec. 7(a) and for the National Labor Relations Act—as a whole—but not for a part of its interpretation and its administration at the hands of the National Labor Relations Board; for the right to strike and against antipicketing and compulsory investigation laws such as have obtained in Canada, and compulsory-arbitration acts, such as that enacted in Kansas in 1920; for the right to boycott and against antiboycott legislation; for injunction limitation laws and against government by injunction, but for cease and desist orders in the enforcement of National Labor Relations Board decisions; against state police systems and suability laws. All of this is done in the interest of freedom "to aspire and to fight" and of collective bargaining.

The Federation has been less immediately interested in other types of labor legislation. It has, however, been actively concerned with laws to improve the conditions of workers where these conditions are quite dependent upon the law, as in the case of seamen, and with laws to meet certain important problems beyond the capacity of the unions to cope with directly. Examples are found in child-labor laws and in workmen's compensation legislation, where, from the beginning in the one case and from an early time in the other, the Federation took advanced ground. Other examples are found in public education for the masses, which has always been stressed, and in restrictive immigration legislation. Bills providing shorter hours for women have been supported, although at first with some hesitation; the legal minimum wage was not officially endorsed at all previous to the NIRA. Under the New Deal, however, the Federation stood for fixing maximum hours as well as minimum wages. It also, in "the deep depression," urged the adoption of the Black thirty-hour-week bill and similar measures. In the field of social insurance, except in the case of workmen's compensation for industrial injuries, the Federation was slow to move. Only some twenty years ago did it come to espouse the cause of noncontributory old-age pensions. It was really sharply divided on the question of compulsory sickness insurance, which has occupied a prominent place in the legislative program of most labor movements, and in the early 1920's disposed of the

---

[1] For a standard discussion of the matters here dealt with, see Mollie Ray Carroll, *Labor and Politics*. See also American Federation of Labor *Reconstruction Program* (1919), in David J. Saposs, *Readings in Trade Unionism*, Part VIII, and *Labor, Its Grievances, Protests and Demands* (1919).

subject, for the time being, in a manner designed to remove it from the floor of the conventions. Some years ago, however, it began to call attention to the need for such legislation to round out the social security program.[1] In its program to meet the problem of unemployment, as reformulated at different times, government insurance found no positive place until 1932, but since then the Federation has supported the unemployment-insurance movement.[2] The Federation has opposed an independent labor party, claiming its nonpartisan policy to be superior and fearing that the attempt to establish and maintain such a party would lead to dissension and interfere with efforts on the industrial field.

As has been implied, the Federation's policies relate to many things in addition to politics and labor legislation. One of these has been production problems. Some thirty years ago, it was stout in its opposition to "scientific management," which, among other things, was regarded as a speeding device, but it stood for "science in management," which would eliminate waste and improve management in handling personnel and production problems. For more than fifteen years, it has taken positive ground in favor of cooperation in solving production problems when efficiency plans have not been merely for the profit of the employer. It has also warmly espoused the cause of union-management cooperation, best known in the case of the Baltimore and Ohio Railroad shops.

These brief observations are designed to describe the A.F. of L. and to give some idea of how it functions in the American labor movement. One of its main functions has been and is to form policies and to try to induce their acceptance. In this connection it has been and is a positive influence. To an extent it has led the American labor movement. And it has been and is interested in leading it along certain paths and in checking any tendency to travel others. One example of this is found in the strong opposition the Federation has shown to any communistic developments. In every situation its policy has been and is to be "safe and sane."

THE CONGRESS OF INDUSTRIAL ORGANIZATIONS

How the Committee for Industrial Organization came into existence in 1935 has been explained.[3] The eight cooperating internationals then

---

[1] See vol. II, pp. 323, 340–341. In 1939, the Executive Council (*Report*, pp. 162–164) recommended that provision should be made for compensation in the case of disabling sickness, and, in general, for the Federal health program submitted by the Inter-departmental Committee in 1937 and incorporated in the Wagner bill (S. 1620). However, the Executive Council made it clear that, in its opinion, the legislation must be federal and that the service should be financed otherwise than by a payroll tax. The Council's recommendations were approved by the convention.

[2] *Ibid.*, pp. 142, 146.

[3] *Supra*, pp. 201–222.

had a membership of approximately 1,000,000.   By October, 1937, as a result of the transfer of allegiance by several other internationals from the A.F. of L. to it, and its successful organizational efforts, the Committee claimed to have represented 3,718,000 workers.[1] A year later, October, 1938, the corresponding figure was 4,037,877,[2] and by the autumn of 1942 it was 5,000,000.   At the time of the First Constitutional Convention in November, 1938, John L. Lewis reported that attached to the C.I.O. were 42 internationals, 675 directly chartered local industrial unions, 23 state industrial councils, and 164 district, county, and city industrial councils.   Save for the International Ladies' Garment Workers, which decided not to join a formally organized rival of the A.F. of L.,[3] these were the organizations represented in the convention[4] which, preserving the letters C.I.O., adopted a constitution and gave the Congress of Industrial Organizations its present organization and government.   In October, 1943, affiliated to the Congress were 40 nationals, internationals, and organizing committees, 368 directly chartered local unions, 35 state industrial councils, and 228 district and local industrial councils.   The Congress may be presented in diagrammatic form as follows:

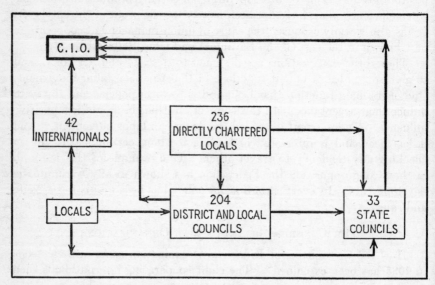

CHART B.—The Congress of Industrial Organizations.

[1] Congress of Industrial Organizations, *Proceedings of the First Constitutional Convention*, p. 36.

[2] *Ibid.*

[3] The International Ladies' Garment Workers' Union has since become a member of the A. F. of L.

[4] Held in Pittsburgh, where the A.F. of L. had been organized fifty-seven years previously.

The Congress is new and still in the organizing stage. The councils created by it have not taken set form and do not have such definite relationships as are found in the A.F. of L. Almost everything is elastic; industrial union councils are to be organized "as may be deemed advisable by the Executive Board and shall be composed of the locals of national unions, international unions and organizing committees, and local industrial unions and local industrial union councils within the territorial limits of such council." As in the case of the A.F. of L., internationals are "to direct their locals to affiliate with proper industrial union councils." "The Executive Board shall issue rules governing the conduct, activities, and affairs of industrial union councils."[1] Roughly, the organizations under the Congress function as do the several types of organizations affiliated to the A.F. of L. One outstanding difference between the diagrams of the two federations, it will be noted, is the absence of departments in the case of the C.I.O. Departments, as has been explained, were established by the A.F. of L. more than a generation ago to meet special problems, these for the most part developing out of the craft form of organization.

Similar to that of the A.F. of L., the government of the C.I.O. is vested in the annual convention, an executive board, and certain administrative officers, including the president, nine vice-presidents,[2] and a secretary.

Representation in the convention, which is to be held annually in October or November, corresponds roughly to the A.F. of L. pattern explained above. Each international and each organizing committee, such as the P.W.O.C., is entitled to from two to ten delegates according to its membership,[3] and each local industrial union and each industrial union council to one delegate. On roll call each international and each organizing committee is entitled to one vote for each member, industrial local unions and industrial councils to one vote each. This means, of course, that voting power is somewhat more highly centralized in C.I.O. internationals and organizing committees than it is in the A.F. of L. internationals.[4]

---

[1] *Constitution*, Art. III, Sec. 4. It should be noted that the Executive Board is authorized (Art. VI, Sec. 2) to "establish bureaus and departments and [to] create such committees as may be necessary to the affairs of the organization."

[2] When first organized, the C.I.O. had two vice-presidents—Philip Murray and Sidney Hillman. At the 1939 convention, however, the number of vice-presidents was increased to six, in 1942 to nine.

[3] Up to 5,000 members, 2 delegates; 5,000 to 10,000 members, 3 delegates; 10,000 to 25,000 members, 4 delegates; 25,000 to 50,000 members, 5 delegates; 50,000 to 75,000 members, 6 delegates; 75,000 to 100,000 members, 7 delegates; 100,000 to 150,000 members, 8 delegates; 150,000 to 200,000 members, 9 delegates; over 200,000 members, 10 delegates. It is to be noted, however, that "members," not the average upon which per capita taxes have been paid during the year, serve as the basis of representation. *Constitution*, Art. VII, Secs. 5 and 6.

[4] *Cf. supra*, pp. 253–257.

The president of the Congress in advance of the convention appoints appropriate committees, but these are subject to approval by the convention. "All resolutions, appeals, and constitutional amendments to be considered by the convention shall be sent not less than ten days prior to the opening date of the convention to the Secretary, who shall sort and distribute them among the chairmen of appropriate committees,"[1] which committees shall then proceed to consider them.[2]

While the Executive Council of the A. F. of L. consists of the president, the secretary-treasurer, and thirteen vice-presidents elected by the delegates in convention, the Executive Board of the C.I.O. formerly consisted of a variable number, for each international and organizing committee nominated one member to serve on it. In the case of the Executive Council, each of the fifteen members had one vote. In the case of the Congress on the other hand, until 1942 each member of the Board was entitled to as many votes as his organization had members.[3] On any stoutly contested issue, therefore, the large internationals, such as the Miners, the Steel Workers, the Automobile Workers, and the Amalgamated Clothing Workers, could exercise much power in the Board as well as in the annual convention. At present, however, the Executive Committee is like that of the A. F. of L. except that it has only eleven members, the president, the secretary-treasurer and the nine vice-presidents. As in the case of the Executive Council, the Executive Committee is vested with extensive powers, for not only does it have power to make decisions and determine policies between conventions, but it also has "power to adopt such rules, not inconsistent with the Constitution, as it may deem necessary to carry out its duties and powers."[4] Yet, in certain respects, explained no doubt by its recent establishment, its powers do not extend so far as those of the Executive Council and the A.F. of L. convention. For example, in connection with disputes between affiliated organizations it has power only to recommend settlements and to report to the convention.[5]

Of course in the usual situation strong leaders have the largest hand in determining the policies of a labor organization. Because of their resourcefulness, courage, and ability, former President Lewis,[6] President Murray, Sidney Hillman, and others have played an unusually large role in determining what the C.I.O. should be and do.

---

[1] *Constitution*, Art. VII, Sec. 13.

[2] *Ibid.*, Sec. 14.

[3] The six vice-presidents had no vote, and the president had a vote only in the case of a tie.

[4] *Constitution*, Art. VI, Sec. 12.

[5] "Any dispute between two or more affiliates may be submitted to the Executive Board which shall make such recommendations to the parties in dispute as it shall deem advisable and report to the convention." *Constitution*, Art. VI, Sec. 6.

[6] In 1942, the United Mine Workers, "John Lewis's organization," withdrew, from the C.I.O. and is now one of more than forty nationals and internationals unaffiliated with the A. F. of L. or the C.I.O.

In order to carry on its work vigorously, the C.I.O. levies much heavier taxes than does the A.F. of L. American Federation of Labor internationals pay a per capita tax of 1.5 cents a month on all dues-paying members up to 300,000, and 1 cent a month on those over 300,000, while the C.I.O. per capita tax is 5 cents a month. In the case of directly affiliated industrial unions the per capita tax is 50 cents a month, the A.F. of L. levy 35.5 cents a month. And, as against the $10 a year levied upon each A.F. of L. state federation and city central, the C.I.O. levies $25 upon each of its corresponding bodies.[1]

These heavy per capita taxes levied by the C.I.O. were rather strongly protested in the organizing convention of 1938. In view of the low dues-paying capacity of their members, it was asserted that many of the affiliated organizations would face difficult problems because of revenues inadequate to meet their needs. On the other hand, it was argued that any such financial difficulty could be met by exonerations at the hands of the Executive Board. The fact is that some of the internationals have at times paid per capita taxes to the central organization either at a reduced rate or on a mere fraction of their dues-paying membership. Only in one way or the other are the deviations between payments made to certain internationals and to the Congress to be explained. Evidently the taxes were, until recently, heavier than could well be borne when the rank and file were working only part time in many of the industries.

The C.I.O. is a young organization and, as has been said, is, in the absence of any amalgamation with the A.F. of L. in the near future, still in the making. In the longer run, it will no doubt function in as many ways as has the A.F. of L., but with a somewhat different emphasis, for it has a different strategy, a somewhat broader interest, and, in part, different policies.

Its organizing and strike activities have been discussed in an earlier chapter.[2] Here it need only be repeated that in the one connection it has been both vigorous and successful, while in the other it has been militant and resourceful.

Some of the policies of the C.I.O., particularly those pertaining to the political sphere of action, contrast to an extent with those of the A.F. of L. But basically the functional character of the two organizations is much the same. This is true with reference to the matters of wages and hours; the wage theory and economic assumptions of the C.I.O. are in substance those of the A.F. of L., and its objectives with reference to the here-and-now situation are much the same.[3] Likewise policies are much the same with reference to

---

[1] *Constitution*, Art. VIII, Secs. 1–5.

[2] Chap. V.

[3] Within the C.I.O. membership as a whole, it might be said that the wage policy looks less toward differentials—more toward a leveling up of the scale for the entire membership

eligibility of nonunion workers for employment. The C.I.O. has, it is
true, had to accept many agreements covering only its own members, not
covering the entire working personnel in the bargaining unit or excluding
nonmembers from employment. But this acceptance is explained for
the most part by necessity.[1] As the initial organizing stages passed,
as collective bargaining and contractual relations were accepted by
employers to a greater extent, and gains were not so likely to be jeopardized by insistence upon the closed or union shop—the C.I.O. unions
began to press for it. As it has been necessary to say many times in the
preceding pages, the one outstanding difference between the two federations on the economic front is that the C.I.O. most frequently stands for
the industrial form of organization in order that it may include the
semiskilled and unskilled, while the A.F. of L. has usually been organized
along craft lines, since its original foundation was based upon the notion
that the "natural" unit of organization is one of workers in a particular
craft, with the consequent predominant position of strong craft internationals with restricted interests.[2] On the economic front, the chief
difference between the two organizations relates to the range of classes
of workers and to the persons whose interests are to be defended and
furthered through organization and collective bargaining.

The C.I.O. has represented a segment of labor whose interests necessarily have involved greater resort to the political instrumentality than
have those of the A.F. of L. constituency; and the leadership, accordingly,
has been more politically minded and more aggressive upon the political
front. Several specific factors, some of them historical in character,
account for the Congress's emphasis upon legislation. Trends in American industrial life have made the Federation's predominant emphasis
upon job control applicable to the needs of a decreasing proportion of the

---

—than does the wage policy of the A.F. of L. But this is a consequence chiefly of the fact
that the C.I.O. is composed largely of industrial unions, the memberships of which are
doing the same or more nearly the same kind of work than are different groups of craftsmen,
whereas the Federation has to a greater extent been composed of craft unions, each pushing
vigorously for higher earnings for its own members. Differences in the success of the
various craft groups have resulted in a more highly differentiated wage structure within
the membership of the A.F. of L.

[1] The acceptance of the preferential shop by the Amalgamated Clothing Workers is a
widely known fact, but in part this acceptance was necessary in different markets in order
to obtain control of contractual relations; in other words it is explained by the same fact
that explains acceptance by the newer C.I.O. unions of agreements covering only their own
members.

[2] It may be remarked in passing that on the whole there has appeared to be more willingness among C.I.O. affiliates to engage in labor-management cooperation to eliminate wastes
and solve technical problems of industry than has been evidenced by the affiliates of the
A.F. of L. In part differences in this regard are to be explained more by circumstance than
by policy, but nevertheless some of the leaders of the C.I.O. have manifested a keenly
intelligent appreciation of the need, once organization has been effected, of making the
union a cooperative agent in solving plant problems.

nation's labor supply, and criticism of the lethargy of the Federation in seeking needed legislation—in some cases of its opposition to legislation on the ground that it would cause workers to look less frequently to the trade unions for their economic salvation—was one of the factors in the background of general dissatisfaction and dissent which focused in 1935 upon the essential issue of industrial organization in many of the unorganized segments of industry. Several of the leaders of the C.I.O.— John L. Lewis, Sidney Hillman, and others—had for years experienced the difficulties of competition with nonunion areas, and accordingly had had impressed upon them the need for a modicum of state control in order to prevent undermining of standards.[1] Their organizations had needed legislative support in Guffey Acts and industrial codes, as well as in injunction-limitation and anti-"yellow-dog"-contract legislation, and statutes establishing the workers' right to organize without interference, restraint, or coercion on the part of employers or their agents. It is likely, also, that the majority of C.I.O. leaders, many of whom did not receive their trade-union education in the ideological school of Gompers, were intuitively more favorably disposed toward a broad political program. Moreover, industrial unionists have fewer economic-front interests the trade-union control of which is likely to be jeopardized when the state does things for the workers, instead of merely giving them a free hand to organize and bargain collectively, than have craft unionists.

To an extent the differences between the C.I.O. and the A.F. of L. in the matters of political action and legislative programs have been differences in kind, but for the most part they have been differences in degree. Some of the C.I.O. leaders had for years been keenly interested in a broad social security program; on the other hand, with the exception of its support of workmen's compensation legislation, the Federation looked with no little fear upon the introduction of a social security program comparable in scope to the system that England had evolved by the end of the First World War period. It was, indeed, not until 1932[2] that the Federation finally endorsed state unemployment insurance. Federation endorsement of organized medical care and sickness benefits took place only shortly before the present rift in the American labor movement. While during the second half of the 1930's both organizations supported—with, of course, proposals for modification and improvement—the Social Security system established in 1935, C.I.O. interest in broadening and liberalizing the Act for a time was greater, and support of these ends more vigorous, than those of the Federation.[3] More recently,

---

[1] This aspect of C.I.O. development is discussed in more detail *supra*, pp. 233–234.

[2] American Federation of Labor, *Proceedings*, 1932, pp. 335–336, 360.

[3] Some of the liberalizations introduced by the 1939 amendments [Public no. 379, 76th Congress, 1st Session, Chap. 666 (H. R. 6635), Aug. 10, 1939] were in accordance with

however, the two organizations have had no differences concerning social security legislation. Likewise the C.I.O. has fought more aggressively for extensive plans of government work and employment than has its rival. In the matter of federal wages and hours legislation, also, the attitudes of the two organizations have differed somewhat. While the Congress had desired more extensive regulation, higher wage minima, and lower hours maxima than the Administration regarded as appropriate when the Fair Labor Standards Act of 1938[1] was enacted, it has on the whole warmly supported the New Deal wages and hours program. The opinions of A.F. of L. spokesmen differed somewhat, but on the whole, in contrast to the Congress, the Federation gave evidence of fear of injury to its affiliated organizations and their wages and hours standards, and supported—but none too strongly—the proposed legislation only after certain revisions had been made.

---

recommendations made by the C.I.O., and some of its leaders have in fact become well versed in different aspects of the subject of social security and have been able to assist Congress in working toward amendment and improvement of the Act.

[1] Public no. 718, 75th Congress, 3d Session, Chap. 676 (S. 2475), June 25, 1938.

CHAPTER VII

TRADE-UNION INSTITUTIONALISM

By trade-union institutionalism is meant the broad welfare, recreational, and educational activities of trade unions, the variety of benefit features provided for their members, and the business institutions they have established for profit or other purposes. The term "institutionalism" itself is, of course, merely a convenient catchall, employed to designate those union activities other than collective bargaining and political effort. The line of demarcation between these types of activities is, however, not always clear. For example, benefits may be instituted to increase loyalty and to strengthen the morale of the members during strikes, and the educational program may be closely linked with political activity.

Trade-union institutionalism as it now exists is the result of the growth and decay of a wide variety of influences, the importance of which has differed among different unions and at different periods of union history. Acting independently, trade-union locals have, for example, established producers' cooperatives following lost strikes, and internationals have established benefit funds. The particular institution may, on the other hand, represent the participation of the union in a nationwide movement, as did the establishment of producers' cooperatives in the 1880's and of labor banks in the 1920's. An examination of the objectives of trade unions in establishing these various institutions, as might be expected, reveals numerous purposes and aims. If any generalization as to objective is possible, it is that these institutions are a part of the effort of unions to provide greater security for their members, to further their welfare, and to make them more loyal to and dependent upon the union.

Trade unions are frequently social as well as business organizations, although the social phase of union activity is less important than it was a generation or two generations ago, when the local was often the center of the social life of the worker and to an extent of that of his family. Even now, in spite of the opportunities presented by motion pictures, reading rooms, social settlements, public parks, and outings made possible by cheap transportation or by automobile, many unions have open meetings, dances, card parties, picnics, suppers, and the like. Not infrequently there are auxiliary organizations for the wives. Gymnasiums and bowling alleys are sometimes made available, and, now and then, as in the case of the Ladies' Garment Workers in New York, camps or other vacation centers are provided.[1] The fullest development of social activities is found, of course, where labor temples have been built, as they have been in forty-eight or more cities.[2] Although some of these, as their chief or exclusive function, house union offices and provide halls for union meetings, others are also important centers of social activity.

One of the most important activities of all unions is that of obtaining favorable publicity and of providing information to their members as well as to the public. Trade unionists have frequently charged that the public press is largely under the control of big advertisers, whose anti-union bias prevents the workers and the public from obtaining accurate information about the labor movement. This bias is particularly strong in times of industrial dispute, when the outcome of the struggle depends so much upon the attitude of the public and the morale of the rank and file,[3] and it constitutes one of the chief reasons why so many of the internationals and some of the city centrals publish their own journals or papers. In addition to these publications, reports of conventions, weekly news letters, and propaganda pamphlets on various subjects are published, sometimes in tremendous quantities. This literature serves the purpose of educating the trade-union members themselves as well as of giving favorable publicity to the trade-union cause. The need for educational literature is particularly great during organizing campaigns, such as those of 1933–1934 and 1936–1937, which bring into the unions many thousands of new members who are unfamiliar with the purposes and policies of trade unions.

WORKERS' EDUCATION

Workers' education, as the term is commonly used, does not mean vocational or trade education; rather it refers to training given to workers, as workers, in a broad range of subjects, ranging from courses on trade-union tactics and institutions, psychology, and economics to art and literature. The scope and aim, however, vary considerably among

[1] A description of some of the more important recreational activities of trade unions may be found in "Beneficial Activities of American Trade Unions," U. S. Bureau of Labor Statistics, *Bulletin* 465, pp. 85–114. The activities of the International Ladies' Garment Workers' Union are described in *Growing Up*, a book prepared by the Educational Department of this union in 1938.

[2] The U. S. Bureau of Labor Statistics in 1928 (*ibid.*, pp. 104–108) reported on forty-eight labor temples. Ordinarily these had been financed by subscriptions to stock made by the locals concerned. The forty-eight temples represented an investment of $3,793,273.

[3] As one example, the great steel strike of 1919 may be cited. Selig Perlman believes that one of the chief causes of the loss of that strike was the failure of the unions to provide sufficient prolabor propaganda to offset the antiunion press of the employers. *A History of Trade Unionism in the United States* (1922), p. 293.

different countries and according to the period and the union carrying on the work. The activity may be directed primarily to supplying the workers with the same sort of education as is received by those who remain longer in school; it may be used in an effort to prepare workers for the advent of, and for life in, a better social order; it may attempt chiefly to strengthen the trade unions' bargaining power[1] by increasing loyalty and stimulating interest of members in union affairs, by encouraging them to take an active interest in labor legislation, and by giving the leaders knowledge of the type that will be helpful in organizing and bargaining.

In Great Britain workers' education, development of which began in the nineteenth century, became a national movement with the formation of the Workers' Educational Association in 1903. This Association was formed by the university extension movement, the cooperatives, and the trade-union movement, all of which had already been engaged in workers' education. All these groups have continued to participate in the work of the Association, although there has been a tendency for trade-union control to increase relative to that of the other groups.[2] In the years following the foundation of the Association, workers' residential colleges, summer schools, tutorial classes,[3] as well as shorter courses, correspondence courses, and scholarships for workers to attend the regular universities were established.[4]

Workers' Education in England.—Although the desire to strengthen unionism has always been present, the main objective of workers' education in Britain has been to provide for workers the courses others, more fortunate than they, have had in school.[5] There has not, however, been

[1] See E. E. Cummins, "Workers' Education in the United States," *Social Forces*, vol. 14 (1936), pp. 601–604.

[2] The grants-in-aid provided by the government have not meant governmental control; in Great Britain and the Scandinavian countries government aid is given to voluntary agencies with little or no exercise of control accompanying the grants [Eleanor G. Coit, "Workers' Education and Government Support," *Journal of Adult Education*, vol. 8 (1936), pp. 263–266]. Among the material on workers' education in Great Britain, reference may be made to T. W. Price, *The Story of the Workers' Educational Association from 1903 to 1924* (1924); J. J. Senturia, "The Trades Union Congress and Workers' Education," *American Economic Review*, vol. 20 (1930), pp. 673–684; Paul Blanshard, *An Outline of the British Labour Movement* (1923), Chap. 12; John H. Nicholson, "Workers' Education in Great Britain," *International Labour Review*, vol. 29 (1934), pp. 656–674; "Workers Education in Great Britain," *American Federationist*, vol. 37 (1930), pp. 982–985; Barbara Wootton, "Reflections on the Present State of the British Workers' Educational Association," *Workers' Education*, vol. 13, no. 4 (October, 1936), pp. 21–23.

[3] The tutorial classes devote three years, of twenty-four lectures each, to one subject, the members doing outside studying and writing papers in connection with the courses.

[4] Relatively few workers apply for these scholarships, however.

[5] The lack of emphasis on training to increase the power of the unions, compared with the emphasis in the United States, may be explained by the fact that, on the whole, British workers have been more class conscious and that trade unions have been more or less

agreement within the workers' education movement as to the desirability of stressing this general education; indeed, it was disagreement on this question of emphasis that split the education movement. One group, desiring workers' education to be different in content and aim from that for other classes—to be used to prepare for a different economic and social order—split with the Workers' Educational Association and formed the Plebs League and, after the World War I, the National Council of Labour Colleges.[1] The National Council demanded that the working class should have complete control of workers' education, that the work be financed by trade unions, independent of capitalist and government support and control, and that more emphasis should be placed on theoretical Marxian economics. These two groups are both represented in the Trades Union Congress, and the persistence of the quarrel between them has greatly hampered the workers' education movement.[2]

After the War the Workers' Educational Association, with the aid of government grants-in-aid for its classes, was able to expand its activities, while the National Council of Labour Colleges, which refused to seek financial aid from the government or cooperation with the universities, experienced financial difficulties, with the result that its residential college in London was closed in 1929 and its other classes were hampered.[3] During the postwar period the trade-union interest in workers' education has been more active. In some cases the unions have conducted their own correspondence courses and have, through the Workers' Educational Trade Union Committee, in turn working through the Workers' Educa-

---

accepted. No doubt the limitations of the public free school system in Britain enter into the explanation.

[1] The Plebs League was formed after a spectacular strike in 1909 of the students of Ruskin College for workers against the alleged tendency of the College to become less of a workers' institution and more like other "bourgeois" institutions. The National Council of Labour Colleges was formed in 1921.

[2] Because of the quarrel, the educational work of the Congress has been very limited. In the United States, the interest in workers' education as a means to change the social and economic order has been almost entirely outside the trade-union movement, whereas in Great Britain the fight has been within the trade-union movement. It should be pointed out that the interest in a general education for workers on the part of many of the supporters of the Workers' Educational Association is explained by a feeling that such an education is necessary for an evolution to a different social and economic order. See J. J. Senturia, *op. cit.*, p. 683.

[3] See *Labour Monthly*, vol. 18 (1936), p. 209, where T. D. Smith, a member of the first executive council of the National Council of Labour Colleges says that "little is done apart from mild W.E.A. classes." Besides the direct effect of the financial difficulties on the classes of the National Council, the closing of the school decreased the supply of teachers. Unlike the Workers' Educational Association, many of whose teachers are university people, the National Council of Labour Colleges classes have been taught by workers, many of them drawn from the London school. See J. J. Senturia, *op. cit.*, p. 682, where he also points out that the quality of teaching in National Council of Labour Colleges classes has been poorer than that of the Workers' Educational Association.

tional Association, set up week-end schools and one-year and three-year courses, paid fees of members for the correspondence courses of Ruskin College, and provided scholarships to the residential and summer schools. With increased interest on the part of the unions has come more emphasis on shorter courses and on the training of union officials.[1]

Workers' Education in the United States.—The workers' education movement developed later in the United States than in Great Britain or in some of the Continental countries. Moreover, because of greater educational opportunities for the masses, different ideologies, and, on the whole, a functionally and ideologically different kind of unionism, workers' education in the United States has differed somewhat in objectives, methods, finance, and control from that of European countries. While, as in the case of the Ladies' Garment Workers and certain other internationals, there has been a desire to compensate for educational opportunities missed or to give workers education for its own sake, and while the more radical unionists have striven above all else to mold the curricula and methods in preparation for a new economic and social order,[2] emphasis in the United States on the whole has been upon the type of training that would add strength to unionism and further organized labor's more or less immediate legislative interests. The emphasis on that kind of education designed to further the unions' power has influenced the methods and forms of education adopted. Courses, conferences, and pamphlets to teach leaders organizing methods and to make them more effective bargainers have been stressed, while the courses, for both the leaders and the rank and file, have more often been on trade-union history and institutions and less often on literature and art than in Great Britain.[3]

[1] In the 1930's a summer school was started for union officials at Ruskin. Another development since the War has been the use of radio for workers' education. Since radio programs are not a by-product of advertising, the radio is used much more extensively for educational purposes in Great Britain than in the United States. Local trade-union study groups can purchase a receiving set and listen to lectures by competent speakers; this may be supplemented by reading lists prepared by workers' educational agencies and even by periodic visits of traveling lecturers.

[2] The socialists and the communists look upon workers' education largely as preparation for a new order. Controversy between a group desiring fundamental changes and those interested in education to protect and further business unionism was responsible for the withdrawal of A.F. of L. support from Brookwood College.

[3] Although there are resident colleges and summer schools, this country has not developed anything like the tutorial classes in Great Britain. There are shorter courses, less formal in character, taught usually by people within the labor movement. Indeed, a good deal of the educational activity has taken the form of lectures and plays presented at union meetings and articles on subjects of current interest in labor publications. This is particularly true at times of great organizational activity. Although series of lectures have been presented over the radio, as in Great Britain, the radio, too, has probably been used more for talks on subjects of great current interest and for organizing activity than for discussions of general educational subjects.

Although the cooperation of outsiders has been sought, control of workers' education in this country has been jealously guarded by the trade unions as their own prerogative.[1] Related to the question of control has been that of finance. Until the advent of the New Deal and its emergency relief expenditures, workers' education had not received government grants.[2]

As has been indicated, interest in workers' education developed later in the United States than in foreign countries; it was not, indeed, until the struggle of unions for recognition and position had been in a measure successfully fought that the organized-labor movement could interest itself in developing its own educational agencies.[3] While the International Ladies' Garment Workers had made progress in its educational efforts prior to the end of the War period, and while it was the success realized by that organization more than anything else that aroused the interest of the American Federation of Labor and its affiliated organizations, the real development of workers' education has been a product of the years since about 1918.

The first manifestation of real interest in workers' education on the part of the A.F. of L. occurred at the 1918 convention, where a committee was appointed to investigate the subject. After a favorable report, submitted the following year, the Federation voted to sponsor workers' education as an integral part of the organized-labor movement, and city central bodies were urged, where they were unable to get the public-school authorities to provide liberally conducted classes in desired subjects, to proceed to establish such classes themselves. Between 1919 and 1921 a number of labor colleges were organized by city centrals in different parts of the country; and in 1921 unions affiliated with the A.F. of L. and other interested groups formed the Workers' Education Bureau and founded Brookwood Labor College, the first resident workers' college in the United States. Although the A.F. of L. later withdrew its official support from Brookwood, mainly because of the left wing tendencies of the college and alleged continuous criticism of the Federation's leader-

---

[1] The resident schools have been an exception to this rule. They have generally been outside the control of trade unions, although the latter have indirect influence when students, who are often union members, have voice in running the schools.

[2] Although jealous of outside control, the unions, through the Workers' Education Bureau, have accepted support from educational foundations interested in education and have, in general, welcomed government support. Indeed there has been advocacy, at least by representatives of the American Federation of Labor, of permanent government aid. See *Workers' Education*, vol. 13, no. 4 (October, 1936), p. 38; *Report of the Executive Council of the American Federation of Labor . . . 1937*, p. 127.

[3] Of course the trade unions throughout their history have been active in behalf of a free public-school system. The early provision of a tax-supported educational system and the great progress in public education have in no small measure been due to the efforts put forth by labor organizations.

ship, Brookwood remained until 1937[1] an active institution, concerned primarily with the training of union members for leadership. In its later years it enlarged its activity through extension work and by offering correspondence courses in industrial problems, labor history, trade-union problems and policies, and public speaking.[2]

In 1923 a plan was put into effect whereby the Workers' Education Bureau became subject to the general supervision of the A.F. of L. and as a result came to be the educational arm of the Federation, although maintaining a formal autonomy.[3] In addition, the Federation's Committee on Education continued to encourage local unions to appoint educational committees and urged the city central unions to take an active part in local school matters. It also recommended the establishment by state federations of educational departments, with directors, to cooperate with the Workers' Education Bureau. The work of the Bureau has included the development of joint educational programs between state federations and universities; the promotion of lectures and study courses in local and central labor unions; the encouragement of summer schools for workers; the holding of regional and local conferences and institutes on economic and social problems that affect workers; the provision of loan libraries; aid in producing radio programs; research and informational service for unions; the preparation of educational literature and the publication of books at prices that workers can afford.[4]

[1] In October, 1937, Brookwood was closed because of inadequate financial support, resulting from the depression and the devotion of union funds to organizing activities and to forms of workers' education that contributed immediately to furthering organization. In addition to financial difficulties, it was reported that unions were unable to spare their "best people" to attend the college during the organizing effort, and that the WPA classes and the work of the International Ladies' Garment Workers made Brookwood less necessary. *New York Times*, Nov. 21, 1937, Pt. II, p. 6.

[2] *Bulletin of the Extension Department of Brookwood, Inc.*, 1930–1931; *Workers' Education*, vol. 13, no. 4 (October, 1936), p. 11; *American Federationist*, vol. 44 (1937), p. 272.

[3] Part of the financial support of the Bureau has come from the A.F. of L. and the affiliated internationals that have had separate memberships in the Bureau. Private endowments and the American Association for Adult Education have also contributed to it. With the financial support from the A.F. of L. came a change in the constitution of the Workers' Education Bureau, by which control over it was lodged in the A.F. of L. and its larger internationals. *Workers' Education*, vol. 3, no. 1 (May, 1925), p. 2.

[4] It has published the *Workers' Bookshelf* series. The Bureau's books and pamphlets cover such subjects as the American and British labor movements, American history, cooperatives, agriculture, and how to conduct a union meeting [see *Workers' Education*, vol. 13, no. 4 (October, 1936), pp. 45–46, for a list of its publications]. More recently the Bureau has been publishing skits to increase interest in workers' education and to give information on subjects of current interest to workers. Two skits, showing the benefit of education and research in collective bargaining, may be found in the *American Federationist*, vol. 44 (1937), pp. 81–85, 191–196. A series of seven short plays has been prepared to explain the Social Security Act. These have been presented at union meetings and over the radio and have been well received. See Mollie Ray Carroll, "Cooperative Workers' Education," *Journal of Adult Education*, vol. 9 (1937), pp. 184–186.

A second national workers' education agency is the American Labor Education Service (formerly the Affiliated Schools for Workers), which grew out of the summer-school movement, starting as a loose federation of these schools. Its work gradually expanded to cover a multitude of services offered all types of workers' education groups. Financed by trade unions, foundations, and individuals, and dependent also to a considerable degree on volunteer help, it offers advice and aid in organizing classes, in getting materials and teachers, and in dealing with the many problems faced by trade unions. It publishes pamphlets, study materials, and bibliographies. It has compiled a national teachers' registry. It organizes sectional and national conferences on workers' education and its relation to union activities and public relations. The 1941 Midwest Conference was attended by representatives of seventy-four organizations, including forty-seven A.F. of L. and C.I.O. nationals and internationals. Serving all branches of the labor movement, the American Labor Education Service acts as a clearinghouse for information on workers' education. It also cooperates with various adult-education groups, with libraries and cooperatives, with settlement houses and church groups. Finally, at the request of the school's Board of Directors, it conducts the Summer School for Office Workers, and, of course, works with the other resident workers' schools.[1]

There were in 1941 six of these schools; the Summer School for Office Workers, Highlander Folk School, Hudson Shore Labor School (formerly Bryn Mawr Summer School), the Southern School for Workers, the Pacific Coast Labor School, and the Wisconsin School for Workers at the University of Wisconsin.[2] In addition to their resident terms—mostly in the summer—all the schools, except the Summer School for Office Workers, carry on other work, such as winter institutes and classes and sectional conferences. Under a two-year grant from the state legislature, Wisconsin from 1937 to 1939 conducted a year-round program of classes in rural and urban communities. From the students of these schools have been recruited many of the teachers for local workers' education classes. The schools have also provided advice and training for teachers.[3]

---

[1] For American Labor Education Service activities, see the annual *Reports of the Director* and *Workers' Education in the United States*, ed. Theodore Brameld (1941), pp. 93–94.

[2] See the annual reports of the various schools and *Workers' Education in the United States*, pp. 97–102.

[3] Besides the activities that have been outlined, there have been the educational, propaganda activities of the radical groups, which began before the First World War. Ruskin College, now out of existence, was originated by the socialists in 1900, while the Rand School of Social Service was organized to spread socialism but was also intended to provide workers with education as well as with propaganda and to aid the trade-union movement. It has cooperated with other workers' educational agencies. The Workers' School of the Communist Party was established in 1924. See E. E. Cummins, *op. cit.*, pp. 597–598; *Journal of Adult Education*, vol. 9 (1937), p. 67.

Several of the international unions have developed their own educational programs, which are of varying scope and effectiveness. Outstanding is that of the International Ladies' Garment Workers, begun in 1914 and carried on, with increasing scope, ever since. Some of the early local unions in the clothing industry had grown out of educational clubs or societies for education and self-improvement, and, together with the educational efforts of the socialists and radicals, played an important role in the early history of the Union. It was not until the biennial conventions of 1914 and 1916, however, that the Union laid the foundation for its permanent educational structure. In 1914, it appropriated $1,500 for courses to be given at the Rand School, and in 1916 an Educational Committee was appointed, an Education Department set up, and the appropriation for educational activity increased to $5,000. The primary purposes of the educational program were (1) the enlightenment of the rank and file upon general labor questions and the methods and aims of trade unionism, and (2) the training of the ablest members of the organization for official duties. Moreover, the Union has probably been more interested than most others in this country in education to supplement the limited public-school education most of the workers have been able to obtain.

In order to carry out this educational program, local unions were urged to establish permanent committees on education and funds were solicited for a workingman's college. In 1918 the Union obtained the use of the public schools in New York City to establish four Unity Centers and a Workers' University, where more systematic studies of labor problems, American government, and history could be pursued.[1] In 1922 the Union appropriated $17,500 to its Department of Education, which was gradually organizing and extending its work. With the NRA and the concomitant union expansion, the International Ladies' Garment Workers' Union, being in position to proceed further, devoted $100,000 to the work in 1933. The interest grew during the renewed organizational activities of the later thirties, the Union reporting 22,050 students in 620 classes in 1937–1938 and expenditures for that year of $200.000.[2] In the following years, expenditures remained at the same high level. In the 1939–1940 season, over 18,000 participated in some 800 classes, music, dramatic, dance, and athletic groups.[3]

[1] Louis Levine, *The Women's Garment Workers* (1924), pp. 488–489. Chapter 36 of this book gives an excellent and detailed account of the educational work of this union. For more recent accounts, see Mark Starr, "A Trade Union Pioneers in Education," *American Federationist*, vol. 43 (1936), pp. 54–60; *New York Times*, Aug. 28, 1938, Pt. II, p. 4; *School and Society*, vol. 48 (1938), p. 330; and *Growing Up*, published in 1938 by the Educational Department of the International Ladies' Garment Workers Union to commemorate its twenty-one years of work.

[2] *New York Times*, Nov. 21, 1937, Pt. II, p. 6; Aug. 28, 1938, Pt. II, p. 4.

[3] Joel Seidman, *The Needle Trades* (1942), p. 283.

As stated by the Education Department, its "educational activity is carried on in three general divisions: Mass Education, Class Education, and Training for Trade Union Service. The first of these three divisions includes lectures, excursions and visits to museums, art galleries, and other places of interest, and all kinds of recreational and cultural opportunities—games, sports, dancing, choruses and mandolin clubs, dramatics. The second division provides systematic study of such subjects as economics, social history, labor problems, history of the American movement and of the ILGWU itself, and 'tool courses' in English, journalism, public speaking, and parliamentary law. The third division offers practical training for union members who are likely to assume positions of responsibility, paid or unpaid, in local unions."[1]

The 1937 International Ladies' Garment Workers' Union convention ruled that, before running for a paid office, a candidate who has not previously served must have completed a special course of study, in localities where such courses are available. Fulfilling this ruling, Officers' Qualification Courses were introduced in New York City in the fall of 1938. The subjects included trade-union techniques, the history of the International Ladies' Garment Workers' Union, and the economics of the garment industry. By 1940, 271 students from twenty locals had completed all the courses. Similar courses have been carried on elsewhere. Special classes for new members are also features of the Union's educational program in a number of cities.[2]

Only less extensive than the educational, cultural, and recreational activities of the International Ladies' Garment Workers' Union have been those of the Amalgamated Clothing Workers of America.[3] Its educational department, first established in the fall of 1920, has carried on extensive work of this sort. Three thousand students have enrolled in the correspondence courses that were initiated in 1938 to promote better understanding of such questions as the economics of the clothing

[1] Quotation from *Growing Up*.

Among the publications that the union has put out to further these activities are copies of union songs, guides for teachers of WPA classes for workers, a carefully worked-out handbook for organizers, pamphlets on the conduct of union meetings, on the structure and function of the International Ladies' Garment Workers' Union. The handbook for organizers grew out of a course of training for union officials. The union organized "Labor Stage" in 1936; this organization produces plays, one of these being *Pins and Needles*, which ran on Broadway from the Fall of 1937 until late in 1940. Road companies also toured the country. Garment workers filled practically all parts in the productions. See *Consumers' Cooperation*, vol. 24 (1938), pp. 92–93; *New York Times*, July 24, 1938, Pt. IX, p. 1; *Growing Up*.

[2] See *Training for Union Service*, published in 1940 by the Education Department of the International Ladies' Garment Workers' Union.

[3] See "Unionism—A Way of Life: The ACWA Program of Cultural Activities" in *The Amalgamated Today and Tomorrow* (1939), pp. 97–102; and *The Advance*, vol. 26 (1940), no. 5.

industry, collective bargaining, and democracy. Classes in subjects of economic, political, and cultural concern are also conducted by the locals, which have sports, music, drama, and dance groups as well. From 1938 to 1940, the sports and recreation program attracted 5,000 union members; 3,000 were in dramatics, music, and dance groups. Other features of the Amalgamated Clothing Workers program include the Officers' Training Institute and Town Hall Meetings held over week ends. In 1940, 3,500 workers participated in a series of Active Workers' Schools and Officers' Institutes held in ten cities.[1]

Other unions that have emphasized workers' education for a number of years include the Textile Workers and the United Mine Workers, one form of activity sponsored by the latter organization being the labor chautauqua in isolated mining districts.[1]

Several developments of recent years have affected all the agencies for workers' education. Among these are the advent of and the great enthusiasm for radio communication; the organizational drive of the trade unions, beginning in 1933; the split between the C.I.O. and the A.F. of L.; and the depression of the 1930's.

Earliest among these recent developments, and not least important, has been the development of radio to a place where it rivals the newspaper as a means of providing information. Labor has not been slow to recognize this growing importance of radio, and since 1926 the Chicago Federation of Labor has sponsored WCFL, while "the militant voice of labor"—WEVD—was established in New York the following year.[3] These stations, as well as time on other stations, have been used for lectures on subjects of interest to labor[4] and for expression of labor's viewpoint to its members and to the public, particularly in times of industrial dispute[5] and during organizational campaigns.[6]

The organization drive that began in 1933 stimulated the interest of trade unions in workers' education; during such drives many organizers must be trained, and the unions are interested in using any method that

---

[1] Workers' Education in the United States, p. 104.

[2] See Paul W. Fuller, "Workers' Education in the Mining Industry," Workers' Education, vol. 2, no. 3 (November, 1924), pp. 23–25.

[3] U. S. Bureau of Labor Statistics, Bulletin 465, pp. 180–185.

[4] The Workers' Education Bureau cooperates with the National Advisory Council on Radio in Education in broadcasts of discussions of current social problems. In 1937 WPA dramatic groups presented the Bureau's skits explaining the Social Security Act. There has been less use of the radio than in Great Britain for education in general as well as for workers' education, and, like other agencies of education, the use of the radio has reflected the difference in aims of workers' education in the two countries.

[5] In the great textile strike in 1934, for example, the radio was used to present to the public labor's side of the controversy. American Federation of Labor, Proceedings, 1934, p. 467.

[6] The C.I.O., like the A.F. of L., has used the radio to aid in organization, to broadcast labor news, and to fight the opposing group.

will add to membership and that will hold the new members and make them interested participants in the union. The intensive organizing efforts have also resulted in increasing emphasis on the primary aim of workers' education in this country—the strengthening of the unions. Activities contributing directly to arousing interest in, and loyalty to, the unions and to training organizers and administrators quickly and effectively have been stressed to an even greater degree since 1933 than in the past. At central labor schools, week-end institutes, and summer camps, officers of the Textile Workers' Union, the United Rubber Workers, the United Auto Workers, and the Steel Workers' Organizing Committee have received instruction in grievance-adjustment procedure, management relations, public speaking, union bookkeeping, and related subjects. In the summer of 1939, more than a thousand C.I.O. officers were being trained in administrative techniques at a Pennsylvania camp.[1] Combined with education in the functions and history of unions and training in participation in the union have been social activities to make the union a center of interest. Other examples of educational activities to cope with current or immediate problems are: strike committees to publicize developments, keep the members informed, and raise money; health committees to study the problems and methods of control of occupational diseases; training in job analysis and time and motion studies; and development of plans for union-management cooperation to increase plant efficiency.[2]

The formation of the C.I.O. and its controversy with the A.F. of L. have had a marked effect on workers' education. The trade-union movement for workers' education, like the trade-union movement itself, has become divided. The Workers' Education Bureau, controlled by the A.F. of L., has been weakened.[3] Most of the internationals that have been active in workers' education in the past and are continuing their activities are now affiliated with the C.I.O., while the unions that started educational departments in the late 1930's were, in the main, other C.I.O. unions.[4]

[1] See Morris Llewellyn Cooke and Philip Murray, *Organized Labor and Production* (1940), p. 227. See also pp. 229–230 for reference to the joint union-management conferences initiated by the Steel Workers' Organizing Committee and to the course for union leaders sponsored by the Paraffine Companies, Inc., at its California plant.

[2] *Workers' Education in the United States*, pp. 122ff.

[3] The Workers' Education Bureau constitution contains a provision that labor organizations "not dual or seceding in character" are eligible to membership. It is true that the A.F. of L. increased its appropriation for education from $5,000 to $7,500 at its 1937 convention, but the Workers' Education Bureau had lost the financial support of the C.I.O. unions that had had individual memberships in the Bureau.

[4] In addition to the unions with established workers' educational activities already referred to, mention should be made of the American Federation of Hosiery Workers. The United Automobile Workers have also devoted a good deal of attention and money to workers' education; the appropriation has been 5 per cent of revenues. A summary of

The depression of the 1930's tended to increase interest in workers' education,[1] but, as contrasted with the effect of the organizing campaign, its effect was probably to increase the emphasis on educational activities less closely related to furthering trade unionism. With this renewed interest in workers' education came increased financial support through Federal Emergency Relief Administration and Works Progress Administration funds for adult education and for workers' education. The unions, both A.F. of L. and C.I.O., the Workers' Education Bureau, and the American Labor Education Service cooperated in setting up classes and in training the unemployed teachers provided.[2] This government aid has led to a desire on the part of representatives of the A.F. of L. for permanent federal grants-in-aid for workers' education.

TRADE-UNION BENEFITS AND INSURANCE

Benefit features were one of the first trade-union devices to develop, and they still are undoubtedly the most important of the various welfare activities undertaken by unions. As has been pointed out, not all unions are equally interested in benefit schemes, and some have no formal benefit system at all. All but a few of the left-wing unions,[3] however, regard strike funds as essential to their existence. This phase of trade-union activity may be discussed more advantageously elsewhere in this volume. Other benefits, such as sick, old-age, disability, and unemployment benefits, which can properly be regarded as types of insurance, have been discussed in vol. II of this series. A summary of the available data relating to the number of unions that have made various kinds of benefit payments, and of the amounts so spent, is presented in

---

recent workers' education activities conducted by both groups of unions may be found in the *New York Times*, Nov. 21, 1937, Pt. II, p. 6; of C.I.O. activities in Mark Starr, "Workers' Education—C.I.O. Model," *The Social Frontier*, vol. 4 (1938), pp. 110–113. See also *New York Times*, Aug. 28, 1938, Pt. II, p. 4; and *Workers' Education in the United States*, Chaps. 5 and 6.

[1] The Workers' Education Bureau reported that, both in the range of interests and in the number of workers involved, the year 1933–1934 established the high-water mark since the Bureau's organization in 1921 (American Federation of Labor, *Proceedings*, 1934, p. 465). In March, 1937, the number enrolled in WPA classes for workers was about 70,000. *Monthly Labor Review*, vol. 45 (1937), pp. 141–142.

[2] Both in this country and in Great Britain the problem of finding capable teachers for workers' education has been a pressing one and the FERA and WPA classes, because of a good deal of ineffective teaching, have frequently been none too effective agencies for workers' education.

[3] The I.W.W. has seldom accumulated any strike funds, partly because the members have been suspicious of their own leaders, and partly because they have believed that "a man fights best on an empty stomach." Such a policy may work fairly well when the membership of a union is composed largely of single men, but when the members of a union have families, strike benefits must be provided to keep dependents from hunger.

TABLE 6.—NUMBER OF UNIONS PAYING, AND AMOUNTS PAID FOR VARIOUS TYPES OF, TRADE-UNION BENEFITS, 1920–1940[1]

Year	Death benefits		Sick benefits		Disability benefits		Old-age benefits		Unemployment benefits		Miscellaneous (excluding strike benefits)		Total	
	No. of unions	Amount	No. of unions	Amount	No. of unions	Amount	No. of unions	Amount	No. of unions	Amount	No. of unions	Amount	No. of unions	Amount
1920	59	$ 9,904,355	20	$1,690,163	11	$1,909,017	a	a	10	$ 319,485	8	$ 33,792	b	$14,650,527
1925	47	9,783,517	15	1,540,692	12	5,240,597	a	a	5	151,820	3	10,009	b	16,726,635
1929	81	17,598,297	33	2,831,937	23	2,707,188	14	$4,883,028	12	276,718	29	3,945,288	87	32,242,440
1930	86	18,527,095	46	3,649,703	26	3,234,067	15	5,910,995	30	3,311,280	43	2,064,840	92	36,697,980
1931	86	17,132,023	41	2,220,975	28	3,671,380	20	6,090,743	38	9,146,724	49	1,700,028	91	39,661,873
1932	85	17,674,384	38	2,308,040	25	4,006,891	19	6,148,302	35	19,970,557	41	1,340,175	93	51,448,349
1933	84	14,780,206	30	1,665,266	20	4,837,730	16	4,678,636	24	13,784,043	42	946,231	85	40,692,113
1934	82	15,011,044	31	1,023,314	18	3,176,014	15	3,912,940	23	4,467,802	38	1,409,530	87	28,840,645
1935	74	12,650,303	28	1,047,011	16	3,379,276	12	3,684,954	17	3,356,276	39	1,990,787	82	26,108,606
1936	68	12,821,607	23	1,272,818	10	2,588,506	16	5,288,906	13	10,990,104	41	1,646,750	71	34,608,692
1937	70	13,390,755	29	2,277,903	14	2,623,918	12	4,600,056	11	1,671,139	38	2,547,454	73	27,111,225
1938c	69	13,125,853	21	1,306,768	16	1,641,091	14	5,334,207	14	2,582,543	37	1,595,827	69	25,586,289
1939	67	12,928,510	24	1,519,559	18	1,766,064	12	2,073,327	9	1,815,784	38	1,591,961	71	21,695,205
1940	64	13,090,352	22	1,553,369	13	1,362,930	12	1,712,597	14	2,365,292	39	3,045,165	69	23,129,705

a Old-age and disability benefits not reported separately in 1920 and 1925.

b Number not available.

c For 1938 (see *Report of the Executive Council of the American Federation of Labor* . . . 1939, pp. 35–42) the report is far from complete because the internationals affiliated with the C.I.O. and certain other unions, formerly included, were no longer covered by it. The same is true for 1939 and 1940.

[1] Adapted from reports of the Executive Council of the American Federation of Labor, except that the figures for death, sick, unemployment, and disability benefits for the years 1920 and 1925 were taken from the "Handbook of Labor Statistics, 1931 Edition," U. S. Bureau of Labor Statistics, *Bulletin* 541, the other figures for 1920 and 1925 from the American Federation of Labor, *Proceedings*. The statistics as given by the A. F. of L. do not separate in all cases the payments made by local unions from those made by the internationals. Sometimes only local unions of the international pay a particular kind of benefit, but the report is made by the international and therefore the international is reported as paying the benefit. It is therefore impossible to estimate the proportion of benefits paid by local unions as compared with international unions. It is also known that not all benefits paid by locals are reported, and therefore the figures are incomplete and understate the amount of benefits paid by unions.

Table 6 in order to make more clear the relative importance of the different kinds of benefits.[1]

Death benefits have consistently been paid by more unions than have any other kind, and except for the year 1932, when payments for unemployment benefits and relief rose sharply, they have exceeded in amount any other payments. Until 1932, in fact, death benefits constituted approximately one-half of all welfare benefits paid by trade unions. Payments for unemployment benefits and relief rose sharply with the increase of unemployment, but after reaching a peak of nearly $20,000,000 in 1932 dropped sharply. The drop was due more to the exhaustion of trade-union unemployment benefit and relief funds than to a decline in need for assistance among union members. Payments for old-age and disability benefits have fluctuated less greatly than those for unemployment and for a time increased in importance relative to death benefits.

The total expenditure by trade unions for various kinds of benefits has been small in comparison with the needs of the membership. The inadequacy of the protection furnished is more obvious when it is realized that the bulk of the payments have been made by a few unions, particularly the Railway Brotherhoods, and that many unions report only insignificant payments and some none at all. It was, indeed, the recognition that their voluntary benefit systems have been at best only a partial success in providing security for their members against the hazards of unemployment, sickness, disability, and old age which caused the unions to develop an enhanced interest in social insurance legislation.

Closely related to the benefit or insurance funds of unions are the insurance companies sponsored by a union or a group of unions. In the United States there are two such institutions. The Union Cooperative Insurance Association, started by the International Brotherhood of Electrical Workers in 1924, writes both participating and nonparticipating policies for individual and for group life insurance. The Union Labor Life Insurance Company, established by the A.F. of L. in 1925, is cooperative to the extent that the number of shares of stock which any one individual or union can hold is limited, that all policies are participating, and that dividends on stock are limited to 6 per cent, the profits remaining after provision is made for surplus being returned to policyholders.[2]

---

[1] The data in Table 6 on benefits paid during the two decades, 1920–1940, do not take account, as the footnote accompanying the table indicates, of benefits paid by the new C.I.O. unions during the second half of the 1930's. Such data are virtually impossible of procurement. However, the omission is not of great consequence so far as indication of the importance of trade-union benefits on the whole, and of the relative importance of different kinds of benefits, is concerned. Benefit features have occupied—and still do occupy—a much larger place in the activities and programs of A.F. of L. unions than in those of the new industrial unions. The table indicates with substantial accuracy the situation during the years between the two world wars.

[2] U. S. Bureau of Labor Statistics, *Bulletin* 465, p. 200. On Dec. 31, 1934, the Union

Trade unions are encouraged by this company to provide for sickness, death, and old age through it rather than to maintain their own funds on a haphazard nonactuarial basis.[1] The majority of unions continue to write insurance through their own special insurance departments, but in some cases, especially where group insurance is carried, the insurance is secured from one of the union insurance companies. In 1928 group life insurance protection was obtained by six unions and group disability by one union through regular commercial insurance companies.[2]

COOPERATIVE BUSINESS ENTERPRISE

In addition to institutions providing a variety of benefits or insurance, trade unions have, at one time or another, become interested in cooperative business enterprise. The cooperative movement, however, has been, and, in spite of some recent revival of interest, still remains relatively weak among trade unionists in the United States. In several European countries, on the other hand, it has been comparatively strong.[3] The role of the cooperative movement in the development of nineteenth-century American unionism has already been discussed.[4] The movement has had a much greater and more stable development in England than in the United States, but there, as here, it has of course been much more than a trade-union movement. Cooperation has been particularly strong in the Scandinavian countries, but there again much of the movement has been outside of the trade unions.[5]

Producers' Cooperatives.—Workers' cooperatives are of two different types—consumers' cooperatives and producers' cooperatives. At times in the nineteenth century the latter were regarded by many enthusiasts as the ultimate solution of labor's problem.[6] The wage system was not so firmly fixed as it later came to be and it was hoped that a cooperative system would replace it. Intellectuals and philanthropists as well as workers shared in the popular enthusiasm for cooperatives, which they hoped to establish either through founding model communities, such as New Harmony and Brook Farm, or through producers' cooperatives in the communities in which they lived. Sometimes the workers were moved to undertake a cooperative project, not so much by idealism

---

Labor Life Insurance Company had a total of $52,560,379 insurance in force (*The Insurance Almanac*, 1935, p. 778). The record of the company is reported to be excellent.

[1] U. S. Bureau of Labor Statistics, *Bulletin* 465, p. 201.

[2] *Ibid.*, p. 21.

[3] For a review of cooperatives in Europe, see *Report of the Inquiry on Cooperative Enterprise in Europe, 1937*. Statistics as to number, membership, volume of sales, etc., of various kinds of cooperative societies in different countries of the world may be found there, pp. 272–308, and in "Development of the Cooperative Movement throughout the World," *Monthly Labor Review*, vol. 37 (1933), pp. 1404–1416.

[4] *Cf. supra*, pp. 52–53, 68–69.

[5] *Report of the Inquiry on Cooperative Enterprise in Europe, 1937*, pp. 71, 224, 229.

[6] See Chap. II.

as by the failure of a strike. In the United States the National Labor Union launched cooperative ventures in the 1870's, and a little later the Knights of Labor became the greatest propaganda agent for the movement[1] and its local assemblies participated in attempts to establish cooperative factories, mills, and mines. Almost without exception, these producers' cooperatives were failures. When they did prosper, they tended to lose their cooperative features, for the original members disliked to share the profits of the organization with new workers and therefore tended to take them in, not as partners, but as ordinary wage earners. Thus, if the project prospered and expanded, the original members became the owners and profit takers and the "cooperative" gave way to capitalism. This tendency to move toward noncooperative capitalist enterprise remains today one of the chief weaknesses of the producers' cooperative movement.

Often producers' cooperatives have been started in industries in which there was little chance of success. They were sometimes started by handicraftsmen in a decaying industry or an industry revolutionized by the introduction of machinery, for example, hand-blown window glass[2] or handmade cigars. At other times workers have taken over abandoned mines or entered highly competitive industries such as the shingle industry in the Northwest. The reason for the discontent of the workers or the failure of the strike that led to the establishment of the cooperative may have been the inability of the employer to pay satisfactory wages. The workers must select a manager for their cooperative enterprise, and, unless he has unusual ability, the new manager in turn may not be able to pay higher wages than the private employer. If he does have unusual ability he is often unwilling to remain with the organization on a cooperative basis.

In the more recent years, producers' cooperatives have been used by trade unions chiefly in connection with strikes and lockouts.[3] Here, the aim has been, not to supplant capitalism, but to give employment to

[1] This phase of the labor movement of the 1870's and 1880's is discussed in some detail *supra*, pp. 68–69. *Cf.*, also N. J. Ware, *The Labor Movement in the United States*, 1860–1895 (1929), p. 327, and Commons and Associates, *History of Labor in the United States* (1918), vol. 2, pp. 430–438.

[2] A Bureau of Labor Statistics study of cooperatives in the United States in 1933 found that none of the once numerous cooperatives manufacturing hand-blown window glass remained in existence. *Monthly Labor Review*, vol. 40 (1935), p. 258.

[3] There has also been some interest in producers' cooperatives to provide for unemployment resulting from business cycles and the migration of industry. The *American Federationist*, vol. 43 (1936), pp. 157–159, contained an article about a cooperative shoe plant to be opened in Milwaukee by the union in order to provide for members thrown out of employment by shoe companies leaving the city during the depression. The *C.I.O News*, Mar. 19, 1938, p. 8, announced a plan of the Amalgamated Clothing Workers to open a factory to manufacture inexpensive neckties, in order to provide employment for members of the Men's Neckwear Union.

needy strikers and to help build up morale during a struggle for better wages and working conditions. Cooperative cigar factories, laundries, milk-distribution agencies, and bakeries have been started during strikes and sold or abandoned after they have served their purpose.[1]

The Bureau of Labor Statistics, after a survey of producers' cooperatives in the United States, reported that there were only eighteen workers' productive organizations in active operation at the end of 1933.[2] Moreover, the majority of these were no longer strictly cooperative enterprises, for they employed nonshareholding wage earners. The eight organizations for which information was available reported 1,181 shareholders, of whom 447 were employed in the cooperative enterprise, along with 650 nonshareholder employees. On a business of $3,629,470 the losses exceeded profits by $86,938 in 1933. While the report did not indicate which of these cooperatives were sponsored by labor organizations, only one of the eight was limited to members of a trade union.[3]

Consumers' Cooperation.—Consumers' cooperatives, while now much more numerous than producers' cooperatives in the United States, have not on the whole been markedly successful. During the 1930's and early 1940's, however, there was a revival of interest in and a development of consumers' cooperatives in this country.[4] The most common

---

[1] U. S. Bureau of Labor Statistics, *Bulletin* 465, p. 213. An example of a cooperative initiated as the result of a strike and later abandoned is that started in Milwaukee, Wis., in 1928, by the Amalgamated Clothing Workers. The largest men's clothing manufacturer in Milwaukee in that year tried to break off relations with the union, and during the strike that followed decided to go out of business. The union was able to shift some of its workers to other plants, but about 400 members continued to draw strike benefits. With the cooperation of the Chicago membership, the Amalgamated met this situation by establishing a clothing factory of its own. For a time the cooperative was a financial success, but by 1935 the members had been largely absorbed by private shops and the enterprise was reorganized on a noncooperative basis. The shop was run, in 1935, by a union official to provide employment for the sixty to seventy people who had not yet found employment in other shops.

[2] Producers' cooperatives have likewise not been of great importance in European countries, although they have been relatively more significant than those in the United States. They were most important in Czechoslovakia, France, and Great Britain. In Great Britain few of them have been exclusively workers' organizations; the producers were often outnumbered by consumer members, so that they were in fact consumers' cooperatives. In Denmark, many of the cooperative bakeries were established with the aid of trade-union funds, while the cooperative mechanics' leagues grew out of a lockout in 1899. These leagues took the same sort of jobs as private contractors and maintained wages and working conditions as examples when there were labor disputes with private contractors. *Report of the Inquiry on Cooperative Enterprise in Europe, 1937*, pp. 6, 178, 213–214.

[3] "Operation of Cooperative Productive Enterprises in 1933," *Monthly Labor Review*, vol. 40 (1935), pp. 257–265. Since there is an incentive in the case of producers' cooperatives to limit membership, the fact that only one limited its membership to trade unionists would indicate that it was probably the only one of which trade unionists were in control.

[4] Statistics of consumers' cooperatives for 1933 may be found in the *Monthly Labor*

type of cooperation is the general store of the Rochdale plan.[1] These stores have been initiated for a variety of reasons but most commonly have been the result of an attempt to reduce living expenses in such periods of high prices as that during and following the First World War. During the War period, many labor organizations, including the A.F. of L., endorsed the principle of cooperative stores. Others, like the United Mine Workers of America, went so far as to advance union funds for the organization of such stores. In Illinois alone, the miners' unions invested $500,000 in 1919–1921 in two cooperative wholesale and seventy branch stores operated on the American-Rochdale plan. For a brief time the movement expanded and seemingly prospered, and hopes for a cooperative movement in America were revived, but by 1922 the miners' cooperative structure had collapsed.[2] Thus most of these miners' ventures have run their course. Nevertheless, there are still a number of cooperative stores in mining districts, some of which have been used during strikes or lockouts to free the miners from dependence upon the company store. In 1928 most of the cooperative stores that were successfully doing business had been converted into genuine Rochdale societies and were not union organizations.[3]

The few cooperatives that remain in the mining towns of Illinois and Pennsylvania have suffered from the depression of the 1930's, from the difficulties from which the coal industry suffered after World War I, and from miners' strikes.[4] Nevertheless, one of the most successful cooperatives in the United States is that started at Dillonvale, Ohio,

---

Review, vol. 39 (1934), pp. 1041–1066, and, for a more limited group, for 1934 and 1935, in *ibid.*, vol. 43 (1936), pp. 1187–1191. The entire study made by the Bureau of Labor Statistics of cooperatives, both producers' and consumers', in 1933 is summarized in "Consumers,' Credit, and Producers' Cooperation in 1933" by Florence E. Parker, U. S. Bureau of Labor Statistics, *Bulletin* 612 (1935), while articles based on a more recent study by the Bureau may be found in the *Monthly Labor Review*, vols. 45 and 46 (1937 and 1938). Operations of retail cooperatives during 1936 are summarized in *ibid.*, vol. 46 (1938), pp. 1068–1084. A summary of the growth of consumers' cooperation in the United States may be found in Florence E. Parker, "Consumers' Cooperation in the United States," *The Annals of the American Academy of Political and Social Science*, vol. 191 (May, 1937), pp. 91–102. See *ibid.*, pp. 97–102, for a summary of the recent movement.

[1] The Rochdale plan has four basic features: (*a*) democratic government, with all shareholders having equal voting power without regard to the number of shares held by them; (*b*) sales for cash, at the usual prices; (*c*) the distribution of profits to purchasers on the basis of purchases made by them; and (*d*) payment of a fixed—not residual—return to capital.

[2] For the reasons for the rise and collapse of this movement, see Colston E. Warne, *Consumers' Cooperative Movement in Illinois* (1926), pp. 70–94.

[3] U. S. Bureau of Labor Statistics, *Bulletin* 465, p. 204. There are still some cooperative burial associations formed by coal miners' unions in mining localities. *Monthly Labor Review*, vol. 46 (1938), p. 647.

[4] *Monthly Labor Review*, vol. 46 (1938), pp. 1070, 1076.

by a coal miners' union after the War.[1] Another, started by a trade union after the War and still doing a successful business, is the Franklin Cooperative Creamery in Minneapolis, Minn.[2]

Paralleling the more recent growth of consumers' cooperation, there has been some revival of interest in the movement on the part of American trade unions. Workers' educational agencies and labor publications have given it increased attention.[3] Resolutions approving cooperation and aid to the movement have been passed by various state federations of labor,[4] while the Executive Council of the American Federation of Labor in its reports for 1936 and 1937 paid a good deal of attention to the movement. In the 1936 report the Council said:

"Labor welcomes the growth of this movement. . . . The labor movement should work in close alliance with the movement for consumers' cooperatives and credit unions, so that cooperation may be fortified by strong labor organization and union members may be assured honest value when they spend their wages and may increase their purchasing power by eliminating waste and middlemen's profits."[5]

Yet there is fear on the part of trade unionists that cooperation may be used to keep money wages down. As expressed in the 1936 report of the Executive Council, "There is real danger in this country that if the growth of cooperation is not paralleled by growth of labor organization, the cooperative might become merely a means of helping wage-

[1] Its sales for 1936 were $639,476 [*Monthly Labor Review*, vol. 46 (1938), p. 1080]. For information on this cooperative, see also *Consumers' Cooperation*, vol. 22 (1936), p. 193; vol. 23 (1937), pp. 27, 152; and Wallace J. Campbell "The Consumers' Cooperative Movement, a Factual Survey," *New Frontiers*, vol. 5, no. 5 (May, 1937), p. 42.

[2] This was started as a result of a strike of milk drivers in Minneapolis in 1919, followed in 1920 by a lockout. Operations began in 1921, and the cooperative grew rapidly. Its employees are members of trade unions, and it has strengthened the milk drivers' union in the city. It has apparently been able to reduce the price of dairy products to its patrons, and in 1936, when it claimed to do from 30 to 40 per cent of the dairy business of Minneapolis and St. Paul, had sales of $2,827,560. Both this cooperative and that at Dillonvale are open to people outside the trade-union movement. It is to the advantage of consumers' cooperatives to have a large membership. This is particularly true of the Franklin Creamery, which was started to give employment to union milk drivers. For information on this cooperative, see Budd L. McKillips, "The Milk Drivers Find the Way," *American Federationist*, vol. 33 (1926), pp. 1183–1186; *Monthly Labor Review*, vol. 46 (1938), p. 1080; *Report of the Executive Council of the American Federation of Labor* . . . 1937, p. 119.

[3] The *American Federationist* has included numerous articles and editorials in recent years. See also James Myers, "Consumers' Cooperation and the Labor Movement," *Annals of the American Academy of Political and Social Science*, vol. 191 (May, 1937), p. 62. This article gives a good summary of the interrelationships between trade unions and the consumers' cooperative movement.

[4] James Myers, *op. cit.*, vol. 191; *Consumers' Cooperation*, vol. 21 (1935), p. 199.

[5] *Report of the Executive Council of the American Federation of Labor* . . . 1936, pp. 126–127. Some of the C.I.O. unions have endorsed consumers' cooperation. *Consumers' Cooperation*, vol. 24 (1938), p. 69.

earners to exist on low wages."[1] William Green wrote, "There is real danger in the United States, where powerful interests are constantly seeking to keep wages at the lowest possible level, that cooperatives may become merely the means of helping low-paid workers to exist on a mere pittance. Wage standards must be buttressed by strong trade union organization if cooperators are to have income to spend in their stores."[2] There is also fear that employees of cooperatives will be exploited.[3]

Whatever the reasons may be, the role played by trade unions in the recent cooperative movement has been small and, in general, relatively few trade unionists have been active in the recent undertakings. Nevertheless, there are a few cooperatives that have been set up mainly by trade unionists during the recent revival of interest.[4]

COOPERATIVE HOUSING

Trade unions in the United States have generally not become actively interested in cooperative housing. More of their interest has focused upon low-cost financing of individual homes,[5] and, since the depression

[1] *Report of the Executive Council of the American Federation of Labor* . . . 1936, p. 126.

[2] *Consumers' Cooperation*, vol. 22 (1936), p. 194.

[3] See *Report of the Executive Council of the American Federation of Labor* . . . 1937, pp. 118–119; *Monthly Labor Review*, vol. 45 (1937), p. 448. In general, cooperatives in this country have not been careful to maintain high labor standards for their employees or to purchase union-made goods, partly because the membership of cooperatives has been drawn largely from farmer, and to some extent from urban middle-class, groups, and partly because the feeling that cooperatives are desirable leads members to justify and employees to accept low standards. For discussions of cooperatives' labor standards and attitudes toward unions in this country, see James Myers, *op. cit.*, p. 66; *New Frontiers*, vol. 5, no. 5 (May, 1937), p. 13; *Monthly Labor Review*, vol. 45 (1937), p. 557. In Europe, where cooperatives are more important and trade unionists are an important element of the membership, most of the cooperatives make collective agreements with unions representing their employees. Jacob Baker points out that where there is a general strike in an industry, the employees of cooperatives in the industry stay at work and are granted the benefits of the settlement from the beginning of the strike [*Cooperative Enterprise* (1937), p. 174.] The *Report of the Inquiry on Cooperative Enterprise in Europe*, 1937 (p. 65) concludes that "Cooperatives are 'good employers,' and set standards of wages, hours and other conditions higher than those generally existing in private business of the same kind, without, however, being able to raise such standards in general to any determinable degree." See also Jacob Baker, *op. cit.*, pp. 171–173.

[4] The cooperative in Racine, Wis., started in 1934–1935 by representatives of various local unions and still mainly composed of trade unionists, may be found described in Wallace J. Campbell, *op. cit.*, pp. 51–52, and in *Consumers' Cooperation*, vol. 22 (1936), pp. 117–119; vol. 23 (1937), p. 46; also in the *American Federationist*, vol. 44 (1937), pp. 851–855. For other cooperatives that have been started, see *Report of the Executive Council of the American Federation of Labor* . . . 1937, p. 119. See, also, the discussion of cooperative housing, below, for a discussion of cooperatives developed in connection with trade-union housing programs.

[5] The U. S. Bureau of Labor Statistics reported that in 1928 there were eight trade-union home-loan organizations (*Bulletin* 465, p. 115).

of the 1930's, upon federal low-cost housing projects. Prior to 1928 actual housing work had been done by only two labor unions and one group of unionists of various trades.[1] The Amalgamated Clothing Workers, through the Amalgamated Clothing Workers' Corporation, administers cooperative apartments in which more than $5,000,000 has been invested and which house 861 families.[2] Two-thirds of the cost of these cooperatives was raised by a first mortgage and the rest from a stock subscription by tenants. Since the tenants were as a rule unable to pay $500 per room at once, they were required to pay immediately a minimum of $150 per room and were loaned the difference by the Amalgamated Bank of New York on a ten-year repayment plan. The bank in turn was protected by deposits, earmarked against these loans, made in it for this purpose by interested public institutions and individuals.[3] The Amalgamated Clothing Workers realized that these projects, in themselves, would not solve the housing problems of the 700,000 wage earners in New York's metropolitan district, but hoped that they would serve as a model and as a challenge to other unions to provide good living quarters for their members.

The United Workers' Cooperative Association in New York City was initiated a number of years ago by a small group of workers, who purchased a small apartment building. A very considerable saving in rent was effected and other workers were attracted. The Cooperative expanded until in 1928 it owned six blocks of land, on two of which cooperative apartments with a total of 2,017 rooms had been built. It is a trade-union project in the sense that all applicants must be members of a trade union in order to lease apartments.[4]

One other housing project deserves mention, because it indicates a possible means of more extensive trade-union activity. The Carl Mackley Apartments, dedicated at Philadelphia, Jan. 5, 1935, constitute the first housing program jointly undertaken by a labor union and a governmental agency. The project was sponsored by the American Federation of Hosiery Workers and erected by the Public Works Administration. The 209 apartments rent for about $10 a room, including heat, light, and refrigeration. About one-third of the apartments have been rented by the members of the Union, another third by workers in other industries, and the rest by professional people, clerical workers, and small businessmen.[5]

In connection with these three projects there has also been developed the cooperative buying of milk and other food, as well as cooperative

[1] *Ibid.*
[2] *Report of the General Executive Board and Proceedings of the Tenth Biennial Convention of the Amalgamated Clothing Workers of America* (1934), p. 130.
[3] *Ibid.*
[4] U. S. Bureau of Labor Statistics, *Bulletin 465*, p. 129.
[5] *Monthly Labor Review,* vol. 45 (1937), p. 312.

recreation. In the Mackley Apartments the tenants have in addition formed a credit union and have a cooperative parking lot.[1] In the Amalgamated apartments, the tenants formerly bought electric light and power cooperatively at a wholesale rate; as a result of the threat of the utility company to break the contract, they built their own generating plant in 1937, the plant being expected to save them from $10,000 to $15,000 a year.[2]

COOPERATIVE FINANCIAL ENTERPRISES

Credit Unions.—Local unions have shown much interest in institutions designed to furnish an avenue of credit for workingmen, many of whom have no banking connections. Such institutions have appeared in much larger number in Europe than in the United States, where the most important of these financial institutions have been credit unions[3] and labor banks.

The first labor credit union in the United States was organized in 1915.[4] By 1934 all but nine states had enacted legislation authorizing the formation of such societies, and in that year the federal Congress authorized the incorporation of credit societies on a federal instead of a state basis.[5] In 1928, 150 labor credit unions were reported, all but 14 per cent of which had been organized since 1922. Of the 150, 83 had been organized by the National Federation of Postal Employees, and 41 by the Brotherhood of Railway Clerks. Reporting for 1927, 105 of the 150 credit unions had 24,370 members, a paid-in share capital of $1,502,274, and for the year had made loans aggregating $3,979,856.[6] In 1938, only sixty-six credit unions were reported by the Bureau of Labor Statistics as limiting their membership to specified labor organizations.[7] The resultant savings to the workers are difficult to estimate,

[1] *Ibid.*, pp. 312–315, reviews cooperative activities in the Mackley Apartments.

[2] *Annals of the American Academy of Political and Social Science*, vol. 191 (May, 1937), p. 142; *New Frontiers*, vol. 5, no. 5 (May, 1937), p. 50. For an early picture of cooperative activities in the Amalgamated projects, see *Report of the General Executive Board and Proceedings of the Ninth Biennial Convention of the Amalgamated Clothing Workers of America*, p. 53.

[3] Credit unions are cooperative organizations, issuing shares in small denominations; every member is required to own at least one share, and the funds received by the union are loaned to its members in small amounts. A large proportion of the loans are unsecured, and interest rates are low.

[4] A brief history of the development of credit unions, with references to more extensive studies, is given by Lewis A. Froman, "Credit Unions," *Journal of Business of the University of Chicago*, vol. 8 (1935), pp. 284–296.

[5] "Cooperative Credit Societies in 1933," *Monthly Labor Review*, vol. 39 (1934), p. 551.

[6] U. S. Bureau of Labor Statistics, *Bulletin 465*, pp. 194–196.

[7] *Monthly Labor Review*, vol. 46 (1938), p. 1359. This number may not include all credit unions sponsored by trade unions, but indicates that only a few of the 4,034 credit unions reported at that time were exclusively trade-union cooperative societies. Whether the interest exhibited by the American Federation of Labor in credit unions will result in

but there is no doubt that many of those who secured loans through the credit union would otherwise have had to resort to "loan sharks" and pay exorbitant rates of interest. One of the chief dangers to the credit union and, indirectly, to the union itself, is that union politics may be mixed with business, for, as a result of personal pressure on the loan officers, loans are sometimes made on doubtful risks. This fear may be exaggerated, however, since trade unions would probably be as careful in this respect as other credit unions; and the record of bad loans for credit unions in general is in fact remarkably low. In the depression year of 1933 only 158 credit unions (out of 1,038 reporting) had any uncollectible debts, and these averaged less than $\frac{1}{4}$ of 1 per cent of all credit-union loans. This percentage of loans is an understatement, however, for some 50 per cent of the societies had beeen started between 1931 and 1933, and at the time of their reports may still have been counting many of their loans as collectible that would eventually be defaulted. That there was a rather high degree of instability in credit-union societies is indicated by the fact that 300 credit unions were reported as having ceased operations between 1925 and 1933. At the same time (1925–1933) the total number of credit unions (chiefly nontrade-union societies) increased from about 400 to more than 2,000.[1]

Labor Banks.—During the 1920's labor banks (those owned to the point of control by a union or by cooperating unions) in the United States attracted widespread attention.[2] Not all trade unions were, however, equally enthusiastic about this form of institutionalism; in fact it was greeted with hostility by most left-wing unions and with coolness by the A.F. of L. One of the first union proposals to establish labor banks in the United States was made at the 1904 A.F. of L. convention. This proposal was rejected. In 1910 and again in 1914 the A.F. of L. rejected proposals to enter the financial field. In 1921 a plan for a central bank,

any marked increase in trade-union participation in them remains to be seen [see *Report of the Executive Council of the American Federation of Labor* . . . 1937, pp. 121–122; also *American Federationist*, vol. 43 (1936), pp. 355–356]. In this connection, it might be noted that the Amalgamated Association of Street and Electrical Railway Employees started twenty-four credit unions in Chicago during the year 1937–1938, covering its entire membership of over 20,000 on the Chicago elevated and surface lines. *Report of the Executive Council of the American Federation of Labor* . . . 1938, pp. 114–115.

[1] *Monthly Labor Review*, vol. 39 (1934), pp. 551, 553. At the end of 1936, the number was 5,400, loans outstanding $112,134,577. Of course only a small percentage of these credit unions had been started by labor unions. See U. S. Bureau of Labor Statistics, *Bulletin* 659 (1938).

[2] Excellent accounts of the subject may be found in *The Labor Banking Movement in the United States*, prepared by the Industrial Relations Section, Department of Economics and Social Institutions, Princeton University (1929); U. S. Bureau of Labor Statistics, *Bulletin* 465, pp. 188–194; and E. W. Morehouse, "Labor Institutionalism: Banking," Chap. 28 of J. B. S. Hardman and Associates, *American Labor Dynamics* (1928).

the capital of which would be raised by assessment, was voted down.[1] The attitude of the officials of the A.F. of L. was consistently one of caution toward having its unions engage in financial experiments. Perhaps because of this, the labor banking movement in the United States, both in its initiation and in its later developments, was largely outside of the A.F. of L. constituency.

The first labor bank, opened in Washington, D. C., on May 15, 1920, by the officers of the National Association of Machinists, did not attract much attention to its labor-cooperative features, and it was not until the opening of the Brotherhood of Locomotive Engineers' Cooperative National Bank in Cleveland, Ohio, in November, 1920, that the labor banking movement gained its first real impetus. The Brotherhood retained 51 per cent of the capital stock and sold the rest to its members. The cooperative features were stressed, dividends on capital stock were limited to 10 per cent, and dividends to savings depositors could be authorized at the discretion of the board of directors. The bank received wide publicity and was immediately successful. Within two months its deposits reached $1,000,000, and they grew steadily for the next four years until on June 30, 1924, they totaled $26,016,688.[2]

From 1920 to 1926 interest in labor banking became increasingly widespread. Among labor unions sponsoring and owning labor banks during this period were the Amalgamated Clothing Workers, the New York State Federation of Labor, the Brotherhood of Railway Clerks, the International Printing Pressmen's and Assistants' Union, the Order of Railroad Telegraphers, the American Flint Glass Workers' Union, and the International Ladies' Garment Workers. Local labor groups in different parts of the United States were also influenced by outside speakers and propagandist literature to promote banks.

The reasons for the enthusiasm of trade unions for labor banks and the purposes of the banks were many and diverse. In some cases the chief aim was to obtain a safe and profitable investment of large union funds accumulated during the period of War activity. Of more general importance, perhaps, was the reaction of the unions against the alleged participation of the regular banks in the open-shop drive of 1920–1921. Nonunion employers had used their resources in an effort to break the unions and reduce wages. The sympathy of the bankers was naturally with their largest customers, the employers. In some cities, the financial power of the banks became an important factor in deciding the result of the open-shop conflict.[3] In the labor press and in their meetings, the

[1] William Green, "What Labor Thinks of Its Banks," *American Bankers' Association Journal*, vol. 19 (1927), p. 732.

[2] *The Labor Banking Movement in the United States*, pp. 17–21.

[3] *Ibid.*, p. 61.

unions denounced the sympathy and cooperation of the bankers with open-shop employers.

Many of the leaders and workers thought that it would be possible for labor banks to finance a union in case of strike or lockout, but loans to unions for such purposes have not been an important function of labor banks. It is generally recognized that financing strikes is not banking. Some enthusiasts saw in labor banks a means of mobilizing the savings of the working class to support union employers,[1] or even to finance and control certain basic industries in the interest of organized labor.[2] In such a scheme labor leaders might become important figures as representatives of banks and of stockholders. This higher strategy so appealed to Grand Chief Warren Stone of the Engineers that he declared that the day of the strike was past—and for a time the members of his union apparently believed it.

Some of the more practical and farsighted leaders, such as Sidney Hillman, saw in labor banks less grandiose but more certain ways of advancing the labor movement. Aid to the cooperative movement was thought to be one of the most important of these possibilities. Many cooperatives had found it difficult to get credit, presumably because of the unfriendly attitude of banks toward the cooperative movement. As a matter of fact, labor banks have not helped the situation much. With the exception of those of the Amalgamated, few labor banks have been willing to accept the risk involved in such loans.[3]

It was also hoped that labor banks would further the labor movement by aiding the individual members and that they would make the workers' financial position more secure in several ways. One was in providing small "character" loans at lower rates of interest than those charged by other loan organizations, without collateral but on the endorsement of two reliable union members.[4] Loans and advice to home builders were expected to save workers from real estate sharks and exorbitant commission charges. The banks were also expected to perform a useful service by keeping hours more convenient for wage earners, and by giving advice to small investors that is usually available only to those with large sums to invest. Another beneficial feature was expected to be found in the cooperative sharing of profits by the limitation of dividends on shares.

With the success of the first labor banks, other, and some times less laudable, motives began to play a part in the rapid expansion of the movement. Not only were advantages for the union sought, but also

[1] While here and there labor banks have extended loans to union employers in order to protect the union, these cases are exceptional. Labor banks have generally made commercial loans without reference to the labor policy of the borrower.

[2] For a highly imaginative discussion of this subject, see Richard Boeckel, *Labor's Money* (1923).

[3] *The Labor Banking Movement in the United States*, p. 269.

[4] Some labor banks have emphasized such a service.

personal gains, such as the chance of position as bank officers with good salaries. The extreme example of this is offered by the banking and other cooperative enterprises of the Brotherhood of Locomotive Engineers after 1923, in which the interest in salaries and commissions kept the projects expanding more than did such motives as the earnings for the Brotherhood or the advancement of the labor movement.[1] Closely

TABLE 7.—NUMBER, CAPITAL, SURPLUS AND UNDIVIDED PROFITS, DEPOSITS, AND RESOURCES OF LABOR BANKS IN THE UNITED STATES, 1920–1941[1]

Date	No. of banks	Share capital	Surplus and undivided profits	Deposits	Total resources
Dec. 31					
1920	2	$ 960,000	$ 194,446	$ 2,258,561	$ 3,628,867
1921	4	1,280,000	225,869	9,970,961	12,782,173
1922	10	2,050,473	742,689	21,901,641	26,506,723
1923	18	4,222,230	1,353,022	43,324,820	51,496,524
1924	26	6,441,267	1,891,757	72,913,180	85,325,884
1925[a]	36	9,069,072	3,467,829	98,392,592	115,015,273
1926	35	8,914,508	3,837,377	108,743,550	126,533,542
1927	32	8,282,500	3,747,176	103,290,219	119,818,416
1928	27	7,537,500	3,821,205	98,784,369	116,307,256
June 30					
1929	22	6,687,500	3,807,579	92,077,098	108,539,894
1930	14	4,112,500	3,105,336	59,817,392	68,953,855
1931	11	3,912,500	2,952,878	50,949,570	59,401,164
1932	7	2,537,500	905,896	22,622,514	28,564,797
1933[b]	4	1,725,000	436,421	15,338,505	18,653,355
1934	4	1,725,000	313,433	15,899,849	19,168,718
1935	4	1,725,000	326,943	17,262,281	19,692,385
1936	4	1,725,000	376,676	20,302,297	22,858,772
1937	4	2,189,671[c]	....	21,679,590	24,359,340
1938	4	2,483,745[c]	....	21,438.903	24,166,706
1939	4	2,544,538[c]	....	22,923,861	25,813,638
1940	4	2,684,911[c]	....	23,847,294	26,931,651
1941	4	2,851,116[c]	....	26,914,510	30,192,066
Dec. 31					
1941	4	2,955,040[c]	....	29,068,608	32,292,188

[a] Amalgamated Bank of Philadelphia not included. The existing labor banks in January, 1942, were the Amalgamated Bank of New York, the Amalgamated Bank of Chicago, the Union National Bank of Newark, and the Telegraphers' National Bank of St. Louis.

[b] Dec. 31.

[c] Capital, surplus, and undivided profits.

[1] Data for 1920 to 1936 from *Monthly Labor Review*, vol. 43 (1936), p. 1192, those for 1937–1941 supplied by the Industrial Relations Section, Department of Economics and Social Institutions, Princeton University.

related to this factor was the possibility of promoters' profits. Ballyhoo experts, possibly with more interest in personal profits than in the promotion of the labor movement, began to take advantage of the enthusiasm of the workers by selling them stocks in unsound or shady bank projects. For a time the movement was "in the air" and it was necessary to show a man why his union should *not* start a labor bank rather than to give him good reasons for starting one.

[1] *Ibid.*, p. 59.

As the result of these several factors, rational and otherwise, the number of labor banks in the United States grew rapidly from 1920 until 1926. This growth, and the almost equally precipitous decline that followed, are shown in Table 7.

The reasons for the decline of the labor banking movement are almost as varied as were the reasons for its growth. In the first place, bank failures were not confined to labor banks—it was a period of crises for the commercial banking system. The number of active banks in the United States declined from 29,417 in 1921 to 13,864 on June 30, 1933. In the single year ended June 30, 1933, there were 1,783 bank suspensions (receivers appointed) or 12.86 per 100 active banks.[1] It was not an auspicious period in which to enter the banking business, but unfortunately the failure of all but a very few of the forty-five labor banks cannot be entirely explained by such general circumstances. In fact, roughly half of those opened in the earlier years had failed or been sold before the end of 1929. A more detailed analysis is necessary to understand why the labor banking movement was not successful.

One of the important points to bear in mind is that many of the banks (eleven) were sponsored by one union, the Brotherhood of Locomotive Engineers, and the collapse of the financial enterprises of that one organization did much to discredit the labor banking movement as a whole. In June, 1927, just before the convention of the Brotherhood, its Philadelphia bank was sold because of lack of success. The disclosure at the convention that year of the huge losses, errors of judgment, betrayals of confidence, nepotism, inefficiency, and extravagance were blows from which the labor banking movement did not recover. The Brotherhood voted to make no further investments and gradually liquidated its holdings. The sale in February, 1930, of the once-emulated Cleveland bank marked the close of a financial system that had at one time impressively stretched from coast to coast.[2]

Another failure that jarred labor banking enthusiasts was that of the Federated Bank and Trust Company of New York City on Oct. 30, 1931. This bank was by far the largest of the existing labor banks and was supposed to have been one of the most prosperous. From June 30 to Oct. 30, 1931, more than $4,500,000 of deposits were withdrawn, and when the bank was forced to close it was revealed that loans had been unwisely selected and distributed and that large losses had been sustained on securities that the bank had purchased.[3]

Of the factors that contributed to the failure of labor banks, union politics was perhaps of first importance. In some of the stronger and more successful banks this factor was of negligible importance, but in

[1] C. B. Upham and E. Lamke, *Closed and Distressed Banks* (1934), p. 247.
[2] *The Labor Banking Movement in the United States*, pp. 46, 250.
[3] *New York Times*, Oct. 31, 1931.

others it prevented adherence to sound banking practices. Union politics expressed itself in desire for prestige of the union, in personal ambition of its officers, and in emphasis upon personalities. Sometimes offices, loans, and commissions were arranged with an eye to advancing the group in power in the union, or nepotism and jealousy of outside banking interests prevented the appointment of a trained and competent executive officer. The failure of directors of many labor banks to choose competent managers was, however, only in part due to union politics. There was a real scarcity of men who were both trained and intelligent bankers and also interested in furthering the labor movement. The seriousness of this problem of personnel is shown by the fact that, according to a study made at Princeton in 1929, in one-half of the labor banks the men selected at one time or another for the key positions were not qualified to fulfill their duties and responsibilities.[1] It is not to be assumed that petty politics and incompetent officers were an exclusive feature of labor banks, but supporters of labor banks did not generally anticipate these difficulties.

Most of the labor banks had difficulty in building up sufficient business to be in proper relation to their fixed costs. Despite convenient hours, higher interest rates on deposits, encouragement of deposits by mail, and special services to small investors, labor banks (with one or two exceptions) were not able to compete successfully with regular banks for deposit accounts. The unions had entered a highly competitive field with more enthusiasm than preparation. Several banks were established in places already oversupplied. Moreover, competing banks tended to take over the features of labor banks, raised interest rates on deposits, and in some cases influenced clearinghouse associations to discriminate against labor banks. In many cases the workers gave their bank poor support, because it was inconveniently located or because of their lack of enthusiasm for the movement. Other reasons were the advantages of established banking connections, fear of failure of the new bank, and hostility of large commercial depositors to labor banks.

From a banking standpoint the failures of labor banks have far outweighed the successes. The rate of failure has been very high, even when consideration is given to the fact that during this period the rate of failure of nonlabor banks was also high. The return on investment of labor banks, taken collectively, was not the 10 per cent or more which was commonly expected. The average returns on investment of banks remaining in business during the relatively prosperous years of 1926, 1927, and 1928, were 3.77, 3.67, and 3.61 per cent respectively. If the losses through failures or forced sales of banks were deducted from these returns, little, if any, net return would remain for those years.[2] Dividends

---

[1] *The Labor Banking Movement in the United States*, p. 153.

[2] *Ibid.*, pp. 233–234.

on deposits were also not so great as was expected. Indeed, only the Hammond, Ind., bank (since closed) was paying such dividends in 1928.[1] Of course, the banking crisis of 1933 entirely changed this and it is no longer a question as to whether a bank should pay dividends to small depositors, but whether they will accept such accounts at all. The Amalgamated Bank in Chicago now prides itself that it maintains lower deposit balances than other Chicago banks and thus makes it possible for workers to obtain banking facilities not provided by nonlabor banks.

The problem of assessing all the gains and losses to the labor movement of union experiments in banking is not an easy one, yet the balance is unquestionably heavily against the labor banks. Some unions, particularly the Brotherhood of Locomotive Engineers, lost heavily. Large sums that could have been well used in building up benefit funds and strengthening the position of the unions in collective bargaining were diverted into unprofitable investments. The energy and time of paid officials and of members were diverted from other and more fruitful methods of furthering the labor movement.

The labor banking movement was not a revolutionary one and it did not make the strike obsolete. In exceptional cases only was substantial aid given to cooperatives. Only a few labor banks were able to help union employers over a period of financial strain, and these cases involved union-management cooperation as well as loans. In most cases, the prestige of owning a bank was negated by the lack of success or by the failure of the enterprise. Labor banks formed such a small part of the whole credit system that open-shop employers were completely independent of them, and therefore labor banks could not have had much influence in checking the open-shop movement.

Not all the elements or factions of the labor movement expected such impressive results from labor banking as did its advocates. The cautious attitude of the officers of the A.F. of L., however, was due to quite different reasons from those which provoked the denunciation of labor banking by the left-wing leaders. The A.F. of L. officials feared, and with good reason, the possible financial losses from banking enterprises. The position of the radicals, as expressed by W. Z. Foster, was that the labor bank is only a part of the insidious movement of class collaboration expressed in employee stock ownership, trade-union life insurance, and labor investment corporations. These, they held, are mere palliatives that paralyze the class-conscious labor movement. According to Mr. Foster, laborers must be brought to realize that the great task is not to gather together the meager savings of the skilled workers, but to defend the economic interests of the great mass of poverty-stricken workers, to fight for the whole working class.[2]

[1] *Ibid.*, p. 96.

[2] W. Z. Foster, *Misleaders of Labor* (1927), p. 331.

The radicals have asserted that workers became interested in stocks and bonds and acquired property interests and that leaders tended to become conservative bank officials and hesitated to call strikes that might injure profits by cutting down deposits. The banks themselves tended to become more like other banks. The removal, in 1925, of the 10 per cent limit on stock dividends by the New York State Federation bank was pointed to as typical of this tendency. "Very few [labor banks] can lay just claim to features that distinguish them from the common run of small, privately owned and operated commercial banks."[1]

Liberals, such as Messrs. Budish and Soule, were, on the other hand, much less sweeping in their condemnation of labor banking. They contended that the value of a labor bank depends upon the type of leadership and controlling philosophy of the union. A successful bank in the hands of conservative "old" unionism would hopelessly compromise unions, making them dependent on a profitable business and enslaving their members. In the hands of adherents to the "new unionism," however, the control of credit might be an effective force for beneficial social reconstruction.[2]

It is rather difficult to check on the truth of this assertion, for the policies of the few labor banks that remained in existence during the depression were dictated more by the necessities of an economic crisis than by the differences between a liberal and a conservative union ownership. The emphasis was upon policies that would assist in survival of the bank rather than upon advancement of the labor movement. The banks of the Amalgamated Clothing Workers in Chicago and New York City, which are unquestionably as interested in the advancement of the labor movement as any of the labor banks were, make no loans to men's clothing shops, require union officials to offer the same security as other applicants for loans, and have stressed the safety and liquidity of the bank's assets rather than cooperative features. The strong position of these banks is in part due to the support of the union and to the fact that the union has encouraged the banks to make safer investments that yield a lower return rather than more speculative and possibly more profitable loans. The Amalgamated banks have furnished some special services to workers, such as Russian remittances, small loans, and cooperative housing loans,[3] but that these are not now the most important part of their business is rather conclusively shown in their statement of condition.[4]

[1] Leo Wolman, "Labor Banking after Ten Years," *The New Republic*, vol. 60 (1929), p. 10.

[2] J. M. Budish and George Soule, *The New Unionism* (1920), p. 251.

[3] *Report of the General Executive Board and Proceedings of the Tenth Biennial Convention of the Amalgamated Clothing Workers of America*, p. 132.

[4] As of Dec. 32, 1938, the Amalgamated Trust and Savings Bank of Chicago had outstanding $443,354 in "character loans" as against a total of $683,474 in demand and time

It is hardly possible that in the immediate future a revived labor banking movement will assume an important role in the labor movement as a whole. Few people now expect that labor banks will assume any such important function in transforming the capitalist system as was expected by many in the early 1920's. Perhaps one of the most important effects of labor's ventures into this type of institutionalism will be to discourage further excursions into the field of business enterprise and to foster concentration of the attention of trade unions upon legislation and collective bargaining.

---

loans. "Character loans" are usually made on two signatures. Between 25 and 30 per cent of the amount outstanding was against members of the Amalgamated Union, between 70 and 75 per cent against nonmember borrowers. Most of the loans are in sums of $50, $100, $150, $200, and $300.

Chapter VIII

THE UNION IN INDUSTRY: THE THEORY OF COLLECTIVE BARGAINING[1]

Unions have a variety of interests and may function in a number of ways. The great majority of unions, however, are interested above all else in the worker's position in his trade or industry. This is especially true of unions of the business type, which have limited interest in matters of reform and no active interest in effecting radical changes in the essentials of the existing economic order; it is almost as true of the less impatient of the "new" or "revolutionary" unions, which also emphasize matters of the trade or industry. Though these latter may wish to establish a new order in "our own time" or later on, they are very immediately interested in jobs, wages, and working conditions. For the most part they are of the view that a new order must be the product of an evolutionary process, not of sudden change. Hence the great majority of the "revolutionary" unions join with the business unions in such a country as the United States in an effort to control wages, hours, and working conditions and to safeguard employment in the craft or industry as their primary task. Nearly all unions stress collective bargaining and rule making and informal regulation, the methods to which they naturally turn in their effort to secure higher wages, shorter hours, security of tenure of the job, protection in matters of discipline, and good working conditions in general. But collective bargaining, and its accompanying rule making and regulation, it should be pointed out, may mean to the unionists something real in addition to better wages, hours, and working conditions. For it means a new "government in industry," "democracy in industry," "citizenship in industry," to employ only a few of the more frequently used terms. Participation in the government of one's industry may have the same appeal as participation in political affairs. The demand for recognition and collective bargaining is not a demand for economic ends alone.[2]

---

[1] In this connection, it will be helpful for the reader to consult vol. I, Chap. IV, where a survey of wage theory is presented.

[2] Nor from the public point of view is the case for organization and collective bargaining entirely economic. Unless democratic procedures can be developed and successfully operated in industry, it is unlikely that the masses of the people will receive that training in discussion, patience, tolerance, and acceptance of majority decision necessary for the development of a stable and efficient representative government.

Collective bargaining means that the representatives of the workers meet with the representatives of the firm or firms to consider and determine wages, hours, and other matters in the domain of industrial relations. If they agree upon the issues involved, what is called a "joint" or "collective" agreement results. This is ordinarily reduced to written form and commonly runs for a specified period of time—six months, a year, two years, or possibly five years.[1] The joint agreement may specifically provide for the conciliation or arbitration of disputes over the interpretation of its clauses and their application in concrete cases during the life of the contract. It may also provide for the arbitration of disputes arising in the formulation of a new agreement to replace the old. Some of these matters will be developed at a later point in our discussion.[2]

An additional point needs to be touched upon in connection with collective bargaining. In many instances the provisions of the joint agreement relate to only a part of the subjects that arise in the employment relationship. Other matters are disposed of according to the rules of management, or become subject to control by formal or informal rule of the union, or are disposed of in conference as they develop.[3] In many trades, for example, that of the compositor, there are a variety of union rules that become implicit parts of the joint agreement, such as those relating to the membership of the foreman in the union, the filling of "situations," the laying off and discharge of workmen, etc. Moreover, it is possible that additional rules may be made effective during the life of an agreement. Thus the scope of collective bargaining may be broad and fairly inclusive, or it may be narrow and accompanied by a variety of rules made by management or the labor organization. These rules we shall consider in the next two chapters.

Union Theory of Collective Bargaining

Three stages, or shifts of emphasis, are discernible in the evolution of the union theory of collective bargaining.[4]

Its first or simplest form emphasized the need of equality of bargaining power between employer and employee. Labor spokesmen stressed

---

[1] In exceptional cases either party may end the agreement or substitute a modified one on notice of a month or sixty days. In other exceptional cases, the agreement is indeterminate and is changed from time to time in conference or by arbitration. Such cases have been found most frequently in the shoe industry.

[2] See Chap. XIII, pp. 706–719.

[3] It is rather common for new subjects to be agreed upon during the life of an agreement and made a part of it. Collective bargaining is, therefore, frequently more or less of a continuous process.

[4] This and the three following paragraphs were previously published by H. A. Millis in "The Union in Industry: Some Observations on the Theory of Collective Bargaining," *The American Economic Review*, vol. 25 (1935), pp. 2–4.

the view that the wage earner under modern industrial conditions is a weak and incompetent bargainer, possessed of little more than an ineffective veto power in the refusal to accept employment on the terms offered and in the right to quit the job when dissatisfied. The individual worker, as compared to the employer, they have said, is ignorant of the market situation and of employment opportunities; he has little or no reserve power in funds in hand; he fears to push a claim vigorously for fear of discrimination or loss of job; he is likely to reason that it is better to accept or retain employment on adverse terms than to lose working time altogether; he finds himself pitted against other seekers of work, and the cheaper man is the successful bidder; if he has employment, the terms of his contract, like the railway timetable, are "subject to change without notice."

Naturally enough, the average unionist's case for collective bargaining has run largely in terms of the concrete instance, the personal factor, big business versus the economically small workman, and the short run.[1] But, thanks largely to intellectual friends such as Mr. and Mrs. Webb, and to experience in a complicated world, the union spokesmen have had more and more regard for the longer run and for market considerations. Thus their second stage has brought them to a realization of the need for control owing to industrial and market organization and the pressure of market competition. They realize that the average employer, however appreciative he may be of the value of good working conditions and the needs of his workers, is under the necessity of reducing costs because of the moneysaving, chiseling practices of his less socially minded competitors. Competition frequently prevents employers from doing what they would like to do in labor matters. Hence, nowadays, we hear not absolutely but relatively less of balancing bargaining power between the employer and his employees, and more of the need for standardization and control, of placing all firms in a market on pretty much the same plane of labor costs, and of having competitive success depend largely upon managerial ability, sound organization, and the like.

To this statement of the case, now decades old, the American unions have added a third argument[2]—that wages must be increased in proportion to increases in industrial efficiency in order to balance consumption and production and to maintain the necessary market outlet for industrial products.[3] Officially adopted as a labor doctrine by the American

---

[1] See, for example, John Mitchell, *Organized Labor* (1903), Chaps. 1 and 12.

[2] This argument will be considered more fully in Chap. IX. See also vol. II, pp. 42–50.

[3] American unions are not exceptional in their adherence to this doctrine. For years the German unions, at any rate the "free unions," took much the same position. It is also espoused by the organized-labor movements of other countries, notably that of Australia. *Cf.* O. de R. Foenander, *Towards Industrial Peace in Australia* (1937), pp. 116*ff.*, and W. B. Reddaway, "Australian Wage Policy, 1927–1937," *International Labour Review*, vol. 37 (1938), pp. 314–337.

Federation of Labor in 1925, it has been accepted by many businessmen, not a few economists, and obviously by many persons holding public office. The same is true of a related doctrine to the effect that in depression maintaining or increasing wages is necessary to maintain or to effect an increase in purchasing power, which is the appropriate road to recovery. The role these doctrines have of late been playing in public affairs is well known.[1]

While there have been shifts in the emphasis that unions have placed upon the announced purposes of collective bargaining, the fundamental assumptions upon which collective bargaining is based have remained largely unaltered. The three most important assumptions upon the basis of which the union organizes, seeks recognition at the hands of employers, and proceeds in support of its interest in wages, hours, and working conditions are:

1. That the members of the worker group have an important common interest rather than conflicting, competitive interests;

2. That the interests of their employers, as seen and acted upon by them, and the interests of the workers of the group are frequently, if not generally, conflicting;

3. That wages, hours, and working conditions are largely a matter of the relative bargaining strength of the two sides; that without organization and concerted action there will be a tendency toward undesirable, if not the worst possible, conditions for the workers; that no adequate safeguard is found in the operation of the factors at work in the unorganized trade; that there is a flexible, changeable situation and that by means of organized effort positive improvement can be secured in wages, hours, and other important details of the labor contract and in their administration.[2]

The union spokesman of course recognizes that a wage earner may within limits, work out his individual problems by his own efforts. He may, by individual effort, merit, or favor, rise to the rank of foreman or superintendent, or he may graduate into the employing class. Or he may become a shopkeeper, a professional man, a bond salesman, or an insurance agent. Not a few wage earners do this, especially in a new country like the United States, where custom and status count for little. But in an advanced industrial society most wage earners remain wage earners indefinitely. "Once a wage earner always a wage earner" per-

---

[1] The National Labor Relations Act [Public no. 198, 74th Congress, 1st Session, Chap. 372 (S. 1958), July 5, 1935], passed by Congress in 1935 to encourage collective bargaining, rests largely upon these arguments. See Chap. XI, pp. 522–533.

[2] Though they are not always explicitly stated, these assumptions are found in preamble after preamble to trade-union constitutions, and in the speeches and writings of trade-union leaders. Perhaps nowhere are they stated more effectively than in John Mitchell's *Organized Labor*. See, especially, Chaps. 1 and 12.

haps contains an increasing element of truth.[1] And while wage earners remain wage earners, those in the associated group are under pretty much the common rule with respect to hours, tenure, and general working conditions; they are tied to the same wage scale and rate structure. Hence the important common interests of the wage earners of the group.

With reference to the second assumption, one frequently reads in union documents and literature of a harmony of employer and worker interests, of the necessity for the spirit of cooperation,[2] but there is no demand for union recognition and collective bargaining or for regulation by union rule that does not rest upon the assumption of a conflict of interest—not at all points, but at some, and precisely at those points which it is desired to bargain about or make the subject of union regulation. The cooperation spoken of must be under the terms of the collective agreement or by acceptance of union rules. Such control assumed, it may be argued that high wages, short hours, the employment of union men, security of tenure, and good working conditions are in the interest of the employer as well as the employees. But after all, there is the fundamental assumption that there is conflict of interest as things go— that the employer will seek the largest output at the least cost; that, if free to follow his own devices, he will hold down or seek to reduce wages; that he will maintain long hours and attempt to prolong them by overtime requirements; that he will speed up the workers and will perhaps seek to cut into earnings by fines and otherwise; that he may maintain working conditions dangerous to health and limb; that he will introduce changes in equipment, processes, and working force without proper regard for the rights and necessities of the workers; perhaps that he will discriminate unfairly in employment, wages, work assignments, etc.; in any event that the terms and conditions will be much inferior to those that can be obtained by means of organized control.

While in such countries as the United States there has been a remarkable advance in managerial and supervisory practices, while there has been a development of a "science of management," there has been and there still remains much seeming basis in fact for the view that such problems as have been indicated tend to develop in the absence of concerted worker control. To this we shall return presently.

The third assumption receives great emphasis in typical union theorizing. For example, John Mitchell, who was a competent and typical spokesman, said: "Trade unionism starts from the recognition of the fact that under normal conditions the individual, unorganized workman cannot bargain advantageously with the employer for the sale of his labor. Since the workingman has no money in reserve and must sell his labor immediately, since, moreover, he has no knowledge

[1] Cf. vol. I, Chap. I, pp. 32–38.
[2] For example, see the preface to John Mitchell's *Organized Labor*.

of the market and no skill in bargaining, since, finally, he has only his own labor to sell, while the employer engages hundreds or thousands of men and can easily do without the services of any particular individual, the workingman, if bargaining on his own account and for himself alone, is at an enormous disadvantage. Trade unionism recognizes the fact that under such conditions labor becomes more and more degenerate, because the labor which the workman sells is, unlike other commodities, a thing which is of his very life and soul and being. In the individual contract between a rich employer and a poor workman, the laborer will secure the worst of it; he is progressively debased, because of wages insufficient to buy nourishing food, because of hours of labor too long to permit sufficient rest, because of conditions of work destructive of moral, mental, and physical health, and degrading and annihilating to the laboring classes of the present and the future, and, finally, because of danger from accident and disease, which kill off the workingman or prematurely age him. The 'individual bargain,' or individual contract, between employers and men means that the condition of the worst and lowest man in the industry will be that which the best man must accept. . . . There can be no permanent prosperity to the working classes, no real and lasting progress, no consecutive improvement in conditions, until the principle is firmly and fully established, that in industrial life, especially in enterprises on a large scale, the settlement of wagers, hours of labor, and all conditions of work, must be made between employers and workingmen collectively and not between employers and workingmen individually."[1]

It is characteristic of union spokesmen to emphasize the weakness of the individual bargainer and to argue for concerted action on the ground of defense. They put much less emphasis on the other side of the picture and generally fail to mention at least some phases of it. Under collective bargaining, the representative of the workers may not only be free from any fear of injury at the hands of the employer of his clients, but he may be, and very frequently is, the better informed and more skillful bargainer of the two in so far as labor matters are concerned. Moreover, the local officials and negotiating committee may have the benefit of data brought together by the international organization[2] and, in important cases, the assistance of the international officers—of Sidney Hillman of the Amalgamated Clothing Workers, President Baker of the International Typographical Union, President Brown of the Electrical Workers, President Tobin of the Teamsters. The union can have recourse to the strike and the boycott. The local, by providing strike

---

[1] *Ibid.*, pp. 2–4 (American Book and Bible House, Philadelphia, 1903).

[2] A good example is found in the *Service Bureau News Bulletins* of the International Printing Pressmen and Assistants' Union of North America. A similar service is provided by the International Typographical Union.

benefits—perhaps financed largely or wholly by the international—gives reserve power and ability to wait; and, just as important, by preaching solidarity and building up and sustaining moral, it may develop the will as well as the power "to see it through." The supply of labor may be controlled and competition for work restricted in a variety of ways. The main object, of course, has been to keep the supply of labor short relative to the supplies of management, capital, and natural resources. As Professor Hansen has said:

"No one is more firmly convinced that a commodity must be scarce in order to be dear than are trade unionists. For this and other reasons they seek to control the supply of labor in their own specialized markets by such devices as the closed shop, high initiation fees, limitation of apprentices, [prohibition of team work and subdivision of labor, restrictions upon the introduction of machinery, reduction of the hours of labor, restrictions upon piece work],[1] and a minimum wage. Whether or not these devices are socially desirable is another question, but at any rate so far as the trade unions are concerned, they are not applying the remedy to the symptom of the disease; they are applying it to the cause; they are seeking to bring about that condition of relative scarcity without which high wages cannot obtain.

"The closed shop with the rigidly closed union constitutes a perfect monopoly control over the supply of labor. The closed shop with the doors of the union open but through which entrance can be gained only over a 'tariff wall' of high initiation fees or an unnecessarily long term of apprenticeship restricts very decidedly the supply of labor but does not completely limit it. The closed shop with the perfectly open union or the open shop with a union agreement as to minimum wages also restricts the supply of labor that can work in that trade. . . . If a trade union is able to maintain a certain minimum wage it by that very fact fixes the number of people who can engage in that trade because only a limited number will be employed at the established wage. If wages are raised fewer laborers will be employed and the rest will have to go elsewhere for employment. Thus the establishment of a minimum wage serves to limit the number of laborers in the trade."[2]

The policies back of some of these devices mentioned have been noted in Chap. VI; the policies back of others will be dealt with in the chapters immediately following this one. To complete the summary statement needed at this point, it should be said that under the collective agreement the terms of employment are not readily changed to the disadvantage of the workers without due notice and consent.

[1] These bracketed clauses have been added by the authors because of their importance in this connection.

[2] A. H. Hansen, "The Economics of Unionism," *Journal of Political Economy*, vol. 30 (1922), pp. 523–524.

As seen by the trade unionist, who acts upon a bargaining theory of wages, there is a tremendous difference between the results of unrestrained individual bargaining and the results to be obtained through concerted action. The language quoted above from Mitchell is typical. He adds, "trade unionism thus recognizes that the destruction of the workingman is the individual bargain, and the salvation of the workingman is the joint, united, or collective bargain."[1]

COLLECTIVE BARGAINING AND ECONOMIC THEORY

But does not the case for collective bargaining and regulation as made by organized labor and its sympathizers prove too much? Is the picture presented a complete one? Are there not in the situation important economic factors wholly neglected or given too little emphasis? What have the nonlabor economists to say about the theory of collective bargaining and the possibility of controlling wages, hours, and working conditions to advantage?

No one has disputed the fact that in the concrete case presented by a trade or industry or locality unions can by concerted action, at least for the time being, raise wage rates, reduce the hours of work, and change and improve working conditions. The fact that they have done so is too well known to everyone to permit of denial. It has been established by experience. What concerted action can effect in the immediate situation needs only to be illustrated by facts at hand. If the organized group possesses sufficient power, matters can be carried to the point where the public is exploited. It is frequently said that this has been true of the building trades in some localities and of certain other trades also. But what are the limits of such control? How is it conditioned? What of the long run? Can control be exercised in the interests of *all* labor with the same result as it can be exercised in the interests of a limited group?

Economists' View of Collective Bargaining.—Most economists have been more or less adversely critical of the union theory and practice of collective bargaining. For fifty years or more, down to about 1875, trade unions in England were widely attacked by the economists of the time as generally futile if not mischievous.

Looking at wages throughout industry, rather than at wages in one organized trade, the wages-fund theorists could find no case for collective bargaining. As put by J. R. McCulloch, "the rate of wages in any given country, at any specified period, depends on the ratio between the portion of its capital appropriated to the payment of wages, and the number of its labourers."[2] Laborers were everywhere regarded as the divisor, capital

---

[1] Quoted from John Mitchell, *op. cit.*, p. 4.

[2] Article on wages in *A Treatise on the Circumstances Which Determine the Rate of Wages* (1868), p. 8.

the dividend. This was not conceived of as the truism that the average of wages was to be found by dividing the fund by the number of laborers sharing in it. Real wages depended on capital, defined as the quantity of goods and services habitually consumed by the workers, and this quantity was fixed in the sense that it was necessarily predetermined by the economic circumstances of the community at the time. The total to be paid in real wages was practically unalterable; if as a result of concerted action the workers in certain trades obtained higher wages, the workers in other trades must be content with so much the less. Trade unions were therefore helpless except to alter wages as between one group and another. As put by an early American economist after this doctrine had been abandoned as unsound by most of the English theorists: "There is no use in arguing against any one of the four fundamental rules of arithmetic. The question of wages is a question of Division. It is complained that the quotient is too small. Well, then, how many ways are there to make a quotient larger? Two ways. Enlarge your dividend, the divisor remaining the same, and the quotient will be larger; lessen your divisor, the dividend remaining the same, and the quotient will be larger."[1]

Though it contained a larger element of truth a hundred years ago than in recent times, the wages-fund theory was not wholly sound. During a period of twelve months there was even in the England of a century ago no definite and fixed quantum of commodities and services set apart for the exclusive use of the laboring classes, all of which they collectively would get and more than which they could not get as their real wages. The facts relating to output of goods and services have become so different that we now think of these in terms of "flows," not in terms of "funds." And, within limits, flows may be enlarged or diminished. The situation is dynamic. Moreover, a large part of the flow of the products of industry and of services is purchased and used by the members of different classes, not by those of any one class. Real wages, if money wages are increased and the volume of employment remains substantially the same, can increase at the expense of other real income.

The wages-fund doctrine was characteristically applied to a short period of time—"during the year," "at any given time," "at any particular moment." But it was reinforced by a doctrine of saving and capital accumulation and investment. If, as a result of concerted action, wages were increased at the expense of profits in a given trade, the amount of capital (here defined in the usual sense) upon which wages depended would, in the course of time, decrease, with dire effect upon the workers. For capital would likely be diverted from the less profitable trade to other employments; moreover, any diminution of profit would result in less saving by those who had less to save. Employment or

[1] A. L. Perry, *Elements of Political Economy* (1875), p. 154.

rate of wages in the trade, or both employment and rate of wages, would be adversely affected. And, if for any reason, wages in all trades increased at the expense of profits, saving and investment would be curtailed and labor would have to accept a lower wage. Any such gain must be temporary. As one writer put it: "There is only a certain produce to be divided between capitalist and labourer. If more be given to the labourer than nature awards, a smaller amount will remain for the capitalist; the spirit of accumulation will be checked; less will be devoted to productive purposes; the wage-fund will dwindle, and the wage of the labourer will inevitably fall. For a time, indeed, a natural influence may be dammed back; but only to act, ultimately, with accumulated force."[1] But, *per contra*, if wages were low and the rate of profit high, more rapid accumulation would take place with the result that wages would rise. Thus, it was contended that wages were dependent in the longer period of time on profits and saving by profit takers. Hence it was to the interest of the workers to "make the position of employers as pleasant and profitable as possible."[2]

This theory of capital formation and investment was narrow and none too realistic in the English situation of a century ago. Certainly it cannot be accepted as wholly valid today when savings are made from incomes of diverse kinds and when there is difference of opinion as to the relation between gains to be realized from investments and the savings that will be made.

Still a third doctrine was employed in the critical discussion of the possibility of increasing wages. This was the celebrated doctrine of population, to the effect that numbers tend to outrun the means of subsistence. Only by the exercise of prudential restraint could low wages be avoided, and any hope for the exercise of such restraint was a slight one, for it would have to extend to the whole wage-earning class. Combining the doctrine of population with the capital accumulation and wages-fund doctrines, it was said that, "if combination were for a time to raise wages, the growth of the wage-fund would be unnaturally retarded, while a fictitious stimulus would be given to population, by the momentary enrichment of the labouring class. A diminished demand for labor would coincide with an increased supply. The labourer's wage would be forced down to starvation-point; and his last state would be worse than his first."[3]

The doctrine of population was a rather extreme one in the peculiar condition obtaining in England at the time the doctrine was formulated. It is now recognized that a higher level of living may be accompanied by a

---

[1] James Stirling, *Unionism: With Remarks on the Report of the Commissioners on Trades' Unions* (1869), pp. 26–27.

[2] T. S. Cree, *A Criticism of the Theory of Trade Unions* (1895), p. 31.

[3] James Stirling, *op. cit.*, p. 29.

lower birth rate. In advanced countries population growth does not turn on mere means of subsistence. It is true also that efficiency is as important as numbers in the labor supply and that efficiency has direct bearing upon productivity, which must be given consideration in explaining wages.

But the older doctrines were effectively used in an effort to demonstrate the futility and the uneconomic character of unionism. As Mr. and Mrs. Webb have said, "With so complete a demonstration of the impossibility of 'artificially' raising wages, it is not surprising that public opinion, from 1825 down to about 1875, condemned impartially all the methods and all the regulations of Trade Unionism. To the ordinary middle-class man it seemed logically indisputable that the way of the Trade Unionists was blocked in all directions. They could not gain any immediate bettering of the condition of the whole wage-earning class, because the amount of the wage-fund at any given time was predetermined. They could not permanently secure better terms even for a particular section, because this would cause capital immediately to begin to desert that particular trade or town. They could not make any real progress in the near future, because they would thereby check the accumulation of capital. And, finally, even if they could persuade a benevolent body of capitalists to augment wages by voluntarily sharing profits, the 'principle of population' lay in wait to render nugatory any such new form of 'out-door relief.' "[1]

With the passing of time the economic theorists generally have become less adversely critical of trade unions and their methods. Indeed, a considerable number of them find a not unimportant case for collective bargaining. Many others, however, emphasize the limited control that can be exercised except at the expense (in amount of employment) of the members of the organized group themselves or at the expense of their fellows, and a considerable number hold that there is practically no opportunity for control if injurious results are not to follow.[2]

Most economic theorists, when discussing the matter, have been at pains to show the one-sidedness and superficiality of the case usually made for collective bargaining. They emphasize particularly that there is a demand, and a competitive one, for labor and maintain that this is largely, when not entirely, effective in giving the workers substantially what their work contribution is worth.

The theory of wages held by most economists runs largely in terms of marginal productivity. Earlier in this treatise the productivity theory

[1] Sidney and Beatrice Webb, *Industrial Democracy*, (1897), pp. 615–616.

[2] An extreme statement of the adversely critical views may be found in an article by S. S. Garrett, "Wages and the Collective Wage Bargain," *American Economic Review*, vol. 18 (1928), pp. 670–683. See, also, the positions of W. H. Hutt, *The Theory of Collective Bargaining* (1930), J. R. Hicks, *The Theory of Wages* (1932), Maurice Dobb, *Wages* (1939), and Z. Clark Dickinson, *Collective Wage Determination* (1941).

of wages has been discussed,[1] and the discussion does not need to be repeated here. According to it, each employer has reason to hire labor and to purchase other factors needed in his business up to that point where the value of the contribution of the last unit of labor or of any other factor is substantially the same as its cost. In an ideal state and in the absence of friction, there is active competition for labor until this results, not only in the given plant but in all plants in all industries. Hence, whatever the forces affecting the supply of labor and of the other factors in production, and whatever determines price of products, wages tend to settle at this particular point because of the nature of the demand for labor.[2]

Thus the economist emphasizes a factor—demand—not sufficiently emphasized by the labor spokesman or by the majority of labor economists. And this factor must be emphasized. The facts in the history of wages in the United States during the last hundred years or during the last generation cannot be adequately explained without great emphasis upon the effects of invention, increasing capital, and better utilized resources upon the demand for labor. An increasing number of workers have been absorbed into industry at increased—not the same or lower—wages as the generations have passed.[3] Yet the tendency for wages, because of the demand for labor, to approximate labor's contribution does not necessarily mean that the tendency works out fully or that collective bargaining with reference to wages is futile or mischievous. Still less does it mean that hours and working conditions, in the absence of concerted control, will be as good as they might be from the point of view of labor's welfare.

Factors Other than Wages.—It is a rather curious fact that, with exceptions, it has been characteristic of the economists to discuss collective bargaining, the need for it, and what it can and what it cannot accomplish, in terms of wages only. But wages are only one detail in the labor contract and employment situation. Though wages are certainly of first consideration, hours of work, tenure, and general working conditions are by no means to be neglected. The question arises, do economic forces operate in such a way as to conserve these interests of the workers as they are supposed to do as regards wages? We address our attention to this question, after which we shall return to the question of wages.

Industry affords an abundance of evidence that a competitive demand for labor does not go far to protect the workers against long hours,

---

[1] Vol. I, Chap. IV, pp. 177ff. of this series.

[2] The theory is clearly and accurately stated by J. R. Hicks, *op. cit.*; see especially Chaps. 1 and 2. *Cf.* vol. I, Chap. IV of this treatise, and Paul H. Douglas, "Wage Theory and Wage Policy," *International Labour Review*, vol. 39 (1939), pp. 319–359.

[3] See Chaps. II, III, and IV of vol. I of this treatise.

excessive overtime, fines, discharge without sufficient cause, and objectionable working conditions. The explanation is found in part in the fact that employers as a rule are not actively interested in the long-run effects of hours and working conditions because of a lack of accurate knowledge of these effects and because the labor contract is ordinarily terminable at will. Only exceptionally is the employer dependent upon particular workmen. Of course, there is growing appreciation of these matters on the part of management, but a broad long-run policy in these connections is still in its early stages. Then, too, in so far as the hours of labor are concerned, there is fear of reduced output if a reduction in working time is made, or that one reduction will develop interest in another, and a knowledge that it is exceedingly difficult to return to a regime of the longer day or week when a shorter has been in use.[1]

The explanation is found in part also in the fact that workers accept employment chiefly in view of rate of pay and possible earnings and of accessibility of the place of employment. In fact, workers may know little or nothing in advance of employment concerning anything except location, wage rate, and usual hours of work. Long hours, much overtime, discrimination, inconsiderate discipline, and bad working conditions may give rise to a large turnover of labor, but such a turnover has not caused management generally to ascertain causes and to remedy them adequately.[2] It would appear that it has been chiefly in periods of distinct labor shortage or when unions were making a serious effort to organize the industry that any large number of employers have actively interested themselves in the matters that concern us here and have introduced better standards and practices to an extent that would go far to protect the workers' welfare.

Finally, the explanation is found in part in the fact that there is usually keen competition in the market for the product as well as competition for labor. In order to extend business, to hold business, to meet the needs and whims of customers with reference to style and delivery, to make favorable prices, and to maintain profits and dividends, these things are likely to be "taken out of labor." In the dress industry, for example, there may be hand-to-mouth buying, the workers being employed first long and then short hours per day or week within a period of a couple of months.[3]

[1] Nevertheless, when the NRA codes were invalidated by the Supreme Court of the United States, many open-shop employers increased hours from forty to forty-four per week, and usually without increasing wages in those cases in which they were on a weekly or monthly basis.

[2] It is surprising to find so many firms keeping records of turnover and so few using the data to ascertain and remedy causes.

[3] Two extreme, but not isolated, examples may be cited. The payrolls of a Chicago manufacturer of dresses showed wide fluctuations in hours worked per week during the busy season—from less than forty to more than seventy. The explanation was found in

If there is monopoly control and keen competition is not present in the labor market, the workers may be exploited for the sake of more profit, as illustrated by the former policy of the "steel trust" with respect to the twelve-hour day and seven-day week so long maintained in the face of a strong adverse public opinion. Experience shows that, in the interest of labor and the general social welfare, control must be exercised at many points by law or otherwise and that in some cases legislative enactments cannot well be applied.

Thus the authors find themselves at this point in agreement with Mr. Hutt, who states that these important matters under discussion "are *not* adequately determined by the market process . . . hours of work and conditions of work are things that intimately concern workmen and are best decided collectively."[1]

Further Observations on Wages.—To return to the discussion of wages and collective bargaining, it is to be noted that according to the economic theory briefly stated above, there is a *tendency* for wages to equal the marginal value product of labor. Economists generally do not contend, however, that this tendency fully safeguards the wage interest of the workers. Professor Clark, whose contributions to the productivity theory of distribution were so important, was of the opinion that "natural" wages were not realized in the actual world because of the unequal bargaining strength of worker and employer in the absence of organization and collective bargaining. Collective bargaining between union and employer, he thought, might correct this inequality and effect an increase in wages.[2] Professor Slichter, whose background in concrete fact is unusually good, makes the point that a competitive demand for labor does not necessarily bring wages up to marginal value product in a changing and advancing situation, for the employer makes advances in wages cautiously.[3] With expanding national income advances are

---

the order book. Salesmen, traveling chiefly in the Northwest, sent in orders for specified garments to be delivered "at once," within three days, within a week, within two weeks. The total of sales fluctuated widely. Manufacture was rushed. In numerous instances the payroll showed women workers, in violation of the state law, working more than seventy hours, men more than eighty hours per week. The other example is taken from the manufacture of men's clothing to order. The general rule in Chicago was to ship a suit or overcoat within a week of receipt of the order. Wishing to extend its business, a certain company advertised a three-day service. This begot severe competition such that in one or more cases shipment was promised within twenty-four hours. The actual hours worked came to vary from only a few to twelve or more per day. Such instances and practices have all but disappeared with very effective union organization and standardization at the hands of the International Ladies' Garment Workers and the Amalgamated Clothing Workers.

[1] W. H. Hutt, *op. cit.*, p. 107.
[2] See John Bates Clark, *Essentials of Economic Theory* (1907), Chap. 25.
[3] *Cf.* vol. I, Chap. IV, and vol. II, Chap. 1, p. 50.

usually made at rather long intervals. Moreover, the employer hesitates to hire more labor at a wage above that which he has been paying, for it would call for advances in the wages of those already employed. It may be more profitable for him to employ only those already on the payroll at the wages they receive than to add more labor, pay higher wages generally, and do a larger volume of business.[1]

Thus the economic theorists speak in terms of a tendency; they recognize the element of friction in a dynamic situation.[2] Some attach very much more importance to friction than do others. In the opinion of the authors it is of greater importance than has generally been indicated in the literature. Or, put in other words, the demand for labor is not so effective in safeguarding the worker's interest in wages as many of the economic theorists contend.

In a boom period, when prices are rising and profits in prospect are good, business is very active and bidding for labor generally becomes keen. It may develop even to the point of stealing help. At such times

---

[1] See Sumner H. Slichter, *Modern Economic Society* (1931), Chap. 24.

[2] Usually not all the assumptions accompanying the productivity theory are explicitly stated and substantiated. With regard to these, see vol. 1, Chap. IV, of this treatise and Paul H. Douglas, *op. cit.*, pp. 339–340. Douglas's statement merits quoting at length. He says: "Let us now, however, face the fact that in real life the conditions of perfect and pure competition are seldom, if ever, fully met. At least two sets of conditions are presupposed. The first set exists where there are (1) an almost infinite number of producers of a commodity, so that changes in the output of any one unit have no effect on the price of the article, causing the demand curve for the products of that establishment, therefore, to have infinite elasticity—this is an example of perfect competition among sellers—and (2) an almost infinite number of buyers of labour power, so that changes in the amount of labour power purchased by any one enterprise will have no effect on the supply price of labour. The supply price of labour for any one establishment will, therefore, under these conditions have an infinite elasticity. This is perfect competition between buyers.

"The second set of conditions which are essential for completely pure competition are the following: (1) There is free and complete competition among the employers for labour. (2) There is free and complete competition among wage earners for work. (3) Capital is mobile and can be transferred from industry to industry and from place to place. (4) Labour is mobile and can be transferred from industry to industry and from place to place. (5) Either all labour is employed or the only cause for the unemployment of labour is a wage in excess of the marginal productivity of labour. (6) Either all capital is employed or the only cause for the unemployment of capital is an interest rate in excess of the marginal productivity of capital. (7) The employers and entrepreneurs—whether consciously or unconsciously—are able to measure the marginal contributions of labour and capital, and govern their payments for wages and interest accordingly. (8) The bargaining powers of labour are equal to those of the owners of capital and those of the entrepreneurs. To the degree that these assumptions do not describe the facts of real life, the conclusions which have thus far been drawn from the deduction aspects of the productivity theory require serious qualifications."

These assumptions have been noted and discussed in vol. I, Chap. IV. Our discussion in the present chapter bears on the more important of them.

rates of pay advance rapidly.[1] But in more "normal times," though
progress is then being made and most workers are finding employment,
wage advances are hesitantly made, and there is more or less room for
underpayment, even for a considerable degree of exploitation; for there
are groups with limited mobility, and new accessions to the labor supply
and displaced workers are more or less eagerly seeking employment on
such terms as their limited individual bargaining ability will secure for
them. It may then well be, especially in the case of women workers,
that there are no well-defined standards of wages in certain industries and
in many localities. For long periods labor tends to be absorbed into the
industry or locality with limited relation to wages paid elsewhere. In
such cases wages depend largely upon the policies of the employers—as
so many experienced investigators have found when investigating the
wages of women in concrete situations. So it has been most of the time
in the needle trades in the absence of collective bargaining. Coal mining
provides another illustration.

Not only are there important limitations upon mobility as between
localities and plants.[2] The piecework system, so important in many
industries, also interferes more or less in the development of a wage rate
structure such as most price theories assume is rather readily approached.
While much has been done by management to adjust piece rates for
operations requiring different skills and training and for work of different
qualities and requiring different amounts of effort, such standardization
has not been made in desirable degree in many cases. The maladjustment is still greater among competitive plants, not only in different but
also in the same localities. The piece-rate structure is frequently accompanied by much unfairness because of incidents in hiring and separations,
differences in quality, machinery, speed, and the limited knowledge
possessed by the workers of the differences in opportunity to earn in
different plants. Beyond this there may be important differences in
charges exacted by management for this and that, such as materials,
equipment, and accessories. These differences are not at all closely
reflected in piece rates. A more or less scientific standardization of piece
rates produces a substantially different wage-rate structure.

Again, the economic theorist, proceeding from competitive assumptions, takes too little cognizance of the presence of a monopolistic element

---

[1] Nevertheless they ordinarily do not advance as rapidly as prices, the cost of living, and
profits.

[2] Of course the mobility of labor would in the course of time be substantially increased
by a very efficient system of labor exchanges. Yet, because of family, church, and other
ties, home ownership in many cases, uncertainties connected with a new environment and a
new job, the costs incidental to moving, uncertainty as to support when "evil times" come,
and other things, labor cannot well be made sufficiently mobile to alter in any large measure
the statements herein made.

in the demand for labor.[1] An employer, or a group of employers acting
in concert or just individually fearing to create problems, may dominate
the employment situation in a community. So it was in the mining
of anthracite coal between the middle seventies and the turn of the
century. Wages were pegged; payment for timbering and "dead work"
was reduced or eliminated altogether; coerced purchases at company
stores charging high prices and powder sold at a profit of 200 per cent
took the larger part of the wages earned by the miners. Some years ago,
wages in a certain Indiana city depended primarily upon wages paid by a
large manufacturer of harvester machinery, and the wages paid there
had no immediate and ascertainable relationship to wages paid in other
localities or in other harvester plants except in times of labor shortage
in the Middle West. In an Illinois city the numerous manufacturers
have had a common labor policy, including wages, and have been successful in maintaining it. It is not surprising to have common wage rates
in packing towns resulting from concerted action and to find that wages in
non-packing plants round about are the same, or a few cents per hour
more when it becomes necessary to entice workers away from the gates
of the largest firms. Former wages in steel towns are in point. And how
many instances are there in which, as a result of association vote, wages
are fixed in terms of maxima, as in the case of an important industry
in Chicago, where some years ago a maximum wage for women was fixed
at the same figure as the minimum set by the arbitrator in the men's
clothing industry and the maximum for skilled men was fixed at 68 cents
per hour? Similar cases are on record, as in the publication of newspapers in a large city, where the maximum to be paid unorganized men
in a certain occupation was for some years together, including years of
rising prices and wages, $18 per week. How many such instances there
are no one can know, but there is good reason to believe that they are not
so highly exceptional as the uninitiated think and that they have significance in the real world of employment. But, of course, it is true
that, while imperfect, a competition for labor exists. And, of course,
the elements of truth in the productivity theory of wages, as set forth
elsewhere in this treatise,[2] are too real and powerful to be ignored; they
describe a "portion of reality." The point is that the element of friction,
as the theorist regards it, is of considerable significance in connection with
wages, where the operation of market forces is more likely to conserve
the workers' welfare than it is to conserve their interest in hours and
working conditions.

Other aspects of our subject remain to be discussed. For the most
part what has been said bears upon the need of organization for labor's
defense against low wages, long hours, and bad working conditions. But

[1] See vol. I of this series, pp. 191–195.
[2] See vol. I, Chap. IV.

trade unions are not primarily on the defensive against substandard wages, hours, and working conditions; most frequently they are on the offensive to secure something better than they or their fellows round about them have had or have. With what results? The question is best answered in a discussion running as far as possible in concrete terms. Some concluding observations on the control of wages may then be added.

Some of the Economic Effects of Collective Bargaining

By means of concerted action trade unions, as a rule, seek not only to protect the type of living and the wage rates they have attained, but also to obtain positive advances in wages. In this they are generally more or less successful, at least for the time being, because of the weight of arguments advanced[1] and the power of the strike and the boycott to which recourse may be made. The changes effected may be quite moderate; in some trades and industries, however, very substantial gains are secured. In the men's clothing industry, for example, aided by the curbing of the immigrant inflow and by a favorable market situation, the Amalgamated Clothing Workers were successful during and immediately following the First World War in obtaining high wages in what had been a sweated trade. The full-time weekly earnings of the workers employed by one of the largest manufacturers were in 1920 fully 217 per cent higher for men and 239 per cent higher for women than they had been in 1911, while the hours per week had been reduced from fifty-four to forty-four.[2] These do not represent the total gains, for at the inception of the joint agreement, ending a prolonged strike, hours had been reduced from ten to nine per day without decrease in pay. This concrete case was not untypical of what transpired in the poorly paid needle trades generally as the unions were recognized and functioned in an unusually favorable situation. The story of coal is known to the well-informed reader; with unionization and prosperous times wages and earnings of miners increased from a subsistence to a high level. In the skilled and better paid trades the gains have generally been less, but a study of concrete cases leaves no one in doubt as to the power of unions, each in turn, to secure increases in wages.

It must be pointed out also that the gains realized in the shorter workday and work week by union action have been equally and possibly more substantial. Increases in wages have been accompanied by reductions in hours and payment for overtime at penal rates—time-and-a-quarter, time-and-a-half, etc. Moreover, these more obvious things have been accompanied by the acceptance of working rules that in some

---

[1] For types of argument employed see Chap. IX.
[2] The cost of living had scarcely more than doubled.

cases are more significant than increases in wages and reductions in hours. In our next two chapters this aspect of the subject will be developed incidental to a discussion of union policies. In this chapter we discuss collective action and wages with only such references to other matters as a dynamic situation makes necessary.

For the purposes of our analysis it is to be pointed out, finally, that while an effort to equalize and standardize wages and hours in the market may not be made in the first instance, it is likely to appear sooner or later in a unionized trade. Indeed, in many instances the standardization of wages on the basis of the standards already observed by some of the employers is the primary objective. Obviously the problem presented to employers and some of the results flowing from union action differ according as the changes are a percentage of existing wages or so many cents per hour or dollars per week added to them, or whether the changes made call only for the application of minimum piece rates or wages per hour, day, or week. In the one case the payrolls of all the employers concerned would be affected in substantially equal measure. In the other case, this would not be true because ordinarily the wages that have been paid have differed substantially as between companies, especially for certain classes of labor. Indeed, the better employers may in such cases have to change few wage rates in order to meet the requirements of the minima fixed.

If it may be accepted as fact that unions in their concrete situations secure higher wages per unit of time than would be forthcoming without concerted action, the question arises, how does this affect labor cost and total cost of producing goods or providing a service?[1] It is only because of effects upon such costs that the businessman has an economic, as against a sentimental, interest to concern himself about unionism.

Perhaps the first thought will be that any increase in the rate of pay per hour is directly and fully reflected in increased labor costs and in increased total costs. Employers, confronted by a demand for an increase or making a demand for a reduction, are likely to assert that such a relationship is a fact. The union leader, on the other hand, will assert that it is not necessarily so, and possibly that an increase in wages will not be accompanied by any increase in total costs that will create a problem in marketing the product. The fact is that, in a dynamic situation, many factors may enter to offset the effect of an increase in wage rates upon labor costs; and the same is true of the effect of an increased labor cost upon total cost. What will happen when concerted action effects a change in wage rates depends upon a variety of conditions, as the following summary analysis will attempt to show.

---

[1] Of course the general analysis applies equally well to most changes wrought as well as to wages.

Of considerable importance is the fact that an increase in wage rates may lead the employer, and especially the employer who has been paying relatively poor wages, to select his workers more carefully and employ them with less waste of time; a high (time) wage does not necessarily mean expensive labor.   Then, too, when the union comes in the turnover of labor is generally reduced to a fraction of what it has been; the cost of acquiring new workers and of training them and the losses from interrupted operation due to unbalanced sections are reduced; there are gains because more of the workers have become adapted to the situation, adjusted to the work, and more experienced in the operations to be performed.   Generally the cost of supervision is also reduced.[1]   Again, the union may cooperate in introducing or extending piecework where all previous attempts have been unsuccessful, as in a Chicago instance. Here, in spite of the dilution of the labor supply during a labor shortage, the firm found that, after piecework had been introduced with the cooperation of the union, the output of suits and overcoats per worker in a given unit of time increased 60 per cent in one shop, 40 per cent in a second, and 20 per cent in a third.[2]   And if there is union-management cooperation, as in the Baltimore and Ohio, the Northwestern, and the Chicago, Milwaukee and St. Paul railway shops, efficiency may be stimulated as well as various economies effected.   Stabilization of employment and other labor gains have promoted morale and built up personal qualities and attitudes that have found expression in more and better work as well as in cooperation in reducing waste in its various forms.[3]

But, on the other hand, the union shop may be accompanied by enhanced labor costs exceeding any increase in wage rates obtained. Possibly management loses adequate control over hiring, layoff, and discharge.   Vacancies may be filled by the union upon requisition filed by the employer; possibly the force is to be reduced not by laying off or discharging the least efficient and least tractable, but by laying off those last hired.   Or, there may be a requirement of equal distribution of work during the slack season, perhaps accompanied by some administrative inconvenience, some loss of efficiency due to transfers of workers to tasks involving change in operations, and a tendency for the better and more ambitious workers to leave the trade and for the less efficient to remain.

[1] One large clothing firm says that in its experience it is one-fifth of what it was twenty years ago, in open-shop days.

[2] Of course this 60 per cent gain is exceptional; ordinarily piecework is accompanied by an increase in output of 20 to 30 per cent.   It should be said that, in this concrete case, a part of the saving was in labor, a part in overhead costs.

[3] For an excellent account of union-management cooperation, see Louis Aubrey Wood, *Union-management Cooperation on the Railroads* (1931).   A small western railway company substituted a union for a company union shop; in spite of some increase in wages involved, it saved $60,000 in repair work the first year.

Discharge may be for cause only or for specified causes, making it difficult to weed out the less desirable. Perhaps with security of tenure, week workers will apply themselves less carefully when there is a shortage of work in order to avoid layoffs.[1] More frequently than they cooperate in the extension of piecework unions oppose it; seldom are bonus systems tolerated in the organized trades. The presence of the union may be accompanied by bad morale, owing to failure to realize all its objectives, a militant attitude on the part of the workers accompanying a strong feeling of solidarity, or the spread of "cockiness." Limitations may be placed directly or indirectly upon the amount of work that one may do in a given time, or upon details of operation, such as the height of lays or the piling of mixed fabrics in the cutting room of the clothing firm. Helpers may be forced out, the number of apprentices limited, and limitations placed upon the subdivision of work in the union shop. The introduction of new types of machinery and of more economical processes may also be restricted.[2]

Thus, there are differences between the conditions obtaining in union and nonunion shops as well as between union and nonunion workers such as to make any conclusions as to labor costs based upon a comparison of wage rates quite insecure. The effect of higher wages accompanying unionization of the workers must be studied in concrete situations, and the results differ widely from one case to another. In one extreme case, as a result of union cooperation in introducing piecework, reducing the turnover of labor, and maintaining discipline, the wage advances were more than offset and the labor cost of manufacturing a suit of clothes reduced approximately 10 per cent though the earnings of the workers more than doubled. In other known cases, even in the same industry, the labor cost increased more than would be indicated by the increases in wages and reductions in hours. But most frequently an increase in wages on a time basis and almost always an increase in wages on a piece basis means some increase in labor cost. Such must be the conclusion of the student whose investigations of concrete cases are of necessity limited to the short run. Perhaps the long-run effects may differ somewhat because of the favorable effect of higher wages on efficiency.

Turning to the question of total cost, it may be, as stated above, that increased labor cost will be offset in part or in its entirety by savings effected in other costs. Possibly with labor made more expensive, less of it and more of capital will be employed, total cost not being increased

---

[1] For example, in the men's clothing industry in Chicago the cutters rather generally in 1921 limited their output in order to avoid layoffs under the "equal division of work" provision of the agreement. Limitation had been practiced in preunion days also. Even after production standards were introduced, some cutting forces continued to limit output when work was slack and accepted individual wage reductions as the penalty.

[2] These matters are discussed at some length in Chaps. IX and X of this volume.

as much as it otherwise would have been—and the amount of employment reduced. With the possibility of paying low wages eliminated, management may be "tightened up" generally. With wages standardized and increased, a problem is presented to weak management. If it is not solved, the firm is sooner or later forced to the wall and production concentrated in the hands of the more efficient plants. But the mortality of firms with unionization is not so great as one might expect, for in the real world necessity is frequently the mother of invention. Waste in the layout of the shop or in the flow of work may be reduced, with consequent saving in overhead, or the purchasing department may be more efficiently conducted or the marketing organization improved. Low wages and long hours may be a tax, higher wages and shorter hours a premium upon efficiency of organization and management.[1]

It must be pointed out that the possibility of offsetting increases in labor costs depends to a considerable extent upon the relative importance of labor costs in total costs. Labor costs may run as low as 5 per cent in some or as high as 60 per cent in other industries. Obviously it would be a much greater problem to offset a 10 or 20 per cent increase in an item amounting to 50 per cent of total cost than in one amounting to 10 or 25 per cent. It may be noted, also, that in many service industries the opportunities for savings are less than in most branches of manufacture— in terms of which we are more or less accustomed to think. For these reasons it is as dangerous to generalize about the possibility of offsetting an increase in labor costs and of keeping total costs down as it is erroneous to assume that other things remain equal, that they do not undergo change.

Thus only the most intensive and extensive investigation would establish the relation between wages increased by union appeal and pressure and labor cost and total cost of producing a commodity or of providing a service. And certainly such investigation would yield diverse results. This is true where higher union standards replace lower non-union standards. It may in a measure be true also where higher standards are introduced in an already unionized establishment or industry, for, while distinct limitations upon capacity for adjustment appear,

[1] In this connection, see J. W. F. Rowe's discussion in his *Wages in Practice and Theory* (1928), Chaps. 10, 11, and 12. It is his thesis that management in England requires pressure if it is to interest itself to a desirable degree in efficiency and that unionism supplies this pressure. He of course recognizes that unions frequently have policies and practices which militate against efficiency and that, by applying too much pressure, they may discourage investment and enterprise. He suggests that what is needed is for unions generally, and at all times, to use their power to fix wages slightly above the marginal value of labor. By following such a policy, as well as by standardization and prevention of exploitation, unions can increase wages. Though the profit motive is keener and enterprise more vigorous in the United States than in England, the thesis is essentially sound for this country also.

seldom do other things remain the same. Nevertheless, it is true that unionization most frequently means some increase in labor costs and in total costs as well, and sometimes the increase is a relatively large one. It is generally true that it costs more to mine coal, to manufacture clothing, to distribute milk, to provide janitor service, to construct buildings, and to conduct a barbershop or a restaurant or a laundry under union than under nonunion conditions.

If this is true—where and when this is true—the question arises, who loses what organized labor gains in wages and working conditions? Do higher costs spell higher prices paid by consumers of the product or service, or do they come out of profits? In either event, and especially in the second, what is the effect on business enterprise and the volume of employment for union men? And this suggests the further question as to the limits upon increases in wages and the permanency of any increase that adds to costs. Is increased cost likely to set forces at work that decrease the volume of employment and thus limit the effectiveness of union effort as regard wages?

It is frequently said by ill-informed persons that all gains in wages are reflected in increased costs and that the increased costs are carried forward through higher prices and the consumers of the commodity or service pay the bill. In other words, any increase in wages secured through trade-union action is, through enhancement of prices, generally diffused throughout the community of consumers. Or it may be thoughtlessly said that what is gained by labor in wage rates is lost by labor in higher prices. Were it all so simple as this employers would react less than they do when confronted by wage demands; if wages bills were shifted more or less automatically through prices, employers would not worry at all about them except in so far as the quantities purchased by consumers at high prices would be reduced—this varying with the elasticity of demand—and the volume of their business curtailed.

But in such statements, noted because they are so frequently made, there are important errors. First, there is not always an increase in labor cost; if there is nothing to be passed on through higher prices, no problem arises. Secondly, and more frequently, there may be no increase in total cost, for in a dynamic situation increased labor costs may be offset by paring down other costs. Thirdly, there is error in thinking that when there is increased total cost and correspondingly increased prices, labor loses through higher prices all that it gains through a larger pay envelope. For barbers do not spend all their income on haircuts, laundry workers do not lose all their wage gains when paying their laundry bills, building tradesmen do not lose all their wage gains because they may pay higher rents for the houses or apartments they occupy. Organized worker groups and consumer groups are not identical. The consumers of a product or service may be workers in general, or professional people of all types, or businessmen, or retired persons living on pensions or charity or income drawn from investments of some kind or other. In short, an increase in prices may cut into incomes of various sorts—wages, profits, and returns from property. Price increases resulting from wage increases may, and frequently do, rest in large part on incomes from other sources than wages.

But what about this passing on of any increase in total cost through higher prices paid by consumers, whoever they may be in the concrete situation? Is it true that it is passed on and that consumers collectively pay the bill? The answer is that the increase will or will not be reflected in prices according to the circumstances involved in the concrete case. Moreover the short-run may be substantially different from the long-run effects. It is possible here to point out only some of the more important factors involved, such as the presence or absence of rate control by public authority, the extent of organization with reference to the area of the market, the nature of the market, the state of business, and the elasticity of the demand for the product or service. Incidental to answering the questions put, observations may be made on other matters of importance.

In the short run it makes a difference whether the industry under consideration is or is not regulated in respect to prices and service. The railways and other public utilities are nowadays very generally closely regulated with the result that it is rather difficult to shift any increase in cost due to increases in wages, to increased cost of supplies and materials, or to increased taxes. Though it may be offset by economies effected, any additional burden will remain where it is placed unless it is shifted through a change in the service or through a change in rates. But a change in rates requires time and may be disallowed by the regulatory authority unless the necessity for relief is clear. Perhaps this is only less important than fear of strikes in explaining the attitude of some of the outstanding public-utility companies toward labor unions. It was only natural that American railways at one time strongly advocated combining the function of arbitration and that of rate control in the Interstate Commerce Commission in order that questions of wages and rates would be considered together.

When we pass to industries the prices of whose products are not authoritatively controlled, the most important single condition is whether effective labor organization is or is not coextensive with the market area. If labor in the building trades of Chicago is generally organized and seeks and secures increases in wages, the fact is almost always quickly and fully registered in the contractors' prices and in the rents tenants must pay for housing,[1] for the market is local and outside competition in building construction is not present in any large measure; with most construction

---

[1] If rents cannot be satisfactorily readjusted as costs increase, investment becomes unattractive.

work let to the lowest bidder among qualified contractors and the contractors submitting bids on the basis of labor and materials costs—with margin added—the industry is on a cost-plus basis; with the growth of urban population and the expansion of business, additional housing is required; the demand is relatively inelastic; the consumers are unorganized and unrepresented in the situation. Hence, except in time of depression, the traffic will bear much in wages and labor cost. Of course high wages are attractive to young persons coming into the labor supply, but the building-trades unions can and usually do protect their position by apprentice rules, relatively high initiation fees, and, possibly, other restrictive devices.[1]

The story of bituminous coal has been very different in certain respects. When the miners revolted in the Central Competitive District (Illinois, Indiana, Ohio, western Pennsylvania, and, at times, a part of the territory to the south) and succeeded in securing an agreement in 1898, piece rates for mining and loading were advanced, and a part of the day wages increased and standardized in specific sums for the entire district, the company store was outlawed by requiring payment in cash, the weighing of coal was checked at the tipple, payment on favorable terms was secured for all "dead work" (shoveling rock, dirt, etc.), and charges for powder and smithing were brought under control. With setbacks now and then, the regime lasted for a generation. From time to time wage increases were made, these being determined under more or less union pressure. Piece rates after 1920, when averaged, were more than two and a half times what they had been under the agreement of 1898, while the day wages of drivers, motormen, trackmen, trappers, and inside laborers were roughly four times what they had been.[2] These increases greatly exceeded the increase in the cost of living—as they should have[3] in view of the inadequacy of miners' wages previous to 1898

[1] Local markets make it possible for the traffic to bear much in wages of janitors, laundry workers, milk-wagon drivers, and cleaners and dyers. The main problem is to build up effective organizations, which the janitors, milk distributors, and cleaners and dyers have succeeded in doing in Chicago. The organizations have succeeded in extracting high wages, as tested by what comparable labor receives in wages. High prices charged by barbers have been more than shaves would bear, but the patronage of women has made good the loss in employment that would otherwise have been sustained. In this policy of high wages and high prices the master cleaners and the unions overreached themselves, however, for many patrons sent their work out of town rather than pay what they regarded as "extortionate" prices. In this case a readjustment has been made in prices and in labor costs in view of what the traffic would bear. Even so, there is a problem of preventing nonunion competition from developing in the Chicago area, and undermining the control set up.

[2] See *Report of the United States Coal Commission* (1925), Pt. III, p. 1057, and Isador Lubin, *Miners' Wages and the Cost of Coal* (1924).

[3] The authors do not pass judgment on the appropriateness of the *actual* increase in real wages realized.

to support anything more than the most sordid living and in view of the great progress made in the United States since 1898 and the increase in national income. Inevitably labor cost and total cost of producing coal increased. In 1898 and at most other times until about 1921, this increased cost was passed on through higher prices. But, within five years of the renewal of the agreement system in 1898, a factor making for difficulty became evident. This was the premium placed upon mining in West Virginia and other localities where the union did not succeed in keeping the miners effectively organized. The First World War had the effect of stimulating the industry greatly, with the result that for almost twenty years it had excess capacity and upwards of 200,000 more miners than were needed—a part of the excess of workmen being due to the increased output of coal per man. Though the union was fairly effective through the War period, it did not remain so. Much of the territory marketing coal in competition with the Pennsylvania, Ohio, Indiana, and Illinois product became or remained nonunion and generally received the protection of the "yellow-dog" contract. Naturally (until the NRA), more and more of the output was derived from the nonunion areas, for, after the War period, wages and labor costs were lower, and most of the time very much lower, there than in the organized territory, where the union insisted upon and succeeded in maintaining wage rates.[1] The majority of union operators in Illinois and other states could not adjust the price of coal to the cost of mining or the cost of mining to the price of coal. This fact, when combined with others that cannot be specifically mentioned here, made it almost inevitable that the interstate agreement should break down and near-chaos develop. Union wages proved to be higher than the traffic would bear in the changed situation and were reduced, drastically in some areas.[2]

As has been stated,[3] the unions in the clothing trades, operating under favorable conditions for a time, succeeded in lifting wages from a sweatshop to a relatively high level. In the manufacture of men's cloth-

---

[1] During the period 1915–1921, Pennsylvania, West Virginia, Kentucky, Alabama, Illinois, Ohio, and Indiana produced 84 per cent of the United States output; in 1929 the percentage was 88. West Virginia's share increased from 16.4 to 26.4 per cent, Kentucky's from 5.9 to 11.6 per cent, Alabama's from 3.3 to 3.4 per cent. On the other hand, Illinois' share decreased from 14.9 to 11.5 per cent, Indiana's from 4.8 to 3.4 per cent, Ohio's from 7.6 to 4.5 per cent, Pennsylvania's from 31.1 to 27.2 per cent. The shifting of source of supply from union to nonunion areas was much greater than these figures would indicate, for much of Pennsylvania always remained unorganized and organization in Ohio was badly disrupted several years ago.

[2] After the advent of NRA, the union was able to extend its membership and agreements to cover nearly the entire industry and the previous wage differentials were greatly reduced. If it can maintain itself in these formerly nonunion areas, the chances of stability in the industry are greatly improved. This is of course an object of the present federal legislation on coal.

[3] *Supra*, p. 370.

ing, at least, there was no corresponding increase in labor cost or total cost, for much waste was eliminated and efficiency increased. Nevertheless, both labor costs and total costs increased in the experience of most manufacturers. In boom times it was not difficult to readjust prices and shift the burden to the consumers. That was not true, however, after 1921. Cheap clothing would not bear high prices; because of the strain they were under, many manufacturers of "tropicals" and low-quality woolens, as well as manufacturers of children's clothing, sought to operate nonunion shops in the organized cities or in other places. A ready supply of green or slightly experienced labor was available at relatively low wages. The industry therefore showed a tendency to become relocated and widely diffused and it was necessary for the Amalgamated to stress organization of small shops in the old centers and of the industry as it developed in Philadelphia, Cincinnati, Los Angeles, and elsewhere. Its organization work has been unusually efficient and successful, but it did not succeed to the extent that it was possible for the typical union manufacturer to sell his product at profitable prices. This was true even before depression developed in 1930.[1] Hence it became necessary for the Union to give unusual attention to the cost of manufacture under union conditions and to make concessions, while attempting to organize the nonunion shops.

The Amalgamated Clothing Workers began in 1939 to apply a new policy in an effort to stabilize the men's clothing industry. This policy is to establish a uniform labor cost for each of the six grades into which clothing is classified. Thus the labor cost on a grade A suit will be uniform whether produced in New York, Philadelphia, Rochester, Cincinnati, or elsewhere. Obviously, while placing a premium on efficiency of management and other factors affecting costs, this stabilization device changes the terms of competition between plants in different areas, and to an extent those between plants in the same area, from what they have been.

That the success of such a policy is dependent upon an effective organization such as the Amalgamated enjoys is shown by the full-fashioned-hosiery industry. During the 1920's there was extensive organization in the Philadelphia area, in which, along with New Jersey and the Middle West, the industry then centered. The demand for the product was then expanding so rapidly that, though mill capacity increased greatly, a ready market at favorable prices was at hand. The Union employed the "army game," obtaining in wages, hours, and conditions what the traffic would bear. And it would bear much. Good

---

[1] The NRA was of temporary assistance to the Union in its effort to keep down cost differentials between union and nonunion shops, but after the *Schechter* decision the Amalgamated Clothing Workers was again forced to rely largely upon its own resources. Of course some assistance is now being received from the Fair Labor Standards Act.

knitters—skilled workers—frequently received in wages $125 or more per week. When depression appeared and lasted on during the 1930's, however, the case was different. Reduced demand and the appearance of new mills, especially in the South, to which the industry has been migrating in search of lower costs, jeopardized jobs, caused unemployment and part-time work, and, between 1929 and 1933, necessitated in union mills reduction in wage rates of as much as 60 per cent. Moreover, for the most part the union mills continued to operate with the old equipment, while the new ones, located increasingly in the South, had the advantage of new types of machinery.

This situation caused the Union to realize that stubborn facts must be faced if it was to maintain a position in the industry and if its members were to have employment. It was realized that wage rates must provide employment, profits, and a flow of new and modern equipment to union mills. Hence the Union and the manufacturers dealing with it adopted a policy of uniform labor costs in all union mills in all areas throughout the country and this policy was more or less systematically applied. But it did not solve the problem, because a large part of the industry remained nonunion and usually this part enjoyed the advantages of both lower labor costs and better equipment. Therefore a new wage policy was adopted, that being observed under the present three-year national agreement. Not only are union wages being adjusted to what the traffic will bear in labor costs, but also so adjusted as to enable mills presenting acceptable plans to modernize their plants. This is designed to give the members of the Union opportunity for employment where they live, not only for the present but in the years to come.[1]

Space limitations preclude the presentation of further detail bearing upon the conditions under which increased costs per unit of product due to increased labor costs may be shifted to the consumers. When they are not so shifted, they come out of profits and may impair the capital account and reduce the value of fixed property, such as the coal mine. Enterprise and capital under such conditions seek other outlets; the unprofitable industry wanes and with it the volume of employment provided by it. In so far as capital is mobile, and most of it is in the long run, it will seek the most attractive investment. In the long run it will demand a "fair return" from the unionized industry or seek investment elsewhere, or, possibly, not be invested at all.

If this partial analysis is correct, certain things are obvious:

1. If the union regime in an industry does not adversely affect costs, it presents no economic problem. If, however, there is increased cost,

---

[1] Some of the facts relating to the hosiery industry have been drawn from the chapter by Professor George Taylor of the University of Pennsylvania in *How Collective Bargaining Works* (Twentieth Century Fund, 1942). *Cf.* Gladys L. Palmer, *Union Tactics and Economic Change* (1932), Chap. 5, especially pp. 99–103.

there is a problem of price or/and profit, accompanied perhaps by other problems. Hence the importance of union-management cooperation and regard for efficiency.[1]

2. Higher costs may or may not be charged up to the consumer through higher prices. In so far as higher wages per unit of time or product are not absorbed or offset but are passed on through higher prices, the real incomes of consumers, whether workers or others in the population, are diminished. Most unions increase the cost of living. There is, of course, no implication that this is necessarily wrong. It is just a fact. But the fact gives point to the observation that unions should "have a heart" and give consideration to the question whether the needs of consumers more needy than the unionists are being or will be sacrificed.[2]

3. When higher costs are not shifted to the consumers, they come out of profits and this produces strain. Though under collective bargaining wages, hours, and working conditions are more or less stabilized for the period covered by the agreement, attempts are made to break down the union when concessions are not readily forthcoming. Moreover, capital tends to be shifted to better investments or to other localities and the organized industry wanes.

4. When union labor costs are substantially out of line with nonunion labor costs the nonunion shop tends to develop and to present an organization problem.

5. It is rather probable that higher wage rates secured by union action, either because they depress the organized industry due to lack of acceptable profit or because they are accompanied by enhanced prices adversely affecting sales, will reduce the volume of employment for the union men. The development of nonunion plants to share the market may further adversely affect the volume of work for them. Again, in the absence of restrictive devices, more workers may be attracted to the union and the well-paid occupation, and this, combined with the tendency for union members to remain in the organized trade paying relatively high wage rates, may result in excessive numbers and irregular employment, as in the bituminous coal industry during the 1920's. High wage rates do not necessarily mean fat pay envelopes. The quantity of labor used in a trade will vary with its price. In the sense that its price and the amount bought are determined by supply and demand factors, labor is a commodity. A restrictive union may be quite content with

---

[1] With some experience in industry most unions develop more or less appreciation of efficiency, unless they must remain on a fighting basis because of the desire of employers to displace or weaken them. Unfortunately most American unions, unlike the British, have operated under such conditions. It is only after the life of the union is no longer threatened that it can be cooperative.

[2] *Cf.* Walton H. Hamilton and Stacy May, *The Control of Wages* (1923), Chap. 7.

high wages and regular employment for a limited number, but an open union with low dues must heed what the traffic will bear in wages. The final outcome may be different from the initial effect.

THE EFFECTS OF COLLECTIVE BARGAINING UPON THE WAGES AND EMPLOYMENT OF NONUNIONISTS

Trade unionists generally assert that in securing better wages, hours, and working conditions they are improving the lot of workingmen generally and that the nonunionist and the antiunionist in large measure share the gains. But, as we have seen, the economists of an earlier time were rather generally of the view that the gains of the one were necessarily at the expense of the other. More significant, many of the present-day economists are of the view that as one of their important effects trade unions obtain differentials in wages for their members at the expense of other wage earners. Though explanations may differ, the view with respect to the consequence is pretty much the same. The questions therefore arise, what of the relationship between wages in the organized trades and wages in the unorganized trades, and what of the effect of union endeavor on the general level of wages and the distribution of the national income?

Upon analysis it becomes clear that the effect of higher wages secured for some by union effort upon the wages of others is a mixed one, for forces are set in action, some of which have one tendency, others a contrary one. In so far as nonunion men are admitted to and work in organized plants, they commonly reap the full benefit of any improvement secured by union effort,[1] for they work the same hours and receive substantially the wages paid the union men. Moreover, the workers in nonunion plants in an industry with an active unionism may also secure gains, for if the nonunion employers pay too low wages and maintain too long hours the task of union organizers will be made easy. Thus, in the book- and job-printing industry in Chicago the open-shop employers have been careful not to depart too far from union standards.[2] So has it been also in the coal industry except in times of depression and a surplus of labor. But of course this relationship is not so true where the workers, say Negroes or an immigrant group, are difficult to organize or in places far removed from union centers in point of distance and contact. Again, union standards may be extended to the benefit of other workers under government "fair wages" clauses, which have been so conspicuously used in Great Britain and have appeared in the United States in recent years. For fair wages is frequently interpreted as the union rate. And, finally, in the absence of fair wages clauses, the union wage undoubtedly plays a part in determining what is a fair wage

---

[1] Of course this may not be true of security of the job.

[2] See Emily Clark Brown, *Book and Job Printing in Chicago* (1931), pp. 216–221.

for workers hired in nonunion establishments in the partly organized localities.

But where the closed shop is maintained the nonunion workman is excluded, and under the preferential shop he is handicapped in securing and retaining employment. The excluded man must find employment elsewhere. Moreover, the effect of unionism, as we have seen, may be to restrict an industry because of the smaller quantities of its product that will be purchased at higher prices or because of curtailment of profit. Where and when this is so some of those who under other conditions would perhaps have become union members and found employment in the trade must look elsewhere. Thus, in either of these ways nonunion men may be excluded from the organized trade and caused to seek employment in increased numbers in other trades. This of course has the tendency to reduce the wages they and their fellow workers will be able to get.

In still another way the nonunion man will be sacrificed by union activity—once more provided it involves higher costs and higher prices. All workers, union and nonunion, like professional and businessmen, are sacrificed as spenders of their money incomes by any enhancement of prices. Thus the nonunionist may be doubly sacrificed—in employment and wage rate and as a consumer.

At this point, a word may be introduced concerning the oft-made statement that the primary end and result of union endeavor is to secure differential advantages, especially in respect to wages, for union members. Criticism of the standardization of wages is seldom advanced; but there is much criticism of "unjustified differentials." Without question, some unions secure such differentials. Unionism may thus result in an uneconomic distribution and use of a nation's resources. Examples of this are well known, but it should be pointed out that such conditions may exist without unionism and may even be corrected by it. Without control through collective bargaining or through law, sweated wages and sweated industries are not highly exceptional, and they frequently persist indefinitely unless control is exercised. Sweated industries are uneconomic. Attention may be directed to coal in the 1890's, the needle trades, the laundries, and the candy factories. It would appear that collective bargaining has almost as frequently reduced negative differentials by bringing wages in an industry up to an acceptable level as it has resulted in uneconomic differentials. Moreover, in many cases high wages for some occupational groups have been sacrificed in order to increase the wages of lowly paid groups. This practice has been well exemplified in the needle trades and it has been witnessed elsewhere.[1] In any event, the fact of unjustified differentials secured does not necessarily argue against collective bargaining. It argues rather for the

[1] Indeed, it has been of common occurrence in industries where labor has been organized along industrial lines.

industrial union so that craft wages will not be unduly out of line with wages of the unskilled, and for government action to provide needed data and efficient conciliation and arbitration machinery in order that a more appropriate wage-rate structure may be obtained.

Effect of Union Effort on the General Level of Wages[1]

Since the effect of union endeavor on the general level of wages has been touched upon only briefly, further consideration is called for. Union spokesmen frequently, if not generally, assume that complete organization can extend the benefits of unionism to all workers. But could all do with the same result what a limited number of groups can do? Can trade unions effect any substantial change in the distribution of the national income as between wages and the other shares? And, equally important, are they not likely to discourage investment and increase unemployment and consequently reduce the size of the national income?

Years ago, in the case of *Plant v. Woods*,[2] Justice Holmes made the following statement: "I think it pure phantasy to suppose that there is a body of capital of which labor as a whole secures a larger share by that means [*i.e.*, the strike]. The annual product, subject to an infinitesimal deduction for the luxuries of the few, is directed to consumption by the multitude, and is consumed by the multitude, always. Organization and strikes may get a larger share for the members of an organization, but, if they do, they get it at the expense of the less organized and less powerful portion of the laboring mass. They do not create something out of nothing."

Were this taken as a complete statement, which it was not intended to be, it would be incorrect. For, among other things, it neglects the dynamic aspects of the situation, and erroneously identifies the "multitude" with the "wage earners." Do unions add to or subtract from the national income (the total of commodities and services)? Can they alter its sharing out as between workers as a whole and other groups? It is only by enlarging the national income (on a per capita basis) or by altering its sharing out to the advantage of labor that unions could raise the general level of wages.

The exploitation of individuals and groups that undoubtedly occurs can be reduced or eliminated, and the lag between actual and "natural"

---

[1] Among the books which may be consulted to advantage in this connection are: Sumner Slichter, *Modern Economic Society;* Maurice Dobb, *Wages;* Walton H. Hamilton and Stacy May, *The Control of Wages;* J. W. F. Rowe, *Wages in Practice and Theory;* Paul H. Douglas, *The Theory of Wages* (1934); J. R. Hicks, *The Theory of Wages;* Joan Robinson, *Essays in the Theory of Unemployment* (1939); and J. M. Keynes, *General Theory of Employment, Interest, and Money* (1936).

[2] 176 Mass. 492 (1900). Quotation at p. 505.

wages when industrial progress is being made can be reduced or taken up if wages and hours are standardized and appropriately readjusted from time to time. This possibility is important in connection with the total of wages. Moreover, it is possible that, as a result of better levels of living gained or eagerly sought, the growth of population resulting from a high birth rate will be retarded, to the advantage of labor, whose productivity is enhanced with a smaller labor supply.[1] Better living should in turn reflect itself in greater efficiency.

But can the share[2] of the national income paid out in wages be increased at the expense of the "normal" return to property and management and salary payments? There is valid reason for believing this could be done under certain conditions, for what is commonly regarded as the "normal" return to capital and management is not something fixed, but depends to a considerable extent upon what can be had. Within limits, about the usual supply of capital and entrepreneurial ability would probably be forthcoming if their returns were gradually and generally reduced as the result of pressure systematically and effectively applied. There can be little doubt that wages could be slightly increased in this manner also at the expense of "fancy" salaries and bonuses that are conspicuously found though the excess in them constitutes only a very small part of the national income.

There is, however, great difficulty in exercising such pressure successfully in a system of free enterprise and investment. With the mobility of capital the returns in any given country are not independent of possible returns in other countries. Of course, the unsettled condition of international relations and the instability of currencies since the First World War have severely limited the normal movement of capital between countries. Nevertheless the flow of capital has not ceased to be a reality. Moreover, if labor becomes dearer and capital becomes cheaper, capital will be substituted to an extent for labor. With the greater proportion of capital used, the share of the total return going to labor will tend to decrease. Finally, though not inevitably so,[3] the control exercised to increase wages may be such as to require prospect of even more than the usual returns to enterprise and investors as a condition of necessary supply.

Though the distribution of the national income is not fixed and unalterable, under a system of free enterprise there are distinct limitations upon the degree of change that may be effected in it. The possibility of alteration is not nearly so great as the union spokesman ordinarily assumes. Certainly, acting within the limitations of the existing eco-

---

[1] *Cf.* Sumner H. Slichter, *op. cit.*, p. 645.

[2] See vol. I, Chap. III, for detailed factual material on wages and other distributive shares.

[3] See *supra*, pp. 375–377.

nomic organization, there are more promising ways of raising the general wage level and the level of living than by increasing wage rates through collective bargaining. One of these ways is to increase the national income out of which workers, management, and investors secure their returns; another is to change the system under which public revenues are obtained and the uses to which these revenues are put.

The general level of wages depends primarily upon the value product of labor. The great increase in wages witnessed during the last generation or century is explained chiefly in this way. And, as in the past, under our economic organization, so in the future: Great strides have been made in solving the problems of production, but no doubt the opportunities lying on beyond are equally great. For the most part, to embrace these opportunities is the responsibility of management. Nevertheless, it is to an extent a responsibility of labor also. What role have the unions played in this connection? What contributions might unions make?

In our earlier discussion of wages and costs we have noted some of the gains in production that may accompany unionization. Some of these are the reduced turnover of labor, the efficiency resulting from apprentice training that employers have been all too prone to neglect, here and there the extension of piecework, and the elimination of waste in certain forms. Then, too, necessity resulting from union pressure has frequently been a spur to better management and better plant organization and routine. Finally, there have been the substantial gains realized from union-management cooperation in certain cases in the United States, to an extent in Germany in years past, and perhaps more extensively in Great Britain. Waste in various forms has been eliminated and efficiency encouraged.[1]

Nevertheless, there is the generally current opinion that unions are more of a hindrance than a help in industry and that they frequently stand in the way of progress. Whether this opinion is correct or false, whether on the whole unions make for or retard industrial advance, there have been and are numerous union practices that involve waste and inefficiency. These practices and the policies out of which they develop will be dealt with in permissible detail in the next two chapters. At this point it suffices to note that, while they may be justified on certain grounds, the frequent opposition of unions to piecework and their rather general opposition to bonus systems may reduce the efficiency of labor, at any rate in the short run. So may the greater security of tenure of jobs accompanying unionization and also the psychology of the organized group. Rather frequently there are formal or informal limitations upon

[1] See Louis Aubrey Wood, op. cit. For a brief account of the Mond Conferences in Great Britain, see B. H. Selekman, British Industry Today (1929), Chap. 8. See also J. W. F. Rowe, op. cit.

the day's work. These may protect against exploitation of the workers and shortening of their industrial lives—with resultant sacrifice of their contributions in the longer run. But, on the other hand, unions may enforce custom as regards output or the manning of machines and processes when the effort required has been reduced, say by technical or organizational change. Then, too, there are cases of make-work, where no question of strain or health arises. Limitations upon the number of apprentices and the work they may do, whatever the long-run results of apprentice training, limitations upon the employment of handymen and improvers, limitations upon the subdivision of work and changes in machinery and processes, likewise limitations upon hiring and discharge may and frequently do stand in the way of the most productive allocation of labor and its most efficient use. And, of course, the hours of work may be shortened at the expense of production in the longer as well as in the shorter run, while the mobility of labor, if not of industry, is reduced when unionism enters or becomes general.

Of course what has been said above implies no judgment as to the soundness or unsoundness of most of the union policies and practices involved, for these must be considered from different points of view and in relation to the concrete situations in which they find place. In the chapters immediately following they will receive further consideration and some evaluation.

Attention may again be called to the influence of trade unionism on the size of the national income through its effect on the allocation of resources. In so far as trade-union activity eliminates sweating, its results are beneficial, even if workers are forced out of the hitherto sweated trades and industries; the national income is increased by their transference to other industries. Similarly beneficial is the reduction of unjustified wage differentials between occupational groups within an industry. On the other hand, the creation of uneconomic wage differentials reduces the national income. And the general maintenance of unduly high wages also decreases its size by forcing workers (and capital) into unemployment.

Reference has been made elsewhere in this series to the fact that several per cent of the worker's income takes the form of free service, in part through government provision.[1] With the extension and enrichment of the public-school system, with the provision of public libraries, public parks, and much else, this form of income has measurably increased with the passing of time. Nevertheless, as was emphasized in the *New Social Order* (a British Reconstruction Program), it would be possible for free or partly-paid-for government service to be further, and materially, extended to the benefit of the common people. More adequate social

---

[1] *Cf.* vol. I, Chap. II, p. 134.

insurance,[1] with only a part of the cost covered by worker contributions, good housing provided under a systematic program, more and better parks and playgrounds, free textbooks, are only a few of the things that might be introduced or more emphasized than they have been in bringing warmth and opportunity to the workers' families.[2] The use of more of the public funds in the ways suggested, and the use of less on armaments and as salaries of those professional politicans who give no equivalent for the moneys they receive, would be of distinct assistance in improving the standard of living, particularly of the underprivileged.

And, on the other hand, by changing the public revenue system a share of the burden, which certainly in the United States has rested in undue amount upon them, could be lifted from the shoulders of the workers and placed upon the shoulders of others with more ability to contribute to the public purse.[3] Certainly protective tariffs, such as those which have been in effect in this country, add to the cost of living in great disproportion to the revenues they yield. They are usually an expensive indirect subsidy. Excise taxes or "internal revenue duties" on articles of general consumption rest regressively and unduly burden those of small means. So do poll taxes. It is a notorious fact that the general property tax frequently if not usually works out regressively. General sales taxes, now used to an increasing extent, are highly regressive. Taking the American system of taxation as a whole, it has certainly been regressive and there is no reason for believing that there has been a sufficient readjustment of wages to offset its regressivity. Whatever its effects on saving and production, a system of taxation, progressive as regards incomes out of which taxes are ordinarily paid, combined with a policy of seeking out monopoly profits and discriminating against unearned gains of various kinds, would have the effect of leaving in the pockets of persons of small means much of what is now taken, directly or indirectly, for the support of the public services and for subsidies to various private groups.

[1] See the several chapters in vol. II.

[2] Of course heavy taxation may prove to be a burden on industry and opportunity for employment. Whether it is burdensome or not depends as much upon the types of taxes levied as upon the amount exacted. Moreover, payroll taxes, such as are employed in connection with old-age annuities and unemployment compensation, are likely, in the long run, to rest upon wages as a result of shifting processes. *Cf.* vol. II, Chap. III, pp. 178–182.

[3] *Cf.* Henry C. Simons, *Personal Income Taxation* (1938).

Chapter IX

SOME TRADE-UNION POLICIES AND PRACTICES

From a discussion of the theory of collective bargaining we turn to a consideration of the policies of unions respecting wages, hours, and other details in the employer-worker relation of importance in collective bargaining and union regulation. Among concrete matters, wages are of first concern to most unions. They, therefore, are discussed first.

The Control of Wages: The Standard Rate

Now and then a newly recognized union agrees that wages being paid shall continue without change or that the wage of each of its members shall be advanced, say, 10 per cent, or 5 cents per hour, or in the sum of one or more dollars per week. But usually this is a temporary and short-lived arrangement, for wages must be standardized if hiring rates are to be controlled as vacancies in the force and new jobs are filled and if wages are to be more or less equalized and a more nearly uniform floor in labor costs is to obtain throughout the organized industry. Hence, unions usually seek to control wages through the device Mr. and Mrs. Webb have spoken of as the "Standard Rate,"[1] but which most union men in the United States speak of as "the scale,"[2] for one reason because an agreement usually provides for standard rates in two or more occupations. By the standard rate is meant a rate, occupational and usually local in its application, established by collective bargaining, or, now and then,[3] adopted by the union and observed by employers individually as a condition of securing the services of union men.

The scale usually consists of piece rates or prices for given operations or results, or of rates of wages per hour, day, week, or month, or of a combination of time and piece rates. When a standard rate takes the

---

[1] For the nature and significance of the Standard Rate, see Sidney and Beatrice Webb, *Industrial Democracy* (1920), Pt. II, Chap. 5, and D. A. McCabe, *The Standard Rate*, Johns Hopkins University Studies, Series 30 (1912), pp. 213–453.

[2] The "scale" comprises the one or more standard rates in the concrete case and also hours of work. The worker, however, may speak of the standard rate applicable to him, when on a time basis, as his "scale."

[3] In earlier history, unions frequently voted scales and pledged their members, under penalty, not to accept less. Naturally, if the union was maintained and its members employed, conferences soon followed and the scale was arrived at in conference. Some survivals of the earliest practice have been met with in recent years.

form of a piece rate, it is the rate at which the workers are paid per unit for their output. It differs from the piece rate paid in the nonunion shop in (a) that it is fixed by joint action;[1] (b) that it is usually higher; (c) that it is very likely to be adjusted more accurately to the work to be done;[2] (d) that it is likely to be more stable, because it cannot be changed except by joint action or by violation of the agreement; and (e) that it is frequently defended against indirect reductions such as occur in non-union shops when work requirements are increased or output to be paid for is undermeasured. When, on the other hand, the standard rate takes the form of a time wage, it is a sum per hour, day, week, or month less than which the employer may not pay but more than which he may be permitted to pay the workmen of the group specified or described. There will be one rate for the full-fledged journeymen in the given occupational group, and possibly two or more rates for workmen with different periods of service, another rate for handymen and helpers, still another for common labor, and a special scale for apprentices, whose individual wages will increase during the period of apprenticeship. Beyond this, arrangements may be made under a "permit" system for the remuneration of old and handicapped workers at substandard figures. Thus, under an agreement recently in effect in Chicago, the minimum wage per hour of machinists on the day shift was $1.00; of tool- and die-makers, $1.13; of automatic and hand screw-machine hands, $1.00; of specialists, 72 cents; of helpers, 63 cents; of apprentices, 33, 43, 52, 68, and 76 cents for the first, second, and third years, and for the first and last six months of the fourth year of apprenticeship, respectively. In addition, the agreement provided that "to men receiving over the minimum rate of wages, a corresponding increase shall apply."

The Standard Rate: Criticisms and Problems.—The standard rate on a time basis is frequently the subject of adverse criticism. Most important among these criticisms, the employer may complain that it requires him to pay some workers more than they are worth, and, possibly, others less than they are worth, with the result that the needed premium on individual application and efficiency is removed. The less efficient workers may complain that it handicaps them in securing and retaining employment. The more efficient and faster workers, on the other hand, may complain that the standard rate tends to hold their wages down,

---

[1] In industries long unionized piece rates are almost always set by joint action but in industries newly organized, such as automobiles, rubber, and steel, they are frequently, if not generally, set by management but are subject to revision under the grievance procedure.

[2] In the typical union garment factory, for example, there will be scores and perhaps hundreds of differentials for additional or harder work that find little or no place in the piece rate lists of the typical nonunion plant. There will be extra payment for belts, Norfolk straps, peak lapels, and a great number of variations from the standard garment. These may accumulate into a rather substantial increase in remuneration of the pocket maker, presser, or other operator.

possibly to the minimum; that they could earn higher wages if there was no union or scale.

To the complaint of the employer, the typical union spokesman and, with qualifications, Mr. and Mrs. Webb[1] reply that he is not required to hire or keep in his employ anyone not worth the standard rate, and that he may pay the more efficient as much more than the scale requires as efficiency warrants—in short, that by refusal to hire, by culling out, and by individual bargaining, the employer is able to adjust wages to the different worths of the several workers employed. Obviously, the validity of the answer made depends upon (a) whether the employer is unrestricted in the hiring and discharge of workers; and (b) whether he is really free to grade wages upward from the scale in various amounts. What are the facts in unionized industries?

In unionized industry in the United States the employer is sometimes unfettered in the selection and retention of workers, but perhaps just as frequently he is limited in his action more or less seriously. The stove manufacturer has generally been free to hire union or nonunion molders of his own selection but has been required to pay those hired at least "the scale." He has been free also to lay off or discharge molders except that he has not been permitted to discriminate because of union activity. The same, except for a rather prevalent closed-shop limitation, has been the general rule in the building trades and in many others that might be named. But in the composing room of the newspaper office certain "rights" find expression. The foreman must be a member of the union; each "regular" man is protected in his "situation" against discharge except for a limited number of causes other than reduced production; when a "regular" is absent, his place is filled by a substitute of his selection; when a situation becomes vacant by death, discharge, or quitting, the first qualified "sub" on the office's list is entitled to it. Again, when the composing force is being reduced, those last employed are the first to be laid off. A number of other instances in which seniority right is important in filling positions might be cited. More important are those cases in which the desire to prevent discrimination against union men in general or against individual workers, the desire to give all members work in their turn, and, perhaps, the desire to develop in the minds of the members a greater sense of dependence upon the union, has led to hiring only through the union except when it is unable to fill requisitions. The brewer has requisitioned the union for help and hired the man or men assigned. When in need of a worker, the Chicago clothing manufacturer requisitions the Amalgamated employment exchange, and the worker at the top of the waiting list is sent. Ordinarily, this

[1] See *op. cit.* (1920 imprint), Pt. II, Chap. 5, pp. 281*ff.*

worker must be accepted and given a trial.[1] If retained more than two weeks, he becomes a regular employee, is entitled to share in the work in slack season, and may be discharged only for cause. Similar arrangements are found in the needle trades rather generally, and to an extent in other trades.

As suggested, these rules are in part the result of discrimination practiced by employers against union members in general or against individuals in an effort to weaken the union. Many of them, however, reflect the feeling of brotherhood and the desire for equal opportunity so strong in what has been called the "new unionism" in the needle trades and elsewhere. Moreover, they to an extent reflect an emphasis upon solidarity. It is evident that they are not without reason and that they serve a purpose. It is equally evident that they interfere with the customary rights the employer has exercised in the nonunion shop. The filling of positions from a compulsory waiting list has the effect of returning the less competent temporarily, if not regularly, to industry. Neither the union list nor the list of "subs" carries a guarantee that the best workers available in the market will be hired. At the same time, equal division of work during slack seasons, layoffs in inverse order of hiring, and limitations upon discharge make it difficult for the employer to weed out the less desirable, and possibly the undesirable, on the force. Moreover, it may be added that the great degree of security of tenure that may be felt may itself result in diminished performance. In the building trades, with freedom of discharge as the general rule, output increases when jobs are scarce, partly as a result of the weeding out of the less competent workers, partly because of more strenuous application on the part of workers to make sure of their jobs. At times, undue strain may be involved. In certain other industries, with security of tenure and equal division of work, the performance of workers in slack times may be substantially reduced.

In some cases, the union employer is free by individual bargaining to make an upward adjustment of wages to efficiency and thereby call forth performance, but in other cases he is not. In the building trades, there are generally many men who, because of superior ability, are paid above the minimum. There is little or no objection by the unions to it. Indeed, there are craftsmen who seldom, if ever, accept work at the scale, and there are contractors who employ only superior men at wages above scale in order to secure and keep a good crew. Photoengravers are paid various wages, from the standard rate up; some superior craftsmen employed in newspaper offices may receive almost double the minimum. In sections of the garment industry, to mention only one

---

[1] If, however, the worker sent is obviously unfit to do the work involved, or is intoxicated, or has been discharged by the firm for cause, or has quit his job with the firm when serious charges against him were pending, he need not be accepted and given a trial.

more important industry, the average of wages may be several per cent above the minimum. But in many organized industries there is a distinct tendency for the standard rate to become the actual rate paid; few receive more. This may happen incidental to increases in the minimum, for many employers fail to increase the wages of those who have been paid above the scale, thus reducing previous differentials presumably based upon efficiency. More likely, in some of the trades the employer fears that if some journeymen are paid more than others it will be a cause of dissatisfaction, that pressure will be exerted to secure increases for others, or that the better paid workers will become marked men. And sometimes the uniform or nearly uniform payment is due to union policy that, in the interest of solidarity, may favor uniformity, or that, because of fear of speeding, may frown upon departures from the scale. As Professor McCabe has said, "In general, the sentiment . . . is against a few men receiving more than the others on the job simply on account of greater speed."[1] The result is that in many instances union men do about the same amount of work; higher wages are paid only to those who have special competency or who are assigned to special kinds of work. But whatever the explanation, there is a tendency toward uniformity of payment. While no evidence of it may be found in certain concrete cases, in many others there is much less dispersion in wage rates in union than in nonunion shops, after due allowance has been made for the elimination of low rates of pay by establishing a standard rate.

Thus, it must be admitted that there is a tendency toward uniformity in payment and that a premium on efficiency is lessened or removed. Hence, the question, frequently asked, why should not the union, when standardizing wages, group its members into classes on the basis of efficiency and establish a series of minima rather than one minimum time wage?

A considerable number of instances of grading are, in fact, to be found in unionized industries. For example, the motorman or conductor on the street-railway car may have one rate of pay per hour during his first three months of service, a second during the next nine months, and a third thereafter. Such scales are, however, usually the remnants of an older classification of workers in open-shop days, one requiring a much longer, and, perhaps, an unduly long, period of service before the final, highest rate of remuneration was gained. Then there are instances in which a related arrangement is found—one in which a second minimum rate of pay is provided for craftsmen who have been "out of their time" for more than a stipulated number of months or years.[2] Of course, both

[1] D. A. McCabe, *The Standard Rate*, Johns Hopkins University Studies, Series 30 (1912), p. 108.

[2] The Newspaper Guild has many contracts in which wage minima for editors and other

types of provision relate remuneration required to probable efficiency or competency in the course of time. Beyond this, there have been many unions that have graded their members directly on the basis of competency. Thus, to give one concrete case, a local of woodcarvers formerly divided its members into four classes, whose respective standard rates were $5.00, $4.50, $4.25, and $3.75 per day. To begin with, each workman was permitted to select his class, but the classification was revised in view of the knowledge gained by the shop delegate. The grading of workmen on the basis of competency was formerly found among carpenters, painters and decorators, and machinists, among others, but such practices are now only very exceptionally found, when they obtain at all. More than one international organization has frowned upon it or legislated against it, because, in the language of the Carpenters, "we deem the same demoralizing to the trade and a further incentive to reckless competition, having the ultimate tendency when work is scarce, to allow the first-class men to offer their labor at third-class prices." In concrete cases, criticism and dissension developed. Hence, various unions, like the Carpenters', "hold . . . the plan of fixing a minimum price for a day's work the safest and best, and let the employers grade the wages above that minimum."

The student of the subject is inevitably led to the conclusion that in concrete instances the standardization of wages, combined with regulations in effect, is accompanied by results affording ground for the employer's complaint that a needed premium on efficiency is removed.[1] The removal of any premium upon efficiency is, however, incidental to standardization to control wages and to the securing of certain union ends, such as the safeguarding of tenure and opportunity to find employment. In general, unions are not opposed to efficiency.[2] On the contrary, as we shall see presently,[3] they have in increasing number shown interest in efficiency, and, in significant instances, have cooperated in promoting it. A good example is found in union-management cooperation in railway shops. Another example of cooperation is found in production standards that are now not uncommon in certain branches of the clothing industry and are found to an extent elsewhere. A study of these standards impresses the investigator with their importance in trades whose work is capable of measurement and whose personnel is

occupational groups advance year after year with experience. Thus in two agreements effective in Chicago offices, the standard rates per week for reporters and certain related groups are for the first, second, third, and fourth years of experience, $25, $33, $41, and $50. For other examples, see American Newspaper Publishers' Association, *Bulletin* 4335 (July 15, 1938).

[1] The student will find also that, in a large proportion of nonunion shops, wages are not so adjusted as to provide incentive.

[2] They are, of course, opposed to speeding.

[3] *Infra*, pp. 464–470.

allocated by the union, shares in the work during the slack season, and can be discharged only for cause. The alternative, if satisfactory performance is to be guaranteed, lies in piecework, a matter to be discussed presently.

The problem of the older or handicapped union worker in securing and retaining employment is not always successfully met under a system of permits, for these are ordinarily limited to "pensioners." As the science of personnel administration is developed and practiced, however, such persons find it increasingly difficult to secure employment on any terms in unorganized industry. It may be observed, also, though the fact has been mentioned already, that the filling of positions from a union compulsory waiting list has, and in part is designed to have, the result of returning the older and less competent workers to employment.

That the more rapid worker, and especially the "speeder," finds less room to profit from his speed in the union shop is frequently true— when he is employed on a time wage. Though, as in the case of the machinists described above, his differential may be protected by a proportional increase of wages above scale when the scale is changed, the differential in his wage may be smaller than it would be under nonunion conditions. This does not necessarily or generally mean, however, that the union regime costs him something in wages, for he profits from the increase contained in the standard rate; his wage is usually higher than would be obtained by individual bargaining in the absence of the union and collective bargaining.

Piece Rates.—The standard rate on a time basis may give rise to problems and criticism because of lack of adjustment of pay to individual performance or capacity. The piece rate, on the other hand, though it is fixed initially by joint action or is subject to adjustment under the grievance procedure and the workers are paid according to measured output, has problems connected with it. Growing out of these problems, custom and vested right, and the idea of a lump of labor, there has been opposition to piecework by much of organized labor, both in the United States and elsewhere. This opposition has given rise to no little criticism of trade unions by employers and others and has been a cause of important strikes and lockouts.

In 1912, Professor McCabe surveyed the prevalence of piecework in American organized industry and the attitudes and policies of the great majority of the international unions toward it.[1] At that time, approxi-

---

[1] See D. A. McCabe, *op. cit.*, pp. 185–232. Corresponding data for British unions have been supplied by Sidney and Beatrice Webb, *op. cit.*, pp. 286–287. There were then in Britain forty-nine unions, with 573,000 members, which insisted on piecework, twenty-four, with 140,000 members, which recognized, in various departments, both piecework and timework, and thirty-eight, with 290,000 members, which insisted on timework. The analysis herein made is in terms of attitudes of internationals. Perhaps then as now there

mately one-fourth of the members of the unions covered were engaged on piecework. Of the 121 organizations, there were 24 in whose industries the piece system widely prevailed and which did not question it at all. There were nine others in which, though it did not prevail so widely, piecework found place and was acceptable. Fifty-eight unions were in trades in which all the workers were paid on a time basis and there was no plan to change from it, and therefore no issue. Among these fifty-eight unions were some, however, that had succeeded in eliminating piecework from their trades at an earlier time. Over against the three groups thus far mentioned, there were two others. In the one there were twelve unions, more than three-fourths of whose members were on piecework, which, while not satisfactory, was not a live issue at the time, partly because of the weakness or precarious existence of some of the organizations. In the other, and final, group, were eighteen unions, a fifth of whose members were still working by the piece, but which were making active efforts to eliminate the system altogether.

During the last thirty years, the use of piecework in the several industries and the attitudes and policies of some of the unions toward it have undergone great change. Opposition has developed in some quarters where there had been none, while in others opposition has given way to acceptance. While union opposition to piecework appears to have become less than it was a generation ago, it is frequently found.[1] A new survey would reveal such groups as have been mentioned. Why do some unions favor, possibly even insist on, payment by the piece, and why do some unions oppose it and regard its elimination as a great victory, as did the Ladies' Garment Workers at the end of World War I?[2]

Before answering these explicit questions attention should be called to the fact that, as indicated by Professor McCabe's analysis, differences between management and unions over payment by the piece are not the general rule as so many appear to think, but rather the exception.

Of course, other things equal, employers are interested in substituting piece or other incentive wages for the time system of remuneration. While experience varies rather widely, under piecework output per employee can usually be expected to increase between 20 and 30 per cent over what it would be under time wages in an uncontrolled situation. This has the twofold effect of reducing direct labor costs more or less and of spreading overhead costs over a larger number of units. Total

were differences in attitudes between locals affiliated with an international, and, of course, neither an international nor a local reflects the varying attitudes of its members.

[1] For an extended and excellent discussion of union attitudes, toward piecework, see Sumner H. Slichter, *Union Policies and Industrial Management*, (1941), Chaps. 10 and 11.

[2] See Louis Levine, *The Women's Garment Workers: A History of the International Ladies' Garment Workers' Union* (1924), pp. 322–328.

costs are therefore reduced. Moreover, under piecework direct labor costs are rather definitely known; management has a better basis for estimating total costs and for setting the price of the product or service. It is largely because of these advantages that employers have in many industries preferred piecework to straight timework. But this does not mean that employers in all industries, or even in most industries, have had an active interest in "payment by result." Other things are not equal. In many industries work is so organized that the employee must accomplish his task or single himself out to be dispensed with. Good examples are found where the conveyer system is employed or where the speed of the power-driven machine virtually determines the amount of work the operator must do, as in some parts of the textile industry. Again, in the pressroom of the daily newspaper there is control of the performance of the crew by publication schedule; the edition must appear on time. In such cases as these, and they are numerous, not only is the piece-rate system accompanied by little benefit, but the tendency is for the gains from minor and gradual technical and other improvements to accrue to the workers, whereas otherwise they accrue, initially at any rate, to the company. In other cases, rapid work, induced by incentive wages, involves more or less waste of materials, or wear of machinery, or impairment of quality of product. Again, piece-rate setting involves time and the administration of piece prices involves extra clerical work. Moreover, piece rates frequently beget worker dissatisfaction, undermine morale, and increase labor turnover, with heavy costs. Thus, while most employers in numerous industries have had a preference for piecework, employers in other industries have rather generally been more impressed by its disadvantages.[1]

Unions, like employers, differ as to the desirable method of remuneration. To repeat the specific question raised above, why do some unions oppose piece work outright or conditionally, while others positively favor it?

One usually finds a combination of factors in the concrete case. The influence of custom has frequently been strong when piecework has been proposed as a substitute for timework, less so when piecework is to be displaced by another method of remuneration. Workers are greatly influenced by custom and are more or less suspicious. Their attitudes are basic in the determination of union policy.

Among the rational factors, there may be no well-defined and durable unit to be priced; joint determination of rates is then difficult, when at all practicable. The manufacture of specialties and the repair work in a shop may give rise to such a variety of tasks that new prices must be

---

[1] It should be noted also that during the last generation many employers have been interested in the bonus system and other incentive devices, instead of, or in addition to, piecework. Such systems and devices are discussed *infra*, pp. 407–408.

set all the while, perhaps job by job, which means that the foreman and the worker set them or that the foreman dictates them. Not only does collective bargaining on wages break down under such circumstances, but also the individual worker is likely to react against piecework because he makes much lower earnings on some jobs than on others. The opposition of certain metal-trades organizations to payment by the piece in jobbing foundries and in railway repair shops, when there may be no such opposition to the system by the same organization when it is applied under other conditions, is largely explained in this way.

In many cases it is the procedure employed, not the piece system itself, that is objected to. In the so-called mass-production industries rather generally, and in many sizable plants in other industries also, job analysis and time study have been widely employed in fixing rates. Unions are frequently suspicious of the methods and results. As a minimum they want an adequate number of studies made of typical men working under typical conditions, and due allowances for time lost between operations, for getting materials, adjusting the machine, and the like, and for loss of time away from the work station. These allowances are frequently more important in figuring the appropriate total than is the actual operating time and in many cases are of such nature and so variable that the "loading" is a matter of judgment. As everyone at all versed in time study knows, there is considerable room for honest differences of opinion. Even neutral parties may arrive at materially different conclusions. The union may wish to be represented or to participate in making the time studies. In any event, it wants the rates set to be tentative and to be tested by earnings realized. If the earnings are not regarded as satisfactory, the union wants to have the rates adjusted under the grievance procedure or by bargaining. It desires to have an effective voice in piece-rate determination. Unless such matters can be satisfactorily adjusted, the union has reason to oppose the piece system.

Perhaps the flow of work through the plant is not regular; the workers object to waiting in the shop on their own time. There may be "crippled machines"; under piecework management tends to neglect or to delay needed repairs. Or, perhaps along with others, there may be machines of an inferior type. Absence of opportunity to make fair earnings on such machines becomes a cause of dissatisfaction.

Again, jobs may not be properly analyzed and appropriate piece prices set for work on different styles or on different materials. In the clothing industry it is to be expected that organized workers will object to a flat rate for all work as it comes; they will probably insist on differential rates on the pressing of ulster overcoats or on other work involving distinctly more effort than the average. Many score of such differential rates will be found in any coat shop that has been conducted on a union basis for more than a few years.

What has just been said suggests that much of the opposition may have been carried over from open-shop days and become articulate with labor organization. Very likely the piece-rate structure, *i.e.*, one rate compared to others in the shop, has been bad and glaring injustices have been revealed by earnings in the pay envelope. Even more likely, the rates give unequal opportunity for earnings in different shops. In open-shop situations bad piece-rate structures find expression in labor turnover or in bad morale; in union shops they beget opposition to payment by the piece or to effective demands for reform of the piece-rate structure.

Very likely, in the interest of lower labor costs in competitive industry or in the interest of more profit, management has widely engaged in piece-rate cutting, and, while inducing more speed and greater output, has attempted to limit earnings to little more than on daywork. It would scarcely exaggerate the importance of this as a factor to say that it has been the cause of causes of opposition to piecework in American industry, appearing long in advance of union organization.[1] Many managements have, of course, become aware of this. For years considerable effort has been expended by efficient management to make comparatively sound piece rates and then permit them to stand except as revisions are called for by changes in the work or in the cost of living; cutting of piece rates in the light of earnings realized or to induce greater speed have been more and more widely discouraged. Nevertheless, much of the old order still obtains in many unorganized industries.

Naturally, and related to the matter just discussed, piece rates have been closely associated with speeding, to which workers, whether unorganized or organized, object. The objection becomes all the stronger when management points to and uses the earnings of the fastest workers to justify its position that wages or piece rates should not be increased or that they should be reduced. And associated with faster work or speeding is the greater risk of work injury and overstrain, which compositors and others formerly emphasized in their struggles to secure "straight time"; health and earning capacity must be conserved.

Most of the opposition of the workers to piecework may, therefore, be said to have developed from the unsuitability of piecework for joint administration in some industries and to the abuses of the system as it has been applied by management. But there have also been other reasons for opposition. The "lump of labor" idea is widely entertained by working

---

[1] The writer cites from personal experience, when serving as chairman of a Citizens' Committee, the following extreme case from the dress industry in Chicago. A strike developed in and spread from an unorganized plant; a union was organized and week work demanded. The trouble began in one section of the shop, where, as the employer stated, piece rates had been reduced four times within a year. The foreman had watched the earnings of the girls and reduced rates when earnings exceeded by more than 5 or 10 per cent the week wages previously paid.

people, they feel that piecework means fewer jobs or a longer slack season because the pieceworker will turn out more work. There will be seven or eight full-time jobs where otherwise there would be ten. Years ago Machinists and Garment Workers emphasized this in their active opposition to the system.[1]

Still other factors have contributed to the opposition to piecework in some unionized industries. As a rule, the more competent and the faster workers are inclined to favor piecework, for under it they make higher earnings, which is an important consideration with all workers. It may be distinctly otherwise with the slower and the newer workers in the trade; while they are less secure in their jobs and more likely to be "bothered by the boss," they feel that they are better off on week work. Union policy reflects such views, this way or that. Again, the new unions, stressing brotherhood and solidarity, may oppose piecework because it is thought to make for rivalry; it certainly does beget jealousy and enmity. Indeed, unless the rule of "turn and turn about" is practiced in giving out work, brawls sometimes occur in garment factories over the fact that workers "grab bundles" when there is little to do and each feels that he must get as much work as he can. Finally, a very different cause of opposition should be noted. When piecework is employed, subdivision of processes and specialization are in the interest of both employer and individual worker. The interest of the craft organization may, however, be very different; to it specialization means diversion of work from the journeymen, loss of craft jobs, and a weakening of the union. Perhaps it was more for this reason than all others that the Machinists and some other organizations years ago fought so stoutly the piecework system.

While there is evidence of present-day union opposition to piecework under prevailing conditions, and even under any circumstances, there is also evidence of union acceptance of it, or even preference for it, provided the job units are such that there is an adequate basis for rate determination and that certain problems are met. The meeting of these problems, the development of techniques, appreciation that certain policies can be furthered, combined with the passing of time and the desire of many workers for the earnings to be realized by superior effort, enter into the explanation of the fact that no small number of unions have become reconciled to piecework or favor it.

Particularly as they gain experience, unions may realize that, with proper techniques and conditions, piecework has distinct advantages. Standardization and stabilization appeal to them; the "army game" of extracting from each employer as much as can be had is surrendered. If

---

[1] With reference to the piece rate issue in women's wear, see Louis Levine, *op. cit.*, pp. 322–329, 343*ff.*, and Julius Henry Cohen, *Law and Order in Industry* (1916), especially pp. 95–100.

time wages prevail in an industry, labor costs may differ greatly.   With uniform piece rates, on the other hand, labor costs are equalized.   This appealed so strongly to the Hosiery Workers some years ago that uniform piece rates were introduced in all plants.   More recently steps have been initiated to introduce standard piece prices for each class of garment in the men's clothing industry.   In the bituminous coal industry, tonnage rates for mining and loading have been favored not only because of the influence of custom and the conditions under which the work is done, but also because of the interest in cost equalization.   The tonnage rates are not uniform as between one area and another but are fixed in the view of marketing costs as well as of character of the coal deposits and other factors.   Though compromises are made to meet the needs of mines adversely circumstanced, cost equalization is furthered and supported as it would not be by time wages.[1]   These instances in hosiery, clothing, and coal are only a few of a considerable number in which piecework has been favored because it was thought to promote the more general interest and welfare of the union and its members.

It should be pointed out, however, that the policy applied in such instances as these has not always proved to be satisfactory.   Costs of living differ; so may equipment, organization, and management, with the result that earnings may not be at all in proportion to effort.   More important, a premium may be placed upon neglectful management.

Along with the desire to equalize costs in a local market or throughout a wide area, there is the natural desire in established industry to observe what the traffic will bear.   A decent firm should not be forced out of business because of some handicap under which it labors; and perhaps a different type of firm should not be given too much reason to move elsewhere.   Moreover, different kinds of products may not be able to bear the same labor costs (for example, children's suits, tropicals, low-priced as against high-priced garments).   Adjustments required to meet such problems are much more easily made by altering piece rates here or there or rather generally than by changing time wages.   Variations and changes in week wages are quite evident; not so variations and more or less indirect changes in piece rates.   Moreover, when week wages are reduced earnings suffer, while if piece rates are cut the workers may maintain their earnings in part or in full by greater effort or more careful application.   Excellent illustrations are found in the men's clothing industry, where many problems have called for solution along practical lines.

Related to what has just been stated, some unions have favored piecework because it affords the workers an opportunity to protect their earnings somewhat in times of trade adversity and at all times to increase

[1] Of course "company men" (others than miners and loaders) are paid by the day, at uniform occupational rates over a wide area or bargaining district.

their earnings by producing more. It may be a comparatively easy matter to secure wage increases to start with but the general experience is that this usually becomes more difficult as time elapses because of the limits upon what the traffic will bear. The traffic will bear more in wages if the workers produce more—a matter which unions may appreciate, as well as any problem presented by speed-up.

Thus, union policies with regard to piecework differ. Moreover, as already mentioned in passing, policies undergo change. This is a very significant fact, and one explained largely by the further fact that relatively little of the opposition found is absolute. Most of it is conditional. A few examples, presented in summary fashion, not only show this but also suggest ways by which the course of collective bargaining may be smoothed.

The Stove Industry.—Stove molding has always been known as a piecework industry. Previous to the 1890's, the molders were strongly opposed to the system. There were no official lists of piece prices; molders frequently claimed that they were not paid the proper rate, in some instances, indeed, that the earnings of molders were figured by the foreman on different rates for identical stove parts. Frequently a shop's rates on different parts did not afford opportunity for equal earnings from the same effort. Some rates were relatively high, others relatively low. The piece rates between different shops were often very unequal. Again, molders were discounted for poor castings due to the cold or "dull" iron provided or to impurities in it as well as for bad work. Even breakages after the parts had been taken from the molder's bench or floor might be charged against him. There was no normal time for beginning or quitting work; some workers made high earnings by starting at three or four o'clock in the morning or by working late into the night, or by both beginning early and working late. Then perhaps the manufacturer would cite the high individual earnings thereby realized to justify refusal of the workers' demand for an increase in wages or in justification of a demand for a reduction. For these, and possibly other, reasons the molders became strongly opposed to the piecework system. Frequently they limited output by limiting earnings per day or by requiring that the excess over a certain sum be paid into the local union treasury.

Under the so-called arbitration agreement entered into by the International Molders' Union and the Stove Founders' National Defense Association in 1891 and continued to the present time, these causes of complaint were considered in the conferences, usually held once a year, and steps taken to remove acknowledged injustices. Steps were also taken to solve the problem of unequal labor costs among stove manufacturers who conducted union shops.[1] In 1892 the rule was laid down

[1] As used here the term "union shop" means only that management recognized and

that "the present price of work in any shop should be the basis for the determination of the price of new work of similar character or grade."[1] In the following year, it was voted that "any existing inequality in present prices of molding in a foundry or between two or more foundries should be adjusted as soon as practicable . . . " and steps were taken without delay to improve and to equalize the rates within each shop and as between shops.[2] Approximate equality in direct labor costs of the several manufacturers was secured. Because of differences in efficiency, the latter could not, of course, be obtained by the standardization of wages on a day basis. The molders were enabled to know where they "were at" with regard to piece rates for the several types of castings by an official shop price list provided for in 1899.[3] The work to be done by the journeyman was made clear, and the tools, equipment, and materials necessary were to be provided by the manufacturer. "Gangway count" (as the castings were finished) was quickly voted, and discounts brought under control. Attempts were made to protect the molder against discounts for bad castings due to dull or dirty iron, but, while the rules adopted in 1896 and 1906 served this function, they were subject to abuse by the workers and changed in the 1920's.[4] The length of the workday was standardized in 1902.[5] At the same conference it was "conceded by the members of the M. P. and D. A. that the earnings of a molder should exercise no influence upon the molding price of work which is set . . . " according to the principle of equal pay for equal effort. With hours standardized and limited and with individual earnings not to be cited in conferences on wage issues, the Molders conceded that "the placing of a limit upon the earnings of a molder should be discountenanced in shops of members of the M. P. and D. A."[6]

With these steps taken and these and some other minor conditions established, the stove molders, even before the end of the 1890's, ceased to question seriously the piecework system while their fellow members in the other metal trades continued to display stout opposition to it.[7]

---

bargained collectively with the union. The old demand for the closed shop disappeared; for a generation, at least, the closed shop was demanded of only one manufacturer, because he discriminated against employees on account of union membership or union activity.

[1] Conference Agreements between I. M. U. of N. A. and M. P. and D. A. (the *Manufacturers' Protective and Development Association*, as the Defense Association has been renamed), issued Jan. 1, 1937, Clause 7.

[2] *Ibid.*, Clause 8.

[3] *Ibid.*, Clause 14.

[4] *Ibid.*, Clause 11, adopted in 1896, amended in 1906 and 1922, and the molder's responsibilities explained in an explanatory note added in 1924.

[5] *Ibid.*, Clause 15, adopted in 1902 and amended in 1916, 1918, 1919, 1921, 1927, and 1930.

[6] *Ibid.*, Clause 16, adopted in 1902.

[7] From time to time "board prices," as the piece rates are called, were advanced and on a few occasions reduced. In the depression of the early 1920's a deadlock developed in

The Needle Trades.—At the time the Amalgamated Clothing Workers was recognized and agreements entered into, the piece-rate system prevailed in the coat, pants, and vest shops in most of the "markets." Though it has insisted that certain conditions must be observed, the Union has been one of those favoring piecework primarily because it soon developed the view that the manufacturers and their employees were "in the same boat." Between them they obtained neither more nor less than the entire return from the business done. One way to raise wages was to increase efficiency and output. The Union therefore cooperated in extending piecework until—except for cutting and trimming—it has become all but universal in the shops of almost every market of importance in the industry and even in New York City.[1] At the same time the Union expected and has exacted piece rates yielding earnings that are higher than week wages in the same occupations.[2]

All piece rates are made by a representative of management and a Union deputy, functioning under and with the Union's price maker. These representatives know the job operations and rates rather thoroughly. Only occasionally are time studies made. In the event of failure to agree, which for years has rarely occurred, at any rate in some of the markets, the price or prices are set by the impartial chairman. The objective is so to price a particular operation that the workers' usual hourly earnings will not be affected. Put in other language, the principle applied is "equal pay for equal effort." Any price set is tentative; if hourly earnings are reduced readjustment is called for.[3] This is now of infrequent occurrence for piece-rate setting is almost always competently done.

What has been said relates to fixing rates on changed or new work. In the earlier days, efforts were made to adjust appropriately rates for work in different "sections," this including some advantages to the occupational groups with the lower earnings. This was one form of

---

conference on the manufacturers' demand for a 20 per cent wage reduction. The thirty-year-old national agreement seemed to be on the point of breaking down. The deadlock was finally broken, however, when most piece rates were reduced 10 per cent and the work and obligations of the molders changed in certain respects so as to make a total saving of 20 per cent in direct labor cost. The significance lies in the fact that the union could accept reduction in wages in the sense important to industry more easily than it could have under a system of time wages.

[1] For years week work was maintained in New York City because management and conditions were such that the piece system in the view of the Union could not operate in a satisfactory manner.

[2] See *How Collective Bargaining Works,* The Twentieth Century Fund (1942), Chap. 8, Father Francis J. Haas, *Shop Collective Bargaining* (1922); and The Chicago Joint Board, Amalgamated Clothing Workers of America, *Clothing Workers of Chicago,* 1910–1922 (1922), Chap. 13.

[3] Seldom is a rate reduced because it proves to be too favorable. The reaction that might result constitutes one reason for this.

leveling, which could most advantageously be effected when conditions were favorable and wages rising. Likewise, in the interest of a reduced turnover of labor and of opportunity to earn, there was partial leveling of rates among the houses in a given market.

As the years have passed, new problems have appeared. In some instances methods of manufacture, processes, and rates have been changed in view of what the traffic would bear. In one well-known instance an x and a y brand of clothing were manufactured, the Union accepting the estimate of what nonlabor costs would be and fixing piece prices for the many operations in view of what was left of the proposed wholesale price. This alleviated the problem of an important firm. Then there has been the problem of unequal labor costs as between markets, due largely to different levels of wages as the Union was recognized in one locality after the other. The stabilization plan recently adopted is designed to equalize direct labor costs in all markets. A fixed amount is set for the many operations involved in making a garment or a suit of a given class (there are six classes); unless an exception is made, each piece rate must be made in the light of the fixed total.

These principles and policies have been very satisfactory to the manufacturers generally; efficiency has been stimulated, output increased, and labor costs made low as compared to the workers' earnings. With a newly hired or transferred worker placed on an hourly rate until he has had time to "get his hand in," they have met with the approval of the employees generally. With security of tenure, they desire fair rates or the best the house can bear and provide desired employment and an opportunity to secure larger earnings with careful and intelligent application.[1]

Unlike the Amalgamated Clothing Workers, the International Ladies' Garment Workers' Union for many years was actively opposed to piecework. Strong, though not unanimous, sentiment for abolishing it developed about 1916, as a result of dissatisfaction with the way the system had functioned under the collective agreements. Some union leaders argued that piecework led to dissension and division among the workers, to speeding and a shorter working season, that individual

---

[1] What has been said relates to the making of the garments, not to cutting and trimming. These operations are usually done on week work. In certain markets and notably in Chicago, however, production standards have been introduced, and wages are adjusted periodically in view of individual efficiency records. The system was developed by the Union, the manufacturers, and the impartial chairman. The standards have been readjusted from time to time in the light of experience, but as they now stand they call for the payment to cutters (of woolens) of wages varying between $32 and $50 a week of thirty-six hours according to the relation between time consumed and time allowed on measured jobs. Between each class and the next, the wage varies by $2. This sum is approximately one-half the amount earnings would vary were the workmen paid straight piece rates. This modified piece or bonus plan has mildly stressed output and has been acceptable to the manufacturers and the Union.

shop bargaining over prices caused unequal labor costs and diversion of work from "inside shops" to the smaller contract shops, where lower prices prevailed. Time wages, they thought, would tend to equalize competition by eliminating shop bargaining. Other leaders, however, opposed this line of reasoning, arguing that there would be just as much variation and speeding under a timework system, that the time scales would be minimum scales and many or most workers would be paid higher rates, with plenty of room for individual bargaining. The opponents of piecework finally won out when the May, 1918, Union convention endorsed time work. In the following year, the Union succeeded in introducing timework in most of the important centers of the cloak and suit (or coat and suit) industry, where it was maintained for almost a decade and a half.

But time work did not prove satisfactory. By 1933 the Union had reversed its position. The depression brought increased pressure from employers, particularly the larger ones, to reintroduce piecework in order to increase efficiency. Union leaders, moreover, had become convinced that only under piecework could labor costs be made more nearly equal—a prime objective in the highly competitive coat and suit industry. Timework had aggravated, not mitigated, the problem of unequal costs. In addition, the speeding drive had continued in the smaller shops, and under a timework system the workers did not get the benefit of any increased productivity. So in the 1933 NRA coat and suit codes, piecework was reinstated, with certain guarantees against the return of previous evils. The codes included both minimum hourly rates and average hourly rates, piece prices being set so as to yield the latter to the average worker. No one's earnings could fall below the minimum. A small proportion of the workers—among them, cutters, examiners, and sample makers—remained on timework.

Though a few shops, mostly better grade, are now entirely on a timework basis, the piecework system as set up under the codes has continued in effect. After the NRA was declared unconstitutional, the National Coat and Suit Industry Recovery Board was established to insure continued observance of "fair labor standards" and "fair commercial practices." The Board represents the Union and almost all the trade associations in the industry.

In the New York metropolitan area standards are administered by the Labor Bureau, which is part of the impartial-chairman setup and dates back to code days. This Bureau has defined and classified the standard garments, according to workmanship required. For example, the operations necessary to make each of six different grades of coat bodies have been listed. Then, after the average time needed to perform each operation in each grade has been computed, piece rates have been set so as to yield the average hourly rates in the agreements. There are also a series of miscellaneous rates—for buttonholes, belts, pockets, and so on—which may be added to any individual garment.   At the beginning of each season these piece rates are applied to the separate shops by committees representing the Union and management (manufacturers or jobbers).   If a committee cannot agree on the grade in which a garment falls or on miscellaneous rates not covered by the Labor Bureau's listing, the dispute goes to the Bureau for settlement.

While there has been some chiseling on rates and some variation in costs owing to lack of complete product standardization, both employers and workers have been rather generally satisfied with the operation of the system.   Earnings, of course, vary, but labor costs are substantially uniform in New York City and intramarket competition has been greatly reduced.   Out-of-town competition has been minimized in recent years, partly because of the Recovery Board's efforts to maintain some degree of national equality in labor standards.   Disputes among employees at the end of a season, with each racing to get a larger share of work, are not a problem, since all work is shared as equally as possible during slack periods.   There has been no recent move to eliminate piecework.

Bonus Systems; Protecting the Standard Rate

Straight time wages or ordinary piece rates have been found almost to the exclusion of other forms of remuneration in unionized industry. Bonus systems, task systems, and the like, though for a time accepted in newly organized shops, are seldom long tolerated, for they are regarded as speeding devices.[1]   Moreover, unions have stood for "a fair day's pay for a fair day's work"; they want time rates or payment at the full piece rate for any increase in output, not merely a part thereof as under the majority of bonus systems.   Of course, as already stated, production standards are accepted in some industries—indeed, increasingly so—and in a sense these are an exception to what has just been said.   But only two bonus systems are known to exist in organized industry in Chicago. One of these is found in the composing rooms of the daily newspapers, where it has obtained for more than forty years but has for more than a decade been opposed by the union.

Finally, in closing this discussion of the methods used in controlling wages, it should be noted that in almost all collective agreements a larger or smaller number of provisions are incorporated to define or to protect the standard rate and to keep it undiminished and to safeguard the workers' earnings.   Most likely, wages are to be paid weekly or twice a month,

---

[1] It appears that here and there agreements resulting from the recent expansion of unionism in certain industries contain incentive plans of one kind or another.   Securing an agreement was the great thing for the time being.   Whether such plans remain in effect long and the workers become reconciled to them, or whether the plans are discarded remains to be seen.

in cash or other prescribed form. Fines may be imposed, if at all, only under certain conditions. In a coal agreement, the miner's and loader's ton is defined as so many hundredweight; the car is to be delivered at a certain point; the miner is to be appropriately paid for timbering, shoveling rock and dirt, and other specified operations; powder is to be provided at cost or at a prescribed figure; the charge for smithing tools shall not exceed a certain percentage of earnings or so many cents per ton; hospital dues are not to exceed so much per month; the miners are permitted to have a checkweighman at the tipple to check on the weighing of the coal. In the clothing agreement, it may be provided that the manufacturer is to provide without charge the power used, to provide all findings free, and not to require deposits in excess of a certain figure, as well as to pay wages in cash at stipulated times. Possibly in employments requiring uniforms, the agreement provides that these shall be supplied on specified terms. In some cases, such regulations as those mentioned have afforded great protection and added much to the earnings realized in preunion days. This has certainly been true in coal mining, some branches of the needle trades, stone molding, and in the manufacture of glass.

The Policies of Unions with Respect to Wage Levels and Wage Changes

The discussion of wages in the immediately preceding chapter needs to be supplemented by an answer to the questions, what do unions want in wages, and what are the arguments advanced in support of claims made?

The answer to the first of these questions has most frequently been that "labor wants a fair day's pay for a fair day's work," but this is, of course, almost a meaningless statement. The only outstanding thing has been that, as Mr. Gompers used to say, "the object of the trade union is to bring to the workers more and ever more of the product of their toil." But the "more and ever more" has had various degrees of emphasis placed upon it, varying from all that can possibly be had in wages for the time being with little regard to the number who will be employed to something distinctly less than that. But whatever the degree of emphasis it has received, the "more and ever more" has usually been desired with, and because of, an appreciation of what increased earnings may mean in terms of living—housing, food, clothing, schooling of the children, and, perhaps, provision for the future. The demand has commonly been accompanied also by a deep-seated feeling that the workers have received too little, others too much—a feeling deepened and confirmed by living conditions dictated by necessity, by the existence of large fortunes and "big business," which make a deep impression upon the rank and file, and by the writings of intellectuals who deplore the grossly unequal distribution of income and property and the presence of very large and partly unearned profits. The relatively high wages exacted by groups occupying strategic positions have been defended on the ground that "everybody is doing it," *i.e.*, everyone is out to make the most of his opportunities, whether he be an operator of public utilities, a coal operator, a lawyer, or a corporation executive. What labor wants is intimately related to the economic situation in which it carries on and to what others strive for and get.

As one follows collective bargaining in concrete cases, one finds significant detail bearing upon the question of what labor wants, as well as upon the positions taken in support of its claims. Here, as in other connections, the union is sometimes found acting in defense of what it has had; sometimes, and much more frequently, it is taking the offensive in an effort to secure better standards. The claims advanced in these connections throw more or less light on the content the unions would put into the standard rate.

Unions nearly always press for increases in wage rates when the cost of living increases, such as the period from 1900 to 1914, during the First World War, and between early 1941 and January, 1944. The claim is that the standard of living should not be undermined, a claim properly accepted by arbitrators unless there is something unusual in the concrete situation, as there was at the time of this writing, when it was proposed to devote half the national income to prosecution of the War. But it is frequently a poor rule that works both ways. While reluctantly conceding a reduction in rates of pay now and then because of general depression or because of a state of bad trade in the given industry, or because the cost of living has fallen, unions have usually opposed any reduction in rates of pay.[1] A number of reasons may enter in to explain the position taken, and seldom are they found singly. First of all, there is almost always present the feeling that all along labor has been getting too little in wages. If it is the cost of living that has fallen, the fact is likely to be unreal in the experience of the workers, because expenditures and the plane of living are prone to expand with any leeway given and the balance left after bills have been paid is perhaps the same as before. And, if it is clear that the cost of better living has offset the reduced cost of a given type of living, what should be done about it? As an intelligent worker said to an arbitrator who showed that the workers' case was of this kind, "What of it? Would you have me take my children and move from my steam-heated apartment to the old unheated, run-down apartment in that filthy

---

[1] An excellent example is found in the coal miners, who for years refused to accept reductions in wages and had as their slogan "no backward step." Another good example is found in the building trades, where the opposition to wage cuts has been very stout. In the building trades, however, it has frequently been union policy, especially in depression years, to require observance of the scale on large jobs and government work and to "wink" at low, nonscale wages paid on other construction and repair work.

locality where I did live? Never." If it is business that is bad, the argument is likely to be, "Should labor share business losses? When did labor share profits?"[1] Frequently there is a feeling that if any concession is made to meet a state of bad trade in the particular industry or a state of general depression, a new start must be made on a lower rung of the ladder, that old territory must be fought over once more in securing a better type of living. Then, too, the union leader knows that a wage reduction is hard on union morale; a reduction will usually be accepted only because, and after, employment is jeopardized. And, finally, since the 1920's, the theory has been increasingly emphasized that it is only by keeping wages up or by increasing them that prosperity can be restored or maintained. Hence, unions generally assert a claim to wage increases when industrial advance is being made or when the increased cost of living tends to undermine standards of living, and, on the other hand, only less generally oppose reductions in wage rates when the cost of living decreases or a bad state of trade develops.

Depression Wage Theory.—This official trade-union wage theory requires special discussion from the point of view of depression conditions.[2] For many years organized labor has adhered with tenacity to the thesis that business depressions, with their concomitant unemployment, are basically caused by improper distribution of income—by the fact that consumers (and especially wage earners) do not receive purchasing power sufficient to lift off the market the goods that have been produced. The moral, if trade unionism's basic assumption as to the cause of depression be accepted, is obvious: that wages should be increased at a more rapid rate than they have been in the past when industry is expanding and physical and value output per employed person is increasing; that wage rates should be maintained if depression does come, in order to provide a foundation in consumer purchasing power that will prevent business activity, and, therefore, the volume of employment, from falling to very low depths; and that one means of recovery is to be found in a general increase in wages, such as was attempted under the NRA of 1933–1935.

A brief critical evaluation is immediately in point, but it may be observed in passing that upon few questions is theoretical analysis, unless subjected to the sternest and most rigid scrutiny of all its assumptions and postulates, more likely to lead to unwarranted conclusions,

---

[1] Perhaps, however, the workers will see the matter in a different light if it is reasonably certain that a reduction in wages will increase the volume of employment and the amount of money in the pay envelope. In 1933, numerous local unions in Chicago readily accepted reductions in the hope that lower costs would induce more business and increase the amount of work.

[2] *Cf.* discussions of certain aspects of the subject in vol. I, Chaps. IV and VI, and vol. II, Chap. I, especially pp. 29, 42–43. There is a considerable repetition in the following pages of what has been said in vol. I, but it has been thought best for readers of the separate volumes that the subject should be discussed as it is in each volume.

and that wage-policy history proves rather little to one groping for ultimate truth in the matter. Indeed, both the wage maintenance-underconsumption doctrine and the orthodox theory that when other prices drop wages must also come down have had their manifestations in public policy since 1929, and in neither case can it be said that experience has proved the validity of the analysis. When business entered its downswing in 1929, the position taken by the Hoover Administration was that wage reductions would only make a bad situation worse by decreasing the purchasing power of the masses; and, as is indicated elsewhere in this treatise,[1] both the frequency and the severity of rate reductions were not so great during the first year of the depression as during the comparable period of other depressions. Had revival come shortly, there is little doubt that the theory of "riding through" a cyclical downswing by maintenance of wages would have been regarded as vindicated, and that for a generation or so the idea of wage-rate maintenance during depression periods would have been entrenched in the economic thinking of the American people. But the depression was not short-lived, and by 1931 and 1932 the wage cuts that many businessmen and "orthodox" economists had regarded as inevitable from the beginning were much in evidence. Had recovery of substantial proportions come, say, toward the end of 1932, it is almost equally certain that the doctrine of wage reductions as a causal factor in recovery would have been believed vindicated, and that for a generation or so the wage maintenance-underconsumption notion would have been viewed as a disreputable outcast from the family of sound economic doctrines. Again, however, recovery did not arrive at a time opportune for the drawing of the *post hoc, ergo propter hoc* conclusion, and the policy of rate cutting was no more vindicated beyond question by practical experience than was the policy of wage maintenance. After 1933, the high-wage policy again had its innings under the National Recovery Administration, and once more experience failed to prove beyond peradventure of doubt that the economically efficacious policy had been adopted.

The trade-union position on the matter can be summarized very briefly. The essential element of the problem—the fact that consumer incomes are insufficient to lift off the market the goods that are produced —dictates not only maintenance of, or increases in, money wages during depressions, but also a progressive stepping up of wages during more normal periods. As the American Federation of Labor phrased it in 1925:

"We hold that the best interests of wage earners as well as the whole social group are served, increasing production in quality as well as quantity, by high wage standards which assure sustained purchasing power to the workers, and, therefore, higher national standards for the

[1] Vol. I, Chap. II, p. 117.

environment in which they live and the means to enjoy cultured opportunities. We declare that wage reductions produce industrial and social
unrest and that low wages are not conducive to low production costs.

"We urge upon wage earners everywhere: that we oppose all wage
reductions and that we urge upon management the elimination of wastes
in production in order that selling prices may be lower and wages higher.
To this end we recommend cooperation in study of waste in production. . . .

"Social inequality, industrial instability, and injustice must increase
unless the workers' real wages, the purchasing power of their wages,
coupled with a continuing reduction in the number of hours making
up the working day are progressed in proportion to man's increasing power
of production."[1] If wages are not increased "in proportion" to productive advancement, constantly greater inequality in income distribution
will result, with its inevitable concomitant—even more disparity between
productive capacity and the nation's capacity to purchase.

It need hardly be said that this theory has had little standing in
orthodox economic thought. In an exchange economy general overproduction is impossible, production and demand being merely the
obverse and reverse of the same phenomenon;[2] and, since it is impossible,
the fundamental premise in the trade-union argument that high wages
are a causal factor in preventing maldistribution of income and therefore
depressions, in putting the brakes on the downswing of business, and in
initiating revival from depression falls to the ground. The sequence of
events, businessmen and frequently economists have insisted, is not
that assumed in the trade-union case. The profit situation governs the
demand for labor; when the money income of a business declines the value
productivity of labor to the employer declines. The presence of large
numbers of unemployed men is *ipso facto* evidence that labor is over-
priced; reduce this price and more of it will be taken off the market.
In order to effectuate a better relationship between the component parts
of the price structure, and therefore to bring about fuller utilization of

---

[1] American Federation of Labor, *Proceedings*, 1925, p. 271.

[2] It may be observed in passing that the classical economic position on this matter is,
for the most part, a generalization and an extension to a money and credit economy of the
laws enunciated for a barter economy by Jean Baptiste Say in 1802. Since production and
demand are merely the obverse and reverse of the same phenomenon, a fundamental disparity between them cannot occur. Put in money terms, this principle of course implies
that savings build up the demand for productive equipment (and therefore for the services
of the workers immediately and remotely connected with making productive equipment) to
exactly the same extent that they diminish demand for labor in the consumer-goods industries. So-called overproduction brings, not a diminution in the aggregate demand for
labor, but only a change in the direction of this demand. The implicit assumption—which
obviously cannot be discussed at this point—is that of almost instantaneous shifts in purchasing power.

both human and nonhuman resources, the labor cost of doing business must be reduced during depression. Only then will it be economically advantageous for employers to hire more labor. And to raise wage rates during a period of business depression is only to engage in a futile attempt to pull ourselves up by our bootstraps—if not, indeed, to engage in sheer economic madness. Since under the existing economic system investment and business enterprises are motivated largely by the prospect of profit, the saddling of business with higher costs can result only in discouraging its employment of labor.

As is true with respect to most abstract or theoretical reasoning, the cases that have been set forth in the immediately preceding paragraphs are considerably simpler than the facts of economic life. The large element of validity in the orthodox case for wage cuts during depressions can be accepted—as the authors do accept it when, as in these paragraphs, it is abstracted from the numerous complicating elements constantly appearing as part of the very substance of economic relationships—but at the same time it must be recognized that thousands of "disreputable accidents," to use Professor Edgeworth's phrase,[1] may occur and prevent the theoretical effects of a high-wage policy or a low-wage policy from working themselves out. It is convenient to turn, first, to the circumstances that may prevent depression-period wage reductions from bringing as their logical consequence fuller employment; second, to evaluate briefly the doctrine that wage rates should not only be maintained but that they should actually be increased during depression periods; and, third, to make a few observations on the general labor thesis that economic balance can be maintained only by wage advances "in proportion to increases in productivity."

The conditions, circumstances, and causal sequences that may prevent the beneficial effect (*i.e.*, fuller employment) of wage cuts from actualizing itself are many. Where demand for a product is very inelastic, the response in increased consumer purchases, and therefore in greater demand for labor, will be slight.[2] In the second place, the assumption that prices will decline when wages are reduced cannot be allowed to pass without comment. It is true that wage reductions without corresponding (or even without any) reductions in prices may enable firms on the verge of insolvency to keep going and thus prevent further diminution in the volume of employment; but an increase in the volume of employment presupposes more consumer purchases, and these

---

[1] F. Y. Edgeworth, *Mathematical Psychics* (1881), p. 46.

[2] If wage cuts were to occur almost simultaneously throughout all of industry, and were of approximately the same magnitude, the immediate effect (assuming prices to decline when wages were reduced) would be greater purchases, with the industries the demand for whose products was most elastic enjoying more of the benefit than those the demand for whose products was only moderately elastic or rather inelastic. The counteracting tendency would be, of course, lower wage-earner incomes.

are dependent upon lower prices. In the depth of a depression, when hoarding is a factor of importance and every price reduction is taken by potential buyers as a signal that prices will go still lower and that post-ponement of delayable purchases is therefore desirable, producers may see no additional market for their goods at almost any price, and they may not pass on the lower labor costs in the form of price reductions unless they have to. They may not have to. Price-fixing schemes of all degrees of ingenuity, the entrenchment of conventional or customary prices, the imperfection of competition in the market, or other forces may enable enterprisers to maintain prices after wages have been cut. In the third place, the proportions of labor costs and other costs must be taken into account. Where the former, per unit of product, are low relative to the latter, the magnitude of the price reductions, increase in purchases, and increase in employment may be slight. The examples might be multiplied. Enough has been said, however, to indicate that numerous institutional impediments may thwart realization of the bene-ficial effect of wage reductions that is theoretically to be expected. Three conclusions can be stated with a fair degree of certainty: that in spite of the numerous institutional impediments to a working out of the theoretical effect, wage maintenance *as a general policy* during depressions may increase the volume of unemployment;[1] that the desirability of any given wage cut depends on the concrete case; and that in any event it is not socially desirable that wages should be cut until management has reduced such forms of waste and unnecessary expense as are within its control—which means that wage cuts must not be too easily made.

In addition to expressing the view that a main objective of trade unions is the securing of "unjustified differentials" in wages for their members,[2] many economists have held unions responsible for much of the rigidity in the economic system that is said to prevent the needed quick readjustments necessary for the maintenance of a desirable balance and for needed opportunities for employment. The rigidity referred to is due to the maintainance of wage rates when value productivity has decreased, particularly in a depression. This matter has been discussed elsewhere in this treatise[3] as well as here. The position here taken is that ordinarily wage maintenance is one of the less objectionable forms of price maintenance. Some of the critics of trade unionism might, indeed, be more careful to criticize other cases of price maintenance as well as

[1] It will be remembered (see vol. I, Chap. II) that while hourly wage rates declined somewhat throughout industry in general between 1929 and 1932, they did not decline more than did the cost of living and that real hourly earnings were, if anything, a little higher by the latter year than in the former. The argument certainly is tenable that unemployment would not have been so widespread in 1932 had hourly rates of pay fallen more than they did.

[2] *Cf. supra*, pp. 360–364.

[3] *Cf.* vol. II, pp. 42–50.

that connected with unionism. All too frequently, also, there has been a facile assumption that the presence of unemployed persons is evidence that wages are too high. An appropriate analysis of types of unemployment (casual, technological, seasonal, as well as cyclical) may indicate that wage rates are not necessarily the chief or immediate cause. So may an examination of price-maintenance plans and a considerable variety of conditions, unless it is assumed that wages alone should undergo such readjustment as to set the wheels of industry turning.

We may now turn to the second case assumed earlier: that of increasing wages during a depression period in the expectation or hope that this action will be a causal factor in recovery. Here the theoretical issues, centering around the matters of costs, prices, purchases, and necessary labor force, are in their fundamentals the same as those just discussed in connection with the question of whether wage rates should be cut during depressions—the difference is merely that of the force and extent of the application of the purchasing-power-maintenance policy. It need only be said that while under ordinary circumstances the policy of trying to restore prosperity by saddling business enterprise with higher costs might seem—in a system of capitalistic free enterprise—to be a policy insuring defeat of its own end, there may be circumstances under which this policy would promise short-run success. In the spring of 1933, for example, when the NRA policy of increasing hourly wage rates in order to offset decreases in weekly earnings due to reductions in hours was instituted, the demand curves for labor in many lines of enterprise were probably extremely inelastic. Working forces in some cases had been cut to about the technologically irreducible minimum if operations were to continue at all, and it seemed likely that increases in hourly rates of pay would not diminish so greatly as in more normal periods the number of labor hours employers would purchase. As is suggested elsewhere in this treatise,[1] most of the traditional avenues of escape from depression—especially those that opened up after the great nineteenth-century depressions—were closed. Unable to turn to the ameliorative forces of the past, the American people took a gambling chance on the outcome of the race between the beneficial effect of an increase in consumer incomes and the retarding effect of higher costs of doing business. Under conditions such as these, there was at least a possibility that a quick "pump priming" might be given to business through the increases in total money wages.[2] There may, indeed, be other circumstances in a depression period when a general raising of money earnings will increase rather than diminish the volume of employment. But such circumstances are likely

[1] Vol. I, Chap. VI, pp. 360–361.

[2] As is pointed out (ibid., pp. 357–361), it is probable that, for reasons there suggested, the purchasing-power theory as applied to special depression conditions was not given a very real test under the NRA.

to be rather special (even for depression periods), and wage increases that are not simultaneous with those of other producers or that occur at a time psychologically unfavorable to business expansion are likely to be disastrous to the industrial producer making the raises and, therefore, to his contribution toward reemployment.

Wages and Prosperity.—We still have for discussion those more typical cases where unions in a normal or expanding business situation demand higher wages. Before completing the critical observations on labor's typical wage policy, however, it will be most convenient to refer to other arguments advanced in support of higher wages.

It is to be noted that in the low-paid trades, say coal mining, slaughtering, and the manufacture of clothing, the newly formed unions have claimed a "living wage." This claim generally meets with public approval and is usually valid, for industry can normally afford to pay a living wage when it is defined in terms appropriate for the given country. That is to say, to be tolerated, an industry should pay wages that are not out of line with what the class of workers employed receive in industries round about. But, when a "living wage" has been realized in clothing and elsewhere, its realization has been followed by a claim to a "decent standard of living," an "American standard of living," a "saving wage." In general, it may be said that these claims are valid or invalid according as wages are brought to or carried beyond that point the economy of the country can afford with little labor left unemployed—except, perhaps, for seasonal or technological causes, or "leakage" in a poorly organized labor market.

Labor asserts a right to wages paid workers employed elsewhere in the trade or paid to comparable workers in other trades. Hence, in conference and in arbitration proceedings, wage data are placed in evidence, designed to show that wages being paid the group concerned are less than fair. Beyond this, labor in general asserts a claim to increased wages as industrial advance is made, a claim to share in the results of progress. Most emphatically, it is not satisfied with a fixed status. This is most strikingly true in the United States. As stated in 1920 in a document entitled *Labor, Its Grievances,* by representatives of the A. F. of L. and its affiliated organizations:

"There is a widespread belief that wages should be fixed on a cost of living basis. This is pernicious and intolerable. It means putting progress in chains and liberty in fetters. It means fixing a standard of living and a standard of life and liberty which must remain fixed. America's workers cannot accept that proposition. They demand a progressively advancing standard of life. They have an abiding faith in a better future for all mankind. They discard and denounce a system of fixing wages solely on the basis of family budgets and bread bills. Workers are entitled not only to a living, but modern society must provide more than what is understood by the term 'a living.' It must concede to all workers a fairer reward for their contribution to society, a contribution without which a progressive civilization is impossible."

Allusion has already been made to the "new wage policy" enunciated by the A. F. of L. in 1925. Assuming that the future would witness a continuation of the past increase in per capita production, the Federation declared that social inequality, industrial instability, and injustice must increase unless real wages increase in proportion to man's power over production. The doctrine or theory was put forth as a departure from and in opposition to the "law of supply and demand," the doctrine of a "living wage," a "decent wage," a "saving wage." As presented, the "new wage policy" was unclear and indefinite, and, of course, it could be of little value in concrete cases of collective bargaining. Wages could not be adjusted in full correspondence with the progress made in the given industry, for, were this done, an impossible situation would quickly develop, since some industries improve rapidly, others slowly, and some not at all. Nevertheless, there is much to commend in the practical policy to which the Federation's nor too clearly elucidated "new wage policy" points—that of increasing, or at least maintaining, labor's share of the value product of industry when prices and production are rising. It is under such circumstances, in fact, rather than during depression periods, that the organized-labor argument of high wages as a maintainer of economic balance is most valid. Had wages been stepped up more than they were during the second half of the 1920's, a considerable inflation of profits, the speculative orgy that preceded the depression, and injudicious investments of capital might have been minimized. One need not accept in its bald and—to many—untenable form the overproduction hypothesis to recognize that higher wages may act as a brake upon a type of expansion that must ultimately be followed by collapse.[1]

Evidently all that the Federation meant when it set forth its wage policy in 1925 was that the level of wages, *i.e.*, wages in industry after industry, should be stepped up (and in proportion) as progress in production was realized and the national income expanded. Of course, the general advance being made is impossible to measure at all accurately. Moreover, the economist may question advances in wages "in proportion" without regard to how the gain is realized—say, as the result of the use of more capital in the form of machinery and other mechanical aids. In such a case, relatively more of the joint product may necessarily have to be distributed to investors.[2] Nevertheless, the principle is attractive and has a degree of merit, for increasing inequality in income is accompanied by problems. Of what value is an augmentation of the national

[1] *Cf.* vol. II, Chap. I, pp. 42–50.
[2] *Cf.* vol. I, Chap. IV, pp. 214–215.

income, of what value is "progress," unless the economic basis of living on the part of the masses is elevated in substantial measure? Moreover, with great inequality in incomes, more of the national income for the year is saved and invested in productive enterprise than would be under a more equal distribution. General overproduction, which labor has feared and the technocrats have made so much of, does not result, but the chance for miscalculation and misdirection of investment is increased. Hence, industrial breakdown is more likely to occur from time to time.[1]

Sliding Scales.—In closing this section of our discussion, brief reference should be made to the union attitude toward the sliding scale and any claim to share in profits.

The sliding scale was formerly rather generally incorporated in union agreements in the manufacture of iron and steel products and the mining of coal and other minerals in the United States, Great Britain, and some of the Continental countries. The arrangement made was to fix a wage or rate per ton when the price realized for the product was a stipulated figure, and then to increase or reduce wages periodically according to the number of points the price realized exceeded or fell below the stipulated figure. Perhaps the scale had a "bottom," i.e., wages were in no event to fall below a specified figure. The thought was, of course, to relate wages to what the traffic would bear, to have wages and prices and, presumably, profits rise and fall together. While such arrangements are still found in unionized industry, they are limited in number and are for the most part survivals of an old device. Put in other words, the sliding scale has been eliminated in many cases in which it was in vogue a generation or so ago. Most frequently this elimination was due to a change in attitude on the part of the unions concerned. The reasons for the change in attitude differed somewhat, of course, from one case to another. Perhaps friction developed over the precise scale, and most frequently over the minimum, or over the administration of the system. Perhaps, as in the mining of anthracite early in this century, there was complaint that the scale was too complicated; the workers could not understand it. Perhaps there was a feeling that production was rushed when wages were lowered. The chief reasons, however, appear to have been the desire of the workers for certainty of wage rate, disinclination to share losses, and the development of the doctrine of a living wage.[2]

In the last twenty-five years, a sliding scale has developed in a new form, linking wage rates and the cost of living as shown by cost of living

---

[1] H. G. Moulton, and Associates *The Formation of Capital* (1935).

[2] For an interpretation of the partial elimination of sliding scales in England, see J. W. F. Rowe, *Wages in Practice and Theory* (1928), Chap. 8. The elimination of the sliding scale has of course removed most of the elasticity in wage rates, under agreements in effect, and made for increased rigidity in unstable industry.

indexes. Partly because of the position taken by the International Joint Conference Council, such an arrangement was rather widely employed in the book- and job-printing trade in the United States during the later World War I years and for a year or two immediately following. Under the scale arrangements entered into, wages were advanced from time to time as the cost of living increased. As prices began to fall, in 1920–1921, however, the unions became dissatisfied because of readjustment of wages downward, and in most cases the use of the sliding scale ended with the joint agreements in effect.[1] Following the War, similar arrangements were agreed upon in British unionized industries employing some 3,000,000 workers. In more recent years, however, this feature has been eliminated from agreements or the agreements themselves have broken down, so that it was a few years ago found in unionized industries employing not more than 1,500,000 British workers.[2]

Unions generally do not make a direct claim to share in profits because, naturally, they do not wish to share losses. Not often is an argument for wage increases based mainly upon the fact that profits are

[1] For a brief account of the arrangement in the industry in Chicago, see Emily C. Brown, *Book and Job Printing in Chicago* (1931), Chap. 6. For a fuller discussion, see Francis H. Bird, "Cost of Living as a Factor in Recent Wage Adjustments in the Book and Job Branch of the Chicago Printing Industry," *American Economic Review*, vol. 11 (1921), pp. 622–642.

[2] Finding place just now in a few unionized plants in this country are newly adopted arrangements under which the total of wages is fixed as a percentage, say 20, of the gross business done. In addition to making wages elastic, this device is designed also to further management-labor cooperation in those factors making for success in business in which both profit and (money) wages find their source. Whatever may be said concerning the underlying theory and whatever the position of unions generally toward it may be, such an arrangement has more or less obvious advantages. One of the most interesting of these is the Nunn-Bush Shoe Company plan, which has been incorporated in agreements with several classes of employees in the works at Milwaukee and Edgerton, Wisconsin. One feature of the plan is a fifty-two weeks' guarantee of employment for those who have been employed for a specified time. The feature of interest in the present connection is described as "a method of safe-guarding the interests of production employees through self-adjusting, continuous remuneration based directly on product value." Inasmuch as the wages fund— a fixed percentage of the value of product—cannot be determined until the end of the year, each employee has a drawing account and receives payment each of the fifty-two weeks in the year, the weekly pay checks being based on a company estimate of the probable volume of business over a stipulated contract period. When, at the close of the period, the fund exceeds payments made, the excess is paid out pro-rata as adjusted compensation. If there is a deficiency, this is carried forward. In 1936, the workers received additional compensation amounting to 4.8 per cent. In 1937, with business and prices of product increasing, the workers received 5.2 per cent in addition to the drawing accounts. With recession, however, the rates were reduced in January, 1938. Hence the employer and workers share gains and losses under a system that divides the product value in fixed proportions. Wages rise and fall with this product value, not directly with prices, as under the usual sliding-scale arrangement. Wages are made flexible. See *The Nunn-Bush Plan, An Address by H. L. Nunn, President, Nunn-Bush Shoe Company,* delivered in Boston, Apr. 22, 1938, published in a pamphlet of twenty pages.

exceedingly good.[1] Nevertheless, much may be said in conference concerning profits in rebuttal of the employer's contention that the industry cannot bear the wages requested. And, of course, in an effort to secure better wages, requests are made chiefly when profits are good, because it is then that such requests are most likely to be granted.

The Hours of Labor[2]

Second only to the interest of trade unions in wages is that in the length of the workday and the work week. Here an effort is made to secure a "progressive decrease of working hours."

As has been indicated elsewhere in this treatise,[3] the immediate objective in the matter of hours has changed with the progress made, and at any given time has differed somewhat from union to union because of differences in circumstances. But, speaking in general terms, American unions during the later 1820's and the 1830's sought to substitute the ten-hour day for that of "sun to sun." With the ten-hour day secured in most organized trades, a movement for the nine-hour day followed. Additional interest in the hours of work was stimulated when, in the 1860's, Ira Steward formulated his philosophy of the eight-hour day, in which he advanced the theory that the only certain way in which to increase wages was to reduce hours. "Whether you work by the piece or by the day, reducing the hours increases the pay," the couplet ran. As a result of Steward's propaganda, existing unions were greatly stimulated, and new labor unions, as well as eight-hour leagues, were organized. The enlarged interest in hours and the new philosophy found expression in demands by many unions for shorter hours. In the middle of the 1880's, when the ten-hour day was still prevalent, plans for a general movement for the eight-hour day were made and strikes were planned for May 1, 1886. Though the movement largely miscarried, a few of the internationals (for example, the Cigar Makers and the Brewery Workmen) were successful during the 1880's in securing a day of eight hours. In more recent years, this became an objective of most other American unions, as their circumstances permitted it, and the A. F. of L. gave them at least its moral support in an effort to secure the general adoption of the eight-hour day, first with the forty-eight- and then with the forty-four-hour week. Shortly before the outbreak of the First World War, certain unions became interested in the five-day week, or the seven-hour day, but the position taken by the A. F. of L., when its support was requested, was that, while any union interested in a further reduction of hours in its trade should have moral

---

[1] From 1941 to 1944, however, high profits realized under the defense and War program were frequently the main talking point of unions trying to get increased rates.

[2] See also vol. I, Chap. IX, and vol. II, Chap. II.

[3] Vol. I, Chap. IX, pp. 465ff.

support, an effort should first be made to reduce the hours of work to eight where they were in excess of that number.[1] The Federation, after the World War, first weakly endorsed the five-day week, and then carried on strong propaganda for it.[2] While the week of forty hours became a most active union interest, some labor organizations also made plans to secure a normal day of less than eight hours. In 1931, a number of unions, some of the Railroad Brotherhoods among them, actively advocated a six-hour day. The A. F. of L. endorsed the six-hour day, thirty-hour week, in emphatic language at its 1932 convention.[3] New impetus to the movement for shorter hours was given by those who wished to spread available employment. The Black Thirty-hour-week Bill, which passed the Senate on Apr. 6, 1933, but was displaced on the legislative program by the NIRA, had as its primary motive the sharing of employment. The A. F. of L., however, supported the thirty-hour week as a basic recovery measure, not merely as a share-the-work scheme. With the failure of industry to absorb all the unemployed under the shortened hours provided in the codes, the A. F. of L. became insistent that the hours permitted by the codes be drastically reduced. The general average established in the codes was around forty hours per week (with wide variations and exemptions), and William Green, as spokesman for the A. F. of L., demanded a 25 per cent reduction to thirty hours per week. The thirty-hour-week issue again became important in the spring of 1935 but was severely and effectively criticized,[4] and, despite pressure from the Federation, temporarily dropped out of the legislative picture.[5]

In other countries, as in the United States, the unions have striven for progressively shorter hours.[6] Moreover, it has almost always been true that the struggle in the organized trades has been for a shorter day than was sought for women workers through legislation. This fact

[1] See, for example, American Federation of Labor, *Proceedings*, 1913, p. 285, and 1914, pp. 340–341.

[2] In 1919 (*Proceedings*, 1919, p. 454), the report of the Committee on Shorter Workday read, in part, "in cases where the work week can be reduced to less than 44 hours . . . it would be of advantage to the worker to so have these hours distributed as to provide for a full Saturday holiday, making the work week a 5-day week, still with a maximum eight-hour day." A stronger position was taken in 1926 (*Proceedings*, 1926, pp. 197–198), since which time the Federation has stressed the five-day week as much as it did the eight-hour day after 1886.

[3] *Proceedings*, 1932, p. 285.

[4] The arguments against the thirty-hour proposal are well summarized in the Brookings Institution pamphlet by H. G. Moulton and M. Leven, *The Thirty Hour Week* (1935).

[5] The position of the A. F. of L. is stated by William Green in his *The Thirty Hour Week* (1935).

[6] The forty-hour week has been rather prevalent in organized industry in Great Britain and several other countries. A law enacted in France provided for it, but as the present War approached, it was set aside.

indicates one of the functions performed by organized labor; through its efforts, it sets new goals to be attained for others.

Organized labor has had a substantial degree of success in the reduction of the hours of work, and in a great majority of cases without concessions in weekly wages.[1] Hours per day and hours per week in unionized industry were, on the eve of the great depression, in great contrast to those of a generation ago and in considerable contrast to those of fifteen years ago.[2] A survey made by the A. F. of L. showed that of 109 international unions covered, only two (the Firefighters and the Seamen), had in 1929 a prevailing week of more than fifty-six hours.[3] Four reported a week of fifty-four or fifty-six hours, and twenty-five a week of forty-eight, forty-nine, or fifty hours. Over against these, twenty-nine internationals reported a forty-four, and six[4] (Painters, Garment Workers, Granite Cutters, Structural Iron Workers, Wood Carvers, and Asbestos Workers), a forty-hour week. A large number of other unions reported less than forty-four hours, and among them were forty-two with the forty-hour week in effect in certain localities. According to an A. F. of L. report, 555,738 union workers, or approximately a seventh of the total, had a five-day normal week in 1931,[5] two years in advance of the adoption of codes that had the effect of making the five-day, forty-hour week the normal in most American industries. Union agreements effective in 1937 were about as likely to call for a week of less as they were to call for one of more than forty hours. The seven-hour day, five-day week became rather general in the organized needle trades and bituminous coal, and made its appearance and in some instances considerable headway in several other industries, for example, in some of the building trades, especially in cities west of the Mississippi River. Indeed, in a few cities, among them Seattle, Portland, Butte, and New York, a six-hour day became the general rule.[6] The six-hour day, five-day week also was won in a part of the unionized rubber industry.[7]

Of special interest are the reasons advanced by organized labor for a progressive reduction in the hours of labor. These reasons have passed

[1] Usually organized labor has not been willing to make concessions in wages in order to secure shorter hours.

[2] For several years the U. S. Bureau of Labor Statistics has published data in its bulletins on union scales of wages and hours of labor. Comparative data will be found also in the reports of the Executive Council of the A. F. of L. (see Convention Proceedings).

[3] American Federation of Labor, *Proceedings*, 1930, pp. 68–71.

[4] Excluding the Teachers.

[5] *American Federationist*, vol. 38 (1931), p. 1287.

[6] See Florence Peterson and C. F. Rauth, "Union Scales of Wages and Hours in the Building Trades, May 15, 1936," U. S. Bureau of Labor Statistics, *Bulletin* 626.

[7] With the urgent need for greater production in the last two years, the trend toward shorter hours came to an end, and, of course, actual hours worked have in many cases far exceeded the standard.

through an evolutionary process, and emphasis placed upon some of them has changed from time to time, owing to economic and other conditions.

In the demand for shorter hours, as has been indicated in more detail in an earlier chapter,[1] is to be found an interest in leisure, rest and recreation,[2] more family life, social opportunity, and self-advancement; in all of these connections, there is a vast difference between the ten- and the eight- or the six-hour day. The shorter workday is very desirable in so far as production needs are not interfered with too seriously, for leisure time, with few exceptions, has a positive value. The ideal is to secure such a balance between time devoted to earning a living and time available for living outside of the job as will give the fullest measure of life. Although frequently, in current discussions of the length of the workday, the largest possible production is assumed to be a sound objective, it is not a sound one in peacetime.

But most of all, as Mr. and Mrs. Webb have observed,[3] the insistence upon the shorter workday is to be accounted for by the general feeling among the workers that shortening the work period both increases wages and contributes toward a solution of the problem of the unemployed. Labor's theory of the causal relationship between the length of the workday, on the one hand, and the wage level and volume of employment,

[1] Vol. I, Chap. IX.

[2] It is interesting to note that manual wage earners in the United States and elsewhere, particularly in Great Britain, have recently developed an active interest in vacations with pay, so frequently accorded office workers and management personnel. The Executive Council of the American Federation of Labor in its 1937 *Report* (pp. 25–28) stated that "Many unions are including vacations in their agreements this year for the first time, and it is reported that employers in increasing numbers are granting this benefit voluntarily." Reports from internationals in response to a questionnaire sent out showed that a part or all of the members of thirty-nine such internationals had vacations of from one to three weeks, with part or full pay, the total of such members, as reported, being 746,893. Of these, 383,000 were employed by Federal Government or state governments, while 363,900 were employed in private industry. In approving this development, the Executive Council said, "As modern industrial techniques shorten work time, vacations with pay should become part of the program for shortening work-hours. Also, they may lessen seasonal unemployment by substituting paid holidays for a lay-off in dull seasons.

"In this day of automobiles, well paved roads, trailers, inexpensive bus tours to national parks and places of interest, a vacation of one or two weeks has more to offer than ever before. A working man and his family may step out of their daily routine into a life full of new interest, mentally stimulating, with a chance to learn something of the world outside of the shop and home. Such an opportunity is of immense value to wage earners; it gives perspective and sends a man back to his work with a new outlook. Now that workers are organizing and, as union members, are taking a more responsible part in the affairs of their industry, such a broadening of outlook is particularly important. A weekend is not long enough to give it." *Ibid.*, p. 25.

It may be added that vacations with pay are as characteristic of C.I.O. as of A.F. of L. agreements.

[3] *Industrial Democracy*, Pt. II, Chap. 6, "The Normal Day."

on the other, has already been discussed in detail in vol. I;[1] and a brief reference to the predominant notions that have been adhered to from time to time must suffice here. As has been pointed out, labor's nineteenth-century work-fund concept has expanded somewhat as the years have passed, but in substance it has remained much the same: that the amount of work to be done is limited, that available work should be divided among the workers through shorter hours, that higher hourly rates can and must be paid if the basic reason for reducing hours is increasing per capita productivity, and that the workers are entitled to increased leisure as one of the benefits due them from the increased efficiency of industry. For a time during the nineteenth century, again as has already been pointed out in more detail elsewhere,[2] labor accepted a somewhat more elaborate version of the thesis that shorter hours and higher incomes go hand in hand than its homespun "make-work" theory. Two basic premises underlay the doctrine of Ira Steward: that wages tend, within reasonable limits and over fairly long periods, to follow the prevailing standard of living, and that technological progress was steadily increasing the per capita productivity of labor. Shorten hours and output would expand in consequence of the stimulation to technical progress, while at the same time rising standards of living and increased wages would furnish a market for the enlarged output. But, important as was the influence of Stewardism, the typical trade-union leader and the rank and file have for the most part thought in somewhat different—and simpler—terms. In an early A.F. of L. pamphlet, Samuel Gompers[3] set forth in all its comforting simplicity the argument that if hours were reduced from ten to eight, five workers would be needed where four had theretofore sufficed, the unemployed and even the unemployables would be hired, and yet a deficient labor supply would cause wages to rise. The thinking of the majority of workers has been to the same effect. Of course, two unexamined and incorrect assumptions are involved in the argument, viz., that a worker will do the same amount of work per hour whether he works ten hours or eight, and that there is and will be just so much work to be done, regardless of the terms on which it is performed.

The most appealing reason for shorter hours, especially when unemployment is a widespread fact, is the belief that additional workers will be taken on with any reduction in the hours of labor. The rank and file are tremendously interested in assurance of regular employment, with the result that new demands for shorter hours per day and per week, and perhaps also demands for the elimination of piecework, appear at times of bad trade. In 1939, for example, there was a very active interest

---

[1] Vol. I, Chap. IX, pp. 493–497, 502–516.

[2] *Ibid.*

[3] *The Eight-hour Workday: Its Inauguration, Enforcement and Influences* (1897).

in the six-hour day on the part of many American unions. With reference to shorter hours as a solution of the problem of the unemployed, it will be generally agreed that a wide distribution of the work available in time of depression is socially and economically desirable, other things remaining unchanged.[1] Indeed, considerable effort has been expended to effect that end, either by reducing the length of the workday or by reducing the length of the work week, or by staggering the work. But there may be, and frequently is, failure to recognize that what is of advantage in a given situation may prove to be undesirable under different conditions. As a permanent arrangement, the six-hour day or the five-day week must be accepted or rejected in view of the desirable balance between leisure and production. In other words, the effect upon production, from which we collectively obtain our living, must be considered along with the value of additional leisure time. Once a shorter schedule is introduced, it will have little effect upon the recurrence of unemployment. Certainly the history of the hours of work and of industrial breakdowns would lead one to the conclusion that there is little relation between the length of the workday and the frequency or severity of depression.[2] Nor, if the position taken in the preceding chapters is correct, can there be any substantial relation between hours of work and the level of wages except that established by those effects which are reflected in productivity.

For a time, it was fairly general for labor, even perhaps while contending that shorter hours would solve the problem of unemployment, to contend that a reduction of hours to eight per day would increase output and be the most profitable arrangement. This argument seems to have gained currency from the struggle in legislative bodies when these had under consideration measures calling for shorter hours, especially for women workers. The proponents of such legislation built up this defense against the argument so emphasized by employers that a reduction in hours would reduce the workers' output per day and therefore increase costs. At any rate, the position that, as a general rule, the eight-hour day is most economical has found a large place in contemporary thinking and in the literature on the subject. Experience shows, however, that the most productive day, at least in the measurable short run, varies greatly with the kind of work—heavy or light—the type of workers employed, numerous working conditions, etc. This matter has been discussed in an earlier chapter and does not require further discussion here.[3]

[1] See vol. II, Chap. II, pp. 119–120.

[2] This relates to depressions as they recur. Of course, as already stated, shortened hours may not only alleviate a depression situation but also affect the chances of recovery.

[3] See vol. I, Chap. IX, pp. 499–501, where certain quantitative evidence on the relation of the length of the working day and week to daily and weekly output is presented.

In recent years, the argument has not run so much in terms of the most productive day, but more and more in terms of the possibility of reducing hours, now that invention and improved organization and techniques have so greatly increased output per worker—a fact broadcast through production indexes and by knowledge of concrete cases. "The justification and advisability of shortening the hours of labor are not entirely those of fifty years ago. It is no longer necessary that men should work as many hours as formerly so that all might live in comfort and abundance. The use of power to replace human brawn and of machinery to replace the skilled craftsman should give the mass of the people a much greater opportunity to enjoy the recreations and the opportunities which modern civilization affords."[1] This argument to the effect that with the greatly increased output that has accompanied industrial advance we can afford more leisure must be accepted as sound, in a peacetime economy, but not when prosecuting a war.[2]

A logical implication, or a reciprocal, of this argument is the contention that unless hours of labor are reduced as production increases, unemployment will inevitably become a serious problem. Selecting only one of many statements in recent trade-union writings: "Technical progress means that workers with better tools can do their work in less time. The whole point in improving the technique of the work process is to 'save labor.' Unless this is done by reducing the work hours rather than by reducing the number of workers employed, technical progress results in unemployment and business depression."[3] In this connection, it may be observed that as important technological changes are introduced, having the effect of "saving labor," the time is very appropriate for such reduction in hours as the general situation in industry makes desirable. But the fact that the long-run may differ from the short-run consequences is frequently overlooked in this connection. In fact, the "lump of labor" idea is frequently present in the minds of the leaders as it so generally is in the minds of the rank and file. It is true that in concrete cases the amount of labor is reduced, as in the glass-bottle industry, where the number of blowers has been reduced to a mere fraction of the former figure by the Owens automatic and other machines, but for industry in general there is no "lump of labor." Revolutionary changes in technique and organization are likely to be accompanied by a lack of balance that requires readjustments, but they do not give rise to

[1] Quoted from an article by John P. Frey, "The Economics of Wages and Hours," *American Federationist*, vol. 38 (1931), pp. 290–291.

[2] This is of course fully realized by organized labor. This is shown by the acceptance at this time of longer shifts and a longer work week.

[3] Quoted from an editorial in *American Federationist*, vol. 38 (1931), p. 677. See also *Report of the Executive Council of the American Federation of Labor* . . . 1939, pp. 132–137.

general overproduction so much feared and said to be inevitable unless the hours of labor are reduced.[1]

Another argument used has been that hours must be reduced in order to protect health and length of working life. It has been used in concrete cases almost, if not quite, from the inception of the shorter hours movement. For many years, it has received great emphasis at the hands of the Cigar Makers and other groups whose experience as regards sickness and death rates has been frequently submitted in evidence by other organizations. More recently, with briefs submitted to legislative bodies and courts and with the increased amount of repetitive and monotonous work, it has been greatly and very generally emphasized in the shorter hours movement. The American Federation of Labor Committee on Shorter Workday, reporting in 1926, said, in part: "Modern methods of production, the high tension of machine operation, the specialization which forces thousands to perform the same meaningless operation thousands of times per day has placed a strain upon the worker's nervous system which is more enervating, more conducive to physical and mental fatigue than many more hours of labor would be where the work called for the constant use of the worker's creative power. Modern methods of production more and more tend to make a machine of men. For this reason, in addition to many others, it is essential that not only should the daily hours of labor be reduced, but in addition, that the number of days per week should be shortened. For social reasons, as well as those of an economic character the American Federation of Labor is justified in declaring for a shorter work week as energetically as it did in the past for the establishment of the eight-hour day. . . . "[2]

Scientists have shown that monotonous and repetitive operations produce fatigue and nervous strains, leading to a higher morbidity rate.[3] Shorter hours are called for when and as increased strain becomes

---

[1] For a discussion of technological unemployment and the position of the technocrats, see vol. II, Chap. I, pp. 27ff.

[2] American Federation of Labor, *Proceedings*, 1926, p. 198. In the Committee's report in 1925 (*ibid.*, 1925, p. 259), it was stated that "In industry the development of giant power which in turn is applied to the marvelous automatic and semi-automatic machinery of today has created conditions surrounding production in industry undreamed of a few short decades ago. Industrial processes have placed a much greater strain upon the worker's vitality. Many of these processes tend to seriously injure and sometimes destroy the workers' health if labor is continued for an eight-hour period. Already, as in the case of caisson workers, four hours and sometimes less is all that heart and lungs can stand. In many of our industrial processes, the conditions under which labor must be performed make it mandatory for humane considerations alone that the hours of labor should be reduced below eight, and the week's work to not more than five days."

[3] See Josephine Goldmark, *Fatigue and Efficiency* (1912, reprinted 1919), H. M. Vernon, *Industrial Fatigue and Efficiency* (1921), and *Health and Efficiency of Munitions Workers* (1940), Harrington Emerson, *Twelve Principles of Efficiency* (1924), and H. W. Heinrich, *Industrial Accident Prevention* (1941).

involved, as it so frequently does. The facts, however, argue quite as strongly for appropriate rest periods as for shorter hours. Investigation shows also that general working conditions may be as important as hours of work in their effects on health. But, while the health argument will not support any given length of workday or work week throughout industry, it is sound in its application in many concrete cases.

We have seen in the preceding section that the standard rate may be accompanied by a number of incidental provisions. So it is with the normal day and the normal week. In order to protect the normal day and the normal week and to secure their effective operation, unions generally insist upon the incorporation of incidental provisions in joint agreements. Perhaps normal beginning and quitting times and the period allowed for lunch are set down specifically, as they not infrequently are in laws relating to the hours of work of women. Very generally, there are one or more provisions relating to overtime, for the normal day (or normal week) is seldom absolute in its requirements. The very general provision is that ordinary overtime (that in excess of the stipulated number of hours of work or that after normal quitting time) shall be paid for at the rate of time and a quarter, or time and a half, or double time, or some combination of these rates. Such an arrangement the union regards as fair to both employer and employee, for it permits the one to continue production to meet the necessities of the case as dictated by raw materials used or by the market for the wares and gives the other extra remuneration for work performed when he is fatigued or when he is put to inconvenience. Much more important, without such penal rate of pay, the normal day becomes merely a basic day and the standard is all too frequently exceeded, because the employer is likely to work his force longer hours in order to spread nonwage costs over a larger output, while the worker may be quite agreeable to working long hours for the sake of the larger earnings realized.

In many and in an increasing number of cases, agreements have provided (in prewar years) for restrictions in addition to penal rates for overtime. In the clothing industry, for example, the agreement may prohibit overtime so long as the union can supply additional help, provided the shop has machines that might be placed in operation. Or, the agreement may prohibit overtime during certain months of the year. The first of these additional restrictions Mr. and Mrs. Webb[1] explain as due to the readiness of employers to pay penal rates because they can save on nonwage costs, and of workers to work beyond normal quitting time because of the additional earnings to be realized. In brief, the explanation runs in terms of the inadequacy of the penalty. Without question, the desire to defend the standard goes far to explain the increasing number of instances in which specific restrictions have been

[1] *Industrial Democracy*, Pt. II, Chap. 6, pp. 345–353.

applied. Other factors, however, may enter in. For example, in the needle trades, where the feeling of brotherhood and the desire for a wide distribution of work are strong, additional restrictions may have the object in view of absorbing the unemployed on the waiting list. And in the needle trades, the prohibition of overtime work during certain months of the year is designed to shorten the slack season.

The question may be raised whether unions have generally not been too intent on protecting established standards. Heavy penal rates for and direct limitations on overtime tend to cause employers, especially in seasonal industries, to hire and retain employees with considerable reference to peak needs. When this is done, part-time work becomes a larger problem in normal and slack months than it would otherwise be. Much is to be said for the element of elasticity provided by permission to work longer hours without penalty during certain seasons or under certain conditions.

Most unions insist upon higher rates of pay for work performed on Sunday, Saturday or Saturday afternoons, or legal holidays than for other overtime. Perhaps the rule will call for double time. The explanation is, of course, that the normal week must be protected[1] and that these particular days have a high leisure and recreational or social value.

Machinery and Improved Processes

While wages and hours, our concern in the preceding pages, have been almost universally emphasized, union interest is not in these alone. Rather, the union interests itself in almost anything connected with the welfare of its group—acting defensively or otherwise as the case may be. Unions frequently become actively interested in the introduction of machinery and improved processes; now and then they seek to retain in use needless processes or uneconomical methods; not infrequently, they concern themselves with the union or nonunion source of materials used; very generally, the craft organizations interest themselves in the employment, training, and work assignments of apprentices, helpers, improvers, and the like; some unions take action with reference to the subdivision of work in the shop; practically all unions interest themselves more or less in the hiring and discharge of workers, and a substantial majority of them demand the closed or the preferential shop; rather frequently, unions interest themselves in the spreading of available work among their members or in securing recognition of seniority rights; and, finally,[2] at

[1] In the early months of 1942 there was much criticism of the demand made by some unions for penal rates of pay for (all) Sunday labor involved in the worker's five- or six-day shift. Of course penal rates cannot be contended for as a protective device when it has been agreed that production shall be continuous, seven days a week. Sunday then becomes a part of the worker's normal shift. This has been recognized by most unions and double time for Sundays and holidays is being rapidly abandoned.

[2] Of course, a considerable number of unions are actively interested in other matters,

times, unions become actively interested in output and the intensity of work. They interest themselves in such matters because they wish to protect jobs, skill, and wages, or because they wish to protect health or life and limb, or because they desire to control the supply of labor, or for other reasons that will appear as one point after another is discussed.

Our discussion of the several interests enumerated may be prefaced by an observation. Wages and hours are almost always disposed of by collective bargaining in the unionized trades. This, as a matter of history, has been increasingly true of these other matters also, but in many cases they are disposed of by union rule that becomes implicit in the joint agreement when the organization is recognized. Hence, in our discussion we shall have to do incidentally with the rule-making phase of the situation in the organized trades.

Union Attitudes and Policies.—Unions are as appreciative as most other groups of the advantages to society of better mechanical aids and improved processes.[1] As John Mitchell said, more than a generation ago: "Trade unionists recognize that machinery has enormously multiplied the productive power of the community. They realize that the work done at present in the United States could not, without the aid of machinery, be performed by three times the present population. They acknowledge that machinery has cheapened all manner of products and that the artisan can now purchase at a moderate price a variety of necessary, useful, and beautiful articles, wholly unattainable a century or even a generation ago. Finally, the trade unionists believe that machinery has not permanently deprived large masses of the population of the opportunity to work, and they recognize, amid the evils of machinery, great and enduring benefits."[2]

But usually the initiative in the substitution of machinery for hand tools, the introduction of new types of machinery, and the adoption of new processes is in the hands of management. The chief exception is found in those cases where union-management cooperation is effective and employment stabilized.[3] The records there show a number of

---

such as sanitary conditions in the shop, but these are incidentally discussed in other chapters of this treatise.

[1] For a discussion of machinery and improved processes and technological unemployment, see vol. I, Chap. IX, pp. 494–496, 509–513, and vol. II, Chap. I, pp. 27–39.

[2] *Organized Labor* (1903), pp. 246–247.

[3] Another example is found in the hosiery industry. Though in specific cases issues developed over the introduction of new types or the manning of machines, more recently it has become union policy to encourage the introduction of the best types of machinery available. This policy is explained, at least in part, by the unequal competition between the largely union older mills in the North and the largely nonunion newer mills in the South and the tendency of the industry to move from the one to the other area. The hosiery workers have accepted drastic reductions in wages on the condition that the employers would modernize their equipment. Modernization, it was thought, would increase productivity, save jobs, and support a better standard of living.

instances in which the introduction of superior equipment or laborsaving devices has been requested by the workers. Nevertheless, and almost inevitably, the typical situation has been such that the union could not actively function except by defending its members against the "evils" involved in technological change and in securing such gains as it could at the time.

From the point of view of the craftsmen, whose wages, employment, and mode of life were seriously threatened by the introduction of machinery and the factory system in the textile trades in England more than a century ago, the evils of machinery were great. The reaction of unions was strong; they quickly gained the reputation of being opposed to machinery. And in more recent years, in England and elsewhere, similar but perhaps less revolutionary changes have aroused organized opposition. But the active hostility of unions of workers confronted by these "evils" has become less great as the decades have come and gone. The explanation of this fact is found in a number of things: changes have become less revolutionary, taking the field of employment as a whole, for the introduction of the machine effects the great revolution; the craftsmen have become relatively fewer, labor as a whole more adaptable; the workers have become more familiar with the long-run advantages resulting from improvements of different kinds; experience has shown that machinery and improved processes will make their way into the trades when they reduce costs, and if they are not accepted by the union will place a premium on the open shop. Nevertheless, there are unions that are now charged, or in recent years have been charged, with opposing the introduction and use in industry of improved mechanical aids and better processes.

The unions in question typically oppose concrete changes, or accept them only on certain conditions, in an effort to avoid or minimize "evils" as seen by the workers immediately concerned. Like other articulate groups, they attempt to protect their interests. Manufacturers or farmers may seek to protect themselves against new competition by securing a protective tariff; commercial insurance companies may oppose compulsory sickness insurance or a state insurance fund in the operation of workmen's compensation; the doctors may oppose socialized medicine; the small shopkeepers may fight the department store and then the chain store. The union, like other groups, may try to protect its members against worsement. A few concrete cases will present the problem involved and indicate union policies adopted.

Concrete Cases.—The first case may be taken from the glass-bottle industry, which was revolutionized before the end of the First World War.[1] Semiautomatic machines in glass blowing appeared toward the

[1] For an excellent account of this case, see George E. Barnett, "Chapters on Machinery

close of the nineteenth century in the manufacture of widemouthed bottles and jars. The union tried unsuccessfully to compete with the machines by accepting wage cuts. This policy was soon abandoned for one of control, the union persuading manufacturers to employ its members on the machines, though they had to accept nonunion rates. No great problem developed, for, with expansion of the industry, the men displaced by the laborsaving device were quickly absorbed, and with improvements in the machine and the worker's skill, earnings before long equaled those of handworkers. But in the years after 1905 the union was also confronted with the Owens automatic, which requires only a semiskilled attendant and which enables one man to do the work otherwise requiring a large number. In this case, the union concentrated on an effort to make the hand and semiautomatic plants competitive, by drastic wage reductions and other concessions. In addition it took jurisdiction over all workers in the industry not subject to another union. Shortly after, during World War I years, the feed and flow device displaced the last of the skilled workers in the semiautomatic plants. Again the union accepted large wage cuts in order to control the feeders. However, many employers even then refused to recognize union control of the machine. In 1924, fewer than 2,000 members of the union, as against some 10,000 in 1910, were employed in the trade; the employees were largely operatives receiving semiskilled and unskilled wages. Of 4,185 members of the organization, 2,252 were then employed outside of the industry. The machine had largely destroyed the craft, displaced many workers, and greatly reduced union membership.

In the same way the compositors were confronted by the linotype machine, which became a commercial success about fifty years ago, and, as introduced, threatened the "sits" of three of each four workers. Was it to be manned by the skilled men in the offices, paid the current wage for hand composition, or was it to be manned by quickly trained workers brought into the trade, receiving lower wages—a selling point of the manufacturer?[1] The International Typographical Union took the position that jobs would inevitably be sacrificed, but that the hand compositors should have an opportunity to become machine operators, and, after acquiring speed, should receive in wages the equivalent of the standard rate paid hand compositors. In this instance, the union's position prevailed; consequently, hand compositors and machine operators have had substantially equivalent scales in the same offices and localities. For a few years the introduction of the machine was accompanied by a considerable amount of unemployment, but then, with the

---

and Labor," in *Quarterly Journal of Economics*, vol. 39 (1925), pp. 544–574; also Sumner H. Slichter, *Union Policies and Industrial Management*, pp. 232–234, 245, 249–252.

[1] For an excellent account of this case, see George E. Barnett, *The Printers* (1909), pp. 196–208.

upturn of the business cycle and the expansion of the printing industry (largely due to the growth of advertising), the supply of labor and the demand for it came into adjustment and the unemployed were absorbed by the trade. This fortunate result convinced not only the compositors but also pressmen and others that "machinery is a good thing," and that the policy of the Typographical Union in this instance was the sound one. Though the view of the printers was widely opposed and only reluctantly accepted by their employers, they, too, found it to be satisfactory, for, though work in the composing room has changed in detail, the need for intelligent, literate, and experienced compositors has continued. In other words, the type of worker needed has not essentially changed, and any displacing effect of the machine was accepted by the union.

A great majority of American unions, when confronted by the machine, have, like the compositors, not opposed it outright, but have sought to man it at the old rate of pay. The argument has been, "it is a poor machine that cannot make its way without reducing wages."[1] But the rate of wages is only one issue that becomes involved. Another is the displacing of men. As regards this, most unions have accepted the loss in the number of jobs, as did the compositors, but some have taken the position that, as a condition of the introduction of a new appliance or process, displaced workers must be provided with suitable employment elsewhere in the shop—i.e., work that will yield them their accustomed earnings. Such was the position once taken by the clothing workers in Chicago and by the arbitrator in the famous pressers' case.[2]

There have been unions, however, that for a time declined to permit the machine to enter the shop. This was the position taken by the Molders for some years.[3] Here, the mechanical devices threatened to reduce the number of jobs substantially. Moreover, they increased the proportion of heavy work, for the number of ladles of molten metal to be handled in the course of the day would be greatly increased. Finally, the skilled workers were of the opinion that the quality of the work would suffer, and, much more important, they feared that there would be an effort to supplant them by workmen who were inferior in the trade but

---

[1] As phrased in the Chicago clothing industry.

[2] The manufacturer proposed to introduce steam pressing machines in his vest shop and to man them with cheaper help than had been employed on hand pressing. The union contended that the machines should be manned by those who had been doing the work, that their piece rate should yield the same earnings as had been realized, and that those no longer needed in the pressing section should be provided with suitable and equally remunerative jobs elsewhere in the plant. By a two-to-one vote, the Board of Arbitration upheld the union's contentions.

[3] See Margaret L. Stecker, "The National Founders' Association," in *Quarterly Journal of Economics*, vol. 30 (1916), pp. 352–386, and F. T. Stockton, *The International Molders Union of North America*, Johns Hopkins University Studies, Series 39 (1921).

who could more easily adapt themselves than they to the requirements of the molding machine. But as the new appliances made headway in the open shops, the union found that it could no longer ignore them. Therefore, in 1899, it took the position that had been taken some years previously by the compositors. There was difference of opinion, however, over the question of what type of worker should man the machine and at what rate of pay, and in some cases in which the skilled hand molders were placed on the machine, the results were unsatisfactory, either because of the inadaptability of the molders or because of their disinclination to give the machine a fair trial. Failure to solve satisfactorily the problem presented by the molding machine was one of several reasons for the breakdown of the national agreement between the Molders and the National Founders' Association in 1904. In the stove industry, however, where the union's position was the same, the arrangement effected was quite satisfactory.

Though exceptional, there have been not a few instances in which unions have long refused to accept the machine. For example, the Cigar Makers for years refused to accept the suction table that aids in placing the wrapper on the cigar.[1] They asserted that only the handmade cigar was good. They feared, however, that an inferior type of labor, used in nonunion shops, would find a larger place in the trade and that the skilled men would be confronted by a new competition. The Stone Cutters' Association in 1902, instructed its members not to use the stone pick, on the grounds that it required only brute strength and that it reduced the already inadequate amount of work for skilled men. Many locals of this union refused to accept the planer for dressing stone, but others did accept it on such varied terms as they could secure.

The old "one man, one machine" rule of the Machinists' Union has been made well known by the voluminous literature relating to machinery and the restriction of output. A provision was long ago inserted in this union's constitution, reading, "Any member running more than one machine in any shop where such is not the practice, unless such introduction is upon the decision and advice of the local lodge, shall be expelled."[2] This rule was not applied in the operation of automatic machines, but was applied in the operation of lathes, planers, shapers, slotting machines, drill presses, etc. Professor Commons reports that it made a difference of some 10 per cent in the number of machinists required in a Chicago union shop.[3] One reason for the restrictive rule was the increased

[1] The ban on the "machine" was removed at the 1923 convention.
[2] The constitution (effective April, 1929) provides: "In shops where it is not now a practice no member of a local lodge is permitted to accept piecework, operate more than one machine, or accept employment under the premium, merit, task, or contract systems."
[3] U. S. Department of Commerce and Labor, "Regulation and Restriction of Output," *Eleventh Special Report of the Commissioner of Labor* (1904), p. 109.

strain and greater risk of accident involved in operating two machines of the types enumerated; another was the effect upon the number of machinists required. No doubt the latter was the more important. In his address at the Machinists' Convention in 1902, the then president said, "We prevented the introduction of the two-machine system in 137 shops, employing 9,500 men. It is safe to say that if this system had been introduced, the force of men would be reduced one-eighth; hence, in this we have saved the positions of 1,188 men, whose wages would amount to $2,613.60 per day, or $818,056.80 per year."

Many unions, because of the influence of custom, or the effect on the number of jobs, or the strain involved if more machines were manned by an operator or if the size of a crew on a machine were reduced, have opposed arrangements proposed by the employers, or have sought to exercise control by union rule. Years ago, the Pressmen required much larger crews in New York and Chicago newspaper offices than were used on octuple and other presses in open shops. They justified their rules as necessary to prevent undue strain, while the employers accused them of making jobs and restricting output. More recently, such issues have been disposed of in conference or submitted for decision by an arbitration board. In the textile trades there have been many disputes growing out of the attempts by manufacturers to increase the number of machines to be supervised by an operator. The workers have been influenced by custom and the desire to avoid strain and/or a reduction in the volume of employment, while the manufacturers have wished to take advantage of the fact that the machinery had been improved, or to speed the workers, or to introduce a more economical organization of the work. At Kenosha, Wis., for example, an attempt was made in the late twenties to substitute a skilled worker, aided by two helpers, on a pair of machines for the old system of an unaided skilled worker on each machine. This attempt was opposed by the organization (of skilled workers only), perhaps almost entirely because the volume of employment for skilled workers would be reduced by half, and a protracted strike ensued. Likewise, though it involved materially different considerations, an attempt by copper-mine operators to substitute a one-man drill for a two-man drill was one of the grievances of the workers in the Northern Michigan strike of 1913.[1]

These few concrete cases are sufficient to indicate the issues involved in connection with the introduction of improved appliances and processes in unionized industries.[2] Employers, seeking profit, wish to make changes, which perhaps require more speed, or involve greater accident-risk, or reduce the number of jobs, or introduce a "new competition."

[1] See "Michigan Copper District Strike," U. S. Bureau of Labor Statistics, *Bulletin* 139 (1914).

[2] For a fuller discussion of unions and technological change and the reasons for adoption of certain policies and their results, see Sumner H. Slichter, *op. cit.*, Chaps. 7–9.

The workers, on the other hand, are influenced by custom, they fear change, and they dislike to bear the very real sacrifice that may be incidental to it. Their largest concern is in jobs and wage rates jeopardized. Nearly all the union activity in this connection has been of a defensive character.

Two questions may be raised at this point. Should hourly earnings be maintained as a condition of introducing improved appliances and processes of such character that a cheaper type of worker might be successfully employed? Should an employer be required to provide suitable employment elsewhere in his plant for those who would be displaced as a condition of changing appliances and processes?

In arriving at a conclusion with reference to the first of these questions, it is to be noted that if hourly earnings are maintained the plane of living of workers retained (or newly employed) is protected, but at the expense of higher labor costs than are inevitably involved, and perhaps at the expense of the consumers of the product. Like a tariff rate, in so many cases, it is a question of the immediate welfare of the smaller group as against the loss of the larger group—unless the employer would pocket any saving in costs. The second of the two questions raises the same issue, plus the additional one of what labor is to be employed—the workers already on the payroll or those in the labor market looking for jobs. Most employers have come to the view that it is good management to make changes slowly, and, in so far as practicable, to transfer acceptable workers and to continue them on the payroll. Whatever may be said concerning these matters when looked at from other points of view, the maintenance of earnings and the provision of employment elsewhere in the plant for those displaced as a result of changes introduced have the effect of preventing opposition to changes in appliances and processes in the union shop and of maintaining and improving the morale of the workers, whether union or nonunion.

A final question arises as to the results of union policy concerning machinery and improved processes: that of whether unionism accelerates or retards industrial progress.

It is obvious that the policies of certain unions have retarded the introduction of improved appliances and processes. But a final conclusion cannot be arrived at as regards the net effect without giving proper weight to other factors in the situation. One of these is that higher wages, due to union pressure, place a premium upon the use of relatively more capital and in such forms as to save labor. Another is that unions usually will not make concessions to those firms in the industry who cannot afford to pay standard wages because of their out-of-date equipment and processes. As a condition of remaining in industry, they must oust the union or improve their equipment and management. Hence, while the union is retarding technical progress in some concrete cases, its policies may be encouraging progress in other concrete cases. Then, too, there have been cases in which employers have been positively encouraged to introduce new and better types of equipment[1]—types calling for the use of fewer workers.

UNION POLICY AND USELESS PROCESSES AND UNECONOMICAL WORK ORGANIZATION[2]

Of examples of useless processes imposed by unions there are relatively few. The best known is in the newspaper industry, where, if printing is done from matrices obtained from another office, it may be required that after publication the copy shall be reset, and the proof read and corrected, within a stipulated period. The rule generally applies only to matter exchanged locally. Such a requirement was extensively introduced years ago, when compositors were paid by the piece, and it was designed to protect against loss of the most profitable jobs. Today the union is interested in it as a make-work device. In many cities, the requirement was long ago dropped or "traded out," but it still obtains in certain cities and is a source of much irritation and a subject of complaint. The rule is said to cost one metropolitan daily $125,000 a year.

Of uneconomical ways of doing work, retained because of union insistence, many examples may be found. In the men's clothing industry, where, fortunately, disputes are settled by arbitration, there have been questions of height of lay (number of plies of cloth to be cut together), the piling of mixed fabrics, the elimination of odd sizes, etc.[3] The matter of increased strain on the worker enters into some of these issues, but, aside from the influence of custom, it has been largely a question of volume of work in a seasonal industry versus cost of getting the work done.

Over against those situations in which the union, circumstanced as it typically is, is likely to act in an obstructive, defensive way, one finds other unions, with employment stabilized, cooperating with the employer in an effort to eliminate waste in its different forms. Such efforts stand out in those cases in which union-management cooperation has been adopted.

UNIONS AND THE SOURCES OF MATERIALS

Frequently, the rules of building-trades unions have prevented employers from securing materials in the cheapest way or cheapest

---

[1] For example, under the current National Agreement with the manufacturers, the Hosiery Workers are accepting lower wages where the mills will introduce modern equipment.

[2] For an extensive discussion of make-work rules and policies, see Sumner H. Slichter, *op. cit.*, Chap. 6.

[3] It has become a policy of the Amalgamated Clothing Workers to eliminate or reduce these restrictions, which had usually been introduced by the manufacturers, in the interest of lower costs, or to "trade" them out, say, for higher wages.

market. Thus a Plumbers' rule provided that all brass and nickel waste, flush and supply pipe should be prepared by the plumber who installed it. It was required, moreover, that several enumerated things should be manufactured in the shop, not purchased from firms in a position to manufacture in quantity and at low cost. The motive was to keep work for the craftsmen in the trade.

Much more important are the rules (or agreements) frequently found forbidding the members of the union to make use of nonlabel materials. Thus, years ago in San Francisco, nonlabel lumber, brick, mantels, and other materials were not to be used in building construction. Similar rules have found place in the building industry elsewhere, as in New York and Chicago. In the latter city, it was a three-party (carpenters, contractors, and materials-men) agreement not to use nonunion millwork that was involved in the famous Brims case,[1] in which the federal court found a conspiracy to interfere with interstate commerce. The union object in such cases may be to further the organization of labor in the manufacturing plant. Carpenters, for example, have jurisdiction over planing mills and sash and blind factories, as well as over construction work. Hence, in the Brims case, the union was attempting to aid and protect organization and to provide business for "fair mills"—those employing its members. In addition to this motive, a rule requiring union-made materials may have the effect of discouraging the purchase of finished materials instead of preparing them at the point of erection. Of course, in the building trades much work has been diverted from the building site to the mill. Finally, behind a few of the regulations there has seemingly been nothing more than union feeling, the organization itself having nothing to gain in volume of work or membership.

Here, again, one has to do for the most part with situations analogous to those behind protective tariffs. Hence nothing further needs to be said except that no small part of the graft in the building trades has grown out of bans on nonunion materials.[2] Contractors are prone to buy in the cheapest market and thus violate union rule or agreement. If the materials have been installed, they must be replaced or a fine paid. Perhaps the latter is preferred. Possibly the money does not find its way into the union treasury, or possibly an acceptable settlement is made with the business agent before nonunion materials can be installed in violation of rule or agreement.

[1] *U. S. v. Brims*, 272 U. S. 549 (1926). This is only one of scores of cases growing out of union bans on nonunion materials.

[2] Most of the rest of it has taken the form of strike insurance.

CHAPTER X

SOME TRADE-UNION POLICIES AND PRACTICES
(*Concluded*)

UNIONS, APPRENTICES, AND HELPERS

Organizations of diverse types are more or less prone to attempt to exercise control over the situation confronting them, in order to protect themselves against the development of problems and to secure a positive advantage. Unions are no exception to the rule. Hence we find many of them seeking, among other things, to regulate the supply of labor through the control of apprentices, helpers, handymen, and the like, and their requirements for admission to membership.

Apprenticeship, as Professor Douglas has said, is "the normal correlative of handicraft labor."[1] The institution appears to have been prevalent in all countries—among them, Greece, Rome, China, England and other Northwestern European countries, the American Colonies and the United States, when and in so far as their industries were in the handicraft stage. Indeed, the embrace of apprenticeship has extended far beyond the confines of industry.[2] But in handicraft industry, the normal working group consisted of master, one or more journeymen, and one or more apprentices. Apprenticeship was a matter of custom, or, as in England, was controlled by guild ordinance or by local or national law. Not infrequently it was regulated by law, as under the Statute of Artificers (England, 1562), for the government was interested in solving the problems of willful idleness, orphanage, and dependency, as well as in training for the crafts and in the minimum of general instruction and religious training. But with the partial breaking down of the crafts by the factory system and the subdivision of labor, there was an inevitable obsolescence of the system of apprenticeship. And, with the less general need for craft training, with the development of educational and other social institutions, and with the spread of the policy of *laissez faire* in matters involving industry, the state largely ceased to control or regulate apprenticeship. England repealed her old statute in 1814.

Though apprenticeship was not so important or so much emphasized in this country as in the older ones, the American Colonies and then the states of the early period under the Constitution did have laws applying

[1] Paul H. Douglas, *American Apprenticeship and Industrial Education*, Columbia University Studies in History, Economics and Public Law, vol. 95, no. 2 (1921), p. 16.
[2] *Ibid.*, Chap. 2.

to the system in trades, and frequently in agriculture and services as well. With the development of the country and of the factory system, however, the greater part of this legislation became obsolete and disappeared. Until the appearance of the New Deal the only states with legislation designed to develop modern apprentice systems were Wisconsin and Oregon, this legislation being enacted in the two states in 1911 and 1931 respectively.[1] In the former state, with employers, labor, and the public schools cooperating with the Industrial Commission, a considerable number of apprentices have been trained in a variety of trades.[2] Since 1933, fourteen states and one territory[3] have enacted laws on apprenticeship and established apprenticeship councils. Nine other states have set up apprenticeship councils only. Much of this action has been taken as a result of the encouragement given by the Federal Government, which for several years has been interested in the subject.

Apprenticeship Programs.—The depression beginning in 1929 created a temporary surplus of skilled men in most occupations and removed most of the incentive employers and trade unions had had in the training of young workers. Under the codes of fair competition adopted in 1933 and 1934, there was for a time a demand for apprentices, but since the codes almost completely neglected to provide for proper apprentice training, it was suspected that many employers were using the term "apprentice" to cover learners who were not being taught a trade but simply the operation of a single machine. The fear that permission to employ "apprentices" and learners would result in the exploitation of youths, at the expense of unemployed adults, led NRA officials to impose restrictions that for a time practically ended the employment of new apprentices. Then even during the depression, shortages of skilled labor appeared in certain industries. Moreover, it was evident that when recovery was attained there would be a dearth of properly trained craftsmen. Steps were therefore taken to provide for proper apprentice training under the codes, and when these were dissolved by the decision of the Supreme Court in the Schechter case,[4] the federal apprentice

---

[1] Wisconsin Laws (1911), Chap. 347; Oregon Acts (1931), Chap. 301.

[2] On Aug. 1, 1930, for example, 3,350 live apprentice contracts were on file. Between 1915 and 1930 a total of 2,567 indentured apprentices completed their terms of training, these averaging about four years. Definite training schedules, combining schooling with work on the job, had been developed in more than sixty trades, including automobile machinists, barbers, blacksmiths, boilermakers, bricklayers, carpenters, electricians, engravers, photoengravers, patternmakers, painters, plumbers, printers, and toolmakers (see *Biennial Reports*, Wisconsin Industrial Commission).

[3] Arizona, Arkansas, California, Colorado, Kentucky, Louisiana, Massachusetts, Minnesota, Montana, Nevada, New York, North Carolina, Virginia, Washington, and Hawaii.

[4] *Schechter Poultry Corporation v. United States*, 295 U. S. 495 (1935).

program was carried on under Executive Order. The Federal Committee on Apprenticeship has secured the cooperation of employers and unions in various industries and of the councils in the several states,[1] these councils usually representing employers, labor, and the public, sometimes just employers and labor.

The federal and state programs are not mandatory; the Committee and councils encourage adoption and standardization of apprenticeship systems by cooperating groups in industry. Basic standards are suggested with regard to age, part-time schooling, schedule of work processes to be learned, an increasing scale of wages during apprenticeship, etc.[2] Under the national defense program this work enormously expanded. At the same time attention came to be centered on critical war industries —aircraft, shipbuilding, tanks, and antiaircraft guns. The Committee's field staff grew from 37 in August, 1940, to 200 in the winter of 1942.[3] The number of approved apprentice-training programs more than doubled from June, 1940, to February, 1942, when more than a thousand were in effect, including some five hundred in plants producing war materials. These plans vary in scope; in some cases they cover only one plant, sometimes a series of plants, and in a few instances they are company-wide. In so far as possible they are set up cooperatively, with the participation of both management and employees.

While public interest and participation in the training of apprentices has thus recently been revived, the prevailing policy for decades was to

[1] The activities are carried on under the Fitzgerald Act, Public No. 308, 75th Congress, approved Aug. 16, 1937.

[2] See *infra*, p. 444–445, 450 for reference to national standards of apprenticeship in the building industry. The Federal Committee has as its functions: to promote the adoption of labor standards necessary to safeguard the welfare of apprentices; to extend the application of such standards by encouraging their inclusion in contracts of apprenticeship; to bring together employers and employees for the formulation of standards of apprenticeship in their trade; to cooperate with state agencies in the formulation and the promotion of standards of apprenticeship; to cooperate with the National Youth Administration and with the Office of Education in services to apprentices; to conduct research in various trades concerning the labor standards of apprenticeship and to publish information; to act as a clearinghouse for information, so that national, state, and local employer and labor organizations may benefit from the experience of similar groups in other sections of the country; and to serve in a technical, consulting, and advisory capacity to all agencies concerned with apprenticeship [*cf.* Special Release no. 3 (February, 1939) and other releases and publications of the Committee]. It is interesting to note that in Australia (*Industrial and Labour Information*, May 18, 1936, p. 186), in parts of Canada (U. S. Department of Labor, Division of Standards, *Survey of Labor Administration*, May, 1937, p. 7), and elsewhere, the same problem is being attacked in a more or less similar manner.

[3] Part of the work of this staff has centered on short-term training programs made necessary by the need for supplying trained workers in as short a time as possible. In these programs, which involve upgrading, breaking down skills, making job descriptions and inventories of skills, etc., the Committee has cooperated with the Training-within-Industry Division of the War Production Board—recently transferred to the Federal Security Agency.

leave the matter to industry itself, to the trade unions, and to industry and unions jointly to deal with. With departure from custom and disappearance of government control, the craft unions became actively interested. It is the policies and practices of these labor organizations in which we are primarily interested. In order to give a clear picture of the subject, however, a few observations on the training policies and practices of management may be made.

Management Policies.—The crafts have been extensively broken down and subdivision of work introduced wherever the factory system and its analogues have been developed. In the United States this has occurred more extensively than in any other country. Yet even in mass industry skilled jobs remain, and the factory system and invention have developed new ones. Examples are found in the skill required in connection with the installation and maintenance of costly appliances and in the development of such arts as modern photoengraving. Moreover, the training of persons for supervisory positions, such as that of foremen, has become an increasingly important problem.

Industry today combines the old handicraft system and subdivided and narrowly specialized work in varying proportions. Especially since it became impossible to rely largely upon the older type of immigrant for necessary skilled labor, and since efficiency has come to be appreciated and the limitations upon fitting jobs to men as they are have become more clearly recognized, management has been active in the training of workers. Some of this training has been done in connection with the workplace and some of it in trade schools, these sometimes operated by employer associations.[1]

Though unaffiliated employers in industries with many establishments have frequently been prone to look entirely to the labor market for the skilled workers they need or to rely upon helpers picking up the details of the crafts from those with whom they are associated at work, open shops have usually employed apprentices. Many large corporations, particularly, have developed systems for training craftsmen as well as systems for job training or for the training of supervisors and executives.[2] Sometimes the training of craftsmen has been very much the same as in the unionized shop. Very frequently, however, the training has been narrowed to fit more directly into the immediate work to be done. Moreover, a considerable number of employers' associations have had as one of their functions to support, if not to operate, trade schools for training skilled labor independently or in conjunction with work in the productive plants. For example, a number of such associations con-

[1] It is not in point here to say anything concerning training by management for supervisory or executive positions, of which there is a great deal, or for cultural or Americanization purposes.

[2] As in the case of R. R. Donnelly and Sons, where excellent training systems are found.

tributed to the support of the Winona School formerly conducted in Indianapolis.[1] Examples of association schools operated to avoid the development of a union psychology, as well as to augment the supply of skilled workmen, are the photoengraving school operated by the associated printers and the school for all printing crafts operated by the open-shop book and job printers in Chicago. The one school trains workers by instruction and supervised work in the plant operated by it; the other adds instruction in various subjects to experience on the job in the production plants. Finally, there are instances, exemplified by the National Metal Trades Association, in which employers' associations have encouraged their members to employ apprentices and to train them under approved systems.

In most industries, however, the larger number of workers are not to be trained as craftsmen or near-craftsmen but for particular jobs. For this purpose the main systems used are the vestibule school, operated in conjunction with the plant but not on the work floor, and supervised work in the production process itself.

Union Objectives and Policies.—The objectives of unions in training for jobs have been different from those of management. Moreover, their systems, while they have undergone change, have been greatly influenced by custom.

Certain early American unions sought to control the situation to the end that those who entered the trade should have training such that they would not hamper their organizations in securing good wages or prove to be a burden upon them because frequently unemployed. In many instances, too, the unions had to meet the problem presented by employers who hired large numbers of young, untrained persons at low wages and then used them on such parts of the work as they were qualified to do. If the problem were not met, some fraction of the volume of work for the journeymen would be taken from them. Hence the adoption of local union apprentice rules requiring training for a number of years and in all parts of the craft, and union prohibition of the employment of cheap "boy labor" or partly trained adults on specialized jobs. It was only at a later time that limitations were placed upon the number of apprentices that might be taken.

The apprentice rules, as they developed, had the three objectives indicated: to insure adequate training, to safeguard against the employment of cheap "boy labor," and, through numerical limitations, to control the number becoming journeymen in the trade. Apprenticeship was one of the main interests of the local craft unions; indeed, the desire to regulate through apprentice rules was an important factor leading to the organization of labor in the crafts.

[1] *Cf.* Clarence E. Bonnett, *Employers' Associations in the United States* (1922).

Local rules, even now, occupy an important place in the control of apprenticeship. This is particularly true in the building trades, where there is a strong feeling for local autonomy and where competition between cities is of small concern.[1] This is true, also, where strong locals are affiliated with a weak international or have no international affiliation at all. But in many cases, especially where there is need for uniformity as between firms and localities competing in a wide or general market, the control of apprenticeship has been transferred to (or assumed by) the international. Indeed, the need for such central control was an important reason for organizing some of the international unions. And, finally, there are trades, such as printing, in which the international legislates on apprenticeship and leaves the locals free to adopt such further regulations as they wish, provided these are not out of harmony with "international law." Thus the International Typographical Union urges its locals to secure the privilege of governing apprentices, lays down rules as to training and the work the apprentices shall do in the shop, and furnishes a splendid set of lessons for use in the training of apprentices, but leaves the locals free to make regulations limiting the number of apprentices to be employed.[2] Such compromise arrangements, in which the control is shared by international and local, are explained in part by internal question as to division of authority, in part by the advantages of elasticity so that adjustments to local situations can be made.

Owing to the importance of the building trades and certain other craft organizations in unionism as a whole and to the great consideration given to matters pertaining to the job, American unions have for some decades emphasized apprenticeship more than have the labor organizations of most other countries. In 1904, since which time the general situation in this country has not changed, in the older areas of organization, except in a few respects to be mentioned later, Professor Motley found[3] that 70 of 120 internationals investigated maintained apprentice rules and enforced them in their respective trades in so far as they were able to do so. The remaining fifty, with 46 per cent of the membership, laid down no rules. Among these fifty international unions were (a) a number of organizations

---

[1] But cf. infra, p. 450.

[2] "Local unions are required to fix the ratio of apprentices to the number of journeymen regularly employed in any and all offices, but it must be provided that at least one member of the typographical union, aside from the proprietor, shall be regularly employed in the composing room before an office is entitled to an apprentice." Book of Laws, 1938, General Laws, Art. I, Sec. 19.

[3] James M. Motley, Apprenticeship in American Trade Unions, Johns Hopkins University Studies in Historical and Political Science, Series 25 (1907). With the amalgamation of craft organizations the number of internationals now regulating apprenticeship is around sixty. Of course the total number of internationals has increased, most of the new ones being industrial unions or unions of white-collar workers in government or private employment.

of professional persons whose training most obviously takes a different form; (*b*) about an equal number of organizations, such as Locomotive Engineers and Railway Conductors, whose members are highly skilled, but who are recruited and trained in such manner that no problem calling forth organized control has developed; and (*c*) a much larger number of organizations, most of whose members, owing to minute subdivision of labor, are unskilled and only the briefest experience is required to give them the necessary training for the work they engage in.[1]

The details of union apprentice regulations differ widely among trades, and to some extent among locals in the same trade.   As a generalization, however, it may be said that the employer takes the initiative by employing the youth, who is normally expected to serve his time in the given shop.   Usually there are regulations concerning age that must be observed; the initiate must be old enough, say sixteen, to be responsible and to "stand the work," but not so old as to be tempted to leave his training before it is completed and attempt to secure employment as a journeyman.   The period of apprenticeship may be as short as one year or as long as seven, but most frequently it is from four to six years.[2] Whatever its length, it is likely to be fixed as much in the light of custom as in view of the time needed to learn the trade; and in some cases it is made considerably longer than is required to gain necessary proficiency because of a desire to discourage young persons from entering the trade.[3] Especially in the seasonal and waning trades, there is great fear of an excessive labor supply.   This fear may find expression in the direct control of numbers also.   A small labor supply insures more regular employment at relatively high wages.   The number of apprentices may be fixed at one per shop, or it may take the form of a ratio to journeymen, or, again, it may be one per shop with one or more added for a stated number of journeymen over a certain figure.   If it takes the form of a ratio, as is usually the case, it may be one apprentice for each two or four or seven or ten journeymen, or it may be that, while increasing, the number of apprentices is not permitted to exceed a specified figure.   Thus, on Chicago daily newspapers, "The proportion of apprentices to regular journeymen [compositors] shall be as follows: for ten journeymen or less, one apprentice; for every additional ten or fractional part thereof, one apprentice . . . ; but no office shall have more than eight apprentices at one time (not including machine tender's apprentices). . . . "   The period of training is five years.   In the pressroom

---

[1] For lists of unions in different groups, see *ibid.*, pp. 53*ff.*   It may be noted that local craft organizations in semiindustrial unions frequently develop apprenticeship systems.

[2] See Sumner H. Slichter, *Union Policies and Industrial Management* (1941), p. 12.

[3] But an unnecessarily long term also encourages training by employers, who profit by paying apprentice wages to boys almost as skilled as journeymen.   Moreover, apprentices are tempted to leave before completion of their term and seek employment in nonunion shops.

one apprentice is allowed for each press crew. The Plumbers allow one apprentice per shop, without regard to size; the Sheet Metal Workers one to three journeymen, two to five, and three to eight; the Tile Layers one for the first seven regularly employed and one additional for each fifteen journeymen in excess of seven; the Plasterers one to five men regularly employed and one additional for each twenty. It is evident that the numerical limitations differ widely.[1] It should be added that in not a few instances local unions have placed a ban upon any apprentices being taken on, unless, perhaps, the sons of journeymen. For the most part such action is explained by the presence of an excessive supply of journeymen in the trade concerned.

Apprentice training has consisted chiefly of learning by watching and doing, with such "pointers" as journeymen and foreman might give. All of the details of training may be left to custom or chance, but most frequently the rules will provide that the apprentice shall have opportunity to learn all parts of the craft or some defined part of the industry and the journeymen are generally admonished to be helpful to the apprentice. Here and there, as in the case of the International Typographical Union, a course of study has been laid down and the apprentice is required to complete it.

A scale of wages for apprentices is ordinarily provided, in specified sums per week or in percentages of the regular scale, but in any event related to the journeyman's wage and stepped up periodically. Thus, in the composing rooms of Chicago daily newspapers, the wage of the apprentice is for the first year 25 per cent; the second, 30 per cent; the third, 40 per cent; the fourth, 60 per cent; the fifth and last year, 80 per cent of the scale for journeymen. Finally, in describing union apprentice systems, it is to be noted that the apprentice is presumed to become or to be made familiar with unionism and that in some cases he is admitted to at least junior membership in the union before he has completed his training.

Much of the adverse criticism of American unions has centered in these apprentice rules, which are observed in union shops. The rules are said to deprive the American boy of opportunity to learn a trade. Not infrequently, limitations upon numbers and period of apprenticeship have been used in an effort to show that their combined effect is unduly restrictive and responsible for a shortage of adequately trained journeymen. While plausible, such argument is likely to be quite misleading, for how many recruits need to be trained for a trade or industry depends upon a number of factors—the rate of expansion or contraction of the trade, the number who enter the trade without formal apprenticeship, the number who die or leave the trade, the average of the working life in the employment, etc. If a not extreme case may be cited as an

[1] For provisions in a sample of 611 trade agreements, see S. H. Slichter, *op. cit.*, p. 11.

example, years ago the period of apprenticeship in the printing trade was five years and the union ratio in Chicago was one apprentice to seven journeymen. Were all recruits to the trade to be trained by being apprenticed in Chicago, thirty-five years would have been required to replace the journeymen employed in union shops. The requirements were said to be restrictive, and the employers wished to have the ratio changed to one to five. The parties in interest finally agreed to set up a joint committee to investigate and report on the proper ratio. Taking into consideration such factors as those noted above, the committee, by unanimous vote, recommended that the ratio should be one to ten. The ratio indicated has now been in effect for years, and, with the migration of workers into Chicago, has been satisfactory.[1]

Without question, restrictive union rules may deprive a youth of opportunity to train for the trade of his choice. At the same time it is no doubt true that many of the critics of unionism have been less interested in appropriate industrial education than in criticizing and weakening the unions and in giving the employer unlimited opportunity to hire boys and use their labor as suits his wishes and convenience. The greatest effect of apprentice rules has been to prevent subdivision of labor in union shops much beyond the work of journeyman and apprentice. This has at times, as formerly in the stove trade,[2] placed the union employer under a handicap in competing with the open-shop employer.

Were the union strongly enough organized, it might use apprentice rules to give it a monopolistic control of the supply of labor. However, relatively few unions have been able to make the serving of an apprenticeship under its system a condition of admission to membership in them and of entrance to the trade; the trade may generally be picked up in an open shop or in small cities and towns, where such unions as exist are usually weak and unable to regulate apprenticeship. Nearly all unions find themselves, therefore, under the necessity of admitting to membership men who without formal training succeed in securing employment. Nor can most unions be charged with primary responsibility for an inadequate supply of properly trained men in their trades. In exceptional cases, it is true, the union shop has relatively fewer apprentices than are employed in the open shop. This was formerly true in the stove industry and in photoengraving. In most other instances, however, investigation has shown that the open shops had relatively the fewest apprentices and in spite of lower wages paid.[3] If the need for apprentice training is assumed, the neglect of unorganized industry

---

[1] For rough tests of the reasonableness of union apprenticeship limits, see *ibid.*, pp. 16–28. Slichter concludes (p. 18) that "typical union agreements fall slightly short of, permitting sufficient replacements to maintain a stationary working force."

[2] See James M. Motley, *op. cit.*, pp. 42–50.

[3] See S. H. Slichter, *op. cit.*, pp. 32–33.

has been worse than the limitations imposed by unions.[1] While union practices have really been restrictive in some known cases, the training of an inadequate number for skilled employment has been due more in the United States to the average employer's desire to use boys on boy's work and to hire skilled men trained at the expense of another, to the preference of parents and youths for the larger immediate earnings to be realized from a regular job in industry, and to the disinclination of youths to train for manual work that exposes them to dirt and grease.

The real case against the usual set of union apprentice rules is that for the most part the rules are the product of custom, whim, and guess-work; that they are not the result of investigation and are not adjusted to the real needs of the situation; and that they are undemocratically imposed upon the trade in so far as the unions wield power in the closed shops. Fortunately there have been an increasing number of instances in which employers and unions democratically and jointly have worked out improved systems of training, and an increasing number of instances in which large employers have developed forward-looking training systems.

In certain of the building trades in Chicago, as in steam-fitting and electrical work, the associated contractors and the unions have developed more or less mutually satisfactory apprenticeship systems. In the electrical trades, for example, all apprentices of the local have been required to serve a four-year period, subject to a reduction to three years and nine months when the youth has had an unusually good record. Apprentices have attended a continuation school one day every two weeks, the contractors being required to pay the apprentice $2 for the day spent in school. Instruction has been given by teachers in the employ of the Board of Education, while the necessary equipment has been provided by the union and contractors. The annual enrollment, until the long depression developed, averaged between 550 and 600; the training has included layout and electrical installation projects, laboratory and shopwork, mathematics, and electrical drawing. This has of course been supplementary to the training secured in the shop.

Perhaps the most interesting jointly developed or administered local apprentice systems have been found in the printing trades. Apprentice-ship in composing rooms of union book and job shops in Chicago has for years been controlled by the provisions of successive joint agreements; the system has been administered by the Joint Apprenticeship Committee

---

[1] In recent months, unions have relaxed their restrictions on apprentice employment. Where plant quotas are filled and there is need for additional apprentices to meet the requirements of the defense program, they have freely granted exceptions. The Machinists for example, have agreed in many cases to a ratio of one apprentice to every five journey-men, though their constitution calls for a ratio of one to ten. "Out of Crisis, Opportunity!" *Bulletin* 43 (revised, September, 1941), Federal Committee on Apprenticeship, U. S. Department of Labor, p. 25.

of two representatives from the Franklin Association and two from Typographical Union No. 16. Under the agreement the ratio is one apprentice to ten journeymen. The Joint Apprenticeship Committee "is responsible for the selection of apprentices. . . . Candidates for apprenticeship must fulfill certain requirements and have been examined and approved by the committee. In practice they are hired by the plants, but they cannot be put to work until they are approved by the Joint Apprenticeship Committee. All apprentices are registered with the union, and are issued apprentice cards.

"The Committee endeavors to assure an all-around training of the apprentice. No employer is entitled to an apprentice, therefore, unless he has a plant and equipment sufficient to enable an apprentice to become a finished compositor at the end of his term. . . . The apprentice term is five years. The first year is one of probation during which the further employment of the apprentice may be protested by either the union or the employer, and at the end of which, if in the judgment of the Committee he is proved incapable, he shall be refused further work at the trade. Definite regulation of the type of work that the apprentice is to do in each year is included. The apprentice is required to study the I.T.U. Lessons in Printing, completing a certain number of lessons each year, before he is entitled to the apprentice card for the next year and the regular increase in pay. Apprentices after their fifth year are not eligible to journeyman membership in the union until they have completed the lessons to the satisfaction of the I.T.U. Commission on Apprenticeship and have passed a satisfactory examination before the Joint Apprenticeship Committee."[1]

Even more interesting and important is the joint control of apprentice training by the unions and the Printers' League of New York, with the cooperation of the Board of Education.[2] The plan covers both composing and pressrooms. The details are similar to those, mentioned above, in Chicago's printing industry, but here the training is divided between the shops and part-time schools that have been jointly directed. School attendance for six hours per week is compulsory, half of it on the employer's, half on the apprentice's, time. The apprentices are thus enabled to secure a broader and sounder training than by acquiring knowledge on the job and from prepared lessons alone. A class in photo-offset platemaking has also been cooperatively given at the pressmen's school. In the winter of 1942 around three hundred pressmen, compositor, and photoengraver apprentices were being trained under this plan in New

[1] Quoted from Emily C. Brown, Book and Job Printing in Chicago (1931), pp. 296–297. For the apprentice provisions of the joint agreement, see pp. 345–350 of that book.

[2] For an excellent account of the arrangement, see "Joint Industrial Control in the Book and Job Printing Industry," U. S. Bureau of Labor Statistics, Bulletin 481 (1928), pp. 118–124.

York. In addition about an equal number of journeymen were attending
the schools on their own time.

One more instance of progressive interest in apprenticeship in industry
may be cited. In line with the methods adopted by the Federal Committee on Apprenticeship, the United Association of Journeymen Plumbers and Steam Fitters agreed nationally upon minimum standards for the
employment and education of apprentices with the Master Plumbers
Association. Corresponding standards were developed and approved
for painting and decorating,[1] and later for steam fitting, carpentry, hand
plastering, and electrical construction. The standards agreed upon are
minima recommended to local parties in interest for their guidance. Any
standards become effective only by adoption by the parties in interest.

The jointly established systems mentioned are a few of the more
important established by organized employers and unions, which have
operated in a satisfactory manner. But, naturally, employers of union
workmen have frequently questioned some features of the union regulations that still prevail. Naturally, too, the issues raised have been
considered in numerous conferences. In some cases only the ratio has
been adjusted so as to be mutually satisfactory. Such was the case in
the stove industry, where, after thirteen years of investigation and
conference, the Molders' Union changed its ratio from one to eight
to that of one to five, and at the same time made further provisions to
enable the union employer to secure an adequate supply of labor and to
place him on a more nearly equal footing with his nonunion competitor.
More recently, however, more thoroughgoing systems have been jointly
developed and administered, in increasing numbers. Rule making has
to that extent given way to collective bargaining. The resulting systems
find a logical place in industrial training for employments in which
prolonged training, chiefly on the job, is needed.

Helpers.—More or less closely related to the apprentice is the helper,
improver, assistant, or whatever he may be called in the particular trade.
The apprentice, as Dr. Ashworth has stated,[2] "is one who, by promise,

---

[1] The standards approved for plumbing and painting and decorating are essentially
the same (cf. Federal Committee on Apprenticeship, Bulletins 16 and 23). Applicants for
plumbing apprenticeship must be between sixteen and twenty-one years of age; the term
shall not be less than five years; the minimum hours of work and related school instruction
shall not be less than 9,500, the hours of schooling being not less than 720; the work training
is scheduled for each year; the scale of wages rises from 25 per cent of the prevailing
journeymen's wage rate for the first six months to 80 per cent of that wage during the last
six months of the indenture; the advancement in the work schedule and remuneration rests
upon the results of periodic examinations; the ratio is one apprentice per eligible shop and
one additional apprentice for each five journeymen, but the total per shop is not to exceed
four.

[2] John H. Ashworth, The Helper and American Trade Unions, Johns Hopkins University
Studies, Series 33 (1915), pp. 22–23.

indenture, or covenant, for a specified time, is being taught the trade by a master of the trade or some one in his employ." A helper, on the other hand, is "any person employed to help the skilled journeyman or journeymen under whose supervision he works." Though there may be differences in age and in other respects, "the only essential distinction between the two classes . . . lies in the purpose of employment. The helper, though he may be a learner of a trade, is primarily employed because he supplies an economic need, and in fixing his wages nothing is deducted for instruction given. On the other hand, an apprentice may assist a journeyman, but the primary purpose for which he is engaged is that he may be taught the trade, though he may incidentally supply an economic need."

The helper may be employed and paid by the journeyman whom he assists or he may be hired and paid by the employer. He may team with a journeyman on work requiring two or more persons, as on some plumbing jobs, or he may have a more or less independent job, as is frequently the case in some branches of manufacture. If he is really an assistant to the journeyman, he incidentally in the course of a few years gains knowledge of and experience in the trade, and the supply of skilled labor is added to in this way. The line to be drawn between the helper and the apprentice then becomes thin and may be negligible. Indeed, serving as a helper may become the chief or exclusive method of training, as in the case of firemen on the way to become locomotive engineers or in the case of piecers who become spinners. And while the helper is gaining knowledge and experience, the volume of journeymen's work may be affected, for journeymen could be used exclusively to help one another out where teamwork is necessary. In those cases where the helper's job is a more or less independent one, there may be some opportunity to pick up a trade, though it is, of course, much less good than that of an apprentice. The main fact that concerns us here, however, is that the presence of such a helper working, as his regular job, on the less difficult parts of the work to be done means that subdivision of labor has been introduced and that no longer are journeyman and apprentice found alone.

It is obvious that, from the point of view of a labor organization interesting itself in apprenticeship, the helper is likely to present a problem, for he may add to the supply of skilled men, he curtails the amount of work available for the journeymen, and he may be used to replace the journeymen when a strike or lockout develops. The unions have adopted different policies in meeting the problems presented. Some craft unions, like the industrial unions, have placed no limitation upon the number of helpers the employer may engage or upon any consequent division of labor but have freely made place for the helper in their membership and permitted things to take their course. Much more likely, however, they have resorted to a policy of restriction, possibly with the helper in the union, possibly with him excluded.

Years ago the unions of journeymen coatmakers and other clothing workers in New York City attempted to abolish the team system altogether or to limit the number of helpers to a fraction of the number of journeymen employed. Likewise, for many years, the cigar makers in some of the cities attempted to exclude the helper and to prevent any subdivision of labor, but this has become a matter of history. The same policy was pursued by some of the Plumbers' locals, but in New York the helper was accepted without limitation. The Molders' Union fought the system of employing "berkshires," in addition to apprentices, in the stove industry and, for a time, succeeded in eliminating them from the union shop. In still other cases, the limitation took the form of defining precisely what the helper might do or of limiting the tools he might use. For example, in bricklaying the helper was limited to the shovel; the journeyman alone might use the trowel.

The helper system may be extended to the point where it ceases to be such, and the situation is to be thought of merely in terms of division of labor within the shop. Thus in the trimming room of one Chicago clothing manufacturer the work is divided into many processes, varying from picking to order pieces (100 pockets, say) from a bin to operating a band saw. Some of the occupations are of such character that they can be filled by almost anyone, while others, employing relatively few of the trimmers, are of such character that they require a high degree of skill. Naturally wage rates vary greatly from one occupation to another; the lowest wage rate may be less than half that of the band-sawyer. Certain other large manufacturers in Chicago at one time wished to introduce a similar division of labor into their trimming rooms but this was successfully opposed by the Amalgamated Clothing Workers, a semiindustrial union in which the local of cutters and trimmers, craft-minded, finds place. The union objected to the reduction in the volume of work for skilled men that would have been involved; it objected to the introduction of low-paid jobs that would doom workers to a low standard of living unless they were permitted to graduate out of such jobs; it objected to a subdivision of labor with graduation from one job to another, because, in the course of years, this would give rise to an excessive supply of skilled men. In Chicago, except in the one house, the union stood for a trimming room in which only journeymen body, sleeve, and lining trimmers and apprentices found place. In another city, Rochester, however, the subdivision of labor was accepted under a plan that grouped the several occupations into three and required that the worker be permitted to graduate from one type of job to another until he received all-around training, but also required that the trained man should be paid according to the level of work he was prepared to do, rather than according to the skill and experience required for the work to which he was actually assigned.

Obviously the question arises whether control should be exercised to protect the interests of journeymen in the trade in a sufficient volume of work and to protect a situation in which a goodly number will have an opportunity to maintain the standard of living of the skilled worker; or whether the employer, in the interest of profit, low cost, and low prices to be paid by consumers, and better opportunity for the unskilled to secure employment, shall be free to organize his work in such manner that he can make use of workmen of different degrees of ability, experience, and skill, paid different rates of wages. The principle involved is the same as the principle involved in connection with opposition to use of new machinery and improved processes, raised in the immediately preceding chapter.

HIRING, PROMOTION, AND DISCHARGE

From the subject of apprentices, helpers, and subdivision of labor, we turn to hiring, promotion, and discharge. In our discussion of the standard rate in the preceding chapter something has been said concerning this. The discussion of the closed-shop issue, at a later point,[1] also bears upon the matter. A few observations in order to give a more concrete view of the types of control attempted will therefore suffice at this point.

Hiring and Other Rules.—In many if not in most agreements, as a minimum, one will find a prohibition of discharge or discrimination because of union membership or union activity. A considerable number of unions go no farther than to try to protect their members against such treatment. With this exception, the employer is left free in hiring and discharge, unless hirings must be of members of the union or preference be given to them, which is frequently the case. In the Chicago building trades, for example, the standard agreement provides that "the employers are at liberty to employ whomsoever they see fit," to which may be added, or carried by implication, "it being understood that such employees are members of the party of the second part" (the union).[2] Many unions, however, insist upon having a hand in hiring and in the determination of cause for discharge. Thus the requirements of the International Typographical Union, noted above,[3] find place in the agreement

---

[1] *Infra,* pp. 470–484.

[2] In hiring workers the building-trades employer is almost always limited to members of the union. It is chiefly outside of building construction that the preferential shop is found among such crafts as masons and carpenters.

[3] An examination of 748 typographical contracts in the book and job and the newspaper industries shows only 29 preferential shops. The others provide for the closed shop.

now effective in the composing rooms of Chicago daily newspapers, as in most other composing room agreements.

"The employer shall employ members of the Union in good standing to do the work of its composing rooms. The Union shall furnish a sufficient number of journeymen printers to perform the work of the Employer required to be done under the terms of this Agreement" (Paragraph 1). "The foreman," who must be a member of the union, "shall be the judge of a man's competency as a workman and of his general fitness to work in the office" (Paragraph 8). "The foreman shall have the right to employ help, and may discharge (1) for incompetency, (2) for neglect of duty, (3) for violation of office rules (which shall be conspicuously posted) and (4) to decrease the force, such decrease to be accomplished by discharging first the person or persons last employed, either as regular or as extra employes, as the exigencies of the matter may require. Should there be an increase in the force competent employes displaced by prior reduction shall be reinstated in the reverse order in which they were discharged, before other help may be employed. Upon demand, the foreman shall give the reason for discharge in writing. Persons considered capable as substitutes by foreman shall be deemed competent to fill regular situations, and the substitute oldest in continuous service shall have prior right in the filling of the first vacancy" (Paragraph 9). It should be added that discharge for specified cause is contestable on the ground of unfairness or unduly severe discipline.

Agreements covering pressrooms, photoengraving departments, and other offices in the printing industry are almost always somewhat less restrictive than those effective in composing rooms. More or less typical there, though in many cases the employer is left free to secure his union help as best he can, are the provisions of the agreement between the Pressmen and the Chicago Newspaper Publishers, which read,

"The Employer shall employ members of the Union in good standing in the operation of its presses. The Union shall furnish a sufficient number of competent and satisfactory skilled journeymen pressmen to perform the work of the Employer required to be done under the terms of this Agreement" (Sec. 1).

"When journeymen are called for by an office, it shall make such request for such help to either the president or other officially named officer of the Union, at a convenient place in Chicago, to be designated in writing by the Union. The Union agrees to furnish such help within four hours after receipt of such request.

"If such help is not furnished by the Union within ample time to prevent delay in doing the work, the office shall have the right to secure such help from any source, and any such person or persons may be permanently employed. Such help shall receive the journeyman's rate of wage, except in the case of apprentices."

In the brewing industry, help is generally to be secured from the union and it is not permissible to have nonunion men employed when union help is to be so secured, but the local of the place where help is wanted is to secure members from the next or nearest union.[1] Furthermore, the International makes it mandatory that a clause be inserted in all agreements entered into that in times of dull business the workingmen shall be laid off in rotation, but that no one should be laid off longer than a week, nor less than one day at a time.[2]

The officers of unions and the business agents serve as employment agents. In the building and many other trades they usually keep a waiting list of those who want jobs. Use of this list by the employer may be optional, in which case it is a mere convenience, but frequently the use of it is compulsory, as in the case of the Pressmen cited above. In the clothing industry the regulations covering hiring and discharge vary from one branch to another and from one city to another, but the use of the compulsory waiting list is not infrequently found. Thus in the men's clothing industry in Chicago, when an employer desires help he makes application to the Union's Employment Exchange, specifying the number and kind of workers needed. The union is given a reasonable time (two working days) to supply the specified help, and if it is unable or for any reason fails to furnish the required help, the employer is at liberty to secure it in the open market as best he can. The Exchange is expected to send the worker (or workers) at the top of its waiting list (in the appropriate occupational division, of course), and he must be given an opportunity to work unless obviously unfit, or reports in an intoxicated condition, or has been recently discharged for cause by the employer concerned, or has quit the firm's employment to avoid discharge for cause. If retained for more than two weeks, unless otherwise agreed, the union worker secures permanent tenure and may be discharged only for cause. "Cause" is defined by the impartial chairman in cases coming before him for review. Until the closed shop was adopted, when it became necessary to reduce the force, or to work short time, the nonunion workers were discharged first. With some exceptions, made several years ago to meet the problem of an excess of workers, regular workers may not be dismissed (except for cause), but during the slack season share in the work available as nearly equally as practicable.

Seniority Rules.—The regulations of some of the newer unions in particular are evidence of the feeling of brotherhood and the desire to

[1] Constitution of the International Union of Brewery Workmen of America, Art. IV, Sec. 33.

[2] *Ibid.*, Sec. 28. At least some of the locals have not attempted to fill peak needs with union men but have granted temporary permits to nonmembers, the object being to give members of the union fairly steady employment throughout the year. See John R. Commons *et al.*, *Industrial Government* (1921), Chap. 18.

give all members an equal opportunity. On the other hand, those of some of the old-line unions, and currently of many of the new unions as well, reflect priority rights and run in terms of seniority privileges. This may have been noted in connection with composing-room regulations, in which the rules relating to reduction and increase of the force are quite specific.[1] Seniority right is best known in the railway world. It has long been enforced by the brotherhoods, where tenure, selection of "runs," layoffs, recalls to work and rehirings have been determined in view of it.[2] Seniority right has been carried by the worker in case of merger.[3] During the Federal operation of railways the principle of priority was recognized by the government and extended to most branches of the railway service.[4] The issue of seniority rights was one of the stumbling blocks encountered in the settlement of the Switchmen's Strike in 1922. Priority finds place in the rules of the street and electric railway employees also. Until recently amended, a rule read, "The preference of runs shall always belong to the man holding the longest period of continuous service at his barn, station or division . . . The same rule shall apply to all shops and departments, giving each class of workers seniority in their respective departments."[5]

Unions with seniority rules have until recently been rather exceptional in the United States. With the frequent layoffs during the depression of the 1930's, however, the desire for recognition of seniority became strong. More important, the struggles over the right to organize during the years of the New Deal brought to the fore seniority rights as a method of protecting union members or active union men from being discriminated against and weeded out. Hence we find now, in contrast to some years ago, a relatively large number of

---

[1] *Supra*, pp. 432–433, 453–454.

[2] In the operative division the locomotive engineers have the right to displace or "bump" firemen and the conductors have the right to displace trainmen.

[3] For example, Sec. 62 of the Constitution, Statutes, and Rules of Order of the Order of Railway Conductors, Revised and Adopted by the 41st Grand Division, May 7th, 1934, provides that "whenever one railroad is absorbed or leased by another railroad the conductors on the road absorbed or leased shall retain their right and seniority as heretofore on the road absorbed or leased. When it becomes necessary to readjust the service of the merged roads, the trains and runs shall be manned by conductors of the respective roads in proportion, as nearly as practicable, to the mileage run on the territory of each . . . ."

[4] See H. D. Wolf, *The Railroad Labor Board* (1927), pp. 38*ff*.

[5] Amalgamated Association, *Constitution and General Laws* (1927), Sec. 154. Under the New York agreement [quoted from Bureau of Labor Statistics, Serial no. R. 824, *Seniority Provisions in Collective Agreements* (1939), p. 12] "the selection of runs for city and suburban service shall be in accordance with seniority of continuous platform service . . . , the oldest men to have the first choice of run and so on down the entire list until all runs are filled. This includes utility cars to be operated by motormen, conductors, one-man car operators and bus operators . . . . The selection of runs will take place at least twice a year, May 1 and November 1, or when time tables change or when vacancies occur."

joint agreements containing seniority clauses.[1] A recent analysis of
current agreements showed that 55 of 57 in the rubber industry, 116
of 147 in the auto industry, 266 of 305 in the iron and steel industry, all
of 16 in the flat-glass industry, all of 15 in the hosiery industry, 19 of 156
in the brewing industry, and 39 of 211 in the baking industry contained
seniority provisions.[2]

Seniority provisions are found in great variety.[3] Seniority rights
may extend to all workers, or to all union workers, or to workers who have
served for a stipulated period.   Union officials or union representatives
may or may not have a preferential right as against other employees.
There may be company-wide preference, or plant preference, or departmental preference, or job preference. Seniority applies to layoffs;
it may apply to rehirings, promotions, transfers, and work shifts, even
to vacations and the like.   In layoffs it may apply generally or only
after the work has been shared to a specified extent.[4]   But, when it does
apply, and in the strictest form, those persons youngest in the service of
the company or in the plant, department, or occupational group are the
first to be laid off, and of those laid off those with the greatest seniority
are usually first to be called back to work.   But finally, it is to be pointed
out that in many cases seniority rights under collective agreements are
conditioned also by "merit" or by ability, family status, number of
dependents, place of residence, etc.

The answer as to objectives, already given in part, is found in the
following quotation from *Seniority Provisions in Collective Agreements*.[5]
"The emphasis on youth and speed in many industries has often led to
the adoption of seniority as a protection of the older workers.   By

---

[1] Curiously enough, many of the more liberal unions, standing for brotherhood and
equality, have been insistent upon recognition of seniority rights.   Under Sec. 7 (a) of the
NIRA and under the National Labor Relations Act, which prohibited discrimination and
interference with the right of self-organization, seniority rights and problems assumed
added importance in union policy.   Seniority became one of the important tests as to
whether the employer had discriminated against union members in the hiring and discharge
of his employees.   When an employer could not satisfactorily explain replacements of
union workers by nonunion workers with a shorter record of employment, a presumption
was likely to be created of interference with the organizing activities of workers of a type
interdicted by the statute.

[2] From data supplied by the Bureau of Labor Statistics, making an analysis of some
thousands of collective agreements current in the late thirties.   For a comparison of the
prevalence of seniority provision in the thirties and the twenties, see S. H. Slichter, *Union
Policies and Industrial Management*, pp. 105–107.

[3] See U. S. Bureau of Labor Statistics, Serial no. R. 824, for many illustrative quotations;
see also S. H. Slichter, *op. cit.*, pp. 110–111, 115*ff.*, and Chap. 5, for a discussion of the
problems connected with and the effects of seniority rules.

[4] Sharing work is combined with seniority right in 97 of 1,083 agreements carrying
seniority privileges examined in detail.

[5] U. S. Bureau of Labor Statistics, *op. cit.*, p. 2.

granting increased job tenure on the basis of length of service, employment advantages are given to the older, more experienced workers. Seniority is also a defence against discriminatory firing, whether based on personal prejudice or intended to break up union organization. Because of its mechanical, impartial operation, seniority also affords protection in rehiring. In the absence of a closed or preferential shop, it is a protection against union discrimination by the employer. When hiring is done through the union it precludes favoritism by union officials. When the system is automatic and easily understood, it may be a factor in reducing the number of disputes and misunderstandings between employees and management."

Such a statement of objectives makes the advantages of seniority rights obvious. As is shown by their own rules, some of these rights have been appreciated by employers. The fact is that seniority rights, independent of union rule or demand, have been recognized by an increasing number of employers, though the rules have generally been qualified and consideration given to skill, efficiency, number of dependents, etc. Yet management may strongly object to union rules laid down or to specific demands made upon it.

⌈Management's opposition to these rules or specific demands is explained in part by the fact that they are regarded as too absolute, that they may not allow for differences in ability, number of dependents, and other considerations it may regard as important. If length of service is the rule and is strictly observed, the less efficient workers cannot be weeded out; moreover, the plant becomes oversupplied with older workers. Again, employees who have the protection of seniority rights may have less incentive to exert their best efforts. Seniority practice may, therefore, not be compatible with efficient plant administration.

From the worker's point of view, seniority means security of the job. But security of the job does not necessarily mean opportunity to earn a living. For, with changing volume of employment, with technological, seasonal, and cyclical changes and the success or lack of success of the individual enterprise, those who are at or near the bottom of the seniority list are sacrificed in the amount of employment they secure and the earnings they make, especially in depression periods.⌋ In the light of the report made by the Railway Retirement Board on payments made to persons who had been paid by First Class Roads for work done in 1937,[1] the President's Emergency Board found the distribution of earnings was strikingly unequal within an occupational group. It observed that "such unemployment as is experienced in the railroad industry appears to be rather unevently spread among workers within a classifica-

[1] See *Railroad Wages and Months of Service for 1937—Number of Employees Classified by Amount of Wages Credited under the Railroad Retirement*, . . .

tion,"[1] and "that with seniority rules, widely observed in railway employment, layoffs are more likely to occur than in many branches of manufacture where the work is regularly shared in some way or other."[2] The uneven distribution of work and earnings would have been even greater than it was in 1937 had several of the unions, aware of an excessive supply of labor and the problem of inadequate earnings in depression, not shared work to an extent by limiting earnings or number of runs or by some other device. The experience of other unions has been similar. To meet the problem presented, and for strategic reasons, the printing-trades internationals and/or locals rather generally during the long depression introduced the five-day week or resorted to some other work-sharing plan.[3] After all, the difference in policy of the needle trades and other unions, thinking in terms of solidarity, requiring discharge for cause only, and insisting upon equal division of work, and the unions insisting upon seniority rights is not so great as one might be inclined to think.

The concrete data suggest the types of control of hiring, assignment to jobs, and discharge found in a large part of organized industry in the United States—a control much more frequently found in English-speaking countries than in pre-Fascist Continental Europe.

DIRECT RESTRICTION AND REGULATION OF OUTPUT

The advantages of standardization and stabilization under collective bargaining may be very great, but, on the other hand, some of the regulations we have reviewed may not only be galling to employers who have been accustomed to manage the details of their plants as they saw fit, but may also be uneconomical because of their effect on output and labor cost. For a variety of reasons a number of unions oppose piecework and practically all of them oppose bonus systems and contract work such as so frequently find place in the open shop. The effect of a minimum wage on a time basis, we have seen,[4] may be to remove a desirable premium on individual application and performance. Machinery may be kept out of the trade or the size of crews per machine or the number of machines per operative may be regulated in order to protect jobs, to avoid strain, to continue custom in effect, or for other reasons. Through rules relating to apprentices, helpers, and the subdivision of labor, the employer may be hampered in securing the best working force and work organization from the point of view of output and labor cost. Limitations

[1] *Report of the Emergency Board to the President, in re Atchison, Topeka and Santa Fe and other Class I Railroads and Certain of Their Employees* (1938), p. 53.

[2] *Ibid.*, pp. 43–44.

[3] Some of the printing-trades unions developed an interest in the four-day week as a work-sharing device.

[4] *Supra*, pp. 390–391, 394.

on hiring, layoff, and discharge may stand in the way of the individual employer who desires to secure the most efficient, best disciplined, and most plastic labor force.

The most serious charge against British unionism, especially before the First-World War, was that it restricted output. Indeed, it was charged by many writers with responsibility for great losses sustained in the prewar export trade. In the United States, in spite of the prevalent British view that our unions are not restrictive, the charges have been only less serious. They were so persistently made against a large number of strong organizations that the U. S. Bureau of Labor Statistics almost forty years ago made an investigation, the results of which were set out in its Eleventh Special Report, the *Restriction and Regulation of Output*. Of course an enormous literature has been developed on the subject.[1]

An examination of details in support of the indictment that unions restrict output shows that much of the evidence runs in terms of the regulations we have been discussing, which, for the most part, have been designed to accomplish other ends but which incidentally affect the output an individual employer can get from a work force of a given size at a given time. But, in addition to this largely indirect restriction or regulation, there has been, chiefly in Great Britain and the United States, not a little restriction or regulation of a direct kind—of output with a given personnel, equipment, work organization, and the like. It is such direct restriction or regulation that we now discuss.

No well-informed person will say that restriction originated with unions or that they alone practice it. Unorganized workers not infrequently practice it in so far as they dare with no security of tenure and the probability that any suggestion looking to slowing down will be reported to the employer. In fact there has been an enormous amount of withholding of effort by unorganized workers, and for the same reasons that effort may be withheld by union workers.[2] Organized labor is more articulate and may dare to go further, but with the ordinary union willing to cooperate with the employer in getting the customary day's work, and with a considerable amount of positive union-management cooperation developed during the 1920's and 1930's, it is not at all clear

[1] Excellent summary discussions will be found in G. G. Groat, *An Introduction to the Study of Organized Labor in America* (1916), Chap. 19, and Warren B. Catlin, *The Labor Problem* (rev. ed., 1935), Chap. 15.

[2] For an excellent statement, see Stanley B. Mathewson, *Restriction of Output among Unorganized Workers* (1931). As is stated in the *Monthly Labor Review*, vol. 33 (1931), pp. 77–85, there are three immediate stimuli to restriction by unorganized workers. One is rate cuts, retiming of jobs, which require the worker to deliver more work at lower rates of pay. A second is layoffs, part-time work, and unemployment over indefinite periods. The third is the result of unintelligent management that depends on a driving system or other dictatorial methods.

that the charge of direct restriction of output will lie more against unions as a whole than against nonunion workers.

It may be noted, also, that restriction is frequently advocated or practiced by businessmen and other groups, with the result that interesting parallels to what is decried in union practice are easily found. The protective tariff is a restrictive device, indirectly limiting a nation's output, at least in the short run and perhaps always in the long run, but tariffs are eagerly sought by groups of manufacturers and by farmers. Bottling up and keeping important inventions out of use restricts output, however profitable it may be to an individual or a group immediately concerned. High monopoly prices restrict output of the goods so priced because of the effect on the quantity that will be purchased. Lax and lazy management affects output quite as much as lazy workers.[1] The restriction in these cases is indirect, but direct restriction or regulation is advocated and practiced. An association of manufacturers, say, restricts and apportions the amount to be produced in order to maintain prices. Or tobacco growers attempt to limit the acreage planted. Only recently our Federal Administration has vigorously limited planting in order to restore profitable prices of wheat and cotton, and some years ago two Southern states sought, under penalty, to restrict cotton acreage to a specified fraction of what it had been. The object in citing these details is not to justify union restrictions or regulation or to condemn restriction by other groups; it is only to suggest that nonunion groups, in meeting their problems and in furthering their interests, resort to practices closely paralleling those found among labor organizations.

Pertinent evidence can be presented to show that not all unions, or groups of union men, but nevertheless a considerable number of them have practiced direct restriction or regulation of output. Where such practice is found, it is to be explained in different ways.

First of all to be mentioned, though it is not sufficiently important to be emphasized as against other causes of limitation, is the changed psychology of newly organized workers. Not infrequently they are told by the organizers that they have been overworked and underpaid and badly mistreated, with the result that their attitude toward the employer and the task is changed and this change in attitude is reflected in their performance. This cannot be said to be a result of union policy; nevertheless it may be and frequently is a fact in the concrete situation. Perhaps the union must undertake to undo what its organizers have done.

The influence of custom is very great among both union and nonunion workers. They may continue to turn out about the same amount

---

[1] The Committee on Elimination of Waste in Industry of the Federated American Engineering Societies [*Waste in Industry* (1911), p. 9] estimated that more than 50 per cent of the responsibility for waste in industries studied was attributable to management and less than 25 per cent was attributable to labor.

per day although with changing processes and equipment equal application would result in a larger product. There have been instances in which the customary day's work has been recognized by a union as a standard. For example, union lathers may put on so many bundles, the faster helping out the slower men, and the day's work may end at two or three in the afternoon when the standard number of bundles have been put on. Among bricklayers, the laying of so many bricks may be recognized as a day's work. If just so much work is actually and always done, the time wage, in a sense, becomes a piece wage.

A considerable part of the restriction of output by American unions has been a product of the fixing and administration of piece rates. The employers, as we have seen,[1] may insist on cutting piece rates when they yield earnings regarded as too high as tested by a daily wage, even, possibly, when the high earnings are due to the unusual application or efficiency of the workers engaged on the process. One of the authors witnessed four reductions within a year in piece rates for the operations of a section engaged in the manufacture of dresses. Of course speeding gave rise to restriction and also to attempted union organization. Years ago in the steel industry there were union rules limiting the output of certain pieceworkers. The chief object was to protect against rate cutting. For the same reason, it was said, the Stove Mounters' Union of Detroit at one time forbade its members to earn more than $4.50 per day. It was only after the Stove Founders' National Defense Association agreed that the earnings of a molder should exercise no influence upon his piece rate but that this should be set by comparison with the rates paid for other work of like kind, that the Molders' Union agreed that "the placing of a limit upon the earnings of a molder should be discountenanced in shops of members of the S.F.N.D.A."[2] For a generation before the arbitration agreement was entered into, the molders had limited output, primarily to protect piece rates, and the practice continued under the agreement until Clause 16 was adopted (1902). These are only a few of many cases that might be cited in which limitation was resorted to in order to prevent rate cutting. Then, over against these, there are cases in which workers "go slow" for a time in order to secure a favorable piece rate—one on which they can make "good money."

Timeworkers may be speeded up by a foreman or superintendent making use of "drive" methods. Pace setters, or workmen employed under such circumstances that they serve in that capacity, may be used. Local union rules frequently enjoin their members against pace setting or speeding and provide penalties for violation. It was said that the

---

[1] *Supra*, p. 399.

[2] See Clarence E. Bonnett, *Employers' Associations in the United States*, p. 55 (Clause 16 of the agreement).

Chicago Plumbers' rules with reference to what should constitute a day's work, in effect in the late 1890's, developed out of the use of speeders paid above scale. A historic case of limitation to prevent speeding and undue strain was found in a large part of Chicago's packing industry at the turn of the century.[1] Those in the initial processes were induced to set a fast pace and the other workers had to keep the carcasses moving, or they came to the attention of the foreman and were perhaps discharged. In the not wholly typical case of the splitters in the cattle-killing department of one company, the five splitters in 1884 split 800 cattle in a ten-hour day, while ten years later the four then comprising the "gang" split 1,200. The average per man had increased from sixteen to thirty per hour; the task remained the same and was performed with the same tool. But when the workers organized they placed limitations upon output—these taken from performance in competing plants. Without question the speeding system constituted a real grievance. Skilled men are known who at age forty, or even younger, were reduced to unskilled work or discharged because, though they were in good health, they could no longer keep up with the pace set. Cases of this general type are greatly emphasized by union spokesmen in discussing limitation of output.[2] Indeed, labor spokesmen are likely to assert that practically all union restriction is designed to cope with the problem of undue speeding; other limitations are disclaimed as a part of trade-union policy.

In spite of this disclaimer, however, there has been not a little restriction of output designed to spread work, to extend the busy season, and to prevent layoffs or discharge. It may be asserted that, in general, the "lump of labor" assumption is erroneous, but the workers in the building trades, in the clothing industry, and in other seasonal employments know it to be a fact—at the time and in the place and in the occupation that interest them. When confronted by the prospect of no work just ahead, the union or the nonunion worker on a time wage is likely to spread the work and make it go further—if he is not in too much danger of discharge for slowing down. If, however, the individual worker wishes to be retained in employment or rehired later on, he may do most work

---

[1] See John R. Commons, "Labor Conditions in Meat Packing," *Quarterly Journal of Economics*, vol. 19 (1904), pp. 1–32, reproduced as Chap. 9 of his *Trade Unionism and Labor Problems* (1921 ed.).

[2] For example, see John Mitchell, *Organized Labor* (1903), p. 29. In 1939 the rate of speed was an important bone of contention in the assembly plants of automobile manufacturers. Under the system there employed, the individual worker has no control over the amount of work to be done by him. All parties regard speed as a matter which may call for consideration. Some of the companies take the position, however, that while excessive speed is a proper subject for union complaint, any adjustment should be at the discretion of management. On the other hand, the Auto Workers take the position that it is a matter for decision in joint conference. This was one of the issues involved in the Chrysler strike of October, 1939.

when there is least to do, a practice generally true in the building trades in time of depression.   But the timeworker with security of tenure, as in the needle trades, is very likely to slow down when confronted by slack work, partly because of custom in the trade, but chiefly because the penalty of unemployment is so great.

Finally, there is the policy of "ca' canny" that has found a place in the policy of some unions, as well as among nonunion men.   Ca' canny was widely advertised and accepted by some British unions when the Dockers some fifty years ago took the view that if their members could not secure proper remuneration they should limit their output to fit the wage received.   This doctrine has been fought by most unions, but has been accepted by some of the radical organizations, such as the Industrial Workers of the World, which at one time preached sabotage.   But, though ca' canny is generally disclaimed as a union policy, many persons experienced in unionized industry know of instances in which unadjusted grievances have been followed by limitation of output by all types of unionists as a method of retaliation.   The stoppage is another incident to be explained chiefly in the same way.   They also know of instances in which small articulate groups, perhaps contrary to union policy, have slowed down in order to secure an increase in wages or some other positive gain.   Not all ca' canny is of the retaliatory type.

Union Attitudes toward Production, and Union-management Cooperation

This summary review of union policies and practices in industry has been designed to bring to the attention of the reader certain matters that may, and sometimes do, loom large in unionized trades.   It should serve also to exemplify the fact that there are many problems in industrial relations other than wages and hours—problems of tenure, regularity of employment, technological change, speed and effort, and others.   The data introduced bring to the fore the negative, restrictive, and obstructive side of unionism, with only a bit of relief here and there.   Union rules and practices, which may be made effective in the concrete situation, are frequently crude, unduly restrictive, and uneconomic, but they cannot be dismissed or ruled out as without reason in human nature and the conditions under which men secure and hold jobs and work.   In considerable measure, it is evident, they find explanation in the insecurity of the job, irregularity of employment, a threatened standard of living, or the imperiling of organization by the practices of management.   Nor are union rules and regulations cruder than many of the rules and practices of management that may be arrayed against them.   But fact does not cancel fact, however far one fact may go to explain another.

Yet one must hold in mind that most union policies and practices subject to criticism are not common to all unions.   One must also realize how many provisions there are in joint agreements similar to that in the stove trade to the effect that, a scientific basis for piece-rate making having been agreed upon and placed in effect, restriction of output was to be discountenanced. Many instances could be cited in which similar provisions have been introduced under collective bargaining, showing, as a rule, not that one side had abjectly surrendered to the other, but that the problems lying behind imposed rules and practices had been considered and dealt with jointly. If there is a case for collective bargaining, and few will deny it, it is a case for collective bargaining about many things in addition to wages and hours and matters incidental to them.

It is important to note that, in the United States at least, restrictive, obstructive unionism has been losing ground, owing to improvements in management that eliminate or alleviate problems and to the change in thought union leaders have been undergoing—with recognition of the union, the right of collective bargaining, and what have been called "elementary human rights." Outstanding union leaders in England[1] and the United States have come more and more to advocate and stress constructive policies. For example, Mr. Gompers wrote in 1920 that "the trade union movement welcomes every thought and plan, every device and readjustment that will make expended effort more valuable to humanity."[2] On a number of occasions, William Green, Mr. Gompers's successor as president of the American Federation of Labor, has gone on record as to union responsibility to industry and as to the importance of efficiency. Thus, "What has been accomplished under union-management co-operation on the Baltimore and Ohio is concrete evidence that good business is not in conflict with humanitarian idealism and that mobilization of the creative capacities of all working together in an industrial undertaking is the greatest asset of that undertaking . . . unions are normally constructive agencies . . . [which can] function as partners in work problems."[3] "The union is just as necessary for the newer function—cooperation—as it is for defensive and bargaining purposes. Cooperation furthers mutual interests and it must be preceded by adjustments in which any element of exploitation is excluded and common purposes agreed to. . . . Cooperative relationships are possible only after the union and management have gone through the experiences necessary to establish collective bargaining as an accepted practice and to see the advantages of utilizing the experience and judgment of those

---

[1] Note, for example, the presidential address and action taken at the Trades Union Congress at Edinburgh in 1927, and the Mond Conferences that began some months later. With reference to these see B. H. and Sylvia Selekman, *British Industry Today* (1929), Chap. 8.

[2] *Annals of the American Academy of Political and Social Science*, vol. 91 (1920), p. x.

[3] *American Federationist*, vol. 37 (1930), p. 149.

who handle tools and materials. Cooperation comes with development and maturity. It rests upon acknowledged strength and utilized wisdom, experience and initiative."[1]

This attitude has found more and more frequent expression in the reports and actions of the Federation itself. In 1929, for example, the Executive Council, in its report, stated, "The background of economic thought brings out clearly that real partnership should exist between groups engaged in production and the service which trade unions can perform in developing the method and spirit of partnership. It is only organization of workers that can use this opportunity to develop the constructive spirit of partnership and thus avert the *impasse* which results in class conflict between workers and management. Development of satisfactory human relations in industry has not kept pace with progress on the material and technical sides. Industry is just beginning to realize the waste from not coordinating the full creative power of wage earners into the channels of thought control that constitute management in industry. The elimination of this waste of human intelligence will make it possible to gear industry to new standards of output and excellence of work."[2] And in setting out its program for meeting the problem of unemployment it stated in its 1930 report, "All producers are part of our business society, individuals in business to get profits on their investments. Some invest capital, others technical capacity to direct operators, others technical capacity to carry on the production processes. All are directly concerned in increasing the total sum accruing from their joint efforts so the share of each may be larger. There is mutual obligation for efficiency and mutual right to demand efficiency."[3]

The C.I.O., too, as is evidenced by the position of President Philip Murray, sees in union-management cooperation the mature stage of industrial relations. After real acceptance of the principle of unionism and collective bargaining, management "has the right to expect the union . . . not only to comply fully with the terms of the agreement, but to cooperate in achieving efficient plant operation."[4] "If the labor movement fails to develop an adequate sense of responsibility for output, the alternative will be increasing tension and bitterness over 'wages, hours and working conditions,' reducing the opportunity for constructive accommodation and community of interest between management and union."[5]

Former President Broach of the Electrical Workers, President Sidney Hillman of the Amalgamated Clothing Workers, and other union

[1] *Ibid.*, vol. 36 (1929), p. 153.
[2] *Report of the Executive Council of the American Federation of Labor* . . . 1929, p. 44.
[3] *Ibid.*, 1930, p. 31.
[4] Morris Llewellyn Cooke and Philip Murray, *Organized Labor and Production* (1940), p. 188.
[5] *Ibid.*, pp. 214–215.

leaders have stressed the need for their organizations to take a constructive position in meeting production problems. One international president has said that the union must interest itself in efficiency in industry and that a union should not and cannot hope to succeed unless, with due regard to the interests of consumers, it can serve the employers and the industry as well as, or better than, the open shop.

It may be confidently asserted that though management has not been noticeably active in inviting the participation of labor in meeting production problems, unions are cooperating to that end much more frequently than the public is aware. The Pressmen, for example, stand ready to give advice where presswork is not of good quality and to advise with reference to equipment.[1] Only the few close to the situation can realize the extent to which the Amalgamated has gone in solving problems of clothing manufacturers in Chicago, Rochester, and elsewhere.[2] In its activities it evidences recognition of the fact that a firm and its workers are "in the same boat," and that the workers cannot expect to have regular employment at good wages unless the employer has a chance to make a satisfactory profit. As a result of advice given by the union, a new type of garment is produced, needless processes on a coat are eliminated, routing is improved, deficiencies in organization of the work are corrected—even at times at the temporary sacrifice of some workers, but of course only because the welfare of the larger group will be conserved. Still other unions might be mentioned that have functioned in analogous ways,[3] and, perhaps without new machinery or committees being set up, over a period of years beginning before the expression "union-management cooperation" came into vogue.

Brief reference should be made to the position set forth by the Steel Workers' Organizing Committee (now the United Steel Workers of America) for the consideration and guidance of lodges in the steel industry.[4] The position taken is to the effect that once the union has been

---

[1] For an account of cooperative relations in printing, see Phillips L. Garman, "How Organized Labor Can Cooperate with Management," *Conciliation and Cooperation in Collective Bargaining*, Personnel Series No. 44, American Management Association (1940), pp. 3–18.

[2] See Morris Greenberg, "Working with Sidney Hillman's Union," *Personnel Journal*, December, 1938, pp. 200–205; and "Practical Pointers on Union Relations," *ibid.*, pp. 206–211; Sidney Hillman, "Labor Leads toward Planning," *Survey Graphic*, March, 1932, pp. 586–588; *How Collective Bargaining Works*, The Twentieth Century Fund (1942), Chap. 8.

[3] See *ibid.*, Chap. 9; other references will be found in *Union-management Cooperation with Special Reference to the War Production Drive*, Bibliographical Series no. 68, Industrial Relations Section, Department of Economics and Social Institutions, Princeton University (1942).

[4] See *Production Problems, A Handbook for Committeemen of Local Lodges of S.W.O.C.*, Publication 2 issued by the Steel Workers Organizing Committee (1938). This is a rather remarkable pamphlet, and one which will at most points withstand critical examination.

recognized and has found place in the industry the militancy of the organizing period must be put into the background and cooperation in reducing waste, improving techniques, and increasing efficiency emphasized. The province of management is recognized, as is the fact that increased output and reduced costs mean more to be divided between employer and men. Production standards, scientifically set, are approved. Among the several concrete suggestions made is this more or less typical one: "Make a call for suggestions from the union membership. This call should ask the workers to report delays and, so far as possible, what appears to cause them; and also to report on wastes of materials or time which are either serious or of long standing. Lack of suitable trucks for removing materials, or of specific instructions, or of assignment of work, or preventable spoilage—all these are possible bottlenecks, causing loss."

Until recently, the most publicized union-management cooperation has been in the railroad industry.[1] Applied in a Baltimore and Ohio shop in 1923, it was soon introduced into Baltimore and Ohio shops generally. With that beginning, it was soon adopted by the Canadian Pacific, the Northwestern, and the Chicago, Milwaukee and St. Paul systems, these four systems operating about one-sixth of the combined railway mileage of the United States and Canada. First applied in maintenance of equipment, the plan was later applied to one or more of the other departments of at least two of these companies.[2] At the same time it has found some application in industrial plants.[3]

Union-management cooperation, as it functions, is related to the cooperation realized under employee-representation or shop-committee plans, as in the shops of the Pennsylvania and other railroads. But its history has been rather independent of the employee-representation movement, which is discussed in a later chapter. While its effective beginning dates from 1923, union-management cooperation as an idea or ideal had its beginning some years before. It connects up with scientific management as it evolved. It was, in a way, the product of our experience in meeting transportation problems during the federal operation of railways. And, like other social inventions, it was the product of certain men, chiefly W. H. Johnston, for years president of the Machinists, William Jewell, and Otto S. Beyer, an engineer who had had a varied experience, was interested and experienced in production problems, and had developed a live interest in labor-management cooperation.

---

[1] For a full, systematic account, see Louis Aubrey Wood, *Union-management Cooperation on the Railroads* (1931); see also S. H. Slichter, *Union Policies and Industrial Management*, Chaps. 15–16.

[2] Louis Aubrey Wood, Chap. 19.

[3] *Ibid.*, Chap. 20.

Union-management cooperation is something in addition to collective bargaining as commonly found in the organized trades. Preceding it and remaining along with and independent of it, are the usual procedures for bargaining with reference to wages, hours, apprentices, etc., and for settling grievances. Union-management cooperation interests itself in other matters. The representatives of management and of workers, forming local and more general committees, consider the elimination of waste, the increase of efficiency, improvement in working conditions, the stabilization of employment, the maintenance of the volume of work, acquisition of new business, etc. Suggestions from the workers are encouraged and given consideration; a very large percentage of the suggestions made have been adopted and used. It is not necessary, however, to present precisely what has been done and in what way. The important thing is that management and organized workers pool their knowledge and make cooperative attack upon problems. Joint, constructive effort is substituted for the truce that so frequently obtains under collective bargaining, especially when newly introduced.

A generalized statement of what is involved in union-management cooperation may be quoted from Mr. Beyer.

"When the Baltimore & Ohio experiment was first inaugurated the idea underlying the proposal to cooperate was rather general as was also the objective aimed at. The unions were to play a constructive part in shop operation and the employes were to share in the benefits resulting. As the program unfolded and more and more experience was acquired, the basic requirements of a sound cooperative program for industry became clear. These requirements may be summarized briefly as follows:

"*First.*—Full and cordial recognition of the standard labor unions as the properly accredited organizations of the employes.

"*Second.*—Acceptance by management of these unions as helpful, necessary and constructive in the conduct of industry.

"*Third.*—Development between unions and managements of written agreements governing wages, working conditions and the prompt and orderly adjustment of disputes.

"*Fourth.*—Systematic cooperation between unions and managements for improved service, increased efficiency, and the elimination of waste.

"*Fifth.*—Willingness on the part of managements to help the unions solve some of their problems in return for the constructive help rendered by the unions in the solution of some of management's problems.

"*Sixth.*—Stabilization of employment.

"*Seventh.*—Measuring and sharing the gains of cooperation.

"*Eighth.*—Provision of definite joint union and management machinery to promote and maintain cooperative effort."[1]

[1] From O. S. Beyer, "Management and Labor Cooperation on the Railroads," *Industrial Management*, vol. 73 (1927), p. 267.

Though a number of experiments have been abandoned, the results of union-management cooperation have been satisfactory to most of those immediately concerned. While many of the gains cannot be measured in pecuniary or other definite terms, the companies have profited from the elimination of a good deal of waste, greater efficiency, reduced turnover of labor, and good will, while the workers have benefited from stabilization of employment, a greater degree of security in the job, and a more dignified position in industry.[1]

Under the current War program, union-management cooperation has made great strides. First urged by various trade unions, then by the War Production Board, joint committees or councils have been set up in many plants to increase war production and maintain or improve morale. By the middle of April, 1942, 500 had been established.[2] Among the unions in the forefront of this drive, has been the United Electrical, Radio and Machine Workers of America, which has published a set of basic rules for production councils.[3] Much publicized has been the Beat the Promise campaign of Radio Corporation of America, run jointly by the management and the Electrical, Radio and Machine Workers of America.[4]

The Closed, the Preferential, and the Open Shop

In the discussion of union policies and practices, we come, finally, to the closed-shop issue, which has received such great emphasis on the public platform and in print in the United States, particularly at certain times in the early years of the century,[5] in 1921,[6] and again in 1941–1942.

Development and Character of the Issue.—It is a significant fact that, contrary to the widespread popular belief that it is comparatively new, the union-closed shop appeared in both England and the United States practically with the appearance of unionism itself. The explanation of its appearance and persistence is to be found in the natural preferences and feelings of union men, and in the fact that the closed shop increases the security and hold of the union and assists it in insuring observance of the scale and working rules.[7] But whatever the explana-

---

[1] See S. H. Slichter, *op. cit.*, Chap. 19, for discussion of the obstacles to and the outlook for union-management cooperation.

[2] For examples, see *Union-management Cooperation with Special Reference to the War Production Drive*, pp. 26–27.

[3] *Ibid.*, pp. 14–15.

[4] *Ibid.*, pp. 23–25.

[5] *Cf. supra*, pp. 95–102.

[6] *Cf. supra*, pp. 165–171.

[7] During the last several years of bitter A.F. of L.–C.I.O. conflict, an additional strong factor has been the desire to secure protection against rival unions. Frequently the employer has agreed to the closed shop to promote stability or to protect the union he favors.

tion may be, even before 1800 certain American local unions were requiring their members to refrain from working in shops not employing union workmen exclusively. The union-closed shop widely prevailed during the 1830's and was partly responsible for the setting up of employers' associations to oppose unionism. It was also a center of attack in early conspiracy cases brought against labor organizations. By 1850, most American local unions had adopted the policy of attempting to bring about the exclusion of nonunionists from work in the organized trades. This has been the policy of most of our unions throughout the decades since.[1] It may be pointed out, also, that for two generations, the internationals in increasing number have accepted the principle of the closed shop and required their locals to enforce it in so far as possible. However, some organizations, such as the railroad brotherhoods, have been exceptions all the while; they have never demanded the closed shop.[2] The explanation of this exceptional position is found in the fact that the place of these unions in the industry has not been seriously questioned, that the workers could not be easily or quickly replaced, and that the insurance features of the organizations have been sufficient to attract the workers and hold them in membership. It is to be noted, also, that a considerable number of unions have, willingly or unwillingly, accepted the preferential shop. Still others have secured "percentage" contracts or maintenance of membership arrangements. In spite of these exceptions, however, the typical American union has sooner or later demanded that the employer engage only workers who have membership in it, or, short of this, discharge those who, within a specified time after being hired, do not affiliate with it.[3]

[1] It may be observed, however, that partly because of the protection afforded by the National Labor Relations Act and partly because the most important thing at the time was to secure recognition and an agreement, many of the unions organized in recent years have not demanded the closed shop but have accepted agreements that covered their members only or gave preference in hiring and discharge. Such open or preferential shops have, however, almost always been accompanied by agreement on the part of management that there would be no discrimination against workers because of union membership or union activity. Indeed, in some cases management has agreed to advise employees to join and to support the union.

[2] This has not been true of some of the railway unions. Since 1934, however, the Railway Labor Act has placed a ban on closed-shop contracts. This, it is interesting to note, was not aimed at "legitimate" unions but at "company unions," with which some of the railways were interested in dealing on a closed-shop basis. It may be added that by 1942 some of the railway unions had become dissatisfied with this ban and desired to secure the closed shop.

[3] This suggests two types of provision in joint agreements. The one type is the usual union-closed shop; the other is now generally known as the "union shop." Their relative importance is shown in an analysis of 250 agreements negotiated between 1923 and 1929 and of 400 negotiated between 1933 and 1939; 168 in the former group and 215 in the latter were of these two types. S. H. Slichter, *op. cit.*, p. 57.

There has been and still is in the United States a great deal of opposition to trade unions; and an outstanding reason assigned for this opposition has been the demand for the closed shop. In this connection it is significant that in all periods marked by a vigorous labor movement in this country, there has been much organization of employers into associations—at first local, but since 1900[1] many of them national—some to enter into contractual relationships with the unions while holding union demands in check, others to combat organizations or to oppose certain union objectives. The fact of organization of belligerent employers' associations was true in the 1830's and in the 1850's and has been more or less continuously true during the last forty-five or fifty years. It may be noted, also, that in this respect the United States stands, and for decades has stood, in contrast to other important industrial countries. In Britain, for example, trade unionism is generally taken for granted. And the closed shop has not been an issue for years.[2] Perhaps the attitude toward unionism in Germany, prior to 1918, was nearest to that in the United States. Previous to the First World War there were in Germany large industrial groups that fought trade unions and set up company unions, with more or less of the usual accompanying explanation and propaganda. After the revolution of 1918, however, organization for collective bargaining became fairly general; discrimination against union men was prohibited by law; nonunion men might not be excluded from employment; if there was a collective agreement, it was the basis for contracts with nonunion as well as with union workers, and its terms were enforceable at law; under certain conditions a collective agreement might be extended to and made binding upon parties in addition to those who entered into it. Obviously the issue of unionism and the issue of the open vs. the closed shop were largely disposed of in pre-Hitler Germany by legislation.

Types of Union Status.—The literature relating to the closed shop has unfortunately been confusing because of the use of the same terms in different senses, as well as because of the inadequacy of the analysis of different types of situations and of the efforts to accomplish desired ends

[1] Of course some of the existing national associations had appeared before 1900, as, for example, the Stove Founders' National Defense Association and the National Founders Association.

[2] In general, British unions have for decades not emphasized the closed shop as much as American unions have. This was very properly explained by Professor Commons, years ago, by the fact that, with few exceptions, British employers have taken union organization and collective bargaining for granted and have not attempted, by discrimination or otherwise, to weaken and to destroy the labor organizations. *Cf.* John R. Commons, "Causes of the Union-shop Policy," *Papers and Proceedings*, Pt. I, *Publications of the American Economic Association*, Third Series, vol. 6 (1905), pp. 140–159. Another fact of importance is that in Britain the workers stand together much better than they do in the United States, so that the nonunionists are more likely to cooperate fully in strike situations.

through misleading propaganda. Also, the terms finding place in the literature—particularly the terms "union shop" and "closed shop"—have come, to an extent, to be used in somewhat different senses in recent years from those employed in the earlier years. A brief mention of the meaning of terms—of the types of situation they have described in the past and of their current usage—is accordingly in point here.

To the spokesmen of labor organizations in the past, the term "union shop" referred to a situation of recognition of the union on the part of the employer and collective bargaining with it; the "nonunion" shop, in his terminology, was one in which the union was not recognized and, of course, collective bargaining did not obtain. Employers, on the other hand—particularly those of antiunion predilections—preferred to use the terms "closed shop" and "open shop" (or in the years following the First World War "closed shop" and "American plan"). It is patent that under the "union shop" as just defined two general types of situation might prevail: the requirement of union membership as a condition of employment, or—although the union was recognized and the employer bargained with it—the absence of this requirement. Employers when speaking of the "closed shop" generally referred to the former of these two situations. For the most part, neutral persons in the past tended to adopt the employers' terminology, the "closed shop" meaning one in which only union men could secure and retain employment, and the "open shop" (or "American plan") one in which nonunionists were not excluded from employment.[1] It should be noted, however, as part of the story of terminological misleadingness, that the open shop in the just-mentioned employer-neutral-person usage might be one in which there was recognition of the union and collective bargaining, the union being bargaining agent for all employees or only for its own members—i.e., the open shop in the employer-public meaning might be a union shop in the labor spokesmen's sense of recognition and collective bargaining. But the types of shops and the situations existing have long been more numerous than these terms suggest, and in the last few years new types have appeared. It will be advantageous, therefore, to classify plants or shops from different points of view.

From one point of view, there has been not only the "simple" closed or all-union shop, but also "joint" and "extended" closed shops.[2] In the first of these, the requirement of union membership has extended

---

[1] It is interesting to note that the terms "closed" and "open" shop were coined by the unions. Originally the closed shop was one in which union men were forbidden to work, an open shop one in which they were permitted by the union to accept employment. Later on, however, the unions came gradually to use the term closed shop to mean that the shop was closed to nonunion men, the open shop one in which nonunion workers found employment. This usage has been accepted by union critics with the result that labor organizations have for many years insisted upon the terms "union" and "nonunion" shop.

[2] Terms used by Frank T. Stockton in *The Closed Shop in American Unions*, Johns

only to those engaged in one craft or occupational group—carpenters, plumbers, or electricians. The "joint closed shop," on the other hand, has been one where the several organized crafts have insisted that all crafts be fully unionized; in other words, the members of one craft would not work if "scabs" were hired in the other crafts. Under the "extended closed shop" the requirement has obtained that not only all workers immediately concerned be members of the union, but also that the materials (sash, doors, mantels, brick, for example) used by them be union made.

When the matter of terms employed and conditions obtaining is viewed from another angle, a variety of types may be noted. There has been, in the first place, the plain nonunion shop: the one in which no union workers have been employed and in which there is of course no collective dealing by employer and a union. Within this group, however, are to be found shops radically different in character. There have been, on the one hand, nonunion shops where the trade or trades have not been organized nor has there been attempt at organization. Standing over against these have been many open shops, in which the nonunion condition has been explained by the refusal of management to hire or retain in employment union men. Many of them have made use of the "yellow-dog" or the individual contract, stipulating that the worker is not a member of a union and will not become one while in the employ of the firm (and possibly for a specified time on beyond); that if he desires to join the union he will first quit his employment.[1] But whether or not such individual contracts have been used, these have been employers' closed shops—shops closed to union men. Some of them have, indeed, been extended employers' closed shops, inasmuch as they have refused to sell their products to employers who used union men in construction work. In the United States for decades before the NRA and its Sec. 7 (a), and then the National Labor Relations Act, were adopted, there were perhaps more workers in employers' closed shops than in union-closed shops. These shops presented the issue of the right to organize and to bargain collectively, with which the National Labor Relations Act comes to grips. Such was the situation in large segments of the metal trades, in a large part of the soft coal trade, in most Southern textile mills, in candy manufacture in Chicago, in parts of the clothing industry in Chicago and elsewhere, and in many other cases. Here was and to a limited extent remains the open shop Mr. Dunne had in mind when he wrote "Mr. Dooley on the Open Shop."[2] Until recently

Hopkins University Studies, Series 29 (1911), pp. 431–611. This is the best study of the subject.

[1] For a discussion of the "yellow-dog" contract, see *infra*, pp. 511–520.

[2] Published in the *Literary Digest*, Nov. 27, 1920, but reproduced in many places, among them, P. H. Douglas, C. E. Hitchcock, and W. E. Atkins, *The Worker in Modern Economic*

at least, most of the employers' fight has been to thwart unionization and collective bargaining, and with that object in view employers have maintained their own closed shop.   Mr. Gompers only exaggerated when he maintained that this was practically all that was involved in the closed-shop issue.[1]

Next in order have been the open shops in which union men have been tolerated and employed but in which there has been no recognition of the union or collective bargaining.   Here the issue, if any, has been one of recognition and collective dealing.   Another type, sometimes called the "true open shop," has been that in which both unionists and nonunionists have been employed on an agreed-upon scale of wages and hours and in which perhaps some of the shop rules were jointly determined.   The manufacture of men's clothing in Rochester was twenty years ago on this basis, but with some 98 per cent of the workers members of the union.   Another example is found in the anthracite coal trade, where the arbitration board, almost forty years ago, decided in favor of the "open-shop principle," and until 1939 its award formed the basis for the several agreements subsequently concluded.   And, of course, as already noted, many examples of the open shop are now found in which the union is the sole collective bargaining agent or bargains for its members only, with the worker deciding whether or not he shall be a member of it.

The preferential shop is still another type.   Though it had been developed elsewhere at a much earlier time, it was brought to public

---

Society (1925), pp. 610–611, and L. T. Beman, *The Closed Shop* (1921), pp. 117–118.   Mr. Dunne wrote:

"'What's all this that's in the papers about the open shop?' asked Mr. Hennessey.

"'Why, don't ye know?' said Mr. Dooley. 'Really, I'm surpized at yer ignorance, Hinnissey. What is th' open shop? Sure, 'tis where they kape the doors open to accommodate th' constant stream av min comin in t' take jobs cheaper than th' min what has th' jobs. 'Tis like this, Hinnissey: Suppose wan av these freeborn citizens is workin' in an open shop f'r th' princely wages av wan large iron dollar a day av tin hour. Along comes anither son-av-a-gun and he sez t' th' boss, "Oi think Oi could handle th' job nicely f'r ninety cints." "Sure," sez th' boss, an th' wan dollar man gets out into th' crool woruld t' exercise his inalienable roights as a freeborn American citizen an' scab on some other poor devil. An' so it goes on, Hinnissey. An' who gits th' benefit? Thrue, it saves th' boss money, but he don't care no more f'r money thin he does f'r his right eye.

"'It's all principle wid him. He hates t' see men robbed av their indipindence. They must have their indipindence, regardless av anything else.'

"'But,' said Mr. Hennessey, 'these open-shop min ye menshun say they are f'r unions if properly conducted.'

"'Shure,' said Mr. Dooley, 'if properly conducted. An' there we are: An' how would they have thim conducted? No strikes, no rules, no contracts, no scales, hardly iny wages, an' dam few mimbers.'"

[1] Samuel Gompers, *Open Shop Editorials* (reprint of editorials in the *American Federationist*, 1903–1904).

attention by the Protocol adopted in the cloak industry in New York in 1910. In that case, it was incorporated at the suggestion of Mr. Brandeis as a compromise to solve the closed-shop-open-shop issue which had proved a stumbling block in negotiations. There are, however, different types of preferential shops. In the Protocol, the definition ran in terms of hiring;[1] one of the issues arising under it was that of discrimination in laying off workers. Under the agreement in the Chicago men's clothing industry, on the other hand, until a few years ago when the closed shop was granted, it ran in terms of preference in hiring, layoff, and tenure.[2]

Then, there are the union shop and the closed shop,[3] in which only union men are regularly employed. These may be, and most frequently are, required by the agreement, but, in the absence of such provision, they may result from the refusal of union workers to work with "scabs," this not infrequently being accompanied by tactics designed to cause nonunionists to seek employment elsewhere. It is well known that there is more than one way to exclude "scabs."

During the last ten years a considerable number of compromise arrangements have appeared in American industry, designed to meet employer wishes and to give union security. One of these is the simple maintenance of membership contract under which union members must remain in good standing as a condition of employment. It is designed to aid in dues collection and to protect against inroads by competing labor organizations. Maintenance of membership has become increasingly prevalent as a result of National Defense Mediation Board and National War Labor Board decisions. Another type of compromise is the percentage contract formerly used by Trainmen and now by other organizations, requiring the employer at all times to have among his employees a minimum of union men. If the proportion

[1] "Each member of the manufacturers is to maintain a union shop, a 'union shop' being understood to refer to a shop where union standards as to working conditions, hours of labor, and rates of wages as herein stipulated prevail, and where, when hiring help, union men are preferred; it being recognized that, since there are differences in degrees of skill among those employed in the trade, employers shall have freedom of selection as between one union man and another, and shall not be confined to any list, nor bound to follow any prescribed order whatever." Sec. 14.

[2] In recent years many preferential agreements have been entered into. The detail varies greatly. In addition to such differences as are noted in the text, some agreements provide that in no case shall the nonunion employees exceed a certain percentage, say ten, of the whole. Of 2,651 agreements in the Department of Labor files in 1939, twenty provided for the open shop, 130 for a preferential shop of some type or other, and 1,733 for the closed shop. Related to this, of 768 nonclosed-shop agreements, largely in the radio, steel, rubber, and automobile industries, 470 recognized the union as the sole bargaining agency while the other 298 recognized it as an agency for bargaining for its members only.

[3] See *supra*, pp. 473–474 for the distinction between the two.

becomes low further hirings are limited to applicants in good standing in the union. Still another is a modified closed shop, which protects the preferences of employees who do not wish to join the union but which requires members to remain in good standing as a condition of employment and limits hirings to union men. Such compromises are, however, usually rather short-lived. As they have found place and gained strength in industry, most American unions have sought the closed shop.

Prevailing Union-status Arrangements.—This discussion of different situations, and of the terms used to describe these different situations, may advantageously be closed with a summary of the relative importance, in point of the number of organized workers covered, of the arrangements with reference to union status and the eligibility of nonunion men to work in American industry at the end of 1942, even though such a summary repeats a bit of what has already been said.[1] Reference is here made only to situations in which there is some form of union recognition, and the terms are used in the senses in which they have come to be used in rather recent years. These types of situation will be considered: (1) the closed and the union shop; (2) the preferential shop; (3) the maintenance-of-membership arrangement; (4) recognition of the union as sole bargaining agent; and (5) recognition of the union as bargaining agent for its own members only.

1. A closed or a union shop is one, in the usage here employed, in which membership in the union is a condition of employment. As the term "closed shop" has come to be rather narrowly defined in recent years, it is one in which not only is complete union membership of all employees covered by the agreement required, but also one in which all new employees must be hired through the union or must be members at the time of employment. The term "union shop," in contrast, refers in more recent usage to the situation in which the employer has complete control over the hiring of new employees, who need not be union members at the time of hiring, but all persons hired must join the union as a condition of continued employment, usually after a probationary period.[2] In late 1942 and early 1943, an estimated 6,000,000 wage earners, or more than 45 per cent of all workers under union agreement, were

---

[1] The terms used are those of the Industrial Relations Division, U. S. Bureau of Labor Statistics, in "Types of Union Recognition in Effect in December, 1942," *Memorandum 5* (1943), and the data on percentages of workers covered by the different types of union recognition are taken from this study.

[2] As the Industrial Relations Division of the U. S. Bureau of Labor Statistics has pointed out (*ibid.*, p. 3), the distinction between a closed and a union shop is sometimes nore theoretical than real. If, for example, a union not having a closed-shop contract does not have prohibitive initiation fees and is willing to accept as members all persons whom the employer wishes to hire, the situation does not differ materially from that existing under a closed-shop provision. Likewise if a union-shop agreement also provides that members be given preference in hiring, the situation approximates a closed shop.

covered by closed- or union-shop provisions.[1] Nearly 3,000,000 of these were in manufacturing and over 1,500,000 were in building construction. About half a million coal miners and over 700,000 public-utility and transportation workers (the latter confined almost entirely to motor and electric transportation, since railroad agreements do not provide for the closed or union shop) were covered by either the closed or the union shop.

2. The nature of the preferential shop has been explained above. Its essential feature is that preference is given to union members in hiring and layoff, although preference may also be given them in such matters as promotion and seniority rights. Under this arrangement there is no compulsion upon union members to join the union or remain in good standing, but its effect is to encourage continued union membership because of the handicap upon nonmembers. About 500,000 workers, or less than 5 per cent of all persons covered by agreement, were under preferential shop conditions at the end of 1942.[2] While a varying number of agreements throughout almost all industries provide that preference in hiring be given to union members, these provisions are most common in the maritime industry.

3. Maintenance-of-membership arrangements have also been mentioned above. Their essential feature is provision that all employees members of the union at the time the agreement was signed or who later affiliate with the union must retain their membership during the duration of the agreement. In the majority of maintenance-of-membership orders issued by the National War Labor Board in 1942 and 1943, however, provision was made for a fifteen-day "escape" period, during which present members might resign from the union if they desired to do so. This type of union recognition usually has been instituted as a compromise between the union's demand for a closed or a union shop and the employer's opposition to this demand.[3] At the end of 1942, more than 15 per cent of all workers under agreement were covered by maintenance of membership clauses.[4]

4. About 35 per cent of all workers under agreement at the end of 1942 were covered by provisions granting the union sole bargaining rights but no other form of union security. Such agreements prevent the employer from dealing with any rival labor organization, and non-

---

[1] This on the U. S. Bureau of Labor Statistics estimate that about 13,000,000 wage earners and salaried workers were covered by collective-bargaining relationships at the end of 1942.

[2] U. S. Bureau of Labor Statistics, *op. cit.*, p. 8.

[3] The majority of workers now covered by such provisions are in the basic iron and steel, electrical-equipment, shipbuilding, aircraft, rubber-products, farm-equipment, and paper industries.

[4] U. S. Bureau of Labor Statistics, *op. cit.*, p. 6.

union as well as union employees work under the terms of the agreement. This limited form of recognition differs from maintenance-of-membership and preferential provisions in that the union is not protected against membership losses among present employees, since no penalty is imposed upon those who drop their membership and refuse to pay dues; and unlike closed- and open-shop provisions, the right of sole bargaining alone does not provide security against both resignations and losses occasioned by changes in plant personnel.

5. Only a negligible number (less than 1 per cent) of all workers under agreement are today covered by provisions that recognize the union as the bargaining agency for its members only. Such limited recognition can, as a practical matter, exist only under a rather limited range of circumstances.[1]

Some Questions of Justifiability.—No one has publicly advocated the employers' closed shop, as defined earlier, except, perhaps, as a measure to avoid the all-union shop. On the contrary, the right to organize without employer interference has been generally recognized and incorporated in legislation. The main questions are, therefore, why have most unions insisted upon the exclusion of nonunionists and why have so many employers insisted upon the "true" or a "bogus"[2] open shop? These questions should be answered prior to some observations on the preferential shop, and perhaps they are best answered by noting and commenting on the arguments that have been advanced in the running debate so outstanding in American discussion.

The unions demanding the closed shop have for many years been compelled by a more or less hostile public opinion to assume the burden of proof. This they have done and have offered as their main contention that the closed union shop is indispensable to the existence of effective organization and collective bargaining. It places the union in position to insure its existence and to secure observance of standards set. In its absence, nonunionists may accept lower wages or act as pace setters. They may bargain secretly with management for favored positions, for promotion, and the like. Again, and important, the unionists will tend to permit their membership to lapse; disorganization is likely to result.[3]

---

[1] Such as the situation where only a minority of the employees belong to a union and therefore cannot (if the employment is within the jurisdiction of the National Labor Relations Act) act as representative of all workers in the unit, or in an intrastate industry not subject to a state labor-relations act, or where the union, although including a majority of the employees, has not exercised its rights under the National Labor Relations Act to secure exclusive bargaining rights.

[2] Meaning one in which there is no collective bargaining or one closed to union workers and therefore standing over against the "true" open shop.

[3] It has in fact been a not uncommon experience for new unions, though obtaining contracts, to disintegrate rapidly when the organization fever subsides. Some fail to pay dues; many others then do likewise. The union must again organize or succumb.

By far most important of all, the union spokesman has asserted that the employer would discriminate and weed out the union workers so as to be in the most favorable position when one agreement ended and a new one was to be entered into or collective bargaining refused. When new demands are made the nonunionists are likely to remain at work and form a nucleus of the necessary working force, with the result that the strike is broken or the lockout won. In short, the union spokesman has contended "that the closed-shop question is one of the life-and-death necessities of trade unionism . . . that where the one goes, the other goes with it."[1] It is a matter of union security.

There is certainly much evidence to support this union contention. Experience shows that the closed shop is of importance in securing the observance of agreements in effect. It shows, also, that unless it is a condition of employment many members of the union will permit their membership to lapse[2] or will not join the union at all. Again, there has been a wealth of evidence that management may take advantage of the possibility of hiring nonunionists and of getting rid of union workers. Professor Lewis quotes a Chicago manufacturer as saying years ago: "When unions are weak I would make individual contracts with nonunionists who were often willing to start at almost any wage. I could then play these men against the union, eventually break the contract, and defy the union." He quotes another as saying, "If the union would permit us to employ non-union men we would do so, and the union could demand anything it chose. It could demand ten dollars a day if it wanted to." He quotes still a third employer, who stated, "A year or so ago, before the formation of the Alliance, I had 297 union men. I have succeeded in eliminating all but 6, and I hope before long to have, not an open shop, but a closed shop—closed to the union."[3] Such have been the possibilities. By no means all employers with agreements are of the type just noted, but, without question, many of them have been. Economic necessity, from the union viewpoint, has been the great factor explaining the appearance and spread in organized industries of the closed shop. Impartial students were long ago forced to this conclusion. While the "true open shop" has operated successfully in the case of the Brotherhoods, and also in most stove plants, it has generally fallen short of meeting organized labor's needs.

[1] H. T. Lewis, "The Economic Basis of the Fight for the Closed Shop," *Journal of Political Economy*, vol. 20 (1912), p. 932.

[2] The checkoff of dues, and perhaps of assessments and other obligations, has long been employed in the bituminous coal industry. Its adoption is explained in part by a desire to avoid the collection of dues at the workplace and "button strikes," in part by the fact that it keeps dues paid up and protects against loss of membership in the union. In recent years the checkoff has been more and more widely applied. It may accompany a provision for the closed shop but it is frequently incorporated in contracts of other types.

[3] Quoted from H. T. Lewis, *op. cit.*, pp. 933–934.

When disorganization follows organization, there is much commotion, distrust, and dissension among employees. Nowadays there are many appeals for union security in order to avoid these problems and to permit the union to become cooperative and helpful in solving production and other problems in the plant and in the industry. The automobile and the steel industries may be cited from a large number in which this has occurred.

It will be noted that in his argument the union spokesman has not stressed the closed shop as an organizing aid—a device requiring all who want to obtain jobs or to hold the jobs they have to join the union. No doubt such aid has been very much desired—and not entirely to enable the union to maintain discipline, to avoid squabbles between workers, and to assist in administering a grievance procedure and in furthering the solution of production problems. Nor has the union spokesman said anything directly concerning the shift of power—from management to union—that may take place with the acceptance of the closed shop.

The typical spokesman for employers opposing the union-closed shop usually reckons with his audience and asserts that the closed shop is un-American, that it keeps the nonunion man out of work or compels him to join the union in order to secure employment. This, he says, deprives the worker of an inalienable right. Of course, this is largely twaddle. Under ordinary circumstances, most employers evidently have not cared about anyone's right to work or about coercion applied to the man they have not wished to employ. They perhaps have wished to have unlimited right of discharge, and the chances are that, while denouncing union compulsion, they, individually or in association, have attempted to compel nonunionism or company unionism. Of course, when a closed-shop demand has been made upon him, an employer may have objected to parting with the services of valuable employees who were not eligible for or did not wish to belong to the union.[1] But the employer may have wished quite as much to have a source of worker information and tale-bearing.[2] When one reaches the facts in the case, he usually finds, when any, two important employer objections to the closed shop. The first of these is that, as he sees it, it means a numerically stronger union, higher wages, and shorter hours, and perhaps higher costs of production. Usually higher costs mean less profit because the trade is generally not fully organized and not all the competitors are placed on the same level.

[1] The preferences of non-union employees are not infrequently protected under modified closed-shop contracts that permit them to remain outside of the union while requiring members to remain members as a condition of employment and limiting hirings to union men.

[2] Experience indicates that there has, at times, been an exaggerated interest in the anti-union man.

If, however, the trade is thoroughly organized and costs are easily passed on to the consumer, the employers are unlikely to find "a principle" in the closed shop. The building trades, among others, provide cases in point. And if a union organization can be used to build up and protect a monopoly situation, as in the manufacture of common brick in Chicago during the 1920's, or if it is helpful in legislative matters, as in the brewing industry of earlier days and for many years also in the pottery trade, collective bargaining is liked, the closed shop is quite acceptable, and few questions are raised.

But, especially when unionization is new, the most important reason for employer opposition to the closed shop is found in the application of union work rules. These mark a break with the customary rights of management and present too great a shift in control. Speaking for the metal trades, Mr. W. H. Pfahler has said, "In the union shop, the union, without invitation, with no endorsement as to its qualification, for no ostensible reason except to exercise accidental power, attempts to limit the owner or employer in the exercise of his right and judgment as to the proper use of that which is his and to put the workingman under the dictation of a walking delegate." And, further, "Change from an open shop to a union shop gives the union entire control."[1] Professor Barnett was correct, when, in explaining the strong open-shop movement early in this century—in which Mr. Pfahler participated—he observed, "the closed shop has become the center of an attack, primarily directed against the shop rules of the union."[2]

The nature and variety of union-shop rules have been set forth earlier in this chapter, and an attempt has been made to explain and, in a measure, to evaluate them. It is only necessary to say here that seldom have they had "no ostensible reason except to exercise accidental power"; they find explanation in human nature and the conditions under which men work; taken collectively, union-shop rules have reasons behind them just as management rules have reasons behind them. The essential difference is that management rules emanate from the customary source.

In the running debate that has been carried on, the plight of the youth deprived of an opportunity to learn a trade and the plight of the non-union man who wishes to work when, where, and as he will have been placed in the foreground. Because of the successful appeal thus made to an uninformed public, the union spokesman has had to take note of the argument in his rebuttal. Nothing need be added here to our discussion of apprenticeship rules.[3] With reference to the plight of the nonunion

[1] "Free Shops for Free Men," *Papers and Proceedings, Publications of the American Economic Association*, Third Series, vol. 4 (1903), p. 186.

[2] "Discussion on the Open or Closed Shop," *Papers and Proceedings, Publications of the American Economic Association*, Third Series, vol. 6 (1905), p. 209.

[3] *Supra*, pp. 439–453.

man who is excluded from employment or forced to join the union in order to get work, the spokesman for the union points out that he has a chance to work elsewhere than in the union shop and that he may join the union. That he may be forced to join the union in order to secure employment or to avoid criticism involves no wrong. The nonunion man in an organized trade is usually, it is said, simply apathetic or misinformed; when he joins the union he becomes a good union man and is happy in his new relationship. Moreover, the worker is under a moral obligation to join the union, pay dues, and assist in carrying on, because the results are valuable to all. To do less is to fail to meet one's moral obligation. Finally, it is asserted that upon analysis it will be found that many in the nonunion group are not deserving of public sympathy. Such are the professional strikebreakers, who are not heroes. In the language of Frank K. Foster, this type of worker is "an industrial thief, a social renegade, a moral leper, and as such merits, and fortunately often receives, the penalty of being set aside in practical isolation from honorable men."[1]

In this connection it has frequently been pointed out that a conscripted union membership may be a source of union weakness as well as a source of numerical strength. This is true; not all union members are fully assimilated and become union men at heart.[2] All too frequently they give rise to problems in the union and in the trade. What is said concerning the professional strikebreaker is true, but what of the workers who cannot pay the high initiation fees sometimes charged, and of those who are not accepted by a restrictive or closed union? There are, as has been noted, some unions of this kind. Finally, it may be observed that whether there is or is not a moral obligation to join the union greatly depends upon the character of the union and what it attempts to do.

As Professor Groat[3] has said, the closed shop, like every other human institution, is inherently neither right nor wrong. Nor is a fundamental principle involved. One's decision as to the closed shop, likewise its related types, must be arrived at in view of the details in the given situation. The argument of defense of organization is generally well taken. That the closed shop aids organization is to be viewed as usually a good thing. The argument of moral obligation is strong. But in all

---

[1] Frank K. Foster, *Has the Non-unionist a Right to Work How, When, and Where He Pleases?* (issued by the American Federation of Labor, 1904), p. 5.

[2] In more than one concrete instance when cards have been checked to settle questions of representation, as high as 10 per cent of the union members have asserted that they belonged to the union only because they had to. Now and then in National Labor Relations Board elections, a considerable number vote against the union of which they are members and to which they are paying dues, nor is this limited to cases in which a second union has come forward and is contesting for recognition.

[3] G. G. Groat, *An Introduction to the Study of Organized Labor in America* (1916 ed.), p. 281.

cases the conclusion will be greatly influenced by the character of the union and its deeds. Certainly a closed shop with an open and unrestrictive union is one thing, a closed shop with a closed or an unduly restrictive or a racketeering union is another. This observation leads to a consideration of the charge often made that the unions use the closed shop for monopoly gains for their members or that the closed shop leads to monopoly, which is assumed to run counter to sound public policy.

In admission to membership, unions most frequently adopt the principle of inclusiveness. But it cannot be denied that a great many unions have charged high initiation fees and discouraged and restricted apprenticeship in an effort to limit the supply of labor. Some have closed their books. Indeed, most established unions are not really open in time of depression, for they must then protect their members against unemployment, but over against these there have been some that have closed their books in order to realize monopoly gain.[1] It must be added, also, that the closed shop tends to beget a closed or restrictive union.

Finally, in the running debate, particularly before the New Deal legislation, the employer's spokesman has asserted that the closed shop was unlawful, to which the union spokesman retorted "If and when true, so much the worse for the law." The facts with reference to the law of the closed shop as well as to the question of what the law should be must be left for later discussion.[2]

The preferential shop has been adopted, in most cases at least, to effect a compromise between employers who refused to grant the closed shop and an organization that would not accept the open shop. The success realized under it has varied widely. Its one service in the cloak industry in New York was that it made negotiation to a successful conclusion possible. Within a short time, however, the issue of hiring and firing raged and was an important cause of the breakdown of the agreement. The manufacturer was not limited to any list when seeking help; there was no explicit rule relative to layoffs and the reorganization of shops.[3] The agreement in the men's clothing industry in Chicago, where the preferential feature was incorporated to break a deadlock in a Hart, Schaffner and Marx conference, was explicit with regard to all these matters.

As already stated, the Chicago manufacturer in need of help requisitioned the union; workers were hired "outside" only when the union

[1] Supra, pp. 250–264.

[2] Infra, pp. 560–565. Nothing further needs to be said concerning the "union shop," as the term is being currently used, for it varies only slightly from the all-union shop. It has the advantage, however, that management may obtain the services of good men who are, at the time hired, outside the union, and then retain them in employment provided they become members of the union.

[3] Louis Levine, The Women's Garment Workers (1924), Chap. 27, and Julius Henry Cohen, Law and Order in Industry (1916), Chaps. 11, 12, and 13.

could not provide them within a reasonable time; when work became slack nonunionists were discharged and the regular (union) help shared the work available as nearly equally as practicable. Under this arrangement the supply of labor was given some elasticity, but seldom was it necessary to hire nonunion workers. The members of the union were vigorous salesmen of unionism to any nonunion workers. The latter usually joined the union because otherwise they would be laid off at the close of the busy season. For the same reason, if not the better one of appreciation of and loyalty to the Amalgamated, the union members endeavored to keep their dues paid up and to remain in good standing.[1] The result was alert and vigorous unionism in the Chicago locals, with few, when any, nonunion workers in the shops.

Maintenance of membership is a compromise formula accepted and widely applied by the boards set up to deal with disputes in defense (later, war) industries. It gives a union almost as much security as does the union shop—a guaranteed membership and income, at least during a period of relatively full employment. Also, like the union or closed shop, it gives labor organizations disciplinary powers over their members; expulsion from the union means loss of employment. On the other hand, a membership-maintenance clause involves less coercion, particularly when, as in recent War Labor Board decisions, it does not go into effect until members are given a certain period in which to withdraw. Those who remain are more likely to be true union men at heart than under a closed or union shop, where everyone is forced to belong.

The same, or even greater, financial security results from a universal, compulsory checkoff, which involves assessing the cost of maintaining a union as a going concern and dividing this sum, on a uniform basis, among all employees covered by the agreement, members and nonmembers alike. Such a "poll tax" was agreed to in the summer of 1942 by one of the large tobacco companies. This type of arrangement spreads union costs equally over those who benefit from the collective-bargaining agreement but leaves individuals free to participate in the union, or not, or to form other unions.

[1] In 1939 the checkoff of dues was adopted.

CHAPTER XI

TRADE UNIONS, THE LAW, AND THE COURTS

In the preceding chapters an attempt has been made to show how in industrially advanced countries trade unionism has become prevalent and also to portray the methods it employs to further its objectives. Recourse is made to collective bargaining to replace individual bargaining, at least in part. Collective bargaining is accompanied by more or less union regulation of apprenticeship and other details, this regulation standing over against the practices and orders of management. In the United States, in contrast to many other countries, very great emphasis has been placed upon the methods of direct action as against legislative standardization and control. In this and the immediately following chapter we shall discuss what the law relating to trade unions is and what the law should be from the point of view of what is here conceived to be sound public policy. The subject is a large and intricate one, but, because of the limitations of a general treatise on the organization of labor, the discussion must be rather summary in character; some interesting points must be dismissed with the briefest reference, while others must be passed over altogether.

Though there are employers who are frank defenders of individual bargaining, the principle of collective bargaining has been very generally accepted as sound procedure in modern industry. But, if there is to be collective bargaining, there must be organization in some form or other. An important source of contention in the United States has been the question of how the workers should organize—whether organization should be through trade unions or through some other machinery for employee representation. The President's Industrial Conference, consisting of public men and employers, reported that it was "in favor of the policy of collective bargaining. It [saw] in a frank acceptance of this principle the most helpful approach to industrial peace. It believe[d] that the great body of employers of the country accept[ed] this principle. The difference of opinion appear[ed] in regard to the method of representation."[1]

---

[1] *Report of Industrial Conference called by the President*, March 6, 1920, p. 31. The members of the conference were William B. Wilson, chairman; Herbert Hoover, vice-chairman; Martin H. Glynn, Thomas W. Gregory, Richard Hooker, Stanley King, Samuel W. McCall, Henry M. Robinson, Julius Rosenwald, George T. Slade, Oscar S. Straus, Henry C. Stuart, Frank W. Taussig, William O. Thompson, Henry J. Waters, George W. Wickersham, and Owen D. Young. The secretaries were Willard E. Hotchkiss and Henry R. Seager.

It was upon this question as to the method of representation that the President's First (1919) Industrial Conference had divided, the representatives of the public and the unions, then participating, declaring in favor of representatives of the workers' own selection, this statement being an endorsement of trade unionism when desired by the workers, those of the employers favoring works councils or representation plans. The issue thus raised in 1919 long continued to be debated and played a leading part in the great struggle incident to the adoption of the National Labor Relations Act.[1] It will be discussed incidentally in this chapter but must be left for further consideration in a later chapter, where employee-representation plans will be described and evaluated.[2]

POLICY IN OTHER COUNTRIES

In most countries other than the United States the place to be occupied by unions has long been made more or less clear by statute law.[3] With the advance of "democracy," i.e., representative government, the decades have witnessed a rather general movement from suppression, to cautious and limited acceptance, to recognition of unions as having a "normal" place in industry. Indeed, in a considerable number of countries trade-union organization has in more recent years been positively encouraged by government, and in some of them labor organizations have been given a preferred status at law. Under the revised arbitration act adopted by the Labour Government in New Zealand in 1936, union membership is generally required of workers in industries under compulsory arbitration awards. In Mexico, the law, contrary to that of the pre-revolutionary order, has more recently placed few limitations upon union activity but many and far-reaching limitations upon what employers may do.[4] In Russia labor unions have really been an integral part of the Soviet machinery for standardization and control.[5]

[1] Public no. 198, 74th Congress, 1st Session, Chap. 372 (S. 1958), July 5, 1935.

[2] See Chap. XV.

[3] For an analysis of the laws of different countries as they stood some years ago, see International Labour Office, Freedom of Association [Studies and Reports, Series A (Industrial Relations), nos. 28–32], 1927–1930.

[4] See Marjorie Ruth Clark, Organized Labor in Mexico (1934).

[5] See Calvin B. Hoover, The Economic Life of Soviet Russia (1931), p. 260, where he says: "The government is not thought of simply as representing the workers, but it is the organ of the dictatorship of the workers, which, therefore, always has in view only the interests of the labourers and does not represent any other class. Since the Communist Party constitutes the leadership of the dictatorship of the proletariat, it is considered logical that it should guide and dominate the labour unions. The labour unions, on the other hand, are one of the institutions upon which the Party relies to maintain its contact with the proletariat, and we thus find a system of interlocking relationships between the labour unions, the Soviets, and the Party which is unique in its closely knit quality." For other references see: Robert W. Dunn, Soviet Trade Unions (1928); S. P. Turin, From Peter the

The development in statutory law from suppression or limited toleration toward general acceptance and few restrictions has of course not proceeded so far in some countries as in others. Nor has the development always been in the direction of more ready acceptance. At times there have been "backward swings," accounted for, in part, by the manner in which newly acquired rights have been exercised. And, more important at this time when what is known as "democracy" is being widely challenged, unionism is also being challenged as out of harmony with the general welfare or with the interests of the state. Italy, Germany, and Japan provide examples of suppressed and displaced labor organizations of the usual types.

In Italy, organization after the First World War was largely mandatory, but along fascist lines; all was designed to further a certain regime; the former free trade unionism was displaced.[1] The German government, following the revolution of 1918, did much to further and maintain unions freely set up by workers and clerks and to give them opportunity to function in industry. Not only was there freedom to organize; joint agreements were recognized at law and their terms were to be observed by employers in making contracts with nonunionists as well as with unionists. Moreover, if conditions fixed by an agreement predominated in an area, the agreement might be extended to and made binding upon the industry throughout the area. Finally, the official conciliation and arbitration boards were regarded not so much as instruments for settling strikes and lockouts as agencies for the initiation and continuation of collective agreements.[2] This supporting legislation was helpful in maintaining an unusually extensive organization of workers and clerks in Germany and goes far to explain the fact that in 1930 collective agreements were in effect in approximately 800,000 establishments, employing about 12,000,000 or three-fifths of the 20,000,000 workers and clerks.[3]

The German policy of encouragement of trade unionism was, however, abandoned and an entirely new labor program promulgated by the

---

Great to Lenin (1935); Amy Hewes, "The Transformation of Soviet Trade Unions," *American Economic Review*, vol. 22 (1932), pp. 605–619; and Sidney and Beatrice Webb, *Soviet Communism: A New Civilization* (1936), especially vol. 1, Chaps. 3 and 4.

[1] See Carmen Haider, *Capital and Labor under Fascism* (1930). Recognizing the impossibility of functioning under the legislation and orders adopted in 1926, the Confederation of Labor transferred its headquarters to Paris. See Haider, Chap. 10, "Extralegal Labor Associations."

[2] See Nathan Reich, *Labour Relations in Republican Germany* (1938); William T. Ham, "The German System of Arbitration," *Journal of Political Economy*, vol. 39 (1931), pp. 1–24; and Wladimir Woytinsky, "New Statistics of Collective Agreements in Germany," *International Labour Review*, vol. 23 (1931), pp. 506–532.

[3] Hans Lehmann, "Collective Labor Law under the German Republic," *Wisconsin Law Review*, vol. 10 (1935), pp. 324–339, also Nathan Reich, *op. cit.*, Chap. 3.

National Socialist Party on Jan. 20, 1934.[1] Trade unionism and collective bargaining based upon a recognition of a difference of interests between the employer and his employees were denounced and replaced by a system assuming a harmony of interests. Trade unions and employers' associations were dissolved and their property seized and turned over to the Labor Front. The Labor Front, to which all manual and clerical workers must belong, is an organ of the National Socialist Party designed to form "a real national and working community of all Germans."[2]

The order of Jan. 20, 1934, provided that each owner or employer should become the leader (*Führer*) of his salaried employees and wage earners and that the employer and his employees should work together for the furtherance of the purposes of the establishment and for the common needs of the people and the State. The leader (employer) was given the right to fix wages[3] and to decide all other matters pertaining to the establishment and was to care for the well-being of his followers (employees), from whom loyalty was expected. The National Socialist Party was to select advisers to assist the leader. If the leader was found by the Social Honor Court to have violated his "social" duties, he might be fined or, in extreme cases, removed from leadership of his establishment. On the employee side, "malicious agitation" and "frivolous and unfounded complaints" or other actions that would endanger the industrial peace of the community became offenses against "social honor."

It is obvious that in the troubled post-World War I situation, prolific of new ideologies and movements, more differences in government policy on trade unionism have developed than at any earlier time.

Having made these few observations, we shall for the most part limit our discussion to the law in Great Britain and the United States and to questions of public policy in democratic countries.[4] The English law has influenced the law of many countries. It is of particular interest to American students of unionism, for the American law developed largely out of the earlier English common law, while in recent decades unions in this country desired the comparative freedom from restriction enjoyed by the British unions under the Industrial Disputes Act of 1906.

[1] The text of the German National Labor Law may be found in the *Monthly Labor Review*, vol. 38 (1934), pp. 1104–1116. Perhaps it is unnecessary to mention that appropriation by the Party of the word "Socialist" as part of its name should not result in confusing it with the kind of parties whose relations to trade unionism in the United States have been discussed earlier.

[2] *Monthly Labor Review*, vol. 40 (1935), pp. 356–357.

[3] As a matter of fact, standards of wages and hours have been widely set by official machinery established for the purpose.

[4] For the place occupied by trade unions in Sweden, see report of the President's Commission on Industrial Relations, *Labor Relations Reporter*, *Supplement*, vol. 3, no. 4 (Sept. 3, 1938). See also Paul H. Norgren, "Collective Wage-making in Sweden," *Journal of Political Economy*, vol. 46 (1938), pp. 788–801, and James J. Robbins, *The Government of Labor Relations in Sweden* (1942).

THE DEVELOPMENT OF THE ENGLISH LAW

British policy and law relating to labor combinations have undergone an interesting development—from stout opposition and attempts at outright suppression to limited acceptance and toleration, then to general acceptance and comparatively few restrictions. This evolution may be sketched in the briefest manner.[1]

The Ordinance of Labourers of 1349 and the Statute of Labourers of 1351, with the several amendments to the latter designed to make the provisions effective, which attempted to establish wage maxima, and hence rendered unlawful concerted efforts to increase wages, were in thorough harmony with the social and economic philosophy and the dominant interests of the time. It was only to be expected, therefore, that as journeymen combined and attempted to employ their collective power these efforts would encounter legal opposition. Beginning even earlier than the Black Death, ordinances were enacted against concerted action by workmen. With Parliamentary statute, as distinguished from local ordinance, becoming more important as the centuries passed, there was little change in policy until the end of the first quarter of the nineteenth century. Nor did the attempts at control remain merely a matter of ordinance and statute; there was also the common law developed by the courts in deciding cases brought before them.

Naturally enough, the philosophy and dominant interests of the time being what they were, the decisions of the courts in applying the common law were usually as restrictive of concerted action as were the statutes. The trial courts had, indeed, been developing a common law of labor long before its outstanding legal doctrines were clearly articulated or generally recognized. In other words, the better known developments of the eighteenth century were not altogether new; nor were the doctrines developed farfetched as tested by the control and suppression that had long been attempted. Be this as it may, the doctrines of criminal conspiracy and of restraint of trade developed as unionism expanded. "By the end of the eighteenth century," Dr. Mason has said, "conspiracy had come to cover, at least in the opinion of certain judges, not only a combination of two or more persons for an unlawful act by any means or for a lawful end by unlawful means, but also a combination of persons for an immoral, a malicious end; the ruin of a third person, for example, or injury to the public."[2]

---

[1] The student will find a scholarly historical summary in James M. Landis, *Cases on Labor Law* (1934), Chap. 1.

[2] Alpheus T. Mason, *Organized Labor and the Law* (Duke University Press, 1925), p. 36. The doctrines of conspiracy and restraint of trade are discussed in the next section of this chapter. The discussion here is limited rather closely to a development of English statute law.

Combination Acts and Later Legislation.—During the eighteenth century the British unions were limited and harassed not only by the common law but also by about twoscore statutes enacted to suppress specific organizations. Then, at the turn of the century, through the Combination Acts of 1799 and 1800, which confirmed a viewpoint toward labor centuries old, all concerted action by workers or employers was outlawed by statute. Though equally applicable to combinations of employers and to combinations of employees, the Acts overlooked the fact that with the development of large-scale production a single employer might have many employees and be a sort of combination in himself, with the result that there was inequality of bargaining power. Moreover, the penalties provided were different for employers and workers, and the procedure and circumstances were such that from its inception the statute was a dead letter in so far as concerted employer action was concerned. Whether or not the law was enforced against labor organizations was very much at the will of employers concerned; in some industries and trades collective bargaining and trade agreements went unquestioned, but frequently the prohibitions of the law were vigorously enforced against an opposed unionism. On occasion action was taken under the common law as well.[1] The unequal application of the law and the severe penalties imposed in certain cases became a source of labor discontent and protest. Furthermore, the limitations imposed upon labor and not upon employers aroused the active interest of persons of ability and prestige outside the ranks of labor, among whom were Francis Place and David Hume. In considerable measure these two men were responsible, or should be given credit, for the adoption of the Combinations Act of 1824.[2]

The Act of 1824 marked a tremendous change from the legislation that preceded it. The Combination Acts of 1799 and 1800 were repealed, the common law was set aside, and unions were accepted and empowered to function with few limitations. The Act has been admirably summarized by Dean Landis, as follows: "It repealed all the earlier combination laws and provided further that workmen combining to obtain an advance in wages, to lessen their hours of work or to decrease the quantity of work, to induce others to depart from their work, or to regulate the mode of carrying on the trade, should not be subject to indictment or prosecution for conspiracy under common law or under statute. Similar liberty was accorded combinations of masters. Persons, however, who used violence or threats or intimidation wilfully or maliciously to induce

---

[1] J. M. Landis observes (*op. cit.*, p. 15), "The period from 1800 to 1824 is replete with prosecutions of collective labor tactics of all kinds. Many of these were prosecutions brought under the Combination Act of 1800; but many, generally more severe in character, were still prosecutions at common law for conspiracy."

[2] 5 George IV, Chap. 95.

others to leave their work or not to accept work or to accomplish other similar ends were still to be criminally punishable. Conspiracies to effect these ends by such means were also outlawed."[1]

But the victory of Place and Hume in achieving enactment of the Combinations Act of 1824 was short-lived. The import of the Act had not been fully understood. Moreover, the measure was far in advance of the thought and contrary to the interests of the classes dominating political life, and the unions, many of them newly organized and inexperienced, all too frequently made awkward and crude use of their privileges. An inevitable reaction quickly resulted in new legislation. The Combinations Act of 1825,[2] which repealed that of 1824, took away part of the rights acquired the year before. Workers were expressly permitted to combine and consult with reference to the determination of rates of wages or hours of work and to enter into agreements with employers covering these matters; but the closed shop and concerted action to obtain objectives relating to matters other than those of wages and hours were placed under a ban. The picketing provisions of the Act of 1824 were elaborated and modified somewhat, the new statute making it a crime if "any person shall by violence to the person or property, or by threats or intimidation, or by molesting or in any way obstructing another, force or endeavor to force any journeyman, manufacturer, workman or other person hired or employed in any manufacture, trade or business, to depart from his hiring, employment or work, or to return his work before the same shall be finished, or prevent or endeavor to prevent any journeyman, manufacturer, workman or other person not being hired or employed from . . . accepting work or employment. . . . "[3] But the most important change resulting from the new law, as interpreted, was to restore the effect of the common law in so far as it was not modified by the positive provisions incorporated in the Act.

With the partial restoration of the common law and with the restrictions and language of the statute most frequently narrowly interpreted by the courts, the unions were harassed, prosecuted, and limited only less than formerly, while employers victimized union men, and used the "iron clad" or "the document," more latterly known in the United States as the "yellow-dog" contract, to maintain nonunion shops. Though numerous all the while, prosecutions for conspiracy in restraint of trade were most frequent in the decade of the 1850's, when more and more of the unionism had come to be of the "new model," stressing benefits and

---

[1] J. M. Landis, *op. cit.*, p. 16.

[2] 6 George IV, Chap. 129.

[3] As J. M. Landis says (*op. cit.*, pp. 17–18), "Any type of picketing was unlawful. Not only was it unlawful to persuade workmen to break their contracts of employment, but to pay them not to work was equally illegal, as well as merely to persuade them to leave the employment of their master."

attempting through trade agreements to bring the poorer employers up to the standards observed by the better. It was then, also, that labor organizations found themselves by court decision without legal protection of their funds. It is true that there was legislation before the 1870's designed to remove some of the limitations resting upon labor organizations. There was, for example, the Molestation of Workmen Act of 1859, which was designed to legalize peaceful picketing outlawed by the courts in so many cases. This Act sought to legalize peaceful persuasion in connection with strikes involving wages and hours only, provided that no inducement of a breach of contract was involved. For the old Masters and Servants Acts, which tied the worker to his employer, were not relaxed until 1867.[1] Moreover, a court decision[2] soon left the legalization of peaceful persuasion without the little significance it might otherwise have had.

Legislative Enlargement of Labor's Self-help Area.—Union discontent with and agitation against the limitations of the law aroused interest and sympathy sufficient to secure the appointment of a Royal Commission of Enquiry in 1867. Though quite aware of what are regarded as the disadvantages connected with unionism, the Commission found that the law was uncertain in many respects, unequal in its application to employers and employees, and unduly restrictive of concerted action. The report of this Commission (1867), followed by the extension of the franchise to urban workers (1867), the formation of the Trades Union Congress (1868), the pledging of candidates for seats in the House of Commons, the establishment of local representation leagues in the early 1870's, and twenty years of experience with a well-disciplined and conservative unionism as the uppermost fact in the labor movement, resulted in the enactment of laws, 1871–1876, which had the effect of replacing the common law by statute law, of clarifying the legal position of trade unions, and of removing all limitations on the activity of two or more acting in concert which would not apply equally to an individual acting alone.[3]

A summary of the new legislation, which has afforded the basis for most of the British law since the 1870's, may be quoted, in part:

"The Trade Union Act of 1871 clarified, modified, and at certain points liberalized the law as it had been developed by statute and court decision. It eliminated the previous common-law doctrine that a trade union, by being in restraint of trade, was a criminal conspiracy. This

---

[1] Under the Masters and Servants Acts, a master could be sued only civilly for breach of contract, while a workman who committed a like offense could be proceeded against criminally and imprisoned.

[2] In *Regina v. Druitt*, 10 Cox C. C. 592 (1867).

[3] This legislation has been reviewed by several writers, among them J. M. Landis, *op. cit.*, pp. 21ff., and H. A. Millis, "The British Trade Disputes and Trade Unions Act, 1927," *Journal of Political Economy*, vol. 36 (1928), pp. 305–329.

act also provided for the voluntary registration of trade unions, safeguarded union funds, and provided a legal basis for the conduct of union affairs. This legislation was, however, accompanied by the Criminal Law Amendment Act which had the effect of outlawing and placing drastic penalties upon all picketing in the conduct of strikes and lockouts.

"This limitation on picketing was relaxed and the law made more liberal in other respects by the Conspiracy and Protection of Property Act of 1875, in which much of the law still effective is to be found. As to conspiracy, the general principle was established that, in the furtherance of a trade dispute, what one may do, two or more may do when acting in concert . . . trade unions had been legal per se, but now their members were free from danger of punishment as criminals or of action for damages for their collective acts if such acts performed by them individually would have been legal. . . . The following qualifications, however, should be pointed out: ordinary conspiracy against the state, riot, unlawful assembly, breach of the peace, or sedition remained punishable. Moreover, penalties were imposed upon anyone breaking a contract of service if the result would be to cut off a supply of gas or water or to inflict serious injury on life or property. . . . [1]

"Under this Act of 1875, the prohibitions of the Criminal Law Amendment Act of 1871 were repealed, and securing and communicating information were legalized in the conduct of industrial disputes; but violence, intimidation, hindrance to work, watching, and besetting were left under the ban. Such acts were to be punishable by fine not exceeding twenty pounds, or by imprisonment not exceeding three months, with or without hard labor. To make it clear that limited picketing was not to be regarded as unlawful, the section provided that 'attending at or near the house where a person resides, or works, or carries on business, or happens to be, or the approach to such house or place, in order merely to obtain or communicate information, should not be deemed a watching or besetting within the meaning of this section.'

"The net effect of this legislation of the 1870's was to remove any doubt as to the lawfulness of trade unions; to recognize them and to provide for their registration; to provide for the protection of their funds, and to give them the necessary basis for the conduct of their business; to legalize picketing . . . ; and to provide necessary conditions for the use of the method of collective bargaining."[2]

As the years passed, some of the freedom given under this legislation was nibbled away by the courts, particularly in cases involving picketing.[3]

---

[1] In 1919, extended to the supply of electric current also.

[2] H. A. Millis, *Journal of Political Economy*, vol. 36, pp. 307–309.

[3] As J. M. Landis says (*op. cit.*, p. 24), "Judges soon found ways and means to impose severe restrictions upon labor activities. Though it was the obvious purpose of the Act of 1875 to legalize that type of conduct loosely described as peaceful picketing, in 1876 Baron

Nor did the legislation go unchallenged at the hands of others when considering public policy, especially after the appearance of the vigorous and assertive New Unionism at the end of the eighties. In 1891, when reaction against union activity was strong, several members of a commission that had been set up recommended that trade unions should be compelled to incorporate and that they should be bound by agreements entered into with employers, but no legislation resulted from the propaganda carried on. However, after some decisions approaching the position that unions should be regarded as legal entities, the Law Lords in the Taff Vale case in 1901 saddled upon unincorporated trade unions a responsibility for property losses due to unlawful union activity;[1] and in the same year it was held[2] that workingmen acting in combination with intent to injure another were civilly liable despite the Act of 1875.

Taff-Vale Decision and the Act of 1906.—In the railway strike out of which the Taff Vale case developed there had been breach of contract and loss of property and business. An injunction was secured and a suit for damages was brought against the union, as distinguished from the individual members who might be shown to have committed the tortious acts. Though the union was unincorporated, the Law Lords held that it was liable for damages and costs. The principle underlying the decision was that where there is power there must be a corresponding responsibility.[3]

The Taff Vale decision, by placing the unions under a collective civil responsibility, affected strike policy and organizational effort. In the view of the trade unions, their very existence was imperiled by this corporate responsibility, the injunction, and the damage suit. A strong propaganda was begun for a change by statute that would remove the effect of the Taff Vale decision and liberalize the law in other respects, especially in respect to picketing. The Conservative Government of the day was opposed to setting aside the Taff Vale doctrine, but in 1903 it did establish a Royal Commission to consider the points involved and to report with recommendations. "In its report, submitted in 1906, the Commission approved of the decision of the Law Lords, both from the point of view of law as it had developed and from the point of view of underlying principle. Their unanimous opinion was that trade unions

---

Huddleston (in *Regina v. Bauld,* 13 Cox C. C. 282) found it to be criminal to watch and beset for the purpose of persuading men to quit work even though no truly intimidatory means were employed."

[1] *The Taff Vale Railway Company Appellants and the Amalgamated Society of Railway Servants, Respondents,* L.R.A.C. (1901), p. 426.

[2] In *Quinn v. Leathem,* A.C. 495 (1901).

[3] This principle is discussed in Chap. XII. In his comment on the Taff Vale decision, Landis observes that "after some thirty years of immunity assumed to have been possessed by trade unions under the Acts of 1871 and 1876, [it] came as a surprise to the legal profession as well as trade unionists." J. M. Landis, *op. cit.,* p. 24.

should rest under a corporate responsibility.[1]   Before the Commission had reported, however, the political situation had changed, and shortly afterward, a statute shaped by political expediency was enacted—a statute conforming closely to the wishes of the unions.   In the election of 1906, Labour had pledged so many of the candidates, both Conservative and Liberal, who were returned to Parliament, and had secured the return of such a large number of its own candidates, that the unwilling (now Liberal) government found it expedient, if not necessary, to place the Industrial Disputes Act upon the statutes."[2]

The Act of 1906, amending the earlier legislation, perhaps gave organized labor the least restrictive labor code till then known.   It dealt with all the questions that had been mooted.   The effect of the Taff Vale decision was eliminated; the Act provided that an "act done in pursuance of an agreement or combination by two or more persons shall, if done in contemplation or furtherance of a trade dispute, not be actionable unless the act, if done without any such agreement or combination, would be actionable."   Courts, moreover, could no longer entertain suits by members of a trade union against their own organization in respect to corporate acts.   Sympathetic, as well as primary, strikes were now included in the term "trade dispute."   The right to picket was modified somewhat, the act providing that it should be "lawful for one or more persons, acting on their own behalf or on behalf of a trade union or of an individual employer or firm in contemplation or furtherance of a trade dispute to attend at or near a house or place where a person resides or works or carries on business or happens to be, if they so attend merely for the purpose of peacefully obtaining or communicating information, or of peacefully persuading any person to work or abstain from working."   In this connection, it is interesting to note that, as Dean Landis points out,[3] the Royal Commission had opposed the legalization of picketing on the grounds that any picketing must "savour of compulsion" and that peaceful picketing "is really a contradiction in terms."   It is to be noted, also, that though the question was raised in the Commons, no direct limitations were placed upon the number of pickets, though in this connection numbers make a difference.

The Act of 1927.—The labor code was revised in important respects following the "general strike" of 1926.   Under the Act of 1927,[4] general strikes were outlawed, and also such sympathetic strikes and lockouts as have "any object other than or in addition to the furtherance of a trade dispute within the trade or industry in which the strikers [or employers

[1] See *Report of the Royal Commission on Trade Disputes and Trade Combinations* (1906, Cd. 2825).   The recommendations of the Commission were all the more interesting because Sidney Webb was one of the five members.

[2] Quoted from H. A. Millis, *Journal of Political Economy*, vol. 36, p. 310.

[3] J. M. Landis, *op. cit.*, p. 26.

[4] 17 and 18 Geo. V, Chap. 22.

locking out] are engaged; and . . . [are] designed or calculated to coerce the Government either directly or by inflicting hardship upon the community."[1] Engaging in such strikes, except by merely quitting work or refusing to accept employment, was made illegal and punishable by fine or imprisonment. Unions were forbidden to discipline their members for failure to participate in strikes made unlawful. Mass picketing and picketing of a person at his residence were also placed under the ban of the law. Moreover, picketing was further limited by a redefinition of "intimidate," which now means to cause in the mind of a person a reasonable apprehension of injury to him or to any member of his family or to any of his dependents or of violence or damage to any person or property. This definition contrasted sharply with the old rule of behavior, which implied a threat of personal violence. Because some unions of civil servants were affiliated with the Trades Union Congress and three of these had in 1926 authorized the General Council to call their members out on sympathetic strike, provisions were incorporated in the Act to effect, with minor exceptions, the withdrawal of organizations of civil servants from affiliation to organizations whose members were non-civil servants, the severance of all political connections with the Labour or other party, and the eventual establishment of independent unions—if there was organization at all.[2] Next to be noted, the law had permitted unions, for political purposes, to levy upon those of their members who did not formally protest. Under the Act of 1927, levy can be made only upon such members as individually authorize it. Finally, the Act introduced the principle of neutrality. Public authorities were prohibited from discriminating between union and nonunion men in employment, and, when purchasing from private parties, from making it a condition of any contract that the parties to it should employ only union men.

When the Labour Party again (1929) became "The Government," notice was given of the introduction of a bill to remove some of the limitations imposed by the Act of 1927. Such a measure was brought forward in 1930, but it failed to receive the support of the Liberals, and, after being amended in unacceptable ways, was withdrawn.[3] Hence the law remained as revised in 1927.

[1] At the time the Act was passed there was some uncertainty as to its application to sympathetic strikes.

[2] Of a total of 300,000 or 400,000 civil servants, some 130,000, a majority of whom were telephone and telegraph operators and others employed in the postal service, had membership in seven organizations affiliated with the Trades Union Congress and the labor party.

[3] The two main objects of the measure were to legalize sympathetic strikes once more and to permit civil servants to have membership in ordinary unions. Revolutionary or political strikes were to remain unlawful. It should be pointed out, however, that doubt as to the lawfulness of the ordinary sympathetic strike has been removed. The Commis-

The English law of labor is of course today somewhat more restrictive, from the viewpoint of labor organizations, than it was during the years 1906 to 1927, and it is equally patent that some of the restrictions in effect since 1927 express a tendency in public policy toward labor combinations somewhat contrary to that of the United States during the 1930's.[1] Indeed some of those convinced that the newly created legal rights of labor combinations in this country necessitate the imposition of "corresponding responsibilities" have found a pattern for their suggestions in the British law. Even with the recently imposed restrictions, however, present English governmental policy toward labor combinations stands out in sharp contrast to that in effect during the first three-quarters of the nineteenth century and is in general one of freedom of combination on both sides. The notion that combinations are wrongful when they attempt to control employment conditions has been abandoned, the conspiracy doctrine set aside, and neither the fact of combination nor the motives of those combining have any weight (except the motives interdicted by the 1927 law) in determining the legality of acts in trade disputes. Action cannot be brought against unions for wrongful acts alleged to have been committed in their behalf, the individuals guilty of these acts, not the union or members unconcerned with them, being held responsible. In contrast to the United States, where despite statutory enactments of recent years the frequently uncertain common law still widely obtains, there is definite statutory prescription of the rights of the contending parties in labor disputes and of the restrictions applicable to them.

The Law of Trade Unionism in the United States

In most countries, as in Great Britain, one can ascertain with a fair degree of accuracy what the law relating to trade unions and their activities is—what purposes and methods are permissible, what ones are not—for it is for the greater part laid down in statute law. This has not for the most part been true in the past of the law in the United States.

---

sion on Industrial Relations in Great Britain states in its report, "We found a complete unanimity of opinion that the Act of 1927 does not forbid or destroy the immunity of unions from suit in the case of sympathetic strikes extending beyond a given industry, unless such strikes are also designed or calculated to coerce the Government, either directly or by inflicting hardship upon the community." See U. S. Department of Labor, *Report of the Commission on Industrial Relations in Great Britain* (1938), p. 10.

[1] For example, there are in the United States no restrictions upon the affiliation of unions of civil servants with general labor organizations; restraints placed upon employers by Sec. 8 of the Wagner Act of 1935 do not have their counterpart in English law; and the legally required neutrality of public officials in the matter of hiring union or nonunion workers and letting contracts to, or purchasing goods from, firms employing nonunion workers is not in accordance with the policy pursued during the 1930's by the Public Works Administration and other government agencies or with the general intent of measures like the Walsh-Healey Act of 1934.

We have not only the statutes enacted by Congress and the forty-eight state legislatures, but also the common law, which has, for the greater part, been taken from England and adapted and developed by the courts. In fact a considerable part of the effective law is still the common or court-made law, and this type of law has varied more or less from one jurisdiction to another because of the different attitudes and philosophies of the courts. It has frequently been confused, uncertain, and inconsistent; much of it has rested unequally upon unions and employers and employers' associations. Much of the statute law enacted has also been restrictive. In many respects the American law has been illiberal as compared to the laws of many other countries. But, on the other hand, under the New Deal, Congress and some of the states have attempted to protect and further unionism and have imposed important limitations and responsibilities upon employers. Important, also, is the fact that in recent years many of the courts have become receptive of new views, and their decisions have been remaking the law. At the present time, American labor law is in a state of flux, and at many points there is confusion and not a little conflict.[1]

The Common-law Basis.—The two legal doctrines that dominated the attitude of the courts toward collective action on the part of labor, especially before the enactment of modern legislation, were those of conspiracy and restraint of trade. Each is an old concept, applied in other fields of law, and possibly it is superfluous to record the fact that neither was concocted to injure labor or to hold it in subjection. They emerged out of conditions and relationships and applied to cases vastly different from the conditions obtaining, and the kind of cases to which the doctrines apply, today. Both theories worked themselves into American law and became the basis for later statutory enactments.[2]

The Conspiracy Doctrine.—The basic public-policy proposition underlying the conspiracy doctrine is that a number of persons acting in concert or combination possess power for wrongful accomplishment not possessed

---

[1] While the Federal Government and some of the states have enacted liberal, if not very liberal, statutes, the rather conservative common law and conservative statutes remain in effect in many jurisdictions. Indeed, recent years witnessed the adoption of very restrictive laws against picketing and other union activities by scores of cities and other local governments. Somewhat related laws were subsequently adopted by various states. Likewise, while the Supreme Court of the United States and other courts have laid down liberal doctrines, some of the state supreme courts and a considerable number of the inferior courts have continued to render decisions like those generally rendered a generation or more ago. Illustrations of these facts will be found in various connections in the pages that follow, as will also a brief summary of legislation enacted after the United States, in 1941, became a participant in World War II.

[2] Until about the 1880's, the majority of legal actions taken in American labor disputes were criminal prosecutions for conspiracy. In later years, the more usual procedure has been to bring suit for damages or to seek an injunction, or both, but in support of the claim of damage or the application for injunction, conspiracy has usually been charged.

by individuals.[1] "A combination of men is a very serious matter. No man can stand up against a combination; he may successfully defend himself against a single adversary, but when his foes are combined and numerous he must fall."[2] This power of combined numbers affords, in turn, logical basis for the principle that when men combine to accomplish a wrongful end, the mere combining is itself unlawful. In other words, if the purpose of the combination is one the law condemns, the crime of conspiracy is complete when a group of men have agreed to try to accomplish that purpose, even though as yet they have done nothing more than so to agree. In most other fields of law, no cognizance is taken of the plans of men until they have done something to put them into execution, but in the field of conspiracy the unexecuted intent to do wrong is itself unlawful. From the same fundamental premise—that the group, by the very fact of union, is more powerful and dangerous than are a number of isolated individuals—there ensues the second of the basic dicta of the conspiracy doctrine: that purposes lawful in the case of an individual are not necessarily lawful in the case of a number acting in concert. It is lawful for one to vent his ill will or spite toward another by withholding patronage or by urging a third party not to become an employee of him toward whom the ill will is directed, but the purpose of reducing the volume of someone's sales or of preventing someone from consummating a contract of employment at will may become unlawful because it is the purpose of a number acting in concert. Not only does combination to accomplish a wrongful end constitute in itself the substantive crime of conspiracy, but the wrongful character of the end may, in turn, be a consequence of the fact of combination. A third of the component dicta of the conspiracy doctrine, that when an illegal plot has been engaged in all the conspirators are responsible for the acts of any one of them, of course inheres in the conception and definition of conspiracy; while a fourth dictum, that when the purpose of a combination is illegal every act done in pursuance thereof is rendered illegal, though the act be innocent of itself, is an application of the general rule of law that all things done to perpetrate a tort or crime are *ipso facto* parts of the tort or crime. Finally, a criminal conspiracy may obtain if the means used by the members of the combination are unlawful, even if the lawfulness of the purpose is not questioned.

Both the great uncertainty surrounding the application of the conspiracy doctrine to the purposes and methods of labor combinations and

---

[1] For excellent discussions of the conspiracy doctrine and its development, to which these summary paragraphs are greatly indebted, see Alpheus T. Mason, *Organized Labor and the Law* (Duke University Press, 1925), pp. 22–37; E. E. Witte, *The Government and Labor Disputes* (McGraw-Hill Book Company, Inc., 1932) pp. 46–54; and Commons and Andrews, *Principles of Labor Legislation*, (Harper's, 1936), pp. 372–388.

[2] From the opinion of the court in *People v. Wilzig*, 4 N.Y. Crim. 403 (1886).

the reasons the application has been obnoxious to a considerable body of jurists as well as to labor and labor's friends should have been suggested by the exposition of the doctrine in the immediately preceding paragraph. Mere combinations are not repugnant to the common law, even though their existence constitutes something of a modification of the individualistic conditions that the courts and other government agencies have tried to maintain. It is only when the end in view or the means used, or both, are unlawful that the combination is to be deemed a conspiracy. But everything then depends upon what ends and means are deemed lawful, what ones unlawful. A labor combination is lawful under conspiracy-doctrine principles when its aim is the mutual benefit of its members but is a conspiracy if the purpose is injury to the reputation or property of an employer, or interference with the employment opportunities of a non-union man, or obstruction of the channels of trade to the injury of the general public, or interference with the legally recognized rights of others. This general distinction is characterized, however, chiefly by its susceptibility to varying—sometimes almost diametrically opposed—concrete applications as between one judicial mind and another. Whether the purpose of a combination engaged in an industrial dispute is legitimate mutual aid on the part of the members or injury to others is a question the answer to which depends on subtle evaluations, necessarily subjective in character. The rights, interference with which constitutes a wrongful purpose, are themselves in part creatures of the common law, and their content and color may vary greatly from time to time and from jurisdiction to jurisdiction, in spite of verbal unanimity in their enunciation by the courts. Responsibility of all conspirators for the acts of any one of them, while a logical implication of the conception of conspiracy, has been regarded by organized labor and by some jurists as unrealistic under modern conditions, since these members frequently are widely scattered, many neither knowing about nor having personal participation in the acts of their officers and agents; and the interdiction, frequently by means of the writ of injunction, of the doing of lawful things—sometimes the exercise of constitutionally guaranteed rights—because the doing was in furtherance of a wrongful end was increasingly criticized as time passed in consequence of the uncertainty and contradictory judicial opinions as to what ends were, after all, unlawful and therefore what combinations were criminal conspiracies. The conviction that the system of customs and precedents provided by the common law did not conform to reason or expediency in commonwealths experiencing the social and economic changes brought about by the Industrial Revolution, that the body of rights and obligations it incorporated was much more simplified and undifferentiated than the relationships to which these rights and obligations applied,[1] gradually crystallized and in time expressed itself in

[1] For good discussions of the premises of the common law and the public policy these

judicial expansion, restatement, and modification of the conspiracy and
other common-law doctrines, as well as in statutory enactments, the purport and policy of some of which departed widely from those of the
common law.[1]

---

premises dictate under modern economic arrangements, see Ernst Freund, *The Police
Power, Public Policy and Constitutional Rights* (1904), Roscoe Pound, *The Spirit of the
Common Law* (1921), and Benjamin B. Cardozo, *The Nature of the Judicial Process* (1921).

[1] The conspiracy doctrine has been discussed in this and the immediately preceding
paragraph only as the broad and inclusive doctrine into which it evolved, not in terms of
its historical evolution. A bit of historical recapitulation is, however, in point. As
Professor Mason has observed, the origin of the conspiracy concept in Anglo-Saxon
law remains a matter of conjecture on the part of, and of disagreement among, legal
historians, some claiming for it a common-law origin and others believing that the crime
of conspiracy was first created by several ordinances during the reign of Edward I. (See
A. T. Mason, *op. cit.*, especially pp. 24–30.) It is certain, however, that in its original form
the term "conspiracy" had a very limited and technical meaning, in contrast to its later
denotation of combination for the purpose of doing any wrong. In the 1304 ordinance of
Edward I that summed up pre-existing law, the crime of conspiracy was a specific rather
than a general offense; the ordinance was directed against those combinations whose purpose was to pervert justice by false and malicious indictments. Also, the doctrine as
defined during the early stages of its development applied only to cases that could be
definitely ascertained—*i.e.*, the crime of conspiracy to secure a false indictment was not
complete until the person whom the combination conspired falsely to indict had been tried
and acquitted (Alpheus Mason, *Organized Labor and the Law*, pp. 22–24). Statutes were
also enacted directed at combinations for treasonable purposes, for breaches of the peace,
and then against merchants combining to disturb the market or fix prices and against
combinations by specific groups of workers to raise wages or shorten hours. The offenses
were, however, specific and designated, and still the laws applied only to cases that could be
definitely ascertained. The process of expansion of the specific offense of conspiracy into
the comprehensive conspiracy doctrine of a later day was, of course, a gradual one. By
the time of the Poulterer's Case of 1611 (9 Coke 55, A. Mason, *op. cit.*, p. 25), mere agreement falsely or maliciously to indict was the gist of the offense, the rule that a conspiracy to
indict was not complete until he against whom it was directed was tried and acquitted
having been dropped. In other words, as between combination to do criminal acts and the
acts themselves, the offense of conspiracy was in the agreement or combination and not in
the actual commission of the crime. The other great development was the expansion of
the doctrine so that it included not merely combination to perpetrate specific legal offenses,
but combination for any purpose that might be deemed malicious in its nature. In accordance with the general tendency to broaden the law so that it covered immoral as well as
illegal acts, judicial opinion had come by the seventeenth and early eighteenth centuries to
hold that a combination might be criminal even though the acts proposed by it would not
be criminal in the absence of a combination, but only tortuous or wrongful. In 1716, in
Hawkins's *Pleas of the Crown*, there appeared the statement that "there can be no doubt
but that all confederacies whatsoever wrongfully to prejudice a third person are highly
criminal at common law," this statement apparently expressing the preponderant, although
not entirely unanimous, position of jurists of the period. In the case of labor combinations, the most frequent wrongful purpose for which combinations were formed was restraint
of trade. At common law it was unlawful, independently of all combination, for one to
restrain another in the exercise of his trade or calling, and under the expanded meaning of
conspiracy any combination to restrain trade became a criminal conspiracy. Later (1832),
under Lord Denman's antithesis, a combination was regarded as criminal if unlawful means

Early American Conspiracy Cases.—The antimonopoly, economic-freedom philosophy of the conspiracy doctrine harmonized well with the ideological and industrial environment of early American labor relations, and, as has been said, the doctrine worked itself thoroughly into American law, the jurists for the most part going to English courts for their precedents and in some cases basing their decisions upon the more extreme cases in the mother country. In the Philadelphia Cordwainers case of 1806[1] the court, with untroubled simplicity, declared that "a combination of workmen to raise their wages may be considered from a twofold point of view; one is to benefit themselves, the other to injure those who do not join their society. The rule of law condemns both." This extreme position never, however, became unchallenged law in the United States. Three years later, in a New York case involving indictment of journeymen for substantially the same offense, the court admitted the right of workers "to meet and regulate their concerns," avoided committing itself on the question of the legality of combinations to raise wages, and decided the case adversely to the journeymen on the ground that the means employed were coercive,[2] and in 1821 a Pennsylvania court foreshadowed later American formulation of the conspiracy doctrine, with its entrenchment of the test of motive or intent, when it said: "Where the act is lawful for an individual, it can become the subject of a conspiracy when done in concert only where there is a direct intention that injury shall result from it, or where the object is to benefit the conspirators to the prejudice of the public or the oppression of individuals, and where such prejudice or oppression is the natural and necessary consequence."[3] Some courts followed this dictum during the years following 1821, others rendered decisions more nearly approaching that of the Philadelphia Cordwainers case of 1806, and the problem of public policy toward labor combinations was obviously most puzzling to the jurists. The 1820's and 1830's witnessed a series of indictments and convictions for criminal conspiracy, but nearly all of them also presented elements of coercion and intimidation.[4] With the clarifying opinion in the 1842 case of *Commonwealth v. Hunt*,[5] in which the purpose of establishing a closed shop was held not to be wrongful, however, the extreme position that combinations seeking to raise wages were unlawful per se was definitely rejected and the tests of motive and means were recognized as controlling

---

were employed, regardless of its object. When this element had been included, the conspiracy doctrine had evolved into the broad, inclusive doctrine discussed in the foregoing paragraphs. (*Ibid.*, pp. 35–37.)

[1] Recorded in J. R. Commons and Others, *Documentary History of American Industrial Society*, vol. 3 (Arthur H. Clark and Co., Glendale, Calif.) p. 59 and quoted by A. T. Mason, *op. cit.*, p. 56.

[2] A. T. Mason, *op. cit.*, p. 57.

[3] *Pennsylvania v. Carlisle, Brightley's Rep.* 36 (Pa., 1821).

[4] For a summary and discussion of these cases, see A. T. Mason, *op. cit.*, pp. 61–66.

[5] 4 Metcalf 111, 45 Mass. 111.

ones. "Without attempting to review and reconcile all the cases, [of the various courts prior to 1842] . . . a conspiracy must be a combination of two or more persons, by some concerted action, to accomplish some criminal or unlawful purpose, or to accomplish some purpose not in itself criminal or unlawful by criminal or unlawful means." After *Commonwealth v. Hunt,* the history of American labor law was a steady accumulation of instances in which the line was drawn between purposes and acts permitted and those forbidden.

Modifications of the Conspiracy Doctrine.—The factors responsible for modification by judicial restatement of the conspiracy doctrine, as it has been discussed up to this point, have already been suggested in part. Some cognizance had to be taken of such realities as the increasing extent of organization in many segments of economic life, the development of large-scale production, the corporation, and the employers' association, and the not infrequent cases in which a combination did not have greater power than a single person, especially if the person chanced to be a corporate entity. The mere fact of combination no longer seemed adequate to serve as a starting point in decisions condemning the activities of laborers in controversy with employers. By the late nineteenth and early twentieth century it had become less common for the courts to hold that numbers made unlawful purposes that would have been lawful in the absence of numbers acting in concert. There was, moreover, the virtual impossibility of determining what the motive of members of labor combinations was—the legitimate one of benefiting themselves or the wrongful and malicious one of injuring the employer or someone else—even if the fact of numbers was excluded as a determinant of the lawfulness of motive. Motives of workmen on strike, it was recognized, are almost always mixed. In a concrete act, such as a strike or boycott, the workers intend to injure in order to accomplish a purpose of benefit to themselves. Both the increasing inadequacy of the fact of numbers as a test of whether a purpose was legally tolerable and the difficulty in probing into, and discovering ultimate truth about, the purpose of a combination underlay the modifications made by the courts in the common-law doctrine of conspiracy.

These modifications took various forms,[1] but they were all more or less related. Some courts attempted to meet the difficulties by drawing a distinction between "motive" and "intent," the former being the ultimate object and the latter the immediate purpose of the combination. Courts making this distinction declared that motive had no causal influence upon the lawfulness of a combination; only the intent had legal significance. But the distinction between motive and intent has to be a somewhat arbitrary one. In most labor disputes several questions, of differing degrees of immediacy or ultimateness, are at stake; the argument

---

[1] Cf. E. E. Witte, *op. cit.,* pp. 49–53 and Commons and Andrews, *op. cit.,* pp. 380–388.

is postulatable that since all strikes attempt to bring immediate economic pressure upon the employer (*i.e.*, immediately to injure his business or property) the immediate purpose or intent of all of them is malicious; and the distinction between motive and intent therefore still left upon the courts the burden of summoning enough transcendent wisdom or intuition to ascertain what was *the* purpose in a bundle of inextricably interwoven purposes.

A second modification of the conspiracy doctrine emerged from courts drawing a distinction between *malice in law* and *malice in fact*. The former determines legality and may be defined as intentional infliction of injury without justification. Whether there is malice in fact—ill will, spite, delight in the economic embarrassment of the employer—is without legal significance. The question before the court therefore is whether the workers have "just cause" for seeking to attain a certain end and resorting to certain actions to effect its attainment. They do have if they are exercising a right equal or superior to the rights that their action necessarily trenches upon; the purpose or motive of the combination is therefore lawful; and the injury to the employer is only a necessary incidental in the exercise of the workers' rights. Here again, however, the courts must exercise judgment without having absolutes upon which to fall back. If intentional infliction of injury without justification is unlawful, everything turns upon the question of what is sufficient justification—of whether the workers have just cause for their action. Accordingly, the courts must evaluate the rights of the parties, and this evaluation once more has to be in part a subjective thing.[1] The initial proposition with which they must start is that everyone is entitled to free, unobstructed access to the commodity market and to the labor market, intentional interference with these rights being *prima facie* a wrongful act; and this presumption of a wrongful act can be rebutted only by proving that there is just cause for the interference. Almost always, in cases arising out of labor disputes, interference with the expectancies of the employer, the nonunion workers, or someone else takes place, and there is therefore a presumption of illegality that can be rebutted only by proof to the court that the inter-

[1] It is interesting to note that, in the two labor cases in which the just-cause theory was first logically developed (*Vegelahn v. Guntner*, 167 Mass. 92, and *Plant v. Woods*, 176 Mass. 492), both the majority and the minority espoused and ably expounded the just-cause theory but reached exactly opposite conclusions on the legality of the workmen's conduct in question. These cases, like many others, illustrate the truth of the observation of Justice Oliver Wendell Holmes in the article in which, years ago, he first presented the just-cause theory: "The ground for decision really comes down to a proposition of policy of rather a delicate nature concerning the merit of the particular benefit to themselves intended by the defendants and suggests a doubt whether judges with different economic sympathies might not decide a case differently when brought face to face with the same issue." "Privilege, Malice, and Intent," *Harvard Law Review*, vol. 8 (1894), p. 114, quoted by E. E. Witte, *op. cit.*, p. 52.

ference was justified. It is worthy of note, moreover, that when the courts engage in the process of evaluating the rights of the parties, and therefore of deciding whether the interference is justified, they are confronted on the one hand by employer property rights in the expectancies of business that have long been entrenched in the law of property and contracts, and on the other hand by the rights of the workers (such as any conception of a property "interest" in their jobs that the court may accept, the right to select representatives for purposes of collective bargaining, protection in the contract of employment at will against certain types of employer discrimination) that developed later and whose specific content has been on the whole less certain.

The position of still a third group of courts should be mentioned in connection with these modifications by judicial dicta. These courts—an increasing number in recent years—have abandoned the attempt to probe into the motives of workers acting in concert and have placed their emphasis upon the means used.[1] The fact that acts are done in pursuance of a combination does not affect their legality, nor can motive render unlawful acts that otherwise would be lawful. When this position is adopted, the very foundations are obviously swept from under the conspiracy doctrine—but the uncertainty of the law is far from dissipated. Combination and persuasion are lawful, but such means or methods as violence, force, threats, coercion, and intimidation are unlawful. The content of these terms, as applied to the field of labor relations, is anything but specific, and more than once, without doubt, courts have looked—consciously or subconsciously—to the purpose or end in order to decide whether a particular act should be regarded as threatening or coercive. "The lawfulness of threats," Justice Holmes once observed, "depends on what you threaten." Drawing the line of demarcation between persuasion and intimidation and reading specific content into the words "coercion" and "intimidation" are again matters of judicial judgment, and in consequence the law has not been made much clearer or more uniform as between one jurisdiction and another by the tendency to look to the means used by, rather than the purposes of, labor combinations.

The Restraint-of-trade Doctrine.—The close interrelationship of the doctrine of conspiracy and the other doctrine most frequently invoked in labor cases, restraint of trade, has already been suggested. In the majority of early American conspiracy indictments, restraint of trade was the wrongful or unlawful end that transformed a lawful combination into a criminal conspiracy. During more recent decades, the charge of restraint of trade has been made chiefly in cases arising under the federal antitrust laws. These cases are discussed in some detail later, and it therefore suffices at this point to suggest the substance of the

[1] Cf. *ibid.,* pp. 53–54.

the restraint-of-trade doctrine at common law.[1] Since, according to the underlying public-policy premise, each person has individually, and the public has collectively, a right to require that the course of trade be kept free from unreasonable obstruction, the law must secure to every man, whether employer or employee, the right to employ his talents or exchange his money for the services of others as he pleases, free from the dictation of others, and must secure to the public the right to demand that the volume of trade should not suffer from unreasonable diminution, irrespective of who enters into the agreements or engages in the acts causing the diminution. At common law all contracts to restrain trade were regarded as against public policy and were unlawful in the sense that they were void and unenforceable;[2] and when two or more combined to enforce an agreement or arrangement for the restraint of trade (*i.e.*, to prevent others from selling their services as they wished or to inflict upon the public the hardship of unreasonable diminution of the volume of trade), the end sought was wrongful and the combination likely to be regarded as a criminal conspiracy.[3] Not all restraints effected by labor combina-

---

[1] See the excellent account of the development of the restraint of trade doctrine in A. T. Mason, *op. cit.*, pp. 38–50. The indebtedness of the authors to this account will be apparent to anyone reading it.

[2] Under the Sherman Antitrust Act of 1890 the entering into restraining contracts that at common law had been merely void and unenforceable of course became an indictable and actionable offense irrespective of the element of combination.

[3] Like the conspiracy doctrine, the restraint-of-trade doctrine originally was limited in its application and technical in its meaning, and gradually evolved into the broader and more comprehensive doctrine that it was when written into federal statute in the United States. Originally the phrase seems to have had reference primarily to contracts whereby a merchant or manufacturer agreed to sell to a competitor the good will of his business, such sale being accompanied by a covenant on the part of the vendor to refrain from competition. These covenants, it will be noted, were incidental to another and principal transaction. In a few English jurisdictions they may have been positively illegal, but in general, as is said above, they were unlawful only in the sense that they were void and unenforceable. Changes took place with the passing of time. Courts began to inquire whether the restraint was "reasonable" or "unreasonable," an affirmative answer to the question of "reasonable" making the contracts enforceable like other contracts. Reasonableness was, of course, a general and most elastic concept, depending upon such factors as the extent of the restraint effected, the effect upon the public interest, just cause in the exercise of other rights on the part of those effecting the restraint, the circumstances of the parties, and the nature of the business. The other great change in the concept of restraint of trade was its expansion to include many restraints imposed by means other than an agreement not to enter a trade or business made incidentally to another and principal transaction. When so expanded restraint of trade came to signify the setting aside of the rule and practice of competition with the intent to control the market (*i.e.*, came to approach closely the common-law conception of monopoly). In its expanded latter-day meaning, restraint of trade was subject to a rule of reason in some jurisdictions, and in others it was not. For an excellent summary of the development of the restraint-of-trade doctrine, from which much of the material in this footnote, and some of the facts about the development of the conspiracy doctrine, have been drawn, see A. Mason, *Organized Labor and the Law* (Duke University Press), pp. 22–50.

tions were, however, indictable and actionable; indeed, every strike involves to a greater or less degree restraint of trade or restriction of competition, and, even in the early period of application of the restraint-of-trade doctrine to the activities of labor groups, criteria of differentiation developed. These criteria appeared in somewhat different verbal garbs, but in general they involved the test of whether members of the combination endeavored by unlawful coercion to enforce upon unwilling persons performance in accordance with the terms of a trade-restraining agreement or arrangement (an obstruction of the rights of these other persons)[1] and the test of reasonableness. Coercion accordingly became the element that stamped a combination in restraint of trade as an indictable or actionable conspiracy, and the restraint had to come within the judicial conception of the unreasonable. If the combination in seeking to gain its ends violated no rights of others by attempting to force upon them lines of conduct necessary for the achievement of its ends, but merely peacefully persuaded them, no element of coercion was present; if, on the other hand, it sought to gain its ends by resort to force, intimidation, or violence, or struck or boycotted for the purpose of gratifying a malice toward others, coercion had intervened and the combination had become a conspiracy in restraint of trade. In view of the vagueness of the term "coercion," a matter commented on earlier, and the necessity for judicial determination of when the extent of, and public inconvenience occasioned by, a restraint were great enough to put it within the "unreasonable" category, the uncertainty as to what combinations were at common law conspiracies to restrain trade is patent.

Such, in general, has been the common law as it developed and underwent modifications at the hands of the courts of the United States. Only in comparatively recent years has it been extensively limited or replaced by statutory enactments. At present, with its variations, it applies narrowly or widely in the various states according as it has or has not been extensively limited or replaced by statute. What the combined common law and statute law at present is will be indicated in the discussion of various union and employer activities in the following pages.

[1] That is, to develop the criterion more fully, at common law one person had the right to choose whether he would labor or not, and the terms upon which he would labor if he did so elect, as well as to declare his purpose in respect of these matters; and a number after consultation with each other could exercise the same right, including the making of a simultaneous declaration of their choice or election. They could not, however, create a legally binding obligation upon each other not to work except upon the terms allowed by the combination (or in the case of a boycott not to purchase, or in the case of a combination of employers not to employ), since such an arrangement was legally void on account of restraint of trade. And when the attempt was made to enforce by unlawful coercion the terms of the agreement, the restraint of trade became actionable and the members of the combination criminal conspirators.

The Right to Organize.—Trade unions have for many decades been held to be lawful per se and numerous declarations to that effect are to be found in statutory law. The typical labor organization, like the typical employers' association, has had a right to exist.[1] This right of the workers to organize, with prescribed freedom from interference, restraint, or coercion by employers, has been incorporated in the Railway Labor Act, Sec. 7(a) of the National Industrial Recovery Act, the National Labor Relations Act,[2] and the "baby Wagner Acts" of several states. Prior to consideration of this more recent legislation, however, the background of earlier state and federal legislation and of court rulings upon that legislation should be traced.

An Indiana statute of 1893 may be taken as an example of legislation, adopted in a number of the states years ago, to protect the right of workers to organize and to check employers in their antiunion activities, particularly in their use of the antiunion contract.[3] The Indiana law read:

"It shall be unlawful for any individual, or member of any firm, agent, officer, or employee of any company or corporation to prevent

[1] Certain statutory restrictions were, it is true, placed upon particular types of unions. During and after the First World War, statutes were enacted in a number of the states of this country making it a felony to organize or to hold membership in any organization advocating criminal syndicalism. Under the California Act of 1919 [*Stat.* (1919), Chap. 188, p. 281, and *General Laws*, Title 590, Act 8428, p. 3498] criminal syndicalism was defined as "any doctrine or precept advocating, teaching, or aiding and abetting the commission of crime, sabotage . . . or unlawful acts of force and violence or unlawful methods of terrorism as a means of accomplishing a change in industrial ownership or control, or effecting any political change"; and any person who by spoken or written words or personal conduct advocated criminal syndicalism as thus defined or attempted to justify it, or who printed, published, edited, circulated, or publicly displayed any book or other form of printed matter advocating it, or organized or assisted in organizing or becoming a member of any organization, society, or group of persons advocating or teaching it, or who committed any act advised, advocated, or taught by that doctrine with intent to accomplish a change in industrial ownership or control or to effect any political change, was declared to be guilty of a felony punishable by not less than one or more than fourteen years. Under this statute, a large number of members of radical organizations have been convicted and imprisoned. One of the worst features of legislation of this type has been its more or less indiscriminate application to members of radical organizations and to strikers and their sympathizers (as in Harlan County, Kentucky) where organization has been attempted under conditions such that violence was practiced by others as well as by the workers and their sympathizers.

[2] The Railway Labor Act, Public no. 257, 69th Congress, 1st Session, Chap. 347 (H.R. 9463), May 20, 1926; the National Industrial Recovery Act, Public no. 67, 73d Congress, 1st Session, Chap. 90 (H.R. 5755), June 16, 1933; and the National Labor Relations Act, Public no. 198, 74th Congress, 1st Session, Chap. 372 (S. 1958), July 5, 1935.

[3] Other states that passed similar laws included such important industrial ones as Illinois, Massachusetts, New York, Ohio, Pennsylvania, and Wisconsin. A complete list of the fourteen states passing such laws, with citations, may be found in "Labor Laws of the United States," U. S. Bureau of Labor Statistics, *Bulletin* 148 (1914), Pts. I and II.

employees from forming, joining and belonging to any lawful labor
organization, and any such individual member, agent, officer or employee
that coerces or attempts to coerce employees by discharging or threatening to discharge from their employ or the employ of any firm, company
or corporation because of their connection with such lawful labor organization, and any officer or employer, to exact [who exacts] a pledge from
workingmen that they will not become members of a labor organization
as a consideration of employment, shall be guilty of a misdemeanor, and
upon conviction thereof in any court of competent jurisdiction, shall be
fined in any sum not exceeding one hundred dollars ($100), or imprisoned
for not more than six (6) months, or both, in the discretion of the court."[1]

Court Decisions.—State laws, such as the one just quoted, were
declared invalid in a series of decisions by several state courts,[2] and
eventually by the Supreme Court of the United States. The Supreme
Court case, *Coppage v. Kansas,*[3] arose as a test of a Kansas statute[4]
similar to the Indiana law just quoted. A railway employee was discharged for refusing to sign a pledge to withdraw from the Switchmen's
Union. Had the employee withdrawn from the union he would have
sacrificed insurance benefits to the amount of $1,500. On the basis
of this and other evidence, the Kansas Supreme Court held the exaction
of the pledge to be coercion, and upheld the statute.[5] The Supreme
Court of the United States, however, reversed the decision of the Kansas
court and declared that an employer had a constitutional right to require
that his employees sign antiunion contracts. The Supreme Court
held that a state law which deprived him of that right interfered with his
freedom of contract and violated the Fourteenth Amendment.[6] The
Court said that in the portion of the Kansas statute under consideration,
"there is no object or purpose, expressed or implied, that is claimed to
have reference to health, safety, morals, or public welfare, beyond the
supposed desirability of leveling inequalities of fortune by depriving one
who has property of some part of what is characterized as his 'financial

---

[1] Acts (1893), Chap. 76, Sec. 1, p. 146; *Burns Annotated Indiana Statutes* (1933), 10:
4906.

[2] Some of the leading state court cases are *State v. Julow,* 129 Mo. 163 (1895); *Gillespie v.
the People,* 188 Ill. 176 (1900); *People v. Marcus,* 185 N.Y. 257 (1906). Although "dead
letters," laws of this type are still found in the statutes of four states—New Hampshire,
Connecticut, Nevada, and Idaho—where they have not been declared invalid by the
supreme courts of these states.

[3] 236 U. S. 1 (1915).

[4] Session Laws (1903), Chap. 222; Gen. Stat. (1909), Secs. 4674–4675.

[5] *State v. Coppage,* 87 Kansas 752 (1912).

[6] The second paragraph of the Fourteenth Amendment, adopted to protect the rights
of the freed Negro, reads: "No State shall make or enforce any law which shall abridge the
privileges or immunities of citizens of the United States; nor shall any state deprive any
person of life, liberty, or property, without due process of law; nor deny to any person
within its jurisdiction the equal protection of the laws."

independence.' In short, an interference with the normal exercise of personal liberty and property rights is the primary object of the statute, and not an incident to the advancement of the general welfare."[1]

In the Coppage case the Supreme Court quoted extensively from the Adair case[2] in which, by majority decision, it had declared unconstitutional Sec. 10 of the Erdman Act,[3] which made it unlawful for an interstate carrier to discharge an employee because of membership in a labor union.[4] The Erdman Act was a federal statute providing for the voluntary arbitration of interstate railway disputes, and the provision forbidding discrimination against union men was thought by the Congress to be helpful in maintaining industrial peace. A worker was discharged because he did not elect to relinquish membership in his union. When the case came before it, the Supreme Court was of the opinion that the Act in question had no logical connection with the power to regulate commerce as the Constitution vests this power in Congress; moreover, and more important since it provided the precedent in deciding the Coppage and other important cases, that the Act deprived the carrier of freedom of contract guaranteed by the Constitution. The employer had a constitutional right to refuse to hire, or to discharge, because of union membership; his right was unqualified.

"*Yellow-dog*" *Contracts.*—These decisions of the courts nullified the earlier attempts of the state and federal legislatures to protect the right of workers to organize although they did not—as the later Hitchman decision did—declare antiunion contracts to be protectable by injunctions. The center of the attack of the courts upon this legislation was that it unduly restricted freedom of contract, which included the right of the employer to make individual antiunion contracts with his employees. When this type of contract was first used in the United States is unknown. Suffice it to note that it was used by stove manufacturers when organizing local associations and fighting the Molders' Union in the 1870's. The extensive state legislation against its use and the numerous court cases indicate that it had become a real social problem before the end

[1] 236 U.S. at p. 18.

[2] *Adair v. United States*, 208 U.S. 161 (1908).

[3] Fifty-fifth Congress, 2d Session, Chap. 370, June 1, 1898. Section 10 of the Erdman Act read in part " . . . any employer . . . who shall require any employee, or any person seeking employment, as a condition of such employment, to enter into an agreement . . . not to become or remain a member of any labor . . . organization . . . ; or shall threaten any employee with loss of employment, or shall unjustly discriminate against any employee because of his membership in such a labor . . . organization . . . is hereby declared to be guilty of a misdemeanor, and, upon conviction . . . shall be punished for each offense by a fine of not less than one hundred dollars and not more than one thousand dollars."

[4] A critical examination of this case and of the Coppage and Hitchman cases was made by Thomas Reed Powell, "Collective Bargaining before the Supreme Court," *Political Science Quarterly*, vol. 33 (1918), pp. 396–429. Found also in John R. Commons, *Trade Unionism and Labor Problems* (1905), Chap. 39.

of the nineteenth century. Both the Adair and the Coppage cases involved these individual antiunion contracts, and these decisions unfavorable to statutes prohibiting such contracts unquestionably increased their use. It was not, however, until after the Supreme Court of the United States by its decision in the Hitchman case[1] established that such contracts might be protected by injunction, defiance of which by union organizers constituted contempt of court, that the individual antiunion contract was very extensively used and the term "yellow-dog" contract became a familiar term. Within a few years "yellow-dog" contracts came to be used in American plants employing a total of at least several hundred thousand wage earners. On a percentage basis, the number employed under such contracts was of course small. This, however, was not so important, for such contracts were in use in a relatively large percentage of cases in which unions had been attempting to gain a foothold and the employers were opposed to organization or to recognition of such organization as existed. The significant fact is that the use of "yellow-dog" contracts was widespread at the growing points of union organization and where attempts were made to initiate collective bargaining. While used most widely in the bituminous coal fields of West Virginia, Tennessee, Kentucky, and elsewhere, the antiunion individual employment contract found place in many industries, among them the manufacture of shoes, glass, full-fashioned hosiery, and men's and women's garments, the various metal trades, commercial printing, and the operation of street railways. It was even applied here and there to prevent organization of public-school teachers.[2]

"Yellow-dog" contracts have taken various forms. Some, like that first employed by the Hitchman Coal and Coke Company, have been oral, as is the usual employment contract. A great majority, however, have been carefully worded, printed slips, which must be signed by the workers as a condition of securing or retaining employment. But that some have been oral and others written is of no real significance at law. Of real significance are the essential nature and object of these contracts and the more or less important differences found in their provisions.

"Yellow-dog" is a rather loose term applied by the workers, and now by many others also, to somewhat different types of contracts. As Professor Witte has said,[3] it lacks precise definition. "Most commonly, it is applied to written promises in which a workman as a condition of

---

[1] *Hitchman Coal and Coke Co. v. Mitchell*, 245 U.S. 229 (1917).

[2] It is interesting to note that some of the unions have employed a parallel device in fighting communism and other forms of radicalism. In isolated instances they have used the "yellow-dog" contract requiring an employer to sever his connection or remain out of affiliation with an employers' organization. For the fullest account of the history and use of the nonunion contract, see J. E. Seidman, *The Yellow Dog Contract*, Johns Hopkins University Studies in Historical and Political Science, Series 50 (1932).

[3] E. E. Witte, " 'Yellow Dog' Contracts," *Wisconsin Law Review*, vol. 6 (1930), p. 21.

employment obligates himself not to join a labor union." Sometimes
the "yellow-dog" contract has taken on a more restrictive form and
stipulated that during the period of employment, which might be "at
will" or for a specified period of time, the worker would have no dealings,
communications, or interviews with the officers, agents, or members of
any labor organization. The term has been applied also to other individual employment contracts, particularly agreements not to go on
strike, or not to do anything that would interfere with the employer's
conduct of a nonunion shop. Usually the contract has been limited
to the duration of the employment relationship, but in a considerable
number of instances it has provided that its prohibitions should be
observed for a specified time beyond that, the typical provision in that
case being, "In case my employment is terminated, I will for one year
thereafter in no way annoy, molest or interfere, directly or indirectly,
with your customers, property, business or employees." It is to be
noted, finally, that the contract may contain nothing but restrictions
upon the "rights" of the worker, or it may, in addition to such restrictions, obligate the employer to do specified things presumed to be of
benefit to the worker.[1] But, whatever the form or content of the
"yellow-dog" contract, it has been designed primarily, when not solely,
to erect a legal wall around the employer's plant in order to prevent it
from being unionized.

The "yellow-dog" contract is a peculiar one. As Senator Wagner
has observed, "No employer has ever sued any employee for violating
it. No employer ever expects to do so. That is not its purpose. Its
utility lies solely in the fact that it affords a basis upon which to apply
for an injunction restraining anyone from attempting to persuade the
employees to unionize." For years previous to 1932, because of such
individual contracts, numerous injunctions were issued prohibiting
efforts to organize.[2]

The Hitchman Decision.—Prior to the Hitchman decision of 1917, it
is true, such contracts were not enforceable in courts of equity. In this
decision, however,[3] such contracts were held by the Supreme Court of
the United States to be entitled to injunctive protection. The United
Mine Workers, in order to extend union influence and to protect conditions secured through collective bargaining in Ohio and other competitive territory, made an effort to organize the miners in West Virginia.
The operators of the Central Competitive District had insisted that this

---

[1] As in the Interborough case discussed below (pp. 516–517). Even in this case, though
certain privileges were extended to the employees, the court found that the element of
mutality presumed to be found in a contract was deficient.

[2] It should be added that the "yellow-dog" contract may be effective in the absence of
a restraining order; it may affect the worker's psychology and keep him from joining the
union.

[3] 245 U.S. 249.

must be done if collective bargaining were to continue. The Hitchman Company, operating in West Virginia as well as in Ohio, recognized the Union and entered into an agreement with it. The relationship, however, did not prove to be satisfactory in certain respects, and the company decided not to renew the agreement upon its expiration. A strike followed. Finally, the miners, not in receipt of strike benefits and with no means of support, sought re-employment by the company. The superintendent hired the miners individually, and to each who applied for employment he explained the conditions, which were that, while the company paid the wages demanded by the union and as much as anybody else, the mine was being run nonunion and would continue to be so run; that the company would not recognize the United Mine Workers of America; that if any man wished to become a member of that union he was at liberty to do so, but that he could not be a member of it and remain in the employ of the Hitchman Company; that if he worked for the company, he would have to work as a nonunion man. To this each man hired gave his assent. Subsequently organizers attempted to secure the promise of these men to join the union, not at once but at a later time. On request of the company, an injunction was granted restraining all organizing activity; the issue was carried from the District Court to the Circuit Court of Appeals and then to the Supreme Court of the United States. The Supreme Court, by majority decision, held that, in spite of the fact that membership had not been consummated, the union's efforts to organize the miners working under the oral contract were equivalent to inducing breach of contract and that an injunction to prevent action inducing breach of contract was appropriate.

The reasoning of the court may be presented largely in the language of its decision:

"That the plaintiff was acting within its lawful rights in employing its men only upon terms of continuing non-membership in the United Mine Workers of America is not open to question. . . . The same liberty which enables men to form unions, and through the union to enter into agreements with employers willing to agree, entitles other men to remain independent of the union and other employers to agree with them to employ no man who owes any allegiance or obligation to the union. . . .

"Plaintiff, having in the exercise of its undoubted rights established a working agreement between it and its employees, *with the free assent of the latter*, is entitled to be protected in the enjoyment of the resulting status, as in any other legal right. That the employment was 'at will,' and terminable by either party at any time, is of no consequence. . . . "[1]

Explaining the property right to be protected, the court said:

"In short, plaintiff was and is entitled to the good will of its employees, precisely as a merchant is entitled to the good will of his customers

[1] 245 U.S. at pp. 250-251. Italics ours.

although they are under no obligation to continue to deal with him. The value of the relation lies in the reasonable probability that by properly treating its employees, and paying them fair wages, and avoiding reasonable grounds of complaint, it will be able to retain them in its employ, and to fill vacancies occurring from time to time by the employment of other men on the same terms. The pecuniary value of such reasonable probabilities is incalculably great, and is recognized by the law in a variety of relations. . . .

"Defendants set up, by way of justification or excuse, the right of workingmen to form unions, and to enlarge their membership by inciting other workingmen to join. The right is freely conceded, provided the objects of the union be proper and legitimate, which we assume to be true, in a general sense, with respect to the Union here in question. . . . The cardinal error of defendants' position lies in the assumption that the right is so absolute that it may be exercised under any circumstances and without any qualification; whereas in truth, like other rights that exist in civilized society, it must always be exercised with reasonable regard for the conflicting rights of others."[1]

In the opinion of the court the fact that the miners only *agreed to join* the union made no difference; the object was to call a strike when a sufficient number had so agreed.

"Upon all the facts, we are constrained to hold that the purpose entertained by defendants to bring about a strike at plaintiff's mine in order to compel plaintiff, through fear of financial loss, to consent to the unionization of the mine as the lesser evil, was an unlawful purpose, and that the methods resorted to by [Organizer] Hughes—the inducing of employees to unite with the Union in an effort to subvert the system of employment at the mine by concerted breaches of the contracts of employment known to be in force there, not to mention misrepresentation, deceptive statements [which, one may infer from the decision in the later *American Steel Foundries* case, had much influence on the Court in arriving at its decision], and threats of pecuniary loss communicated by Hughes to the men—were unlawful and malicious methods, and not to be justified as a fair exercise of the right to increase the membership of the Union."[2]

In his dissenting opinion, which was concurred in by Justices Holmes and Clarke, Justice Brandeis saw in the situation only an incident in the plan of the union to organize every mine on the continent and thus protect its organized territory and was of the opinion that the desire and purpose were not unlawful. "They were part of a reasonable effort to improve the condition of workingmen engaged in the industry by strengthening their bargaining power through unions, and extending the

[1] *Ibid.*, at pp. 252–254.
[2] *Ibid.*, at p. 259.

field of union power."[1] With reference to the coercion exercised by the union against the company, he maintained that "coercion, in a legal sense, is not exerted when a union merely endeavors to induce employees to join a union with the intention thereafter to order a strike unless the employer consents to unionize his shop. Such pressure is not coercion in a legal sense. The employer is free to accept the agreement or the disadvantage. Indeed, the plaintiff's whole case is rested upon agreements secured under similar pressure of economic necessity or disadvantage. If it is coercion to threaten to strike unless plaintiff consents to a closed union shop, it is coercion also to threaten not to give one employment unless the applicant will consent to a closed non-union shop. The employer may sign the union agreement for fear that *labor* may not be otherwise obtainable; the workman may sign the individual agreement for fear that *employment* may not be otherwise obtainable. But such fear does not imply coercion in a legal sense."[2] Justice Brandeis was of the opinion that there had been no breach of contract; to agree to join the union at a later time was not joining it. Moreover, the employment was "at will." There had been no threat, violence, or intimidation; to induce workers to leave employment "at will" for the purpose of improving the miners' conditions was lawful.

The decision in the Hitchman case, following the Adair and Coppage decisions, definitely established the fact that the "yellow-dog" contract was a contract at law that would be protected in the federal courts. The rule of law laid down in these leading cases was followed in numerous other cases, largely in the coal-mining industry. The same general position was taken by the supreme courts of most of the states in which the issue of the "yellow-dog" contract was litigated.[3] In only two states— New York and Ohio—[4] did the courts rendering decisions on the issue fail to recognize such a document as a contract to be protected at law. As Professor Witte has said:[5] "The New York courts, from an entirely different approach [from that of the federal and most of the state courts], have completely destroyed the value of yellow dog contracts to non-union

[1] *Ibid.*, at p. 268.

[2] *Ibid.*, at p. 271. Italics in original.

[3] For citations of "yellow-dog" cases (to 1930) see E. E. Witte, *op. cit.*, pp. 21–32; and the same author's *The Government in Labor Disputes* (1932), pp. 226–227. See also Donald MacDonald, "The Constitutionality of Wisconsin's Statute Invalidating 'Yellow Dog' Contracts," *Wisconsin Law Review*, vol. 6 (1931), pp. 86–100.

[4] The leading cases are: *Exchange Bakery Co. v. Rifkin,* 245 N.Y. 260 (1927); *Interborough Rapid Transit Company v. Lavin,* 247 N.Y. 65 (1928); *Interborough Rapid Transit Co. v. Green,* 227 N.Y. Supp. 258 (1928); *La France Electrical Construction & Supply Co. v. International Brotherhood of Electrical Workers,* 108 Ohio St. 61 (1923). In both New York and Ohio the courts had in other cases recognized the "yellow-dog" contract as one to be protected by the courts.

[5] E. E. Witte, " 'Yellow Dog' Contracts," *Wisconsin Law Review,* vol. 6, p. 26. See also his *The Government in Labor Disputes,* p. 225.

employers.[1] The Court of Appeals in two cases refused injunctions
sought against organizing activities of unions on the strength of written
non-union agreements, on the ground that these promises did not constitute enforcible contracts. Although having substantially the same
provisions as the yellow dog 'contracts' which have figured in other
cases, they were in these cases [*Exchange Bakery*[2] and *Interborough v.
Lavin*[3]] held to be a mere understanding, lacking the essential element of
contracts, consideration. Much the same conclusion was reached in a
third case [*Interborough v. Green*[4]], which in intrinsic importance and in
degree of preparation is the most outstanding yellow dog case ever to
have come up. . . . This was an action brought by the Interborough
Rapid Transit Co. against the American Federation of Labor and all its
affiliated unions to restrain them from interfering with 'contracts,'
running for two years, requiring the complainants' employes not to join
any labor union. These contracts were artfully drawn, obligating on
their face the employer as well as the employes. Upon proof that the
employer's promises did not afford the employes any real protection, and
opinions from many of the leading students of labor problems of the
country condemning yellow dog contracts as anti-social, the court found
that no valid contract existed; and that, hence, no action lay against the
unions for seeking to persuade employes to join them."

Subsequent Legislation.—In the case of the "yellow-dog" contract two
rights recognized at law came into conflict—the employer's common-law
right to hire and discharge for any reason that was in his opinion sufficient,
and the workers' privilege to organize for the purpose of acting in concert
to promote their own economic and social welfare. The decisions that
have been briefly reviewed, like the decisions on many other issues, make
it clear that which privilege was protected and which was sacrificed
depended very much upon the attitudes and philosophies of the higher
courts. Certainly the courts attached substantially different weights to
the various details involved in the concrete situations out of which litigation arose. But, whatever the merit of rulings on it, the "yellow-dog"
contract was usually accepted as a contract to be protected by restraining
order and proved to be a great stumbling block in the path of American
unions. It seriously interfered with the organizing efforts of the typical
union; it proved to be one more factor encouraging the revolutionary
union; it was a tax upon collective dealing in industry. It was but
natural, therefore, that organized labor protested vigorously and appealed

---

[1] The reader must keep in mind that Professor Witte, writing before 1932, was describing
a situation that obtained prior to enactment of the Norris-La Guardia, the National Labor
Relations, and the recent New York anti-injunction and "little Wagner" acts. These
laws, and court decisions in cases involving them, are discussed *infra*, pp. 522–534, 591–593.

[2] *Exchange Bakery and Restaurant v. Rifkin*, 245 N.Y. 260 (1927).

[3] *Interborough Rapid Transit Co. v. Lavin*, 247 N.Y. 65 (1928).

[4] *Interborough Rapid Transit Co. v. Green*, 227 N.Y.S. 258 (1928).

to Congress and the state legislatures to enact measures undoing what the majority of the courts had done by recognizing the "yellow-dog" contract as one enforceable at law.[1]

Congress and the state legislatures were faced with a difficult task of meeting the insistent demand for legislation that would curb the use of the "yellow-dog" contract and yet fall within the limitations on legislative power imposed by the Adair, Coppage, and Hitchman decisions. The first two of these cases had made it clear that individual nonunion employment contracts were valid, but, until the Hitchman decision of 1917, it did not follow that such contracts must be protected by injunctions in case they were violated. The legislation enacted between 1932 and the National Labor Relations Act of 1935 was, for the most part, an attack upon the usefulness of such "yellow-dog" contracts to employers rather than a direct ban upon them. The wording of a majority of these laws was to the effect that such contracts were "contrary to public policy and wholly void, and should not afford any basis for the granting of legal or equitable relief by any court."[2] Similar provisions are found in the language of the "anti-yellow-dog" contract laws which had been enacted in almost half of the states by the first half of the 1940's.[3] The federal policy as declared in the Norris-La Guardia

---

[1] In connection with the "yellow-dog" contract, it is to be held in mind that neither at common law nor by statute had corresponding limitations been placed upon the establishment and conduct of employers' associations and participation in their activities—frequently to maintain the employers' closed shop.

[2] Quoted from the Wisconsin law of 1929. That law provided [Wis. Stat. (1929), Sec. 103.46]:

"Every undertaking or promise hereafter made, whether written or oral, express or implied, constituting or contained in either: (1) A contract or agreement of hiring or employment between any employer and any employe or prospective employe, whereby (a) either party to such contract or agreement undertakes or promises not to join, become or remain, a member of any labor organization or of any organization of employers, or (b) either party to such contract or agreement undertakes or promises that he will withdraw from the employment relation in the event that he joins, becomes or remains, a member of any labor organization or of any organization of employers, . . . is hereby declared to be contrary to public policy and wholly void and shall not afford any basis for the granting of legal or equitable relief by any court."

The Ohio statute, however, simply declared that the "yellow-dog" contract was contrary to public policy. It is to be noted also that in Louisiana, in addition to the denial of legal or equitable relief, the making of a "yellow-dog" contract is made subject to penalty. Act of 1934, Chap. 10.

[3] Arizona, Acts (1931), Chap. 19.
California, Acts (1933), Chap. 566.
Colorado, Acts (1931), Chap. 112; Acts (1933), Chap. 59.
Connecticut, Laws (1939), Sec. 6209.
Idaho, Acts (1933), Chap. 215.
Illinois, Acts (1933), p. 588.
Indiana, Acts (1933), Chap. 12.
Louisiana, Acts (1934), Act no. 202.

Anti-injunction Act was to the same effect.[1] The justification of these laws from the point of view of social policy has been ably stated by Professor Witte:[2]

"It is only on the assumption that labor unions are socially undesirable that yellow dog contracts can be defended. This assumption is contrary to numerous pronouncements both in the statutes and court decisions. As Chief Justice Taft so clearly developed in the *Coronado Coal & Coke Co.* case, labor unions have, heretofore, been regarded not only as lawful but as desirable and necessary, and have been accorded many governmental favors. To now throw the weight of government behind the anti-union employers in their efforts to destroy the unions represents a reversal of a long-established policy. . . . .

"The right to discriminate in hiring and firing against union members gives employers all of the powers with which they can safely be entrusted. They stand in no need of governmental assistance in combatting labor unions. The weak position of the unions in the manufacturing industries

---

Maryland, Acts (1935), Chap. 574.
Massachusetts, Acts (1933), Chap. 351.
Minnesota, Acts (1933), Chap. 416.
Nevada, Laws (1929), Sec. 10473.
New Hampshire, Laws (1926), Chap. 176, Sec. 29.
New Jersey, Acts (1932), Chap. 244.
New York, Acts (1935), Chap. 11, also, Acts (1936), Chap. 447, Sec. 876 *f*(2).
North Dakota, Acts (1935), Chap. 247.
Ohio, Acts (1931), Chap. 562.
Oregon, Acts (1931), Chap. 247; Acts (1933), Chap. 355.
Pennsylvania, Acts (1933), Chap. 219, also Acts (1937), Chap. 308, Sec. 6(*b*).
Rhode Island, Laws (1941), Chap. 299.
Utah, Acts (1933), Chap. 15.
Washington, Acts (1933–1934) (ex. ses.), Chap. 7.
Wisconsin, Stats. (1931), Secs. 103.46 and 268.19.

[1] Public no. 65, 72d Congress, 1st Session, Chap. 90 (H.R. 5315), Mar. 23, 1932. Section 3 of the Norris-La Guardia Act reads:

"Sec. 3. Any undertaking or promise, such as is described in this section, or any other undertaking or promise in conflict with the public policy declared in section 2 of this Act, is hereby declared to be contrary to the public policy of the United States, shall not be enforceable in any court of the United States and shall not afford any basis for the granting of legal or equitable relief by any such court, including specifically the following:

"Every undertaking or promise hereafter made, whether written or oral, expressed or implied, constituting or contained in any contract or agreement of hiring or employment between any individual, firm, company, association, or corporation, and any employee or prospective employee of the same, whereby

"(*a*) Either party to such contract or agreement undertakes or promises not to join, become, or remain a member of any labor organization or of any employer organization; or

"(*b*) Either party to such contract or agreement undertakes or promises that he will withdraw from an employment relation in the event that he joins, becomes, or remains a member of any labor organization or of any employer organization."

[2] E. E. Witte, "'Yellow Dog' Contracts," *Wisconsin Law Review*, vol. 6, pp. 31–32.

of this country bears testimony that the employers are not underdogs in the industrial struggle. The right to discriminate carries with it the power to blacklist, despite all the laws we have against blacklisting. To give employers, plus all this, the right to bar unions from attempting to organize their employes is to vest them with power approaching economic dictatorship.[1]

"The crux of the entire problem is the attitude which government should assume toward labor unions. It is most unneutral to put the power of government behind the anti-union employers in their efforts to destroy the unions. . . . "

These new laws have been tested in only a few of the higher courts, but it is clear that they will not be declared invalid. That there is no constitutional obstacle to statutes declaring "yellow-dog" contracts unenforceable was demonstrated when the United States Supreme Court upheld orders of the National Labor Relations Board requiring employers to reinstate with back pay employees discharged for union membership or activity.[2] In the case of Carlisle Lumber Company, a "yellow-dog" contract was held to be an unfair labor practice under the National Labor Relations Act.[4] To the same effect was the decision of the Supreme Court in the Phelps Dodge case,[4] where it was ruled that an employer may not refuse to hire workers because of their affiliation with a labor organization.

Protection under the Railway Labor Act and New Deal Legislation.—The Norris-La Guardia Act and the similar state laws had the effect of lessening the handicap to trade-union organization wrought by the "yellow-dog" contract. The Congress and several of the state legislatures did not, however, remain content with such negative protection of organization and collective bargaining, but once more enacted legislation restricting the right of employers to discriminate against employees because of their trade-union membership or activities. These laws have the same intent as those declared void in the Adair and Coppage cases.

The Railway Labor Act of 1926 provided that, in negotiations for settling railway disputes, representatives should be designated "by the respective parties in such manner as may be provided in their corporate organization or unincorporated association, or by other means of collective action, without interference, influence, or coercion exercised by either

---

[1] The argument in this paragraph is, of course, no longer applicable to those industries which fall within the jurisdiction of the National Labor Relations Act or the "baby Wagner acts." Nevertheless, it supports the adoption and enforcement of such acts.

[2] See Calvert Magruder, "A Half Century of Legal Influence upon the Development of Collective Bargaining," *Harvard Law Review*, vol. 50 (1937), pp. 1071–1117. This is an excellent review of court decisions and legislation relating to the right to organize, a considerable part of the article relating to the National Labor Relations Act.

[3] 2 N.L.R.B. 248, 94 Fed. (2d) 138 (C.C.A. 9, 1937), cert. den. 304 U.S. 575 (1938).

[4] 313 U. S. 177 (1941).

party over the self-organization or designation of representatives by the other."[1]   By inducement and coercion the Texas and New Orleans R.R. Co. sought to introduce an employee-representation plan and to rid itself of the necessity of dealing with the Brotherhood of Railway Clerks. The Supreme Court approved an injunction against company coercion, etc., and upheld as constitutional the provision of the law in question.[2]   In this case the court was not particularly impressed with common-law rights, but saw in the provision of the statute one recognizing an existing union situation and attempting to provide for the maintenance of industrial peace.   It said:

"In reaching a conclusion as to the intent of Congress, the importance of the prohibition in its relation to the plan devised by the Act must have appropriate consideration.   Freedom of choice in the selection of representatives on each side of the dispute is the essential foundation of the statutory scheme.   All the proceedings looking to amicable adjustments and to agreements for arbitration of disputes, the entire policy of the Act, must depend for success on the uncoerced action of each party through its own representatives to the end that agreements satisfactory to both may be reached and the peace essential to the uninterrupted service of the instrumentalities of interstate commerce may be maintained."

This decision, technically reconcilable[3] with the Adair and the Coppage rulings, but in fact conceding to organized labor rights that those decisions had denied, gave rise to the hope that legislation similar to that of the Railway Labor Act would he held valid for workers other than those employed in railway service.   It was partly in this hope that Congress in 1933 included Sec. 7(a) in the National Industrial Recovery Act.[4]   This section, which applied to all employers in industries operating under codes of fair competition, read as follows:

---

[1] Sec. 2, paragraph 3.

[2] *Texas & New Orleans Railway Company et al v. Brotherhood of Railway & Steamship Clerks et al.*, 281 U.S. 548 (1930).   For an excellent review of this case in relation to earlier decisions, see Edward Berman, "The Supreme Court Interprets the Railway Labor Act," in *American Economic Review*, vol. 20 (1930), pp. 619–630.

[3] In the Texas and New Orleans case, the appellant (the railroad company) contended that the interdictions against discrimination were unconstitutional in view of the precedent already established in the Adair case.   Chief Justice Hughes, in rendering the unanimous decision in the 1930 case, found the substantive issue in the earlier cases and in the instant one to be different and the Adair and Coppage precedents therefore not applicable.   Specifically, the Chief Justice observed that in the earlier cases the issue had been the employer's right to hire and fire, whereas in the Texas and New Orleans case the issue was the employees' right to organize and bargain through representatives of their own choice without interference or coercion on the part of employers.   Nevertheless it should be noted that the practical effect of the decision was to deny the railroad corporations a prerogative they enjoyed under the Adair ruling.

[4] The interpretations placed upon Sec. 7(a) of the NIRA by the National Labor Board and the National Labor Relations Board of 1934–1935 are discussed *infra*, pp. 750–761.

"Every code of fair competition, agreement, and license approved, prescribed, or issued under this title shall contain the following conditions: (1) That employees shall have the right to organize and bargain collectively through representatives of their own choosing, and shall be free from the interference, restraint, or coercion of employers of labor, or their agents, in the designation of such representatives or in self-organization or in other concerted activities for the purpose of collective bargaining or other mutual aid or protection; (2) that no employee and no one seeking employment shall be required as a condition of employment to join any company union or to refrain from joining, organizing, or assisting a labor organization of his own choosing; and (3) that employers shall comply with the maximum hours of labor, minimum rates of pay, and other conditions of employment, approved or prescribed by the President."

The National Labor Relations Act.—Section 7(a) was interpreted in many cases coming before the National Labor Board and the (first) National Labor Relations Board.[1] In 1935 these interpretations were in large part incorporated into the specific provisions of the National Labor Relations Act relating to unfair labor practices. That Act, which applies to all industries and trades involving or affecting interstate commerce, reads, in part:

"Sec. 7. Employees shall have the right to self-organization, to form, join, or assist labor organizations, to bargain collectively through representatives of their own choosing, and to engage in concerted activities, for the purpose of collective bargaining or other mutual aid or protection.

"Sec. 8. It shall be an unfair labor practice for an employer—

"(1) To interfere with, restrain, or coerce employees in the exercise of the rights guaranteed in section 7.

"(2) To dominate or interfere with the formation or administration of any labor organization or contribute financial or other support to it: *Provided,* That subject to rules and regulations made and published by the Board pursuant to Sec. 6(a), an employer shall not be prohibited from permitting employees to confer with him during working hours without loss of time or pay.

"(3) By discrimination in regard to hire or tenure of employment or any term or condition of employment to encourage or discourage membership in any labor organization: . . .

"(4) To discharge or otherwise discriminate against an employee because he has filed charges or given testimony under this Act.

---

[1] See *Decisions of the National Labor Board,* Pts. I and II (1934); *Decisions of the National Labor Relations Board,* Pt. I (July 9–December, 1934), and Pt. II (January 1–June 16, 1935).

"(5) To refuse to bargain collectively with the representatives of his employees, subject to the provisions of Sec. 9(a)."[1]

This newer federal legislation is designed to support such organization as the worker may desire, to the end that collective bargaining may be both extended and stabilized. Not only does it prohibit discrimination by discharge or otherwise for union membership or activities; it also, in order to protect "legitimate" labor organizations against "company unions," makes it an unfair labor practice for an employer to dominate or interfere with the formation or administration of any labor organization or contribute financial or other support to it; finally, it makes it an unfair labor practice for an employer to refuse to bargain collectively with the properly accredited representatives of a majority of his employees in an appropriate unit. In the event there is a question concerning the appropriate organization for collective bargaining, the National Labor Relations Board is authorized to determine the matter by election or by checking of membership lists or authorization cards against the payroll.

The support intended to be given labor organization is stouter than that given in almost any other country except those with revolutionary governments. As would be expected, the statute was attacked on constitutional grounds. Though declared invalid in some respect or other, or *in toto*, by several of the inferior courts, in April, 1937, it was sustained and given broad coverage by the Supreme Court in several cases.[2]

Constitutionality of the National Labor Relations Act.—Determination of the coverage or application of the Act rested upon interpretation of the federal power to regulate interstate commerce. On the one side, argument ran in terms of previous narrow interpretations of the commerce power, on the other in terms of factual situations and in terms of the flow of commerce found in the Stockyards case.[3] While the Supreme

---

[1] Under the NIRA the penalty for violation of Sec. 7(a) was removal of the Blue Eagle and criminal prosecution at the hands of the Department of Justice. Enforcement under the National Labor Relations Act is through cease-and-desist orders.

[2] *Associated Press v. National Labor Relations Board*, 301 U.S. 103; *National Labor Relations Board v. Jones & Laughlin Steel Corp.*, 301 U.S. 1; *National Labor Relations Board v. Fruehauf Trailer Co.*, 301 U.S. 49; *National Labor Relations Board v. Friedman-Harry Marks Clothing Co.*, 301 U.S. 58; and *Washington, Virginia & Maryland Coach Co. v. National Labor Relations Board*, 301 U.S. 142 (all decided in April, 1937). On Feb. 28, 1938, the Supreme Court handed down opinions on two cases involving the issue as to whether or not the National Labor Relations Board could order the disestablishment of company unions found to have been initiated or dominated by the employer [*National Labor Relations Board v. Pennsylvania Greyhound Lines, Inc., et al.*, 303 U.S. 261 (1938); *National Labor Relations Board v. Pacific Greyhound Lines, Inc.*, 303 U.S. 272 (1938)]. In both cases the Supreme Court overruled decisions of the circuit courts. It ruled that the disestablishment orders were justified under the provision of the Act empowering the Board to "take such affirmative action . . . , as will effectuate the policies of this Act."

[3] *Stafford v. Wallace*, 258 U.S. 495 (1921).

Court of course takes the position that each case must be decided in the light of pertinent circumstances, it held by majority vote in the cases decided in March, 1937, that the National Labor Relations Act was predicated upon a proper conception of Congress's power to regulate interstate commerce and was applicable to all the cases before it.[1]

The Associated Press, with head office in New York and doing business far and wide, discharged one Watson, a rewrite man. The order of the National Labor Relations Board that he should be reinstated was contested. One contention was that interstate commerce was not involved in the rewrite and transmission work done by Watson in the New York office. The Court held otherwise. Citing, among others, the Texas and New Orleans case, Justice Roberts said, "We think . . . it is obvious that strikes or labor disturbances amongst this class of employees would have as direct an effect upon the activities of the petitioner as similar disturbances amongst those who operate the teletype machines or as a strike amongst the employees of telegraph lines over which petitioner's messages travel."[2]

In the Jones & Laughlin case, involving a huge, vertically integrated steel business, with wide interstate ramifications,[3] the Chief Justice observed that, "When industries organize themselves on a national scale, making their relation to interstate commerce the dominant factor in their activities, how can it be maintained that their industrial labor relations constitute a forbidden field into which Congress may not enter when it is necessary to protect interstate commerce from the paralyzing consequences of industrial war?"[3] Much of American manufacture—automobile, meat packing, harvester machinery, etc.—falls into the same category as this part of the steel industry.

Scope and Application of the National Labor Relations Act.—The Fruehauf and the Friedman-Harry Marks cases were decided on the authority of the Jones & Laughlin case. Large size or volume of business was not an essential condition, for, as the four dissenting justices[5] pointed

---

[1] 301 U.S. 1–147. In the Washington, Virginia & Maryland Coach Company cases the interstate operation of busses was involved. No contention was made that the petitioner was other than an instrumentality of interstate commerce.

[2] 301 U.S. at p. 129. Another contention was that the statute, as applied to the petitioner, abridged the freedom of the press as guaranteed in the First Amendment, for it deprived it of the right to select unhampered employees who would edit the news without bias. This was dismissed as an unsound generalization and irrelevant, the petitioner having contended that Watson's discharge was "solely on the grounds of his work not being on a basis for which he has shown capability."

[3] For details concerning organization and business activities and relationships, see *Decisions and Orders of the National Labor Relations Board*, vol. 1 (1936), pp. 504–509.

[4] 301 U.S. at p. 41.

[5] Justices McReynolds, Van Devanter, Sutherland, and Butler. Citing numerous decisions, they held that manufacturing concerns, whether large or small, are not engaged in interstate commerce. As the first step in their operations, they secure raw materials;

out, both of these manufacturing concerns were relatively small. Fruehauf had only one plant, employed 900 persons, and had annual receipts
of about $3,000,000. The clothing concern was even smaller, employing
in its one plant some 800 workers and having a business of approximately
$2,000,000 per year. It was one concern among 3,300 and had only
½ of 1 per cent of the business in this highly competitive industry. If
the plant were closed, "the ultimate effect on commerce in clothing obviously would be negligible." But, as Professor (now Judge) Magruder
has pointed out,[1] "The controlling factor in *Friedman-Harry Marks* was
that the company, though small, was part of one of the most important
national industries." While a strike in any one factory in this widely
unionized industry "would, in itself, have a negligible effect on interstate
commerce, unsatisfactory labor conditions throughout the industry might,
in the aggregate, produce effects of nationwide concern."[2] Later decisions have clarified the scope and application of the Act. Mining has
been held to be within the jurisdiction of the Board, though its processes
are not preceded by the gathering of raw materials, as is manufacture.[3]
In an early public utilities case,[4] it was held that the Act applied though
all the service was supplied within the state of New York, with only the
smaller part of it going to railroads and others engaged in interstate
commerce. Jurisdiction extends also to newspaper offices[5] and to the
telegraph service.[6]

These are some of the early cases in which the courts held that the
Act applied. Further sampling of the types of businesses covered by the
Act will indicate the broad scope of the Board's jurisdiction now recog-
nized by the courts. As in the Fainblatt case, the Supreme Court in
National Labor Relations Board v. Bradford Dyeing Association[7] held the
Act applicable to a small processor of goods moving in interstate com-

---

next is the manufacturing process; beyond this is the shipment of product, which is commerce. They were of the opinion that manufacture is a local matter and that it was
"unreasonable and unprecedented to say the commerce clause confers upon Congress power
to govern relations between employers and employees in their local activities." 301 U.S.
at p. 99.

[1] Calvert Magruder, *op. cit.*, p. 1094.

[2] *Ibid.* It is significant that the National Labor Relations Board's characterization of
industry and its relationships was freely quoted in the majority opinion.

[3] *National Labor Relations Board v. Good Coal Co.*, 12 N.L.R.B. 136 (1939); 110 Fed. (2d)
501 (C.C.A. 6, 1940); *National Labor Relations Board v. Sunshine Mining*, 7 N.L.R.B. 1252
(1938), 110 Fed. (2d) 780 (C.C.A. 9, 1940).

[4] *Consolidated Edison Company v. National Labor Relations Board*, 95 Fed. (2d) 390
(C.C.A. 2d, 1938); 305 U.S. 197 (1938).

[5] *National Labor Relations Board v. Star Publishing Co.*, 97 Fed. (2d) 465 (C.C.A. 9,
1938).

[6] *National Labor Relations Board v. Mackay Radio & Telegraph Co.*, 87 Fed. (2d) 611
(C.C.A. 9, 1937); 304 U.S. 333 (1938).

[7] 310 U.S. 318 (1940).

merce. Questions of possession or transfer of title or other commercial
practices are not relevant to the determination of the question of the
Board's jurisdiction over goods moving in interstate commerce. The
Jones & Laughlin and other cases already mentioned are examples of
manufacturing where interstate movement precedes and succeeds manufacturing. The lumber industry, as well as mining, is an example of an
industry where interstate movement succeeds production and is subject
to the Act.[1] From the standpoint of the Board's jurisdiction, it does not
make any difference whether manufacturing precedes or succeeds the
interstate movement.[2] Businesses having incoming interstate shipments
and virtually none outgoing are subject to the Act. In *National Labor
Relations Board v. Schmidt Baking Co.*,[3] the Act was held applicable to a
bakery having no outgoing interstate sales, but only incoming interstate
shipments. Not only manufacturing industries, but also merchandising
businesses of this type are subject to the Act. In *National Labor Relations
Board v. Suburban Lumber Company*[4] the Act was held applicable to a
retail lumber dealer having only 1 per cent of its outgoing but most of its
incoming shipments interstate. In *National Labor Relations Board v.
Levaur, Inc.*[5] the Act was held applicable to an automobile distributing
company. In *National Labor Relations Board v. Green Inc.*[6] a wholesale
and retail establishment selling construction material was held subject
to the jurisdiction of the Board. Within the purview of the Board's
jurisdiction have also been held to be department stores[7] and chain stores.[8]
The Board, however, has not, in its administrative discretion, accepted
jurisdiction indiscriminately in the retail merchandising field, even
though constitutionally it might have been justified in doing so. Department stores and chain stores because of their national ramifications and
organization are peculiarly appropriate for the exercise of the Board's
powers of jurisdiction.

Within the purview of the Act have also been held the businesses
described as "of local character" but operating across state lines. Typi-

---

[1] *National Labor Relations Board v. Carlisle Lumber Co.*, 2 N.L.R.B. 248 (1936), 94 Fed.
(2d) 138 (C.C.A. 9, 1937), cert. den. 304 U.S. 575 (1938).

[2] *Newport News Shipbuilding & Drydock Co. v. National Labor Relations Board*, 8
N.L.R.B. 866 (1938), 101 Fed. (2d) 841, 843 (C.C.A. 4, 1939).

[3] 27 N.L.R.B. 864 (1940); 122 Fed. (2d) 162 (C.C.A. 4, 1941).

[4] 121 Fed. (2d) 829 (C.C.A. 3, 1941); cert. den. 314 U.S. 693 (1941).

[5] 17 N.L.R.B. 1034 (1939), 115 Fed. (2d) 105 (C.C.A. 1, 1940), cert. den. 312 U.S. 682
(1941).

[6] 33 N.L.R.B. 1184 (1941); 125 Fed. (2d) 485 (C.C.A. 4, 1942).

[7] *Marshall Field*, 34 N.L.R.B. 1 (1941); *Blatt Co.*, 38 N.L.R.B. 1210 (1942); *May
Department Stores*, 39 N.L.R.B. 471 (1942); *Goldblatt Bros.*, 41 N.L.R.B. 741 (1942).

[8] *First National Stores*, 26 N.L.R.B. 1275 (1940); *Kroger Grocery & Baking Co.*, 27
N.L.R.B. 250 (1940); *A. & P. Stores*, 33 N.L.R.B. 1103 (1941); *National Tea Co.*, 35
N.L.R.B. 340 (1941).

cal of this type of business was a laundry and dry-cleaning establishment.[1]
Because they serve as a link in interstate communication, businesses
operating wholly within a state have been held subject to the Act.[2]

In applying the Board's jurisdiction to a business, departmentalization
of employees so as to remove some of them from the protection of the Act
where the business as a whole is subject to the Act is not countenanced.
In the Texas Company case[3] the Board took jurisdiction of building-
maintenance employees working in a building occupied by offices of a
company engaged in interstate commerce.   In *Virginia Electric and Power
Company v. National Labor Relations Board*[4] the employees of the company working in the artificial-gas-manufacturing and street-railway
departments were held subject to the Act where the company as a whole
was engaged in interstate commerce, the court saying, "A sufficient
answer to this position is the unitary character of the company's business,
which has resulted, notwithstanding the division into these departments,
in the organization of a single association of its employees.   It is clear
that wage controversies or unfair labor practices in any department of
such a business will have repercussions in other departments; and strife
affecting the interstate commerce in which the company is engaged will
be avoided only if the rights of all employees are properly safeguarded."
From the standpoint of jurisdiction, a business is considered as a unit
where it is so operated.[5]

The Board must, however, examine the specific work of the employees
involved and draw a line of demarcation between agricultural and other
employees, since Sec. 2 (3) of the Act excludes from the term "employee"
"any individual employed as an agricultural laborer."   Progress in the
application of machine production to agriculture and the transfer of farm
operations to packing and processing plants have made it extremely
difficult to draw a distinction between agricultural and other laborers.
The Act has been held applicable to packing employees working in the
sheds of the Citrus Fruit Growers Association[6] and to lettuce-packing
workers.[7]   But, it is interesting to note, that while it might have been

---

[1] *National Labor Relations Board v. White Swan*, 19 N.L.R.B. 1079 (1940), 118 Fed. (2d)
1002 (C.C.A. 4, 1941), 313 U.S. 23 (1941).

[2] *National Labor Relations Board v. Central Missouri Telephone Co.*, 15 N.L.R.B. 798
(1939), 115 Fed. (2d) 563 (C.C.A. 8, 1940).

[3] 21 N.L.R.B. 110 (1940).

[4] 20 N.L.R.B. 911 (1940), 115 Fed. (2d) 414, 415 (C.C.A. 4, 1940), rev'd on another
point, 314 U.S. 469 (1941).

[5] *National Labor Relations Board v. Schmidt Baking Co.*, 27 N.L.R.B. 867 (1940); 122
Fed. (2d) 162 (C.C.A. 4, 1941).

[6] *North Whittier Heights Citrus Ass'n v. National Labor Relations Board*, 10 N.L.R.B.
1269 (1929), 109 Fed. (2d) 76 (C.C.A. 9, 1940); cert. den. 310 U.S. 632 (1940).

[7] *American Fruit Growers, Inc.*, 10 N.L.R.B. 316 (1938).   To the same effect is *National
Labor Relations Board v. Tovrea Packing Co.*, 12 N.L.R.B. 1063 (1939), 111 Fed. (2d) 626
(C.C.A. 9, 1940), cert. den. 311 U.S. 668 (1940).

within its power the Board has refused to take jurisdiction over lemon pickers[1] and employees of a nursery engaged in the planting, budding, and preparation of nursery stock[2] working on farms.

Another type of determination relevant to the question of the Board's jurisdiction is made necessary by Sec. 2(2) of the Act which excludes from the term "employer" "the United States, or any State or political subdivision thereof." An independent contractor carrying mails for the United States was held to be within the Board's jurisdiction,[3] as was also a company leasing a cannery owned by the United States Government.[4] On the other hand, a harbor district formed pursuant to a state law providing for the improvement of harbors was held to be a political subdivision of the state and not subject to the Board's jurisdiction.[5]

As interpreted, the National Labor Relations Act has a tremendous scope. In some of the industrial states perhaps more than 80 per cent of workers other than agricultural laborers and domestic servants, who are specifically excluded, are so employed that they come within the protection of the National Labor Relations and the Railway Labor Acts.

The Import of Various Provisions.—In the earlier cases involving construction of the Act, the Supreme Court approved of the reinstatement with back pay of men discharged because of union activity or membership, in the interest of industrial peace, and of cease-and-desist orders against further discrimination. In none of the first five cases was the promotion, domination, or financing of company unions involved, but on this unfair labor practice the Court had already provided a precedent in the Virginian Railway case[6] in an application of a provision common to the Railway Labor and Wagner-Connery acts. During the last several years a considerable percentage of the decisions of the National Labor Relations Board have required the disestablishment of company-dominated and/or company-assisted labor organizations, *i.e.,* "company unions."[7] A smaller number of decisions have declared agreements between employers and assisted "affiliated" unions to be valid.

[1] *Saticoy Lemon Association,* 41 N.L.R.B. 243 (1942) and *Seaboard Lemon Association,* 41 N.L.R.B. 248 (1942).

[2] *Stark Bros. Nurseries,* 40 N.L.R.B. 1243 (1942).

[3] *National Labor Relations Board v. Carroll,* 29 N.L.R.B. 343 (1941); 120 Fed. (2d) 457 457 (C.C.A. 1, 1941). See also *National New York Packing & Shipping Co.,* 1 N.L.R.B. 1009 (1936); *Cosmopolitan Shipping Company,* 2 N.L.R.B. 759, 762 (1937), and *Panama Railroad Co.,* 2 N.L.R.B. 290 (1936).

[4] *Alaska Salmon Industry, Inc.,* 33 N.L.R.B. 727 (1941).

[5] *Oxnard Harbor District,* 34 N.L.R.B. 1285 (1941).

[6] *Virginian Railway Co. v. System No. 40,* 300 U.S. 515 (1937).

[7] See Chap. XV.

Most questioned on administrative and constitutional grounds were the matters of majority rule and the last of the five unfair labor practices contained in the National Labor Relations Act.[1] The extension and stabilization of collective bargaining was, however, the primary objective of the Act. Corresponding provisions had been upheld in the Virginian Railway case. In Jones & Laughlin, the company asserted its right to conduct its business in an orderly manner without being subject to arbitrary restraints. The Supreme Court, however, found nothing arbitrary in the requirements under the Act. After reference to Virginian Railway, the Chief Justice said:

"The decree which we affirmed in that case required the Railway Company to treat with the representative chosen by the employees and also to refrain from entering into collective labor agreements with anyone other than their true representative as ascertained in accordance with the provisions of the Act. We said that the obligation to treat with the true representative was exclusive and hence imposed the negative duty to treat with no other. We also pointed out that, as conceded by the Government, the injunction against the Company's entering into any contract concerning rules, rates of pay and working conditions except with a chosen representative was 'designed only to prevent collective bargaining with anyone purporting to represent employees' other than the representative they had selected. It was taken 'to prohibit the negotiation of labor contracts generally applicable to employees' in the described unit with any other representative than the one so chosen, 'but not as precluding such individual contracts' as the Company might 'elect to make directly with individual employees.' We think this construction also applies to § 9(a) of the National Labor Relations Act."[2]

There has been much discussion as to precisely what Sec. 8(5) of the Wagner-Connery Act requires of employers. It was intended to require them to confer in good faith with properly accredited representatives on such matters connected with employment relations as their representatives might seek to present. Conference in good faith can result in agreement and promote industrial peace, but agreement is not required.[3] In upholding the provision of the Act in question, the

---

[1] Section 8(5), quoted on p. 523. See William H. Spencer, *The National Labor Relations Act*, Studies in Business Administration, vol. 6, no. 1, The School of Business, The University of Chicago (1935), especially Chaps. 4 and 5.

[2] 301 U.S. at pp. 44–45. Section 9(a) is the one specifying that representatives selected by the majority in a unit appropriate for collective bargaining shall be the representatives for collective bargaining of all in that unit.

[3] The import of Sec. 8(5) has now been rather fully determined. The National Labor Relations Board has made rulings including:

  a. A refusal to meet or negotiate with the representatives of the employees is a refusal to bargain collectively [*In the matter of Surbuban Lumber Company and International*

Chief Justice said, in none too happy language (note third sentence):
"The Act does not compel agreements between employers and employees.
It does not compel any agreement whatever. It does not prevent the

---

*Brotherhood of Teamsters, Chauffeurs, Stablemen, and Helpers of America, Local Union No.
676*, 3 N.L.R.B. 194 (1937)]; but a meeting with the employees' representative is not
necessarily collective bargaining. *In the matter of Atlas Mills Inc., and Textile House
Workers Union No. 2269, United Textile Workers of America*, 3 N.L.R.B. 10 (1937).

    b. "Collective bargaining means more than the discussions of individual problems and
grievances with employees or groups of employees. It means that the employer is obligated
to negotiate, in good faith with his employees as a group, through their representatives, on
matters of wages, hours, and basic working conditions, and to endeavor to reach an agreement for a fixed period of time." *In the matter of Atlanic Refining Company and Local
Nos. 310 and 318 International Association of Oil Field, Gas Well, and Refinery Workers of
America*, 1 N.L.R.B. 359, at p. 368 (1936). See also *Consolidated Edison Co. v. N.L.R.B.*,
305 U.S. 197 (1938) and *In the Matter of Globe Cotton Mills and Textile Workers Organizing
Committee*, 6 N.L.R.B. 461 (1938). The position of the Board was upheld by the United
States Supreme Court in *N.L.R.B. v. Harnischfeger*, decided June 6, 1940.

    c. "The act imposes upon employers the duty to meet with the duly designated
representatives of their employees, to bargain in good faith with them in a genuine attempt
to achieve an understanding on the proposals and counter-proposals advanced, and finally,
if an understanding is reached to embody that understanding in an agreement." *In the
matter of St. Joseph Stock Yards Company and Amalgamated Meat Cutters and Butcher
Workmen of North America, Local Union No. 159*, 2 N.L.R.B. 39, at p. 54 (1936); see also
In the matter of United States Stamping Company and Enamel Workers Union No. 18630,
5 N.L.R.B. 172 (1938).

    d. As to what constitutes the process of collective bargaining, no general rule can be
made to cover all cases. The process required varies with the circumstances in each case.
"The question whether an employer has failed in his affirmative duty to bargain collectively with the representative of his employees has meaning only when considered in connection with the facts of a particular case. The history of the relationships between the
particular employer and its employees, the practice of the industry, the circumstances of
the immediate issues between the employer and its employees are all relevant factors which
might be given weight." *In the matter of Birge and Sons Company and United Wall and
Paper Crafts of North America*, 1 N.L.R.B. 731, at p. 739 (1936); see also *In the matter of
Sands Manufacturing Company and Mechanics Educational Society of America*, 1 N.L.R.B.
546 (1936).

    e. "An employer is not required to sign the specific agreement presented to him by
representatives of his employees. Nor is he obligated to agree to any of the demands solely
for the sake of reaching some agreement when genuine accord is impossible, although both
sides are acting in good faith." *In the matter of St. Joseph Stock Yards Company and
Amalgamated Meat Cutters and Butcher Workmen of North America, Local Union No. 159*,
2 N.L.R.B. 39, at p. 55 (1936).

    f. Furthermore, the employer may cease to bargain collectively when negotiations
already held make plain that to do so would be futile [*In the matter of Trenton Garment
Company and International Ladies' Garment Workers' Union, Local 278*, 4 N.L.R.B. 1186
(1938)]. However, "Every avenue and possibility of negotiations must be exhausted
before it should be admitted that an irreconcilable difference creating an impasse has been
reached" [(*In the matter of The Sands Manufacturing Company and Mechanics' Educational
Society of America*, 1 N.L.R.B. 546, at p. 557 (1936)]. If new situations arise, or new issues
are introduced, the employer must again resume his collective bargaining. *In the matter*

employer 'from refusing to make a collective contract and hiring individuals on whatever terms' the employer 'may by unilateral action

---

*of Kuehne Manufacturing Company and Local No. 1791, United Brotherhood of Carpenters
and Joiners of America,* 7 N.L.R.B. 304 (1938).

g. Dilatory tactics on the part of the employer are evidence of a lack of good faith.
In the matter of S. L. Allan and Company, Inc., and Federal Labor Union Local No. 18526,
1 N.L.R.B. 714, at p. 727 (1936); see also *In the matter of Bell Oil and Gas Company and
Local Union 258 of the International Association of Oil Field, Gas Well, and Refinery Workers
of America,* 1 N.L.R.B. 562, at p. 584 (1936).

h. Statements of inability to pay the wages demanded, if accompanied by refusal to
prove this claim or to have it verified, come in the same category. *In the matter of Pioneer
Pearl Button Company and Button Workers' Union, Federal Local No. 20026,* 1 N.L.R.B.
837 (1936).

i. That the employees have gone on strike does not absolve an employer from his
obligation to bargain collectively [*In the matter of Columbian Enameling and Stamping
Company,* 1 N.L.R.B. 181, at p. 196 (1936); see also *In the matter of Black Diamond Steamship Corporation and Marine Engineers' Beneficial Association Local No. 33,* 3 N.L.R.B. 84,
at p. 92 (1937)]. This is true both of the strike that is the result of an employer's unfair
labor practice and the strike that is not [*N.L.R.B. v. Black Diamond Steamship Corporation,*
94 Fed. (2d) 875 (1938)]. But workers may lose their rights as strikers by unlawful behavior
after an employer has engaged in an unfair labor practice. See *N.L.R.B. v. Fansteel
Metallurgical Corporation* (306 U.S. 601, 1939), where the Supreme Court overruled the
National Labor Relations Board and held that because the workers had engaged in a
stay-in strike they had lost the rights the statute was designed to protect. Having discharged them for this unlawful act, the employer was within his right when he refused to
rehire them. See also *In the matter of Republic Steel Corp.,* 9 N.L.R.B. 219 (1938); 107
Fed. (2d) 472 (C.C.A. 3, 1939).

j. That the employees have violated an agreement in the past does not absolve the
employer from his obligation under Sec. 8(5). It is therefore unnecessary to decide
whether or not there has been a breach of the alleged agreement. "The Act imposes an
unconditional duty upon an employer to bargain collectively. . . . [The employees'] misconduct, for which appropriate remedies exist under State laws, does not justify the . . .
[employer] in ignoring Federal law by . . . [his] refusal to bargain collectively with the
Union" [*In the matter of Kuehne Manufacturing Company and Local No. 1791, United
Brotherhood of Carpenters and Joiners of America,* 7 N.L.R.B. at p. 321 (1938)]; though the
union may have misconducted itself, it has a *locus poenitentiae;* if it offers in good faith to
treat, the employer may not refuse because of its past sins [*N.L.R.B. v. Remington Rand,
Inc.,* 94 Fed. (2d) 862 (C.C.A. 2, 1938)].

k. Nor does the character of the union make a difference—the employer must meet
and negotiate with the representative chosen by a majority of his employees in an appropriate unit. It is an unfair labor practice for the employer to impose his preference as to
the representatives of his employees or to insist upon representatives of a certain character
as a condition precedent to negotiation [*In the matter of Fansteel Metallurgical Corporation
and Amalgamated Association of Iron, Steel, and Tin Workers of North America, Local 66,*
5 N.L.R.B. 930 (1938)]. The employer cannot legally refuse to negotiate with the union
because he prefers another. His "duty is to negotiate in good faith with whatever agent
or agency a majority of . . . [his] employees have selected." *In the matter of Louisville
Refining Company and International Association, Oil Field, Gas Well, and Refinery Workers
of America,* 4 N.L.R.B. 844, at p. 858 (1938).

l. For an employer to refuse to sign a written agreement embodying the terms reached
in collective bargaining is a violation of his duty to bargain collectively [*H. J. Heinz Co.,*

determine.' . . . The theory of the Act is that free opportunity for negotiation with accredited representatives of employees is likely to

---

10 N.L.R.B. 963 (1939), 311 U. S. 514, 523–526 (1941)]. So is advance announcement of refusal to sign [*Art Metal Construction Co.*, 12 N.L.R.B. 1307 (1939), 110 Fed. (2d) 148, 150, (C.C.A. 2, 1940), *Highland Park Mfg. Co.*, 12 N.L.R.B. 1238 (1939), 110 Fed. (2d) 632 (C.C.A. 4, 1940)]. Among the requirements of a written contract is that it contains a recognition clause [*McQuay-Norris Mfg. Co.*, 21 N.L.R.B. 709 (1940), 116 Fed. (2d), 748 (C.C.A. 7, 1940), (2d) 748 (C.C.A. 7), cert. den. 313 U.S. 565] and that the union be a signatory to it [*National Seal Corp.* 30 N.L.R.B. 27, May 5, 1942 (C.C.A. 2)].

m. It is not illegal to refuse to bargain with a minority; indeed it may under certain conditions be unlawful to bargain with it. The obligation is to bargain collectively with a majority of the employees in an appropriate unit; the Act requires negotiations by an employer with the view to reaching an agreement with the organization representing the majority of his employees to the exclusion of all other possible representatives. By express provision, such a majority representative is the exclusive representative of all the employees [*In the matter of United Stamping Company and Enamel Workers' Union No.* 18630, 5 N.L.R.B. 172 (1938)]. However, the majority is one of employees who have designated representatives for that purpose; a majority of employees do not have to be members of the union. Ordinarily issues as to which of the organizations claiming it has a majority and is to be recognized is decided by election held by consent or under National Labor Relations Board order. In the earlier cases, the Board ruled that a majority means a majority of all those in the appropriate unit eligible to vote, but in a subsequent case in which only 3,163 votes were cast by 9,752 employees eligible to vote, the Board ruled that "the organization receiving a majority of the votes cast at an election shall be the exclusive representative for collective bargaining" [*In the matter of R.C.A. Manufacturing Company Inc. and United Electrical and Radio Workers*, 2 N.L.R.B., at p. 179 (1936)]. This ruling was in line with the decision of Judge Way, of the U. S. District Court, in *System Federation No. 40 v. The Virginian Railway Company*, 11 Fed. Supp. 621, 1935, arising under the Railway Labor Act. The Circuit Court of Appeals affirmed Judge Way's decision, holding that, as in political elections, provided there was opportunity for all eligible persons to vote, the required majority was a majority of those actually voting.

n. If an employer has an honest doubt regarding the appropriateness of the unit claimed by the union or about the wishes of the majority of the employees with regard to a bargaining representative, he does not have to bargain until this doubt is authoritatively removed. But the employer's doubt must be advanced in good faith if he is to be excused from the duty of bargaining collectively [*In the matter of McNeely and Price Company and National Leather Workers' Association Local No.* 30 *of C.I.O.*, 6 N.L.R.B. 800 (1938)]. The duty to bargain collectively includes a duty to cooperate with the union in a reasonable effort to determine its claim to represent all of the employees. *In the Matter of Burnside Steel and Foundry Company and Amalgamated Association of Iron, Steel, and Tin Workers of North America*, 7 N.L.R.B. 714 (1938).

o. The subject matter of collective bargaining may be said to cover all the problems arising in the employer-employee relationship. Thus, the employer is required to bargain, as requested, concerning arbitration provisions [*Boss Mfg. Co.*, 3 N.L.R.B. 400 (1937) and 11 N.L.R.B. 432 (1939), 107 Fed. (2d) 574 (C.C.A. 7, 1939)]; bonuses [*Singer Manufacturing Company*, 24 N.L.R.B. 444 (1940), 119 Fed. (2d) 131, 136 (1941)]; checkoff [*Reed & Prince Mfg. Co.*, 12 N.L.R.B. 944 (1939) 118 Fed. (2d) 874,883 (C.C.A. 1, 1941)], closed and preferential shop [*National Licorice Co.*, 7 N.L.R.B. 537 (1938), 309 U.S. 350, 360 (1940)]; interpretation or modification of current contract provisions [*Sands Mfg. Co.*, 306 U. S. 332, 342 (1939), *Rapid Roller Co.*, 33 N.L.R.B. 557 (1941) 126 Fed. (2d) 452, 456 (1942), *Highland Shoe, Inc.*, 23 N.L.R.B. 259 (1940), 119 Fed. (2d) 218 (C.C.A. 1,

promote industrial peace and may bring about the adjustments and agreements which the Act in itself does not attempt to compel."[1]

State Labor Relations Acts.—The present federal legislation concerning the right to organize and to be recognized, and the majority rule, as interpreted and upheld by the Supreme Court, represents a marked change from the common-law and valid statutes of pre-New Deal days.

1941)]; settlement of grievances [*Bachelder*, 21 N.L.R.B. 907 (1940), 120 Fed. (2d) 574, 577–578 (C.C.A. 7, 1941)]; seniority provisions [*Highland Park Mfg. Co.*, 12 N.L.R.B. 1238 (1939), 110 Fed. (2d) 632, 635 (C.C.A. 4, 1940)]; Sunday and holiday provisions [*Singer Mfg. Co.*, 24 N.L.R.B. 444 (1940), 119 Fed. (2d) 131, 136 (C.C.A. 7, 1941)]; paid vacations [*Singer Mfg. Co., supra.*]; and wages, hours, and conditions of employment [*Whittier Mills Co.*, 15 N.L.R.B. 457 (1939), 111 Fed. (2d) 474, 478 (C.C.A. 5, 1940), *Westinghouse Airbrake*, 25 N.L.R.B. 1312 (1940), 120 Fed. (2d) 1004 (C.C.A. 3, 1941)].

p. Among the requirements of collective bargaining must be considered recognition as bargaining representative [*Louisville Refining Co.*, 4 N.L.R.B. 844 (1938), 102 Fed. (2d) 678, 680–681 (C.C.A. 6, 1939), *Griswold*, 6 N.L.R.B. 298 (1938), 106 Fed. (2d) 713, 715 (C.C.A. 3, 1939)]; recognition as exclusive representative, recognition for membership not being enough [*Biles-Coleman Lumber Co.*, 4 N.L.R.B. 679 (1937), 98 Fed. (2d) 18, 22 (C.C.A. 9, 1938), *Hartsell Mills Co.*, 18 N.L.R.B. 268 (1939), 111 Fed. (2d) 291, 292 (C.C.A. 4, 1940), *McQuay-Norris*, 21 N.L.R.B. 709 (1940), 116 Fed. (2d) 748, 750–751 (C.C.A. 7, 1940)]. The following have been held to constitute denial of recognition: dealing with company union [*Good Coal Company*, 12 N.L.R.B. 136 (1939), 110 Fed. (2d) 501, 505 (C.C.A. 6, 1940)]; dealing with minority union [*National Motor Bearing Co.*, 5 N.L.R.B. 409 (1938), 105 Fed. (2d) 652, 660 (C.C.A. 9, 1939)]; negotiations with individual employees [*Acme Air Appliance Co.*, 10 N.L.R.B. 1385 (1939), 117 Fed. (2d) 417, 420 (C.C.A. 2, 1941)]; and refusal to include recognition clause in contract [*McQuay-Norris, supra.*].

q. A most significant requirement of collective bargaining is that the employer should not go over the heads of the representatives seeking to bargain. Among the practices that have been considered as going over the heads of the representatives are: unilateral change of working conditions or announcements or offers thereof while the union seeks to bargain, whether or not these terms are favorable to the employees [*Chicago Apparatus Co.*, 12 N.L.R.B. 1002 (1939), 116 Fed. (2d) 753, 756 (C.C.A. 7, 1940), *Pilling*, 16 N.L.R.B. 650 (1939), 119 Fed. (2d) 32, 38 (C.C.A. 3, 1941), *Oughton*, 20 N.L.R.B. 301 (1940), 118 Fed. (2d) 486, 498 (C.C.A. 3, 1940), *Whittier Mills Co.*, 15 N.L.R.B. 457 (1939), 111 Fed. (2d) 474, 478–479 (C.C.A. 5, 1940)]; addressing reply to union proposal directly to employees [*Acme Air Appliance Co.*, 10 N.L.R.B. 1385 (1939), 117 Fed. (2d) 417, 418–419 (1941), *National Licorice Co.*, 7 N.L.R.B. 537 (1938), 104 Fed. (2d) 655, 656 (C.C.A. 2, 1939)]; bargaining with individuals [*Highland Shoe Company*, 23 N.L.R.B. 259, (1940), 119 Fed. (2d) 218, 221 (C.C.A. 1, 1941), *Hopwood Retinning Company*, 4 N.L.R.B. 922 (1938), 98 Fed. (2d) 97, 100 (C.C.A. 2, 1938)]; bargaining with other representatives [*Piqua Munising Wood Products Co.*, 7 N.L.R.B. 782 (1938), 109 Fed. (2d) 552, 556 (C.C.A. 6, 1940)]; meeting with employees [*Schmidt Baking Co.*, 27 N.L.R.B. 864 (1940), 122 Fed. (2d) 162, 163–164 (C.C.A. 1941)]; conducting elections or canvasses after receipt of bargaining request [*American Manufacturing Co.*, 5 N.L.R.B. 443 (1938), 106 Fed. (2d) 61, 63 (C.C.A. 2, 1939), *Kiddie Kover Co.*, 6 N.L.R.B. 355 (1938), 105 Fed. (2d) 179, 181–182 (C.C.A. 6, 1939)].

For a fuller presentation of "principles" enunciated by the Board and further citations of cases, see its several annual reports, particularly its *Fourth Annual Report* (1938–1939), pp. 56–111, and Joseph Rosenfarb, *The National Labor Policy and How It Works* (1940).

[1] 301 U.S. at p. 45.

This legislation has now been complemented by state laws—and also attacked on several grounds. Our discussion may be concluded by brief comment on the industrial-relations acts adopted by several of the states in 1937 and more recently[1] and the charges of unfairness made against the federal Act.

The avowed purpose of the state acts adopted in Utah,[2] Wisconsin,[3] Massachusetts,[4] New York,[5] and Pennsylvania[6] in 1937, like that of the National Labor Relations Act, was to diminish the causes of labor disputes and to guarantee the right of collective bargaining. The unfair labor practices prohibited were the same as those prohibited by federal law, except that the Wisconsin and New York acts went farther and definitely outlawed espionage and black-listing by employers.[7] In only one instance, that of the Massachusetts law, were unfair practices by labor organizations prohibited; there the "sit-down strike" was declared to be unlawful and made punishable on the same terms as unfair labor practices committed by employers.

Since 1937 only one state, Rhode Island, has enacted a law of the Wagner Act type. This 1941[8] statute contains the rights of employees and the unfair labor practice prohibitions of the federal law. It is administered by a board of three members in the Department of Labor, one representing labor, one industry, and one the public. Like the National Labor Relations Board, it settles representation disputes, but where the majority of the employees in a particular craft shall so desire the craft unit is mandatory.

"Wagner Acts" Challenged.—It was expected in 1937 that states other than the five mentioned above would in the near future enact similar legislation. While bills with that object in view were introduced in a large number of states, the legislative sessions of 1939 were marked

[1] An excellent discussion of the five "baby Wagner Acts" adopted in 1937 may be found in Paul H. Douglas, "American Labor Relations Acts," *American Economic Review*, vol. 27 (1937), pp. 735–761.

[2] Chap. 55, Laws of Utah (1937).

[3] Chap. 51, Laws of Wisconsin (1937).

[4] Chap. 436, Acts of Massachusetts (1937).

[5] Chap. 443, Laws of New York (1937).

[6] Act 294, Laws of Pennsylvania (1937).

[7] In the laws enacted by these two states it was made unlawful for employers "to spy upon or keep under surveillance any activities of employees or their representatives in the exercise of the rights" guaranteed. Moreover, in Wisconsin it was made unlawful for an employer to inform any person of the exercise by any individual of his right to join a union and to bargain collectively when this was done "for the purpose of preventing individuals so blacklisted from obtaining or retaining employment." Finally, under the Wisconsin Act, the Board was authorized to conciliate and arbitrate disputes, appoint labor organization and employer committees to investigate unethical practices, and to enforce collective-bargaining agreements through publication of violations and reference to the committees for appropriate action.

[8] Rhode Island General Laws (1938), Title 28, Ch. 281, amended by Ch. 1066 (1941).

by the introduction and in some cases the enactment of measures of a
different—a restrictive—type. In Wisconsin, the Act of 1937 was
repealed and a new statute enacted; in other states the existing laws were
amended more or less extensively, particularly in Pennsylvania; Minnesota and Michigan, which had had no "industrial relations statutes,"
adopted such measures but, on the whole, of a conservative type. A
second chapter in the history of labor-relations acts has since 1939 been
in process of being written.

The explanation of the amendatory proposals and of the new statutes
is found in the recurrence of depression in 1937, in the reaction against
much of the reform measures finding place under the "New Deal," in
dissatisfaction with the National Labor Relations Act and its administration—a dissatisfaction due more to misunderstanding and misrepresentation than to shortcomings and injustices—in a divided labor movement
and certain union practices, some of them unfortunate. Bills modeled
upon proposals to amend the federal Act and upon the Oregon popularly
voted Act of 1938 and strike-limitation measures have been introduced
in the various legislatures.

Bills introduced in the Congress in 1939, while retaining in whole or in
large part the present declared unfair labor practices, would amend the
National Labor Relations Act in numerous respects.[1] Indeed, some of
the measures,[2] if enacted, would radically change the law. The several
measures cannot be analyzed, much less discussed on their merits, in this
treatise.[3] Only some of the more important changes proposed can be

---

[1] Save for a few footnotes, these paragraphs (from here to p. 547) are published as they
were written in August, 1940. Because he is now serving as Chairman of the National
Labor Relations Board, the writer of these paragraphs does not care to discuss the various
bills more recently introduced into Senate or House but not enacted into law. Nor is it
important that such measures should be dealt with for they have incorporated no significant
new ideas and it is the purpose of this volume to present and evaluate ideas rather than to
record legislative history in detail.

[2] The bills introduced into the Senate or the House may be grouped into three general
classes. One group, such as S. 1550 and H.R. 4400, would modify the National Labor
Relations Act little or not at all except that "agricultural labor" would be broadly defined
so as to exempt certain classes from its embrace. Another group, such as S. 1000, H.R.
4749, and H.R. 9195, would modify the Act and limit the National Labor Relations Board
or its substitute so as to be more favorable to the A. F. of L., which organization has
claimed that the Board had discriminated against it and favored the C.I.O. The third
group, such as S. 1264 and H.R. 4990, would modify the Act in numerous respects, incorporate unfair labor practices the commission of which by employees or labor organizations
would constitute complete defense against charges of employer unfair practices, and limit
trade-union activities. The bills of the third type are in general accord with the views of
the National Association of Manufacturers, the U.S. Chamber of Commerce, the League
for Industrial Rights, and other organizations opposed to legislation of the Wagner Act
type.

[3] The testimony taken by the Senate and House Committees is very voluminous, and
trade and other publications are replete with articles. The reader will be particularly

noted incidental to analysis and discussion of industrial-relations laws more recently adopted by a number of the states.

Some of the proposed measures[1] would broaden the definition of "agricultural laborer" so as to exempt creameries, canneries, fruit-packing plants, and other establishments processing or handling agricultural products from the coverage of the Act, as is desired by agricultural pressure blocks. Such redefinition would limit somewhat the area in which the Act would apply. Then, a very different type of change, the Walsh bill,[2] the Barden Bill,[3] and the Hartley Bill[4] would withdraw from the jurisdiction of the Board all disputes over jurisdiction and the like within a labor organization or between organizations with a common affiliation, say to the American Federation of Labor.

The law now in effect requires the employer to be neutral on the question of whether the workers shall be organized, and, if so, what organization shall represent them, and it forbids him to act in such manner as "to interfere with, restrain, or coerce employees" in the right of self-organization. The Walsh bill omits the word "interfere"; only employer restraint and coercion would still be prohibited. Moreover, this bill and the Smith Bill[5] would give the employer the right of "expression of opinion" on matters of organization and the like, so long as such expressions of opinion were not accompanied by acts or threats of discrimination. Important to note also is the fact that under the former of these measures an employer would not be responsible for the acts of those of his supervisory force not vested with the right to hire and fire. Inasmuch as in many cases hiring and firing are highly centralized, this would remove responsibility now resting upon the employer for unfair labor practices at the hands of many foremen and others among the supervisory staff. The Burke bill would likewise permit the employer

---

interested in the analyses and discussions contained in two articles in the *International Juridical Association Monthly Bulletin*, vol. 7, pp. 73, 76–84, and 85, 91–100 (January and February, 1939). The analyses cover many proposals made by private organizations and persons as well as by members of Congress. The proposals are discussed in light of the decisions rendered by the National Labor Relations Board and the interpretations made of the Act. See also Joseph Rosenfarb, *op. cit.*

[1] S. 1264 (the Burke Bill), S. 1550 (the Logan Bill), and H.R. 4400 (introduced by Congressman Lea), all of which were introduced during the 1st Session, 76th Congress.

[2] S. 1000, Sec. 9(c). This bill was introduced by Senator Walsh at the request of the A.F. of L. This and the "five-man board bill" later introduced at the request of the A.F. of L., are designed chiefly to protect the A.F. of L. and to handicap the C.I.O. in the struggle between these two organizations. In this struggle the A.F. of L. became opposed to the Board and adversely critical of certain parts of the Act that do not redound to its advantage. At the time of its enactment, the Act met with hearty support from the A.F. of L.

[3] H.R. 4749.

[4] H.R. 5231.

[5] H.R. 9195.

to "counsel or advise" in matters of organization, the clause permitting this not being directly qualified by prohibition of restraint or coercion. Furthermore, it is to be noted that the Walsh bill is so drafted as to permit the employer to favor one organization as against another. For example, it would amend Sec. 8(2) so that the employer could lend support to a labor organization, provided he did not finance it, compensate anyone for services performed in its behalf, or contribute to it money, services, or materials, and provided, further, that it was not a company union. The probable net result would be that an employer would be permitted under these amendments to do lawfully many things he cannot now do to interfere with a labor organization he does not like or wishes to destroy, or to encourage one organization as against another. The proposals would mark a departure from the principle of neutrality to be observed by the employer and his representatives and the doctrine that workers should be permitted to organize when and as they please without employer influence,[1] interference, restraint, or coercion.

If a word of comment may be introduced in this connection, the wisdom of such proposals may well be questioned. They are foreign to the assumptions and spirit of the Act. The right of freedom of speech and expression of opinion are not now limited except where there is such behavior as more or less seriously interferes with the right of self-organization. Both the Board and the courts have recognized that the employer is a somewhat interested party, but they have placed a ban on, but only on, such "expressions of opinion" and "counsel and advice" as, in their opinion, were intended to prevent or discourage organization or to favor one organization as against another.[2]

[1] It is interesting to note that the Railway Labor Act adds "influence" to "interfere" and "coercion."

[2] The leading case decided by the Supreme Court is *National Labor Relations Board, Petitioner, v. Virginia Electric and Power Company*, 314 U.S. 469 (1941). The Court said: "Neither the Act nor the Board's order here enjoins the employer from expressing its view on labor policies or problems, nor is a penalty imposed upon it because of any utterances it has made. The sanctions of the Act are imposed not in punishment of the employer but for the protection of the employees. The employer in this case is as free now as ever to take any side it may choose on this controversial issue. But certainly conduct, though evidenced in part by speech, may amount *in connection with other circumstances* to coercion within the meaning of the Act. *If the total activities of an employer restrain or coerce his employees in their free choice, then those employees are entitled to the protection of the Act, and in determining whether a course of conduct amounts to restraint or coercion, pressure exerted vocally by the employer may no more be disregarded than pressure exerted in other ways.*" (Italics ours). Since the decision in the *Virginia Electric and Power Company* case the Second Circuit Court of Appeals has upheld the right of an employer to express opinions concerning labor organizations whether favorable or unfavorable so long as they are unaccompanied by other antiunion conduct or do not form part of an integral pattern of antiunionism. *N.L.R.B. v. American Tube Bending Company*, 134 Fed. (2d) 993. Where the statements of an employer, however, are made in a context of intimidation or coercion

In safeguarding against unfair labor practices, the Board had by March, 1939, deemed it necessary to invalidate sixteen contracts or joint agreements with "outside unions" and sixty-two contracts with "inside" or company unions. The most important reasons were that although the favored union did not have a majority of the employees it had received a closed-shop contract, with the effect that the majority were denied representation by those of their choice, or that it was the smaller of two unions seeking an agreement, or that it had benefited from the employer's unfair labor practices. The object of the Board has been to re-establish the original status where there have been unfair practices and to safeguard the right of self-organization.[1] The American Federa-

---

the constitutional guarantee has been held inapplicable. *N.L.R.B. v. Trojan Powder Company*, 135 Fed. (2d) 603. In both cases the Supreme Court refused to entertain petitions for certiorari. The Third Circuit Court has also recently held in a contempt case that the right of freedom of speech extends to protect an employer found to have engaged in unfair labor practices by the National Labor Relations Board and by that Court. The employer, at the same time that it posted notices required by the Board's order as enforced by the Court, sent letters to all its employees expressing an unfavorable opinion of the union which represented them. The Court declared: "The Wagner Act does not purport to authorize a restraint upon freedom of speech in any circumstances. . . . Had there been such a provision in the statute it would have been invalid as in contravention of the first amendment. . . . Accordingly, it is our opinion that it was not the intention of Congress to forbid an employer from expressing opinions as to labor unions or to anything else so long as his expressions do not constitute, or contribute to, acts or threats of discriminations, coercion or intimidation in denial of his employees' free and untrammeled exercise of their rights as guaranteed by the Act." *N.L.R.B. v. Edward G. Budd Manufacturing Company*, decided May 13, 1944.

In view of the absence of a definitive pronouncement by the Supreme Court, the question of whether and under what circumstances an employer's antiunion statements may be considered outside the protection of the constitutional guarantee of freedom of speech, even though unaccompanied by other antiunion conduct, is not yet settled. In view of what is said in the text, it is important to note that in two important circuits the Courts have found that the Board's decisions, though in line with its decisions all the while, had been too restrictive. It may be added that at the present time (1944), "Tube Bending" speeches and letters are used by employers in many Board elections in an effort to defeat the union or to assist one union competing with another, and that not infrequently these speeches and letters are not of a mild type. More and more employers are ceasing to be neutral in matters of employee organization and representation.

[1] The Supreme Court decided adversely in some cases in which the Board had held a trade union-employer contract to be invalid. The best known of these cases is that of *Consolidated Edison Company v. National Labor Relations Board* [305 U.S. 197 (1938)]. The Edison Company had adopted an employee-representation plan. Early in 1937, the United, a C.I.O. union, was carrying on organizing activities. When the National Labor Relations Act was upheld by the Supreme Court, there was a conference between management and the President of the Electrical Workers, an A.F. of L. affiliate, out of which came a short agreement covering the members of the Electrical Workers only. Some members of the C.I.O. organization were discharged. The company cooperated in shifting membership from the Plan to the locals established by the Electrical Workers, unusual facilities were given the one set of organizers to carry on their activities, the agreement was spoken

tion of Labor has reacted strongly in some of the fifteen cases in which the contentions of its affiliates have not been accepted by the Board, and one of the bills[1] has sought such modification of Sec. 8(3) as would protect closed-shop contracts though made with a labor organization established, maintained, or assisted by the employer's unfair labor practices, provided, of course, that the organization was not a company union, and that the contract did not by its terms deprive the representative designated by a majority of exclusive bargaining rights.

The requirement of the Act that the employer shall bargain collectively with the properly accredited representatives of the appropriate unit has raised a number of issues. One of these has been whether the unit shall be the industrial group or a craft group contained therein. This issue is important in the struggle between the A.F. of L. and C.I.O., a struggle that began primarily over the question of industrial unionism. In deciding what units were appropriate in cases coming before it for decision, the Board has considered a number of factors, such as the

---

of as an exclusive one, it was announced that the company would deal with the Electrical Workers only, and a request made for conference by the United was denied. The United filed a complaint of violations of the Act. Hearings were held and, before the issues before the National Labor Relations Board had been decided, regular contracts with the Electrical Workers locals were consummated. The Board ruled that because of company unfair practices these agreements, though not made with a company union, were invalid and should not be given effect until such time as the workers had freely selected a collective-bargaining agency. This particular part of the decision was not accepted by the Supreme Court. In its opinion, other parts of the decision were sufficient to end such unfair labor practices as had occurred, and it was wrong to deprive a legitimate labor organization of the fruits of a contract whose terms were in harmony with the law. The court did not see in the case, as had the Board, a sort of conspiracy by the company and a lawful labor organization to interfere with organizational and collective-bargaining rights guaranteed by the Act.

In a later case [*International Association of Machinists; Tool and Die Makers Lodge No. 35, etc., v. National Labor Relations Board*, 311 U.S. 72 (1940)], the court upheld invalidation of a closed-shop contract with the A.F. of L. Machinists on the grounds that "there was substantial evidence that petitioner [the union] had been assisted by unfair labor practices of the employer. . . . " The "unfair labor practices" involved were not unlike those in *Consolidated Edison Company v. National Labor Relations Board*. Although the Machinists' case differs from the other in involving a closed-shop contract with a labor organization assisted by unfair labor practices, some of the court's language is difficult to reconcile with the Consolidated Edison decision. Upholding the Board's order directing the employer to bargain exclusively with a C.I.O. industrial union, the court said: "Where as a result of unfair labor practices a union cannot be said to represent an uncoerced majority, the Board has the power to take appropriate steps to the end that the effect of those practices will be dissipated. That necessarily involves an exercise of discretion on the part of the Board—discretion involving an expert judgment as to ways and means of protecting the freedom of choice guaranteed to the employees by the Act. It is for the Board not the courts to determine how the effect of prior unfair labor practices may be expunged."

[1] S. 1000, 76th Congress, 1st Session.

previous history of collective bargaining, if any, management practices with reference to wage adjustments and the like, relations between the occupational groups, the desires of the workers concerned, and the numerical importance of the special groups. In most cases subsequent to its Globe Machine and Stamping Co. decision[1] in 1937, however, the Board has applied the so-called "Globe doctrine"; but it has not applied it as an inelastic and invariable rule. The "Globe doctrine" permits the employees in the craft group, by vote or other expression of their wishes, to decide for themselves whether they desire to be in a separate craft unit or to be part of a larger unit including the craft group. If a majority of the craft employees express their preference for the craft union, then the Board holds the craft unit to be appropriate; on the other hand, if a majority of the craft employees express a preference for the union claiming the larger unit, then the Board includes the craft employees in the larger unit. In the opinion of the Board and in the opinion of many who have studied the matter realistically, this rule is fair, or perhaps more than fair,[2] to the craft unions, which may have interests not appreciated by workers over whom they seek jurisdiction. Though the A.F. of L. has on not infrequent occasions sought recognition of industrial groups, in some cases as against narrower groups supported by the C.I.O., it seeks in the so-called Walsh bill to obtain an inelastic rule and to deprive the Board of all discretion in the matter. The amendments, as revised since

[1] 3 N.L.R.B. 294.

[2] The Globe doctrine was first applied because the factors arguing for one union and those arguing for separate organization of the craft about balanced in the case. The Board said "let the workers decide." This, of course, meant let the craft workers who were interested decide. For a considerable time there appears to have been a tendency for a majority of the Board to apply the doctrine rather freely. Perhaps there has been too little consideration of the effect of separate organization of craftsmen upon the effective rights of the other employees to self-organization and to collective bargaining. Separate organization may weaken, even destroy, the organization of the noncraftsmen among the employees. The mandate of the Congress seems to be clear if "employees" is to be read as "all employees." The Act requires that a unit must be determined which will "insure to employees the full benefit of their right to self-organization and to collective bargaining." Cf. "N.L.R.B. Divides on Appropriate Bargaining Unit," in International Juridical Association Monthly Bulletin, vol. 8 (1939), pp. 31–37.

While accepting the Globe doctrine as applicable during the original organizing stage, Dr. Leiserson has recently contended that once recognition has been obtained and an agreement secured, the form of organization has been decided and the Board cannot or should not change it. The workers have decided and the Board is without power. This would have the effect of freezing in perpetuity any form of organization once it had been successfully used, unless "thawed out" without Board ruling. The wisdom of such a policy is very debatable, for the employment situation does and will change and union structure should at times be readjusted. No small block should make readjustment impossible. While emphasizing stability, as Dr. Leiserson does, room for change and adjustment finds place in sound policy. Dr. Leiserson's position, which was not accepted by the other members of the Board, was first stated In the Matter of American Can Company, 13 N.L.R.B. 1252 (1939).

S. 1000 was introduced, also H.R. 9195, provide that if a majority of employees in any craft group signify that such is their desire, the Board must designate the craft group as the appropriate bargaining unit. In badly phrased language, the Burke bill attempts the same modification of the Act; it reads, "Sec. 9(b) . . . *provided,* that if the majority of any craft union within a plant or employer unit signify its wish for the craft unit, the Board shall designate the craft unit as the unit appropriate for the members of that union."

If, here again, an opinion may be expressed, it may be said that these proposals are too favorable to craft organization. All too frequently employers have found that dealing with a number of unions is time consuming, and troublesome. Again, there is a strong tendency for each craft union to demand for its members a more favorable differential in wage rates than it has had, so that great pressure is exerted to gain increases and to avoid reductions in wages. This may work injury to the wage interests of the noncraft employees. The most important criticisms of the proposal, however, are that difficulty is involved in defining a craft, and that unconditional acceptance of the crafts as the bargaining units places a premium on the breaking away of minority groups from the parent organization and the formation of organizations of their own.[1] Existing craft, and especially multiple-craft, organizations might find their welfare and existence endangered. Finally, the proposals would, as perhaps they are intended to do, handicap labor organization along industrial lines. With technological change and economic advance, the industrial form of organization merits more recognition than it has, until recently, generally received in the United States.[2]

Another issue is that of whether the plant, or the company, or some more extended group should be accepted in determining the bargaining unit. Most collective agreements have been between an employer or corporation and the union and have covered one or more of the plants involved in the business, but in rather numerous and important cases they have been between the union and the associated employers of the locality, the district, or the nation. A number of reasons enter into the explanation of departures from the more general practice. In deciding whether the single plant or the employer's several plants, or the associated employers' plants, should be regarded as the appropriate unit for the selection of the labor agency for the purpose of collective bargaining, the National Labor Relations Board has in the overwhelming number of cases decided in favor of the plant or the associated plants of the given

---

[1] The most outstanding example of this is found in the case of the welders, who have sought to secure independence of the Boiler Makers, the Machinists, and other metal-trades organizations in shipbuilding and other industries. The welders have become an increasingly important craft.

[2] *Cf.* Chap. VI.

employer as the appropriate unit. In special cases, however, such as in water shipping, where the workers are engaged for short times by one employer and then by another, and where collective bargaining has been on a district-wide basis, it has decided in favor of a larger unit.[1] One organization has been certified as the collective-bargaining agency for the workers employed in the several associated plants, whereas in some plants another agency would have received a majority vote had the rule applied been plant by plant. Protests have been made. The Walsh, the Burke, and the Smith bills would eliminate the Board's discretion in the matter. The first of these provides "that an appropriate unit shall not embrace employees of more than one employer" [but] that "Two or more units may, by voluntary consent, bargain through the same agent . . . ," the second "That . . . if the majority of the employees of any plant . . . signifies its wish for the plant unit for voting or representation . . . the Board shall designate the plant unit as the unit appropriate for collective bargaining for the employees of that plant." Such modifications would in concrete cases place a premium on dual unionism in the industry and would in some instances militate against effective collective bargaining.

The determination of appropriate units and of appropriate organizations is incidental to the effectuation of collective bargaining. The Wagner Act (Sec. 9a) provides for majority rule. To repeat, for the sake of convenience: "Representatives designated or selected for the purposes of collective bargaining by the majority of the employees in a

---

[1] Among the cases so decided by the National Labor Relations Board are *In the matter of Shipowners' Association of the Pacific Coast* [and others] . . . *and International Longshoremen's and Warehousemen's Union, District* 1, 8 N.L.R.B. 1002 (1938), and *In the matter of Alston Coal Company and Progressive Mine Workers*, 13 N.L.R.B. 683 (1939). Both of these decisions have been vigorously criticized by the A.F. of L. In the first of the two cases the shipping industry of the entire Pacific Coast was taken as the appropriate unit because collective bargaining had in fact been on a coast-wide basis. While the C.I.O. organization received a minority of votes in some localities, it was certified because it received a majority of the total vote cast. In the Alston case, the company belonged to an association that had entered into agreements with the United Mine Workers. Its employees shifted allegiance to the Progressive Miners. The Board ruled that the United Mine Workers was the appropriate bargaining agency because of the history of collective bargaining in the district. These rulings are final. In *American Federation of Labor et al. v. National Labor Relations Board*, 309 U.S. 401, and in *National Labor Relations Board v. International Brotherhood of Electrical Workers et al.*, 308 U.S. 413 (both decided Jan. 2, 1940), the Supreme Court of the United States held that Congress had vested the Board with discretionary power to certify representatives and the courts have no right of review.

It is to be noted that in 1941, with a somewhat changed membership, the Board modified its earlier ruling in the first case mentioned so as to make three excepted ports separate units. For a discussion of this and other debated rulings, see Emily C. Brown, *The Employment Unit for Collective Bargaining in* "National Labor Relations Board Decisions," *Journal of Political Economy*, vol. 50 (1942), pp. 321–356.

unit appropriate for such purposes, shall be the exclusive representatives of all the employees in such unit for the purposes of collective bargaining in respect of rates of pay, wages, hours of employment, or other conditions of employment: *Provided*, that any individual employee or a group of employees shall have the right at any time to present grievances to their employer." Majority rule, without which collective bargaining cannot well succeed and instability and strife be avoided, was vigorously opposed in 1935 by those organizations opposed to effective unionism and collective bargaining. The opposition is once more articulate. Two of the pending bills[1] would abolish majority rule.

The Burke bill and the Hoffmann bill (H.R. 4990) strike directly at the provision making it an unfair labor practice for an employer to refuse to bargain collectively. These bills define collective bargaining to mean much less than the term actually means, was expected to mean when the Act was adopted, and the Board has consistently and properly held it to mean.[2] The Burke proposal is: "The phrase 'collective bargaining' for the purpose of this Act shall be understood to mean the meeting together of the employer and his employees, through accredited representatives voluntarily chosen by them, with the full and free opportunity for negotiating concerning the terms or conditions of employment."[3]

In the guise of equalization, attempts were made in 1935 so to amend the Wagner-Connery bill as to impose limitations and saddle responsibilities upon trade unions. Since its enactment the statute has been criticized as "unequal" and "one-sided." Proposals made in 1935, and still others, now find place in the Burke, the Hoffman, and other bills, which appear to meet with general approval at the hands of organizations all the while opposed to the Act. Under the Burke bill, it would be "an unfair labor practice for a labor organization, or any officer or officers of a labor organization, or any agent or agents of a labor organization, or any one acting in the interest of a labor organization, or for an employee, or for employees acting in concert:

1. "To interfere with, restrain, or coerce employees in the exercise of the rights of [self-organization, etc.] guaranteed in Section 7";

2. "To threaten, intimidate, restrain by force or threat, or coerce any employee, directly or indirectly, for the purpose and with the intent of compelling him to join or not to join any labor organization, to continue or to cease his employment, or to influence or affect his selection of representatives for the purpose of collective bargaining";

3. "To resort to or engage in, during the course of any labor dispute, any act or practice which is a violation of any civil or criminal law effective in the jurisdiction in which such act or practice occurs";

[1] S. 1580 and H.R. 4990.
[2] *Cf. supra*, pp. 529-533.
[3] Sec. 2 (14).

4. To interfere with the employer's business by jurisdiction disputes, etc.;

5. "To strike except in pursuance of an affirmative vote of a majority of the employees in the appropriate unit, the vote to be taken by secret ballot"; or

6. "To strike in violation of a valid contract or agreement."

Though coercion by labor is forbidden by the Railway Labor Act, it is of doubtful wisdom to insert it into a law applicable to industry in general, for one reason because of the meaning that might be given the word "coercion," for another because coercion is already under the ban of state law and local ordinances and regulations, and, for still another, because the National Labor Relations Board cannot handle police matters. The existing law relating to coercion by labor should be appropriately enforced. Number 3 of the above is very definitely objectionable because it would give recognition and application to many severe antiunion laws and ordinances that should be appropriately revised, as well as to acceptable civil and criminal law. Then, too, the federal Act would be different in its application in the several states.

The other paragraphs of the Burke bill are directed against certain types of strikes. Though at certain points corresponding behavior on the part of employers would be an unfair labor practice, no attempt is made to impose equal limitations and responsibilities upon employers and labor. Moreover, those clauses would provide opportunity for an employer to escape responsibility for any unfair labor practice of his own by engaging in strike-producing behavior. Section 10(c) of this proposed measure provides that any unfair labor practice on the part of labor, even by one worker, shall serve as a complete defense against prosecution for an employer's unfair labor practice. In practice most employers could proceed with any unfair practice because almost always some member or members of a labor organization will have engaged, or can be provoked or induced to engage, in some unfair practice as defined in this bill. If one or more members, say, should violate some picketing ordinance, the employer would have a complete defense for his unfair labor practice in discharging all the union men found in his plant. From the point of view of fairness, law enforcement, and sound industrial relations, the several proposals are not well conceived. From the point of view of administration at the hands of a board, they are bad. There would be charges and counter charges, important and trivial; cases might be endlessly drawn out where time is exceedingly important, and the Act would become unworkable. Though questions of motive should generally be avoided, there may be truth in the charge that it is desired so to amend the Act that it would break down in practice.

The Burke bill would further weaken the protection afforded labor and reduce the penalties and responsibilities imposed by the Act upon offending employers by defining an industrial dispute so that it would be regarded as "current" only until such time as a volume of production sufficient to fill orders as scheduled had been secured, by requiring that complaints could not be filed after the elapse of thirty days from the time the unfair labor practice was engaged in, and, while permitting "severance pay," by barring "reinstatement of employees against the will of the employer."[1] This last provision, while avoiding undesirable situations sometimes involved in reinstatements, would, when combined with limited severance pay, make it possible for employers at little cost to discharge union leaders and active union members. It would tend strongly to defeat a primary object of the Act, and one receiving real or pretended acceptance by almost everyone.[2]

With little justification evident in its decisions, the National Labor Relations Board has been severely and widely criticized as prounion and, as between rival organizations, pro-C.I.O. Unfounded or only slightly founded rumor, misunderstanding, and positive misrepresentation have been followed by proposals to disestablish the Board, or/and to change procedures, to curtail the authority of the Board, even to revise the Act so that the Board's powers and procedures would cause the Act to be quite different from what it is—these in addition to the proposals already noted.

An A.F. of L. bill[3] has called for a new five-man board; the Burke bill[4] calls for a new three-man board consisting of an employer representative, an employee representative, and a public representative.

The Burke bill[5] and also the Hoffman bill would permit any person against whom a proceeding is brought at any time within twenty days of filing of complaint to secure removal of the case to the district court of the judicial district in which such person resides or engages in business. With such removal, the Board would be shorn of all responsibility and power. Were this proposal adopted, most cases would almost certainly be removed to the courts. Not only would diverse interpretations and applications of law result, but the calendars of the courts would be more crowded than they now are, unless, as would probably occur, the aggrieved parties concluded that it was worthless to press complaints in many districts in which the judges are less vigilant and more conservative than almost any specialized, national, semijudicial board would be. The Burke bill, as well as several others, would also change the law or rule

[1] Section 10 (c).
[2] While the Smith bill (H.R. 9195) also introduces limitations, they are much less drastic. No complaint may be filed charging an unfair labor practice more than six months prior, and recovery for loss of wages is limited to one year.
[3] H.R. 4749. Still other House bills, including H.R. 4990 (Hoffman) and H.R. 5231 (Hartley), also provide for a new board to replace the present one.
[4] S. 1264, Sec. 3.
[5] S. 1264, Sec. 11.

with reference to the admission of evidence and in other respects. A section of the Burke bill[1] would provide that "In any such proceeding the rules of evidence prevailing in courts of law shall be substantially followed but shall not be absolutely controlling," a rule more strict and more favorable to aggrieving employers than the rule now in effect and sanctioned by the highest court. The Anderson bill[2] would go farther than the Burke bill in that all cases would be heard and decided by the courts; the Board would be deprived of its judicial functions. The Holman bill[3] would set up wholly new machinery, including a Labor Relations Commissioner in the Department of Labor, who would have administrative and investigatory functions and would bring all actions to restrain violations and to secure enforcement of the law; all litigation would be subject to the direction and control of the Attorney General; hearings would be before and decisions made by a Labor Appeals Board composed of nine members, all but two of whom must be attorneys at law. The Smith bill, likewise the Walter-Logan bill, which would apply to a very large number of federal agencies, are designed to accomplish the same separation of powers.

The former of these two measures would divide the functions of the present National Labor Relations Board between it and an administrator. The administrator would have charge of the regional offices, the investigation and acceptance of charges, and the prosecution of cases before the Board, which, except that it would still handle representation cases, would become a trial court, with the circuit courts having the right to review the facts as well as the legal issues.

An object of this proposed separation of functions and power is to meet the claim that the present Board is "prosecutor, judge and jury," a claim of little merit because of the assignments of duties under the present organization and because only a court can make a decision binding and enforce cease-and-desist orders. The observation may be added that the Federal Trade Commission, the Interstate Commerce Commission, and other quasi-judicial departments of the government are organized and proceed in a manner similar to that prevailing under the Wagner Act, and that delegation of power to an administrative body is in accord with a trend in governmental affairs the underlying principle of which has long been generally approved. The object of the Congress in all these cases has been to secure the most effective machinery and procedures for dealing with specialized and difficult problems.

Further observations may be made on the Smith bill, which was passed by the House but not by the Senate. The measure would result in the establishment of two groups of persons for fact-finding purposes,

[1] Sec. 10 (b).
[2] H.R. 2761.
[3] S. 1392.

the one employed by the Board to serve in representation cases, the other employed by the administrator to investigate charges of unfair labor practice. If it is proper for the Board's agents to investigate representation questions and conduct elections, even though the Board must later decide issues raised by the investigation, why is it not equally proper to have its own agents investigate charges of unfair labor practice?

Really important is the fact that, were the Smith bill enacted, it would tend strongly to make the Board's hearing room a place of contest between lawyers as in an ordinary law court. The administrator's lawyers, to a greater extent than the Board's present legal staff, would try to obtain as many convictions as possible. The Act is misconceived by the authors of the Smith and other bills. It is not a penal statute. It was designed to be merely remedial and educational, as were the measures administered by the Interstate Commerce Commission and Securities Exchange Commission. The remedial and educational objectives of the Act, as Dr. Leiserson has observed, need to be maintained and emphasized more than they have been. The objectives of the Act can only be realized by improved administration and more careful and objective investigations and administration, not by amendments that encourage prosecutions and convictions.

Through such measures as these noted have the National Labor Relations Act and the National Labor Relations Board been challenged— but without legislative change in the Act. Numerous bills introduced in state legislatures during the 1939 and subsequent sessions have contained some of the same or similar proposals. Save in Rhode Island the new state industrial-relations acts have been of a different type from those of 1937; they have been designed to serve interests and have reflected ideas different from those in the ascendancy seven years ago.[1]

As already stated, Wisconsin in 1939 repealed its 1937 statute and adopted a substantially different one.[2] An Employment Relations Board replaced the Industrial Relations Board. The ban on unfair labor practices of employers was weakened—although how far will depend upon court rulings—by the deletion of the word "interference" from the clause "interference, intimidation or coercion from any source" used in the 1937 law to protect the right to organize. An employer was given the right to favor and aid a particular organization of his employees if he does not thereby cause "additional expense to his company." He may petition for an election to determine representation for the purpose of collective bargaining; in holding an election, the Board may, in its discretion, exclude from the ballot "one who, at the time of the

---

[1] In the following general summary of state laws enacted since 1939, the popularly voted Oregon Act is omitted, though its provisions affected measures drafted elsewhere. It is summarized infra, pp. 617-619.

[2] Act 154, approved May 3, 1939.

election, stands deprived of his rights . . . by reason of a prior adjudication of his having engaged in an unfair labor practice"; a craft must be recognized as the appropriate bargaining unit if a majority of those in the craft so elect. Many limitations are placed upon labor activities under listed employee unfair labor practices or otherwise. These unfair labor practices include coercion or intimidation of workers in connection with the exercise of their right to join or not to join a labor organization; coercion of an employer to engage in what would be an unfair labor practice if the employer acted on his own motion; refusal to recognize final determinations of competent tribunals, such as engaging in a strike when another organization has been certified as the collective-bargaining agency; engaging in picketing or boycotting unless a strike has been called by a majority of the employees involved; mass picketing, which had been widely practiced in that state; secondary boycotts (which had already been under the ban of the law); taking unauthorized possession of the employer's property (the stay-in strike); and failure to give a required ten days' notice of intention to strike if the workers are engaged in the production, harvesting, or initial processing of any farm or dairy product. Moreover, since it is now provided that it is an unfair labor practice for employers or employees "to violate the terms of a collective bargaining agreement, including an agreement to accept an arbitration award," collective agreements are recognized and made binding at law. Again, the legality of a closed-shop agreement is conditional on the affirmative vote of three-fourths of the employees in a collective-bargaining unit.[1] The Board is empowered to terminate such a closed-shop agreement when it finds that any union has unreasonably refused to admit workers into membership; and the checkoff of union dues is banned unless authorized by each worker concerned. Finally, in the enumeration of only the more important provisions of the measure, employees who have been found to have committed an unfair labor practice are disqualified from receiving the benefits of the Act. Such are the important new features of a measure designed to protect the "rights" of individual workers, farmers, creameries, employers, and the public from infringement quite as much as to protect the "rights" of workers to organize if and when they wish for the purpose of collective bargaining.

With the impaired status given employees engaging in strikes or guilty of unfair labor practices, with a narrower definition of collective bargaining, with the plant fixed as the appropriate unit, with a craft

---

[1] In 1943 the Wisconsin Employment Peace Act was amended to require approval of a closed-shop agreement by three-fourths of the voting employees, provided such three-fourths constitute a majority of employees in the bargaining unit, instead of by three-fourths of the employees affected, as originally provided. Chap. 465, approved July 7, 1943.

therein made the appropriate unit when desired by a majority, with company unions finding place on ballots while bona fide unions may be disqualified because of unfair practices committed, with a three-quarters majority limitation on the closed shop, and with limitations on the right to strike, this Wisconsin Act is substantially different from the National Labor Relations Act and the older model of state acts.[1] It therefore presents greater possibilities of conflict between state and federal law in its administration than is found elsewhere. Indeed, there is little opportunity for conflict between the federal and the state laws of New York, Massachusetts, Rhode Island, and Utah, for the laws of these states are based upon the Wagner Act and differ from it in no significant respect.

The federal act is, of course, not an exclusive one. The Congress has not limited the application of state law except when the latter is in conflict with the federal, which is the controlling law if and when applied within constitutional bounds. This was no doubt the intent of the Congress and this intent has been made clear by the courts. In the 1942 case of *United Electrical Radio and Machine Workers of America v. Wisconsin Employment Relations Board*,[2] involving an order directed against mass picketing, the Supreme Court held that the State Act was not to be treated as an inseparable whole and found that the particular provision against that type of picketing was not hostile to the policy expressed in the federal Act and the union activities involved were in no way guaranteed by that Act. Mr. Justice Douglas said: "In sum, we cannot say that the mere enactment of the National Labor Relations Act, without more, excluded state regulation of the type which Wisconsin has exercised in this case. It has not been shown that any employee was deprived of rights protected or granted by the Federal Act or that the status of any of them under the federal Act was impaired."

The Wisconsin Act is inclusive in its scope, applying to employment relations in any plant in the state, without regard to whether the business involved is interstate or only intrastate. The State Board has taken jurisdiction in any case over which the National Labor Relations Board has not. Indeed, there have been a few instances in which the Board has entertained cases involving interstate commerce that had been or were before the National Labor Relations Board or has applied state rules in

---

[1] Its administration also differs from that of the federal Act in that field investigations do not precede hearings and that the Board sits as a bench and its legal staff does not participate in a case until the stage of compliance with a Board order is reached. And of course under the Wisconsin Act mediation is emphasized, a function not exercised by the National Labor Relations Board. During the years 1939 to June 30, 1942, the Wisconsin Employment Relations Board handled 825 cases. Of these, 227 were mediation or arbitration, 147 unfair labor practice, and 229 election cases. Of the 147 unfair labor practice cases received, complaint was against employer in 97, against union in 50. Data supplied by Secretary of the Board.

[2] 315 U.S. 740.

conflict with federal provisions applied somewhat later by the National Labor Relations Board in the same cases.[1] Any such problem is, however, now being met, at least in part, by an arrangement for quick clearance of cases by the two boards. Moreover, the recent decision of the Supreme Court referred to above leaves no doubt that, if contested, any state order that deprived a party of a right guaranteed by the Federal Act would be set aside. The following conclusion is an appropriate one: "In short, the State Board *must* give consideration in each case to a factor, which it heretofore has deemed irrelevant: does the proposed state order deprive employees of rights protected by the National Labor Relations Act? If it does, the order is unconstitutional and will not be enforced. In this manner the National Labor Relations Act may prove only less effective as a protection of employees' rights where it is invoked as a check upon intrusions through state law than it has been where the direct remedial assistance of an N.L.R.B. order has been obtained."[2] Nevertheless, it should be said that while much may be learned concerning best policy from experience under somewhat different regulations, the ideal in the immediate situation would be to have federal and state legislation in close harmony and complementary, all of it expressing the best public policy, whatever that may be thought to be.

Unlike Wisconsin, where the act of 1937 was repealed and a new and conservative one substituted, Pennsylvania in 1939 merely amended its 1937 law, but it thereby attained somewhat similar results.[3] Two important changes were made in the section enumerating unfair labor practices of employers. In the prior act all-union shop contracts were expressly exempted from the provision prohibiting discrimination by employers with reference to hire and tenure of employment; now a closed-shop contract is permissible only if the union does not deny membership to anyone employed at the time the contract is made except those who have been employed in violation of any previously existing agreement. Secondly, the checkoff of union dues from wages is now prohibited unless authorized both by a majority of the employees by secret ballot and by each individual affected. In addition, the amended act declares certain acts of employees to be unfair labor practices and those guilty of them are denied the benefits of the act. Among the unfair labor practices are: participation in stay-in strikes; intimidation or coercion of any employee to compel him to join or refrain from joining a labor organization; and intimidation or coercion of an employer with the intent of compelling him to accede to demands made upon him. Further changes made by the act include these: only employers or unions who have not committed unfair labor practices may petition for the certification of representatives;

---

[1] For the particular instances, see International Juridical Association, *Monthly Bulletin*, vol. 10, no. 12 (May, 1942), p. 129.

[2] *Ibid.*, p. 129.

[3] Laws (1939), Act 162.

the Labor Relations Board is limited in ordering affirmative actions by the word "reasonable"; the right to order reinstatement of employees is limited to those discharged in violation of the section prohibiting discrimination in hire or tenure; awards of back pay may not extend beyond six weeks prior to the time the complaint is filed. Moreover, a labor organization filing a complaint of unfair practice must itself present its case before the Board or its examiner; the Board and its agents are not to "serve as prosecutor and judge." Put in other words, complaints are to be treated as private, not as matters of public concern.[1]

Though like the Wisconsin Act in certain respects, the Minnesota Labor Relations Act[2] differs from it in important ways. Under this act the unfair labor practices of an employer are extremely limited. While the statute recognizes the rights of workers to self-organization and to form, join, or assist labor organizations, to bargain collectively through representatives of their own choosing, and to engage in lawful concerted activities, it does not specifically declare it to be an unfair labor practice for an employer to dominate or interfere with the formation or administration of labor organizations or to refuse to bargain collectively. Nor is there an administrative agency designated or empowered to prevent unfair labor practices or even to investigate them. Finally, it is to be noted that the office of Labor Conciliator is created and provisions made for the calling and settlement of strikes along the general lines followed in Canada since 1908.[3] Like the Wisconsin Act, on the other hand, a strike or lockout against a joint agreement is made unlawful; any employer, employee, or organization guilty of an unfair labor practice is without right of benefit under the Act; it is unlawful for any employee or union to compel or to attempt to compel any person to join or to refrain

---

[1] In *Pennsylvania Labor Relations Board v. Heindel Motors Inc.* Mar. 23, 1942, 10 L.R.R. 177, the Supreme Court of Pennsylvania held that the State Board cannot appeal to the Supreme Court from a decision of the Court of Common Pleas setting aside a Board order. Apparently only a party to the dispute, the union or the employer, is empowered to do so.

[2] Chapter 440, Laws (1939), approved Apr. 22, 1939.

[3] A ten-day notice is required of a labor organization or an employer if there is a desire to negotiate a collective-bargaining agreement, to change an existing agreement, or to change rates of pay, rules, or working conditions. It is the duty of employer and employee representatives to "endeavor in good faith to reach an agreement respecting such demand." At the end of the ten-day period, if negotiations have failed, notice of intention to strike or lockout may be served; but it is unlawful to engage in or aid in the conduct of a strike or lockout unless notice is served on the Labor Conciliator and other parties ten days before the effective date. In industries affected with a public interest, such as businesses supplying necessities of life, safety, or health—in addition to the above—the governor shall be notified and he may appoint a commission of three to conduct hearings and file a report. A strike or lockout is unlawful until after a report has been filed or until thirty days after notification of the governor. A 1941 amendment provides that if he fails to appoint a commission within five days, the time limitation is suspended. Of the ten cases in which commissions were appointed during the first year of the Act five were settled before the commissions completed their work. *Chicago Sunday Tribune*, Sept. 21, 1940, Part 1, p. 16.

from joining a union or to strike against his will, by any threatened or actual unlawful interference with his person, immediate family, or physical property; it is unlawful likewise to seize or occupy property during a labor dispute, to picket a place where no strike is in progress, or to have more than one picket at a point of ingress or egress, or for anyone not there employed to picket a place of employment unless the majority of pickets are employees of that place. For determining cases of representation in collective bargaining the Conciliator is to conduct elections and the craft must be recognized as the appropriate unit for the representation of those who are members of it.[1]

The Michigan Act[2] contains a provision similar to those found in Minnesota and Wisconsin permitting workers to organize, join, or assist unions, and to bargain collectively, but it differs from both of these acts in several respects. Not only does it declare certain specified acts of employers to be unlawful, but it makes them punishable as misdemeanors. Among these acts are the creation, encouragement, or domination by employers of company unions. Neither the Minnesota nor the Wisconsin Act limits company unions directly or to any significant extent. Following the recent trend in state legislation, the Michigan Act places many limitations upon labor and its activities. Specific unfair labor practices of employees are established, violation of which is a misdemeanor. These include the use of force, coercion, and intimidation against employees to cause them to join labor organizations or to refrain from engaging in employment. The right to strike is also limited. In case of a labor dispute that the parties thereto are unable to settle, a strike cannot be called until notice is served upon a mediation board, created by the Act. The Board must then be given five days to undertake adjustment of the dispute, and the parties are directed to "undertake a mediation" during this period. The Act gives the Board discretionary power, after tender of notice or on its own motion, to attempt to facilitate a settlement. At the direction of the Governor this duty is mandatory. If the industry is affected with a public interest, a thirty-day notice is necessary before a strike, lockout, or change in normal operations may be undertaken. Under these circumstances the Act provides for the appointment of a special committee by the Governor to attempt mediation. Similar to acts recently passed in other states, the Michigan Act also contains a provision outlawing the stay-in strike, which is here made a misdemeanor.

Likewise the Kansas Labor Relations Act of 1943[3] does not follow the pattern of the earlier state Labor Relations Act, but includes features

---

[1] During the first year's operation of the Act, there were only twenty-five strikes—a reduction of more than 50 per cent from the average of sixty-two strikes for the preceding three years. Over 600 disputes were settled peacefully. Report of the Labor Conciliator as published in *ibid*.

[2] Public Act 176, 1939.

[3] S. 264, 1943.

of the Wisconsin Employment Peace Act as well as of the National Labor Relations Act. Unfair labor practices of employers are defined much as they are in the Wagner Act, but the right of employees to refuse to engage in concerted action receives emphasis equal with their right to engage in such activities.[1] Unlike the federal statute, however, discrimination in hiring and discharging are not prohibited by the Kansas Act of 1943. Among the activities of employees and labor organizations defined as "unfair labor practices" are participation in a strike without authorization of the majority of employees by secret ballot, entering into a closed-shop agreement unless upon authorization of the majority of employees to be governed thereby, and picketing which interferes with the employees' right to work. In addition, jurisdictional disputes, sympathetic strikes, and secondary boycotts are outlawed, and a degree of state regulation of union affairs is established.[2]

Colorado's 1943 "Labor Peace Act"[3] also includes the main features of the Wisconsin Employment Peace Act, as well as others. The State Industrial Commission is charged with determination and certification of representatives for purposes of collective bargaining and with the appointment of mediators. The "Statement of Public Policy" declares that whatever the rights of disputants in industrial controversies, their conduct shall not be permitted to intrude on the primary rights of third parties to earn a livelihood or to transact business. Among the "unfair labor practices" of employees (in addition to those included in the Wisconsin Act) are "sit-down" strikes and demands for the use of "stand-in" employees not required by the employer. Persons committing an unfair labor practice are liable to civil suit and may also be punished by fine for misdemeanor.[4] A Florida 1943 statute,[5] in addition to providing for

---

[1] Provisions of the Kansas Act of 1943 with respect to picketing, the closed shop, and other matters are summarized in the following chapter. For a summary of all the important provisions of this Act, see *Monthly Labor Review*, vol. 56 (May, 1943), pp. 942–943.

[2] See *Infra*, p. 619.

[3] S. 183, 1943.

[4] Other provisions of the Colorado Act 1943, summarized in the following chapter, include the following: the State Industrial Commission may limit picketing which would "tend to disturb"; there must be a thirty-days' "cooling-off" period in the case of threatened strikes involving the production, harvesting, or initial processing of farm and dairy products and a twenty-days similar period in the case of all other industries; prohibition of closed-shop agreements unless these are approved by a three-fourths vote of the employees affirmatively entering into such agreements. Contracts providing for maintenance of union membership are declared to be contrary to public policy and cannot be enforced in the courts. A compulsory incorporation provision was also included in the statute, but was the same year (1943) declared by the Supreme Court of Colorado to be unconstitutional. The statute also provides for audit of union books by the State Industrial Commission, annual election of union officials, and Commission approval or alteration of union dues and fees, and prohibits the use of union funds for political purposes. See *Monthly Labor Review*, vol. 56 (May, 1943), pp. 943–944.

[5] H. 142, 1943. For a summary of the provisions see *Monthly Labor Review*, vol. 57 (October, 1943), pp. 778–779.

regulation and reporting of the affairs of unions,[1] defines "unfair labor practices" on the part of employees along the lines of the 1943 Kansas model. Striking because of an interunion dispute or without majority authorization in secret ballot, picketing beyond the area in which the labor dispute arises or by force or violence in such manner as to prevent ingress or egress, or which interferes with an employee's right to work, and prevention of any union elections or interference with the right of franchise of any union member are declared to be unlawful.

Law of the Strike and the Lockout.—In exerting pressure upon employers to recognize them and to accept their demands, unions, provided argument is unsuccessful,[2] resort to the strike, the boycott, and possibly violence and sabotage. The employers resort to corresponding methods —the lockout, the black list, and violence. Leaving violence, which, it is to be regretted, has not infrequently been used by both workers and employers in the United States, to be discussed presently,[3] we turn to a discussion of the law relating to the strike and the lockout, the boycott and the black list, and to picketing and other incidental matters.

The strike has been and is organized labor's great weapon when differences are not settled by conciliation, mediation, or arbitration. From its use or threatened use the union obtains most of its power on the industrial field. Its counterpart on the employer's side, and matching it fairly accurately, is the lockout.

A strike should be defined or described, not, as some courts formerly did, as a concerted quitting of employment, but as a concerted leaving off or suspension of work, such suspension being intended to be temporary and working relations to be resumed when acceptable conditions are obtained. A lockout should be similarly defined, except, possibly, in those cases where the intention is not to permit the workers who are locked out to return to work under any circumstances—*i.e.*, where it involves a personal black list of all workers concerned, as it has in not a few instances. It then becomes a black list and should be so regarded. It must be noted, however, that these definitions of the strike and the lockout are not entirely adequate, for a suspension has almost always been preceded by formulation and presentation of "demands" and by failure to agree. The formulation and presentation of demands and quitting work involve concerted action. The same is true of the lockout when two or more employers are concerned, which is often the case in the more important suspensions of this type.

Arbitration laws, discussed in Chaps. XIII and XIV, may of course prohibit or place restrictions upon strikes and lockouts, while strikes by

---

[1] See *infra*, pp. 619–620.

[2] Of course cases involving refusal to recognize are now most frequently taken up under the National Labor Relations Act and strikes held in abeyance.

[3] See *infra*, pp. 667–689.

public employees, such as policemen, may be forbidden. In the United States the chief limitations of this kind have been imposed by the compulsory investigation law in Colorado, the restrictive laws recently adopted in Michigan, Minnesota, and Georgia,[1] the Industrial Court Act in Kansas,[2] the federal legislation relating to railway disputes,[3] and the National Labor Relations Act.[4]

Restriction under arbitration laws and other legislation may be reserved for later discussion, and attention here centered, first, upon the law of the lockout and, then, upon that of the strike.

Law of the Lockout.—At common law[5] the lockout may be practiced without legal restriction, whether by a single employer or by a voluntary association of employers directly interested. Numbers make no difference; what one employer may do, two or more may do acting in concert. Indeed, a member may be penalized by his association for failure to observe his obligation to cooperate in its lockout activities.[6] The one exception (at common law) to the principle that the lockout may be practiced by those personally concerned without legal limitation is found in decisions rendered by some courts holding that a lockout in violation of a joint agreement in effect is unlawful. Such was the ruling in New York[7] when the manufacturers locked out the Ladies' Garment Workers in 1921. In that case the manufacturers were enjoined from doing anything in violation of the terms of a joint agreement that was to expire some months later. Decisions of this character have in more recent years been made by the courts in a number of other states.[8] In 1941, California amended its Labor Code[9] to provide that collective agreements between an employer and a labor organization shall be enforceable at law or in equity,

---

[1] *Cf. supra*, pp. 551–553 and *infra*, pp. 619–620.

[2] See Chap. XIV.

[3] See *infra*, pp. 730–748.

[4] There are also special laws against stay-in or sit-down strikes.

[5] Statutory limitations on the lockout, such as under industrial-relations acts, will be discussed presently.

[6] *Associated Hat Manufacturers v. Baird-Unteidt Company,* 88 Conn. 332 (1914). But an association may not coerce a nonassociation member—a third party—to go along with it. Such was the ruling, for example, in *Carpenters' Union v. Citizens' Committee to Enforce the Landis Award*, 333 Ill. 225 (1928).

[7] *Schlesinger v. Quinto*, 201 N.Y. App. Div. 487 (1922); 194 N.Y. Supp. 401. Similar rulings have been made, among others, in *Golden v. Cohen*, 227 N.Y. Supp. 311 (1928); *Farulla v. Freundlich*, 274 N.Y. Supp. 70 (1934); *Ribner v. Racso Butter & Egg Co., Inc.*, 135 Misc. 616, 238 N.Y. Supp. 132 (S. Ct., Kings County, 1929); *Goldman v. Rosenzweig*, Sup. Ct. N.Y. Co. (1928); *Rifkin v. Mandelbaum*, Sup. Ct. N.Y. Co. (1928); and *Dubinsky v. Blue Dale Dress Co., Inc.*, 292 N.Y. Supp. 898 (1936); *Adler & Sons v. Maglio*, 200 Wisconsin 153 (1929); and *Pearlman v. Miller*, Sup. Ct. Suffolk County, Massachusetts (1925). Numerous cases are cited, with summary statements, in Plaintiffs' Trial Memorandum in the case of *Dubinsky v. Blue Dale Dress Co., Inc.*, 292 N.Y. Supp. 898 (1936).

[8] See Chap. XII, pp. 665–666.

[9] Chap. 1188.

and a breach of such agreement by any party thereto shall be subject to the same remedies, including injunctive relief, as are available on other contracts in the state's courts.

Of course the courts would be expected to regard a strike in violation of an agreement as unlawful in those jurisdictions, such as New York, in which they regard the corresponding lockout as unlawful.[1] But beyond this, the courts in applying the common law have placed limitations upon strikes not placed upon lockouts. Nor is this fact explained entirely by the nature of the concrete cases coming to the courts for decision. In California alone, it is said, have all strikes been held to be lawful.[2]

Law of the Strike.—In the case of the strike, numbers and relationships may, under conspiracy-doctrine premises,[3] make a difference. A worker may lawfully leave the job, but it does not follow that what one worker may do lawfully, two or more may do when acting in concert. Where concerted action is involved, the motive and the method are subject to judicial inquiry; a strike may be held to be unlawful because of lack of necessary degree of proximity of interest, or because of unlawfulness of the object in view, or because of unlawful methods employed in its prosecution.[4]

The purely sympathetic strike the courts have generally condemned as illegal because the possible benefit accruing from it has been regarded as remote and indirect. There is not just cause. Injury to employers other than those directly involved has then been regarded as the outstanding fact; in its essence such a strike is like the unlawful boycott of third parties and malicious.[5] But the dividing line between sympathetic strikes and nonsympathetic or primary strikes is not a clean-cut one. Not infrequently struck work is taken over by another employer so that orders may be filled. If the strike then spreads to the plants of other employers, the refusal to do strike-bound work, defensive though it is as seen by organized workers, may be held to be unlawful. Such has been

---

[1] On Dec. 9, 1938, for example, the New York Court of Appeals upheld the validity of the complaint of Nevins, Inc., accusing a waiters' and waitresses' union of violating an agreement not to strike. Overruling the Appellate Division, Second Department, the court ruled unanimously that officers of the local union could be directed by an equity court to live up to their contract. *Nevins, Inc. v. Kosmach*, 18 N.E. (2d) 294 (1938).

[2] The leading California case is that of *Parkinson v. Building Trades Council*, 154 Cal. 581 (1908).

[3] *Cf. supra*, pp. 499–506.

[4] To say that a strike is unlawful does not mean that the rank and file who participate in it may be proceeded against and compelled, under penalty, to work. It does mean that the calling of a strike or the activities of officers may be enjoined and that damage suits may be brought. Anyone who violates an injunction may be cited and punished for contempt.

[5] *Infra*, pp. 583–587.

the view of a considerable number of the courts.   This position, however, now appears to be rather exceptional.[1]

As just indicated, it is a matter of judgment what is of sufficiently immediate and proximate benefit to be lawful, what too remote and indirect with the element of malice likely in consequence to be more apparent.   Just what will be permitted and what regarded as malicious has not been entirely clear, and the views of different courts have differed, but it may be said that there was, from the 1890's to the 1920's, a tendency for the courts to define needed proximity of interest more narrowly than theretofore.   In this connection the Duplex case was important, though the primary issues there were those involving the boycott.[2]

The Duplex Printing Company was engaged in the manufacture of printing presses that were marketed in competition with the products of three companies operating union shops.   These companies complained of an unequal competition due chiefly to substantial differences in wages paid and hours worked per week; to leave the Duplex plant unorganized was to threaten the maintenance of collective bargaining in the manufacture of printing presses.   The machinists, therefore, called an organization strike against the Duplex Company.   Only eleven of some 200 workers employed in the plant located at Battle Creek, Mich., and three road men responded to the call.   Machinists in New York and elsewhere, belonging to locals of the same international and interested in conditions in the industry, came to the strikers' assistance.   There were refusals to install or to repair Duplex presses, a trucking firm was warned not to haul them, and an exposition company was threatened with a strike if it exhibited them.   A restraining order was issued against this behavior and the case thus initiated was carried to the Supreme Court of the United

---

[1] Some courts have granted restraining orders against strikes by union men to avoid doing work transferred from a strike-bound plant [see *Piano & Organ Workers' International Union v. Piano & Organ Supply Company*, 124 Ill. App. 353 (1906); *Schlang v. Ladies' Waist Makers' Union*, 124 N.Y. Supp. 289 (1910); *Barnes v. Chicago Typographical Union*, 232 Ill. 424 (1908)].   Other courts have, however, recognized that to restrain such a strike is to force workers to become strikebreakers, taking over the jobs of members of their own union or occupation [see *Searle Mfg. Company v. Terry*, 106 N.Y. Supp. 438 (1905), and *Iron Molders' Union v. Allis-Chalmers Company*, 166 F. 45 (1908)].   The Norris-La Guardia Act now forbids the granting of restraining orders in such cases [see *infra*, pp. 591–593].   In the building and other trades, in which numerous crafts are found, all the unions have in many cases gone on strike in order to force a general contractor to bring pressure to bear upon a subcontractor in dispute with one craft.   Some courts have held such a strike to be lawful, while others have held it to be an unlawful sympathetic strike.   In New York, the courts have permitted concerted action by the building trades unions against materials trucked by nonunion drivers [*Willson & Adams Co. v. Pearce*, 264 N.Y. 521 (1934)], and, similarly, by the Transportation Trades Council [*New York Lumber Trade Assn. v. Lacey*, 281 N.Y. Supp. 647 (1935)].

[2] *Duplex Printing Co. v. Deering*, 254 U.S. 443 (1921).   For a discussion of *Bedford Cut Stone*, a somewhat related case, see *infra*, pp. 587–588.

States. That court, in a majority opinion, held that the privilege of concerted action was limited to those who were proximately or substantially concerned. Past, present, or prospective employees of the Duplex Company had such interest, but the other members of the union, residing and working in New York, did not.[1]

In some cases lower courts have defined necessary proximity of interest quite as narrowly as, if not more narrowly than, it was defined in the Duplex case. Thus a district court in 1929, relying largely upon the Hitchman and American Steel Foundries cases, held that an organization strike by the Amalgamated Clothing Workers was unlawful on the ground that it was really not for the benefit of the Philadelphia workers being organized, but for that of the workers of New York and other cities whose standards were being threatened by an unequal competition.[2] Statements made in conventions and in official publications left "no doubt whatever [in the mind of the court] that the primary purpose of the campaign for the unionization of the Philadelphia market was the protection of the unionized markets in other states, particularly New York, and that while the improvement of the conditions of the workers in Philadelphia may have been present as a motive, it was at best a secondary or remote one." The court was of the view that "the self-interest of the defendants [was] totally unconnected with the employment interfered with." It held, therefore, that the strike was at common law without justification and actionable.[3] The union was restrained from combining to bring about a strike or strikes in the factories of the complainants by peaceful persuasion. In Cleveland, Ohio, to cite another case, electrical workers went on strike to assist the effort to organize the workers and to secure for them a closed shop in a second plant operated by their employer in Detroit. No doubt some of the work

---

[1] This was the narrower common-law rule. Properly interpreted, the majority opinion held that the Clayton Act, under which the case was decided, did not change the common-law rule, that Congress, in Sec. 20, which limited the granting of restraining orders, "had in mind particular industrial controversies, not a general class war." Justices Brandeis, Holmes, and Clarke dissented from the majority decision, which reversed the rulings of the District Court and the Circuit Court of Appeals. They expressed the view that in an application of the common law, many courts, with "a better realization of the facts of industrial life," had recognized a wide common interest among workers. So had the Congress in the Clayton Act. The refusal of the Duplex Company to deal with the machinists' union and to observe its standards threatened the interest not only of such union members as were in its employ, but even more of all members of the several affiliated unions employed by plaintiff's competitors and by others whose more advanced standards the plaintiff was, in reality, attacking. The parties restrained in this case had a justification in self-interest. "They [had] injured the plaintiff, not maliciously, but in self-defense."

[2] Alco-Zander Co. et al. v. Amalgamated Clothing Workers of America et al., 35 Fed. (2d) 203 (1929).

[3] The court held also that the strike was unlawful under the Sherman Act, because it interfered with the shipment of the product (80 per cent of it) into interstate commerce.

might be done either in Cleveland or in Detroit, but the Court of Common Pleas held that the workers in Cleveland had no interest in the organizing activities in Detroit such as would make the strike lawful.[1]

This narrow conception of a legitimate interest has recently been extensively modified by the limitations placed upon the courts in the granting of injunctions by the Norris-La Guardia Act and by some state laws based directly thereon. The federal law defines "labor dispute" so as to embrace those engaged in the same industry, trade, craft, or occupation in which the dispute concerning terms or conditions of employment occurs or those who have "direct or indirect" interest therein. As a condition of participation the disputants need not "stand in the proximate relation of employer and employee." Under the Norris-La Guardia Act a federal court cannot grant such a restrictive restraining order as was granted in the Duplex[2] and the Alco-Zander cases.

Discussing now more particularly primary or nonsympathetic strikes, the courts may find them to be unlawful because of the objects in view or because of the methods employed in their conduct. Strikes are most frequently undertaken to secure an increase in wages and a reduction in hours or to oppose attempts to reduce wages and to increase hours. Unless in violation of individual or collective contract,[3] such strikes are everywhere held to be lawful at common law. Strikes concerning apprentice regulations, shop rules, and sanitary and safety conditions have also been generally regarded as lawful. Some strikes designed to secure additional work have been held to be lawful, while others have been condemned as unlawful. In brief, certain objects have been regarded as of such direct and obvious benefit to workers immediately concerned that suspensions to secure them have usually been held to be lawful. In such cases the employer is without remedy even though the strike threatens to result, or does actually result, in his financial ruin. On the other hand, there are objects that are usually or always frowned upon by the courts. Although a recent Supreme Court decision may provide precedent for opposite rulings by the state and lower federal courts in the future,[4]

---

[1] *Bellows v. The Electrical Workers' Union, Local No.* 381, commented on in *Law and Labor*, vol. 10 (1928), p. 5.

[2] For a discussion of the Norris-La Guardia Act and the granting of injunctions, see pp. 643–647.

[3] The interrelated matters of enforceability of collective agreements, the lawfulness of strikes in violation of them, and the legally enforceable interests of both workers and employers in them are discussed *infra*, pp. 661–667.

[4] *Senn v. Tile Layers' Protective Union*, 301 U.S. 468 (1937). Senn had refused to sign an agreement with the union because under its rules he could not have worked with his men; a strike and picketing ensued, and an injunction was sought. The Supreme Court of the United States (with four members dissenting) held that there was reasonable ground for the presumption that the closed shop and the union rule prohibiting employers from working were necessary to maintain standards, and for the union to have set aside its rule

strikes to prohibit employers from working on the job have very generally
been held to be unlawful, on the ground that constitutional liberties
include the right to engage in any common occupation of life. Likewise
strikes to compel employers to continue manufacturing operations,[1] to
make them hire more men on given operations than they wished to
employ,[2] or to force them to apportion work during slack seasons[3] have
generally or frequently been held to be unlawful. The same is true of
strikes to collect fines from employers for alleged violation of trade agreements[4] and those to extort money or to do damage to a business. In all
the foregoing and in other types of cases not mentioned, the declaration of
unlawfulness stemmed from application of the two general tests of
whether the purpose was malicious and (not separate from the malice
test, since the test of "malice in law" itself involves evaluation of the
relative rights of the parties) of whether rights of others more important
than the right to strike were being violated.

Strikes for the Closed Shop.—Except for wages, hours of work, and
union recognition, the question most frequently involved in industrial
disputes in the United States has been the closed or all-union shop.[5]

---

in the case of Senn would have been to discriminate against other employers. Prior to the
Senn case, however, as stated above, a strike to prevent an employer from working with his
men had been generally regarded (as the four dissenters regarded it in the Senn case) as a
strike to deprive the employer of constitutional liberties. Cases in point are *Ronaback v.
Motion Picture Operators' Union*, 140 Minn. 481 (1918); *Hughes v. Kansas City Motion
Picture Machine Operators*, 282 Mo. 304 (1920); *Parke Paint and Wall Paper Company v.
Local Union*, 87 W. Va. 631 (1921). On the other hand, the Supreme Court of Washington
in 1933 held that the precedent to the effect that a union cannot dispute the right of a
proprietor to do journeyman's work did not prevail in that state [*Zaat v. Building Trades
Council*, 20 Pacif. (2d) 589 (1933)].

[1] Such strikes have been held to be unlawful in *Welinsky v. Hillman*, 185 N.Y.S. 257
(1920); *Cohen Friedlander & Martin Co. v. Schlesinger*, 193 N.Y.S. 928 (1922); and *Greenberg v. Berlin*, 4 Law and Labor 309 (1922). A contrary ruling was made in *Rutan Co. v.
Hatters'*, 97 N.J. Eq. 77 (1925).

[2] Strikes of this kind have been held to be unlawful in, among other, *Haverhill Strand
Theater, Incorporated v. Gillen*, 229 Mass. 413 (1918); *Edelman, Edelman & Berrie v. Retail
Grocery and Dairy Clerks' Union*, 198 N.Y.S. 17 (1922); and *Yablonowitz v. Korn*, 199 N.Y.S.
769 (1923). Contrary rulings have been made in *Scott-Stafford Opera House Company v.
Minneapolis Musicians' Association*, 118 Minn. 410 (1912), and *Empire Theater Co. v.
Cloke*, 53 Mont. 183 (1917).

[3] Among the cases, *Jaeckel v. Kaufman*, 187 N.Y.S. 889 (1920), and *Benito Roviro Co.,
Inc. v. Yompolsky*, 187 N.Y.S. 894 (1921) may be cited.

[4] Among the cases in which this has been held to be unlawful are: *Carew v. Rutherford*,
106 Mass. 1 (1870); *People v. Barondess*, 133 N.Y. 649 (1892); *Burke v. Fay*, 128 Mo. App.
690 (1908); and *People v. Walczak*, 315 Ill. 49 (1924).

[5] In recent years the labor movement has been seriously divided into two main camps,
and rival organizations have clashed much more frequently than theretofore. In many
instances there has been no real "labor dispute" as that term is most frequently used; the
employer is "placed in the middle." The law bearing upon contests between rival unions
is discussed below (pp. 566 and 580–581) and in Chap. XII, in connection with picketing and

The question has come before the courts in different ways, with diverse rulings as between jurisdictions, and, at times, within the same jurisdiction—rulings that are sometimes difficult, if not impossible, to reconcile. The courts have differed greatly as to what is of direct and sufficient benefit to the union group, what is undue interference with the rights of the employer or of the nonunion man concerned, or what tends unduly or unreasonably toward monopoly.

While the closed-shop cases have come before the state courts in different ways, most of them have involved the discharge of nonunion men or of the members of a rival organization or the reinstatement of a union man. In Massachusetts, where many cases have been litigated, the courts have been most restrictive in interpreting the rights of the union. While the Supreme Court of that state has recognized the right of a union to strike in order to force the discharge of a man against whom there is a legitimate grievance, "in not a single case," Dr. Witte states, "has this court ever found a strike for the discharge of non-unionists to have been justified."[1] Strikes to secure the reinstatement of union men have been held to be unlawful. While agreements for the closed shop voluntarily entered into and not involving monopoly have not been banned,[2] and while strikes to procure the discharge of the members of a rival union have been held not to be unlawful,[3] the court has refused to regard the motive of strengthening the union as just cause for the discharge of the nonunion worker or the reinstatement of the union worker.

---

the legal status of joint agreements. Suffice it to say at this point that while some courts have not been inclined to interfere, more of them have granted restraining orders against strikes held to be unlawful and against picketing in their prosecution.

[1] E. E. Witte, *The Government in Labor Disputes*, p. 24. The leading Massachusetts cases, as cited by Professor Witte, are: *Plant v. Woods*, 176 Mass. 492 (1900); *Berry v. Donovan*, 188 Mass. 353 (1905); *Picket v. Walsh*, 192 Mass. 572 (1900); *Aberthaw Construction Co. v. Cameron*, 194 Mass. 208 (1907); *Reynolds v. Davis*, 198 Mass. 294 (1908); *Folsom v. Lewis*, 208 Mass. 336 (1911); *Deminicio v. Craig*, 207 Mass. 593 (1911); *Hanson v. Innis*, 211 Mass. 301 (1912); *Hotel and Railroad News Co. v. Leventhal*, 243 Mass. 317 (1912); *Fairbanks v. McDonald*, 219 Mass. 291 (1914); *Burnham v. Dowd*, 217 Mass. 351 (1914); *Cornellier v. Haverhill Shoe Manufacturers' Assoc.*, 221 Mass. 554 (1915); *Snow Iron Works v. Chadwick*, 227 Mass. 382 (1917); *Bausch Machine Co. v. Hill*, 231 Mass. 30 (1918); *Smith v. Bowen*, 232 Mass. 106 (1919); *Shinsky v. O'Neil*, 232 Mass. 99 (1919); *Folsom Engraving Co. v. O'Neil*, 235 Mass. 269 (1920); *Plant v. Gould*, 2 Law and Labor 276 (1920); *Mechanics Foundry Co. v. Lynch*, 236 Mass. 504 (1920); *Jackson v. Brown*, 3 Law and Labor 53 (1921); *United Shoe Machinery Corp. v. Fitzgerald*, 237 Mass. 537 (1921); *Stearns Lumber Co. v. Howlett*, 260 Mass. 45 (1927).

[2] *Hoban v. Dempsey*, 217 Mass. 166 (1914).

[3] But in *Plant v. Woods*, 176 Mass. 492 (1900), one union threatened to call a strike because the employer was employing members of a rival union. This was enjoined as unlawful. The court was of the view that equal rights were involved. The rights of the one left off where the rights of the other began. "A legal right [was involved], entitled to legal protection."

The courts of New York have tended to be more receptive of the union point of view in this matter. While some of the earlier decisions[1] closely resemble Massachusetts decisions, for more than forty years the highest court has accepted the motive of strengthening the union through procuring the discharge of the nonunion man as well as members of a rival union as adequate justification. Thus in *National Protective Association v. Cumming*,[2] involving repeated discharge of a worker, Judge Parker held that the closed shop was necessary to assure beneficial results, that the union had a right to make room for the employment of its members, and that its action in this instance was not malicious, but within the bounds of proper competition. This position is in striking contrast to that of the Massachusetts Supreme Court, which more than once has expressed the view that similar behavior was not one of proper trade competition, but malicious and therefore unlawful.

As Dr. Witte has stated, the courts of about half of the states in which decisions have been rendered have accepted substantially the views of the Massachusetts court, while the other half have expressed more liberal views such as have more recently found acceptance in New York. "A majority of the state supreme courts have never passed on the legality of strikes for union recognition or the closed shop. Where this question has come up, the courts have been almost evenly divided between the Massachusetts and New York positions. Strikes for the discharge of non-unionists have been held illegal by the Supreme Courts of Connecticut, New Hampshire, New Jersey, Pennsylvania, and Vermont, and also in an old Maryland case. . . . Strikes for the discharge of non-unionists or of members of rival unions have been sustained by the highest courts in Arkansas, California, Indiana, and Oklahoma, and by the Supreme Court of the District of Columbia (an inferior court)."[3]

---

[1] Thus in *Curran v. Galen*, 152 N.Y. 33 (1897), the agreement provided that, while nonunion men might be employed, as a condition of retention they must join the union within four weeks. The plaintiff in the case refused to join the union and his discharge was forced. This was declared unlawful.

[2] 170 N.Y. 315 (1902).

[3] Quoted from E. E. Witte, *The Government in Labor Disputes*, p. 26. The leading cases, as cited by Professor Witte, are: *Wyeman v. Deady*, 79 Conn. 414 (1906); *Connors v. Connelly*, 86 Conn. 641 (1913); (slightly contrary) *Cohn, etc., Co. v. Bricklayers*, 92 Conn. 161 (1917); *White Mountain Freezer Co. v. Murphy*, 78 N.H. 398 (1917); *State v. Donaldson* 32 N.J.L. 151 (1867); *Blanchard v. Newark Joint District Council*, 78 N.J.L. 389 (1908); *Ruddy v. United Assoc.*, 79 N.J.L. 467 (1910); *Baldwin Lumber Co. v. Local 560*, 91 N.J. Eq. 240 (1920); *Bijur Motor Appliance Co. v. International Assoc. of Machinists*, 92 N.J. Eq. 644 (1920); *Lehigh Structural Steel Co. v. Atlantic, etc., Works*, 92 N.J. Eq. 131 (1920); *Gevas v. Greek, etc., Club*, 99 N.J. Eq. 770 (1926); (contrary) *Mayer v. Journeymen Stone Cutters*, 47 N.J. Eq. 519 (1890) and *Jersey City Printing Co. v. Cassidy*, 63 N.J. Eq. 759 (1902); *Erdman v. Mitchell*, 207 Pa. 79 (1903); *Bausbach v. Rieff*, 244 Pa. 559 (1914); *State v.*

This summary statement of the common law relating to the closed union shop may be concluded with the observation that the courts have been more liberal in their treatment of unions when demanding agreements of employers providing for the closed shop than when the discharge of nonunionists has been immediately involved. Nevertheless, a considerable number of injunctions have been issued against strikes where a closed-shop demand was involved. One of the most restrictive decisions was in the case of *O'Brien v. The People*,[1] where the court said that 'an attempt to compel an employer to sign an agreement to conduct his business by employing only members of labor unions, under threats of ordering a strike, is unlawful, such an agreement being violative of the legal rights of the employer and unjust and oppressive as to non-union employees."[2]

Though there have been recent decisions in which the closed or all-union shop has been held to be illegal and strikes to secure it have been enjoined,[3] there is now apparent a tendency for most of the courts to accept a different view. This changed judicial attitude is evident in recent decisions rendered in such states as New Jersey, Maryland, and Pennsylvania,[4] from which have emerged numerous decisions hostile to the closed shop, and it is most strikingly evident in New York. Though in *Curran v. Galen*[5] the strike was not enjoined, an all-union shop agree-

---

Dyer, 67 Vt. 690 (1895); *Lucke v. Clothing Cutters*, 77 Md. 396 (1893); *Sarros v. Nouris*, 38 Atl. 607 (1927); *Harmon v. United Mine Workers*, 166 Ark. 255 (1924); *Overland Publishing Co. v. Union Lithograph Co.*, 57 Cal. App. 366 (1922); *Greenwood v. Building Trades Council*, 71 Cal. App. 159 (1925); *Shaughnessey v. Jordan*, 184 Ind. 499 (1916); *Roddy v. United Mine Workers*, 41 Okla. 621 (1914); *Bender v. Local Union*, 34 Wash. Law Rep. 574 (1906); *O'Brien v. People*, 216 Ill. 354 (1905); *Kemp v. Division 241*, 255 Ill. 213 (1912); *Cooks, etc., Union v. Papageorge*, 230 S.W. 1086 (1921); *Sheehan v. Levy*, 238 S.W. 900 (1922); (strike for preferential union shop held lawful) *Underwood v. Texas & Pac. R.R. Co.*, 78 S.W. 38 (1915); *National Fireproofing Co. v. Mason Builders' Assoc.*, 169 Fed. 259 (1909); *Tunstall v. Stearns Coal Co.*, 192 Fed. 808 (1911); *Niles-Bement-Pond Co. v. Iron Molders*, 246 Fed. 851 (1917).

[1] 216 Ill. 354 (1905). Among the more recent decisions was one by the highest court in Maine which held that a strike for the closed shop was not lawful [*Keith Theatre, Inc. v. Vachon*, 187 Atl. 692, 134 Me. 392 (1936)]. A similar decision was rendered in New Jersey in 1937 in *International Ticket Company v. Wendrich*, 122 N.J. Eq. 222 (1937).

[2] In *Kemp v. Division No. 241*, 255 Ill. 213 (1912), the Illinois Supreme Court divided equally on the closed-shop issue. There were three opinions, no one of which was accepted by a majority.

[3] As in *Keith Theatre, Inc. v. Vachon*, 187 Atl. 692, 134 Me. 392 (1936), and *International Ticket Company v. Wendrich*, 122 N.J. Eq. 222 (1937).

[4] Compare Maryland decisions in *Lucke v. Clothing Cutters*, 77 Md. 396 (1893), and *Bricklayers', Masons' & Plasterers' International Union v. Ruff*, 160 Md. 483 (1931); Pennsylvania decisions in *Erdman v. Mitchell*, 207 Pa. 79 (1903), and *Kirmise v. Adler*, 311 Pa. 78 (1933); and *Four Plating Co., Inc. v. Mako*, 122 N.J. Eq. 298 (1937).

[5] 152 N.Y. 33 (1897).

ment was condemned by the highest court in New York as militating "against the spirit of our government and the nature of our institutions." This was in 1897. Eight years later, however, the same court in *Jacobs v. Cohen*[1] upheld a contract between a union and an employer providing that the latter was not to "employ any help whatsoever other than those belonging to, and who [were] members" of the union. In 1910, in *Kissam v. United States Printing Company*,[2] and again in 1916, in *Grassi Contracting Co. v. Bennett*,[3] the court again sustained the legality of an all-union shop agreement.

In view of the fact that the element of monopoly, actual or feared, has greatly influenced the thinking of the judges and controlled their decisions in many cases, the more recent case of *Williams v. Quill*[4] is important. Here, an election had been held to determine representation of twelve groups of transport workers. The union received a majority of the votes cast by the members of eleven of these groups and was certified by the New York Labor Relations Board as the exclusive agency for the purpose of collective bargaining. Following certification of the union, a joint agreement was entered into, providing, among other things, that the transit companies would not employ anyone who was not or who did not, within one month of his employment, become a member of the union. Though membership in the union was open to them, six workers refused to join it and sought to have the transit companies and the union enjoined from requiring them, as a condition of employment, to join the union. Inasmuch as the transit companies controlled all transit facilities in the locality, these workers contended that their constitutional rights would be violated and that they would be deprived of a livelihood. The trial court, the Appellate Division, and the Court of Appeals all ruled adversely on the prayer for a restraining order. With reference to the monopoly of jobs entering into the situation, the Court of Appeals said, " . . . if there be an evil in the monopoly of the labor market in a particular industry by labor organizations it is a matter to be considered by legislatures and not by the courts, for the reason that there are two sides to the question—the other side being that the labor organizations, through this means of contracting and negotiating, are enabled to strengthen their representative bodies and to effectuate collective bargaining."[5] The Williams decision represents a marked advance in the judicial recognition of the all-union shop agreement.

---

[1] 183 N.Y. 207 (1905).

[2] 199 N.Y. 76 (1910).

[3] 160 N.Y.S. 279 (1916).

[4] 277 N.Y. 1 (1938).

[5] *Ibid.*, at pp. 9–10. For an interesting article on "The All-union Shop in the Courts," containing many old and new citations of cases, see *International Juridical Association Monthly Bulletin*, vol. 6 (1938), pp. 147, 154–158. This article has been freely used by the authors.

It should be noted also that the Supreme Court of the United States has rendered "liberal" decisions in the Lauf[1] and Senn[2] cases, recently decided. In the Senn case, it held that there is no constitutional objection to a state's refusing to grant injunctive relief against picketing to obtain an all-union shop. This view is likely to be controlling in other states with injunction-limitation laws based upon the Norris-La Guardia Act.[3]

The question as to what the law of the closed shop should be is debatable. The view of the authors is, however, that the courts have generally been too much concerned about the injury to the nonunion workmen and too little inclined in most cases to recognize the necessity of the closed shop if the union is to be effective in collective bargaining and is to secure for the larger group the advantages of organization. In protecting the individual, who has rather generally been brought into the case by the employer to serve his own ends, the courts have certainly aided the employer in effecting his will. The law should rest upon employers and unions as nearly equally as possible. At common law, the employers' closed shop has been lawful everywhere. If the union was to have equal rights, its closed shop should have been legalized. Nor, in the opinion of the authors, could there be substantial objection to the closed shop, provided the union was not unduly restrictive or monopolistic. It should have been easily possible to frame a law legalizing the union closed shop, while at the same time placing a ban on labor monopoly.

Outlawing of Employers' Closed Shop.—Thus far in the discussion of the law of the closed shop no reference has been made to the outlawing of the employers' closed shop under the Railway Labor Act of 1926, Sec. 7(a) of NIRA[1] and the National Labor Relations Act in so far as these laws apply. These several laws have forbidden discrimination because of union membership by employers in hiring or discharge. Indeed, an employer must deal with the representatives of his workers and thus recognize the union when his workers are organized in that manner and, when requests are presented, make a reasonable effort to reach agreement with the representatives as to terms and conditions of employment.

In view of this legislation and the state industrial-relations acts,[5] it has been urged that the union closed shop should now be placed under a

---

[1] *Lauf v. E. G. Shinner & Co., Inc.*, 303 U.S. 323 (1938).

[2] *Senn v. Tile Layers' Protective Union*, 301 U.S. 468 (1937).

[3] *Cf.* discussion of picketing, pp. 613–629, and the injunction, pp. 629–651.

[4] A voluminously documented discussion of the effect of Sec. 7(a) upon the validity of the closed shop may be found in the *Yale Law Journal*, "Effect of Section 7(a) of NIRA on the Validity of a Closed Union-shop Contract," vol. 44 (1935), pp. 1067–1075.

[5] For limitations on the closed shop under state industrial-relations acts, see *supra*, pp. 550–554.

ban as it was in the German labor code adopted after World War I. With the law attempting to safeguard the right to join and be represented by the union, and with the employer's closed shop outlawed, much is to be said for this contention when and in so far as the existing legislation proves to be effective. The National Labor Relations Act, however, because of the contention that Sec. 7(*a*) had the effect of making the union closed shop unlawful in code industries, contains a provision that the other parts of the Act shall not be interpreted to preclude an employer from making an agreement with a legally acceptable labor organization requiring membership in that organization as a condition of employment.[1] In other respects the law of the closed shop was left unchanged, because, for one reason, it was regarded as best not to enact a measure that would be in conflict with divergent state laws or court rulings.

As these lines are being written, the Congress has before it for consideration several bills designed to freeze the economic status of unions or to outlaw the closed shop. An object common to these several bills is to prevent strikes during the present war. Some of them are no doubt motivated by antiunionism. Another factor explaining the legislative movement is found in the desire to have a fluid labor supply and to prevent or minimize the evils of high initiation fees all too frequently exacted of applicants for union membership.

Because of competition between unions when the labor movement is divided and of the natural desire of employers with war contracts to have stable industrial relations, it appears that a considerable number of closed-shop contracts have been entered into in advance of hiring any employees or when only a small percentage of the expected number of workers has been hired. Indeed, in some instances collusion is charged. The result is that adherents of the C.I.O. are compelled to join an A.F. of L. union or A.F. of L. adherents are compelled to join the C.I.O. as a condition of obtaining employment at a time when there are great shifts in employment. As would be expected, charges are filed with the National Labor Relations Board of discrimination and violation of the Wagner Act. The closed shop not infrequently presents problems. The general policy of the National War Labor Board, when mediating or arbitrating disputes involving the issue of "union security," is to introduce some form of the compromise found in the maintenance-of-membership arrangement. This is designed, among other things, to meet the union's dues problem and to have unions strong enough to be effective and responsible as agents for the purposes of collective bargaining.[2]

---

[1] The National Labor Relations Act, Sec. 8(3).

[2] Without the closed or preferential shop the union, and particularly a new one, may have a very unstable membership, for some members, for one reason or another, will not keep their dues paid up. Very likely, witnessing this, other members will fail to pay dues.

Labor Disputes and Federal Law.—Thus far our discussion of strikes has been almost exclusively in terms of the common law as interpreted and applied by the state and federal courts. The common law still widely obtains, but nevertheless statute law has more and more taken its place as the determinant of what organized labor may do. Measures bearing upon the strike have been adopted by a number of the states, chiefly antitrust laws, "anti-injunction" laws, and mediation and arbitration laws. Much more important is the federal legislation relating to transporting the mail, trusts, and labor disputes.[1]

The federal statutes forbid interference with United States mail.[2] This prohibition has been used by the government in coping with important railway strikes, such as the Pullman strike of 1894 and the Shop Crafts strike of 1922.[3] It has also been at least twice employed in the prosecution of striking postal employees. In New York City, in 1914, eleven chauffeurs were convicted and sentenced to jail for interfering with the mails through acts of violence. At Fairmount, W. Va., in 1916, the postal employees "resigned" in a body when the new postmaster discharged thirty of their number. Those "resigning" were fined.[4] In his charge to the jury the presiding judge in the New York case expressly stated that it was not unlawful for the men to strike—it was the violence that was unlawful—but the ruling in the Fairmount case suggests that the statutes prohibiting interference with the mails may possibly be construed to forbid all strikes of postal employees.

This operates more or less cumulatively. The union must again devote itself to organizing efforts to the neglect of other functions. Moreover, it is likely to picket the mine or factory to collect dues and to prevent these members who are in arrears from going to work. Assuming that labor organization is desirable, it may be necessary to solve the dues problem if the closed or preferential shop is not to obtain. See discussion of the closed shop, *supra*, pp. 470–485.

[1] The shipping laws are also important. In December, 1937, under a federal statute of 1790, fourteen seamen were convicted on charges of endeavor and conspiracy to revolt growing out of a sit-down strike on the government freighter *Algic* at Montevideo. The court in its charge to the jury expressed the view that seamen have no right to strike against the laws of the United States at any place, at any time, or under any circumstances. The sit-down was in protest against the use of strikebreaking stevedores in loading the vessel.

[2] U. S. Criminal Code, Sec. 201, 35 *Stat.* 1127 (1909).

[3] In both of these cases, the injunctions obtained by the Attorney General restrained interfering with, hindering, obstructing, or stopping any mail train, etc. For these restraining orders, see Felix Frankfurter and Nathan Green, *The Labor Injunction* (1930), p. 253. See also E. E. Witte, *The Government in Labor Disputes*, pp. 76–77.

[4] *Ibid.*, p. 76. The basic issue in this case was not settled since the defendants pleaded *nolle contendere* and agreed to payment of fines, the judge then withdrawing the prison sentences that would have provided the basis of appeal.

The Sherman and Clayton Acts.—Far-reaching in their bearing upon the rights of organized labor are the Sherman Act of 1890 and the Clayton Act of 1914.[1] Their bearing upon the strike alone is discussed at this point. The Sherman Act provided:

1. That "every contract, combination in the form of trust or otherwise, or conspiracy, in restraint of trade or commerce" among the states or with foreign nations, was illegal (Sec. 1).

2. That every attempt to monopolize such trade or commerce, or every actual monopoly of it, was illegal (Sec. 2).

3. That every person guilty of these illegal acts, was, on conviction, liable to a fine not exceeding $5,000, or to imprisonment not exceeding one year, or to both of these punishments (Secs. 1 and 2).

4. That the district attorneys of the United States, under the direction of the Attorney General, might institute proceedings in equity to restrain violations of the law (Sec. 4).

5. That any person injured in his business or property by any action forbidden under the act might sue for and recover threefold the damages sustained, plus the costs of the suit, including a reasonable attorney's fee (Sec. 7).[2]

Thus, certain acts were declared to be criminal offenses; persons guilty of offenses might be indicted and tried; a restraining order might be resorted to; and injured private parties might recover damages.

The Sherman Act was directed at the practices of industrial combinations, which had then begun to present a problem. Whether or not Congress expected it to be applied to labor combinations has been debated almost from its enactment, and perhaps the issue remains in doubt.[3] But, whatever the intent of Congress may have been, federal courts, within a few years of the enactment of the law, ruled that the activities of labor organizations directly and substantially interfering with interstate commerce were within the scope of this law. In 1893 and 1894 there were seven cases in which the statute was invoked against labor unions. Six of the seven grew out of railroad strikes and all of them involved direct interference with interstate commerce and also were accompanied by more or less violence. The courts held that in the several cases there was illegal restraint of trade. Following these cases there was comparatively little litigation involving labor under the Sher-

[1] Sherman Antitrust Act, 51st Congress, 1st Session, Chap. 647, July 2, 1890; Clayton Act, Public no. 212, 63d Congress, 2d Session, Chap. 323 (H.R. 15657), Oct. 15, 1914.

[2] This summary is from Edward Berman, *Labor and the Sherman Act* (1930), pp. 57–58.

[3] For the fullest discussion of the issue and for opposed conclusions, see A. T. Mason, *Organized Labor and the Law*, Pt. III, and Edward Berman, *op. cit.*, Pt. I. For the actual application of the Act, see, among the many references available: E. E. Witte, *The Government in Labor Disputes*, Chap. 4, G. W. Terborgh, "The Application of the Sherman Law to Trade Union Activity," in *Journal of Political Economy*, vol. 37 (1929), pp. 203–224, and Edward Berman, *op. cit.*

man Act until the famous 1908 case of *Loewe v. Lawlor* ended in important decisions by the Supreme Court of the United States.[1]

At the time the Loewe case arose there were some eighty-two manufacturers of men's hats over which the United Hatters of North America claimed jurisdiction. Seventy of the manufacturers conducted union shops; the union undertook to organize the others, including the shop conducted by Loewe at Danbury, Conn. The company refusing to recognize the union, there was the usual organization strike. The strike proving to be ineffective, a boycott was resorted to with the aid of the American Federation of Labor, its affiliated unions, and local labor organizations. The boycott was more or less effectively spread. Loewe hats were sold chiefly outside of Connecticut, in twenty-eight states. Dealers were requested not to patronize the "unfair" firm and in some instances were themselves threatened with boycott in the event they continued to patronize Loewe. The result was that the volume of sales was reduced; the company, it averred, was injured in the sum of $80,000. A restraining order was sought and secured and a suit for damages was instituted. The Supreme Court of the United States, on appeal, held that "the combination described in the declaration is a combination 'in restraint of trade or commerce among the several States,' in the sense in which those words are used in the [Sherman] act. . . . And that conclusion rests on many judgments of this court, to the effect that the act prohibits any combination whatever to secure action which essentially obstructs the free flow of commerce between the States, or restricts, in that regard, the liberty of a trader to engage in business."[2]

In regard to the defense that interstate trade was not directly affected, the court said, "If the purposes of the combination were, as alleged, to prevent any interstate transportation at all, the fact that the means operated at one end before physical transportation commenced and at the other end after the physical transportation ended was immaterial."[3]

Thus it was made clear that a secondary boycott, such as this, was unlawful in the Supreme Court judgment because of its effect upon the volume of goods entering into interstate commerce. The reasoning behind the decision would apply equally well to primary boycotts having or intended to have the same effect. And why not to all strikes also? We shall return to the law of the boycott presently; at this point we shall confine our discussion to some of the federal cases involving application of the Sherman Act to the strike.

The Sherman Act was amended by the Clayton Act, which was passed in 1914. This measure, as is indicated later, modified the law of labor in

---

[1] *Loewe v. Lawlor*, 208 U.S. 274 (1908), and *Lawlor v. Loewe*, 235 U.S. 522 (1915).

[2] 208 U.S. at pp. 292–293.

[3] *Ibid.*, at p. 301. It is worth noting, however, that Judge Platt, in writing the decision of the court immediately below the Supreme Court, held that this fact was material.

certain respects, chiefly in the use of restraining orders, but, as interpreted by the Supreme Court, did not change at all the law with reference to strikes (and boycotts). Contrary to the hopes and expectations of labor leaders, the Clayton Act, as construed until the end of the 1930's, was merely declaratory of what had been lawful and what unlawful theretofore.[1]

The first of the important cases involving the Sherman Act and the strike, selected for brief summarization here, was that of *United Mine Workers v. Coronado Coal Company*,[2] decided by the Supreme Court of the United States in 1922.

The Coronado Coal Company mine was one of a number operating in Arkansas under a Southwestern labor agreement. Approximately three-quarters of the output of the mine was marketed outside of the state. In 1914 the management decided to put its operations on a nonunion basis. The mine was closed down and then shortly reopened with nonunion help secured from outside the state. Anticipating trouble, the manager fenced the properties, hired guards, and purchased rifles and ammunition. Union miners were given notice to vacate company houses. Trouble soon developed in this union stronghold. Guards and nonunion miners were assaulted when a union committee, after a mass meeting, called upon the management in an effort to persuade it not to operate nonunion. Some weeks later a coal washhouse was burned, the defending force driven away, and several nonunion miners killed. Production of coal had of course ceased. Thereupon the company sued the Local, District, and International of the United Mine Workers for damages, under the Sherman Act.

In the District Court the union demurred on the ground that inasmuch as it was an unincorporated association, it could not be sued, and denied that it had interfered with interstate commerce. This demurrer was sustained. The case was then taken to the Circuit Court of Appeals, which held[3] that the union could be sued under the Sherman Act and that the destruction of property was part of the union's policy to organize the whole industry and to handicap the nonunion producers of coal, which constituted an illegal interference with interstate commerce. The case was therefore remanded and the suit in the District Court resulted in an award in the sum of $200,000, this being trebled under the Sherman Act, to which costs and attorney's fees were added. The judgment was

---

[1] *Duplex Printing Press Company v. Deering*, 254 U.S. 443 (1921). As a matter of fact the Clayton Act probably weakened the position of labor by making it possible for private parties, who prior to the enactment of the law could not bring suits in equity, to do so under the antitrust law.

[2] 259 U.S. 344 (1922).

[3] *Dowd v. United Mine Workers of America*, 235 Fed. 1 (1916).

upheld in the Circuit Court of Appeals and the union appealed to the Supreme Court.[1]

The Supreme Court, by unanimous decision, held that the union, though unincorporated, was suable. The reason given was not that the Sherman Act made *associations* suable, but was essentially that given by the House of Lords in the English Taff Vale case of 1901. The reasoning in that case was freely used in the Coronado case. But the Supreme Court found that the lower courts had erred in charging the International with responsibility for the loss of property. The International was therefore absolved from responsibility. With reference to whether interference with interstate commerce had been involved, the court stated that "coal mining is not interstate commerce, and the power of Congress does not extend to its regulation as such. . . . Obstruction to coal mining is not a direct obstruction to interstate commerce in coal, although it, of course, may affect it by reducing the amount of coal to be carried in that commerce"; that the object the union had in view was "unionization of non-union mines not only as a direct means of bettering the conditions and wages of their workers, but also as a means of lessening interstate competition for union operators which in turn would lessen the pressure of those operators for reduction of the union scale or their resistance to an increase"; that the product here was unimportant in the total supply of coal; and that "coal mining is not interstate commerce and obstruction of coal mining, though it may prevent coal from going into interstate commerce, is not a restraint of that commerce unless the obstruction to mining is intended to restrain commerce in it or has necessarily such a direct, material and substantial effect to restrain it that the intent reasonably must be inferred."[2]

Another significant case is that of *United Leather Workers v. Herkert*,[3] decided by the Supreme Court in 1924. In 1920 the United Leather Workers' International Union had tried to secure recognition at the hands of five Missouri manufacturers of bags and other leather goods. Agreement failing, a strike developed, accompanied by mass picketing and some violence. The companies, so they averred, sustained losses amounting to $327,000 because of their inability to fill orders. Nine-tenths of the market was outside of Missouri. Charging conspiracy to interfere with interstate commerce, the companies sought an injunction in the District Court. This was granted and made permanent, the court holding that, though there had been no boycott and though transportation had not been interfered with, there had been unlawful interference

[1] *United Mine Workers v. Coronado Coal Company*, 259 U.S. 344 (1922). See also 268 U.S. 295 (1925).

[2] 259 U.S. at pp. 407–408, 410–411.

[3] 265 U.S. 457 (1924).

with interstate commerce as commerce had been defined.[1] The union appealed to the Circuit Court of Appeals, where the decision of the lower court was sustained by two of the three judges. The union denied all intent to interfere with interstate commerce, contending that it had merely gone on strike to secure the closed shop and certain other demands. At this time the Supreme Court had not ruled in the Coronado case; influenced by the ruling of the Court of Appeals in that case and by the decisions relating to the boycott, Justices Sanborn and Munger said that "the natural and inevitable effect of the prevention by the defendants of the making by the plaintiffs of the articles they had made interstate contracts to sell, make, and deliver was the prevention of their performance of their contracts and the prevention or partial prevention of their interstate commerce, and this result was so evident and unavoidable that the defendants could not have failed to know, to purpose, and to intend that this should be the result."[2]

In his dissenting opinion, Judge Stone pointed out that there had been no boycott or direct interference with transportation; the strike had been designed to prevent manufacture only. "The jurisdictional question turn[ed], therefore, on the point of whether a conspiracy for the sole purpose of unionizing a manufacturing plant [was] a restraint of interstate commerce because some of the articles which [were] prevented from being made [were] intended for interstate commerce and would normally enter therein." He then, in emphatic language, pointed out the possible consequences of the rule laid down in the majority opinion. "The natural, logical and inevitable result will be that every strike in any industry or even in any single factory will be within the Sherman Act and subject to federal jurisdiction provided any appreciable amount of its product enters into interstate commerce. Moreover, if this be true as to the products produced in such industry or factory, it is entirely logical the same rule should apply to the raw materials used in such production if any of them are subjects of interstate commerce. In a practical sense, this would result in all strikes being subject to federal jurisdiction, because scarcely any factory is so small that some of its finished products do not enter into interstate commerce."[3]

The union appealed from the decision of the Circuit Court of Appeals to the Supreme Court, where, with three of the justices dissenting, the decision was reversed, in a ruling in line with its decision in the Coronado case. The dissenting Justices filed no opinion. The majority found no element of intended or probable monopoly or discrimination in interstate commerce. After reviewing the Loewe and other cases cited, Chief Justice Taft said, "This review of the cases makes it clear that the mere

---

[1] *Herkert v. United Leather Workers'*, 268 Fed. 662 (1920).

[2] *United Leather Workers' v. Herkert*, 284 Fed. 446 (1922). Quotation from p. 451.

[3] *Ibid.*, at pp. 464–465.

reduction in the supply of an article to be shipped in interstate commerce, by the illegal or tortious prevention of its manufacture, is ordinarily an indirect and remote obstruction to that commerce. *It is only when the intent or necessary effect upon such commerce in the article is to enable those preventing the manufacture to monopolize the supply, control its price or discriminate as between its would-be purchasers, that the unlawful interference with its manufacture can be said directly to burden interstate commerce.*"[1]

The Chief Justice then quoted, with approval, the statement of Judge Stone as to the logical consequences of the ruling from which appeal had been taken, and added, "We cannot think that Congress intended any such result in the enactment of the Anti-Trust Act or that the decisions of this Court warrant such construction."[2]

In the Herkert case the court did not find the intent to interfere with interstate commerce it had found in the far-flung, presumably coercive boycott in the Loewe case. Yet, in view of the fact that 90 per cent of the leather goods normally found a market outside of the state in which they were manufactured and that the strike would interfere, as the Hatters' boycott had, with shipments, it is rather difficult to harmonize the two decisions unless we assume the substantial difference to have inhered in the acts "after transportation had ceased" which obtained in the Loewe case but not in the Herkert case.

Meanwhile a new suit had been instituted by the Coronado Coal Company against the district organization and the local of the United Mine Workers. In the District Court the judgment was in favor of the Union and, upon appeal, the decision was sustained by the Circuit Court of Appeals.[3] The case was then appealed to the Supreme Court, the company contending, among other things, that new evidence showed the intent of the union to prevent nonunion competition in interstate commerce and that the amount of coal whose production and marketing had been prevented was sufficiently large to have a substantial effect upon interstate commerce. Evidence in union records, etc., showing that an effort was being made to eliminate nonunion competition, with its injurious effect upon the market for the union product, was emphasized in this second trial. It was shown also that the lost output was 5,000 tons daily instead of per week as had been reported in the earlier trial. The Supreme Court, in view of the evidence, now held that the lower courts had erred and that the company's case should have been sustained. The court's view was expressed as follows:

"The mere reduction in the supply of an article to be shipped in interstate commerce by the illegal or tortious prevention of its manufacture or production is ordinarily an indirect and remote obstruction to

---

[1] 265 U.S. at 471 (1924). Authors' italics.

[2] *Ibid.*, at pp. 471–472.

[3] *Finley et al. v. United Mine Workers of America et al.*, 300 Fed. 972 (1924).

that commerce. But when the intent of those unlawfully preventing the manufacture or production is shown to be to restrain or control the supply entering and moving in interstate commerce, or the price of it in interstate markets, their action is a direct violation of the Anti-Trust Act. . . . We think there was substantial evidence at the second trial in this case tending to show that the purpose of the destruction of the mines was to stop the production of non-union coal and prevent its shipment to markets of other States than Arkansas, where it would by competition tend to reduce the price of the commodity and affect injuriously the maintenance of wages for union labor in competing mines."[1]

Reconciliation of this decision with the one in the Herkert case presents some difficulties. The effect on the relative quantity of coal was less than the effect on the relative quantity of leather goods entering into interstate commerce. The object in the two cases was the same— to organize the industries effectively, and have only the union product find place in the market, whether intra- or interstate. But the decision in the second Coronado case did harmonize with that in the Loewe case. And, of course, it was of great consequence to unions in those industries with important interstate markets. As Professor Berman has said, "The significance of such a position [as the one taken in the second *Coronado* case] can hardly be over-estimated. Any strike carried on with a view to secure nation-wide recognition of a union is necessarily intended, in part, to prevent the competition of non-union goods with union goods in the interstate market. If union textile and shoe manufacturers in New England and union clothing manufacturers in Chicago and New York find their business threatened by the competition of non-union manufacturers in other districts, the obviously intelligent and necessary thing for the unions to do in order to protect the wages and conditions of their own members, is to attempt to organize the non-union producers. On the basis of the second Coronado decision, however, if such an attempt seriously obstructed production, it would be a violation of the Sherman Act."[2]

The Supreme Court's interpretation of the Sherman Act in the second Coronado decision was applied by the Circuit Court of Appeals, Seventh District, in the Red Jacket coal cases decided in 1927.[3] For years, the International Union, in order to protect its agreement in the Central Competitive District, had attempted to organize the mines in West Virginia, but had been faced by numerous sweeping restraining orders issued by the Federal District Court, some of which, with modification,

---

[1] *Coronado Coal Company et al. v. United Mine Workers of America et al.*, 268 U.S., at p. 310 (1925).

[2] Edward Berman, *op. cit.*, pp. 129–130.

[3] *United Mine Workers of America et al. v. Red Jacket Consol. Coal & Coke Co.*, 18 Fed. (2d) 839 (1927).

had been approved by the Circuit Court of Appeals. Finally, a large number of cases were combined and heard by the Court of Appeals. On consolidation 316 companies were involved. The total production of their mines was in excess of 40,000,000 tons per year, more than 90 per cent of which found an interstate market. The Circuit Court of Appeals, applying the law as laid down by the Supreme Court in the second Coronado case, was of the opinion that "when the union turns aside from its normal and legitimate objects and purposes and engages in an actual combination or conspiracy in restraint of trade, it is accountable therefor in the same manner as any other organization; and we think that the evidence adduced in this case justifies the conclusion that the defendants have engaged in an actual combination and conspiracy in restraint of trade in a manner quite foreign to the normal and legitimate objects of the union."[1]

The Court stated, further: "Interference with the production of these mines as contemplated by defendants would necessarily interfere with interstate commerce in coal to a substantial degree. Moreover, it is perfectly clear that the purpose of defendants in interfering with production was to stop the shipments in interstate commerce. It was only as the coal entered into interstate commerce that it became a factor in the price and affected defendants in their wage negotiations with the union operators. And, in time of strike, it was only as it moved in interstate commerce that it relieved the coal scarcity and interfered with the strike [in the Central Competitive District, in 1922]. A conspiracy is in violation of the statute, where there exist an intent to restrain interstate trade and commerce and a scheme appropriate for that purpose, even though it does not act directly upon the instrumentalities of commerce. . . . And where the necessary result of the things done pursuant to or contemplated by the conspiracy is to restrain trade between the states, the intent is presumed."[2]

The union petitioned the Supreme Court for permission to appeal from this decision on a writ of certiorari, but the petition was denied. The inference is that, in the opinion of the Supreme Court, the law had been properly applied.

Recent Trends in Sherman Act Construction.—The above cases, it would seem, now have an interest a considerable part of which is historical. A radical departure from its earlier position on application of the Sherman Act to the labor movement, particularly in strike situations, has been made by the "reconstructed" Supreme Court, and emphasis has been shifted to combinations to control prices paid by purchasers or consumers as the test in antitrust prosecution.

---

[1] 18 Fed. (2d) at p. 844.
[2] 18 Fed. (2d) at pp. 845–846.

The first milestone on the new road to the liberation of organized labor from the incubus of the Sherman Act was erected in the Apex case decided by the Supreme Court May 27, 1940.[1] A local union sought recognition at the Apex plant in Philadelphia when its membership was limited to 8 of the 2,500 employees. Recognition having been denied, a "stay-in" strike was inaugurated and continued from May 4, to June 23, 1937, when the plant was vacated under a court order. During the strike, the locks were changed, management was not permitted to enter the plant or to remove stock to fill orders on its books, and considerable damage was done to machines. Following the strike the Apex Company brought suit for damages under the Sherman Act. The jury trial resulted in a verdict for the company in the sum of $237,310, which, as provided in the law, was trebled by the court. The case was appealed to the Court of Appeals for the Third Circuit Court, which reversed the lower court "on the ground that the interstate commerce restrained or affected . . . was unsubstantial, the total shipment of merchandise . . . being less than three per cent of the total value of the output in the entire industry of the country, and on the further ground that the evidence failed to show an intent on the part of respondents to restrain interstate commerce."[2] Appeal to the Supreme Court of the United States resulted in a majority decision[3] affirming the decision rendered by the Circuit Court.

The Supreme Court, in the majority opinion, recognized that the civil and penal laws of the state of Pennsylvania had been violated, but it characterized this as a matter of state concern. Contrary to the contentions of organized labor, it found that labor combinations were within the embrace of the Sherman Act. But the Sherman Act was directed at attempts at price control and restrictions upon competition in the market for commodities, and in this case these were not involved. Of course the strikers had refused to permit the company to remove from the plant any stock to fill the large volume of orders until the strike was settled, but the court held that the policing of transportation was not of federal concern under the Sherman Act. The Court said, "A . . . significant circumstance is that this Court has never applied the Sherman Act in any case, whether or not involving labor organizations or activities, unless the Court was of the opinion that there was some form of restraint upon commercial competition in the marketing of goods or services and finally

---

[1] *Apex Hosiery Company, Petitioner v. William Leader and American Federation on Full-fashioned Hosiery Workers*, 310 U.S. 469 (1940). In this decision, the court majority went to considerable length to demonstrate that previous precedents were not being set aside, but the practical import, as indicated above, is clear.

[2] As stated in the majority opinion of the Supreme Court of the United States.

[3] Chief Justice Hughes submitted a dissenting opinion in which Justice McReynolds and Justice Roberts concurred.

this Court has refused to apply the Sherman Act in cases like the present in which local strikes conducted by illegal means in a production industry prevented interstate shipment of substantial amounts of the product but in which it was not shown that the restrictions on shipments had operated to restrain commercial competition in some substantial way."[1] On the other hand, it had "extended the condemnation of the statute to restraints effected by any combination in the form of trust or otherwise, or conspiracy, as well as contract or agreement, having those effects on the competitive system and on purchasers and consumers of goods or services which were characteristic of restraints deemed illegal at common law, and they gave both private and public remedies for the injuries flowing from such restraints."[2] "This [the *Apex*] is not a case of a labor organization being used by combinations of those engaged in an industry as the means or instrument for suppressing competition or fixing prices. . . . Here it is plain that the combination or conspiracy did not have as its purpose restraint upon competition in the market for petitioner's product. Its object was to compel petitioner to accede to the union demands and an effect of it, in consequence of the strikers' tortious acts, was the prevention of the removal of petitioner's product for interstate shipment. So far as appears the delay of these shipments was not intended to have and had no effect on prices of hosiery in the market, and so were in that respect no more a restraint forbidden by the Sherman Act than the restriction upon competition and the course of trade held lawful in *Appalachian Coals, Inc. v. United States, supra,* because notwithstanding its effect upon the marketing of the coal it nevertheless was not intended to and did not affect market price."[3]

Chief Justice Hughes took sharp issue with this majority opinion. There had been, as was conceded, a direct and intentional prevention of interstate commerce in the furtherance of an illegal conspiracy. This the Sherman Act prohibits, even though, as in the Fainblatt case,[4] the amount of the product be relatively small. The ruling made was accordingly, in the Chief Justice's opinion, out of harmony with the rulings in boycott cases, such as Loewe, Duplex, and Bedford Stone.[5] Again, it applies one rule to labor and another to other combinations, which should be treated alike. Finally, the decisions of the court do not justify the interpretations made of them in this case. "This Court has never heretofore decided that a direct and intentional obstruction or prevention of the shipment of goods in interstate commerce was not a violation of the Sherman Act. In my opinion it should not so decide now. It finds no

---

[1] 310 U. S. 469, at p. 495.
[2] *Ibid.,* at p. 498.
[3] *Ibid.,* at p. 501.
[4] *Supra,* p. 525.
[5] *Supra,* pp. 557–558, 569–570, and *infra,* pp. 587–588, 656.

warrant for such a decision in the terms of the statute. I am unable to find any compulsion of judicial decision requiring the Court so to limit those terms. Restraints may be of various sorts. Some may be imposed by employers, others by employees. But when they are found to be unreasonable and directly imposed upon interstate commerce, both employers and employees are subject to the sanctions of the Act."[1]

As already indicated, the decision rendered in the Apex case reduces the restrictions upon the right to strike theretofore thought to be imposed by the Sherman Act. As the Act was interpreted, the Apex Company was left to seek protection and relief in the courts of Pennsylvania.

The next significant pronouncement of the Supreme Court on the application of the Sherman Act to organized labor was not long in coming. In *Milk Wagon Drivers' Union v. Lake Valley Farm Products, Inc.*,[2] decided Nov. 18, 1940, a union of milk-wagon drivers employed by local dairies in delivering milk picketed a large number of retail stores that sold at cut prices milk bought at wholesale from so-called "vendors," who delivered it by their own trucks from supplies bought from other dairies. The claim of the union was that this system undercut union wages and working conditions and it therefore sought to induce the vendors to join the union. The plaintiffs, in seeking an injunction, contended that there was no labor dispute within the meaning of the Norris-La Guardia Act, but rather an unlawful secondary boycott intended to monopolize Chicago milk. In a unanimous opinion delivered by Justice Black, the Supreme Court ruled that the union in this case could not be enjoined from picketing. The court held that a "labor dispute" existed within the meaning of the Norris-La Guardia Act and that the requirements of that Act for issuance of an injunction were not met. Justice Black pointed out that the Norris-La Guardia Act was adopted with the purpose of reversing the judicial interpretation of the Clayton Act in the Duplex, American Steel Foundries, Bedford, and other cases. For the Supreme Court, he concluded, "to hold, in the face of this legislation, that the federal courts have jurisdiction to grant injunctions in cases growing out of labor disputes, merely because alleged violations of the Sherman Act are involved, would run counter to the plain mandate of the Act and would reverse the declared purpose of Congress."[3]

What appears to be, at least for the time being, the culminating step in this new trend of the Supreme Court was taken in the case of *U. S. v.*

---

[1] *Ibid.*, at pp. 528–529.

[2] 311 U. S. 91.

[3] *Ibid.*, p. 103. Section 5 of the Act, quoted in part by the court, reads: "No court of the United States shall have jurisdiction to issue a restraining order or temporary or permanent injunction upon the ground that any of the persons participating or interested in a labor dispute constitute or are engaged in an unlawful combination or conspiracy because of the doing in concert of the acts enumerated in Section 4 of this Act."

Hutcheson,[1] decided Feb. 3, 1941.   In the opinion of the majority, written by Justice Frankfurter, the facts of the case were summarized as follows:

"Anheuser-Busch, Inc., operating a large plant in St. Louis, contracted with Borsari Tank Corporation for the erection of an additional facility.   The Gaylord Container Corporation, a lessee of adjacent property from Anheuser-Busch, made a similar contract for a new building with the Stocker Company.   Anheuser-Busch obtained the materials for its brewing and other operations and sold its finished products largely through interstate shipments.   The Gaylord Corporation was equally dependent on interstate commerce for marketing its goods, as were the construction companies for their building materials. Among the employees of Anheuser-Busch were members of the United Brotherhood of Carpenters and Joiners of America and of the International Association of Machinists.   The conflicting claims of these two organizations, affiliated with the American Federation of Labor, in regard to the erection and dismantling of machinery had long been a source of controversy between them.   Anheuser-Busch had had agreements with both organizations whereby the Machinists were given the disputed jobs and the Carpenters agreed to submit all disputes to arbitration.   But in 1939 the president of the Carpenters, their general representative, and two officials of the Carpenters' local organization, the four men under indictment, stood on the claims of the Carpenters for the jobs.   Rejection by the employer of the Carpenters' demand and the refusal of the latter to submit to arbitration were followed by a strike of the Carpenters, called by the defendants against the Anheuser-Busch and the construction companies, a picketing of Anheuser-Busch and its tenant, and a request through circular letters and the official publication of the Carpenters that union members and their friends refrain from buying Anheuser-Busch beer."[2]

For these activities, the majority ruled, officials of the union could not be indicted under the Sherman Act for, as Justice Frankfurter declared: "It is at once apparent that the acts with which the defendants are charged are the kind of acts protected by §20 of the Clayton Act.   The refusal of the Carpenters to work for Anheuser-Busch or on construction work being done for it and its adjoining tenant, and the peaceful attempt to get members of other unions similarly to refuse to work, are plainly within the free scope accorded to workers by §20 for 'terminating any relation of employment,' or 'ceasing to perform any work or labor,' or 'recommending, advising, or persuading others by peaceful means so to do.'   The picketing of Anheuser-Busch premises with signs to indicate that Anheuser-Busch was unfair to organized labor, a familiar practice in these situations, comes within the language 'attending at any place

[1] 312 U. S. 219.
[2] *Ibid.*, at p. 227.

where any such person or persons may lawfully be, for the purpose of peacefully obtaining or communicating information, or from peacefully persuading any person to work or to abstain from working.' Finally, the recommendation to union members and their friends not to buy or use the product of Anheuser-Busch is explicitly covered by 'ceasing to patronize . . . any party to such dispute, or from recommending, advising, or persuading others by peaceful and lawful means so to do.'"[1]

To the argument that the defendants could not invoke the Clayton Act because outsiders to the immediate dispute were also involved, Justice Frankfurter replied that the Norris-La Guardia Act definition of a "labor dispute" has superseded any previous rulings of the courts interpreting the Clayton Act. Of course, the Norris-La Guardia Act referred only to the equity phase of the remedies of the Sherman Act and did not touch upon the criminal side. "But to argue, as it was urged before us, that the *Duplex* case still governs for purposes of a criminal prosecution is to say that that which on the equity side of the court is allowable conduct may in a criminal proceeding become the road to prison. It would be strange indeed that although neither the Government nor Anheuser-Busch could have sought an injunction against the acts here challenged, the elaborate efforts to permit such conduct failed to prevent criminal liability punishable with imprisonment and heavy fines. That is not the way to read the will of Congress, particularly when expressed by a statute which, as we have already indicated, is practically and historically one of a series of enactments touching one of the most sensitive national problems. Such legislation must not be read in a spirit of mutilating narrowness.

"The underlying aim of the Norris-La Guardia Act was to restore the broad purpose which Congress thought it had formulated in the Clayton Act but which was frustrated, so Congress believed, by unduly restrictive judicial construction . . . The Norris-La Guardia Act reasserted the original purpose of the Clayton Act by infusing into it the immunized trade union activities as redefined by the later Act."[2]

This reassertion of Congress compelled the court to review its interpretations of the Clayton Act, and the Duplex and Bedford decisions were overruled as not consonant with the congressional conception of the Clayton Act as reaffirmed in the Norris-La Guardia Act.[3]

[1] *Ibid.*, at p. 233.
[2] *Ibid.*, at p. 234.
[3] Justice Stone concurred in the result on the basis of the holding in the Apex case that restraints upon interstate commerce flowing from strikes and picketing and incidental to strikes are not within the purview of the Sherman Act. Declared Justice Stone: "It is a novel proposition that allegations of local peaceful picketing of a manufacturing plant to enforce union demands concerning terms of employment accompanied by announcements that the employer is unfair to organized labor is a violation of the Sherman Act whatever effect on interstate commerce may be intended to follow from the acts done" (*ibid.*, at p.

The wide latitude this decision gives labor's right to strike, picket, and boycott is not limited by a jurisdictional strike. In the words of Justice Frankfurter, "There is nothing remotely within the terms of §20 that differentiates between trade union conduct directed against an employer because of a controversy arising in the relation between employer and employee, as such, and conduct similarly directed but ultimately due to an internecine struggle between two unions seeking the favor of the same employer. Such strife between competing unions has been an obdurate conflict in the evolution of so-called craft unionism and has undoubtedly been one of the potent forces in the modern development of industrial unions. These conflicts have intensified industrial tension but there is not the slightest warrant for saying that Congress has made §20 inapplicable to trade union conduct resulting from them."[1]

Labor's freedom from the traditional restrictions of the Sherman Act is coextensive with labor's activities dictated by "self-interest." And within that realm, the courts may not exercise any judgment. As Justice Frankfurter declared, "So long as a union acts in its self-interest and does not combine with non-labor groups, the licit and the illicit under §20 are not to be distinguished by any judgment regarding the wisdom or unwisdom, the rightness or wrongness, the selfishness or unselfishness of the end of which the particular union activities are the means."[1] Labor's "self-interest" and isolated action will then become the future criteria for the courts to appraise in judging of the applicability of the Sherman Act to the activities of organized labor. Such judgment, however, will not liberate the court from evaluating labor policy.

The Boycott and the Black List.—In the boycott trade unionists have found a second weapon, but a less powerful one than the strike. It has accompanied many strikes and has been resorted to in many cases where the workers employed by the aggrieving party were not unionized and strikes were therefore virtually impossible. Moreover, it has frequently been applied, especially in the building industry, to nonunion materials.

The Boycott.—The word "boycott" has been given different meanings by the courts and by different writers.[2] Some have described it in concrete terms but have declared it to be impossible of accurate definition; others have defined it in different ways. Perhaps the most useful defini-

---

241). The dissent of Justice Roberts, in which Chief Justice Hughes concurred, turned in the main on the proposition that the Norris-La Guardia Act did not affect the indictment aspect of the Sherman Act and that, therefore, the prior Supreme Court decisions were still controlling.

[1] *Ibid.*, at p. 232.

[2] For a comprehensive listing of the various (and frequently irreconcilable) definitions, see Edwin Stacey Oakes, *The Law of Organized Labor and Industrial Conflicts* (1927), pp. 602*ff*.

tion for the lay reader is that given by Adams and Sumner: "The boycott, as used in modern labor disputes, may be defined as a combination to suspend dealings with another party, and to persuade or coerce others to suspend dealings, in order to force this party to comply with some demand, or to punish him for noncompliance in the past."[1] The main defect in this definition is that it runs too much in personal terms. One type of boycott is that of nonunion materials where the personal element may be entirely absent. But this type, sometimes called a "producers' boycott," really consists of a strike against nonunion materials.

By means of the ordinary strike the union attempts to withdraw the employer's supply of labor and thus bring pressure to bear upon him by rendering it impossible for him to continue his business until an agreement is reached. By means of the personal boycott, the union attempts to curtail the demand for the employer's product or service and thus, through a contraction of demand, injure his business. By means of the boycott of nonunion materials, the union attempts to limit the market to union firms, the primary object being to extend organization and to protect collective bargaining.

While in many countries the union boycott has found little acceptance by trade unions it has been used most extensively in the United States.[2] It was employed as early as in the 1830's in the Baltimore hat trade and now and then during the next four decades. It was during the 1880's, however, that its use became widespread. Frequently it was levied with little reason and in many cases spread beyond reasonable limits. Such radical use and the multiplicity of boycotts became sources of weakness in the labor movement. This weakness and the restrictive rulings of the courts finally led to attempts by both the Knights of Labor and the American Federation of Labor to bring the levy of boycotts under control. The procedure adopted by the A.F. of L., and imposed by it upon its city central bodies, was to refer requests for endorsements of boycotts to an appropriate committee for investigation and to attempt to secure adjustment of the grievances. Further negotiation frequently proved successful. Only in the event of failure to adjust a grievance was a central body allowed to endorse and assist in the spreading of a boycott. This procedure had the double effect of greatly reducing the number of local boycotts and restricting the number of those without adequate cause. The greatest factor making for more conservative use of the boycott, however, has been the common and statute law.

Labor boycotts, as has been indicated, have been classified in different ways. Witte makes the useful distinction, implied in our discussion

---

[1] Thomas S. Adams and Helen L. Sumner, *Labor Problems* (1905), pp. 196–197.

[2] Full accounts of the boycott are to be found in Harry W. Laidler, *Boycotts and the Labor Struggle* (1914) and Leo Wolman, *The Boycott in American Trade Unions*, Johns Hopkins University Studies, Series 34 (1916).

above, between "consumers'" and "workers'" boycotts.[1] The one is "a collective refusal to purchase boycotted commodities," the other "a refusal to work upon or with boycotted materials" carried out through strikes or threat of strike. Laidler has spoken of primary, secondary, and tertiary boycotts on the basis of whom they are levied against in the chain of persons. The classification made by another writer is into the label, the unfair list, the primary, and the secondary boycott.[2] It may be said, however, that the label, unless demanded in connection with materials, is not a boycott at all but an appeal for patronage, and that the unfair list is just what the name indicates, viz., a means of calling attention to and spreading a boycott. The distinction made by the courts, when a distinction is made at all, is between primary and secondary boycotts.[3] The line of distinction between the two has not, however, always been the same. For example, the Supreme Court of the United States and most of the state courts have regarded the workers' boycott of materials as a secondary, while the New York courts regard it as a primary boycott.

The primary or simple boycott is one in which the aggrieved party resolves not to patronize a firm or firms or its product and appeals to its friends to withhold their patronage. The usual secondary boycott is one in which, in addition to the above, coercion, loss of business, etc., are resorted to or threatened to cause third parties to sever business relations. For example, in a well-known Los Angeles case the printers, on strike, resolved not to purchase copies of the newspaper or to insert advertisements in it and appealed to the "friends of labor" to withhold their patronage from the aggrieving publisher. As would be expected, the measure was quite ineffective. Later on, in an effort to make the union's action effective, its representatives demanded that stores and patent-medicine manufacturers withdraw their advertisements under threat of boycott. With attempted coercion of third parties the boycott took on the secondary or "compound" form, based upon coercion, intimidation, or threat of loss of business. Primary boycotts of restaurants, stores, barbershops, and the like, may be effective, but these are exceptional cases. Most boycotts have been of the secondary or compound type, for the union must secure the withdrawal of patronage of "third parties" if the boycott is to be effective.

The legality of the boycott, under the common law, has depended upon (1) the lawfulness of the object in view, and (2) the lawfulness of the means employed. The courts have not all viewed the matter in the same way, but, with very few exceptions, they have held the secondary boycott,

---

[1] E. E. Witte, *The Government in Labor Disputes*, p. 38.

[2] Frank T. Carlton, *History and Problems of Organized Labor* (1911), p. 167. In a revised edition (1920), however, the label disappeared from the list (p. 180).

[3] Sometimes the word "compound" is used interchangeably with "secondary."

as described above, to be malicious and unlawful. The reasons assigned for this view are that by threat and coercion a third party is deprived of his right to patronize whom he pleases and/or that a breach of contract is induced. In only a few states have the courts approved of secondary boycotts generally.[1]

A very important form of boycott is found in the refusal of union men to work on nonunion materials or on materials handled by nonunion workmen. Refusal to work on nonunion materials has been of frequent occurrence in many trades but most strikingly in building construction. As to the lawfulness of this type of boycott the courts have been divided. In most jurisdictions they have declared it to be unlawful on the grounds already noted, *viz.*, that it interferes with the business rights of third parties or involves breach of contract.[2] In other jurisdictions, however, the courts have refused to grant restraining orders in such cases, because they have accepted the view that the working groups concerned had a common interest such as has now been recognized in the Norris-La Guardia Act.   In California, years ago, the Supreme Court ruled that it was not unlawful for the members of a union to refuse to use materials provided by an aggrieving firm, even though breach of contract was involved.[3] Similar rulings have been made by the supreme courts of North Carolina and New York.[4] Indeed, the New York courts have gone far in legalizing the secondary boycott. For not only have they sanctioned the boycott, say, of nonunion lumber by carpenters who claim jurisdiction over millwork as well as construction work;[5] they have also sanctioned the boycott by building tradesmen of materials because serviced by nonunion teamsters[6] and by dock workers of freight because hauled by nonunion drivers.[7]

---

[1] The California Supreme Court has held that trade unions have a legal right to carry on either primary or secondary boycotts. *P. M. Lisse, et al. v. Local Union No.* 31, *Cooks, Waiters and Waitresses et al.*, 2 Cal. (2d) 312 (1935).

[2] Of the numerous decisions, the following may be cited: *Mears Slayton Lumber Company v. United Brotherhood of Carpenters and Joiners*, 156 Ill. App. 327 (1910); *Anderson & Lind Manufacturing Company v. Carpenters' District Council*, 308 Ill. 488 (1923); *Stearns Lumber Company v. Howlett*, 260 Mass. 45 (1927); *Lohse Patent Door Company v. Fuelle*, 215 Mo. 421 (1908); *Pacific Typesetting Company v. International Typographical Union*, 125 Wash. 273 (1923).

[3] *Parkinson Company v. Building Trades Council*, 154 Cal. 581 (1908).

[4] *State v. Van Pelt*, 136 N.C. 633 (1904); *Bossert v. Dhuy*, 221 N.Y. 342 (1917); *Newton Co. v. Erickson*, 126 N.Y.S 949 (1911) affirmed in 129 N.Y.S. 1111 (1911) and in 221 N.Y. 632 (1917); *Aeolian Co. v. Fischer*, 27 Fed. (2d) 560 (1928).

[5] This in New York is regarded as a primary boycott. A leading case in New York is *Bossert v. Dhuy*, 221 N.Y. 342 (1917).

[6] *Willson & Adams Co. v. Pearce*, 264 N.Y. 521 (1934).

[7] *New York Lumber Trade Association v. Lacey*, 269 N.Y. 595 (1935). See also *Reardon, v. Caton*, 178 N.Y. S. 713 (1919), and *Reardon v. International Mercantile Marine Co.*, 178 N.Y.S. 722 (1919).

Very frequently unions have advertised the product or products of an aggrieving firm as "unfair" and have attempted to persuade or coerce consumers to withhold their patronage. In recent years, picketing dealers in the product or products in question has furnished occasion for court decisions, the most interesting of which is that in *Goldfinger v. Feintuch*.[1] Here, the union had not succeeded in organizing the poorly paid workers of a New York firm manufacturing the "Ukor" meat products. It therefore began to picket the retail distributors of these products—but not the entire business of these stores. After the manufacturer had failed to secure an order restraining this picketing, a distributor, one Goldfinger, tried to do so. He was denied relief.[2] The New York Court of Appeals, in upholding the denial of relief, said: "Within the limits of peaceful picketing . . . picketing may be carried on not only against the manufacturer but against a *non-union product* sold by one in unity of interest with the manufacturer who is in the same business for profit. Where a manufacturer pays less than union wages both it and the retailers who sell its products are in a position to undersell competitors who pay the higher scale, and this may result in an unfair reduction of the wages of union members. . . . Where the manufacturer disposes of the product through retailers in unity of interest with it, unless the union may follow the product to the place where it is sold and peacefully ask the public to refrain from purchasing it, the union would be deprived of a fair and proper means of bringing its plea to the attention of the public."[3]

In this case the boycott prosecuted was regarded as a primary boycott, for only the "Ukor" meats were advertised as unfair. Of course the picketing would probably injure other parts of the distributor's business, but the boycott was not compounded, as it frequently has been, by extension to the entire business. Had it been so extended, the court was careful to state in its opinion, it would have been unlawful. In line with this observation, in *Canepa v. "John Doe,"* in which a dealer, ignorant of the situation, had bought a neon sign from a firm having labor difficulties and had had his entire business boycotted, the Court of Appeals held that an unlawful secondary boycott was involved.[4] Thus, in New York, where the courts have been unusually careful to make needed distinctions, the position taken on this subject has been stated as follows: "If the banners [carried by pickets] are considered to be directed merely against the unfair product, the picketing will be permitted; but if the retailer

---

[1] It was said several years ago that only four cases of picketing of a distributor of "unfair" manufacturers' products had been found in reported cases outside of the State of New York. *International Juridical Association Monthly Bulletin*, vol. 6 (1938), p. 89.

[2] 288 N.Y. Supp. 855 (Supreme Court, N.Y. County, 1936).

[3] 276 N.Y. at 286 (1937).

[4] *Canepa v. "John Doe" as President of Sheet Metal Workers' International Association*, 277 N.Y. 52 (1938).

himself is called 'unfair,' and the public is asked not to patronize him, the courts generally have enjoined the picketing."[1]

The law of the primary boycott may be said to be the same as the law of the ordinary (direct or non-sympathetic) strike. As has been said:

"It is generally not unlawful for a combination of working people to withhold their patronage from a dealer or manufacturer against whom they have a grievance. Usually also it is not unlawful for them to ask and persuade others to join them in withholding patronage. In all cases, however, the purpose of the persons conducting the boycott must be one which the courts regard as justifiable, and the means employed to make the boycott effective must be free from physical violence, coercion, or intimidation. In the conduct of a boycott, there must also be no interference with ingress and egress to the boycotted premises. When pickets are stationed in front of the boycotted establishment, they must not interfere with the prospective customers, and their very presence may be unlawful if it tends to attract crowds."[2]

In the absence of prohibitive legislation, such as that enacted in Illinois and in certain other states and in some cities, it has not been illegal to call attention to a lawful boycott by the distribution or display of cards, handbills, placards, and banners. The statements made, however, must not be false or libelous; they must not convey a threat; nor may they arouse in third parties a fear of physical or economic injury. Not infrequently, also, courts have held that terming employers "unfair" implied a threat and was therefore illegal.[3] On the other hand, some of the state courts have held that because of the right of free speech (and publication), the unfair list may be employed to spread an unlawful boycott. This has not, however, been the view of most of the state courts or of the Supreme Court of the United States. In the Bucks Stove and Range Co. case the Supreme Court of the United States held (as an abstract proposition) that the constitutional guarantee of free speech and free press was not absolute and was of no avail when spoken or written words were employed in the prosecution of an unlawful boycott.[4] Recently, however, the Supreme Court has rendered decisions of a different character, which interpret the constitutional guarantee in such

---

[1] As stated in "Secondary Boycotts in Labor Disputes," in *International Juridical Association Monthly Bulletin*, vol. 6 (1938), p. 89.

[2] E. E. Witte, *The Government in Labor Disputes*, p. 40.

[3] Cases upholding the right to refer to employers as "unfair," as cited by Professor Witte, are: *People v. Radt*, 15 N.Y. Crim. 174, 71 N.Y.S. 846 (1900); *State v. Van Pelt*, 136 N.C. 633, 49 S.E. 177 (1904); *Steffes v. Motion Picture Operators*, 136 Minn. 200, 161 N.W. 524 (1917); *Clark Lunch Co. v. Cleveland Waiters*, 22 Ohio App. 265, 154 N.E. 363 (1926). Cases in which the opposite position has been taken are: *Seattle Brewing and Malting Co. v. Hansen*, 114 Fed. 1011 (1905); *Henrici v. Alexander*, 198 Ill. App. 568 (1916); *Martin v. Francke*, 227 Mass. 272, 116 N.E. 404 (1917); *Campbell v. Motion Picture Operators*, 151 Minn. 220, 186 N.W. 781 (1922).

[4] *Gompers v. Bucks Stove & Range Co.*, 221 U.S. 418 (1911). This case arose under the

manner as to deprive the states and minor political divisions of power to
prohibit the circulation of unfair lists or to require a license as a condition
of distributing them.[1] The use of unfair lists and the display of cards,
handbills, placards, and banners are now lawful, provided that the statements are not false, or libelous, or coercive in nature, and provided that
the end in view is lawful.

Such, briefly, is the common law developed and applied to the boycott
in the United States. The federal antitrust laws and the federal and
state anti-injunction laws also have had very important bearing in this
connection. How the Sherman Act was applied in the Loewe and Duplex
cases has been told in the preceding section of this chapter, incidental to
the discussion of strikes and restraint of interstate commerce.[2] It
remains to note briefly a few other cases in order that the significance of
the antitrust laws may be adequately appreciated and then to discuss the
bearing of anti-injunction legislation of the Norris-La Guardia type upon
the use of the boycott.

As Professor Berman has said, "The Supreme Court decision in the
Bedford case [of 1927] may be considered as the capstone of the long
development in the application of the Sherman Act to labor."[3] During
the World War I period collective bargaining obtained in the quarrying of
limestone in the Bedford-Bloomington, Ind., District. In 1921, however, the parties in interest were unable to agree upon a new contract,
relationships were broken, the union went on strike, and the firms set
up organizations of their "scab" employees. In 1924 the Journeymen
Stone Cutters' Association of North America, which claims jurisdiction
over both the quarrying and the installation of stone on buildings and
with which the local union was affiliated, began to enforce a provision
of its constitution prohibiting its members from handling stone "cut
by men working in opposition" to it. Those members and those locals
of stonecutters not inclined to observe this provision of the constitution
were threatened with penalty. Thus, in an effort to bring pressure to
bear upon the stone companies, building operations were interrupted by
strikes in various parts of the country. With 75 per cent of their product

---

Antitrust Act, not under the common law which is our immediate concern, but the ruling on
freedom of speech is in point here.

[1] *Lovell v. City of Griffin*, 303 U.S. 444 (1938). In this case, a city ordinance, prohibiting
the distribution of leaflets and circulars without a license, was invalidated on the ground
that the right to distribute pamphlets and leaflets is a part of the liberty of the press and
may not be infringed by states and municipalities, except to safeguard against indecency,
etc. In recent years local ordinances had increasingly limited the distribution of circulars.
See "Ordinances Restricting Leaflet Distribution," *International Judicial Association
Monthly Bulletin*, vol. 5 (1937), p. 147. See also *Hague, Mayor, et al. v. Committee for
Industrial Organization et al.*, 307 U.S. 496 (1939).

[2] *Supra*, pp. 557–558, 569–570.

[3] Edward Berman, *Labor and the Sherman Act*, p. 179.

finding a market outside of Indiana and with sales more or less diminished because of the fear of building contractors of difficulty with their workmen, the companies sought a restraining order in the District Court. This was denied, and the decision of the court was upheld by the Circuit Court of Appeals. The case was then carried to the Supreme Court of the United States, where by majority decision the earlier ruling was reversed.[1]

The union contended in this case that it had not interfered with the transportation of stone and that its sole purpose was to organize the cutters and carvers of stone at the quarries. As in its rulings in earlier cases, the court held that the presence or absence of direct interference with transportation was immaterial. With reference to the second contention, it conceded that organization of the workers was the ultimate end in view but ruled that its accomplishment was sought by the unlawful means of restricting interstate commerce.

"The strikes, ordered and carried out with the sole object of preventing the use and installation of petitioners' product in other states, necessarily threatened to destroy or narrow petitioners' interstate trade by taking from them their customers. That the organizations, in general purpose and in and of themselves, were lawful and that the ultimate result aimed at may not have been illegal in itself, are beside the point. Where the means adopted are unlawful, the innocent general character of the organizations adopting them or the lawfulness of the ultimate end sought to be attained cannot serve as a justification."[2]

In this case Justice Brandeis, with the concurrence of Justice Holmes, dissented in a vigorous opinion. Among other things, he pointed out that the court in the Standard Oil, the American Tobacco, and other cases had held that only *unreasonable* restraints of trade were prohibited by the Sherman Act. The union's action in this case, Justice Brandeis thought, had been reasonable. It was defending itself against mighty employers controlling 70 per cent of the cut-stone industry. There had been no trespass, breach of contract, violence, or intimidation. The workers, acting under a provision of a constitution they had subscribed to when joining the union, had, in different localities, only refused to set stone purchased from their industrial enemy. This was the only means of self-protection against a combination of militant and powerful employers. To restrain the union from doing these things, he said, "smacks of involuntary servitude."

The Brims case,[3] decided by the Supreme Court of the United States in 1926, is important, for it declared illegal an agreement of a type fre-

---

[1] *Bedford Cut Stone Company v. Journeymen Stone Cutters' Association,* 274 U.S. 37 (1927).

[2] *Ibid.,* at p. 55.

[3] *United States v. Brims,* 272 U.S. 549 (1926).

quently found in the building trades and only less frequently in other trades as well. The agreement was one between the carpenters, the building contractors, and the manufacturers of millwork in Chicago, providing that the manufacturers and contractors would employ union carpenters only and that the carpenters would not install millwork produced under nonunion conditions. One object was to extend organization of millworkers by excluding the cheaper product from the local market; another was to enlarge the volume of business done by local millowners; the consumer was expected to bear the additional cost of building involved. The agreement was satisfactory to the contractors because they were given liberal discounts on their purchases of materials from the union firms.

In 1921, the manufacturers, contractors, and officers of the union were indicted and some of them convicted of conspiracy to violate the Sherman Act. The judgment was overruled by the Court of Appeals for the Seventh District on the ground that the restriction was not directed against the shipment of millwork into Illinois but against nonunion millwork produced in or outside of Illinois and that, therefore, the evidence did not sustain the indictment of conspiracy to restrain interstate commerce. But when the case was taken to the Supreme Court, the decision of the Court of Appeals was overruled and the decision of the District Court sustained. By unanimous decision[1] it was declared that "as intended by all the parties, the so-called outside competition was cut down and thereby interstate commerce directly and materially impeded," and that "the crime of restraining interstate commerce through combination is not condoned by the inclusion of intrastate commerce as well."[2]

A third important case applying the Sherman law is that of *Industrial Association of San Francisco v. U.S.*, decided by the Supreme Court of the United States in 1925.[3] This case involved the charge that the Association, whose members were building contractors and other business men, was restricting interstate commerce as a result of the permit system used in the purchase of building materials.

After collective bargaining had obtained many years in the building industry in San Francisco, it broke down in 1921 and the so-called "American Plan," or open shop, was inaugurated. The Industrial Association was organized and a permit system adopted that made it practically impossible for building contractors not going along with the open-shop plan to secure necessary building materials. In 1923 the government filed suit against the Association, charging that it was engaged in a conspiracy to restrain interstate commerce in building

[1] Justice Stone did not participate.
[2] 272 U.S. at pp. 552–553.
[3] 268 U.S. 64.

materials. The District Court rendered a verdict for the government, holding that, however little interstate commerce was interfered with, the plan adopted was a violation of the Sherman Act. This decision was, however, overruled by the Supreme Court. It found that the permit required was effective only as to plaster that had already been brought into the state and, as Justice Sutherland phrased it, had "commingled with the common mass of local property, and in respect of which, therefore, the interstate movement and the interstate commercial status had ended." The lower court had found, also, that the permit system had reduced the amount of plumbing supplies brought into the state. The Supreme Court, however, was of the view that the effects upon and interference with interstate trade, if any, "were clearly incidental, indirect or remote"; the "thing aimed at and sought to be attained was not restraint of interstate sale or shipment of commodities, but was purely a local matter, namely, regulation of building operations within a limited local area, so as to prevent their domination by the labor unions. Interstate commerce, indeed commerce of any description, was not the object of attack." Thus, the decision involving employers' activities ran in terms of the decisions in the first Coronado and the Herkert cases rather than in terms of later decisions—those rendered since 1925 and subsequent to the decision in this particular case.[1] The comment should also be made that while the number of parties involved in the activities alleged unlawfully to restrain interstate commerce was fewer, the effect upon interstate commerce less, and perhaps the intent to restrain trade less apparent here than in the Brims case, the two cases had much in common. The methods in both cases had as their natural consequence curtailment of trade that was partly interstate in character. Interstate commerce was no more the object of attack in the one case than in the other. It may be observed also that basing the decision that interstate commerce had not been interfered with upon the fact that the materials had come into the state and commingled with other materials was hardly in point in view of the already discussed decisions on interference with interstate commerce.

It is difficult to reconcile some of the decisions of the Supreme Court in defining and applying the provisions of the Sherman Act in strike and boycott situations. It would appear that, for years, and certainly down to the end of the 1920's, interpretations were, on the whole, increasingly severe in the limitations they placed upon labor organizations in these connections. Only with the recent decisions in the Apex, Milk Wagon

---

[1] In January, 1938, a large number of officials and members of the Progressive Miners in Illinois, and a few other persons, were convicted in the United States District Court of violation of the Sherman Act and also of interference with the mails, by bombings and other violent acts. These acts had been committed incidental to the war between this organization and the United Mine Workers.

Drivers, and Hutcheson cases[1] were the limitations on the strike and boycott relaxed. Because they must ordinarily take the initiative in industrial disputes, labor organizations principally, rather than employers' associations, were handicapped. The far-flung boycott was outlawed; the strike by coal miners and others was crippled. And for what reason? Is there any more logical reason for outlawing or crippling a boycott or strike by coal miners or other interstate groups than a strike by some other group resulting in equal loss and public inconvenience? And, if a strike or a lockout is limited or crippled, is there not an obligation to create adequate public machinery for the purpose of seeing that justice is done? Is it not evident that economic interests frequently transcend state boundaries? Whether Congress did or did not intend that the Sherman Act should apply to labor combinations and employers' associations, it is unfortunate that it was applied as it was in some of these cases.[2]

The Norris-La Guardia Immunities.—In turning to the bearing of anti-injunction legislation upon the phases of labor law we have been discussing, it is to be noted that, contrary to the hope of labor, the substantive law was not changed by the Clayton Act of 1914,[3] as that measure was interpreted by the Supreme Court through the twenties and thirties. The Norris-La Guardia Act of 1932,[4] as interpreted and applied, however, removed many of the former restrictions on strike and boycott activities, and in the early 1940's the Clayton Act provisions were reconciled with it by the Supreme Court.[5] Had it been in effect, the Duplex, Bedford, and other important cases could not have been decided as they were, for, among other things, the Norris-La Guardia Act provides:

"Sec. 4. No court of the United States shall have jurisdiction to issue any restraining order or temporary or permanent injunction in any case involving or growing out of any labor dispute to prohibit any person or persons participating or interested in such dispute (as these terms are herein defined) from doing, whether singly or in concert, any of the following acts:

---

[1] *Supra*, pp. 575–581.

[2] It is not intended to imply that monopolies should be protected if labor organization is involved. The point is that in some of these cases organized labor was rendered ineffective merely because a strike or boycott interfered with interstate commerce. The illiberality is found in unequal treatment of unions differently circumstanced with reference to the market. Unlike other organizations, some must function in wide markets if they are to be effective, and as they function in these wide markets they may not affect the public more adversely than it is affected by strikes in many local situations.

[3] *Supra*, pp. 569–570 and *infra*. pp. 615–616.

[4] This act will be discussed at some length in Chap. XII. It is necessary, however, to discuss its bearing upon strike and boycott activities at this point.

[5] *U.S. v. Hutcheson*, 63 Sup. Ct. 463 (1941).

"(a) Ceasing or refusing to perform any work or to remain in any relation of employment; . . .

"(e) Giving publicity to the existence of, or the facts involved in, any labor dispute, whether by advertising, speaking, patrolling, or by any other method not involving fraud or violence.

"(f) Assembling peaceably to act or to organize to act in promotion of their interests in a labor dispute;

"(g) Advising or notifying any person of an intention to do any of the acts heretofore specified;

"(h) Agreeing with other persons to do or not to do any of the acts heretofore specified; and

"(i) Advising, urging, or otherwise causing or inducing without fraud or violence the acts heretofore specified. . . . "

In short, the Norris-La Guardia Act has placed a ban on the granting of restraining orders or injunctions by the federal courts in labor disputes unless fraud or violence is involved. The term "labor dispute" was much more broadly defined than it had theretofore been defined or conceived of by most of the courts. The definition is found in Sec. 13, which reads: "When used in this Act, and for the purposes of this Act—

"(a) A case shall be held to involve or to grow out of a labor dispute when the case involves persons who are engaged in the same industry, trade, craft, or occupation; or have direct or indirect interests therein; or who are employees of the same employer; or who are members of the same or an affiliated organization of employers or employees; whether such dispute is (1) between one or more employers or associations of employers and one or more employees or associations of employees; (2) between one or more employers or associations of employers and one or more employers or associations of employers; or (3) between one or more employees or associations of employees and one or more employees or associations of employees; or when the case involves any conflicting or competing interests in a 'labor dispute' (as hereinafter defined) of 'persons participating or interested' therein (as hereinafter defined).

"(b) A person or association shall be held to be a person participating or interested in a labor dispute if relief is sought against him or it, and if he or it is engaged in the same industry, trade, craft, or occupation in which such dispute occurs, or has a direct or indirect interest therein, or is a member, officer, or agent of any association composed in whole or in part of employers or employees engaged in such industry, trade, craft, or occupation.

"(c) The term 'labor dispute' includes any controversy concerning terms or conditions of employment, or concerning the association or representation of persons in negotiating, fixing, maintaining, changing or seeking to arrange terms or conditions of employment, regardless of whether or not the disputants stand in the proximate relation of employer and employee."[1]

The changes in the law effected by the Norris-La Guardia Act, in so far as injunctive relief is concerned, are clear when one recalls the judicially made law as found in limitations on the number of pickets in the American Steel Foundries case,[2] and in the limitation of rights to past, present, and prospective employees in the Duplex case,[3] and when one recalls also the common membership of the stone setters and the stonecutters in the Bedford Cut Stone case,[4] and employment in the same industry in Philadelphia and New York as set forth in the Philadelphia clothing workers' case.[5] The possibility of criminal prosecution under the Sherman Act has also been drastically reduced by the Supreme Court's reinterpretation of the Clayton Act.[6] Such judgments as that in *Loewe v. Lawler* are apparently no longer possible.

In 1943 seventeen[7] of the states had anti-injunction laws based upon the Norris-La Guardia model. Save that the Wisconsin Act expressly declares that it does not "legalize a secondary boycott," these laws contain the same provisions as, or provisions similar to, those of the Norris-La Guardia Act. Hence in equity cases the right to strike and the right to boycott are now protected in a number of important industrial states, as they are in the jurisdiction of the Federal Government.

Such is the American law relating to the labor boycott. What more, if anything, is called for to bring the law into harmony with sound public policy? More specifically, should the secondary boycott, which is unlawful in most of the states, be legalized? Before attempting to answer this specific question, however, it will be well to discuss the black list briefly for in much of the literature the use of the black list is given as a reason for the legalization of all secondary boycotts.

The Black List.—The black list is an employers' boycott of workers. Earlier in our discussion reference has been made to the exclusion of all union men in the maintenance of the employer's closed shop. Here, however, we shall discuss the more personal black-listing of union leaders and "agitators" and others giving offense, in order to keep them out of

---

[1] Sec. 13.
[2] *Infra*, p. 616.
[3] *Supra*, pp. 557–558.
[4] *Supra*, pp. 587–588.
[5] *Supra*, p. 558.
[6] *Supra*, p. 578.
[7] Colorado, Connecticut, Idaho, Indiana, Louisiana, Maryland, Massachusetts, Minnesota, New Jersey, New York, North Dakota, Oregon, Pennsylvania, Utah, Washington, Wisconsin, and Wyoming.

employment and perhaps to force them out of the community in search of a livelihood. Of such black-listing there has been a great deal, and, though it has been accompanied by much secrecy, the established instances of it would lead one to believe that, say, ten years ago it was more prevalent than it had been theretofore. The chief difference evident between older and more recent practice is that, for the most part, it has in more recent years been done otherwise than through a circulated list of names. As Professor Witte has said, "In this day, the old-fashioned blacklist is *passé*. Reports about union agitators are conveyed by telephone, letter, or word of mouth, through a central hiring hall, or the record system of an employers' association."[1] Exchanges for the allocation of labor and central files have been successfully used by anti-union clothing manufacturers, open-shop printers' associations, and associations in the metal trades. Very frequently these methods have been fortified by employment of the labor spy.[2]

Under the common law an employer may discharge a worker for any reason, and upon the request of another he may give his reason for so doing; but he may not hound or libel a man in order to secure his discharge or to keep him out of employment. The common law had, however, by 1932 been replaced or fortified by general anti-black-listing statutes in more than half of the states.[3] Six states, including four of those with general anti-black-listing laws, then provided penalties where employers, upon demand, refused to give discharged employees a truthful statement of the reasons for discharge.[4] The doubt as to the constitutionality of some of this legislation seems to have been removed by decisions of the Supreme Court of the United States.[5]

State laws against black-listing have, however, been of little avail. According to Professor Witte, "Only two successful criminal prosecutions for blacklisting are known, and there have been less than a dozen cases in which strikers or union men have recovered damages, with but one instance of an injunction issued against a blacklist. Nearly all of these cases are old and are greatly outnumbered by unsuccessful actions."[6] The explanation of the lack of success realized is found largely in the techniques employed, the secrecy with which black-listing may be done, and the extreme difficulty in securing the evidence necessary to sustain conviction for conspiracy or a damage suit.

[1] E. E. Witte, *op. cit.*, p. 217.
[2] See Chap. XII, pp. 606–608.
[3] E. E. Witte, *The Government in Labor Disputes*, p. 213.
[4] Florida, G. L. 1927, ss. 6608–6610; Indiana, A. S. 1926, ss. 9350, 9351; Montana, R. C. 1921, ss. 3094, 11219; Nebraska, C. S. 1922, ss. 7666–7668; Ohio, G. C. 1920, s. 9012; Oklahoma, C. S. 1921, s. 7266.
[5] *Prudential Insurance Company v. Cheek*, 259 U. S. 530 (1922); *Chicago, Rock Island & Pacific Railway Company v. Perry*, 259 U.S. 548 (1922).
[6] E. E. Witte, *op. cit.*, p. 215.

The prohibition of black-listing, indeed of all discrimination because of union activity or membership, contained in the Railway Labor Act and the National Labor Relations Act have been referred to in our discussion of the "yellow-dog" contract. Section 7(a) of the National Industrial Recovery Act contained a like prohibition. In the experience of the present National Labor Board and the former (1934–1935) National Labor Relations Board, complaints of discrimination because of union membership or activity were very numerous; indeed they numbered 1,440 cases in a grand total of 4,794 filed with the latter board and its district boards between July 9, 1934, and May 31, 1935. A very large percentage of these complaints were filed in behalf of officials, committee members, and others most active in the unions. Needless to say, the prohibition of discrimination was not very effective, for the feeling against and fear of unionism remained strong; in many instances the behavior and tactics of union spokesmen left much to be desired; guilt of discrimination is difficult to establish, for clever strategy and pleadings were resorted to; the chance that effective penalties would be imposed was not great;[1] and the constitutionality of NIRA and its Sec. 7(a) was doubtful and being contested in the courts. The enforcement of the law was therefore less successful than it would have been under other circumstances and perhaps had its operation continued over a longer period. As we have seen, the same prohibitions have been incorporated in the National Labor Relations Act (1935)[2] and enforced by the present National Labor Relations Board. Of 23,936 complaints filed with this board by June 30, 1941, 14,945 or 62 per cent alleged discrimination in regard to employment. In numerous cases the reinstatement of workers with pay for time lost has been ordered, with cease-and-desist orders against further discrimination. Through national laws of wide embrace and with similar legislation in some of the states, a far more effective attempt is being made to protect workers against discrimination because of union activity—by black list or otherwise—than had been witnessed theretofore. In spite of management strategy, the legislation is at least somewhat effective in protecting workers in the jobs they hold. Perhaps no legislation can be really effective in preventing discrimination against offending union men in the filling of new positions, for there are numerous ways to conceal reasons for choices made. Nevertheless, the National Labor Relations Act is the most effective black list legislation yet devised; the black list is taboo and an employer may not refuse to hire a worker because of his union affiliation.[3]

[1] The penalties in case of conviction were reinstatement of the worker, possibly with "back pay," removal of the Blue Eagle by NRA, and criminal prosecution at the hands of a reluctant Department of Justice.

[2] Also in the statutes of some of the states.

[3] *Phelps-Dodge Corp.*, 19 N.L.R.B. 547, 313 U.S. 177; *Waumbec Mills*, 15 N.L.R.B. 37, 14 Fed. (2d) 226 (C.C.A. 1).

In their essence the black list and the labor boycott are the same. Yet in practice the one may be much more pernicious than the other.[1] The boycott may be accompanied by great abuse, but, unless it is of the impersonal form levied against materials, there are decided practical limitations upon its effective use. The personal boycott must work openly; it is more or less dependent upon public opinion. If decidedly unjust, it may create a hostile public opinion with the result that the union's unfair list may become other people's fair list. This has frequently been true of boycotts against restaurants, barbershops, and stores. In extreme instances the boycott has really been courted because of the value of advertising thereby obtained. Many union leaders deprecate the use of this instrument because, they say, it cannot be effectively used. The black list, on the other hand, is secret and is almost independent of public opinion because there is no effective basis for its formation in the concrete case. Moreover, there is some difference in motive. The boycott may be malicious, the participants in it seeking revenge for a real or fancied grievance and desiring to bankrupt the employer and to "put him out of business." Yet this is exceptional. In most instances the desire is to secure the right to organize or to extend organization, to gain recognition, and/or to secure certain specific demands. The injury is then incidental to something regarded as immediately beneficial to the union. But, in the case of the personal black list, the desire is usually to drive workers out of the trade because they have given offense as active union men. Ordinarily, unless the worker has definitely shown that he no longer has a union interest or membership, the employer does not wish to subdue him and then employ him on favorable terms. The element of malice is clearly much more evident in the black list than in the boycott. If one believes in the right to organize and in collective bargaining, he must approve of prohibitions of discrimination against union men, such as are contained in the Railway Labor Act and the National Labor Relations Act.

Public Policy and the Secondary Boycott.—Reverting to the question whether or not the secondary boycott of different types should be legalized in the United States, we may note that the question has received an affirmative answer at the hands of many persons well versed in industrial relations and labor law. For example, six of the nine members of the United States Commission on Industrial Relations advocated the legalization of all boycotts as well as of all strikes. In his argument in support of this position, Professor Commons, a member of the Commission and dean of American students of labor problems, stated that a ban on the

---

[1] For that reason a part of Professor N. P. Gilman's argument is not well taken—see *Methods of Industrial Peace* (1904), pp. 274–275—that in which he invited Mr. Gompers and others to substitute "boycott" for "black list" in their speeches and writings, because they were essentially the same instruments.

secondary boycott "does not seem to be equal treatment of the employers' blacklist which interferes with the unionists' right to have uninterrupted access to all employers, and the employees' boycott which interferes with the employers' right of access to the commodity market."[1] J. W. Bryan, an outstanding authority on certain aspects of labor law, has advocated legalization of the secondary boycott. The unions employing it, he says, merely demand that the third party choose between the two parties to a dispute. This is true. The coercion exercised he speaks of as coercion only in "a figurative sense." He asserts: "The unions are fairly entitled to all the benefits, direct or indirect, derivable by them from a bestowal of their patronage where they will—to deal with those whom they consider their friends rather than with those whom they regard as allied with their enemy."[2]

Perhaps the most comprehensive argument for the legalization of all boycotts, the secondary as well as the primary, was made years ago by Dr. Laidler. Not to legalize them, he contended, was to leave the law resting unequally upon unions and employers who used the black list, spies, and similar methods. If deprived of the use of the boycott, the unions would be driven to secret practices and the tactics of radical unions, such as the I.W.W. Legalization of the boycott would increase the strength of unionism and further collective bargaining. In closing, Dr. Laidler summarized his argument as follows:

"In view of the effectiveness of the boycott in many trades, in strengthening the hands of labor, and thus, indirectly, in advancing social welfare; in view of the weapons which are constantly being brought into play against the laborer in his struggles, necessitating the use of weapons additional to the strike and the picketing; in view of some of the substitutes which may be resorted to if the boycott is not available; in view of the decreasing likelihood of any great abuse in the employment of the boycott, and the laws on the statute books which take due care of many of the perversions complained of; and in view of the great number of peaceful settlements which would probably result from its potential use, the writer is in favor of legalizing this weapon. By this he means that neither the injunction nor the civil nor the criminal process should be employed against the primary or the secondary boycott, nor against that form of the compound boycott which involves only the threat to injure the business of another by the withdrawal of patronage or labor. He, of course, would not include in this exemption the threat of actual violence to person or property.

[1] United States Commission on Industrial Relations, *Final Report*, vol. 1 (64th Congress, 1st Session, Senate Document 415, 1916), pp. 217–218. Only the three employer representatives dissented and opposed the legalization of the secondary boycott.

[2] J. W. Bryan, "Proper Bounds of the Use of the Injunction in Labor Disputes," in *Annals of the American Academy of Political and Social Science*, vol. 36 (1910), pp. 288–301. Quotation from p. 293.

"In advocating this legalization, he believes that there will probably be some abuses in the employment of the boycott, as there are in the exercise of every right; that at times the use of this weapon is less effective than that of others at the disposal of labor; but that such abuse and such occasional ineffectiveness do not constitute any sufficient argument for rendering the boycott illegal."[1]

Much of the case made for legalizing all boycotts may be questioned. Increasingly and with a measure of success, as we have noted, workers are now being protected against discrimination by black list or otherwise. Moreover, it may be contended that the black list in its strict sense has stood and stands over against the primary boycott and that complete legalization of the primary boycott and the boycott of nonunion materials and products would do full justice to labor in so far as that instrument is concerned.   The counterpart of the personal secondary boycott is found in those comparatively infrequent instances in which employers' associations, by exercising pressure, prevent independent employers from getting necessary materials or bank credit.   But such interference with the course of trade is unlawful[2] and should remain so if labor's secondary boycott is not legalized.   The problem is to free the unions to fight the aggrieving employer and his product, and the nonunion product, on even terms and at the same time to conserve the rights of third parties.   Is to threaten loss to those who do not side with the union coercion only in a figurative sense?   Does the history of the boycott establish that or the contrary?   Is it any worse for the third-party businessman to decline to join in a boycott than for a worker to disregard labor's stand and to accept a struck job?   Few persons advocate withholding protection from the nonunion man who is unamenable to persuasion and works as a "scab."   If legalized, would the secondary boycott be used sparingly or does its radical use in some instances while it is illegal point to a different conclusion?   Of course, complete legalization of the boycott would increase the power of the union, but if the instrument were not conservatively used, would it aid collective bargaining or would it tend to create a still greater hostility to unionism, with the contrary result?   Would not the legalization of all forms of the boycott tend to develop "class war"?

The authors are among those who remain unconvinced of the soundness of the case made for the legalization of more than the primary boycott, including the workers' boycott of nonunion materials and products. Most of the distinctions and positions arrived at by the New York courts in recent years are persuasive.   The distinction between the primary and lawful and the secondary and unlawful boycott made by them is generally

---

[1] H. W. Laidler, *op. cit.*, pp. 350–351.
[2] *The Carpenters' Union v. The Citizens Committee to Enforce the Landis Award et al.* 333 Ill. 225 (1928).

well taken. It may be added that the issue of constitutionality would be raised were all secondary boycotts protected by statute.

The War Labor Disputes Act of 1943.—The provisions of the War Labor Disputes Act of 1943,[1] a measure the stated purpose of which is to prevent interruptions in production, constitute to an extent, and for the duration of the War,[2] modifications of the law of labor as already discussed, and particularly with respect to the legally permissible area of labor organization activities discussed in the immediately following chapter. A wartime measure, the Act has authorized government action when industrial disputes arise, or threaten to arise, far beyond the scope of what has been regarded as desirable or constitutionally permissible during peacetime. It should be kept in mind, however, that the right to organize and bargain collectively as provided for in the National Labor Relations Act, the machinery for determining the representatives of the workers' own choosing, the unfair labor practices of the federal Act, the operative meaning that the National Labor Relations Board has read into the provisions of that Act, and the court precedents with respect to the lawfulness of concerted action per se and of the policies and methods which labor organizations may utilize in peacetime remain intact. While some of the provisions of the 1943 federal statute impinge more directly upon matters constituting the subject matter of the following chapter than upon those matters already discussed, they may most conveniently be summarized at this point.

When the United States, late in 1941, became a participant in the second World War, the officialdom of organized labor gave to the President and to the public labor's "no-strike" pledge—a pledge adhered to, on the whole, commendably well—and the machinery for adjustment of disputes described in Chap. XIII was established by executive order early in 1942. Not until a year and one-half later did Congress enact legislation governing wartime labor relations. The more important provisions of this legislation, the War Labor Disputes Act, are the conferring of power upon the President to take possession of establishments when strikes or other labor disturbances threaten to interrupt production; the requirement that union officials give notice of disputes or threatened disputes that might interrupt production, with the *status quo* being maintained for thirty days after such notice and a strike being lawful only if approved by the majority of the workers to be affected in an election conducted by the National Labor Relations Board; the conferring of statutory status upon, and the defining of the powers and duties of,

---

[1] Public No. 89, Chap. 144, 78th Congress, 1st Session. The bill was passed over the veto of the President on June 25, 1943.

[2] The Act, by its own provision, is to cease to be effective six months after the termination of hostilities, as proclaimed by the President, or on the date of the passing of concurrent resolution to that effect by Congress.

the National War Labor Board; and the imposition of restrictions upon political contributions by labor organizations. Only the first two of these four provisions are our present concern.[1]

Government possession and operation of establishments threatened by labor disputes which would interrupt production was regarded by the framers of the Act as the most important deterrent of stoppages of production. The Act[2] empowers the President to take possession of and to operate "plants, mines, and facilities" upon his finding and proclamation that there is a threatened or actual interruption of operations because of a strike or other labor disturbance as a result of which the war effort is being, or would be, unduly impeded or delayed. Establishments and facilities possession of which is taken for this reason are to be returned to their owners as "soon as practicable," and in no event more than sixty days after restoration of the productive efficiency that prevailed before

[1] The status of the N.W.L.B., which was established for peaceful settlement of disputes early in 1942 and which had, by the time of the enactment of the War Labor Disputes Act, been charged with effectuation of the wartime wage stabilization policy, is discussed in Chap. XIII, and a brief summary is sufficient here. When the U. S. Conciliation Service certifies that a dispute "may lead to substantial interference with the war effort and cannot be settled by collective bargaining or conciliation," the Board has power to summon both parties to the dispute before it (or before panels or hearing officers designated by it) and conduct a hearing. The Board may also take action on its own motion. The statute specifically authorizes the Board to decide such labor disputes and to provide by Directive Order the wages, hours, and other items and conditions to govern the relations of the parties. In making its decisions, the Board is required to conform to the provisions of the Fair Labor Standards Act of 1938, the National Labor Relations Act, and the Emergency Price Control Act of 1942. It is authorized to issue subpoenas, to require the attendance of witnesses and the production of any material paper, documents, or records, and to apply to any federal district court for an order requiring obedience to its subpoenas.

The provisions with respect to political contributions are—as developments of 1944 showed—far from being free from ambiguity. It may be observed in passing that inclusion of provisions intended to curb labor's political activities in a statute enacted to prevent disputes in plants essential to the war effort appears to be somewhat gratuitous. The War Labor Disputes Act amended the Federal Corrupt Practices Act so as to render it unlawful for any labor organization to make a contribution in connection with any election at which presidential electors, a senator or a representative in Congress, or a delegate or resident commissioner to Congress are to be voted for. Labor organizations violating this provision are subject to fines of $5,000, and every officer who consents to a contribution by an organization in violation of the section is subject to a fine of up to $1,000 and/or imprisonment for not more than one year. The construction placed upon the political-contributions section of the War Labor Disputes Act by organized labor—particularly by the C.I.O. and its Political Action Committee, described in Chap. V—has been that while the section prevents unions from making direct financial contributions to candidates for federal office, it does not—and could not constitutionally—prohibit members of a union, through the medium of the union or an associated effort of unions such as the Political Action Committee, from exercising their rights of free speech by making known their views with respect to candidates for public office, whether at union or other meetings or public gatherings, through the medium of leaflets and newspapers, or by other methods.

[2] As an amendment to the Selective Training and Service Act of 1940.

the seizure. Establishments and facilities taken over must be operated under the terms and conditions of employment obtaining when the action was taken, but the government agency operating them may apply to the National War Labor Board for a change in wages or conditions of employment and the Board, in turn, may authorize changes which it finds to be reasonable and not in conflict with law. Whenever a plant or facility has been taken over by the government, it is an offense punishable by fine (of not more than $5,000) and/or imprisonment (of not more than one year) for anyone to "coerce, instigate, induce, conspire with, or encourage any person to interfere by lockout, strike, slowdown, or other interruption with the operation of such plant, mine, or facility," or to aid such action "by giving direction or guidance thereof or by providing funds thereof or for the payment of strike, unemployment, or other benefits to those participating therein."

The statute also provides that in order that the President may be apprised of labor disputes which threaten seriously to interrupt production and in order that "employees may have an opportunity to express themselves, free from restraint or coercion, as to whether they will permit such interruption in wartime," the representatives of the employees of a "war contractor"[1] shall notify the Secretary of Labor, the National Labor Relations Board, and the National War Labor Board of such dispute, the notification being accompanied by a statement of the issues giving rise to the dispute. For not less than thirty days after the notice, the "contractor" and his employees must continue production under the conditions prevailing when the dispute arose. Unless the dispute has been settled within this thirty-day period, the National Labor Relations Board must take a secret ballot of the employees on the question of whether they wish to strike,[2] and a strike becomes lawful only if approved by the majority. Jurisdiction is conferred upon the district courts of the United States to hear and determine proceedings instituted under this section of the Act, and violation subjects a person to liability for damages to any person injured and to the United States if injured.

The provisions of the Act summarized in the immediately preceding paragraph have been adversely criticized on a number of grounds. The provision for a strike vote, it has been asserted, does not harmonize well with the authorization of government seizure of plants threatened with industrial disturbances. The purpose of seizure is to prevent strikes or other interruptions of production, but the government could not con-

---

[1] Defined in Sec. 2 (c) as a "person producing, manufacturing, reconstructing, installing, maintaining, storing, repairing, mining, or transporting under a war contract or a person whose plant, mine, or facility is equipped for the manufacture, production, mining of any articles or materials which may be required in the prosecution of the war or which may be useful in connection therewith."

[2] This procedure does not apply to establishments possession of which has been taken by the United States.

sistently take possession of a plant—maintaining the *status quo* unless this were changed by the National War Labor Board, and with all persons attempting to instigate strikes being subject to fine and/or imprisonment—when the strike had been approved by the employees in an election held in accordance with the provisions of the statute. Organized labor and a number of impartial observers have emphasized that in contrast to labor's "no-strike" pledge the legal machinery for wartime strikes has been established by the Act; that "it is not easy to determine whether such notice by representatives of employees of labor disputes threatening to interrupt production is viewed as a notice of the intention of the labor organization to strike or whether they [labor organizations] might nevertheless be required to file such a notice in situations where employer provocation or other circumstances were such that an interruption of production might possibly result despite efforts of the union to prevent such an eventuality;"[1] that the means has been created whereby obstructive minorities might seek to instigate strike votes because of the provocative effects of such votes; and that the provisions relating to notification of threatened labor disputes—particularly whether local or national officials are so charged—are vague. Other criticisms have been or might be, advanced. It is, in the opinion of the authors, highly questionable whether the War Labor Disputes Act of 1943 constituted as practicable and workable an approach to the problem of maintaining uninterrupted wartime production as might reasonably have been hoped for.

[1] Report of President Philip Murray to the Sixth (1943) Constitutional Convention of the Congress of Industrial Organizations, p. 32.

Chapter XII

TRADE UNIONS, THE LAW, AND THE COURTS
(Concluded)

We turn from the law of the strike, the lockout, the boycott, and the black list to other matters involved in industrial contests. Unions appeal to the public, hold assemblies and strike meetings, pay strike benefits, resort to picketing and now and then to parade, and, incidental to picketing or independently of it, not infrequently indulge in sporadic or organized violence. Now and then they have gone so far as to take possession of the workplace. The employer or employers, on the other hand, have likewise appealed to the public, have sought to fill vacated positions from local applicants or workers secured through association offices, employment agencies, or detective agencies, perhaps have hired guards, and rather commonly have sought injunctions in an effort to protect their property and business relations. Not infrequently in important struggles employers also have had important connections with citizens' committees or law and order leagues, when they have not taken the initiative in their formation. Some of these activities will be briefly discussed in this chapter.

Some Employers' Activities[1]

In some of the European countries, and in Great Britain particularly, where unions have been strongly entrenched and where there have been

---

[1] The largest mass of detail concerning these and industrial policing may be found in *Violations of Free Speech and Rights of Labor, Hearings before a Subcommittee of the Committee on Education and Labor, United States Senate . . . Pursuant to S. Res.* 266 (74th *Congress*), 74th Congress, 2d Session, 75th Congress, 1st, 2d, and 3d Sessions, and 76th Congress, 1st, 2d, and 3d Sessions; by May, 1942, the hearings had been published in seventy-five parts, and, in addition twelve reports had been issued [*Violations of Free Speech and Rights of Labor: Preliminary Report Pursuant to S. Res.* 266 *of the 74th Congress* (75th Congress, 1st Session, Senate Report 46); *Report . . . [on] the Chicago Memorial Day Incident* (75th Congress, 1st Session, Senate Report 46, Pt. II); *Report . . . [on] Industrial Espionage* (75th Congress, 2d Session, Senate Report 46, Pt. III); *Interim Report* (75th Congress, 3d Session, Senate Report 46, Pt. IV); *Report . . . [on] Strikebreaking Services* (76th Congress, 1st Session, Senate Report 6); *Report . . . [on] Private Police Systems* (76th Congress, 1st Session, Senate Report 6, Pt. II); *Report . . . [on] Industrial Munitions* (76th Congress, 1st Session, Senate Report 6, Pt. III); *Report . . . [on] Labor Policies of Employers' Associations Part I, The National Metal Trades Association* (76th Congress, 1st Session, Senate Report 6, Pt. IV); *Report . . . on Labor Policies of Employers' Associations, Part II, The Associated Industries of Cleveland* (76th Congress, 1st Session, Senate Report 6, Pt. V); *Report . . . [on] Labor Policies of Employers' Associations, Part III, The*

relatively few attempts "to go open shop," employers' activities have differed materially from those so well known in connection with important industrial contests in the United States.   In these countries it has become common to suspend business until an acceptable arrangement has been effected with the union.   While this practice has frequently obtained in the building and other trades in the United States, there have been many cases in which unions conducting organization strikes[1] were not recognized or in which the employers were not content to wait until acceptable terms could be secured from unions they did recognize.   Hence employers, frequently and generally with little delay, have proceeded to fill vacated positions—or to show evidence of doing so.   The most common practice has been, of course, to hire new workers applying at the gate, to make use of records of former employees and applicants for work, and to search for help in the locality.   To such a labor market the law has always, and appropriately, given employers free access.[2]

Employer Methods.—Not infrequently, if organized, employers have had the assistance of the associations to which they have belonged in breaking strikes.   In the Chicago book- and job-printing industry, for example, the local open-shop association, which long operated an employment bureau, might search for workers far and near and distribute them among the struck plants of its members.   Perhaps recruits would be secured, also, from schools being conducted in the trade.   In some strongly organized industries the belligerent associations[3] have kept

---

National Association of Manufacturers (76th Congress, 1st Session, Senate Report 6, Pt. VI); *Report . . .* [on] *Labor Policies of Employers' Association, Part IV, The "Little Steel" Strike and Citizens' Committees* (77th Congress, 1st Session, Senate Report 151); *Appendix to Senate Report 151 . . .* [and] *Senate Report 6, Part 3; Report . . .* [on] *Employers' Associations and Collective Bargaining in California, Part I, General Introduction* (77th Congress, 2d Session, Senate Report 1150, Pt. I)].   The hearings will be cited here as: La Follette Committee, *Hearings,* with the appropriate part listed; the second, third, and fifth reports as: La Follette Committee, *Report on the Chicago Memorial Day Incident, Report on Industrial Espionage,* and *Report on Strikebreaking Services,* respectively.   For additional information on espionage activities of employers, see Clinch Calkins, *Spy Overhead* (1937), Leo Huberman, *The Labor Spy Racket* (1937), *Labor Spy* (1937) by GT-99 and Edward Levinson, *I Break Strikes* (1935).

[1] Of course the National Labor Relations Act and the state laws based upon it make it obligatory upon the employer to recognize the union and to confer with the representatives of his employees, provided certain conditions have been met.   Though this legal obligation is still disregarded in many cases, the new legislation is changing the organizational situation and reducing the relative number of "organization strikes."   More and more representation issues have, on petition, been decided by Labor Board elections.

[2] Positions so filled may, however, be vacated when the federal and state industrial-relations acts have been violated.   In many cases the National Labor Relations Board has ordered strikers restored to their jobs, displacing new employees if necessary.

Clarence E. Bonnett, in his *Employers' Associations in the United States* (1922), classifies associations into "negotiatory" and "belligerent" associations.   The reader is referred to that book for an account of the activities of several of the best known associations.

available at all times a supply of key men around whom new working forces could be built.   Thus, the National Founders' Association, providing a variety of services for its members in trouble, formerly retained, on annual or sixty-day contracts, men who could be sent to any point and set at work.   These men manned the key positions and assisted in training "green hands" until an acceptable working force was secured. Among other belligerent employers' associations functioning in a similar manner has been the open-shop branch of the American Newspaper Publishers' Association, with headquarters in Philadelphia.[1]

Employers individually or in combination have also frequently advertised for help in trade or other publications.   The only restriction upon this practice has been found in the statutes of about a fourth of the states, providing that in such advertising mention must be made of the existence of labor troubles.[2]   Such legislation is desirable for the information and protection of those seeking employment.

On occasion employers seeking new help have resorted to the public employment offices now to be found in all the larger industrial centers of the country, or to the large number of private employment agencies conducted for profit.   The laws of most of the states have for years required the public offices to inform persons referred to jobs of any labor difficulty.   This requirement has now become universal because of the rules laid down for the administration of offices operated in cooperation with the Federal Government.   The object of such a requirement is, of course, not to protect the jobs of striking union workers but to give valuable information concerning working conditions to those who seek employment.   Less frequently the same requirement is made of private employment agencies conducted for profit.   The requirement should be made effective in every state.

[1] The National Metal Trades Association, an open-shop organization since 1901, has worked in cooperation with the National Founders' Association.   It has been very active in combating union activities.   Although it says that the employees of its members have a right to organize and to bargain collectively (La Follette Committee, *Hearings*, Pt. III, pp. 835–836, 900–901), it has furnished its members with undercover men to report on union activities (*ibid.*, pp. 822–824, 846, 862, 868–869), and it has maintained an employment service, one function of which, if one may conclude from correspondence concerning the union activities of persons listed, has been to weed out undesired persons (*ibid.*, pp. 893–895).   The Association has also provided strike insurance and furnished strikebreakers and guards when this was regarded as the best method of combating a strike.   It has paid all of the expenses of the guards, and the cost of recruiting, transporting, and, if necessary, feeding and lodging the strikebreakers (*ibid.*, pp. 845–846, 848, 850, 859).   Moreover, during strikes the Association's representatives have advised the employer, being in fact in charge of fighting the strike; the administrative council must approve any settlement, the penalty for disregarding advice given being payment of the expenses incurred by the Association, and expulsion from and forfeiture of dues paid to the Association (*ibid.*, pp. 846–847).   *Cf.* also C. E. Bonnett, *op. cit.*, Chap. 4.

[2] See E. E. Witte, *The Government in Labor Disputes* (1932), p. 209.

Employers also have made use of the so-called detective agencies.[1] In Great Britain and in the Continental countries generally detective agencies have been detective agencies; they have not engaged in "industrial work." In the United States, however, there are many detective agencies that have served employers of labor. They have served them throughout the year with a "spy service"; in time of trouble they have supplied "guards," assisted in securing strikebreakers, and, in the more recent years, provided "missionaries" to visit the homes of strikers and to further back-to-work movements. Among other large and many small agencies, numbering, all told, approximately 200, which have functioned, at least until recently, in some or all of these ways, may be named the W. J. Burns Agency, Bergoff, the Pinkerton Agency, Sherman Service, Inc., Corporations' Auxiliary, Railway Audit, and Baldwin-Felts. The largest of these agencies have maintained offices in many cities and have done a large business.[2] In addition to furnishing "spies," they have functioned in a large percentage of strikes.[3] Some of these agencies have advertised openly that their chief service was to break strikes.

Industrial Espionage.—Industrial espionage has been widespread in the United States. Many of the local employer associations have provided for it through an officer operating under some such title as "corporation adjuster."[4] The provision of spies for their members has been a part of the regular service rendered by some of the belligerent national employers' associations. This, as already stated, has been a part of the service the independent agencies rendered their patrons. When provided by these outside agencies, as Professor Witte has said:

"The inside operatives carry on the work of industrial espionage while working for the client employer under assumed names as ordinary mechanics or workmen, or in some other capacity. They do their daily work and draw their pay checks like other workmen, and their fellow employees and immediate superiors—often the superintendents themselves—have no inkling that they are spies. But every day they make a

[1] An indication of the widespread use of the services of detective agencies is found in the fact that Corporations' Auxiliary had 200 clients, while an incomplete list of Pinkerton clients, 1933–1936, included more than 300 industrial firms. La Follette Committee, *Hearings*, Pt. IV, p. 1113, Pt. V, pp. 1853–1858.

[2] Pinkerton has had offices in twenty-eight cities, Burns in twenty-six. La Follette Committee, *Hearings*, Pt. II, p. 663, Pt. VIII, pp. 2730, 3065.

[3] For an excellent, brief account of the matter, see E. E. Witte, *op. cit.*, Chap. 9. See also La Follette Committee, *Hearings*. A list of agencies is found on pp. 72–76 of Pt. I.

[4] Such an adjuster was for years employed by a large open-shop association in Chicago, whose members did 75 per cent of the business of that industry in the city. He maintained a representative on each floor of each plant and had two spies in the union who reported the activities of each meeting of that organization. In addition to regular wages received as workers, each representative was paid $10 per week (on corporation adjuster's payroll). All union members, all "troublemakers," and all dissatisfied workers were reported on and weeded out.

report to the detective agency, and this agency in turn reports to the employer. Practically never do the operatives report directly, the roundabout method of reporting being represented to the employer as necessary to preserve secrecy, but it is no doubt primarily resorted to to enable the home office to make the employer think that he is getting a valuable service."[1]

There has, of course, been opportunity to make work for the agency by stirring up trouble and by false reporting. The spy may gain membership in the union and at times even serve as a union official.[2] The primary purpose of this espionage has been, of course, to enable the employer to get rid of "agitators" and "troublemakers" and perhaps all persons interested in unionism. As would be expected, spies are generally a low class of men. Mr. Burns has frequently been quoted as saying that "as a class, they are the biggest lot of blackmailing thieves that ever went unwhipped of justice." Of all persons they have been the most hated by workingmen.

In addition to supplying guards for private police duty, most of the detective agencies with "industrial departments" have assisted in recruiting in the bigger cities large numbers of strike guards and strikebreakers and in transporting them to struck mines, railway shops, and factories. Excellent examples are found in the copper strike in Northern Michigan in 1913, in the teamsters' strike in Chicago in 1905, in numerous strikes in West Virginia coal mines, in the Herrin and Coronado affairs, in the railway shopmen's strike of 1922, and in the Remington-Rand struggle of 1936. Drawing high rates of pay and perhaps fed and lodged, the strikebreakers have functioned, at least to the extent of causing the plant to appear to be operating with many employees, until the strike was broken, when they have usually quickly disappeared. The natural unionist attitude of hostility toward them has frequently been heightened by their uncivil conduct, as when, in the Chicago teamsters' strike, armed with hickory clubs and jeering, they were hauled through the streets of Chicago. Frequently violence has first manifested itself with the appearance of groups of strikebreakers. Union hatred of the professional strikebreaker, all strangers brought in being so regarded, has been extreme. Frank K. Foster has said, "He is an industrial thief, a social renegade, a moral leper, and as such merits, and fortunately often receives, the penalty of being set aside in practical isolation from honorable men."[3]

[1] E. E. Witte, op. cit., p. 185.

[2] As in the Fruehauf case, 1 N.L.R.B. 68, at p. 73 (1936). Of Pinkerton secret agents at least 331 were trade-union members. Of thirty operatives attached to the Cleveland office of Corporations' Auxiliary, twenty-three were union members. La Follette Committee, Hearings, Pt. IV, p. 1148, Pt. V, p. 1616, note 1. See also La Follette Committee, Report on Industrial Espionage, pp. 26–28, 75–79.

[3] Frank K. Foster, Has the Non-unionist a Right to Work How, When, and Where He Pleases? (an American Federation of Labor propaganda pamphlet, 1904), p. 5.

Strike guards provided by the agencies have provoked even more trouble than have strikebreakers. Usually armed and directly interested in prolonging disputes and in provoking trouble in order to insure employment for themselves in large numbers, they have in many cases resorted to violence or have provoked it by extending their activities beyond the plant, as they did in the Berger case in 1935.[1]

On occasion there has been strong public reaction against the importation of strikebreakers into a state, especially when they have been guarded by armed men, and legislation has been adopted to prevent it. Such was the case in Illinois[2] when certain coal operators refused to abide by the scale agreed upon and imported Negroes from Alabama, under the protection of men armed with repeating rifles, to take the places of the striking miners. The legislation enacted shortly thereafter was declared unconstitutional.[3]

Organized labor would like to have detective agencies prohibited from engaging in industrial work. Because of labor's protest and because of the problems developing out of the activities of these agencies in concrete cases, a number of the states and the Federal Government have in recent years enacted laws providing for more or less extensive regulation.

Regulation of Detective Agencies.—In some of the states, as in California[4] and Illinois,[5] detective agencies must be licensed. To secure a license in these two states an agency must satisfy the regulatory authority of its good character and must post an indemnity bond. The acts do not require the licensing or registration of the individual guards or operatives employed by an agency, as do the statutes of Wisconsin and New York.

The Wisconsin legislation, as amended in 1935,[6] is far-reaching and has greatly limited the activities of the agencies. It provides that any

---

[1] For an account of the Berger and many other cases and the views of the La Follette Committee, see that Committee's *Hearings*, Pts. XXIII and XXIV, and especially *Report on Strikebreaking Services*.

[2] See Laws of 1899, p. 139. For an account of the episode, see Earl Beckner, *A History of Labor Legislation in Illinois* (1929), pp. 68–70.

[3] In *Josma v. Western Steel Car and Foundry Company*, 249 Ill. 508 (1911). Anyone having armed men to bring workmen into the state or to move them from one place to another within the state, and any person coming into Illinois armed with deadly weapons for any such purpose, without written permission of the governor, was to be imprisoned for a period of one to five years. The State Supreme Court in the Josma case declared the act invalid on the ground that it imposed upon persons employing workmen coming from another place to the place of employment a different measure of liability, both civil and criminal, for deceit and misrepresentation from that imposed upon other persons. The court did not regard the act as a proper or necessary police measure, but as special legislation.

[4] *Deering's General Laws* (1937), vol. 1, Act 2070a.

[5] *Illinois Laws* (1933, as amended in 1937), Smith-Hurd Ann. Stats, Secs. 608b–608z.

[6] *Wisconsin Statutes* (1937), Sec. 175.07.

agency providing guards and all individuals acting or serving as guards must be licensed by the Secretary of State. A prospective guard must be endorsed by five reputable citizens and the fire and police commissions of the city in which he plans to work.

The Massachusetts law of 1937[1] amended an act of 1879, which had already been amended in 1919. Agencies must be licensed, but the act does not require that strike guards, who are most frequently the source of trouble, shall also be licensed. An earlier law,[2] however, provides that no employer may hire armed strike guards from an unlicensed agency during the continuance of a strike or lockout and that armed guards employed through a licensed agency must be citizens of the state and must not have been convicted of felony. Pennsylvania also enacted a law in 1937[3] but of a different type from any of those just mentioned. This law made it a misdemeanor for any person, firm, or corporation "not directly involved in a labor strike or lockout" to recruit any persons to take the place of employees in an industry where a strike or lockout is in effect. Still more limiting is a Utah law that provides that every person must register with the State Industrial Commission before starting to work for an employer whose employees are on strike. The act also prohibits the deputizing of any employee of a struck plant.[4]

Accepted by the La Follette Committee as a model for state legislation[5] is the New York law adopted in 1938.[6] Under that act detective agencies, which must be licensed, are prohibited from employing any person who has been convicted of a felony, or any offense involving moral turpitude, or any specified misdemeanor. Finger printing and comparison of finger prints with those in the file of the Bureau of Criminal Identification are also required. The act then proceeds to make it unlawful for a detective agency to furnish strikebreakers and strike guards[7] or to engage in industrial espionage.[8]

---

[1] *Acts and Resolves of Massachusetts*, Chap. 437 (1937).

[2] Chap. 149, Sec. 23A, *Gen. Laws* 1932; Chap. 233 L. 1934.

[3] *Pennsylvania Laws* (1937), No. 391.

[4] Utah Revised Statute Supplement, Secs. 49-1-18 and 20 (1939).

[5] La Follette Committee, *Report on Strikebreaking Services*, p. 132.

[6] *Cahill's Consolidated Laws of New York* (1938 Supplement), Chap. 21, Sec. 81.

[7] The act reads, in part: "It shall be unlawful for the holder of a license or for any employee of such licensee, knowingly to commit any of the following acts within or without the State of New York . . . to advertise for, recruit, furnish, or replace or offer to furnish or replace for hire or reward, within or without the State of New York any help or labor, skilled or unskilled, or to furnish or offer to furnish armed guards, other than armed guards theretofore regularly employed for the protection of payrolls, property or premises, for service upon property which is being operated in anticipation of or during the course or existence of a strike, or furnish armed guards upon the highways, for persons involved in labor disputes." Quoted from La Follette Committee, *Report on Strikebreaking Services*, pp. 131–132.

[8] Other states with legislation relating to matters here reviewed are Minnesota, Oregon,

What is perhaps the beginning[1] of far-reaching federal regulation of strikebreaking and of detective agencies engaging in industrial work is found in an act passed by Congress in 1936.[2] The law provided that "whoever shall knowingly transport or cause to be transported, or aid or abet in transporting, in interstate . . . commerce any person with intent to employ such person to obstruct or interfere . . . with the right of peaceful picketing during any labor controversy affecting wages, hours, or conditions of labor, or the right of organization for the purpose of collective bargaining, shall be deemed guilty of a felony and shall be punishable by a fine not exceeding $5,000, or by imprisonment not exceeding two years, or both, in the discretion of the court."

The labor movement regarded this (the Byrnes) Act as a very important one. The Act was, however, badly drafted. For one thing the significance of the clause relating to interference with the "right of organization for the purpose of collective bargaining" was not clear. Again, with the incorporation of the word "intent" the Act could be expected to have little effect. In the one case tried in the federal courts the interpretation of the Act and the instructions given the jury were such that the defendants were acquitted.[3] Following this, in 1938, the

---

and Tennessee. Minnesota prohibits the maintenance of a private detective agency for the purpose of supplying armed guards [Minnesota Statutes, Sec. 10501 (1927)]. An Oregon statute prohibits the employment or organization of any body of armed men in any city to perform the duties of the regular police [Oregon Annotated Code, Title 14, Sec. 14–446 (1930)]. Tennessee makes it a felony to hire armed guards [Tennessee Code, Sec. 11363 (1932)]. Moreover, there are fourteen states which entirely prohibit the procurement of armed guards from within or without the state or require the governor's permission before they can be procured. These states are Arkansas, Colorado, Idaho, Indiana, Kentucky, Massachusetts, Minnesota, Montana, Oklahoma, South Carolina, South Dakota, Texas, Utah, and West Virginia.

[1] With a view to further legislation, evidence was in 1937 taken by the La Follette Committee on the activities of detective agencies, etc. Of course espionage is unlawful under the National Labor Relations Act and the state "baby Wagner Acts," because it is designed to interfere with labor organization. This is true of espionage carried on both by agents of an employer or the agents of an employers' association and by the agents of a detective agency. After the National Labor Relations Act was upheld by the Supreme Court and after the Senate (S. Con. Res. 7, 75th Congress, 1st Session, Apr. 7, 1937), with the House of Representatives concurring, resolved " . . . That the so-called industrial spy system breeds fear, suspicion, and animosity, tends to cause strikes and industrial warfare, and is contrary to sound public policy . . . ," some of the agencies and the National Metal Trades Association announced that they were discontinuing this branch of their service. See La Follette Committee, *Report on Industrial Espionage*, p. 74, and also pp. 121–122, where an order sent out to its agents by Pinkerton's National Detective Agency, Inc., is reproduced.

[2] Public no. 776, 74th Congress, 2d Session, Chap. 746 (S. 2039), June 24, 1936. For discussion of this act, see "Industrial Strikebreaking—The Byrnes Act," *University of Chicago Law Review*, vol. 4 (1937), pp. 657–666.

[3] *U. S. v. Bergoff-Rand*, U. S. D. C. Conn. (1937). The indictment charged that Mr. Rand, president of Remington Rand, Inc., and Mr. Bergoff, head of a detective agency, had

Act was amended,[1] so as to remedy some of its defects.   The first section of the law reads: "It shall be unlawful to transport or cause to be transported in interstate or foreign commerce any person *who is employed or is to be employed* for the purpose of obstructing or interfering by force or threats with (1) peaceful picketing by employees during any labor controversy affecting wages, hours, or conditions of labor; or (2) the exercise by employees of any of the rights of self-organization, and collective bargaining."[2]

It was the opinion of the La Follette Committee[3] that further federal legislation was needed.   It was also its opinion that, for administrative reasons and because the employer who engages the services of detective agencies should accept responsibility, the law should represent a different attack from that found in state legislation, which is directed at the agency and its operatives.   Therefore, early in 1942, Senators La Follette and Thomas introduced a bill[4] directed at certain "oppressive labor practices"—the use of labor spies, strikebreakers, or strikebreaking agencies; the employment of private armed guards off company property (except where necessary for protection against theft of goods or money in transit) or of guards convicted of crimes of violence; the use or possession of industrial explosives in or about a place of employment or during a labor dispute; acting in concert to injure or intimidate any persons in order to interfere with their right to organize and bargain collectively—a provision aimed at physical attacks on union organizers, breaking up union

---

taken fifty-seven men from New York to Middletown, Conn., when a strike was on against a Remington Rand factory, the intent being to break the strike by giving the false impression that the factory was to be dismantled.   Advertised as millwrights, the miscellaneous crew mixed among the pickets, elbowed them off the sidewalk, etc.   The court interpreted the act to mean that the "intent" must be to interfere physically with peaceful picketing. In its charge to the jury, the court said, in part: "The only obstruction and interference with peaceful picketing which is denounced by the statute shall be a physical obstruction or interference as distinguished from such interference as might arise from any words or device not involving direct physical violence. . . . If he [the employer] suspects that the pickets, though seemingly or ordinarily peaceful, are, in fact intimidating possible employees, it is not unlawful for him to test his suspicions by causing strangers, whether from within or without the state, to come to the factory through the picket lines, on the ostensible mission of seeking work, provided, of course, he neither instructs nor intends that such persons shall by word or act attempt to provoke violence or other evidence of intimidative tactics."

[1] Public no. 779, 75th Congress, 3d Session, Chap. 813, June 29, 1938.

[2] Italics the authors'.   The law was also amended so that strikebreakers themselves are liable to the penalties provided.   "Any person who wilfully violates or aids or abets any person in violating any provision of this section, and any person who is knowingly transported in or travels in interstate or foreign commerce for any of the purposes enumerated in this section, shall be deemed guilty of a felony and shall, upon conviction thereof, be fined not more than $5,000 or be imprisoned not more than two years, or both."

[3] *Report on Strikebreaking Services*, pp. 137–138.

[4] S. 2435, 77th Congress, 2d Session.   The provisions obviously overlapped those of the National Labor Relations Act.

assemblies, and other forms of vigilantism; the use of black lists, "yellow-dog" contracts, and agreements by employers not to engage in collective bargaining; acting in concert with a group of employers to injure or intimidate other employers, or employees, in order to prevent collective bargaining; conspiring to commit any of the above; acting as an officer or employee of an employers' association, knowing that it has failed to register with the National Labor Relations Board. Any person who engaged in oppressive labor practices where interstate commerce was involved, or assisted in their commission through furnishing industrial munitions or services, would have been subject to a penalty of a fine of $10,000 or imprisonment of six months. So would any person using the mails or the instrumentalities of commerce to procure, furnish, or offer industrial munitions or services for engaging in any oppressive labor practice. The bill also provided for injunctive remedies, to be invoked only by the Secretary of Labor.[1]

Citizens' Committees.—Important in connection with employer activities, as these have developed in many strike situations—in the rubber and automobile strikes of 1936–1937, in the "Little Steel" strikes of 1937, in textiles, in water shipping and elsewhere—are the local citizens' committees formed to maintain or to re-establish law and order, perhaps to promote back-to-work movements, and to build up and strengthen a popular opinion favorable to the employer interest. From such activities was the well-publicized Mohawk Valley Formula developed.[2] The activities of such committees are important in connection with the conduct of strikes and industrial policing, which will be discussed presently.[3]

---

[1] The Congress expired without taking action on the La Follette-Thomas measure.

[2] The Mohawk Valley Formula was an elaborate strikebreaking scheme. Introduced by James Rand in the 1936 strikes of Remington Rand employees, it was later successfully utilized in the steel strike of 1937 and widely publicized as the Johnstown Plan. The elements in the "formula" have, of course, varied in its different applications. In essence, however, the original scheme comprised about nine steps: (1) conducting of a strike ballot by an employer, with misrepresentation of the issues involved and the strength of the union; (2) labeling the union leaders "agitators" and "radicals"; (3) economic pressure on the community, through threats to move the plant, in order to stimulate the formation of a citizens' committee by means of which public opinion could be crystallized against the strikers; (4) the amassing of a large police force to preserve "law and order" and intimidate the strikers; (5) emphasis on the violent aspects of the strike to hide the employment of strikebreakers; (6) the organization of a back-to-work movement accompanied by extensive advertising; (7) a theatrical opening of the struck plant; (8) the combined show of police force and pressure by the Citizens' Committee; (9) the complete cessation of publicity once the plant was operating at near-capacity. [See Robert R. R. Brooks, *When Labor Organizes* (1937), pp. 133–149; *Decisions and Orders of the National Labor Relations Board*, vol. 2 (1937), pp. 664–666; National Association of Manufacturers, *Labor Relations Bulletin* 19 (1937), p. 10; National Labor Relations Board, *Second Annual Report* . . . 1937, pp. 59–62.]

[3] *Infra*, pp. 674–689.

SOME UNION ACTIVITIES

If a strike is to be effective or a lockout defeated, the union usually must resort to picketing, pay strike benefits, and through meetings and otherwise build up and maintain a will to "see it through." As already indicated, the union or its individual members may also resort to coercion and violence.

Strike Benefits.—Well-financed unions always provide strike benefits covering the minimum cost of living, at least in the case of the needy. Even poorly financed unions at least attempt to provide relief in some form.[1] In the case of prolonged disputes large sums of money may be collected and disbursed. For example, the International Typographical Union paid out more than $16,000,000 during the strike for the forty-four-hour week that began in 1921. The members at work were assessed for many months, for a time as much as 10 per cent of wages, to provide the necessary funds.

That a union may pay strike benefits, not only to its members but also to nonmembers who leave the job or who refuse employment, is accepted law. This, of course, assumes that the strike is lawful, for a lawful means may not be used to accomplish an unlawful end. In fact, many injunctions, as the one issued in the Shopmen's case in 1922, have forbidden the payment of strike benefits. Some courts have restrained the levy of assessments to replenish the defense fund or have restrained the employers from using the checkoff. Nor, as we shall see in a later section of this chapter, has the strike to which these financial arrangements were incidental always been unlawful. One of the elements in the injunction problem has been that not infrequently the doing of lawful things has been prohibited.[2]

Picketing.—There are a few unions, such as the Locomotive Engineers, so fully organized and so circumstanced that they do not need to picket in order to win a strike or lockout. But most labor organizations need representatives to see to it that workers inclined to hesitate actually leave their jobs and that those who weaken do not return to work; by persuasion or otherwise, they also try to prevent others from accepting the struck jobs.[3] Hence picketing usually begins with the inauguration of

[1] Some years ago the Federal Emergency Relief Administration adopted the policy of granting relief to persons in need even though the need was due to the fact that they were on strike. This policy was of great assistance to weakly financed unions. With such aid many strikes were prolonged far beyond the time they otherwise must have been ended and the workers returned to their jobs.

[2] See discussion of the injunction, pp. 629–651.

[3] In recent years the "sit-down" or, better, the "stay-in" strike has been resorted to by a number of "standard" American unions. Of course it had previously been employed now and then by radical organizations and on rare occasions by other unions. It, no doubt, assists in acquiring new members, for many workers who hesitate to join a union

the strike or lockout. What picketing is in fact differs greatly from one case to another. The number of pickets may be one, or a few, or so many as to cause the activity to be known as mass picketing—in recent years a widespread fact. Again, the pickets may simply by word or placard call attention to the charge that the firm is "unfair" to labor, they may converse with prospective workers in an effort to persuade them not to accept employment, or they may call names and make threats, indeed resort to physical violence. Picketing may also be accompanied by following and "dogging" workers and by visiting them in their homes, with or without threat.

Thus far picketing has been described as a detail in the conduct of strikes, as it is commonly thought of by the public. In the United States, however, picketing has also been employed in the conduct of boycotts of nonunion stores, restaurants, and barbershops, when no strike was in progress. Moreover, it has recently been increasingly employed as an aid to organization. A union that has failed to secure a favorable response from the workers of a firm may then request the employer to exert his influence upon them to conduct an all-union shop and pickets his place of business if he does not do so. Also, what is

---

when approached will participate in a stay-in strike and then join the union. From the point of view of tactics, this form of strike is a double-edged sword, for, whatever its short-run accomplishments, it tends to undermine union discipline of working groups and to be followed by stoppages in violation of agreements entered into. Our chief interest here, however, is to point out that for the time being it renders ordinary picketing unnecessary. By remaining in the plant, the men, even a comparatively small group, not only cause production in related departments to cease, but also prevent the introduction of strikebreakers to take their places. See "Sit-down Strikes: A New Problem for Government," *Illinois Law Review*, vol. 31 (1937), pp. 942–959; an excellent reading list on stay-in strikes may be found in the *New York Public Library Bulletin*, June, 1937, pp. 480–484. Of course it was to be expected that the courts would rule that stay-in strikes are unlawful. They have done so in a number of cases. In the first case to come before the federal courts, it was held that a stay-in strike involving the seizure of property and acts of violence constituted an unlawful means of conducting a strike. Because of its effect upon interstate commerce, the court ruled that it amounted to a conspiracy in restraint of trade, within the meaning of the Sherman Act, intent being implied from the knowledge that the seizure and retention of property would prevent that property from entering into the flow of interstate commerce [*Apex Hosiery Co. v. Leader*, 90 Fed. (2d) 155 (1937)]. Although the Circuit Court of Appeals of the Third District overruled this decision, it, too, condemned the stay-in strike [108 Fed. (2d) 71 (1939)]. Recently the U. S. Supreme Court outlawed the stay-in strike as a "high handed proceeding without shadow of legal right" [*N.L.R.B. v. Fansteel Metallurgical Corporation*, 59 Sup. Ct. 490 (1939)]. It was also to be expected that laws would be passed relating to the matter. By the end of 1939, at least eight states had passed such measures, outlawing stay-in strikes: Massachusetts, Acts (1937), Chap. 436, Sec. 8a; Vermont, Acts (1937), Chap. 210; Tennessee, Acts (1937), Chap. 160; Michigan, Acts (1939), Public Act no. 176, Sec. 15; Washington, Revised Statute, Sec. 2563–2564 (1939); Wisconsin, Acts of (1939), Chap. 57; Minnesota, Laws (1939), Chap. 440; and Pennsylvania, Laws (1939), Act no. 162.

described as secondary picketing has been employed in support of a boycott of one product purchased and sold by the firm picketed.[1]

Until the World War I years the rules with reference to picketing were usually laid down by the courts in an application of the common law or they were made by local authorities. Only slowly and tardily had they been established by statute or ordinance. As a result, the law varied considerably with the views of the judges. Judges of the inferior courts in not a few instances in the past ruled that there could be no lawful picketing because they conceived of a strike as definitely terminating employment relations. The strikers were in such cases regarded as "strangers to the plant," without rights to protect by picketing. As one Chicago jurist said in reply to the arguments advanced in a contempt case, "What rights do the workers have? By striking they have definitely ended their employment and become strangers to the plant. They have no rights to protect; the employer has a right of access to the labor market and prospective workers have a right of access to jobs. There can be no lawful picketing."

The position just described has usually not been regarded by the courts as a correct one. Most judges have always regarded a strike as a suspension, not a quitting, of employment. In general the courts have ruled that picketing that is not peaceful is unlawful and that peaceful picketing is lawful, provided, of course, that the end in view is lawful— all acts in furtherance of an unlawful end are unlawful. But not a few of the courts in years past defined "peaceful" so narrowly as to make picketing unlawful in the usual meaning of the word or else had such experience with it that they ruled there was, in fact, no peaceful picketing. In this manner all picketing came to be placed under the ban in a number of states, among them California.[2]

While the Federal Government and almost half of the states some years ago expressly legalized peaceful picketing, or, more frequently, provided that it should not be enjoined, this legislation was, until rather recently, so construed that in fact picketing was narrowly restricted. Section 20 of the Clayton Act provided that "no restraining order or injunction [granted by a Federal court] shall prohibit any person or persons, whether singly or in concert, from terminating any relation of employment . . . or from recommending, advising, or persuading others by peaceful means so to do; or from attending any place where any such person or persons may lawfully be, for the purpose of peacefully obtaining

[1] See *Goldfinger v. Feintuch*, 288 N.Y.S. 855 (1936), *supra*, p. 585; also *Fortenbury v. Superior Court of California*, S.F. No. 16408, Oct. 14, 1940 (7 L.R.R. 220).

[2] *Pierce v. Stablemen's Union*, 156 Cal. 70 (1909). Among similar decisions, see *Beck v. Railway Teamsters' Protective Union*, 118 Mich. 497 (1898) and *Jonas Glass Co. v. Glass Bottle Blowers*, 66 Atl. 953 (1907). Though the courts later became more liberal than they had been in such matters, as late as 1936 the Supreme Judicial Court of Maine held that no picketing is legal (*Keith Theatre v. Vachon*, 187 Atl. 692).

or communicating information, or from peacefully persuading any person
. . . to abstain from working . . . ."[1] But in the American Steel
Foundries case[2] the Supreme Court, following the practice of judging
each case "on its own circumstances," held that here large numbers of
pickets involved intimidation, and though Congress had safeguarded
peaceful persuasion, new employees and strikebreakers had a right to
"a clear passage on an unobstructed street," free from "following and
dogging." Therefore, only one picket would be permitted at each factory
entrance, these pickets to have "the right of observation, communication
and persuasion but with special admonition that their communication,
arguments and appeals [should] not be abusive, libelous or threatening,
and that they [should] not approach individuals together but singly
. . . ."[3] A few weeks later in *Truax v. Corrigan*[4] the court handed down
a similar ruling.

These Supreme Court decisions served as precedent for the lower
federal courts and were widely accepted by state courts in interpreting
and applying state statutes, which before 1932 were largely modeled on the
Clayton Act. Most of the courts placed a firmer ban on mass picketing,
limited the number of pickets—though not always to one—and in other
ways interpreted the law of picketing in the light of the "circumstances
of each case." The effect was to place more narrow limitations on
picketing than had theretofore been enforced by the courts in some
jurisdictions.

A few states[5] and more cities[6] have at some time gone further than
these decisions by prohibiting all picketing. Other statutes and ordinances have been almost as restrictive, for example, the measure adopted
in Los Angeles in September, 1938, by a popular vote of 198,507 to
152,065.[7] This ordinance provided that pickets must be employees of
the firm against which the strike was directed and might be used only
when there was a bona fide strike. The term "bona fide strike" meant
and included "any cessation of work by at least a majority of all employees
of all classes [not, say, of those in one craft] of an employer in order to
obtain or resist a change in wages, hours, or conditions of their employment after demands therefor on such employer, which cessation of work
has taken place after a majority of all of the bona fide employees [with
a minimum of 30 days service] of all classes of such employer have by

---

[1] Public no. 212, 63d Congress, 2d Session, Chap. 323 (H. R. 15657), Oct. 15, 1914.

[2] *American Steel Foundries v. Tri-city Central Trades Council*, 257 U. S. 184 (1921).

[3] *Ibid.*, at pp. 206–207.

[4] 257 U. S. 312 (1921).

[5] Among them, Alabama, Colorado, Kansas, Michigan, and Nebraska.

[6] For example, Indianapolis.

[7] The ordinance may be conveniently found in *Labor Relations Reporter*, vol. 3, no. 4
(Sept. 26, 1938), pp. 7–8.

secret ballot voted to strike."[1] Picketing for other objectives or in connection with strikes otherwise called was proscribed, as well as any picketing involving threats, misrepresentation, etc. So, also, was picketing of any plants of an employer other than the one or ones involved in the dispute. Pickets had to be duly designated and had to carry their credentials. With a minimum of two, the number of pickets might not exceed one for each place of ingress or egress, and no two of them might be within twenty-five feet of each other.[2] Loud talk and "indecent, obscene, profane, opprobrious, libelous, slanderous, or derogatory epithets, words or language" were forbidden, and any banner displayed might not exceed twenty by thirty inches, and had to be limited to specified things. The penalty for violation was a fine not to exceed $500 or a jail sentence not to exceed six months, or both fine and imprisonment. This ordinance remained in effect only a brief time, however, for it was declared invalid in 1939, as unreasonable and arbitrary, and a violation of the Fourteenth Amendment.[3]

The year 1938 witnessed attempts in the three Pacific Coast states to secure the adoption by popular vote of very restrictive laws, based more or less directly on the Los Angeles ordinance. All these states had been sorely tried by struggles incidental to the attempts of workers to organize, by the awkward and questionable activities of newly established unions, by the activities of alleged racketeers, by the stopping off of work by unions contesting for power, by hostile employers' associations not at all inclined to share power with labor or to observe in good faith the National Labor Relations Act, and by farmers angered by labor activities of almost any kind. The less immoderate measures placed on the ballot by initiative in California and Washington failed, but the very restrictive measure placed on the ballot in Oregon carried by a substantial majority. Under this Act,[4] picketing, boycotting, and other labor activity were outlawed in connection with all disputes except where a majority of the employees of an employer were involved in issues directly relating to their wages, hours, and working conditions. Strikes, picketing, and boycotting incidental to other issues, among them disputes between labor organizations, became unlawful. It was specifically made "unlawful to boycott directly or indirectly any employer . . . not directly involved as a party in a labor dispute" as just described. Specifically, also, it was made "unlawful for any person, persons, association or organization to obstruct or prevent . . . the lawful buying, selling, transporting, receiving, delivering, manufacturing, harvesting, processing,

[1] Sections 1 (c) and 1 (d).

[2] Section 4.

[3] *People v. Gidaly,* Superior Ct., Los Angeles County, July 18, 1939; *People v. Garcia,* App. Dept., Sup. Ct., Los Angeles County, Dec. 29, 1939.

[4] Oregon Laws (1939), Chap. 2, adopted at the general election, November, 1938.

handling, or marketing of any agricultural or other products." All conflicting laws, such as Oregon's injunction-limitation law[1] of the Norris-La Guardia type, were set aside in disputes not recognized by this Act, and the courts were given a free hand in the granting of restraining orders and injunctions. Moreover, the courts might take such further steps as were "necessary" or "appropriate" to carry out and enforce each and every provision of the Act. All acts prohibited and restrainable became misdemeanors and were punishable as such. Beyond this, it was made unlawful for any labor organization "to make any charge, or exaction for initiation fees, dues, fines or other exactions, which [would] create a fund in excess of the legitimate requirements of such organization, association, or person, in carrying out the lawful purpose of activities of such organization." Accurate, itemized accounts had to be kept and these were to be subject to inspection by any member at any time. The law applied to labor organizations only. Limitations were not placed upon the corresponding rights and activities of management.

This badly drafted Act remained in force only until the fall of 1940, when in a five-to-one decision the Oregon Supreme Court declared it to be unconstitutional.[2] Before its invalidation, however, the Act was very restrictive of labor activities, at any rate as tested by most state and federal law.[3]

The Oregon law has influenced both recent state legislation and decisions rendered by the courts. The Minnesota Labor Relations Act[4] prohibits picketing where no strike is in effect and limits the number of pickets to one at each place of ingress or egress. Picketing by "strangers" (persons not involved as employees) is not permitted unless a majority of the pickets are employees. In Wisconsin, the new Industrial Peace Act prohibits mass picketing and restricts picketing to strikes called by a

---

[1] *Infra*, p. 649.

[2] *A.F. of L. v. Bain, et al.; C.I.O. v. Bain et al.*, 106 Pac. (2d) 544.

[3] According to Herbert Harris (*Labor's Civil War*, 1940, pp. 215*ff.*) under the law, as interpreted and enforced, "Clerks and other workers in an A & P store in Oregon [could not] withdraw their labor-power unless more than fifty per cent of the clerks and other workers of all A & P stores in the United States signif[ied] their intention of doing the same thing"; "craft-type unions [were] especially hard hit. . . . in a small factory of a hundred employees, ten of them machinists, the machinists [could not] go on strike unless they [could] persuade the other ninety workers to join them"; "the law likewise for[bade] any strike over union recognition," also over an issue of jurisdiction because rival unions were involved. He also states that "more than one hundred collective-bargaining agreements in Oregon and California were formally destroyed two months after the passage of initiative 316-X and more than half of all others are being ignored or chiseled at informally." Again he says, "The result has been that union gains, achieved slowly, step by step over the past half-century, have melted away in Oregon like butter in the sun. Loggers in the pine forests, stevedores along the waterfronts, weavers in the knitting mills, tuna fishermen in the Pacific, all labor in the state, have taken wage-cut after wage-cut, without resistance. They cannot resist."

[4] Laws (1939), Chap. 440.

majority of the employees involved.[1]   Again in 1943, several of the states enacted legislation limiting picketing and placing other restrictions upon trade unions.[2]   The main provisions of this legislation are summarized in the appended footnote.[3]

[1] Wisconsin Laws (1939), Chap. 57.

[2] For convenient summaries of this recent state legislation, see *Monthly Labor Review*, vol. 56 (May, 1943), pp. 941–944 and vol. 57 (October, 1943), pp. 778–780.

[3] Arkansas' 1943 "Anti-Violence Act" (S. 65), almost identical with laws enacted by Texas in 1941 and Mississippi in 1942, declared it to be unlawful for any person, by use of threat of force or violence, to prevent or attempt to prevent any person from engaging in a lawful occupation or for any person acting in concert with others to assemble for that purpose at or where a labor dispute (defined as including any controversy between an employer and two or more of his employees concerning terms or conditions of employment or the association or representation of persons in negotiating terms and conditions of employment) exists.

Idaho (S. 95) and South Dakota (H. 185) that same year (1943) enacted similar laws, directed in large part against unionization of farm labor and of employees in processing plants.   Under the provisions of both of these statutes, representatives of labor organizations may not, without the consent of the owner, enter "any ranch, feed yard, shearing plant, or other agricultural premise" to solicit members, collect dues, or promote a strike; and picketing of such premises and boycotting of agricultural products are prohibited. The South Dakota Act includes an "anti-racketeering" clause which forbids solicitation or acceptance of emoluments from employers for services rendered or claimed to have been rendered to them because of labor-union connections or associations; and both the Idaho and South Dakota laws require unions to file annual financial statements with the Secretary of State.

Texas, as has been said, in 1941 adopted an anti-picketing law similar to that of Arkansas.   In 1943 it enacted a registration law (H. 100) under which unions must be registered and must file information on their officers and finances with the Secretary of State.   All labor organizers must obtain identification cards from the Secretary of State before they may solicit members, union accounts must be open to members, union officers must be elected annually by majority vote in secret elections with aliens and persons convicted of felonies ineligible for union office, and fees which would create a fund in excess of the "reasonable requirements" of the unions are prohibited.   The Kansas Labor Relations Act of 1943 (Sec. 164), referred to in the preceding chapter, provides for the regulation of unions in a manner closely approximating that set forth in the Texas statute.

The Colorado Peace Act of 1943 (S. 183), also referred to in the preceding chapter, authorizes the State Industrial Commission to limit picketing which might "tend to disturb," provides for the "cooling-off" periods there mentioned, requires approval of closed-shop agreements by three-fourths of the employees to be affected thereby, subjects dues and fees to approval of the Commission, and requires annual elections and annual audit by the Commission of union books.   Alabama in 1943 enacted a law (S. 341) containing an "anti-violence" clause similar to that of the Arkansas statute, summarized above, and with provision for supervision of union affairs patterned upon the Texas registration statute. Striking is forbidden (as it is also under legislation enacted by Kansas and Florida in 1943) unless approved by a majority of the employees to be governed by the decision to strike, and acceptance of executive or professional employees into membership of unions open to other employees is prohibited.

A Florida statute of 1943 (H. 142) limits, as was noted incidentally in the preceding chapter, picketing beyond the area of the industry in which a labor dispute arises, picketing by force or violence or in a manner to prevent ingress and egress, and picketing which inter-

Laws outlawing all picketing and much of the more restrictive statutes and local ordinances, to which reference has been made, may now be expected to be invalidated as a result of two decisions[1] rendered by the Supreme Court of the United States on Apr. 22, 1940. Indeed, in its decision declaring unconstitutional the Oregon antipicketing law, the State Supreme Court said that no other alternative was possible.[2]

Under Sec. 3448 of the Alabama Code of 1923, one Thornhill had been convicted when he, as a member of a group of six to eight pickets, had, without threat, or calling of names, appealed to workers not to continue to work in a struck plant. His conviction had been sustained by the Court of Appeals, and the State Supreme Court had declined to issue a writ of certiorari. The Supreme Court of the United States held, however, that as it had been interpreted and applied by the state courts,[3]

---

feres with an employee's right to work. Paid agents of unions must be licensed annually, prevention of any union elections and interference with the right of franchise of union members are made unfair labor practices on the part of the employees, and annual reports must be made to the Secretary of State on the organization and officers and an accounting to members on financial matters. The Act also provided for submission to the voters in 1944 of a constitutional amendment to bar closed-shop agreements.

Minnesota's Labor Relations Act, referred to in the preceding chapter, was amended in 1943 (Laws, chap. 624) to prohibit hindering by threats, force, or intimidation the transportation, processing, or marketing of farm products and conspiracy to injure any processor or marketing organization by secondary boycotts. The 1943 Minnesota amendment extends, however, beyond agriculture. Interference with the free and uninterrupted use of streets and highways is made unlawful, and strikes may not be called unless they have been approved by a majority of the voting employees in a collective-bargaining unit composed of employees of the employer or association of employers against whom the strike is directed. Whenever an interunion controversy becomes the ground for picketing, boycotting, or striking, the governor is empowered to appoint a labor referee to resolve the conflict, and pending the referee's determination there may be no strike, boycott, or picketing. A separate Minnesota enactment of 1943 (Chap. 625) requires the election of union officers for terms not exceeding four years, and charges the responsible officer of each labor organization with the duty of making financial statements to members. Unions not complying with these requirements are disqualified from representing employees in collective bargaining. Michigan in 1943 enacted a law (Public Act 24) making it a criminal offense, punishable by fine or imprisonment, to stop or hinder the operation of any vehicle transporting farm or commercial products in order to delay the transportation, loading, or unloading of such products.

[1] *Thornhill v. Alabama*, 310 U. S. 88, and *Carlson v. California*, 310 U. S. 106. It has already been noted that the Los Angeles ordinance was previously invalidated on the same grounds.

[2] On Dec. 10, 1940, the Michigan Supreme Court upheld the legality of peaceful picketing in two cases, thus overruling a forty-two-year-old precedent. *Book Tower Garage, Inc. v. Local No.* 415, C. C. H. Labor Law Service, Par. 60,187, 295 N. W. 320; *People v. Bashaw*, C. C. H. Labor Law Service, Par. 60,184.

[3] As interpreted, the statute left room for no exceptions based on the number of persons engaged in the activity, the peaceful character of their demeanor, the nature of their dispute with an employer, or the restrained character or the accuracy of the terminology used in notifying the public of the facts of the dispute. Indeed, it had been applied by the state

the statute was invalid because in conflict with the Fourteenth Amendment of the Federal Constitution, which protects freedom of speech and press from abridgement by the states. "The freedom of speech and of the press guaranteed by the Constitution embraces at the least the liberty to discuss publicly and truthfully all matters of public concern without previous restraint or fear of subsequent punishment." Though there is a justifiable area in which to exercise the police power, "the danger of breach of peace or serious invasion of rights of property or privacy at the scene of a labor dispute is not sufficiently imminent in all cases to warrant the legislature in determining that such place is not appropriate for the range of activities outlawed by Section 3448."

Carlson was one of twenty-nine men engaged in picketing on a public highway in front of a tunnel project. The picketing consisted of displaying small banners, such as one with the legend "This job is unfair to C.I.O.," as the pickets walked to and fro, without threat and without interference with traffic. He was convicted under an ordinance of Shasta County, California, rather characteristic of a mushroom crop of restrictive ordinances adopted in many parts of the country, especially on the Pacific Coast. Among other things, the ordinance prohibited any person in a public place, "to picket in front of, or in the vicinity of, or to carry, show or display any banner, transparency, badge or sign in front of, or in the vicinity of, any works, or factory, or any place of employment, for the purpose of inducing or influencing, or attempting to induce or influence, any person to refrain from entering such works, or factory, or place of business, or employment," or "to refrain from doing or performing any service or labor" in such works. The Court declared the ordinance invalid for the same reasons it had given in the Thornhill case. It said, "for the reasons set forth in our opinion in *Thornhill v. Alabama* . . . , publicizing the facts of a labor dispute in a peaceful way through appropriate means, whether by pamphlet, by word of mouth or by banner, must now be regarded as within that liberty of communication which is secured to every person by the Fourteenth Amendment against abridgment by a State."

Injunctions against picketing that is associated with acts of violence have not, however, been held to be in conflict with the Fourteenth Amendment. Such was the ruling of the Supreme Court on Feb. 10, 1941, in the case involving the Chicago Milk Wagon Drivers Union.[1] "It was in order to avert force and explosions due to restrictions upon rational modes of communication," said the court, "that the guarantee

___

courts to prohibit a single individual from walking back and forth on the public sidewalk in front of the premises of his employer without speaking to anyone, merely because he carried a sign or placard stating that the employer did not employ union men.

[1] *Milk Wagon Drivers' Union of Chicago v. Meadowmoor Dairies, Inc.*, 312 U. S. 287 (1941).

of free speech was given in generous scope.   But utterance in a context of violence can lose its significance as an appeal to reason and become part of an instrument of force.   Such utterance was not meant to be sheltered by the Constitution." This doctrine leaves wide discretion to the judges.   For while it is clear that the Supreme Court did not mean that picketing can be prohibited where violence is only sporadic or where union responsibility is not clearly established, how much violence there must be and the degree of union responsibility required will be up to the judges.   Such a result is, of course, inevitable, unless it is held that the right to picket is absolute.

The three preceding cases show that the right to picket is protected by the Constitution, but that it is not entirely immune from regulation or restriction; it must at least be peaceful before the Fourteenth Amendment can be invoked.   The question then arises as to how far peaceful picketing can now be regulated.   Can certain ends, such as the closed shop, be sought through picketing?   What persons can picket, and where, and in how great numbers?

The narrow limitations placed on picketing under court interpretations of the Clayton Act were substantially reduced a number of years before the Thornhill and Carlson decisions by the Norris-La Guardia Anti-injunction Act,[1] which regulates the power of the federal courts to grant injunctions—a power conferred upon the lower courts by the Congress and therefore one which the Congress can limit or regulate. The right of peaceful picketing was strengthened by limiting the issuance of injunctions restricting it.   The Act provides, as already pointed out, that the courts shall not issue any restraining order or injunction forbidding: "Giving publicity to the existence of, or the facts involved in, any labor dispute, whether by advertising, speaking, patrolling, or by any other method not involving fraud or violence."   There are also various procedural requirements to be observed in granting restraining orders and injunctions.[2] The seventeen state antiinjunction acts, modeled upon the Norris-La Guardia Act, similarly reduced the power of state courts to issue restraining orders restricting picketing.

There are now a number of decisions indicating how far the Norris-La Guardia Act and the similar state acts go in protecting the right to picket and how far in the absence of such laws, the right to picket is protected by the Fourteenth Amendment.   In *Senn v. Tile Layers' Protective Union*,[3] the Supreme Court upheld the right of a union to picket for the purpose of inducing an employer to sign a closed-shop contract that would forbid him, as an employer, to work with his hands and tools.   The Court said:

[1] Public no. 65, 72d Congress, 1st Session, Chap. 90 (H.R. 5315), Mar. 23, 1932.
[2] For procedural requirements see pp. 645-647.
[3] 301 U. S. 468 (1937).

"The State may, in the exercise of its police power, regulate the methods and means of publicity as well as the use of public streets. If the end sought by the unions is not forbidden by the Federal Constitution the State may authorize working men to seek to attain it by combining as pickets, just as it permits capitalists and employers to combine in other ways to attain their desired economic ends. The Legislature in Wisconsin has declared that 'peaceful picketing and patrolling' on the public streets and places shall be permissible 'whether engaged in singly or in numbers' provided this is done 'without intimidation or coercion' and free from 'fraud, violence, breach of the peace or threat thereof.'"[1] "In the present case the only means authorized by the statute and in fact resorted to by the unions have been peaceful and accompanied by no unlawful act. It follows, that if the end sought is constitutional—if the unions may constitutionally induce Senn to agree to refrain from exercising the right to work in his business with his own hands, their acts were lawful." The end sought was found to be a reasonable rule for the protection of those employed owing to demoralized conditions in the tile-laying industry, and picketing for the purpose of inducing Senn to accept a closed-shop agreement was not an "effort to induce Senn to do an unlawful thing." Moreover, picketing to induce a competing self-employer himself not to work was declared to be as legitimate as picketing to organize nonunion employees.[2]

The American Steel Foundries decision, with its ruling that "each case must turn on its own circumstances," had left the law uncertain on the legality of picketing "in numbers." The Wisconsin Act provided that picketing should be "lawful whether engaged in singly or in numbers." Although there was no finding of fact as to how many pickets were involved, there was testimony that picketing was conducted by at least four pickets; hence, it would appear that the decision, particularly with respect to state statutes of the Norris-La Guardia type, sanctions the legality of picketing by at least four pickets in similar circumstances.[3]

In cases involving only the closed shop, or the unionization of workers, court decisions have been diverse, but on the whole have tended to become more favorable to organized labor. In *Levering & Garrigues Co. v. Morrin*,[4] a case in which some of the employees were unionized but no controversy existed as to hours or wages, the court held that a dispute

---

[1] *Ibid.*, at pp. 478–480. The Wisconsin law was amended in 1939. See *supra* pp. 618–619 and *infra* pp. 627–628.

[2] For a discussion of this, the constitutional right to work, and the issue of equal protection of the laws, see *International Juridical Association Monthly Bulletin*, vol. 6 (1937), p. 16; *Thompson v. Boekhout*, 273 N.Y. 390, 7 N.E. (2d) 674 (1937); and *Harvard Law Review*, vol. 50 (1937), p. 1295.

[3] But a state may also limit the number of pickets, by forbidding mass picketing, as does the present Wisconsin Act. See *infra*, p. 627.

[4] 71 Fed. (2d) 284 (C.C.A. 2d Circuit 1934); certiorari denied, 293 U. S. 595 (1934).

existed since picketing by the union for the closed shop was an attempt "to arrange terms or conditions of employment" within the provisions of the Norris-La Guardia Act. In reply to the argument advanced in *Cinderella Theater Co. v. Sign Writers' Local Union*[1] that no labor dispute could justify picketing where the single employee involved was satisfied with his conditions of employment, the court declared that the persons agitating and picketing need not be employees.

The decision of the Supreme Court in the Lauf case[2] is important in this connection and also as showing the position of that tribunal toward the observance of the procedural requirements of the Norris-La Guardia Act. The employer involved operated five meat markets in Milwaukee with thirty-five employees. None of these was a member of the union. Nevertheless the union demanded that the employer unionize his stores and sign a closed-shop contract. The employer refused to comply with the demand on the ground that his meat cutters did not wish to join the union. Picketing began and a restraining order was sought. The District Court found, among other things, that, inasmuch as there was no dispute between the employer and his employees, there was no industrial dispute that would bring the matter within the limiting provisions of the injunction-limitation law. Of course the pickets were not employees. The District Court therefore restrained the defendants from (1) "in any wise picketing the premises of the complainant," (2) advertising, stating, or pretending that the complainant was "in any wise unfair to said defendants or organized labor generally," and (3) "persuading or soliciting any customers or prospective customers of the said complainant to cease patronizing the complainant at its meat market."

The action of the District Court was affirmed by the Circuit Court of Appeals for the Seventh District,[3] but the Supreme Court, on appeal, ruled otherwise. In line with the decision in the Senn case, the majority[4]

---

[1] 6 Fed. Sup. 164 (District Court, Michigan, 1934).

[2] *Lauf et al. v. E. G. Shinner & Co., Inc.*, 303 U. S. 323 (1938). *Cf.* article on the decision in *International Juridical Association Monthly Bulletin*, vol. 7 (1938), pp. 111, 119–122.

[3] 90 Fed. (2d) 250 (1937).

[4] Justices Cardozo and Reed did not participate: Justices Butler and McReynolds dissented. Justice Butler in his dissent, Justice McReynolds concurring, was of the opinion that the interpretation of the Norris-La Guardia Act by the majority of the court was wrong. The declaration of policy, explicitly set out to assist in the interpretation of the Act, states that the individual unorganized worker, " 'though he should be free to decline to associate with his fellow workers,' should 'have full freedom of association, self-organization, and designation of representatives of his own choosing.' " Lauf's employees had membership in an association; when approached by an organizer they had refused to join the union. Thereupon, the union demanded that the employer coerce them into joining on threat of discharge. This he declined to do, but stated that the employees were entirely free to do as they liked. Because he declined to accept the demands of the union he was falsely advertised as "unfair" to labor, etc. In brief, he was declared unfair for not doing what the Act forbade him to do. The Justice was of the opinion also that there was no "labor

were of the view that there was an industrial dispute within the meaning of the statute. It also held that the District Court erred in granting any restraining order without observing the procedural requirements of the statute.[1] The case was referred back for further proceedings in conformity with the opinion.

In addition to the federal cases, there have been recent decisions by state courts that also liberalize the law. Among these are a few which, contrary to many rulings,[2] recognize the right in connection with organization effort to picket nonunion establishments in the absence of a strike or dispute between an employer and his employees.[3] This position was again affirmed by the U. S. Supreme Court in the Swing case,[4] this time on the grounds that issuance of an injunction to restrain peaceful picketing in such cases is inconsistent with the constitutional guarantee of freedom of speech—reasoning in line with its decision in *Thornhill v. Alabama*.[5]

In its decision in *Bakery and Pastry Drivers and Helpers v. Hyman Wohl*, the Supreme Court about a year later threw further light on the extent to which the right to picket is constitutionally protected. In attempting to unionize the peddlers who distributed bread to the retailers, a bakery union picketed the bakeries who sold to the peddlers. The union also contemplated picketing the retail establishments. The trial court had held that there was no labor dispute within the meaning of the New York statute and that therefore no constitutional right was involved. Overruling this decision, the Supreme Court, speaking through Justice Jackson, stated: "One need not be in a 'labor dispute' as defined by state law to have a right under the Fourteenth Amendment to express a grievance in a labor matter by publication unattended by violence, coercion, or conduct otherwise unlawful or oppressive." And though a state need not under all circumstances tolerate even peaceful picketing,

---

dispute" in the proper sense of the term, or in the sense in which the highest court in Wisconsin used it.

[1] For these, see *infra*, pp. 645–647.

[2] Among these were *Waitresses' Union, Local No. 249 v. Benish Restaurant Co., Inc.*, 6 Fed. (2d) 568 (1925); *Moreland Theatres Corporation v. Portland Moving Picture Machine Operators' Protective Union*, 140 Ore. 35, 12 Pac. (2d) 333 (1932).

[3] *Blumauer v. Portland Moving Picture Machine Operators' Protective Union*, 17 Pac. (2d) 1115 (1933); *Stillwell Theatre, Inc., v. Kaplan*, 182 N.E. 63 (1932); *Music Hall Theatre v. Moving Picture Machine Operators*, 61 S.W. (2d) 283 (1933); *Schuster v. International Association of Machinists*, 293 Ill. App. 177 (1937); *McKay v. Retail Automobile Salesmen's Union*, C.C.H. Lab. Law Serv., Par. 60,098 (1940); *C. S. Smith Metropolitan Market Co. v. Lyons*, C.C.H. Lab. Law Serv., Par. 60,099 (1940). See also *Klein's Restaurant Corporation v. McLain*, 293 Ill. App. 54 (1937).

[4] *A.F. of L. v. Swing*, 312 U. S. 321 (1941).

[5] *Supra*, pp. 620–621. Shortly before, the Washington Supreme Court had held that *Thornhill v. Alabama* did not prevent a state court from enjoining such picketing. *J. E. Shively and W. W. Frisby v. Garage Employees' Union, Local 44* (1941).

"so far as we can tell, respondents' mobility and their insulation from the public as middlemen made it practically impossible for petitioners to make known their legitimate grievances to the public. . . . except by the means here employed and contemplated; and those means are such as to have slight, if any, repercussions upon the interests of strangers to the issue."

The significance of this decision is that it extends the right to picket to the boundaries of the industry involved, including those who produce and distribute the "unfair product." That this case perhaps marks the outward limits of a "labor dispute" within which picketing is constitutionally protected is indicated by the important decision in *Carpenters' and Joiners' Union of America v. Ritter's Cafe,* handed down Mar. 30, 1942, the same day as the bakery decision.

In this case, a man named Ritter awarded a contract for the construction of a building to a contractor who employed non-union carpenters and painters. Ritter also owned a restaurant, apparently in no way connected with the new building, and free from any labor dispute. But in their efforts to organize the construction project, the carpenters' and painters' unions picketed the restaurant. Under the Texas antitrust law, picketing was enjoined. The Supreme Court upheld the injunction on the grounds that a state has the right to restrict picketing "to the area of the industry within which a labor dispute arises."

"It is true that by peaceful picketing workingmen communicate their grievances. As a means of communicating the facts of a labor dispute peaceful picketing may be a phase of the constitutional right of free utterance. But recognition of peaceful picketing as an expression of free speech does not imply that the states must be without power to confine the sphere of communication to that directly limited to the dispute. Restriction of picketing to the area of the industry within which a labor dispute arises leaves open to the disputants other traditional modes of communication. To deny to the states the power to draw this line is to write into the Constitution the notion that every instance of peaceful picketing—anywhere and under any circumstances—is necessarily a phase of the controversy which provoked the picketing. Such a view of the Due Process Clause would compel the states to allow the disputants in a particular industrial episode to conscript neutrals having no relation to either the dispute or the industry in which it arose."[1]

It has been seen that the Constitution and acts of the Norris-La Guardia type protect picketing, when peaceful and restricted to the limits

---

[1] This case must, of course, be distinguished from *Goldfinger v. Feintuch* [159 Misc. 806; 288 N.Y.S. 855 (1936)], where the New York Court of Appeals held peaceful picketing to be lawful if directed, not against the retailer Goldfinger, but only against the Ukor products he was handling. For a rather severe criticism of the Ritter decision, see *International Juridical Association Monthly Bulletin,* vol. 11 (1942), pp. 1–6, where it is argued that this decision marks a wide retreat from the position taken in the Thornhill case.

of the industry involved, even when it is directed against nonunion establishments where there is no controversy between the employer and his employees.[1] But what of the right of a dual organization to picket an already unionized establishment?

In *Mann v. Rainist*,[2] the New York courts declared that the right to picket "is not lost because the controversy is one between the members of rival unions, and not, as happens oftener, between unions and employers."[3] The Circuit Court of Appeals, Seventh District, on the other hand, took the view in *United Electric Coal Companies v. Rice*[4] that the employer was an innocent by-stander in the controversy between the Progressive Miners and the United Mine Workers and that restraint of picketing was not limited by the Norris-La Guardia Act. In *Hotel, Restaurant and Soda Fountain Employees v. Miller*, an inferior court in Kentucky in 1939 held unlawful the picketing of a place of business by a rival union, to which none of the employees belonged. And in June, 1942, in an important four-to-three decision, the New York Court of Appeals declared illegal picketing by unions defeated in State Labor Relations Board elections.[5] In this case, an alleged company union was absorbed by an A.F. of L. local, later won an election conducted by the New York State Labor Relations Board, and was certified as exclusive bargaining representative. Shortly thereafter, it entered into an agreement with the employer. The rival union, a C.I.O. local, continued to picket the stores involved. The Court of Appeals said: "When the contract was executed by appellants and the duly certified agent of the employees and went into effect, any labor dispute within the provisions of the New York State Labor Law ended . . . " and "it was unlawful . . . for the defendants to continue or renew or threaten to continue picketing of appellants' shops for the reason that the minority were dissatisfied with the result of the election and with the terms of the contract duly negotiated and entered into between the appellants and the duly certified representative of the employees."

As has been noted, some of the most recent legislation has placed strikes between rival unions, and the picketing incidental to them, under the ban of the law.[6] Thus in Wisconsin[7] picketing and boycotting have become unlawful in the absence of a "labor dispute." As the term was defined, minority unions are deprived of the privilege of picketing and must confine themselves to persuasion of employees until enough have been weaned away from a rival majority organization to constitute a new

---

[1] But *cf. supra*, pp. 616–619.

[2] 255 N. Y. 307 (1931).

[3] *Ibid.*, at p. 314.

[4] 80 Fed. (2d) 1 (1935).

[5] *Florsheim Shoe Store Co. v. Retail Shoe Salesmen's Union.* 288 N Y. 188.

[6] *Cf.* Walter Galenson, *Rival Unionism in the United States* (1940), especially Chap. 8.

[7] Laws (1939), Chap. 25, Sec. 103.535.

majority. In Minnesota,[1] a majority of pickets must be employees of the firm involved, while in Pennsylvania[2] the limitations placed on the use of the injunction are removed when disputes involve rival unions.

Whether the recent decision of the New York Court of Appeals and this state legislation would be upheld by the U. S. Supreme Court is highly problematical. That court did uphold two orders of the Wisconsin Employment Relations Board forbidding picketing. But in one case the picketing involved violence,[3] and in the other[4] the order was directed against mass picketing, threats of physical injury, and the like. Bans on rival union picketing, and requirements that strikes must be called by a majority of employees before they and the concomitant picketing are lawful, seem to be in conflict with the recent decisions of the Supreme Court.[5]

Desirable Public Policy regarding Picketing.—In the interest of sound policy, the law should permit peaceful picketing in the conduct of lawful strikes and boycotts and define it accurately by statute in so far as possible. Justice and equal treatment under the law require this. In fairness the law must permit both employers and workers to present their cases to those in the labor market and leave it to those in the labor market to decide to accept or to reject employment or to decide how they shall bestow their patronage. But, in fairness to those in the labor market and in the interest of peace and order, picketing must be limited. In this connection numbers may make a difference. Unfortunately, what numbers are appropriate varies with circumstances; no explicit rule can be soundly applied unless it is that pickets must not be less than so many paces apart.[6] Unless some such rule as has just been suggested is practicable, leeway must be given and those who are charged with industrial policing and the courts must be permitted to decide the question of numbers under standards established by law. While picketing should be permitted "by numbers," mass picketing should not be tolerated. Not only is it unduly coercive; in many cases it makes bad matters worse. "Peaceful" should be defined as accurately as possible, but realistically and not

---

[1] Laws (1939), Chap. 440, Sec. 11 (*d*).

[2] Laws (1939), Act. no. 163.

[3] *Hotel & Restaurant Employees' International Alliance v. Wisconsin Employment Relations Board*, 315 U. S. 437 (1942).

[4] *United Electrical, Radio and Machine Workers of America v. Wisconsin Employment Relations Board*, decided Mar. 30, 1942.

[5] But the court during its 1942 term declined to review two Ohio decisions upholding bans on picketing an establishment where none of the employees were on strike. It also refused to review a Wisconsin decision banning picketing in a situation similar to that in the Wohl case (*Supra*, pp. 625–626). See *Internatinal Juridical Association Monthly Bulletin*, vol. 11 (1942), pp. 5–6.

[6] In New Jersey pickets must be stationed at least ten paces apart. New Jersey Revised Statute, Sec. 2:29–77, 1937.

too narrowly. Actual intimidation, really abusive language, and the like should be forbidden, as well as violence, actual or threatened. Except for these limitations and avoidance of interference with use of the streets or annoyance of customers, picketing in the conduct of lawful strikes and boycotts should not be restricted.

In days of divided unionism, such as those beginning in 1935, more than occasional picketing of an unoffending business by two competing unions may be expected. Permitting such picketing leads to undesirable situations and leaves innocent employers without needed protection. It would be better if each state had a "baby Wagner Act" and if the union to be recognized were determined thereunder by secret ballot of the employees. With such procedure provided for settling the issue between two contesting unions, picketing should be prohibited, or subject to cease-and-desist orders issued by the board making certifications.[1]

THE INJUNCTION IN LABOR DISPUTES

Reference has already been made, in passing, to the injunction in labor disputes. The problem of the labor injunction and the important issues growing out of its employment should, however, be presented in some detail at this point.

The injunction is a very old instrument of the courts, originating centuries ago and developing and finding extended application in the course of social evolution.[2] In Great Britain it was first applied in a labor case in 1868;[3] in the United States it appeared in a number of the states during the 1880's—in Baltimore, Md., in 1883, in Georgia and Iowa in 1884–1885, in Illinois in 1886, in Massachusetts in 1888. In 1891, for the first time, a federal court issued a labor injunction. It was not widely advertised and brought into frequent use, however, until the Pullman strike of 1894. From that time to the earlier 1930's, for reasons indicated below, the injunction was widely and increasingly employed in labor disputes in this country.

The labor injunction has been essentially an American problem. Little use of it has been made in the countries of Continental Europe. In Great Britain, some years after the Springhead case of 1868, the Court of Appeals rendered a decision that had the effect of restricting the use of the injunction in that country. Indeed, the Taff Vale[4] case of 1901 is the one

---

[1] This was recommended by the New York State Joint Legislative Committee on Industrial and Labor Relations in its Report (Legislative Document 57, published in January, 1940). See also Professor Galenson, *op. cit.*, pp. 289–295.

[2] For a historical account of the injunction, see Felix Frankfurter and Nathan Greene, *The Labor Injunction* (1930), pp. 2–47. For a labor account, see John P. Frey, *The Labor Injunction* (1923).

[3] *Springhead Spinning Company v. Riley*, L. R. 6 Equity 551 (1868).

[4] *Cf. supra*, pp. 495–496.

outstanding instance in which it has been employed in subsequent years. The infrequent use there is explained by the public and employer attitude toward labor organizations; by the general respect for law and the efficient enforcement of law through the ordinary channels; by the British view of the part the courts should play in government, a view very different from that held in this country; and by the little labor activity that was unlawful and actionable under the Industrial Disputes Act of 1906. Though that law was revised and made more restrictive upon labor in 1927, the government alone may now seek a restraining order.

In the United States, on the other hand, the courts have played an increasing role in government; injunctions, until ten or fifteen years ago, became more and more numerous, sweeping, and restrictive in labor disputes. This is, of course, equally true of the injunction in other connections, such as in the enforcement of the prohibition laws, the anti-trust laws, and other laws. The frequent recourse to restraining orders has in a way justified the expression "government by injunction."

Extent of the Use of the Injunction.—Professor Witte has been a most painstaking student of the labor injunction in the United States. With reference to the extent it has been used, he says:

"The exact number of injunctions in labor disputes is unascertainable. This results from the fact that most injunctions are issued by the inferior courts, whose decisions are not noted in any series of official or unofficial reports.

"Some idea of the number of injunctions can be gathered from the fact that the author has definite reference to 508 cases in federal courts and 1,364 cases in state courts in which injunctions were issued prior to May 1, 1931, on the application of employers.[1] In addition, there were 32 federal cases and 191 state cases in which injunctions were known to have been sought without being allowed.

"On the author's list are injunctions in every state except South Carolina, but with the great industrial states predominating, particularly New York, Massachusetts, and Illinois. The unreported cases exceed the reported cases in the ratio of five to one. Of the grand total of 1,845 injunctions, 28 were issued in the 1880's, 122 in the 1890's, 328 from 1900 to 1909, 446 from 1910 to 1919, and 921 between Jan. 1, 1920, and May 1, 1930. Very probably this list includes a larger percentage of all injunctions in the last two decades than in earlier periods, and for the last ten years is swelled by the large number of injunctions issued in the railroad shop crafts strike of 1922. Yet the author believes the impression of a steadily increasing number of injunctions, created by the figures cited, to be substantially correct. In the last six or eight years there has

---

[1] Labor organizations also occasionally apply for injunctions. Some of these are sought against employers, perhaps because they violate union agreements, but it would appear that most often they are sought by one union, or one union group, against another.

probably been a decrease in absolute numbers, but this is believed to have been smaller than the reduction in the number of strikes."[1]

For almost a generation and a half, from the 1890's to the early 1930's, it may be said that the power of the courts was invoked to assist in defeating most of the more important strikes—among them, the Pullman strike of 1894, the coal strike of 1919, the shopmen's strike of 1922— and only a smaller proportion of the relatively less important ones. Although the number of cases was much smaller, the injunction was used relatively as frequently to prevent the successful spreading of labor boycotts. And after the Hitchman decision in 1917, it was frequently used in an effort to prevent organizing activities where the workers were engaged under individual nonunion or "yellow-dog" contracts.

The labor view is that the injunction has been a great handicap to the organized-labor movement. Years ago, John Mitchell said "no weapon has been used with such disastrous effect against trade unions as has the injunction in labor disputes." John Walker, for many years president of the Illinois State Federation of Labor, spoke of it "as the most perfect and modern strike-breaking agency there is on earth." These views have been shared by most labor leaders. The alacrity with which employers have sought restraining orders at the hands of the courts would indicate that there has been much reason for the views expressed. Nevertheless, as Professor Witte contends,[2] both employers and labor have exaggerated the importance of the injunction in connection with the outcome of industrial disputes.

In strike situations the injunction has frequently not struck terror and it has more and more frequently been ignored. Indeed, it may develop and strengthen the feeling of solidarity and the determination of the workers to win. It may have the effect of advertising and spreading a boycott. But, on the other hand, it cannot be doubted that it may break the spirits of the rank and file and undermine a strike, especially one by workers inexperienced in such matters. It may restrict picketing and render it ineffective; and it may stop the publication and distribution of the "unfair list." It certainly has the effect of "dragging" strike leaders into court at the cost of their time and effort in the field. It also involves the unions in substantial outlays for legal counsel. Nor can it be doubted that the injunction frequently has had a decided effect upon the policing of industry. While it has had the general effect of weakening the enforcement of law through the ordinary channels, it has also certainly had the

[1] E. E. Witte, *The Government in Labor Disputes*, p. 84. See also P. F. Brissenden, "Campaign against the Labor Injunction," *American Economic Review*, vol. 23 (1933), pp. 42–54, and J. F. Christ, "The Federal Courts and Organized Labor," *Journal of Business of the University of Chicago*, vol. 5 (1932), pp. 283–300.

[2] E. E. Witte, *The Government in Labor Disputes*, Chap. 6, and the same author's "Value of Injunctions in Labor Disputes," *Journal of Political Economy*, vol. 32 (1924), pp. 335–356.

effect of causing the police to be unusually active and severe in handling many concrete strike situations. Beyond this, it would appear that the injunction has been more effective in handicapping the union organizers in their activities when the workers were under individual nonunion contracts than in defeating strikes and boycotts. Finally, it may be noted that much of the restrictive court-made law has been developed in injunction cases. In the absence of the injunction the law applying to labor organizations might have been less restrictive than it became with reference to what labor might lawfully do. Indeed, all too frequently the courts have issued restraining orders going quite beyond the bounds of the law—a point to be discussed presently.

Theory and Nature of the Injunction.—The theory of the injunction is that it will issue only in extraordinary cases where there is no adequate remedy at law for an impending or threatened injury to property rights if things are permitted to take their usual course, and that the party seeking injunctive relief comes into court with "clean hands." The inadequacy of the remedy at law—that is, damage suits—may be due to the pecuniary irresponsibility of the restrained, or to the multiplicity of suits that would have to be brought, or to the difficulty involved in ascertaining the identity of the guilty parties, or to the impossibility of measuring and compensating for the loss if sustained. In labor difficulties there are many such cases—under the law as it has been and in many jurisdictions still is. Unlawful boycotting may work great injury, as it did in the Danbury Hatters' case. So may violent picketing, intimidation, destruction of property, and other unlawful acts accompanying many strikes and lockouts. So may unlawful strikes also.[1] These all give rise to losses for which, as we shall see later,[2] the employers have usually had no adequate means of obtaining compensation through damage suits. The injunction has been designed to serve the purpose of preventing injury, just as binding over to keep the peace is presumed to make for order. The logic of its application to labor disputes is evident.

As has been stated, the injunction is designed to serve as a substitute for the damage suit where such suit would not afford an adequate remedy.[3] It also came to be used as an aid in the enforcement of criminal law. In the older theory it did not extend to crimes punishable under common or statute law. This limitation has always remained the common practice in Great Britain, but in the United States the injunction has been extended to cover criminal acts where the injury to property or business

---

[1] See *Barnes & Co. v. Berry*, 156 Fed. 172 (1907); *Gilchrist v. Metal Polishers, etc. Union*, 113 Atl. 320 (1919); *Meltzer v. Kaminer*, 227 N. Y. S. 459 (1927).

[2] For a discussion of the damage suit, see pp. 651–657.

[3] Of course the injunction has been more than a substitute for the damage suit. It has not been highly exceptional to seek an injunction and to file suit, on the theory that the suit would not afford an adequate remedy.

rights would be continuous and irreparable. In fact, many of the acts restrained in labor disputes have been criminal. The legality of the extension of the injunction to such acts was once much debated, but it was upheld by the Supreme Court of the United States in the Debs[1] and subsequent cases. The position of the courts has been that the jurisdiction of a court of equity is due to the pecuniary injury that may result from the criminal act. The fact that the act involving loss is a crime makes no difference. If the act stopped at crime, or if the injury threatened could, if done, be actually compensated in damage, equity would not interfere.[2] More will be said concerning this aspect presently in a statement and examination of the injunction problem.

An injunction is a restraining order issued by an equity court, commanding certain named or described persons to refrain from doing certain specified things.[3] The labor injunction carries with it the expectation that union leaders will cooperate with the court in securing observance of the order. Occasionally, the injunction is more than a restraining order; incidentally, on the theory that the doing of the things commanded is necessary in order to achieve the main objective, it may command the doing of specified things. If the order is violated, there may be citation for contempt of court. Those found guilty of contempt are, at the common law, punishable by fine or imprisonment, or both, at the discretion of the offended court. Under the common law those cited for contempt do not have a right to change of venue or to jury trial.

Procedure in Injunction Cases.—Injunction procedure is so important that it must be briefly described as it has developed in the United States.[4] At a later point in our discussion modifications made by statute will be noted.

A case starts with the filing of a complaint, duly supported by recitation of unlawful acts and perhaps by affidavits, a statement that unless prevented irreparable injury for which there is no adequate remedy at law will be sustained, and a prayer for a restraining order or a notice to the parties to be restrained for a hearing on a request for a temporary injunction. Though less frequent in recent years than formerly, it is rather common practice to seek a temporary restraining order without notice or hearing, on the ground that protection is urgently and immediately needed. To grant or to refuse to grant an order without a hearing is within the discretion of the court, but the courts have usually been compliant, because a hearing may be had upon order of the court or

---

[1] *In re Debs, Petitioner*, 158 U. S. 564 (1895).

[2] For an early decision on the point, see *Farmers' Loan & Trust Co. v. Northern Pacific R. Co. et al.*, 60 Fed. 803 (1894).

[3] A number of labor injunctions are reproduced in Frankfurter and Greene, *op. cit.*, in John Frey, *op. cit.*, and in Duane McCracken, *Strike Injunctions in the New South* (1931).

[4] For excellent descriptions of procedure, see Frankfurter and Greene, *op. cit.*, Chaps. 2 and 3, and E. E. Witte, *op. cit.*, Chap. 5.

application of the restrained parties.[1] Frequently matters have gone no further than the restraining order—no trial has been held; or the hearing may have been delayed; possibly, after a hearing, decision has been tardily made. Unless limited in time, as it now frequently is,[2] the temporary restraining order remains in effect until a hearing is held and a decision is rendered.

The temporary restraining order is presumed to be and may be followed by a hearing on the question of whether or not a temporary injunction shall issue. Or, as indicated above, there may be no temporary restraining order; in such a case the first step is to secure a temporary injunction. This involves a hearing, which is described briefly but accurately by Professor Witte as follows:

"The preliminary hearings in injunction cases are generally conducted without oral examination of the witnesses in court, being confined to the complaint, answer, and affidavits, with arguments by opposing counsel. No jury is impanelled, the judge determining all questions of fact as well as law. This throws upon him the burden of determining where the truth lies amid the contradictions of the affidavits presented by the contending parties,[3] without opportunity to see or question any of the witnesses.

"After the preliminary hearing and consideration of the claims and counterclaims of the respective parties, the judge renders a decision allowing or refusing a temporary (interlocutory) injunction. This may be merely a continuance or modification of the temporary restraining order, or an entirely new writ."[4]

It may be added that frequently the temporary injunction, as well as the restraining order, has run in the language of the prayer submitted, or with only slight modifications thereof.

Of course the temporary injunction is intended to control the parties only until a full hearing, with witnesses and cross-examination, is held, at which time the writ is dissolved or made permanent with or without modification. The fact is, however, that in most labor cases the stage of the full hearing involved in the permanent injunction has never been reached. The permanent injunction has been exceptional; the temporary

---

[1] As Frankfurter and Greene state, some courts have refused to grant temporary restraining orders where doubtful as to the merits of the case. "For the most part, however, courts have granted the injunction despite grave doubt, on the theory that the preliminary injunction does not pass finally on the merits of the controversy." *The Labor Injunction*, p. 78.

[2] *Cf. infra*, pp. 641 and 645–646.

[3] Frequently the affidavits—offered in about equal numbers by the parties in interest—are flatly contradictory. Frequently, also, they run in stereotyped language. They cannot be regarded as good evidence of the facts in the case. See Frankfurter and Greene, *op. cit.*, pp. 105–108.

[4] E. E. Witte, *op. cit.*, pp. 92–93.

restraining order and the temporary injunction have been the typical and usual writs.[1]

At common law, there is no right of appeal from a temporary restraining order. Appeals from injunctions are time-consuming, for ordinarily they have had no special preference. Sometimes the decision of a supreme court is rendered months, even years, after the writ appealed from has been issued by an inferior court. Of course the writ appealed from remains in effect meanwhile.

Upon appeal, the record alone is reviewed; no further testimony is taken. The higher court will set aside or modify the decision only if the trial court has been clearly wrong. It is an interesting fact that the higher courts have set aside or modified a considerable proportion of the decisions appealed to them, but, as a rule, the dispute had long since become a matter of history.

With the background in injunction theory and procedures thus provided, we may proceed to examine the injunction problem as presented by the labor spokesman.

The Injunction Problem.—One of the much used arguments against the labor injunction has been that it has deprived the accused of certain constitutional guarantees, such as the right of jury trial in criminal cases. In contempt cases (except where procedure has been modified by statute), the trial is by the offended court who punishes at his discretion. The technical answer made to the objection is that the trial and punishment are for contempt of court only; in criminal cases the accused may still be indicted, tried by jury, and punished as prescribed by law. The fact is that the offended court has often fixed the punishment according to the heinousness of the act committed. Seldom have there been the contempt trial and also prosecution for a criminal act. The answer made is, therefore, not wholly satisfactory to the layman. Nor is it entirely satisfactory to many lawyers. As a House Judiciary Committee has said: "That complaints have been made and irritation has arisen out of the trial of persons charged with contempt in the Federal Courts is a matter of general and common knowledge. The charge most commonly made is that the courts, under the equity power, have invaded the criminal domain, and under the guise of trials for contempt have really convicted persons of substantive crimes for which, if indicted, they would have had a constitutional right to be tried by jury."[2]

Objection has been made to injunctions when they have taken the so-called "blanket" form, restraining specified persons and "all others." The first blanket injunction is said to have been issued by Judge Jenkins in the *Northern Pacific*[3] case (December, 1893); in addition to persons

---

[1] See Frankfurter and Greene, *op. cit.*, pp. 64, 200–201, and Appendix II.

[2] Quoted from Frankfurter and Greene, *op. cit.*, p. 191.

[3] 222 U. S. 370.

named, it restrained "all persons generally." In the Debs[1] case the writ was directed against eighteen defendants named "and all persons combining and conspiring with them, and all other persons whomsoever." Judge Wilkerson, in the Shopmen's[2] case (1922), restrained many persons specified and "all of their attorneys, servants, agents, associates, members, employers and all persons acting in aid or in conjunction with them." Writs against specified persons are served upon them personally, but the service upon "all persons generally" must take impersonal form. Perhaps the injunction is read at a street corner (as in the Chicago Teamster's strike of 1905), posted on light and telephone poles or on buildings or delivery trucks, or published in the newspapers. In contempt proceedings it has been necessary, however, to show that those who had not been personally served had actual knowledge of the injunction or were so circumstanced that they should have had and probably did have such knowledge.

The legality of the blanket injunction was once seriously questioned, but the question was long ago disposed of by the courts—and adversely to labor's contention. It is evident that the injunction must take that form in most labor cases if it is to be effective; otherwise pickets and other personnel might be shifted. It is frequently said, as by the Anthracite Coal Strike Commission (1902), that persons who obey the law will not be injured by the issuance of a blanket injunction restraining the doing of unlawful things. There is, however, one substantial objection to the blanket injunction as it has worked out in practice. This lies in the fact that it may widen the range of persons restrained and stand in the way of expressing class or public opinion.[3] If, in a strike situation, a town barber voluntarily puts up a card to the effect that "scabs" will not be served and is cited for contempt, has not the injunction been carried too far?

The greatest objection to the injunction, according to labor, is that it has frequently prohibited the doing of lawful things. Judge Jenkins in the Northern Pacific case, in 1893, issued a writ so sweeping as to forbid the workers to leave their employment.[4] Some of the restraining orders issued by Judge Dayton and by Judge McClintock in West Vir-

[1] 158 U. S. 564.

[2] 283 Fed. 479.

[3] See Frankfurter and Greene, op. cit., pp. 125–126.

[4] Farmers' Loan & Trust Co. v. Northern Pacific R. Co. et al., 60 Fed. 803 (1894). Among other things, the District Court enjoined the Locomotive Engineers from "so quitting the service of the said receivers, with or without notice, as to cripple the property or prevent or hinder the operation of said railroad." Upon appeal [Arthur v. Oakes, 63 Fed. 310 (1894)], the Circuit Court of Appeals ruled that this clause should be eliminated from the injunction on the ground that "equity will not compel the actual, affirmative performance of merely personal services, or (which is the same thing) require employes, against their will, to remain in the personal service of their employers."

ginia forbade the doing of lawful things. To cite only one more of many cases that might be cited, the federal court of the Northern District of Illinois in the Shopmen's case[1] restrained persons far and near (most of them outside of the district) not only from doing many unlawful things, but also from doing lawful things. The following clauses may be quoted:

"1(d) inducing or attempting to induce by the use of threats, violent or abusive language, opprobrious epithets, physical violence or threats thereof, intimidations, display of numbers or force, jeers, entreaties, argument, persuasion, rewards, or otherwise, any person or persons to abandon the employment of said railway companies, or any of them, or to refrain from entering such employment. . . .

"1(i) in any manner by letters, printed or other circulars, telegrams, telephones, word of mouth, oral persuasion, or suggestion, or through interviews to be published in newspapers or otherwise in any manner whatsoever, encourage, direct or command any person whether a member of any or either of said labor organizations or associations defendants herein, or otherwise, to abandon the employment of said railway companies, or any of them, or to refrain from entering the service of said railway companies or either of them;

"2(a) [Directed against the officers of the unions] issuing any instructions, requests, public statements or suggestions in any way to any defendant herein or to any official or members of any said labor organizations constituting the said Federated Shop Crafts, or to any official or member of any system federation thereof with reference to their conduct or the acts they shall perform subsequent to the abandonment of the employment of said railway companies by the members of the said Federated Shop Crafts, or for the purpose of or to induce any such officials or members or any other persons whomsoever to do or say anything for the purpose or intended or calculated to cause any employee of said railway companies, or any of them, to abandon the employment thereof, or to cause any persons to refrain from entering the employment thereof to perform duties in aid of the movement and transportation of passengers and property in interstate commerce and the carriage of the mails;

"2(b) using, causing, or consenting to the use of any of the funds or monies of said labor organizations in aid of or to promote or encourage the doing of any of the matters or things hereinbefore complained of."[2]

Some of these restraints quoted above are interesting in view of the fact that the Clayton Act had been in effect almost eight years. Section 20 of that Act read, in part:

---

[1] *United States v. Railway Employees' Department of American Federation of Labor et al.,* Temporary Injunction, 283 Fed. 479 (1922), Final, 290 Fed. 978 (1923).

[2] See Frankfurther and Greene, *op. cit.,* pp. 253–259; *Harvard Law Review,* vol. 37 (1924), pp. 1101–1109.

"And no such restraining order or injunction shall prohibit any person or persons, whether singly or in concert, from terminating any relation of employment, or from ceasing to perform any work or labor, or from recommending, advising, or persuading others by peaceful means so to do; or from attending at any place where any such person or persons may lawfully be, for the purpose of peacefully obtaining or communicating information; or from peacefully persuading any person to work or to abstain from working; or from ceasing to patronize or to employ any party to such dispute, or from recommending, advising, or persuading others by peaceful and lawful means so to do; or from paying or giving to, or withholding from, any person engaged in such dispute, any strike benefits or other moneys or things of value; or from peaceably assembling in a lawful manner, and for lawful purposes; or from doing any act or thing which might lawfully be done in the absence of such dispute by any party thereto; nor shall any of the acts specified in this paragraph be considered or held to be violations of any law of the United States."

It should be added that all the above-mentioned injunctions were modified, upon appeal, because in the opinion of the higher courts they transcended the law. The modifications, however, were made after the strikes had been broken.

The numerous instances of granting restraining orders forbidding the doing of lawful things is explained in part by the fact that the law has frequently been uncertain. It is explained in part, also, by the inadequacies of the procedure. A third factor has also entered into the explanation. This is the bias or economic and social predilections of the court. This factor has been given additional room to express itself because of the opportunity frequently available to the party seeking an injunction to elect as between judges. The bias of the court, when any, has usually been in favor of the employer. That, however, has not always been the case. At times employers have had to seek injunctions at the hands of judges with a prolabor bias.

There is, however, much in connection with the complaint made by labor that does not lie on the surface. The larger part of the complaint that the courts have forbidden the doing of lawful things is due to the feeling that pickets and others have certain unlimited rights—say to freedom of speech. But in most cases the courts have merely restrained actions in accordance with established law. It may be that the limitations imposed have been unreasonable, but, if so, it has usually been the fault of the law laid down by the higher courts, not the fault of the courts issuing the injunctions. Over a period of thirty years a number of judges in Chicago were labeled "injunction judges" and fought by organized labor. Some of them in fact merely granted stereotyped injunctions every part of which had been approved by the (State) Supreme Court in earlier cases, and generally they were not severe in handling contempt cases. After all, the main difficulty has been with the law, not with the injunction as an instrument for its enforcement. Labor has at times been altogether too tardy in grasping this fact.

Labor has complained bitterly, and properly, of procedure in injunction and restraining-order cases, and especially of the procedure employed in granting temporary restraining orders. Without a hearing, the restraining of the doing of lawful things has been made more likely; moreover, false statements have become "news" and prejudiced the public and the court. It is now generally appreciated that the restraining order, granted without a hearing, should be issued, if at all, only in a case presenting a real emergency,[1] and that a hearing should then be held without delay.

Two objections to the labor injunction, both very important but not generally appreciated, some time ago came to be emphasized by leading thinkers on the subject.

The first of these, and the most important evil connected with the problem, is that the injunction weakened and undermined the courts. Partly because of the bias of a minority of the judges, but chiefly because of an unclear and in many respects an unfair and unduly restrictive labor law, organized labor years ago lost much of its faith in, and became strongly hostile to, the courts. It is not too much to say that respect for law and government has been undermined.

The other objection involves the emphasis placed upon the right to do business as against the right to work. The courts have included both of these among property rights. It is of little importance that the right to work (to retain or to get a job) is held to be a property right; until recently it has received scant protection. At common law, the right to work does not entitle one to a job at the hands of the employer or protect one against discharge, for reason or without reason. The right to labor is protected in only a few connections. The first of these is in connection with blacklisting, where, as we have seen, the protection has been very ineffective. Another is the protection of the nonunion man against oppression at the hands of a union enforcing the closed shop.[2] In most of the closed-shop cases coming before the courts the protection really sought has been that of the employer who has induced the complainant workman to go into court and seek protection of his right to work. The other type of case is where one union is prevented from keeping the members of a rival organization out of employment. Hence the right to work has usually received no protection[3] in the sense in which the

---

[1] This has, of course, been the theory always, but temporary restraining orders have frequently been granted when there was no emergency in fact.

[2] Of course unions have frequently interfered with the right to work. See, particularly, the discussion of the closed shop and of picketing.

[3] But in these stirring times, marked by heated struggle between A.F. of L. and C.I.O. organizations, protection of the right to work may have more significance than it has had.

organized-labor movement has conceived it. Not so the right to do
business, which is presumed to parallel the right to work. The great
majority of injunctions in labor disputes have been designed not to
protect tangible property from loss or destruction but to protect business
—as the employer wishes to conduct it—from being interfered with.

In some connections important limitations are placed upon the right
to do business and to realize profit, with the object in view that gains
may be forthcoming only where there is a social benefit. Generally
this fact has been lost sight of in labor disputes. Though, as is pointed
out later, attitudes have rather generally undergone change in labor
disputes, the courts have frequently regarded the right to do business
as almost unlimited. The employer's working conditions might be
good, bad, or indifferent—it mattered not. Most persons will agree
that as the law has been applied, the protection of business, as against
the efforts of labor to obtain better standards, has been carried too far.
The courts have done much through the injunction to retain the *status quo*
when labor has wished a change and to effect what the employer has
attempted to do when he has wished a change. Though in recent years
there have been an increasing number of exceptions, seldom have the
courts required the employer, when seeking an injunction, to come with
clean hands, in a broad and the popular sense—in terms of decent wages,
lawful hours, good sanitary conditions, or observance of labor contracts
entered into. A notable exception is found in the injunction issued in
connection with the Adler strike (Milwaukee), where the whole situation
was reviewed and both parties were explicitly directed as to what they
might and might not do.[1]

Legislative Restrictions.—Thus far we have discussed the labor
injunction as it has been developed and applied under the common law.
Injunction evils became so real that it was only to be expected that
organized labor would attempt by statute to circumscribe and regulate
its use or to eliminate the injunction altogether. From the middle of the
1890's down into the 1930's, organized labor almost continuously made
the injunction its most important legislative issue.

More than forty years ago organized labor, led by the American
Federation of Labor, sought relief at the hands of Congress, in so far as
the federal courts were concerned. A number of antiinjunction bills
were introduced and received some attention, but none was enacted into
law.[2] The same was true of conservative bills introduced more or less
as "back fires." Failing to secure the relief sought, the A. F. of L., in
1906, made injunction-limitation legislation one of its legislative demands
served upon the President, the President *pro tem* of the Senate, and the

---

[1] See *Adler Co. v. Maglio*, 228 N.W. 123 (1929).

[2] For historical sketches of the efforts to regulate the labor injunction, see Frankfurter
and Greene, *op. cit.*, Chap. 4, and E. E. Witte, *The Government in Labor Disputes*, Chap. 12.

Speaker of the House.[1]   In 1912 attention began to be centered upon two measures, one relating to the issuance of injunctions, the other to jury trial in contempt cases.   The essentials of these two measures were incorporated in the 'Clayton Act passed in 1914, the provisions of which, in so far as they related to the injunction, were supplemented and in part superseded by the Norris-La Guardia Act, approved in March, 1932.

The Clayton Act was designed to limit and control the granting of temporary restraining orders by the federal courts, to clarify and improve the practice in issuing injunctions, to limit penalties imposed for contempt, and to provide the right of jury trial in cases of criminal contempt.   Moreover, the Act was presumed by many of its sponsors to have changed and liberalized the substantive law of labor.

No temporary order was to be granted without notice to the parties to be restrained except in a real emergency, and the court was to state the facts in the emergency situation.   A hearing was to follow at the earliest possible date.   Moreover, the defendant was given the right to a hearing on two days' notice.   The Act was designed to bring injunction procedure generally up to the level observed by the best courts, and no writ was to issue except to prevent irreparable injury to property, or to a property right, of the party making the application, for which there was no adequate remedy at law.   Such property or property right was to be described with particularity in the application, which must be in writing and sworn to by the applicant or his attorney.   Trial for contempt was, upon demand, to be by jury, but the right to jury trial was limited to cases of contemptuous acts which were also punishable as crimes and was not to be applicable in cases of contempt "committed in the presence of the court, or so near thereto as to obstruct the administration of justice, nor to contempt committed in disobedience of any lawful writ, process, order, rule, decree, or command entered in any suit or action brought or prosecuted in the name of, or on behalf of, the United States."[2]

Organized labor expected the Clayton Act to liberalize the federal law with reference to what it might do.   For example, it was expected to make labor a personal—not a property—right and to protect peaceful picketing, the payment of strike benefits, and all forms of the boycott from being restrained by the federal courts, as they so frequently had been.   These hopes, as we have seen, were for many years largely illusory. The ruling in the Duplex case was that the substantive law had not been changed, while in the American Steel Foundries case a special, limiting rule was laid down with reference to picketing.   Only the sections of the Act relating to jury trial in case of contempt proceedings growing out of refusal to obey an injunction and to the promptitude of hearings in

---

[1] See American Federation of Labor, *Text Book of Labor's Political Demands* (1906), and *supra*, pp. 124–127.

[2] Section 24.

temporary restraining order cases proved to have any value to labor.[1]
The provision of jury trial in contempt proceedings that involved accusations of crime was contested, but was upheld by the Supreme Court as
within the power of Congress to regulate the federal courts.[2]

The early attempts of the state legislatures to check the power of
the courts in contempt cases were not primarily concerned with the use
of the injunction in labor disputes, but as the injunction came to be more
frequently used the question of jury trial in contempt cases growing out of
such disputes became more important. A number of states passed laws
providing for jury trials in cases of indirect contempt, that is, disobedience of or interference with the process of justice not committed
within view of the court or so near as to obstruct the administration of
justice. These laws, however, when tested in the courts, were usually
either declared to be unconstitutional or were so interpreted by the courts
as to produce little or no change from common law, which was held by
the courts to give them an inherent power to punish all cases of contempt.[3]

In some states, however, the courts have now upheld the right of the
legislature to provide for jury trial in cases of indirect contempt. Thus
in a 1935 case the Supreme Court of Pennsylvania upheld the constitutionality of such a statute. After reviewing the history of judicial powers
in Pennsylvania, the court quoted with approval the decision of the
Supreme Court in the Michaelson case,[4] and concluded that "while the
legislature may not abolish the common pleas, it may abolish or change
any or all chancery powers conferred on those courts."[5] Other states,
such as New York,[6] have passed similar laws providing for jury trial in
contempt cases arising out of violation of injunctions issued in labor
disputes. If the courts follow the Pennsylvania precedent rather than
the older precedents when these laws are tested, one of the more objectionable features of labor injunctions will be curbed.

Prior to the appearance of the Clayton bills, a California statute
(1903) had forbidden the use of the injunction in labor disputes,[7] but
the State Supreme Court held that the statute "is somewhat difficult
of construction; but . . . cannot, in our opinion, be construed as under-

---

[1] *Cf.* Frankfurter and Greene, *op. cit.*, pp. 197–198.

[2] *Michaelson v. United States*, 266 U. S. 42 (1924).

[3] *Watson v. Williams*, 36 Miss. 331 (1858); *Hale v. The State*, 55 Ohio St. 210 (1896);
Carter v. Commonwealth, 96 Va. 791 (1899); *Smith v. Speed*, 11 Okla. 95 (1901); *Nichols v.
Judge of Superior Court of Grand Rapids*, 130 Mich. 187 (1902); *State v. Shepherd*, 177 Mo.
205 (1903); *Burdett v. Commonwealth*, 103 Va. 838 (1904); *Ex Parte McCown*, 139 N.C. 101
(1905).

[4] 266 U. S. 42.

[5] *Penn Anthracite Mining Co. v. Anthracite Miners of Pennsylvania et al.*, 318 Pa. at p.
412 (1935).

[6] Chap. 298, Regular Session, 1935, approved Apr. 5, 1935 (effective Sept. 1, 1935).

[7] Statutes of California (1903), Chap. 235.

taking to prohibit a court from enjoining the main wrongful acts [picketing] . . . [and] . . . if it could be so construed, it would to that extent be void because violative of plaintiff's constitutional right to acquire, possess, enjoy and protect property."[1]

With the appearance of the Clayton bills, to which reference has been made, most of the state antiinjunction legislation for approximately twenty years was based largely upon their provisions or upon the Clayton Act itself. The Arizona law, the provisions of which were practically identical with those of the Clayton Act, was upheld by the Arizona courts,[2] but was declared unconstitutional in a majority decision of the Supreme Court of the United States on the ground that, as interpreted by the State Court, it permitted illegal annoyance and obstruction, coercion and conspiracy.[3] The other state laws of the same type were not held to be unconstitutional but were construed in much the same way as was the Clayton Act and were rendered largely ineffective.[4]

Among the laws enacted between 1914 and 1932 was one in New Jersey which provided that contempt cases should be tried before another judge than the one who issued the injunction and, in the discretion of the court, might be tried before a jury.[5] In 1929 Minnesota placed narrow limitations upon the granting of temporary restraining orders and prohibited the granting of injunctions without hearing and notice.[6] New York, in 1930, after a long struggle, passed a measure forbidding the granting of injunctions of any kind without notice,[7] but the length of time after notice was not specified. A similar law was enacted in Pennsylvania in 1931.[8]

The Norris-La Guardia Act.—Because of the adverse decisions of the courts, labor leaders and others sought to eliminate the phrases in the law that had been adversely interpreted by the courts or to frame new statutes that would effectively protect labor from injunctions issued without notice and that were arbitrary not only in the actions they

---

[1] *Goldberg, Bowen & Co. v. Stablemen's Union, Local no.* 8760, 86 Pac. 806 (1906). Massachusetts, in 1914, enacted an antiinjunction law [Acts (1914) Chap. 778] but it was likewise declared unconstitutional [*Bogni v. Perotti*, 224 Mass. 152, 112 N.E. 853 (1916)] and was later repealed.

[2] *Truax v. Corrigan,* 20 Ariz. 7 (1918).

[3] *Truax v. Corrigan,* 257 U. S. 312 (1921).

[4] For a detailed discussion, see 27 *A. L. R.*, 360, 413 (1923). Some of the early laws patterned after the Clayton Act and as yet unchanged are those of Arizona [Code (1928), Sec. 4286], Montana [Revised Code (1921), Sec. 9242], and Illinois [Smith-Hurd, Revised Statutes (1931), Chap. 48, Sec. 2a]. The Kansas Act (*Gen. Stats.* 1923, Secs. 60–1104) provided that no injunction should be issued without previous notice and opportunity to be heard in open court.

[5] New Jersey Laws (1925), Chap. 169.

[6] Minnesota Session Laws (1929), Chap. 260.

[7] New York Laws (1930) Chap. 378.

[8] Pennsylvania Laws, Sessions of 1931, No. 311.

enjoined, but also in the method of enforcement. The most important of the new laws have been the Federal Norris-La Guardia Antiinjunction Act[1] and state acts based upon the same model. Our discussion of the injunction may be closed with an analysis of these acts and mention of some of the court cases in which they have been tested.

With some revision, the Norris-La Guardia Act incorporated the provisions of a bill drafted by a subcommittee of the Senate Judiciary Committee, with the aid of a number of liberal legal scholars.[2] It was designed to remedy the defects of the injunction sections of the Clayton Act—and much more. At first the American Federation of Labor did not approve the bill, but subsequently did so, and it became one of organized labor's measures.

Like the Clayton Act, the Norris-La Guardia Act was designed to change, in effect, the substantive law as enforced through equity proceedings in the federal courts, to limit and regulate the granting of temporary restraining orders and labor injunctions, and to provide for jury trial and possible change of trial judge in contempt cases.

As has been indicated earlier,[3] the "yellow-dog" contract was made unenforceable [Secs. 3 and 4(b)]. Any such undertaking or promise "is . . . declared to be contrary to the public policy of the United States, shall not be enforceable in any court of the United States and shall not afford any basis for the granting of legal or equitable relief by any such court."[4]

The secondary boycott was not legalized, but such decisions as that in the Bedford Cut-Stone case are no longer possible under the law, for the term "labor dispute" was broadly defined.[5] The Act alters the dividing line between direct and sympathetic strikes. It recognizes a considerably wider range of interest than had been recognized by the Supreme Court, and in fact introduces Justice Brandeis's conception of a "community of interest" as set forth in the dissenting opinion in the Duplex case.

Several subsections of Sec. 4 were designed to protect the payment of strike benefits, picketing, and peaceable assembly, which had frequently

[1] For an analysis and criticism of this law, see P. F. Brissenden, "The Campaign against the Labor Injunction," *American Economic Review*, vol. 23 (1933), pp. 42–54. For an excellent discussion of the constitutional questions involved, see J. F. Christ, "Is the Norris Act Constitutional?" *Va. L. Rev.*, vol. 19 (1932), pp. 51–59.

[2] The members of the subcommittee were Senators Norris, Blaine, and Walsh (Montana); the legal experts were Felix Frankfurter, Herman Oliphant, Donald R. Richberg, Francis B. Sayre, and Edwin E. Witte.

[3] *Supra*, pp. 518–519.

[4] Of course the National Labor Relations Act (1935) is more far-reaching.

[5] *Supra*, pp. 592–593, where Sec. 13 is quoted. In fact, with the broad definition of "labor dispute" and the procedural requirements, few labor injunctions can be granted by the federal courts.

been enjoined. The language employed in Sec. 4(e) leaves the number of pickets without specific limitation and intimidation is not mentioned; any method not involving fraud or violence is not to be restrained. The effect of this subsection may, however, depend very much upon the definition of the word "violence" made by the courts.[1]

The granting of temporary restraining orders, not effectively controlled by the Clayton Act, is dealt with (Sec. 7). No restraining order shall be issued except that, if a complainant shall allege that "unless a temporary restraining order shall be issued without notice, a substantial and irreparable injury to complainant's property will be unavoidable, such a temporary restraining order may be issued upon testimony under oath, sufficient, if sustained, to justify the court in issuing a temporary injunction upon a hearing after notice. [But] such a temporary restraining order shall be effective for no longer than five days and shall become void at the expiration of said five days."

Injunctions may not be granted "except after hearing the testimony of witnesses in open court (with opportunity for cross-examination) in support of the allegations of a complaint made under oath, and testimony in opposition thereto, if offered, and except after [certain] findings of fact." Among these findings of fact are the familiar ones that unless a writ is issued substantial and irreparable injury to property will follow and that the complainant has no adequate remedy at law. In addition to these, there are other necessary specific findings that were new in injunction legislation. One of these is "that as to each item of relief granted greater injury will be inflicted upon complainant by the denial of relief than will be inflicted upon defendants by the granting of relief."[2] Another is "that the public officers charged with the duty to protect complainant's property are unable or unwilling to furnish adequate protection."[3] Notice of hearing is to be given to such officers as well

---

[1] Subsection (e) prohibits the restraining of parties to any labor dispute from "giving publicity to the existence of, or the facts involved in, any labor dispute, whether by advertising, speaking, patrolling, or by any other method not involving fraud or violence." (For discussion of this see *supra*, pp. 591–593.)

Subsections (c) and (f) read as follows: "(c) Paying or giving to, or withholding from, any person participating or interested in such labor dispute, any strike or unemployment benefits or insurance, or other moneys or things of value"; "(f) Assembling peaceably to act or to organize to act in promotion of their interests in a labor dispute."

[2] Section 7 (c). Of course this is a statement of the old doctrine of the balancing of rights of the parties involved, a legal rule that had been none too carefully observed. Combined with the statement of policy and other provisions of the Act, it may be regarded as an important provision.

[3] Section 7(e). This section is important in that it throws the duty of protecting physical property back where it belongs—upon the law-enforcement officials—and not upon courts of equity. The strategy of incorporating the provision into the Act is apparent. Few sheriffs or chiefs of police are anxious to take a solemn oath that they are unable to perform one of the duties they were elected or appointed to perform.

as to defendants. Added to this are the further conditions contained in Sec. 8: "No restraining order or injunctive relief shall be granted to any complainant who has failed to comply with any obligation imposed by law which is involved in the labor dispute in question, or who has failed to make every reasonable effort to settle such dispute either by negotiation or with the aid of any available governmental machinery of mediation or voluntary arbitration."

The granting of the blanket injunction is limited by a clause stating that no writ shall be issued "excepting against the person or persons, association, or organization making the threat or committing the unlawful act or actually authorizing or ratifying the same after actual knowledge thereof."[1] Any restraining order or injunction "shall include only a prohibition of such specific act or acts as may be expressly complained of in the bill of complaint or petition filed . . . and as shall be expressly included in said findings of fact made and filed by the court as provided herein."[2]

Protection against delays in review of injunctions is afforded. Upon request of either party to the proceedings, the court shall "forthwith certify as in ordinary cases the record of the case to the circuit court of appeals for its review." Upon filing of the record "the appeal shall be heard and the temporary injunctive order affirmed, modified, or set aside with the greatest possible expedition, giving the proceedings precedence over all other matters except older matters of the same character."[3]

The right of trial by jury has been extended far beyond the limited right under the Clayton Act. The only limitation in the Norris-La Guardia Act is contained in the clause: "That this right shall not apply to contempts committed in the presence of the court or so near thereto as to interfere directly with the administration of justice or to apply to the misbehavior, misconduct, or disobedience of any officer of the court in respect to the writs, orders, or process of the court."[4]

Finally, where contempt arises from an attack upon the character or conduct of the judge issuing a writ, unless the attack is in the presence of the judge or, if elsewhere, so near to the court as to interfere with the administration of justice, the defendant is given the right to have the case transferred to another judge. "Upon the filing of any such demand the judge shall thereupon proceed no further, but another judge shall be designated in the same manner as is provided by law."[5]

This analysis of the Norris-La Guardia Act may be completed by reference to Sec. 6. The limitation therein imposed was designed to

[1] Section 7(a).
[2] Section 9.
[3] Section 10.
[4] Section 11.
[5] Section 12.

prevent mulcting the members of an organization who do nothing more than retain membership in it and pay their dues, as was done in the Loewe case.[1] In that case it was alleged that some of the members had no knowledge of the unlawful boycott for which damages were assessed. Now no officer or member of an organization may be held liable for the unlawful acts of individual officers, members, or agents, "except upon clear proof of actual participation in, or actual authorization of, such acts, or of ratification of such acts after actual knowledge thereof."

The "Baby" Norris-La Guardia Acts.—It is not necessary to review in detail the provisions of those state laws which are patterned after the Norris-La Guardia Act, for the language is in many instances identical. Of the twenty-four states with antiinjunction laws in 1941, seventeen[2] had laws modeled more or less closely after the federal law, three[3] had measures similar to the Clayton Act, while the remaining states[4] had

[1] See *infra*, pp. 652–653.

[2] Colorado, Laws (1933), Chap. 59.

Connecticut, Laws (1939), Chap. 251.

Idaho, General Laws (1933), Chap. 215.

Indiana, Acts (1933), Chap. 12.

Louisiana, Acts (1934), Act. no. 203.

Maryland, Acts (1935), Chap. 574.

Massachusetts, Acts (1934), Chap. 381; *Acts*, 1935, Chap. 407.

Minnesota, Statutes (1927), Sec. 4256, as amended, Laws (1929), Chap. 260; Laws (1933), Chap. 416. The Labor Relations Act of 1939, however, repealed the injunction-limitation provision where unfair practices are committed by labor (*supra*, pp. 551–552).

New Jersey, Laws (1941), Chap. 15, Sec. 1 et seq.

New York, Laws (1935), Chap. 477.

North Dakota, Laws (1935), Chap. 247.

Oregon, Code (1930), Secs. 49–902 to 49–903; Acts (1933), Chap. 355.

Pennsylvania, Acts (1937), Chap. 308. Repealed by Act 163, of 1939, in so far as employees are guilty of any of several specified unfair practices.

Utah, Revised Statutes (1933), Secs. 49-2-6 to 49-2-8; *Laws* (1933), Chap. 15.

Washington, Rem. Revised Statute, Secs. 7612*ff*.

Wisconsin, Statutes (1931), Secs. 133.05-133.08 and 268.18 to 268.30, modified in 1939 (Chap. 25) by a narrow definition of "labor dispute."

Wyoming, Laws (1933), Chap. 37, as amended by Chap. 15, Laws (1937).

Variations are found in the conditions under which injunctions may be granted. That every reasonable effort shall have been made to settle the dispute is not contained in the statutes of Minnesota, North Dakota, and Wyoming. Nor does the Wyoming statute require (1) a finding that greater injury will be inflicted upon complainant by denial of relief than upon defendants by granting of relief, or (2) a finding that public officers are unable or unwilling to give necessary protection.

[3] Arizona, Illinois, and Montana.

[4] Kansas, General Statutes (1923), Secs. 60-1104; Maine, Acts (1933), Chap. 261; Rhode Island, Laws (1936), Chap. 2359; and New Mexico Laws (1939), Chap. 195. The New Mexico law places rather severe limitations on the issuance of temporary restraining orders. Such orders are not to be issued without notice and hearing, and the complainant must "first file an undertaking with adequate security . . . sufficient to recompense those enjoined for any loss, expense, or damage caused by the improvident or erroneous issuance of such order or injunction . . . ."

laws providing that no injunction should be issued without previous notice and an opportunity to be heard in open court. Of these twenty-four states with antiinjunction legislation, only five have failed to enact anti-"yellow-dog" contract laws.[1]

A number of the state antiinjunction laws have gone somewhat further than the federal statute in curbing the labor injunction. For example, some of them have restricted the duration of temporary restraining orders to forty-eight hours[2] instead of to five days, as is provided in the federal statute. Punishment for contempt is limited under a number of the statutes, while under others agreements to join a union, as well as agreements not to join, are made unenforceable.

The language used in some of the state court cases also is indicative of a change in attitude toward antiinjunction legislation. Prior to the passage of the federal Act, proposed antiinjunction legislation had been declared invalid in advisory opinions by the Supreme Court of Massachusetts in 1931,[3] and, somewhat later, by the corresponding court in New Hampshire.[4] Since then, however, the decisions of the higher courts have been more favorable. In Wisconsin the Supreme Court upheld a broad interpretation of the Act of 1929[5] upon the ground that a narrower interpretation was not intended by the Legislature.[6] In two more recent decisions,[7] the Supreme Court of that state not only sustained the constitutionality of this Act, but applied the law to two cases of vigorous unionization campaigns[8] by prohibiting the issuance of injunctions against picketing of establishments by unions in their attempt to unionize

---

[1] Kansas, Maine, Montana, New Mexico, and Wyoming. Rhode Island has adopted a State Labor Relations Act closely modeled after that of New York, which includes in effect a provision against "yellow-dog" contracts.

[2] Colorado, Louisiana, Maryland, Utah, and Wisconsin.

[3] *Opinion of the Justices*, 275 Mass. 580, 176 N.E. 649 (1931).

[4] *Opinion of the Justices*, 86 N.H. 597, 166 Atl. 640 (1933).

[5] Statutes (1931), Secs. 133.05-133.08 and 268.18 to 268.30.

[6] In this case the Supreme Court said, "We cannot give to Section 268.18 such limited effect. That section deliberately declares the public policy of this state as section 2 of . . . the Norris-La Guardia Act declares the public policy of the United States. Both enactments are strikingly similar. . . . When the legislature [Wisconsin] declared 'it is necessary that the individual workman have full freedom of association, self-organization, and designation of representatives of his own choosing . . . .' it intended, in our opinion, that such declaration should have the force of law. To hold otherwise would amount to saying that the Legislature did not intend what it said, but merely intended to write into the statute language pleasing to labor. We can ascribe no such motive or intention to the Legislature." *Trustees of Wisconsin State Federation of Labor v. Simplex Shoe Mfg. Co.*, 256 N.W. 56 (1934); quotation at pp. 60–61.

[7] *American Furniture Co. v. International Brotherhood of Teamsters, Chauffeurs, and Helpers of America*, 268 N.W. 250 (1936), and *Senn. v. Tile Layers' Protective Union, Local no. 5*, 268 N.W. 270 (1936).

[8] For comment, see *International Juridical Association Monthly Bulletin*, vol. 5 (1936), pp. 59*ff.*

employees.[1] The Louisiana Court of Appeals, in upholding the act adopted in that state,[2] relied heavily upon the decisions of the federal courts in the Cinderella Theatre and Levering and Garrigues cases.[3] The New York State law[4] has been referred to in at least four cases that have come before the Supreme Court. In two of these cases the issue of constitutionality was raised, and the court declared that, as far as the issues in the case were concerned, the law was valid.[5] This is all the more significant since the Aberdeen case concerned the right of the employer to hire and fire. More recently, in Indiana[6] and in two cases before the Oregon Supreme Court,[7] legislation patterned after the Norris-La Guardia Act has been declared constitutional. The two Oregon cases arose from the efforts, in the first case, of an American Federation of Labor organizer to form a union among unorganized employees, and, in the second case, of a machinists' union to prevent certain employers from undercutting union wage and hour scales. The court recognized the union's vital and legitimate interest in the wages, hours, and working conditions of unorganized workers as well as in those of its own members, and, consequently, found nothing unreasonable in extending the status of disputants in a labor controversy to interested parties not standing in an

[1] Under somewhat similar circumstances, the Federal Court of Appeals for the Seventh Circuit had held previously that the provisions of the Norris-La Guardia Act were not applicable. See *United Electric Coal Companies v. Rice*, 80 Fed. (2d) 1 (C.C.A. 7th, 1935), cert. den. 297 U. S. 714 (1936); *Newton v. Laclede Steel Co.*, 80 Fed. (2s) 636 (C.C.A. 7th, 1935); *Lauf v. E. G. Shinner & Co., Inc.*, 82 Fed. (2d) 68 (C.C.A. 7th, 1936).

[2] Act no. 203 of 1934.

[3] *Cf. supra*, pp. 623–624. In this case the Louisiana Court of Appeals said: "Under the plain and unambiguous wording of that act the courts of this state are now without jurisdiction to issue injunctions in labor disputes. . . . It limits the right to a remedy. It does not deprive any one of a constitutional right to have an injunction issue, for the reason that the right to an injunction is not a constitutional one, but a right granted by statute and subject to be enlarged or limited at the will of the Legislature." *Dehan v. Hotel and Restaurant Employees and Beverage Dispensers, Local Union*, 159 So., at p. 647 (La. 1935).

[4] Chap. 477, Regular Session, 1935.

[5] *Goldfinger v. Feintuch*, 276 N.Y. 281 (1937); and *Aberdeen Restaurant Corporation v. Gottfried*, Supreme Court New York County, 285 N.Y. S. 832, 94 N.Y. L.J. 18 (July 1, 1935). The court denied an injunction to restrain picketing because plaintiff had not complied with all the provisions of Chap. 477. "Defendants sought an agreement from plaintiff permitting the union to organize plaintiff's employees. Though willing to some extent, the plaintiff unalterably refused to give the union the right to exercise the power of dictating who were to be employed by the plaintiff, commonly called the right to 'hire and fire.' Obviously, this is conceived to be the backbone of union control. Without this authority the control of the union is bloodless."

[6] *National Brothers of Operative Potters et al. v. City of Kokomo et al.*, 5 N.E. (2d) 624 (1937).

[7] *Starr v. Laundry and Dry Cleaning Workers' Local Union No. 101 et al.*, 63 Pac. (2d) 1104 (1936), and *Geo. B. Wallace Co. et al. v. International Assn. of Mechanics, Local No. 1005 et al.*, 63 Pac. (2d) 1090 (1936).

employer-employee relationship.   In the case of a badly sweated industry, asked the court, who would protest if trade unions were so disqualified?   Moreover, as the court observed, a union cannot be expected
to stand idly by and see its standards undermined and its cause defeated
merely because in particular establishments there is no immediate dispute between employer and employee.

These recent favorable decisions reflect a changed attitude on the
part of the courts.[1]   The following statement made in an injunction case
by a New York Supreme Court recognizes that fact:[2]

"Explanation for the present-day liberal judicial attitude towards
labor and labor disputes is not to be discovered, therefore, in statutory
enactment; but rather in judicial determination that unionization and
collective bargaining are so necessary in industrial life and so justified
by public policy, that all peaceful concerted action will be permitted as
justifiable means to accomplish any purpose legitimately associated
with and necessary for their full utilization."

This brief analysis makes clear the far-reaching limitation Congress
and some of the state legislatures have attempted to place upon the
use of the labor injunction and the attitude of the courts in the cases so
far tested.[3]   Such is the answer Congress and the states have given to the
demand for "antiinjunction" legislation.   Constitutionality of the
provisions being assumed, the effectiveness of the laws depends in practice somewhat upon the attitude of the inferior courts and upon their
care, or lack of care, to conform to the requirements of the statutes.
In this connection it may be said that a considerable number of the
inferior courts have shown in these matters a more liberal attitude than
was shown ten or twenty years ago.   Moreover, the Supreme Court of
the United States has in *Lauf v. Shinner*[4] and in *Milk Wagon Drivers v.
Lake Valley Farm Products, Inc.*[5] rendered decisions that make it difficult
for the federal inferior courts to disregard the requirements of the
Norris-La Guardia Act.   In the first case the District Court had granted

---

[1] The lower courts, however, apparently have been reluctant to accept the restrictions
imposed upon their jurisdiction by the New York Anti-injunction Act. See, "Recent
Limitations upon the New York Anti-Injunction Law," *International Juridical Association
Monthly Bulletin*, vol. 5 (1936), p. 5.

[2] *A. S. Beck Shoe Corporation v. Johnson et al.*, 274 N.Y. S. 946 (1934); quotation at p.
952.

[3] It may be noted that on Dec. 6, 1936, the Supreme Court of Washington declared the
injunction act of that state unconstitutional, to be an unwarranted attempt to deprive a
constitutionally created court of equitable jurisdiction expressly conferred upon it. In
most other state constitutions such explicit provisions are wanting.

[4] *Lauf v. E. G. Shinner & Co., Inc.*, 303 U. S. 323 (1938).

[5] *Milk Wagon Drivers' Union, Local No. 753, International Brotherhood of Teamsters,
Chauffeurs, Stablemen and Helpers of America, et al., v. Lake Valley Farm Products, Inc.,
Amalgamated Dairy Workers, Local Industrial Union no. 819, et al.*, 311 U. S. 91 (1940).

an injunction restraining all picketing and related practices without making all the findings explicitly required by the Act. In the language of the court, "The District Court made none of the required findings save as to irreparable injury and lack of remedy at law. It follows that in issuing the injunction it exceeded its jurisdiction."[1] The case was sent back for appropriate action under the law. In the Milk Wagon Drivers case, the Court held that an injunction could not be granted merely because of violation of the Sherman Act.

The effectiveness of the laws depends also upon the interpretation of some of the language employed. Because they were better drafted, the Norris-La Guardia Act and the similar state acts are less likely to have their effectiveness removed by court construction than was the Clayton Act. Nevertheless, such terms as "violence," "so near thereto as," and "failed to make every reasonable effort" are not so definite as one who is not well versed in law might suppose.

The Pecuniary Responsibility of Trade Unions

The injunction has been employed in labor disputes in an effort to safeguard against losses due to violence, interference with business, and destruction of property and to handicap the opposition in various ways. A writ is presumed to issue only in the case where adequate damages cannot without undue difficulty be recovered through suit at law. We, therefore, must review the subject of the pecuniary responsibility of trade unions, chiefly in relation to the employer group.

Damage Suits.—Suits for damages have been much more frequently brought against American trade unions, their officers, and their members than is commonly realized. They have been brought to recover damages for losses sustained in industrial disputes, for losses due to breach of agreement, for losses sustained by workers who have been suspended or expelled from labor organizations and/or deprived of the opportunity to work, and for losses incidental to the nonindustrial business relations of labor organizations.

The first known suit against an American trade union was that brought against the Thompsonville Carpet Weavers in 1834. According to Professor Witte, "There were at least thirty-three damage suits against unions or their members before 1900, including eleven in which the plaintiffs recovered damages."[2] During the last generation such suits have been more numerous than theretofore; Professor Witte ten years ago compiled a list of 314 cases, those previous to 1900 included, in which

---

[1] *Ibid.*, at p. 330. The court also stated, "There can be no question of the power of Congress thus to define and limit the jurisdiction of the inferior courts of the United States."

[2] E. E. Witte, *The Government in Labor Disputes*, p. 139.

damages had been sought against unions or their members for acts committed by, or on behalf of, the union.[1]

The American labor movement showed no great concern over damage suits previous to 1908, when the Supreme Court of the United States handed down its decision in *Loewe v. Lawlor*.[2] It will be recalled that the Hatters had prosecuted a nationwide boycott against the Loewe product. Following the decision that this boycott was unlawful, suit for damages was pressed against 197 members of the hatters' union. The jury, in 1912, awarded the full amount of damages sued for, $240,000, plus costs, and in 1915 the award was sustained by the Supreme Court of the United States.[3] In 1917 the case was settled when, with aid in the sum of $216,000 from the American Federation of Labor, a total of approximately $234,000 was paid. As Professor Witte has said: "The most significant feature of this case is that it was an action against individual members of the hatters' union, who were not sued as representatives of the union but by reason of their individual membership. Only two of the 197 defendants were prominent in the union; nearly all of the others had no prominent part in the boycott. Many of them had not attended a union meeting for years and testified that they did not even know of the existence of the boycott. They were sued solely because they were union members and had property not exempt from execution. At the outset, their savings accounts and homes were placed under attachment. In the final wind-up, they lost their savings accounts, and their homes were returned to them after they had been under attachment for fourteen years, during which no repairs were made on any of them. . . . this suit was an action against individual union members who were held responsible for acts of union officers in which they did not directly participate."[4]

The Loewe case had two effects—to advertise and popularize the damage suit and to alarm the unions. Involving even a larger sum than that involved in the Hatters' case was the Coronado case, which was in the federal courts from 1914 to 1927. This case, it will be recalled, developed out of a strike called against coal operators in Arkansas who undertook to change from a union to a nonunion basis of operation. The mining of coal was interrupted for months; the strike was accompanied by violence and destruction of property. Suit for damages was brought in the federal court against the international union (the United Mine Workers of America), District 21 of that organization, twenty-seven locals of this district and their officers, and sixty-seven individuals directly involved in the trouble. The amount sued for was $2,200,000.

---

[1] *Ibid.*, p. 138.

[2] 208 U. S. 274 (1908).

[3] *Lawlor v. Loewe*, 235 U. S. 522 (1915). *Cf. supra*, p. 569

[4] E. E. Witte, *op. cit.*, p. 135.

A jury trial resulted in an award of $600,000, with attorney's fees, costs, and interest, these bringing the total to $745,000. Upon appeal from the District Court to the Circuit Court of Appeals, the decision was upheld, except for the item of interest that had been allowed.[1] The case was then carried to the Supreme Court, which held that there was insufficient evidence of responsibility on the part of the International; it had not initiated the strike nor had it financed or ratified it.[2] The responsibility was that of District 21 and the local parties. The Supreme Court held further, as we have seen,[3] that the interference with the interstate marketing of coal had not been sufficient to constitute a violation of the Antitrust Act, under which suit had been brought in the District Court. The lower courts, therefore, had erred in assessing damages. The most interesting aspect of the decision, however, was the dictum[4] that an unincorporated union was a legal entity, that it might be sued in its own name, and that its funds accumulated to be expended in conducting strikes were subject to execution in suits for torts committed in the course of a strike. This dictum corresponded closely to the Taff Vale decision rendered in England in 1901; indeed the reasons assigned for the rulings were largely the same. Essentially, the position taken was that, where important and powerful organizations function and are recognized at law, there must be an appropriate accompanying responsibility.

In the first Coronado decision, the Supreme Court, as we have noted, expressed the view that the reduction in the interstate shipment of coal caused by the strike had been insufficient to be regarded as a violation of the federal Antitrust Act. A new suit was instituted in the District Court and additional evidence was introduced to show, among other things, that the reduction in output had been substantially larger than the Supreme Court had thought in view of the evidence submitted earlier. The District Court directed a verdict for the defendant miners. This decision was appealed and finally reached the Supreme Court, which now held that the evidence of intent and interference with coal shipment before it showed a violation of the Antitrust Act. Hence, the case was remanded for a new trial. This time the jury disagreed, and, after a jury was empaneled for a fourth trial but before another trial could be held, a settlement was reached. District 21 paid to the plaintiffs $27,000, and each side paid its own costs.

There have been other important suits in the federal courts developing out of coal strikes. And there have been suits developing out of other

---

[1] *United Mine Workers v. Coronado Coal Co.*, 258 Fed. 829 (1919).

[2] *United Mine Workers v. Coronado Coal Co.*, 259 U. S. 344 (1922).

[3] *Supra*, pp. 570–571.

[4] This dictum was not essential because it was found that the evidence did not establish unlawful interference with interstate commerce.

strikes, but further detail cannot be presented here[1] save for mention of the important Apex case decided in 1940. The Apex Company had opposed the hosiery workers' union; influenced by its president, the local union engaged in a stay-in strike. Charging that to its injury interstate commerce had been interfered with in violation of the Sherman Act, the company brought suit for damages. The District Court found that interstate commerce had been interfered with and the jury found that the union, as distinguished from its individual members, was, because of financing the strike and other activities, responsible. The intent of the union was to interfere with interstate commerce, an unlawful act. Damages were awarded in the sum of $711,932.55.[2] But on Nov. 29, 1939, the Circuit Court of Appeals of the Third District, in a unanimous decision, held that the union had not intended to restrain interstate commerce and that the federal court therefore had no jurisdiction.[3] The decision was affirmed by the Supreme Court in May, 1940.[3]

The number of suits brought against unions, their officers and members in the state courts has been, as one would expect because of the restricted jurisdiction of the federal courts, very much larger. In a considerable number of cases union officers and members have been sued because of losses due to illegal strikes, violence, and other unlawful activities. There have also been a considerable number of suits brought against unions by their members or other workers, charging injury due to unlawful action. Finally, there have been a limited number of cases in which employers have instituted suit for violation of joint agreements in effect.[4] Over against the cases of this last type, there have been a considerably larger number of cases brought by unions against employers, who were alleged to have violated unexpired agreements to the injury of the workers and the union.

A large number of the damage suits instituted have not been pushed to a conclusion. No doubt some of these were instituted as a bluff or to harass the opposition and to tie up its funds; in other cases the matters in dispute were composed and suit dropped. In any event, the successful suit has been rather exceptional. Moreover, the sums recovered, with few exceptions, have been comparatively small. In these facts, the procedural difficulties involved in suing unions, and the difficulty in establishing the connection of a union or its members with unlawful acts, is found the explanation of the failure of the number of

---

[1] For detail and references, see E. E. Witte, *op. cit.*, Chap. 7.

[2] *Apex Hosiery Company v. Leader*, Labor Law Service, C. C. H., vol. 2, p. 18, 769, also 102 Fed. (2d) 702 (1939). The decision of the trial court had the effect of encouraging the bringing of damage suits against labor unions as did the Loewe case years ago.

[3] 310 U. S. 469.

[4] See, among them, *Nederlandsch Amerikaansche Stoomvaart Maatschappij v. Stevedores' & Longshoremen's Benev. Soc. et al.*, 265 Fed. 397 (1920).

damage suits against labor organizations or their members to increase in proportion to applications for restraining orders.[1]

The difficulties just alluded to should be discussed briefly. Those of procedural character have been less great in the federal courts than in most of the state courts. For, in the first place and chiefly, as will be recalled, associations as well as corporations were made suable under the Sherman Antitrust Act (Sec. 8). Moreover, as explained above, the Supreme Court in the first Coronado case ruled that an unincorporated union might be sued in its own name. Yet this procedure has rarely been used in the federal courts,[2] and the precise liability of such an organization has not become entirely clear. The suits actually brought have almost always been under the Antitrust Act, or, as in the Loewe case, against the officers and members of the union, not the union itself. In the Loewe case the fact that workers retained membership in the union was held to be sufficient to make them liable for the unlawful things done. Now, under the Norris-La Guardia Act, the officers and members of unions are accorded a degree of protection against such a ruling.[3]

Suits brought in the state courts have usually not been against unions as such. The state supreme courts have not been inclined to follow the federal ruling in the Coronado case. Of course incorporated unions may be sued like other corporations, but incorporated affiliated unions are very few indeed.[4] It is a general principle of law that, in the absence of statutory provision to the contrary, a mere association, like a partnership, cannot be sued in its own name. Voluntary associations are not, in their collective capacity and name, recognized at common law as having any legal existence apart from their members. The funds, as a matter of law, are the property of the members. Suit must be brought against the members joined. As has been stated, at common law:

"Recovery could be had only against the individual who actually made the contract, or against the individual members of the union who conferred power upon the acting agent, all of whom must normally be named as defendants. . . . If the 'union fund' can be reached at all, it can be reached only as the joint property of the members, who are really joint tenants of all the association property, and not as the property of a distinct legal entity known by the union name. In other words, the union funds, like all other property, belong not to the union, as such,

[1] However, the Apex case encouraged, for a time, the filing of suits, as had the Loewe case years earlier.

[2] The ruling was applied by a District Court in *Christian v. International Ass'n, of Machinists*, 7 Fed. (2d) 481 (1925).

[3] *Cf. supra*, pp. 646–647.

[4] Many of the recently organized so-called "independent unions" have been incorporated, but it would appear that for the most part until very recently they have really been company unions, based upon the theory of harmony of employer-worker interests.

but the individual members who compose it. In suits against individual members their joint union funds can be reached on execution, just as their separate and individual property can be, but only such portion of those funds as belongs to the individual members who can be proved to have authorized the acts for which the suit is brought."[1]

This common-law rule has now, however, been modified in a large minority of the states, including a number of great industrial significance. Five states[2] have statutes permitting a union to be sued by the bringing of action against the officers or selected members as representatives of the entire membership. Fourteen states[3] have adopted laws or have court decisions under which suit may be brought against unincorporated associations in their common name. In these ways the procedural difficulty in damage suits has in part been overcome.

The difficulty of procedure overcome, there is the problem of establishing and defining the responsibility of the union or the members sued. As Professor Witte says,

"The responsibility of unions as entities (where they are so regarded) and of their members for unlawful acts allegedly committed in their behalf must be determined in accordance with the general principles of agency law [as in nonlabor cases]. A relationship of principal and agent must be established between the union and its members on the one hand, and those who personally committed the unlawful acts on the other. Such a relationship can be established either on the grounds of antecedent authorization or subsequent ratification. Unions and their members are liable for unlawful acts committed in behalf of the union when they have directly or indirectly authorized these acts in advance of their commission. Again, they are liable, although these acts were not authorized in advance, if they subsequently ratified them by expressing approval thereof or by accepting without protest the benefits resulting therefrom."[4]

But courts will frequently rule differently on what is authorization or ratification; it is sometimes a matter of opinion, as other questions of fact often are. In the Loewe case there was no explicit authorization of the boycott given by the members of the union sued, but the Supreme Court found authorization in a provision of the union constitution directing the officers to make every possible effort to organize the trade. Nor did the members explicitly ratify what had been done. The Supreme Court, however, found such ratification in the fact that the boycott

---

[1] In note on Coronado Coal Co. case, *Yale Law Journal*, vol. 32 (1922), pp. 60–61.

[2] New York, Ohio, Rhode Island, Washington, and Wisconsin. For citation of laws, see E. E. Witte, *op. cit.*, p. 143.

[3] Alabama, California, Connecticut, Louisiana, Maryland, Michigan, Missouri, Montana, Nevada, New Jersey, South Carolina, Texas, Vermont, and Viriginia. See *ibid.*, p. 142, for citations and explanatory note.

[4] *Op. cit.*, pp. 144–145.

had been discussed in union meetings and in the union journal. It made no difference that some of the members had not attended the union meetings and claimed ignorance of the entire matter; they must or ought to have known what was being done.

There have been many rulings by state courts to the same effect as the ruling in the Loewe case. In a larger number of decisions, however, it has been held that something more than mere membership is necessary to establish liability. Proof has been required that the members sued knew of the unlawful acts and yet continued to remain in the union and to pay dues. Such rulings are of course a distinct handicap to those who bring suit to recover losses due to unlawful acts. At the same time, as Professor Witte states, such rulings leave the union members in "a most hazardous situation." If a member knows of the unlawful acts, "the choice may be one between giving up his insurance in the union, to which he may have contributed for years, and losing his job, or taking a chance upon being mulcted in damages for the unlawful acts committed in behalf of the union; but, however serious the practical consequences may be to him, many cases assert that to avoid liability he must give up membership as soon as his union engages in any unlawful acts."[1]

The courts differ as to the liability of unions as organizations. For example, some courts have held that a union is liable for all acts of violence accompanying a strike that has been called, even though it may not be shown that the acts were committed by its members. Other courts have not gone further than to hold the union liable for the unlawful acts of its pickets. Still others have held that the union is not liable at all except where a campaign of violence has been inaugurated by it or its officers or where the unlawful acts of members or others have been approved in some manner, such as by providing counsel, by paying fines, or by failure to mete out punishment.[2]

The above summary statement of course is inadequate save for indicating the more or less uncertain and unsatisfactory state of the law. Though the alarm of twenty or twenty-five years ago has decreased, the unions fear the possible developments. And there is much in the law as applied in different jurisdictions that they regard as unfair and injurious to their cause. The situation has been equally unsatisfactory to employers, and especially those employers more or less hostile to unionism.

Incorporation of Unions.—The open-shop drive early in the present century was accompanied by a vigorous demand for the compulsory incorporation of unions so that they would have what was alleged to be an appropriate responsibility and would be capable of being sued without the usual difficulties.

[1] *Ibid.*, p. 148.

[2] The reasoning of the Supreme Court of the United States in the Coronado case of 1922 is discussed *supra*, pp. 570–571.

The main arguments in favor of such incorporation were: (1) that organizations wielding so much power should be required to accept legal responsibility for its use; and (2) that it would tend to make for law and order and a desirable, conservative, and constructive unionism. Another argument, to which our attention must be addressed presently, was that incorporation would encourage collective bargaining, since joint agreements could then be legally enforced, to the advantage of the union as well as to that of the employer.[1] Though the demand that unions should be incorporated was largely a product of the open-shop movement, it was voiced by some lawyers sympathetic with unionism, by some "intellectuals," and, indeed, by an occasional unionist. Among the first group, it is interesting to note, was Mr. Brandeis, long a member of the Supreme Bench.[2] Among the second, was Professor Gilman. In discussing the subject, he said: "There is to-day a crying social need for more responsibility in labor disputes. Incorporation corresponds to this need. When the trade-unions repent of their illogical and immoral unwillingness to become incorporated, and take their right position as corporations in that collective bargaining which is to be more and more the custom of the future, the prospect for industrial peace will be much brighter than it is to-day."[3]

In the 1880's the American labor movement was demanding legislation providing for the voluntary incorporation of labor unions. By incorporating, labor organizations expected to improve their position at law, to gain prestige, and to meet problems connected with their benefit funds. Legislation permitting the incorporation of unions was adopted by Congress and in some of the states.[4] However, few unions incorporated, partly because of the problems involved under the laws enacted, more because of a change in attitude. For a generation and more the American unions have, almost without exception, opposed incorporation.[5] When confronted by the demand that they be required to incorporate, they protested vigorously and argued that: (1) the demand was an antiunion one, as it largely was; (2) there was no real problem; unions were conservative and law-abiding, which was, of course, sometimes untrue; (3) unions were not organized for profit and incorporation was accordingly inappropriate in their case; (4) the unions could not hire the attorneys

---

[1] *Cf.* Gordon S. Watkins, *Labor Problems* (1929), p. 478.

[2] See article in *Green Bag*, vol. 15 (1903), pp. 11–14.

[3] N. P. Gilman, *Methods of Industrial Peace* (1904), p. 197.

[4] Public no. 306, 72d Congress, 1st Session, Chap. 524 (S. 4661), July 22, 1932, repealed the Federal Act of 1886 providing for the voluntary incorporation of trade unions. No international had incorporated under this Act, for one reason because it would have had to maintain its headquarters in Washington.

[5] Of course so-called "independent" unions now being organized by "loyal" workers, largely as a substitute for employee-representation plans, frequently seek state charters. See Chap. XVI.

required to match wits with those hired by the employers; (5) damage suits would deplete union funds; (6) the members would be afraid and withdraw from the union, which no doubt contained a measure of truth; (7) internal difficulties would develop because of the changed relationship between members and union; (8) the employers were not responsible in their relations with the union.   This last point will be considered presently in connection with the legal position of the joint agreement.

Recognizing that unions could not be compelled to incorporate, a new demand was made after World War I, *viz.*, for legislation making them capable of suing and being sued in their own name, though unincorporated.   The League for Industrial Rights was foremost in the endeavor to secure such legislation.   Its model bill, presented at many legislative sessions but without desired result, save in Alabama where a suability law was enacted in 1921,[1] read as follows:

"Section 1.   Any voluntary association of seven or more members may sue and be sued in the name of the association.

"Section 2.   Service of process upon any officer, manager or business agent of such association shall constitute service upon the association."[2]

A second bill, one "For the Better Protection of Public Welfare Against Unwarranted Strikes and Lockouts," was also sponsored by the League for Industrial Rights.   It is of interest because of related legislation very actively supported in recent years and of importance because it is indicative of the objectives of the model bill just quoted.   It read as follows:

"Sec. 1.   The phrase 'unwarranted industrial warfare,' as used in this statute, shall mean a strike or lockout when carried on (a) by or in respect to employees whose terms of employment are fixed by the State or the United States, or any political sub-division thereof; (b) in violation of an agreement or for conditions of employment conflicting with an agreement between an employer and his employees, or any employer and any labor union; or (c) in violation of any arbitration award, or for conditions of employment conflicting with the terms thereof; or (d) to enforce terms of employment where a request therefor has not first been presented to the party from whom such terms are sought and a reasonable time given for the consideration; or (e) where there is no trade dispute involving issues of direct benefit to the acting parties.

"Sec. 2.   It shall be unlawful for any person, firm, association or corporation willfully to cause, further or make effective any such unwarranted industrial warfare, or to attempt so to do by any of the following acts, to wit: inducing any person to engage or continue therein; taking any vote or issuing any order relative thereto; paying moneys or furnish-

[1] Alabama Code (1928), Secs. 5723–5728.   A measure was passed in Massachusetts, also, but it was narrowly defeated on referendum vote.
[2] *Law and Labor*, vol. 3 (1921), p. 1.

ing material help of any kind, or agreeing so to do, to any person on condition that such person engage or continue therein; stationing pickets or patrols; displaying or distributing banners, placards or handbills; performing any act for the purpose of inducing any person, firm or corporation to terminate or not to enter into employment or business relations with the person, firm or corporation against whom said warfare is directed.

"Sec. 3. The State or any political sub-division thereof, or any person, firm or corporation, injured, or threatened with injury, by anything forbidden in this act, shall be entitled to all of the appropriate civil remedies in law and equity.

"Sec. 4. If any part of this act shall be adjudged by any court of competent jurisdiction to be invalid such judgment shall not invalidate the remainder thereof."

Suability laws were fought as vigorously by unions as was the demand for compulsory incorporation, and with success. For, as has been incidentally indicated, only one such law (that of Alabama) was added to those previously in effect as a result of the campaign inaugurated.

As the 1930's drew to a close, there were suggestions emanating from many sources—political and industrial—that unions should be required to shoulder pecuniary responsibility by incorporation or otherwise.[1] These recent suggestions are largely a product of the validation of the more important provisions of the National Labor Relations Act and of the high fees and dues exacted by some unions. One thought is that if employers are restrained in their activities, labor unions should carry on in hobbles. What of the issues raised? Should unions be made suable in their own names and be required to shoulder a greater responsibility than they have usually had in the United States?

Unlike the law of Britain, the labor codes of most of the Continental countries have provided for the suability of labor organizations and for a considerable degree of responsibility for losses due to unlawful acts in the

---

[1] Other suggestions made are (1) that unions should be required to register, perhaps with a commission empowered to review constitutions, by-laws, etc., and (2) that they should make annual financial statements, these perhaps to be public. In connection with the first of these suggestions, foreign systems of registration, particularly that of Great Britain, are frequently cited but almost always in an erroneous manner. For example, contrary to what is usually said, in Great Britain the registration of unions is voluntary and many of the unions are not registered. Registered unions report annually to the Registrar of Friendly Societies, showing their financial status. The names of union members are not reported, nor is control exercised over initiation fees, dues, and other union matters. The case for compulsory registration of and reporting by unions alone is a weak one. It is hard to see why any such requirements should not be equally well applied to employer associations and other organizations standing over against labor organizations. Such associations are not incorporated, nor are they regulated, or required to register or to make reports. Practically all the bills introduced in the Seventy-seventh Congress providing for compulsory registration and reporting of dues, fees, membership, etc., applied only to labor organizations.

prosecution of strikes, etc. In the opinion of the authors of this volume there is a sound case for making unions suable for losses due to unlawful acts clearly authorized or ratified by them. On logical grounds such liability cannot be questioned. Moreover, in so far as the New Deal legislation is applicable, employers must accept unions. This places at least a moral responsibility upon labor organizations. But, in imposing any legal responsibility, the matter of agency should be clearly defined, so that the liability would be properly limited.[1] The union, because of its very nature and because of the situation in which it functions, should not, in fairness, be held responsible for all acts committed by union men. To mention only one reason for this precaution, there are too many spies in unions and in industry and too much opportunity for "plants." But assuming that the matter of liability can be properly defined and limited, the authors would question the fairness of directly or indirectly saddling a greater responsibility upon our unions until the law relating to what unions may do is appropriately revised in the particular (state) jurisdiction. Whether or not the particular conclusions drawn earlier in this volume with reference to what the law should permit the unions to do are accepted, the position here taken is that legislative bodies should first accord to labor organizations the rights to which they are entitled in view of sound public policy. That done, the question of whether or not unions should be readily suable for damages becomes an appropriate one in the realm of legislation.

THE LEGAL STATUS AND ENFORCEMENT OF JOINT AGREEMENTS

The discussion thus far has had no direct bearing upon the validity and enforceability of agreements entered into jointly by union and employer or employers. In the literature relating to the incorporation or suability of unions it has frequently been assumed that there was needed, and that were suability instituted there would be, recovery for breach of joint agreement as well as for violence in strikes, unlawful boycotting, and other activities. However, breach of an agreement may be one thing, violent picketing, destruction of property, and unlawful boycotting something materially different from the point of view of law and public policy. In the preceding section we have been discussing recovery for losses due to unlawful acts. Is it unlawful to violate a collective labor agreement? What is the legal position of such a working arrangement? Is it such as to provide a basis for relief through injunction proceedings or through suits for damages? As a matter of public policy, should the collective agreement have the status of a contract at law?

[1] Industry incorporates to limit liability. The demand that unions should incorporate is not accompanied by the suggestion that there should be corresponding limitations upon liability, nor is it usually accompanied by the suggestion that employers' associations should likewise be required to incorporate.

In Great Britain collective agreements have been, and still remain, only morally, *i.e.*, not legally, binding upon the parties entering into them. In France and in most of the other countries on the Continent of Europe, on the other hand, such agreements have for years been and are enforceable at law in so far as trade unions have not been placed under a ban. When an agreement in conformity with the German code in effect until 1934 was entered into, all hirings, of nonunionists as well as of unionists, were required to be made in compliance with its terms. If it was breached by employer or union, there was right of recovery. So it was for many years in France also, though the control of industrial relations there under the Act of 1919 was less far-reaching than that in Germany from 1918 to 1934.[1]

The law of the United States regarding the trade-union agreement, at least as it existed prior to the adoption of the National Industrial Recovery Act, is to be found with a few exceptions in court decisions. The lack of uniform analysis by the courts of the several states, as well as the variety in the character of trade agreements themselves, makes it necessary to guard against generalizing too widely.

With this background in mind, the legal effect of the trade-union agreement in the United States may be reviewed. Efforts to establish rights, and less frequently duties, of individual workers appear to have been the most common cause for bringing trade agreements into litigation.[2] Since 1920, however, efforts have also been made to gain judicial recognition of legal interests vested in the trade union as an organization. An understanding of the American law requires that the cases involving an organization interest be sharply distinguished from those which involve only the interests of individual workers.

Where the issue at stake has concerned an individual workman, no case has been found that has denied the enforcement of the terms of a trade-union agreement where it has been shown that these terms were incorporated in the individual contract of employment.[3] In such circumstances, of course, strictly speaking, the trade agreement is not being enforced. Its terms acquire legal significance only because they

[1] See article by Ralph F. Fuchs on "The French Law of Collective Labor Agreements," *Yale Law Journal*, vol. 41 (1932), pp. 1005–1036, and International Labour Office, *Collective Agreements* (Studies and Reports, Series A, no. 39), 1936, in which the law in the major countries is discussed. For an excellent discussion of the legal status and enforcement of collective agreements in Sweden see James J. Robbins, *The Government of Labor Relations in Sweden* (1942).

[2] Scores of such cases have been decided by the courts, these involving wages, seniority, and discharge.

[3] *Burnetta v. Marceline Coal Co.*, 79 S.W. 136 (Mo., 1904), was an early case, which has been subjected to varying interpretations. The one followed here is that set forth by C. L. Christenson in *Indiana Law Journal*, vol. 9 (1933), pp. 74*ff*. For a rather different interpretation of this case, see *Harvard Law Review*, vol. 44 (1931), p. 584.

have been adopted by individuals in the course of the creation of an employment relationship.[1]

Sometimes American courts have spoken as if the requirement of individual adoption may be waived if "usages" defined by the trade agreement have been observed so long that they may be regarded as "custom." Such language is predicated upon the assumption that where the trade agreement has been in existence for a very long time and has been continuously observed, it may be taken for granted that its terms will be known to all workers and employers in the industry involved. Thus, a federal case[2] of fifteen years ago involved circumstances that led the court in considering it to speak in terms of "custom." In that case, the court permitted a union workman to recover back pay in accordance with the terms of a union agreement, holding that there was "not only a custom so old, notorious, definite, and uniform as to be binding on those within its purview, but one admittedly known to plaintiff in error [employer], and with reference to which plaintiff in error contracted." This would seem to indicate that "custom" was one of the grounds upon which the court based its decision. But no case has been found upon which one may confidently base the conclusion that a court consciously intended to enforce interests of individual workers solely upon the theory that a trade-union agreement was an established custom. On other grounds, however, courts have indicated a willingness under some circumstances to extend further protection. Some relatively early New York decisions showed a disposition to regard the union (or its officials) as agents for the employees in the execution of contracts of employment[3] and there have been similar decisions in other jurisdictions.[4] In such cases the trade agreement may become the formal embodiment of a group of contracts of individual workers. However, cases relying on the "agency" theory are in a distinct minority, and the New York decisions enforcing agreements on behalf of an individual worker now stand on the ground that he is the intended beneficiary of the union's contract, not the principal party to a contract signed for him by the union as agent.[5]

---

[1] The courts have differed on what constitutes adoption. In some cases the existence of a union agreement and knowledge of it by the worker has been regarded as sufficient. In other cases, this plus membership in the union has been the requirement. And, in still other cases, something more, such as individual acceptance, has been required. *Cf.* T. Richard Witmer, "Collective Agreements in the Courts," *Yale Law Review*, vol. 48 (1938), at p. 229, where cases are cited.

[2] *United States Daily v. Nichols*, 32 Fed. (2d) 834 (1929).

[3] *Maisel v. Sigman*, 305 N.Y.S. 807 (1924); *Meltzer v. Kaminer*, 227 N.Y.S. 459 (1927).

[4] For example, *Mueller v. Chicago & N. W. Ry.*, 259 N.W. 798 (Minn., 1935).

[5] Note, 19 N.Y.U. Law Quarterly 315, March 1942, on *Rotnofsky v. Capital Distributors Corp.*, 262 App. Div. 521, 30 N.Y.S. (2d) 536 (1941).

Although this doctrine was first applied in New York in a case involving an agreement made by an incorporated union[1] it has since been adopted by a number of other states in cases where the union was unincorporated.[2] In fact about one-third of the states, a majority of the jurisdictions that have passed on the question, have permitted suit to be brought by individual members. Indeed, the Supreme Court of Mississippi in 1931 went so far as to sustain the claim of a nonunion worker to wages in accordance with the terms of a trade agreement made by an unincorporated union on the ground that it was contemplated that he was to be a beneficiary under the agreement.[3]

It may be worth while to indicate more specifically the significance of the decisions that adopt the third-party-beneficiary doctrine as contrasted with those enforcing interests on the grounds of either "usage" or "agency." First of all, as illustrated in the earliest New York case, *Gulla v. Barton*, it would be possible on the third-party-beneficiary theory for a worker to claim rights under a trade agreement even though he had been working without knowledge of its terms. This could hardly be true if the arrangement were regarded as a mere usage subject to individual adoption or if it was assumed that only such workers as had authorized the union to act for them were entitled to contractual rights. Perhaps more significant is the fact that even nonunion workmen could claim benefits under a trade agreement if it could be shown that the makers of the agreement contemplated that nonunionists were to come within its terms. This fact indicates that courts which follow the third-party-beneficiary line of reasoning treat the union as a competent contracting party, whose contracts require no previously expressed or implied authority or no subsequent adoption or ratification in order to become effective. It is difficult to see how a court once having sustained a workman's claim on this theory could deny a union competency to contract on its own behalf. The implication is that the joint agreement is a contract at law.

It will be noticed that all the preceding discussion is in terms of the justification for the enforcement of workers' rights that may be defined by the terms of a working agreement. Nothing has been said about correlative duties. As a matter of fact, even where the contract of employment is defined by the language of a union agreement, it still has an anomalous character, of which the courts enforcing it have not always been aware. Since no obligation is undertaken for the future in the ordinary "contract" of employment, which is "at will," it can hardly be

---

[1] *Gulla v. Barton*, 149 N.Y.S. 952 (1914).

[2] *Rentschler v. Missouri Pacific*, 253 N.W. 694 (Neb., 1934); *Youmans v. Charleston & W.C. Ry. Co.*, 178 S.E. 671 (S.C., 1935); *H. Blum & Co. v. Landau*, 155 N.E. 154 (Ohio, 1926); *Johnson v. American Railway Express Co.*, 161 S.E. 473 (S.C., 1931); *Levine v. Meizel*, 10 L.R.R. 338 (N.Y. Cy. Ct., 1942).

[3] *Yazoo & M. V. Co. v. Sideboard*, 133 So. 669 (Miss., 1931).

spoken of as a "contract" in the strictest sense. Where the terms of a trade-union agreement are enforced for the benefit of a workman, either on the theory that its terms were adopted by him or that he had authorized the union or its officials to act for him, this anomalous character of the employment relation is not removed merely because a trade-union agreement has become involved. On the other hand, where rights are recognized on the theory that the workman is a third-party beneficiary, the consideration for the enforcement of these rights will pass not from the workman but rather from the union involved. Under these circumstances it is conceivable that a workman might acquire enforceable interests even before he had entered into an employment relation, to say nothing of beginning work.[1]

Most of the protection received by workers is incidental to the enforcement of trade-union agreements with clauses containing schedules of wages and hours, seniority provisions, and the like. But as the law is rapidly changing the courts are developing an appropriate theory that collective agreements neither confer indefeasible rights nor impose duties upon individual workers.[2] Under this theory, the obligations created by the collective contract are neither the individual property nor the individual burden of each union member. A true collective contract grants neither rights to, nor exacts obligations from, the individual employee; his protection is obtained through the union which can, within the limits of its constitution and by-laws, change the terms of an agreement and modify the worker's tenure. The most important question has therefore become, what is the legal position of the trade-union agreement? Is it an enforceable contract against the employer and the union? Does it provide a basis for relief through injunction proceedings or through suits for damages?

While some courts[3] still follow the English precedent and hold that a collective agreement is not a contract at law, others in rapidly increasing number have given it legal status protected by restraining order and suit for damages. The marked change began some twenty years ago. In this connection *Schlesinger v. Quinto*[4] was important. Subsequently

---

[1] Professor J. F. Christ has discovered a case that he has interpreted as holding that partial performance by an employee creates not only a right in the employee but also involves a duty and implies that he will continue to work in accordance with the terms of the employment agreement. See his article "The Federal Courts and Organized Labor," *Journal of Business of the University of Chicago*, vol. 3 (1930), pp. 218–219.

[2] For example, in *Donovan v. Travers*, 285 Mass., 167 (1934) and *Hartley v. Brotherhood*, 283 Mich. 201 (1938) it was held that the union and the employer could modify their agreement and affect members' rights without individual consent.

[3] For example, Kansas [see *Swart v. Huston*, 154 Kan. 192 (1942)] and Iowa [see *Wilson v. Airline Coal Co.*, 215 Iowa 855 (1933)].

[4] 192 N.Y.S. 564 (1921), aff'd 201 App. Div. 489 (1922).

there have been numerous similar decisions by New York[1] and other state courts,[2] some of them against the denouncement of agreements or against runaway shops, others against calling of strikes by unions in violation of agreements. It should be added that collective agreements have recently been recognized and protected by statute in a few states. As already noted, violation of a collective agreement became an unfair labor practice in Wisconsin and Minnesota under the legislation of 1939.[3] In 1940, in a revision of the California Code, collective agreements were given the same status as other contracts. Finally, an amendment to the civil practice act now makes written arbitration agreements legally enforceable in New York.[4]

The consequences of making joint agreements legally enforceable are not entirely clear. Binding agreements mean for the employer that he is dealing with more responsible parties. While the union is more frequently confronted by damage suits or injunctions, it has the right to obtain the assistance of the court in securing observance of an agreement by the employer when its economic power fails, as it so frequently does. Employer and union are more or less checked when inclined to take advantage of changes in the industrial situation. Binding agreements, in certain ways, make for greater stability in joint relations. But such a legal status is not really effective in many cases. An agreement no longer acceptable may become a distinct problem in the workplace. In changing situations the terms of agreements need to be modified now and then; adjustment is necessary; an agreement must be tolerable. Do binding agreements make for standing on one's "rights" when adjustment is needed? Do they tend to place a tax on time agreements of any considerable duration and to make for temporary contracts and radicalism? In these connections Australian experience is interesting.[5] A still further question is whether they tend to bring legal counsel into the

---

[1] Among them, *Segenfeld v. Friedman*, 193 N.Y.S. 128 (1922); *Goldman v. Cohen*, 227 N.Y.S., 311 (1928); *Farulla v. Freundlich*, 274 N.Y.S. 70, 277 N.Y.S. 47 (1934), 279 N.Y.S. 228 (1935); *Dubinsky v. Blue Dale Dress Co.*, 292 N.Y.S. 898 (1936); *Uneeda Credit Colthing Stores v. Briskin*, 14 N.Y.S. (2d) 964 (1939); and *Weiss v. Fields Shops, Inc.*, 8 L.R.R. (N.Y. Sup. Ct. 1941). In the Uneeda case an injunction was issued against a contract-breaking union.

[2] Among other cases, see *Weber v. Nasser*, 286 Pac. 1074 (1903); *O'Jay Spread Co. v. Hicks*, 195 S.E. 564 (Ga. 1938); *Pearlman v. Millman*, 7 Law and Labor 7 (Super. Court, Suffolk Co., Mass., 1925); *Henry v. Century Shoe Co.*, 12 Law and Labor 7 (Mass., 1930); *Mississippi Theatres Corp. v. Hattiesburg Local Union No. 615*, 164 So. 887 (1936); *Hudson Bus v. Hill Bus Co.*, 121 N.J. Eq. 582 (1937); *Leveranz v. Cleveland Home Brewing Co.*, 24 Ohio N.P. (N.S.) 193 (1922); *Harper v. Local Union No. 520, Int. Bro. of Electrical Workers*, 48 S.W. (2d) 1003 (Texas, 1932); *F. F. East Co. v. United Oystermen's Union*, 128 N.J. Eq. 27 (1940).

[3] *Supra*, p. 551.

[4] Chap. 851, approved Apr. 29, 1940.

[5] See Chap. XIV.

bargaining picture and thus render it more difficult to conclude acceptable agreements.

It is quite evident that when joint agreements are made legally binding upon employer and union problems may arise. On the other hand, certain advantages accrue. Moreover, it is to be pointed out that under the National Labor Relations Act and similar state acts the employer must recognize the duly accredited representatives of his employees and bargain with them in good faith on the matters they present. While it is not necessary that an agreement should result, the employer must do all that is reasonable in an effort to meet the demands presented to him or he is likely to run afoul of the law. And, if an agreement does result, he must, in some measure at least, observe it or he may be chargeable with discrimination if not with failure to do something implicit in collective bargaining.[1] Hence, the employer, in so far as the new industrial-relations laws are effective, no longer has the entire freedom he once had. In a sense, the joint agreement is binding upon him.[2] It may well be that, as one thing leads to another, sound policy and equal treatment will call for legislation making joint agreements legally binding contracts to the extent that, without question, injunctive relief may be available or damages may be assessed against those responsible for breach of the collective contract. But mere declaration that agreements shall be legal and binding is not sufficient. Agreements contain a great variety of things. Appropriate legislation must be discriminating and, in order that it may be so, extensive study is required. Moreover, many laws on the statute books would need to be adjusted. Perhaps any legislation on the specific matter should await not only careful study but also the further development of law through decisions made by the courts.

VIOLENCE, LAW ENFORCEMENT, AND THE POLICING OF INDUSTRY

The injunction has been used to check or to prevent unlawful behavior in industrial disputes; the damage suit has been intended to discourage infraction of law as well as to enable parties to recover for losses sustained in violation of law. What of the agencies for maintaining law and

---

[1] The National Labor Relations Board does not enforce collective-bargaining agreements, but leaves that to be done through suit at law. Nevertheless what is said above is correct.

[2] And, on the other hand, the Supreme Court of the United States has made it clear that a union may jeopardize its position and its members' jobs by failure to observe the terms of an agreement in effect. In the case of *National Labor Relations Board, Petitioner, v. Sands Manufacturing Company* (59 Sup. Ct. 508, 1939), the court held that by refusing to work on the conditions incorporated in an agreement, the workers had in effect quit; the employer had no further duty to bargain with their union but was free to enter into an agreement with another union and to employ its members.

order and the machinery for law enforcement? After all, chief reliance should be placed upon these rather than upon the injunction and the damage suit.

All countries have greater or lesser problems of law infraction connected with industrial struggles. This is especially true in the newer countries, with less well settled populations, diverse peoples, and rapid changes, outstanding among them the United States. The contrast between this country and Great Britain in the matters of law observance and law enforcement is very great, that between the United States and most of the Continental countries only less so.

The Reasons for Violence in America.—The story of violence and the like in connection with American labor struggles, either in general or in particular situations, has frequently been recorded in print. It need not be related here except in so far as parts of it illustrate significant phases of the problem. Suffice it to say for the present that there has been much violence in connection with strikes and lockouts, much also in instances where unions have not been able to strike effectively but nevertheless have sought a foothold, and not a little in connection with agreements in effect, in the treatment accorded nonunionists, undesirable competitors, and the like. Most violence and its lesser accompaniments have been spontaneous, being evinced in heated moments, but not a little of it has been premeditated and is to be regarded as a part of union or employer policy. In more recent years, though the total amount of violence has perhaps not increased, planned violence appears to have done so, and "racketeering" and gangsterism have here and there come into the situation.

Why has the United States had more labor violence and other violations of law than, say, Great Britain or the Scandinavian countries? The answer is found in several factors entering into the situation.[1]

The United States is a relatively new country marked by rapid change and an unusually mobile and a restless population. Parts of it are close to the frontier pattern in their ways of settling difficulties. Most of us are restless and wish to "get ahead"; we are not content with a given status and the accustomed standard of living. Law infraction in labor matters does not stand alone. It is only one phase of a more general situation.

History has bequeathed us an extraordinary mixture of races and nationalities, with conflicts of ethical codes, with somewhat different standards and ways of living, and with some unfortunate antipathies not all of which are of domestic origin. There are unfortunate "should nots" and "thou shalt nots" in the situation. Evidence of the conflict is

[1] For an excellent analysis, see E. E. Witte, *The Government in Labor Disputes*, especially Chap. 9.

found in connection with housing and many other things as well as in connection with the business of earning a living.

Another factor is found in the limited amount of labor organization we have had until recently, and the comparative newness of most of it, now that it has greatly expanded. Moreover, the trade union was not preceded by other similar forms of organization as it was in European countries. Individualism has held unusual sway. Through organization, with which most Americans have had no real familiarity, labor has been trying to protect what it has had, to acquire new "rights," and to extend its power. But labor organization has usually not been taken for granted or readily accepted in most branches of industry; indeed various methods have been and are employed to discourage or to prevent it. Witness the one-time many violations of law to exclude organizers from the mining communities of West Virginia and Kentucky, the steel mills and the mill villages of the South. Witness also the numerous denials of the right of peaceful assembly, which are a matter of common knowledge to close observers of the industrial-relations scene.[1]

Another factor is found in the concentration of the employer-worker struggle on the industrial field, where the lines are readily and sharply drawn and where contacts all too readily lead to altercation and violence. There has been in the United States relatively little familiarity with or little interest in socialism, little independent political action, and, until very recently at any rate, limited interest in working things out through legislative channels. The struggle has been pretty much limited to matters of such a nature that the strike, the lockout, the boycott, and the black list have been the usual weapons employed.

Labor violence has been closely connected with the importation and employment of strikebreakers, the employment of guards, spies, and "plug-uglies." Of course violence all too frequently occurs when workers of the same kind as the strikers and drawn from the locality are induced to accept struck jobs. Violence is of such frequent occurrence that it may almost be expected when help is secured through detective agencies and shipped into the community from outside. The same is true when Negroes are rounded up and shipped in or when "foreigners" are supplied by "padrones" or "contractors."

Important, also, chiefly in the past, has been an unjust and unequal labor law and the unquestionable lack of confidence in the courts in general. That the law has been unequally restrictive of the "rights" of workers and employers is a fact, though never so glaring a fact as labor has felt. The feeling of unfairness has become magnified. Largely because of the inequality of the law, but also in part because of the

---

[1] See La Follette Committee, *Hearings*, particularly Pts. IX to XIII on Harlan County.

language, views, and behavior of some of the judges, the workers frequently lost confidence in the courts. That this loss of confidence has not been fully warranted is true, but the fact of lack of confidence remains a fact. The feeling has widely prevailed that "labor must make its fight in its own way."

Closely related to this factor has been the poor policing of industry and a weak or a severe administration of justice, so widespread in the United States. This matter will be discussed later in this chapter. Mere mention of it will therefore suffice for the present.

Racketeering has developed in labor organizations as well as in business and political affairs. The expression "racket" is used so loosely as to include a great variety of things one does not like—violence, graft, monopolistic exactions, etc. Nevertheless, it is a substantial and sinister reality. In Chicago, Al Capone and "Bugs" Moran were induced to come or "muscled" into the cleaning and dyeing industry and were used to protect the master cleaners' "interest" against "unfair competition."[1] The master cleaners insisted that the unions should organize the entire industry and see to it that the proprietor of the little tailor shop that serves as a "stop" or collecting agency did not change from one cleaner to another without the Association's consent. This rule was to make price maintenance and stability in the industry effective. The Union was paid for this and for removing cut-price signs displayed by tailors. How much more was expected of the union and paid for may best be left to be guessed by those who know more or less about the happenings in the industry. The tailors (shopkeepers), like master barbers, frequently saw to it that competitors did not become too numerous or locate too near an existing shop. Shops were bombed, perhaps by officers and members of the Tailors' Association as well as by "professionals" or gangsters who work for anyone at a price, provided there is a degree of assurance that the man who hires will not "squawk."

In some branches of the clothing industry, as well as in the cleaning industry, garments or materials were destroyed by sprinkling acid or by other means. Moreover, there is good reason for believing that gangsters who have been employed for this purpose have also been employed to do "educational work" in the conduct of strikes. Gangsters do not go unremunerated.

The specific instances of racketeering mentioned are only a few of a much larger number that might be cited—in milk price wars,[2] janitor service, and elsewhere. But the cases cited will serve the purposes of this analysis. It is necessary, however, to state emphatically, though the fact

[1] Capone a few years ago completed a prison sentence for evasion of the income tax, but some of his lieutenants did not cease to carry on as best they could.

[2] Note the indictment of fifty-five dairymen (July, 1932) for rioting, etc., incidental to a reduction in price of milk. *Chicago Tribune*, July 17, 1932.

has already been indicated, that labor organizations have by no means had a monopoly on racketeering. Some writers have dwelt upon labor racketeering at such length, or limited their discussions so narrowly to it, that one might think that it finds place in labor organizations almost, if not quite, alone. This is not the case. It looms large in business and finance. It should be added, also, that employers are frequently parties to it where it occurs in the field of industrial relations. In this respect the cleaning industry in Chicago has not stood alone. Businessmen may directly benefit from it; they may aid and abet, indeed instigate it. When unemployment insurance, involving a contribution by the employers running in terms of a percentage of the payroll, was introduced in one industry some years ago, acceptance of the plan was made conditional upon the payment of a quarter of the receipts to the then president of the association.

These are some, if not the chief, factors explaining the excessive amount of violence and other forms of law infraction in the American industrial struggle. But, whatever the explanation may be, there have been many violations of law—by workers, employers, and their agents, and by the police. How many arrests of workers and those allying themselves with them there have been each year no one knows, but they number tens of thousands. Most of those arrested have been charged with misdemeanors, such as disorderly conduct, obstructing traffic, disturbing the peace, trespass, intimidation, picketing, loitering, and holding meetings or distributing handbills without required permit. A considerable number have been arrested for the commission of petty crimes, such as simple assault. Over against these have been major offenses, such as bombing, the more extreme forms of physical violence, and murder, which, though very exceptional, has occurred.

As has been stated, the number of arrests in connection with industrial disputes has been very large. There can be no doubt, however, that the number of arrests gives a greatly exaggerated picture of the number of real offenders among the workers and their sympathizers. For one reason, the inadequacy of laws and ordinances relating to employer-worker activities makes it possible for the police, who have frequently proceeded upon the theory that it is their function to suppress industrial conflicts and to end them quickly, to make arrests on charges for which persons are seldom arrested in the absence of an industrial dispute. Indeed, the police have frequently exceeded any authority in law, sometimes because of bribery or favors of one kind or another. Of course there have been, on the other hand, instances in which the police sympathized with labor and have overlooked its offenses connected with industrial disputes, but these, until recently at any rate, have been of less frequent occurrence. The pro-labor attitude in such instances may be due to a natural feeling, but it is as likely to be explained by "influence" or by the weight of political considerations with those who exercise authority over the police.[1]

The number of arrests is not an accurate measure of the extent of the violation of law. Nor is the number of convictions. These vary greatly according to whether there is or is not trial by jury and whether the police "go the limit" or otherwise. Moreover, many, and sometimes most, of those arrested on not unsubstantial charges have not been tried at all, because the disputes ended, interest disappeared, and the prosecutors and judges wished to clear the calendar. All but extreme cases are therefore commonly dropped when an industrial dispute passes into history. However severe the penalties imposed may be, the number of convictions is as likely to understate as the number of arrests is to overstate the number of infractions of the law.

Concrete Cases.—Some of the matters just mentioned, and the problem presented by excessive bail accompanying drastic policing, may be briefly illustrated by a few concrete cases.

The first concrete case may be mentioned in Professor Witte's terms: "In the strike of waitresses employed by the —— Company, Chicago, in 1914, there were 153 arrests, although Judge McGoorty, who conducted extensive hearings upon this strike, in connection with an application for an injunction, said that 'it is admitted that no acts of violence were committed by any of the pickets.' Bail amounting to as high as $1,400 was exacted from some of those arrested, and the only one of the entire number brought to trial was acquitted."[2]

In the 1924 strike of dressmakers in Chicago, in which some 3,000 workers were involved, there were 1,200 arrests. Four nonunion men, presumably working for hire, were caught in the act of bombing a plant. There were a dozen or so assaults, and some factories were "rushed" in an effort to get the workers to join in the strike. Aside from the bombing and the assault cases, nearly all the arrests were made on the charge of disorderly conduct. Three hundred of those arrested were released because it was admitted that there was no valid case against them— sometimes after they had been held without being "booked." Bail in many disorderly cases was as high as $400. After being continued from time to time, 800 cases were dropped; only about 100 persons were tried, these without jury, and only 2 were convicted. A careful student of this

---

[1] An injunction was granted prohibiting violent picketing (cutting tires, damaging the wares being trucked, etc.) in connection with a strike in a certain city. Activities continued very much as before and there were no arrests or citations for contempt. The police had said there must be no "rough work" within a block of this place; do what you like elsewhere; you must give us a chance. The question as to why this interest should be shown by the police was answered by the responsible representative of the union, "We pay them—up to the City Hall. This is an —— strike" (the name used being that of a well-known union).

[2] E. E. Witte, op. cit., p. 157.

strike concluded that a very large number of the arrests were wholly unwarranted.[1] Indeed, some passers-by, who stopped to read the injunction that had been granted, were arrested. The above arrests, however, were of persons not cited for contempt. An injunction against picketing as well as against unlawful acts was granted, and 258 persons were cited for contempt. Of these, 255 were convicted. The fines imposed, chiefly for picketing, ranged from $10 to $450, and the jail sentences added in some cases ranged upward to six months.

In policing this strike there was a special detail of fifty uniformed policemen, about thirty-five plain-clothes men detailed by the state's attorney but drawn from the city's police force, and about a dozen deputy sheriffs, the last named to serve in connection with the injunction. Moreover, about a hundred guards were employed by the manufacturers. Many of these guards were armed, and, contrary to law in so far as they were not deputized as special police, they undertook, in many instances, to function as policemen and made arrests. It was the opinion of competent representatives of a citizens' committee that most of the violence by strikers was due to the presence and behavior of the company guards and the plain-clothes men, who made three-fourths of the arrests. Both guards and plain-clothes men were abusive and used profane language. Unlike most of the uniformed policemen, they did not stay within the confines of the law in making arrests. Moreover, they used threats and engaged in physical violence—and without penalty. In one extreme case an arrested girl was dragged into a hallway and beaten so violently that she was confined to the hospital for several weeks.[2]

To cite only one more concrete case, in the silkworkers' strike at Paterson, N. J., in 1913, 2,238 persons were arrested on the charge of rioting, and excessive bail was required, with the result that many of them remained in jail for several weeks. Tried without jury, approximately only one in seven of those arrested was convicted.

These cases suggest something of the problem of law infraction and law enforcement in urban strikes. The cases are, however, not entirely typical of those in strike situations generally. For one reason, most of the strikers and pickets were women. Whatever the showing may be as regards arrests and convictions, strikes in the building and iron and steel industries and those of teamsters, where men greatly predominate, are usually accompanied by more numerous assaults and physical violence in the extremer forms.

One thing shown by concrete studies made is that the amount of violence as well as the number of arrests has depended very much upon the quality of policing. And this in turn has depended very much upon

---

[1] H. B. Myers, *The Policing of Labor Disputes in Chicago* (unpublished Ph. D. Dissertation, The University of Chicago, 1929).

[2] The detail given is drawn from H. B. Myers, *ibid.*

the policy of, and the instructions given and the discipline exercised by, those directly in charge. These factors being what they have been and are in most urban communities, the policing of industry presents a distinct and sadly neglected problem.

Policing of Urban Industry.—In urban strike situations it is common practice to increase the number of regular policemen in an area immediately affected. These may or may not be carefully selected, properly officered, and instructed with reference to what they should and should not do, the law, ordinances, and court orders being what they are. Special police may be added, these not infrequently being deputized on the recommendation of interested parties. Deputy sheriffs, also, are not infrequently added, they being deputized in the same way. Deputy United States marshals may function where a federal court intervenes. In exceptional cases, the state militia, or the state constabulary where there is such a force, is called in to cope with the situation. And then, in large strikes, there are the guards, secured directly by the employer or association or more likely through detective agencies. These have only the rights of civilians when off the premises to which they are assigned, but frequently, if not generally, they have functioned on the street, armed, and, in some cases, entirely without authority in law, have made arrests. Such have been the policing forces in strike situations in Chicago and elsewhere.

Dr. Myers's observations on Chicago policing would apply almost equally well to policing in most large urban communities:

"The case studies have shown that the attempts to maintain law and order in Chicago have usually been ineffective and unfair. The municipal police force has been the most important and the most satisfactory policing force employed in Chicago. The patrolmen have usually been courageous and cool, and at times they have used fairly effective policing methods.

"At the same time, the police force has, at best, only a mediocre record. It has been inadequate, poorly disciplined, and poorly trained, and its members have often possessed an insufficient knowledge of their duties and the law. The patrolmen have frequently been biased and partial, and, on numerous occasions, have shown this bias by needless arrests, obscene language, and violence and lawlessness.

"The problem of securing a satisfactory emergency force to assist the municipal police in cases of extraordinary disturbance has not been solved in Chicago. Special patrolmen, deputy sheriffs, and deputy United States marshals are unfit for such duty. These forces are composed, largely or wholly, of untrained men, hastily recruited from the least desirable portion of our population. They are untrustworthy, ignorant of their duties and of the law, and often irresponsible, biased, and violent.

"Privately employed emergency forces have an even worse record. The actions of these men have been substantially the same, whether they were called private guards, private detectives, special policemen, privately employed deputy sheriffs, or privately employed deputy United States marshals. They are wholly untrained, irresponsible, and ignorant of their duties. They are secured, in large part, from the scum of civilization—many of them are thieves, vagrants, criminals, and gangsters. They show a natural partiality toward the employer, who pays them; they consistently violate the law, and they have often engaged in an astounding career of violence and crime. They have consistently increased violence and lawlessness in Chicago labor disputes instead of restoring law and order.

"The state militia, although it lacks adaptability and specialized training, has clearly been the best available emergency force for strike policing in Chicago."[1]

While not all the details required for a sound system for policing industry in urban communities are clear, certain of them are. Indispensable is the removal of the police from politics in the popular sense of the word, from domination by either employing or labor interests, and from any affiliation with gangsterism. In other words, the police force must be cleaned up where necessary and then be kept clean. Beyond this certain things are necessary for successful strike policing. At all times, the police force in industrial centers should be somewhat larger than is absolutely necessary in times of peace. Moreover, there should be a Strike Bureau,[2] with a strong advisory board with effective representation of the employing, labor, and public interests. This bureau should study the problem, arrange for needed training of policemen in labor law and other matters so that they may serve efficiently as members of the

---

[1] H. B. Myers, in *Abstracts of Theses*, The University of Chicago, vol. 7 (1929–1930), pp. 122–123.

[2] Such as was proposed in Chicago in 1915. Most of the suggestions here made were developed at that time. *Cf.* H. B. Myers, *The Policing of Labor Disputes in Chicago.*

The clash between the police and marchers during the steel strike in Chicago (on Memorial Day, 1937) both illustrates what is all too frequently happening in important strikes and shows the significance of what is said concerning a sound system of industrial policing. Those in authority did not give adequate instructions to the commanding officers. For some days these officers were in contact with the management of the plant, but never in direct contact with union headquarters a few blocks away. Instead, they relied upon statements made by unknown civilians over the phone that the strikers planned to capture the plant, etc. At the beginning of the strike, picketing was suppressed and then the number of pickets permitted was limited. Later, the Mayor said that there would be no limitation of numbers, provided picketing was peaceful. The police used were not trained for industrial work; members of the detective bureau trained in the use of tear gas were not present. Save for increasing the number of policemen on duty, no plans were made to cope with the expected trouble. Even the tear gas and hatchet handles used were not provided by the Police Department. With trouble believed to be pending, the only

strike detail, and be helpful in devising methods of maintaining law and order in concrete strike situations. A specially selected and carefully trained strike force should be established. These men would perform routine policing work in times of industrial peace, but would be assigned to strike duty as soon as a labor dispute of any considerable dimensions began. A municipal ordinance should require all policemen engaged in strike duty to be under the direct control of the superintendent of police or his subordinates. A dual system should be avoided. And the strike force should be under carefully selected and well-trained officers.

Policing is public business.[1] It should have no private angle. Therefore, guards privately employed should not be permitted to function

---

instructions given the patrolmen were to form a line and not to use revolvers, and these instructions were given so late that perhaps not all the patrolmen received them. For some days the officers had been in and around the plant and had eaten at the plant cafeteria. This was the background.

At a union meeting it was moved and carried that a march to the plant should be made, to engage, it is claimed, in mass picketing in order to show solidarity. Union members and others, including women and children, took up the march across the vacant land, some of them carrying or picking up sticks, rocks, and other missiles on the way. They were met by the police and ordered to disperse. This order was not complied with; instead, request is said to have been made to permit the mass picketing the Mayor had promised. Who first engaged in violence perhaps rests in doubt, but trouble started. Tear gas was used and almost at once the police used their revolvers. Ten persons, in "the mob," were killed, a majority of them shot from the rear. As the people sought to get away, they were clubbed, in some cases without mercy. The removal and care of the injured was accompanied by much that must be censured. If one makes use only of the evidence given by the police before the La Follette Committee and at the coroner's hearing in Chicago, he is driven to the conclusion that the whole affair was very ineptly handled. The lack of preparation and the nonuse of common sense, rather than the killing of ten people and the maiming of others, is the real indictment against the police, "whitewashed" by the coroner's jury. There is difference of opinion as to the impartiality of the La Follette Committee's report (*The Chicago Memorial Day Incident*), but there can be no difference of opinion as to certain observations made (p. 41) by Senator Elmer D. Thomas. He said, "The following conclusion properly may be made: That the use of police officers in such a way that they seem to be allied with either side of a labor dispute destroys their effectiveness as peace officers representing the public. The moment they are used in defense of a given group they are associated in the minds of the opposing group as partisans to the dispute. Therefore, their very presence in unusual numbers invites disorderly incidents, which in turn magnify themselves into clashes that produce death and beatings. Riot duty is the most difficult task which even a well-disciplined soldier has to perform. Those not trained in this work should not be available to either owner or laborer for the taking of sides in a labor dispute."

[1] Certainly it is not the active, personal business of "law and order leagues," citizens' committees, or vigilante organizations so much in evidence in certain areas, especially a few years ago. Such organizations are pretty much a law unto themselves, and, led by hotheads and swayed by interested parties, their behavior in practically every known case has been more anti-social and contrary to the spirit of the law than the behavior protested against. Only good industrial policing can, with justice and respect for legal rights, minimize intimidation, coercion, and labor violence on the one hand and vigilantism on the other.

except on the employer's premises; it should be quite as much the business of the police to keep such guards within the bounds of the law as it is their business to see to it that strikers and their sympathizers observe the statutes and ordinances. Special patrolmen, privately employed deputy sheriffs, and private detectives should be rigidly excluded from strike areas.

Deputy sheriffs should not be employed on strike duty. In case of emergency, the state militia, or the state constabulary,[1] where such a force is maintained, should be called to the assistance of the regular police force to maintain order. When the assistance of either of these state forces is obtained, the division of work between it and the police should be appropriately arranged and the proper coordination effected.

The law to be enforced should be made as fair and rest as equally as possible upon the parties with conflicting interests. The question of what constitutes desirable labor law has been discussed in earlier pages of this volume. The administration of justice at the hands of the public prosecutors and the courts, in the typical urban community, must be improved and maintained on a tolerable level. This is as important as sound police administration in the maintenance of law and order.

Here, again, what Dr. Myers has said concerning the administration of justice in Chicago can be applied rather generally.

"The public prosecutors and the judges of the lower courts have often been lax, apathetic, biased, or incompetent. The judges of the higher courts, although more able, are frequently unconsciously biased against labor by environment and training. The various administrative officers of the city, county, and state governments have frequently failed to perform the duties required of them by law."[2]

Fundamentally, the general public must be brought to a realization of any evil in the existing situation. In the last analysis, a large part of the problem is that of educating the public and forming an intelligent public opinion and a proper attitude. The courts and prosecutors must be divorced from politics in which they are so frequently enmeshed. While safeguards must be maintained, it is clear that the jury system is not working well in the administration of justice. Courts have become more and more specialized. The establishment of a labor court or courts merits serious consideration. Concentration of responsibility goes far to develop efficiency, fairness, and a sense of responsibility.

Policing of Rural Industry.—More difficult than the urban problem we have discussed is that found in the small satellite cities, industrial towns, mill villages, and rural areas in which industries are so frequently located. While riots and other emergencies have developed in the larger cities, as in the railway riots of 1877, in the street-railway riot in New Orleans

---

[1] See *infra*, pp. 685–688.
[2] H. B. Myers, *Abstracts of Theses*, vol. 7, p. 124.

some years ago, and in the long-shore and general strike in San Francisco in 1934, emergencies have more frequently developed in these other places in connection with industrial disputes in coal and metal mining, steel and textile manufacture, and construction work. Very important there, also, is the administration of justice in nonemergency situations.

Generally speaking, labor has until recently remained unorganized in the rural areas, the mill villages, and the smaller cities, but there have long been important exceptions. Most important among these exceptions have been the coal and the metal miners. At times, also, construction workers have been organized to an extent. And since World War I important efforts have been exerted to organize the textile workers of the South, as the old paternalism in management showed signs of decay and especially as Northern manufacturers tended to relocate in the area and to introduce efficiency methods, including the "stretch-out" system, in order to operate more profitably. And, of course, the NIRA and the National Labor Relations Act aroused great interest in unionization in cotton textiles and the timber industry.

Most of the miners in the North and West have been foreigners, representing many races; in the South they have been largely composed of native hill people, Negroes, and a variety of people who have migrated to the new mining areas as they developed. With exceptions, such as that of southern Colorado, paternalism and welfare work have found small place in mine management. Housing has, of course, been provided because it has been necessary; the company store has been opened, and sometimes medical and certain other services arranged for. The restrictions and exactions connected with these and the low wages prevailing in unorganized competitive industry have produced discontent and caused many of the miners to be receptive to the suggestions of the union organizers as they sought to extend unionism to the point where it would be effective in raising and maintaining the standard of living and work of the miners in general. Low wages, relatively long hours, and especially the "drive system" and wage reductions caused many of the Southern textile workers to become discontented and to question paternalistic rule and welfare work, and caused them also to become receptive to the suggestion of labor organization. Indeed, in many concrete instances there have been revolts by Southern millworkers, who, in spite of their fear of outsiders and dislike for "agitators," have requested that organizers be sent to aid them in setting up unions.[1]

Typically, the operators and mill managements have been bitterly opposed to unionization, sometimes because it would be out of harmony with the industrial government to which they were accustomed, sometimes because of desire for profits to be realized, sometimes because of

[1] For an account of the earlier developments in the South, see Broadus Mitchell, *The Industrial Revolution in the South* (1930).

earlier experience with unions. Typically, also, the general public, in so far as there is one in the areas concerned, has been sympathetic with the operators and mill managements rather than with unionism. Not infrequently the reaction against labor organization has been so great that chambers of commerce or "good citizens" have, as at Elizabethton, Tenn., and Gadsen, Ala., deported organizers and "agitators" and perhaps subjected them to physical punishment. Very generally organizations teaching or presumed to be in sympathy with radical doctrines have not been permitted to gain or to keep a foothold. Hence attempts at organization have frequently been accompanied by much violence and infraction of law on the part of the "better element," assisted in some instances by the officers of the law. And, naturally enough under the circumstances, labor organizations established have to a large extent been unstable and their recognition frequently questioned. Union mistakes and shortcomings have added to the trouble. Disputes and bitter strikes have been numerous; industrial war has often developed.

In the smaller cities the public machinery for maintaining law and order consists of the courts and the limited police force; in the towns the town marshal and his aids replace the police. The county sheriff and his deputies are also available for policing industry in city and town; in the rural areas, so important in the mining industry, they constitute the local public provision. Besides the local provision, in all cases[1] is the state militia, frequently made available by the governor, usually upon request of the local authorities, to assist in emergencies beyond the power of the local forces to cope with. And a number of states maintain a system of state police available for strike duty.

Generally speaking, the public protection of property and business has been so inadequate that the large industries have hired police and guards, and/or paid at least a part of the salaries of the deputy sheriffs.[2] The police and guards have been employed directly or through the detective agency, which so frequently has supplied industry with spies at

[1] An exception appears to be found in Nevada, where the law [Compiled Laws (1929), sec. 7140] prohibits the use of the militia in strike situations.

[2] Fairly typical is a case occurring during the textile strike of 1934, when a company operating five mills hired guards from an agency and had 700 persons, largely its own employees, sworn in as deputy sheriffs. The deputies were paid by the company, for the county and city did not have sufficient funds (La Follette Committee, *Hearings*, Pt. VII, pp. 2688-2705). The company alleged that the governor of the state said that protection of the mills and employees during the strike was a matter for local officers to handle (*ibid.*, pp. 2690-2691). For other cases in which the excuse given for hiring deputies was the inadequacy of the publicly paid police force, see *ibid.*, Pt. III, pp. 737, 743-744, 955. For an illustration of the indiscriminate deputization that occurs in some places in time of labor trouble, see the letter written by the sheriff of Monterey, Calif., in reply to an inquiry regarding the deputization of a munitions salesman during the Salinas lettuce war of 1936. He said that the man in question:

". . . may or may not have been (deputized), as there were some 1900 men deputised

all times and with guards and strikebreakers when needed. These guards, many of them of objectionable[1] character, have policed the premises. Rather generally they have also been sworn in as deputy sheriffs and, though privately hired and paid, have had the authority of public officers conferred upon them. In the closed town they and the camp marshal alone have functioned in normal times. Their word has been law.

When disputes have developed into strikes or lockouts, the employers in many cases have sooner or later hired more guards and proceeded to import strikebreakers. The miners, the textile-mill workers, and the steelworkers have then commonly resorted to mass picketing, regardless of what the law on the subject might be. Parades have frequently been held to impress the employers and the community with union power and the determination to win, as well as to educate "scabs." Assemblies have been held in private or public halls or in the open.

What has happened with regard to policing has depended rather generally upon the pressure exerted by local groups and upon political considerations.[2] At Herrin, Ill., where tolerable conditions came only with unionization, where the union therefore became the first considera-tion with the miners, where the people generally sympathized with the miners as against a foreign corporation, and where the prosperity of the tradesmen and townspeople generally depended upon the prosperity of the miners, labor has for many years done about as it pleased. Its record has, however, had only one serious blot upon it, the massacre of 1922.

During the country-wide coal strike of 1922, the superintendent of the Southern Illinois Coal Company decided to operate near Herrin on a nonunion basis in defiance of the union. As the United States Coal

---

in squads of from 50 to 100 at a time who were required to sign their names to a long list and afterwards raising their right hands were sworn in as deputies.

"However, without going over the long list, most of whom have since been revoked, I would say that if he was here in Salinas at the time he was undoubtedly deputised" (*ibid.*, Pt. VII, pp. 2659). Industrial concerns also purchase large quantities of tear gas, machine guns, and other weapons, for the use of their own guards, or in some cases for the use of the local police. *Ibid.*, pp. 2432*ff.*, *passim*, 2603-2628, Pt. II, pp. 402, 566-587, *Hearings before a Subcommittee of the Committee on Education and Labor . . . Seventy-fourth Congress, Second Session, on S. Res.* 266, pp. 48-56.

[1] Of forty-three guards arrested for violence in an Ohio strike, sixteen were found to have police records. This is more or less typical. For this and other cases, see La Follette Committee, *Hearings*, Pt. I, pp. 166, 210-212, Pt. III, pp. 852, 856, 1018-1033, Pt. VII, p. 2384.

[2] The United States Coal Commission [*Report*, 68th Congress, 2d Session, Senate Doc. 195 (1925), Pt. I, p. 175] stated, "That the election of officers by the people has something to do with the administration of justice can not be denied. Where the territory is union-ized and the officials are elected by the vote of the union miners, they naturally have a friendly feeling for the United Mine Workers. Where it is non-union and they are elected by men who are opposed to the union, a like condition of mind necessarily exists."

Commission said, "He was inviting mob violence and flirting with death; he knew it and prepared to meet it. The resentment was spontaneous and instantaneous. He challenged the supremacy of the union"[1] in an industry for almost twenty-five years thoroughly organized throughout the state. Provoked by the challenge and the behavior of the company guards,[2] the miners prepared to give battle. Though urged to do so, the sheriff, because of his sympathy with the union and his candidacy for the office of county treasurer, hesitated to request the aid of the state militia. After some union men had been killed by guards, a mob, including leading union men, formed, armed itself, and took possession of the superintendent and his employees. It was agreed that the mine would be closed and that the imported employees should leave the community. On the march from the mine, the superintendent was killed and his men were told that they would be given "a chance for their lives under fire." As they ran some fifteen were killed and several others wounded. Of those who temporarily escaped, one was caught and hanged and four others were shot in the woods near by. Six others, four of them wounded, were conducted up 13th Street in Herrin, were made to crawl on all fours, were jeered by women and children, and were finally led to the cemetery, where all but one were killed. The sheriff, his deputies, and the police officers of Herrin were notable for their inactivity and never attempted to ascertain who was responsible for the murders or to assist in any way to secure evidence upon which to convict the guilty parties. The inquest resulted in the verdict, we "find that they came to their deaths by gunshot wounds by the hands of parties unknown." The blame was placed largely upon the company; it was recommended by the coroner's jury "that an investigation be conducted for the purpose of fixing the blame personally on the individuals responsible." A grand jury was empaneled; the attorney general took personal charge of its investigation; indictments were returned against seventy-six men, nearly all of whom were members of the union. There were many witnesses of the killings, and hundreds of people had stood on the sidewalks and seen the six doomed men marched through the streets of Herrin, but they would say nothing in court; it was therefore impossible to secure a conviction in the two trials held,

---

[1] *Ibid.*, p. 167.

[2] The company had secured between twenty-five and thirty guards from the Hargraves Detective Agency of Chicago to protect its property and employees, purchased ammunition, and mounted a machine gun. "The guards, when patrolling the property, are alleged to have assumed an arrogant and defiant attitude toward the citizens of the county who passed along the road. Some of the citizens say they were stopped, told to get off the highway, and struck in the face by the guards. Farmers living near the mine said that the guards had trespassed upon their property to get water for the mine, to steal their chickens, and to milk their cows. Some of the farmhouses bear evidence of having been fired upon by the guards." Quoted from J. W. Scott, *The Policing of Non-urban Industry* (unpublished Ph. D. Dissertation, The University of Chicago, 1929), p. 397.

and the attorney general nolle-prossed the other indictments because he was convinced that the spirit in the county was such that a conviction could not be secured.[1] The sheriff was elected to the new county office to which he had aspired.

While Herrin is not absolutely unique in American experience, it is exceptional. It has been very much more common for the companies to be in effective control of the local government and to employ it to realize their objectives.

Harlan County, Ky., affords one among a number of illustrations. In that county, coal mining, employing 68 per cent of those gainfully occupied, has been the only important industry, and its workers have lived in the unincorporated company towns. The coal companies have not only owned the land and houses, but also owned or controlled the schools and even the post office buildings.[2] Until recently, they have dominated the local governments and have paid the salaries of many of the deputies appointed by the sheriff.[3] With a maximum income as sheriff of $5,000 and with little to begin with, one sheriff accumulated property holdings rapidly. His wife and the wife of the county judge owned stock in a corporation that ran the company store of one of the coal companies, the dividends received amounting to 96 per cent annually.[4] A commonwealth attorney was paid monthly retainers by three coal companies, and the grand jury is said to have been composed mainly of coal operators or of others dependent upon them.[5] The sheriff's chief deputy was a brother of the association's secretary.[6]

The coal companies of Harlan County had for fifteen years before 1938 been unyielding in their opposition to any unionization of their employees. More than once, serious trouble developed. In 1931, when, because of wage cuts and other grievances, the miners attempted to organize, the companies hired extra guards and succeeded in defeating the effort. Much violence occurred on both sides; miners were tried on the charge of criminal syndicalism, and more than forty were charged with murder or conspiracy to murder in connection with the deaths of several deputies in a battle occurring in the spring. The president and

---

[1] The authors have here made liberal use of Dr. Scott's manuscript.

[2] In some cases, also the local jail. La Follette Committee, *Hearings*, Pt. X, pp. 3454–3457, 3576–3579; Pt. XI, pp. 3841–3845, 3944–3952.

[3] Of 379 deputies appointed, 154 were paid by private companies or by the coal operators' association (*ibid.*, Pt. X, pp. 3694–3716). Of the 379, 37 had records of one or more convictions and sentences for felonies in the state, 3 had records of federal convictions for felonies, and 64 had been indicted locally one or more times. *Ibid.*, p. 3569.

[4] *Ibid.*, Pt. X, pp. 3545–3553, 3573–3575; Pt. XII, pp. 4145–4174. The judge also independently owned what was alleged to be a company store in another town.

[5] *Ibid.*, Pt. X, p. 3616; Pt. XII, pp. 4297, 4299, 4310, 4312, 4332–4333.

[6] *Ibid.*, Pt. X, p. 3532. The secretary of the Coal Association had served one year as sheriff while working for the Association. *Ibid.*, Pt. X, pp. 3503–3504.

the vice-president of the union were the first to be convicted and sentenced to life imprisonment on the charge of planning the murder of two deputies. At least a dozen miners were killed but none of the deputies was indicted.[1]

According to the evidence on suppression of union organization taken by the La Follette Committee, in more recent years deputies, led by one in the employ of the Coal Operators' Association, carried on a campaign of violence, including the running of organizers out of town, the breaking up of union meetings, the forcing of strikers at the point of guns to return to work,[2] and the killing of active union men.[3]

The deputies committed these acts of violence without fear of punishment, since not only was the sheriff lax in investigating crimes,[4] but the commonwealth attorney secured the dismissal of many cases involving deputies,[5] and the grand jury failed to return indictments.[6] Moreover, witnesses were afraid to testify for fear of being killed or felt that testimony was futile in view of the composition of the grand jury and of the attitude of local officials.[7] In the few cases in which deputies or those hired by them committed violence and were sentenced to prison,

---

[1] For readily accessible accounts of the matter, see *The New Republic*, vol. 69, pp. 32–33, 55, 62–64, 145, 199, 226–227, 280–281, vol. 70, p. 284, vol. 71, pp. 61, 218, 246, 327; and *The Nation*, vol. 134, pp. 30, 485, and vol. 135, p. 21.

[2] The deputies also reported to the operators on union activities, one of the deputies using his position as a union official for this purpose. La Follette Committee, *Hearings*, Pt. X, pp. 3472–3473.

[3] During a three-week period early in 1937, in which there were active organization efforts, there occurred the killing of the son of a union organizer, when the organizer's house was shot into; the shooting at the organizer and his wife while they were on a public highway; the shooting at another organizer's son; the shooting and wounding of three other men, one an organizer, the other two being shot because the one—a deputy—had refused to take part in some of the violence and knew too much; the dynamiting of two organizers' cars; and the gassing of a hotel in which organizers were staying. There is reliable evidence that the deputies were involved in all these crimes, except in the case of the gassing of the hotel, although the gassing occurred at the same time as the dynamiting of the cars. However, after the gassing, the sheriff's supply of tear-gas grenades was missing. It was at this time that the Coal Association paid their chief deputy $2,300 for one month. For information on these and other acts of violence, see *ibid.*, Pt. X, pp. 3487–3494, 3562, 3635–3639; Pt. XI, pp. 3821, 3882–3883; Pt. XII, pp. 4200–4201, 4203–4209, 4212–4213, 4249, 4252–4267, 4290, 4346–4349, 4364–4368; Pt. XIII, pp. 4405, 4422–4423, 4427, 4429–4430, 4434, 4524, *passim*. For information regarding the arrest of twenty-three union men, apparently without cause, see *ibid.*, Pt. XI, pp. 3916–3919, 3926–3927, 3929–3933, *passim*.

[4] *Ibid.*, Pt. XIII, pp. 4425–4427.

[5] *Ibid.*, Pt. XII, pp. 4293, 4322–4327, *passim*.

[6] *Ibid.*, Pt. XII, pp. 4227, 4236.

[7] *Ibid.*, Pt. X, p. 3560; Pt. XII, pp. 4250, 4322–4327; Pt. XIII, pp. 4434–4436, *passim*. One of the witnesses before the Senate Committee was threatened by a coal operator with a long prison sentence for causing the operators trouble by his testimony (*ibid.*, Pt. X, pp. 3644–3646; Pt. XI, pp. 3994–3995). For a note on the killing of one of the witnesses, see *ibid.*, Pt. XII, p. 4288, footnote 1.

pardons were usually granted after a short time, often with the help of
county officials. Imprisonment was no barrier to redeputization after
release.[1]

In numerous communities, as in Harlan County, local police and
sheriffs have frequently been subservient, when not politically owned.
There has been no particular difficulty in having guards and others named
by the companies deputized as public officers. Indeed, at times, all
"loyal employees" have been deputized, as was the case in some of the
steel towns in 1919. Usually little attention has been given to the
requirements of law relative to previous residence in the county or to
the reputations of those deputized. There have even been cases in which
commissions have been turned over to the companies concerned to bestow
as they saw fit.[2] The policing forces thus built up have been biased in
their work; and frequently they have been quite ruthless in their efforts
to break a strike and to destroy the union. So it was in Colorado in
1913–1914, in Pennsylvania towns in 1919, and in most of the coal
counties in West Virginia. Little regard was paid to rights guaranteed
by law. Other examples are found in the Michigan copper strike (1913),
in the steel strike of 1919, in the numerous coal strikes in various parts of
Pennsylvania and West Virginia, and in a long list of other strikes that
might be specifically mentioned.[3] And, it should be added, the militia
has, as a rule, been made easily available and then all too frequently bent
and influenced to aid the companies.

[1] *Ibid.*, Pt. X, pp. 3561, 3696; Pt. XII, pp. 4292–4293. In one case men accused of
dynamiting an organizer's home were paid their wages and lawyer's fees by the Coal
Association's chief deputy while they were in jail. *Ibid.*, Pt. X, pp. 3479–3484, 3492–3494.

[2] As Dr. Scott states (*op. cit.*, p. 9), "Ordinarily the laws of the various states provide
that the sheriff is the supreme policing official in the county, and charge him with the duty
of maintaining the peace and protecting life and property within his jurisdiction. It is the
sheriff, therefore, to whom the employers usually go when they want more protection.
Assistance may be had from various sources, but usually the first increase in the police
force takes the form of an increase in the number of deputy sheriffs. This is frequently
done by issuing a blanket license to the employer under the terms of which he designates
men for the sheriff to deputize and turn back to the employer for instructions, service and
pay. For the most part such deputies are selected from men who have formerly served
as camp marshals or company guards, or from the private detectives who are under contract
with the employer to 'aid in policing the strike.' Then, too, other employees of the companies are sometimes deputized. In some cases, but relatively few in non-urban strikes,
the deputies are commissioned at the will of the sheriff and paid from county funds."

[3] For factual material see U. S. Coal Commission, *Report* [Senate Doc. 195, 68th Congress, 2d Session (1925)]; "Michigan Copper District Strike," U. S. Bureau of Labor
Statistics, *Bulletin* 139 (1914); B. M. Rastall, "Labor History of the Cripple Creek District," *Bulletin of the University of Wisconsin*, no. 198, Economics and Political Science
Series, vol. 3 (1908); G. P. West, *Report on the Colorado Strike*, United States Commission
on Industrial Relations (1915); W. D. Lane, *Civil War in West Virginia* (1921); Commission
of Inquiry, Interchurch World Movement, *Report on the Steel Strike of* 1919 (1921; W. Z.
Foster, *The Great Steel Strike and Its Lessons* (1920). The facts set out in the above, and
much more, may be found in J. W. Scott, *op. cit.*

The state militia is frequently called upon to preserve order in important strikes in nonurban areas. This is especially so in coal and metal mining. The militia, though not well trained for such work, often polices in a fairly satisfactory manner when it first enters the strike area, but it is easily susceptible to the friendly approaches of the employers and is repelled by the antagonistic attitude of the workers until it eventually almost always favors the employers. Moreover, as time passes the militia is likely to suffer from an adverse selection; the more efficient and the more disinterested militiamen are apt to be relieved from further service in order that they may return to their regular duties.[1] At all times the attitude and policies of the officers in charge of the militia and of the governor of the state are very important in connection with the type of policing given. At its worst, as in the Cripple Creek strike of 1903, the militia has been as biased and as harsh as the local police at their worst.

Problems of State Policing.—Fifteen of the states have state-police systems.[2] The constabulary is in normal times engaged principally in patrolling the state highways and the rural communities and is primarily trained in dealing with individuals. In time of strike, however, it is, or may be,[3] used in strike-police duties, supplementing the local police and the sheriff's deputies. In many ways, a state-police system provides the best policing service. It is, or may be, well trained and efficient, as the state militia has not been. It is also immediately available. Provided other emergency police work does not require its attention, it is available as long as needed. Experience has shown, however, that the system is capable of much abuse. While it has worked well in New York and certain other jurisdictions, it has worked badly in a number of the states, and especially in Pennsylvania previous to its reform there several years ago. The constabulary in many cases has been biased, harsh, even brutal, and has frequently acted outside of and in contravention of

[1] Examples of this are found in the Michigan Copper Strike (1913) and the Colorado Coal Strike (1913–1914). At the time of the Ludlow massacre (1914) a large part of the militia consisted of mine guards and the like.

[2] Arkansas, Connecticut, Indiana, Maine, Maryland, Massachusetts, Michigan, Nevada, New Jersey, New York, Oregon, Pennsylvania, Rhode Island, Texas, and West Virginia. There are of course state highway police in some of the other states. Three states (South Dakota, Tennessee, and Wyoming) have provision for some type of reserve or special force for emergency purposes. For an analysis of laws as of August, 1934, see Kansas Legislative Council Research Report, *State Police* (November, 1934), and A. Vollmer and A. E. Parker, *Crime and the State Police* (1935).

[3] The laws of Connecticut, Indiana, Massachusetts, New Jersey, and New York provide that the state police may be used to suppress riots only upon the approval of the governor. Those of Indiana, New Jersey, and New York provide, also, that the state police may be used in cities only upon request of the mayor. In Arkansas, however, no officer or member of the state police may be used for performing police duties on private property in connection with any strike, lockout, or other industrial disturbance.

the law. It is largely because of such behavior that the system has seemingly incurred the undying hatred of organized labor.[1]

Industrial policing is, however, of a far different nature and varies greatly from the functions ordinarily carried out by the state-police system. This system is organized on the assumption that most of its activities will be in connection with individual infractions of the law. For that reason, the police force has had little or no training in policing groups of men such as are involved in industrial disputes. Consequently, the attitudes, tactics, and procedures often followed by the state-police force have tended to increase the resort to violence and destruction rather than to decrease it.

One of the chief abuses of the Pennsylvania state-police system as it existed prior to 1931 was that the law permitted private companies to hire armed men for the protection of their property. Unlike private watchmen, these guards, or "coal and iron police," had police powers and their commissions were issued by the governor. If they abused their authority their employer was not liable for damages unless he had directed them to do something unlawful.[2] These privately paid coal and iron police were so hated by the workers and so frequently abused their powers that, on June 30, 1931, Governor Gifford Pinchot revoked all the outstanding coal and iron police commissions, which then totaled 1,015.[3] The remaining publicly paid state-police force soon gained the reputation of being well trained and impartial in industrial disputes so that one or two state police could ordinarily handle a disorderly crowd of hundreds.[4] This reform, however, was not a real cure for the abuses of the industrial police system, for employers could still hire deputy sheriffs, who were commissioned by the county sheriff but selected and paid for by the companies. Many of the former coal and iron police, in fact, became deputy sheriffs. Their selection and training were no better than formerly, and in time of strike the workers knew that they could be relied upon to support the employer in his efforts to break the strike.

---

[1] Dr. Scott studied firsthand the state-police forces in Pennsylvania and a number of other states. His conclusion was as follows: "In the final analysis the unbiased student is driven to the conclusion that the state police, or the constabulary as it is sometimes called, for one reason or another, has not proved satisfactory as a force to police industrial disturbances. And the clash of crystallized opinion which never fails to develop relative to the utility of the state police in policing industrial disputes indicates the bias of this force. Finally, the terms state police, trooper, or constabulary are in such disrepute with labor that little, if any, advancement toward just policing of industrial troubles can reasonably be expected from any organization that bears such a name." J. W. Scott, op. cit., p. 530.

[2] "Report to Governor Gifford Pinchot by the Commission on Special Policing in Industry," Pennsylvania Department of Labor and Industry, Special Bulletin 38 (1934), p. 18.

[3] Ibid., p. 19.

[4] Ibid., p. 21.

After an examination into the causes of riots and bloodshed in Pennsylvania industrial disputes, the Commission on Policing in Industry made the following recommendations:

"1. *Company Deputies:* We recommend legislation prohibiting any private person or corporation from paying directly or indirectly the salaries of deputy sheriffs or the cost of their uniforms or equipment.

"2. *Roving Deputies:* We recommend legislation providing that deputy sheriffs shall be selected only by the sheriff, with the approval of the county commissioners, with pay and mileage fixed by the county commissioners and paid from county funds. Each deputy should subscribe to an oath of office which should be recorded immediately.

"3. *Coal and Iron Police:* We recommend that the Industrial Police Act of April 18, 1929, shall be repealed.

"4. *State Police:* We recommend that in cases of serious industrial disturbance, the governor should be able to place the State Police in charge and to supersede the authority of all other peace officers. In this event, the county should be relieved of liability for injuries caused by mob violence."[1]

The Pennsylvania legislature in 1935 carried out the Commission's third recommendation, and abolished the coal and iron police by repealing the Industrial Police Act. This action, in effect, ratified Governor Pinchot's action in revoking commissions in 1931, but it did not touch what had subsequently become the heart of the problem—the hiring of deputy sheriffs by private companies. These special deputies continued to be used to terrorize union workers and persistently exceeded their authority in important industrial disputes.[2]

After a long study of strike policing and law enforcement in nonurban areas, involving research on the ground in times of disturbance as well as in the literature, Dr. Scott fifteen years ago came to the conclusion that fair and efficient policing of industrial disputes "had been practically unknown in this country during the past thirty-five years." Moreover, he was of the opinion that little improvement could be expected until the attitudes of those immediately involved in these dis-

---

[1] *Ibid.*, p. 22.

[2] One example of this occurred in the strike of the United Anthracite Miners (an insurgent group that broke away from the United Mine Workers of America) called against the Glen Alden Coal Co., in Luzerne County, Pa., which lasted from February, 1934, to June, 1935. The American Civil Liberties Union reported that the police systematically exceeded their authority, entering workers' homes without warrants, clubbing and arresting them when they were engaged only in peaceful activity, and trying and sentencing them without permitting counsel or witnesses. Incidentally, an injunction was issued in this case ordering the union officials to call off the strike, and restraining all strike activities. When the union leaders refused to abide by the injunction some thirty of them were sent to jail for contempt of court. The strike was broken. Further details are reported in *The New Republic*, Aug. 21, 1935, p. 35.

putes were changed, until the law applicable to such situations was amplified and clarified, and until the necessary precautions were taken to provide a qualified and impartial police force to handle such disturbances.[1] The importance of the attitudes of the employers and organized workers was also emphasized by the United States Coal Commission.[2]

One thing in addition to the foregoing is essential. The county and other local governments are agencies of the state. The state must be looked to in order that a real government of the community may be maintained, especially where closed camps obtain, and that policing may be performed by public servants, selected as such, and paid from public funds, without remuneration from private sources and without obligations except to the public. The private guard must be limited to private policing on the premises, the privately appointed or privately paid deputy sheriff must be eliminated, and the state executive must remove the inefficient, or biased, or politically owned or subservient sheriff. The principle of home rule is not sacred when fundamental human rights become involved.

After all, the state must accept much responsibility for the policing of industry in nonurban areas. The local governments cannot well provide more police than are needed in time of industrial peace. Moreover, the people of the area are frequently practically all divided into two opposed camps. Until relationships are much improved, a state force must frequently be called upon to serve in troubled and troublesome areas. As already stated, it is an unfortunate fact that a state constabulary cannot or usually will not be permitted to meet the need. Generally the state militia must serve that need as well as function in the less frequent emergencies arising in the cities. It can be made to serve much better than it has served in the past. It is suggested that a state industrial commission, fairly representing employers, labor, and the public, should be created in each state where none now exists, with authority to administer all labor laws of the state, including those which apply to the policing of industrial disputes in nonurban areas. In this latter connection it would, however, function in cooperation with the governor. It is suggested, further, that selected members of the militia should be especially trained in industrial policing and that the orders of the governor relative to the use of the militia and the instructions given it should be subject to the approval of the industrial commission. It is suggested, finally, that the industrial commission should be authorized to investigate thoroughly the causes of each important industrial dispute and to

---

[1] See abstract of thesis, published in *Abstracts of Theses*, the University of Chicago, vol. 9 (1930–1932).

[2] See *Report of the United States Coal Commission* [Senate Doc. 195, 68th Congress, 2d Session (1925)], Pt. I, pp. 163–180.

recommend suitable legislation for the relief of undesirable conditions found to exist.

This chapter may be closed with the observation that desirable changes in attitudes in labor matters and the enforcement of law may be greatly aided by the development of efficient machinery for the mediation and arbitration of industrial disputes. Mediation and arbitration are discussed in the next two chapters.

CHAPTER XIII

THE PROBLEM OF STRIKES AND LOCKOUTS: THE CONCILIATION AND ARBITRATION OF INDUSTRIAL DISPUTES

We have considered the organization of labor and the theory and practice of collective bargaining. The strength of the union, we have seen, lies to a large extent in its power to strike and to boycott. The law relating to these weapons and to the employers' corresponding weapons, as well as to organization, assembly, picketing, and other acts or methods, has been examined with reference to what it is and what it ought to be in view of what is conceived to be sound public policy. The conclusions drawn with reference to what the law ought to be must, however, be regarded as tentative and subject to modification, for the chief test applied in our discussion has been that of equal treatment of employers and unions under the law. Both the costs and results of comparative freedom of employer and union to fight and the presence of a third party—"the public"—with its interests, must be given due weight before any final conclusions are drawn. Should a government merely lay down the rules of the game to be observed by contestants and permit matters to take their course, or should it attempt to function in a more positive way through mediation and arbitration of industrial disputes?

Few governments, faced by the problem of strikes and lockouts, have remained content to pursue a negative course; the majority of them have, rather, attempted to smooth the way and to assist in or to require the maintenance or restoration of industrial peace. Some of them have functioned through mediation and voluntary arbitration; some have, in addition, resorted to investigation and report on the issues involved in disputes, in an effort to cause employers and unions to take their responsibilities less lightly than they are frequently wont to do; not a few have placed a ban on suspensions in certain industries until such an investigation has been completed and a report made as to what would be a suitable settlement—as under the Canadian Industrial Disputes Investigation Act; still other governments, in considerable number, have, under compulsory arbitration, provided for the authoritative determination of wages, hours, and working conditions when the parties immediately interested failed to agree; while still other governments have applied various of the foregoing methods in connection with strikes and lockouts in different industries of different degrees of public concern. In the present chapter, and the one immediately following, conciliation, mediation, arbitration, and investigation of industrial disputes will be our main subject for consideration. Experience with different methods of intervention will be presented briefly, in an effort to throw light on proper public policy. First of all, however, the problem presented by strikes and lockouts must be set out in so far as this has not been done in the two immediately preceding chapters.

THE PROBLEM OF STRIKES AND LOCKOUTS

What are the more outstanding statistical facts relating to strikes and lockouts? What do they show with reference to trends as to their frequency, the number of workers involved in them, and the amount of working time lost due to them? What other facts are of importance in stating the problem?

Number and Trend of Strikes.—The Federal Government from time to time published reports on strikes and lockouts occurring in the United States from 1881 to 1905, and has again done so since 1915.[1] The data are not complete and are not wholly comparable for the earlier and the later of the two periods just indicated. The chief shortcoming, however, lies in the less complete recording of the data for the early eighties and again in 1915 and 1916. Never have all minor suspensions been recorded and reported; the more recent practice in reporting has been, in so far as data have been available, to exclude those where the number of workers involved is less than six and the suspension lasts less than one day. In Table 8 the average number of disputes[2] and of workers involved, together with their number relative to the 1881–1885 average, are presented for the years 1881–1905 and 1916–1943.[3]

As is shown in Table 8, the averages for both disputes and workers involved were in the later eighties and in the nineties more than twice

---

[1] Four reports were made on strikes and lockouts for 1881–1905, but the results may be found in the fourth report—*Strikes and Lockouts, Twenty-first Annual Report of the Commissioner of Labor* (1906). The later data have been published in the annual reports of the Department of Labor, also in various numbers of the *Monthly Labor Review* [see particularly, the annual summaries, for example, vol. 34 (1932), pp. 1353–1368, and vol. 46 (1938), pp. 1186–1203]. Both periods are covered in Florence Peterson, "Strikes in the United States, 1880–1936," U. S. Bureau of Labor Statistics, *Bulletin* 651 (1938).

[2] The distinction between a strike and a lockout rests upon which party takes the initiative by walking out or by closing the doors of the plant. Beyond this it has no meaning and the distinction is fraught with so many difficulties that it has generally been discontinued for statistical purposes. The word "dispute" is now commonly used to include both strikes and lockouts and will be so used here.

[3] In his *Strikes, a Study in Quantitative Economics* (1939), Dr. J. I. Griffin has not only presented and evaluated the official data we have used in these chapters but has also attempted to bridge the gap for the years 1906–1915 by making general estimates based upon reports of seven of the states. The volume contains the fullest quantitative study of the subject.

TABLE 8.—ABSOLUTE AND RELATIVE NUMBER OF DISPUTES AND OF WORKERS INVOLVED, BY
PERIODS: 1881–1905, 1916–1943

Period	Average per year		Relative movement of disputes (average 1881–1885 = 100)	
	Disputes	Number of workers involved[1]	Disputes	Workers
1881–1885	528	176,511	100	100
1886–1890	1,406	369,200	266	209
1891–1895	1,436	390,725	272	221
1896–1900	1,390	385,564	263	218
1901–1905	2,901	583,887	549	331
1916–1920	3,727	1,938,112	706	1,098
1921–1925	1,520	910,290	288	516
1926–1930	781	289,058	148	164
1931–1935	1,443	883,641	273	501
1936–1940	2,961	1,017,119	561	576
1941	4,288	2,362,620	812	1,335
1942	2,965	839,961	562	476
1943	3,752	1,981,279	711	1,122

[1] From 1916 through 1926 the number of workers involved was not reported for all disputes. The number of strikes in which the number of workers was not reported was, by years, as follows: 1916, 1,122; 1917, 2,125; 1918, 1,202; 1919, 965; 1920, 1,185; 1921, 600; 1922, 213; 1923, 354; 1924, 351; 1925, 289; and 1926, 252. Included in workers involved are workers within establishments who lost time because of the stoppage whether or not they were among the strikers.

the numbers recorded in 1881–1885, with the number of persons involved increasing less than the number of disputes. A distinctly higher level obtained in 1901–1905, a period marked by rapid organization of labor and the open-shop struggle so bitterly fought during some of those years. The World War I years were marked by many suspensions and a large number of strikers, the former being almost 30 per cent larger than in 1901–1905, the latter slightly more than 3.3 times as large. With the return of peace and the appearance of depression (1921–1922), however, the number of disputes decreased to almost two-fifths, the number of workers involved to less than one-half, of what they had been in the War period. In the seven years 1926–1932 there were still further reductions in both sets of figures.[1] Indeed, the number of disputes during

[1] The number of disputes and workers involved was, for 1926 to 1941, as follows:

Year	Number	Workers involved	Year	Number	Workers involved
1926	1,035	329,592	1935	2,014	1,117,213
1927	707	329,939	1936	2,172	788,648
1928	604	314,210	1937	4,740	1,860,621
1929	921	288,572	1938	2,772	688,376
1930	637	182,975	1939	2,613	1,170,962
1931	810	341,817	1940	2,508	576,988
1932	841	324,210	1941	4,288	2,362,620
1933	1,695	1,168,272	1942	2,968	834,961
1934	1,856	1,466,695	1943	3,752	1,981,279

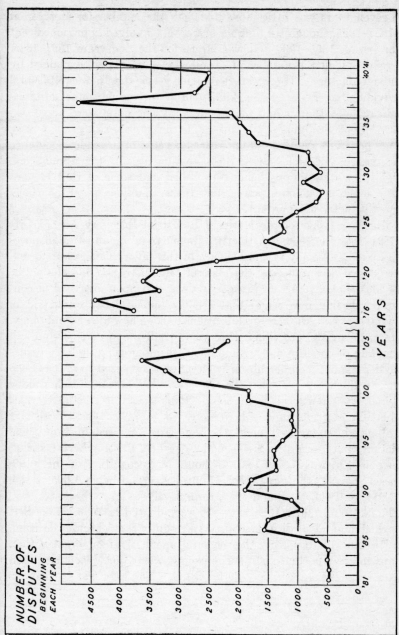

CHART C.—Data for years 1881–1936 computed from U. S. Bureau of Labor Statistics., *Bulletin* 651, p. 21; for the years 1937–1941, from the *Monthly Labor Review*, vol. 52 (1941), p. 1092, and vol. 54 (1942), p. 1109.

those seven years was little more than half the number for any period save 1881–1885, though the number of workers involved approached that for the period 1886–1900 and was larger for the five years 1881–1885. This reduction in the number of disputes was, of course, explained by a number of factors. There were depression years; the "new capitalism," by providing benefits of various kinds and improving personnel administration, reduced the amount of discontent; living costs were fairly stationary, in fact declining a bit, and real earnings were rising; wage rates were not generally reduced, for one reason because of the wide acceptance of the doctrine of high wages; the extent of organization diminished, relatively few new unions being established and some of the old ones suffering losses in economic power; and American unionism, on the whole, became distinctly less militant.[1]

With the passage of the National Industrial Recovery Act, and its Sec. 7(a),[2] in June, 1933, a distinctly different trend in industrial disputes was initiated. Largely in consequence of this favorable legislation, and of the general acceptance by the Federal Administration and the public of the idea that a return of prosperity depended upon a revival of consumer purchasing power and that organization of labor would aid in achieving that end, workers' organizations took on new life and militancy. Whereas during the preceding three years trade-union membership had been falling off rapidly and organizations disintegrating under pressure of the depression, membership in trade unions increased from 3,144,300 in 1932 to 3,608,600 in 1934.[3] The American Federation of Labor alone chartered 1,859 new locals in the period 1932–1935. By the latter year, membership in trade unions had increased to 3,895,700.[4] With this revival of union strength, and the comparative freedom from legal restriction on the right to strike and to picket, the number of strikes for increases in wages, decreases in hours, or recognition of the union increased sharply, the number of disputes recorded being 1,695, 1,856, and 2,014 for 1933, 1934, and 1935, respectively.

The National Labor Relations Act was adopted in 1935. Like Sec. 7(a), which had fallen with the codes as a result of the Schechter decision, it had as one of its effects the encouragement of union organization. Perhaps more important than this encouragement, yet dependent upon the Act, was the appearance of the C.I.O. Not only was it vigorous

[1] See *supra*, pp. 150–162, for fuller discussion of these influences.

[2] Quoted in Chap. XI, p. 522.

[3] The membership in 1933 was only 2,973,000. The failure of the figures of this year to reflect the changed situation is explained by the fact that the National Industrial Recovery Act was not passed until June of that year, while the membership figures are based mainly on reports of the American Federation of Labor, whose figures are an average for the year ending Aug. 31.

[4] As estimated by Leo Wolman, in *Ebb and Flow in Trade Unionism* (1936), p. 238.

in its organizing campaign; its presence and activities aroused efforts on the part of the A.F. of L. perhaps not previously witnessed at any time in the history of that organization. The organization of labor advanced as strikingly as it had during the World War; by the end of 1937, if both non-dues- and dues-paying members are included, the membership in American trade unions had reached an all-time peak of more than 7,000,000, or even 8,000,000. Of course organizing activity was naturally accompanied by many strikes. Adding fuel to the fire, a majority of employers in many important industries, frequently on advice of legal counsel, ignored the National Labor Relations Act until its wide application and the constitutionality of its important provisions were decided by the Supreme Court of the United States in April, 1937. This employer behavior caused the Act, designed to further industrial peace, to make for industrial war. In view of these facts, further industrial recovery, and rising prices, a great increase in the number of industrial disputes was only to be expected. The number increased from 2,014 in the (calendar) year 1935 and 2,172 in 1936 to 4,740 in 1937.[1] This was an all-time peak. The number of workers involved in these strikes in 1937, 1,860,621, exceeded the number for any year save 1919, which had been marked by the great steel and bituminous coal strikes and great struggles in the needle trades and other industries. Then, with business recession in 1937–1938, with less active organizational efforts, with an aroused public opinion against strikes, and with less disregard for law by employers, the number of disputes and persons involved fell strikingly, reaching a low in 1940, when there were only 2,508 strikes and lockouts, involving 576,988 workers. But in the following year, with the defense boom and the highly competitive struggle between the C.I.O. and the A.F. of L., disputes jumped to 4,288 and the number of workers involved to 2,362,620.

The above data must be considered in the light of increasing population, greater industrialization, and an increasing number of wage earners, all of which are matters of common knowledge.[2] In the sixteen years from 1890 to 1905, around 4 per cent of all employed workers were, as Chart D shows, at some time during each year involved in strikes and lock-

---

[1] Beginning in the latter half of 1936, the strike situation became very acute and remained so during the first half of 1937. The number of disputes in 1937 was 2.1 times as large as the number in 1936. The number of man-days lost, as reported, increased from 13,091,956 in 1936 to 28,424,857 in 1937. In 1940, the number of man-days lost fell to 6,700,872, which was only a quarter of the loss in 1937, and the smallest figure since 1930. The 1941 figure of 23,047,556 was almost as large as that for 1937. With the no-strike pledge becoming effective and with the institution of the National War Labor Board, the number of strikes in 1942 decreased to 2,968, the number of man-days idle to 4,182,557. In 1943, however, the number of strikes rose to 3,752, the number of man-days idle to 13,500,529. Cf., Monthly Labor Review, vol. 56, (1943), p. 929.

[2] For details concerning these, see vol. I, Chap. I, of this treatise.

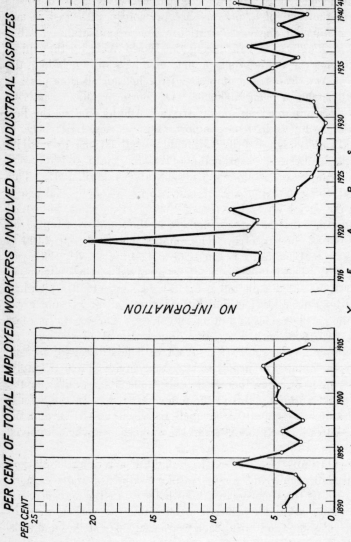

PER CENT OF TOTAL EMPLOYED WORKERS INVOLVED IN INDUSTRIAL DISPUTES

CHART D.—"Total employed workers" includes all employees except those in occupations and professions where strikes rarely occur. In general, the following are excluded: government workers, agricultural wage earners on farms employing less than six, managerial and supervisory employees, and certain other groups such as college professors, commercial travelers, clergymen, and domestic servants. *Monthly Labor Review*, vol. 52 (1941), p. 1092, and vol. 54 (1942), p. 1109.

outs, the percentage fluctuating from year to year; it rose during World War I and the years immediately following. At that time it appeared from American and foreign data that there had been a distinct tendency for strikes and strikers to increase in number more rapidly than population or that part of it engaged in industry.[1] From 1922 to 1932, however, the trend was quite different, but the difference was short-lived for, as already noted, a new peak in industrial disputes was witnessed in 1937 and almost equaled in 1941, though the percentages of all employees involved were far below the 1919 figure. The data raise the question whether or not it is worth while to discuss the general trend that has aroused the interest of more than one writer on the subject.[2] The position here taken is that any discussion should be limited to the factors explaining the variations from one year to another, and, more important, from one period to another.

Some Explanations.—One important factor entering into the explanation of American strike statistics has been discussed by Professor Hansen,[3] among others. This is the business cycle. It affects not only the number, but also the causes and outcome, of disputes. In a period of prosperity, prices rise and the cost of living increases; perhaps unionization makes progress and new groups demand recognition; the financial strength of the unions improves and displaced workers have relatively good opportunity to obtain other employment; though employers may accede to demands rather than lose production when profits may be realized, frequently they do not; strikes for recognition, increases in wages, reductions in hours, and the closed shop distinctly increase. Such was the case for several years beginning with the late 1890's, still more strikingly during the period of the War, again in the recovery years 1934–1937, and during the defense boom of 1941. When business is depressed and prices are falling, unions usually make little progress, are more cautious in initiating strikes, and the number of disputes tends to decrease. But attempts to cut wages at such times are likely to give rise to many defensive strikes and to demands for recognition of unions incidentally and quickly organized.

Another factor determining the number of disputes, is, as already indicated, the progress being made in labor organization and in the extent to which the workers are unionized. Not all strikes involve union men; indeed 2,160 of the strikes occurring in the United States between 1916

---

[1] *Cf.* Paul H. Douglas, *Journal of the American Statistical Association*, vol. 18 (1923), pp. 876–877.

[2] Among them Thomas S. Adams and Helen L. Sumner, *Labor Problems* (1905), pp. 179–185, Ira B. Cross, "Strike Statistics," *Journal of the American Statistical Association*, vol. 2 (1908), pp. 168–194; Paul H. Douglas, *op. cit.*; and J. I. Griffin, *op. cit.*

[3] Alvin H. Hansen, "Cycles of Strikes," in *American Economic Review*, vol. 11 (1921), pp. 616–621.

and 1930 were not connected with unions as against 20,741 that were, but the former were usually short-lived, small flare-ups, and more than 90 per cent of the strikers were involved in union situations.[1] The problem of strikes is practically one of trade-union labor; other things equal, the more widespread unionism is, and, especially, the more rapid its extension, the greater the number of strikes. New unions are usually comparatively undisciplined, unstable, and crudely militant, and have frequently found it necessary to go on strike in order to obtain recognition. It is sufficient to call attention to this matter here; it will be developed presently in a somewhat different connection.

A third, closely related factor, of more importance in explaining differences between countries or between long periods of time than in accounting for variations in a given country year after year or by decades, is found in the type of union, especially as regards attitude toward direct action. The strike history of the Catholic unions in Canada has been very different from the strike history of the Industrial Workers of the World. The appearance of a radical unionism was important in the development of strikes under systems of compulsory arbitration in New Zealand and Australia.

Another factor of importance is found in the policies being pursued by management. These were certainly of great importance in explaining the trend in disputes in the United States during the ten years ending with 1933. Influenced more or less by the labor doctrine that wages must be maintained if the product of industry was to find a favorable market, and then appealed to by the administration at Washington not to cut wages, American management was slow to reduce costs by reducing the workers' remuneration. And just as important, perhaps, was the development of the "new capitalism of the twenties," with its more efficient administration of labor, its stock-sharing schemes, benefit plans, etc. All these reduced discontent, begot patience, and went a considerable distance in "solving" labor problems. These management policies stood in contrast to the crudities so frequently witnessed early in the century, which resulted in an increased number of industrial disputes. Many of the benefit plans alluded to, however, suffered a setback during the depression beginning in 1929, and not a few were abandoned. On the whole, the depression of the earlier 1930's with its cut-throat com-

---

[1] *Monthly Labor Review*, vol. 32 (1931), p. 1293. The percentage of disputes in which unions were involved was a little over 90 from 1934 to 1936, then rose to almost 100 in 1939–1941 [*ibid.*, vol. 42 (1936), pp. 165, 1312; vol. 44 (1937), p. 1233, vol. 50 (1940), p. 1098, and vol. 52 (1941), p. 1108; vol. 54 (1942), pp. 1122–1123]. Dr. Griffin (*op. cit.*, Table XIII, at p. 101) has found that, for the years 1881–1905 and 1916–1937, unions were connected with the low percentage of 47.3 of disputes in 1881 and the high percentage of 92.6 in 1937. The percentage of workers in union strikes was substantially larger, varying between 56.2 in 1881 and 97.5 in 1937.

petition and financial reverses, was a severe blow to the ideals of the "new capitalism."

To mention only one more factor, the absence or the presence and efficient functioning of machinery for conciliating and arbitrating industrial disputes affects the number and duration of strikes. It is unquestionably true that the emergency machinery set up by the NRA to settle labor disputes at first functioned with surprising smoothness and succeeded in preventing a large number of strikes and lockouts.[1] The seriousness of the emergency and the popularity of the appeal of the Administration to avoid disputes and stoppages of work that would hinder the re-employment program were important factors encouraging the use of the government mediation and arbitration machinery. This is a partial explanation of the failure of the wave of stoppages that usually occurs during a recovery period to reach the peaks of previous recovery periods (see Table 8). However, as the depression crisis passed, difference of interests led to more bitter conflicts, particularly in 1936–1937.

Causes.—The percentages of strikes or industrial suspensions due to four sets of causes are shown in Table 9 for the years for which data are available.

The outstanding facts revealed by this table may be briefly noted:

1. Wages have been the issue most frequently involved in industrial disputes.

2. The relative importance of wages as a factor, however, has tended to decrease somewhat, though uncertainly, with the acceptance of unionism in many industries, with the growing importance of other issues, and with the spread of machinery for arbitrating disputes. The median for the percentages of cases in which this issue entered was 71.7 for the period 1881–1885; 52.5 for 1886–1890; 53.6 for 1891–1895; 55.6 for 1895–1900; 40.9 for 1901–1905; 66.0 for 1916–1920; 52.2 for 1921–1925; 47.5 for 1926–1930; 61.3 for 1931–1935; 49.2 for 1936–1940.

3. Much more striking is the fact that in periods of expansion the number of strikes growing out of demands for increases in wages rises; in periods of depression (the early nineties, 1921–1922, 1930–1933) the number falls. The contrary is true of the number growing out of employer demands for reductions in wages, the percentages rising to 25.9 in 1893, 27.3 in 1894, 43.8 in 1921, 28.7 in 1922, and 50.6 in 1932.

4. Hours of labor have been a much less important issue than wages in labor disputes. The number of strikes over demands for reductions in hours has varied greatly with the stages in union development. There was the great eight-hour urge of 1886 and again at the turn of the century. There was the movement for the forty-four-hour week during World War I period; in turn this was followed by the demand for the forty-hour

[1] *New York Times*, Nov. 13, 1933, and Jan. 7, 1934.

TABLE 9.—CAUSES AND RESULTS OF INDUSTRIAL DISPUTES (IN PER CENT OF DISPUTES REPORTED), BY YEARS, 1881–1905, 1916–1943[1]

Year	Number of disputes beginning each year	Causes[a]								Results[b]		
		Wages			Hours			Recognition of union and other union issues	Working conditions	Won by employees	Won by employers	Compromised
		Increase	Decrease	Total	Increase	Decrease	Total					
1881	477	66.0	12.1	78.1	0.2	5.7	5.9	6.7	2.5	61.2	31.8	7.0
1882	476	55.5	16.2	71.7	0.6	4.2	4.8	8.0	4.4	53.2	38.8	8.0
1883	506	46.8	27.5	74.3	0.6	1.7	2.3	10.9	4.3	57.6	27.0	15.4
1884	485	31.3	39.2	70.5	1.2	2.7	3.9	10.3	4.5	54.1	42.5	3.4
1885	695	40.9	28.6	69.5	0.4	3.0	3.4	9.6	4.7	53.2	37.7	9.1
1886	1,572	48.9	9.6	58.5	1.8	16.2	18.0	13.4	4.5	38.3	43.5	18.2
1887	1,503	37.3	12.2	49.5	0.8	9.9	10.7	19.9	3.1	48.7	45.1	6.2
1888	946	30.4	22.1	52.5	1.2	7.7	8.9	17.2	4.3	50.7	43.9	5.4
1889	1,111	33.5	23.1	56.6	0.6	6.1	6.7	15.6	4.8	46.1	34.8	19.1
1890	1,897	36.9	10.9	47.8	0.5	9.4	9.9	16.8	3.1	51.8	38.3	9.9
1891	1,786	33.0	11.6	44.6	1.2	9.1	10.3	18.7	3.0	36.8	54.5	8.7
1892	1,359	33.2	13.5	46.7	1.2	8.6	9.8	19.2	3.6	35.5	53.9	10.6
1893	1,375	27.7	25.9	53.6	1.7	5.6	7.3	18.7	3.1	50.2	39.0	10.8
1894	1,404	33.5	27.3	60.8	0.9	3.1	4.0	14.7	3.0	42.8	44.8	12.4
1895	1,255	46.8	19.1	65.9	0.4	4.1	4.5	17.3	2.8	56.8	33.7	9.5
1896	1,066	34.5	19.3	53.8	0.7	4.3	5.0	27.9	2.0	58.8	33.8	7.4
1897	1,110	41.7	20.2	61.9	0.8	5.0	5.8	17.4	3.7	56.9	15.5	27.6
1898	1,098	43.4	16.0	59.4	0.6	6.3	6.9	21.5	2.4	63.0	30.8	6.2
1899	1,838	49.4	6.2	55.6	0.3	10.0	10.3	25.6	3.3	73.5	12.6	13.9
1900	1,839	46.5	6.0	52.5	0.5	14.7	15.2	22.5	3.5	38.3	45.1	16.0
1901	3,012	38.3	4.6	42.9	0.5	13.3	13.8	33.7	3.8	47.7	34.2	18.1
1902	3,240	35.2	4.1	39.3	0.4	12.7	13.1	32.4	3.3	44.8	33.9	21.3
1903	3,648	44.2	3.7	47.9	0.5	14.8	15.3	32.9	2.5	37.0	42.1	20.9
1904	2,419	30.9	8.1	39.0	1.2	8.1	9.3	39.9	3.9	32.7	50.6	16.7
1905	2,186	35.5	5.4	40.9	0.7	9.0	9.7	36.6	3.5	39.5	46.1	14.4
1916	3,789	56.4	1.1	66.0	0.3	18.8	24.5	22.8	2.2	32.9	32.9	34.2
1917	4,450	53.3	1.0	63.4	0.5	13.9	23.7	21.8	3.2	36.1	22.6	41.2
1918	3,353	57.2	1.2	66.7	0.2	11.6	20.1	20.2	3.2	35.2	26.1	38.8
1919	3,630	50.1	2.5	61.1	0.7	20.6	29.7	25.7	3.6	29.7	32.5	37.8
1920	3,411	54.7	4.7	67.8	0.3	10.7	19.3	20.0	3.7	29.6	42.4	28.1
1921	2,385	6.9	43.8	59.4	0.8	14.8	24.3	16.8	3.7	20.5	56.2	23.3
1922	1,112	16.4	28.7	54.3	1.1	3.6	14.0	19.8	6.9	42.3	40.5	17.2
1923	1,553	34.2	3.3	52.2	0.3	5.0	20.1	21.0	5.4	42.9	39.2	17.9
1924	1,249	25.0	11.6	47.6	0.4	4.2	15.7	21.4	6.9	45.7	36.5	17.8
1925	1,301	25.5	10.1	46.5	0.5	3.0	14.5	18.2	7.4	47.2	34.2	18.6
1926	1,035	30.3	5.4	48.5	0.4	5.9	19.1	20.9	6.7	43.6	34.2	22.2
1927	707	29.1	9.3	43.4	0.4	9.5	12.2	36.0	...	25.5	41.4	24.9
1928	604	21.8	12.4	41.8	0.8	4.6	8.7	36.5	...	27.9	39.3	27.6
1929	921	24.1	14.0	48.4	0.4	11.9	15.9	41.3	...	28.1	41.2	25.2
1930	637	16.8	25.7	47.5	0.7	6.9	9.9	31.8	...	24.0	44.5	23.0

[a] For the years 1927–1943, the causes are given in terms of disputes ending each year.

[b] For all years, the results are given in terms of disputes ending each year.

[1] This table was compiled from data given in *Strikes and Lockouts, Twenty-first Annual Report of the Commissioner of Labor* (1906), pp. 580–613, 763–771; U. S. Bureau of Labor Statistics, *Bulletin 651*, pp. 21, 33,

TABLE 9.—CAUSES AND RESULTS OF INDUSTRIAL DISPUTES (IN PER CENT OF DISPUTES REPORTED), BY YEARS, 1881–1905, 1916–1943.[1]—(Continued)

Year	Number of disputes beginning each year	Causes[a]								Results[b]		
		Wages			Hours			Recognition of union and other union issues	Working conditions	Won by employees	Won by employers	Compromised
		Increase	Decrease	Total	Increase	Decrease	Total					
1931	810	12.6	42.4	61.3	1.6	1.9	5.8	27.8	....	26.6	46.8	18.3
1932	841	14.5	50.6	71.0	1.2	3.4	7.1	19.0	....	27.3	51.9	15.7
1933	1,695	41.5	13.3	68.3	0.2	9.6	14.7	31.9	....	36.9	31.4	26.4
1934	1,856	32.3	6.5	56.7	0.4	6.1	12.2	45.9	....	35.0	28.2	31.4
1935	2,014	23.2	12.5	53.8	5.2	5.4	19.3	47.2	....	44.3	33.4	18.7
1936	2,172	25.9	7.9	63.0	1.3	7.4	25.9	50.2	....	45.9	27.5	23.6
1937	4,740	27.9	1.4	66.1	0.1	9.5	32.2	57.8	....	46.4	17.3	31.8
1938	2,772	17.3	9.9	48.2	0.7	4.1	17.2	50.0	....	40.0	20.9	29.9
1939	2,613	20.4	5.3	45.2	0.6	4.2	14.4	53.5	....	39.7	18.7	32.3
1940	2,508	25.9	3.3	49.2	0.4	4.2	13.6	49.9	....	42.0	17.4	31.8
1941	4,288	33.7	1.7	59.9	0.2	2.8	8.9	49.5	....	41.9	14.5	35.8
1942	2,968	40.5	1.5	64.0	0.3	1.3	23.6	31.2	16.4	34.6	17.0	34.8
1943	3,752	34.7	2.3	56.9	0.3	0.5	20.7	15.7	29.3	30.7	25.7	25.6

34, 39, 40, 62, 69; *Monthly Labor Review*, vol. 46 (1938), pp. 1188, 1200–1201; vol. 48 (1939), pp. 1125–1126; vol. 50 (1940), pp. 1099, 1101; vol. 52 (1941), pp. 1109, 1112; vol. 54 (1942), pp. 1125–1126; vol. 56 (1943), pp. 966, 973, 975; vol. 58 (1943), pp. 934, 937–938.

NOTES ON TABLE

The figures for the period 1916–1926 include disputes in Alaska, Hawaii, Puerto Rico, the Canal Zone, and the Virgin Islands, while the other figures apply only to the states and the District of Columbia. The only years in which the number is increased appreciably because of inclusion of these areas are 1919 and 1920, when the disputes in them numbered 62 and 121 respectively. The total of such disputes from 1916 to 1927 was 282.

Between the periods 1881–1905 and 1916–1943 the Bureau of Labor Statistics changed its classification of the causes of disputes. The classifications, especially in the early period, were much more detailed than in this table, which attempts only to show the major causes of disputes. It was consequently necessary in many instances to combine two or more of the categories given in the Bureau of Labor Statistics classification. The coverage of the data from 1927 to 1943 is also more complete than in earlier years. As a result, the data before and after 1927 are not strictly comparable.

The heading Working Conditions includes disputes listed in the early period as "concerning working conditions and rules combined with other causes" and "concerning working conditions and rules (other than union rules)." In the period 1916–1926 "working conditions" comprises disputes listed as due to "general conditions," by which the Bureau meant working conditions. It does not include "other conditions," by which the Bureau meant miscellaneous causes. When the Bureau revised its classification in 1934, going back to 1927, it dropped the "general conditions" class.

The various causes overlap in the classification, *i.e.*, several factors may enter as causes of one dispute, and each time a cause was a factor in a dispute it was counted in computing the percentage. This accounts for the fact that many of the percentages add up to more than 100. If the other minor causes of strikes, unfair products, jurisdiction, sympathy, and "other conditions" were counted, the percentages would in every year total more than 100.

The figures for *results* of disputes were obtainable for the first period only by establishments, whereas for the period 1916–1943, they are given only by disputes. There is no a priori reason, however, to believe that this should affect comparisons materially when the figures are reduced to a percentage basis.

In the early part of the period 1916–1941, a large number of strikes were reported in which the causes and results were not known. This was not the case in the period 1881–1905, and, in order to make the percentage figures more closely comparable, the causes and results were computed as a percentage of the disputes for which those data were available rather than as a percentage of the total number of disputes. The number of strikes for which causes were not known declined from 631 in 1916 to 48 in 1926. The data have been complete in this respect since 1928. The results of disputes are still unreported in a small number of cases and are not classified as to won, lost, or compromised in a few others.

week. With the depression in 1931 and the years following came the demand for the thirty-hour week, but despite the widespread popularity of the six-hour day and five-day week, few disputes were solely over reductions in hours. The number of disputes over attempts to increase hours has been comparatively small except in 1935.

5. The number of disputes over union recognition, the closed shop, and related issues, has varied greatly with the effort to organize labor and the attempts to prevent the spread of organization or to weaken it. It will be noted that the percentages ran particularly high in the earlier years of the century and again in the nineteen-thirties. From 1936 to 1939 the issue was involved in more than half of the disputes.

It is frequently asserted that labor loses more than it gains by going on strike. In spite of the waste involved in industrial warfare, any such statement is absurd if there is any case at all for unionism. For the strike is a necessary weapon if unionism is to function without compulsory arbitration and authoritative settlement of industrial disputes; also, the possible use of it may be quite effective in situations in which no strike occurs. Moreover, the long-run effects as well as the immediate outcome must be given consideration. These long-run effects do not lend themselves to quantitative measurement. But what have been the immediate results in terms of percentages of strikes won, lost, and compromised? The answer, in so far as it is available in our federal statistics, is contained in Table 9.

One of the outstanding facts is that in the more recent years, when organized labor has become more usual in industry and when there has been more pressure exercised by the public upon disputants, the percentage of compromises has been two or three times as large as in the 1880's and 1890's. The percentages won have, on the whole, exceeded the percentages lost by roughly one-seventh. Very strikingly, the percentages won run high in prosperous years, and low in depression years when the employers' front stiffens and strikes are more easily broken. Or, put the other way around, observe the percentages lost, rising in lean years to 54.5 in 1891, 53.9 in 1892, 50.6 in 1904, 56.2 in 1921, 46.8 in 1931, and 51.9 in 1932.

The Costs of Strikes.—It was once the practice of the Federal Government as well as of the governments of other leading countries to collect and publish data on wage and other losses caused by strikes. The effort to do so has, however, very largely been given up because of the difficulties involved in gathering the data and their shortcomings when obtained. As has been said, "Even an exact statement of the time lost through strikes, and the amount of money losses in wages, interest and profits due to stoppage of work, were such a statement possible, would give a very inadequate idea of their real cost to the worker, the employer, and the community in general, and the elaborate calculations of costs of strikes which make their appearance from time to time, generally under the title of estimates, are but mere guesses by the compiler, not statistical in character, and frequently incorrect in their conclusions."[1]   The wages of those who stop work can of course be calculated from the payroll and the duration of the suspension.   But how many of the strikers obtain other work meanwhile?   On the other hand, how many remain unemployed after a strike has been broken?   How far do successful strikers make up their losses, at least in part, by working more nearly full time or overtime when production is resumed?   What wage losses are visited on nonstriking workers?   Similar questions arise in connection with the employer's losses.   For example, how frequently and to what extent does the employer recoup as a result of sales made at a higher price than he would have realized in the absence of the suspension?   Again, is the employer's business crippled, say, because of loss of market connections, beyond the period of the strike?   Undoubtedly it is even more difficult to estimate the money losses of the "public" when that is undertaken, as it has been in connection with certain railway and other suspensions.

The number of days lost in strikes and lockouts is, however, a significant fact, and most countries report it along with the number of disputes and the number of workers directly involved.   Of course, the total and the average number of days lost vary with the number of disputes, the number of workers involved, and the duration of suspensions.[2]

The number of man-days lost is large, of course, but when it is spread over all industrial wage earners the time directly lost due to industrial disputes has usually been less than 1 per cent of the workdays in the year. This was true during the period 1916–1922, when the number of workers involved was largest in the United States until 1941.   During the early part of the depression and until 1933, the days lost materially decreased, from totals of 26,218,628 and 12,631,863 in 1927 and 1928, respectively, to 5,351,540 in 1929, 3,316,808 in 1930, 6,893,244 in 1931, and 10,502,033 in 1932.   In 1935, 15,456,337 days were lost; in 1936 the days lost receded to 13,901,956.   In 1937, an all-time high of 28,424,857 days was reached, but in 1938, it receded to 9,148,273.   In 1939 it advanced sharply to 17,812,219, only to fall to 6,700,872 in 1940.   The following year saw a tremendous increase to 23,047,556, approaching the 1937 level.[3]

---

[1] E. L. Whitney, "Cost of Strikes," *Monthly Labor Review*, vol. 11 (1920), p. 593.

[2] The average duration of strikes in the United States has been shown by Paul H. Douglas for the years 1881–1921, grouped into periods, *Journal of the American Statistical Association*, vol. 18 (1923), p. 871.   For the years 1916–1932, see *Monthly Labor Review*, vol. 36 (1933), p. 1303; for 1936–1941, see *ibid.*, vol. 44 (1937), p. 1229, vol. 46 (1938), p. 1198, vol. 48 (1939), p. 1128, vol. 50 (1940), p. 1096, vol. 52 (1941), p. 1105; vol. 54 (1942), p. 1121; for 1927–1936, see U. S. Bureau of Labor Statistics, *Bulletin* 651, pp. 51–54.

[3] U. S. Bureau of Labor Statistics *Monthly Labor Review*, vol. 52 (1941), p. 1092; vol. 54 (1941), p. 1109.

Space limitations preclude a corresponding review of the statistics of disputes in leading foreign countries.[1]　Were a review made, the data would present few important contrasts to those presented for the United States.　It is true of course that political strikes have been an interesting phenomenon in some of the European countries; political considerations have played a much more important part in union policy in most countries

[1] The British and German data are fairly typical of those published, year by year, by many of the European governments.　The German statistics of industrial disputes may be summarized as follows, the figures again being averages for the periods into which the years have been divided.　Source: *Reichsarbeitsblatt*, Nr. 6, Teil II, 1932, p. 78, for 1920–1930 data; earlier data from *Statistik des Deutschen Reichs*.

Period	Average number of disputes	Plants involved	Workers involved	Days lost	Days lost per striker
1899–1902	1,290	......	82,828		
1903–1907	2,248	......	214,336		
1908–1912	2,015	......	461,823		
1899–1913	2,114	11,410	510,644	8,006,791	15.7
1920–1925	3,387	40,223	1,538,854	23,322,907	15.2
1926–1930	565	6,725	332,826	6,975,805	21.0

Some students, not realizing the effects of the Taff Vale decision upon the use of the strike and the misleading nature of short-run trends, have drawn unwarranted conclusions from the British figures for the early years of this century.　The data for number of industrial disputes, number of workers directly involved, and total working days lost in Great Britain during the years 1893–1941 are shown in the following table.

INDUSTRIAL DISPUTES IN GREAT BRITAIN, BY PERIODS: 1893–1941[1]

Period	Average annual number of disputes beginning in period	Average annual number of workers involved in disputes beginning in period	Average annual number of working days lost
1893–1896	784	300,000	12,300,000
1897–1900	722	159,000	7,790,000
1901–1904	447	94,000	2,840,000
1905–1908	451	137,000	4,580,000
1909–1912	662	652,000	15,900,000
1913–1916	909	365,000	6,270,000
1917–1920	1,214	1,420,000	18,270,000
1921–1924	669	796,000	31,200,000
1925–1928	384	852,000[a]	43,187,000[a]
1929–1932	416	427,250	6,539,000
1933–1936	549	214,000	1,454,000
1937–1940	966	376,750	1,760,750
1941	1,241	358,000	1,080,000

[a] The averages for the period 1925–1928 were greatly affected by the "general strike" in 1926, in which 2,724,000 workers were directly involved and 162,000,000 days lost.　If 1926 is eliminated, the averages for the period were 224,000 workers involved and 3,505,000 working days lost.

[1] Data computed from International Labour Office, *Conciliation and Arbitration in Industrial Disputes* (1933), p. 159; Ministry of Labour reports; *Statistical Abstract for the United Kingdom for* 1937 (1939), p. 151; *Monthly Labor Review*, vol. 47 (1938), p. 46; *Labor Notes*, Labor Research Association, April, 1942, p. 8.

than they have in the United States and Canada. The data relating to the number of strikes and strikers for other countries, however, show variations from year to year and period to period similar to those occurring in the United States; they do not indicate any definite general trend. They do show interesting changes with the business cycle, the type of unionism, and other things mentioned above. Hence the relatively small number of strikes and strikers in most countries in comparatively recent years, a fact largely accounting for the generally favorable records in postwar as against the later pre-World War I years. But even the years marked by the largest number of strikes generally show a loss of one or two man-days per wage earner when spread over the entire wage-earning population. Thus in Great Britain during the period 1922–1925, the average loss of workers directly involved was something more than twenty days, but the total of man-days involved was only approximately 0.3 per cent of full working time for all wage earners. During the years 1927–1930, the immediate loss, when spread over all wage earners, decreased to one-fourth day per man or roughly to $\frac{1}{12}$ of 1 per cent of working time. In Germany the number of strikes, strikers, and days lost mounted to unusually high figures during the troubled period of 1920–1925. When the days lost are divided by the number of wage earners insured against sickness and unemployment, however, the average number of days lost per wage earner is found to have been roughly $1\frac{1}{2}$ and during the period 1926–1930, when the numbers of strikes, strikers, and days lost were all distinctly less than during the period 1899–1913, the corresponding average loss was less than $\frac{1}{2}$ day per man. Thus, strikes have been a much less important cause of loss of time by wage earners generally than have sickness and unemployment.[1]

The more important statistical detail relating to strikes has been presented in summary form. The strike problem is found in part in the facts given—the number of suspensions, the number of employees directly involved, and working time lost. At times the largeness of all of these, and their increase for some years together, are important factors in the problem. Other things also enter. One of these is the increasing dependence of industry upon industry, of urban community upon rural community and vice versa, and of those engaged in trade upon those engaged in industry, in an economic organization becoming more and more complex with the passing of time. Concrete cases exemplifying this will readily occur to the reader. This last-named factor suggests

[1] The time directly lost as a result of industrial disputes is not substantially different from that resulting from disabling industrial injury. The number of days lost through disabling sickness is very much larger and that through unemployment is several times larger than that directly lost through industrial disputes (cf. vol. II, Chaps. I, IV, and V). This comparison must not be carried too far, however, for there are other losses than of man-days. This is particularly true of losses caused by industrial disputes.

in turn another consideration of importance in stating the problem. It is not so much the number of strikes as important specific strikes that are so important to the public. The Pullman strike of 1894 was accompanied by material losses sustained by shippers, especially of perishable goods. The railway strike threatened in 1916, but prevented by the adoption of the Adamson Act, would have paralyzed the industrial United States. It was only because of the dire prospect confronting the country that this measure was hurriedly enacted by Congress. The coal strike of 1919 resulted in a real emergency; many industries were forced to operate on a short-time basis. The great anthracite strike early in the century undermined the economic activities of many localities in Pennsylvania while placing a burden upon consumers of anthracite coal. A telephone or telegraph strike is accompanied by more inconvenience and loss than one could realize until he had experienced one. A street-railway strike or a bus strike has been a sad experience in the life of the community concerned. It has been such experiences as these more than any one other thing that have begotten a public reaction against industrial warfare and a demand for government intervention in the settlement of industrial disputes, even in time of peace.

In the statistical summary, the relatively small amount of working time lost by strikes has been shown. That, however, does not mean that the sacrifice of those directly involved and their dependents does not become acute in the case of prolonged suspensions. Witness the plight of women and children during the great anthracite strike early in the century, during the many coal strikes in West Virginia and Colorado, and during the steel strike of 1919. The fact that much of the cost is not spread, and that its incidence falls upon a limited number, with crushing weight, is an important phase of the problem.

Still another phase needs only to be mentioned for it has been discussed in the immediately preceding chapter. That factor is found in violation of law, in disorder, in undermined and unrepresentative government, and in substantial direct costs met by taxpayers.

Such are some of the more important considerations entering into a statement of the problem. The matter should not, however, be dismissed without a further observation. The outcome of industrial warfare depends chiefly upon might. Though strikes and lockouts may have a sobering effect, though they may at times "clear the atmosphere" while a government decision may not, might does not guarantee the most reasonable solution. Hence the position of many persons that compulsory arbitration is the better way to dispose of industrial disputes, and especially of those in industries containing a large element of public interest.

SETTLEMENT OF DISPUTES WITHIN INDUSTRY

Of course strikes occur all too frequently among the more radical groups, and especially among those with communistic leanings. Such groups see in the strike the great weapon of the revolution that is their main objective and may wish only breathing spells between suspensions. But the typical union, as well as the typical employer, knows well the costs of industrial warfare; most unions and most employers will ordinarily go far to avoid an open break.   In far more than 90 per cent of their negotiations, employers and unions in such countries as the United States and Great Britain reach agreements without a strike or the intervention of outside parties.   Successful bargaining is the typical, strikes and lockouts the incidental, thing where the law gives freedom to strike.   But a strike may occur (1) when a union seeks recognition at the hands of employers who will not recognize it, or (2) when questions of interpretation or observance of agreements in effect are not agreed upon or settled by machinery established by the parties in interest for that purpose, or (3) when differences as to the terms of a new agreement to replace one expiring are not ironed out, or when employers desire to rid themselves of union relationships and operate on an open-shop basis. It is in one or the other of these several situations that industrial warfare develops.

It is obvious that, unless public authority is exercised, there will be many obstinate fights in industries in which unions are seeking recognition, for most employers desire to continue to manage their businesses as they have in the past, and many of them are afraid of what will happen if they "tie up with the union."   Of course the threat of strike may be sufficient to win union recognition in an industry when business is very prosperous and large profits would be sacrificed by suspensions, as during the World War I period.   Of course, also, threat of strike may be sufficient to secure recognition at the hands of an individual publisher or coal operator or clothing manufacturer when the market is extensively organized and an actual strike would have the effect of diverting business to competitors continuing to operate.   And, finally, in concrete instances employers will readily grant recognition, and even encourage unionism, where the label is of great importance in marketing the product, or where the boycott of nonunion products might be disastrous, or where a monopolistic arrangement may be effected with union support.   Nevertheless, most unions have had to fight in order to secure recognition, as did the anthracite miners forty years ago, the bituminous miners of West Virginia, Kentucky, Colorado, and elsewhere on many occasions, and the clothing workers in scores of instances.   Until the adoption of industrial codes beginning in 1933, the specific industry had no machinery for determining whether union recognition should be granted by independent employers.   A large percentage of the most bitter fights have been over recognition or continued acceptance of unionism.   The issue is non-arbitrable and is most difficult to mediate.   But now, as has been noted in our earlier discussion,[1] under the Railway Labor Act, under the

---

[1] Cf. supra, pp. 520–523.

National Labor Relations Act, and under similar legislation adopted by some of the states, an organization appropriate for the purpose of collective bargaining and employing proper procedures must be recognized and its representatives bargained with. This compulsory recognition and the employer's obligation to bargain, in so far as it is applicable and effective, eliminates this type of dispute at the source. In this one respect at least, this legislation is in the interest of industrial peace.

The recognition of a union and the successful negotiation of a contract with it do not end all occasion for disputes. Indeed, a joint agreement is sometimes accompanied by a multitude of grievances and demands for adjustment. But strikes over differences of interpretation of agreements, over charges of nonobservance caused by different interpretations, and over grievances in general have become exceptional in most industries in which organization and collective bargaining have endured for any length of time. In Great Britain machinery within the trade for settling such disputes appeared generations ago and has long been the usual thing. The absence of such devices is exceptional. In less degree the same may be said of the United States. Here, most collective agreements limit or prohibit recourse to suspension of work and provide machinery and procedures for the settlement of disputes. The provision agreed upon may be for conciliation only, or for conciliation and arbitration. The arrangements made are of different types and differ greatly in detail. Though the subject is both interesting and very important, our discussion of it must be brief. We shall attempt to show and exemplify types of arrangement and explain and evaluate them.

The simple, rather primitive provision found in thousands of local collective agreements is that disputes (and requests for adjustment) shall be taken up by the officers of the union and the employer or employers concerned. Possibly the president of the international to which the local is affiliated will intervene in the more important cases in the event of deadlock.

Widespread, also, is the provision for a standing committee to which disputes and grievances shall be referred. For example, a recent machinists' agreement in the Chicago district provided that:

"Should any difference arise in reference to the rules contained in this agreement that cannot be satisfactorily adjusted by the works superintendent and shop committee, such matters in dispute shall be referred to the proper officer of the company and a representative of the International Association of Machinists, who shall have access to the shop. There shall be no strike or lockout until the two last referred to fail to agree."

A more typical example is found in the joint standing committees provided for in the agreements entered into since 1887 by the several printing-trades unions and the Chicago newspaper publishers. As summarized by Dr. Fagan,

"In all of the agreements both conciliation and arbitration have been provided for. The ordinary course followed in the case of a grievance or a difference in the interpretation of a clause of the agreement has been for the chairman of the chapel to take the matter up with the foreman. An officer of the local union might then take the question to the publisher, or his representative. If a satisfactory settlement could not be secured by such a conference the next step has been to refer the grievance to the Joint Standing Committee. All of the local agreements of all the unions have provided for the appointment of a Joint Standing Committee to consist of two representatives of the associated employers, and two of the Union. All questions of interpretation of the agreement, or of any alleged violations of its terms, have been referred to this committee for adjustment, provided the differences could not be otherwise settled. . . . When the Joint Standing Committee has been unable to reach an agreement, the differences have been referred to arbitration. . . .

"The method of organizing the board of arbitration has been for each party to select a member, or two if the board was to consist of five members, and for these parties to select a chairman."[1]

Such provisions as these are, of course, almost always accompanied by a prohibition of stoppages or strikes. Possibly some penalty for violation is incorporated; more likely the international may have been empowered to inflict penalties upon contract-breaking locals.

The simpler arrangements do not go beyond providing for conciliation. When conciliation fails, as it is obvious that it will more or less frequently, arbitration—with a neutral chairman or, possibly, an entire board of neutral persons—may be resorted to, but in the absence of specific provision to this effect this is purely voluntary, and no explicit requirement of it or machinery for it is provided for. But deadlocks and delays experienced in the settling of disputes have resulted in the addition of arbitration provisions to those relating to conciliation until they have become fairly prevalent.

The building industry of Chicago is rather typical of the industry in the larger cities of the United States, in so far as it is unionized. In Chicago, since 1915, most of the trades have been under so-called standard agreements. These prohibit sympathetic strikes and all stoppages, including those developing out of jurisdiction disputes. Each trade has a board, with equal representation of the union and the associated employers, to which all disputes are to be referred. In case of deadlock, which frequently occurs, an issue goes to arbitration, with a neutral chairman or umpire whose decision is in theory final and binding. There

---

[1] Harrison B. Fagan, *Industrial Relations in the Chicago Newspaper Industry* (unpublished Ph.D. Dissertation, The University of Chicago, 1930), pp. 91–92.

have been, however, some appeals to the Joint Conference Board, which is the conference body and governs the entire industry. The special procedure in the case of a jurisdiction dispute has been indicated elsewhere.[1]

The internationals in the printing trades have generally favored arbitration. Hence many of the local agreements, especially those in the newspaper branch, provide for the conciliation and arbitration of grievances and also of differences on changes in the wage scale arising during the term covered by the contract. Here, again, the Chicago agreements are fairly typical. Those between the Pressmen and the Publishers have for years provided for the conciliation and arbitration of grievances and differences somewhat as follows: A dispute unadjusted in the pressroom is referred to the manager and the Union. If the difference remains unadjusted, it is then referred to the Joint Standing Committee, which consists of two representatives of the Publishers' Association and two representatives of the Union. If this committee deadlocks, as it occasionally does, the unsettled issue is submitted to arbitration, with an outside chairman selected by the interested parties for the specific case. The decision rendered by the board is conclusive and final save for the right of appeal under the International Arbitration Agreement, which, with renewals at the close of five-year periods, has been continuously operative since 1923. This agreement has laid down the provisions and procedures for local arbitration as well as for arbitration, upon appeal, by the International Board. This board has consisted of three direct representatives of the pressmen and three representatives of the publishers and a neutral chairman drawn from a panel of chairmen. Save for the device of a panel, which has avoided delay and friction when a board has had to be established for a specific case, and which at the same time has avoided dependence upon one impartial chairman, this arrangement is essentially the same as that originated by the International Typographical Union and the American Newspaper Publishers' Association in 1901, and, renewed and revised a number of times, maintained until 1922.[2] The agreement was not then renewed, chiefly because the Union refused to submit work rules in its International Laws to arbitration and because of the open-shop movement of the time, centering in Indianapolis, which was headquarters for both the Union and the Association. Following the example of the compositors, the Photo-Engravers' and the Stereotypers' international unions entered into like arbitration agreements with the Association, but these came to an end with the failure to renew the parent agreement. It should be added, however, that, without renewal of the agreement, international arbitrations continued to be resorted to in

[1] See Chap. VI, pp. 290–300.

[2] For an excellent history of this agreement, see David Weiss, "History of Arbitration in the American Newspaper Publishing Industry," *Monthly Labor Review*, vol. 17 (1923), pp. 15–33.

composing-room cases as frequently after, as previous to, 1922. The explanation of this fact is that arbitration is regarded as the reasonable and economical way to correct grievances and to decide differences as to scales of wages and hours in the newspaper industry.

Usually, when recourse is taken to arbitration, a new board is created for each case. This procedure frequently gives rise to much delay, waste of time, and increased discontent because of the difficulty involved in securing agreement upon an arbitrator. There may be a desire to insure a favorable decision when selecting him; in any event the issue is all-important at the time and unusual care is exercised "to avoid mistakes." Sometimes weeks or even months are consumed in securing a neutral chairman. It is obvious that this will be accompanied by friction and dissatisfaction. The feeling being very widespread that, if a permanent chairman is selected, a premium will be placed upon arbitration as against conciliation, which is likely to give better results where technical problems are involved, and that a chairman may become undermined and constitute a problem, most groups doing anything to smooth the way of arbitration have introduced devices for hastening the process of securing a chairman for the given case. Possibly, after a specified number of days have elapsed, a chairman is selected by lot or is selected by a judge or the mayor or someone else. But in the needle trades and in a limited number of other instances, where there is a considerable volume of work to be done and where there is more than the usual faith in arbitration, the device of a standing board and permanent chairman has been adopted.

The best known of these standing boards, with their salaried chairmen, have been those in the men's and women's garment trades. In the men's clothing industry in Chicago, for more than twenty years there was at Hart, Schaffner & Marx, the Trade Board, with a salaried chairman. This board served as the trial court. The chairman served also as chairman of the Cutters' Commission and of the Price Committee, the one having to do with matters pertaining to the cutting room, the other with the setting of piece rates and the recording of work specifications. Over the Trade Board was the Arbitration Board, also with an impartial chairman.[1] This latter board served as an appeal court, as the court of first instance in cases involving the application of new principles, and as the board for deciding contested issues involved in the formulation of new agreements.

In 1919 a second trade board was established to dispose of cases arising in the other clothing shops in Chicago. There was also for six years a standing Arbitration Board, but this was really that functioning at Hart, Schaffner & Marx as well. In New York, Rochester, and other

---

[1] The Board of Arbitration was created in 1911, when the great strike of that year ended and the first agreement was entered into. The Trade Board was instituted later to handle the multitude of small cases.

clothing centers the same general arbitration system has obtained, but only in Chicago and Baltimore has more than one board been maintained.[1] Roughly corresponding machinery and procedures have been employed in the various branches of manufacture of women's wear—chiefly in New York, Cleveland, and Chicago. Thousands of decisions, important and relatively unimportant and on a great variety of things, have been rendered by these impartial chairmen.[2]

The strength and the weakness of standing boards and permanent chairmen have been shown by experience. On the one hand, cases can be disposed of without delay; the impartial chairman becomes qualified because he comes to know the techniques, people, and customs of the trade; with the accumulation of decisions rendered by one or two chairmen, there is more or less consistency in the rulings, certain principles are applied, and a common law of the industry is gradually evolved.[3] But, on the other hand, not all impartial chairmen have functioned so successfully as was desired; the easy accessibility of a court has tended strongly to cause it to become congested with many inconsequential cases and to undermine conciliation, which all admit is the better method of settlement when effective without undue delay—a tendency that the abler impartial chairmen have with more or less success tried to correct; perhaps too much common law has developed; in any event in a changing situation some of it has been eliminated or revised by agreement. On the whole, arbitration, with standing boards, has worked fairly well in the needle trades and in a few others. Nevertheless, most unions emphasize conciliation, and not a few regard arbitration as a necessary evil to be accepted now and then in the administration of collective agreements or as something best avoided altogether.[4]

Before this particular phase of conciliation and arbitration is dismissed, a brief description should be given of the machinery and procedures in the two branches of the coal industry.

Collective agreements, with provision for conciliation and arbitration of grievances and disputes arising under them, have obtained contin-

[1] The two trade boards and the Arbitration Board in the Chicago market were merged into one board some years ago. The one board now serves the entire market, and perhaps not more than a dozen cases go to formal hearing in the course of a year.

[2] The decisions are written and, for the greater part, available in mimeographed or printed form.

[3] This has been discussed by many writers, but best by Paul Wander. See *Clothing Workers of Chicago*, 1910–1922 (Chicago Joint Board, Amalgamated Clothing Workers of America, 1922), Part III.

[4] In the organized stove trade arbitration has been avoided and adjustments made by conciliation. Disputes not settled locally are referred to the presidents of the Molders' Union and the Association. These officials, or their representatives, have settled all but a few disputes, which have then been settled by the full conference board. Peace has been maintained except where an employer has decided to operate on an open-shop basis, as some have in recent years.

uously in the anthracite industry since 1903.[1] There has been a board
of conciliation, consisting of one miner and one operator from each of
the three districts in Pennsylvania, and an umpire or arbitrator, appointed
by one of the judges of the third judicial circuit of the United States.
Under the machinery and procedure developed by 1912, a grievance is
taken up by the workman and the foreman. If not adjusted, the grievance is then submitted to the mine superintendent and the pit committee
of three, perhaps with a local union official or the district union member
of the board of conciliation assisting. If the grievance is not then satisfactorily disposed of, it goes to the board of conciliation, which operates
on a district basis or as a whole. If conciliation fails, the grievance goes
automatically to the umpire, whose decision is final. Formerly there
was much delay in disposing of many cases and this was a source of great
discontent, but for years (since 1923) the requirement has been that
grievances referred to the board of conciliation shall be answered within
fifteen days and heard within thirty days of date of filing. The board
must render a decision within thirty days or refer the dispute to the
umpire, and the umpire must render his decision within thirty days.[2]
All stoppages are prohibited.

Practically all the collective bargaining in bituminous coal mining
has been accompanied by more or less elaborate machinery for the conciliation and arbitration of grievances arising under the various agreements. Indeed, it was in connection with the interesting interstate
agreement of 1886 that elaborate local and interstate machinery for the
settlement of disputes was first experimented with in the United States.
With the renewal of collective bargaining on a fairly stable basis in the
Central Competitive District in 1898, adjustment machinery reappeared,
and it accompanied the extension of agreements in the "outlying territory" in the more recent years. But, unlike the provision in the eighties,
most of the machinery has been on a state or subdistrict basis.[3]

The machinery and procedures established for conciliation and arbitration of disputes in the coal industry have varied from one part of the
country to another and have undergone more or less change in some of
the states. A description of the more recent system in Illinois will,
however, suffice for our purposes.

---

[1] The earlier history of collective bargaining in anthracite does not concern us here.
For it and the matters touched upon in this discussion, see A. E. Suffern, *Conciliation and
Arbitration in the Coal Industry of America* (1915); the same author's *The Coal Miner's
Struggle for Industrial Status* (1926), especially Chap. 9; and Edgar Sydenstricker, "Col-
lective Bargaining in the Anthracite Coal Industry," U. S. Bureau of Labor Statistics,
Bulletin 191 (1916).

[2] These rules are frequently not observed.

[3] For an excellent discussion of the subject, see A. E. Suffern, *The Coal Miner's Struggle
for Industrial Status*, Chap. 9. See also Louis Block, *Labor Agreements in Coal Mines*
(1931).

All stoppages and strikes during the life of the joint contract were prohibited; for a time fines were assessed for violations (under the "penalty clause"). A grievance, say over payment for "dead work," the distribution of cars, the condition of the workplace, or discharge, was taken up by the miner with the mine manager or foreman. If unadjusted, it was taken up with the management by the pit committee. Thence it was handled by the miners' subdistrict president and the manager. If not satisfactorily disposed of at that stage, the grievance was taken up by a member of the Miners' Executive Board and a representative of the Coal Operators' Association and, if they disagreed, then by the full joint board of miners and operators. Reaching this point, it may have been referred to a special commission or have been considered only by the board. Conciliation failing, the grievance was submitted to arbitration.

Perhaps 85 per cent of the complaints, and a still larger percentage of the less important ones, were settled locally and without being recorded. Of those not locally settled and referred in writing to the other, nonlocal agencies mentioned above, there were 6,695 during the twelve years, Dec. 1, 1908, to Nov. 30, 1920. This was an average of some 500 or 600 cases per year, a figure corresponding roughly to the number of Trade Board complaints in the clothing industry in Chicago in the earlier years. More than 90 per cent of these were filed on behalf of the workers. Some 62.6 per cent involved wages (payment for dead work, allowance for loss of time, etc.); 13.1 per cent alleged discrimination in some respect or other (workplace, distribution of cars, etc.); 2.3 per cent involved working conditions (water, ventilation, etc.); 15.7 per cent alleged unjust discharge; 22.2 per cent involved discipline otherwise than by discharge (fines, dockage for loading bone and rock, etc.). Over against these, 6.3 per cent involved strikes and lockouts, the latter few in number, while 2.6 per cent were lodged against union officials. Of the complaints, 4.1 per cent were withdrawn; almost 70 per cent were settled by an executive board member and an operators' commissioner; 24 per cent were settled by the joint executive boards or by special commissions; 1.9 per cent were decided by arbitration. Thus roughly 2 per cent of the cases were settled by arbitration, the great mass by conciliation. Unlike the situation in the clothing industries at times, conciliation has been emphasized in the coal industry as against arbitration. Indeed, because of worker opposition to it, for years the submission of a dispute to arbitration was not automatic in Illinois, but voluntary on the part of union and operator. Interesting, and somewhat in contrast to what has occurred in some other industries, the largest number of the disputes here analyzed, 39.0 per cent, were decided in favor of the operator. A considerably smaller number, 31.7 per cent, were decided in favor of the workers; 16.9 per cent were compromised, the decision holding in part for the operator, in part for the workers.[1]

Without presenting further concrete detail, it may be said that machinery for settling disputes arising under collective agreements and for making necessary adjustments has contributed substantially to the maintenance of industrial peace in industries in which the workers have become articulate through organization. This, however, does not mean that there have been no stoppages or shop strikes or lockouts in violation of explicit provisions of the agreement, for these have occurred in both branches of the coal industry, in building construction, in the printing trades, and in the manufacture of men's and of women's clothing. At times direct action has been resorted to and the contractual requirement of reference of disputes to the machinery established ignored; now and then settlements or decisions arrived at by conciliation or arbitration have been rejected; but it must be agreed that all of these have been exceptional. The fact is that the settlement of even seemingly inconsequential disputes is important in preventing the accumulation of discontent that leads to protest through direct action and that the needed cooperative spirit in industry has been given a better opportunity to develop. Moreover, the use of arbitration in settling disputes and contested changes in the "scale" during the life of a joint agreement has naturally given rise to the question, why not arbitrate differences relative to the terms of a new agreement to replace the one expiring?

Generally speaking, both employers and unions, while agreeing to arbitrate a specific dispute, have not been inclined to bind themselves in advance to arbitrate all differences arising in the negotiation of agreements. Indeed, some union groups whose experience with arbitration awards has been rather or quite unsatisfactory are definitely opposed to compulsory arbitration, even though self-imposed. The anthracite coal miners furnished an example, when, in 1927, they stoutly resisted the operators' proposal to incorporate in the agreement a provision that issues not agreed upon in conference on the terms of the agreement should be arbitrated. The unions in the building trades and many others might equally well be cited. And so might groups of employers; it scarcely needs to be pointed out that the attitudes of employers toward arbitration are determined in much the same way. This does not mean that the unions are definitely opposed to arbitration, but that they wish to be free to reject it; whether or not they will advocate or accept or reject it when an issue arises depends in part upon the degree of radicalism in the union, in part upon past experience, in part upon the relative advantages of striking or arbitrating in the concrete situation. Then there may be fear—and experience in some industries has shown substantial ground

---

[1] The others were withdrawn, referred back, etc.

for it—that an advance arrangement for arbitration of issues in the formulation of a new contract will beget excessive demands and stand in the way of and undermine negotiation in conference. Arbitration may militate against as well as protect and further collective bargaining.

Nevertheless there have been a considerable number of agreements in which compulsory arbitration of the terms of the new agreement has been provided for. In the newspaper industry this arrangement has been fairly common;[1] in the needle trades it has been only less so; in book and job printing and some other industries numerous instances of it will be found, but they are to be regarded as exceptional rather than common features of the joint agreements entered into.

Fairly typical of the newspaper contracts in the larger centers of population[2] are the agreement effective July 1, 1937, to June 30, 1940 between the Publishers' Association of New York and Pressmen's Union No. 2 and the Pittsburgh agreement between the corresponding parties, entered into in 1937. The former read, in part:

"This contract shall become effective July 1st, 1937, and continue for a term of three years ending June 30th, 1940, and thereafter until the contract is changed in the following manner.

"Either party desiring to change the contract after June 30, 1940, shall submit to the other party in writing the changes desired, not less than sixty days nor more than 90 days before June 30, 1940, or any anniversary thereof, and the other party shall, within thirty days after receiving such notice of desired changes, deliver its answer in writing. If at the end of thirty days of conciliation there should remain a difference between the desires of the two parties such differences shall, in the same manner as all other differences, be referred to the Joint Conference Committee hereinafter provided for settlement. In case of inability of the Joint Conference Committee to agree upon the change after 30 days,

---

[1] The greatest factor entering into the explanation of this is the importance to the publisher of continuous and regular publication.

[2] Typographical Union no. 16 (Chicago) consistently opposed the position of the International while the International Arbitration Agreement was in effect and would not accept the arbitration agreement, which was so widely accepted. Its agreement with the Chicago publishers, effective 1927 to 1929, provided in part, that "Four months in advance of the expiration of the three year term hereof, either party may give the other notice in writing of its intention to open negotiations; . . . A conference between the two contracting parties shall be held within ten days from date of such notice, and negotiations shall be begun, which negotiations shall be of a continuous character . . . until finally concluded. *Nothing herein shall be construed as obligating either party hereto to arbitrate differences respecting an agreement to be effective after the expiration date of this agreement.*" It may be added that this agreement expired May 21, 1929, after which time there were conferences, proposals and counterproposals, threat of strike, and consideration of arbitration until an arbitration was held in the later weeks of 1932. During all these months the terms of the expired agreement remained in effect.

the matter shall then, upon motion of either party, be referred to arbitration as hereinafter provided for.

"A Joint Conference Committee, composed of two representatives of the party of the first part and two representatives of the party of the second part, shall be appointed as soon as practicable after the signing of this contract; the members representing the party of the first part shall be selected by the Local Publishers and the members representing the party of the second part shall be selected by the Local Union; and in case of vacancy, absence or refusal of either of such representatives to act, another shall be appointed in his place immediately. To this committee shall be referred all questions which may arise as to the scale of wages provided herein, the construction to be placed upon any clause of this contract, or alleged violation thereof, which cannot be settled otherwise, and such Joint Conference Committee shall meet within five days when any question or difference shall have been referred to it for decision by the executive officers of either party to this contract. All decisions of the Joint Conference Committee shall be final and binding on both parties and it shall require a majority vote of the four members to make a decision. Should the Joint Conference Committee be unable to agree within thirty days, then it shall, upon motion of either party, refer the matter to a Local Board of Arbitration, whose decision shall be final and binding. Said arbitration to be conducted under the Code of Procedure as provided in the agreement between the American Newspaper Publishers' Association and the International Printing Pressmen and Assistants' Union of North America.

"It is understood and agreed that the Joint Conference Committee provided herein has final jurisdiction over any and all disputes arising out of discharge cases.

"It is also agreed that all questions regarding a new contract or scale to become effective at the expiration of this contract which cannot be settled by conciliation shall be decided by arbitration as provided in the International Arbitration Agreement now existing between the A.N.P.A. and the I.P.P. & A.U. The International Arbitration Agreement is made a part of this contract in the same manner as if recited at length over the signatures of the parties hereto. It is agreed that as soon as may conveniently be done, following ratification of this contract, the parties hereto will execute the International Agreement in quadruplicate as provided therein.

"In all cases where appeal is made to the Joint Conference Committee and/or the Arbitration Board, pending the hearing and determination of such issue, any order given by the foreman responsible for such issue shall prevail and be complied with, and all work shall continue without interruption or curtailment."

The corresponding provision of the Pittsburgh agreement reads:

"In the event of any differences arising as to the interpretation of this agreement or any question arising not covered by this agreement which cannot be settled between the Publishers in question and the employee or employees, such differences or dispute shall be submitted to a standing committee hereby created. Such standing committee shall consist of not over three (3) representatives from the Union and not over three (3) representatives from the Publishers. This standing committee shall make earnest effort to come to an agreement upon the matter in dispute, and in the event this standing committee fails to agree within fifteen (15) days after the matter in dispute has been submitted to them, the dispute shall be submitted to arbitration; the plan of arbitration to be the same as provided for elsewhere in this agreement. It is understood that pending completion of such arbitration, all work shall proceed without interruption, but that the decision shall be retroactive.

"In the event the Pittsburgh Newspaper Printing Pressmen's Union No. 9 and the Publishers, parties to this agreement, fail to negotiate a new agreement within ninety (90) days as provided for in this agreement, or the standing committee fails to reach a decision regarding a dispute under the contract, the matter shall then be referred to arbitration; the arbitration board consisting of five (5) members, two (2) to be chosen by the Publishers and two (2) by the Union; the fifth (5th) to be agreed upon by the above four (4) and all work shall proceed without interruption pending negotiation or arbitration. In the event either party is dissatisfied with the award, then an appeal shall be taken in accordance with the International Arbitration Agreement between the American Newspaper Publishers' Association and the International Printing Pressmen and Assistants' Union of North America."

These New York and Pittsburgh agreements, it may be added, ran in terms of the system of arbitration established by the International Union and the American Newspaper Publishers' Association. Though the acceptance of an arbitration agreement is voluntary on the part of both the local union and the publisher or publishers' association, such agreements have become common in the larger cities.

In the needle trades there have been many agreements providing for the arbitration of disputes over the terms of a new agreement when the conference method failed. The agreement between the Amalgamated Clothing Workers and Hart, Schaffner & Marx is a good example. The arrangement was general in the Chicago market for some years, beginning with 1919. Because of the opposition of some of the manufacturers, however, most of the more recent agreements have provided for the arbitration of only those disputes arising under and concerning an existing contract.

Except, possibly, for the arbitration agreement (the Protocol) in the cloak and suit industry of New York, adopted in 1910 and operative for some years, the fullest application of the principle of arbitration has been found in that part of the shoe industry organized under the Boot and Shoe Workers' Union. Owing to the enthusiastic advocacy of the principle by Mr. Tobin, long president of that international organization, it has been common since the early 1890's to sign agreements without termination date, *i.e.*, to run indefinitely, and providing for the arbitration of all grievances and of all disputes over scales not disposed of in conference. In much of the industry concerned it has been customary to select an arbitrator to decide a specific case as it arose, but in Massachusetts, by far the most important area involved, the agreements have stipulated that the State Board of Conciliation and Arbitration should serve in this capacity. To an extent, the unusually good record of that particular state board is explained in this way.

But, as has been stated above, self-imposed compulsory arbitration of the terms of a proposed agreement has remained more or less exceptional. Nor has the trend been altogether in favor of arbitration. In a very considerable number of instances, after a trial, jointly agreed upon compulsory arbitration has been discarded. The history of the New York Protocol presents a case in point. It is doubtful whether, taking American unionized industry as a whole, the acceptance of the principle of arbitration is as widespread as it was during the "honeymoon" period of collective bargaining early in the century. In any event, the emphasis is placed upon conciliation. Yet, in spite of the fact that only after collective arrangements have been effected can any machinery established in industry function, and in spite of the limited acceptance of self-imposed compulsory arbitration and of reversions to direct action, the provision developed within industry for settling disputes is by far the most important for discussion in connection with the methods of industrial peace in the United States, as well as in Great Britain. Quite appropriately, in both of these countries the main efforts of most governmental agencies and semipublic and civic organizations have been designed to strengthen trade machinery for disposing of the trades' disputes and to avoid so functioning as to weaken it.[1]

MEDIATION[2] AND ARBITRATION BY AMERICAN STATE AGENCIES

In spite of what the unions and employers have done to provide for the conciliation and arbitration of disputes in organized industry, the problem stated in the first section of this chapter has remained. The,

---

[1] Wartime is exceptional. Continuous production is then so necessary that wastes of one kind or another are usually not tolerated. State arbitration machinery may then weaken that provided by joint agreements.

[2] The terms "mediation" and "conciliation" are often used interchangeably. Technically, however, conciliation refers to the adjustment of disputes by the parties in interest, mediation to the intervention of an outside person.

at times, large number of strikes, specific strikes giving rise to emergency situations, the hardships experienced and the losses sustained by those involved in industrial warfare, the problem of disorder, and the fact that fighting power does not guarantee satisfactory solution of issues have aroused more or less interest on the part of the public and called forth attempts to cope with the problem through private, civic, and public agencies.

Certain institutions, such as the National Civic Federation in years past and the American Arbitration Association at present, have at times been distinctly helpful in the cause of industrial peace.[1] So, also, have some of the religious organizations. Because of space limitations, we must, however, limit our attention to intervention by governmental agencies.

Without express provision of law, the President of the United States, governors, and mayors have on numerous occasions intervened in disputes in an effort to maintain or to restore industrial peace.[2] An outstanding instance was the role played by President Theodore Roosevelt in the early years of this century in making arbitration possible in the anthracite coal industry. Less well known is the part played by Governor Pinchot (Pennsylvania) in 1927 in ironing out the difficulties in the same industry after all other efforts had failed. Equally outstanding were the activities of Governor Smith of New York in the 1920's and of Governor Murphy, of Michigan, in 1937. In numerous instances mayors have functioned in the same way in connection with strikes of importance in their localities.

State Machinery.—At some time or other almost all the American states have adopted laws providing for intervention in industrial disputes.[3] For the most part, these laws have been enacted when the number of strikes was rapidly increasing, or, and more important, their enactment has followed closely upon outstanding disturbances, such as the riots of 1878, the railway strikes of 1886, the Pullman strike of 1894, the coal strike of 1919, and the upheavals of 1936–1937. With few exceptions the legislation has been the product of an intense but more or less temporary public interest.

---

[1] The American Arbitration Association had in April, 1942, panels of arbitrators in 1,600 cities. In the first few months of 1942, 114 A.F. of L. and C.I.O. unions made use of its facilities, and the number of disputes handled increased 106 per cent over the corresponding period of the preceding year. Almost all these disputes were referred to it in accordance with arbitration clauses in collective agreements. *New York Times*, Apr. 22, 1942.

[2] For an account of interventions by the President, see Edward Berman, *Labor Disputes and the President*, Columbia University Studies in History, Economics, and Public Law, no. 249 (1924).

[3] In 1938, such laws were to be found in thirty-five of the forty-eight states. Since then eight states have enacted such laws, some of them replacing earlier ones. Missouri repealed its law in 1939.

Several different types of measures have been adopted. Viewed in terms of the type of machinery created or employed, it may be noted that a few states, including Kansas and Pennsylvania, years ago made provision for setting up local arbitration boards, these perhaps centering in the county court. Laws have been enacted in Arkansas, Georgia, Indiana, Iowa, Nevada, and other states, authorizing the establishment by the governor or the department of labor of special boards to settle the specific disputes giving rise to their appointment. Arkansas, Georgia, Indiana, South Carolina, South Dakota, and Washington have empowered the commissioner of labor or the chief of the bureau of labor statistics to intervene in an effort to settle labor disputes. In addition, the more recently adopted laws have usually provided for the appointment of one or more mediators to assist the commissioner or bureau in settling disputes. Similarly, a few states have charged other state officials than these with intervention as an incidental function. A large number of the states legislating, including some of those already mentioned, have, however, created standing state boards, generally known as state boards of conciliation and arbitration,[1] or, since 1911, have required the state industrial commission, as in Wisconsin, formerly, and in Massachusetts, to mediate industrial disputes as one division of its work.

With few exceptions, the state boards have consisted of three or five men, representing different economic interests, and paid $3 to $10 per day for the limited number of days they functioned in the course of the year. In Massachusetts alone was there a salaried board functioning continuously through a long period of years—until the industrial commission replaced it. At present the state board in several states is simply a part of the industrial commission, consisting of certain designated officials, or the commission itself. In such cases, the officials are, of course, on regular and, presumably, adequate salaries.

Most of the state legislation, save that creating some of the permanent state boards or industrial commissions, has been all but futile. Seldom were local boards set up; in only one locality (in western Pennsylvania) was anything accomplished by them. The same may be said of nearly all the laws authorizing the appointment of special boards or commissions. The accomplishments of the commissioners of labor or the chief of the bureau of labor statistics have amounted to little, except in a very few states where full-time mediators have been appointed. For the most part, these officials have been minor politicians, meriting little confidence and unfitted for the task of intervention. Moreover, charged with a variety of duties, they have usually regarded the particular task of mediation as an incidental one and have neglected it. Broadly speaking,

[1] Among the states with laws providing for a state board of conciliation and arbitration or a state mediation board are Connecticut, Maine, Maryland, Michigan, Montana, New Hampshire, New York, Oklahoma, and Oregon.

the only serious attempts to cope with the problem of industrial disputes have been made by some of the permanent state boards, the industrial commissions, and the Kansas Industrial Court, which was created to administer the Industrial Court Act of 1920.

Save in a few instances American state legislation has stopped short of compulsory arbitration in any form or of placing a time limitation on strikes. South Carolina, in 1922, enacted a law providing for the compulsory arbitration of street-railway disputes occurring in cities of specified size, provided one of the parties initiated a case. The law has been quite ineffective; nothing more need be said concerning it. The Kansas Industrial Court Act placed a ban on strikes, and much else, in certain industries, and provided for the adjudication of disputes. In connection with our discussion of compulsory arbitration, in a section of the next chapter, we shall have occasion to discuss the Kansas experiment briefly. Likewise, the Colorado act of 1915, modeled after the Canadian act, and the Michigan and Minnesota legislation of 1939 will be noted in the later section devoted to the compulsory investigation of disputes with time limitation on strikes and lockouts.[1] At this point we shall limit our discussion to an examination of the procedures and accomplishments of other states establishing state boards of conciliation and arbitration or state industrial commissions serving as such.[2]

The state board has been empowered to intervene in disputes in an effort to maintain or re-establish industrial peace through its mediation, and, this failing, to attempt to secure agreement to arbitrate the issues involved. In more recent years, the laws of a comparatively large number of states have authorized, and in exceptional cases required, the board to investigate and report on the merits of the issues in the more important disputes in which the other procedures are spurned or fail.

The theory of such laws is that intervention by the board may result in conferences by the parties in interest when none has been held or when those held have been discontinued, or that the mediators will act as go-betweens; that helpful suggestions can perhaps be made looking toward a composing of differences; or that an understanding may be reached with the mediators when one party to the dispute will not recognize or deal directly with the other. A further theory is that, when mediation fails, the parties immediately interested will, under moral

---

[1] Chap. XIV, pp. 791–792.

[2] For discussions of the constitution and functioning of state boards, see: John R. Commons and John B. Andrews, *Principles of Labor Legislation* (1936), Chap. 7; Ting Tsz Ko, *Governmental Methods of Adjusting Labor Disputes in North America and Australasia* [Columbia University Studies in History, Economics, and Public Law, vol. 123 (1926)], Chap. 2; George E. Barnett and David A. McCabe, *Mediation, Investigation and Arbitration in Industrial Disputes* (1916), Pt. 1; Carl Mote, *Industrial Arbitration* (1916), pp. 191–288; N. P. Gilman, *Methods of Industrial Peace* (1904), Chap. 12.

pressure, consent to arbitration—usually at the hands of a board of their own selection. The theory of investigation and report is that, if imminent, it will cause the parties in interest to arrive at an agreement in conference or agree to arbitration; in any event it will inform the public as to the issues involved and cause the parties in interest, and others, in the future to take their moral responsibilities and the public interest more seriously than they otherwise might. In practice by far the greatest emphasis has been placed upon mediation; arbitration has been of minor importance except in Massachusetts and, more recently, in New York. Of investigation and report there has been comparatively little save in Massachusetts, where this step has been taken in important cases when other procedures failed. In the other states investigation and formal report has usually been at the discretion of the board, which generally means that recourse has not been had to it.[1]

There is a striking lack of accurate information as to the degree of success realized by nearly all these boards. Most of the reports are all but meaningless and many of them are open to the suspicion of making claims to results far in excess of accomplishment. It can be said, however, that the accomplishments of many of the boards have been almost nil. Indeed, in a few states no boards have been appointed; in a few others the boards have lapsed, at least for years together; in not a small number they have accomplished so little that the laws providing for them have been repealed. The small accomplishment may be explained by inadequacy of the law, or by poor personnel, or by some act that has aroused strong prejudice; perhaps the boards have not had the needed cooperation of local authorities and have not had information about disputes in time to be really helpful; seldom have they been able to win for themselves or to compel much interest and public confidence.[2]

Results of State Assistance.—But what can be said of the system of mediation and voluntary arbitration in those few states where it has been properly tested? If New York and Wisconsin since 1937 are excepted, the answer given by the available data is: (1) that in a large percentage of the cases the attempts of the mediators have been thwarted by one or the other party to the dispute because it was too strong and the force of public opinion too weak; (2) that many of the cases in which intervention has not been spurned have not been settled, among them a relatively large percentage of important ones; (3) that in a very large percentage of the cases in which disputes have been settled, the settle-

---

[1] During the first two years of the present New York board, investigation was resorted to in only four cases, with report made public in two. It is the theory of this board that, if investigation is expected to follow unsuccessful efforts to mediate, mediation is likely to be jeopardized.

[2] In recent years this machinery has not functioned with any particular efficiency except in a few states, chiefly Massachusetts, New York, and Pennsylvania.

ment has been after a strike or lockout has occurred;[1] and (4) that in a considerable number of cases a settlement has been reached only after the fight has been rather decisive. In other words, a comparatively small number of disputes have been prevented from developing into strikes or lockouts; in a much larger number of cases the duration of strikes and lockouts has been shortened but to an unknown extent; in the remainder of the cases matters have proceeded unaffected.

Brief reference may be made to the experience of the New York and Massachusetts boards, the most effective over a period of years. Quoting Dr. Ko with reference to the experience of the first of these states, "From 1901 to 1925, there were 4382 disputes reported to the Board of Mediation and Arbitration. Of these disputes, 1826 cases [41.7 per cent] were adjusted by direct negotiations, . . . 645 cases [14.7 per cent] by mediation and only 77 cases [1.8 per cent] by arbitration. The remaining 1834 [41.9 per cent] were either deadlocked or adjusted by other means."[2] Unfortunately no record of duration of strikes involved or of terms of settlement are presented. The record for one year, though it cannot be presented as wholly typical, will add something to the partly told story. In 1913, 268 strikes were reported. These involved 304,301 workers, of whom 115,000 were involved in the New York clothing strikes running for ten weeks. The total number of working days lost was 7,741,247. Fifteen of the strikes were in public-service industries. An analysis of 263 of the disputes shows that 130 were settled by direct negotiation; but how important were they, or when were they settled, and on what terms? Sixty-eight were settled on the employers' terms; the strikes were broken. In thirty-five cases the workers were displaced; they lost the strike and their jobs. Thirty were settled as a result of mediation, all in conference, none by arbitration. To take one more year, 1920, 240 strikes were reported, these involving approximately 350,000 workers and a loss of 10,608,000 working days. Of these 240 disputes, the Mediation Bureau settled forty-nine, other agencies ten, while five were disposed of by arbitration. The records for 1927 and 1928 ran in much the same terms, though the numbers were very much smaller.

The record of the Massachusetts board has until recently been the best. The law was well drafted; the personnel of the board, during most of its existence, excellent; cooperation by local authorities has not been lacking. Moreover, the board has had the confidence of and an unusual degree of cooperation from organized labor and employers, especially in

---

[1] Between 1887 and 1900, the then New York board acted upon 402 cases. It positively intervened in 267. It reported success in settling 112 and failure in the other 155. There were only nineteen cases in which there was not a strike or lockout. See Ting Tsz Ko, *op. cit.*, pp. 19–20).

[2] Ting Tsz Ko, *op. cit.*, p. 20.

the shoe industry. Hence, it has served as a board of arbitration in many of the disputes arising under agreements. During the first 16½ years of its operation the independent board acted upon 675 industrial disputes. During most of this period, from 1886 to 1900, C. H. Walcott was umpire of the board and contributed in large measure to its success. All the decisions of the board were accepted, although in a few cases the workers hesitated a few days before accepting. Arbitrations numbered 175, but there were 271 other adjustments brought about by the board's inducing the disputants to make some kind of agreement. Unadjusted controversies numbered 229, and most of them are said to have straightway vanished when the board began inquiries.[1] Under an act adopted in 1919, the associate commissioners of the Department of Labor and Industries came to constitute the Board of Conciliation and Arbitration. During the ten years ending with 1929, this Board arbitrated and decided an average of 244 cases per year, the greater portion being in the shoe industry. The number of cases in which mediation was employed was very much smaller, seventy in 1921 being the largest number.[2] It has been the practice in Massachusetts to investigate and report on all important cases in which the effort to mediate has been balked. The findings have been accepted by the industries concerned in a large proportion of the cases. It should be added, moreover, that, under a provision of the law, a considerable number of applications have been made to the board for "certificates of normality" (*i.e.*, that relatively fair standards are in effect) in advance of suspensions. The investigations following and the findings arrived at have been effective in preventing an open break from developing in from a few to several cases in most of the years.

This does not mean, of course, that Massachusetts has not experienced a considerable number of important strikes, running for weeks, in textiles, in street-railway transportation, on the docks. In 1928, though that was a year marked by a greatly diminished number of disputes, the New Bedford strike, involving 28,000 textile workers protesting a 10 per cent reduction in wages, ran for twenty-five weeks; 6,000 shoe workers at Haverhill struck in protest against an arbitration award; 800 Boston ironworkers were on strike for several weeks. But it would appear that in Massachusetts, where mediation and voluntary arbitration have been applied under favorable circumstances and where investigation has been resorted to, the degree of success realized has been approximately the same as in Canada under the Industrial Disputes Investigation Act, with its time limitations upon strikes and lockouts.

[1] B. F. Supple, *The Peaceful Settlement of Industrial Controversies, Development of the Massachusetts System of State Arbitration* (1904).

[2] *Annual Report of the Department of Labor and Industries for the Year Ending November 30, 1929*, p. 65.

Such until recently was the experience in the two of our states in which most was accomplished. Professor Witte, speaking of the accomplishments of the states collectively, said some years ago, "all told, the work of the state adjustment agencies must be put down as negligible."[1] Of course, much might have been done in most of the states to increase the effectiveness of intervention. At the same time many of them would have been handicapped in comparison with New York and Massachusetts. Moreover, many of the important disputes have been of an interstate character; something more than state machinery is required to cope with these.

Experience now indicates that with state industrial-relations acts of the Wagner-Connery type efficiently enforced so that collective dealing under appropriate conditions cannot be lawfully refused by employers, a state mediation and arbitration service can be made much more successful than it has been in the past. At any rate, the present New York State Board of Mediation, established in 1937,[2] has functioned more successfully than any of the agencies that preceded it. Granted no unusual powers, this Board, with excellent personnel and an active interest in the cause of industrial peace, settled a large majority of the disputes accepted for mediation during the calendar year 1938. Of a total of 223 cases accepted for mediation,[3] 36 were settled in advance of, and 156 with, positive mediatory effort. Of these 156 disputes, 122 were settled before impending strikes were called. Twelve disputes were not adjusted; the remaining nineteen were in process at the end of the year. The record of voluntary arbitration was in still greater contrast to that made in earlier years. In the language of the Industrial Commissioner, "Convinced that its greatest value lies in the field of mediation where no compulsion is used and where no orders or instructions are issued, [the Board] has turned over this second function to a panel of about 75 public spirited citizens informed on industrial matters who are called on to act as arbitrators when designated by the Board in specific cases. The increasing number of requests received by the Board for appointment of arbitrators is an indication of the willingness of unions and employers to submit their disputes for determination by a disinterested person and speaks well for the future of employer and employee relationships. Moreover, many labor contracts executed since the Board came into existence on July 1,

---

[1] E. E. Witte, *The Government in Labor Disputes* (1932), p. 253.

[2] *Laws* (1937), Chap. 443.

[3] Over against the 223 accepted for mediation, 207 were referred to other agencies, and there were 303 that were not within the jurisdiction of the Board or of any state or federal agency. Of the 207 referred to other agencies, 34 were referred to the National Labor Relations Board, 82 to the State Industrial Relations Board, 11 to the U. S. Conciliation Service, 49 to the Industrial Relations Bureau (of New York City), 10 to the District Attorney, and 21 to various other agencies. Release by Executive Secretary Jules S. Freud on Second Annual Report, Jan. 1, 1938, to Dec. 31, 1938.

1937, provide that the Board of Mediation shall designate an arbitrator in the event that the parties thereto cannot adjust their differences through the machinery established in the contract itself."[1] For the year 1938, 237 cases were accepted for arbitration. Awards were made in 212 of these, 11 were settled by mediation after submission, and 14 were settled by the disputants themselves after submission but without award.

THE U. S. CONCILIATION SERVICE[2]

Though the matter had been discussed for some time, the Federal Government did not set up an agency for intervening in industrial disputes, except in the case of the operation of railway trains, until the Department of Labor was created in 1913 and charged with that duty. Little was done in fact until World War I broke out, when a number of "commissioners of conciliation" were added to the staff. In postwar years the number of commissioners increased from about thirty to fifty, the Conciliation Service's budget from roughly $200,000 to $400,000 a year.[3] With the recent defense and war program, the Service expanded greatly; at the end of the fiscal year 1942, commissioners numbered 128, and the budget was $470,900.

The great bulk of the Service's work is mediation of industrial disputes, except those in transportation, for which special agencies have been provided. Mediation may be undertaken at the request of labor, management, or public representatives or initiated by the Service. The commissioners are sent here and there as disputes of any considerable dimension develop, the assignments being made according to the industrial experience and availability of the staff members. Recently nineteen special commissioners have been assigned to certain vital war industries. If mediation fails the commissioner may suggest arbitration and the Service may name or help select the arbitrator; some of the commissioners themselves serve in this capacity. When cases affecting the war program cannot be settled, they are certified to the War Labor Board

[1] Annual Report of the Industrial Commissioner, State of New York, for the twelve months ending Dec. 31, 1938, p. 7.

[2] Early accounts of the Service and its work are found in: Joshua Bernhardt, The Division of Conciliation (1923); and John A. Moffit, "Conciliation in Labor Disputes," in "Proceedings of the Fourteenth Annual Convention of the Association of Governmental Labor Officials," U. S. Bureau of Labor Statistics, Bulletin 455, pp. 119–125. For recent information see "Handbook of Federal Labor Legislation," Bulletin 39, Pt. 2, U. S. Department of Labor, Division of Labor Standards (1941), pp. 57–60; "The Governmental Setup for the Prevention of Strikes," an address by John Meade before the Catholic Conference on Industrial Problems, Mar. 23, 1942, and Kurt Braun, The Settlement of Industrial Disputes, (1944), pp. 71–74 and 145–149.

[3] In the fiscal year 1936–1937, the number of commissioners was fifty-odd and the appropriation for salaries and expenses $408,000. Twenty-fifth Annual Report of the Secretary of Labor, 1937, pp. 14, 41.

(formerly to the National Defense Mediation Board). In addition to its mediatory activities, the Conciliation Service also gives, on request, technical advice on such things as work loads, job analysis, and comparative wage rates.

TABLE 10.—SUMMARY OF CASES, U. S. CONCILIATION SERVICE, 1916–1941[1]

Year	New cases handled	Cases closed without assistance of commissioners	New cases adjusted	Cases unable to adjust	Cases pending end of year
Total	25,800	1,227[a]	18,998	1,824[b]	
1916	227	6	178	22	21
1917	378	41	248	47	42
1918	1,217	66	1,073	71	7
1919	1,780	214	1,442	111	13
1920	802	101	596	96	9
1921	457	47	338	48	24
1922	370	32	266	41	31
1923	534	19	428	27	60
1924	544	69	346	62	67
1925	559	61	392	64	42
1926	551	70	377	61	43
1927	545	69	395	57	24
1928	478	61	307	57	53
1929	522	21	385	40	76
1930	557	45	386	66	60
1931	582	63	385	52	82
1932	759	49	640	55	15
1933	833	17	774	24	18
1934	1,140[c]	41	885	67	13
1935	1,007[d]	79	749	76	23
1936	1,012	56	805	115	36
1937	1,267	.....	1,016		
1938	2,319	.....	1,450[e]	221	
1939	1,678	.....	1,077[e]	146	
1940	1,977	.....	1,341[e]	99	
1941	3,705	.....	2,719[e]	99	

[a] Figures for 1937–1941 not included.
[b] Figure for 1937 not included.
[c] Of these, 134 were referred to other agencies.
[d] Of these, 80 were referred to other agencies.
[e] Incomplete. Includes only signed and verbal agreements. Since 1937, the data have not been presented in the same form as they were formerly.
[1] Annual Report of the Secretary of Labor, 1936, p. 26; 1937, p. 13; 1938, pp. 11–12; 1939, pp. 19–20; 1940, p. 20; 1941, pp. 24–25.

Table 10 presents the number of cases handled and the results of interventions for the fiscal years 1916 to 1941. The figures for the years 1914 and 1915 have not been included, for the Service had not then been fully organized.

During the years 1916–1941, the Conciliation Service intervened in 25,800 labor disputes.[1] The fact is that the Service has attempted to

[1] In recent years many of these disputes have been referred to the National Labor Relations Board, the National Defense Mediation Board, and the War Labor Board.

settle nearly all large disputes throughout the country, and many small ones as well. Its services are almost never rejected, though the division is now overshadowed by the War Labor Board. The claim is made of successful settlement in a substantial majority of the total number of cases of active intervention each year. The percentage of adjusted cases for the twenty-six years was approximately 75.

The figures presented may be so interpreted as to give too roseate a picture of the accomplishments of the Service. In the first place, like other agencies, the Service has at times perhaps made claims of doubtful validity. Again, it appears that in a number of cases state boards or other agencies have cooperated and shared in the results accomplished. Finally, no adequate picture can be formed of the accomplishment of any such agency without taking into consideration how many disputes were settled without strike,[1] the duration of strikes, and, especially, whether the warfare was practically (or wholly) decisive before a settlement was reached.[2] But Professor Witte's observations are in the main[3] quite correct. He says, "This percentage may overstate the value of the Conciliation Service, since it is impossible to say whether settlement would have occurred except for its intervention, but the increasing effectiveness of its mediation cannot be denied. In the early years of the service, it was viewed with considerable suspicion by employers, apparently because many of the conciliators were former trade-union officials. This distrust seems to have vanished, and the Conciliation Service is today (1932) by far the most important agency of mediation in the country. To a very great extent it has taken over work formerly done by state arbitration boards, with their full consent. United States conciliators come into practically all large labor disputes occurring anywhere in the country and, once in the field, stay on the job as long as there is any prospect of bringing the parties together. The great area of the country and the frequent failure of either party to inform the Conciliation Service of pending disputes before they reach the strike stage (when adjustment is, of course, much more difficult) are distinct limitations, but altogether the Conciliation Service represents one of the most constructive activities for the preservation of industrial peace now operative in this country."[4]

[1] There has been a growing trend toward intervention before a strike or lockout develops. In 1941 the Service claimed prevention of 90 per cent of 2,251 threatened strikes and lockouts. *Annual Report of the Secretary of Labor*, 1941, p. 19.

[2] After referring to the statistics for the year 1933, the Twentieth Century Fund [*Labor and the Government* (1935), p. 116] very appropriately observes, "In considering the above statistics, however, it must be borne in mind that sooner or later every labor dispute is in some manner 'adjusted.'"

[3] It is too much to say that the earlier distrust of employers "seems to have vanished," but there is much less of it than, say, twenty years ago.

[4] E. E. Witte, *The Government in Labor Disputes*, pp. 245-246.

Without question, the U. S. Conciliation Service has substantially improved as the years have passed. It is much better than it was ten or fifteen years ago. Nevertheless, further improvement is possible. Its general direction and supervision have for years been good and now, indeed, are excellent. But, after all, the efficiency of any system of mediation depends very largely upon the "conciliators" in the field and upon the cooperation of employers and labor organizations in the several areas and industries. The number of commissioners of conciliation should be still further increased; more important, it will be very generally agreed that the level of personnel should be brought up to that of the best 25 per cent of the commissioners now in the Service. But an efficient system requires more than good commissioners. It is suggested that advantage might be taken of our experience with the several industrial boards and the several regional boards used during 1933–1935. Such boards, consisting of employer, labor, and public representatives, could be set up to cooperate with and to aid the commissioners assigned to different areas and industries.[1] They should be helpful both in maintaining industrial peace and improving industrial-relations practices, and in the development of the most efficient staff of commissioners.

The Adjustment of Railroad Labor Disputes

Another branch of the federal service has been charged with the adjustment of disputes arising in interstate railway service. A suspension of railway service may present an emergency so great that most countries have withdrawn or placed extensive limitations upon the right to strike or to lock out. In the United States, compulsory arbitration has frequently been urged and at times seriously considered by Congress, but because of the strong opposition of the carriers or the unions it has never been adopted.[2]

Early History.—The great railway strikes of the 1870's and 1880's gave rise to serious consideration of the problem presented and to the introduction into Congress of a variety of bills providing for conciliation and arbitration. Organized labor favored arbitration, and to an extent even compulsory arbitration, but the carriers, conscious of their strength, opposed arbitration in its various forms. The final outcome was the enactment of the law of 1888, which applied to all railroad employees.

[1] An approach to this has recently been introduced by Dr. Steelman and has become widely employed. Reference is made to the use of panels to assist in effecting settlements.

[2] The best discussions of mediation and arbitration of railroad disputes are found in: C. O. Fisher, "Use of Federal Power in Settlement of Railway Labor Disputes," U. S. Bureau of Labor Statistics, *Bulletin* 303 (1922); H. D. Wolf, *The Railroad Labor Board* (1927); Ting Tsz Ko, *Governmental Methods of Adjusting Labor Disputes in North America and Australasia*, pp. 54–102; and A. R. Ellingwood, "The Railway Labor Act of 1926," *Journal of Political Economy*, vol. 36 (1928), pp. 53–82.

It made no provision for mediation, the method most emphasized in this country in the settlement of industrial disputes. It did provide for arbitration by special boards to be set up by the parties in interest as disputes arose, and also for the appointment by the President of a commission to investigate and report on any case in the event one of the parties refused the offer of the other to arbitrate. The law was quite ineffective. No proceedings were initiated under it except that, after the Pullman strike had practically failed, a commission of three was established by the President to report on that emergency. With that strike a matter of history, the commission recommended provision for the conciliation of disputes, with a form of compulsory arbitration to be employed in the event conciliation failed.

The Erdman Act.—The Erdman Act of 1898 developed out of the discussions in Congress following the Pullman strike. That Act was narrower in its embrace than and differed materially from the law of 1888 which it replaced. It was narrower in its embrace because it applied only to employees actually engaged in the operation of trains and to those disputes involving the operation of interstate trains—disputes between the carriers and the engineers, firemen, conductors, and like groups. It was also unlike the law of 1888 in that it did not provide for investigation in any case, but did provide for mediation. It provided that, when requested by one or by both disputants, the Chairman of the Interstate Commerce Commission and the Commissioner of the Bureau of Labor Statistics should intervene and attempt to effect a settlement. If mediation failed, arbitration at the hands of a special board set up by the disputants was to be urged. It will be noted that the two officials mentioned had no legal power to initiate proceedings and that conference and arbitration might be rejected by either party.

For several years the Erdman Act was ineffective because the carriers were opposed to intervention. By 1906, however, the situation had changed. The unions had become more powerful and were using their power in a planned way. It was then that the Southern Pacific requested the good offices of the mediators. From this time to 1913, the adjustment machinery, with the mediators frequently taking the initiative, functioned well, within the limited embrace of the law. In all, from 1906 to 1913, some sixty-one controversies were settled without one important strike in the operation of trains. Twenty-six of the sixty-one cases were settled by mediation; ten in part by mediation, in part by arbitration; six by arbitration alone. Most of the other cases were composed by the disputants.

As in other cases of successful mediation, most of the success realized under the Erdman Act was due to the mediators in this case, Mr. Knapp and Dr. Neill. Their personalities and strategy have seldom been equaled among mediators.

Yet not all was well.   The strain upon the mediators, with their other official duties, was too great.   Moreover, the law was too narrow in scope.   At the time of its enactment only the brotherhoods were strongly organized, but early in the century other railway groups organized and there were many strikes, some of them both bitter and important.   Of more immediate importance, the brotherhoods pressed hard for higher wages, shorter hours, and more satisfactory working rules, and succeeded in securing a part of their demands.   Usually arbitration yields something.   The question arose as to how long this process could continue with railway rates controlled and the cost of materials rising.   Hence, the spokesman for the carriers for some years before World War I voiced the opinion that one board or one commission should be empowered to control both railway rates and service and wages and hours.   In the changed situation the companies were more and more favorable to compulsory arbitration, or, short of that, to a time limitation upon strikes and lockouts.

In 1912 a dispute developed between the Engineers and all of the trunks lines north of the Ohio and east of the Mississippi rivers, and mediation failed.   It was finally agreed to arbitrate, but because of the objection of the carriers to a board of three, with the chairman saddled with so much responsibility and inclined to "split the difference," an extralegal board of seven was established.   Seldom has equally good personnel been secured for weighing evidence and making an award.[1] Many weeks were spent in taking evidence and in weighing it, the board aided by able statisticians.   Yet, when the board made its award, it was with apology for guesswork and compromise.   No temporary board could gain command of all the factors involved in making an award on wages and many working rules.   The board reviewed its experience, described the emergencies caused by railway strikes, and advocated compulsory arbitration with adequate machinery for reaching informed conclusions.[2]

The 1913 *Board of Mediation.*—The next year, when another case was to be adjusted, a deadlock developed because the brotherhood involved was adamant in its opposition to an extralegal board, while the carriers opposed a statutory board of three.   The Newlands Act, hastily adopted, was designed to meet the exigencies of this case and to remedy patent defects in the law.   It created a Board of Mediation and Conciliation consisting of four full-time members.   Like the Erdman

[1] The members of the board were Charles R. Van Hise, Oscar S. Straus, F. N. Judson, Albert Shaw, and Otto M. Eidlitz, representing the public; Daniel Willard representing the carriers; and P. H. Morissey representing the Engineers.

[2] The board presented the best argument thus far made in the United States for compulsory arbitration of railway disputes.   See *Report of the Board of Arbitration in the Matter of the Controversy between the Eastern Railroads and the Brotherhood of Locomotive Engineers* (Nov. 2, 1912), pp. 86–109.

Act, this Act applied only to employees engaged in train service.[1] The Board was given the right of initiative; in addition it was required to function upon request. An arbitration board was to consist of six members unless the disputants agreed upon a board of three. The Board was instructed not to go beyond the provisions of the law, which in mediation and arbitration features were practically the same as under the Erdman Act.

From the time of its establishment, in 1913, down to the end of 1917, after which it practically ceased to function in the capacity for which it was originally created, the Board of Mediation was successful in bringing about a settlement of fifty-eight of the seventy-one controversies in which it served. Fifty-two of these disputes were settled by mediation, the remaining six by mediation and arbitration. No important strikes occurred. Nevertheless, there was a great deal of tension, and in 1916 an emergency developed to be solved by the hurried adoption of the Adamson Act. A nation-wide strike was thus avoided.

The 1916 Episode.—This episode of 1916 has been so well summarized by Dr. Wolf that his account of it is quoted in full:

"Certain arbitration awards under the provisions of the Newlands Act, particularly the award in the engineers' and firemen's wage movement in western territory in 1915, resulted in much dissatisfaction among the employees with arbitration as a method of settling controversies. When the four brotherhoods joined forces in December of that year and launched a nation-wide movement for the eight-hour day all efforts to persuade them to submit the matter to arbitration were in vain. 'The eight-hour day,' declared President W. S. Carter of the Brotherhood of Locomotive Firemen and Engineers, 'is not an arbitrable question.' Furthermore, he insisted, the roads had aroused public opinion against the employees' request by an extensive propaganda; the statistical data collected by the roads, although partisan and unscientific, could not be disproved by the employees and would be accepted by the arbitrators; the standards of qualification for neutral arbitrators, as demonstrated by appointments to previous boards of arbitration, were grossly unfair to the employees; precedent would be an obstruction in gaining the eight-hour day through arbitration; and finally, the administration of all wage agreements and awards was in the hands of the roads and would be interpreted in their interests as opposed to the interests of the employees.

"After a number of unsuccessful attempts had been made to effect a settlement of the controversy, President Wilson intervened in an attempt to avert the strike which was threatening. His proposals were declined by the carriers and the country was faced with the prospect of a nationwide strike by all train and engine-service employees, to take place

[1] Public no. 6, 63d Congress, 1st Session, Chap. 6 (S. 2517), July 15, 1913.

September 4, 1916, the date set by the chief executives of the brotherhood organizations.

"On August 29 President Wilson appeared before a joint session of the Senate and the House of Representatives and urged the need of an eight-hour day for all employees engaged in the movement of trains. On September 2, two days before the effective date of the strike, Congress passed the Adamson eight-hour bill which was immediately signed by the President. The act provided for the basic eight-hour day, but payment for overtime was to be at pro-rata rates, rather than time and one-half as the employees had requested. It also provided for the appointment of a commission of three members to study the operation and effects of the eight-hour work day and to report its findings to the President and Congress."[1]

The emergency of 1916, the circumstances under which the Adamson Act was adopted, and the extreme restiveness of the unions while awaiting a decision on constitutional questions by the Supreme Court of the United States[2] begot a strong demand on the part of Chambers of Commerce, the press, and other institutions for the compulsory arbitration of railway disputes. To an extent this carried over into 1920, when the Transportation Act was passed. The President at the time of the emergency felt that some restrictions were needed to protect the public interest and suggested that a law should be enacted based upon the Canadian Industrial Disputes Investigation Act, with its time limitation upon strikes and lockouts. But soon thereafter the United States entered the War, and this was followed by the federal operation of railways, which greatly changed the situation in which industrial relations were to be shaped.

Wartime Railroad Administration.—While the railways were under federal operation[3] there was comparatively little labor trouble, for the administration was (not unreasonably) sympathetic with labor, and the unions were fairly cooperative.[4] Wages were advanced by the Director General and then readjusted. The eight-hour day, with penal rates for overtime, was generally introduced. Work rules were revised, with

[1] H. D. Wolf, *The Railroad Labor Board*, pp. 9–10. A detailed, excellent account of this episode is to be found in C. O. Fisher, *op. cit.*, pp. 57–68.

[2] The circumstances were such that Congressmen felt that the minimum demands of the unions must be granted. The unions "showed their teeth" while awaiting the court's decision, and another emergency was in the offing. In *Wilson v. New*, 243 U. S. 332 (1917), a majority of the Supreme Court held that the Adamson Act was constitutional as an exercise of the power to regulate interstate commerce. Some members of the bench regarded the Act as primarily a regulation of hours, while others regarded it as an appropriate measure for meeting an emergency situation.

[3] December, 1917, to April, 1920.

[4] In 1919 there were, however, some "runaway strikes" due to delay in wage adjustments.

far-reaching effect; piecework was eliminated from the shops, jobs were classified, and many workers secured higher wages from occupational advances; hiring, discharge, and many other matters were placed on a liberal basis. Finally, three national adjustment boards were established, with equal representation of management and unions, and operated so efficiently that the great mass of grievances were effectively settled. But these adjustment boards, on a national basis, the uniform work rules, and rates of wages were to become bones of contention when the railroads were returned to the companies and operated by them in a changed situation at the close of the War.

The Esch-Cummins Act.—When Congress was considering the return of the railroads to the companies in 1920, it was faced with two problems, the one financial, the other relating to industrial relations. Only the latter need concern us here.

In the Senate a strong stand was made for the compulsory arbitration of railway disputes, but in the compromise arrived at between the two houses, provision for it was not made. Under the Transportation Act of 1920[1] carriers and their employees were directed to "exert every reasonable effort" to avoid any interruption of service, and all disputes were to be settled by direct conference if possible. The establishment of adjustment boards by agreement between the carriers and their employees was authorized. Such a board was empowered to hear and decide disputes involving grievances, rules, or working conditions, but not wages, when requested by either party or by the Labor Board, established by the Act, or upon its own initiative. In the event of failure of adjustment by it or in the absence of such a board, a dispute was to be taken to the Railroad Labor Board, consisting of three representatives each of the carriers, the employees, and the public. Or the Labor Board might take the initiative in disposing of a dispute.

The Labor Board alone had authority to determine disputes about wages. Wages were to be just and reasonable, as tested by criteria set down in the Act. Finally, the Labor Board was empowered to suspend the operation of a wage agreement arrived at in conference by the parties immediately in interest when in its opinion any increase in wages would "be likely to necessitate a substantial readjustment of the rates of any carrier." But, contrary to the contentions of some persons at the time, the decisions rendered were not enforceable. As Professor Ellingwood has said, "The scheme stopped just short of full-fledged compulsory arbitration, for there was no legislative command that the decisions of a board be carried into effect, or any provision for judicial process to enforce them. The only sanction contemplated was the pressure of public opinion, for all decisions of the Labor Board were given such publicity as the Board determined, and the Board was empowered, though

[1] Public no. 152, 66th Congress, 2d Session, Chap. 91 (H.R. 10453), Feb. 28, 1920.

not required, to determine whether any railway, employee, or organization had violated a decision, and to make its conclusions public."[1]

As its accomplishments were summarized by the Board,

"From the date of its establishment to December 31, 1925, 13,941 disputes had been referred to the board. Of this number 6,006 were of a local nature, affecting individual roads and their employees in one or more classes of service or possibly two or three railroads at one point; and 7,935 were of a general nature, affecting large groups of railroads and their employees in any or all classes of service, such as general requests for wage increases or wage decreases or general revision of rules governing working conditions. The board during this period disposed of 13,447 of these submissions, 5,549 of which were of local nature and 7,898 of general nature. Of the total number of disputes, 912 did not reach the status of regularly docketed cases."[2]

An examination of the more important decisions rendered by the Board yields little to criticize, though at times the Board was without the needed facts, properly classified, analyzed, and presented. But in spite of the prodigious volume of work of good quality performed by the Board it had come to be regarded as a failure long before 1925, and there was an insistent demand for its abolition, especially by organized labor. The dissatisfaction was due in part to some unfortunate appointments made to the Board, in part also to pronouncements made by one of its chairmen and to a demand for more power to be vested in it. Another factor is to be found in the figures quoted above. A large number of the disputes should never have come to the Board at all, but should have been disposed of by adjustment boards whose creation was authorized by the Transportation Act. But the unions sought national adjustment boards, while the carriers opposed them and sought to have boards established by the carrier and its employees. The result was that little adjustment machinery of this subordinate but important type was established, and this little very tardily, and that conference counted for little, arbitration at the hands of the Board for almost everything, and the Board was overburdened. Again, the Board and its decisions were imposed upon the parties immediately interested; they sought and found ways of avoiding rulings, or frequently ignored them. In this respect some of the companies were grievously at fault. And there was no effective remedy; public opinion was not easily formed; moreover, the Board was not effective in commanding observance. Beyond this there were the open-shop and the shop-committee or -association movements, which caused dissension and aroused suspicion on the part of the unions. But, in the absence of all these, it would have been difficult for any board, created under any law, whatever its powers,

[1] A. H. Ellingwood, *op. cit.*, p. 59.
[2] *Report of the United States Railroad Labor Board*, Apr. 15, 1920–Dec. 31, 1925, p. 9.

to have coped with the situation with which the Labor Board had to deal. In boom times, marked by rising prices, almost any arbitration machinery can function satisfactorily, but in times of deflation arbitration machinery is likely to be wrecked.

The Railroad Labor Board inherited from 1919 the problem of adjusting wages to the increased cost of living and to wage scales in other employments. Early in its history the Board did this in a satisfactory manner. But almost immediately industrial depression set in, railway traffic diminished, the cost of living fell, and there was an insistent demand that wages be deflated. A wage reduction followed, within the reduction in the cost of living and well within the increase in wages that had earlier been granted. Nevertheless, and for obvious reasons, the decision was unsatisfactory. The question of working rules also proved to be a troublesome problem. The companies desired to regain their prewar position in so far as possible, while the unions desired to retain the advantageous and frequently quite profitable rules secured in wartime. The Board handled the problem reasonably well, but of course its action was not accepted as satisfactory. Though there were at times threats to strike, peace was maintained until 1922, when the shopmen struck against a decision rendered. From that time on, and partly because of incidents in the behavior of some of its members, the Board was sadly undermined. Indeed, it could no longer function in an effective manner, and was abolished by the Railway Labor Act of 1926.[1]

The Act of 1926.—While organized labor was attempting to secure the abolition of the Board and the enactment of a new law, the business situation improved and prices became more or less stabilized at a level much lower than that of 1920. Moreover, it was necessary to have grievances settled in some way. Hence the unions and some of the carriers made more use of conferences than they had been making for some time past. Finally, in 1925, conferences began between certain railway executives and union officials with reference to the adoption of a new law. The eventual outcome was a bill enacted into law by Congress, without amendment of any consequence, the Railway Labor Act of 1926. This Act was formulated as it was because of the reaction of both carriers and unions against settlement of disputes by rulings of a national board and a desire to emphasize conciliation and collective bargaining instead.

The Act applied to disputes between any interstate carrier and its employees, "carrier" being defined so as to include "any express company, sleeping-car company, and any carrier by railroad, subject to the Interstate Commerce Act."[2] It declared that it should be the

[1] Public no. 257, 69th Congress, 1st Session, Chap. 347 (H.R. 9463), May 20, 1926.
[2] *Ibid.*, Sec. 1.

duty of carriers and their employees to "exert every reasonable effort to make and maintain agreements concerning rates of pay, rules, and working conditions, and to settle all disputes, whether arising out of the application of such agreements or otherwise, in order to avoid any interruption to commerce or to the operation of any carrier growing out of any dispute between the carrier and the employees thereof. . . . All disputes between a carrier and its employees [should] be considered, and, if possible, decided, with all expedition, in conference between representatives designated and authorized so to confer, respectively, by the carriers and by the employees thereof interested in the dispute."[1]

The above requirements of course rendered some form of organization and representation necessary. Relative to that, the Act provided that "representatives . . . shall be designated by the respective parties in such manner as may be provided in their corporate organization or unincorporated association, or by other means of collective action, without interference, influence, or coercion exercised by either party over the self-organization or designation of representatives by the other."[2] In other words, each party was to have representatives of its own choosing. It was this clause which was interpreted by the Supreme Court of the United States in the Texas and New Orleans case in such manner as to protect the employees in their efforts to organize into trade unions and secure representation through them.[3]

The Act of 1926 replaced the judicial but impotent Labor Board with a Board of Mediation similar to that established by the Newlands Act. This Board of Mediation, an independent agency in the executive branch of the government, consisted of five members appointed by the President.

This legislation made the needed distinction between (1) disputes arising out of "grievances or out of the interpretation or application of agreements concerning rates of pay, rules or working conditions," and (2) "disputes concerning changes in rates of pay, rules or working conditions."

To handle "grievances," as disputes arising out of the interpretation or application of agreements were called, Sec. 3 provided that "boards of adjustment shall be created by agreement between any carrier or carriers as a whole and its or their employees." The membership and scope of these adjustment boards were to be determined by agreement between the carriers and the employees. Section 3 was regarded as making the establishment of adjustment boards compulsory and thus to correct the failure of the 1920 law to make adequate provision for adjustment of grievances. It soon developed, however, that the provision was defective because both parties could work entirely within the pro-

[1] *Ibid.*, Sec. 2.
[2] *Ibid.*
[3] See *supra*, pp. 520–521.

visions of the law and never agree, and so never establish an adjustment board. The carriers usually wanted a local or system board, while the unions generally desired a regional or national board. This controversy in many cases prevented the establishment of any board to consider grievances. The failure to establish adjustment boards became more significant because the Board of Mediation early decided that it could hear grievance cases only on appeal from adjustment boards. This decision was made by the Board to protect itself from a flood of petty grievances such as had impeded the work of the Railway Labor Board, but the result was that in many cases there was no regular means for hearing and disposing of serious disputes arising out of the application or interpretation of agreements.

Thirty days' notice of an intended or desired change in rates of pay, rules, or working conditions must be given the other party by the one seeking such change. The parties must then agree, within ten days, upon the time and place for a conference, which must be within thirty days of the notice. The carrier was not to alter rates of pay, rules, or working conditions involved during the period of the conference or for ten days thereafter. If the parties were not successful in composing their differences, either of them might invoke the services of the Board of Mediation, or this Board might proffer its services on its own initiative. "In either event the said board shall promptly put itself in communication with the parties to such controversy, and shall use its best efforts, by mediation, to bring them to agreement."[1]

In the event its mediatorial efforts failed, it became the duty of the Board to try to persuade the disputants to accept arbitration. Acceptance was, of course, voluntary. If accepted, the arbitration board created for deciding the case was to consist of one or two representatives of each party, and one or two neutrals selected by these direct representatives. In the event of failure to agree upon the neutral member or members, the board was to be completed by the Board of Mediation. The decision of an arbitration board was to be filed, with the record of the case, with the district court, and became binding and enforceable unless appealed. So were decisions on questions of interpretation that must be settled by the board. In the event of a contest, it was to be decided by the district court, which then entered judgment, unless within ten days the case was appealed to the circuit court of appeals, whose decision was final.

But voluntary arbitration might be rejected by either party. If as a result of such rejection an emergency arose, the Mediation Board might bring it to the attention of the President, who then, at his discretion, might arrange for an investigation and report by an emergency board. The investigation and report were to be made within thirty days, during

[1] *Ibid.*, Sec. 5.

which time, and for thirty days thereafter, "no change, except by agreement, [should] be made by the parties to the controversy in the conditions out of which the dispute arose."[1] The results of such an investigation were to be reported to the President; publication of the report and further action were discretionary with him. Such were the essential provisions of the law relating to investigation when conference, mediation, and arbitration failed to maintain industrial peace in interstate transportation.

For a time the Act of 1926 worked rather well, and the United States was practically free from railway strikes. There were a number of reasons for this. Until 1930 railway earnings were more satisfactory than they had been some years before, and prices and wages were fairly stable. More important, there was a strong feeling of moral obligation to observe the law and to make it effective, for the carriers and the unions had agreed upon what the new law, its procedures, and machinery should be.

Table 11 reveals that up to 1930 there were comparatively few cases brought to the Board and these were almost entirely cases involving

TABLE 11.—STATEMENT OF CASES RECEIVED AND DISPOSED OF UNDER THE RAILWAY LABOR ACT, BY FISCAL YEARS, FOR THE EIGHT YEARS ENDED JUNE 30, 1934.[1]

Fiscal year	Cases received during year			Disposition of cases												
				By mediation		By withdrawal		By arbitration		Retired for refusal to arbitrate		Retired for other causes		Total disposed of		
	C.[a]	G.C.[a]	Total	C.[a]	G.C.[a]	C.[a]	G.C.[a]	C.[a]	G.C.[a]	C.[a]	G.C.[a]	C.[a]	G.C.[a]	C.[a]	G.C[a].	Total
1927	265	7	272	57	0	24	0	27	0	0	0	3	0	111	0	111
1928	98	25	123	84	0	45	0	14	0	0	0	2	0	145	0	145
1929	65	37	102	46	18	43	19	10	0	9	0	21	4	129	41	170
1930	112	222	334	25	48	20	66	4	8	3	0	10	1	62	123	185
1931	78	305	383	24	74	21	60	2	113	1	0	5	2	53	249	302
1932	110	282	392	45	94	69	59	4	47	47	33	5	1	170	234	404
1933	117	390	507	23	107	20	103	3	37	39	96	10	1	95	344	439
1934	122	447	569	17	64	26	77	9	260	50	97	9	0	111	498	609
Eight-year total	967	1,715	2,682	321	405	268	384	73	465	149	226	65	9	876	1,489	2,365

[a] C. cases include questions submitted in accordance with Section 5, first (b) and (c) (disputes about new agreements not settled in conference) of the Railway Labor Act. G.C. cases include questions submitted in accordance with Section 5, first (a) (grievances arising out of the interpretation or application of agreements concerning rates of pay, rules, or working conditions).

[1] Adapted from *Annual Report of the United States Board of Mediation* . . . 1934, pp. 4, 5.

changes in rates of pay, rules, or working conditions. The increase in the number of grievance cases from 1930 on is very significant as an indication of the added strain put upon the adjustment boards by the

[1] *Ibid.*, Sec. 10.

depression and of the failure of the boards to adjust disputes satisfactorily. It is significant that in the first five years of operation of the Act there were only thirteen cases closed on account of refusal to arbitrate, and none of these refusals to arbitrate were grievance cases. From 1932 through 1934 there were 362 refusals to arbitrate, and more than one-half of these were grievance cases. In the eight years ended June 30, 1934, the Board of Mediation received 2,682 and disposed of 2,365 cases, 726 by mediation, 538 by arbitration, and the rest by withdrawals by the parties or refusal to arbitrate or "otherwise."

The volume of railway traffic declined sharply after 1929 and railway earnings were sadly undermined. Partially in response to President Hoover's request that wage rates be maintained, and also because of the resistance of the unions, the carriers, with few exceptions, did not reduce wage rates until 1932. After a joint conference, however, an agreement was reached on Jan. 31, 1932, in which the several unions agreed to accept a 10 per cent deduction in wages for a period of one year. In return the carriers agreed "to make an earnest and sympathetic effort to maintain and increase railroad employment." In December, 1932, it was agreed to extend the 10 per cent deduction until October 31, 1933. However, in June the carriers proposed an additional 12½ per cent reduction. The unions were able to prevent this, but again agreed to the extension of the 10 per cent deduction, this time to June 30, 1934. Again in February, 1934, the carriers threatened a 15 per cent cut, while the unions proposed that their basic rates be restored on July 1, 1934, in accordance with the agreement. President Roosevelt intervened and appointed Coordinator Eastman to mediate the dispute. After some weeks of tense controversy an agreement was arrived at, whereby one-fourth of the 10 per cent deduction was to be restored July 1, 1934, another one-fourth on Jan. 1, 1935, and the remainder Apr. 1, 1935. This was regarded as a signal victory for the railway unions.

The machinery for adjusting and changing wages, hours, and working conditions was, then, put under a very severe strain by the depression, but was successful in avoiding any important strikes or lockouts on the railways. For this reason no changes, save the substitution of a board of three for a board of five, were made in this part of the 1926 law when it was otherwise amended in 1934.

Under the 1926 Act approximately 300 system boards of adjustment were finally set up,[1] but in a significant number of cases boards were not established, and there was an increasing tendency for those which were set up to deadlock. In fact the number of deadlocks ran into the hundreds.[2] Another distressing tendency of these bipartisan boards was to side-step

[1] Estimate of George Cook, secretary of the Board of Mediation, Oct. 2, 1934.

[2] Testimony of Joseph B. Eastman, Hearings, *A Bill to Amend the Railway Labor Act*, S. 3266, 73d Congress, 2d Session (1934), p. 17.

issues that threatened to develop into a delicate or dangerous dispute.[1] The Board of Mediation, as previously noted, had decided that it could not pass upon controversies that had not previously been heard by an adjustment board, and hence in many of the most acute controversies there was no agency for hearing the dispute.

The combination of these factors resulted in an accumulation of unsettled disputes and grievances and increasing discontent and resentment on the part of both carriers and employees. The situation became so tense and disturbed that, within a few months prior to the amendments made to the Act in 1934, strike votes had been taken in at least four important instances, for the purpose of creating an emergency that would justify the President in appointing a fact-finding board, so that these grievances and controversies might be passed upon by an impartial body.[2]

By the spring of 1934 both the carriers and the employees were generally agreed that the law must be changed to make compulsory the setting up of adjustment boards. Both sides agreed that more compulsion was necessary to secure the hearing and settlement of grievances, but they were not agreed as to what kind of board they wanted. The "standard" unions, that is the "Big Four" and those organizations affiliated with the A.F. of L., wanted national adjustment boards, while the carriers and the "independent" or company unions preferred local or system boards, but offered a compromise of regional boards, with system boards if the carrier and employees agreed.[3]

Commissioner Eastman's testimony in the controversy favored the establishment of a national board, partly because of the difficulty of appointing and paying the salaries of the multitude of neutral members that would be required if system boards were set up, because with a smaller number of boards more competent men could be obtained, and also in order to obtain more uniform interpretations throughout the entire country. The carriers objected to a single adjustment board on the ground that it would be bogged down by petty disputes and on the ground that only unions that were national in scope could be represented on the Board. Mr. Eastman recognized the possibility of such overloading of one board, but thought that the danger was exaggerated, especially since uniform rulings should soon reduce the number of disputes over interpretations. As for the argument that company unions would be denied representation, he admitted that they would be excluded unless they formed national organizations, but pointed out that they would be permitted to form system boards where the majority of the

[1] Statement of Colonel J. H. Elliott, former member of the Railway Labor Board, Oct. 4, 1934.

[2] Joseph B. Eastman, op. cit. p. 17.

[3] Statement of M. W. Clement, Chairman of the Committee of the Railroads, Hearings on S. 3266, Apr. 12, 1934, pp. 69, 72.

employees in any case freely decided that they wanted such a type of representation.

1934 Amendments.—Despite the opposition of the carriers and the representatives of the company unions, the 1934 amendments to the Railway Act of 1926 provided for the establishment of a National Railroad Adjustment Board, with offices in Chicago. The Board, to be set up within thirty days after approval of the Act, was to be composed as follows: "The said Adjustment Board shall consist of thirty-six members, eighteen of whom shall be selected by the carriers and eighteen by such labor organizations of the employees, national in scope, as have been or may be organized in accordance with the provisions of Section 2 of this Act."[1] The carriers were to prescribe rules under which their representatives would be selected, and the Secretary of Labor and special mediation boards were to settle disputes as to which organization qualified for representation.

Each member of the Adjustment Board is compensated by the party or parties he represents. The Adjustment Board is composed of four divisions, according to class of employee, and each division is independent in its proceedings. "The disputes between an employee or group of employees and a carrier or carriers growing out of grievance or out of interpretation or application of agreements concerning rates of pay, rules or working conditions, including cases pending and unadjusted on the date of approval of this Act, shall be handled in the usual manner up to and including the chief operating officer of the carrier designated to handle such disputes; but failing to reach adjustment in this manner, the disputes may be referred by petition of the parties or by either party to the appropriate division of the Adjustment Board with a full statement of facts and all supporting data bearing upon the disputes."[2]

"Upon failure of any division to agree to an award because of a deadlock or inability to secure a majority vote of the division members . . . , then such division shall forthwith agree upon and select a neutral person to be known as 'referee,' to sit with the division as a member thereof and make an award."[3] Should the division fail to agree upon and select a neutral person within ten days, either party may certify that fact to the Mediation Board. That Board must then name the referee within ten days. The disputes will, as under the original 1926 Act, be heard in the first instance by bipartisan boards, but now a hearing is assured in all cases, and in event of deadlock definite procedure for decision by a neutral member is provided.

---

[1] Public no. 442, 73d Congress, 2d Session, Chap. 691 (H.R. 9861), June 21, 1934, Sec. 3. Most of the provisions of the Act were applied to disputes in air transport by an act approved Apr. 10, 1936.

[2] *Ibid.*

[3] *Ibid.*, (1), p. 7.

The provision for the establishment of a national board instead of system or regional boards was a distinct setback to company unions, and the Act contained other provisions that were an even more direct blow to them. The standard unions complained that despite the decision in the Texas and New Orleans Railroad case,[1] the carriers in many instances continued to interfere with employees' self-organization. The failure of the 1926 Act to eliminate coercion by the carriers was twice recognized by law prior to the 1934 amendment. The first time was in the amendment to the Bankruptcy Act, which became law on Mar. 3, 1933. Paragraph (p) of Sec. 77 of that Act, as amended, read, "no judge or trustee acting under this act shall deny or in any way question the right of employees on the property under his jurisdiction to join the organization of his choice,—or to interfere in any way with the organization of employees, or to use the funds of the railroad under his jurisdiction in maintaining so called 'company unions,' or to influence or coerce employees in an effort to induce them to joint or remain members of such company unions." The Emergency Railroad Transportation Act of June 16, 1933,[2] incorporated this provision and applied it to carriers under private management as well as to those in receivership.

The 1934 amendments to the Railway Labor Act continued this restriction on financial aid of carriers to unions and made the language of the act more specific. Section 2 of the amended act reads in part:

"Third. Representatives, for the purposes of this Act, shall be designated by the respective parties without interference, influence, or coercion by either party over the designation of representatives by the other; and neither party shall in any way interfere with, influence, or coerce the other in its choice of representatives. Representatives of employees for the purpose of this Act need not be persons in the employ of the carrier, and no carrier shall, by interference, influence, or coercion seek in any manner to prevent the designation by its employees as their representatives of those who or which are not employees of the carrier.

"Fourth. Employees shall have the right to organize and bargain collectively through representatives of their own choosing. The majority of any craft or class of employees shall have the right to determine who shall be the representative of the craft or class for the purpose of this Act. No carrier, its officers or agents, shall deny or in any way question the right of its employees to join, organize, or assist in organizing the labor organizations of their choice, and it shall be unlawful for any carrier to interfere in any way with the organization of its employees, or to use the funds of the carrier in maintaining or assisting or contributing to any labor organization, labor representative, or other agency of

---

[1] Cf. supra, p. 521.

[2] Public no. 68, 73d Congress, 1st Session, Chap. 91 (S. 1580), June 16, 1933.

collective bargaining, or in performing any work therefor, or to influence or coerce employees in an effort to induce them to join or remain or not to join or remain members of any labor organization, or to deduct from the wages of employees any dues, fees, assessments, or other contributions payable to labor organizations, or to collect or to assist in the collection of any such dues, fees, assessments, or other contributions: Provided, that nothing in this Act shall be construed to prohibit a carrier from permitting an employee, individually, or local representatives of employees from conferring with management during working hours without loss of time, or to prohibit a carrier from furnishing free transportation to its employees while engaged in the business of a labor organization."

It is difficult to see how the carriers could comply with these provisions and continue to dominate the unions of their employees. The prohibition of financial aid is especially effective since it deprives the company union of many of its chief advantages and is relatively easy to check up on.

The Supreme Court ruled in the Texas and New Orleans case of 1930, that: "The absence of penalty is not controlling. The creation of a legal right by language suitable to that end does not require for its effectiveness the imposition of statutory penalties."[1] Nevertheless it was thought that the Act would be more effective if penalties were imposed and, in fact, very heavy penalties were written into the law. The tenth paragraph of Sec. 2 imposes a fine of not less than $1,000 nor more than $20,000, or imprisonment, or both, for each day of willful violation of the terms of the Act that forbid interference with employee organizations. The imposition of penalties is not dependent upon the Adjustment or Mediation Boards. It is doubtful whether it will ever be necessary to use these drastic penalty clauses, but the teeth are available if any union or worker thinks them necessary.

It was intended that enforcement of awards of the Adjustment Board in favor of employees should rest with the courts. Upon rendering an award in favor of a petitioner, the division directs the carrier to make it effective. If the carrier fails to comply with the order, the petitioner, or any person for whose benefit such an order was made, may, without being liable for court costs, file in a district court a petition setting forth his claims for relief. The findings of the division of the Adjustment Board are prima facie evidence of the facts stated therein.[2] However, such redress has not been sought by the railway unions. When compliance has not been secured within a reasonable time, they have taken

[1] 281 U. S. 569.

[2] Public no. 442, 73d Congress, Sec. 3(p). The Act makes no provision for either carriers or employees to appeal to the courts from awards made against them. Presumably, employees cannot strike against an unfavorable award.

strike votes, leading to the intervention of the Mediation Board and, in several instances, to the creation of an emergency board.[1]

Another important feature of the Act is that it expressly forbids the checkoff and the closed shop.[2] This provision is in keeping with the past policies of the brotherhoods, and prevents the continuance of the checkoff by some of the carriers which had been dealing with "independent" unions. It removes means by which a carrier might favor one group of workers at the expense of another.

Under the present law, an increasing majority of railway employees have become organized through standard trade unions, though representation plans remain conspicuous in railway shops and some other branches of the service.[3] Questions of representation have been important and the Mediation Board has held elections or checked membership lists against payrolls in scores of cases in order to determine and certify what, if any, organization should represent the class of workers concerned.[4]

[1] See William H. Spencer, *The National Railroad Adjustment Board*, Studies in Business Administration, vol. 8, no. 3, The School of Business, The University of Chicago (1938), p. 56. According to Dean Spencer, the carriers have, in a majority of cases, complied with the awards, though somewhat haltingly, and there have been no strikes. However, in a case that he does not mention, failure to apply awards of the Adjustment Board was an issue in a strike (*Annual Report of the National Mediation Board . . . June* 30, 1937, p. 4).

[2] Public no. 442, 73d Congress, Sec. 2, paragraphs 4 and 5.

[3] For the situation concerning labor organization in 1941, see *Annual Report of the National Mediation Board . . .* 1941, Tables 10 and 10A, pp. 30–32. Of the large carriers, only the Pennsylvania and the Santa Fe have had extensive representation plans.

[4] During the year July 1, 1934, to June 30, 1935, the Board issued 273 certifications— 239 to national labor organizations, 31 to system associations, and 3 to other organizations. Excluding 21 cases that involved interunion disputes, 47,511 votes or authorizations were received by national labor organizations, 17,741 by system associations, and 371 by other organizations (*Annual Report of the National Mediation Board . . .* 1935, pp. 16–17). In settlement of disputes between unions and system associations or unorganized employees, in 1935–1936, the Board issued 143 certifications—114 to national unions, 7 to local unions, 22 to system associations; 28,725 voted for or otherwise chose national unions, 18,378, system associations, and 2,184, local unions (*ibid.*, 1936, p. 9). In 1936–1937, 92 certifications were made in cases involving disputes between unions and system associations or unorganized employees. Of these, 76 were of national labor organizations, 12 of system associations, and 4 of local unions. The number of cases of this type was smaller than in the preceding year. In connection with this decline, the Board stated, "The decline in disputes between labor unions and system associations coincides with a marked trend toward representation by national organizations and elimination of system associations" (*ibid.*, 1937, p. 11). In 1937–1938, however, 140 certifications were issued in cases involving such disputes—100 to national organizations that received 16,746 votes or authorizations, one to a local union receiving 153 votes, and thirty-nine to system associations that received 15,830 votes. Fifty certifications were issued in settlement of interunion disputes and one in settlement of a dispute between system associations (*ibid.*, 1938, p. 19). Out of a total of 104 certifications in 1938–1939, 80 were made in settlement of disputes between unions and system associations or unorganized employees. Of these 80, 50 were issued to national organizations, 4 to local unions, and 26 to system associations;

In the seven years from 1934 to 1941, the Board disposed of 911 mediation cases. Over half of these were closed by mediation agreements. A few cases were settled by agreements to arbitrate, while most of the rest were withdrawn. During this period, there were two years (1934–1935 and 1937–1938) with no strikes at all, four with one strike each, and one year (1936–1937) when there were four strikes, two of them very minor stoppages. In the fiscal year 1936–1937, the Mediation Board succeeded in mediating a stubborn dispute over wage advances between the carriers and the several railroad brotherhoods.

In nine cases the President set up special emergency boards, all of which were successful in settling the disputes, as had been almost all of the similar twelve boards created since 1926. However, this was not true of the Emergency Board set up in the fall of 1941, when negotiations over wage increases between the various unions and the carriers broke down. When the unions rejected the board's recommendations, the President recalled it, asking it to serve in a mediatory capacity. The result was a compromise settlement. But although a strike that would have hurt the defense program considerably was thus avoided, this action also diminished Emergency Board prestige, weakening this part of the procedure for settling railway labor disputes.[1]

On the basis of the entire record, it can be said that the mediation of railway disputes is being done with efficiency and success, in spite of the present inadequate personnel to handle the large volume of work. Significant is the fact that the number of mediation agreements signed has increased each year of the operation of the amended Act.

By far the larger number of cases arising have been grievances within the jurisdiction of the four divisions of the National Railway Adjustment

---

although national organizations were thus certified in almost twice as many cases as system associations, the latter received 23,872 votes as against 19,897 votes or authorizations for the former (*ibid.*, 1939, p. 15). In the next two years, out of a total of 239 certifications, 154 settled disputes between unions and system associations or unorganized employees; national unions received 135, system associations 16, and local unions 3 (*ibid.*, 1940, p. 19, 1941, pp. 27–28).

In the absence of an agreement stipulating otherwise, the Board to begin with did not certify an organization unless it obtained the votes of a majority of all employees eligible to vote (see *ibid.*, 1935, pp. 15–24). More recently, however, it has followed the Fourth Circuit Court of Appeals ruling in *Virginian Railway Co. v. System Federation* [84 Fed. (2d) 641 (1936)], so a majority vote of those voting, provided those voting constitute a majority of those eligible to vote, would be conclusive. See *Annual Report of the National Mediation Board* . . . 1936, p. 11.

[1] The procedure was modified somewhat in May, 1942, when the President made provision for creation of emergency boards without the necessity of waiting for a strike vote, as was theretofore the case. A board of three is to be chosen from a nine-man National Railway Labor Panel whenever efforts of the Mediation Board fail and the Panel Chairman finds, after the dispute has been referred to him by the union involved, that failure to settle will interfere with the war effort. The board is to have exclusive and final jurisdiction.

Board.[1] During the year 1934–1935 1,753 cases were received (including more than 200 referred at the beginning of the year by the Mediation Board); 479 awards were made and 104 cases withdrawn, leaving 1,170 cases on the docket at the close of the year. Approximately four-fifths of the decisions were made by the partisan members of the divisional boards, one-fifth by referees called in to decide deadlocked cases. In the next two years, the record was not so satisfactory. Some of the divisional boards deadlocked on many cases upon which they should easily have agreed, and technicalities were too frequently resorted to. The year 1937–1938 saw improvement, 70 per cent of the 1,120 awards being made without calling in a referee, as contrasted with 60 per cent in 1936–1937; but in the next two years only about half were so decided, and in 1940–1941, only about 40 per cent. Instead of diminishing, the number of claims filed has increased; not enough controversies are settled on the property of the carrier. The first division, to which the great majority of the cases are brought, was several years behind in its work in 1941. Unless more of the spirit called for by the Act becomes evident, the actual accomplishments of this industrial court will fall short of what was hoped for.

THE MARITIME LABOR BOARD

On occasion, as during World War I and since 1934, serious disputes have developed in ocean and coastwise shipping. As during the World War I period, so in 1934 was special machinery established to effect adjustments. It was then that a special board was appointed to settle the strike on the Pacific Coast. Agreements between the companies and the unions were finally entered into, but the disputes recurred. In 1934 difficulties, unaccompanied by suspension of work, developed on the Atlantic Coast also. There, with the assistance of the National Labor Relations Board of 1934–1935, agreements between the Seamens' Union and the shipping companies were reached. A few years later relationships became more or less chaotic, owing chiefly, perhaps, to the rapid extension of labor organization, a revolt on the part of the workers against the officials of the international union (as there had been on the Pacific Coast also), and the struggle between the A.F. of L. and the C.I.O., now in the ascendancy in water shipping.

In this situation there were many complaints of the service on shipboard and the near-chaos that obtained, and different types of legislation were proposed. One type was based upon the Railway Labor Act, with its limitations on direct action. Such a measure was supported by the United States Maritime Commission established under the Merchant

[1] See the annual reports of the National Railroad Adjustment Board, in the annual reports of the National Mediation Board.

Marine Act of 1936. The Administration—at any rate, the Department of Labor—and the C.I.O. union were, however, opposed to the limitations and requirements of such a law, with the result that a milder measure was enacted in 1938 to be effective for three years.[1]

The Act, amending the Merchant Marine Act of 1936, applied to "water-borne commerce." In contrast to the Railway Labor Act, questions of unfair labor practices and of representation for the purpose of collective bargaining remained under the National Labor Relations Act and were to be decided by the National Labor Relations Board. A Maritime Labor Board was established and charged with certain duties, the most important of which were mediatory in character. It was to encourage all maritime employers, their officers and agents, and their employees, or the duly selected representatives of such employees, to exert every reasonable effort:

"(1) To make and maintain written agreements concerning rates of pay, hours of employment, rules, and working conditions, which agreements shall provide, by means of adjustment boards or port committees, for the final adjustment of disputes growing out of grievances or the application or interpretation of the terms of such agreements;

"(2) to settle all disputes, whether arising out of the interpretation or application of such agreements or otherwise, in order to avoid any interruptions to transportation of passengers or property in water-borne commerce."

In its capacity as a mediation board, the Maritime Labor Board was required to act upon request and might do so on its own initiative. Under penalty, all agreements or contracts were to be filed with it. The Board was also to submit recommendations for a permanent federal policy for adjustment of maritime labor disputes and stabilization of labor relations.

The stability achieved in maritime employer-employee relations in the years between 1938 and 1941 was probably due in considerable measure to the work of the Maritime Labor Board. In its three years as a mediatory agency, the Board handled 195 cases involving nearly 200,000 workers.[2] Seventy-nine were strike cases, and in twenty, strikes had been authorized in the event of a breakdown of negotiations. In 154 cases, agreement was reached between the disputants, or they were brought together on a working basis, or agreed to arbitration. Only seven cases failed of settlement. Four were dismissed because of

---

[1] Public no. 705, 75th Congress, 3d Session, Chap. 600 (H.R. 10315), June 23, 1938.

[2] Maritime Labor Board, *Supplemental Report to the President and to the Congress*, March 1, 1942, p. 17. Does not include workers involved in "observation" cases, where the mediator merely followed and reported developments without formally participating in the dispute.

lack of jurisdiction. Of the remaining thirty, most were referred to other agencies; a few could not be completed because of the lack of appropriations.[1]

In June, 1941, Congress extended the life of the Board for one year, but it was shorn of its mediatory functions, except in disputes already before it. In spite of the Board's recommendation that a specialized government agency be maintained to further collective bargaining and peaceful relations in the maritime industry,[2] nothing was done by Congress. Instead various improvised measures were resorted to. First the Department of Labor and the Maritime Commission called a conference of licensed officers' unions and offshore steamship operators' associations to formulate a national agreement on war-risk compensation. Then, after Pearl Harbor, the same two government bodies called another conference, representing the unlicensed seamen, radio operators, and longshoremen, as well as the licensed officers and shipowners. This conference agreed that there should be no strikes or lockouts during the War, that War bonuses and insurance should be determined on a national uniform basis, that the right of collective bargaining should not be violated, and finally that a Maritime War Emergency Board should be set up to which all disputes could be appealed.

Labor Disputes Machinery under the NRA and the National Labor Relations Act

In completing the discussion of legislation and machinery for the maintenance and restoration of industrial peace in the United States, that finding place in the New Deal period and the current War years must be surveyed.

The history of the hundreds of codes has been reviewed elsewhere in this treatise.[3] To secure observance of these codes, compliance machinery in each state as well as code authorities were established. The compliance boards served principally in the settlement of disputes over wages and hours. However, until other machinery was established and disputes other than those over wages and hours were transferred to it near the end of 1933, some of the compliance boards did a considerable amount of general mediation work. This was particularly true in New

---

[1] *Ibid.*, p. 20.

[2] Other recommendations of the Board were: unemployment insurance for seamen; and clear and unequivocal definition of their legal status, with reenactment of the provision adopted by Congress in June, 1941, making it the duty of maritime employers and employees to exert every reasonable effort to make agreements and settle peacefully all disputes. The original Act merely said it was the duty of the Board to encourage employers and employees to do so—a "halting recognition of their [the seamen's] capacity for self-government. . . ." *Ibid.*, p. 2.

[3] Vol. I, pp. 357–370.

York City, where, during August, September, and October, 1933, the Compliance Board settled 130 strikes involving 250,000 workers.[1]

Right of Self-organization.—As has been indicated, the National Industrial Recovery Act incorporated Sec. 7(a) and required that it should become a part of every code of fair competition. This section was in harmony with the principles adopted by the first War Labor Board and the provisions of the Railway Labor Act. It was also regarded as a logical extension of the Norris-La Guardia Act of 1932. As has been explained in an earlier chapter,[2] it was designed to safeguard the right of workers to organize without employer interference when and as they might desire, and to protect the individual worker against discrimination because of union membership or activity. Moreover, it had as objectives the stabilization of employment relations, the encouragement of collective bargaining, and the increase of purchasing power, which was regarded as a condition of recovery.[3] Finally, Sec. 7(a) was designed to get rid of the many and most difficult disputes—those over "recognition."

The new restrictions imposed by Sec. 7(a) upon the rights of employers to discharge or to discriminate against workers because of union membership or activity encouraged union organizers to enter industries and communities in which for years they had been unable to gain a foothold. In the wave of enthusiasm for union organization, membership in most old unions increased and new unions were formed at a rate unprecedented in a time of widespread unemployment and rarely equaled in boom times. As would have been expected, many of the newly and hurriedly formed unions proceeded to act in awkward and impolitic ways. And, on the other hand, because of their hostility to or fear of unions, many employers proceeded to establish company unions and employee-representation plans. Numerous conflicts occurred. The struggle over type of organization, the inexperience of the many new unions, the inevitable demand for restoration of or increases in wages when prices and the cost of living were rising, and the failure of many employers to observe Sec. 7(a) resulted in many strikes. There was a rather general fear that a wave of strikes would upset the entire recovery program. It therefore became necessary to establish new governmental agencies to mediate disputes and to interpret and apply Sec. 7(a). These agencies were the various industrial boards, the National Labor Board, and the (first) National Labor Relations Board.[4]

Code Agencies for Dispute Adjustment.—The several industrial boards were designed to complement the code authorities, which, because

---

[1] *New York Times*, Nov. 13, 1933.

[2] Chap. XI, pp. 521-522.

[3] See vol. I, pp. 357-361.

[4] For an excellent account of these agencies, see Lewis L. Lorwin and Arthur Wubnig, *Labor Relations Boards* (1935).

of their very nature, could not function well in settling certain types of disputes, especially those involving Sec. 7(a). In the early stages of the NRA these relatively independent industrial-relations boards were encouraged, chiefly on the theory that such boards had the advantage of familiarity with the techniques, customs, and problems of their industries and therefore could more readily adjust disputes and grievances. Usually these boards were bipartisan with an equal number of members representing employers and employees, and with provision for a neutral chairman. In November, 1933, Senator Wagner, then chairman of the National Labor Board, announced the policy of encouraging industries with their own adjustment machinery to settle as many of their labor disputes as possible.[1] On Mar. 30, 1934, General Johnson, Administrator of the NRA, issued Administrative Order X12, requesting all industries under codes to set up agencies for the handling of labor disputes. After practical difficulties had developed in carrying out this program, however, this order was modified on July 27, 1934, by Administrative Order X69, emphasizing primarily wages and hours complaints and making the procedure for handling Sec. 7(a) disputes optional and subject to approval of the National Labor Relations Board, which had then begun to function.

Despite the early encouragement, by Feb. 1, 1935, only 26 of the industries covered by the first 546 codes and 183 supplemental codes had established agencies for the handling of labor complaints or labor disputes. Only twenty-two were actually handling cases; thirteen were authorized to handle Sec. 7(a) cases, but five of these had restricted jurisdiction only (upon reference by both parties, etc.); four were not bipartisan code boards, but impartial boards established either under Public Resolution 44 (textile, steel, and longshoremen's boards) or under an administrative order. Some of the major reasons why boards were not set up in other industries were: opposition of employers or union, lack of union organization of employees to elect representatives, expense of administration, and difficulty of obtaining competent men to serve as impartial chairmen.

One of the most important of the boards was the one established under the Bituminous Coal Code. In each of the six administrative divisions established by that Code, a divisional labor board was appointed consisting of three members. One member was selected from nominations made by organizations of employees, one from nominations made by the divisional code authority, and one was a wholly impartial representative of the President. The expenses of these boards were to be met by equal contributions from the employers and employees nominating members.

---

[1] *New York Times*, Nov. 2, 1933, p. 15.

The Code provided that in cases of controversy concerning hours, wages, conditions of employment, or the collective-bargaining provisions of the NRA, every effort was to be made to settle the dispute by conference between the duly elected representatives of the employers and employees. In case such controversy could not be settled in this manner and it threatened to interrupt the efficient operation of the mine, it was to be referred to the divisional board. If the divisional board could not adjust the dispute it could be appealed to the National Bituminous Coal Labor Board.

The National Bituminous Coal Labor Board consisted of the members of the six divisional boards, but only the six chairmen representing the President had a vote. The Code provided that the decision of the Board should "be accepted by the parties to the controversy as effective for a provisional period of not longer than six months, to be fixed by the Board."[1]

This machinery set up in the coal industry apparently worked fairly well in the settlement of grievances and disputes, though the divisional boards were so handicapped by inadequate personnel that much of the work of adjusting complaints was actually done by local machinery provided for in contracts of the United Mine Workers with the operators.

The Newspaper Industrial Board, established under Art. VI, Sec. 5, of the Code for Daily Newspaper Publishing, may be taken as another example of bipartisan boards. On this Board there were four publisher members designated by the code authority, and an equal number of members representing the employees selected by the NRA Labor Advisory Board. These eight were to select a permanent panel of five impartial chairmen, from which panel, in event of a deadlock on any question, a ninth member might be chosen by lot. The chairman thus chosen was to cast the deciding vote. The Code provided that the Board had jurisdiction in controversies arising under the Code except where another method of settlement was provided by contract or agreement. Disputes were to be settled locally if possible.

The Newspaper Board was never able to select the required number of impartial chairmen. By April, 1935, it had agreed on only three of the sixteen names submitted, and one of the three was unable to serve. Only one impartial chairman was ever called in. The Board deadlocked on most of the important issues before it, including the question of its own power and the interpretation of the Code provisions under which it was established. The unsatisfactory treatment of issues submitted to it caused the Newspaper Guild and the Typographical Union to refuse to submit any new cases to it. These two unions had previously brought

---

[1] Code of Fair Competition for the Bituminous Coal Industry (Code 24), Art. VII, Sec. 5b.

most of the cases heard and therefore the most important work of the Board ended.

The advantages that such bipartisan boards had in membership familiar with the industry appear to have been more than offset by their disadvantages in handling cases of the type arising under Sec. 7(a). In handling ordinary grievances concerning wages, hours, and working conditions, intimate knowledge of the industry and its personalities might be of considerable assistance in arriving at a satisfactory compromise or adjustment. Such knowledge was, however, of little advantage in adjusting controversies arising under Sec. 7(a). Section 7(a) was a relatively new instrument of social policy and compromise with the principles it established was not possible or desirable. An employer either discriminated against his employees for union activity or he did not; he recognized the elected representatives or he did not; he bargained with such representatives or he did not. Sometimes the meaning of the law was not clear; in some cases there was deliberate refusal to accept the intent of the section. Bipartisan boards showed a distressing tendency to divide and deadlock on questions of principle according to employer and employee membership, or, equally serious, to avoid such issues entirely. Only an impartial, quasi-judicial board could consistently interpret and apply Sec. 7(a).

Another difficulty faced by bipartisan boards established under the codes was that of obtaining compliance with decisions. With such boards, compliance could be enforced only through the compliance division of the Code, upon which the employees usually had no representatives, and, even if the division did remove the Blue Eagle or take other action within its powers, compliance was often not obtained.

When developed in large number, as was once planned, industry boards, whether of the bipartisan or the impartial type, would inevitably involve serious problems. A system of agencies adequate to handle all labor disputes in each industry would require a great deal of time to establish, and the cost of office equipment and salaries of stenographers and other necessary personnel would be high. In a single industrial area several industry boards would be required to handle the disputes that might be adjusted by a single independent and impartial division of a national board. The enormous and unnecessary expense of duplicating boards in separate industries, the difficulty of obtaining competent personnel, and the inevitable confusion in interpreting and enforcing the law by a multitude of semiofficial and uncoordinated agencies, indicated the desirability of closely limiting the number of separate industrial boards with jurisdiction in Sec. 7(a) cases and of creating a central national board.

The National Labor Board.—The National Labor Board was created on Aug. 5, 1933, by presidential appointment following the unanimous recommendation of the Industrial and Labor Advisory Boards of the National Recovery Administration. The President's announcement stated: "This joint appeal proposes the creation of a distinguished tribunal to pass promptly on any case of hardship or dispute that may arise from interpretation or application of the President's reemployment agreement. The advantages of this recommendation are plain and I accept it and hereby appoint the men it proposes whose names will carry their own commendation to the country."[1] The appointees were Senator Robert F. Wagner, chairman; Dr. Leo Wolman, chairman of the Labor Advisory Board; Walter C. Teagle, chairman of the Industrial Advisory Board; Louis E. Kirstein and Gerard Swope, representing employers; and William Green and John L. Lewis, representing labor. The members of the Board served without pay, as did the representatives of industry and labor on the panels of the nineteen regional boards that were gradually set up by the National Labor Board to facilitate local settlement of disputes.

An emergency strike situation existed at the time and the National Labor Board and its local representatives immediately began to act in labor disputes and to make interpretations of Sec. 7(a). Curiously enough, no order delegating any specific powers to the National Labor Board was promulgated until Dec. 16, 1933. On that day, the President issued the following executive order (No. 6511) which was formulated in the light of the apparent dictates of experience:

"By virtue of the authority vested in me under title I of the National Industrial Recovery Act approved June 16, 1933 (Public No. 67, 73d Cong.), and in order to effectuate the purposes of said act, it is hereby ordered as follows:

"(1) The National Labor Board, created on August 5, 1933, to 'pass promptly on any case of hardship or dispute that may arise from interpretation or application of the President's Reemployment Agreement,' shall continue to adjust all industrial disputes, whether arising out of the interpretation and operation of the President's Reemployment Agreement or any duly approved industrial code of fair competition, and to compose all conflicts threatening the industrial peace of the country. All action heretofore taken by this Board in the discharge of its functions is hereby approved and ratified.

"(2) The powers and functions of said Board shall be as follows:

(a) To settle by mediation, conciliation, or arbitration all controversies between employers and employees which tend to impede the purposes of the National Industrial Recovery Act; provided, however, the Board may decline to take cognizance of controversies between employers and employees in any field of trade or industry where a means

---

[1] Quoted from *Decisions of the National Labor Board, August,* 1933–*March,* 1934, p. v.

of settlement, provided for by agreement, industrial code, or Federal law, has not been invoked.

(*b*) To establish local or regional boards upon which employers and employees shall be equally represented, and to delegate thereto such powers and territorial jurisdiction as the National Labor Board may determine.

(*c*) To review the determinations of the local or regional boards where the public interest so requires.

(*d*) To make rules and regulations governing its procedure and the discharge of its functions."[1]

The procedure in case of a complaint was as follows: The employee or union representative first took the matter up with the employer. If the issue was not settled by these direct negotiations, it was taken before the local compliance board (this step was eliminated late in 1933). If serious differences persisted, the dispute could be taken before a regional labor board. The procedure of the regional boards was not standardized, but usually cases were heard by members selected from the panels of employer and employee representatives, with or without a neutral chairman. These hearings were informal, and an effort was made to settle the disputes by mediation.

In case of refusal of one party to comply with a decision of a regional board, or if either party was dissatisfied with a decision rendered in cases involving violation of law, appeal could be taken to the National Labor Board. As a matter of fact, many disputes were taken directly to the National Board itself. The National Labor Board might then refer the cases back to the appropriate regional boards. If a dispute was of importance and a stoppage of work was imminent, the regional board could intervene on its own initiative. The regional boards were required to report new cases daily by telegraph to the National Labor Board, in order that it might maintain the necessary cooperation with the Conciliation Service of the Department of Labor.

In the early days of the NRA, there was considerable confusion and controversy as to the proper procedure for settlement of industrial disputes. This was not surprising in view of the enormous volume and of the variety of cases arising under the NRA and the emergency character of the various governmental and quasi-governmental agencies. It soon became apparent that there were fairly distinct types of cases, which required different treatment. Disputes regarding wages, hours, and working conditions were regarded as cases for the mediatory efforts of the Conciliation Service. If code standards of wages and hours were in question, the compliance division of the code was consulted and requested to take appropriate action. Cases involving alleged violations of Sec. 7(*a*) were taken directly to a regional division of the National

[1] Quoted from *Decisions of the National Labor Board, August,* 1933–*March,* 1934, p. vi.

Labor Board. These distinctions were not clear in all disputes, and, while there was close cooperation between the Conciliation Service and the National Labor Board, there was considerable divergence of opinion and friction between the National Labor Board and the NRA officials. These jurisdictional disputes and different interpretations of Sec. 7(a) by various governmental agencies were among the fundamental weaknesses in the administration of the labor provisions of the NRA.

Effective administration of the provisions of Sec. 7(a) and settlement of labor disputes were hampered by the composition of the National Labor Board itself. It was difficult for the members of the Board to devote to it the time necessary for the expeditious settlement of the disputes that came before it. The chairman was occupied with his senatorial duties and the industry members of the Board were frequently unable or unwilling to attend the hearings. The result was that at an increasing number of the hearings only the labor representatives were present.

A difficulty at least equally serious was that the mechanism for the enforcement of decisions of the Board was cumbersome and ineffective. The industrial crisis was acute and the prestige of the members of the National Labor Board was great, and for a time few employers challenged the jurisdiction or authority of the Board; but this happy situation was short-lived. The Board found that one of the most effective means of settling controversies as to who were the proper representatives of the employees was an election by secret ballot supervised by the government. The original orders establishing the Board did not confer upon it specific powers to conduct such elections and the executive order of Feb. 1, 1934 (No. 6580) was intended to correct this omission. After Messrs. Weir and Budd[1] had shown that the Board could be defied with impunity, however, the National Labor Board found it almost impossible to hold elections without the consent of employers.

It was equally difficult to obtain compliance from recalcitrant employers in the nonelection cases decided by the Board. In the early stages of the NRA, cases were referred to the NRA Administrator who, if he concurred in the findings of the Board, might remove the Blue Eagle. The executive order of Feb. 23, 1934 (No. 6612A) placed the enforcement machinery in the care of the Compliance Division of the NRA and the Attorney General. In some instances the threat of removal of the Blue Eagle was sufficient to obtain compliance. In other important cases, however, the Blue Eagle was of little value to the employer, and in these cases the Board was helpless in its efforts to obtain compliance with its decisions. The Department of Justice was reluctant to push to a decisive test in the courts questions involving the constitutionality of the NRA. In any event, the delays involved in court

[1] See Lorwin and Wubnig, *op. cit.*, pp. 102–106.

procedure made it impossible to carry a court case to a conclusion during the life of the Board. Furthermore, a favorable decision after long delay might be of little value to a union broken by the employer during the delay.

To remedy these weaknesses Senator Wagner in March, 1934, introduced a bill (S. 2926) "to create a National Labor Board." This bill provided for a permanent independent board consisting of seven members, two members representing the employers, two representing labor, and three representing the general public. The employer was prohibited from interfering by any unfair labor practice with the rights guaranteed to his employees by Sec. 7(a). Unfair labor practices were defined to include discrimination, interference, restraint, favor, or coercion of employees by financial contribution to, participation in, initiation, or influence of any labor organization, by lockout, by hiring and discharge policies, or by any other means. Powers to compel attendance of witnesses at hearings, to produce evidence, and to hold elections were also fully provided. Enforcement was to be through the district courts of the United States. The bill aroused a greater storm of protest from employers than any measure considered since the War period. After extended hearings, it was finally reported in amended form in the closing days of Congress. It became clear, however, that the bill could not be passed without delaying the adjournment of Congress, and in order to expedite that event the Administration substituted the less controversial Public Resolution No. 44, under which the National Labor Board was replaced by the National Labor Relations Board.

The National Labor Board was in existence for less than one year (until July 9, 1934). Handicapped as it was in enforcing its findings, and always of the view that agreed settlements were to be cherished above all else, it stressed mediation. During its existence, it and its regional boards received a total of 4,277 cases, of which 3,532, or 83 per cent, were settled. It was estimated that more than 2,000,000 workers were involved in these cases, and approximately 1,800,000 in cases which were adjusted.[1] The boards conducted 183 elections to determine employee representation. In these elections 103,714 votes were counted, of which 69.4 per cent were cast for trade-union representation.[2]

Despite its short existence and the handicaps under which it worked, the National Labor Board performed a highly useful service, not only in the adjustment of disputes, but also in the interpretation and application of the social policy in employer-employee relations expressed in Sec. 7(a). In its interpretations of Sec. 7(a) the National Labor Board

---

[1] Further data are given in National Labor Board Release 6295, July 7, 1934.

[2] A review of these elections was made by Emily C. Brown, "Selection of Employees' Representatives," *Monthly Labor Review*, vol. 40 (1935), pp. 1–18.

outlined policies that were later affirmed and clarified by the National Labor Relations Board of 1934–1935. In its decisions the National Labor Board did not hesitate to order reinstatement of employees who had been discharged for union activity or to order that employers cease interference with the self-organization of employees. When controversies arose as to who were the proper representatives of employees, an election free from employer coercion was usually ordered. The National Labor Board in the Denver Tramway Corporation case upheld the principle of majority rule in the election of employee representatives.[1] The President's Automobile Settlement in March, 1934, which in effect repudiated this decision, was one of the most severe blows to the prestige and effectiveness of the Board. Despite the addition of new members who could devote more time to the work, as chairman and representatives of industry and labor, the N.L.B. was able to do very little effective work during the remaining months of its existence.

The National Labor Relations Board of 1934-1935.—The (first) National Labor Relations Board was created by executive order of the President dated June 29, 1934, pursuant to Public Resolution no. 44 of the Seventy-third Congress.[2] It consisted of three impartial members, who were appointed for a period ending June 16, 1935.[3] Unlike the National Labor Board members, they were salaried employees of the government and devoted full time to the work. The National Labor Relations Board continued the system of regional boards initiated by the National Labor Board, making only those changes necessitated by administrative efficiency. Twenty-four district offices were established in the seventeen districts into which the continental United States was divided. In each of the districts, a regional director was placed in charge, with a small staff. As before, panels of members representing industry, labor, and the public were established; by May, 1935, there were some 650 of these panel members, who served without remuneration.

The Board and the agencies that it might establish were given jurisdiction in all labor disputes arising under Sec. 7(a) or which threatened to burden or obstruct the free flow of commerce and were given power to conduct elections and to enforce orders in the manner prescribed in Public Resolution no. 44.[4] It was also directed to study the activities of such other boards as were created to deal with industrial and labor relations, and to recommend, through the Secretary of Labor, to the

[1] *Decisions of the National Labor Board*, Pt. I, no. 149, p. 64.

[2] The executive order and the resolution may be conveniently found in the book of *Decisions of the National Labor Relations Board, July 9, 1934–December, 1934.*

[3] The original members were Lloyd K. Garrison (chairman), H. A. Millis, and Edwin S. Smith. In November, 1934, Mr. Garrison resigned and was succeeded by Francis Biddle.

[4] The relationship of the National Labor Relations Board to the Department of Labor was not made clear in the executive order, but a working agreement was made between the Board and the Conciliation Service.

President the establishment of special labor boards for particular industries when necessary. It was not expected to function in disputes not involving Sec. 7(a). Hence, under a cooperative arrangement effected, the Board and the Conciliation Service shared the work to be done, the former emphasizing law enforcement, the latter ordinary settlements.

In its interpretations of Sec. 7(a) the (first) National Labor Relations Board, in line with the decisions of the N.L.B., built up a comprehensive body of rules of conduct in collective-bargaining relationships between employers and employees.[1] Its rulings with reference to unfair labor practices and the employer's obligation to recognize labor organization and to confer with its representatives provided the ground for, and were, in essentials, incorporated in, the National Labor Relations Act of 1935.[2] In securing observance of its decisions, however, the Board met with increasing opposition and obstacles, dependent as it was upon the removal of the Blue Eagle—frequently of no value—and prosecutions at the hands of the Department of Justice. Its greatest success was in the settlement of disputes—in accordance with law, at hearings, for the most part conducted by the regional boards.

During the period in which they were active, from July 9, 1934, to May 31, 1935,[3] the twenty-four regional boards of the National Labor Relations Board handled 9,364 cases involving 2,154,000 workers. The boards acted in 1,019 strike cases involving 536,000 workers.[4] Settlements of 703 strikes were effected; 127 cases were transferred to other agencies. During this period the regional boards conducted 151 and the National Labor Relations Board conducted three elections to determine employee representation in disputed cases. In these 154 elections, 58,814 employees were involved.[5]

With NIRA's approaching termination and with the Board's lack of power to enforce its decisions at all effectively, the necessity for new legislation became apparent if the policy of the Administration was to be carried forward. Senator Wagner again introduced a bill to remedy the defects in the existing legislation and to give statutory form to important rulings made by the Board. This bill (S. 1958, 74th Congress, 1st Session) was much more carefully drawn than the proposal of 1934, and the objections of employers to it were much less impressive. The reports

[1] An excellent and thoroughly documented discussion of these interpretations appeared in "The Decisions of the National Labor Relations Board," *Harvard Law Review*, vol. 48 (1935), pp. 630–659.

[2] *Supra*, pp. 522–523.

[3] The regional boards continued in existence after the Schechter decision but were without power and hence heard no new cases after May 27, 1935.

[4] This figure does not include a number of important disputes, such as the A. & P. strike in Cleveland, which the National Labor Relations Board itself handled.

[5] For the results of these elections, see George Wheeler, "Employee Elections Conducted by National Labor Relations Board," *Monthly Labor Review*, vol. 40 (1935), pp. 1149–1154.

of the Senate and House committees to which the bill had been referred strongly supported the provisions of the measure[1] and it was enacted into law.[2]

As indicated in an earlier chapter, the National Labor Relations Act was designed to clarify and extend the law relating to labor organization and collective bargaining, in so far as Congress had jurisdiction. The present National Labor Relations Board,[3] established under it, was expected to serve as a quasi-judicial body and to enforce rights established by law; it was not expected to serve as a mediating agency.[4] The regional offices have been maintained for the acceptance and investigation of charges and petitions, but the regional boards, with their employer-labor-public panels, have disappeared. Nevertheless, a considerable number of disputes are disposed of incidental to investigation of charges of unfair labor practices. Though less of a mediatory body than the National Labor Relations Board that preceded it, just as that Board was much less of a mediatory body than the National Labor Board, the present Board and its representatives, in the course of investigation, have settled a large percentage of all the disputes brought officially to its attention. Such settlements are far more numerous than the decisions rendered, in spite of the fact that the attitude of employers toward the Board has, on the whole, been more or less hostile.[5] It must be borne in mind, moreover, that an effective establishment of rights and a minimization of unfair labor practices have the effect of stopping many disputes at

[1] 74th Congress, 1st Session, Senate Report N. 573, to accompany S. 1958, and same, House of Representatives Report no. 972 (Committee on Labor).

[2] National Labor Relations Act, Public no. 198, 74th Congress, 1st Session, Chap. 372 (S. 1958), July 5, 1935. For the "rights" of labor under the Act, see *supra*, pp. 522–523.

[3] The Board appointed in August, 1935, consisted of J. Warren Madden (chairman), John Carmody, and Edwin S. Smith. After serving for several months Mr. Carmody resigned and Donald W. Smith was appointed to fill the vacancy. Upon the expiration of his term (June, 1939), Dr. William Leiserson succeeded Mr. Donald Smith. In 1940, H. A. Millis replaced Mr. Madden as chairman, and in 1941 Gerald D. Reilly succeeded Edwin S. Smith. In February, 1943, John M. Houston succeeded Dr. William Leiserson.

[4] To protect the Conciliation Service and to prevent overlapping and friction between the Board and the Department of Labor, a sentence was inserted in Sec. 4(a) reading, "Nothing in this Act shall be construed to authorize the Board to appoint individuals for the purpose of conciliation or mediation (or for statistical work), where such service may be obtained from the Department of Labor."

[5] Up to May 31, 1944, a total of 66,670 cases had been handled by the NLRB and its twenty-two regional offices. Of these 64,136, or more than 96 per cent, had been closed; 2,534 were pending on May 31. Taking the 64,136 cases closed, 30,335 or 47 per cent, had been closed by agreement between the parties; 16,642 or 26 per cent, were withdrawn; and 9,551 or 15 per cent were dismissed by the Board and its regional directors. The remainder were closed in some other way, including certification and compliance with Board decisions or the Trial Examiners' Intermediate Reports.

Between October, 1935 and June 30, 1943, 14,319 elections were conducted of which 9,949 were consent and 4,370 were ordered and stipulated.

the source. Though the law has been flouted by many employers in many industries, it has prevented some disputes from arising and is now preventing many more relating to failure to recognize or bargain collectively with labor organizations.[1] With the main provisions of the Act upheld and given wide application by the Supreme Court, observance of the law has become the general fact; enforcement is less difficult. While the Act encourages labor organization and therefore begets disputes, in the longer run it has proved to be an important instrument of industrial peace.

WORLD WAR II MACHINERY

Months before the United States entered World War II, it was clear that achievement of uninterrupted production for the defense program made necessary additional public machinery to cope with the problem of industrial disputes. In March, 1941, a tripartite body, the National Defense Mediation Board, was given investigatory and mediatory powers to deal with disputes in defense industries. The Board handled only cases certified to it by the Secretary of Labor after mediatory efforts of the Conciliation Service had failed, and legally it had only the weight of its prestige and public opinion to enforce its recommendations. Two major issues faced it—wages and union security. The National Defense Mediation Board never formally announced any policy on either of these issues but attempted to decide each case on its merits.

Although until the entrance of the United States into the War, the number of strikes was high, the Mediation Board for several months experienced a good deal of success.[2] In few instances were strikes called after a dispute was certified to it, and there were few failures to abide by its recommendations, which, naturally enough under the circumstances, incorporated, at least in part, the reports made by the unions involved. But its career came to an end when in November, 1941, it rejected the United Mine Workers' demand for a union shop in the steel companies' captive mines. As a result of this decision the C.I.O. members resigned and the Board's usefulness was destroyed. During its life, the Mediation Board closed ninety-six cases.[3]

[1] The following figures provided by the National Labor Relations Board are not without significance. For 1938, as compared with 1937, the number of strikes in industries in which the Board had taken jurisdiction decreased 48 per cent, the number of workers involved in them 66 per cent, man-days of idleness, 71 per cent. The corresponding, substantially smaller percentages in other industries were 29, 52, and 51.

[2] During the latter half of 1941, the Board was aided in settling defense-plant disputes by the labor division of the Office of Production Management. The work of the latter overlapped that of both the Mediation Board and the Conciliation Service and some confusion was inevitable.

[3] See the study prepared by Louis L. Jaffe and William Gorham Rice, Jr., *Report on the Work of the National Defense Mediation Board March 19, 1941—January 12, 1942*, Bureau of Labor Statistics, *Bulletin* 714, (1942).

After the United States entered the War in December, 1941, the trade unions pledged uninterrupted production, and strikes declined to a low level. There was still, however, urgent need for machinery to settle the many disputes arising as production accelerated, plants were converted to war work, the cost of living rose sharply, and labor continued its organizing efforts. Within a month of the declaration of War, the President called an industry-labor conference, which agreed on a no-strike, no-lockout policy and the creation of a new agency to adjust disputes but deadlocked on whether this agency should handle union demands for security. Overruling management's stand on the latter issue, the President on Jan. 12, 1942, established by Executive Order a twelve-man National War Labor Board to have final power to determine all disputes certified to it by the Secretary of Labor. The Board's membership was equally divided among public, employer, and labor representatives,[1] and it was given authority to settle disputes by mediation and by arbitration under rules established by it.

As originally constituted, the National War Labor Board was in considerable part a revamped, but more powerful, National Defense Mediation Board. Like the latter, the new Board was the ultimate vehicle employed by the government for the mediation of labor disputes. More powerful than its predecessor, however, it was given express authority to require arbitration. Some of the personnel of the old Board continued to serve on the new. Similar procedures were likewise adopted. Thus, after a case was certified to the National War Labor Board and the Board accepted jurisdiction,[2] the case as a rule, as was formerly true, was assigned to a mediation panel consisting of a neutral chairman, an employer representative, and a union representative. Settlements were reported to the Board for its approval. If the mediatory efforts of the panel failed, the case went to the Board for arbitration or decision. Thus, the basic pattern of mediation continued.

Like the National Defense Mediation Board before it, the National War Labor Board in the beginning avoided pronouncements of policy and made its determinations on a case-to-case basis. It was inevitable, however, from the composition of the Board, from the frequency with which similar problems were presented to it for disposition, and from the pressure accompanying the increasing number of disputes submitted, that basic policies would develop. Most important, of course, were the policies developed in the controversial issues of union security and wages.

[1] Alternates were also appointed for each of the employer and labor representatives. In 1944, the number of full-time public members was increased from four to eight.

[2] The Board has usually declined to handle cases where reconsideration of another agency's decision is involved, where the employer is a governmental agency or a municipality, where procedure under a collective-bargaining contract has not been exhausted, or where alteration of a contract is sought in the absence of provision for alteration.

Though in its early decisions the Board made clear its support of the principle that majority unions should be protected from hostile employers and rival unions, the formative nature of its position was manifest both in the gradual easing of the requirements for the award of security and in the wide variation in type of clause applied. In the earlier stages of the Board's history, maintenance of membership was granted only where the need for security—under strict application of the protection principle—had been demonstrated. As months passed, however, the Board came to deny security only when the requesting union failed to demonstrate its responsibility in adhering to the no-strike pledge.

Concurrently, the security clause itself underwent a gradual evolution. At one extreme was a decision merely requiring employer assurance that he favored unionization of his employees. Other decisions went farther, granting some form of "maintenance of membership."[1] In one such case, the security clause was made elective, in another, withdrawable for "legitimate reasons." In another case, all union members as of a given date, and all future members, were required to remain in good standing, but the local union involved was required to waive claims to dues and initiation fees that accrued prior to Apr. 1, 1942; it was not to increase dues or initiation fees by its own action, nor was it to coerce any employee into joining.[2]

One of the most widely discussed of National War Labor Board decisions was that handed down in the International Harvester case.[3] There, with the four employer members of the Board dissenting, the union was granted maintenance of membership on the condition that a majority of the union employees, voting in a secret election, approved. The experience with the Harvester formula proved so expensive and cumbersome, however, that the formula was abandoned. In June, the Board majority developed a basic formula that for a time seemed on the verge of being accepted by the employer members. This formula, subsequently dubbed the Norma-Hoffman clause, provided for maintenance of membership to go into effect after the expiration of a fifteen-day period during which employees could, if they so wished, resign from union membership.[4] The Norma-Hoffman clause has come to be known

---

[1] The Board has also frequently ordered the checkoff. Except when granted in connection with a maintenance-of-membership clause, it has been voluntary and revocable on the part of the employee. The National War Labor Board has never come out for a closed or union shop, as did the Defense Mediation Board in one case, but it has granted the union shop in particular cases [as in *Harvill Aircraft Die Casting Corp.*, Case 163 (Feb. 12, 1943), 6 War Lab. Rep. 334], where such had been the form of contractual relationship between the parties prior to the outbreak of the War.

[2] *Walker-Turner Co.*, Case 17 (Apr. 10, 1942), 1 War Lab. Rep. 101.

[3] *International Harvester Co.*, Case NDMB-4, 4-A, 89 (Apr. 15, 1942), 1 War Lab. Rep. 112.

[4] *Norma-Hoffman Bearings Corp.*, Case 120 (Aug. 24, 1942), 2 War Lab. Rep. 433.

as the Board's standard maintenance-of-membership provision and, with few exceptions to meet special industrial situations, has been applied in every case where security has been granted.[1]

On April 1, 1944, the War Labor Board announced in the Humble Oil and Refining Company case[2] a definitive policy with respect to maintenance-of-membership awards. Stated briefly, the Board's policy established the following criteria which would govern the automatic grant of its standard clause: (1) whether the union is responsible and has abided by its no-strike pledge; (2) whether the union conducts elections of officers which are open to participation of its members; (3) whether the union makes audited financial reports to its members. The policy is justified by the Board on the theory that since labor has given up its right to strike for union security and wage increases, the award of maintenance of membership is of national necessity for stabilization of union-management relations during the war and is an equitable industrial necessity in view of the wage stabilization program enacted by Congress.

Similarly, the Board's wage policy has emerged gradually from the application of multifarious criteria to a particularized, highly specialized and markedly singular formula which, designed as it was to implement the developing national wage stabilization policy, has had a profound effect upon the entire nature of the Board's activities. The Board's policy toward wage increases emerged in concrete form first in the International Harvester[3] decision, which proposed "reasonable" protection of real wage levels arrived at through collective bargaining and the elimination of inequalities and substandard rates that failed to provide a "decent" standard of living. This ruling, in effect, meant that wages in the lower brackets should move upward faster than the cost of living but that not all those in the higher brackets should be expected to keep pace with the cost of living. Demands for increases were to be appraised with reference to changes in living costs since the last wage adjustment and to other factors, such as the employer's ability to pay, rates for similar jobs elsewhere, the effect of increases on prices, and employee morale.

---

[1] In the case of the *Interstate Steamship Co. et al.*, the Board, in order to meet the special conditions of the shipping industry on the Great Lakes, modified its traditional clause by requiring the Company to employ a specific proportion of union employees during the shipping season. *Interstate Steamship Company, Inland Steel Company, Bethlehem Transportation Company, and the International Harvester Company*, Case 376 (Feb. 2, 1943), 6 War Lab. Rep. 263, 567. See also the decision of the Board in *Allis-Chalmers Mfg. Co.*, Case 211 (Mar. 18, 1943).

See discussion on union security in *Summary of Decisions of the National War Labor Board, Volume 1; January 12, 1942, to February 15, 1943*, 1943, pp. 3–37.

[2] In re *Humble Oil and Refining Company* decided on April 1, 1944, and reported in 15 W.L.R. 380 (1944).

[3] 1 War Lab. Rep. 112.

With the President's enunciation of the stabilization policy in April, 1942, however, the new National War Labor Board wage policy began to evolve. In July, 1942, clarification of the new position came with the decision in "Little Steel."[1] Demands for wage increases were to be considered, not in the light of increases in the cost of living since the last wage adjustment, but of increases since Jan. 1, 1941. Prior to that date living costs had, for several years, been relatively stable. Thereafter, to May, 1942, there had been a 15 per cent rise. Real hourly wages as of January, 1941, were to be maintained and there were to be no other increases except to iron out inequalities and eliminate substandard rates. Peacetime standards, the Board argued, should be maintained as a contribution to efficient production and maintenance of employee morale. In a later decision denying any increase to employees whose hourly rates kept up with the 15 per cent rise in the cost of living, the Board estimated that about two-thirds of all American workers had received similar increases and were not eligible for more under the formula.

In October, 1942, however, with the passage of the act to amend the Price Control Act and the promulgation of the President's Executive Order 9250 "Providing for the Stabilizing of the National Economy," the wage policy of the Board became, to all intents and purposes, the wartime wage-stabilization policy of the Federal Government. The effect on the character of the Board's work was profound. From an agency designed chiefly to settle labor disputes, the Board became in addition the government's most important wage-stabilization agency. With few exceptions, no wage increase (or decrease) could thenceforth be put into effect without prior authorization from the Board.[2]

In order to administer its new function, the Board established 10 regional offices throughout the country and called upon the some 100 field offices of the Wage and Hour and Public Contracts Divisions of the Department of Labor for assistance in the preliminary processing of approval requests. As originally established, the regional offices were empowered to handle wage agreements only. Thus employers and unions seeking approval of proposed wage increases first secured from their nearest Wage and Hour office preliminary rulings on whether their agreements required Board approval, and, where the rulings were in the affirmative, assistance in the preparation of the necessary papers required by the Board in ruling upon the approval requests. Regional directors,

---

[1] *Bethlehem Steel Corp., Republic Steel Corp., Youngstown Sheet and Tube Co., Inland Steel Co.* (also referred to as "Little Steel Companies"), Cases 30, 31, 34, 35 (July 16, 1942), 1 War Lab. Rep. 325.

[2] The exceptions included employees in agriculture, employees in executive, administration, and professional capacities, and employees receiving salary payments in excess of $5,000 a year.

aided by tripartite advisory councils, were empowered to make final determinations in the great bulk of agreement cases. In addition, in order to stabilize certain industries as well as to maintain prevailing industry wage patterns, the Board appointed a number of industry commissions and "special panels."[1] The determinations of the commissions, as distinct from determinations of the "special panels," were final, subject, however, to ultimate review by the National War Labor Board on its own motion, while determinations of the "special panels" were submitted to the Board, nonwage cases as well as cases in which the parties were unable to reach an agreement on their wage problems continuing to be referred to the Washington office for handling in the customary fashion.[2]

On Apr. 8, 1943, however, the wage policy of the Board was subjected to sudden and drastic revision. On that day the President issued his "Hold the Line" Executive Order (9328). This order, with some minor exceptions, left to the Board the discretion only to grant such increases as were designed to meet the 15 per cent increase in the cost of living (the so-called "Little Steel" maladjustment formula), to eliminate substandards, and to make such minor adjustments as might be occasioned by promotions, reclassifications, merit increases, and the like.[3] The net effect of the order was to make wage increases impossible in a considerable percentage of the cases then pending on the calendars of the Board throughout the country. For about three weeks, on orders from the National Board, inequality cases were dismissed by Board offices in the various regions. Late in April, 1943, however, the National Board ordered the regions to hold up processing their inequality cases pending clarification of the new order by the Director of Economic Stabilization.

---

[1] These included the West Coast Lumber Commission, Nonferrous Metals Commission, Trucking Commission, Shipbuilding Commission, War Shipping Panel, Tool and Die Commission, and the Newspaper Publishing Panel.

Similarly, the Wage Adjustment Board for the Building Construction Industry, which had been created after the May, 1942, industry wage-stabilization agreement, was required to take no action inconsistent with the stabilization policy of the Board.

The same requirements were imposed on state, county, and municipal authorities, the National Mediation Board, the special emergency railroad boards, the Department of Agriculture, and various so-called "delegated agencies" such as the OPA, the Navy, the Tennessee Valley Authority, the National Housing Agency, and the Pan American Union, to whom the Board had delegated the right to make wage adjustments. See *First Monthly Report of the National War Labor Board* [to the U.S. Senate], *Jan.* 12, 1942, *Mar.* 31, 1943, *May* 10, 1943 (mimeographed), pp. 7, 10.

[2] For the various general orders adopted by the Board to implement its wage-stabilization policy see "Wage Stabilization General Orders and Interpretations under E. O. 9250" issued by the National War Labor Board Division of Public Information, Apr. 1, 1943.

[3] See White House press release of Apr. 8, 1943, incorporating the President's statement and the text of Executive Order 9328.

But major labor organizations expressed open opposition to the directive, and, to many observers, the future of the Board looked precarious. On May 12, 1943, clarification was forthcoming in a statement from the Director of Economic Stabilization. The effect of the clarification was to return to the Board in more stringent definition substantially the discretion it had formerly possessed. Thus, though the Stabilization Director reaffirmed the denial of the Board's authority to eliminate inequalities, the clarification permitted the Board to make adjustments up to the minimum going rate in given occupational groups and in given market areas. In order to implement such powers, the Board was authorized to establish as rapidly as possible a series of wage-rate brackets for such going rates in particular occupational groups and labor market areas. Except as exceeded by application of the "Little Steel" formula, these rates were to be considered stabilized rates, not subject to change. In "rare and exceptional" cases, the Board was authorized to fix rates above the minimum in the wage-rate bracket. In addition the Board was authorized to approve increases designed to maintain job classification differentials. All wage adjustments that might call for increases in price ceilings or, conversely, cause resistance to decreases in such ceilings, still required approval of the Director of Economic Stabilization. The effect of the clarification was immediately to ease a good deal of the tension surrounding the Board's activities.[1]

In the spring of 1944, however, the "Little Steel" formula came under direct attack from organized labor. Seeking adjustments in wages, particularly in the steel industry, both the A.F. of L. and C.I.O. hotly contested the bases upon which continued application of the formula was justified by the Board. The issue crystallized in hearings before the Board during April and May and the question of a revision in the formula was taken under advisement. Primary among contentions urged upon the Board by labor spokesmen was the inaccuracy of statistics published by the Bureau of Labor Standards which reflected a rise in the cost of living since Jan. 1, 1941 of approximately 20 per cent. The percentage increase, labor contended, was approximately double that figure.

[1] In the Everbest Engineering Corporation case the Board issued its first decision under the "Hold the Line" Executive Order, awarding a wage increase to correct "substandards of living." In that case the average earnings in the plant, located in the New York City area, ranged from 35 to 72.3 cents per hour, making an over all average of 42.3 cents per hour. *Everbest Engineering Corporation*, Case 551 (May 25, 1943).

For discussion of the Board's wage policy up to Apr. 8, 1943, see *Summary of Decisions*, vol. 1, pp. 3 and 56–76. A later discussion of the Board's wage policy to Apr. 8, 1943, as well as a statement of the effect of this policy on prices and the cost of living may be found in the *First Monthly Report* (to the Senate), pp. 2–13 and 18–20. See also Chairman Davis's letter to Vice-president Wallace, transmitting this report. For discussion of the wage policy after Apr. 8, 1943, see *Second Monthly Report* (to the Senate), June 1, 1943, pp. 3–7 and 14–17.

Of less immediate public interest in a war economy, but perhaps all the more far-reaching for what may prove to be their effect on postwar collective relations, are the policies which the Board has developed on issues other than those of union security and wages. In a number of cases, it has recognized the usefulness of arbitration as the final step in grievance procedures, has equalized the pay of men and women engaged in comparable work, has recognized the desirability of vacations, has established plant-grievance procedures for unions representing less than a majority of the employees, has extended governmental assistance to organized labor in industries heretofore excluded from the benefit of national and state labor statutes, has introduced job classification and evaluation as a method of placing plant-rate structures on a more scientific basis, has demonstrated the use of area determinations in the fixing of proper wage rates, and has, where necessary, enforced decisions made by the National Labor Relations Board.

Although some of the Board's policies have proved less successful than others, it seems hardly likely that the less successful will be abandoned in principle but rather that their mechanics of application will be redefined. Thus, the great volume of disputes as to membership in good standing arising under the Board's standard union security clause may result in some restatement of the clause to eliminate inconsistencies in its administration; but it does not seem likely that the security principle itself will undergo alteration. Similarly, a good deal of difficulty has been experienced with the establishment of grievance procedures for minority unions, especially where rival unions in the plant had been found by the National Labor Relations Board to be company-dominated. In the Sun Shipbuilding case, for example, both the C.I.O. and the A.F. of L. unions were granted such interim grievance procedures on the theory that the independent union that had originally been party to a contract with the company had been disestablished by National Labor Relations Board order.[1] Reversal of the National Labor Relation Board's order by the circuit court made it necessary for the War Labor Board to withdraw its original directive. Then, too, unions have shown themselves prone to utilize such interim grievance procedures not in order to settle disputes but rather to create them in the interest of organizing the employees. Prior to 1944 the Board was most reluctant to grant such minority grievance procedures and it probably will not do so where the situation is similar to that at Sun Ship. On the other hand, the Board does not seem averse to applying this interim grievance formula where the facts clearly support its use and, particularly, where the petitioning union has demonstrated its good faith.

The extension of governmental assistance to employees who, traditionally, have been outside the pale of federal and state trade-union

---

[1] *Sun Shipbuilding and Drydock Co.*, Case 427 (Oct. 1, 1942).

protection is too new a policy to have brought with it serious complications. In so far as the Board has acted in the place of the National Labor Relations Board or state labor boards in determining questions of representation, it has raised questions of jurisdiction and of employer right to court review under the National Labor Relations Act. In at least two cases, its agents have held elections (though in at least one, the Board availed itself of the facilities of the National Labor Relations Board) and have certified bargaining representatives.[1]

The provisions of the 1943 War Labor Disputes (Smith-Connally) Act under which the War Labor Board derives statutory recognition include a mandate to that Board that its administration must not impinge upon the jurisdiction of the National Labor Relations Board. Demarcation problems arising from this Congressional recognition of the correlative importance of preserving the full vigor of the Wagner Act during wartime have arisen chiefly in situations where employers have questioned, at the termination of a contract term, the majority status of the union previously certified as exclusive representative. Since, under the Wagner Act, enforcible collective bargaining rights accrue only to majority representatives, employers have questioned the legality of continued recognition of unions concerning whose majority status they entertain doubt. On this ground a number of employers have resisted War Labor Board orders extending contracts pending full settlement of disputed issues between the parties. Met by this apparent conflict in the application of its procedures with existing law under the Labor Relations Act, the War Labor Board, in the Chicago Transformer Corporation case,[2] decided in March, 1944, announced that questions concerning representation were peculiarly and solely within the jurisdiction of the National Labor Relations Board and that, in the absence of special circumstances which indicate a loss of majority status, it would continue to honor a previous certification of the Labor Relations Board. Such special circumstances have not as yet been clearly categorized, but factors such as a large rate of turnover during the contract period and a marked decrease in the number of voluntary check-off authorizations have received attention from the War Labor Board as evidence of loss of majority status. Possible solution of this problem in the form of a proposed amendment

---

[1] *Darr School of Aeronautics* (Case 3369-CS-A) and *Austin Company* (Case 4264-D). In the Darr case the parties requested the Board to appoint an arbitrator for the purpose of determining the exclusive bargaining representative. The arbitrator determined to hold an election, and on Mar. 17, 1943, reported his findings, certifying the union as exclusive representative. Since the parties had agreed that the award of the arbitrator would be final and binding, no decision by the Board was necessary. In the Austin Company case, a decision of the Sixth Regional War Labor Board in Chicago, certifying three A.F. of L. unions following a War Labor Board election, was subsequently upheld by the National Board (Apr. 10, 1943).

[2] In re *Chicago Transformer Corporation*, 14 W.L.R. 666 (1944).

to the rules and regulations of the National Labor Relations Board was pending before that Board in the second half of 1944. Under the proposed change, employers entertaining bona fide doubt as to the majority status of a union would have been granted the privilege of filing petitions for representation elections. While the question thus remained open, it is significant that the number of employers who had urged this contention before the War Labor Board was quite small.

It is significant that in the application of the policies discussed above, the Board has maintained essentially harmonious relationships with the National Labor Relations Board. Problems of interagency relations have been carefully discussed in joint conferences. In a number of cases, in order to settle disputes, the War Labor Board has acted to enforce decisions of the National Labor Relations Board. Thus, the War Labor Board has stated that decisions of the latter Board would be given "full faith and credit . . . at whatever stage they may have reached" and would be "assumed to be valid unless and until . . . reversed by a superior authority."[1] Employees found by the National Labor Relations Board to have been illegally discharged have been ordered reinstated;[2] company-dominated unions have been held nonexistent and their contracts without force;[3] and collective-bargaining determinations have been accepted as valid and conclusive.[4]

As the Board grew older its administrative organization underwent a marked change. In October, 1942, as was mentioned above, the Board, in order to administer the President's first wage order, created a country-wide field organization with offices in ten regions. Once such an organization was established, it was not long before the pattern of decentralization was applied to the Board's entire administrative structure. By January, 1943, the step was inevitable with the staggering increase in case load, the piling up of a large blacklog of unsettled cases, and the resultant public demands for more expeditious handling of labor disputes. Two new regions were added to the ten established in October, and, in the twelve subdivisions thus created, tripartite regional War Labor Boards, patterned after the National Board, supplanted the regional directors and advisory councils. Each Board was empowered to settle labor disputes in the same manner as the National Board and in each office the responsibility for carrying on the wage-stabilization program was transferred from the former regional directors to newly designated directors of wage stabilization. Voluntary wage agreements continued to be submitted to the regions by the Wage and Hour field offices; simi-

---

[1] *Lebanon Steel Company*, Case No. 333 (Aug. 17, 1942), 2 War Lab. Rep. 283.

[2] *Western Cartridge Co.*, Case 491 (Nov. 25, 1942), 4 War Lab. Rep. 427.

[3] *Sun Shipbuilding and Drydock Co.*, Case 427.

[4] *Shell Oil Company*, Case 92. For discussion of relations with the N.L.R.B., see *Summary of Decisions*, vol. 1, pp. 47–52.

larly, dispute cases continued to be certified by the U.S. Conciliation Service to the National Board. All but interregional cases and important policy cases were forwarded to the appropriate regional office for handling. Regional cases, as well as the so-called "blue ribbon" cases retained in the national office, continued to be handled in most instances by tripartite mediation panels. Directive orders issued by regional War Labor Boards have been final, except that the National Board may at any stage of the proceedings assume jurisdiction over a dispute. Appeals from orders issued by regional boards are heard by the National Board only if novel and important questions are presented, if the order of the regional board has been unfair to the petitioner or caused him substantial hardship, or if the order either exceeds the jurisdiction of the Board or contravenes the Board's established policies.[1]

A tremendous number of cases have been referred to the National War Labor Board—many more per month than were referred to the National Defense Mediation Board. From Jan. 12, 1942, to Apr. 30, 1943, the National War Labor Board closed 872 dispute cases involving approximately 3,250,000 workers.[2] But over 2,000 dispute cases affecting more than 2,340,000 workers were still pending. In addition, from Oct. 3, 1942, through Apr. 30, 1943, at least 46,148 voluntary wage-adjustment cases were received for processing. Only some 23,779 of these cases had been approved or disapproved.[3]

From its creation to May, 1944, the War Labor Board, according to Chairman Davis, had successfully handled 6,750 dispute cases involving nearly 8,500,000 employees. Only eighteen cases had been referred to the President for executive action, eight because of employer noncompliance, and ten because of union refusal to accept War Labor Board orders. In seven cases Government seizure resulted from employer defiance and five from union noncompliance.

The authority of the Board would seem so far practically beyond successful challenge. The methods the Board may employ in seeking compliance are four: (1) referral to the President, (2) referral to the War Department for the cancellation of contracts and blacklisting, (3) referral to the War Production Board for denial of priority, and (4) referral to the Bureau of Internal Revenue for the disallowance of deductions for wages paid in violation of Board orders. When a large corporation

---

[1] For a general discussion of the Board's procedure see "War Labor Board Procedures" by Harry Shulman, Associate Member of the Board, in "Wartime Trends in Employer-employee Relations," American Management Association, *Personnel Series* 66 (1943), pp. 3–10.

[2] Of these, 422 were resolved by Board order, 83 were settled through mediation, 27 by arbitration, after certification, and 87 by other means. In only nine cases has the Board refused to accept certification from the Secretary of Labor. Unpublished figures secured from the Administrative Research Section of the National War Labor Board.

[3] *Second Monthly Report* (to the Senate), Table 2.

refused to comply with an interim order, the Board held a public hearing on the declaration of the company, at which the latter quickly fell in line. In some six cases the Board had, by 1943, been obliged to refer its compliance problems to the President.[1] In only one case, that of the Baltimore Transit Company, was an injunction sought against the Board, and in that case, after conference with the judge of the District Court, the company decided not to file a complaint. A subsequent complaint filed by the company against certain federal officials in Baltimore who would be called upon to enforce the Board's order was dismissed.[2] More recently the Circuit Court of Appeals for the District of Columbia has held that orders of the War Labor Board are not reviewable.[3] The Court's conclusion was specifically based upon three conclusions: (1) "It is clear and undisputed that no statute authorizes review of the War Labor Board's orders;" (2) "The legislative history of the War Labor Disputes Act implies a positive intention that these orders should not be reviewed;" and (3) "General equitable principles" do not authorize review.

The general strike situation in the country has been good. During the year 1942 only .05 of 1 per cent of industry man-days were lost through strikes. During the first four months of 1943 the strike picture was as follows: January, .06 per cent; February, .02 per cent; March, .03 per cent; and April, .08 per cent.[4] During March, 1944, .06 per cent of industry man-days was lost through strikes; in April, .08 per cent and in May, 19. The Smith-Connally Act, which requires strike notice with election conducted by the N.L.R.B. on the thirtieth day thereafter, has probably had no appreciable effect with respect to minimizing the number of strikes. Partial statistics in this connection reveal that by the end of June, 1944, 1,083 strike notices were received by the appropriate governmental agencies. Through May, 1944, 212 strike votes had been taken and 733 notices had been withdrawn. Only twenty-nine elections were held in which the vote was against striking. There had been no accurate report by that date of the actual number of strikes which had

[1] *Montgomery Ward & Company*, Case 192, 1 War Lab. Rep. 280 (June 29, 1942), 4 War Lab. Rep. 276 (Nov. 5, 1942), and 5 War Lab. Rep. 80 (Dec. 8, 1942); *General Cable Company*, Case 247, 2 War Lab. Rep. 228 (Aug. 5, 1942); *Celanese Corporation of America*, Case 374, 7 War Lab. Rep. 95 (Mar. 16, 1943); *S. A. Woods Machine Company*, Case 160, 2 War Lab. Rep. 159 (Aug. 1, 1942); *Toledo, Peoria & Western Railroad Company*, Case 48, 1 War Lab. Rep. 46 (Feb. 27, 1942), and 4 War Lab. Rep. 276 (Nov. 4, 1942); and *Operators Negotiating Committee, Appalachian Joint Conference and Operators Negotiating Committee, Southern Appalachian Joint Wage Conference*, Case 111–1284 (May 25, 1943).

[2] *Baltimore Transit Co.*, Case 522 (Nov. 18, 1942), 4 War Lab. Rep. 363. See Press release of National War Labor Board, May 25, 1943, p. 2.

[3] See *Employers Group of Motor Freight Carriers* v. *War Labor Board et al.*, No. 8680 decided June 2, 1944, and reported in 14 L.R.R. 456 (1944).

[4] The relatively large figure for April was principally due to the bituminous coal stoppage shortly prior to the expiration of the coal contract.

occurred after an election had been conducted but they were few as compared to strike actions voted or to strikes occurring without the required notice.

There has been some criticism of the administrative organization of the Board, particularly because mediation has been practiced before the Conciliation Service as well as before the Board, and, most important, because there is delay in securing final determinations. Many critics have been of the opinion that all mediation except that purely incidental to arbitration proceedings should be carried on by Commissioners of the Conciliation Service. Recently, however, the Conciliation Service, in order to avoid duplication of function between itself and the Board, abandoned the policy of submitting disputes to its own panels.

Differences of opinion among the Board's public, employer, and labor representatives are to be expected. They have appeared in connection with the union security and wage issues particularly. Compromises must be resorted to or majority and dissenting opinions become numerous. The view has been advanced that while employer and labor representatives are more or less essential in mediating disputes, decisions should be made by men who represent only the public. This has been the rule applied to other compulsory arbitration agencies. Yet much can be said for representative boards in a situation such as that confronting the War Labor Board, where policies have not been fully laid down by statute or executive order. Moreover, in other countries, like Australia, it has been found necessary to add mediation panels to the Arbitration Court[1] in order to cope with wartime industrial-relations problems.

The War Labor Board has on the whole been very successful in the handling of disputes in spite of the fact that its organization and the tremendous and increasing volume of work have caused many cases to await decision for weeks and months. This delay has been a tax on worker morale. Moreover, policies have undergone change, chiefly as orders have been issued in connection with the stabilization program. Patient and cooperative groups have been irked by change in policies while their cases have been before the Board. Many have concluded that the more militant and the impatient have fared better than they.

The Board really began to undergo its big test when the responsibilities of the stabilization program were imposed upon it. The task was exceedingly difficult. Price control and rationing did not meet with the hoped-for degree of success. In many industrial areas housing facilities and food supplies were inadequate; rents and retail prices defied effective control. The cost of living rose during 1942 and 1943. A second difficulty inhered in worker ideas as regards rates of pay. As has been stated earlier in this volume, trade-union feeling has been strong that wage rates must generally be adjusted to any substantial increase in

[1] See Chap. XIV.

the cost of living. With thorough indoctrination of the idea in time of peace, it was rather generally assumed that this adjustment can and should be made in time of war, when an increasing proportion of the nation's effort must be directed to products other than the usual consumable goods and conveniences of life. And it appears to make little difference in attitude that those who have been employed lose less time and in fact work much overtime, with the result that the figures for earnings become much more favorable than those of rates of pay. In addition to this, millions who have not been employed have found place on pay rolls, adding to the money incomes of millions of families. Unless the increased purchasing power of "quick spenders," as most wage-working families commonly are, is drained off by taxation or by bond purchases, and this has taken place only in part, the enlarged purchasing power finds place in the markets and becomes an inflationary factor.

Any stabilization plan is more difficult to achieve because employers, faced by a shortage of labor and in many cases able to shift onward any added labor cost, are eager to raise wages in order to attract or to hold workers.[1] It is a meaningful fact that the great majority of wage cases brought to the War Labor Board are filed by employers requesting permission to make increases. The workers can only be expected to ask, Why should we not have wage increases when the employer of his own volition offers them?

Another important and complicating factor has been found in the divided organized-labor movement. Dissatisfied workers have been prone to change their affiliations, since not a few organizers have appeared to be as intent upon securing the adherence of those already organized by a union with a different affiliation as upon organizing the unorganized. Many an organization has attempted to outbid another. The effort to stop "raiding" has not been as effective as one would desire.

Thus the great test the Board has had to meet has been due to the fact that it must play a part in the stabilization program necessary if great inflation was to be avoided. Perhaps all that can be done by any board in time of war is to place a brake upon wage increases, pressing it down and releasing it somewhat in turn as good judgment and the situation as regards the control of prices and government needs and government financial arrangements permit.

---

[1] Of course, the widespread government price controls of the World War II period have limited greatly the extent to which added labor costs could be shifted onward.

Chapter XIV

THE PROBLEM OF STRIKES AND LOCKOUTS: MEDIATION AND ARBITRATION OF INDUSTRIAL DISPUTES (*Concluded*)[1]

In Great Britain

Mediation and arbitration of labor disputes have had a long and interesting history in Great Britain.[2] In contrast to that of many other countries, the history there has shown a movement from compulsory arbitration to mediation and voluntary arbitration. Significant, also, is the prevailing view during the last three or four decades that industrial peace must have a firm foundation in an acceptable standard of living and appropriate recognition of trade unions.

We are concerned here primarily in the agencies for mediation and arbitration since 1896, when the Conciliation Act was passed. With reference to the earlier history, however, mention may be made of the Cotton Arbitration Act of 1800, under which a successful system of compulsory arbitration was operative for several years; the Arbitration Act of 1824, which, in the language of Dr. Chang, "applied the principle of compulsory arbitration to the settlement of all disputes arising between employers and workmen engaged in any trade, except disputes concerning future wage rates,"[3] but which became ineffective as the unionism of the Engineers' model became prevalent and disputes centered more in wages and hours; the Councils of Conciliation Act of 1867 under which representative councils might be established and licensed to settle disputes by mediation and, this failing, by enforceable arbitration award; and the Arbitration (Masters' and Workmen's) Act of 1872, popularly known as the Mundella Act. This last-mentioned measure, with its complicated machinery, like the others mentioned, contained a provision for arbitration with binding awards. It proved to be quite ineffective, for one reason because the view came shortly to obtain that disputes should be settled by agencies established within the trade or industry, rather than

---

[1] With certain exceptions this chapter deals only with developments to 1939.

[2] The best histories of mediation and arbitration in Great Britain are: Lord Amulree, *Industrial Arbitration in Great Britain* (1929); and Ducksoo Chang, *British Methods of Industrial Peace* (1936). See also J. H. Richardson, *Industrial Relations in Great Britain*, International Labour Office, Studies and Reports, Series A (Industrial Relations), no. 36 (1933).

[3] D. Chang, *op. cit.*, p. 37.

by agencies created and governed by legislative enactments. More recent history has witnessed the adoption and use of compulsory arbitration only during World Wars I and II[1] when it was agreed that the extraordinary emergency required measures neither acceptable nor desirable at other times.

The Conciliation Act of 1896 marked a new start in government intervention in industrial disputes. It reflected the maturer opinion of the time and also recognized the fact that voluntary boards of conciliation and arbitration had grown greatly both in number and influence and that they were proving effective while, as Dr. Chang states, "the existing Acts of compulsory arbitration had seldom been put into operation, very few people even knowing of their existence."[2] To quote this writer further,

"The Conciliation Act . . . definitely buried the past and ushered in the full forces of the new age. It repealed the three existing compulsory arbitration Acts of 1824, 1867, and 1872, and took a positive step toward helping and encouraging the growth of voluntary boards of conciliation and arbitration by the simple means of registration with the Board of Trade; such registration carried no special power or privilege with it. Provision was made also for informal consultation with those immediately concerned on the advisability of establishing trade or district boards of conciliation and arbitration (clauses 1 and 4). The Act charged the Central Government with the duty, or privilege, of intervention in trade disputes, and provided, for the purpose, a wide and very flexible method in order to meet every set of circumstances. The Board of Trade was authorized (1) to inquire into the causes and circumstances of any existing or impending trade dispute, (2) to take steps expedient for the purpose of enabling the parties to meet under an impartial chairmanship to be mutually agreed upon or to be appointed by the Board of Trade, (3) to appoint a conciliator or board of conciliation on the application of either party, or (4) to appoint an arbitrator upon the application of both parties to the dispute (clause 2). In brief the Act provided the means of public inquiry, conciliation, and arbitration upon a purely voluntary basis, as each particular case might require."[3]

As a result of the impetus given by the Act, and with an increasing number of trades and industries unionized and on a collective-bargaining basis, the number of (voluntary) Trade Boards increased from eighty-three in 1896 to 310 in 1913, while District and General Boards, arising in less developed situations and at a time when other agencies were fewer,

---

[1] For an account of arbitration during World War I years, see, in addition to the references already cited, G. R. Askwith, *Industrial Problems and Disputes* (1920). The current War measure is described in the *Monthly Labor Review*, vol. 54 (1942), p. 601.

[2] D. Chang, *op. cit.*, pp. 45–46.

[3] *Ibid.*, pp. 47–48.

decreased from twenty-two to fifteen. Moreover, provision was increasingly made in trade agreements for the appointment by the Board of Trade of a mediator or arbitrator in case of deadlock.[1] As the years passed, the number of requests by one or both parties for government intervention increased. Yet, there were many cases in which intervention was not requested or in which intervention was not successful; and shortly after the turn of the century the number of strikes and lockouts and the number of workmen involved in them greatly increased. In an attempt to strengthen its efforts by assuring that the arbitrators would have adequate knowledge of any technical aspects involved in disputes before them, the government in 1908 made provision for tripartite boards of three members, a chairman and representatives of industry and labor, drawn from employers' and workmen's panels formed by the Board of Trade. The new device, however, worked none too well, for the panel members were called upon too infrequently to become experienced and their trade knowledge was largely limited to the one with which they had been connected. To overcome these difficulties and to cope with a situation marked by serious strikes of railwaymen, transport workers, and others, and involving much strain, an Industrial Council was established in 1911, to serve as a Parliament of Industry and as a body to which important disputes might be taken for settlement. The Council consisted of thirteen representatives of employers' organizations and an equal number of union officers, with Sir George Askwith as chairman.[2] The Council failed, however, as a Parliament of Industry, perhaps because it was not adequately representative, and was also unsuccessful in the settlement of the few disputes placed before it. No appointments were made to the Council in 1913 and it quietly disappeared.

As Dr. Chang points out[3] in his discussion of the operation of the Conciliation Act from 1896 to 1913, there were 11,492 strikes and lockouts, involving 6,312,000 workers. Of these cases, 949, involving 1,432,000, or less than a quarter of the workers, were settled by mediation or arbitration; the others were sooner or later settled by direct negotiation, on some terms or other. Of the 949 cases, 739 were settled by (voluntary) Trade Boards and other agencies, 210 under the Conciliation Act. During the same period, also, 328 disputes not involving stoppages were settled under the Act.

Since 1913 the mediation service has continued to serve in much the same way as theretofore and with not dissimilar result. In other respects, the law and the agencies established have been changed. During World War I compulsory arbitration, with prohibition of strikes, was widely

---

[1] The number increased from two in 1897 to 121 in 1913. *Ibid.*, p. 51.

[2] *Ibid.*, pp. 52–54.

[3] *Ibid.*, pp. 58–59.

employed; after the War the policy recommended by the Whitley Committee was accepted and the Industrial Court established.[1]

As its starting point, the Whitley Committee assumed an extensive organization of labor as both a fact and a thing to be desired. In urging adequate organization for collective bargaining, it said:

"The essential condition of securing a permanent improvement in the relations between employers and employed is that there should be adequate organization on the part of both employers and workpeople. The proposals outlined for joint co-operation throughout the several industries depend for their ultimate success upon there being such organization on both sides; and such organization is necessary also to provide means whereby the arrangements and agreements made for the industry may be effectively carried out."[2]

The Whitley Committee recommended:

1. The establishment of National Joint Industrial Councils, district councils, and works committees in well-organized industries (interpreted by the Minister of Labour to mean 75 per cent organized).

2. Extension of the trade boards[3] (or wages boards) to less extensively organized industries.

3. The establishment of a standing arbitration tribunal, authorization of *ad hoc* bodies to inquire into and report on disputes, and the continuation of the existing voluntary boards of conciliation in different industries.

The reaction of employers and the unions to this report was so favorable that the provisions were quickly put into operation. Between 1918 and 1921 joint industrial councils were established in seventy-three industries. In addition, thirty-three Interim Reconstruction Committees were set up to serve a similar purpose pending formation of Trade Boards in the less well-organized industries. In 1919 a standing arbitration tribunal, the Industrial Court, was established in accordance with the third Whitley recommendation. Provision was also made for the setting up of courts of inquiry as needed in emergencies due to actual or threatened strike. The functions and accomplishments of the joint industrial councils, the Industrial Court, and the courts of inquiry may be noted briefly.

One of the fundamental aims of the Whitley system was the prevention of disputes between employers and employees. The mutual interests of employers and their workers were stressed, much as they have been in this country by those interested in personnel administration. It was

[1] The Whitley Councils are also discussed in connection with the development of employee-representation plans in Chap. XV.

[2] Quoted by International Labour Office, *Conciliation and Arbitration in Industrial Disputes* [Studies and Reports, Series A (Industrial Relations), no. 34 (1933)], p. 150.

[3] For a description of the trade boards, see vol. I of this treatise, Chap. VI.

originally hoped that trade unionism would be so encouraged that there would be a declining need for trade boards in theretofore poorly organized industries and an increase in the number of joint industrial, or Whitley, councils. There were several reasons why this hope was not unreasonable. Even prior to the War, membership in the 1,269 British trade unions was 4,135,000, and under the stimulation of the War period it reached a peak of 8,339,000 in 1920. Furthermore, there was a general willingness on the part of British employers to accept collective bargaining as a means of settling controversies.

It was intended that the joint industrial councils should meet regularly for the consideration of problems affecting their industries, thus affording the workers a greater opportunity to participate in industrial government. For the most part, however, the councils have accomplished little save to make more regular and formal the ordinary negotiating machinery of unions and employers' associations.[1] In some cases, as in the printing industry, the councils left wage negotiations to the unions and employers' associations and confined their activities to other less time-consuming matters, such as health, unemployment, and apprenticeship. Organized workpeople and employers in many of the chief industries, such as iron and steel, cotton, and coal, preferred their own joint agencies and either abandoned or never established Whitley councils. On the railways a voluntary agreement has provided that all disputes must be settled by conciliation, or, that failing, by arbitration by a joint board with a neutral chairman. Joint arrangements for the settlement of disputes in the cotton industry have been in operation for more than forty years. In 1934 the Cotton Manufacturing Industry (Temporary Provisions) Act modified the prior voluntary machinery in the weaving section of the industry by making joint agreements concerning wages applicable to the entire section, upon request of a majority of the workers and employers and upon unanimous recommendation of a board appointed to consider the request.

In the coal industry there appeared in the late thirties to be little room for compromise and cooperation. The employers refused to bargain on a national basis. Many of the mines were economically unable to pay a living wage, and the unions contended that the only solution for the ills of the industry was government ownership and operation.[2] In the face of such controversies joint industrial councils are helpless, as they were in the crisis and general strike of 1926. The failure of this strike, however, did much to discredit class-conscious unionism and to

---

[1] For a detailed description of the machinery for settling disputes and effecting collective agreements, see Ministry of Labour, *Report on Collective Agreements between Employers and Workpeople in Great Britain and Northern Ireland* (1934).

[2] Under legislation enacted in September, 1938, the government was to come into the ownership of the mines by 1942. This was in process in July, 1942.

turn attention again to cooperation through joint industrial councils. The membership in unions declined to 4,441,000 in 1932.[1] These facts, coupled with continued industrial depression until 1935, account for much of the decline in time lost as a result of industrial disputes and make it difficult to estimate the effectiveness of the joint industrial councils in preventing strikes and lockouts. It is significant, however, that the number of councils had decreased from seventy-three in 1921 to forty-one in 1938.

The Industrial Court consists of three groups, viz., of representatives of employers, of workmen, and of the public, all of whom are appointed by the Minister of Labour. The President of the Court and the chairmen are selected from the public group. In the absence of an agency in the trade in which a dispute arises, and/or with the consent of both parties, the Minister of Labour may refer the dispute to the Industrial Court (or to a single arbitrator appointed by him, or to a special board of arbitration). According to its importance the case, if referred to the Court, is heard by the President or by a chairman. The Court's decision, though generally accepted, is not enforceable unless this is agreed to in advance.[2]

The Industrial Court between 1919 and 1932 handled 1,573 cases, involving wages in about half of these, interpretation of awards in more than a fourth, and working conditions in between a tenth and a ninth, with about the usual results in terms of "favorable to the employers," "favorable to workers," and "compromises."[3] Of this total, no fewer than 540 were handled in 1920, a year marked by very unsettled economic conditions and by a large and rather militant trade unionism. Some 43 per cent were handled in the six-year period 1921–1926, and some 18 per cent in the six-year period 1927–1932. As these data indicate, the number of cases handled declined greatly—to twenty-eight in 1932. This decline is explained by several factors, including the bad state of trade, less extensive labor organization, a less militant unionism following the general stoppage of 1926, the establishment by legislation of special agencies in important industries alluded to above, and the preference of many trades for their own machinery or their disinclination to refer cases to the Industrial Court. In recent years the most important work of the Court has been in government departments, the civil service, and such government industries as the naval dockyards.[4]

[1] Ministry of Labour, *Twenty-first Abstract of Labour Statistics of the United Kingdom* (1919–1933), p. 135. By 1936, however, it had increased to 5,308,000. U. S. Department of Labor, *Report of the Commission on Industrial Relations in Great Britain* (1938), p. 122.

[2] In a few cases the courts held that decisions made by the Industrial Court were enforceable. This had the effect that some of the trades became opposed to reference of disputes to the Court and militated against its success.

[3] For statistical tables, see D. Chang, *op. cit.*, pp. 152–153, 167–168.

[4] Now, however, civil service cases, formerly referred to the Court, are handled by a

The Industrial Court, as it decided cases, was expected to establish and observe sound principles in the determination of wages and other issues, and also to be helpful in coordinating wages so as to build a consistent wage rate structure, as well as to serve directly as an agency of industrial peace. In neither function has it been successful; it could not be expected to be. In determining wages it has considered, but none too consistently, what the industry could afford to pay, the cost of a desirable standard of living, changes in the cost of living, and other factors commonly recognized; it not been able to advance the knowledge of wage determination already possessed. Nor has it been able to coordinate and standardize wages because it could not, consistently with common sense, always regard a living or other wage as a first charge upon industry.[1]

As has already been stated, the government is authorized to set up courts of inquiry as needed in cases of actual or threatened stoppages. The purpose is to reach helpful findings of fact and through publicity enlist public sympathy so as to effect the settlement of disputes of great moment to the community at large. As Dr. Chang observes,[2] "The power to appoint a court of inquiry has been used with great reserve and only in cases of great disputes on matters of exceptional importance."[3] In the entire eighteen-year period from 1920 to 1937, only twenty-three courts of inquiry were appointed to deal with disputes affecting such important industries as coal mining, transport, building, engineering, and the woolen textile trades. These courts appear to have been established more frequently by Labour than by other governments, if allowance is made for their respective time in power. In approximately half of the cases settlements have been reached along the lines suggested in the reports made; in a few cases the necessary cooperation in the inquiry has not been given or the report made has been ignored.[4]

Thus Britain has maintained a diversified and flexible system for maintaining or restoring industrial peace, a system embracing a mediation service, an Industrial Court, courts of inquiry, and special agencies in certain

---

special tribunal similar in form to the Court. "It has an independent chairman, one member selected from a Government panel, and another from the staff side of the national Whitley council. Cases coming up for arbitration include claims for wages, hours, and leave of absence. Consideration is given to claims affecting a group but not an individual. Awards are given effect by the Government subject to the overriding authority of Parliament." Quoted from *Monthly Labor Review*, vol. 47 (1938), p. 51.

[1] For analyses of decisions and more or less critical appraisals of the work of the Court, see D. Chang, *op. cit.*, especially pp. 154–166, and Mary T. Rankin, *Arbitration Principles and the Industrial Court* (1931). See also Lord Amulree, and Allan G. B. Fisher, *Some Problems of Wages and Their Regulation in Great Britain* (1926), Chap. 6.

[2] D. Chang, *op. cit.*, p. 135.

[3] See summary by D. Chang, *ibid.*, p. 136.

[4] The reports are made to Parliament. No limitations are imposed on strike or lockout when a court of inquiry is established.

industries. Joint industrial councils and trade machinery have also been encouraged. Britain has felt that peace is promoted by the existence of strong organizations of employers and employees, negotiating jointly. And, as already indicated, she has realized that in large degree maintenance of industrial peace depends upon the maintenance of wholesome conditions as regards wages and other matters of importance in industrial relations. Social security and the regulation of wages as well as joint industrial councils find place in the British system for maintaining and promoting industrial peace.

THE CANADIAN INDUSTRIAL DISPUTES INVESTIGATION ACT AND RELATED STATE LEGISLATION[1]

Since 1907 the so-called system of compulsory investigation in Canada has aroused more interest and has been the subject of more discussion than any other device employed in the settlement of industrial disputes, except, possibly, the compulsory arbitration systems of Australia and New Zealand. Moreover, the principle has been incorporated into the legislation of a number of other countries,[1] and of the state of Colorado, and, in a measure, of Michigan and Minnesota.

Canada had experimented with a conciliation law enacted in 1900, based directly upon the British legislation of 1896, and with a railways disputes act passed in 1903. Under these measures about the usual percentage of disputes had been settled, with or without strike, as had been settled elsewhere under similar measures. Early in the century much industrial warfare developed, the most bitter fights being between the miners, who organized and sought recognition for the purpose of collective bargaining, and their employers. Developing in a long series of bitter strikes was the strike in 1906 at Lethbridge, Alberta, the source of the coal supply for a large population in western Canada. The strike

---

[1] In the vast literature relating to the Canadian Act, the following books, monographs, and articles are particularly valuable: B. M. Selekman, *Postponing Strikes* (1927); the same author's *Law and Labor Relations: A Study of the Industrial Disputes Investigation Act of Canada*, Publications of the Graduate School of Business Administration, Harvard University, vol. 23, no. 1 (1936); H. A. Logan, *The History of Trade-union Organization in Canada* (1928); G. R. Askwith, *Industrial Problems and Disputes*, Chap. 24; W. L. Mackenzie King, *Canadian Method of Preventing Strikes and Lockouts* (pamphlet, 1912); B. M. Squires, "Operation of the Industrial Disputes Investigation Act of Canada," U. S. Bureau of Labor Statistics, *Bulletin* 233 (1918); B. M. Squires, in John R. Commons, *Trade Unionism and Labor Problems* (New Series, 1921), Chap. 44; F. A. Acland, "Canadian Legislation concerning Industrial Disputes," *Labour Gazette*, vol. 16 (1916), pp. 1111–1119; C. E. Dankert, "The Canadian Industrial Disputes Investigation Act," *Journal of Political Economy*, vol. 36 (1928), pp. 141–163. For official and current reports, see Dominion of Canada, Department of Labour, *Labour Gazette* (published monthly), and the Department's annual reports.

[1] For countries legislating along these lines see the International Labour Office, *Conciliation and Arbitration of Industrial Disputes* (1933), p. 535.

dragged on for months, fuel was lacking, the efforts of the mediator failed because of the refusal of the operators to recognize or deal with the union. His efforts to restore peace having been balked, Mr. King, then Deputy Minister of Labour and more recently Premier, took the ground in his report on the case that private rights end where they become public wrongs, and held that where the public is dependent upon a service it should be rendered or the disputants should give way to others who would render it. At any rate, he contended, the public has a right to know what the dispute is about and what a competent board would regard as a fair settlement of it. He concluded his report by suggesting that strikes and lockouts should be made unlawful in industries with a large element of public interest or necessity until a "conciliation board" had settled the dispute, or, that failing, had investigated and reported on the merits of the issues involved. Striking a sympathetic chord, the suggestion was incorporated in a government bill, which was quickly enacted into law. These are the essentials in the early history of the Lemieux Act,[1] approved Mar. 22, 1907.

The Act has always applied to disputes arising in the operation of coal and metal mines and of public utilities of all sorts. During World War I it applied also to disputes in munitions works. As a result of another amendment it was applied to disputes where a government unit was the employer. To complete the legislative history, it must be pointed out that in 1925 the Act was declared by the British High Court to exceed the Dominion Government's powers contained in the British North America Act; the power being exercised in the specific case, it was held, belonged to the several provinces except in so far as interprovincial disputes were concerned. Almost immediately a new act was passed, designed to meet the views of the court. This legislation now applies to disputes in certain industries with a large degree of public interest, when the government is involved or the disputes are interprovincial, or, though provincial, if the province has authorized the Dominion to proceed under the Act.[2] By the end of 1932 all the provinces except Prince Edward Island had given the Dominion this authority. More recently, however, Alberta and British Columbia rescinded their authorization and provided for the creation of provincial machinery for dealing with disputes falling within the jurisdiction of the province.[3] Likewise, Manitoba and New Brunswick now have similar legislation, which—although the

---

[1] So known because Lemieux was then Speaker of the House. Organized labor in the United States has frequently referred to it as the "Lemon Act."

[2] The Act is available also to disputants in other industries. A limited number of such disputes have been settled under it. By an Order in Council of November, 1939, the Act was extended to cover all war production industries—all those which in the judgment of the Minister of Labour are essential for the war needs of the country.

[3] Alberta, 2 Geo. VI, Chap. 57 (1938); British Columbia, 1 Geo. VI, Chap. 31 (1937) and 2 Geo. VI, Chap. 23 (1938).

enabling acts have not been repealed—in large measure supersedes the Dominion law.[1]

The Canadian law requires that employers and employees coming within the jurisdiction of the law must give thirty days' notice of an intended or desired change in wages or hours. If such proposals result in a dispute that is likely to end in a strike or lockout, such strike or lockout may not be declared and no change in wages or hours may be made until the dispute has been dealt with by a board. The side proposing the change must make application for a board.[2] If a grievance over discharge or conditions of employment other than hours or wages threatens to result in a strike or lockout, the dispute also goes to a board. An application for the establishment of a board accompanied by a statement of the nature of the dispute must be filed with the Registrar of Boards of Conciliation, who notifies the Minister of Labour, and a copy must be sent to the other party to the dispute. The latter party is given opportunity to reply. Upon receipt of application and answer, the Minister of Labour proceeds, within his discretion, to have a board set up for mediation, investigation, and report.[3] A new board is established for each dispute. Each side is to select its representative on the board, and these two are to select a third, who serves as chairman. In the event either disputant refuses or neglects to select a representative, or in the event of failure to agree upon the third member, the board is completed by appointment by the Minister of Labour. In fact, one or more appointments are frequently made by that official. During the five years 1920–1924, the workers in three cases, and the employers (sometimes a government unit) in twenty-four cases failed to select their representatives. In eighty-eight cases the chairman was appointed by the government; in forty-four cases he was agreed upon by the other two members of the board.[4]

The boards thus constituted have the powers of a court to summon witnesses and to call for records and other data and may adopt such procedure as they see fit.[5] Most of them in fact proceed quite informally

[1] Manitoba, 1 Geo. VI, Chap. 40 (1937) and 3 Geo. VI, Chap. 63 (1939); New Brunswick, 2 Geo. VI, Chap. 68 (1938) and 3 Geo. VI, Chap. 41 (1939).

[2] Prior to 1925 the party deciding to strike or lock out was required to do so.

[3] During the War beginning in 1939, provision was made for an Industrial Disputes Inquiry Commission of three to make a preliminary investigation of any threatened dispute and try to settle it.

[4] Perhaps it has been increasingly difficult to agree upon a chairman. In any event, during the years 1907–1918, 103 chairmen were agreed upon as against 111 appointed by the Minister of Labour, while during the subsequent years to 1925, 78 chairmen were agreed upon and 128 appointed.

[5] Once established, they are not directed or supervised by the Labour Department. Since December, 1940, however, they have, in wage cases, been required to follow certain principles laid down by the Dominion Government. No wage rate that is "fair and reasonable" can be raised above the highest level paid by the employer in question from

and with the hope that the disputants will come to an agreement. Conciliation, as the term is popularly used, is the largest element in the Canadian system. When it succeeds the agreement becomes the report of the board. Only when conciliation fails is there investigation and independent report, with recommendation.

Between Mar. 22, 1907, and Mar. 31, 1940, 976 applications were made for the setting up of boards, and 594 boards were actually established.[1] To summarize results in the first 421 of these (those of 1907–1925): there was unanimous agreement and report (nearly always the disputants agreed and the agreement became the finding) by 230, and agreement except on minor points by 25 others. Thus, in approximately three-fifths of the cases a satisfactory settlement was reached. In eighty-seven, or 20.7 per cent, of the cases, the workers' representatives dissented, in fifty-three, or 12.6 per cent, of the cases, the employers' representatives dissented, while in a limited number of cases (three) there were as many findings as members of the board.[2] But it is found that, after all, the majority findings are usually accepted and, possibly with some changes, made the basis of settlement of the disputes. Though it is not unlawful to strike after a report has been gazetted,[3] there were during the thirty-three years ending in 1940 only forty-one cases in which boards were established and strikes were not averted or ended[4] (see Table 12).

1926 to Dec. 15, 1940, except for a cost-of-living bonus. In November, 1941, this wage policy was extended to all except a few industries, and employers were forbidden to increase the basic rates paid on Nov. 15 without permission from the National War Labor Board, established to administer the order. For further details, see *Wartime Regulation of Wages and Hours in Canada*, U. S. Department of Labor, Wage and Hour Division (December, 1941).

[1] *Report of the Department of Labour* [Canada] *for the Fiscal Year Ending March* 31, 1940, p. 29. A few of the boards dealt with two or more applications. *Ibid.*

[2] For the period 1907–1935, the extent of agreement among the members of the boards was practically identical with that in the eighteen years ending in 1925 (see B. M. Selekman, *Law and Labor Relations*, p. 38, and the same author's *Postponing Strikes*, p. 65).

[3] Under an amendment passed after the outbreak of World War II, the Minister of Labour must be notified of any intent to strike. He may order a strike vote under the supervision of the Department of Labour. It is then unlawful to strike unless a majority so vote.

[4] Of course most of the threats are threats to strike. This being so, it is not difficult to explain why in so many cases in which the workers dissent, there should be no strike. One fact is that, as likely as not, the workers have secured some gain anyway. Another, and an important, fact is that the delay involved in the procedure must ordinarily work to the advantage of the employer and to the disadvantage of the workers. In this connection it may be pointed out that of the 408 cases disposed of down to 1925, the days elapsing between application for a board and report did not exceed 30 in 55 and did not exceed 60 in 240. On the other hand, the time elapsing exceeded 60 days in 168 cases, 75 days in 111 cases, and 90 days in 71 cases or, roughly, 1 case in 6. During the thirteen years 1925–1938, of 118 cases, 2 were disposed of within 30 days and 26 within 60 days, while the time elapsing exceeded 60 days in 92 cases, 75 days in 73 cases, and 90 days in 67 cases.

TABLE 12.—PROCEEDINGS UNDER CANADIAN INDUSTRIAL DISPUTES INVESTIGATION ACT BY
INDUSTRIES, FROM MAR. 22, 1907, TO MAR. 31, 1940[1]

Industries affected	Number of applications for boards received	Number of strikes not averted or ended
I. Disputes affecting mines, transportation and communication, other public utilities, and war work:		
1. Mining and smelting:		
Coal..	106	13
Metal...	22	5
Asbestos..	1	0
Salt..	2	1
2. Transportation and communication:		
Steam railways......................................	262	7
Street and electric railways........................	154	7
Motor transportation...............................	17	0
Express...	14	1
Shipping..	69	0
Telegraphs..	36	1
Telephones..	12	0
3. Miscellaneous:		
Light and power and waterworks....................	65	3
Elevators...	13	0
4. War work...	32	1
II. Disputes not falling clearly within the direct scope of the Act	171	2
Total...	976	41

[1] *Report of the Department of Labour* [Canada] . . . 1940, p. 31.

This seemingly remarkable record must, however, be materially discounted for reasons the government has not been at pains to point out in its reports. It is certainly erroneous to say, as it has been so frequently said or implied, that in a specified number of cases (the total minus the number of lawful stoppages) strikes have been averted. As Dr. Squires has pointed out, boards have been applied for but not set up in a large number of cases, and strikes have seldom followed. The weight of this fact is not entirely destroyed by the further fact that to an increasing extent the mediators attached to the Department of Labour have sought to compose disputes before the government has proceeded to establish boards. As Dr. Selekman has said, "As soon as the Department of Labour receives an application for a board, it attempts wherever possible to bring about a settlement through mediation and conciliation and thus to avert the necessity for establishing a board."[1] Of 305 cases within the scope of the Act, arising during the fifteen years ending in 1940, agreement was achieved by Department action or by the resumption of negotiations without board procedure in 122 cases.[2] Evidently most

[1] B. M. Selekman, *Law and Labor Relations*, p. 34.

[2] During the thirty-three years ending in 1940, there has been a decline in the proportion of cases in which boards were set up. (*Report of the Department of Labour* [Canada] . . . 1940, p. 32). In the cases in which boards were not set up, either the machinery provided

of the settlements resulted from the intervention of the Department. Over against this significant figure, board reports embodied agreements in twenty-nine cases and were the basis of agreements in sixty-eight others. In twenty-six cases the reports of the boards were rejected but agreements reached by resumed negotiation or as a result of further mediation by the Department's mediators.[1] But conceding that most of the cases in which boards were not established were exceptional, no one would believe that suspensions would have occurred in all the other cases had there been no intervention. Voting to strike in order to secure intervention is one thing, voting with the expectation of suspending work is another. In organized industry a large proportion of the strike votes do not result in actual suspensions. No one could possibly state how many strikes have been averted in Canada by the provisions and requirements of the Industrial Disputes Investigation Act.

To turn to a slightly different aspect of the case, investigation has shown that the law, with its time limitations and penalties, has been as frequently ignored or openly violated as it has been observed. The facts have been, at least partially, revealed by Dr. Squires, Dr. Selekman, and others. Thus, according to Selekman,[2] strikes were either "averted or ended"[3] in 589 of a total of 638 disputes referred to boards in the fields of

TABLE 13.—ESTIMATED NUMBER OF STRIKES OCCURRING IN PUBLIC UTILITY INDUSTRIES IN VIOLATION OF THE CANADIAN INDUSTRIAL DISPUTES INVESTIGATION ACT, BY INDUSTRY, MAR. 22, 1907, TO MAR. 31, 1935[1]

Industry	Strikes in violation of the Act		
	1907–1925	1925–1935	Total
Railroads	51	3	54
Street railways	25	1	26
Other municipal	30	1	31
Coal mining	198	154	352
Shipping	58	17	75
Other mining	38	4	42
All other	72	5	77
Total	472	185	657

[1] B. M. Selekman, *Law and Labor Relations*, p. 9. In 52 of these 657 cases, application for the establishment of boards was made but strikes preceded this or occurred before proceedings were completed.

by the Act could not be utilized or settlements were effected by other agencies. *Ibid.*, p. 29.

[1] B. M. Selekman, *Law and Labor Relations*, pp. 33–34, and Reports of the Department of Labour (Canada) for 1936, 1937, 1938, 1939, and 1940.

[2] B. M. Selekman, *ibid.*, p. 8.

[3] "Averted" does not always mean averted. "Ended" means that contrary to law, strikes had occurred before boards had been set up or before proceedings had been finished. There were few, some forty-seven, of these unlawful strikes.

public utilities and mining, down to 1935. Over against this figure, in addition to the lawful, there were 657 unlawful strikes. The record in mining and shipping has been particularly bad, as is shown by Table 13.

The details call for no further comment, except the observation that the Canadian record has perhaps been no better than that of the Massachusetts state board. But the large number of unlawful strikes raises the question, what steps have been taken to secure observance of the law? Some moral pressure has been exerted upon disputants to comply with the law, and there has been occasional threat of prosecution, but there have been few prosecutions for its violation and, at least until 1941, none by the government itself. In only a few instances have penalties been inflicted. The explanation is that in a democratically governed country it is impolitic to prosecute and impose penalties upon workers for going on strike. Very soon after the adoption of the Act the penalty clauses became almost dead letters.[1]

Though the test of strikes "averted" and of unlawful strikes occurring in Canada is important to apply, it is exceedingly difficult to measure the degree of success of any conciliation or arbitration law. Little value attaches to comparisons between one country and another, for the situations are not the same, and what will work in a given way in the one is not likely to work in precisely the same way in the other. Even comparison of experiences under different laws in a given country has limited value because the situation changes with the lapse of time. Perhaps as good a test as any of a law is found in attitudes of the various groups affected by it.

It is interesting to observe that there have been no differences between the Liberal and the Conservative parties as to the soundness of the Canadian Act. It has been administered with the same sense of responsibility regardless of which party has been in power. The public generally, though apparently not well informed as to its operation, is favorable to the Act because it is supposed to safeguard somewhat against turmoil and to be a conservative influence.

Some of the railway managers were opposed to the Act at the outset, but they soon changed their position. The die-hard western coal operators were hostile to it and remained so until their association was dissolved in 1925. But employers generally have always favored the law "in principle," although they have at times opposed its application to any other industries than public utilities. The time given for considering demands made upon them and for making adjustments has been advan-

---

[1] Under Secs. 58, 59, and 60 of the Act of 1907, employers declaring an unlawful lockout were liable to a fine of from $100 to $1,000 per day of its duration; and each employee unlawfully striking was liable to a fine ranging from $10 to $50 for each day of the strike. Moreover, penalties ranging from $50 to $1,000 might be imposed on any person inciting, encouraging, or aiding unlawful strikes or lockouts.

tageous to them. Yet, as would be expected, they have complained of
details in its operation and have lost enthusiasm for it since the First
World War, as labor has had better standing with the government and
has come to advocate an extension of the scope of the Act.[1] Following
1925 they also complained of the tardiness of wage reductions when
needed.

Organized labor has always been divided on the subject of the Disputes Investigation law, but since 1918 a great majority of the unions have
distinctly favored it. While the Catholic unions, always opposed to
strikes, and a considerable number of other unions have always favored
the Act, the miners and many others, especially those in close touch
with the unions of the United States, were bitterly opposed to it. They
complained of delays and of chairmen not being impartial; they saw in
the time limitations injury to them and benefit to the employer; they
expressed fear lest, as in Norway, compulsory investigation would lead
to compulsory arbitration. But during and since the First World War,
there has been a distinct change in the attitude of many of the unions
formerly quite hostile. This is explained perhaps by the recognition of
labor during the War and most of the subsequent years, the degree of
protection given to wage standards developed in time of labor shortage
and high cost of living, and the amendment of the Act so that employers
must (since 1925) give notice of changes desired, and, if these are protested, make application for the establishment of a board. An additional
factor is found in a rather important change in policy. In the earlier
years union recognition, questions of worker representation, and related
issues were generally treated as not proper issues for government intervention. In more recent years, however, such issues have generally been
taken up and treated as liberally as the exigencies of the cases would
permit. The principles of collective bargaining, of unlimited selection
of their representatives by the workers, and majority rule have generally been recognized and accepted by the boards and the Ministry of
Labour. This has been of substantial value to the newer and weaker
unions.[2] But whatever the factors entering into the explanation may

---

[1] Among the complaints have been: (1) agreements resulting have not settled matters
for any length of time as compulsory arbitration is supposed to do; (2) poor chairmen in
concrete cases; (3) the amendment of 1925, requiring them to hold desired action in abeyance and to request that a board be set up.

[2] For an excellent discussion of this phase of the matter, see B. M. Selekman, *Law and
Labor Relations*, pp. 23–24. It is to be noted in this connection that in recent years statutes
have been enacted in Canada somewhat related to the so-called Wagner Acts found in the
United States. The Dominion Government, in 1939, made punishable by fine or imprisonment both discrimination against employees because of union affiliation and the use of
threats, intimidation, or actual reprisals to prevent employees from joining a labor organization. Similar provisions, which in a majority of cases were enacted in connection with, or
incidental to, the setting up of machinery for conciliation and arbitration, are contained

be, there has been an interesting change in attitude, taking organized labor as a whole. Formerly there was much denunciation of the Act at the annual sessions of the Canada Trades Congress, with which a majority of the unions have been affiliated, but since World War I the Congress has on more than one occasion expressed approval of it and voted in favor of extending its scope.[1]

The Canadian law, as has already been said, has served as a basis for legislation in a number of countries, in Colorado,[2] and, in a measure, in Michigan, Minnesota, and Iowa.[3] Little detail need be presented, however, for it would add nothing significant in appraising this type of legislation. Suffice it to say that in Colorado, where the Industrial Commission is charged with the administration of the law and functions

---

in the laws of no less than seven provinces. It should be noted, however, that the Manitoba law penalizes only the use of threats or intimidation. The laws of Nova Scotia, British Columbia, and Alberta impose penalties on employers who refuse to bargain with the representatives chosen by a majority of the employees concerned; the others, with the exception of Quebec, which ignores the question, merely assert the lawfulness of collective bargaining. Unlike the National Labor Relations Act, none of these provincial acts clearly outlaws company unions, and all save that of Nova Scotia penalize coercion by employees as well as by employers. But while the Quebec legislation definitely outlaws the closed shop, the laws of four other provinces follow the National Labor Relations Act to the extent of stating that their provisions shall not invalidate closed-shop agreements. Quebec alone provides penalties in the event of the dismissal of any employee for complaint or testimony in an investigation or prosecution under the two acts concerned; moreover, any employee illegally dismissed has the right to claim damages. See Alberta, 2 Geo. VI, Chap. 57 (1938); British Columbia, 1 Geo. VI, Chap. 31 (1937), and 2 Geo. VI, Chap. 23 (1938); Canada, 3 Geo. VI, Chap. 30 (1939); Manitoba, 1 Geo. VI, Chap. 40 (1937); New Brunswick, 2 Geo. VI, Chap. 68 (1938), and 3 Geo. VI, Chap. 41 (1939); Nova Scotia, 1 Geo. VI, Chap. 6 (1937); Quebec 1, Geo. VI, Chaps. 49 and 50 (1937), 2 Geo. VI, Chaps. 52 and 53 (1938), 3 Geo. VI, Chaps. 61 and 62 (1939); Saskatchewan, 2 Geo. VI, Chap. 87 (1938).

[1] For example, in a resolution passed in 1920, the Congress asked that the Act be extended to all industries upon the application of either an organization involved, an employer, or a municipality and that the compulsory clauses restraining the right to strike pending decision of a board be eliminated so "as to preserve full liberty of workers and employers during sitting of the board." Trades and Labour Congress of Canada, Report of Proceedings (1920), p. 182.

[2] For an analysis of the Colorado law, description of procedure under it, and discussion of accomplishments, see C. E. Warne and M. E. Gaddis, "Eleven Years of Compulsory Investigation of Industrial Disputes in Colorado," Journal of Political Economy, vol. 35 (1927), pp. 657–683.

[3] An Iowa law [Iowa Code (1935), Secs. 1496, 1497, 1500, 1507] provides for boards of conciliation and arbitration to be appointed by the Governor on written application of either party to a dispute, the mayor or county chairman, the labor commissioner, or twenty-five citizens. Strikes and lockouts are thus forbidden during a ten-day period of investigation by the board. Decisions are binding for a year if both parties have agreed to be so bound.

In 1941, Georgia passed a law prohibiting any strike until after thirty days' written notice to the employer, except in the case of seasonal industries and unions under the Railway Labor Act.

as mediator, the records of strikes "averted" and of unlawful strikes
have been not unlike the record in Canada as presented above.

The legislation in Michigan and Minnesota finds place in the labor-
relations acts passed in 1939, acts quite as much concerned about strikes
and lockouts and unfair practices by labor as about the right of workmen
to organize and to bargain without employer interference.[1]

In the former of these two states a Board of Mediation is provided
for, and the governor is empowered to appoint special commissions to
hold hearings and report on disputes affecting public utilities, hospitals,
and other institutions or industries affected with the element of public
interest. Notice of intention to strike or to lock out in any industry
must be given the Board of Mediation by union or employer; it is a
misdemeanor to strike or lock out for five days after such notice is
given, and the parties are required to confer in an effort to reach an
adjustment. The Board is empowered to undertake mediation. In
the case of industries affected by the element of public interest, going
on strike or locking out is made unlawful for a period of thirty days after
notice is given.

The related Minnesota statute provides that when a change in a labor
agreement or in wages, hours, and working conditions is desired by union
or employer, it (or he) shall give written notice thereof to the other party.
The parties must then endeavor in good faith to iron out their differences.
If no settlement is reached within ten days, ten days' notice must be
given the state conciliator by the union of any intention to strike or by
the employer of an intended lockout. Thereupon it is the duty of the
conciliator to hold conferences and to attempt to mediate a settlement.
Strikes or lockouts are, of course, under a ban during the ten-day period.[2]
In the case of disputes in industries with a public interest, the stay upon
suspensions, the machinery established, and the procedures laid down
are essentially the same as are found in Michigan.

COMPULSORY ARBITRATION OF INDUSTRIAL DISPUTES: NEW ZEALAND

We turn to a discussion of compulsory arbitration of industrial disputes,[3] a method which has been adopted in several countries.[4] The

[1] Michigan, Public Act no. 176, *Acts* (1939); Minnesota, *Laws* (1939), Chap. 440.

[2] Under a 1941 amendment, unless a strike or lockout is begun within ninety days of
service of notice, it is necessary to serve a new notice. The ninety-day period may be
extended by written agreement of both parties, filed with the conciliator.

[3] In connection with this discussion of compulsory arbitration in New Zealand and
Australia, our discussion of the regulation of wages may be consulted. See vol. I, Chap. VI.

[4] Considering modern times only and omitting wartime regulations, compulsory arbitration has been adopted by the following countries: New Zealand, 1894; New South Wales
and West Australia, 1902; Australia (Commonwealth), 1904; South Australia and Queensland, 1912; Norway, 1916; Kansas, 1920; Mexico, 1925; Italy, 1926; France, 1936, 1938.
Germany had a system of quasi-compulsory arbitration from 1923 to 1934. See Nathan
Reich, *Labor Relations in Post-War Germany*, especially Chap. 4.

laws have been of different types. Some have provided for an inclusive system of arbitration, others for arbitration of disputes in certain industries with a large element of public interest; some have made recourse to the court mandatory, while others have left the initiation of proceedings to one of the disputants; some have prohibited all strikes and lockouts, while others have prohibited strikes only after proceedings looking toward a settlement have been begun. The following discussion will emphasize the experience of New Zealand and Australia, where compulsory arbitration has been longest and most thoroughly tested and where it can be studied with most benefit. Brief reference will, however, be made to the short-lived experiment in Kansas.

Environmental Factors.—As Sir John Findlay has pointed out,[1] compulsory arbitration in New Zealand must be studied in the light of such factors as her population, industry, government, and system of social control. The population is largely of British origin and is unusually homogeneous. In 1940 it had grown to something over a million and a half (1,634,500); it was scattered over the inhabited parts of the two islands with an area of nearly 105,000 square miles. The density of population is therefore less than that of the state of Kansas, but, owing to the conditions of settlement and sources of livelihood, some 50 per cent of the people live in urban areas. The basic industry is agriculture and stock raising, but distance from other countries and a system of protective tariffs have permitted a considerable amount of secondary manufacture to develop in addition to that using farm products as raw materials.

Recent figures on the distribution of wage earners among branches of employment are unavailable. But of the 414,673 wage earners in 1926, about one-eighth (52,010) were engaged in agricultural and pastoral pursuits, and about 2 per cent (8,106) in mining and quarrying. Over against these, approaching one-fourth (90,025) were engaged in slaughtering and meat packing and various other branches of manufacture, with more than 5 per cent (22,822) engaged in building construction. More than 10 per cent (44,645) were engaged in shipping and transportation. The others (197,065) were employed in the operation of local public utilities, in banks, in stores, in domestic and personal service, etc.

Because of the nature of their country and the conditions surrounding its settlement, the New Zealanders have not thought in terms of "eternal principles," but in terms of concrete and immediate problems and have been guided by experience. Naturally enough, they have attacked many problems through state and local governments. As Sir John Findlay has said,

---

[1] Sir John Findlay, "Industrial Peace in New Zealand," *International Labour Review,* vol. 4 (1921), pp. 32–46.

"The state has not hesitated to embark on any enterprise that promised a reasonable measure of success and of general good. It not only owns, and has in the main constructed, the railways, but has adopted the settled policy of prohibiting the construction and working of any railway by private enterprise. Nearly all of our city and borough tramways are municipally owned and operated. The state has acquired, to a substantial extent by compulsion, large pastoral estates and divided them among landless would-be settlers. It has lent these settlers money for farming purposes at the lowest possible rates of interest and on the most favorable terms. It has engaged extensively in ordinary banking. It has opened and worked coal mines. It has erected and conducted saw-mills for the supply of a portion of its requirements. It has extensively engaged in life and fire insurance. It has acquired land and erected many houses thereon for workmen generally. It has co-operated as a helpful and unremunerated partner with those engaged in nearly every branch of production."[1]

It is these and other experiments about which Le Rossignol and Stewart wrote in *State Socialism in New Zealand* and which Professor Condliffe has interpreted in his *New Zealand in the Making*.[2]

Compulsory arbitration in New Zealand was just another experiment and was undertaken without a foreseeing of all that would be involved in that form of intervention and control. The maritime strike (1890) had spread from Australia to New Zealand, where it interrupted shipping and paralyzed much of industry for several weeks. Then, too, owing to the course of industrial development, the lot of the laborer had for some time been a hard one, and the unions had become rather ineffective in safeguarding the workers' interests. The Minister of Labour, W. Pember Reeves, reviewed the experience of other countries to see what might be done to improve the situation, but found no satisfactory answer. He concluded that a solution, if to be found in any plan, was to be found in a system of mediation and compulsory arbitration. With the employing interests vigorously opposing, with organized labor supporting, and with the farmers not greatly interested but "going along" with labor, a government bill was finally enacted in 1894.

Arbitration Policies and Machinery.—The law enacted provided that New Zealand should be divided into eight industrial districts, in each of which a standing board of conciliation should be established. This board was to consist of one or two members selected by the associated employers, of the same number selected by the organized workers, and of one or two selected jointly by these direct representatives. Bargaining was expected to obtain as theretofore, but, in the event of deadlock, either

[1] Quoted from Sir John Findlay, *op. cit.*, p. 43.
[2] J. E. Le Rossignol and W. D. Stewart, *State Socialism in New Zealand* (1910); J. B. Condliffe, *New Zealand in the Making: A Survey of Economic and Social Development* (1930).

party might seek the good offices of the district board. If neither party saw fit to do so, the dispute would take the usual course; there was no general prohibition of strikes or lockouts. If an application was made to a district board, however, a strike or lockout was prohibited. The board was expected, first, to make an effort to bring about a compromise agreeable to the two parties, which was to be recorded and to constitute a legally binding and enforceable contract. If mediation failed, it then became the duty of the board to render a decision according to the merits of the case and with a view to substantial justice. This award, or "recommendation" as it was called, was binding upon the parties, subject to appeal within one month to the Arbitration Court.

The Arbitration Court was composed of a judge, having the qualifications of a judge of the Supreme Court, and two associate members, one nominated by the registered workers' unions[1] and the other by the employers' unions and appointed by the governor. The court was expected to render a decision on the appealed case within one month. From its decision there was no right of appeal to the ordinary courts except on questions of law.[2]

Provision was made for the enforcement of recommendations and awards. The parties, frequently large groups, were specified in them and they were bound, subject to such modification as might be made, for the duration of the award and until a new agreement or award was made. The penalty for violation was a fine not to exceed £500, assessed upon the offending employer or union, this being paid to the injured party. If a union's funds were not adequate to pay a fine, the penalty was to be assessed against the individual members but was not to exceed £10 as against any one worker. Prosecution was initiated at first by the other party, but later by the factory inspectors. Evasion by dissolving an organization was protected against. Individuals (employers or employees) might leave the trade, but if they remained in it, they were bound by the provisions of an agreement, recommendation, or award.

The intent of the law was, accordingly, to induce organized workers and employers to bargain collectively and competently and to permit them to bargain as they saw fit. In the event of failure to arrive at an agreement in the first instance, however, they were to mediate and attempt by further negotiation to reach an agreement acceptably fair to both sides. Then—in the case of failure—as a last resort and in the exceptional case, there was to be authoritative decision as to what would be fair as a working relationship between the disputants and to enforce it. The outstanding fact was that more and more of the conditions

---

[1] Unions must be registered in order to bring cases to a board or court.

[2] The law provided that: "No award or proceeding of the Court shall be liable to be challenged, appealed against, reviewed, quashed or called into question by any court of judicature on any account whatsoever."

obtaining in organized industries were established by the Arbitration Court.

The "conciliation boards" were not effective. For one thing some of them were weak. For another, the struggle between employers and workers militated against mediation. But most important, the employers were inclined to carry issues to the court of last resort, because of their opposition to the legislation and because the law was not altogether clear. Pember Reeves had thought that not more than one case in a hundred would ever come before the Arbitration Court. When the bill was under discussion in the Assembly, it was stated that in all probability the Arbitration Court would not hear a case in twenty years. The facts proved to be quite different. Down to 1901, 156 cases arose. Forty-three of these were fully settled and two were partly settled by further negotiation or by board "recommendation"; seven were withdrawn. The other 104, or exactly two-thirds of the entire number, were appealed to the Arbitration Court for final decision. This fact, the delay incidental to original hearing and appeal, and the unsatisfactory state of a number of the conciliation boards[1] led to an amendment of the law in 1901, so that cases might be taken directly to the Arbitration Court. After this was permitted the conciliation boards found little to do and the Court more than it could do expeditiously and with a full-time president. Between 1902 and 1905, the "conciliation boards" dealt with only twenty cases; in 1906, with only two; in 1907, with none at all. A ban had been placed upon the appearance of attorneys, but by this time secretaries and union officials had become specialists in presentation and defense. The outstanding thing, except in those organized trades where collective bargaining had been working smoothly, was litigation in the specialized court.

Results.—Further detail is required to complete the picture of the system of control established through this system of arbitration. The scope of the Act was not clear, but, by court decision and amendment in 1901, it came to apply to labor disputes rather generally except in rural occupations. Eventually it found limited application there—to shearmen and like groups.

Within a few years after the inauguration of the system there was complaint that favorable terms granted under awards handicapped the employers bound by them in competing with other employers. This problem became so pressing that in 1900 the Arbitration Court was authorized, upon petition, to extend the terms of an award and to make it binding upon employers not parties to the dispute occasioning the award. Eventually authority was given to extend an award to and

---

[1] In one industrial district no board had been established.

make it binding upon all employers in a competitive industry throughout New Zealand, but this authority was not really effective until 1920. After that date a limited number of awards had country-wide application. Thus the Court was not merely a judicial body deciding disputes, but a legislative authority prescribing more or less special, limited laws relating to rates of wages, hours of work, sanitary conditions, preference to unionists, and other matters.

The number of registered unions, with privilege of initiating cases, increased from 65 in 1896 to 325 in 1908; the number of employers' associations from 1 to 122, many of them with paid secretaries. With the more extensive registration of unions, recommendations and awards became more numerous and applied to more industries. By Mar. 31, 1907, 535 agreements, recommendations and awards had become effective and binding in some 78 branches of industry. Of these, 135 were effective on the date mentioned. Thus state regulation through the machinery created had to a considerable extent replaced private contracts and collective bargaining. What was the nature and what were the effects of the regulation?

Needless to say, a great variety of things may become issues in the field of industrial relations. A rough analysis shows that in the early years more than seventy types of issues had developed—preference to unionists, rates of wages, hours, discharge, use of a time clock, division of work, whether it was too wet to work, and many others.

The first case coming before the Arbitration Court raised the issue of the union shop. Inasmuch as the law predicated organization and registration of unions, the Court ruled that preference should be given to members of the union. This was soon incorporated into the law. Incidentally questions arose as to restrictive union practices with regard to admission to membership and as to suspensions and expulsions. Consequently there has been some control of unions. On the other hand, unions have been protected and their membership expanded, especially through the support given by the Court in fixing higher wages than the weaker unions had bargaining power to obtain and the preference in employment granted by the Court to union members.

Wages were of course most frequently an issue in disputes. The rates awarded were minimum rates, designed to prevent sweating and to correspond to what fair employers in the region were paying for the type of worker in question.[1] The Court regarded it as its duty to set and from time to time to revise wage rates so as to conserve the purchasing power of wages as of the turn of the century. It did not act with the object in view of sharing profits or altering the distribution of income or

---

[1] *Cf.* vol. I of this treatise, pp. 280–282.

wealth. In other words, the general policy was to fix minima that would be fair and then protect them against being undermined by any substantial increase in the cost of living.[1] The eight-hour day was accepted as a sound principle. The Court favored good working conditions.

Within ten years of the inauguration of this system, the attitude of employers toward it changed from one of strong opposition to one of acceptance. This was more than the effect of time and the adaptation of business to the regulations. Business was expanding, profits were good, the control of wages, in the long run, was rather conservatively exercised. There were no strikes. Investment and business enterprise were not discouraged. And, not unimportant, the changed attitude of organized labor was a further cause of the change in attitude of the employers.

Generally speaking, the attitude of the unions immediately concerned[2] changed from enthusiasm to weakened enthusiasm, and then to one of more or less disappointment. Discontent developed with it some outright opposition to arbitration and espousal of direct action by some unions. There were delays in securing decisions. Once wages were standardized, it was difficult to secure further increases except as an offset to a material increase in prices. "The consistent refusal of the Court to consider anything resembling compulsory profit-sharing meant in effect that the workers were bound by the arbitration legislation to accept nominal wage rates based upon the standard of living of 1900. . . . The substantial benefits which they secured from industrial peace, continuity of employment, the tendency for wages to advance beyond the minimum wage rates, improvements in holidays, hours, and labour conditions, did little to counteract the psychological effect of their feeling that they were tied to inadequate standards of living as expressed in wages." Moreover, "the growing tendency to legalism, inevitable in a tribunal which had accumulated precedents and rules of procedure, was a source of constant irritation."[3] But the explanation of the changing attitude, and more particularly the outright opposition, is found to a considerable extent in the appearance of radical I.W.W. unions. These were few in number, but they were active in certain occupations and industries, and

[1] During the War period it was the policy to maintain the purchasing power of wages as of 1914. Basic wages for the unskilled were increased as the cost of living increased; the semiskilled and the skilled retained their differential rates. At times increases took the form of bonuses. After the War these were twice reduced. In 1925 there were increases in wages that brought the basic rate up to the War maximum. There was no further general change until the most recent depression appeared, when a general reduction was ordered, along with reductions in capital obligations and interest charges.

[2] There were always strongly entrenched craft unions that relied upon their economic power and that were not much interested in the system of compulsory arbitration.

[3] The quotations are from J. B. Condliffe, *New Zealand in the Making*, p. 338.

of course always vocal.   The Court was criticized and denounced; there were demands for change in its selection and personnel.

For twelve years New Zealand had been "A Country without Strikes,"[1] but, with the radical unionism and the discontent, the era of industrial peace ended in 1906.   In that year and in 1907, there were seven strikes, mostly in the slaughtering industry.   Though comparatively few workers were directly involved, the fact that there were strikes and other clouds on the horizon presented the first of three emergencies, each followed by amendatory legislation.   The earlier system having been described and its effects indicated, most of what follows will relate to the appearance of new problems and the amendatory legislation.

Later Modifications.—With the Arbitration Court on trial, three changes were made in the law in 1908.   The first of these was made in an effort to revive the mediation procedure that had failed.   The district boards were abolished; in place of these the governor was authorized to appoint four "conciliation commissioners," one for each of four districts. Moreover, he was authorized to appoint special commissioners as needed to help out, and also to set up "conciliation councils" for settling inter-district disputes.   A commissioner was expected to take the initiative, as the standing boards could not, and to serve as chairman of the special board set up in each case.   The other members of the board were to be representatives of the parties in interest.   Such a board was given essentially the same powers as had been vested in the standing boards—plus that of the initiative; the intent, which was realized in practice, was that the new machinery should use mediation and binding agreement more, the making of binding recommendations and awards very much less.   Of course, the Arbitration Court, with its full-time president, remained in the background with all its former powers, but it was now to become, and to remain, a court of appeals.   Unlike the procedure from 1901 to 1908, a dispute was required to pass through the hands of a "conciliator"; after 1908 it did not come to the Arbitration Court directly.   Peace by agreement was wanted; compulsion was limited to the minimum regarded as essential.   This amendment, it may be observed, was the expression of an interesting verdict on how to proceed in maintaining industrial peace.

In order to meet the challenge of the Arbitration Court's authority, the penalties for violation of its awards were increased, and a clause was inserted by which registration of an industrial union could be suspended for calling an illegal strike.   During the period of suspension a union could participate in neither mediation nor arbitration proceedings, nor could a new union covering the same industry be registered.

A third important amendment prohibited strikes and lockouts in the operation of gas, electric, water, tram, and railway systems until after

[1] Title of Henry D. Lloyd's interesting book (1900).

fourteen days' notice had been given. The object of this time limitation on suspensions was to provide a cooling-off period, and to give the conciliators a better opportunity for functioning in disputes of most serious concern to the public.

The effectiveness of this new legislation will be discussed presently. Suffice it to say at this point that it cleared the atmosphere temporarily. The dissatisfaction previous to the adoption of the amendments had been accompanied by the deregistration of some unions intent upon avoiding compulsory arbitration. This now ceased for the time being; and during the first year of operation of the new system there was only one strike. Yet, in 1912–1913, a second emergency developed. This was caused largely by the growth of "red" unionism and the involvement of other unions in industrial disputes as a result of the setting up of a common federation. Direct action was preached by miners, waterfront workers, and others.

In 1912 there was a strike by the Waiki Miners' Union, running from May to the end of November. This radical organization had canceled its registration. When the engineers organized independently, the Miners' Union denounced them as scabs and went on strike. The strike was lost; a considerable number of the leaders served prison sentences.

A much larger strike, involving 13,000 workers, occurred in 1913. The issue was whether the workers employed by an engineering firm at Wellington should travel by boat from the old location of the works to the new, requiring some thirty minutes, on their own or on the firm's time. The strike spread until it involved building tradesmen, miners, and others, some of them under binding agreements or court awards. At Auckland a general strike was called and participated in by 5,916 workers. Some of the strikers remained away from work for weeks. There were clashes between strikers and their sympathizers and the police. Deregistration of unions had been renewed and now proceeded rapidly.

To meet this situation the law was, in 1913, amended in one interesting respect. The amendment came from the Canadian experience. It applied to unregistered unions and provided that notice should be given of any proposed strike or lockout. Then dispute commissions were to be formed as in Canada, except that each party might appoint one, two, or three representatives who, with the neutral chairman, would constitute boards of three, five, or seven. If mediation failed, investigation and report with recommendation were to follow. No strike was to be permitted for seven days thereafter and until an election had been held under the supervision of the government, at which a majority of the workers voted to suspend work.

These "hobbles" placed upon unregistered unions, together with the formation or threat of formation of "loyal" unions, solved the problem of deregistration. In relatively few instances was it necessary to apply the new provisions of the law.[1] During the next twenty years there were few cancellations of registration; most unions were registered.[2]

After 1908 mediation was successfully used. Approximately two-thirds of the cases in which the government intervened were settled completely by mediation and roughly half of the remaining third were settled in part. Unsettled cases alone went to the Arbitration Court. It must be held in mind, however, that agreements reached were at least colored by the awards of the Court, and these awards were not few or unimportant. About a half-dozen awards were applied in the more recent years to as many industries throughout both islands. It is not too much to say that the wage structure and many details in the field of industrial relations continued to be based largely upon the principles and decisions of the Arbitration Court.

Effectiveness in Preserving Industrial Peace.—The system of arbitration as it developed in New Zealand should be regarded as primarily a system of regulation of the various aspects of industrial relations rather than as a device for preventing strikes. This is necessarily true of compulsory arbitration when applied to industry generally. But what of the system as tested by the record of strikes?

The total number of strikes and lockouts from 1906 to 1939 inclusive was 1,247.[3] These disputes involved 205,271 workers. The number of workers involved declined from 14,815 in 1924 to 2,323 in 1935, then rose to 15,682 in 1939. Most of the suspensions were both small and short-lived, but some of them involved a large number of workers (for New Zealand) and were of considerable duration. Again, a large proportion

---

[1] In forty-two cases to the end of 1923.

[2] The number of registered unions and members were as follows:

Year	Number of unions	Number of members
1901	202	23,768
1921	418	97,719
1928	403	103,980
1932	400	79,283
1933	407	71,888
1934	404	74,391
1935	410	80,929
1936	487	185,527[a]
1937	499	232,986
1938	466	249,231
1939	442	254,690

[a] The reason for this large increase in membership is found in the provision of the Industrial Conciliation and Arbitration Act of 1936 that all workers subject to an award or industrial agreement registered under the Act must become members of a union.

No data are given for unregistered unions. *New Zealand Official Year-book,* 1927, 1932, 1938, 1941.

[3] See footnote at the bottom of page 802.

of the strikes were lawful; yet a large number, including some important suspensions, were in violation of law. The question arises, what steps were taken to enforce the law?

Each year there were some hundreds of prosecutions for violation of agreements and awards—"failing to pay award rate," "accepting less than award rate," "failing to pay overtime rate," "employing too many apprentices," "failing to pay wages weekly," and other types of violation. Though there were times when workers were prosecuted for participating in unlawful strikes, the number of such prosecutions was small—and necessarily so. In 1913–1914, for example, out of a total of 437 prosecutions, 349 were of employers and 88 of workers; and of the 88 only 6 were for taking part in a strike. Inevitably the enforcement of standards was much more vigorous than the enforcement of prohibitions against unlawfully striking or locking out. Many disputes were fought until one party was decisively defeated or until a compromise was reached. Miss Rankin has used exaggerated language in this connection, but what she has said contains an element of truth.

"The settlement of strikes in New Zealand has, without exception, been arrived at by ignoring the Arbitration Court and its awards, and by mutual agreement between the parties concerned; the details of the agreement and the extent of concessions depending on the relative strength of their bargaining power. Out of the total of 63 strikes, 49 were settled by employers granting concessions to workers. In the other 14 cases employers stood firm and the strike collapsed or gradually 'fizzled out.'

INDUSTRIAL DISPUTES IN NEW ZEALAND[1]

Year	Disputes	Workers involved
1906–1925	695	101,455
1926	59	6,264
1927	38	4,476
1928	39	9,253
1929	47	7,151
1930	38	5,467
1931	24	6,356
1932	23	9,355
1933	15	3,558
1934	24	3,773
1935	12	2,323
1936	43	7,354
1937	52	11,411
1938	72	11,388
1939	66	15,682
1906–1939 inclusive	1,247	205,271

[1] New Zealand Official Year-book, 1927, p. 880, 1937, p. 719, 1938, p. 813, 1941, p. 757. Figures for number of workers involved before 1921 are incomplete.

With regard to the 29 strikes cited as important, 27 were settled by concessions to workers, and out of the 27, 20 were illegal."[1]

An examination of New Zealand's experience with compulsory arbitration yields significant conclusions. (1) The system probably reduced the amount of open industrial conflict, but it did not provide a specific solution for the problem of strikes and lockouts. New Zealand did not remain for long a country without strikes. Important strikes, in the operation of railways, for example, occurred. (2) There was the problem of protesting minorities—a very difficult problem to deal with, especially when class-conscious groups are involved. (3) New Zealand came to be of the opinion that mediation and agreements are much to be preferred to litigation and court award. (4) The system, as was inevitable when it was applied to competitive industries, became primarily a system for regulating wages, hours, and other matters involved in industrial relations. It does not provide a simple device easily limited in its application when it is given wide legal embrace. (5) The regulation solved the problem of sweating, gave a more consistent wage rate structure and a better one from the point of view of the needs of the various working groups, and had the effect of improving a variety of working conditions. (6) The system of regulation, for better or for worse, stabilized wage rates and real wages; but it made wages comparatively inelastic in the country's economy.

More Recent Developments.—In the 1920's, the New Zealand system aroused considerable opposition, chiefly as a result of the effect of the depressed condition of the export trades. The farmers and stock growers in particular voiced their dissatisfaction. Though, as has been noted, the regulation had found only limited application in agricultural and pastoral pursuits, the system of compulsory arbitration was charged with causing wage rates and labor costs in these callings to remain too high, because of the effect of regulation upon the general wage level of the country, and with compelling the farmers and stock growers to pay high prices for the domestic commodities they purchased. For many years the agricultural interests had sided with labor on compulsory arbitration and other issues arising out of problems in industry. More recently, however, these interests were found in the forefront among those demanding a change.

In 1927 the government brought forward a bill designed to meet some of the criticism lodged against the system of labor regulation, but, because of the opposition it aroused, decided to postpone further action on the bill and to summon a conference of all parties interested.[2] At the conference various views were expressed by economists and others as to what the effects of the regulation had been and as to any responsibility it had had

---

[1] Mary T. Rankin, *Arbitration and Conciliation in Australasia* (1916), pp. 174–175.

[2] For an excellent account of this conference, see W. H. Cocker, "Industrial Arbitration in New Zealand," *The Economic Record*, vol. 4 (1928), pp. 227–238.

for the fact that agriculture and other pursuits were out of balance with
each other. It is clear, however, that state regulation of wages had been a
comparatively unimportant factor in creating the farmers' plight. The
world chaos, mortgage indebtedness, and taxation had been very much
more important. Moreover, it is clear that the lack of balance between
agriculture and industry obtained in less degree than in many other
countries. Finally, it may be added that it is possible that in the
absence of state regulation union-controlled wages and working rules
might have been such as to create a larger problem in the depression
situation.

As regards changes of policy wanted, the agricultural interests desired
that the whole system should be disestablished. They demanded at
least that it should have no application whatever to disputes in agricultural and pastoral pursuits and that the farmers should be recognized,
along with unions and employers, when industrial disputes were being
mediated or arbitrated. The employers in industry were by no means
in agreement among themselves. In general, however, they wished
regulation to continue but with the system changed so as to eliminate the
element of compulsion in a goodly proportion of the cases. The unions
also disagreed somewhat among themselves, but, in general, they opposed
any weakening of the system of regulation. On the contrary, they desired
it to be applied more vigorously.

The representatives of these different groups disagreed and the
conference of 1928 adjourned without a program of legislation to recommend. But in 1932 several minor amendments and one very important
one were made to the Act of 1925.[1] Minor amendments authorized the
appointment for periods not exceeding twelve months of additional
commissioners (additional to the four regular commissioners whose
appointment had been authorized) to assist in mediation in special cases
and authorized the appointment of a somewhat larger number of "assessors," i.e., representatives of the disputants, in cases involving one district
or two or more districts. The important amendment was one which
greatly changed the system of arbitration. Under the law as it had stood
for years, when mediation failed cases went to the Arbitration Court for
authoritative award.[2] Under the Act of 1932, this was no longer so;
cases were then referred to the Court only by agreement of the assessors.[3]

---

[1] Act assented to Apr. 27, 1932. Published by International Labour Office, in *Legislative Series*, 1932, N. Z. 1.

[2] Subsection 6 of Sec. 58 had read, "If a full settlement of the dispute is not effected by
the Council the dispute shall be referred to the Court for settlement."

[3] Where there were four assessors on either side in a dispute confined to a district, a
case was referred only upon affirmative vote of at least three assessors on each side. If the
number of assessors was less than four, then unanimous vote to refer was required. Where
there were six or more assessors on either side in a case involving two or more districts, a
case was referred only upon affirmative vote of at least five assessors on each side. If the

Voluntary arbitration replaced compulsory arbitration of deadlocked cases. If a deadlocked case was not referred to the Court, any previous binding arrangement lapsed at the end of one month. Where a case involved women workers, however, the Arbitration Court might fix minimum wages for such workers, effective for a specified period of from six months to two years.

Thus, after more than thirty-five years, New Zealand extracted most of the teeth from her system of compulsory arbitration and made recourse to the Court voluntary. Industrial depression was the chief factor in dethroning a system of regulation that was adjudged to stand in the way of necessary adjustment.

The all but complete elimination of compulsory arbitration, however, proved to be short-lived, for a Labour government was returned in 1935, and it proceeded to restore, with amendment, the former system and to add to it other features designed to protect and further the interests of the wage earners. Hence, since June, 1936, arbitration has again been obligatory, and awards may be extended to cover all firms in a competitive area. So, also, has the fixing of basic wages been reintroduced, for a standard family consisting of a man, wife, and three children.[1]

The restoration of compulsory arbitration and wage fixing was accompanied by the general introduction of the forty-hour week, effective in September, 1936. It was to prevail except where sufficient reason was found for a different rule.[2] Agreements in effect were to be amended accordingly, and any reduction in hours was to be accompanied by increases in hourly wages to maintain weekly earnings undiminished. Ordinarily, the forty-hour week was to be one of five days, eliminating Saturday employment in so far as possible.

The new legislation also made union membership compulsory for workers of eighteen years and over who receive adult minimum rates and for such minors as are similarly paid, in so far as they are employed under Arbitration Court Award. The prices of food and gasoline were brought under control and likewise rents for a short period (until September, 1937).

---

number of assessors was less than six, unanimous vote to refer was required. International Labour Office, *Conciliation and Arbitration in Industrial Disputes* (Studies and Reports, Series A, no. 34), p. 651.

[1] See Arbitration Amendment Act, 1936. Its provisions and the early operations under it, in relation to all that had happened prior to 1936, are covered by E. J. Riches' excellent article, "The Restoration of Compulsory Arbitration in New Zealand," *International Labour Review*, vol. 34 (1936), pp. 733-771. See also "Labor Program in New Zealand," in *Monthly Labor Review*, vol. 43 (1936), pp. 1172-1175.

[2] Most of the awards in effect May 1, 1938, provided for the forty-hour week, but some provided for forty-eight hours, and a few, effective in agricultural or maritime occupations, provided for the fifty-two-, fifty-six-, or sixty-hour week. See New Zealand, *Report of the Department of Labour*, 1938, pp. 4-6.

Finally, extensive public works and housing programs were provided for. In short, compulsory arbitration was restored in its pristine strength[1] and was accompanied by various measures constituting a "new deal." In 1940–1941, 22 industrial agreements were filed, and 165 awards made. The total number of agreements and awards in effect Mar. 31, 1941, was 528.

The basic weekly wages fixed in 1936 were £3, 16s. for adult males, and £1, 16s. for adult females. The hourly rates for casual workers were 2s. 6d. for males, 1s. 3d. for females. At the end of 1936, the unions expressed disappointment because the Court had fixed these basic wages at the 1931 level while, partly as a consequence of large public outlays and expanding business, prices had advanced and wages then paid would buy no more than had the former wages. Many unions for a time were vigorous in the demand for the removal of the judge who took up the position that higher basic wages were inappropriate in view of the state of industry.[2]

Australian Experience with Compulsory Arbitration

A study of Australian experience leads to much the same significant conclusions as have been recorded for New Zealand, except for the addition of the influence of the political factor, which has been so important there, and also of the problem presented by a governmental organization involving states and a Commonwealth government superimposed upon them.

Beginning with New South Wales in 1901, compulsory arbitration has been adopted by the several Australian states except Victoria and Tasmania and by the Commonwealth Government shortly after its establishment. Victoria and Tasmania have wages boards through which a system of control has been worked out. Other states, Queensland, for example, also had wages boards before provision was made for compulsory arbitration. And in some of the states, New South Wales, for example, boards somewhat similar to wages boards have been introduced under the arbitration court. Hence, in most of the Australian states a combination of boards of some type in the different industries and of compulsory arbitration is now found; extensive regulation finds place in

---

[1] Shortly before World War II broke out, additional penalties were imposed for participating in illegal stoppages. Later, the Minister of Labour was given power to suspend the provision of any act, award, or industrial agreement; strikes and lockouts were forbidden; and provision was made for Emergency Disputes Committees to deal with industrial disputes.

[2] In 1937–1938 the number of industrial disputes was sixty-three, as against forty-two in 1936–1937. The issues in most of these disputes were rates of pay and weekly hours in excess of the generally prevailing forty. See New Zealand, *Report of the Department of Labour*, 1938, p. 8. In 1940, wage rates under all awards and agreements were increased 5 per cent.

all of them and to this is added the regulation applied by the Common-wealth Government.   Space limitations do not permit us to do more than to summarize briefly the experience with compulsory arbitration in New South Wales and in the Commonwealth.[1]

New South Wales.—When, in 1901, the most advanced Australian state, New South Wales, prohibited all strikes and lockouts and created a court to decide authoritatively industrial disputes of any and all types, the action was taken with a background of failure in mediation and voluntary arbitration, and with New Zealand's compulsory arbitration system as an example.   In its ban on strikes and again in its omission of district conciliation boards, however, the New South Wales law differed from that in effect in New Zealand.   But the burden placed upon the Arbitration Court was too great; by 1906, 146 cases had been submitted to the Court and seventy-five of these remained to be heard.   Some of these unheard cases were of long standing; the Newcastle miners, for example, had waited four years for an award.   In such delays at a time when the cost of living was increasing is found one of the factors giving rise to a growing discontent.   By 1908 the whole system seemed to be on the point of breaking down.   Then, as in New Zealand, the legislature came to the rescue with amending legislation.

On the one hand, the amending legislation increased the penalties for striking or locking out and for other violations of the law.   Imprisonment, as well as fines, was made a penalty for violation.   On the other hand, to protect the Court and to relieve it of a share of its burden, provision was made for the establishment of industrial boards in each industry to deal with questions of wages, hours, and apprentices.   The pattern for this was found in the wages boards in the sister state of Victoria, but in New South Wales, the boards were legalistic in their procedure, and really arms of the Arbitration Court.   Within a short time, upwards of two hundred of these boards were established, to function in conjunction with the Arbitration Court.   And the Arbitration Court that had func-tioned through one judge came to have four.

In New South Wales after 1908 radical labor organizations multiplied and presented a greater problem than in New Zealand.   In no year were there fewer than a hundred strikes, some of them important and pro-longed.   In 1912 there were eighty strikes in mining alone.   Tom Mann and other radical labor leaders were imprisoned—and became martyrs to

---

[1] For the legislation and the application of its provisions to the great variety of cases, see George Anderson, *Fixation of Wages in Australia* (1929).   For an excellent account, not of a semilegal character, see E. M. Burns, *Wages and the State* (1926).   The Common-wealth legislation and experience under it have been well covered by Orwell de R. Foenan-der in his *Towards Industrial Peace in Australia: A Series of Essays in the History of the Commonwealth Court of Conciliation and Arbitration* (1937).   A good statement of Queens-land's experience may be found in Chief Justice T. W. McCawley, "Industrial Arbitration in Queensland," *International Labour Review*, vol. 5 (1922), pp. 385–409.

the cause.   The industrial question got into politics, and when labor came
into power the arbitration law was changed and liberalized (in 1912).
Prison sentences were eliminated by the new Act, and, as in New Zealand,
machinery for the mediation of disputes was introduced.   The number
of boards was reduced (from 213 to 135).   For the purpose of mediation,
the office of commissioner was established; provision was made also for the
creation of conciliation committees of five in different areas.   The new
machinery established met with a degree of success.   Nevertheless, in
spite of this and in spite of the ban on industrial warfare, New South
Wales continued to experience more strikes than almost any other
country, when due allowance is made for differences in the number of
persons engaged in industry.   In 1913, the number of strikes reported
was 169; the figures rose to 313, 314, and 344, for 1914, 1915, and 1916,
respectively; in 1917 there were 296 strikes.   In the last year mentioned,
a crisis occurred in a great railway strike, on government-owned lines.
Other workers, increasing the number of strikers to 76,000, went out in
sympathy; the trouble lasted for ten weeks and involved a wage loss
of $8,500,000.

In 1918 the Conservatives, on issues connected with the War, regained
power.   Then came drastic amendment of the arbitration law, by a party
that had been less sympathetic with labor than had been the party it
had displaced.

The legislation of 1918 contained three provisions of importance.   For
one thing, as in 1912, it provided for a basic wage to be observed in all
awards and agreements, and created a Board of Trade, consisting of six
members with the judge of the Arbitration Court as president, to fix this
and periodically to revise wage scales established by awards and agreements in effect.[1]   The thought was that the lagging of wages behind the
cost of living was the great cause of the widespread discontent.   Revisions
in wages have been made periodically in the light of changes in the cost
of living.[2]   For another, the conciliation machinery was revised in order
to extend the method of conciliation in industrial disputes.   Significant,
and of more interest even than these changes, was the lifting of the ban
from strikes under certain conditions.   Theretofore, all strikes had been
unlawful.   Under the Act of 1918 those involving government work
remained so, but others ceased to be unlawful unless there was failure to
give fourteen days' notice or unless they were against an award in effect.
And even in the last eventuality, a strike was not unlawful if it was
against an award in effect for twelve months and if voted by a majority
of two-thirds, with at least two-thirds of those involved voting.

---

[1] The Arbitration Court had been fixing basic wages since 1914, under authority of the
Act of 1912.

[2] For basic wages declared at different times, see *New South Wales Industrial Gazette*,
vol. 50 (1936), p. 1632, and other issues of this publication.

The strike record in New South Wales remained bad.   In 1920, there were 349 strikes and lockouts in a grand total of 554 in all Australia.[1] Among these was that of the firemen and enginemen employed by the municipal gasworks of Sydney, lasting between six and seven weeks.   Of course it was unlawful.   In the same year, 30,000 shearmen struck unlawfully when under award and remained out from July to September. Then there was the strike in shipping, likewise unlawful because of an award in effect.   A fourth unlawful strike may be mentioned, though it began in 1919.   It was that by the turbulent miners at Broken Hill, running for a year and a half and ending in compromise in November, 1920.   The wage loss involved was $8,000,000.   The large number of unlawful suspensions in New South Wales is significant in its bearing upon the effectiveness of compulsory arbitration in maintaining industrial peace.

The state machinery and the provisions of the arbitration acts were amended in important respects in 1926 and 1928,[2] the earlier machinery being disestablished and new machinery set up.   Provision was made, on the one hand, for conciliation committees, on the other for an Industrial Commission with broad administrative and regulatory powers. Standing committees, the members holding office for three years, were set up in as many industries as might need them.   At the close of 1939, there were over 300 of these.   Employers and workers[3] have equal representation on a committee; each committee is presided over by one of the commissioners, of whom there are nearly thirty.   The Industrial Commission, which replaced the Board of Trade and the Arbitration Court, has four members.[4]

Strikes and lockouts are prohibited or limited very much as under the Act of 1918.   A dispute goes to a committee for consideration.   It is its function to mediate.   If mediation is successful, the resulting agreement is legally binding.   If, however, the employer-worker members of the committee deadlock, there are two possible procedures.   One is that

---

[1] The number of strikes for the years 1923 to 1927 were 200, 416, 413, 256, and 339.

[2] For a summary of the provisions of the law as then amended, see George Anderson, *op. cit.*, pp. 84–89.   The Industrial Arbitration (Amendment) Act, approved May 25, 1936, was of minor importance.   It related to apprentices and trainees, the composition of the Industrial Commission, eligibility for appointment to conciliation committees, and prescribed that the living wage for adult females should be 54 per cent of the living wage for adult males, calculated to the nearest sixpence.

[3] The legislation had provided for the appointment of persons "who are or who have been engaged in the industry or calling."   In 1936 there was added to this "or who are acquainted with the working of the industry or calling."

[4] The Industrial Commission had consisted of three judges.   In 1936 provision was made for the addition of a fourth.   The Commission was empowered to delegate matters to a single member for determination.   Appeal from his decision is to the other three, three members always constituting the Commission for the purposes of hearing appeal cases.

the commissioner-chairman will be empowered to decide the issue or issues in dispute. In the event he is not so authorized by the committee, the dispute is referred by him to the Industrial Commission. In any event, all cases must go through the hands of the appropriate committees; there is no direct access to the Industrial Commission. Unlike the early arbitration court, the Commission is only a court of appeal and an authority to decide cases in which the attempt at mediation ends in deadlock.

Regulation in New South Wales extends to a great variety of matters. Basic wages are declared;[1] no lower wage may be stipulated in any agreement or award; upon these, secondary wages and the wages of women and minors are based; upon application, wage rates may be altered in view of changes in the cost of living, but not oftener than once in a period of six months. Significant in connection with wages is the fact that here, as well as in other parts of Australia, the condition of the industry must be given consideration in arriving at decisions. Control extends to the hours of work, overtime, and holidays, to apprenticeship, to working conditions, and to preference to unionists, but the law forbids the requirement of membership in a union as a condition of securing or of retaining employment and any requirement that workers shall be secured through a union office. With such broad possibilities, many of the awards made are quite detailed and extensive, paralleling agreements arrived at through collective bargaining.[2]

In 1939 there were in effect in New South Wales 155 enforceable industrial agreements and 566 awards.[3] A corps of inspectors is employed for the enforcement of agreements and awards, and infractions of the law are tried in magistrate courts established in 1912; heavy fines and, in some cases, prison sentence may be imposed.[4] The enforcement has been colored by the political situation; in recent years certain phases of this system of regulation have been an important political issue.

These have been the outstanding facts about New South Wales's system of compulsory arbitration. We may conclude this discussion by a summarization of some of the more significant of these facts.

The original idea was not to regulate industry widely, but to put an end to strikes and lockouts by legal proscription and to have matters in dispute determined by a court. This policy did not work satisfactorily, so the government (1) eased up on the prohibition of strikes (1918), and (2) attempted to introduce mediation as far as possible (1908, 1912, 1918,

---

[1] Under an amending law passed in 1937, the basic rates determined by the Commonwealth Court are to be used under the direction of the Commissioner.

[2] Agreements and awards may be found listed in full in any issue of the New South Wales *Industrial Gazette*, published monthly by the Department of Labor and Industry.

[3] *The Official Yearbook of New South Wales*, 1938–39, p. 659.

[4] The maximum penalty for being concerned in a lockout is £1,000, and for an illegal strike is £500 in case of a union, and £50, or six months' imprisonment in the case of an

1926). But court or commission award has been and remains more
general than collective bargaining or mediated agreement. Awards
dominate in the field of industrial relations. Possibly strikes have been
reduced in number, but they have not been eliminated. Important
unlawful strikes occur. Instead of being in fact primarily one for strike
control, the system has become one for the regulation of wages, hours,
overtime, vacations and holidays, apprenticeship, hiring, and discharge.
Emphasis has been placed on a living wage, with differentials for skill
and other factors. But the attempt to establish a living wage has had
to reckon with the industrial situation and the requirements of industry.
The law has been revised so as to require specifically that the industrial
situation be taken into account in fixing wages. With industrial relations
extensively and minutely controlled, of course, the scheme has been in
politics. An outstanding question between the Labour Party and its
opponent has been, what shall be done in this particular province, especially as regards wages.

Commonwealth of Australia.—Compulsory arbitration was found at
its best in the settlement of interstate disputes under the law of the
Commonwealth of Australia down to about 1920, when matters became
complicated, pressure and politics entered in, and the outstanding President of the Court resigned. The success realized must perhaps be
accredited largely to Justice Higgins, who served as president of the
Court from 1907 to 1920, and to the then favorable state of trade and to
rising prices.

The principal Commonwealth Act of 1904 had by 1930 been amended
no fewer than thirteen times, and radically so in certain respects, in 1928

individual. Statistics of strikes and lockouts reported were as follows:

Year	Strikes	Workers involved	Days lost
1927	457	178,920	841,702
1928	276	100,937	470,546
1929	330	100,676	3,209,761
1930	185	52,045	339,783
1931	99	26,772	103,661
1932	122	45,183	92,743
1933	92	23,409	59,002
1934	171	50,780	211,406
1935	224	50,766	262,853
1936	281	84,407	383,514
1937	511	183,848	567,995
1938	480	182,961	917,789
1939	532	211,565	446,985

In 1939 there were an estimated 831,600 wage and salary workers employed in New
South Wales. In 1938 the 181 registered trade unions had some 275,000 members. *The
Official Yearbook of New South Wales*, 1935–36, p. 804; 1938–39, pp. 632, 659.

and 1930, when it was the great political issue. The history of compulsory arbitration in the Commonwealth must be treated in its earlier, and, then, in its more recent phases.

The Act of 1904 provided for mediation and arbitration in an effort to decide interstate disputes[1] on their merits and to prevent strikes and lockouts. Those within the province of the Commonwealth were prohibited under penalty and remained so until 1930, when the absolute ban was removed. As the principal piece of machinery, an Arbitration Court, consisting of a president, assisted by deputies, was established. The Court, it is true, was empowered to set up special conference boards to handle cases and to refer cases to boards of referees to implement awards. It also had power to call compulsory conferences of parties in interest. All these powers were employed on occasion, but not with important result. Although boards of referees have been frequently used, the Court itself has done most of the work, even since special machinery for mediation was introduced. It was Justice Higgins's view that procedure should be rather informal and that mediation should be emphasized; awards were made only when agreement could not be reached. Mediation, with Justice Higgins as mediator, was rather effective, as is shown by the fact that at one time there were in effect 454 agreements as against 141 awards—a ratio of more than three to one. Agreements and awards were to operate for a stipulated period not exceeding five years and until denounced by one party or the other. While in effect, all agreements arrived at and all awards made were binding and all their provisions enforceable at law.

By laying down principles as it decided cases, the Court gradually evolved an extensive labor code, and one dominating throughout the country in so far as wages were concerned.[2] The unskilled laborer should have a wage sufficient to support a wife and three children[3]—the "standard family"; appropriate differentials should be provided for skill, arduousness of work, and other factors of importance. In general, the forty-eight-hour week was accepted and applied.[4] Contrary to the more common rule in Australasia, preference to unionists was not granted

[1] Disputes extending beyond the limits of any one state. Since 1920 the Act has applied also to industrial disputes arising in the operation of the government instrumentalities of the states, such as railways. During the present War, the Acts coverage has been broadened, so that it can be applied wherever necessary in the interests of "national security."

[2] The best accounts of this phase are found in Justice Henry Bournes Higgins, *A New Province for Law and Order* (1922), and in Orwell de R. Foenander's *Towards Industrial Peace in Australia.*

[3] First prescribed by the Court in the Harvester Case (1907).

[4] The forty-eight-hour week was extensively observed. "Generally accepted by agreement or custom," Justice Higgins applied the forty-eight-hour week, so arranged as to give Saturday afternoon off, unless there was special reason for a longer or shorter week.

except where necessary to prevent discrimination against them.[1] As a rule no limitations were introduced in connection with apprentices; the minimum of restriction upon management was desired.

From the point of view of the public peace at least, the system of mediation and arbitration operated very satisfactorily down into the period of World War I; till then only two or three strikes involving the Commonwealth law had occurred. During the War, however, discontent spread, owing chiefly to soaring prices, enlarged profits, and lagging wages. Serious difficulties developed in mining, in the operation of railways, and in shipping. In some cases the Government (in the English sense of the word) intervened; promises were made in order to restore peace, extralegal tribunals were set up. Then, in 1920, the law was amended so as to authorize the setting up of special tribunals at the instance of the government, to deal with special cases. Such special tribunals made twenty-one awards in 1921, all, presumably, in important cases. This meddling of course placed a premium on the exercise of pressure and threatened to undermine the Arbitration Court. Reacting strongly against the government interference, Justice Higgins resigned.[2]

Since 1920 the system has not worked as well as formerly because of the activities of pressure groups, changed personnel of the Court, the disaffection of important organized groups of workers accounted for in part by tardy awards, the—at times—adverse industrial condition of the country, legalistic procedure, and the conflicts and differences between state and Commonwealth awards. Great struggles have been witnessed in the attempts to amend the law to meet the problems and to satisfy the interests of opposed groups. The chief amendments were made in 1928 and 1930.

In the years since World War I a number of strikes have occurred in defiance of law, such as that by the Seamen some years ago. It appears also that the number of cases multiplied in which awards were not observed and in which union officers and union members counseled and urged their fellows not to keep or accept employment on award terms. The situation became far from satisfactory, except possibly to radical labor groups. Hence, when the election of 1927 resulted in a Conservative victory, the Government proceeded to "put teeth" into the law and still more into its administration. It almost at once (1927) practically eliminated the granting of preference to unionists that had occurred in some cases and eliminated from awards any provision for the procuring of workers from union headquarters. And this was followed, in 1928, by the enactment of a substantially strengthened law.

---

[1] Section nine of the Act prohibits discrimination against workers because of union membership or activity.

[2] See his *A New Province for Law and Order*, pp. 172–176, for statement made by him on announcing his resignation, Sept. 25, 1920.

The primary object of the legislation of 1928 was to saddle effectively a responsibility upon the unions, to make decisions of the Court effective, to avoid strikes, and to protect the public interest. Heavy penalties were to be imposed on persons advising refusal to work on award terms and upon unions or employers not accepting awards.[1] Individuals at fault might be expelled from membership in an organization and become ineligible for union office. Union responsibility for its officers and committees was made clear and definite. Bond in a sum not to exceed £500 might be required for the observance of an award. Union rules must be registered fourteen days before becoming effective and, if in conflict with law or an order, were null and void. Other provisions were added to the same effect, all intended to make the system effective against unions and union men. Moreover, with the same end in view and in order to thwart sectional strikes, of which there had been a considerable number, the Court was empowered to declare the existence of a strike, and the aggrieved party might then apply, to the full, economic pressure on the entire group. And, it should be added, inspectors of agreements and awards were provided for; till then the inspection had been largely by union agents.

The Act of 1928 directed the Court to make its decisions as nearly uniform and as consistent as possible. It also directed the Court to take the economic effects of a proposed decision into consideration, unless the basic wage was involved. Of course the Court had always given some consideration to the industrial effects of a proposed decision, but this statute expressed a desire for a change in emphasis. This was symptomatic of a change of view in Australia, finding expression in Queensland and elsewhere. For some years there appears to have been a growing feeling that too much emphasis may be placed upon wages based upon needs and the standard of living; more emphasis on their production effects was desired. In addition, the Court was directed by the 1928 Act to safeguard the public interest. In this connection it was empowered to refuse to register agreements deemed to be in conflict with that interest. Finally, and very significant in connection with procedure, mediation as against arbitration was emphasized more in the legislation of 1928 than it had been in the principal Act.[2] Specifically, the governor general was empowered to appoint as many conciliation commissioners as were needed. In practice this made little difference; only one such commissioner was appointed.

---

[1] Some excessive penalties were, however, reduced in order that they might be assessed against workers.

[2] The Act has always run in terms of conciliation and arbitration. An amendment passed in 1926 had provided for the appointment of a conciliation commissioner. This marked the renewal of emphasis upon mediation, which had come to count for less since Justice Higgins's presidency.

Before discussing the legislation of 1930, it is necessary to note a problem arising in Australia's experience, owing to a political organization corresponding closely to that of the United States.

The concrete standards incorporated in state and in Commonwealth awards have differed more or less, especially in respect to wages.[1] This absence of uniformity caused uncertainty and confusion as to what standard was to be observed, inequality as between plants in overlapping industries and operating under different awards, and discontent and criticism. As Mr. Foenander says, there has been "duplication and overlapping of effort that at times is little short of the ludicrous."[2] Moreover, varying awards were accompanied by efforts to secure an award from the authority whose standards would be most favorable. For frequently a choice was to be had by organizing so as to involve parties in two or more states, thus bringing an issue within the purview of the Commonwealth tribunal, or vice versa. Attempts were made to correct this situation by conference and more than once[3] by amendment of the Commonwealth constitution, but only to fail. The Act of 1928, however, provided that in the event of a state or industrial authority dealing with a dispute or a part thereof that was already before the Commonwealth Court or was a subject involved in proceedings before the Court, the Commonwealth Court might restrain the state authority from dealing with such matter and, in addition, any award or order of the state authority was to be void. This amendment was not entirely effective in meeting the problem. Because of this fact and because of other problems, the Government took up the position that the Commonwealth system of arbitration should be restricted to the maritime trades only. This became the issue in the election of 1928, when the Government was defeated and the Labour Party was returned to power.

The Arbitration Amendment Act of 1930 was the result of Labor's efforts to eliminate the harshness and limitations introduced into the law

[1] In 1929, for example, the basic wage per week was fixed by state and Commonwealth authorities in the following sums:

City	State tribunals			Commonwealth tribunal		
	£.	s.	d.	£.	s.	d.
Sydney	4	5	0	4	14	6
Brisbane	4	5	0	4	0	6
Adelaide	4	5	6	4	8	6
Perth	4	7	0	4	6	6

[2] Orwell de R. Foenander, op. cit., p. x.

[3] On four occasions—in 1911, 1913, 1919, and 1926—amendments to the Constitution providing for the centralization of authority in the Commonwealth Court had been voted down.

in 1928.[1]   The Labour Party wanted nonlegalistic procedure and "courts of the people," less drastic penalties, less responsibility, and fewer restrictions placed upon unions, and universal preference for unionists. But there was division between the lower and the upper houses; and the measure adopted was the product of compromise agreed upon by "managers" representing the Government and the Nationalists.   Some parts of the Act passed were declared unconstitutional, the most important of these being the part providing for the setting up of conciliation committees with power to make final awards except as regards basic wages and hours of labor.[2]   The law was, however, made less drastic; the absolute ban on strikes and lockouts was removed; penalties were reduced, the suspension and expulsion clauses of 1928 directed at the unions were eliminated,[3] and attorneys, permitted to appear by the Act of 1928, were excluded from the Court unless their appearance was assented to by both parties.   The provision of the bill giving universal preference to unionists was defeated, but under the law as it now stands preference may be granted in special cases.   The provision of the Act of 1928 requiring the Court before making an award or certifying an agreement to consider the probable economic effect was dropped, but this was unimportant for the Court has evidently continued to emphasize what the traffic would bear when exercising control over wages and hours.[4]

Before stating the significant conclusions to be drawn from Australia's experiments with compulsory arbitration, it remains to note briefly how the powers of the Commonwealth Court have been exercised in the control of hours and wages, which are the most important elements in employment relations.

As has been said of the Court's policies during the presidency of Justice Higgins, the forty-eight-hour week having been extensively applied as a result of agreements or custom, a week of that length, so arranged as to allow Saturday afternoon off, was usually incorporated in

---

[1] For an account of this law, see George Anderson, "The Commonwealth Conciliation and Arbitration Act, 1930," *Economic Record* (1931), pp. 82–99; and Orwell de R. Foenander, *op. cit.*, Chap. 4.

[2] In 1931 a bill relating to conciliation committees was brought forward but was defeated in the Senate, which was controlled by the opposition party.

[3] However, under the 1930 Act, no official or agent of an organization shall advise or incite or encourage a member to refrain from offering for employment, or from accepting employment, or from carrying on work in pursuance of the terms of an award.

[4] Further amendments came in 1940, when the present War was more than a year old. The National Security Act extends the powers of the Court, so that it can make awards apply to a whole industry.   In addition, any industrial matter likely to lead to unrest may, by the Minister or the parties involved, be referred to the Court for decision, or the Court may exercise jurisdiction on its own initiative.   Conciliation commissioners are also empowered to investigate whenever a dispute threatens and may be directed by the Court or the Minister to hear and determine the dispute.   Provision is also made for appointment by the Court of boards of reference with the same powers as commissioners.

awards. It was not long, however, before the forty-four-hour week became an issue and it was for years fought over in the Court. Until 1920, the Court, realizing that any substantial loss in production, forecast by employers, would be unfortunate, stood firm against any change in the general norm. That year, however, Justice Higgins reconsidered the whole subject and granted the forty-four-hour week in the famous Australian Timber case, and followed this up by granting the same hours to the Engineers. He also announced his intention to be guided by the action in these instances as other cases came before the Court. Shortly after these decisions, however, Justice Higgins resigned. Much more important in this immediate connection, the Commonwealth Legislature, influenced by business recession in the early twenties, amended the Arbitration Act so as to require a decision by the full Court (as against one justice) to reduce hours below or to increase them above forty-eight per week. The more recent policy of the Court was arrived at in 1926 in the famous Engineers' case, decided by majority vote. The question of policy with reference to hours was carefully considered. The Court was reluctant to reduce hours if in consequence output would be reduced or the cost of production would be increased. On the other hand, it was appreciative of the fact that by state law,[1] agreement, or court award, one-half of the population had by 1926 come under the forty-four-hour standard. Moreover, it was interested in the relation between strain, monotony, and working conditions and health and efficiency. In the more recent years, it has granted the forty-four- or the forty-six-hour week in a large number of cases. On the other hand, it has refused to grant a week of less than forty-eight hours in other cases.[2] Its action, as compared to that taken by legislative bodies, has been rather conservative. It has not been at all receptive of the forty-hour week more recently demanded by the trade unions, which saw in the shorter week a measure that would help to absorb the unemployed.

For more than a generation, Australia, to a greater extent than any other country, has been wedded to the principle of the living wage.[3] This has been accepted by the state and Commonwealth governments and applied by wages boards and arbitration courts. It is estimated that in 1924 nearly three-fourths of the workers were employed in industries with wages regulated by such instrumentalities. The same is true today. The number of state and Commonwealth awards and agreements in effect in 1913 and 1939 is shown in Table 14.

---

[1] Forty-four-hour-week laws had been adopted in Queensland in 1924 and in New South Wales in 1925. Special legislation relating to the hours of employment in government industries had also been adopted.

[2] For a full and excellent account of the whole matter, see Orwell de R. Foenander, *op. cit.*, Chaps. 7 and 8.

[3] *Cf.* vol. I of this treatise, Chap. VI, pp. 280–286.

TABLE 14.—WAGES BOARDS AUTHORIZED AND AWARDS AND AGREEMENTS IN FORCE IN AUSTRALIA, 1913 AND 1939[1]

Particulars	Dec. 31	Commonwealth Court	New South Wales	Victoria	Queensland	South Australia	Western Australia	Tasmania	Total
Boards authorized.....	1913	...	216	135	75	56	...	23	505
	1939	...	323	192	...	76	29	60	680
Awards and determinations in force	1913	17	265	127	73	54	18	21	575
	1939	209	572	213	271	132	177	60	1,688
Industrial agreements in force	1913	228	75	...	5	11	82	..	401
	1939	113	158	...	159	51	192	10	673
Commonwealth Court awards in force in each state	1913	...	13	17	15	16	9	13	
	1939	...	128	157	65	117	46	87	
Commonwealth agreements in force in each state	1913	...	132	129	68	62	57	61	
	1939	...	24	44	20	14	13	37	

[1] Taken from the Commonwealth Bureau of Census and Statistics, *Labour Report*, 1939, p. 51.

In recent years the wage standards applied by state boards and courts have been very much influenced by those applied by the Commonwealth Court. Indeed, wages in unregulated trades have been greatly influenced by the general system of regulation. Allusion has already been made to Justice Higgins's award in the Harvester case in 1907.[1] He took as his standard for an adult male "the normal needs of the average employee regarded as a human living in a civilized community." In 1909 he expressed the view that "it is necessary to keep this living wage a thing sacrosanct, beyond the reach of bargaining."[2] Basic wages for women were related to those for men; minima for workers engaged in occupations other than common labor contained differentials to cover cost of training, responsibility, and other circumstances that vary among occupations.

In general, the Arbitration Court has throughout the last thirty-five years adjusted basic wages of men so as to give them the purchasing power of the 7s. per day awarded in the Harvester case. It is true that in the earlier years the minima established tended to exceed the figures necessary to provide the same purchasing power as the Harvester wage; real wages increased somewhat. During World War I, on the other hand, the adjustments made, though great, were on the whole insufficient to offset the increase in the cost of living. This, as we have noted, was an important cause of the discontent that led to the use of special boards, the resignation of Justice Higgins in protest against the undermining of the Court by these boards, an investigation of the actual cost of living, and a

---

[1] *Supra*, p. 812.

[2] Quoted from F. C. Benham, in *London Essays in Economics: In Honour of Edwin Cannan* (1927), p. 222.

promise to institute a real living wage based upon its findings. The investigation showed, however, that a living wage, as defined, was greatly in excess of what could be paid out of current national income. Besides some adjustments made by changing indexes of the cost of living, the Court in 1921 limited itself to adding 3s. per week to the basic wage (the so-called Powers' 3s.).

Except for recession in the early 1920's, the state of business in Australia was generally good, and, with the industrial progress under way, there was little complaint by employing interests that wages were too high. In the later 1920's however, industry, and particularly that part of it dependent upon the export market, was greatly crippled. Wage reduction was demanded by employers as a necessity, but was protested by labor, which argued that purchasing power would be reduced and unemployment increased. The Court was loath to reduce wages except to adjust them to the reduced cost of living, but in 1931 did so, the reduction, over and above the reduction in the cost of living, being 10 per cent. This, however, was only a part of a government program to spread among all groups the loss the country had sustained. Moreover, the Court was then more conscious than it had previously been of the necessity of observing the principle of what the traffic would bear. A balanced situation was the objective sought.[1]

With some improvement in the state of trade in the early 1930's, the Court was soon pressed to restore wages to the former level. New orders were issued in 1933 and 1934, eliminating the Powers' 3s. and making "a new start." "In their cumulative effects, the awards of May, 1933, and April, 1934, were tantamount to the restoration of about 6% of the reduction in the real wage effected in January, 1931. As 'Powers' 3/.' may be said to represent about 4½% of the basic wage, the worker was, in approximate terms, in receipt of the Harvester Equivalent before, at the end of 1921, Mr. Justice Powers decided to add his 3/."[2] With recovery, increased national income, and higher prices, there was a further increase in basic wages in June, 1937.[3]

It is evident that, once wages were placed upon a higher level by its earlier decisions, the Court, if not conservative, has not been extremely liberal. Besides the initial increases, the chief effects of its awards have been to standardize wages within and between plants in an industry and thus prevent exploitation of workers, and to stabilize wages and to make

[1] See Orwell de R. Foenander, op. cit., Chap. 6, and W. R. MacLaurin, Economic Planning in Australia, 1929–1936 (1937), especially Chaps. 4, 5, and 6.

[2] Quoted from Orwell de R. Foenander, op. cit., p. 98. In Chaps. 5 and 6 of that book will be found an adequate recital of details and an excellent statement of policies contended for and of the Court's position.

[3] Monthly Labor Review, vol. 44 (1937), pp. 697–699. See also W. B Reddaway, "Australian Wage Policy, 1927–1937," International Labour Review, vol. 37 (1938), pp. 314–337.

the wages bill the employers would have to pay and their labor costs more nearly certain through a period of time. This stabilization and a degree of assurance as to wages to be paid, together with the beneficial effects of standardization upon the turnover of labor and morale, have been appreciated by employers generally. Compulsory arbitration has frequently been charged with making wages inelastic. This charge, however, cannot be sustained against the Commonwealth Court as well as it can be against the state tribunals, which have been still more cautious in reducing wages in time of depression.[1]

What has been said thus far concerning wages has related to "primary" or "basic" wages or those paid to common labor. The story of "secondary" wages, those paid to semiskilled and skilled workers, has been somewhat different.

When setting wages in his Harvester award in 1907, Justice Higgins fixed minima for semiskilled and skilled workers in view of the differentials that had obtained. Of course the Court then had no alternative other than to accept as a guide "the practices which [had] been established as a result of long years of experience." Differentials once set, in terms of so many shillings per week, were, however, generally carried along without change as primary wages were increased. Put in other language, the increase in the cost of living was not commonly applied to the differentials in secondary wages. This omission of the cost of living factor had the effect of reducing the difference between the wages of skilled and unskilled, particularly when prices and the cost of living increased enormously during the World War I period. This fact gave Justice Higgins much concern and in his Engineering Award of 1921 "he acted on the rough guide that margins should be increased in proportion to rises in the basic wage. But the Court, as constituted after his resignation, disagreed with this principle, and refused to follow it."[2]

By the late 1920's, the Court had changed its mind on the issue, but the bad state of trade that had developed, as well as the absence of any accurate basis for valuing training, skill, and other elements entering into differentials, stood in the way of adjustments. In 1931, secondary, as well as primary, wages were reduced 10 per cent—over and above the adjustment for changes in the cost of living.[3] When wages were again advanced, however, a full 10 per cent was added to secondary wages. Perhaps this was motivated by the fact that during the depression many workers had left their callings, and, with the return of a measure of prosperity, there was a shortage of skilled labor. More recently, as in

[1] In 1931, for example, except for those of two of the states, the state tribunals were tardy and hesitant in adopting the policy of the Commonwealth Court.

[2] Quoted from Orwell de R. Foenander, *op. cit.*, p. 82.

[3] The total reduction was about 20 per cent.

1935, for example, there have been wage decisions discriminating in favor of skilled labor.[1]

Clearly, a number of significant conclusions can be drawn from Australia's state and Commonwealth experiments with compulsory arbitration.

1. In Australia compulsory arbitration was initially conceived of primarily as a method of preventing strikes. Though it has perhaps had the effect of reducing the number of industrial suspensions, this is not capable of statistical proof. In any event, strikes have neither been eliminated nor reduced to negligible numbers.

2. Penal clauses against strikes cannot be vigorously enforced. Enforcement has been attempted, in New South Wales and at the hands of the Commonwealth Government, for example, only to be ineffective and to create too much dissatisfaction. Vigorous enforcement of penalty clauses has usually been followed by amendment or by relaxation in administration of the law.

3. As to form of intervention, it may be said that, in general, the desire has been to substitute mediation for arbitration in so far as practicable. Nevertheless, in Australian thought, compulsory arbitration finds a legitimate place and is not to be eliminated.[2] And, accompanying the change in emphasis from arbitration to mediation, there has been a reaction against the litigious atmosphere that developed in connection with the former of the two methods of settling industrial disputes.[3]

4. A general system of compulsory arbitration evolves into a far-reaching, and, perhaps, a dominating system for regulating wages and the great variety of things in the field of industrial relations. Binding agreements and, still more, court awards are controlling factors in the Australian situation. Compulsory arbitration has provided "a new province for law and order."

---

[1] Hence the relatively small differentials shown by F. C. Benham, *op. cit.*, pp. 231–241, have been altered somewhat.

[2] Australian thought on the subject is stated by Orwell de R. Foenander (*op. cit.*, p. 13) as follows: "By no means can it be said that there is a unanimity of opinion in the community that industrial relations form a fit and proper province for the activities of the Judicature. . . . But there is every reason to believe that, in Australia, those who hold such views are in a decided minority and that their numbers are decreasing." A few years ago an attempt to make a place for voluntary arbitration in the system met quick defeat.

[3] Foenander, who writes sympathetically about the Australian system, says, "Nevertheless, as the Attorney-General said, industrial peace still remains 'an ideal devoutly to be wished for.' What is ultimately desired lies in the direction of more expeditious and less costly methods, and their divorce from irritating and confusing legalisms. A system that does not operate on these principles cannot command in sufficiently full measure the confidence of the people, and without that confidence it is idle to say that it rests on secure foundations" (*ibid.*, p. 65). Also, "The increasing resort to conciliation is, after all, the surest way of divesting the system of excessive and bewildering legalisms, and of melting the frigidity of the Court-room." *Ibid.*

5. Finally, a system of government involving states and Commonwealth tends to introduce problems when control is exercised.

COMPULSORY ARBITRATION IN KANSAS[1]

These reviews of compulsory arbitration in New Zealand and Australia are sufficient to give the reader a conception of what such a method of intervention is when generally applied, of its advantages, and of the problems connected with it.[2] It will be well, however, to present briefly the experience of our own state of Kansas in order to make clear the special difficulties involved in a system of authoritative intervention in the United States.

Except for numerous irritating stoppages and short strikes by the militant coal miners, Kansas had been practically free from industrial warfare until the great coal strike occurred in 1919. Then, with the coal supply shut off at the beginning of winter, a serious situation developed. Steps were taken to conserve the fuel on hand, but even then many schools and industrial plants were forced to close down, and a number of hospitals were threatened with lack of fuel. Power plants, business houses, and practically all industries not closed down operated on a part-time basis. The reaction to the problem presented was strong and fairly general on the part of Kansas, a state that had adopted prohibition, a "blue sky law" to control the sale of securities, and restrictive legislation applying to railways and other corporations. A truce failing, the coal properties were placed in receivership and the state proceeded to mine coal with volunteer help, protected by troops. The miners' union still stubbornly rejecting all overtures, the legislature was called into special session and the Industrial Court Act was passed (January,

[1] The following are among the many discussions of the subject: Henry J. Allen, *The Party of the Third Part* (1921); William L. Huggins, *Labor and Democracy* (1922); Samuel Gompers, "Labor's Protest against a Rampant Tragedy," *American Federationist*, vol. 27 (1920), pp. 521–532; Frank P. Walsh, "Henry Allen's Industrial Court," *The Nation*, vol. 110 (1920), pp. 755–757; J. S. Dean, "The Fundamental Unsoundness of the Kansas Industrial Court Law," *American Bar Association Journal*, vol. 7 (1921), pp. 333–336; "Kansas Court of Industrial Relations," U. S. Bureau of Labor Statistics, *Bulletin* 322 (1923); Herbert Feis, "The Kansas Court of Industrial Relations," *Quarterly Journal of Economics*, vol. 37 (1923), pp. 705–733.

[2] An excellent account of the German system of arbitration as it existed from the War until the Nazi regime is found in W. T. Ham, "The German System of Arbitration," *Journal of Political Economy*, vol. 39 (1931), pp. 1–24. The system found place in the Republic's program to protect and further organization of labor and collective bargaining and to stabilize the industrial situation. Conciliation committees and conciliators were available for mediation when no machinery was available in the industry concerned or when the machinery available was not effective in disposing of differences over the terms of an agreement being negotiated. The committees and conciliators had the right to take the initiative. When it was in the public interest, compulsory awards could be made. Though a very small percentage of cases arising ended in such compulsory awards, a large percentage of important cases involving wages did so end.

1920) in the face of opposition by employers' associations and organized labor, but with few dissenting votes in Assembly or Senate.[1]

The object of the Industrial Court Act was to protect the public and individual against organized oppression, to safeguard individual liberty, to settle differences on their merits and in the light of sound principles, and to maintain industrial peace.   Unlike the legislation in New Zealand and in Australia, the Act applied only to specified essential industries. These industries were (1) the manufacture or preparation of food products; (2) the manufacture of clothing and all manner of wearing apparel in common use by the people of the state; (3) the mining or production of any substance or material in common use as fuel, either for domestic, manufacturing, or transportation purposes; (4) the transportation of any and all of the above, from the place where produced to the place of manufacture or consumption; (5) all public utilities and all common carriers. In these several industries, strikes, lockouts, picketing and similar things, also shutdowns and restrictions of output by employers, were prohibited. Violations of the Act were punishable by fine or imprisonment or both.

The Kansas law also differed from foreign arbitration laws in other respects.   Arbitration, with representatives of the parties in interest participating, was regarded as undesirable; the law provided for the adjudication of disputes by a Court of Industrial Relations, consisting of three neutral persons.   No special qualifications, such as legal training, were required for membership on the board or Court and this left the door open for political appointments, which later militated against the effectiveness of the Court.   Again, organization of the workers into unions was not presupposed, as is so generally true elsewhere; individuals and groups of workers, individual employers, and organizations were given equal privileges under and had equivalent obligations imposed upon them by the law.   Finally, the Court of Industrial Relations was not vested with the full powers of a court; subpoenas, restraining orders, and the like were to be sought and obtained from the ordinary courts.   Moreover, under our governmental framework, the right of appeal from the findings of the Court to the ordinary courts must be accorded.   In the last analysis, the final authority was, therefore, in the hands of the courts of law, chief among them, in important cases, the Supreme Court of the United States.

The Court of Industrial Relations was also empowered to mediate and to investigate and report, but its chief function was to adjudicate or arbitrate disputes and to assist in making the prohibitions of the Act

---

[1] The Court was in fact a public service commission also. The Act that created it abolished the Kansas Public Utilities Commission and imposed its duties on the Court. The 1921 legislature restored the Public Utilities Commission, abolished the position of Commissioner of Labor, and saddled the duties of the Department of Labor and Industry upon the Court.

effective. A case might be brought before the Court by an individual complainant, by a group, or by an organization, or it might be brought by the attorney general as a representative of the public. During the years 1920–1922, fifty-three cases were presented to the Court. Of these, seven were brought by the attorney general, ten by employers, twelve by unorganized workers, the remainder by unions, these for the most part being local organizations. Though cases were most frequently brought by unions, the Miners and various other labor organizations consistently refused to present cases to the Court or to participate in proceedings before it.

For the most part the Court, in spite of changing membership and some poor personnel, reached decisions not subject to serious adverse criticism. Rates of pay were most frequently the matter in dispute; here the Court, according to the nature of the cases, applied its estimate of a living wage, attempted to decide upon rates that would be fair in view of wages being paid for comparable work, or increased or reduced rates in view of changes in the cost of living. It accepted the principle of the eight-hour day but in some instances prescribed a longer day when the exigencies of the employment apparently required it. Working conditions were regulated in view of the needs for economy and efficiency and in view of the health and welfare of the workers. The Kansas Court also recognized the right of collective bargaining and guaranteed to workers the right to representation of their own choice, but without the right to strike or picket these were rather useless liberties.

Though a considerable number of cases were decided satisfactorily by the Court and an unknown number of strikes thereby prevented, there were a number of important situations in which the Court proved to be impotent. Indeed, its presence was the real cause of some strikes in coal mining. Four cases may be cited to illustrate the problem presented by protesting minorities and the ineffectiveness of a state law in important interstate cases.

Primarily to show his disrespect for the Court, the district president of the Miners, Alexander Howat, announced a strike in the coal industry to occur in April, 1920. This was enjoined by a county court upon petition of the Court of Industrial Relations. After a number of skirmishes with the Court two small strikes were called by Howat in defiance of the law and the restraining order, and in September, 1921, Howat was sentenced to jail for contempt of court. Although no general strike order had been issued, a spontaneous walkout of a majority of the miners in the district followed this action. The Court was at a loss as to how to proceed. It could take no action against any individual since the walkout was apparently a voluntary individual matter. After some violence, however, the National Guard was called out and the strike quickly came to an end.

The second case was that of the strike in the meat-packing industry, which was about 50 per cent unionized in Kansas City. During the War Judge Alschuler, as arbitrator, had maintained peace in the industry and settled disputes as to wages, hours, etc. In 1921 the agreement under which the arbitration plan had been developed expired, and the packers decided to conduct their business on an open-shop basis. Wages were reduced and the reduction was accepted for a time, but in the following December the Amalgamated Meat Cutters called a strike against all the large firms, those operating in Kansas City as well as in Chicago and other packing centers. The Attorney General of Kansas brought a case before the Industrial Court, but the packers contended that the reduction had been accepted and that there was no dispute. The workers in Kansas City were not actively interested in pressing a case. It was within the power of the Industrial Court to restore wages and, after a hearing, to make a finding. But because production was continuing with no particular loss in volume, because the attitude of the workers was as described, and, if one may guess, because it would have been almost absurd to have made an award when the dispute was nation-wide, the Court limited its activity to suppressing picketing of the plants.

The same observation may be made with reference to the handling of the Switchmen's strike in 1922. The dispute was nation-wide; the appropriate settlement in Kansas would depend upon the outcome elsewhere. The Court confined its activities to eliminating picketing—which, naturally, assisted in breaking the strike.

Earlier in the same year (1922) a nation-wide bituminous coal strike occurred. The strike was called by union officials outside the State and beyond the jurisdiction of the Court. The Court found that the supply of coal on hand in Kansas was adequate for the months to come, and a majority of its members decided that nothing should be done by it to terminate the strike. These last three strikes had clearly indicated the inability of the Court to cope with industrial disputes that were interstate in extent.

It is apparent that a new interpretation of the law was implicit in some of these cases. The earlier interpretation, squaring with the language of the statute, had been that every strike in any of the five essential industries was unlawful. Under the new interpretation a strike (or a restriction of output) was unlawful only if it created a problem by reason of rather seriously interfering with the needed supply of a commodity or service. At the same time labor was handicapped by the fact that all picketing in connection with a strike, lawful or unlawful, in an essential industry was under the ban. Thus was an inconsistency introduced into the law. In all these cases the Court took the position that, in leaving their jobs, the strikers had severed all employer-employee relationships and had no standing under the law. The Court regarded it as its duty to insure continuous production where such seemed to be demanded in the interest of the public welfare. This it accomplished to a marked degree by prohibiting picketing.

Unfortunately appointment to membership on the Court was in some instances influenced by politics. In Kansas, as in some of the Australian states, the Act became "a football in politics." Its repeal was one of the main issues in the election of 1922. The candidate elected as governor was pledged to the elimination of compulsory arbitration, but repeal was prevented by the opposition party, which had a majority in the legislature and which, no doubt, reflected the dominant opinion of the state in so far as this particular issue was concerned. Repeal was balked, but the administration of the law was weakened and more or less undermined. This phase of the matter is significant because of the probability that politics will enter into the operation of any system of control established by the American commonwealths.

The enormous number of strikes in 1919 and 1920, including such great struggles as the steel strike and the coal strike of 1919, caused many persons and organizations to be very receptive to compulsory arbitration. In 1920 and 1921 it seemed that a number of the states would try the Kansas experiment. Then acute depression appeared and with it a change in the employment situation and numerous reductions in wages. In this new situation the interest in compulsory arbitration rapidly waned. Then, in 1921, the Kansas Act was in large part declared unconstitutional by the Supreme Court of the United States.

In 1921 the Wolff Packing Company reduced wages. Its unionized employees, numbering some 300, filed a complaint with the Court of Industrial Relations against the company respecting the reduced scale. The case was heard and a decision was rendered increasing wages over the figures to which the company had recently reduced them. The employer refused to comply with the decision and a ruling by the State Supreme Court followed. That court ruled that, because of the element of public interest, the food industry was not improperly within the embrace of the Act; nor was the Act unconstitutional on the ground that action taken under it involved the taking of property without due process of law.[1] The issue was then carried to the Supreme Court of the United States, which, by unanimous decision,[2] held that the fixing of wages in a competitive industry such as meat packing contravened the Fourteenth Amendment to the Federal Constitution. Subsequently a second issue was

---

[1] The Court of Industrial Relations v. The Wolff Packing Company, 109 Kansas Reports 629 (1921). The Kansas Supreme Court had made a decision in an earlier case in harmony with that in the Wolff case. [The State, ex rel. The Court of Industrial Relations v. Howat, 107 Kansas 423 (1920)].

[2] Wolff Packing Company v. Court of Industrial Relations of the State of Kansas, 262 U. S. 522 (1923).

raised concerning control of the hours of labor, and the Supreme Court ruled[1] that the hours provision, combined as it was with other matters, was likewise unconstitutional. The Supreme Court was of the view that:

"The Industrial Relations Act of Kansas, which seeks to promote continuity of operation and production in the industries to which it relates by compelling employer and employees to submit their controversies to compulsory settlement by a state agency, is, as applied to a manufacturer of food products, unconstitutional, not only so far as it permits compulsory fixing of wages . . . but also, and for the same reasons, in the provision for compulsory fixing of hours of labor, since the compulsion in both these features alike is but part of a system by which the Act seeks to compel owner and employees to continue in business on terms not of their own making, which infringes the rights of property and liberty of contract guaranteed by the due process of law clause of the Fourteenth Amendment."

The Supreme Court observed that three types of business had been regarded as sufficiently affected by the element of public interest to bring them under a large degree of control. These were (1) businesses which operate under privileges extended by the government and which impose certain duties upon them (railroads and other public utilities, for example); (2) certain exceptional occupations to which public interest has attached from very early times (keepers of inns, taverns, gristmills, etc.); and (3) such businesses as banks, elevators, warehouses, and insurance companies, which, though not affected with a public interest at their inception, have since come to be regarded as so affected.[2] Any such division of businesses into those sufficiently affected by the element of public interest and those not so affected was of course not regarded as unchangeable, but the case was strong against additions to the regulatable list. It was not sufficient for a legislative body to declare that an industry was so essential that steps should be taken to secure continuity of production or service.

These adverse decisions related to the food industry alone. The views expressed and the language used, however, would indicate that in the absence of more drastic reversal of Supreme Court opinion than constitutional lawyers believe to have occurred, compulsory arbitration of disputes would be unconstitutional if applied outside of the field of public utilities.

[1] *Wolff Packing Company v. Court of Industrial Relations of the State of Kansas*, 267 U. S. 552 (1925).

[2] It may be recorded in passing that in all probability the Supreme Court's conception of "affected with a public interest" has been sufficiently broadened since 1924 to make this threefold enumeration no longer sufficiently inclusive. But recent decisions in cases involving the police power and due process issues do not establish with certainty that a case exactly the same as the Wolff case would today be decided differently, unless the statute involved were a war-time measure.

SOME CONCLUDING OBSERVATIONS

Governments cannot ignore the problem presented by strikes and lockouts and the incidents so frequently connected with them. But how, and to what extent, should a government intervene in an effort to deal with the problem?

It is obvious that provision for mediation is required by sound policy. The experience of different countries shows that great, if not the main, reliance must be upon this method. But if this, or any other method, is to be effective, the personnel must be good and the procedure such as to secure the cooperation of employers and workmen. It is scarcely too much to say that personnel is more important than any other one thing, including the nature of the power with which that personnel is vested.

Likewise, it is clear that investigation of and report on important disputes is needed when mediation fails. Moreover, certainty of investigation and report adds greatly to the efforts of the mediator. Time limitation on strikes and lockouts until opportunity has been given for mediation, investigation, and public report involves, however, questionable policy. A time limitation may provide a salutary cooling-off period, but, on the other hand, it may be ineffective in crucial cases,[1] and nonobservance may undermine respect for law. In any event, such a limitation is a greater restriction upon the workers than upon the employer in the usual employment situation. And, most important of all, the effect of limitations upon worker morale must be kept in mind. Low morale may become a greater problem than a considerable number of strikes.

The encouragement of voluntary arbitration, chiefly by suggestion from mediators and by legal provisions designed to guide and smooth the way of the boards established, is of course to be approved.

Experience teaches caution with regard to a general system of compulsory arbitration in time of peace,[2] with or without mediation as the first method of attack upon the problem of strikes and lockouts. But of course it is true that the answer to the question of what to do about the problem of strikes and lockouts will and should be different for different countries and perhaps for different phases of the problem. If a country has an extensively controlled economy, compulsory arbitration fits into the situation better than if it is following a general policy of limited control.

In any event, a general system of compulsory arbitration develops problems of its own and is not the simple thing in practice it has so generally been supposed to be. There is almost inevitably the problem

[1] It appears that in Michigan and Minnesota the time limitations upon strikes have been generally respected.

[2] Compulsory arbitration cannot be regarded as inappropriate in wartime, provided other measures prove to be inadequate.

of protesting minorities, a problem never adequately solved. If parties to a dispute in a competitive industry are to be bound by a decision rendered by a court, fairness requires that they shall be protected from unequal competition at the hands of others not parties to the dispute. Hence the extension of awards so common in Australasia. Regulation of wages and hours becomes an extensive fact. Much can be said for the resulting standardization. Much can also be said against it, because of relative inelasticity of wage rates, undemocratic imposition of standards, and possibly unsound and uneconomic policy pursued. Beyond this, it is by no means clear that a strike is more injurious than the bad morale and uncooperative behavior that so frequently accompany arbitration decisions made without the freely given consent of the workers. Again, a system of compulsory arbitration, with wide application, is rather likely to get into politics.

After all, most strikes and lockouts do not present any great problem in so far as public convenience is concerned. There is therefore no logical or practical reason why disputes should be dealt with in the same manner in all industries. Perhaps compulsion should be reserved for use in connection with disputes in industries of such nature that the general public is really vitally concerned. And even in connection with such disputes, in such a country as the United States it would appear to be wise to adopt compulsory arbitration only after other possible methods have been fairly tried and have failed to yield reasonably satisfactory results.

A final word is called for. However carried out, constructive efforts should be put forth to remove the causes of the discontent that finds expression in strikes and lockouts. Government has a responsibility for meeting the grosser problems of wages, hours, and working conditions. Prevention is better than emergency intervention, however good the machinery for, and techniques of, intervention may be. Moreover, if there is to be representative government in industry when it is desired by the workers, government must protect the right to organize. Whatever may be said of certain other aspects of such laws as the National Labor Relations Act, they should have the effect of minimizing the number of wars over organization and recognition, which are most difficult to mediate and to arbitrate.

CHAPTER XV

EMPLOYEE-REPRESENTATION PLANS AND INDEPENDENT UNIONS

No discussion of the organization of labor is complete without a summary treatment and evaluation of employee-representation plans, associations, and "independent unions" as forms of organization standing over against the "regular," "legitimate," or "outside" unions with which we have thus far been concerned. Inasmuch as approximately 2,500,000 American workers[1] were in 1935 covered by such plans and associations, the importance of an analysis and evaluation of company unionism is apparent.

There is no general agreement upon a satisfactory name for the diverse types of employee organization. The general term "company union" may, however, be used throughout this discussion to describe organizations variously called "employee-representation plan," "friendship association," "shop committee," "shop council," "Leitch Plan," "industrial democracy," "employee industrial association," "good-will club," "protective association," "cooperative association," "joint conference plan or committee," "works council," "company union," and even a tainted "independent union."[2] This term, "company union," is widely known, generally understood, and is most commonly used in public discussion and in government publications; it has appeared in the bankruptcy acts of 1933 and 1934, in the National Industrial Recovery Act of 1933, in the Bituminous Coal Conservation Act of 1935, in the bulletins of the United States Bureau of Labor Statistics,[3] and in the indexes to the reports and decisions of the National Labor Relations Board. Consequently the term "company union" is used here, as by the Bureau of Labor Statistics, "generically and without implying prejudgment."[4]

Company unionism has been for the most part an American development of comparatively recent origin. It is true, however, that the shop-

---

[1] Twentieth Century Fund, *Labor and the Government* (1935), p. 79.

[2] International unions (*i.e.*, the Railroad Brotherhoods, etc.) which are unaffiliated with the A.F. of L. or the C.I.O., and their locals are of course not considered as "company or independent" unions in this discussion.

[3] See especially "Characteristics of Company Unions," U. S. Bureau of Labor Statistics, *Bulletin* 634 (1938).

[4] "Types of Employer-employee Dealing," *Monthly Labor Review*, vol. 41 (1935), p. 3. See also "Characteristics of Company Unions," U. S. Bureau of Labor Statistics, *Bulletin* 634, p. 3.

committee idea dates back to the middle of the nineteenth century and that company unions were set up on the Continent during the last quarter of the nineteenth century.[1] In Germany, an industrial-representation plan was presented by the Industrial Commission of the German Constitutional Assembly in 1849, and plans were introduced in a number of plants decades later.[2] There were also in Germany before the First World War company or "yellow" unions, especially in the cartelized, antiunion steel industry.[3] Then, after World War I, when collective bargaining was supported by the revolutionary government, there was an extensive development of works councils and a struggle developed over the place to be occupied by them as against that by the trade unions.[4] In this struggle the trade unions were successful and the councils were by law reduced to a subordinate position and authorized to function within the area of plant problems only. Industrial councils were experimented with in Belgium and Italy also. Attracting much attention and arousing much interest were the Whitley Councils established in Britain at the conclusion of the War, but these were based upon trade-union organization and were designed to function in such a manner as to stabilize industrial relations over an entire industry.[5] Whatever their exact nature and role, most of these foreign councils or representation plans were different from rather than like those in the United States.

Viewed broadly, the American company unions have been a product of the open-shop struggle, large-scale business and its reaction to government policies and laws, a new and powerful "welfare" capitalism, and the lack of a coherent philosophy on the part of the employees.

[1] C. R. Daugherty, *Labor Problems in American Industry* (1936), p. 778.

[2] For a bibliography relating to foreign works councils, see Paul H. Douglas, "Shop Committees: Substitute for, or Supplement to, Trade-unions?" *Journal of Political Economy*, vol. 29 (1921), pp. 89–90.

[3] Membership in these "yellow" (nonmilitant) unions ran as high as 300,000 before the War, then fell to 45,000 in 1918 because the employers' associations after the revolution pledged themselves to discontinue the support they had given these organizations. Nevertheless the organizations not only survived but in 1925 were reported to have approximately 250,000 members. Although they were not based on trade-union principles, they founded the National Federation of German Professional Unions (Nationalverband Deutscher Berufsverbände). See R. R. Kuczynski, "Postwar Labor Conditions in Germany," U. S. Bureau of Labor Statistics, *Bulletin* 380 (1925), p. 82.

[4] See Boris Stern, "Works Council Movement in Germany," U. S. Bureau of Labor Statistics, *Bulletin* 383 (1925).

[5] For a discussion of the Whitley Committee, see *Reports of the Committee* (March, 1917); also "Joint Industrial Councils in Great Britain," U. S. Bureau of Labor Statistics, *Bulletin* 255 (1919), and A. B. Wolfe, "Works Committees and Joint Industrial Councils" (U. S. Shipping Board Emergency Fleet Corporation, Industrial Relations Division, 1919). See also Ministry of Labour, *Directory of Joint Standing Industrial Councils, Interim Industrial Reconstruction Committees and Trade Boards* (1920); and "Joint Industrial Councils," *Bulletin* 3 (September, 1920). *Cf.* also *supra*, pp. 779–780.

THE DEVELOPMENT OF COMPANY UNIONISM IN THE UNITED STATES

Early and Prewar Period.—The earliest representation plan in the United States was introduced in the Filene Store in Boston, where the Filene Cooperation Association was launched in 1898 and functioned as a welfare committee until the council was formed in 1905.[1] The idea took hold slowly, and only a few plans were introduced during the first decade of this century.[2] Among the pioneers were the Nernst Lamp Company plan, set up in 1903, with purely consultative and advisory functions, the plan of the American Rolling Mill Company of Middletown, Ohio, adopted in 1904, and the more elaborate organization of the Nelson Valve Company of Philadelphia, instituted in 1907.

Important developments occurred in the five years, 1911 to 1915. The Dennison Manufacturing Company plan and the "cooperative welfare plan" of the Philadelphia Rapid Transit Company[3] were inaugurated in 1911, and the Mutual Benefit Association of the Milwaukee Electric Railway and Light Company was established in 1912. In 1913 and 1914 the Leitch Plan[4] of Industrial Democracy, which became famous during World War I years, was first installed in the works of the Packard Piano Company and the Printz-Biederman Clothing Company. A "shop forum" was also established by the White Motor Company of Cleveland in 1914.

Great interest was aroused by the employee-representation plan adopted by the Colorado Fuel and Iron Company in 1915.[5] Formulated by William Lyon MacKenzie King, this plan was introduced in the company's mines and steel mill to meet the need for better industrial relations and the demands of a public opinion created by the investigations of the turbulent industrial warfare in Colorado.[6] Since this plan covered far more employees than any other plan of the pre-World War I period and

[1] This plan is the oldest in the United States and is still successfully functioning. See Mary La Dame, *The Filene Store; A Study of Employes' Relation to Management in a Retail Store* [Russell Sage Foundation, Industrial Relations Series (1930)].

[2] See Carroll E. French, *The Shop Committee in the United States*, Johns Hopkins University Studies in Historical and Political Science, Series 41 (1923); Earl J. Miller, *Workmen's Representation in Industrial Government*, University of Illinois Studies in the Social Sciences, vol. 10, nos. 3 and 4 (1924); E. R. Burton, *Employee Representation* (1926); and the National Industrial Conference Board, *Works Councils in the United States* (1919).

[3] *Cf.* J. J. K. Caskie, "The Philadelphia Rapid Transit Plan," *Annals of the American Academy of Political and Social Science*, vol. 85 (1919), pp. 119–130.

[4] See John Leitch, *Man to Man: The Story of Industrial Democracy* (1919).

[5] For description of this organization, see *infra*, p. 858. *Cf.* also B. M. Selekman and Mary Van Kleeck, *Employes' Representation in Coal Mines* (1924), and B. M. Selekman, *Employes' Representation in Steel Works* (1924).

[6] See "Report of the Colorado Coal Commission on the Labor Difficulties in the Coal Fields of Colorado during the Years 1914 and 1915," 64th Congress, 1st Session, House Document 859, in *House Documents*, vol. 145 (1916).

was introduced by the large and important Rockefeller interests at this early date, it served as a model for many plans and has often been regarded as the beginning of the employee-representation movement. So great was the departure from the former policies of the company and also from the usual form of labor organization that the Colorado Coal Commission said:

"Your commission knows of nothing just like it in force anywhere. The importance of it, as an effort on the part of a large corporation to regulate its relations with its own employees, by contracting with them instead of through a trade agreement made with a labor union, justifies your commission in discussing this plan with great care."[1]

The World War I Period.—The employee-representation-plan movement might better be said, however, to have had its real beginning in the United States during World War I, when great impetus was given to the introduction of works councils by agencies of the government. In a setting of strikes, a short labor supply, an increased demand for labor, a large turnover of labor, and a need for uninterrupted production, the Federal Government encouraged the inauguration of employee representation where labor was unorganized, in an effort to locate responsibility and to promote stability. The Shipbuilding Labor Adjustment Board and the National War Labor Board set out to establish machinery for conciliation and arbitration in troubled industrial establishments. Works councils or shop committees were stipulated as tools of collective bargaining in awards of these boards; more than 125 awards provided for the establishment of some form of employee representation.[2] The type of organization prescribed by the boards varied in the several cases and ranged from the simple department committee plan in the first case (the General Electric Company Plant in Pittsfield, Mass.)[3] to the more elaborate plans set up in establishments at Bridgeport, Conn.[4] Included also in the plans established under government supervision during this period was the unique 4L Plan in the timber industry of the Northwest.[5] In some cases, however, the government boards challenged an intra-company association imposed on the workers by management as constituting interference with the workers' right of organization.[6]

[1] *Ibid.*, p. 6.

[2] Don D. Lescohier, *Working Conditions*, vol. 3 of John R. Commons and Associates, *History of Labor in the United States* (1935), p. 342.

[3] Carroll French, *op. cit.*, pp. 24–26.

[4] *Ibid.*, p. 36.

[5] See *infra*, pp. 868–869. See also Cloice R. Howd, "Industrial Relations in the West Coast Lumber Industry," U. S. Bureau of Labor Statistics, *Bulletin* 349 (1923), and E. B. Mittelman, "The Loyal Legion of Loggers and Lumbermen," *Journal of Political Economy*, vol. 31 (1923), pp. 313–341.

[6] In Case 283, for example, the War Labor Board stated, "It must be ruled that the employees of the [New York Consolidated Railroad] company who desire to become mem-

The attitudes of different groups varied on the question of the introduction of these works councils. For the most part, the employers immediately affected opposed or grudgingly accepted these government-sponsored bodies.[1] Organized labor, on the other hand, then looked with favor on their installation except in the case of the strongly organized shipyards.[2]

In addition to the government-sponsored works councils, others were established, in part because of the stimulus given by the Whitley Report in Great Britain. In line with this report,[3] joint national industrial councils of trade unions and employers' organizations, joint district industrial councils, and joint plant works councils were set up in England, based, of course, on the acceptance of trade unionism. In the United States, however, the individual industrial works council, though inspired in part by the British report, was complete unto itself in each plant or company,[4] and was almost always completely divorced from trade unionism.[5] While employers frequently objected to plans devised and imposed by the government, they did not object to this form of organization instead of the trade union. Indeed, though fewer in number than those sponsored by government agencies, many nongovernmental plans were instituted during the War period, including those of Standard Oil of New Jersey and Indiana, Westinghouse, Joseph Feiss, the Plimpton Press, Nunn Bush and Weldon, Goodyear, Procter and Gamble, Midvale Steel, Yale and Towne, and International Harvester.[6] The growth of

---

bers of the Brotherhood of Locomotive Engineers, or any other legitimate labor organization, shall be permitted to do so without denial, abridgement, or interference upon the part of the company." See "History of the War Labor Board," U. S. Bureau of Labor Statistics, *Bulletin* 287 (1922), pp. 263–264.

[1] National Industrial Conference Board, *Collective Bargaining through Employee Representation* (1933), pp. 8–9.

[2] Mr. Gompers wrote, on the occasion of the Bethlehem award, as follows: "Through assistance from the outside the Bethlehem steel workers may be enabled to make their shop committee the nucleus of an industrial constitution that will result in just as thorough an organization of that side of production in this plant which concerns employes as has existed on the side of the management. A shop committee for the Bethlehem steel workers may mean the beginning of industrial freedom.

"The same benefits may be established for the workers in every other place where a shop committee is inaugurated; nor, is it necessary to wait for an award from the War Labor Board. Shop Committees can be established through the initiative of the workers themselves." See *American Federationist*, vol. 25 (1918), p. 810.

[3] *Second Report of the Committee of the Ministry of Reconstruction on the Relationship of Employers and Employed, Great Britain Command Papers*, 9002 (1918).

[4] The 4L Plan, organized by the War Department in November, 1917, was an exception. It covered the timber industry of Washington, Oregon, and Idaho, and was later extended to the East.

[5] See Paul H. Douglas, *op. cit.*, pp. 90–91.

[6] C. Miller, *op. cit.*, p. 43, and U. S. Bureau of Labor Statistics, *Bulletin* 634, pp. 10–18. For a discussion of the company unions in the petroleum industry, see D. Horowitz, *Labor*

shop committees at this time is evidenced by the fact that 87, or 14.7 per cent, of the 592 company unions found by the Bureau of Labor Statistics in its 1935 survey of 14,725 establishments, had been formed during the War period.

The situation at the end of the War period has been summarized by one writer, although, it may be observed, with too much emphasis upon government influence, as follows:

"The local shop committee has been planted so well and so broadly throughout industry by these various governmental adjustment agencies as hardly to seem eradicable. Promoted from the onset by the Ship-building Labor Adjustment Board, later by the President's Mediation

TABLE 15.—REPRESENTATION PLANS AND COVERAGE, 1919–1932[1]

Classification	1919	1922	1924	1926	1928	1932
Number of plans in effect[a]	196	725	814	913	869	767
Number of companies with plans.................	145	385	421	432	399[b]	313[c]
Number of companies introducing plans since preceding date............	......	317	173	59	14	7
Number of companies discontinuing plans since preceding date..........	......	77	137	48	41	86
Net increase or decrease in number of companies with plans.............	......	240	36	11	−33	−79
Number of workers covered	403,765[d]	690,000[e]	1,240,704[f]	1,369,078	1,547,766[g]	1,263,194[g]

[a] In industrial companies with more than one establishment, each plant coming under the employee-representation plan has been counted separately. In public-utility companies, each employee association has been counted as a separate unit.

[b] Information on status of plans not received from six companies previously reported as having them. These plans not counted as either active or abandoned during the period 1926–1928.

[c] Information on status of plans not received from seven companies.

[d] Information on number of employees not obtainable for fourteen companies, of which eight were in wartime industries and went out of business shortly after the 1919 report was published. Of the remaining six, three reported a very small force employed in 1919.

[e] Information on number of employees not obtainable for forty-five companies, of which thirty-eight were closed down because of business depression.

[f] Information on number of employees not obtainable for one company.

[g] Information on number of employees not obtainable for two companies.

[1] National Industrial Conference Board, *Collective Bargaining through Employee Representation*, p. 16.

Commission in the Arizona Copper District and in the packing establishments, firmly established subsequently by the War Labor Board in widely divergent fields of industrial activity which had never known its use, and finally made a thoroughly integrated part of a machinery for adjust-

Relations in the Petroleum Industry (WPA Project), New York, 1937, pp. 28–45. See also *Report of the Petroleum Labor Policy Board*, vol. I, p. 81 (1937).

ment extending over the entire American railroad system, the shop committee has secured a strong position."[1]

Postwar Years to the New Deal.—In spite of the fact that most of the plans introduced by the government during the War period did not endure, and in spite of some reverses, company unionism made marked progress in general in the postwar years. By 1926, there were 432 companies with 913 plant plans covering 1,369,078 employees.[2] Then, as many smaller and a few large firms discontinued their plans, the number of companies and the number of plants with company unions decreased until 1933, though the number of employees covered remained more stable, except for the rise in 1928. As reported by the National Industrial Conference Board, the relevant facts are shown in Table 15.

While the coverage of company unions was increasing during the 1920's, the total membership in trade unions was in most years decreasing.[3] In 1932, company-union plants had 1,263,194 employees as against 403,765 in 1919—an increase of 213 per cent. During the same period the per capita taxpaying membership in trade unions affiliated with the A. F. of L. dropped from 3,260,068 to 2,532,261, a decrease of 22 per cent.[4] The loss in membership in all trade unions was slightly larger.[5] The data on membership trends of company unions and of trade unions are brought into relationship in Table 16. In 1919, the coverage of company unions was to the trade-union membership of the United States as 9.8 to 100. In 1932, the corresponding ratio was as 40.1 to 100. In other words, in 1919 the coverage of company unions was approximately one-tenth as large as the trade-union membership; in 1932 it was four-tenths as large.

The factors explaining the growth of company unionism and the decline in trade unionism were largely, though by no means entirely, the same.[6]

[1] L. B. Wehle, "War Labor Policies and Their Outcome in Peace," *Quarterly Journal of Economics*, vol. 33 (1919), p. 336.

[2] National Industrial Conference Board, *Collective Bargaining through Employee Representation*, p. 16. The National Industrial Conference Board figures cover plans known to that organization; the coverage may not have been complete.

[3] *Cf. supra*, p. 163.

[4] *Report of the Executive Council of the American Federation of Labor* . . . 1937, p. 10. The figures include membership in locals in Canada and the insular possessions as well as membership in locals in the continental United States. It is to be held in mind, of course, that not all employees in company-union plants were members of the membership organization maintained or had the right to vote under representation plans.

[5] According to Leo Wolman [*Ebb and Flow in Trade Unionism* (1936), pp. 138–139], the total membership in trade unions in the United States was 4,125,200 in 1919 and 3,144,300 in 1932. The loss had, therefore, been 23.8 per cent.

[6] For a discussion of the reasons for the decline of trade unionism, see pp. 150–162. Of course the introduction of representation plans was one reason why trade unionism waned. This, however, is not meant to imply that the workers always preferred employee-representation plans or that they always voluntarily accepted them.

By 1919 much of industry, forced by War precedent and by public opinion to accept the principle of collective bargaining, and more or less appreciative of constructive personnel policies, had come to prefer company unionism to trade unionism. For the most part, articulate industry opposed trade unionism and approved company unionism on the

TABLE 16.—GROWTH OF COMPANY-UNION COVERAGE AND OF TRADE-UNION MEMBERSHIP, 1919–1932

Year	Company unions[1]	American Federation of Labor[2]	Total trade union[3]	Company-union membership as percentage of total trade-union membership
1919	403,765	3,260,068	4,125,200	9.8
1922	690,000	3,195,635	4,027,400	17.1
1924	1,240,704	2,865,799	3,536,100	35.1
1926	1,369,078	2,803,966	3,502,400	39.1
1928	1,547,766	2,896,063	3,479,800	44.5
1932	1,263,194	2,532,261	3,144,300	40.1

[1] National Industrial Conference Board, *Collective Bargaining through Employee Representation*, p. 16.
[2] *Report of the Executive Council of the American Federation of Labor* . . . 1937, p. 10.
[3] Leo Wolman, *Ebb and Flow in Trade Unionism*, p. 16.

occasion of the President's First Conference on Industrial Relations, held late in 1919.[1] Then, and for years thereafter, the National Industrial Conference Board espoused properly limited and wisely guided works councils as against trade unions. In September, 1920, the United States Chamber of Commerce published the results of a referendum vote of its members, showing that a large majority of them endorsed open-shop dealings with shop committees.[2] It is only in recent years that the Chamber and large employers' associations generally have ceased to express publicly their preference for company unionism as against trade unionism.

During the World War I period many employers had reacted against the power exercised by the trade unions. Then deflation and depression appeared in 1920 and 1921, and wage cuts and cost and price reductions became the order of the day. In many branches of industry unionism was not wanted. A well-organized, well-financed, and well-directed open-shop drive was instituted; many unions were evicted from their place in industry; and in not a few instances, representation plans were introduced for fear the public would react adversely against denial to the workers of a voice in determining the terms of their employment.[3] In

[1] For statement of principles submitted, see *Proceedings of the Conference*, pp. 80–82. As a matter of fact, the position taken by the employer members, voting as a unit, was largely formulated by the National Industrial Conference Board.
[2] "Employment Relations, Referendum Number Thirty-one," U. S. Chamber of Commerce, *Special Bulletin*, September, 1920.
[3] Note that, between 1919 and 1922, 317 companies introduced representation

these years there were several outstanding cases of refusal to recognize
trade unions and of the introduction of company unions as the machinery
for the adjustment of grievances, if not for collective dealing. In 1920,
the Pullman Company introduced an employee-representation plan to
replace the Brotherhood of Sleeping Car Porters. In August, 1921, the
large meat-packing companies introduced representation plans to replace
the unions with which, under government pressure, they had very reluctantly dealt under an arbitration plan. The failure of the shopmen's
strike of 1922 and the loss of prestige by the Railroad Labor Board[1] gave
many companies the opportunity they sought, and, following the example
set by the Pennsylvania Railroad in 1921, sixteen roads, with nearly one-
fourth of the country's total mileage, formed company unions for their
shopmen in 1922.[2] It was during this period, also, that the unique plans
in the printing industry were established, with joint representation of the
workers and employers of a group of plants instead of a single plant.
Following the great 1921 strike, the American Guild of the Printing
Industry was set up in Baltimore, the Graphic Arts Industrial Federation
in Boston, and the Open Shop Edition Book Binders Council in New
York City.[3]

While representation plans in considerable number were discontinued
because of loss of interest, because of failure to work well, because of no
immediate use as a protective device, or because of the necessity of recognizing a trade union, company unionism continued to grow after deflation
and the stout open-shop struggle had come to an end. For there was
proselyting to follow patterns set, there was a desire to insure against an
undesired trade unionism, and there was the development of the "new
capitalism" into which representation plans frequently would fit well.[4]
Encouraged by the National Industrial Conference Board, the National
Association of Manufacturers, the American Management Association,
and other organizations, company unions were established in many large
plants. Among those introduced were that of the General Electric Company at its Schenectady plant, that of the Amoskeag Manufacturing
Company, and that of the Pacific Mills Company of Lawrence, Mass. It
may be observed, also, that by 1924 the majority of the plans started by
the government during the War period had been either abandoned or
superseded by plans drawn up by the employers themselves.[5] The repre-

---

plans. This represented a high peak, exceeded only by that established in 1933–1934.
See Tables 15 and 16.

[1] See H. D. Wolf, *The Railroad Labor Board* (1927), pp. 295–329.

[2] U. S. Bureau of Labor Statistics, *Bulletin* 634, p. 20.

[3] See Emily Clark Brown, "Joint Industrial Control in the Book and Job Printing
Industry," U. S. Bureau of Labor Statistics, *Bulletin* 481 (1928), pp. 1–2.

[4] The "new capitalism" has been discussed in Chap. IV, and only its connection with
the growth of company unionism requires mention at this point.

[5] See Don D. Lescohier, *op. cit.*, p. 350.

sentation-plan movement after the War was an employers' movement. The government had become neutral. The trade unions, naturally enough, had become extremely hostile, because the representation-plan movement was for the most part antiunion.[1] At its 1919 convention, the A.F. of L. passed resolutions declaring:

"We disapprove and condemn all such company unions and advise our membership to have nothing to do with them . . . we demand the right to bargain collectively through the only kind of organization fitted for this purpose, the trade union."[2]

The earlier thirties, marked by greater and still greater depression and by a weakened and, on the whole, an ineffective and discouraged trade unionism, also witnessed a recession in the company-union movement.[3] Nevertheless, company unions continued to hold a conspicuous place in oil refining, electrical manufacture, public utilities of various kinds, and especially in the telegraph and telephone industry, meat packing, manufacture of farm machinery, and some branches of the metal trades. They continued to be useful in settling grievances and in readjusting wages as reductions in costs became necessary. Perhaps more than ever, they found place in plants operated by very large companies. In 1932, according to the National Industrial Conference Board, 13 companies, with more than 15,000 employees each, or 7.6 per cent of a total of 172, accounted for 63.1 per cent of the 1,263,194 employees covered by representation plans,[4] while 118 companies, each employing 1,000 or more workers, accounted for 97.5 per cent of the employees covered.[5]

[1] Of course, not all companies introducing company unions were opposed to trade-union organization. For example, the Columbia Conserve Company and the Filene Company, which protected the right of employees to retain membership in and deal through trade unions, were not opposed. These are only two of several companies that were not opposed to trade unionism.

[2] American Federation of Labor, *Proceedings* . . . 1919, p. 303. The President's First Conference on Industrial Relations came to an end when Mr. Gompers and the other labor representatives withdrew because industrialists insisted on recognition of works councils. Since 1919 and 1920, the Federation has of course passed resolutions strongly denouncing company unions. The weight of organized labor was used to secure the greatest limitations upon, if not the outlawing of, company unions when the Railway Labor and National Labor Relations acts were adopted by the Federal Government.

[3] On the railways the prohibitions of the Railway Labor Act of 1926 were given meaning by the decision of the Supreme Court of the United States in the case of *Texas & New Orleans Railroad Company v. Brotherhood of Railway and Steamship Clerks* [281 U. S. 548 (1930)]. See Chap. XI, pp. 520–521. Yet company unionism did not wane quickly in railway transportation until after the Emergency Transportation Act of 1933 and the Railway Labor Act Amendment of 1934 were passed. Taking industry as a whole, the decline in company unionism in general was not so great as the recession in business and employment.

[4] National Industrial Conference Board, *Collective Bargaining through Employee Representation*, p. 17.

[5] *Ibid.* The National Industrial Conference Board said, "As the decade came to a close, employee representation was strongly established. Many comparatively small plants that

LABOR ORGANIZATION AND THE "NEW DEAL"

As has been observed in Chap. V, both the trade-union and the company-union movements were greatly affected by the policies of the Roosevelt Administration and the adoption of the NIRA.[1] Collective bargaining was stressed, and under Sec. 7(a) of the NIRA the workers were to have freedom to organize as and when they desired and were to be protected against discrimination because of union activity.[2] Labor organization was thus encouraged, and membership in coal mining, the needle trades, and many other industries or trades increased rapidly. Labor unions also appeared in many places where there had been none, at least for years.   In 1932, union membership had fallen to approximately 3,144,000;[3] early in 1935, it was estimated at 4,200,000.[4] After allowance is made for the losses incurred by unions in the first half of 1933, it can be said that within less than two years under the New Deal, they added to their membership more than a million and a quarter. Individual employers and employer groups, including many comparatively small firms, also became much more actively interested than they had been in the organization of their employees into company unions, primarily as insurance against advent of the trade union.   In many cases new representation plans were introduced, and not a few of them even before the Recovery Act was actually passed.   With industrial combinations, institutes, and associations playing a leading role, with suggestions made to the more or less detached employers by their group insurance carriers, with lawyers and industrial-relations experts prepared to advise employers and employees on what to do, and with the great weight of authority and the power of the purse possessed by employers when the mass of the workers were without a coherent philosophy and were concerned above all else with security of their jobs, the efforts of management were more successful than the efforts of the American Federation of Labor and other "legitimate" labor organizations.   As against a company-union coverage of 1,263,194 employees reported by the National Industrial Conference Board for 1932, the Twentieth Century Fund, as a result of its survey, estimated it at 2,500,000 in early 1935.[5]   The gains by company unions and trade unions in number of adherents had been approximately equal, but the coverage of the former had about doubled, while the

---

had organized works councils as a general aid to better understanding had found them unnecessary, and sometimes cumbersome, and had abandoned them.   On the other hand, larger organizations that had introduced them experimentally in a few departments or plants had extended them to other units." *Ibid.*, p. 14.

[1] Also by the Railway Labor Act of 1926 and the later amendments thereto.

[2] See *supra*, pp. 521–522, for quotation of Sec. 7(a).

[3] Leo Wolman, *op. cit.*, p. 139.

[4] By the Twentieth Century Fund, in *Labor and the Government*, p. 24.

[5] Twentieth Century Fund, *op. cit.*, pp. 79–80.

membership in trade unions had increased about one-third. Hundreds of representation plans had been introduced. It was only to be expected that the National Industrial Conference Board should report that 61.3 per cent of the company unions found in manufacturing and mining had been introduced subsequent to the adoption of the NIRA.[1] A study made by the United States Bureau of Labor Statistics, in April, 1935, covered 592 plans, and of these, 378, or almost two-thirds, had been adopted in or subsequent to 1933.[2]

Table 17 shows the relative positions of company and trade unions in 1932 and 1935. During these three years company-union coverage increased from approximately 40 per cent to almost 60 per cent of the estimated trade-union membership.

TABLE 17.—ESTIMATED COVERAGE OF COMPANY UNIONS AND TRADE UNIONS, 1932 AND 1935

Year	Company-union coverage	Total trade-union membership	Company-union coverage as per cent of union membership
1932	1,263,194[a]	3,144,300[b]	40.1
1935	2,500,000[c]	4,200,000[c]	59.5

[a] National Industrial Conference Board, *Collective Bargaining through Employee Representation*, p. 16.
[b] Leo Wolman, *Ebb and Flow in Trade Unionism*, p. 34.
[c] Twentieth Century Fund, *Labor and the Government*, pp. 79–80.

The areas occupied by the plain open shop, the union shop, and the company union are both important and interesting. The facts as of the spring of 1935 are most accurately portrayed by tables resulting from the investigations made by the Bureau of Labor Statistics, to which reference has been made (Tables 18 and 19).

It will be noted that 42.5 per cent of all the workers covered in this survey[3] were in establishments dealing with the employees individually. Most conspicuous for their high percentages in operating without any arrangement for collective bargaining were the wholesale and retail trades, the service industries, the manufacture of cigars, textiles, and lumber and allied products. On the other hand, mine operators, the manufacturers of stone, glass, and clay products, and the manufacturers of wearing apparel most frequently dealt with unions for a part or all of their employees. Company unions were in 1935 very prevalent in the iron and steel, chemical, transportation-equipment, and miscellaneous

[1] National Industrial Conference Board, *Individual and Collective Bargaining under the N. I. R. A.* (1933), p. 23–24.
[2] *Bulletin* 634, p. 50.
[3] The survey by the U. S. Bureau of Labor Statistics covered 14,725 establishments with 1,935,673 employees and constituted the largest sample used in any investigation in this field thus far.

manufacturing industries. Table 19 requires no comment except the statement that while the Railway Labor Act of 1926 and the later legislation, as well as the Texas and New Orleans decision by the Supreme

TABLE 18.—DISTRIBUTION OF WORKERS BY INDUSTRY AND TYPE OF INDUSTRIAL RELATIONS, APRIL, 1935[1]

| | Percentage of workers in establishments dealing | | | | | |
| | | With some or all workers through trade unions | | | | |
	With employees individually	Total	Estimated percentage covered by trade unions	Estimated percentage not covered by trade unions	Through company unions	Through company union and trade union
All industries covered	42.5	30.2	26.1	4.1	19.9	7.4
All manufacturing industries	42.5	24.1	19.5	4.6	24.9	8.5
Durable goods	39.8	16.8	12.2	4.6	34.0	9.4
Iron and steel	29.1	13.6	10.6	3.0	49.3	8.0
Machinery	39.6	10.8	7.0	3.8	39.6	10.0
Transportation equipment	20.7	19.9	16.9	3.0	39.7	19.7
Nonferrous metals	58.2	14.8	11.8	3.0	23.0	4.0
Lumber and allied products	74.9	11.3	8.8	2.5	12.1	1.7
Stone, clay, and glass products	22.7	63.5	42.4	21.1	5.9	7.9
Nondurable goods	45.5	30.8	26.1	4.7	16.0	7.7
Textiles	60.7	30.8	28.1	2.7	6.3	2.2
Fabrics (except hats)	68.1	22.7	19.6	3.1	6.7	2.5
Wearing apparel (except millinery)	37.5	55.9	54.6	1.3	5.4	1.2
Leather	36.9	45.4	35.8	9.6	17.7	....
Food	45.3	35.7	28.6	7.1	8.0	11.0
Cigars	74.0	26.0	25.0	1.0	....	....
Paper and printing	37.8	44.8	33.4	11.4	16.8	0.6
Chemicals	25.4	14.0	13.0	1.0	54.9	5.7
Rubber products (except boots and shoes)	12.5	8.8	7.2	1.6	13.1	65.6
Miscellaneous nondurable goods	28.7	71.3	71.3	....	....	....
Miscellaneous manufactures	22.3	9.6	7.7	1.9	59.0	9.1
Service	86.0	11.6	6.4	5.2	2.3	0.1
Public utilities	27.4	50.6	47.7	2.9	15.2	6.8
Mining	9.9	87.2	86.6	0.6	2.4	0.5
Retail trade	73.0	11.4	0.9	10.5	5.8	9.8
Wholesale trade	94.6	5.0	3.5	1.5	0.4	....

[1] Adaptation by Leo Wolman (*Ebb and Flow in Trade Unionism*, p. 128) from Table 2 (pp. 1450–1451), *Monthly Labor Review*, vol. 41 (1935); for explanatory notes and discussion, see the article in that issue, pp. 1441–1466, and *Bulletin 634*, pp. 36–45.

Court,[1] had discouraged company unionism in a measure, system associations were still conspicuous in 1935 in railway shops, dining cars, and certain other departments.

[1] *Texas & New Orleans Railroad Co. et al. v. Brotherhood of Railway and Steamship Clerks et al.*, 281 U. S. 548 (1930).

TABLE 19.—DISTRIBUTION OF EMPLOYEES ON CLASS I RAILROADS, BY CRAFT AND TYPE OF INDUSTRIAL RELATIONS, APRIL, 1935[1]

Craft or class	Total number of workers	Estimated number and percentage of workers covered by agreements with				Estimated number and percentage of workers not covered by agreements	
		Trade union		System association			
		Number	Percentage of total	Number	Percentage of total	Number	Percentage of total
All crafts or classes............	909,249	646,169	71.1	218,885	24.1	44,195	4.8
Engine and train service.........	158,716	156,514	98.6	1,286	0.8	916	0.6
Yard-service employees..........	54,730	51,826	94.7	665	1.2	2,239	4.1
Clerical and station employees....	180,817	125,796	69.6	49,811	27.5	5,210	2.9
Telegraphers....................	43,892	37,447	85.3	5,687	13.0	758	1.7
Signalmen......................	11,620	11,152	96.0	198	1.7	270	2.3
Train dispatchers...............	3,321	1,966	59.2	378	11.4	977	29.4
Maintenance of way.............	192,482	143,421	74.5	42,153	21.9	6,908	3.6
Shop crafts....................	244,999	115,015	47.0	114,240	46.6	15,744	6.4
Dining-car service..............	9,481	2,736	28.9	2,969	31.3	3,776	39.8
Miscellaneous..................	9,191	296	3.2	1,498	16.3	7,397	80.5

[1] Adaptation by Leo Wolman (*Ebb and Flow in Trade Unionism*, p. 130) from table appearing in the *Monthly Labor Review*, vol. 41 (1935), p. 1466.

THE LABOR BOARDS AND COMPANY UNIONISM

Section 7(a) of the National Industrial Recovery Act, though designed to protect the right of workers in code industries to organize as and when they might wish, actually stimulated more than it checked the introduction of company unions. While many employers observed Sec. 7(a), thousands of them did not. Nor was it merely a matter of misinterpretation of the meaning of the statute, though in many cases that occurred. In any event, many employers in no small measure influenced their employees to adopt representation plans, or presented to their employees representation plans they themselves had formulated for approval at meetings or at elections fairly or unfairly held, or imposed plans by mere announcement; furthermore in most cases the employers paid the incidental bills.[1] There was also, by discharge, layoff, transfer, or

[1] Examples of these types of activity by the employers are found in many Labor Board cases. In the S. Dresner and Son case, the National Labor Board said:

"Since the strike a company union has been formed. At the hearings before the National Labor Board the attorneys for the company claimed authorship of the plan of employee representation under which the company union was established. It is patent that the new union is the creature of the company and not of its employees." *Decisions of the National Labor Board, August, 1933–March, 1934*, at p. 27.

Then, in the Standard Tailoring Company case, the National Labor Relations Board referred to the plan as "a well coordinated puppet show with all the strings pulled by the company." *Decisions of the [first] National Labor Relations Board*, vol. 2, at p. 426.

In addition, see Danbury & Bethel Fur Company (*ibid.*, vol. 1, pp. 195–200); North

demotion, much discrimination against trade-union workers, especially the officers, the members of committees, and others of the more active among them. Contests between trade unions and company unions, and charges of unlawful discrimination against workers because of trade-union membership or activity were involved in a large share of the cases filed with the National Labor Board (August, 1933–July, 1934), the (first)

Carolina Granite Corporation (*ibid.*, pp. 89–93); Ely & Walker Dry Goods Company (*ibid.*, pp. 94–98); Houde Engineering Corporation (*ibid.*, pp. 35–44).

Reporting on 126 company unions surveyed rather than studied at length in the field, the Bureau of Labor Statistics arrived at some interesting conclusions on these matters. With some allowances for the fact that a majority of the plans studied had been hurriedly established upon the appearance of the New Deal and that these usually differed in considerable measure from such outstanding plans as had been established earlier by International Harvester, Standard Oil, and certain other companies, the conclusions are both correct and important. They therefore merit quoting at length.

"The great majority of company unions were set up entirely by management. Management conceived the idea, developed the plan, and initiated the organization. In a number of cases one or more employees played a part in the initiation of the company union. In some of these, however, employee initiative was more apparent than real. In some, the company accepted an employee's suggestion that such an agency be set up and then pushed through the organization. In only a few instances, generally where a trade-union had failed to win the confidence of the workers, was the organization set up primarily through the action of employees. Almost never was it established without some assistance from management.

"Where management set up company unions or supported their establishment, it sometimes exerted no pressure other than stating its own wish in the matter. More frequently, however, it applied varying degrees of additional pressure, including in some cases discharge of trade-union members and threats to close down the plant unless the company union was established. Since in so many instances the presence of a trade-union had inspired the movement to organize a company union, one phase of the work of setting up a company union was to attack the trade-union or to hamper it by delay and manipulation.

"The existence of a company union was almost never the result of a choice by the employees in a secret election in which both a trade-union and a company union appeared on the ballot. In a third of the cases the employees were offered a chance to vote in secret election for or against the company union. In some of these cases the company union was set up even when the vote was in the negative." From *Bulletin* 634, p. 199.

For more recent cases, *cf. Yates-American Machine Company*, 7 N.L.R.B. 627 (1938); *Metropolitan Engineering Company*, 4 N.L.R.B. 542 (1937). In the latter case the Board found that the manager suggested the shop-representative plan to the salesman and that the plan was initiated by the head of the shipping department and other employees. In the *Fletcher Company* case [5 N.L.R.B. 729 (1938)], the Board held the plan to be company-dominated and described the plan as follows:

"The works council is plainly the creature of the respondent, subject to its desires and checked by the procedural restraints embodied in the plan. Composed of equal numbers of representatives of both employer and employees, the works council is limited in its activity to the requirement of a two-thirds vote of its membership. Nor can the employees, through their elected representative, amend, alter, or repeal the plan, since such action would require a three-fourths vote of the council. Any action of the works council is therefore always predicated upon the approval of the respondent's representatives who can frustrate the employees' desires whenever they are so instructed by the respondent."

National Labor Relations Board (July, 1934–June, 1935), the National Mediation Board (railway cases), and the several special-industry boards.[1]

The National Labor Board of 1933–1934 established a hazy dividing line between what was lawful and what was unlawful for employers to do in introducing representation plans, by using certain tests, such as (1) whether there had been or was interference, restraint, or coercion, and (2) whether there had been opportunity for the workers to accept or reject plans submitted. The Board found some of the plans not to have been, but others to have been, unlawfully introduced.[2] Where, however, there was a contest between a trade union and a company union, the practice was developed of holding elections to ascertain the will of a majority of the workers concerned—this generally without any special reference to how the "inside" union had been established or was being operated. What a majority of the workers regarded as acceptable was acceptable to the Board. Although many elections were held by consent, and some by order, after such power had been conferred by executive order, the holding of others was stayed by legal proceedings brought by the employers.[3]

With changes in detail, history repeated itself when the (first) National Labor Relations Board, established under Public Resolution No. 44, 73d Congress, replaced the National Labor Board in 1934. The report of the new Board on its operations for the first six months stated that "our records show that in 30 per cent of the 86 cases heard by the Board, company unions were a primary or attendant cause of the dispute."[4] The experience of the regional boards, most of whose cases did not come to the National Labor Relations Board by reference, or on appeal, or for enforcement proceedings, was much the same. In a number of cases the Board found that, because of extreme employer domination or/and support, the company union was not an acceptable organization under Sec. 7(a)[5]. In

---

[1] Special-industry boards included the National Bituminous Coal Labor Board, the Automobile Labor Board, the National Longshoremen's Board, the Newspaper Industrial Board, the Petroleum Labor Policy Board, the National Steel Labor Relations Board, and the Textile Labor Relations Board. For a discussion of cases before the National Labor Board and the National Labor Relations Board see U. S. Bureau of Labor Statistics, *Bulletin* 634, pp. 230*ff.*; see also Lewis L. Lorwin and Arthur Wubnig, *Labor Relations Boards* (1935).

[2] For example, the National Labor Board's decisions were favorable to the companies in the Federal Knitting Mills and the Cleveland Worsted Mills cases. *Decisions of the National Labor Board*, Pt. I, pp. 69–70, and Pt. II, pp. 17–19.

[3] See *U. S. v. Weirton Steel Co.*, 10 Fed. Supp. 55 (1935). For other problems, *cf.* Lorwin and Wubnig, *op. cit.*, pp. 102–117.

[4] National Labor Relations Board, "Report for Six Months' Period," *Release*, Feb. 13, 1935, pp. 4–5.

[5] As in the second Firestone case, *Decisions of the [first] National Labor Relations Board*, vol. 2, pp. 291–293, in Weyerhaeuser Timber Company case, (*ibid.*, pp. 303–306), and in North Carolina Granite Corporation case, (*ibid.*, vol. 1, pp. 89–93).

such cases, the Board ruled that, as a condition of operation as an agency
for collective bargaining, specific changes should be made in the representation plans and/or in their operation, or that the plan would not be
accepted at all and that the trade union was to be recognized.   More
frequently, however, the Board took the position, as had the National
Labor Board, that where there was a contest between a trade union and
a company union, even though the latter's nature, introduction, or
provisions were questionable, the matter should be disposed of by an
election supervised by the government.[1]   For example, in the Kohler
case, where the election resulted in the certification of the company
union, the Board said,[2]

"Thus it is clear that the company participated in forming and
engaged actively in promoting the new organization [Kohler Workers
Association], that the workers had no opportunity of expressing an
unfettered choice as to whether or not they wished to belong to it, and
that the company not only indicated its favorable attitude toward the
organization, but stood ready to finance its existence. . . . *The wrong
done by the company can, however, be remedied by an election.*"[3]

Not only did the (first) National Labor Relations Board, as time
passed, secure a decreasing number of consent elections in contests
between trade unions and company unions, but it also had its election
orders in increasing number contested in the courts.[4]   Nevertheless,
numerous elections were held.   Table 20 shows the total and distribution
of votes cast at elections held under the auspices of the National Labor
Board, the National Labor Relations Board, and the several industrial
boards, August, 1933, to September, 1935.[5]

The National Labor Board conducted 183 elections in 546 plants or
other industrial units.   The trade unions won 74.7 per cent of these;

[1] As the Board said in the first Firestone case, "Since the election is to determine a
choice of representatives for collective bargaining, we may, in extreme cases, be justified
in refusing a place on the ballot to an organization or plan of representation which by its
very terms is incapable of serving as a collective bargaining agency.   This, however, we
should rarely have occasion to do, since ordinarily the choice, good or bad, is for the
employees to make" (*Decisions*, vol. 1, at pp. 175–176).   In connection with this and other
cases, it should be noted, however, that the Board was careful to point out wrong practices
of the company and to indicate what would be desirable.

[2] *Decisions*, vol. 1, at p. 75.

[3] Italics ours.   This position was modified in the second Firestone case (*Decisions of the*
[first] *National Labor Relations Board*, vol. 2, pp. 291–293).   *Cf.* first Firestone case (*Decisions*, vol. 1, pp. 175–176).

[4] On Apr. 2, 1935, the following cases involving company unions were in the courts:
Acme Machine Company; Bendix Products Corporation; Kelsey-Wheel Company; Fire-
stone Tire and Rubber Company; Goodrich Rubber Company; L. Grief and Company;
Hoosier Manufacturing Company; and International Nickel Company.

[5] For reasons given in the text (p. 848), the results of elections held under the auspices
of the Automobile Labor Board are not included in this table.

TABLE 20.—REPRESENTATION ELECTIONS HELD BY FEDERAL LABOR BOARDS, AUGUST, 1933–SEPTEMBER, 1935[1]

Name of board	Approximate period covered	Total valid votes cast[a]	Votes for					
			Trade union		Company union		Others[b]	
			Number	Percentage of total	Number	Percentage of total	Number	Percentage of total
National Labor Board[c]	Aug. 5, 1933–[d] July 9, 1934	103,714	71,931	69.4	29,644	28.5	2,139	2.1
National Labor Relations Board[e]	July 10, 1934– June 16, 1935	45,287	26,478	58.5	15,060	33.2	3,749	8.3
Petroleum Labor Policy Board[f]	Mar. 8, 1934–[d] Feb. 28, 1935	11,463	7,220	63.0	1,951	17.0	2,292	20.0
Bituminous Coal Labor Boards[g]	Apr. 18, 1934–[d] Dec. 28, 1934	4,571	2,104	46.0	2,262	49.5	205	4.5
National Mediation Board[h]	July 21, 1934– Sept. 7, 1935	84,878	60,212	70.9	24,666[i]	29.1		
National Steel Labor Relations Board[j]	Sept. 6, 1934[d]	378	237	62.7	134	35.4	7	1.9
National Longshoremen's Labor Board[k]	Oct., 1934[d]	977	733[l]	75.0	220	22.5	24	2.5
Textile Labor Relations Board[m]	Dec. 27, 1934[d] Feb. 27, 1935.	1,352	910	67.3	303	22.4	139	10.3
Total, all boards		252,620	169,825	67.2	74,240	29.4	8,555	3.4

[a] Excludes all blank, void, and destroyed ballots. The figures, therefore, do not indicate either the total number eligible to vote or the total number of votes cast.

[b] Votes for no representation, individuals, other organizations, etc.

[c] Emily Clark Brown, "Selection of Employees' Representatives," *Monthly Labor Review*, vol. 40 (1935), pp. 1–18. Does not include five elections.

[d] Experience here reported covers the entire life of the board; dates given indicate the period during which elections were conducted.

[e] George Shaw Wheeler, "Employee Elections Conducted by National Labor Relations Board up to June 16, 1935," *Monthly Labor Review*, vol. 41 (1935), pp. 956–959.

[f] David A. Moscovitz, "Employee Elections Conducted by the Petroleum Labor Policy Board," *Monthly Labor Review*, vol. 41 (1935), pp. 951–956. Includes certifications based on sixteen checks of authorizations against payrolls as well as those based on thirty-four elections held.

[g] Based on elections held under the Bituminous Coal Labor Board, Divisions 1, 4, and 5 only.

[h] Tabulated directly from the Board's reports of certifications. Includes certifications based on checks of authorizations.

[i] Covers all votes and authorizations other than those cast for a standard union.

[j] Covers the only election held by the Board, the one at the West Virginia Rail Co. in Huntington, W. Va.

[k] Data from American Federation of Labor, *Weekly News Service*, Jan. 12, 1935. These are the results of balloting among unlicensed personnel on tanker fleets on the Pacific Coast up to Oct. 23, 1934.

[l] Comprises 709 votes for the International Seamen's Union and twenty-four for the Communist Marine Workers.

[m] Covers the two elections held by the Board.

[1] Reproduced, with adaptations and the publisher's permission, from Leo Wolman, *Ebb and Flow in Trade Unionism*, National Bureau of Economic Research (1936), Table 18, pp. 79–80.

69.4 per cent of the ballots cast were for trade unions, 28.5 per cent for company unions. The National Labor Relations Board conducted 154 elections in 579 units. The trade unions won in 58.2 per cent of these units; of the ballots cast, 58.5 per cent were for trade unions, 33.2 per cent for company unions. At the many elections held by the several boards, approximately a quarter of a million valid votes were cast. Of these votes slightly more than two-thirds were for the trade unions, slightly less than three-tenths for the company unions involved.

In addition to the elections covered by Table 20, the Automobile Labor Board held elections from Dec. 19, 1934, to Apr. 19, 1935, with 154,780 valid votes cast. Of this number, 111,878, or 72.3 per cent, were votes not showing affiliation, 2,177, or 14.0 per cent, were for employee associations, and 21,128, or 13.6 per cent, were for trade unions.[1] These elections have not been included in Table 20 because the manner of voting did not lend itself readily to the designation of an organization as the representative, for the voters here, in contrast to other cases, voted for individuals whose affiliation was not stated.[2] Furthermore, there were differences in the origins of the elections, in the character of the ballot, and in the size and composition of the voting district.

Though not so strikingly true in 1935 as it had been earlier, the carefully conducted elections showed that in most cases a substantial majority of the workers, when given the opportunity of a secret ballot, favored the trade union as against the representation plan.[3] However, elections did not as a rule end the matter. While the result of a consent election was usually accepted by the employer and the defeated "inside" or "outside" union waned or entirely disappeared, the results of elections held by the boards without such consent were frequently ignored or else only slight changes were made in representation plans in order to remove crudities in their provisions or in their operation. One reason for this was that the removal of the Blue Eagle was generally not an effective penalty, especially during the later months of the NRA, and that few prosecutions were undertaken by the Department of Justice. The decisions rendered by the several boards were on the whole ineffectual in bringing fostered company unions into harmony with Sec. 7(a) as interpreted and applied. And this was increasingly so up to May, 1935, when the NIRA was declared unconstitutional in the Schechter case[4] and the National Labor Relations Board was thereby shorn of all power.

By the end of 1934 the operations of the National Labor Relations Board, and also those of most of the industrial boards established under

---

[1] *Final Report*, Automobile Labor Board, Aug. 6, 1935.

[2] For differences in elections of the various boards, especially the Automobile Labor Board, see Leo Wolman, *op. cit.*, pp. 78–83; Twentieth Century Fund, *op. cit.*, pp. 94–95; Lorwin and Wubnig, *op. cit.*, pp. 372–381.

[3] The results of these elections, however, are not conclusive and present some bias as regards the preference of employees for trade unions over company unions. The elections that were held at the request of the unions (except under the Automobile Labor Board) were usually petitioned for when the unions felt they had a reasonable chance of winning the election.

[4] *Schechter Poultry Corporation v. United States*, 295 U. S. 495 (1935).

the NIRA, had noticeably bogged down. It was in this situation that the Wagner-Connery bill was drafted and, with amendments, enacted into law some months later. The National Labor Relations Act of 1935 was designed to confirm the principles laid down by the National Labor Board and the National Labor Relations Board, to impose definite limitations on company unions, and to provide adequate machinery for the enforcement of decisions rendered by the new National Labor Relations Board to be established under it. Moreover, it was designed to make the provisions of law independent of codes and a permanent part of the labor statutes. Certain aspects of the National Labor Relations Act have been discussed elsewhere in this volume.[1] Only those parts of it relating to company unions are pertinent for discussion here.

The National Labor Relations Act does not place a ban on all "company" or "independent" unions, but it does make it an unfair labor practice for an employer "to dominate or interfere with the formation or administration of any labor organization (including company unions) or to contribute financial or other support to it."[2] Thus the Board has dismissed charges against employers charged with dominating a company union unless there has been more than a mere prima facie case of violation of Sec. 8(2).[3] In addition, the Board has held closed-shop agreements with independent unions valid if there was no interference or domination by the employer.[4] Factors which the present Board has considered in determining whether there has been domination or interference by the employer include the following: "Active solicitation on behalf of a labor organization by officials and other supervisory employees, lack of opportunity for the employees to accept or reject a particular organization proposed to them, the disparagement by supervisory employees of any rival labor organization which may be attempting to organize the employees, the linking of benefits arising from group insurance plans and other such activities with membership in the favored organization, and the advance of money by foremen to employees unable to pay their membership fee."[5] Other actions include threats, moral sup-

---

[1] See *supra*, pp. 522–533. For two summary chapters of early company-union cases before the National Labor Relations Board, see Joseph Rosenfarb, *The National Labor Policy and How It Works* (1940), pp. 103–135, and 534–540.

[2] Section 8(2) of the Act. The section also contains a proviso which states: "Provided, that subject to rules and regulations made and published by the Board pursuant to section 6(a), an employer shall not be prohibited from permitting employees to confer with him during working hours without loss of time or pay." The Board, however, has not found it necessary to issue any specific rules or regulations on this provision. See *Fourth Annual Report of the National Labor Relations Board* . . . 1939, p. 69.

[3] *Wisconsin Telephone Company*, 12 N.L.R.B. 375 (1939); *Eastern States Petroleum Co.*, 15 N.L.R.B. 450 (1939); *Brewer-Titchener Corporation*, 19 N.L.R.B. no. 22 (1940).

[4] *Aeolian-American Corp.*, 8 N.L.R.B. 1043 (1938); *J. Wiss and Sons Co.*, 12 N.L.R.B. 601 (1939); *Simplicity Pattern Co., Inc.*, 16 N.L.R.B. 291 (1939).

[5] National Labor Relations Board, *Summary of Third Annual Report of the National Labor Relations Board, Release* R1438, p. 24.

port, and discrimination in favor of the company union and against the trade union by granting the use of company property and facilities only to the former organization.[1]

The present National Labor Relations Board has dealt with many company-union cases in complaint charges. From October, 1935, to June, 1943, charges alleging violation of Sec. 8(2) were filed in 4,873 cases, these constituting 15 per cent of the total charges of unfair labor practices received by the Board or its regional offices.[2] It is fair to say that, contrary to public impression, a substantial number of these charges have been withdrawn or dismissed in the early stages of the proceedings.[3] In others, the regional offices have secured settlements and compliance with the Act. Approximately 10 per cent of the cases have gone to the Board for formal actions.[4] Of the latter group, the Board has by formal orders found violations of Sec. 8(2) in more than 90 per cent, while it has dismissed the charge in slightly less than 10 per cent of the cases.[5] In

[1] The use of these various devices for employer domination was set forth in the Stackpole Carbon Company Case, where the Board held: "From the facts as presented above it is clear that the Association was brought into being originally at the instigation of and under the guidance of the respondent. Since its resurrection, the respondent has continually interfered with the administration of the Association and contributed encouragement and support to it. Meetings of the Association have been and are being held on the respondent's property during working hours. . . . The respondent has aided in the intimidation and coercion of its employees to join the Association. It encouraged membership in the Association by assuring its members that none of them would lose by removal of part of its plant to Johnsonburg. It climaxed its support to the Association by recognizing it as the exclusive representative of its employees and by signing an agreement with it pursuant to such recognition." 6 N.L.R.B., at pp. 184–185 (1938).

[2] Compiled from National Labor Relations Board, *First Annual Report* (1936), p. 34; *Second Annual Report* (1937), p. 19; *Sixth Annual Report* (1941), p. 24; *Seventh Annual Report* (1942), p. 77; and *Eighth Annual Report* (1943), p. 85.

[3] For the only periods in which specific data are available, the following figures are worthy of note: (1) In the forty-five-month period from October, 1935, to June, 1939, the regional offices dismissed or secured withdrawal of 765 charges of "company domination" of the company union (information furnished authors by the Division of Economic Research of the National Labor Relations Board); (2) for the period October, 1935, to December, 1938, a total of 653 charges of violation of Sec. 8(2) were dismissed without formal action by the Board or withdrawn by the complaining party. See *Hearings before the Committee on Education and Labor*, U. S. Senate, 76th Congress, 1st Session, on Bills to Amend the National Labor Relations Act (1939), Pt. 2, p. 316.

[4] During the first six years ending June 30, 1941, there were 21,684 unfair labor practice cases of all types closed by the Board or its agencies. Of this total, 91.7 per cent were closed without formal action, *i.e.*, the issuance of complaint and notice of hearing. See *National Labor Relations Board Sixth Annual Report*, 1941, p. 2. From 1935 to 1939, approximately 43 per cent of all charges were withdrawn or dismissed before complaints and approximately 50 per cent were settled; only 8 per cent required formal action by the Board. See National Labor Relations Board, *Report of The Attorney General's Committee on Administrative Procedure* (1941), Pt. 5, pp. 6–8.

[5] From October, 1935, to June, 1939, the Board handed down 275 formal decisions involving Sec. 8(2) of the Act; in 252 orders, or 92 per cent of these cases, the company

summary, it has been estimated that from 1935 to 1941 the Board and its agencies found violations of Sec. 8(2) of the Act in approximately 1,200 cases, or less than one-third of the cases where charges were filed.[1]

In addition to the complaint cases, the Board in representation cases has ordered and conducted elections involving company unions where there was a contest between outside labor organizations and the company unions over recognition for the purpose of collective bargaining. The company unions and the national unaffiliated unions were usually placed on the ballot in these elections held by the Board from October, 1935, to June, 1941; in these cases, they lost more frequently than not to the "legitimate" trade unions.[2]   If, however, a charge was filed that an employer was violating Sec. 8(2) and the charge sustained by the Board, the present National Labor Relations Board, unlike the National Labor and the (first) National Labor Relations Boards,[3] has ordered that the company union be disestablished as an agency for collective bargaining.[4]

Since the Supreme Court decisions of April, 1937,[5] the Act, as interpreted and applied by the Board, has produced a marked change in the extent, structure, and characteristics of company unionism.   Moreover, the establishment of new company unions by interested employers has been drastically reduced.   Finally, a considerable number of company unions have become regular trade unions.[6]

---

was ordered to stop violating the Act, while in 23 cases, the charge was dismissed (information furnished authors by the Division of Economic Research of the National Labor Relations Board).   For the period October, 1935, to December, 1938, the Board handed down formal decisions in 200 cases in which violation of Sec. 8(2) was charged; of these, the Board found 126 violations of the Act, entered into stipulations in 60 cases whereby it could issue consent orders requiring the employer to cease and desist interference and/or domination, and dismissed 14 charges.   *Hearings before the Committee on Education and Labor, op. cit.*, Pt. 2, p. 137.

[1] Estimated by Mandal R. Segal from Board data.   Specific figures are available only for certain years: (1) For the fiscal year 1938–1939 employers ceased dominating and interfering with labor organizations of their employees in 245 cases [National Labor Relations Board, *Fourth Annual Report* (1939), p. 23]; (2) In the fiscal year ending June 30, 1940, there were 220 disestablishments of company unions [National Labor Relations Board, *Fifth Annual Report* (1940), p. 17]; and (3) In 1940–1941, there were 502 disestablishments [National Labor Relations Board, *Sixth Annual Report* (1941), p. 18].

[2] See *infra*, Table 21, p. 853.

[3] See *supra*, pp. 843–848.

[4] *International Harvester Company*, 2 N.L.R.B. 310 (1936); *Bemis Brothers Bag Company*, 3 N.L.R.B. 267 (1937); *Falk Corporation*, 6 N.L.R.B. 654 (1938).   In the fiscal year ending June 30, 1941, there were 502 company unions disestablished and consequently these would be denied a place on the ballot in any immediate Board election.   See National Labor Relations Board, *Sixth Annual Report* (1941), p. 36.

[5] See supra, pp. 523–524; also National Labor Relations Board, *Third Annual Report* (1938), p. 144, and especially footnote 4.

[6] See *infra*, pp. 862–863.

The statistical record of company unions in elections under the Wagner Act is worthy of note. From the time it first started to function, in October, 1935, through June 30, 1941, the National Labor Relations Board conducted 5,952 elections, of which 4,243 were consent and 1,709 were ordered. Company or independent unions won 545, or 9.2 per cent of the total.[1] As shown in the following table, however, they participated in only 1,101 of the elections won by some labor organization. This is in sharp contrast to the record of A.F. of L. and C.I.O. unions, which participated in 3,291 and 3,486 elections respectively. The table further shows that company unions and independents fared less well than the affiliated organizations, for the former won only 545, or 49.4 per cent of the elections in which they participated, while A.F. of L. unions won 1,939, or 58.9 per cent of their elections, and C.I.O. unions won 2,325, or 66.7 per cent of the elections in which they participated. Company unions and independents have polled approximately 200,000 votes, or 12 per cent of the total valid votes cast in all elections.[2] Recently the standard independents, which represent more than one plant or company, have become increasingly important in comparison to the old company unions, but they have fared less well than the old type of company union.[3] In general, then, the employees still favor company unions in many instances as they did during the time of the previous Labor Boards.[4]

There is available no statistical record of the number of company unions that have been dissolved without Board intervention because of the limitations contained in the Wagner Act as well as because of decisions rendered by or elections held under the supervision of the National Labor Relations Board. Although approximately 1,200 cases of violation of Sec. 8(2) were found by the board or its agencies from 1935 to June,

[1] See National Labor Relations Board, *Annual Reports*, 1936–1941. For the period October, 1935, to December, 1937, for which statistics are available, company unions were more fortunate in consent than in ordered elections, for they won 13 per cent of the consent elections and only 8 per cent of the ordered elections. See E. Marks and M. Bartlett, "Employee Elections Conducted by National Labor Relations Board," *Monthly Labor Review*, vol. 47 (1938), p. 37.

[2] See *Monthly Labor Review*, vol. 47 (1938), p. 36; National Labor Relations Board, *Fourth Annual Report* (1939), p. 54; *Fifth Annual Report* (1940), p. 30; and *Sixth Annual Report* (1941), pp. 19–20.

[3] From July 1, 1937, to June 30, 1941, standard independent unions appeared on the ballot on 389 occasions, winning 169 elections, or 43 per cent of the total in which they participated. Local company unions appeared on the ballot on 686 occasions, winning 350 elections, or 51 per cent of the total in which they participated. See National Labor Relations Board, *Annual Reports*, 1938–1941.

For the period October, 1935, to December, 1937 standard independents participated in 25 elections, winning 14, or 56.0 per cent. Company unions or local independents appeared on the ballot on 212 occasions, winning 103, or 48.6 per cent. See *Monthly Labor Review*, vol. 47 (1938), p. 36.

[4] See *supra*, Table 20, p. 847.

TABLE 21.—ELECTIONS[a] UNDER THE NATIONAL LABOR RELATIONS BOARD, OCTOBER, 1935–JULY, 1941[1]

Type of labor organization	Total appearances on ballot	Elections won		Elections lost	
		Number	Percentage of appearances	Number	Percentage of appearances
Unions affiliated with A.F. of L.........	3,291	1,939	58.9	1,352	41.1
Unions affiliated with C.I.O...........	3,486	2,325	66.7	1,161	33.3
Independents[b]......................	1,101	545	49.4	556	50.6

[a] Includes only those elections which were won by some form of labor organization.

[b] Includes standard independents or national unaffiliates that represent more than one plant or employer, and local independents or company unions that represent one plant or company.

[1] The table was compiled by Mandal R. Segal from *Monthly Labor Review*, vol. 47 (1938), p. 36; *Labor Relations Reporter*, vol. 2 (1938), pp. 215 and 675; National Relations Board, *Fourth Annual Report*, p. 54, *Fifth Annual Report*, p. 30, *Sixth Annual Report*, p. 19.

1941,[1] not all the company unions involved were ordered disestablished.[2] In many of these cases, as a result of settlements, the employer agreed to cease dominating and interfering with the company unions.[3] Dissolutions, however, have been carried out in many cases, especially in the manufacture of harvester machinery, and the automobile, rubber, oil, and steel industries. In some instances dissolution has been followed by the organization of "independent unions," with few basic changes from the old company-dominated union and with suspicious circumstances beclouding their origin.[4] In other cases new "independent" unions without company-union backgrounds have been organized. Along with the new independent unions has also come incorporation of these unions. Other company unions have not been dissolved but have sunk into a state of innocuous desuetude or have limited their scope to social and welfare activities. Where the Board has ordered the disestablishment of the union as an agency for collective bargaining, it has held that the social and welfare activities of the company union were not thereby affected.[5] Practically all the large number that survive have undergone reorganiza-

[1] See *supra*, p. 851.

[2] See National Labor Relations Board, *Fourth Annual Report*, p. 23.

[3] The 142 settlements involving Sec. 8(2) in 1938–1939 involved "agreement to cease dominating and interfering with these labor organizations." No mention is made of disestablishment. *Ibid.*, p. 21.

[4] The National Labor Relations Board issued a report on sixty "independents" which were investigated between May 1, 1938, and Feb. 1, 1939, and found to be company-dominated. Seventeen of these had "developed from admittedly employer-dominated unions." National Labor Relations Board, *Characteristics of 60 Company-dominated Unions*, Research Memorandum 10 (December, 1939), p. 2. See also National Labor Relations Board, *Fifth Annual Report*, p. 94.

[5] *Central Truck Lines, Inc.*, 3 N.L.R.B. 317 (1937); *Utah Copper Company*, 7 N.L.R.B. 928 (1938); and *Duffy Silk Company*, 19 N.L.R.B. No. 11 (1940).

tion or modification in order to bring them more or less into harmony with the law.

Thus partly as a result of these decisions by the labor boards and of the New Deal legislation, there have been marked changes in the nature and character of company unions.[1] Not only have the old company unions been readapted and changed from the early employee-representation plans to associations,[2] but many new independents have appeared on the scene where there was no company union previously.[3] The situation was well summarized by Mr. Saposs, who pointed out in 1935:

"A combination of factors since the advent of the 'New Deal' is responsible for a tendency to readapt 'company unions.' The new legislation, guaranteeing the right of workers to self-organized, self-directed, and self-financed labor organizations for the purpose of collective bargaining, is materially affecting the nature and character of employee representation plans. The ruling by most of the labor boards intrusted with the enforcement of this legislation, that labor organization is the sole concern of the workers, has been an additional stimulus to the readaptation of 'company unions.' The simultaneous assertiveness of the trade-union movement, with its spread of union activity to important industries in which it had been previously quiescent, and the general public sentiment that workers should have a right to organize for collective bargaining have accentuated this tendency. The desire of certain employers to provide a more cohesive and representative agency through which they can deal with their workers has been another contributory factor.

"Some of these adaptations are so fundamental that a new type of 'company union' appears to be emerging. The new features introduced are designed to give the 'company union' distinct organizational machinery and a considerable degree of independent financial status. In general the changes and added features seem to be modeled after trade-union organization and procedure."[4]

In the railroad industry, there have been some marked changes in the company-union situation as a result of the Railway Labor Act of 1926, the decision of the Supreme Court in the Texas and New Orleans case, the amendments to the Federal Bankruptcy Act of 1933, and the 1934 amendments to the Railway Labor Act. Owing to the provisions of the law that prohibit carriers from influencing or coercing the employees

---

[1] For a detailed discussion of these changes see David J. Saposs, "Organizational and Procedural Changes in Employee Representation Plans," *Journal of Political Economy*, vol. 44 (1936), pp. 803–811. See also National Labor Relations Board, *Fifth Annual Report*, pp. 51–52, 94–96.

[2] See *infra*, pp. 855–862, for a description of the various types of company union plans.

[3] See *infra*, pp. 886–889.

[4] David J. Saposs, *op. cit.*

in their organization and that make it unlawful for carriers to use their funds in maintaining, assisting, or contributing to any labor organization, the company unions or shop associations have lost ground.[1] The national labor organizations in recent years have steadily increased the proportions of total mileage upon which they represent employees, while the unaffiliated system associations have lost portions of the mileage for which they were the representatives of the employees in the past.[2] This has been especially true in the shop crafts, where the company unions formerly had their chief support. National organizations represent almost all the train- and engine-service and clerical and telegraph employees.

Description and Characteristics of "Company Unions"

From the beginning, there have been different types of company unions. One broad distinction that may be made is between (1) membership organizations—associations with members, meetings, etc., and (2) plans for the election of committees or representatives with the employees of the plant being voters without membership in anything. Prior to the advent of the New Deal, associations had been rather exceptional, representation plans the general rule. But with the enactment of the NIRA, with its Sec. 7(a) and labor boards, many changes have occurred. While as a result of these recent changes the detail relating to types and to much else has lost considerable of its interest and importance, something further needs to be said. Holding in mind the distinction made between nonmembership and membership organizations, we may discuss briefly the different types of representation plans.

Representation plans have ranged from the Leitch Industrial Democracy Plan to three forms of committee plans, *viz.*, (1) joint councils or "committees," (2) employee committees, and (3) "combination forms."[3]

---

[1] See *supra*, pp. 520–521.

[2] National Mediation Board, *Seventh Annual Report* (1941), pp. 28–29. Of the total agreements covering rates of pay, rules, and working conditions on file with the National Mediation Board on June 30, 1935, national labor organizations held 2,222, system associations held 718. Six years later, the number held by national organizations had increased to 3,727, while the number held by system associations had decreased to 442. Agreements with air-line carriers are not included in these totals. *Ibid.*, p. 40.

[3] These committees have in fact been common to association and mere representation plans. Under either plan, (1) a council consisting of employee representatives and management representatives has been established, or (2) an employee committee has been available for meeting with the officers of the company, or (3) a combination of council and committees has been established. For a more detailed description of the various types of company-union plans, *cf.* C. R. Daugherty, *Labor Problems in American Industry*, pp. 774–791; Don D. Lescohier, *Working Conditions*, in vol. 3 of Commons and Associates, *History of Labor in the United States*, pp. 337–342; National Industrial Conference Board,

The *Leitch Plan*, which lost vogue years before the New Deal was inaugurated, was modeled after the government of the United States. The Leitch idea of Industrial Democracy, based on "Justice," "Cooperation," "Economy," "Energy," and "the capstone . . . Service," was "the organization of any factory or other business institution into a little democratic state, with a representative government which [should] have both its legislative and executive phases."[1] There were, therefore, a "house" of elected employee representatives, responsible to their shop constituencies, a "senate" of lower executives appointed by management, and a "cabinet" consisting of the firm's higher officers, presided over by the president of the company.[2] The "house" and the "senate" held separate meetings, elected their own officers, and appointed their own committees to consider and report on proposed legislation. Any one of the three bodies might initiate legislation, but for a measure to become law it had to pass both houses and be approved by the cabinet, which usually had final power. Consequently, the houses served more or less in an advisory capacity.

Such was the basic plan. However, in order to simplify them, some of the Leitch plans eliminated the senate or combined the senate and the cabinet into a single planning board. Furthermore, in some cases a committee arrangement was introduced to supplement the "federal" organization and a small number of representatives from the two houses might confer with an equal number of cabinet members on important matters. Short cuts were established in an effort to overcome the difficulties involved in an overelaborated structure.

The Leitch Plan was originally worked out at the plant of the Packard Piano Company in 1913. It attracted considerable attention, and within five years some twenty companies installed this type of organization.[3] Perhaps the Plan has been best known in connection with the Goodyear Tire and Rubber Company and the Printz-Biederman Clothing Company, two of the companies in which it found place in the more recent years.[4] In most instances the Plan did not continue to appeal because it was too

---

Collective Bargaining through Employee Representation, pp. 19–43; Twentieth Century Fund, *Labor and the Government*, pp. 69–73; Carroll E. French, *The Shop Committee in the United States*, pp. 33–52.

[1] John Leitch, *Man to Man: The Story of Industrial Democracy*, pp. 39*ff.* Original in italics.

[2] It is obvious that the plan differed from the pattern provided by the Federal Government, for both the President and the Senators are elected by the people and do not serve ex officio or by appointment.

[3] E. R. Burton, *Employee Representation*, p. 23. See also Carroll E. French, *op. cit.*, p. 17.

[4] It was dropped by the Printz-Biederman Company a number of years ago when an agreement was entered into with the International Ladies' Garment Workers.

elaborate. By 1933 it remained in use in only seven cases known to the National Industrial Conference Board.[1]

Far more numerous than the Leitch plans, and least far removed from them, have been the *works council*, *joint-council*, or *joint-committee* plans.[2] Here, typically, the workers, by departments, districts, or other units, have elected a stipulated number of representatives, who, as a committee, have met on occasion with an equal number of representatives of management for the consideration of general problems and for the disposition of matters not disposed of by the agencies underneath. These agencies underneath have most frequently been the representative or representatives in a department whose function it has been to take up worker grievances with the foremen or the superintendent, and committees on safety and perhaps a number of other things. The superintendent or other management representative has most frequently presided at council meetings, but under some plans the presiding officer has been elected by the councilmen. Some joint-council plans have permitted each worker or management representative to vote individually, in which case the necessary majority vote has usually been two-thirds or three-quarters of those present and voting. Other joint councils have had unit voting. In such cases perhaps the representatives on either side have met separately for determining how their vote should be cast. But however arrived at, the decisions of the joint councils have most frequently not been definitive. Of course, in practice most council decisions have been accepted by the company, but most frequently the company has retained veto power. In reporting the results of one of its surveys, the National Industrial Conference Board stated,

"Only seven employee-representation plans are known to invest the council with final authority over matters properly brought before it, and even in these cases a unanimous or large majority vote is required. . . . Approximately 46% of the joint plans make the council only an advisory body, and its decisions are subject to revision or veto by the proper company official."[3]

Nevertheless, it is true that in line with the International Harvester Plan, the joint-council plans, as formulated during the 1920's, increasingly provided for arbitration to end deadlocks or/and as a check on management's veto power. Such arbitration provisions were found in 41 per

[1] National Industrial Conference Board, *Collective Bargaining through Employee Representation*, p. 19.

[2] It was reported that, in 1926, 70 per cent of the representation plans were of this type. See F. M. Dee, *Employee Representation Technique*, American Management Association, Production Executives Series, no. 49. See also L. Fairley, *The Company Union in Plan and Practice* (pamphlet, 1936), p. 14.

[3] National Industrial Conference Board, *Collective Bargaining through Employee Representation*, p. 26.

cent of the joint council plans analyzed by the National Industrial Conference Board in 1933.[1]

The plans adopted by Colorado Fuel and Iron, Standard Oil of Indiana and of New Jersey, International Harvester, Du Pont de Nemours, Armour, and Swift companies were, among others, of this joint-council type. The Colorado Fuel and Iron Plan, widely publicized for several years, may be used for illustrative purposes.[2] Provision was made for the election by secret ballot of workers' representatives, who were to meet periodically with an equal number of management representatives "to discuss freely matters of mutual interest and concern to the company and its employees, embracing a consideration of suggestions to promote increased efficiency and production, to improve working and living conditions, to enforce discipline, avoid friction, and to further friendly and cordial relations between the company's officers and employees." The company operated coal and ore mines in many localities and a steel plant at Minnequa. Provision was made for joint annual meetings of the councils established in the several places. In addition, there were standing local joint committees on sanitation, health, housing, recreation and education, and safety and accidents; and industrial cooperation and conciliation machinery was established for taking grievance cases step by step, if necessary, from the foreman in the mine or mill to the president of the company. If adjustment was not thus reached, a case might go to the Joint Committee on Industrial Cooperation and Conciliation, and, thence, to an umpire or board of arbitration.

The *employee committee* is another type of representation plan. Used in numerous instances prior to 1933, and most popular with the smaller companies, it became very prevalent under the New Deal largely because of the restrictive requirements of Sec. 7(a).[3] Such plans typically provided for the election of representatives or committeemen by eligible worker votes, perhaps by departments or districts. These representatives were to function in connection with grievances and problems in their respective precincts, and, as a whole, to function as a works committee to represent the workers in conferences with management on the more general issues raised by the one party or the other. The workers' representatives could meet together, whether or not the plan so provided. In

---

[1] *Ibid.*

[2] For a detailed description, see B. M. Selekman and Mary Van Kleeck, *Employes' Representation in Coal Mines*, and B. M. Selekman, *Employes' Representation in Steel Works.*

[2] In the steel industry, for example, it was found that a majority of the new plans were of this type. See C. R. Daugherty, M. G. de Chazeau, and S. S. Stratton, *The Economics of the Iron and Steel Industry* [University of Pittsburgh Bureau of Business Research Monographs, no. 6 (1937)], vol. 2, p. 1022. Most of the company union cases coming to the attention of the National Labor Relations Board revealed hurriedly adopted committee plans.

exceptional cases specific provision was made for meetings of the workers, if these were desired.[1] As regards the allocation of power, what was said concerning joint councils, is, with two exceptions, applicable here. The function of the committee was, still more frequently than in the case of the joint councils, only advisory. Related to this, it would appear that provision for the arbitration of issues remaining unsettled was of considerably less frequent occurrence under this committee than under the more elaborate joint-council plans.[2]

In several instances, as in the case of Carnegie-Illinois Steel, the features of the joint council and those of the committee plan were combined in some manner in an effort to realize the advantages of the two. It is unnecessary to present the varying details.

Whatever the type, the representation plan ran largely in terms of eligibility to vote for representatives, eligibility to serve as a representative, holding of elections under joint auspices, the representatives' functions, and the functions of the committee or of the joint council, rather than in terms of a labor organization. Perhaps meetings were not mentioned in the constitution or outline of the plan, for the arrangement was one of voting for representatives. Very infrequently was anything said concerning dues, for the company almost invariably paid the small incidental bills and perhaps provided all clerical service needed. If worker meetings were held during working hours perhaps the loss of time was taken care of by the timekeeper. Representatives were not to be docked for time spent on their official duties. Indeed, in a considerable number of cases they were paid a small salary, over and above their wages, presumably to compensate them for services rendered outside of plant working hours.[3]

Standing over against these representation plans of different types there have been, all the while, *association plans* operating on a membership basis. Found in exceptional cases from the origin of the movement, they have, as has been observed, recently become the prevailing form of

---

[1] But possibly attended by officers of the company also.

[2] It would seem fair to say that several of the large companies, such as International Harvester, in introducing joint-council plans had a desire to attack certain, and even a wide range of, problems in a constructive manner. On the other hand, many of the larger companies that had not followed a liberal policy and many of the smaller ones introduced the committee plan largely as a protective device. Frequently they were willing to concede only the very minimum required by the situation in which they acted.

[3] The Bureau of Labor Statistics reports (*Bulletin* 634, p. 124), "About one-third of the company unions paid the employee representative something above his regular earnings, making the position a source of extra income to him. In 10 cases, the extra compensation amounted to $50 or more a year; in 1, to as much as $15 a week. . . . In some instances [the representatives] were paid out of company-union treasuries to which management regularly contributed," but "in the great majority of cases the employer paid representatives directly."

"independent" or "company unionism."[1] The earlier ones, such as the Filene Plan, it would appear, resulted largely from a desire for industrial democracy when no trade unionism was imminent, or were built around benefit plans in effect or to be introduced. Most of those now operating have resulted from reorganization to conform to the provisions of federal law.

A description of the association form of organization by a prominent industrial-relations manager is as follows:

"A company union (association in our case) presupposes organization, officers, memberships, insignia, everything that in a sense any regular trade union would have. It is simply a local union confined to membership in one plant or company, and more or less dominated or controlled by the company management."[2]

TABLE 22.—FREQUENCY OF COMPANY-UNION GENERAL MEMBERSHIP MEETINGS[1]

Frequency of meeting	Total with company unions			Company unions only			Company unions and trade unions		
	Estab-lish-ments	Workers		Estab-lish-ments	Workers		Estab-lish-ments	Workers	
		Number	Per cent		Number	Per cent		Number	Per cent
Provision for regular meeting..........	275	188,225	35.6	227	150,121	38.9	48	38,104	26.7
Weekly.............	10	10,323	1.9	9	9,716	2.5	1	607	0.4
Semimonthly.......	21	9,802	1.8	10	4,981	1.3	11	4,821	3.4
Monthly............	158	105,204	19.9	130	76,289	19.8	28	28,915	20.3
Quarterly..........	14	4,609	0.9	12	4,284	1.1	2	325	0.2
Semiannually.......	20	10,418	2.0	20	10,418	2.7			
Annually...........	52	47,869	9.1	46	44,433	11.5	6	3,436	2.4
No provision for regular meeting.......	221	265,738	50.3	192	178,959	46.4	29	86,779	60.9
On call.............	135	76,016	14.4	117	62,853	16.3	18	13,163	9.2
No provision........	86	189,722	35.9	75	116,106	30.1	11	73,616	51.7
Not reported.........	96	74,570	14.1	77	56,874	14.7	19	17,696	12.4
Total..............	592	528,533	100.0	496	385,954	100.0	96	142,579	100.0

[1] U. S. Bureau of Labor Statistics, *Bulletin* 634, Table 21, p. 67.

After satisfying requirements as to age, citizenship, and length of service with the company, the worker has under a majority of association plans applied for membership. In other words, membership has been

[1] For the most part this is explained by the fact that the association plans come closer to being legally "acceptable" under the National Labor Relations Act.

[2] C. R. Dooley, American Management Association, Personnel Series, no. 19 (1935), p. 4. Quoted in "Types of Employer-employee Dealing," *Monthly Labor Review*, vol. 41 (1935), pp. 1442–1443.

voluntary. The evidence shows, however, that not uncommonly the pressure exercised by foremen and others in "signing up" workers has been such as to leave a thin line between voluntary and compulsory membership. But in some cases, as under the Filene Plan, membership was made compulsory; the eligible workers have come into membership automatically at the time of employment or when the required length of service has been attained.

The association has usually collected dues to cover incidental operating expenses or/and profit payments. As a rule, the dues have been low, partly because there is no need for contributing to national organizations, and partly because the company has perhaps housed or directly or indirectly financed the organization; and there has been no strike or defense fund.[1] The larger part of the revenues derived from dues has generally been used to finance benefits of one kind or another, not to pay the bills incidental to the operation of a labor organization.[2]

Provision has been made by the typical association for membership meetings. Especially in medium and small plants, the working force in each shop has presumably had some opportunity to discuss or vote on matters of common interest. It may be observed, however, that the personnel director or other representative or representatives of management have frequently attended the meetings held.

Unfortunately, in the analysis of the data collected in the survey made by the United States Bureau of Labor Statistics, no distinction was made

---

[1] As shown in the following table, the U. S. Bureau of Labor Statistics in its survey of company unions found that in approximately 80 per cent of the cases in which dues were collected these dues were 40 cents or less per month, while in only seven cases, with 5.3 per cent of the workers covered, were they in excess of 80 cents per month.

Monthly dues	Establishments	Workers	
		Number	Per cent
Not to exceed 20 cents	45	46,240	44.0
21 to 40 cents	62	38,051	36.2
41 to 80 cents	20	11,315	10.8
81 cents to $1	5	4,142	3.9
More than $1	2	1,435	1.4
Assessments only	2	392	0.4
Other provision	10	1,889	1.8
Amount not stated	9	1,613	1.5
Total	155	105,077	100.0

Adapted from U. S. Bureau of Labor Statistics, *Bulletin* 634, Table 15, p. 62.

[2] The U. S. Bureau of Labor Statistics survey showed that in 90 of the 140 plans with optional membership and dues provisions the payment of dues entitled a member to benefits. In some cases profit-sharing has been associated with representation and association plans *Bulletin* 634, p. 63.

—relative to employee meetings—between mere representation plans and membership organizations. Such a distinction would have been pertinent in connection with the collection of dues as well as with the holding of meetings. Table 22 presents an analysis of provisions for meetings made by all the plans studied, whether of the association or of the other type.

RECENT CHANGES IN COMPANY UNIONS

Recently, there have been great changes in company unions, changes due not so much to experience with them in operation as to the necessity of conforming more or less closely to the requirements of Sec. 7(a) of the NIRA and, more particularly, since 1935, to the requirements of the National Labor Relations Act.[1] Many company unions that were unsuccessful in Board elections have become inactive. Other company unions have divorced themselves from industrial matters, many have been dissolved, some have become "regular," and many have been reorganized and changed in certain respects. Since the Board under Sec. 8(2) has proscribed any form of employer participation in the formation or administration of a labor organization, supervisory officials and foremen have become less active in the sponsorship of these inde-

[1] The many cases before the Labor Boards illustrate these changes. As pointed out in the *Chicago Motor Coach Company* case, "The amendments to the bylaws, following the passage of the Recovery Act, eliminate many of these objectionable features and expressly designate the Fraternity the collective-bargaining agency for its members" (*Decisions of the National Labor Board*, Pt. II, at p. 75). Then, in the *Fifth Avenue Coach Company* case, "the company enlarged the scope of the Fifth Avenue Coach Association which had, until that time, been a benefit society. The functions of this Association were changed so as to include 'collective bargaining.' At the same time, the company appointed additional officers of the Association to hold office until the next Coach Association election . . ." (*ibid.*, at p. 8). See also especially Acme Machine Products Company (*Decisions of the [first] National Labor Relations Board*, vol. 2, p. 74); Houde Engineering Corporation (*ibid.*, vol. 1, p. 37); and Johnson Bronze Company (*ibid.*, p. 106).

The case of Swift and Company is also typical. In 1933 Swift and Company established an employee-representation plan at its plant in Evansville, Ind., but with the constitutionality of the Wagner Act affirmed by the Supreme Court in April, 1937, the company notified the plant assembly that "it is not possible to continue the present representation plan." As a result a so-called "independent union" was formed and named Evansville Meat Packers, Local 400. The entire situation was described by the National Labor Relations Board as follows:

"The continuity of events which followed the official dissolution of the plan on April 20, 1937, clearly shows that the formation of the Evansville Packers was the natural sequel to the acts of the respondent substantially inviting the formation of an 'inside' organization, and while it was yet in an inchoate state, to the presence and participation of Becker, the plant superintendent" [*Swift & Company*, 7 N.L.R.B. 287 (1938)]. Other cases of changes in the employee-representation plans following the Supreme Court decision include *Falk Corporation*, 6 N.L.R.B. 654 (1938); *Hoover Company*, 6 N.L.R.B. 688 (1938). See also National Labor Relations Board, *Fifth Annual Report*, pp. 94–96; and *Sixth Annual Report*, pp. 90–91.

pendent unions. In addition there have been many cases of revision of admittedly company-dominated labor organizations, purportedly to bring them within the terms of the Act.[1] In a few cases, the National Labor Relations Board has found that the only change in the new organization was the removal of financial support by the company;[2] in other cases the company reorganized a whole series of company-dominated organizations.[3] Some of these new organizations have been found by the Board to be company-dominated,[4] while others have been found to be truly independent.[5] Moreover, the disestablishment of many of the old representation and association plans has been followed by the formation of a considerable crop of independent unions. Then, too, some independent unions have been organized in plants where there had been no company representation plan or association. The changed plans and such independent unions as are independent in name only present a company unionism different in certain respects from that described above.

The typical company union functioning in matters of industrial relations, if in an industry within the scope of the Railway Labor Act or the National Labor Relations Act, is now a membership organization or association.[6] Mere voting privileges have been extensively replaced by membership in an organization. Moreover, membership in it is presumed to be voluntary and without employer pressure or undue influence. With minor exceptions, membership is, however, open only to workers on the payroll of the given plant or in the employ of the given company; separation from the payroll is accompanied by withdrawal from membership. The organization finances itself and therefore collects dues. The dues, however, remain low—practically the same as before—for the operating expenses are small and ordinarily there is no provision for a strike or defense fund. Indeed, there may be a specific provision that there shall be no such fund. Provision is now made for regular and special membership meetings, but representatives of management may be invited to attend them. There are union officers corresponding more or less closely to the officers of the ordinary local union, but in some cases these officers are selected by the elected representatives, not by the members directly. Yet, the constitutions of these organizations contain much relating to the selection of representatives by departments or districts, and

---

[1] See *supra*, p. 522.

[2] *Bethlehem Shipbuilding Corporation*, 11 N.L.R.B. 105 (1939).

[3] *Republic Steel Corporation*, 9 N.L.R.B. 219 (1938).

[4] *Ibid.*, see also National Labor Relations Board, *Fourth Annual Report*, pp. 71–72.

[5] *Wisconsin Telephone Company*, 12 N.L.R.B. 375 (1939); *Mohawk Carpet Mills, Inc.*, 12 N.L.R.B. 1265 (1939).

[6] For an analysis of typical "independent union" constitutions and by-laws, see Noel Sargent, National Association of Manufacturers, *Labor Relations Bulletin* 23 (July 23, 1937), pp. 20–26.

relating also to how these representatives, selecting a chairman or president and other officers, shall constitute a committee or council for dealings with management.

Among the purposes specifically mentioned in the recent constitutions and by-laws is that of collective bargaining for the determination of wages, hours, and working conditions. Earlier, the settlement of grievances had been provided for rather widely, but collective bargaining only exceptionally. More recently, written agreements have in most cases been entered into, frequently with provisions for a closed or preferential shop in favor of company-union members. However, the National Labor Relations Board has held that a company-union agreement, whether or not it provided for the closed shop, was invalid if there was indication of company domination.[1] In many cases the document will perhaps contain all the pious statements of yesterday concerning harmony or unity of interest, cooperation with management, etc.[2] Though in many cases structure, financing, and other details have undergone noteworthy changes, it is fair to say that the changes have generally not extended beyond what was deemed necessary in order that the institution might qualify for functioning under the federal statutes. Although the typical company union of today stands in considerable contrast to the typical company union of 1932 or 1920, in so far as structure, support, and announced scope of activity are concerned, the new organizations—"employees' associations," "protective associations," "independent unions" or whatever they may call themselves—remain company unions in their essential features and characteristics.

[1] Cf. Clinton Cotton Mills, 1 N.L.R.B. 97 (1935); Ronni Parfum, Inc., 8 N.L.R.B. 323 (1938); and Third Annual Report of the National Labor Relations Board . . . 1938, pp. 212–213.

[2] Noel Sargent, op. cit., p. 20. Typical statements may be quoted.

Article II—Purpose.

"Section 1. To adjust grievances and prevent injustice, and to serve as a means for collective bargaining on wages, hours, and working conditions. "Section 2. To protect the interests and desires of employees."

"Section 1. The purposes are to coordinate the efforts of the employees of the XYZ Company in dealing with the management of the Company on matters pertaining to hours of employment, wages and working conditions, to facilitate necessary cooperation between the employees and their employer, and to encourage and develop good fellowship among the members. . . ."

"The purposes are to promote cooperation between the employees and the management; to give employees a voice in matters of mutual interest, including wages; hours of work, safety, sanitation and other working conditions; to provide an orderly and expeditious procedure for the prevention and adjustment of differences; and to afford a means through which employees may be furnished information of mutual interest by the management."

"This society being convinced that the spirit of conciliation and arbitration should form the fundamental basis of relationship between employer and employee, pledge themselves to adopt at all times the method of conciliation and arbitration in all the problems that may confront them as employees of the ABC Company."

Of new importance in connection with the present independent unions has been the role of the lawyers, city officials, and officers of the local chambers of commerce. Many of the cases before the National Labor Relations Board have illustrated this increasing importance of the lawyers and local officials and their appeals to loyalty and participation in back-to-work movements. Typical of six cases[1] during the year 1937–1938 is *Cating Rope Works, Inc.,*[2] where the Board found that the industrial secretary of the Brooklyn Chamber of Commerce was active in advising the employer who was found guilty of dominating and interfering with the labor organization. Other cases where city officials were prominent include *Remington Rand, Inc.,*[3] and *Regal Shirt Company.*[4] In the latter case the Board held:

"The association was the creature of the Mayor and the City Builders, who were impelled by fear that the factory would move if the Amalgamated organized the employees. It was their desire to form a labor organization that would be amenable to the respondents and would at the same time have the effect of keeping a legitimate labor organization out of Moorehead City."[5]

In addition, in recent years, and particularly those marked by a divided labor movement and competitive organizing campaigns, not a few truly independent unions have arisen without company-union backgrounds. These organizations have regular monthly general meetings, moderate dues, written agreements, voting privileges, and sometimes full-time organizers. For the most part the representatives have raised money to defray the small incidental expenses of the organizations by sponsoring picnics, parties, raffles, and group meetings. In contrast to the old company unions, the new independents stress collective bargaining on wages, hours, and working conditions, rather than settlement of grievances or welfare, social, and recreational activities. Although trade unions have contracts with the companies in some areas, the independents have also sprung up in the same area and even in the same plants.[6] Membership in these independents is still almost invariably

---

[1] In addition to *Cating Rope Works, Inc.,* the cases are *Metropolitan Engineering Company,* 4 N.L.R.B. 542 (1937); *Jacobs Bros. Co.,* 5 N.L.R.B. 620 (1938); *David E. Kennedy, Inc.,* 6 N.L.R.B. 699 (1938); *Art Crayon Company, Inc.,* 7 N.L.R.B. 102 (1938); *National Licorice Company,* 7 N.L.R.B. 537 (1938).

[2] 4 N.L.R.B. 1100 (1938).

[3] 2 N.L.R.B. 626 (1937).

[4] 4 N.L.R.B. 567 (1937).

[5] 4 N.L.R.B. 567; see also *Sunshine Mining Company,* 7 N.L.R.B. 1252 (1938), where the respondent through the aid of public officials broke the strike and formed a second company-dominated organization to succeed the original company plan.

[6] In the Firestone Rubber plants, for instance, an independent labor organization, called the Firestone Employees Protective Association, became active at the end of 1937 and continued as a rival union to the local of the United Rubber Workers of America, a

limited to the employees of a given plant, or, occasionally, to those of a given firm. Aided by outside legal help, statistics furnished by the Department of Labor, and sympathy from the local community, these independents represent a third form of company or inside union as contrasted with the early nonmembership representation plans and the association organizations. Incorporation of independent unions has also been a new step that differentiates them from the old company-union plans.[1]

One further detail in the description and characterization of company unions remains to be mentioned. For the most part the plans, councils, or associations have been those of the individual company. Even where a company has operated several plants, it has frequently been the practice to introduce a plan or similar plans in plant after plant and to operate them independently. But, on the other hand, there have been numerous instances in which a tie-up has been effected of plans operative in two or more plants of the given company. Incidental reference has been made to the annual meetings provided for by the former Colorado Fuel and Iron Company Plan. In the International Harvester Plan, which has been dissolved, there was provision for the calling by the president of the company of a general council for the consideration of matters common to the several plants. The shop-committee representatives of three works of Standard Oil of New Jersey have had annual meetings with the company officials for the discussion of matters affecting the entire industry. A similar arrangement has obtained in the oil industry in California also. In the meat-packing industry the one-time Armour Company Plan provided for calling together a general conference board by the general superintendent for the consideration of matters of common concern in the several plants operated by the company.[2] Likewise the disestablished Swift and Company Plan authorized the president of the company to call a general assembly whenever important matters affecting a number of plants arose.[3] To mention only one more example, the local

---

C.I.O. affiliate, which has a contract with the company and which won the March, 1938, election, petitioned for by the independent union. See *How Collective Bargaining Works*, The Twentieth Century Fund (1942), Chap. 12, pp. 653–654.

[1] In an analysis of eight-five independents in July, 1937, the Division of Economic Research of the National Labor Relations Board found that in thirty-two of the forty-five cases on which information was available the company union was incorporated. Division of Economic Research of the National Labor Relations Board, Research Memorandum 1, *Statistical Analysis of 85 "Independent" Unions and Readapted Company Unions* (Mar. 14, 1938).

[2] Carroll E. French, *The Shop Committee in the United States*, p. 38. See also constitutions of the various plans.

[3] The constitution of the original Swift Plan is given in P. H. Douglas, C. N. Hitchcock, and W. E. Atkins, *The Worker in Modern Economic Society*, pp. 754–760.

associations of railway employees, as in the case of the Pennsylvania Railroad Company, have been drawn together after the general pattern of the divisional and system organizations found among the trade unions.

In all these instances, and other similar ones, the coordination has been of local plans effective in plants of the same company. It remains to note briefly the councils and conferences, sometimes intercompany, established by representatives of the workers in company union plants, and a few instances of intercompany representation plans adopted in the timber industry of the Northwest and in the graphic arts.

To mention first the movements of employee representatives to get together for common action in the several plants of a given company: In December, 1936, the representatives from three Chrysler plants were exchanging minutes and holding meetings for the formulation of demands. In the steel industry it has been stated[1] that by the middle of 1934 informal contacts with employee representatives of other plants were found in more than 40 per cent of the sixty-seven company unions studied. In the various subsidiaries of U. S. Steel contacts between employee representatives of different plants had become well established by 1935. Representatives from twelve mills of the American Sheet and Tin Plate Company held a convention in September, 1935, and formulated demands; then a second convention was held in 1936. A central committee of Carnegie Illinois Steel representatives was established early in 1936. Although recognition of this committee was at first refused, the movement eventuated in the creation of the Pittsburgh District General Council as a part of the representation plan in November of that year. In the Chicago-Gary area, the Calumet Council was set up in 1934 by employee representatives from U. S. Steel mills, and, although never recognized by the Corporation, lasted, with lapses, until trade-union organization was effected. A Chicago District Council of employee representatives of the American Steel and Wire Company was in operation in the fall of 1936.

Here and there intercompany councils were also established. In Detroit there was for a time an Officers' Association of Automobile Employee Representatives, but it disintegrated with the growth of independent and A.F. of L. unions in 1935. Such movements were quite extensive in the steel industry. In 1935–1936, in the Chicago-Gary area, there was an informal organization of employee representatives from plants of U. S. Steel, Republic, Youngstown Sheet and Tube, Inland Steel, Wisconsin Steel, and other companies. In the autumn of 1936, there were representatives' councils in the Youngstown-Cleveland and the Pittsburgh areas, through which representatives from plants of all the major companies agreed upon demands to be presented.

[1] *Cf.* C. Daugherty, M. Chazeau, and S. S. Stratton, *The Economics of the Iron and Steel Industry*, vol. 2, p. 1029.

Some of the earlier efforts at coordination by employee representatives appear to have been designed to make the company union a more effective agency for presenting, and securing action on, the desires of the employees. The steps taken are explained in part, also, by the influence of the organized-labor movement. It will be noted that most of the developments cited occurred when trade-union organization was advancing rapidly.

In contrast to these attempts at coordination, developing unexpectedly out of company plans, there have been at least four instances in which representation plans were organized on an industry-wide basis. The 4L Plan (Loyal Legion of Loggers and Lumbermen), instituted during the First World War, found place in the timber industry in the northwestern states—chiefly Washington, Oregon, and Idaho. Originally[1] it was an organization of employers and workers, and operated through local and district joint committees and a board of directors, with headquarters in Portland. Joint local committees were elected in logging camps and mills. Representatives from these committees constituted joint district councils, and these in turn sent delegates to the central council or board of directors. Norms were established for wages and hours, by occupation as well as by branch of the industry. This plan has been described by the (first) National Labor Relations Board in one of its decisions as:

"An employer-employee organization on an industry-wide basis in the Northwest, with the avowed purpose of maintaining cooperation between employers and employees. It is supported by joint contributions by employer and employee members. An employer member must consult a conference committee of employees before making any 'general change in the going wage, work shifts or operating time.' Certain appellate machinery exists, but need not be described in detail. Problems which affect a number of locals or which are of industry-wide scope are dealt with by a District Board of Directors consisting of an equal number of employers and employees. In the event of a deadlock, the decision rests with the impartial president of the 4L."

Organizations based upon or resembling in important respects the 4L Plan have found place in the book- and job-printing industry.[2] The American Guild of the Printing Industry, organized by the employing printers of Baltimore, the Graphic Arts Industrial Federation, set up by the employers in Boston, and a general council and series of shop councils inaugurated by the Open Shop Edition Book Binders in New York City, were three exceptional instances of employee-representation plans covering several plants or companies. These plans differed in

---

[1] A few years ago the 4L Plan gave way to the Industrial Employees' Union, Inc., in which employers were no longer members and did not participate in the conduct of the organization. In 1941 the union was dissolved and most of the locals were taken over by the A. F. of L.

[2] *Decisions of the [first] National Labor Relations Board*, vol. 2, at p. 294.

their provisions, for the Graphic Arts Federation of Boston was a democratic plan for consultation by the representatives of both groups with the final veto power in the hands of the employers' organization, while in Baltimore the American Guild of the Printing Industry provided for arbitration in case of disagreement.

In addition to these organizations in the lumber and printing industry and the sporadic early attempts in steel, federations of independent unions have recently developed. Many different types of federations have been appearing, ranging from the convention to the individual promoter type.[2] For the most part these federations have been limited to a given area or district, such as the American Association of Independent Labor Unions in and about Houston, Tex., the National Independent Unions of America in Indiana, and the Federated Industrial Union which concentrates around Buffalo, N. Y. On the other hand, there was the Industrial Employees' Union Inc., which was a readaptation of the 4L's in the Western lumber industry and even included the retail trade groups in the lumber towns. In one instance, *viz.*, the Christian Labor Association, the organization was formed on a religious basis, all the members being inhabitants of the town of Holland, Mich., and holding membership in the Dutch Reformed Church. This union has already won five consent elections in plants in the town. Many of the federations of company unions, however, have never gone beyond the convention or organization stage, such as the California League of Independent Unions, or have become almost completely defunct, as in the case of the Berks County Employees Association. On the other hand, several federations, such as the American Association of Independent Labor Unions, have organized on a stable federated basis.

SPONSORSHIP AND OBJECTIVES

Some representation plans have been formulated and some associations have been organized by workers acting independently and then have

---

[1] For a detailed discussion of these organizations see "Joint Industrial Control in the Book and Job Printing Industry," U. S. Bureau of Labor Statistics, *Bulletin* 481 (1928). Thirteen, forty-two, and seventeen plants, respectively, were included in the three organizations.

[2] Included among the latter group have been the plans set up by the Hamilton Labor Bureau. The constitutions of all the unions are substantially identical and proclaim the right to bargain either individually or collectively through representatives of their own choice. A strike can be called by a vote of three-fourths of the membership in secret ballot. Under this Hamilton Plan, the unions have had company-union features whereby the company contributed to the union through a contract to pay the union for services performed; in this way the payment became a legal consideration and was an essential part of the Hamilton Plan. Partly through adroit legal maneuvering, the Hamilton Plans in several instances have avoided the condemnation of the Board, although in the Calco case the National Labor Relations Board found some of these unions to be company dominated. See *Calco Chemical Company, Inc.*, 12 N.L.R.B. 275 (1939).

been brought to management for acceptance. Moreover, many of the "independent unions" have been organized without stimulation or inducement by the employer and even without any knowledge by him of what was being contemplated. No doubt, workers, acting independently or taking the initiative, have, in some instances, actually sought a mechanism for the solution of their problems and have preferred an "inside" union to a trade union. Or, perhaps they have thought that the company would be more receptive to a representation plan or an unaffiliated organization than to a trade union. Possibly it was thought that the formation of a plant organization would redound to the personal advantage of the active organizers and that it would add to their prestige. Perhaps the leaders were themselves hostile to trade unions and desired in so far as possible to insure against their gaining a foothold in the plant. Yet, the mass of evidence now available from different sources shows that in the overwhelming proportion of cases company unions have been definitely conceived and imposed, or conceived and their adoption either induced by one or more of various methods, or insured by more or less coercive methods, by management. Certainly, though acceptance has frequently been gladly given or regarded as a matter of course, the installation of company unions by management has been accompanied by more fear and coercion than have entered into the organization of trade unions, where fear and coercion have not been altogether absent.[1] This was particularly true in the period 1933–1935.

Why the widespread interest on the part of management in company unionism? Some of the reasons for the great activity and interest displayed have been mentioned or have been implicit in earlier pages. In order to secure a more adequate basis for discussing company unions at work, however, it will be helpful to answer the question just raised more definitely.

---

[1] The U. S. Bureau of Labor Statistics, in reporting the results of its study, states that an employee or a group of employees were reported to have been actively connected with the formation of about 20 per cent of 126 company unions covered by field investigation. Of course, as the records of the National Labor Relations Board show, "actively connected" may mean any one of a number of things. It is fair to say that in far more than 80 per cent of the cases company unions have had their origin in the minds of management. The following table presents the results of the Bureau's findings. *Bulletin* 634, p. 86.

Sponsor	Number of plans	Per cent
Management	96	76.2
Management and employees	18	14.3
Primarily employees	8	6.3
War Labor Board (World War I)	1	0.8
No information	3	2.4
Total	126	100.0

Anyone who is at all conversant with the subject knows that in respect to objectives there have been "company unions and company unions." It is also known that a mixture of motives is to be found behind them, that both negative or obstructive and positive or constructive possibilities have appealed, and that both possibilities have been actualities in a great majority of cases.

In part these organizations have arisen as a response to the need for some form of management-employee communication and contact in the plant. With the increase in the number of large-scale enterprises and with corporate organization and the development of mass-production methods of manufacture since the turn of the century, the old personal relations between employer and employee have tended to weaken and disappear. Grievances and local conflicts have been placed in the hands of foremen, who have often been high-handed in their methods and not adept in meeting problems of human relations. In part, then, the original employee-representation plan arose as an attempt to replace the old personal relationships and in part to give the worker a more satisfactory position in his relations with his immediate superior, in order to avoid strife and dissatisfaction.[1]

In a limited number of cases management has been interested in introducing a form of industrial democracy in the workplace. Out of a larger number of such companies, three may be mentioned—Filene, the Columbia Conserve Company, and the Nash Clothing Company. Such cases have, however, been exceptional. Management has not generally wanted to share much power with the workers. It has usually desired only a more or less limited representative government, when not a slightly checked dictatorship.

Though here and there firms with company unions in their plants have at the same time willingly or unwillingly dealt with trade unions, and though there have been other firms with no animus against such labor organizations, the broad fact is that company unionism has generally been an open-shop device. Indeed, the evidence shows that in a large majority of cases at all times and in a still larger majority of cases in times of stress and strain, as in 1921–1922 and in 1933–1935, an important reason for the introduction of company unions has been to insure against an undesired trade unionism. As Professor Lescohier has said,

"Every investigator, whether pro-employer, pro-labor, or neutral, seems to agree that the company unions have interested a majority of the employers because of their potentialities in combating unionism."[2]

---

[1] In some instances, even in early days, the employer was confronted with opposition in his attempt to introduce an employee-representation plan. This was especially true in the General Electric plants in the electrical manufacturing industry. See Chap. 14 in *How Collective Bargaining Works*.

[2] Don D. Lescohier, *Working Conditions*, in vol. 3 of Commons and Associates, *History of Labor in the United States*, p. 354. The investigators referred to included: proemployer,

Similarly, a well-known personnel manager and industrial-relations counselor, one who was, moreover, a proponent of representation plans, said,

"After all what difference does it make whether one plant has a 'shop committee,' a 'works' council,' a 'Leitch Plan' . . . or whatever else it may be called? . . . They can all be called 'company union' and they all mean the one fundamental point: *The Open Shop.*"[1]

Detailed research abundantly reveals the following facts: (1) many company unions have been introduced during or upon the conclusion of trade-union strikes, for the purpose of meeting the demands of public opinion or/and dividing labor and keeping the union out; (2) others have been set up when unionism was imminent and perhaps making headway in the plant—the cases Dean Garrison had in mind when he said that many of the plans had been formed "for the palpable purpose of checking or destroying incipient union organization";[2] (3) many have been established when organization of labor in the plant was not imminent but was active and spreading in the community.[3] The 126 cases studied in detail by the United States Bureau of Labor Statistics give some indication of the influences and strains which have led to company-union

---

National Industrial Conference Board (*Reports*, 1919–1933); prolabor, R. W. Dunn, *Company Unions* (1923); neutral, reports published by Russell Sage Foundation; Earl J. Miller, *Workmen's Representation in Industrial Government*, Carroll E. French, *The Shop Committee in the United States;* J. R. Commons and Associates, *Industrial Government* (1921).

[1] Dudley Kennedy, "Collective Bargaining in Practice," *Industrial Management*, vol. 59 (1920), p. 152.

[2] Lloyd K. Garrison, "7-A and the Future," *Survey Graphic*, vol. 24 (1935), p. 54. He spoke in the light of his experience as chairman of the (first) National Labor Relations Board. See many of the decisions of that Board, for example, Shell Oil, Samson Tire, Kelsey-Hayes Wheel, Union Overall, North Carolina Granite, and Fifth Avenue Coach cases. In addition, more recent cases under the present National Labor Relations Board include *Industrial Rayon Corporation*, 7 N.L.R.B. 877 (1938); *Regal Shirt Company*, 4 N.L.R.B. 567 (1937); *American Manufacturing Company*, 5 N.L.R.B. 443 (1938); *Precision Castings Company*, 3 N.L.R.B. 212 (1937).

[3] The advent or threat of a union with outside affiliations has enhanced the importance of the company union to the employer in many cases. It has often caused the employer to deal seriously with the employee representatives, to meet with them, and to grant wage increases and concessions formerly denied, in an endeavor to continue to control the employee organization. In the *American Potash Chemical Corporation* case, 3 N.L.R.B. 140 (1937), the Association attempted fruitlessly from September, 1934, to March, 1936, to obtain adequate housing facilities and a general wage increase; in April, 1936, after a union affiliated with the A. F. of L. had become active, the company appropriated funds to relieve the housing shortage, arranged for regular meetings with the Association, and granted a general increase in wages. In the *Idaho-Maryland Mines Corporation* case, 4 N.L.R.B. 784 (1938), the company approached "the League" and signed a written agreement recognizing it as the agent for its members only after a union had become active in the vicinity. See also *Ford Motor Company*, 31 N.L.R.B. 994 and *G. Sommers & Co.*, 3 N.L.R.B. 992 (1937).

organization, and in most instances they show trade-union activity in the situation. Thus, of 125 company unions where the facts were obtained, 28 had been established when strikes were in progress or had been only recently settled; 52 when the trade union was making headway in the locality or plant; 31 had been incidental to NIRA; while 14 had been due to a desire of the company to improve personnel relations.[1]

In addition to the above reasons, other motives help explain the development of the new independents. Many workers distrust trade unions because of bitter experiences in the past with union organizers, strikes, layoffs, lockouts, and unemployment in the vicinity. In addition, employees are wary of many union tactics and methods, of sympathetic strikes, rackets, and radical union leaders. Furthermore, they are reluctant to join and pay high dues to a distant national organization, whose immediate benefits the job-conscious workers cannot see. Along with these factors, many employees, because of sentiment in the community or because of loyalty to management and to the company itself due to past concessions, prefer local independent organization as contrasted with national unions, which the employees know, in many instances, are looked upon with disfavor by the community and the company. Thus the plans have in not a few cases originated with the employees, rather than with management.

But, whatever their origin, most company unions have not been merely obstructive organizations or an insurance against trade unionism. For they have usually had as an objective positive or constructive functions of one kind or another. Company unionism has found place in the industrial relations and personnel setup, which during the fifteen years immediately preceding the great depression, and especially during the 1920's, made such great advance in large plants in American industry.[2] In general, it was desired that cooperation and understanding should be developed—rather than the "class war" many businessmen have been prone to associate with trade unions in industry. The company union, it was hoped, would provide a channel of communication and expression and a substitute for the old intimate personal contacts between workers and employer. It would serve as an agency for handling grievances of various kinds so important as a cause of discontent, high turnover of labor, low production, and poor quality of product. It would serve as an agency for improving the piece rate and the hourly wage structures. Perhaps it might serve as a collective-bargaining agency. Furthermore, safety campaigns, recreational activities, benefit and welfare plans could be tied in with it.[3]

[1] U. S. Bureau of Labor Statistics, *Bulletin* 634, pp. 80–82.

[2] *Cf. supra*, pp. 159–160.

[3] It was only to be expected that the Bureau of Labor Statistics should find that two-thirds of the companies whose plans were studied had benefit features as an element in their industrial-relations systems.

These objectives, together with the influence of patterns provided by large companies and the critical guidance of such organizations as the National Industrial Conference Board, explain most of the detail concerning committees, conferences, and the like found in representation and the old association plans. They serve also as an introduction to a more detailed discussion of company unions as they have functioned.

COMPANY UNIONS AS THEY HAVE FUNCTIONED

In 1935 the Bureau of Labor Statistics secured schedules[1] for 592 company unions. Table 23 presents an analysis of these schedules, by purported[2] function.

TABLE 23.—MATTERS REPORTED DISCUSSED BY COMPANY UNIONS WITH MANAGEMENT, 1933–1935[1]

Matter discussed or negotiated	Total company unions			
	Establishments		Workers	
	Number	Per cent	Number	Per cent
Individual grievances and complaints.................	455	76.9	467,777	88.5
Health and safety.....................................	386	65.2	420,739	79.6
General wage increases or decreases..................	384	64.9	371,474	70.3
Wage rates for specific occupations....................	377	63.7	426,895	80.8
Changes in weekly or daily hours.....................	357	60.3	368,168	69.7
General rules and regulations.........................	334	56.4	374,810	70.9
Methods of sharing or rotating work..................	317	53.5	365,591	69.2
Discharge of an employee or employees................	288	48.6	377,554	71.4
Rules of seniority....................................	253	42.7	348,602	66.0
Type of wage payment (piecework, bonus, etc.).........	244	41.2	322,841	61.1
Other..	12	2.0	34,512	6.5
Both general wage changes and changes in hours........	294	49.7	323,041	61.1
Neither of two principal matters[a]....................	142	24.0	99,415	18.8
General wage changes, type of wage payment, and changes in hours...................................	178	30.1	260,562	49.3
None of three principal matters[b].....................	79	13.3	63,902	12.1
All establishments with company unions.............	592	....	528,533	

[a] General wage changes, changes in hours.
[b] General wage changes, type of wage payments, changes in hours.

[1] U. S. Bureau of Labor Statistics, *Bulletin* 634, Table 23, p. 70. The 592 establishments with company unions in this total include 496 with company unions alone and 96 establishments with both company and trade unions.

Company unions have, of course, functioned in ways not noted in this table. For example, they have, as already observed, provided a

[1] Usually filled out by management.

[2] Such investigations as have been made and the experience of one of the authors as a member of the first and the present National Labor Relations Boards indicate that not infrequently there has been a substantial difference between purported and actual performance, indeed a greater difference than is found in the operation of most social and economic institutions.

channel of communication between workers and management.[1] The workers have frequently thereby learned of the problems of management and the condition of the company. This knowledge has made for tolerance and patience, removed or minimized misunderstanding and discontent, been more or less effective in improving morale, and tended to make for economy and efficiency. But such results have depended upon how the plan was introduced, how it was operated, and what the company's policies were. Where the plan has been primarily antiunion and obstructive, as it so frequently has, or where it has been imposed upon the workers, or where the employer has been "hard boiled" in respect to wages and hours, or in hiring, layoff, and discharge, such desirable results have been minimized when secured at all. No plan of industrial relations functions automatically; the machinery of industrial relations is not self-operative. As the National Industrial Conference Board has so frequently warned, plans must be fair and operated intelligently and with an active sense of justice if they are to be successful.[2]

Other examples of the ways in which some plans have functioned, not specifically indicated by the analytical table, are found in connection with benefits of one kind or another, recreational facilities and agencies, and social and educational affairs. In these fields company unions have been of some importance and have functioned fairly well. For a generation large industry has been more or less actively interested in health and safety, especially the latter. Hence approximately two-thirds of the plans surveyed, with four-fifths of the coverage, were designed to function in that connection. A majority of the plans have therefore provided for a committee on health and safety to cooperate in safety first programs and other matters. The Bureau of Labor Statistics concluded that company unions had achieved their greatest success in connection with health and safety work.[3]

---

[1] As the Bureau of Labor Statistics reported (*Bulletin* 634, p. 102), "Company-union constitutions emphasized the improvement of mutual relations between workers and management. More than two-thirds of the 97 constitutions included such statements of purpose as: 'To provide a means of friendly and lasting cooperation . . . ' or 'to promote good feeling, harmony, and full cooperation. . . . '

"The desire to establish a means of communication between management and employees found expression in the statement of purpose in 40 constitutions."

[2] National Industrial Conference Board, *Collective Bargaining through Employee Representation*, pp. 41–63. The Conference Board said, "A plan of employee representation conceived or administered insincerely cannot be expected to be successful. . . . A company is better off with no plan for collective consultation and negotiation than with one that is not genuinely representative. . . . Any plan involving joint action by two parties or groups must have the approval and cordial support of both groups if it is to function successfully. . . . No plan for harmonizing human interests and relationships can be genuinely successful unless the spirit as well as the letter of its provisions is scrupulously observed. Employee representation is no exception to this rule."

[3] *Bulletin* 634, p. 201.

The plans have most frequently provided machinery for handling individual grievances and complaints. Indeed, the desirability of such machinery is so great and so much emphasis has been placed upon it by the proponents of company unions that one may well be surprised not to find the settlement of grievances and complaints reported by all or nearly all of the 592 plans. Perhaps the explanation of the percentage recorded above, 76.9, is found in part in the frequency of organization primarily as insurance against trade unionism, in part by the fact that many small companies have not felt the need for the laying down of definite rules relative to the matter, and in part by the fact that in many cases well-known and accepted procedures had already been operative and it was not regarded as necessary to incorporate them in the constitution of any formal representation or association plan introduced. The fact is that the settlement of grievances has been the most generally performed function of those company unions that have really done anything.

It has been the procedure in most open-shop plants for an employee to present any grievance he might have to the foreman before presenting it, if at all, to the superior officers for adjustment. Under approximately one-third of the plans surveyed by the Bureau of Labor Statistics this initial step was still required before a representative could be called upon to become active in the adjustment of a worker's grievance. In the other two-thirds of the cases, however, a worker could present his grievance at once to his representative, who was thereupon expected to take it up with the foreman and other company officials in order, and, if necessary,[1] to bring it up in committee or joint conference. In a large majority of cases, therefore, a company-union plan, if it did not create the needed machinery, made the adjustment procedures known to the workmen and also supplied assistance in securing adjustments in meritorious cases. Moreover, such plans have tended to remove fear of discrimination if grievances were presented.

The evidence available, drawn from different sources, would lead one to conclude that the most important single function performed by company unions has been the disposition of individual grievances. Some companies have published in plant magazines or elsewhere reports on the operation of their representation plans, which show the large number of such grievances adjusted.[2]

---

[1] Typical of a considerable number of company unions was one cited by the National Industrial Conference Board in its *Collective Bargaining through Employee Representation*, pp. 23 and 29. In the experience of this company 85 per cent of the grievances were settled in the initial stage where the workers' representative informally discussed them with the foreman, whereas only 2.5 per cent reached the Executive Board. Improvement in plant morale was said to be the "outstanding contribution of employee representation: . . . It appears in a better esprit de corps, which acts as a lubricant for smooth and effective functioning of the organization." *Ibid.*, pp. 39–40.

[2] In most reports, however, the analysis runs in such terms that individual grievances

While the evidence is impressive, one should not rush to exaggerated, questionable conclusions as to the efficiency with which the adjustment function has been performed under company-union plans. For, in the first place, no doubt many of these grievances would have been settled, and frequently with the same result, had there been no company union. Yet, there can be no more doubt that in the typical plant many of them would have been "nursed" and endured had the special machinery not been established. Indeed, the machinery established, the right specifically accorded to use it, and the assistance given by the workers' representative have multiplied the number of grievances brought into the open —frequently to the surprise of alert and well-disposed management. In the second place, the evidence shows many instances in which the sense of fear has not been removed by representation plans, and still others in which the workers have failed to obtain satisfactory adjustments of cases regarded as meritorious. Indeed, there have been some instances in which, according to report, the workers generally have felt that it was no use to bring up grievances for adjustment under plans purporting to accord the privilege or right.[1]

The conclusions concerning the settlement of grievances arrived at by the Bureau of Labor Statistics from its field study of 126 company unions merit quotation. The Bureau found instances, even where plans had been functioning for a long time, in which fear remained and there was hesitancy lest the displeasure of foremen or management be incurred. Concerning the efficiency with which grievances were adjusted, it stated:

"In view of the emphasis placed upon the company union as an agency for adjusting individual grievances, it is significant that one-third of the company unions handled no such matters. According to persons interviewed in company unions which did take up individual grievances, approximately one-third of this group did so effectively, another third with limited effectiveness, and the remainder ineffectively. The company unions which were effective in handling grievances included most of those with full-time officials as well as most of those which showed some ability to negotiate with management regarding wages. They also included a relatively large proportion of companies with personnel departments."[2]

It is obvious that the analysis presented in Table 23 contains overlapping categories. For example, discipline, layoff, or a piece rate may

---

are not listed. For tabular reports, see E. R. Burton, *Employee Representation*, pp. 268–274, various numbers of *Personnel*, and American Management Association, Production Executives' Series.

[1] *Cf.* Twentieth Century Fund, *Labor and the Government*, pp. 326–327, and B. M. Selekman and Mary Van Kleeck, *Employes' Representation in Coal Mines*, p. 188.

[2] *Bulletin* 634, p. 201.

constitute an individual grievance. Discussing some of these briefly, it may be observed that, according to the analysis, consideration of "discharge of an employee or employees" was reported by 48.6 per cent of the establishments reporting on their company-union plans. Thus the workers had the right of review and a degree of protection in their jobs in almost half of the cases. At the same time it must be noted that under the constitutions or outlines of plans many companies reserved unto themselves unfettered right to hire and fire. It can be said that much less generally than in unionized plants the workers have had the right of review in hiring and discharge.

Related to this is the matter of seniority rules in layoff and recall to work. It has been observed at an earlier point in our discussion,[1] that a limited number of "new" trade unions have insisted upon the sharing of work available and discharges of regular employees only for cause; that many unions have not insisted upon or obtained any rule relating to the matter; but that an increasing number have insisted upon and obtained seniority rights. In the upheaval of 1933–1934 many newly organized trade unions, primarily in order to protect their officers and most active members against discrimination, demanded security of tenure and seniority in layoffs and in recall for work when work became available. Though they had not been conspicuous from the inception of the company-union movement, seniority provisions were, naturally enough, incorporated in a considerable number of the plans introduced or revised in the days of the New Deal. It was therefore reported that, in 42.7 per cent of the establishments for which the schedules distributed by the Bureau of Labor Statistics were filled out, "rules of seniority" had been subjects "discussed or negotiated." The evidence available does not show how frequently practice conformed to the rules laid down. The evidence does show, however, that seniority rules in effect were usually qualified in one way or another, as, for example, by "efficiency" or by "family status." In most cases, it would appear, management had retained a large measure of discretion.[2] Indeed, as already noted, some constitutions specifically reserved to management full authority over hiring, discharge, and related matters.[3]

---

[1] *Supra*, pp. 455–457.

[2] This does not imply that any particular arrangement is to be preferred or that there should be no element of discretion. It means only that the seniority rules were generally different from those some trade unions have insisted upon.

[3] The Bureau of Labor Statistics reported (*Bulletin* 634, p. 103) that: "Fifteen company-union constitutions specifically included discharge, lay-off, and transfer among the matters to be taken up by the company union. . . . On the other hand, 11 company-union constitutions specifically reserved to management the authority over hiring and discharge. The most common form of reservation, found identically in nine constitutions, was as follows: 'The management of the works and the direction of the working forces, including the right to hire, suspend, or discharge for proper cause, or transfer, and the right to relieve employees

According to the schedules returned to the Bureau of Labor Statistics, a substantial majority of company unions discussed or negotiated with reference to hours and wages, and a large minority with reference to method of wage payment. The analysis, in terms of establishments and percentages, is presented in Table 23.

In many cases the company union has played an important part in the adjustment of individual rates of pay and has expressed the workers' views on proposed piece rates. It has frequently been helpful in developing more satisfactory hourly-rate and piece-rate structures. At the same time it can be said that company unions have had much less real influence upon general changes in wages and hours than the percentages shown in Table 23 would indicate. For the most part, they have not been like trade unions, which above all else seek time agreements with respect to wages, hours, and job protection. Indeed, it was only during the years 1933–1934, which witnessed the introduction of Sec. 7(a) and which were marked by struggles between company union and trade union for position in many plants, that most company unions claimed themselves to be agencies for the purpose of collective bargaining on wages, hours, and basic working conditions. The claims then and subsequently made in this connection have, however, been much exaggerated. Certainly this is true if one makes a distinction between the adjustment of grievances day after day and collective bargaining with reference to wage and hours standards to run through a period of time—a distinction very properly made by the various labor boards as well as by labor experts and economists.

SHORTCOMINGS OF COMPANY UNIONS

The exaggerated claims made for company unions as collective-bargaining agencies[1] are explained in considerable part by the rather general failure of their proponents and defenders, when speaking if not when thinking, to make a distinction between (1) mere adjustment of details to other details or to work and employment rules, and (2) bargaining on general changes in levels of wages and hours and in work and employment rules. They are explained in part also by the failure to make a

---

from duty because of lack of work, or for other legitimate reasons, is vested exclusively in the management; and, except as expressly provided herein, these rights shall not be abridged by anything contained herein.'"

[1] It is true that indirectly the company unions aided collective bargaining, for many company unions proved to be the training grounds for many "leaders" in the subsequent unions in the industry. This was especially true in the steel and electrical industry. In addition, "it facilitated collective bargaining to the extent that it had familiarized the employees with the techniques and procedures for negotiating with management and adjusting grievances." See Chaps. 10 and 14 of *How Collective Bargaining Works*.

distinction between (1) conference or discussion and (2) negotiation or bargaining.[1] Discussion may leave management free to do as it likes. It is only when conference is for the purpose of reaching an agreement on the matters discussed, which will be mutually satisfactory and which is not subject to change during the period it is to run except by further conference and agreement, that collective bargaining obtains. Successful collective bargaining results in a joint agreement.[2] In some unionized trades, for example, newspaper publication, the agreement as executed is generally spoken of as a "contract."

In this connection, the (first) National Labor Relations Board may be quoted as follows:

"Collective bargaining . . . is simply a means to an end. The end is an *agreement*. And, customarily, such an agreement will have to do with wages, hours, and basic working conditions, and will have a fixed duration. The purpose of every such agreement has been to stabilize, for a certain period, the terms of employment, for the protection alike of employer and employee. By contrast, where all that transpires is a demand by employees for better terms and an assent by the employer, but without any understanding as to duration, there has been no *collective agreement*, because neither side has been bound to anything."[3]

Collective and signed agreements had been entered into up to the end of 1939 by relatively few company unions other than independent unions organized since 1935.[4] The Bureau of Labor Statistics found in 1935 that there were only 82 agreements in effect, to which 13.9 per cent of the 592 plans were parties, these agreements including 10.5 per cent of the workers covered by the survey. Most of these agreements were not signed and were not of stated duration. Moreover, not all of them

[1] It has been this hasty attempt since 1935 to make the employee-representation plans sole collective-bargaining agencies rather than pure grievance committees and administrators of the welfare plans, as originally intended in many instances, that has caused a good deal of the strife in many labor situations. As Justice Stone stated in the case of *Virginian Railway Co. v. System Federation no. 40* (300 U. S. 515), "Experience had shown, before the amendment of 1934, that when there was no dispute as to the organizations authorized to represent the employees, and where there was willingness of the employer to meet such representatives for a discussion of their grievances, amicable adjustment of differences had generally followed and strikes had been avoided. On the other hand, a prolific source of dispute had been the maintenance by the railroads of company unions and the denial by railway management of the authority of representatives chosen by their employees."

[2] 10 N.L.R.B. 963 (1939).

[3] Houde Engineering Corporation, *Decisions of the [first] National Labor Relations Board*, vol. 1, at pp. 35–36. Italics ours.

[4] Attention should be called to the evidence that only eighteen of the sixty "independents" covered by the National Labor Relations Board study of company-dominated unions had formal agreements. All these unions were organized or readopted after May 31, 1935; and most of them were new organizations claiming independence from their inception. National Labor Relations Board, *Release R 2351*.

covered wages, hours, and basic working conditions. Somewhat earlier the Twentieth Century Fund studied eight-five plans, with corresponding results.[1] Of course, as indicated by the Twentieth Century Fund and as shown by the cases coming before the National Labor Relations Boards for hearing and decision, general changes in wages, hours, and basic working conditions had been discussed by management and works representatives in a large proportion of the establishments, but, as the conclusion of the discussion, management in most cases remained free to exercise its discretion as to what should be done. It may be said, then, (1) that company unions were conceived of as providing channels for the communication to management of what was on the workers' minds, and as machinery for settling grievances, chiefly individual; (2) that early in the movement, largely as a result of the pattern provided by the International Harvester Company, provision for collective bargaining was made in exceptional instances; and (3) that under the New Deal such instances became less exceptional but did not come to constitute the rule, as some would have us believe.

Except for some of the firms hurriedly adopting company-union plans during the last decade, most of the companies introducing such plans have been relatively good employers. It has been their policy, with or without conference with representatives of the workers, to introduce the better hours prevailing in the industry or in the community and to pay at least the market rate of wages, and perhaps the wages paid by the "better" employers in the industry or in the locality. With little bargaining, they have raised wages in accord with this policy when the market situation has been favorable. If the matter of wages was discussed in conference, the company union has commonly been given credit for the increase made.[2] On the other hand, there have been many instances in

---

[1] Twentieth Century Fund, *Labor and the Government*, pp. 100–102.

[2] Concerning this, the Bureau of Labor Statistics stated that: "Company unions were less effective in handling general questions of wages and hours than in handling other matters. In nearly half of the [126] cases, no general wage increases were requested or negotiated by the company union between January, 1933, and July, 1935. This does not mean that there were no wage increases in these plants. Since it was a period of rising prices and business improvement, some of these concerns gave increases but the company unions played no part in securing these increases.

"Such wage adjustments as did take place following requests by company unions were in most cases not a result of any process which might be termed negotiation and collective bargaining. In some instances, it appeared that the wage increase which management had decided to make was announced through the company union in order to increase the prestige of the company union. Many requests for increases were refused by management without any negotiation, management simply stating that conditions did not warrant an increase or that wages were above those in other plants.

"A small number of the company unions engaged in a procedure which approximated negotiation. Some of these negotiations resulted in wage increases. Analysis of the internal structure and strength of these organizations leads to the conclusion that their

which, in adversely affected markets, employers have made general wage
reductions without conference with the official representatives of the
workers lest this should discredit these representatives and the company
union.[1] Nevertheless, there have also been many instances in which
wage cuts have been made after conference, the workers' representatives
perhaps being helpful to the employers where the action taken was
desirable or necessary.[2]

In industries largely unionized the situation has in some respects been
different. For example, under the Colorado Fuel and Iron Company
Plan it was the common practice in the coal mines to accept the scales
adopted by union operators and the United Mine Workers.[3] In steel
works, on the other hand, changes were based upon changes made by the
United States Steel Corporation.[4] Among the company-union agreements studied by the Bureau of Labor Statistics there were a number
that ran in terms of the trade-union agreements effective in another
department or in other plants.

The above paragraphs cover company-union collective bargaining in
a broad way. It remains to note that in some instances union men have
said that they fared better under a company-union than they had previously under a trade-union regime. Perhaps, as is said to have happened
in one instance, wage adjustments really wanted had been made because
of the strategy of making unacceptable demands for other things. But,
while here and there strategy has been an important factor in securing
what was really wanted, the evidence available supports the conclusion

---

aggressiveness was due to the activity of trade-union members within the company union
or to encouragement by a management favorably inclined toward the idea of a vigorou.
union of its own employees but independent of outside affiliation." *Bulletin* 634, pp
201–202.

[1] In a number of instances in which companies had accredited wage advances to com
pany unions, cuts were later made without the consultation the company-union constitution
seemed to call for.

[2] This is said in the light of details presented in a number of National Labor Relation
Board cases heard in 1934–1935. On this matter the National Industrial Conferenc
Board has said, "The investigation of the Conference Board shows that where employer
have discussed with the employee representatives on their Works Councils the reasons for
proposed reduction in wages, a curtailment of the working force, or a change in work hou
schedules, the representatives in a vast majority of cases have appreciated the cogency c
the circumstances . . . and have concurred with the employers in the proposed change:
. . . The management was able to prepare the minds of the employees for acceptance of th
economies in wages that would sooner or later have to be effected." Quotation fron
Experience with Works Councils in the United States, Research Report 50 (1922), p. 8
See also Carroll E. French, *The Shop Committee in the United States*, pp. 57–58.

[3] There was only one exception. In this case wages were reduced when there was n
reduction in union wages.

[4] B. M. Selekman, *Employes' Representation in Steel Works*, pp. 90ff., and B. M. Selek
man and Mary Van Kleeck, *Employes' Representation in Coal Mines*, p. 387. See als
How Collective Bargaining Works, Chap. 10.

of the Bureau of Labor Statistics that company unions have been less effective in handling wages and hours than in handling other matters.[1] The evidence forces one to the general conclusion that, although collective bargaining has been found in exceptional cases, there has not been much of it in the past between company unions and management in the proper sense of the term.   After more or less discussion, when there has been discussion at all, what management has wanted to do has usually been acceptable to the company unions.   In any event, the company unions have generally acquiesced.   In only a limited number of cases have the workers strongly protested, much less revolted and gone on strike or changed the company union over into a really independent and a more or less militant trade union.

All this one would expect, even without the substantial evidence found in the many National Labor Relations Board cases, for it is quite obvious that, even when expected to function as a collective-bargaining agency, the company union is in several respects weak as compared to the typical trade union.   In the typical case, the working assumptions are against the presentation and stout support of what the workers may really want and feel they are entitled to in respect of wages and hours.[2]   Most company unions have been organized and operated for the purpose of cooperating, not bargaining, with management.   In so far as there is truth in the oft-made statement that a union cannot cooperate effectively because of the emphasis placed upon collective bargaining, there is truth in the statement that a cooperating organization cannot bargain effectively.

[1] *Bulletin* 634, p. 201.   Cf. also Twentieth Century Fund, *Labor and the Government,* p. 331.

[2] This does not apply to some independent unions organized within the last few years. In some instances they have been legally competent bargainers.   Nor does it apply accurately to all company unions during the last six or eight years.   The following factors have been important: (1) increased management interest and willingness to deal with the company union, in a final effort to forestall trade unionism; (2) increased activity by some employee representatives who thought that company unionism might be made to work better than it had and be preferable in some respects to trade unionism (there was some of this activity in Carnegie-Illinois plants and at the Dodge plant of the Chrysler Company); (3) the influence of independent unions that worked through the works councils—electing men who became very active in pushing demands (this was true in the two cases just mentioned and in the tractor works of International Harvester); and (4) the influence of individual union men or of locals of the C.I.O. or A.F. of L., working, in 1936–1937, in close contact with union organizing campaigns (the program was to work through the works councils, using them as a means of contact for organizing purposes, and at the same time to push very actively the demands of the rank and file in an effort to convince the workers that the company union was an ineffective mechanism for collective bargaining and that a real trade union was needed).   While this is true, it cannot be regarded as important in evaluating the company union as an independent mechanism for the purpose of collective bargaining.   The situation was extraordinary; the functioning of company unions, also of independent unions, was influenced by the militant organized-labor movement in unusual degree.

Another source of weakness is found in the fact that in the typical case the company union has had no outside help in handling its problems and no outside contact with other labor organizations. While it is true that now and then it has had the advice and counsel of a person not in the employ of the company, this has been very exceptional. Indeed, few company unions have had the assistance and leadership of a full-time officer.

The fact that in almost four cases in five the company union has been an isolated institution, without outside contacts,[1] is an important one. Unlike a local trade union affiliated to an international, it has not had the advantage of definite policies that have been adopted, or of the aid of the president and other officers of an Amalgamated Clothing Workers, a United Mine Workers, or a Teamsters' Union, or even of the officers of a city central body. It has not had the advantage of the researches into wage scales, cost of living, and other matters as has a pressmen's or a compositors' local. On the contrary, it has typically been limited to the employees of the given firm for leadership, and the leaders have usually been inexperienced and lacking in adequate knowledge of standards elsewhere in the market area. As a rule, also, these leaders have been cautious in what they did lest they should "get in bad." The rank and file, usually meeting irregularly, if at all, perhaps have developed no general view of what they really wanted. Usually the representatives have been largely dependent upon their ordinary contacts for such knowledge as they have had as regards this; seldom have they been fortified by a vote on the wages and hours upon which the workers were prepared to insist. For the most part, the members of company unions have been inarticulate. With exceptions, it is trade unions, not company unions, that have presented "demands."[2]

The company union is usually not in position to make demands and to withdraw the labor of its members. The underlying doctrine, usually made explicit in company-union constitutions, is that of a harmony of interests in the employer-employee relationship. When there is a difference in respect to what should be, and more or less frequently there will be differences because of the conflict that lies alongside any harmony of interests, it is to be disposed of by discussion—or by arbitration, which though it may be provided for, has seldom been resorted to. Generally

[1] The Bureau of Labor Statistics found (*Bulletin* 634, p. 73) that only 22.1 per cent of the 592 plans covered by its survey claimed to have any contact, direct or indirect, with other company unions in the same company, while only 8.3 per cent claimed to have such contacts with company unions in plants of other companies. The Division of Economic Research of the National Labor Relations Board found that only three of the eight independents on which information was available covered more than one company. Research Memorandum 1, *Statistical Analysis of 85 "Independent" Unions and Readapted Company Unions.*

[2] It is significant that company-union terminology is usually "request," not "demand."

speaking, company unions are nonstrike organizations.[1] Though strikes have occurred now and then, the instances are very exceptional. One reason for this is that the company union has been financially weak, when not financially dependent upon the employer. Dues, when any, have, as we have seen, been low; disposable reserves have not been built up. Isolated, the company union has not had an international upon which to draw in case of financial need or even a city central body to "pass the hat." Thus circumstanced, what the workers have wanted could not really be pressed for otherwise than by argument, and thus they have been at a distinct disadvantage under company-union organization.[2] Nor has the boycott weapon been available for use by such an organization. Under company unionism, any employer fear that may have been effective has not been of boycott or strike, but of loss of cooperation and good will, and, perhaps, in extreme cases, of embarrassment because of possible outside knowledge that the plan has not worked to the satisfaction of all parties.

Not only is it true that, as Mr. Lewisohn said, "it is a great mistake to consider this device as a means of balancing the power of management by the power of another group,"[3] but it is also true that wages and hours are most frequently matters of the local, district, or national market, not matters in and limited to a given plant or the several plants of a given firm. Both the employer and his employees may have to carry on in a limiting market situation. A market situation can be brought under control only by an organization coextensive with the market.

Years ago, Professor Seager pointed out that, while a properly devised and fairly operated company union might function more or less effectively in such monopolistic industries as the supply of gas, electric current, and local transportation, it could not, because of its usual limitations, function well in a competitive industry with perhaps many plants operated by a considerable number of firms.[4] The reason is obvious. What effective control could one clothing manufacturer and his company-union employees exercise over wages and hours? Very little, for each firm is very much limited by the wages paid and hours worked by other firms

[1] As the Bureau of Labor Statistics has stated (*Bulletin* 634, p. 202), "Practically all of the organizations specifically or by inference disavowed the use of the strike and a negligible number had funds sufficient to carry a strike for any length of time."

[2] The Bureau of Labor Statistics observed (*ibid.*, p. 205), "So rarely was strike action even considered that the threat of withholding their labor played virtually no part in negotiations with their employers."

[3] S. A. Lewisohn, *The New Leadership in Industry* (1936), p. 127. The quotation continues, "It should rather be regarded as a mechanism which the management officials utilize to assist them in their function of leadership. It is a technique for making leadership compatible with democratic ideals."

[4] H. R. Seager, "Company Unions vs. Trade Unions," *The American Economic Review,* vol. 13 (1923), p. 11.

and by the prices at which they sell the product. Would not each plant or firm group differ from the "social shop"[1] only in size, and would it not likely undercut all others in an effort to get more of the business to be had in a seasonal industry? Did not union organization in the needle trades come into existence primarily to limit that competition and to meet the problems presented by "sweated industry"? The coal, the cleaning and dyeing, the textile, the shoe, and many other industries cannot standardize, stabilize, and exercise much control without a market mechanism. Be the outcome good or bad in its various aspects, it is only a labor organization with the structure and the relations of the trade union that can exercise control over matters not of plant or firm origin.

Thus far the company union has been considered almost entirely as an agency for collective bargaining and the adjustment of grievances, but as Professor Douglas years ago said, "The labor question cannot be settled on the economic field alone. Protective legislation has been found necessary to protect men as well as women from the effects of unrestricted competition. Such legislation is generally opposed by the organized employers and its passage and subsequent enforcement depends largely upon the efforts of labor itself, together with that of the independent humanitarian groups."[2] In contrast to trade unions, company unions, organized to deal with matters primarily on a plant or company basis, have seldom shown any interest in labor or welfare legislation, and, in the rare instances in which they have, they have usually reflected the employer point of view.[3] In so far as they have had any influence on such legislation it has been largely negative and obstructive.

INDEPENDENT UNIONS OF RECENT YEARS

Of late, however, as has been stated, there have developed many new independent unions. In some cases these have been reformed or readapted company unions;[4] in other cases they have resulted from subtle

[1] As the term is used in the garment trades.

[2] Quotation from Paul H. Douglas, "Shop Committees: Substitute for, or Supplement to, Trades-unions?" *Journal of Political Economy*, vol. 29 (1921), p. 99.

[3] It is significant to note that most of the company-union plans whose representatives testified before the Senate Committee on the hearings for the Wagner Act have been found "company dominated" under Sec. 8(2) by the National Labor Relations Board.

[4] This development was particularly true in the "Little Steel" part of the steel industry where independent unions continued to function for a time because of: (1) the distrust of the employees of the tactics, methods, and leaders of the Steel Workers' Organizing Committee, (2) the influence and prestige achieved by employee-representation plans from concessions and wage increases, (3) the close and intimate relationship (not necessarily domination) of management and the independents, (4) the liberal treatment of employee through welfare plans sometimes associated with the employee-representation plan, (5) the low overhead expenses and dues of these independents as contrasted with the national organizations, and (6) their "parasitic" dependence on the Steel Workers' Organizing

employer influence that has not been discovered by the National Labor Relations Board or the courts; and in some cases these independent unions have arisen from the employees themselves. This latter group has taken on a new position in the industrial-relations field. Formed in many cases by employees who distrust trade-union organizations, for reasons already enumerated,[1] many independents have recently developed with the guidance of outside legal help and local independent organizers. In some cases, particularly in the steel industry, these independents have assumed a militancy in collective bargaining that belies any charge of company domination.[2] These independents in some instances are in a strategic position: in some organized industries they are in a "parasitic" situation and follow the standards worked out by the national trade union; in other industries, the employer has dealt with the independent and has been forced to grant concessions in excess of trade-union demands in order to prevent union organization. Thus in some cases these new independents have truly assumed the role of independence with organizers, legal advice, dues, and meetings. In a few instances, some attempts at federation of these company unions have been started,[3] while in others, after the original drive and impetus has worn off and the limitations discovered, these independent unions have turned to trade-union affiliation.[4]

One further recent type of local independent should be mentioned, *i.e.*, the radical local. In many cases, it has seceded from a national labor organization because of its own radical tendencies. In other cases it represents an old radical association that has never affiliated with the two large labor organizations and has maintained an independent existence for some time. In a few cases, it controls a small market area or community. Although these organizations are truly independent and

---

Committee, as well as their collective-bargaining power derived from the existence of the Steel Workers' Organizing Committee and the relative profitability of some of the "Little Steel" companies. In spite of these developments, the independents in steel had the following inherent weaknesses: (1) they were isolated and could count on little outside help in time of strike, (2) they lacked means of investigating wages and working conditions in competing companies, (3) their legal status was uncertain owing to the past history and origin of many of the plans, (4) they were in an unstable position, since the employer feared making a closed-shop agreement with the independent because of a possible charge of company domination, and (5) they were weak politically.

[1] See *supra*, pp. 870–872.

[2] The National Labor Relations Board has recognized that a genuine independent labor organization, completely distinct from the previous company-dominated union, meets the requirements of the National Labor Relations Act and is not illegal under Sec. 8(2). *Wisconsin Telephone Company*, 12 N.L.R.B. 375 (1939), and *Mohawk Carpet Mills, Inc.*, 12 N.L.R.B. 1265 (1939).

[3] In the steel industry, for instance, the organizations in plants of the Republic Steel Corporation have belonged to a federation or central delegate council.

[4] This has been particularly true in the large companies of the steel industry, and partly in the electrical industry. See *How Collective Bargaining Works*, Chaps. 10 and 14.

are not company dominated, their functions as trade organizations are limited.

In spite of the independence and legality of these new unions, the discussion above regarding the representation and association plans that predominated until very recently applies with minor qualifications to them. For while they may have and may display a measure of independence, they are largely isolated, financially weak, and usually have a membership limited to the employees of a given plant or firm. Their very existence is dependent in many instances on the presence of a national organization in the industry and on the standards established by a national union. Not only are they isolated and economically weak, they are also politically impotent. Scarcely more than the other older types of company unions can they by themselves be expected to balance the power of management. Only in so far as there is no need for collective bargaining on a large area or industry scale and no need for standardization or stabilization, or in so far as trade unions cover the major part of the particular industry, can these independent unions function as effective collective-bargaining agents.

The limitations of company unions are apparent even in areas where the company union has been organized on a large local market basis. In printing in Baltimore and Boston, as we have noted, company unions were not restricted to the individual concern but were organized on a local market unit. But even here, Miss Brown reported, "The chief weakness of these open-shop organizations is the narrow territory covered. . . . The organizations are therefore unable to affect standards widely and follow the union standards for the most skilled workers, while the open-shop scales, whether they are considered minimum scales or 'normal scales,' are not objectively defined and can not be universally enforced even within the organization. . . . Since these organizations depend for their success fundamentally upon the active interest and consent of the employers they have developed no power to enforce widely their standards and policies."[1]

Though the facts have not been as conclusively established, it appears that the same may be said of the 4L Plan in the timber industry of the Northwest. While it set minima or norms for wages in different occupations, these were closely related to what market forces were establishing in the several localities. And, it would appear, in the absence of an independent trade unionism, these standards were frequently not observed by some of the companies.

The weaknesses of the individual company union as well as the company unions organized on a market basis in the parts of the printing and lumber industry apply for the most part to the few existing federated

[1] Emily Clark Brown, "Joint Industrial Control in the Book and Job Printing Industry," U. S. Bureau of Labor Statistics, *Bulletin* 481, pp. 193–194.

independent unions. It may be that stable federated independent unions with genuine plans for collective bargaining will play a more important role in the field of industrial relations in the future, inasmuch as this type of plan overcomes the weaknesses of the old individual company unions and employee-representation plan. The federation may provide trained leaders, a permanent staff, a large treasury, outside assistance in time of dispute, certain political power in the area, a more welcome reception from the employer than A.F. of L. or C.I.O. unions, and a new appeal untainted in some instances by the radical views and racketeering of certain union leaders. Hence, those federations which are legal under the Wagner Act may stand over against the affiliated unions as legitimate organizations with definite possibilities for collective bargaining. However, many of the present federations of independent unions have been composed of individual company-dominated unions,[1] are often the cloak for an individual's money-making activities, are still subtly dominated by employers' associations, and are still sham collective-bargaining agencies of doubtful legality.

Concluding Observations

Company unions and their independent successors are, for the most part, by-products of the so-called "legitimate" labor movement. But, whatever the origin in different cases, as collective-bargaining agencies they function under serious handicaps. The case for collective bargaining is sound, and the legitimate union must be regarded as the normal and desirable form of workers' organization in industry.

This statement is true in spite of the numerous union problems to which reference has been made in the foregoing pages and chapters of this volume: problems of a divided and to an extent a warring labor movement, of defective organization, of occasionally undemocratic government, of inferior leadership in more cases than one, of one form or another of racketeering, of poor judgment and impatience, of mistaken policies, of an excess of obstruction and a deficiency of cooperation. All these problems are to be found in exceptional cases, and some of them are rather widespread. The answer or solution to these problems lies, however, not in replacement of trade unions by company unions, but rather in solutions, in so far as is possible, under a democratic regime. Attainment of industrial democracy or real representative government in industry is possible only where labor organizations are uncoerced, unassisted, and undominated.

[1] Several of the organizations in the American Association of Independent Labor Unions, the National Independent Unions of America, Inc., and the California League of Independent Unions have been ordered disestablished by the National Labor Relations Board.

The case for representative government in industry has been examined and discussed in the foregoing chapters. Yet a final observation remains to be made: one that is, in the belief of the authors, of tremendous importance, particularly in these days of contest over what our "way of life" shall be. Oligarchic management of labor and representative government in the political sphere are inharmonious. In the political sphere, stable and efficient representative government cannot be realized and maintained unless the great mass of the electorate becomes accustomed to, and experienced in, a joint solving of its many common problems. In the economic sphere, where lie the most immediate and continuous interests of the average person, trade unionism can contribute mightily in training for the democratic way. There is, in addition, the feeling engendered of "belonging" and of enhanced status stemming from individual membership and participation in the affairs of an active and successful union. In the greater emotional security resulting from group solidarity is to be found a truly important contribution to social stability and the maintenance of a democratic political system. Trade unions are, moreover, one of the most important political supports of democratic government. They have a stake in the perpetuation of a free-enterprise economy—the parallel in the industrial sphere of political democracy— and in the perpetuation of democratic processes. A free-enterprise economy is, in fact, the only kind in which they can really bargain with employers and function as the representatives of the workers' free choosing; and a democracy is the only form of government in which they can have effective voice in securing political and social gains for themselves and their members. A well-organized, well-led, and experienced trade-union movement is an essential part of the foundation for that democracy in government in which we believe and to which we are pledged.

NAME INDEX

Acland, F. A., *cited*, 783n.
Adamic, Louis, *cited*, 49n., 64n.
Adams, John Quincy, 24
Adams, Thomas S., and Sumner, Helen L., *cited*, 582, 697n.
Allen, Henry J., *cited*, 822n.
Alliance for Labor and Democracy, 138
Alschuler, Judge, 825
Altgeld, Governor, 64n., 72, 81n.
American Academy of Political and Social Science, *cited*, 343n.
American Alliance for Labor and Democracy, 137
American Anti-boycott Association, 96
American Arbitration Association, 720
American Association for Adult Education, 327n.
American Economic Association, *cited*, 482n.
American Engineering Council, 292
American Institute of Architects, 291, 292
American Management Association, 838; *cited*, 467n., 877n.
American Newspaper Publishers' Association, 605, 710, 717, 718
Amulree, Lord, *cited*, 776n.
Amulree, Lord, and Allan J. B. Fisher, *cited*, 782n.
Anderson, George, *cited*, 807n., 816n.
Anderson, Judge, 145n.
Andrews, J. B., *cited*, 46n., 49n., 50n., 52n., 53n., 54n., 55n., 62n.
Anthracite Coal Strike Commission, 636
Ashworth, Dr. J. H., *cited*, 450
Askwith, G. R., *cited*, 777n., 783n.
Askwith, Sir George, 778
Association for the Protection of Industry and for the Promotion of National Education, 26
Atkins, W. E., *cited*, 866n.
Automobile Labor Board, 845n., 846n.; 848; *cited*, 848n.

Baer, George F., 97n.
Baker, C. M., 358
Baker, Jacob, *cited*, 341n.
Bakunin, Michael, 56n., 57n.
Baltimore and Ohio Railroad, 44, 173n., 313, 372, 465, 468, 469
Barnett, George E., 482; *cited*, 94n., 431n., 432n.
Barnett, George E., and David A. McCabe, *cited*, 722n.
Bates, Harry C., 220n.
Beard, Charles A., 47; *cited*, 24n., 40n.
Beard, Mary, *cited*, 24n.
Beckner, Earl, *cited*, 608n.
Belmont, August, 101n.
Benham, F. C., 818n.; *cited*, 821n.
Bentham, Jeremy, 26n.
Berger, Victor, 113, 114, 137n.
Berman, Edward, *cited*, 61n., 475n., 521n., 568n., 574, 587, 720n.
Bernhardt, Joshua, *cited*, 727n.

Bernstein, Eduard, 114
Berry, George L., 235n.
Beyer, Otto S., 468; *cited*, 469
Biddle, Francis, 759n.
Bird, Francis H., *cited*, 419n.
Bismarck, 56n.
Bituminous Coal Commission, 145n.
Black, Justice, *cited*, 578
Blaine, Senator, 644n.
Blanqui, Auguste, 57n.
Blanshard, Paul, *cited*, 323n.
Block, Louis, *cited*, 713n.
Blum, Solomon, *cited*, 274n.
Board of Trade (Great Britain), 777–778
Boeckel, Richard, *cited*, 346n.
Bonnett, Clarence E., *cited* 443n., 462n., 604n. 605n.
Boston Prison Discipline Society, 24n.
Bowers, Claude, 47
Brameld, Theodore, *cited*, 328n.
Brand, Carl, *cited*, 12n.
Brandeis, Justice, 476, 558n., 588, 644, 658; *cited*, 515–516
Braun, Kurt, *cited*, 727n.
Brissenden, Paul F., *cited*, 115n., 117n., 118n., 119n., 121n., 631n., 644n.
Brookings, Robert S., *cited*, 158n.
Brooks, Robert P. R., *cited*, 247n., 612n.
Browder, Earl, 240n.
Brown, Emily Clark, *cited*, 382n., 419n., 449n., 542n., 758n., 838n., 847n., 888
Bryan, J. W., *cited*, 597
Bryan, W. J., 68, 113, 114n., 126
Budd, E. G., 757
Budish, J. M., and George Soule, *cited*, 253n., 351
Bugniazet, G. M., 212n., 215n., 218n.
Burns, A. R., *cited*, 151n., 607
Burns, E. M., *cited*, 807n.
Burns, W. J., Agency, 606
Burton, E. R., *cited*, 832n., 856n., 877n.
Butler, Justice, 524n., 624n.

Calkins, Clinch, *cited*, 604n.
Calumet Council, 867
Campbell, Wallace J., *cited*, 340n., 341n.
Canadian Pacific Railway, 468
Capone, Al, 670
Cardozo, Justice, Benjamin B., 624n.; *cited*, 502n.
Carey, James B., 215n.
Carlton, Frank T., *cited*, 583n.
Carmody, John, 761n.
Carrazo, Mike, 249n.
Carroll, Mollie Ray, *cited*, 124n., 126n., 312n., 327n.
Carter, W. S., 733
Carver, Thomas N., *cited*, 158n.
Caskie, J. J. K., *cited*, 832n.
Catchings, Waddill, *cited*, 160n.
Catholic Conference on Industrial Problems, 727n.
Catlin, Warren B., *cited*, 460n.

891

SUBJECT INDEX

A

Act of 1927, English Trades Disputes, 496–497
Actors' Equity Association, 245
Aberdeen case, 649
Aberthaw Construction Co. v. Cameron, 561n.
Acme Air Appliance Co. case, 533n.
Acme Machine Products Co. case, 846n., 862n.
Adair case, 167n., 511, 512, 516, 518, 520, 521
Adamson Act, 130, 706, 733, 734
Adler & Sons v. Maglio, 555n., 640n.
Adler strike, 640
Advance, The, cited, 330n.
Aeolian-American Corp. case, 849n.
Agency law, 656
Agrarianism, 27, 29, 34, 40, 47, 86
Agreements, in Australia, 812, 814, 816, 818, 821
  in Canada, 786, 788
  as chief goal of unionism, 9
  for closed shop held valid by National Labor Relations Board, 849
  on closed and union shop, 471n.
  under collective bargaining, 354
  and company unions, 864, 872n., 880–881
  for compulsory arbitration, 716
  and conciliation and arbitration, 708
  damage suits brought for violation of, 654
  defined, 880
  filed with National Mediation Board, 855n.
  in France, 662
  in Germany, 488, 822n.
  and hiring, 453–455
  of independent unions, 865
  in Kansas, 825
  legal status and enforcement of, 661–667
  matters covered by, 430
  in Minnesota, 792
  in needle trades, 718
  in New South Wales, 809, 810
  in New Zealand, 795, 796, 797, 799, 801, 802, 803, 805, 806
  in newspaper industry, 716–718
  in railroading, 747
  rule out restriction of output, 465
  seniority clauses in, 457
  in shoe industry, 719
  in stove industry, 93n.
Agricultural Implement Workers, initiation fees, fines, and benefits of, 267
Aircraft Workers, initiation fees, fines, and benefits of, 267
Agricultural labor, 527–528, 535n., 536
  organization exclusive of, in 1930, 202
Agriculture, 620n.
Air transport, 743n., 885n.
Aircraft industry, 199n.
Alabama laws, 619n., 620–621, 659, 660

Alaska Salmon Industry, Inc., case, 528n.
Albany, N. Y., 19
Alberta, 784, 791n.
Alco-Zander case, 558n., 559
Allan, S. L., and Company, Inc., and Federal Labor Union Local No. 18,526, 531n.
Allied trade organizations, 271–272, 278
Allis-Chalmers Mfg. Co. case, 765n.
Alston case, 542n.
Aluminum industry, 195n., 206
Aluminum Workers, 198
Amalgamated Association of Iron and Steel Workers, 146n., 174, 175n., 198n., 210, 212n., 223, 224, 227
Amalgamated Association of Street and Electrical Railway Employees, 344n., 456n.
Amalgamated Bank of Chicago, 347n., 350
Amalgamated Bank of New York, 342, 347n.
Amalgamated Clothing Workers, 134n., 180n., 198n., 199n., 228, 235n., 244, 256, 264, 273n., 274, 275, 278, 279, 280n., 316, 318n., 337n., 338n., 345, 346, 347, 358, 366n., 370, 466, 467, 884
  banks of, 351
  of Brooklyn, 865
  of Chicago, 271, 391, 452, 485, 718
  and the C.I.O., 210
  form extensive trade agreements, 258
  and housing, 342, 343
  initiation fees, dues, and benefits, 267
  organizational work of, 379
  of Philadelphia, 558
  and piecework, 404–405
  policy of, toward work organization, 437n.
  and preferential shop, 318n.
  wage policy of, 379–380
  and workers' education, 330–331
Amalgamated Clothing Workers Corp., 342
Amalgamated Society of Engineers of Great Britain, 117n.
Amalgamated Textile Workers, 134n.
Amalgamated Today and Tomorrow, The, cited, 330n.
Amalgamated Trust and Savings Bank of Chicago, 351n.
Amalgamation, 94
  agitated for, by Communists, 178n.
  as a constructive answer to problem of craft and industrial unionism, 278–279
Amalgamations, 105, 291, 300
American Association of Independent Labor Unions, 869, 889n.
American Brotherhood of Steamboat Pilots, 80n.
American congress of labor proposed, 220
American Federation of Hosiery Workers, 332n., 342
American Federation of Labor, 55, 59n., 69, 70, 78, 127, 161n., 163, 176, 177n., 184, 190n., 199, 579, 839, 847n., 889
  and arbitration, 720n.
  Atlantic City convention of, in 1935, 208–212
  and automobile industry, 867